Collins

SCRABBLE™
BRAND Crossword Game
TRAINER

Published by Collins
An imprint of HarperCollins Publishers
Westerhill Road
Bishopbriggs
Glasgow G64 2QT

First Edition 2016

10 9 8 7 6 5 4 3 2 1

© HarperCollins Publishers 2016

ISBN 978-0-00-814650-4

Collins® is a registered trademark of
HarperCollins Publishers Limited

SCRABBLE™ and associated trademarks and
trade dress are owned by, and used under
licence from, J. W. Spear & Sons Limited,
a subsidiary of Mattel, Inc. © 2016 Mattel, Inc.
All Rights Reserved.

www.harpercollins.co.uk/scrabble

Typeset by Davidson Publishing Solutions,
Glasgow

Printed in Great Britain by Clays Ltd, St Ives plc

If you would like to comment on any aspect
of this book, please contact us at the given
address or online.
E-mail: puzzles@harpercollins.co.uk
facebook.com/collinsdictionary
@collinsdict

AUTHOR
Allan Simmons

EDITORS
Robert Groves
Mary O'Neill

COMPUTING SUPPORT
Kris Siwiec

FOR THE PUBLISHER
Gerry Breslin
Kerry Ferguson

Contents

Introduction

Collins Scrabble Trainer is the companion volume to *Collins Official Scrabble Words* (CSW), the official wordlist for Scrabble. While *CSW* contains the complete list of words that are valid in Scrabble, this book presents sets of words derived from CSW in a form that is geared towards learning and improving one's Scrabble vocabulary. With over 276,000 words eligible for play in Scrabble, it is virtually impossible for anyone to learn them all. This book provides the best of the words – those that are most useful in the game – in a manner in which they can be easily learned and remembered for Scrabble situations. Essentially, *Collins Scrabble Trainer* is a collection of lists, each of which groups together words with similar attributes for exploiting a particular type of rack of letters or aspect of the game.

What sort of lists are in this book?

You will find straightforward lists of all the two-, three-, and four-letter words, where you'll also be introduced to the concept of word families; lists of words using the power tiles, JQXZ; lists of words beginning with particular prefixes, and ending with particular suffixes; words with unusual endings and beginnings; and lists of words for offloading excessive vowels or awkward combinations of consonants. There are also extensive lists of hook words, showing how a single letter can be added before or after a word. There are lists of six-letter stems – groups of six letters which are particularly productive in combining with a seventh letter to form valid seven-letter bonus words. And there is also a selection of the most useful seven-letter stems yielding eight-letter words worth noting. There are lists of variant spellings – which should help you with recalling if, for example, a particular word is spelled COSEY, COSIE, COSY, COZEY, COZIE, or COZY (all six are valid!). And there's a miscellany section including personal names and place names that are valid, and examples of words from overseas English. All of the lists in this book bring to the fore a great many words that will be unfamiliar to most people, and even to most Scrabble players. By adding these words to their vocabulary, players are equipping themselves with a powerful arsenal that they can deploy to improve their game, no matter at what level the game is played.

Generally, definitions have been excluded because they are not essential for the function of this book, but have been included for added interest for some of the useful short words and very unusual words. Notes have been added occasionally where there is something of interest to draw attention to.

All the definitions of words in this book can be found in *Collins Ultimate Scrabble Dictionary and Wordlist.*

Foreword

Of course, there are now many online and computer resources related to words, but not many people have the time or the inclination to devote to using them. Collins has done all of that hard work for you by producing *Collins Scrabble Trainer*. Call me old-fashioned, but I'd always rather have something tangible that I can hold in my hand anyway.

There are all of the essentials here to enhance your playing ability – hooks, unusual words with J, Q, X, and Z, short words, vowel-heavy words, etc. etc. There's more than that, though: *Collins Scrabble Trainer* not only gives you the words, but there are comprehensive sections taking you through the required approach for learning that will help you turn your newfound knowledge into higher scores and better play.

I particularly admire some of the lists in *Section 9, Miscellaneous lists*. Something that surprised me was the sheer number of place names that are valid: a couple worth knowing are ORLEANS and WORTHING. Then, when you get to personal names, there are loads of excellent ones to learn, such as LOUIE, HENRY, or SPENCER. Personally, I find it a lot easier to remember whether a word is playable in Scrabble if it's already familiar to me. It's excellent that a lot of the words in this section are defined; that should reassure you that you're playing a proper game based on the English language, rather than just remembering letter strings.

Section 4, Beginnings and endings is superb, particularly the 'endings', which are not easily obtained from just reviewing a dictionary. Even an expert like me was flabbergasted to find out that there are over 100 seven-letter words ending in -OID. Pretty much all of these are worth knowing: some particularly high-probability words include AGATOID and LIANOID. I also had a chuckle at two of the more bizarre-sounding ones – ERICOID and OIDIOID.

Not everyone can be a champion, but you will increase your scores and become a better player by browsing this book.

Philip Nelkon
www.tripleword.co.uk

Other Scrabble resources

Associations

World English-Language Scrabble Players Association (WESPA) – www.wespa.org

The WESPA website also provides access to an Initiation Kit, highlighting major differences between the 2011 third edition of *Collins Official Scrabble Words* and the 2015 fourth edition.

Association of British Scrabble Players (ABSP) – www.absp.org.uk

The ABSP website includes details of UK Scrabble clubs and UK tournaments Schools Scrabble contact – youthscrabble@absp.org.uk

Mindsports Academy – www.mindsportsacademy.com

Facebook

Scrabble Facebook Fan Page – www.facebook.com/scrabble

Play Online Scrabble on Facebook – search for Scrabble Worldwide

Interactive Scrabble games

Internet Scrabble Club (ISC) – www.isc.ro

Mobile phone – Real Networks

Sky Interactive – Sky TV platform

iTouch / iPhone / Android / iPad – Electronic Arts (EA)

Scrabble App

Download *Collins Official Scrabble Checker and Solver* app from the iTunes Store

SECTION 1

SHORT WORDS

....

- While seven and eight-letter words in Scrabble will get you 50 bonus points – and spectacular words of up to 15 letters in length can be formed by extending existing words – the shorter words (twos, threes and fours) are the bread and butter of the game.

- A player's best chance of consistently high game scores is often founded on eking out the most points from short words, forming parallel plays in tight situations.

- Short words are easy to squeeze onto the board and can score well if they contain one of the higher-scoring letters in conjunction with premium squares.

- The short words containing only or mostly vowels also serve to help resolve a vowel-heavy rack (eg **AI**, **OU**, **EAU**, **AIA**, **ILIA**, **UNAU**).

Two-letter words

Two-letter words are vital to the Scrabble player. While very few two-letter words afford big scores in their own right, they are crucial linking elements in the game. Essentially, two-letter words are the nuts and bolts of the game, allowing longer words to be played parallel to each other or can be used for slotting in a high-scoring letter on a premium square to form words in two directions. There are 124 valid two-letter words in Scrabble, all of which are listed in this section, also showing which of them can have an –S added. Definitions are given for these, but sometimes it will be the more unusual definition, especially if it is only the unusual one that allows the –S plural. A summary of the twos without the definitions is given after the initial list.

AA s   type of volcanic rock
AB s   abdominal muscle
AD s   advertisement
AE   one
AG s   agriculture
AH s   exclamation expressing surprise, joy, etc
AI s   three-toed sloth of South America
AL s   Asian shrub or tree
AM   form of 'be'
AN s   additional condition
AR s   the letter R
AS s   ancient Roman unit of weight
AT s   Laotian monetary unit
AW   Scots variant of all
AX   US spelling of axe
AY s   expression of agreement
BA s   symbol for the soul in Ancient Egyptian religion
BE s   exist or live
BI s   bisexual person
BO s   exclamation uttered to startle or surprise someone
BY s   a pass to the next round of a competition
CH   obsolete form of I
DA s   Burmese knife
DE   of or from
DI s   a plural of deus
DO s   party, celebration
EA s   river
ED s   editor
EE   Scots word for eye
EF s   the letter F
EH s   exclamation of surprise or inquiry

EL s	American elevated railway
EM s	square of a body of any size of type
EN s	unit of measurement half the width of an em
ER s	sound made when hesitating in speech
ES s	the letter s
ET	(dialect) past tense of eat
EX	former husband, wife, etc
FA s	fourth note in a musical scale
FE s	variant of Hebrew letter pe
FY	exclamation of disapproval
GI s	white suit worn in martial arts
GO s	a board game
GU s	type of violin used in Shetland
HA s	exclamation of triumph, surprise, or scorn
HE s	male person or animal
HI s	hello
HM	sound made to express hesitation or doubt
HO s	derogatory term for a woman
ID s	mind's instinctive unconscious energies
IF s	uncertainty or doubt
IN s	way of approaching or befriending a person
IO s	exclamation of triumph
IS	form of 'be'
IT s	player whose turn it is to catch the others in children's games
JA	yes
JO	Scots word for sweetheart
KA s	(in ancient Egypt) type of attendant spirit
KI s	vital energy
KO s	(in New Zealand) traditional digging tool
KY	Scots word for cows
LA s	musical note
LI s	Chinese measurement of distance
LO s	exclamation meaning 'look'
MA s	mother
ME s	third note in a musical scale
MI s	third note in a musical scale
MM	expression of enjoyment of taste or smell
MO s	moment
MU s	12th letter in the Greek alphabet
MY	belonging to me
NA s	no
NE	nor
NO s	answer or vote of 'no'
NU s	13th letter in the Greek alphabet

NY s	variant of nigh
OB s	expression of opposition
OD s	hypothetical force
OE s	grandchild
OF	belonging to
OH s	exclamation of surprise, pain, etc
OI s	grey-faced petrel
OM s	sacred syllable in Hinduism
ON s	side of the field on which the batsman stands
OO s	Scots word for wool
OP s	operation
OR s	gold
OS	mouth or mouthlike part
OU s	South African word for man, bloke, or chap
OW	exclamation of pain
OX	castrated bull
OY s	grandchild
PA s	fortified Māori settlement
PE s	17th letter of the Hebrew alphabet
PI s	16th letter in the Greek alphabet
PO s	chamber pot
QI s	vital energy
RE s	second note in a musical scale
SH	hush
SI s	seventh note in a musical scale
SO s	fifth note in a musical scale
ST	exclamation to attract attention
TA s	a thank you
TE s	seventh note in a musical scale
TI s	seventh note in a musical scale
TO	indicating movement towards
UG s	hate
UH	expression of hesitation
UM s	hesitate while speaking
UN s	spelling of 'one'
UP s	increase or raise
UR	hesitant utterance used to fill gaps in talking
US	refers to the speaker or writer and other people
UT s	syllable used musical notation
WE	the speaker or writer and one or more others
WO s	archaic spelling of woe
XI s	14th letter in the Greek alphabet
XU	Vietnamese currency unit
YA s	an Asian pear

YE s   you
YO   expression used as a greeting
YU s   jade
ZA s   pizza
ZO s   Tibetan breed of cattle

Two-letter words summary for learning
A: AA AB AD AE AG AH AI AL AM AN AR AS AT AW AX AY
B: BA BE BI BO BY
C: CH
D: DA DE DI DO
E: EA ED EE EF EH EL EM EN ER ES ET EX
F: FA FE FY
G: GI GO GU
H: HA HE HI HM HO
I: ID IF IN IO IS IT
J: JA JO
K: KA KI KO KY
L: LA LI LO
M: MA ME MI MM MO MU MY
N: NA NE NO NU NY
O: OB OD OE OF OH OI OM ON OO OP OR OS OU OW OX OY
P: PA PE PI PO
Q: QI
R: RE
S: SH SI SO ST
T: TA TE TI TO
U: UG UH UM UN UP UR US UT
V: –
W: WE WO
X: XI XU
Y: YA YE YO YU
Z: ZA ZO

Three-letter words

Three-letter words are a natural progression from two-letter words. They are an essential weapon in every Scrabble player's armoury. It's worth trying to become familiar with them all, but if that's a tall order then you should at least focus on those that can be formed as one-letter extensions (hooks) of two-letter words (before or after) and strive to be familiar with those that contain a higher-scoring letter (three points or more).

There are 1,341 valid three-letter words in Scrabble, all of which are listed in this section, showing which can take an –S extension. The list includes plurals of two-letter words to emphasise these. Not all the threes are valuable in Scrabble but are all listed here for completeness.

AAH s	ALL s	AUA s	BIB s	CAA s
AAL s	ALP s	AUE	BID s	CAB s
AAS	ALS	AUF s	BIG s	CAD s
ABA s	ALT s	AUK s	BIN s	CAF s
ABB s	ALU s	AVA s	BIO s	CAG s
ABO s	AMA s	AVE s	BIS	CAL
ABS	AME s	AVO s	BIT s	CAM s
ABY s	AMI s	AWA	BIZ	CAN s
ACE s	AMP s	AWE s	BOA s	CAP s
ACH	AMU s	AWK s	BOB s	CAR s
ACT s	ANA s	AWL s	BOD s	CAT s
ADD s	AND s	AWN s	BOG s	CAW s
ADO s	ANE s	AXE s	BOH s	CAY s
ADS	ANI s	AYE s	BOI s	CAZ
ADZ	ANN s	AYS	BOK s	CEE s
AFF	ANS	AYU s	BON	CEL s
AFT	ANT s	AZO	BOO s	CEP s
AGA s	ANY	BAA s	BOP s	CHA s
AGE s	APE s	BAC s	BOR s	CHE
AGO	APO s	BAD s	BOS s	CHI s
AGS	APP s	BAG s	BOT s	CID s
AHA	APT s	BAH	BOW s	CIG s
AHI s	ARB s	BAL s	BOX	CIS
AHS	ARC s	BAM s	BOY s	CIT s
AIA s	ARD s	BAN s	BRA s	CLY
AID s	ARE s	BAP s	BRO s	COB s
AIL s	ARF s	BAR s	BRR	COD s
AIM s	ARK s	BAS s	BRU s	COG s
AIN s	ARM s	BAT s	BUB s	COL s
AIR s	ARS	BAY s	BUD s	CON s
AIS	ART s	BED s	BUG s	COO s
AIT s	ARY	BEE s	BUM s	COP s
AJI s	ASH	BEG s	BUN s	COR s
AKA s	ASK s	BEL s	BUR s	COS s
AKE s	ASP s	BEN s	BUS s	COT s
ALA s	ASS	BES	BUT s	COW s
ALB s	ATE s	BET s	BUY s	COX
ALE s	ATS	BEY s	BYE s	COY s
ALF s	ATT	BEZ	BYS	COZ

CRU s	DIS s	EDH s	EVE s	FLU s
CRY	DIT s	EDS	EVO s	FLY
CUB s	DIV s	EEK	EWE s	FOB s
CUD s	DOB s	EEL s	EWK s	FOE s
CUE s	DOC s	EEN	EWT s	FOG s
CUM s	DOD s	EEW	EXO	FOH
CUP s	DOE s	EFF s	EYE s	FON s
CUR s	DOF	EFS	FAA s	FOO s
CUT s	DOG s	EFT s	FAB s	FOP s
CUZ	DOH s	EGG s	FAD s	FOR
CWM s	DOL s	EGO s	FAE	FOU s
DAB s	DOM s	EHS	FAG s	FOX
DAD s	DON s	EIK s	FAH s	FOY s
DAE s	DOO s	EKE s	FAN s	FRA s
DAG s	DOP s	ELD s	FAP	FRO s
DAH s	DOR s	ELF s	FAR s	FRY
DAK s	DOS s	ELK s	FAS	FUB s
DAL s	DOT s	ELL s	FAT s	FUD s
DAM s	DOW s	ELM s	FAW s	FUG s
DAN s	DOY s	ELS	FAX	FUM s
DAP s	DRY s	ELT s	FAY s	FUN s
DAS	DSO s	EME s	FED s	FUR s
DAW s	DUB s	EMO s	FEE s	GAB s
DAY s	DUD s	EMS	FEG s	GAD s
DEB s	DUE s	EMU s	FEH s	GAE s
DEE s	DUG s	END s	FEM s	GAG s
DEF	DUH	ENE s	FEN s	GAK s
DEG s	DUI	ENG s	FER	GAL s
DEI	DUM	ENS	FES s	GAM s
DEL s	DUN s	EON s	FET s	GAN s
DEN s	DUO s	ERA s	FEU s	GAP s
DEP s	DUP s	ERE s	FEW s	GAR s
DEV s	DUX	ERF	FEY s	GAS
DEW s	DYE s	ERG s	FEZ	GAT s
DEX	DZO s	ERK s	FIB s	GAU s
DEY s	EAN s	ERM	FID s	GAW s
DIB s	EAR s	ERN s	FIE	GAY s
DID	EAS	ERR s	FIG s	GED s
DIE s	EAT s	ERS	FIL s	GEE s
DIF s	EAU s	ESS	FIN s	GEL s
DIG s	EBB s	EST s	FIR s	GEM s
DIM s	ECH	ETA s	FIT s	GEN s
DIN s	ECO s	ETH s	FIX	GEO s
DIP s	ECU s	EUK s	FIZ	GER s

GET s   GUT s
GEY   GUV s
GHI s   GUY s
GIB s   GYM s
GID s   GYP s
GIE s   HAD s
GIF s   HAE s
GIG s   HAG s
GIN s   HAH s
GIO s   HAJ

Note

It is worth nothing that any vowel, including Y, can go between H and P to form a valid three-letter word. There are two other patterns that have a similar property: S_N and T_G. There are a lot more examples that can have any vowel, but not Y, as a central letter, eg V_G.

GIP s	HAM s	HMM	HUT s	JAM s
GIS	HAN	HOA s	HYE s	JAP s
GIT s	HAO s	HOB s	HYP s	JAR s
GJU s	HAP s	HOC	ICE s	JAW s
GNU s	HAS s	HOD s	ICH s	JAY s
GOA s	HAT s	HOE s	ICK s	JEE s
GOB s	HAW s	HOG s	ICY	JET s
GOD s	HAY s	HOH s	IDE s	JEU
GOE s	HEH s	HOI s	IDS	JEW s
GON s	HEM s	HOM s	IFF	JIB s
GOO s	HEN s	HON s	IFS	JIG s
GOR s	HEP s	HOO	IGG s	JIN s
GOS s	HER s	HOP s	ILK s	JIZ
GOT	HES	HOS s	ILL s	JOB s
GOV s	HET s	HOT s	IMP s	JOE s
GOX	HEW s	HOW s	ING s	JOG s
GOY s	HEX	HOX	INK s	JOL s
GRR	HEY s	HOY s	INN s	JOR s
GUB s	HIC	HUB s	INS	JOT s
GUE s	HID	HUE s	ION s	JOW s
GUL s	HIE s	HUG s	IOS	JOY s
GUM s	HIM s	HUH	IRE s	JUD s
GUN s	HIN s	HUI s	IRK s	JUG s
GUP s	HIP s	HUM s	ISH	JUN
GUR s	HIS s	HUN s	ISM s	JUS
GUS	HIT s	HUP s	ISO s	JUT s
			ITA s	KAB s
			ITS	KAE s
			IVY	KAF s
			IWI s	KAI s
			JAB s	KAK s
			JAG s	KAM
			JAI	KAS
			JAK s	KAT s

Note

IWI is the only three with two Is and, with that awkward W, is a popular three-letter word among club and tournament players.

KAW s	LAR s	LOU s	MET s	NAE s
KAY s	LAS s	LOW s	MEU s	NAG s
KEA s	LAT s	LOX	MEW s	NAH
KEB s	LAV s	LOY s	MHO s	NAM s
KED s	LAW s	LUD s	MIB s	NAN s
KEF s	LAX	LUG s	MIC s	NAP s
KEG s	LAY s	LUM s	MID s	NAS
KEN s	LEA s	LUN s	MIG s	NAT s
KEP s	LED	LUR s	MIL s	NAV s
KET s	LEE s	LUV s	MIM	NAW
KEX	LEG s	LUX	MIR s	NAY s
KEY s	LEI s	LUZ	MIS s	NEB s
KHI s	LEK s	LYE s	MIX	NED s
KID s	LEP s	LYM s	MIZ	NEE
KIF s	LES s	MAA s	MMM	NEF s
KIN s	LET s	MAC s	MNA s	NEG s
KIP s	LEU	MAD s	MOA s	NEK s
KIR s	LEV s	MAE s	MOB s	NEP s
KIS s	LEW	MAG s	MOC s	NET s
KIT s	LEX	MAK s	MOD s	NEW s
KOA s	LEY s	MAL s	MOE s	NIB s
KOB s	LEZ	MAM s	MOG s	NID s
KOI s	LIB s	MAN s	MOI	NIE s
KON s	LID s	MAP s	MOL s	NIL s
KOP s	LIE s	MAR s	MOM s	NIM s
KOR s	LIG s	MAS s	MON s	NIP s
KOS s	LIN s	MAT s	MOO s	NIS
KOW s	LIP s	MAW s	MOP s	NIT s
KUE s	LIS	MAX	MOR s	NIX
KYE s	LIT s	MAY s	MOS s	NOB s
KYU s	LOB s	MED s	MOT s	NOD s
LAB s	LOD s	MEE s	MOU s	NOG s
LAC s	LOG s	MEG s	MOW s	NOH
LAD s	LOO s	MEH	MOY s	NOM s
LAG s	LOP s	MEL s	MOZ	NON
LAH s	LOR	MEM s	MUD s	NOO
LAM s	LOS s	MEN	MUG s	NOR
LAP s	LOT s	MES s	MUM s	NOS
			MUN s	NOT
			MUS s	NOW s
			MUT s	NOX
			MUX	NOY s
			MYC s	NTH
			NAB s	NUB s

Note

NYS is not actually a plural of NY but an old word meaning 'is not'.

NUG s	OOH s	PAR s	POS s	REC s
NUN s	OOM s	PAS s	POT s	RED s
NUR s	OON s	PAT s	POW s	REE s
NUS	OOP s	PAV s	POX	REF s
NUT s	OOR	PAW s	POZ	REG s
NYE s	OOS	PAX	PRE	REH s
NYM	OOT s	PAY s	PRO s	REI s
NYS	OPA s	PEA s	PRY s	REM s
OAF s	OPE s	PEC s	PSI s	REN s
OAK s	OPS	PED s	PST	REO s
OAR s	OPT s	PEE s	PUB s	REP s
OAT s	ORA	PEG s	PUD s	RES
OBA s	ORB s	PEH s	PUG s	RET s
OBE s	ORC s	PEL s	PUH	REV s
OBI s	ORD s	PEN s	PUL s	REW s
OBO s	ORE s	PEP s	PUN s	REX
OBS	ORF s	PER	PUP s	REZ
OCA s	ORG s	PES	PUR s	RHO s
OCH	ORS	PET s	PUS s	RHY
ODA s	ORT s	PEW s	PUT s	RIA s
ODD s	OSE s	PHI s	PUY s	RIB s
ODE s	OUD s	PHO s	PWN s	RID s
ODS	OUK s	PHT	PYA s	RIF s
OES	OUP s	PIA s	PYE s	RIG s
OFF s	OUR s	PIC s	PYX	RIM s
OFT	OUS	PIE s	QAT s	RIN s
OHM s	OUT s	PIG s	QIN s	RIP s
OHO	OVA	PIN s	QIS	RIT s
OHS	OWE s	PIP s	QUA	RIZ
OIK s	OWL s	PIR s	RAD s	ROB s
OIL s	OWN s	PIS s	RAG s	ROC s
OIS	OWT s	PIT s	RAH s	ROD s
OKA s	OXO	PIU	RAI s	ROE s
OKE s	OXY	PIX	RAJ	ROK s
OLD s	OYE s	PLU s	RAM s	ROM s
OLE s	OYS	PLY	RAN	ROO s
OLM s	PAC s	POA s	RAP s	ROT s
OMA s	PAD s	POD s	RAS	ROW s
OMS	PAH s	POH s	RAT s	RUB s
ONE s	PAK s	POI s	RAV s	RUC s
ONO s	PAL s	POL s	RAW s	RUD s
ONS	PAM s	POM s	RAX	RUE s
ONY	PAN s	POO s	RAY s	RUG s
OOF s	PAP s	POP s	REB s	RUM s

RUN s	SEZ	SOW s	TAU s	TRY
RUT s	SHA	SOX	TAV s	TSK s
RYA s	SHE s	SOY s	TAW s	TUB s
RYE s	SHH	SOZ	TAX	TUG s
RYU s	SHO	SPA s	TAY s	TUI s
SAB s	SHY	SPY	TEA s	TUM s
SAC s	SIB s	SRI s	TEC s	TUN s
SAD s	SIC s	STY	TED s	TUP s
SAE	SIF	SUB s	TEE s	TUT s
SAG s	SIG s	SUD s	TEF s	TUX
SAI s	SIK	SUE s	TEG s	TWA s
SAL s	SIM s	SUG s	TEL s	TWO s
SAM s	SIN s	SUI	TEN s	TWP
SAN s	SIP s	SUK s	TES	TYE s
SAP s	SIR s	SUM s	TET s	TYG s
SAR s	SIS s	SUN s	TEW s	UDO s
SAT	SIT s	SUP s	TEX	UDS
SAU	SIX	SUQ s	THE	UEY s
SAV s	SKA s	SUR	THO	UFO s
SAW s	SKI s	SUS s	THY	UGH s
SAX	SKY	SWY	TIC s	UGS
SAY s	SLY	SYE s	TID s	UKE s
SAZ	SMA	SYN	TIE s	ULE s
SEA s	SNY	TAB s	TIG s	ULU s
SEC s	SOB s	TAD s	TIK s	UMM
SED	SOC s	TAE s	TIL s	UMP s
SEE s	SOD s	TAG s	TIN s	UMS
SEG s	SOG s	TAI s	TIP s	UMU s
SEI s	SOH s	TAJ	TIS	UNI s
SEL s	SOL s	TAK s	TIT s	UNS
SEN s	SOM s	TAM s	TIX	UPO
SER s	SON s	TAN s	TIZ	UPS
SET s	SOP s	TAO s	TOC s	URB s
SEV s	SOS s	TAP s	TOD s	URD s
SEW s	SOT s	TAR s	TOE s	URE s
SEX	SOU s	TAS s	TOG s	URN s
SEY s	SOV s	TAT s	TOM s	URP s
			TON s	USE s
			TOO	UTA s
			TOP s	UTE s
			TOR s	UTS
			TOT s	UTU s
			TOW s	UVA s
			TOY s	VAC s

Note

UTU is a very useful three-letter word for dumping surplus Us, but watch out for the T and K front hooks.

VAE s	WAE s
VAG s	WAG s
VAN s	WAI s
VAR s	WAN s
VAS	WAP s
VAT s	WAR s
VAU s	WAS

> ### Note
> YEH is the only spelling of the words meaning 'yes' that doesn't have an –S plural. YAHS, YAYS, YEAS, and YEAHS are all allowed.

VAV s	WAT s	WON s	YAY s	YUP s
VAW s	WAW s	WOO s	YEA s	YUS
VEE s	WAX	WOP s	YEH	ZAG s
VEG	WAY s	WOS	YEN s	ZAP s
VET s	WAZ	WOT s	YEP s	ZAS
VEX	WEB s	WOW s	YER	ZAX
VIA s	WED s	WOX	YES	ZEA s
VID s	WEE s	WRY	YET	ZED s
VIE s	WEM s	WUD s	YEW s	ZEE s
VIG s	WEN s	WUS s	YEX	ZEK s
VIM s	WET s	WUZ	YEZ	ZEL s
VIN s	WEX	WYE s	YGO	ZEP s
VIS	WEY s	WYN s	YID s	ZEX
VLY	WHA	XED	YIN s	ZHO s
VOE s	WHO	XIS	YIP s	ZIG s
VOG s	WHY s	YAD s	YOB s	ZIN s
VOL s	WIG s	YAE	YOD s	ZIP s
VOM s	WIN s	YAG s	YOK s	ZIT s
VOR s	WIS s	YAH s	YOM	ZIZ
VOW s	WIT s	YAK s	YON	ZOA
VOX	WIZ	YAM s	YOU s	ZOL s
VUG s	WOE s	YAP s	YOW s	ZOO s
VUM s	WOF s	YAR	YUG s	ZOS
WAB s	WOG s	YAS	YUK s	ZUZ
WAD s	WOK s	YAW s	YUM	ZZZ s

Four-letter words

Four-letter words are generally less valuable than three-letter words. The ones that are most useful during play tend to be those that can be formed by hooking three-letter words before or after (eg ALOW, LOWE), those that contain awkward combinations of letters (eg VEHM) or three vowels (eg HIOI) that help to resolve problems. **All the four-letter words are listed here except for those that are plurals of three-letter words and those that contain the power tiles (JQXZ).** This makes the list less cluttered and the JQXZ fours are given under their own section and best learnt separately, so don't need to be repeated here.

ABAC s	AGLU s	ALOE s	ARCH	AVER s
ABBA s	AGLY	ALOO s	ARCO s	AVID
ABBE s	AGMA s	ALOW	AREA s	AVOW s
ABED	AGOG	ALSO	ARED	AWAY s
ABER s	AGON s	ALTO s	AREG	AWDL s
ABET s	AGRO s	ALUM s	ARET s	AWED
ABID	AGUE s	AMAH s	AREW	AWEE
ABLE s	AHED	AMBO s	ARGH	AWFY
ABLY	AHEM	AMEN s	ARIA s	AWNY
ABRI s	AHOY	AMIA s	ARID	AWOL s
ABUT s	AIDA s	AMID s	ARIL s	AWRY
ABYE s	AIDE s	AMIE s	ARIS	AYAH s
ACAI s	AIGA s	AMIN s	ARLE s	AYIN s
ACCA s	AINE	AMIR s	ARMY	AYRE s
ACED	AIRN s	AMLA s	ARNA s	BAAL s
ACER s	AIRT s	AMMO s	AROW	BABA s
ACHE s	AIRY	AMOK s	ARPA s	BABE s
ACHY	AITU s	AMYL s	ARSE s	BABU s
ACID s	AKED	ANAL	ARSY	BABY
ACME s	AKEE s	ANAN	ARTI s	BACH s
ACNE s	AKIN	ANCE	ARTY	BACK s
ACRE s	ALAE	ANEW	ARUM s	BADE
ACRO s	ALAN s	ANGA s	ARVO s	BAEL s
ACTA	ALAP s	ANIL s	ARYL s	BAFF s
ACYL s	ALAR	ANKH s	ASAR	BAFT s
ADAW s	ALAY s	ANNA s	ASCI	BAGH s
ADDY	ALBA s	ANNO	ASEA	BAHT s
ADIT s	ALBE	ANOA s	ASHY	BAHU s
ADRY	ALCO s	ANON	ATAP s	BAIL s
AEON s	ALEC s	ANOW	ATMA s	BAIT s
AERO s	ALEE	ANSA	ATOC s	BAKE s
AERY	ALEF s	ANTA s	ATOK s	BALD s
AESC	ALEW s	ANTE s	ATOM s	BALE s
AFAR s	ALFA s	ANTI s	ATOP	BALK s
AFFY	ALGA s	ANUS	ATUA s	BALL s
AFRO s	ALIF s	APAY s	AUGH	BALM s
AGAR s	ALIT	APED	AULA s	BALU s
AGED	ALKO s	APER s	AULD	BANC s
AGEE	ALKY	APOD s	AUNE s	BAND s
AGEN	ALLY	APSE s	AUNT s	BANE s
AGER s	ALMA s	APSO s	AURA s	BANG s
AGHA s	ALME s	ARAK s	AUTO s	BANI
AGIN	ALMS	ARAR s	AVAL	BANK s
AGIO s	ALOD s	ARBA s	AVEL s	BANT s

BAPU s	BELL s	BIRL s	BODY	BOUK s
BARB s	BELT s	BIRO s	BOEP s	BOUN s
BARD s	BEMA s	BIRR s	BOET s	BOUT s
BARE s	BEND s	BISE s	BOFF s	BOWL s
BARF s	BENE s	BISH	BOGY	BOWR s
BARK s	BENI s	BISK s	BOHO s	BOYF s
BARM s	BENT s	BIST	BOIL s	BOYG s
BARN s	BERE s	BITE s	BOKE s	BOYO s
BARP s	BERG s	BITO s	BOKO s	BRAD s
BASE s	BERK s	BITT s	BOLA s	BRAE s
BASH	BERM s	BLAB s	BOLD s	BRAG s
BASK s	BEST s	BLAD s	BOLE s	BRAK s
BAST s	BETA s	BLAE s	BOLL s	BRAN s
BATE s	BETE s	BLAG s	BOLO s	BRAP
BATH s	BETH s	BLAH s	BOLT s	BRAT s
BATT s	BEVY	BLAM s	BOMA s	BRAW s
BAUD s	BHAI s	BLAT s	BOMB s	BRAY s
BAUK s	BHAT	BLAW s	BONA	BRED s
BAUR s	BHEL s	BLAY s	BOND s	BREE s
BAWD s	BHUT s	BLEB s	BONE s	BREI s
BAWK s	BIAS	BLED	BONG s	BREN s
BAWL s	BIBB s	BLEE s	BONK s	BRER s
BAWN s	BIBE s	BLET s	BONY	BREW s
BAWR s	BICE s	BLEW	BOOB s	BREY s
BAYE s	BIDE s	BLEY s	BOOH s	BRIE s
BAYT s	BIDI s	BLIN s	BOOK s	BRIG s
BEAD s	BIEN	BLIP s	BOOL s	BRIK s
BEAK s	BIER s	BLIT s	BOOM s	BRIM s
BEAL s	BIFF s	BLOB s	BOON s	BRIN s
BEAM s	BIGA	BLOC s	BOOR s	BRIO s
BEAN s	BIGG s	BLOG s	BOOT s	BRIS s
BEAR s	BIKE s	BLOT s	BORA s	BRIT s
BEAT s	BILE s	BLOW s	BORD s	BROD s
BEAU s	BILK s	BLUB s	BORE s	BROG s
BECK s	BILL s	BLUE s	BORK s	BROO s
BEDE s	BIMA s	BLUR s	BORM s	BROW s
BEDU	BIND s	BOAB s	BORN	BRRR
BEEF s	BINE s	BOAK s	BORT s	BRUT s
BEEN	BING s	BOAR s	BOSH	BUAT s
BEEP s	BINK s	BOAT s	BOSK s	BUBA s
BEER s	BINT s	BOBA s	BOTA s	BUBO
BEET s	BIOG s	BOBO s	BOTE s	BUBU s
BEGO	BIRD s	BOCK s	BOTH	BUCK s
BEIN s	BIRK s	BODE s	BOTT s	BUDA s

> ## *Note*
> A good way to learn the fours is to play a solo game using this list and the JQXZ list, limiting yourself to just the four-letter words.

BUDI s	CADE s		CHEF s	CLAD s
BUDO s	CADI s		CHEM s	CLAG s
BUFF s	CAFE s		CHER	CLAM s
BUFO s	CAFF s		CHEW s	CLAN s
BUHL s	CAGE s		CHIA s	CLAP s
BUHR s	CAGY		CHIB s	CLAT s
BUIK s	CAID s	CAST s	CHIC s	CLAW s
BUKE s	CAIN s	CATE s	CHID	CLAY s
BULB s	CAKE s	CAUF	CHIK s	CLEF s
BULK s	CAKY	CAUK s	CHIN s	CLEG s
BULL s	CALF s	CAUL s	CHIP s	CLEM s
BUMF s	CALK s	CAUM s	CHIT s	CLEW s
BUMP s	CALL s	CAUP s	CHIV s	CLIP s
BUNA s	CALM s	CAVA s	CHOC s	CLIT s
BUND s	CALO s	CAVE s	CHOG s	CLOD s
BUNG s	CALP s	CAVY	CHON s	CLOG s
BUNK s	CAMA s	CAWK s	CHOP s	CLON s
BUNN s	CAME s	CEAS	CHOU	CLOP s
BUNT s	CAMI s	CECA	CHOW s	CLOT s
BUOY s	CAMO s	CEDE s	CHUB s	CLOU s
BURA s	CAMP s	CEDI s	CHUG s	CLOW s
BURB s	CANE s	CEIL s	CHUM s	CLOY s
BURD s	CANG s	CELL s	CHUR	CLUB s
BURG s	CANN s	CELT s	CHUT s	CLUE s
BURK s	CANT s	CENS	CIAO	COAL s
BURL s	CANY	CENT s	CIDE s	COAT s
BURN s	CAPA s	CEPE s	CIEL s	COBB s
BURP s	CAPE s	CERE s	CILL s	COCA s
BURR s	CAPH s	CERO s	CINE s	COCH
BURY	CAPI	CERT s	CION s	COCK s
BUSH	CAPO s	CESS	CIRE s	COCO s
BUSK s	CARB s	CETE s	CIRL s	CODA s
BUST s	CARD s	CHAD s	CIST s	CODE s
BUSY	CARE s	CHAI s	CITE s	COED s
BUTE s	CARK s	CHAL s	CITO	COFF s
BUTT s	CARL s	CHAM s	CITY	COFT
BYDE s	CARN s	CHAO s	CIVE s	COHO s
BYKE s	CARP s	CHAP s		
BYRE s	CARR s	CHAR s		
BYRL s	CART s	CHAT s		
BYTE s	CASA s	CHAV s		
CABA s	CASE s	CHAW s		
CACA s	CASH	CHAY s		
CACK s	CASK s			

COIF s	COST s	CULT s	DARN s	DELI s
COIL s	COSY	CUNT s	DART s	DELL s
COIN s	COTE s	CURB s	DASH	DELO s
COIR s	COTH s	CURD s	DATA	DELT s
COIT s	COTT s	CURE s	DATE s	DEME s
COKE s	COUP s	CURF s	DATO s	DEMO s
COKY	COUR s	CURL s	DAUB s	DEMY
COLA s	COVE s	CURN s	DAUD s	DENE s
COLD s	COWK s	CURR s	DAUR s	DENI s
COLE s	COWL s	CURT	DAUT s	DENT s
COLL s	COWP s	CUSH	DAVY	DENY
COLT s	COWY	CUSK s	DAWD s	DERE s
COLY	CRAB s	CUSP s	DAWK s	DERM s
COMA s	CRAG s	CUSS	DAWN s	DERN s
COMB s	CRAM s	CUTE s	DAWT s	DERO s
COME s	CRAN s	CYAN s	DEAD s	DERV s
COMM s	CRAP s	CYMA s	DEAF	DESI s
COMP s	CRAW s	CYME s	DEAL s	DESK s
COMS	CRAY s	CYST s	DEAN s	DEUS
COND	CRED s	CYTE s	DEAR s	DEVA s
CONE s	CREE s	DAAL s	DEAW s	DEVI s
CONF s	CREM s	DACE s	DEBE s	DEVO s
CONI	CREW s	DACK s	DEBT s	DEWY
CONK s	CRIA s	DADA s	DECK s	DHAK s
CONN s	CRIB s	DADO s	DECO s	DHAL s
CONY	CRIM s	DAFF s	DEED s	DHOL s
COOF s	CRIP s	DAFT	DEEK	DHOW s
COOK s	CRIS	DAGO s	DEEM s	DIAL s
COOL s	CRIT s	DAHL s	DEEN s	DICE s
COOM s	CROC s	DAIS	DEEP s	DICH
COON s	CROG s	DALE s	DEER s	DICK s
COOP s	CRON s	DALI s	DEET s	DICT s
COOT s	CROP s	DALT s	DEEV s	DIDO s
COPE s	CROW s	DAME s	DEFI s	DIDY
COPY	CRUD s	DAMN s	DEFO	DIEB s
CORD s	CRUE s	DAMP s	DEFT	DIED
CORE s	CUBE s	DANG s	DEFY	DIEL s
CORF	CUED	DANK s	DEGU s	DIET s
CORK s	CUFF s	DANT s	DEID s	DIFF s
CORM s	CUIF s	DARB s	DEIF	DIKA s
CORN s	CUIT s	DARE s	DEIL s	DIKE s
CORY	CUKE s	DARG s	DEKE s	DILL s
COSE s	CULL s	DARI s	DELE s	DIME s
COSH	CULM s	DARK s	DELF s	DIMP s

DINE s	DONE	DRAM s	DURA s	EGAD s
DING s	DONG s	DRAP s	DURE s	EGAL
DINK s	DOOB s	DRAT s	DURN s	EGER s
DINO s	DOOK s	DRAW s	DURO s	EGGY
DINT s	DOOL s	DRAY s	DURR s	EGIS
DIOL s	DOOM s	DREE s	DUSH	EGMA s
DIPT	DOON	DREG s	DUSK s	EHED
DIRE	DOOR s	DREK s	DUST s	EIDE
DIRK s	DOPA s	DREW	DUTY	EILD s
DIRL s	DOPE s	DREY s	DWAM s	EINA
DIRT s	DOPY	DRIB s	DYAD s	EINE
DISA s	DORB s	DRIP s	DYED	EISH
DISC s	DORE s	DROP s	DYER s	EKED
DISH	DORK s	DROW s	DYKE s	EKKA s
DISK s	DORM s	DRUB s	DYNE s	ELAN s
DITA s	DORP s	DRUG s	EACH	ELHI
DITE s	DORR s	DRUM s	EALE s	ELMY
DITT s	DORT s	DUAD s	EARD s	ELSE
DIVA s	DORY	DUAL s	EARL s	EMEU s
DIVE s	DOSA s	DUAN s	EARN s	EMIC s
DIVI s	DOSE s	DUAR s	EASE s	EMIR s
DIVO s	DOSH	DUCE s	EAST s	EMIT s
DIYA s	DOST	DUCI	EASY	EMMA s
DOAB s	DOTE s	DUCK s	EATH	EMMY s
DOAT s	DOTH	DUCT s	EAVE s	EMPT s
DOBE s	DOTY	DUDE s	EBON s	EMYD s
DOBY	DOUC s	DUED	ECAD s	EMYS
DOCK s	DOUK s	DUEL s	ECCE	ENEW s
DOCO s	DOUM s	DUET s	ECCO	ENOL s
DOCU s	DOUN	DUFF s	ECHE s	ENOW s
DODO s	DOUP s	DUIT s	ECHO s	ENTS
DOEK s	DOUR	DUKA s	ECHT	ENUF
DOEN	DOUT s	DUKE s	ECOD	ENVY
DOER s	DOVE s	DULE s	ECRU s	EOAN
DOFF s	DOWD s	DULL s	EDDO	EORL s
DOGE s	DOWF	DULY	EDDY	EPEE s
DOGY	DOWL s	DUMA s	EDGE s	EPHA s
DOIT s	DOWN s	DUMB s	EDGY	EPIC s
DOLE s	DOWP s	DUMP s	EDIT s	EPOS
DOLL s	DOWT s	DUNE s	EECH	ERED
DOLT s	DRAB s	DUNG s	EEEW	EREV s
DOME s	DRAC	DUNK s	EELY	ERGO s
DOMY	DRAD	DUNT s	EERY	ERHU s
DONA s	DRAG s	DUPE s	EEVN s	ERIC s

ERNE s	FAIN s	FERE s	FLAN s	FORD s
EROS	FAIR s	FERM s	FLAP s	FORE s
ERST	FAKE s	FERN s	FLAT s	FORK s
ERUV s	FALL s	FEST s	FLAW s	FORM s
ESES	FAME s	FETA s	FLAY s	FORT s
ESKY	FAND s	FETE s	FLEA s	FOSS
ESNE s	FANE s	FETT s	FLED	FOUD s
ESPY	FANG s	FEUD s	FLEE s	FOUL s
ESSE s	FANK s	FIAR s	FLEG s	FOUR s
ETAT s	FANO s	FIAT s	FLEW s	FOWL s
ETCH	FARD s	FICE s	FLEY s	FRAB s
ETEN s	FARE s	FICO s	FLIC s	FRAE
ETHE	FARL s	FIDO s	FLIM s	FRAG s
ETIC s	FARM s	FIEF s	FLIP s	FRAP s
ETNA s	FARO s	FIER s	FLIR s	FRAT s
ETUI s	FART s	FIFE s	FLIT s	FRAU s
EUGE	FASH	FIGO s	FLOB s	FRAY s
EUGH s	FAST s	FIKE s	FLOC s	FREE s
EUOI	FATE s	FIKY	FLOE s	FRET s
EURO s	FAUN s	FILA	FLOG s	FRIB s
EVEN s	FAUR	FILE s	FLOP s	FRIG s
EVER	FAUT s	FILK s	FLOR s	FRIS
EVET s	FAVA s	FILL s	FLOW s	FRIT s
EVIL s	FAVE s	FILM s	FLUB s	FROE s
EVOE	FAWN s	FILO s	FLUE s	FROG s
EWER s	FEAL s	FIND s	FOAL s	FROM
EYAS s	FEAR s	FINE s	FOAM s	FROW s
EYED	FEAT s	FINI s	FOCI	FRUG s
EYEN	FECK s	FINK s	FOEN	FUCI
EYER s	FEEB s	FINO s	FOGY	FUCK s
EYNE	FEED s	FIRE s	FOHN s	FUEL s
EYOT s	FEEL s	FIRK s	FOID s	FUFF s
EYRA s	FEEN s	FIRM s	FOIL s	FUGU s
EYRE s	FEER s	FIRN s	FOIN s	FULL s
EYRY	FEET	FISC s	FOLD s	FUME s
FAAN	FEHM	FISH	FOLK s	FUMY
FACE s	FEIS	FISK s	FOND s	FUND s
FACT s	FELL s	FIST s	FONE	FUNG s
FADE s	FELT s	FITT s	FONT s	FUNK s
FADO s	FEME s	FIVE s	FOOD s	FURL s
FADY	FEND s	FLAB s	FOOL s	FURR s
FAFF s	FENI s	FLAG s	FOOT s	FURY
FAIK s	FENT s	FLAK s	FORA	FUSC
FAIL s	FEOD s	FLAM s	FORB s	FUSE s

FUSK s	GAUD s	GINN	GOER s	GREY s
FUSS	GAUM s	GIRD s	GOEY	GRID s
FUST s	GAUN	GIRL s	GOFF s	GRIG s
FYCE s	GAUP s	GIRN s	GOGO s	GRIM
FYKE s	GAUR s	GIRO s	GOLD s	GRIN s
FYLE s	GAVE	GIRR s	GOLE s	GRIP s
FYRD s	GAWD s	GIRT s	GOLF s	GRIS
GABY	GAWK s	GISM s	GOLP s	GRIT s
GACH	GAWP s	GIST s	GONE	GROG s
GADE s	GEAL s	GITE s	GONG s	GROK s
GADI s	GEAN s	GIVE s	GONK s	GROT s
GAED	GEAR s	GLAD s	GOOD s	GROW s
GAEN	GEAT s	GLAM s	GOOF s	GRRL s
GAFF s	GECK s	GLED s	GOOG s	GRUB s
GAGA	GEED	GLEE s	GOOK s	GRUE s
GAGE s	GEEK s	GLEG	GOOL s	GRUM
GAID s	GEEP s	GLEI s	GOON s	GUAN s
GAIN s	GEIT s	GLEN s	GOOP s	GUAR s
GAIR s	GELD s	GLEY s	GOOR s	GUCK s
GAIT s	GELT s	GLIA s	GORA s	GUDE s
GALA s	GENA s	GLIB s	GORE s	GUFF s
GALE s	GENE s	GLID	GORI s	GUGA s
GALL s	GENT s	GLIM s	GORM s	GUID s
GAMA s	GENU s	GLIT s	GORP s	GULA s
GAMB s	GERE s	GLOB s	GORY	GULE s
GAME s	GERM s	GLOM s	GOSH	GULF s
GAMP s	GERT	GLOP s	GOTH s	GULL s
GAMY	GEST s	GLOW s	GOUK s	GULP s
GANE	GETA s	GLUE s	GOUT s	GULY
GANG s	GEUM s	GLUG s	GOWD s	GUMP s
GANT s	GHAT s	GLUM s	GOWF s	GUNG
GAOL s	GHEE s	GLUT s	GOWK s	GUNK s
GAPE s	GIBE s	GNAR s	GOWL s	GURL s
GAPO s	GIED	GNAT s	GOWN s	GURN s
GAPY	GIEN	GNAW s	GRAB s	GURU s
GARB s	GIFT s	GNOW s	GRAD s	GUSH
GARE s	GIGA s	GOAD s	GRAM s	GUST s
GARI s	GILA s	GOAF s	GRAN s	GYAL s
GART	GILD s	GOAL s	GRAT	GYBE s
GASH	GILL s	GOAT s	GRAV s	GYMP s
GASP s	GILT s	GOBI s	GRAY s	GYNO s
GAST s	GIMP s	GOBO s	GREE s	GYNY
GATE s	GING s	GOBY	GREN s	GYPO s
GATH s	GINK s	GOEL s	GREW s	GYRE s

GYRI	HART s	HERM s	HOLE s	HUER s
GYRO s	HASH	HERN s	HOLK s	HUFF s
GYTE s	HASK s	HERO s	HOLM s	HUGE
GYVE s	HASP s	HERY	HOLO s	HUGY
HAAF s	HAST	HESP s	HOLP	HUHU s
HAAR s	HATE s	HEST s	HOLS	HUIA s
HABU s	HATH	HETE s	HOLT s	HUIC
HACK s	HAUD s	HETH s	HOLY	HULA s
HADE s	HAUF s	HEWN	HOMA s	HULE s
HAED	HAUL s	HICK s	HOME s	HULK s
HAEM s	HAUN s	HIDE s	HOMO s	HULL s
HAEN	HAUT	HIED	HOMY	HUMA s
HAET s	HAVE s	HIGH s	HOND s	HUMF s
HAFF s	HAWK s	HIKE s	HONE s	HUMP s
HAFT s	HAWM s	HILA	HONG s	HUNG
HAGG s	HEAD s	HILD	HONK s	HUNH
HAHA s	HEAL s	HILI	HOOD s	HUNK s
HAIK s	HEAP s	HILL s	HOOF s	HUNT s
HAIL s	HEAR s	HILT s	HOOK s	HURL s
HAIN s	HEAT s	HIND s	HOON s	HURT s
HAIR s	HEBE s	HING s	HOOP s	HUSH
HAKA s	HECH	HINT s	HOOR s	HUSK s
HAKE s	HECK s	HIOI s	HOOT s	HUSO s
HAKU s	HEED s	HIPT	HOPE s	HUSS
HALE s	HEEL s	HIRE s	HORA s	HWAN
HALF s	HEFT s	HISH	HORE	HWYL s
HALL s	HEID s	HISN	HORI s	HYED
HALM s	HEIL s	HIST s	HORK s	HYEN s
HALO s	HEIR s	HIVE s	HORN s	HYKE s
HALT s	HELD	HIYA	HORS	HYLA s
HAME s	HELE s	HMMM	HOSE s	HYLE s
HAND s	HELL s	HOAR s	HOST s	HYMN s
HANG s	HELM s	HOBO s	HOTE	HYPE s
HANK s	HELO s	HOCK s	HOUF s	HYPO s
HANT s	HELP s	HOED	HOUR s	HYTE
HAPU s	HEME s	HOER s	HOUT s	IAMB s
HARD s	HEMP s	HOGG s	HOVE s	IBIS
HARE s	HEND s	HOGH s	HOWE s	ICED
HARK s	HENT s	HOHA	HOWF s	ICER s
HARL s	HEPT	HOIK s	HOWK s	ICKY
HARM s	HERB s	HOKA s	HOWL s	ICON s
HARN s	HERD s	HOKE s	HOYA s	IDEA s
HARO s	HERE s	HOKI s	HUCK s	IDEE s
HARP s	HERL s	HOLD s	HUED	IDEM

IDLE s	KADI s	KEET s	KING s	KORO s
IDLY	KAED	KEIR s	KINK s	KORU s
IDOL s	KAGO s	KEKS	KINO s	KOTO s
IDYL s	KAGU s	KELL s	KIPE s	KRAB s
IFFY	KAID s	KELP s	KIPP s	KRAI s
IGAD	KAIE s	KELT s	KIRK s	KRAY s
IGLU s	KAIF s	KEMB s	KIRN s	KRIS
IKAN s	KAIK s	KEMP s	KISH	KSAR s
IKAT s	KAIL s	KENO s	KIST s	KUDO s
IKON s	KAIM s	KENT s	KITE s	KUDU s
ILEA	KAIN s	KEPI s	KITH s	KUEH
ILIA	KAKA s	KEPT	KIVA s	KUFI s
ILKA	KAKI s	KERB s	KIWI s	KUIA s
ILLY	KALE s	KERF s	KLAP s	KUKU s
IMAM s	KALI s	KERN s	KLIK s	KULA s
IMID s	KAMA s	KERO s	KNAG s	KUNA
IMMY	KAME s	KESH	KNAP s	KUNE
IMPI s	KAMI s	KEST s	KNAR s	KURI s
INBY	KANA s	KETA s	KNEE s	KURU s
INCH	KANE s	KETE s	KNEW	KUTA s
INFO s	KANG s	KETO	KNIT s	KUTI s
INGO	KANS	KEWL	KNOB s	KUTU s
INIA	KANT s	KHAF s	KNOP s	KVAS s
INKY	KAON s	KHAN s	KNOT s	KYAK s
INLY	KAPA s	KHAT s	KNOW s	KYAR s
INRO	KAPH s	KHET s	KNUB s	KYAT s
INTI s	KAPU s	KHOR s	KNUR s	KYBO s
INTO	KARA s	KHUD s	KNUT s	KYLE s
IOTA s	KARK s	KIBE s	KOAN s	KYND s
IRED	KARN s	KICK s	KOAP s	KYNE
IRID s	KARO s	KIEF s	KOBO s	KYPE s
IRIS	KART s	KIER s	KOEL s	KYTE s
IRON s	KATA s	KIEV s	KOFF s	LACE s
ISBA s	KATI s	KIFF	KOHA s	LACK s
ISIT	KAVA s	KIKE s	KOHL s	LACY
ISLE s	KAWA s	KILD	KOKA s	LADE s
ISNA	KAYO s	KILL s	KOLA s	LADY
ITCH	KBAR s	KILN s	KOLO s	LAER s
ITEM s	KECK s	KILO s	KOND	LAIC s
IURE	KEEF s	KILP s	KONK s	LAID s
KAAL	KEEK s	KILT s	KOOK s	LAIK s
KAAS	KEEL s	KINA s	KOPH s	LAIN
KACK s	KEEN s	KIND s	KORA s	LAIR s
KADE s	KEEP s	KINE s	KORE s	LAKE s

LAKH s	LEEP s	LIME s	LOGY	LUDE s
LAKY	LEER s	LIMN s	LOID s	LUDO s
LALL s	LEET s	LIMO s	LOIN s	LUES
LAMA s	LEFT s	LIMP s	LOIR s	LUFF s
LAMB s	LEHR s	LIMY	LOKE s	LUGE s
LAME s	LEIR s	LIND s	LOLL s	LUIT
LAMP s	LEKE	LINE s	LOMA s	LUKE
LANA s	LEKU	LING s	LOME s	LULL s
LAND s	LEME s	LINK s	LONE	LULU s
LANE s	LEND s	LINN s	LONG s	LUMA s
LANG	LENG s	LINO s	LOOF s	LUMP s
LANK s	LENO s	LINT s	LOOK s	LUNA s
LANT s	LENS	LINY	LOOM s	LUNE s
LARD s	LENT	LION s	LOON s	LUNG s
LARE s	LEPT	LIPA s	LOOP s	LUNK s
LARI s	LERE s	LIPE s	LOOR	LUNT s
LARK s	LERP s	LIPO s	LOOT s	LUNY
LARN s	LEST s	LIRA s	LOPE s	LURE s
LASE s	LEUD s	LIRE	LORD s	LURK s
LASH	LEVA s	LIRI	LORE s	LUSH
LAST s	LEVE s	LIRK s	LORN	LUSK s
LATE	LEVO	LISK s	LORY	LUST s
LATH s	LEVY	LISP s	LOSE s	LUTE s
LATI	LEWD	LIST s	LOSH	LWEI s
LATU s	LIAR s	LITE s	LOST	LYAM s
LAUD s	LIAS	LITH s	LOTA s	LYCH
LAUF s	LICE	LITU	LOTE s	LYME s
LAVA s	LICH	LIVE s	LOTH	LYNE s
LAVE s	LICK s	LOAD s	LOTI	LYRA
LAWK s	LIDO s	LOAF s	LOTO s	LYRE s
LAWN s	LIED	LOAM s	LOUD	LYSE s
LEAD s	LIEF s	LOAN s	LOUN s	LYTE s
LEAF s	LIEN s	LOBE s	LOUP s	MAAR s
LEAK s	LIER s	LOBI	LOUR s	MABE s
LEAL	LIEU s	LOBO s	LOUT s	MACE s
LEAM s	LIFE s	LOCA	LOVE s	MACH s
LEAN s	LIFT s	LOCH s	LOWE s	MACK s
LEAP s	LIKE s	LOCI s	LOWN s	MADE
LEAR s	LILL s	LOCK s	LOWP s	MAGE s
LEAT s	LILO s	LOCO s	LOWT s	MAGG s
LECH	LILT s	LODE s	LUAU s	MAGI
LEDE s	LILY	LOFT s	LUBE s	MAHA
LEED	LIMA s	LOGE s	LUCE s	MAID s
LEEK s	LIMB s	LOGO s	LUCK s	MAIK s

MAIL s	MAUT s	MEVE s	MOAI	MORT s
MAIM s	MAWK s	MEWL s	MOAN s	MOSE s
MAIN s	MAWN s	MICA s	MOAT s	MOSH
MAIR s	MAWR s	MICE	MOBE s	MOSK s
MAKE s	MAYA s	MICH	MOBY	MOST s
MAKI s	MAYO s	MICK s	MOCH s	MOTE s
MAKO s	MEAD s	MICO s	MOCK s	MOTH s
MALA s	MEAL s	MIDI s	MODE s	MOTI s
MALE s	MEAN s	MIEN s	MODI	MOTT s
MALT s	MEAT s	MIFF s	MOER s	MOTU s
MALL s	MECH s	MIGG s	MOFO s	MOUE s
MALM s	MECK s	MIHA s	MOHO s	MOUP s
MALT s	MEED s	MIHI s	MOHR s	MOVE s
MAMA s	MEEK	MIKE s	MOIL s	MOWA s
MANA s	MEER s	MILD s	MOIT s	MOWN
MAND	MEET s	MILE s	MOKE s	MOYA s
MANE s	MEFF s	MILF s	MOKI s	MOYL s
MANG s	MEGA	MILK s	MOKO s	MUCH
MANI s	MEIN s	MILL s	MOLA s	MUCK s
MANO s	MELA s	MILO s	MOLD s	MUFF s
MANY	MELD s	MILT s	MOLE s	MUGG s
MARA s	MELL s	MIME s	MOLL s	MUID s
MARC s	MELT s	MINA s	MOLT s	MUIL s
MARD	MEME s	MIND s	MOLY s	MUIR s
MARE s	MEMO s	MINE s	MOME s	MULE s
MARG s	MEND s	MING s	MOMI	MULL s
MARK s	MENE s	MINI s	MONA s	MUMM s
MARL s	MENG s	MINK s	MONG s	MUMP s
MARM s	MENO	MINO s	MONK s	MUMU s
MART s	MENT	MINT s	MONO s	MUNG s
MARY	MENU s	MINY	MONY	MUNI s
MASA s	MEOU s	MIPS	MOOD s	MUNT s
MASE s	MEOW s	MIRE s	MOOI	MUON s
MASH	MERC s	MIRI	MOOK s	MURA s
MASK s	MERE s	MIRK s	MOOL s	MURE s
MAST s	MERI s	MIRO s	MOON s	MURK s
MASU s	MERK s	MIRV s	MOOP s	MURL s
MATE s	MERL s	MIRY	MOOR s	MURR s
MATH s	MESA s	MISE s	MOOT s	MUSE s
MATT s	MESE s	MISO s	MOPE s	MUSH
MATY	MESH	MIST s	MOPY	MUSK s
MAUD s	META	MITE s	MORA s	MUSO s
MAUL s	METE s	MITT s	MORE s	MUST s
MAUN	METH s	MITY	MORN s	MUTE s

MUTI s	NEEP s	NOIL s	NYAS	OLIO s
MUTT s	NEIF s	NOIR s	NYED	OLLA s
MWAH	NEMA s	NOLE s	OAKY	OLPE s
MYAL	NEMN s	NOLL s	OARY	OMBU s
MYNA s	NENE s	NOLO s	OAST s	OMEN s
MYTH s	NEON s	NOMA s	OATH s	OMER s
NAAM s	NERD s	NOME s	OATY	OMIT s
NAAN s	NERK s	NONA s	OBEY s	OMOV s
NABE s	NESH	NONE s	OBIA s	ONCE s
NABK s	NESS	NONG s	OBIT s	ONER s
NACH	NEST s	NONI s	OBOE s	ONIE
NADA s	NETE s	NOOB s	OBOL s	ONLY
NADS	NETT s	NOOK s	OBVS	ONST
NAFF s	NEUK s	NOON s	OCCY	ONTO
NAGA s	NEUM s	NOOP s	OCHE s	ONUS
NAIF s	NEVE s	NOPE	OCTA s	OOFY
NAIK s	NEVI	NORI s	ODAH s	OONT s
NAIL s	NEWB s	NORK s	ODAL s	OOSE s
NAIN	NEWT s	NORM s	ODEA	OOSY
NALA s	NGAI	NOSE s	ODIC	OPAH s
NAME s	NICE	NOSH	ODOR s	OPAL s
NAMU s	NICK s	NOSY	ODSO	OPED
NANA s	NIDE s	NOTA	ODYL s	OPEN s
NANE	NIDI	NOTE s	OFAY s	OPPO s
NANG	NIED	NOTT	OFFA	OPUS
NANO s	NIEF s	NOUL s	OFFY	ORAD
NAOI	NIFE s	NOUN s	OGAM s	ORAL s
NAOS	NIFF s	NOUP s	OGEE s	ORBY
NAPA s	NIGH s	NOUS	OGLE s	ORCA s
NAPE s	NILL s	NOUT	OGRE s	ORDO s
NARC s	NIMB s	NOVA s	OHED	ORFE s
NARD s	NINE s	NOWL s	OHIA s	ORGY
NARE s	NIPA s	NOWN	OILY	ORLE s
NARK s	NIRL s	NOWT s	OINK s	ORRA
NARY	NISH	NOWY	OINT s	OSAR
NAVE s	NISI	NUDE s	OKAY s	OSSA
NAVY	NITE s	NUFF s	OKEH s	OTIC
NEAL s	NOAH s	NUKE s	OKRA s	OTTO s
NEAP s	NOCK s	NULL s	OKTA s	OUCH
NEAR s	NODE s	NUMB s	OLDE	OULD
NEAT s	NODI	NURD s	OLDY	OULK s
NECK s	NOEL s	NURL s	OLEA	OUMA s
NEED s	NOES	NURR s	OLEO s	OUPA s
NEEM s	NOGG s	NYAH	OLID	OUPH s

OURN	PARE s	PENI s	PING s	POKE s
OUST s	PARK s	PENK s	PINK s	POKY
OUTA	PARP s	PENT s	PINT s	POLE s
OVAL s	PARR s	PEON s	PINY	POLK s
OVEL s	PART s	PEPO s	PION s	POLL s
OVEN s	PASE s	PERC s	PIOY s	POLO s
OVER s	PASH	PERE s	PIPA s	POLT s
OVUM	PAST s	PERI s	PIPE s	POLY s
OWED	PATE s	PERK s	PIPI s	POME s
OWER	PATH s	PERM s	PIPY	POMO s
OWLY	PATU s	PERN s	PIRL s	POMP s
OWRE s	PATY	PERP s	PIRN s	POND s
OWSE	PAUA s	PERT s	PISE s	PONE s
OYER s	PAUL s	PERV s	PISH	PONG s
PAAL s	PAVE s	PESO s	PISO s	PONK s
PAAN s	PAWA s	PEST s	PITA s	PONS
PACA s	PAWK s	PFFT	PITH s	PONT s
PACE s	PAWL s	PFUI	PITY	PONY
PACK s	PAWN s	PHAT	PIUM s	POOD s
PACO s	PEAG s	PHEW	PLAN s	POOF s
PACT s	PEAK s	PHOH	PLAP s	POOH s
PACY	PEAL s	PHON s	PLAT s	POOK s
PADI s	PEAN s	PHOT s	PLAY s	POOL s
PAGE s	PEAR s	PHUT s	PLEA s	POON s
PAID	PEAT s	PIAL	PLEB s	POOP s
PAIK s	PEBA s	PIAN s	PLED	POOR
PAIL s	PECH s	PICA s	PLEW s	POOT s
PAIN s	PECK s	PICE	PLIE s	POPE s
PAIR s	PEED	PICK s	PLIM s	PORE s
PAIS	PEEK s	PIED	PLOD s	PORK s
PALE s	PEEL s	PIER s	PLOP s	PORN s
PALI s	PEEN s	PIET s	PLOT s	PORT s
PALL s	PEEP s	PIKA s	PLOW s	PORY
PALM s	PEER s	PIKE s	PLOY s	POSE s
PALP s	PEGH s	PIKI s	PLUE s	POSH
PALY	PEIN s	PILA	PLUG s	POST s
PAND s	PEKE s	PILE s	PLUM s	POSY
PANE s	PELA s	PILI s	POCK s	POTE s
PANG s	PELE s	PILL s	POCO	POTT s
PANT s	PELF s	PILY	POEM s	POUF s
PAPA s	PELL s	PIMA s	POEP s	POUK s
PAPE s	PELT s	PIMP s	POET s	POUR s
PARA s	PEND s	PINA s	POGO s	POUT s
PARD s	PENE s	PINE s	POGY	POWN s

PRAD s	PULY	RAIT s	REEL s	RING s
PRAM s	PUMA s	RAKE s	REEN s	RINK s
PRAO s	PUMP s	RAKI s	REFI s	RIOT s
PRAT s	PUMY	RAKU s	REFT	RIPE s
PRAU s	PUNA s	RALE s	REGO s	RIPP s
PRAY s	PUNG s	RAMI s	REIF s	RIPT
PREE s	PUNK s	RAMP s	REIK s	RISE s
PREM s	PUNT s	RANA s	REIN s	RISK s
PREP s	PUNY	RAND s	REKE s	RISP s
PREY s	PUPA s	RANG s	RELY	RITE s
PRIG s	PUPU s	RANI s	REND s	RITT s
PRIM s	PURE s	RANK s	RENK	RIVA s
PROA s	PURI s	RANT s	RENO s	RIVE s
PROB s	PURL s	RAPE s	RENT s	RIVO
PROD s	PURR s	RAPT	RENY	ROAD s
PROF s	PUSH	RARE s	REPO s	ROAM s
PROG s	PUTT s	RARK s	REPP s	ROAN s
PROM s	PYAT s	RASE s	RESH	ROAR s
PROO	PYET s	RASH	REST s	ROBE s
PROP s	PYIC	RASP s	RETE	ROCH
PROW s	PYIN s	RAST	RHEA s	ROCK s
PRUH	PYNE s	RATA s	RHUS	RODE s
PSST	PYOT s	RATE s	RIAD s	ROED
PTUI	PYRE s	RATH s	RIAL s	ROID
PUBE s	PYRO s	RATO s	RIBA s	ROIL s
PUCE s	RABI s	RATU s	RICE s	ROIN s
PUCK s	RACA	RAUN s	RICH	ROKE s
PUDU s	RACE s	RAVE s	RICK s	ROKY
PUER s	RACH	RAWN s	RICY	ROLE s
PUFF s	RACK s	RAYA s	RIDE s	ROLF s
PUGH	RACY	READ s	RIEL s	ROLL s
PUHA s	RADE	REAK s	RIEM s	ROMA
PUIR	RAFF s	REAL s	RIFE	ROMP s
PUKA s	RAFT s	REAM s	RIFF s	RONE s
PUKE s	RAGA s	REAN s	RIFT s	RONG
PUKU s	RAGE s	REAP s	RIGG s	RONT s
PUKY	RAGG s	REAR s	RILE s	ROOD s
PULA s	RAGI s	RECK s	RILL s	ROOF s
PULE s	RAGU s	REDD s	RIMA	ROOK s
PULI s	RAIA s	REDE s	RIME s	ROOM s
PULK s	RAID s	REDO s	RIMU s	ROON s
PULL s	RAIK s	REED s	RIMY	ROOP s
PULP s	RAIL s	REEF s	RIND s	ROOT s
PULU s	RAIN s	REEK s	RINE s	ROPE s

ROPY	RUSH	SARK s	SEER s	SHIM s
RORE s	RUSK s	SASH	SEGO s	SHIN s
RORT s	RUST s	SASS	SEIF s	SHIP s
RORY	RUTH s	SATE s	SEIK	SHIR s
ROSE s	RYAL s	SATI s	SEIL s	SHIT s
ROST s	RYFE	SAUL s	SEIR s	SHIV s
ROSY	RYKE s	SAUT s	SEKT s	SHMO
ROTA s	RYND s	SAVE s	SELD	SHOD
ROTE s	RYOT s	SAWN	SELE s	SHOE s
ROTI s	RYPE	SCAB s	SELF s	SHOG s
ROTL s	SAAG s	SCAD s	SELL s	SHOO s
ROTO s	SABE s	SCAG s	SEME s	SHOP s
ROUE s	SACK s	SCAM s	SEMI s	SHOT s
ROUL s	SADE s	SCAN s	SENA s	SHOW s
ROUM s	SADI s	SCAR s	SEND s	SHRI s
ROUP s	SADO s	SCAT s	SENE s	SHUL s
ROUT s	SAFE s	SCAW s	SENT s	SHUN s
ROVE s	SAFT	SCOG s	SEPS	SHUT s
ROWT s	SAGA s	SCOP s	SEPT s	SHWA s
RUBE s	SAGE s	SCOT s	SERA	SIAL s
RUBY	SAGO s	SCOW s	SERE s	SIBB s
RUCK s	SAGY	SCRY	SERF s	SICE s
RUDD s	SAIC s	SCUD s	SERK s	SICH
RUDE s	SAID s	SCUG s	SERR s	SICK s
RUDI s	SAIL s	SCUL s	SESE	SIDA s
RUDY	SAIM s	SCUM s	SESH	SIDE s
RUED	SAIN s	SCUP s	SESS	SIDH
RUER s	SAIR s	SCUR s	SETA	SIEN s
RUFF s	SAKE s	SCUT s	SETT s	SIES
RUGA	SAKI s	SCYE s	SEWN	SIFT s
RUIN s	SALE s	SEAL s	SHAD s	SIGH s
RUKH s	SALL	SEAM s	SHAG s	SIGN s
RULE s	SALP s	SEAN s	SHAH s	SIKA s
RULY	SALT s	SEAR s	SHAM s	SIKE s
RUME s	SAMA s	SEAT s	SHAN s	SILD s
RUMP s	SAME s	SECH s	SHAT	SILE s
RUND s	SAMP s	SECO	SHAW s	SILK s
RUNE s	SAND s	SECT s	SHAY s	SILL s
RUNG s	SANE s	SEED s	SHEA s	SILO s
RUNT s	SANG s	SEEK s	SHED s	SILT s
RURP s	SANK	SEEL s	SHEN	SIMA s
RURU s	SANT s	SEEM s	SHET s	SIMI s
RUSA s	SARD s	SEEN	SHEW s	SIMP s
RUSE s	SARI s	SEEP s	SHHH	SIND s

SINE s	SLED s	SNOW s	SOUP s	STAY s
SING s	SLEE	SNUB s	SOUR s	STED s
SINH s	SLEW s	SNUG s	SOUT s	STEM s
SINK s	SLEY s	SNYE s	SOWF s	STEN s
SIPE s	SLID	SOAK s	SOWL s	STEP s
SIRE s	SLIM s	SOAP s	SOWM s	STET s
SIRI s	SLIP s	SOAR s	SOWN	STEW s
SIST s	SLIT s	SOBA s	SOWP s	STEY s
SITE s	SLOB s	SOCA s	SOYA s	STIE s
SITH	SLOE s	SOCK s	SPAE s	STIM s
SKAG s	SLOG s	SODA s	SPAG s	STIR s
SKAT s	SLOP s	SOFA s	SPAM s	STOA s
SKAW s	SLOT s	SOFT s	SPAN s	STOB s
SKED s	SLOW s	SOHO	SPAR s	STOP s
SKEE s	SLUB s	SOIL s	SPAT s	STOT s
SKEG s	SLUE s	SOKE s	SPAW s	STOW s
SKEN s	SLUG s	SOLA s	SPAY s	STUB s
SKEO s	SLUM s	SOLD s	SPEC s	STUD s
SKEP s	SLUR s	SOLE s	SPED	STUM s
SKER s	SLUT s	SOLI	SPEK s	STUN s
SKET s	SMEE s	SOLO s	SPET s	STYE s
SKEW s	SMEW s	SOMA s	SPEW s	SUBA s
SKID s	SMIR s	SOME	SPIC s	SUCH
SKIM s	SMIT s	SOMY	SPIE s	SUCK s
SKIN s	SMOG s	SONE s	SPIF s	SUDD s
SKIO s	SMUG s	SONG s	SPIK s	SUED
SKIP s	SMUR s	SOOK s	SPIM s	SUER s
SKIT s	SMUT s	SOOL s	SPIN s	SUET s
SKOG s	SNAB s	SOOM s	SPIT s	SUGH s
SKOL s	SNAG s	SOON	SPIV s	SUGO s
SKRY	SNAP s	SOOP s	SPOD s	SUID s
SKUA s	SNAR s	SOOT s	SPOT s	SUIT s
SKUG s	SNAW s	SOPH s	SPRY	SUKH s
SKYF s	SNEB s	SORA s	SPUD s	SULK s
SKYR s	SNED s	SORB s	SPUE s	SULU s
SLAB s	SNEE s	SORD s	SPUG s	SUMI s
SLAE s	SNIB s	SORE s	SPUN	SUMO s
SLAG s	SNIG s	SORI	SPUR s	SUMP s
SLAM s	SNIP s	SORN s	STAB s	SUMY
SLAP s	SNIT s	SORT s	STAG s	SUNG
SLAT s	SNOB s	SOTH s	STAP s	SUNI s
SLAW s	SNOD s	SOUK s	STAR s	SUNK s
SLAY s	SNOG s	SOUL s	STAT s	SUNN s
SLEB s	SNOT s	SOUM s	STAW s	SUPE s

SURA s	TAIG s	TEAM s	THEY	TIRR s
SURD s	TAIL s	TEAR s	THIG s	TITE
SURE s	TAIN s	TEAT s	THIN s	TITI s
SURF s	TAIT s	TECH s	THIO	TIVY
SUSU s	TAKA s	TEDY	THIR	TIYN s
SWAB s	TAKE s	TEED	THIS	TOAD s
SWAD s	TAKI s	TEEK	THON	TOBY
SWAG s	TAKY	TEEL s	THOU s	TOCK s
SWAM	TALA s	TEEM s	THRO	TOCO s
SWAN s	TALC s	TEEN s	THRU	TODY
SWAP s	TALE s	TEER s	THUD s	TOEA s
SWAT s	TALI	TEFF s	THUG s	TOED
SWAY s	TALK s	TEGG s	THUS	TOEY
SWEE s	TALL s	TEGU s	TIAN s	TOFF s
SWEY s	TAME s	TEHR s	TIAR s	TOFT s
SWIG s	TAMP s	TEIL s	TICE s	TOFU s
SWIM s	TANA s	TEIN s	TICH	TOGA s
SWOB s	TANE	TELA	TICK s	TOGE s
SWOP s	TANG s	TELD	TIDE s	TOHO
SWOT s	TANH s	TELE s	TIDY	TOIL s
SWUM	TANK s	TELL s	TIED	TOIT s
SYBO	TAPA s	TELT	TIER s	TOKE s
SYCE s	TAPE s	TEME s	TIFF s	TOKO s
SYED	TAPU s	TEMP s	TIFT s	TOLA s
SYEN s	TARA s	TEMS	TIGE s	TOLD
SYKE s	TARE s	TEND s	TIKA s	TOLE s
SYLI s	TARN s	TENE s	TIKE s	TOLL s
SYNC s	TARO s	TENT s	TIKI s	TOLT s
SYND s	TARP s	TEPA s	TILE s	TOLU s
SYNE s	TART s	TERF s	TILL s	TOMB s
SYPE s	TASE s	TERM s	TILT s	TOME s
SYPH s	TASH	TERN s	TIME s	TOMO s
TAAL s	TASK s	TEST s	TINA s	TONE s
TABI s	TATE s	TETE s	TIND s	TONG s
TABU s	TATH s	TETH s	TINE s	TONK s
TACE s	TATT s	THAE	TING s	TONY
TACH s	TATU s	THAN s	TINK s	TOOK
TACK s	TAUT s	THAR s	TINT s	TOOL s
TACO s	TAVA s	THAT	TINY	TOOM s
TACT s	TAWA s	THAW s	TIPI s	TOON s
TAED	TAWT s	THEE s	TIPT	TOOT s
TAEL s	TEAD s	THEM	TIRE s	TOPE s
TAHA s	TEAK s	THEN s	TIRL s	TOPH s
TAHR s	TEAL s	THEW s	TIRO s	TOPI s

TOPO s	TROG s	TYED	URAO s	VELE s
TORA s	TRON s	TYEE s	URDE	VELL s
TORC s	TROP	TYER s	URDY	VENA
TORE s	TROT s	TYIN	UREA s	VEND s
TORI	TROU	TYKE s	URGE s	VENT s
TORN	TROW s	TYMP s	URIC	VERA
TORO s	TROY s	TYND	URSA	VERB s
TORR s	TRUE s	TYNE s	URUS	VERD
TORT s	TRUG s	TYPE s	URVA s	VERS
TORY	TRYE	TYPO s	USED	VERT s
TOSA s	TRYP s	TYPP s	USER s	VERY
TOSE s	TSAR s	TYPY	UTIS	VEST s
TOSH	TUAN s	TYRE s	UVAE	VETO
TOSS	TUBA s	TYRO s	UVEA s	VIAE
TOST	TUBE s	TYTE	VADE s	VIAL s
TOTE s	TUCK s	UDAL s	VAGI	VIBE s
TOUK s	TUFA s	UDON s	VAIL s	VIBS
TOUN s	TUFF s	UGLY	VAIN	VICE s
TOUR s	TUFT s	ULAN s	VAIR s	VIDE
TOUT s	TULE s	ULNA s	VALE s	VIED
TOWN s	TUMP s	ULVA s	VALI s	VIER s
TOWT s	TUNA s	UMBO s	VAMP s	VIEW s
TOWY	TUND s	UMMA s	VANE s	VIFF s
TOYO s	TUNE s	UMPH s	VANG s	VIGA s
TRAD s	TUNG s	UMPY	VANT s	VILD
TRAM s	TUNY	UMRA s	VAPE s	VILE
TRAP s	TURD s	UNAI s	VARA s	VILL s
TRAT s	TURF s	UNAU s	VARE s	VINA s
TRAY s	TURK s	UNBE	VARY	VINE s
TREE s	TURM s	UNCE s	VASA	VINO s
TREF	TURN s	UNCI	VASE s	VINT s
TREK s	TURR s	UNCO s	VAST s	VINY
TREM s	TUSH	UNDE	VATU s	VIOL s
TRES s	TUSK s	UNDO s	VAUT s	VIRE s
TRET s	TUTU s	UNDY	VEAL s	VIRL s
TREW s	TWAE s	UNIT s	VEEP s	VISA s
TREY s	TWAL s	UNTO	VEER s	VISE s
TRIE s	TWAT s	UPAS	VEGA s	VITA s
TRIG s	TWAY s	UPBY	VEGO s	VITE
TRIM s	TWEE	UPDO s	VEHM	VIVA s
TRIN s	TWIG s	UPGO	VEIL s	VIVE s
TRIO s	TWIN s	UPON	VEIN s	VIVO
TRIP s	TWIT s	UPSY	VELA	VLEI s
TROD s	TYDE	UPTA	VELD s	VLOG s

VOAR s	WANG s	WEKA s	WIFE s	WORN
VOID s	WANK s	WELD s	WIKI s	WORT s
VOIP s	WANT s	WELK s	WILD s	WOST
VOLA	WANY	WELL s	WILE s	WOVE
VOLE s	WARB s	WELS	WILI s	WOWF
VOLK s	WARD s	WELT s	WILL s	WRAP s
VOLT s	WARE s	WEMB s	WILT s	WREN s
VOTE s	WARK s	WENA	WILY	WRIT s
VRIL s	WARM s	WEND s	WIMP s	WUDU s
VROT	WARN s	WENT s	WIND s	WULL s
VROU s	WARP s	WEPT	WINE s	WYCH
VROW s	WART s	WERE	WING s	WYLE s
VUGG s	WARY	WERO s	WINK s	WYND s
VUGH s	WASE s	WERT	WINN s	WYNN s
VULN s	WASH	WEST s	WINO s	WYTE s
WAAC s	WASM s	WETA s	WINY	YAAR s
WAAH	WASP s	WHAE	WIPE s	YABA s
WACK s	WAST s	WHAM s	WIRE s	YACK s
WADD s	WATE	WHAP s	WIRY	YAFF s
WADE s	WATT s	WHAT s	WISE s	YAGE s
WADI s	WAUK s	WHEE	WISH	YAGI s
WADT s	WAUL s	WHEN s	WISP s	YALD
WADY	WAUR s	WHET s	WIST s	YALE s
WAFF s	WAVE s	WHEW s	WITE s	YANG s
WAFT s	WAVY	WHEY s	WITH s	YANK s
WAGE s	WAWA s	WHID s	WIVE s	YAPP s
WAID	WAWE s	WHIG s	WOAD s	YARD s
WAIF s	WAWL s	WHIM s	WOAH	YARE
WAIL s	WEAK	WHIN s	WOCK s	YARK s
WAIN s	WEAL s	WHIO s	WOKE	YARN s
WAIR s	WEAN s	WHIP s	WOLD s	YARR s
WAIT s	WEAR s	WHIR s	WOLF s	YATE s
WAKA s	WEED s	WHIT s	WOMB s	YAUD s
WAKE s	WEEK s	WHOA	WONK s	YAUP s
WAKF s	WEEL s	WHOM	WONT s	YAWL s
WALD s	WEEM s	WHOP s	WOOD s	YAWN s
WALE s	WEEN s	WHOT	WOOF s	YAWP s
WALI s	WEEP s	WHOW s	WOOL s	YAWY
WALK s	WEER	WHUP s	WOON s	YBET
WALL s	WEET s	WICE	WOOT	YEAD s
WALY	WEFT s	WICH	WORD s	YEAH s
WAME s	WEID s	WICK s	WORE	YEAN s
WAND s	WEIL s	WIDE s	WORK s	YEAR s
WANE s	WEIR s	WIEL s	WORM s	YEBO

YECH s	YEST s	YLKE s	YONI s	YUCK s
YEDE s	YETI s	YMPE s	YONT	YUFT s
YEED s	YETT s	YMPT	YOOF s	YUGA s
YEGG s	YEUK s	YOCK s	YOOP s	YUKE s
YELD	YEVE s	YODE	YORE s	YUKO s
YELK s	YGOE	YODH s	YORK s	YUKY
YELL s	YIKE s	YOGA s	YORP s	YULE s
YELM s	YILL s	YOGH s	YOUK s	YUMP s
YELP s	YIPE s	YOGI s	YOUR s	YURT s
YELT s	YIRD s	YOKE s	YOWE s	YWIS
YEOW	YIRK s	YOLD	YOWL s	
YERD s	YIRR s	YOLK s	YUAN s	
YERK s	YITE s	YOMP s	YUCA s	
YESK s	YLEM s	YOND	YUCH	

SECTION 2

POWER TILES

....

- The highest-scoring tiles in the game are J, Q, X, and Z, with J and X scoring eight points each, while Q and Z are worth ten. These four are often referred to as 'power tiles'.

- These power tiles are the most potent weapons in the Scrabble player's arsenal, but need to be carefully deployed. This isn't always a matter of using them in a long word – a carefully positioned short word maximizing use of premium squares can be just as good a move.

- You should also remember that, on average, in a two-player game you are only likely to get each one every other game so it isn't worth concentrating just on these words at the expense of learning other short words or bonus-scoring words.

- This section lists all of the power-tile words of two and three letters, with a brief definition for each, and showing where an –S can be added. These are followed by lists of words of four to six letters.

- It's worth learning all the twos and threes as they can be tremendously useful and being familiar with the definitions of these words will help you commit them to memory.

- The highlighted list of Q words that don't have a U following the Q should be especially noted. The shorter ones are extremely useful.

Using J

There is only one J tile in Scrabble, so for any word with two Js (eg HAJJ or JUJU) a blank is required. When you are trying to use a word with J for parallel play, remember that there are only two two-letter words with J – JA and JO. The J can be as awkward as the Q and is not as flexible as the X and Z so it is wise to try to use it as soon as it arrives on your rack rather than hold onto it, hoping for a better score later. Don't forget unusual combinations like the FJ in FJELD and FJORD, or the DJ in DJIN, DJINN, and their plurals. An examination of the following lists will also reveal a number of words that contain a JR combination, including BAJRA, BAJRI, and HIJRA. Learning some of these more unusual words will give you greater ammunition to make the best use of the J if more common words are unplayable. If there is a Z on the board or on your rack when you have a J, there are several words that could impress your opponent (eg JAZY, ZANJA).

Two-letter words

JA	yes
JO	Scots word for sweetheart

Three-letter words

AJI	s	type of spicy pepper
GJU	s	type of violin used in Shetland
HAJ		pilgrimage a Muslim makes to Mecca
JAB	s	quick punch or poke
JAG	s	period of uncontrolled indulgence in an activity
JAI		victory (to)
JAK	s	device for raising a motor vehicle or other heavy object
JAM	s	pack tightly into a place
JAP	s	splash
JAR	s	wide-mouthed container
JAW	s	one of the bones in which the teeth are set
JAY	s	type of bird
JEE	s	to move aside
JET	s	aircraft driven by jet propulsion
JEU		game
JEW	s	obsolete offensive word for haggle
JIB	s	taunt or jeer
JIG	s	type of lively dance
JIN	s	Chinese unit of weight
JIZ		wig
JOB	s	occupation or paid employment
JOE	s	Scots word for sweetheart
JOG	s	run at a gentle pace

JOL s party
JOR s movement in Indian music
JOT s write briefly
JOW s ring (a bell)
JOY s feeling of great delight or pleasure
JUD s large block of coal
JUG s container for liquids
JUN   North and South Korean monetary unit
JUS   right, power, or authority
JUT s project or stick out
RAJ   (in India) government
TAJ   tall conical cap worn as a mark of distinction by Muslims

Four-letter words

AJAR	JATO s	JILT s	JUBA s
AJEE	JAUK s	JIMP	JUBE s
BAJU s	JAUP s	JINK s	JUCO s
BENJ	JAVA s	JINN s	JUDO s
DJIN s	JAXY	JINX	JUDY
DOJO s	JAZY	JIRD s	JUGA
FUJI s	JAZZ	JISM s	JUJU s
GAJO s	JEAN s	JIVE s	JUKE s
GOJI s	JEAT s	JIVY	JUKU s
HADJ	JEDI s	JIZZ	JUMP s
HAJI s	JEED	JOBE s	JUNK s
HAJJ	JEEL s	JOCK s	JUPE s
JAAP s	JEEP s	JOCO s	JURA
JACK s	JEER s	JOEY s	JURE s
JADE s	JEEZ	JOHN s	JURY
JAFA s	JEFE s	JOIN s	JUST s
JAGA s	JEFF s	JOKE s	JUTE s
JAGG s	JEHU s	JOKY	JUVE s
JAIL s	JELL s	JOLE s	JYNX
JAKE s	JEON s	JOLL s	KOJI s
JAMB s	JERK s	JOLT s	MOJO s
JANE s	JESS	JOMO s	PUJA s
JANN s	JEST s	JONG s	RAJA s
JAPE s	JETE s	JOOK s	ROJI s
JARK s	JEUX	JOSH	SIJO s
JARL s	JIAO s	JOSS	SJOE
JARP s	JIBB s	JOTA s	SOJA s
JASP s	JIBE s	JOUK s	SOJU s
JASS	JIFF s	JOUR s	
JASY	JILL s	JOWL s	

Five-letter words

AFLAJ	JAGIR s	JEUNE	JOLTY
AJIVA s	JAGRA s	JEWED	JOMON s
AJUGA s	JAKEY s	JEWEL s	JONES
AJWAN s	JALAP s	JEWIE s	JONTY
BAJAN s	JALOP s	JHALA s	JORAM s
BAJRA s	JAMBE s	JIBBA s	JORUM s
BAJRI s	JAMBO	JIBED	JOTTY
BANJO s	JAMBU s	JIBER s	JOTUN s
BASIJ	JAMES	JIFFY	JOUAL s
BHAJI s	JAMMY	JIGGY	JOUGS
BIJOU s	JAMON	JIGOT s	JOULE s
BUNJE s	JANNY	JIHAD s	JOUST s
BUNJY	JANTY	JIMMY	JOWAR s
CAJON	JAPAN s	JIMPY	JOWED
CAJUN	JAPED	JINGO	JOWLY
DJINN s	JAPER s	JINNE	JOYED
EEJIT s	JARTA s	JINNI s	JUDAS
EJECT s	JARUL s	JIRGA s	JUDGE s
EJIDO s	JASEY s	JIRRE	JUGAL s
EMOJI s	JASPE s	JIVED	JUGUM s
ENJOY s	JAUNT s	JIVER s	JUICE s
FALAJ	JAVEL s	JIVEY	JUICY
FJELD s	JAWAN s	JNANA s	JUKED
FJORD s	JAWED	JOBED	JULEP s
GADJE s	JAXIE s	JOCKO s	JUMAR s
GADJO s	JAZZY	JOCKY	JUMBO s
GANJA s	JEBEL s	JODEL s	JUMBY
GAUJE s	JEELY	JOINT s	JUMPY
HADJI s	JEEZE	JOIST s	JUNCO s
HAJES	JEHAD s	JOKED	JUNKY
HAJJI s	JELAB s	JOKER s	JUNTA s
HEJAB s	JELLO s	JOKEY	JUNTO s
HEJRA s	JELLY	JOKOL	JUPON s
HIJAB s	JEMBE s	JOLED	JURAL
HIJRA s	JEMMY	JOLLY	JURAT s
HODJA s	JENNY		
JABOT s	JERID s		
JACAL s	JERKY		
JACKY	JERRY		
JADED	JESSE s		
JAFFA s	JESUS		
JAGER s	JETON s		
JAGGY	JETTY		

> ## *Note*
> The words JONES and JOUGS are spelt as if they are plural forms but aren't, so don't be fooled into playing the invalid JONE or JOUG.

JUREL s	NINJA s	RAJES	TAJES
JUROR s	OBJET s	REJIG s	THUJA s
JUTTY	OJIME s	REJON	UNJAM s
JUVIE s	OUIJA s	RIOJA s	UPJET s
KANJI s	POLJE s	ROJAK s	WILJA s
KHOJA s	POOJA s	SAJOU s	WOJUS
KOPJE s	PUJAH s	SHOJI s	YOJAN s
LAPJE s	PUNJI s	SHOJO	ZANJA s
MAJOR s	QAJAQ s	SLOJD s	
MUJIK s	RAJAH s	SUJEE s	

Six-letter words

ABJECT s	DJINNY	INKJET s	JAMBOK s
ABJURE s	DONJON s	JABBED	JAMBUL s
ACAJOU s	EJECTA	JABBER s	JAMJAR s
ADJIGO s	ENJAMB s	JABBLE s	JAMMED
ADJOIN s	ENJOIN s	JABERS	JAMMER s
ADJURE s	EVEJAR s	JABIRU s	JAMPAN s
ADJUST s	FAJITA s	JACANA s	JAMPOT s
AJOWAN s	FANJET s	JACARE s	JANGLE s
BAJADA s	FEIJOA s	JACENT	JANGLY
BAJREE s	FIGJAM s	JACKAL s	JANKER s
BANJAX	FINJAN s	JACKED	JANNEY s
BASEEJ	FRIJOL	JACKER s	JANSKY s
BEJADE s	GAIJIN	JACKET s	JANTEE
BEJANT s	GANJAH s	JACKSY	JAPERY
BENJES	GARJAN s	JADERY	JAPING s
BHAJAN s	GIDJEE s	JADING	JAPPED
BHAJEE s	GOUJON s	JADISH	JARFUL s
BHAJIA	GURJUN s	JAEGER s	JARGON s
BIJOUX	GYTTJA s	JAGAED	JARINA s
BOOJUM s	HADJEE s	JAGGED	JAROOL s
BUNJEE s	HADJES	JAGGER s	JARPED
BUNJIE s	HAJJAH s	JAGHIR s	JARRAH s
CAJOLE s	HAJJES	JAGUAR s	JARRED
COJOIN s	HANJAR s	JAILED	JARVEY s
CONJEE s	HEJIRA s	JAILER s	JARVIE s
CROJIK s	HIJACK s	JAILOR s	JASIES
DEEJAY s	HIJRAH s	JALEBI s	JASMIN s
DEJECT s	HOBJOB s	JALOPY	JASPER s
DJEBEL s	INJECT s	JAMAAT s	JASPIS
DJEMBE s	INJERA s	JAMBED	JASSES
DJIBBA s	INJURE s	JAMBEE s	JASSID s
DJINNI	INJURY	JAMBER s	JATAKA s

JAUKED	JESTEE s	JINXES	JOTTED
JAUNCE s	JESTER s	JIRBLE s	JOTTER s
JAUNSE s	JESUIT s	JISSOM s	JOTUNN s
JAUNTY	JETLAG s	JITNEY s	JOUKED
JAUPED	JETSAM s	JITTER s	JOULED
JAWARI s	JETSOM s	JIVEST	JOUNCE s
JAWBOX	JETSON s	JIVIER	JOUNCY
JAWING s	JETTED	JIVING	JOURNO s
JAYCEE s	JETTON s	JIZZES	JOVIAL
JAYGEE s	JETWAY s	JOANNA s	JOWARI s
JAYVEE s	JEWING	JOBBED	JOWING
JAZIES	JEZAIL s	JOBBER s	JOWLED
JAZZBO s	JHATKA s	JOBBIE s	JOWLER s
JAZZED	JIBBAH s	JOBING	JOYFUL
JAZZER s	JIBBED	JOCKEY s	JOYING
JAZZES	JIBBER s	JOCOSE	JOYOUS
JEANED	JIBING	JOCUND	JOYPAD s
JEEING	JICAMA s	JOGGED	JOYPOP s
JEELED	JIGGED	JOGGER s	JUBATE
JEELIE s	JIGGER s	JOGGLE s	JUBBAH s
JEEPED	JIGGLE s	JOHNNY	JUBHAH s
JEERED	JIGGLY	JOINED	JUBILE s
JEERER s	JIGJIG s	JOINER s	JUDDER s
JEESLY	JIGSAW s	JOJOBA s	JUDGED
JEEZLY	JIHADI s	JOKIER	JUDGER s
JEFFED	JILBAB s	JOKILY	JUDIES
JEHADI s	JILGIE s	JOKING s	JUDOGI s
JEJUNA	JILLET s	JOLING	JUDOKA s
JEJUNE	JILTED	JOLLED	JUGATE
JELLED	JILTER s	JOLLER s	JUGFUL s
JEMIMA s	JIMINY	JOLLEY s	JUGGED
JENNET s	JIMJAM s	JOLLOP s	JUGGLE s
JERBIL s	JIMMIE s	JOLTED	JUGLET s
JERBOA s	JIMPER	JOLTER s	JUGULA
JEREED s	JIMPLY	JOOKED	JUICED
JERKED	JIMSON s	JORDAN s	JUICER s
JERKER s	JINGAL s	JOSEPH s	JUJUBE s
JERKIN s	JINGKO	JOSHED	JUKING
JERQUE s	JINGLE s	JOSHER s	JULIET s
JERRID s	JINGLY	JOSHES	JUMART s
JERSEY s	JINKED	JOSKIN s	JUMBAL s
JESSED	JINKER s	JOSSER s	JUMBIE s
JESSIE s	JINNEE	JOSSES	JUMBLE s
JESTED	JINXED	JOSTLE s	JUMBLY

JUMPED

JUMPER s

JUNCUS

JUNGLE s

JUNGLI s

JUNGLY

JUNIOR s

JUNKED

JUNKER s

JUNKET s

JUNKIE s

JUPATI s

JURANT s

JURIED

JURIES

JURIST s

JUSTED

JUSTER s

JUSTLE s

JUSTLY

JUTTED

JYMOLD

JYNXES

KHODJA s

LOGJAM s

MAJLIS

MASJID s

MATJES

MEJLIS

MOJITO s

MOJOES

MOUJIK s

MUSJID s

MUZJIK s

NUTJOB s

OBJECT s

OBJURE s

OUTJET s

OUTJUT s

PAJAMA s

PAJOCK s

POOJAH s

POPJOY s

POTJIE s

> ## Note
> MUZJIKS is renowned for being the highest possible scoring opening move. If positioned with the S on the centre square it will score 128 points.

PRAJNA s

PROJET s

PUJARI s

PYJAMA s

RAKIJA s

RAMJET s

REJECT s

REJOIN s

RHANJA s

ROMAJI s

SANJAK s

SEJANT

SHINJU s

SOOJEY s

SVARAJ

SWARAJ

TAJINE s

TINAJA s

TRIJET s

UJAMAA s

UNJUST

VEEJAY s

VERJUS

WILTJA s

YOJANA s

Using Q

Along with Z, Q is the highest-scoring letter in Scrabble. Unlike Z, Q can be tricky to use because the majority of words that contain Q also require a U. You shouldn't unnecessarily hold onto the Q and hope for a U to go with it. It is better being played as soon as possible and there are a number of words that contain Q but no U which can help. A complete list of these follows in this section. It's easy enough to learn all of these, especially the more likely shorter ones. There's only one two-letter word with Q, QI, which is very useful as you are either likely to have an I on your rack or one available on the board. It's also worth committing the few three-letter Q words to memory. If you have a Q and U on your rack, or a U is available on the board then the four or five-letter Q words are more likely to get you the best scores. It can help to remember some of them in sets such as (QUAD, QUID, QUOD) and (QUINA, QUINE, QUINO).

Two-letter words

QI s   vital energy

Three-letter words

QAT s white-flowered evergreen shrub whose leaves have narcotic properties
QIN s type of Chinese zither
QUA in the capacity of
SUQ s (in Muslim countries) a marketplace

Four-letter words

AQUA s	QUEP
CINQ s	QUEY s
FIQH s	QUID s
QADI s	QUIM s
QAID s	QUIN s
QOPH s	QUIP s
QUAD s	QUIT s
QUAG s	QUIZ
QUAI s	QUOD s
QUAT s	QUOP s
QUAY s	WAQF s

> ## *Note*
> With so many short Q words taking an –S plural, including the similar word QUOP, it's easy to forget that QUEP does not take an –S. However, it might also be played to trap your opponent into losing a turn.

Five-letter words

AQUAE	QIBLA s	QUASI	QUINO s
BURQA s	QORMA s	QUASS	QUINT s
COQUI s	QUACK s	QUATE s	QUIPO s
EQUAL s	QUAFF s	QUAYD	QUIPU s
EQUES	QUAIL s	QUBIT s	QUIRE s
EQUID s	QUAIR s	QUEAN s	QUIRK s
EQUIP s	QUAKE s	QUEEN s	QUIRT s
FAQIR s	QUAKY	QUEER s	QUIST s
FIQUE s	QUALE	QUELL s	QUITE s
GUQIN s	QUALM s	QUEME s	QUOAD
MAQUI s	QUANT s	QUENA s	QUOIF s
NIQAB s	QUARE	QUERN s	QUOIN s
PIQUE s	QUARK s	QUERY	QUOIT s
QAJAQ s	QUART s	QUEST s	QUOLL s
QANAT s	QUASH	QUEUE s	QUONK s
		QUEYN s	QUOTA s
		QUICH	QUOTE s
		QUICK s	QUOTH
		QUIET s	QURSH
		QUIFF s	QUYTE s
		QUILL s	ROQUE s
		QUILT s	SQUAB s
		QUINA s	SQUAD s
		QUINE s	SQUAT s

> ## *Note*
> Both QURSH and QUYTE are especially difficult to spot because you are unlikely to put anything other than AEIOU after a QU in looking for possible plays.

SQUAW s	SQUID s	TALAQ s	TUQUE s
SQUEG s	SQUIT s	TOQUE s	UMIAQ s
SQUIB s	SQUIZ	TRANQ s	USQUE s

Six-letter words

ACQUIS	NIQAAB s	QUEASY	QUIPPY
ACQUIT s	OPAQUE s	QUEAZY	QUIRED
ASQUAT	PIQUED	QUEBEC s	QUIRKY
BARQUE s	PIQUET s	QUEENY	QUITCH
BASQUE s	PLAQUE s	QUEEST s	QUITED
BISQUE s	PULQUE s	QUEINT	QUIVER s
BOSQUE s	QABALA s	QUELCH	QULLIQ s
BUQSHA s	QASIDA s	QUELEA s	QUOHOG s
CAIQUE s	QAWWAL s	QUEMED	QUOIST s
CALQUE s	QIGONG s	QUENCH	QUOKKA s
CASQUE s	QINDAR s	QUETCH	QUOOKE
CHEQUE s	QINTAR s	QUETHE s	QUORUM s
CHEQUY	QIVIUT s	QUEUED	QUOTED
CINQUE s	QUACKY	QUEUER s	QUOTER s
CIRQUE s	QUAERE s	QUEZAL s	QUOTHA
CLAQUE s	QUAGGA s	QUICHE s	QUOTUM s
CLIQUE s	QUAGGY	QUICKY	QURUSH
CLIQUY	QUAHOG s	QUIDAM s	QUYTED
CLOQUE s	QUAICH s	QUIGHT s	QWERTY s
COQUET s	QUAIGH s	QUINCE s	REQUIN s
DIQUAT s	QUAINT	QUINIC	REQUIT s
EQUALI	QUAKED	QUINIE s	RISQUE s
EQUANT s	QUAKER s	QUININ s	ROQUET s
EQUATE s	QUALIA	QUINOA s	SACQUE s
EQUINE s	QUALMY	QUINOL s	SAIQUE s
EQUIPE s	QUANGO s	QUINSY	SEQUEL s
EQUITY	QUANTA	QUINTA s	SEQUIN s
EXEQUY	QUARER	QUINTE s	SHEQEL s
FAQUIR s	QUARRY	QUINZE s	SQUAIL s
HAIQUE s	QUARTE s	QUIPPU s	SQUALL s
JERQUE s	QUARTO s		
LASQUE s	QUARTZ		
LIQUID s	QUASAR s		
LIQUOR s	QUATCH		
LOQUAT s	QUATRE s		
MANQUE s	QUAVER s		
MARQUE s	QUAZZY		
MASQUE s	QUBYTE s		
MOSQUE s	QUEACH		

Note

While SQUUSH has excellent show-off value, if you had such letters it might well be that a simpler SUQ would be a better play, retaining the other S.

SQUAMA	SQUEAL s	SQUIRL s	TORQUE s
SQUAME s	SQUIER s	SQUIRM s	UBIQUE
SQUARE s	SQUIFF	SQUIRR s	UNIQUE s
SQUARK s	SQUILL s	SQUIRT s	YANQUI s
SQUASH	SQUINT s	SQUISH	YAQONA s
SQUAWK s	SQUINY	SQUUSH	
SQUEAK s	SQUIRE s	TOQUET s	

Q but not U

There are few things more infuriating in Scrabble than having a Q on your rack but no U with which to play it! But this situation needn't be disastrous: there are a surprisingly high number of words that have a Q but not U. A complete list of these words is included here. These have short definitions to help you remember them; it is well worth learning them all, as they can be extremely useful. Note that the A is a key vowel in quite a few of these words, and the D and T appear frequently too.

Two-letter words

QI s   vital energy

Three-letter words

QAT s   white-flowered evergreen shrub whose leaves have narcotic properties
QIN s   type of Chinese zither
SUQ s   (in Muslim countries) a marketplace

Four-letter words

CINQ s   number five
FIQH s   Islamic jurisprudence
QADI s   judge in a Muslim community
QAID s   a chief
QOPH s   letter of the Hebrew alphabet
WAQF s   endowment in Muslim law

Five-letter words

BURQA s   garment worn by Muslim women in public
FAQIR s   Muslim who spurns worldly possessions
GUQIN s   type of Chinese zither
NIQAB s   veil worn by some Muslim women
QAJAQ s   kayak
QANAT s   underground irrigation channel
QIBLA s   direction in which Muslims turn to pray
QORMA s   mild Indian dish
TALAQ s   Muslim form of divorce

TRANQ s   short for tranquillizer
UMIAQ s   Inuit boat made of skins

Six-letter words

BUQSHA s   former Yemeni coin
NIQAAB s   veil worn by some Muslim women
QABALA s   ancient Jewish mystical tradition
QASIDA s   Arabic verse form
QAWWAL s   singer of qawwali
QIGONG s   system of breathing and exercise
QINDAR s   Albanian monetary unit
QINTAR s   variant of qindar
QIVIUT s   soft wool from the muskox
QWERTY s   standard English-language typewriter or computer keyboard
SHEQEL s   monetary unit of Israel
YAQONA s   Polynesian shrub

Seven-letter words

INQILAB s   (in India, Pakistan, etc) revolution
KAMOTIQ s   sled with wooden runners
QABALAH s   ancient Jewish mystical tradition
QAMUTIK s   variant of kamotiq
QAWWALI s   Islamic religious song
TSADDIQ s   Hasidic Jewish leader
TZADDIQ s   variant of tsaddiq

Eight-letter words

MBAQANGA s   style of Black popular music of urban South Africa
MUQADDAM s   person of authority in India
QABALISM s   adherence to Qabala
QABALIST s   adherent of Qabala
QAIMAQAM s   Turkish officer or official
QALAMDAN s   writing case
QINDARKA   plural of qindar
QINTARKA   plural of qintar
QWERTIES   plural of qwerty
SHEQALIM   plural of sheqel

> ## *Note*
> You don't have to worry about which of these words take an –S plural or not because it's only the last four eight-letter examples that don't, and they are unlikely to appear on the board anyway.

Q and K

Looking at the words that contain Q but not U, you may well notice that many are of Arabic or Hebrew origin. Of course, these languages aren't written using the Roman alphabet, so these words are transliterations from a different script. It's an interesting – and helpful – fact that the Arabic consonant that is represented as a Q in Roman script can also be transliterated as a K, which means that many of the Q-but-no-U words can also be spelt with a K. This is useful for two reasons. Firstly, looking at the list of K alternatives will help you remember the Q-only words. Secondly, K is a sort of 'semi-power' tile, scoring five points and being the most valuable letter after the power tiles. Thus it's quite useful to know these unusual words using K for their own sake.

Two-letter words

KI s	QI s

Three-letter words

KAT s	QAT s
KIN s	QIN s
SUK s	SUQ s

Four-letter words

KADI s	QADI s
KAID s	QAID s
KOPH s	QOPH s
WAKF s	WAQF s

Five-letter words

BURKA s	BURQA s
FAKIR s	FAQIR s
KIBLA s	QIBLA s
KORMA s	QORMA s
NIKAB s	NIQAB s
TALAK s	TALAQ s
TRANK s	TRANQ s
UMIAK s	UMIAQ s

Six-letter words

KABALA s	QABALA s
KURUSH	QURUSH
SHEKEL s	SHEQEL s

Seven-letter words

TSADDIK s	TSADDIQ s
TZADDIK s	TZADDIQ s

Eight-letter words

KABALISM s	QABALISM s
KABALIST s	QABALIST s
KAIMAKAM s	QAIMAQAM s

KALAMDAN s   QALAMDAN s
SHEKALIM   SHEQALIM

Using X

X is perhaps the most versatile of the power tiles, simply because of the extensive number of two and three-letter words that contain it. It can reap many points through parallel play, especially if the X falls on a premium square, because there is a two-letter word for every vowel. It is fairly easy to spot words that end in X so it's worth learning a few words that begin with X when a board may not favour X-ending words (eg XENIA, XYST). Of all the power tiles, the X is the only one that it can be worthwhile holding back in the hope of a better score later, providing you can score reasonably well with your other tiles meanwhile.

Two-letter words

AX	US spelling of axe
EX	former husband, wife, etc
OX	castrated bull
XI s	14th letter in the Greek alphabet
XU	Vietnamese currency unit

Three-letter words

AXE s	tool with a sharp blade for felling trees or chopping wood
BOX	container with a firm flat base and sides
COX	coxswain
DEX	dextroamphetamine
DUX	(in Scottish and certain other schools) the top pupil in a class or school
EXO	(Australian) excellent
FAX	electronic system for sending documents
FIX	make or become firm, stable, or secure
FOX	reddish-brown bushy-tailed animal of the dog family
GOX	gaseous oxygen
HEX	evil spell
HOX	hamstring
KEX	any of several hollow-stemmed umbelliferous plants
LAX	not strict
LEX	system or body of laws
LOX	kind of smoked salmon
LUX	unit of illumination
MAX	reach the full extent
MIX	combine or blend into one mass
MUX	spoil

NIX	be careful! watch out!
NOX	nitrogen oxide
OXO	acid that contains oxygen
OXY	analgesic drug
PAX	peace
PIX	variant of pyx
POX	disease in which skin pustules form
PYX	any receptacle for the Eucharistic Host
RAX	stretch or extend
REX	king
SAX	saxophone
SEX	state of being male or female
SIX	one more than five
SOX	informal spelling of 'socks'
TAX	compulsory payment levied by a government on income, property, etc
TEX	unit of weight used to measure yarn density
TIX	tickets
TUX	short for tuxedo
VEX	frustrate, annoy
VOX	voice or sound
WAX	solid shiny fatty or oily substance
WEX	obsolete form of 'waxed'
WOX	obsolete form of 'wax'
XED	marked a cross against
YEX	hiccup
ZAX	tool for cutting roofing slate
ZEX	variant of zax

> ## *Note*
> XED is allowed because it is shown in the source dictionaries in lowercase meaning 'crossed' as in 'crossed out'. However, XING is not allowed because that form is only shown spelt as X-ING, and hyphenated words are disallowed in Scrabble.

Four-letter words

APEX	CRUX	EXUL s	ILEX
AXAL	DEXY	FAIX	IXIA s
AXED	DIXI	FALX	JAXY
AXEL s	DIXY	FAUX	JEUX
AXIL s	DOUX	FIXT	JINX
AXIS	DOXY	FLAX	JYNX
AXLE s	EAUX	FLEX	LANX
AXON s	EXAM s	FLIX	LUXE s
BOXY	EXEC s	FLOX	LYNX
BRUX	EXED	FLUX	MAXI s
CALX	EXES	FOXY	MINX
COAX	EXIT s	GREX	MIXT
COXA	EXON s	HOAX	MIXY
COXY	EXPO s	IBEX	MOXA s

MYXO s	OXES	ROUX	VEXT
NEXT s	OXIC	SAXE s	WAXY
NIXE s	OXID s	SEXT s	WEXE s
NIXY	OXIM s	SEXY	XRAY s
ONYX	PIXY	TAXA	XYST s
ORYX	PLEX	TAXI s	YUNX
OXEN	POXY	TEXT s	
OXER s	PREX	ULEX	

Five-letter words

ADDAX	BOXTY	DIXIT s	FIXIT s
ADMIX	BRAXY	DOXIE s	FLAXY
AFFIX	BUXOM	DRUXY	FLEXO s
ANNEX	CALIX	DUXES	FOREX
ATAXY	CALYX	EMBOX	FOXED
AUXIN s	CAPEX	ENFIX	FOXES
AXIAL	CAREX	EPOXY	FOXIE s
AXILE	CAXON s	EXACT s	GALAX
AXING	CHOUX	EXALT s	GOXES
AXIOM s	CIMEX	EXCEL s	HAPAX
AXION s	CODEX	EXEAT s	HELIX
AXITE s	COMIX	EXEEM s	HEXAD s
AXLED	COXAE	EXEME s	HEXED
AXMAN	COXAL	EXERT s	HEXER s
AXMEN	COXED	EXFIL s	HEXES
AXOID s	COXES	EXIES	HEXYL s
AXONE s	COXIB s	EXILE s	HOXED
BEAUX	CULEX	EXINE s	HOXES
BEMIX	CYLIX	EXING	HYRAX
BOLIX	DEOXY	EXIST s	IMMIX
BORAX	DESEX	EXODE s	INBOX
BOXED	DETOX	EXPAT s	INDEX
BOXEN	DEWAX	EXPEL s	INFIX
BOXER s	DEXES	EXTOL s	IXNAY
BOXES	DEXIE s	EXTRA s	IXORA s
BOXLA s	DIXIE s	EXUDE s	IXTLE s
		EXULT s	JAXIE s
		EXURB s	KEXES
		FAXED	KYLIX
		FAXES	LATEX
		FEDEX	LAXER
		FIXED	LAXES
		FIXER s	LAXLY
		FIXES	LEXES

Note

It's worth drawing attention here to the S and T front hooks of AXMAN and AXMEN listed further on, and under the Hooks section.

LEXIS	OXIME s	SEXER s	VEXER s
LIMAX	OXLIP s	SEXES	VEXES
LINUX	OXTER s	SEXTO s	VEXIL s
LOXED	PANAX	SILEX	VIBEX
LOXES	PAXES	SIXER s	VITEX
LUREX	PHLOX	SIXES	VIXEN s
LUXED	PIXEL s	SIXMO s	VOXEL s
LUXER	PIXES	SIXTE s	WAXED
MALAX	PIXIE s	SIXTH s	WAXEN
MAXED	PODEX	SIXTY	WAXER s
MAXES	POXED	SOREX	WAXES
MAXIM s	POXES	TAXED	WEXED
MIREX	PREXY	TAXER s	WOXEN
MIXED	PROXY	TAXES	WUXIA s
MIXEN s	PYREX	TAXOL s	XEBEC s
MIXER s	PYXED	TAXON s	XENIA s
MIXES	PYXES	TAXOR s	XENIC
MIXTE	PYXIE s	TAXUS	XENON s
MIXUP s	PYXIS	TELEX	XERIC
MOXIE s	RADIX	TEXAS	XEROX
MUREX	RAXED	TEXES	XERUS
MUXED	RAXES	THANX	XOANA
MUXES	REDOX	TOXIC s	XYLAN s
NEXUS	REDUX	TOXIN s	XYLEM s
NIXED	REFIX	TUXES	XYLIC
NIXER s	RELAX	TWIXT	XYLOL s
NIXIE s	REMEX	UNBOX	XYLYL s
NOXAL	REMIX	UNFIX	XYSTI
NOXES	RETAX	UNMIX	YEXED
ORIXA s	RETOX	UNSEX	YEXES
OXBOW s	REWAX	UNTAX	ZAXES
OXEYE s	REXES	URBEX	ZEXES
OXIDE s	SALIX	VARIX	
OXIES	SEXED	VEXED	

Six-letter words

ADIEUX	ANNEXE s	AXEMAN	AXONIC
ADMIXT	ANOXIA s	AXEMEN	AXSEED s
ADNEXA	ANOXIC	AXENIC	BANJAX
AFFLUX	APEXES	AXILLA s	BAXTER s
ALEXIA s	ATAXIA s	AXISED	BEMBEX
ALEXIC	ATAXIC s	AXISES	BEMBIX
ALEXIN s	ATWIXT	AXLIKE	BEMIXT
ALKOXY	AUSPEX	AXONAL	BIAXAL

BIFLEX	DEXTRO	EXONIC	FOXIER
BIJOUX	DIAXON s	EXONYM s	FOXILY
BOLLIX	DIOXAN s	EXOPOD s	FOXING s
BOLLOX	DIOXID s	EXOTIC s	FRUTEX
BOMBAX	DIOXIN s	EXPAND s	GALAXY
BOMBYX	DIPLEX	EXPECT s	GREXES
BONXIE s	DOGFOX	EXPEND s	GUANXI s
BOXCAR s	DUPLEX	EXPERT s	HALLUX
BOXFUL s	EARWAX	EXPIRE s	HANDAX
BOXIER	EFFLUX	EXPIRY	HATBOX
BOXILY	ELIXIR s	EXPORT s	HAYBOX
BOXING s	ETHOXY	EXPOSE s	HEXACT s
BOYAUX	EUTAXY	EXPUGN s	HEXADE s
BRUXED	EXACTA s	EXSECT s	HEXANE s
BRUXES	EXACUM s	EXSERT s	HEXENE s
CALXES	EXAMEN s	EXTANT	HEXING s
CARFAX	EXARCH s	EXTASY	HEXONE s
CARFOX	EXCAMB s	EXTEND s	HEXOSE s
CARNYX	EXCEED s	EXTENT s	HOAXED
CAUDEX	EXCEPT s	EXTERN s	HOAXER s
CERVIX	EXCESS	EXTINE s	HOAXES
CHENIX	EXCIDE s	EXTIRP s	HOTBOX
CLAXON s	EXCISE s	EXTOLD	HOXING
CLIMAX	EXCITE s	EXTOLL s	IBEXES
COAXAL	EXCUSE s	EXTORT s	ICEBOX
COAXED	EXEDRA s	EXUDED	ILEXES
COAXER s	EXEMED	EXUVIA	IMBREX
COAXES	EXEMPT s	FAXING	IMPLEX
COCCYX	EXEQUY	FIXATE s	INFLUX
COMMIX	EXERGY	FIXING s	ISOLEX
CONFIX	EXEUNT	FIXITY	IXODID s
CONVEX	EXHALE s	FIXIVE	JAWBOX
CORTEX	EXHORT s	FIXURE s	JINXED
COWPOX	EXHUME s	FLAXEN	JINXES
COXIER	EXILED	FLAXES	JYNXES
COXING	EXILER s	FLEXED	KLAXON s
CRUXES	EXILIC	FLEXES	LARNAX
DEFLEX	EXITED	FLEXOR s	LARYNX
DEIXES	EXODIC	FLIXED	LAXEST
DEIXIS	EXODOI	FLIXES	LAXISM s
DELUXE	EXODOS	FLUXED	LAXIST s
DENTEX	EXODUS	FLUXES	LAXITY
DESOXY	EXOGEN s	FORFEX	LEXEME s
DEXTER s	EXOMIS	FORNIX	LEXICA

LOXING
LUMMOX
LUXATE s
LUXEST
LUXING
LUXURY
LYNXES
MAGNOX
MASTIX
MATRIX
MAXIMA
MAXING
MAXIXE s
MENINX
MINXES
MIXIER
MIXING s
MUSKOX
MUXING
MYXOID
MYXOMA s
NEXTLY
NITROX
NIXING
NONTAX
NOYAUX
ONYXES
OREXIN s
OREXIS
ORIFEX
ORYXES
OUTBOX
OUTFOX
OXALIC
OXALIS
OXCART s
OXFORD s
OXGANG s
OXGATE s
OXHEAD s
OXHERD s
OXHIDE s
OXIDIC
OXLAND s

OXLIKE
OXSLIP s
OXTAIL s
OXYGEN s
OXYMEL s
PAXWAX
PEGBOX
PEROXO
PEROXY
PHENIX
PICKAX
PINXIT
PLEXAL
PLEXED
PLEXES
PLEXOR s
PLEXUS
POLEAX
POLLEX
POXIER
POXING
PRAXES
PRAXIS
PREFIX
PREMIX
PRETAX
PREXES
PREXIE s
PROLIX
PTYXES
PTYXIS
PYXING
RAXING
REFLEX
REFLUX
REMIXT
REXINE s
RHEXES
RHEXIS
SAXAUL s
SAXIST s
SAXMAN
SAXMEN
SAXONY

> ### *Note*
> MAXIXE is one of only three root
> words of less than ten letters
> containing two Xs. The others are
> XEROX and PAXWAX, which also
> appear in this list. Obviously you'd
> need a blank to play any of those.

SCOLEX
SEXFID
SEXIER
SEXILY
SEXING s
SEXISM s
SEXIST s
SEXPOT s
SEXTAN s
SEXTED
SEXTET s
SEXTON s
SEXUAL
SILVEX
SIXAIN s
SIXISH
SKYBOX
SMILAX
SPADIX
SPHINX
SPHYNX
STORAX
STYRAX
SUBFIX
SUFFIX
SUPLEX
SURTAX
SYNTAX
SYRINX
TAXEME s
TAXIED
TAXIES
TAXING s
TAXITE s
TAXMAN

TAXMEN
SEABOX
TETTIX
TEXTED
TEXTER s
THORAX
TOXINE s
TOXOID s
TOYBOX
TRIMIX
TUTRIX
TUXEDO s
ULEXES
UNAXED
UNFIXT
UNISEX
UNMIXT
UNSEXY
UNVEXT
URTEXT s
VERNIX
VERTEX
VEXING s
VOLVOX
VORTEX
WAXEYE s
WAXIER
WAXILY
WAXING s
WEXING
WRAXLE s
XENIAL
XENIUM
XEROMA s
XOANON

XYLENE s	XYLOSE s	XYSTOS	YUNXES
XYLOID	XYSTER s	XYSTUS	
XYLOMA s	XYSTOI	YEXING	

Using Z

Z scores the same as Q: ten points. But is an easier letter to use primarily because of the two two-letter words (ZA, ZO). Occasionally it may be worth considering holding the Z back if no great scores are immediately available but generally you should look to play it sooner rather than later. It is worth familiarizing yourself with some unusual three-, four-, and five-letter words with the Z, especially those with low-scoring other letters (eg ZEA, ZOA, ZEIN, ZILA, ZONAE, ZANTE). There are a few Z words that also contain another power tile (JAZY, ZANJA, ZAX, ZEX, QUIZ). Although these appear to be very useful, in practice if you have two power tiles on your rack, it can be wiser to assess whether you might be better off playing them separately over two turns. There are also quite a few words with a double Z (BUZZ and FUZZ, for example) so you would need to use a blank to be able to play those.

Two-letter words

ZA s	pizza
ZO s	Tibetan breed of cattle

Three-letter words

ADZ	woodworking tool
AZO	of the divalent group -N:N-
BEZ	part of deer's horn
BIZ	business
CAZ	casual
COZ	cousin
CUZ	cousin
DZO s	variant of zo
FEZ	brimless tasselled cap
FIZ	variant of fizz
JIZ	wig
LEZ	offensive word for lesbian
LUZ	supposedly indestructible bone of the human body
MIZ	misery
MOZ	hex
POZ	positive
REZ	informal word for an instance of reserving
RIZ	(in some dialects) past form of rise
SAZ	Middle Eastern stringed instrument

SEZ   informal spelling of 'says'
SOZ   informal variant of 'sorry'
TIZ   state of confusion
WAZ   urinate
WIZ   short for wizard
WUZ   nonstandard spelling of 'was'
YEZ   yes
ZAG s   change direction sharply
ZAP s   kill (by shooting)
ZAX   tool for cutting roofing slate
ZEA s   corn silk
ZED s   British and New Zealand spoken form of the letter z
ZEE s   US spoken form of the letter z
ZEK s   Soviet prisoner
ZEL s   Turkish cymbal
ZEP s   type of long sandwich
ZEX   variant of zax
ZHO s   variant of zo
ZIG s   change direction sharply
ZIN s   short for zinfandel
ZIP s   zipper
ZIT s   spot or pimple
ZIZ   short sleep
ZOA   plural of zoon
ZOL s   South African slang for a cannabis cigarette
ZOO s   place where live animals are kept for show
ZUZ   ancient Hebrew silver coin
ZZZ s   informal word for 'sleep'

Four-letter words

ADZE s	DAZE s	GEEZ	LAZO s
AZAN s	DITZ	GIZZ	LAZY
AZON s	DOZE s	GRIZ	LEZZ
AZYM s	DOZY	HAZE s	LOLZ
BAZZ	DZHO s	HAZY	LULZ
BIZE s	FAZE s	HIZZ	LUTZ
BOZO s	FIZZ	IZAR s	MAZE s
BUZZ	FOZY	JAZY	MAZY
CAZH	FRIZ	JAZZ	MEZE s
CHEZ	FUTZ	JEEZ	MEZZ
CHIZ	FUZE s	JIZZ	MIZZ
COZE s	FUZZ	KAZI s	MOZE s
COZY	GAZE s	KUZU s	MOZO s
CZAR s	GAZY	LAZE s	MOZZ

MUZZ
MZEE s
NAZE s
NAZI s
OOZE s
OOZY
ORZO s
OUZO s
OYEZ
PHIZ
PIZE s
POZZ
PREZ
PUTZ
QUIZ
RAZE s
RAZZ
RITZ
RIZA s
RONZ
SITZ
SIZE s
SIZY

SPAZ
SWIZ
TIZZ
TOZE s
TREZ
TUZZ
TZAR s
VIZY
WAZZ
WHIZ
YUTZ
YUZU s
ZACK s
ZANY
ZARF s
ZARI s
ZATI s
ZEAL s
ZEBU s
ZEDA s
ZEIN s
ZERK s
ZERO s

> ### *Note*
> MZEE is a fantastic unexpected front hook for ZEE and one to definitely watch out for. It's so easily missed even if you know it.

ZEST s
ZETA s
ZEZE s
ZIFF s
ZILA s
ZILL s
ZIMB s
ZINC s
ZINE s
ZING s
ZITE
ZITI s
ZIZZ
ZOBO s
ZOBU s
ZOEA s

ZOIC
ZONA
ZONE s
ZONK s
ZOOM s
ZOON s
ZOOT
ZORI s
ZOUK s
ZULU s
ZUPA s
ZURF s
ZYGA
ZYME s

Five-letter words

ABUZZ
ADOZE
ADZED
AGAZE
AIZLE s
AMAZE s
ARROZ
ASSEZ

AVIZE s
AVYZE s
AZIDE s
AZIDO
AZINE s
AZLON s
AZOIC
AZOLE s

AZOTE s
AZOTH s
AZUKI s
AZURE s
AZURN
AZURY
AZYGY
AZYME s
BAIZA s
BAIZE s
BAZAR s
BAZOO s
BEZEL s
BEZES
BEZIL s
BEZZY
BIZZO s
BIZZY
BLAZE s

BLITZ
BONZA
BONZE s
BOOZE s
BOOZY
BORTZ
BRAZA s
BRAZE s
BRIZE s
BUAZE s
BUZZY
BWAZI s
CAPIZ
CEAZE s
CEZVE s
CHIZZ
CLOZE s
COBZA s
COLZA s

> ### *Note*
> It's worth being familiar with the handful of four- and five-letter Z words that end in TZ like BLITZ. Write them out from this list to familiarise yourself with them, and note similar forms such as FUTZ, LUTZ, PUTZ and DITZ, RITZ, SITZ.

COOZE s	GAZAR s	LEEZE	PUZEL s
COZED	GAZED	LEZES	PZAZZ
COZEN s	GAZER s	LEZZA s	RAZED
COZEY s	GAZON s	LEZZY	RAZEE s
COZIE s	GAZOO s	LOZEN s	RAZER s
CRAZE s	GHAZI s	MAIZE s	RAZOO s
CRAZY	GINZO s	MATZA s	RAZOR s
CROZE s	GIZMO s	MATZO s	REZES
CUZES	GLAZE s	MAUZY	RITZY
DARZI s	GLAZY	MAZED	ROZET s
DAZED	GLITZ	MAZER s	ROZIT s
DAZER s	GLOZE s	MAZEY	SADZA s
DIAZO s	GONZO s	MAZUT s	SAZES
DITZY	GRAZE s	MAZEY	SCUZZ
DIZEN s	GRIZE s	MEZZE s	SEAZE s
DIZZY	GROSZ	MEZZO s	SEIZA s
DOOZY	GYOZA s	MILTZ	SEIZE s
DOZED	HAFIZ	MIRZA s	SENZA
DOZEN s	HAMZA s	MIZEN s	SIZAR s
DOZER s	HAZAN s	MIZZY	SIZED
DURZI s	HAZED	MOTZA s	SIZEL s
ENZYM s	HAZEL s	MOZED	SIZER s
EZINE s	HAZER s	MUZAK s	SMAZE s
FAZED	HEEZE s	MUZZY	SOYUZ
FEAZE s	HERTZ	NAZIR s	SOZIN s
FEEZE s	HIZEN s	NEEZE s	SPAZA
FEZES	HUZZA s	NERTZ	SPAZZ
FEZZY	HUZZY	NIZAM s	SPITZ
FIZZY	IZARD s	NUDZH	SQUIZ
FORZA	IZZAT s	OOZED	SWIZZ
FORZE	JAZZY	OUZEL s	TAZZA s
FRITZ	JEEZE	OZEKI s	TAZZE
FRIZE s	KANZU s	OZONE s	TEAZE s
FRIZZ	KARZY	OZZIE s	TIZES
FROZE	KAZOO s	PEAZE s	TIZZY
FURZE s	KHAZI s	PEIZE s	TOAZE s
FURZY	KLUTZ	PHIZZ	TOPAZ
FUZED	KRANZ	PIEZO	TOUZE s
FUZEE s	KUDZU s	PIZED	TOUZY
FUZIL s	LAZAR s	PIZZA s	TOWZE s
FUZZY	LAZED	PLAZA s	TOWZY
GAUZE s	LAZZI	PLOTZ	TOZED
GAUZY	LAZZO	PONZU s	TOZIE s
GAZAL s	LEAZE s	POZZY	TROOZ
		PRIZE s	

ULZIEs
UNZIPs
VEZIRs
VIZIRs
VIZORs
VOZHDs
WALTZ
WANZEs
WAREZ
WAZIRs
WAZOOs
WEIZEs
WHIZZ
WINZEs
WIZENs
WIZES
WOOTZ
WOOZY
ZABRAs
ZAIDAs
ZAIDY
ZAIREs
ZAKATs

ZAMANs
ZAMBOs
ZAMIAs
ZANJAs
ZANTEs
ZANZAs
ZANZEs
ZAPPY
ZAXES
ZAYINs
ZAZENs
ZEBECs
ZEBRAs
ZEBUBs
ZENDOs
ZERDAs
ZESTY
ZEXES
ZHOMOs
ZIBETs
ZIGANs
ZILCH
ZILLAs

ZIMBIs
ZINCOs
ZINCY
ZINEBs
ZINGY
ZINKEs
ZINKY
ZIPPOs
ZIPPY
ZIRAMs
ZIZELs
ZIZIT
ZLOTE
ZLOTYs
ZOAEAs
ZOCCOs
ZOEAE
ZOEAL
ZOISMs
ZOISTs
ZOMBIs
ZONAE
ZONAL

ZONDAs
ZONED
ZONERs
ZOOEAs
ZOOEY
ZOOIDs
ZOOKS
ZOOTY
ZOPPA
ZOPPO
ZORILs
ZORROs
ZOWEE
ZOWIE
ZUPANs
ZUPPAs
ZUZIM
ZYGAL
ZYGON
ZYMIC

Six-letter words

ABLAZE
ABRAZOs
ADZING
ADZUKIs
AGAZED
AGNIZEs
AGRIZEs
AGRYZEs
AGUIZEs
ALTEZAs
AMAZED
AMAZONs
APOZEMs
ASSIZEs
AVIZED
AVYZED
AZALEAs
AZERTY
AZIONEs

AZOLLAs
AZONAL
AZONIC
AZOTED
AZOTIC
AZYGOS
BAIZED
BANZAIs
BARAZAs
BAZAARs
BAZAZZ
BAZOOMs
BAZZED
BAZZES
BEDAZEs
BEEZERs
BEGAZEs
BENZALs
BENZILs

BENZINs
BENZOLs
BENZYLs
BEZANTs
BEZAZZ
BEZOARs
BEZZIEs
BEZZLEs
BIZAZZ
BIZONEs
BIZZES
BLAIZE
BLAZARs
BLAZED
BLAZERs
BLAZONs
BLINTZ
BLOWZEs
BLOWZY

BONZER
BOOZED
BOOZERs
BOOZEY
BORZOIs
BRAIZEs
BRAZED
BRAZENs
BRAZERs
BRAZILs
BREEZEs
BREEZY
BRONZEs
BRONZY
BROUZEs
BUZUKIs
BUZZED
BUZZERs
BUZZES

BYZANT s
CEAZED
CHAZAN s
CHINTZ
CIZERS
COROZO s
CORYZA s
COUZIN s
COZIED
COZIER s
COZILY
COZING
COZZES
COZZIE s
CRAZED
CROZER s
CRUZIE s
CUZZES
CUZZIE s
CZAPKA s
DAZING
DAZZLE s
DEFUZE s
DEZINC s
DIAZIN s
DITZES
DIZAIN s
DONZEL s
DOOZER s
DOOZIE s
DORIZE s
DOZIER
DOZILY
DOZING s
DRAZEL s
DZEREN s
ECZEMA s
ENTREZ
ENZIAN s
ENZONE s
ENZYME s
EPIZOA
ERSATZ
EVZONE s

FAZING
FEAZED
FEEZED
FEZZED
FEZZES
FIZGIG s
FIZZED
FIZZEN s
FIZZER s
FIZZES
FIZZLE s
FLOOZY
FOOZLE s
FOZIER
FRANZY
FRAZIL s
FREEZE s
FRENZY
FRIEZE s
FRIZED
FRIZER s
FRIZZY
FROUZY
FROWZY
FROZEN
FUTZED
FUTZES
FUZING
FUZZED
FUZZES
FUZZLE s
GAZABO s
GAZANG s
GAZEBO s
GAZIER
GAZING s
GAZOON s
GAZUMP s
GEEZAH s
GEEZER s
GHAZAL s
GHAZEL s
GIZZEN s
GIZZES

> ## *Note*
> KUVASZ is a beautiful word for Scrabble. Who would have thought it would be possible to use a K, U, V, and Z in a single play?

GLAZED
GLAZEN
GLAZER s
GLITZY
GLOZED
GOZZAN s
GRAZED
GRAZER s
GROSZE
GROSZY
GUIZER s
GUTZER s
GUZZLE s
HALUTZ
HAMZAH s
HAZARD s
HAZIER
HAZILY
HAZING s
HAZMAT s
HAZZAN s
HEEZED
HEEZIE s
HIZZED
HIZZES
HOWZAT
HOWZIT
HUTZPA s
HUZOOR s
HUZZAH s
IMBIZO s
IODIZE s
IONIZE s
IZZARD s
JAZIES
JAZZBO s
JAZZED

JAZZER s
JAZZES
JEEZLY
JEZAIL s
JIZZES
KAIZEN s
KAMEEZ
KHAZEN s
KIBITZ
KLUTZY
KOLHOZ
KOLKOZ
KRANTZ
KUVASZ
KWANZA s
LAZIED
LAZIER
LAZIES
LAZILY
LAZING
LAZOED
LAZOES
LAZULI s
LEZZES
LEZZIE s
LIZARD s
LIZZIE s
LOZELL s
LUTZES
LUZERN s
LUZZES
MAHZOR s
MAMZER s
MATZAH s
MATZOH s
MATZOT
MAZARD s

MAZHBI s
MAZIER
MAZILY
MAZING
MAZOUT s
MAZUMA s
MEAZEL s
MEZAIL s
MEZCAL s
MEZUZA s
MIZUNA s
MIZZEN s
MIZZES
MIZZLE s
MIZZLY
MOMZER s
MOZING
MOZZES
MOZZIE s
MOZZLE s
MUZAKY
MUZHIK s
MUZJIK s
MUZZED
MUZZES
MUZZLE s
MZUNGU s
NAZIFY
NEEZED
NOZZER s
NOZZLE s
NUZZER s
NUZZLE s
NYANZA s
OOZIER
OOZILY
OOZING
OYEZES

OZAENA s
OZALID s
OZONIC
PACZKI s
PANZER s
PATZER s
PAZAZZ
PEAZED
PEIZED
PEZANT s
PHEEZE s
PHIZES
PHIZOG s
PIAZZA s
PIAZZE
PIZAZZ
PIZING
PIZZAZ
PIZZLE s
PODZOL s
POTZER s
POZOLE s
PREZES
PRIZED
PRIZER s
PUTZED
PUTZES
PUZZEL s
PUZZLE s
QUARTZ
QUAZZY
QUEAZY
QUEZAL s
QUINZE s
RANZEL s
RAZEED
RAZING
RAZURE s

RAZZED
RAZZES
RAZZIA s
RAZZLE s
REBOZO s
RESIZE s
REZERO s
REZONE s
REZZES
RHIZIC
RITZES
RIZARD s
RIZZAR s
RIZZER s
RIZZOR s
RONZER s
ROZZER s
SAZHEN s
SAZZES
SCAZON s
SCHIZO s
SCHIZY
SCHNOZ
SCOZZA s
SCRUZE s
SCUZZY
SEAZED
SEIZED
SEIZER s
SEIZIN s
SEIZOR s
SHAZAM
SHIRAZ
SHITZU s
SHVITZ
SIZIER
SIZING s
SIZISM s
SIZIST s
SIZZLE s
SLEAZE s
SLEAZO s
SLEAZY
SLEEZY

SNAZZY
SNEEZE s
SNEEZY
SNOOZE s
SNOOZY
SOZINE s
SOZZLE s
SOZZLY
SPELTZ
SPRITZ
STANZA s
STANZE s
STANZO s
STOOZE s
SUIVEZ
SYZYGY
TARZAN s
TEAZED
TEAZEL s
TEAZLE s
TENZON s
TIZWAS
TIZZES
TOAZED
TOLZEY s
TOUZED
TOUZLE s
TOWZED
TOZING
TREZES
TUZZES
TWEEZE s
TZADDI s
TZADIK s
TZETSE s
TZETZE s
TZURIS
UMFAZI s
UPGAZE s
UPSIZE s
VIZARD s
VIZIED
VIZIER s
VIZIES

Note

SYZYGY is unique in having three Ys behaving as vowels and no AEIOU.

VIZSLA s	ZANANA s	ZIBETH s	ZONING s
VIZZIE s	ZANDER s	ZIGGED	ZONKED
WANZED	ZANIED	ZIGZAG s	ZONOID s
WAZZED	ZANIER	ZILLAH s	ZONULA s
WAZZES	ZANIES	ZINCED	ZONULE s
WEAZEN s	ZANILY	ZINCIC	ZONURE s
WEIZED	ZAPATA	ZINCKY	ZOOEAE
WEZAND s	ZAPPED	ZINGED	ZOOEAL
WHEEZE s	ZAPPER s	ZINGEL s	ZOOIER
WHEEZY	ZARAPE s	ZINGER s	ZOOMED
WHIZZO	ZAREBA s	ZINKED	ZOONAL
WHIZZY	ZARIBA s	ZINNIA s	ZOONED
WIZARD s	ZARNEC s	ZIPOLA s	ZOONIC
WIZIER s	ZEALOT s	ZIPPED	ZOOZOO s
WIZZEN s	ZEATIN s	ZIPPER s	ZORINO s
WIZZES	ZEBECK s	ZIPTOP	ZOSTER s
WURZEL s	ZECHIN s	ZIRCON s	ZOUAVE s
WUZZLE s	ZELANT s	ZITHER s	ZOUNDS
YAKUZA	ZELOSO	ZIZITH	ZOYSIA s
YUTZES	ZENANA s	ZIZZED	ZUFOLI
ZABETA s	ZENDIK s	ZIZZES	ZUFOLO s
ZADDIK s	ZENITH s	ZIZZLE s	ZUZZIM
ZAFFAR s	ZEPHYR s	ZOAEAE	ZYDECO s
ZAFFER s	ZEREBA s	ZOARIA	ZYGOID
ZAFFIR s	ZERIBA s	ZOCALO s	ZYGOMA s
ZAFFRE s	ZEROED	ZODIAC s	ZYGOSE s
ZAFTIG	ZEROES	ZOECIA	ZYGOTE s
ZAGGED	ZEROTH	ZOETIC	ZYMASE s
ZAIDEH s	ZESTED	ZOFTIG	ZYMITE s
ZAIKAI s	ZESTER s	ZOMBIE s	ZYMOID
ZAMANG s	ZEUGMA s	ZONARY	ZYMOME s
ZAMBUK s	ZHOOSH	ZONATE	ZYTHUM s

SECTION 3

WORD FAMILIES

....

a concept developed by Allan Simmons

You wouldn't be reading this book if you weren't interested in learning some useful words for Scrabble! But not everyone finds it easy nor has the patience to learn tedious lists of words. I have always found it ideal to learn words in small, manageable sets that are going to have a high yield on the Scrabble board. To be manageable a list has to be fairly short and restricted to a single page. To have a high yield the list has to focus on words that are more likely to crop up during play.

It was with these criteria in mind that I first created the concept of word families – a sort of mind map of words centred around a short root word. Two- and three-letter words regularly appear on the board, so showing how those words can be developed is very relevant. And because all the words in the 'family' contain the embedded root word, clumps of words with similar patterns naturally occur and these can be grouped together for convenient learning. Through careful arrangement of family members with shorter words near the centre and longer words further away, it is also possible to reflect the natural extension of the shorter words into longer words (hooks). Generally, I try to show the words that start with the root word flowing to the right of each diagram and those that contain the root word flowing to the left, but this will always depend on the number of words in the family that start or end with the root word. The overall aim is to provide an aesthetically pleasing and useful arrangement of words of relevance to the game.

In selecting the best words to use as root words I have analysed the two letter words to ascertain those that produce the more useful and pleasing families. For example, there is little point in using the two-letter word IT because it will generate far too many words, and the 'IT' within longer words will not be a significant component of most of those words. Whereas a root word with a higher-scoring tile or an unusual combination of two-letters (eg KO, ZO, IO) generates shorter lists where the two-letter sequence for the most part remains a key component of the family members. Thus, the word families here are based on these words:

**AA AE AH AX BY CH EH EX FY GU HM IF IO
JA JO KI KO KY MY NY OF OH OX OY QUA UG
UP YO ZA ZO**

The maximum length of words selected for each family is mostly five, but sometimes four or six depending on the volume of words generated in each case. In order to keep the families uncluttered all -S plurals of words have been excluded but a small −S is shown alongside a word where an s can be added. The absence of an −S does not mean that a word cannot be pluralized because in some cases the plural may be something other than an -S. Inflections of verbs and plurals of words that take the form -ES have been included, providing they are within the length criteria.

I trust you find the word families of great use and interest to improve your Scrabble vocabulary. They've also been fun to compile and I'm sure I've learned one or two new words in the process as well. You might like to try and create further families yourself, making use of the extensive lists in this book to find the appropriate words.

Happy Families!

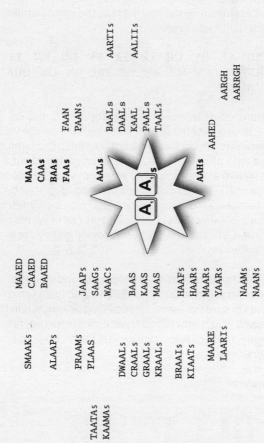

AARTIs
AALIIs

AARGH
AARRGH

FAAN
PAANs

BAALs
DAALs
KAAL
PAALs
TAALs

MAAs
CAAs
BAAs
FAAs

AALs

AAHs

AAHED

MAAED
CAAED
BAAED

JAAPs
SAAGs
WAACs

BAAS
KAAS
MAAS

HAAFs
HAARs
MAARs
YAARs

NAAMs
NAANs

SMAAKs
ALAAPs

PRAAMs
PLAAS

DWAALs
CRAALs
GRAALs
KRAALs

BRAAIs
KIAATs

MAARE
LAARIs

TAATAs
KAAMAs

s = word takes an –**S** extension

PSOAE
STOAE

ANSAE
ANTAE

CAESE

CAECA
FAENAs

TUBAE
PUPAE

ISNAE
ULNAE
URSAE

PILAE
RIMAE
MINAE
VITAE

LAEVO

VIAE
UVAE

PAEDOs

AEROs
AERY

FAERY

AECIA
AERIEs

SETAE
TELAE
VENAE

AQUAE
ZOEAE

NAEVEs
NAEVI

AESIR

AEDES
AEGIS

ZOAEAs

VAEs

FAE

AESC

AREAE
AURAE

KANAEs

ZONAE
COMAE

NAEs
MAEs

SAE

PAEANs
PAEONs

CLAES

BLAER
SPAERs
SPAED

E   **A**

SCRAEs
STRAEs
THRAE

URAEI

CYMAE
GYNAEs

COXAE
NOVAE
VOLAE

KAED
TAED

KAEs
TAEs
DAEs
GAEs

HAEs
WAEs
YAE

AEONs

ALAE

BLAEs
BRAEs
FRAE
SPAEs
SLAEs
THAE
TWAEs
WHAE

ALGAE
BIGAE
NUGAE

GAEN
HAEN
HAEMs
HAETs

GAED
HAED

BAELs
TAELs

BAAED
CAAED
MAAED

HOAED
TEAED

OLPAE

RUGAE
TOGAE

LAERs

POTAEs
PORAEs
PARAE
MORAE
MARAEs

MAERLs

s = word takes an –S extension

A₁ H₄ s

AHA AAHs AHIs YAHs HAHs DAHs FAHs PAHs LAHs RAHs NAH BAH

AHEAD
AHEAP
AHENT
AHINT
AHIND
AHING
AHIGH
AHOLDs
AHULL

AHURUs

SPAHIs

OBEAHs

DAWAHs
SAWAHs
TAVAHs

LATAHs
LOTAHs

AAHED
AHED
AHEM
AHOY

YEAHs

YAHOOs
WAHOOs

BEKAHs
NIKAHs
SOKAHs

MWAH
WAAH

AYAHs
NYAH

RAYAHs
RAJAHs
PUJAHs

TAHRs
TAHAs
MAHA
HAHAs

KAHALs
NAHALs
LAHALs
LAHARs

DADAHs

HORAHs
TORAHs

DAHLs

ODAHs

PRAHUs

ARRAH

GERAHs
MARAHs
SURAHs
SYRAHs

EPHAHs

SHAHs

BLAHs

OPAHs

RAHED

RAHUIs

OMRAHs
UMRAHs

SUBAHs

BAHUTs

BAHUs
BAHTs

NOAHs
WOAH

AMAHs

DONAHs
MYNAHs

ALMAHs
BIMAHs
UMMAHs

BELAHs
SELAHs
SOLAHs
GALAHs

MAHOEs
MAHUAs
MAHWAs

CAHOWs

OMLAHs

SAHIBs
SAHEBs

s = word takes an –**s** extension

ADDAX

GALAX
MALAX
HAPAX
PANAX
LIMAX
BORAX
HYRAX

AXIAL
AXILE
AXITEs

ATAXY

BRAXY
FLAXY

AXING

AXLED

AXIOMs
AXONEs

AXAL
AXELs
AXILs
AXLEs
AXIS
AXONs

AXIOMs
AXIONs

FLAX

AXED

AXEs

SAXEs

AXMAN
AXMEN

COAX
HOAX

FAX
MAX
RAX
TAX
WAX

A_1 X_8

LAX
PAX
SAX
ZAX

FAXES
MAXES
RAXES
TAXES
WAXES

TAXERs
WAXERs
LAXER

LAXES
PAXES
SAXES
ZAXES

FAXED
MAXED
RAXED
TAXED
WAXED

WAXY
JAXY

WAXEN

JAXIEs

TAXA
TAXIs
MAXIs

RETAX
REWAX
RELAX

LAXLY

CAXONs
TAXONs

TAXOLs
TAXORs
TAXUS

MAXIMs

UNTAX
DEWAX

s = word takes an **–s** extension

DEBYEs

OUTBY   BYWAYs
FLYBYs BYLAWs

INBY   INBYE   BYSSI
UPBY   UPBYE

ABYEs   ABYSMs   **BYEs**

BABY   **ABYs**   BYRLs   BYDEs   BYDED
GABY   BYKEs   BYKED
                    B₃ Y₄ s   BYREs
                                    BYTEs

DOBY   ORBY   SIBYLs
GOBY   JUMBY   BILBY
MOBY   LAMBY   RUBY
TOBY   LIMBY   BUSBY
                    RUGBY

DERBY   DEBBY   BOBBY   BUBBY
HERBY   WEBBY   COBBY   CUBBY
                    DOBBY
GLEBY   COMBY
GLOBY   WOMBY   FABBY   FUBBY
                    GABBY
DAUBY   GOBBY   HUBBY
MAUBY   COLBYs   HOBBY
                            LOBBY
CORBY   BARBY   MOBBY
FORBY   CARBY   NOBBY   NUBBY   RIBBY
        WARBY   RUBBY
BOOBY   SUBBY
GOOBY   KIRBY   CABBY   TUBBY
LOOBY
                            TABBY
                            YABBY   YOBBY

s = word takes an −S extension

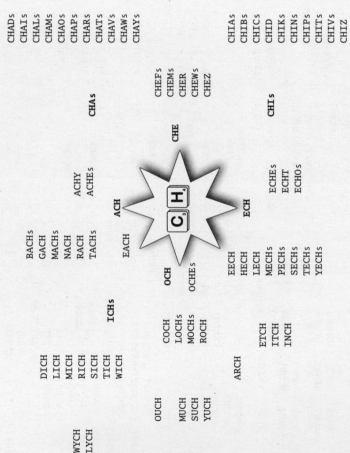

CHA s
CHAD s, CHAI s, CHAL s, CHAM s, CHAO s, CHAP s, CHAR s, CHAT s, CHAV s, CHAW s, CHAY s

CHOC s, CHOG s, CHON s, CHOP s, CHOU, CHOW s

CHUB s, CHUG s, CHUM s, CHUR, CHUT s

CHE
CHEF s, CHEM s, CHER, CHEW s, CHEZ

CHI s
CHIA s, CHIB s, CHIC s, CHID, CHIK s, CHIN s, CHIP s, CHIT s, CHIV s, CHIZ

ACH
ACHY, ACHE s
BACH s, GACH, MACH s, NACH, RACH, TACH s
EACH

ECH
ECHE s, ECHT, ECHO s
EECH, HECH, LECH, MECH s, PECH s, SECH s, TECH s, YECH s

OCH
OCHE s
COCH, LOCH s, MOCH s, ROCH
ETCH, ITCH, INCH
ARCH

ICH s
DICH, LICH, MICH, RICH, SICH, TICH, WICH

OUCH
MUCH, SUCH, YUCH
WYCH, LYCH

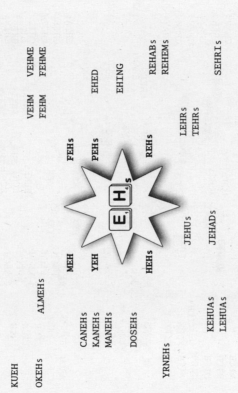

FOEHN s

VEHME
FEHME

VEHM   EHED
FEHM   EHING

REHAB s
REHEM s

SEHRI s

LEHR s
TEHR s

FEH s

PEH s

REH s

E_1 H_4 s

MEH

YEH

HEH s

JEHU s

JEHAD s

KUEH

OKEH s

ALMEH s

CANEH s
KANEH s
MANEH s

DOSEH s

YRNEH s

KEHUA s
LEHUA s

s = word takes an **–S** extension

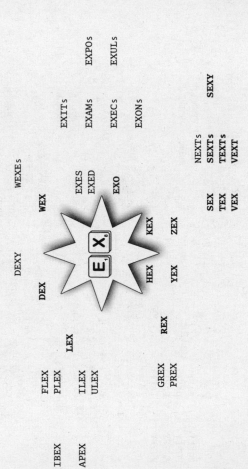

EXPOs
EXULs

EXITs
EXAMs
EXECs
EXONs

SEXY

WEXEs

EXES
EXED

EXO

NEXTs
SEXTs
TEXTs
VEXT

WEX

KEX
ZEX

SEX
TEX
VEX

DEX

HEX
YEX

DEXY

REX

LEX

FLEX
PLEX

ILEX
ULEX

GREX
PREX

IBEX

APEX

s = word takes an **–S** extension

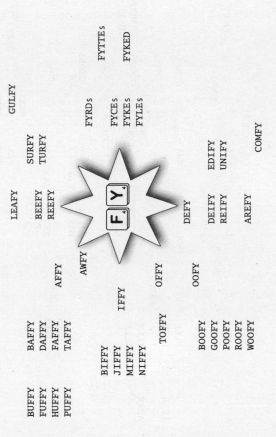

BUFFY
FUFFY
HUFFY
PUFFY

BAFFY
DAFFY
FAFFY
TAFFY

BIFFY
JIFFY
MIFFY
NIFFY

IFFY

AFFY

AWFY

LEAFY

BEEFY
REEFY

SURFY
TURFY

GULFY

FYRDs

FYCEs
FYKEs
FYLEs

FYTTEs

FYKED

DEFY

OOFY

OFFY

TOFFY

BOOFY
GOOFY
POOFY
ROOFY
WOOFY

DEIFY
REIFY

AREFY

EDIFY
UNIFY

COMFY

s = word takes an **–S** extension

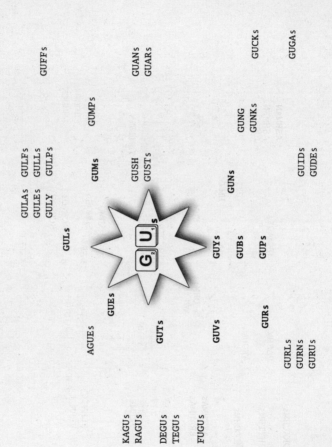

GUFFs

GUANs
GUARs

GUCKs

GUGAs

GUMPs

GULAs GULFs
GULEs GULLs
GULY GULPs

GUMs

GUSH
GUSTs

GUNG
GUNKs

GULs

GUIDs
GUDEs

GUNs

AGUEs

GUEs

GUYs
GUBs
GUPs

GUTs

GUVs

GURs

GURLs
GURNs
GURUs

KAGUs
RAGUs

DEGUs
TEGUs

FUGUs

s = word takes an –**S** extension

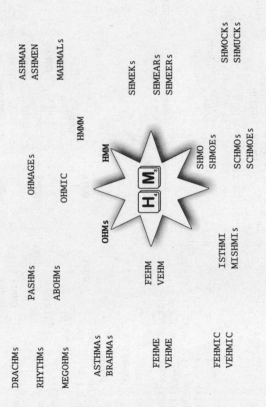

DRACHMs

RHYTHMs

MEGOHMs

ASHMAN
ASHMEN

MAHMALs

OHMAGEs

PASHMs

ABOHMs

OHMIC

HMMM

HMM

SHMEKs

SEIMEARs
SEIMEERs

SHMOCKs
SHMUCKs

OHMs

SHMO
SHMOEs

SCHMOs
SCHMOEs

ASTHMAs
BRAHMAs

FEHM
VEHM

FEHME
VEHME

FEHMIC
VEHMIC

ISTHMI
MISHMIs

s = word takes an –S extension

CLIFTs CLIFFs
GLIFTs GLIFFs
GRIFTs GRIFFs
WHIFTs WHIFFs
SNIFTs SNIFFs

DRIFTs SKIFFs
SHIFTs SPIFFs
SWIFTs STIFFs
        TRIFF

        QUIFFs
        QUOIFs

SPIFs

WIFIEs   FIFTY
                                    FIFTHs
IFTARs   MIFTY
                    NIFTY
BIFFOs   RIFTY

FIFED   FIFEs   BIFFs   WIFTY
FIFERs   LIFEs   DIFFs
LIFERs   NIFEs   JIFFs
         RIFE   KIFF
RIFER   WIFEs   MIFFs   MIFFY
WIFED   NIFFs   NIFFY
WIFEYs   **IFF** RIFFs
                   TIFFs
COIFs   IFFY   VIFFs   BIFFY
CUIFs   BIFFY
          I F s
                   ZIFFs   JIFFY
GIFTs   **GIFs**
RIFTE   **DIFs**
          SIF s **KIFs**
                     RIFs
KNIFEs

RIFLEs

BIFID
        LIFTs
VIFDAs RIFTs
        SIFTs
        TIFTs

        CALIFs   KAIFs
        KALIFs   NAIFs
                 WAIFs
        METIFs
        MOTIFs   WAIFTs

        GONIFs

        SERIFs

DEIFY   DEIF
NEIFs
REIFs
SEIFs

REIFY

EDIFY   ALIFs

UNIFY

PREIFs
TREIF

s = word takes an –S extension

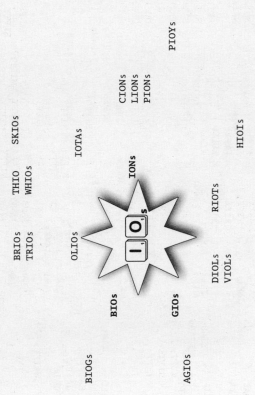

PIOYs

CIONs
LIONs
PIONs

SKIOs

IOTAs

HIOIs

THIO
WHIOs

IONs

RIOTs

BRIOs
TRIOs

OLIOs

DIOLs
VIOLs

BIOs

GIOs

BIOGs

AGIOs

s = word takes an –**S** extension

GANJAs
HODJAs
KHOJAs
NINJAs
OUIJAs
POOJAs
RIOJAs
THUJAs
WILJAs
ZANJAs

PUJAHs

RAJAHs

JALAPs
JALOPs

JAUKs
JAUPs

JAUNTs

JAFFAs

JAGGY
JAGERs
JAGIRs
JAGRAs

JAVELs

JAVAs
JAFAs
JAGAs

JACALs

JACKY

JAGGs

JAGs

JAPs

JAPED
JAPERs
JAPANs

JADED

JAAPs
JAPEs

JADEs

JATOs

JASPEs
JASEYs
JAXIEs
JAZZY

JASPs
JASS
JASY
JAXY
JAZY
JAZZ

JAKEYs

JANEs
JANNs

JANNY
JANTY

JAMMY

JAMBEs
JAMBO
JAMBUs

JAMES
JAMON

JACKs

JARKs
JARLs
JARPs

JARULs
JARTAs

AJAR

HEJABs
HIJABs

JABOTs

JABs

JARs

JAWs

ROJAKs

UNJAMs

JAI
JAKs
JAMs

JAILs
JAKEs
JAMBs

JAYs

JAWED
JAWANs

QAJAQs

BAJANs
YOJANs

PUJAs

RAJAs

SOJAs

| J | A |

s = word takes an –S extension

JODELs

JOCKOs
JOCKY

JOKOL
JOKERs
JOKEY

JONTY
JOTTY

JOLTY
JOLLY
JOWLY

JOCKs
JOCOs
JOKEs
JOKY

JOULEs
JOUALs
JOUGs
JONES

JOMONs

JOSH
JOSS

JOBEs
JOLEs
JOLTs
JOLLs
JOWLs

JOEYs   JOOKs
         JOUKs

JOURs

JOMOs
JOINs
JOHNs
JONGs

JORAMs
JORUMs

JOTUNs

JOYs

JOBs
JOGs

JOLs
JOWs

JOEs

JORs

JOTs

JOTAs

SJOE

DOJOs
GAJOs
SIJOs
MOJOs

FJORDs

MAJORs

JOINTs
JOISTs
JOUSTs

JOWARs

ENJOYs

JOYED
JOBED
JOKED
JOLED
JOWED

BANJOs
GADJOs
SHOJO

BIJOUs
SAJOUs

CAJON
REJON

KAKIs
MAKIs
RAKIs
SAKIs
TAKIs

PIKIs
TIKIs
WIKIs

AKIN

SKIDs
SKIMs
SKINs
SKIPs
SKITs

SKIs
SKIOs

MOKIs
HOKIs

KIDs

KINAs   KINDs
KINEs   KINGs
KINOs   KINKs

KIBEs

KINs

KIPEs
KIPPs

KIPs

KITEs   KISH
KITHs   KISS
        KISTs

KITs

K₃ I₁ s

KIRs

KIRNs   KICKs
KIRKs   KIKEs

KIFs

KIFF

KIWIs

KIVAs

KILD
KILLs
KILNs
KILOs
KILPs
KILTs

KIEFs
KIERs
KIEVs

s = word takes an –**S** extension

K O (tiles)

KOTCH
KOTOWs
KOBANs
KOGALs
KOOKY
KOKERs
KOKRAs
KOKAMs
KOKUMs
KOPEKs

KOALAs
KOLAs
KOLOs KOTOs
KOBOs KOROs
KOOKs
KOJIs

SKOALs
SKOOLs
KOELs
KOANs
KOAPs
KOBs
KONs
IKONs
KOND
KONKs
KONDOs
KONBUs
KOMBUs

JOKOL
SOKOLs
SKOGs
SKOLs

KOSES
KOSS
KOSs **KOAs**
KORs
KORAs
KOREs
KOROs
KORUs
KOORIs
KOURAs

EIKONs
DYKONs
KORAI
KORATs
KORMAs
KORUN

NKOSIs
KOIs
KOPs
KOPHs
KOKAs
KOHAs
KOHLs
KOHEN

SEKOS
ASKOS
ASKOI
KOINEs
KOFFs
KOPJEs
KOPPAs

HIKOIs
KIKOIs
YAKOWs
KOWs
KOFTAs
SKOFFs
SKOSH
SKORTs

DAIKOs
MAIKOs
TAIKOs
PEKOEs

BERKO
MILKOs
SHAKOs

ALKOs
BOKOs
TOKOs
MOKOs
MAKOs
YUKOs

IROKOs
CHOKOs
SMOKOs

DONKOs
BUNKOs
PINKOs
SANKOs
PANKOs

BUCKOs
DECKOs
GECKOs
JOCKOs
SOCKOs
SICKOs
WACKOs
YUCKO

DEKKOs

s = word takes an −S extension

KYNDs
KYNE

KYLEs
KYPEs
KYTEs

KYBOs

KYEs
KYUs

KYAKs
KYARs
KYATs

K Y

SKYFs
SKYRs

SKY

ESKY

FIKY

ICKY
INKY

OAKY

CAKY
LAKY
TAKY

ALKY

COKY
JOKY
POKY
ROKY

PUKY
YUKY

s = word takes an **−S** extension

FOAMY
LOAMY

PREMY

DORMY
GORMY
WORMY

BOOMY
COOMY
DOOMY
ROOMY

BEAMY
REAMY
SEAMY

BLIMY
SLIMY

EMYDEs
EMYS

EMYDs

BALMY
CALMY
MALMY
PALMY

WOMYN

KUMYS

ATIMY
ATOMY
ANOMY

ENEMY

GAUMY

COMMY

GERMY

MOMMY

POMMY

SWAMY

TOMMY

FILMY
FLAMY

PLUMY
SPUMY

PIGMY
PYGYM

STYMY
STIMY

GRIMY
PRIMY

DOMY
HOMY
SOMY

BARMY
ARMY

GAMY

ELMY

LIMY

RIMY

DEMY

SUMY
FUMY
PUMY

AMYLs

MYCs

M₃ Y₄

FEMMY
GEMMY
JEMMY
EMMYs

JIMMY
IMMY

GAMMY
JAMMY

HAMMY
LAMMY
MAMMY

RAMMY
SAMMY
TAMMY

GUMMY
DUMMY
LUMMY
MUMMY
NUMMY
RUMMY

TUMMY
YUMMY

MYAL   MYALLs

MYNAs   MYNAHs   MYLARs

MYTHs   MYTHI
          MYTHY   THYMY

MYXOs

MYSIDs

MYRRHs

MYOIDs

MYOMAs

MYOPEs
MYOPS
MYOPY

s = word takes an −**S** extension

NYAFFs
NYALAs
NYLONs
NYMPHs
NYSSAs

ANYONs

NYAH
NYAS

CANY
MANY
WANY
ZANY

NYEs **NYED**

NYING

ONYX

ANY **NYM**

BONY
CONY
MONY
PONY PUNY
TONY TUNY
LUNY

MINY
PINY
TINY
LINY
VINY
WINY

ATONY

STONY

SNYEs

ONY

SNY

EBONY

SPINY

TWINY

AWNY

DENY
RENY

GYNY

FAWNY
LAWNY
TAWNY
YAWNY

CORNY
HORNY
PORNY

CRONY
DRONY

IRONY

AGONY

SHINY
WHINY

DOWNY
POWNY
TOWNY

TEENY
WEENY

BEANY
LEANY
MEANY

GYNNY

FERNY

BARNY
CARNY

CURNY

GOONY
LOONY
MOONY

BONNY
DONNY
NONNY
SONNY

BANYAs
BUNYAs

NONYLs
VINYLs

GONYS

NOUNY

BRINY
BLINY

PEONY
PIONY

RAINY

MEINY
VEINY

BENNY
FENNY
GENNY
HENNY
JENNY
NINNY
PENNY
TENNY
WENNY

FINNY
GINNY
HINNY
LINNY
MINNY
NINNY
PINNY
TINNY

BUNNY
DUNNY
FUNNY
GUNNY
NUNNY

CANNY
DANNY
FANNY
JANNY
NANNY

PHONY

PUNNY
RUNNY
SUNNY
TUNNY

s = word takes an –**S** extension

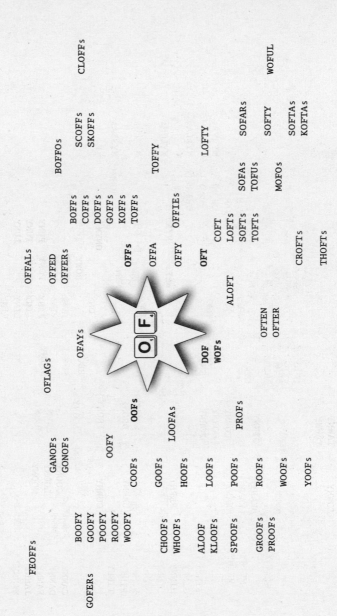

GOFERs

FEOFFs

OFFALs

OFFED
OFFERs

BOFFOs

SCOFFs
SKOFFs

CLOFFs

BOFFs
COFFs
DOFFs
GOFFs
KOFFs
TOFFs

TOFFY

SOFARs

SOFTY

WOFUL

SOFAs
TOFUs

MOFOs

SOFTAs
KOFTAs

OFFIEs

LOFTY

OFFs

OFFA

OFFY

OFT

COFT
LOFTs
SOFTs
TOFTs

CROFTs

THOFTs

ALOFT

OFTEN
OFTER

GANOFs
GONOFs

OOFY

OFLAGs

OFAYs

O₁ F₄

DOF
WOFs

OOFs

LOOFAs

PROFs

BOOFY
GOOFY
POOFY
ROOFY
WOOFY

COOFs

GOOFs

HOOFs

LOOFs

POOFs

ROOFs

WOOFs

YOOFs

CHOOFs
WHOOFs

ALOOF
KLOOFs

SPOOFs

GROOFs
PROOFs

s = word takes an –S extension

ALOHAs
AROHAs

KOHEN
COHENs
COHABs

COHOEs
COHOGs

BOHOs
COHOs
MOHOs
SOHO
TOHO

OHIAs

OHONE
OHING

OHED

OHMIC

ABOHMs

OHMs

OHMs

NOHOW

NOH

OHO

OOHED

HOHs

POHED
HOHED

POHs

HOHA
KOHAs

EVOHE

OOHs

OHO

FOH

PHOH

BUTOHs

BOHEAs

BOOHs
POOHs

BOHs

DOHs

SOHs

FOHNs
JOHNs

DOHYOs

LOHANs

KOHLs
MOHRs

MOHELs
MOHUAs
MOHURs

SOHURs

s = word takes an **–S** extension

			WOXEN
			BOXEN
			BOXERs

		WOX	BOXES	BOXED
		BOX	COXES	COXED
		COX	LOXES	LOXED
		LOX	FOXES	FOXED
COXA		FOX	HOXES	HOXED
MOXAs		HOX	POXES	POXED
		POX		

NOXAL

			NOXES	OXIDEs
BOXY			GOXES	OXIMEs
COXY				OXBOWs
DOXY			OXIC	OXEYEs
FOXY			OXIDs	OXLIPs
POXY			OXIMs	OXTERs
			OXEN	
			OXERs	
			OXES	

O₁ X₈

OXIES

VOXELs

BOXLAs	NOX		SOX
BOXTY	GOX	OXO	VOX

FLOX   OXY

EPOXY

PROXY   DEOXY

	PHLOX
EMBOX	DETOX
INBOX	RETOX
UNBOX	REDOX
	XEROX

TOXICs
TOXINs

COXAE
COXAL
DOXIEs
MOXIEs
FOXIEs

COXIBs

COYED
BOYED
HOYED
NOYED
JOYED
TOYED

DECOYs
UNCOY

COYER
FOYERs
TOYERs

SHOYUs

COYPUs

BOYAU
COYAUs
NOYAUs

POYOUs

COYLY
DOYLY

DOYENs

GOYIM

NOYES

SOYUZ

TOYONs

COYs
DOYs
GOYs
FOYs
JOYs
NOYs

OYEs

OYERs
OYEZ

BOYARs
BOYLAs
BOYSY

BOYFs
BOYGs

BOYOs
TOYOs

POBOYs

BOYs
TOYs
LOYs

MOYLs

HOYAs
MOYAs
SOYAs

BUOYs

TROYs

CLOYs
PLOYs

PIOYs

HOYs
MOYs
SOYs

LOYAL
ROYALs

STROYs

CLOYEs
PLOYEs

PIOYEs
PEEOYs

AHOY

FOYLEs
GOYLEs
HOYLEs
MOYLEs
SOYLEs

ACCOYs
ALLOYs
ANNOYs

ENJOYs
ENVOYs
SAVOYs

DUROYs

SEPOYs
TEPOYs

SLOYDs

FOYNEs
ROYNEs

PROYNs

ROYSTs

POYNTs
POYSEs

EQUANTs
EQUATEs

QUANTA
QUARRY
QUAERES
QUARER

QUANTs
QUARTs
QUARE
QUATEs
QUALE
QUAILs
QUAIRs
QUALMs

QUARTEs
QUARTOs
QUARTZ

QUALIA

QUAYD

QUALMY

QUARKs
QUAKEs
QUAKY
QUACKs

QUAKED
QUAKERs
QUAVERs

QUACKY

QUATREs

QUASARs

SQUAREs

EQUALI

EQUALs

QUAIs
QUAYs

Q U A

QUASH
QUASI
QUASS

QUAINT
QUATCH
QUAICHs
QUAIGHs

SQUAILs
SQUALLs

QUATs
QUADs
QUAGs

QUAFFs

SQUAMA
SQUAMEs

AQUAs

AQUAE

QUAZZY
QUAGGY

QUAGGAs
QUAHOGs

ASQUAT

QUANGOs

DIQUATs
LOQUATs

SQUASH
SQUAWKs
SQUARKs

SQUABs
SQUADs
SQUATs
SQUAWs

s = word takes an **–s** extension

SCUGs
SKUGs

GLUGs
PLUGs
SLUGs

CHUGs
THUGs

SMUGs
SNUGs
SPUGs

DRUGs
FRUGs
TRUGs

LUGEs
HUGE

HUGY

UGLY

LUGs HUGs MUGGs

MUGs
NUGs
PUGs

BUGs TUGs DUGs

UGHs VUGs

AUGH EUGE
EUGHs
PUGH
SUGHs
VUGHs

VUGGs

FUGs SUGs

FUGUs SUGOs

GUGAs JUGA RUGA YUGAs

JUGs RUGs YUGs

U₁ G₂ s

s = word takes an **−S** extension

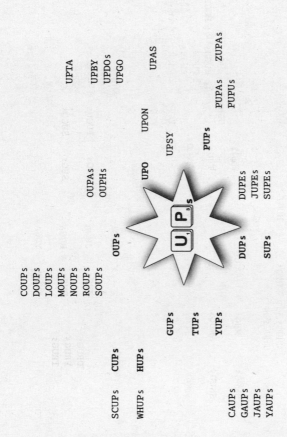

UPTA

UPBY
UPDOs
UPGO

UPAS

PUPAs
PUPUs

ZUPAs

UPON

UPSY

PUPs

UPO

OUPAs
OUPHs

UPO

DUPEs
JUPEs
SUPEs

OUPs

DUPs

SUPs

COUPs
DOUPs
LOUPs
MOUPs
NOUPs
ROUPs
SOUPs

GUPs

TUPs

YUPs

SCUPs

WHUPs

CUPs

HUPs

CAUPs
GAUPs
JAUPs
YAUPs

s = word takes an –S extension

YOJANs

YOGEEs

YOGIC
YOGINs

YOWED
YOWLEs

YODELs
YODLEs

YOGAs   YOKED
YOGIs   YOKERs
YOGHs   YOKELs
            YOKUL

YOWEs   YODE   YOLKY
YOWLs   YODHs
                        YOICKs

DOHYOs   **YOWs**   **YODs**

HYOIDs   YOBBY   YOREs   YOKEs
PYOID   YOBBOs   YORKs   YOCKs
MYOIDs   **YOBs**   YORPs   YOLKs
                                                                    YOLD
PSYOPs   **YOKs**

MYOMAs   YOOFs
MYOPEs   YOOPs
MYOPS   YOND
MYOPY   AYONT   YONT   **YON**
                                    YONIs
GYOZAs   GUYOTs   **YOM**   **YOUs**

            EYOTs   YOURs   YOUNGs
            PYOTs   YOUKs   YOUTHs
BOYOs   RYOTs   YOUSE
TOYOs
            YOMPs
ANYONs
TOYONs   YOMIM   YOURN
RAYONs   YOURTs
SAYONs   KAYOs
            MAYOs

MAYORs
PAYORs

            BAYOUs
            POYOUs

YONKS
YONIC

s = word takes an **–S** extension

ZABRAs

ZANJAs
ZANZAs
ZANZEs

ZAZENs

ZAMIAs
ZAMANs
ZAMBOs

ZANTEs

ZACKs

ZANY

ZARFs

ZAYINs

ZAKATs

ZAIDAs
ZAIDY

ZAIREs

ZARIs
ZATIs

ZAXES

ZAPPY

ZAX   ZAGs   ZAPs

HAMZAs

Z **A**s

RIZAs

HUZZAs
LEZZAs
PIZZAs
TAZZAs

IZARDs

IZZATs

PZAZZ

AZANs

CZARs
TZARs
IZARs

HAZANs

MUZAKs

SIZARs

NIZAMs

SPAZA
SADZAs

SEIZAs
SENZA

COBZAs
COLZAs

FORZA

GYOZAs

BAIZAs

BONZA

BRAZAs

PLAZAs

MIRZAs

MATZAs

MOTZAs

BAZARs
LAZARs
GAZARs

GAZALs

s = word takes an **–S** extension

GINZOs
GONZOs
PIEZO
DIAZOs

BIZZOs
LAZZO
MEZZOs

BOZOs
LAZOs
MOZOs
OUZOs
ORZOs

ZOBOs
ZOBUs
ZOUKs

ZOISMs
ZOISTs

ZOIC

ZOMBIs

ZOWIE
ZOWEE

ZOEAL
ZOEAE
ZOAEAs
ZOOEAs

ZOPPA
ZOPPO
ZOCCOs
ZORROs

ZOEAs

ZOOEY

ZORILs

ZOOIDs

ZOOKs
ZOOTY

ZORIs

ZONAE
ZONAL

ZONED
ZONERs
ZONDAs

Z O s

ZOLs

ZOOMs
ZOONs
ZOOT

ZOA

ZOOs

AZO

DZOs

ZONA

ZONEs

ZONKs

MATZOs

AZOLEs
AZOIC
AZOTHs
AZOTEs

RAZORs
VIZORs

AZONs

GAZONs

GAZOOs
BAZOOs
KAZOOs
RAZOOs
WAZOOs

OZONEs

BEGINNINGS AND ENDINGS

- This section deals with grouping words together according to similar beginnings and endings, to enable players to learn similar words in a more manageable way.

- There are lists of words based on common prefixes and suffixes which are especially useful when you are looking for a bonus word on your rack.

- There are lists of words ending the vowels A, I, O and U which are often less easy to think of during play. Among them will be plenty of common words that are easy to overlook as well as some obscure words and words adopted from foreign languages.

- You may also be fascinated by the list of words that have unique two-letter beginning and endings. You'll probably have no trouble remembering these because they are so unusual in form.

Prefixes

It's very useful to be aware of the common prefixes in English, as these provide a wealth of opportunities for building on words that are already on the board. Moreover, they can help players find bonus words on their rack by forming prefixes and seeing if the remaining letters, maybe using a letter on the board, fit with it to make a valid seven or eight-letter word. The following lists show the most common prefixes in English, along with the valid words of seven and eight letters that they form. Only those words which can be formed by adding a prefix to a valid word are shown. Words that are blatantly not a use of the prefix in question (eg REACHED is not RE-ACHED, and BEDREST is not BE-DREST) are excluded. In some cases the validity of the word for the specific prefix may be arguable, in which case the word is included for completeness.

Words beginning with the prefix ANTI

An s shows that a word can take a valid –S hook.

Words are excluded that happen to take the prefix ANTI but are not genuine ANTI- words. Thus words such as ANTICAL ANTIQUEY (CAL and QUEY are valid words) are omitted.

Seven-letter ANTI words

ANTIAIR	ANTIFOG	ANTILOG s	ANTISEX
ANTIBUG	ANTIFUR	ANTIMAN	ANTITAX
ANTICAR	ANTIGAY	ANTIMEN	ANTIWAR
ANTICLY	ANTIGEN s	ANTIPOT	
ANTIFAT	ANTIGUN	ANTIRED	
ANTIFLU	ANTIJAM	ANTISAG	

Eight-letter ANTI words

ANTIACNE	ANTIGANG	ANTIMINE	ANTIRAPE
ANTIATOM s	ANTIGENE s	ANTIMONY	ANTIRIOT
ANTIBIAS	ANTIHERO	ANTIMUON s	ANTIROCK
ANTIBODY	ANTIKING s	ANTINODE s	ANTIROLL
ANTIBOSS	ANTILEAK	ANTINOME s	ANTIRUST s
ANTICITY	ANTILEFT	ANTINUKE s	ANTISERA
ANTICOLD	ANTILIFE	ANTIPHON s	ANTISHIP
ANTICULT s	ANTILOCK	ANTIPILL	ANTISKID
ANTIDOTE s	ANTILOGY	ANTIPOLE s	ANTISLIP
ANTIDRUG	ANTIMALE	ANTIPOPE s	ANTISMOG
ANTIDUNE s	ANTIMASK s	ANTIPORN	ANTISMUT
ANTIFOAM	ANTIMERE s	ANTIPYIC s	ANTISNOB s

ANTISPAM	ANTITANK	ANTIWEAR	
ANTISTAT s	ANTITYPE s	ANTIWEED	

Words beginning with the prefix BE

An s shows that a word can take a valid –S hook.

Words are excluded that happen to take the prefix BE but are not genuine BE- words. Thus words such as BESTING (BEST+ING) and BEDREST (BED+REST) are omitted.

Six-letter BE words

BEBUNG s	BEGAZE s	BELAUD s	BESEEM s
BECALL s	BEGIFT s	BELEAP s	BESEEN
BECALM s	BEGILD s	BELEED	BESIDE s
BECAME	BEGILT	BELIED	BESIGH s
BECLOG s	BEGIRD s	BELIEF s	BESING s
BECOME s	BEGIRT	BELIER s	BESMUT s
BECURL s	BEGLAD s	BELIKE	BESNOW s
BEDAMN s	BEGNAW s	BELIVE	BESORT s
BEDASH	BEGOES	BELONG s	BESPAT
BEDAUB s	BEGONE	BELOVE s	BESPED
BEDAZE s	BEGRIM s	BEMAUL s	BESPIT s
BEDECK s	BEGULF s	BEMEAN s	BESPOT s
BEDELL s	BEGUNK s	BEMETE s	BESTAR s
BEDROP s	BEHALF	BEMIRE s	BESTIR s
BEDRUG s	BEHAVE s	BEMIST s	BESTOW s
BEDUCK s	BEHEAD s	BEMIXT	BESTUD s
BEDUMB s	BEHELD	BEMOAN s	BESUNG
BEDUNG s	BEHEST s	BEMOCK s	BETAKE s
BEDUST s	BEHIND s	BEMOIL s	BETEEM s
BEDYED	BEHOLD s	BEMUSE s	BETIDE s
BEFALL s	BEHOOF s	BENAME s	BETIME s
BEFELL	BEHOTE s	BENUMB s	BETOIL s
BEFLAG s	BEHOVE s	BEPELT s	BETOOK
BEFLEA s	BEHOWL s	BEPITY	BETOSS
BEFOAM s	BEJADE s	BEPUFF s	BETRAY s
BEFOOL s	BEKISS	BERAKE s	BETRIM s
BEFORE	BEKNOT s	BERATE s	BETROD
BEFOUL s	BELACE s	BEREFT	BEWAIL s
BEFRET s	BELADY	BERIME s	BEWARE s
BEGALL s	BELATE s	BESANG	BEWEEP s

BEWENT   BEWORM s   BEYOND s
BEWEPT   BEWRAP s

Seven-letter BE words

BEBLOOD s   BEGUILE s   BEPAINT s   BESTEAD s
BECAUSE   BEHAVER s   BEPEARL s   BESTICK s
BECHALK s   BEHIGHT s   BEPROSE s   BESTILL s
BECHARM s   BEHOOVE s   BEQUEST s   BESTORM s
BECLASP s   BEHOVED   BERAKED   BESTREW s
BECLOAK s   BEINKED   BERATED   BESTROW s
BECLOUD s   BEJADED   BERAYED   BESTUCK
BECLOWN s   BEJESUS   BEREAVE s   BESWARM s
BECRAWL s   BEJEWEL s   BERHYME s   BETAKEN
BECRIME s   BEKNAVE s   BERIMED   BETAXED
BECROWD s   BEKNOWN   BEROBED   BETHANK s
BECRUST s   BELABOR s   BESAINT s   BETHINK s
BECURSE s   BELACED   BESCOUR s   BETHORN s
BECURST   BELATED   BESHAME s   BETHUMB s
BEDAZED   BELAYED   BESHINE s   BETHUMP s
BEDEVIL s   BELAYER s   BESHONE   BETIDED
BEDEWED   BELEAPT   BESHOUT s   BETIGHT
BEDIGHT s   BELOVED s   BESHREW s   BETIMED
BEDIRTY   BELYING   BESIEGE s   BETITLE s
BEDIZEN s   BEMADAM s   BESLAVE s   BETOKEN s
BEDRAIL s   BEMAZED   BESLIME s   BETREAD s
BEDRAPE s   BEMEANT   BESMEAR s   BETROTH s
BEDROLL s   BEMEDAL s   BESMILE s   BETWEEN s
BEDROPT   BEMETED   BESMOKE s   BETWIXT
BEDUNCE s   BEMIRED   BESPAKE   BEVOMIT s
BEDWARF s   BEMIXED   BESPATE   BEWARED
BEFLECK s   BEMIXES   BESPEAK s   BEWEARY
BEGAZED   BEMOUTH s   BESPEED s   BEWHORE s
BEGLOOM s   BEMUSED   BESPICE s   BEWITCH
BEGOING   BENAMED   BESPOKE   BEWORRY
BEGORED   BENEATH   BESPORT s   BEWRAPT
BEGRIME s   BENEMPT   BESPOUT s
BEGROAN s   BENIGHT s   BESTAIN s

Eight-letter BE words

BECALLED   BECLAMOR s   BECUDGEL s   BEDAMNED
BECALMED   BECLOTHE s   BECURLED   BEDARKEN s
BECAPPED   BECOMING s   BECURSED   BEDASHED
BECARPET s   BECOWARD s   BEDABBLE s   BEDASHES
BECHANCE s   BECRIMED   BEDAGGLE s   BEDAUBED

BEDAZING	BEGUILED	BEMIXING	BESETTER s
BEDAZZLE s	BEGUILER s	BEMOANED	BESHADOW s
BEDEAFEN s	BEGULFED	BEMOANER s	BESHAMED
BEDECKED	BEGUNKED	BEMOCKED	BESHIVER s
BEDEWING	BEHALVES	BEMOILED	BESHROUD s
BEDIAPER s	BEHAPPEN s	BEMUDDED	BESIEGED
BEDIMMED	BEHATTED	BEMUDDLE s	BESIEGER s
BEDIMPLE s	BEHAVING	BEMUFFLE s	BESIGHED
BEDOTTED	BEHAVIOR s	BEMURMUR s	BESLAVED
BEDRAPED	BEHEADED	BEMUSING	BESLAVER s
BEDRENCH	BEHEADER s	BEMUZZLE s	BESLIMED
BEDRIVEL s	BEHOLDEN	BENAMING	BESMILED
BEDUCKED	BEHOLDER s	BENETTED	BESMIRCH
BEDUMBED	BEHOOVED	BENUMBED	BESMOKED
BEDUNGED	BEHOVING	BEPATTED	BESMOOTH s
BEDUSTED	BEHOWLED	BEPELTED	BESMUDGE s
BEDYEING	BEJABERS	BEPEPPER s	BESMUTCH
BEFALLEN	BEJADING	BEPESTER s	BESNOWED
BEFINGER s	BEJESUIT s	BEPIMPLE s	BESOOTHE s
BEFINNED	BEJUMBLE s	BEPITIED	BESORTED
BEFITTED	BEKISSED	BEPITIES	BESOTTED
BEFLOWER s	BEKISSES	BEPLUMED	BESOUGHT
BEFOAMED	BEKNIGHT s	BEPOMMEL s	BESOULED
BEFOGGED	BELABOUR s	BEPOWDER s	BESPICED
BEFOOLED	BELACING	BEPRAISE s	BESPOKEN
BEFOULED	BELADIES	BEPROSED	BESPOUSE s
BEFOULER s	BELAUDED	BEPUFFED	BESPREAD s
BEFRIEND s	BELAYING	BERAKING	BESPRENT
BEFRINGE s	BELEAPED	BERASCAL s	BESTOWED
BEFUDDLE s	BELEEING	BERATING	BESTOWER s
BEGALLED	BELIEVER s	BERAYING	BESTREAK s
BEGAZING	BELIQUOR s	BEREAVED	BESTREWN
BEGEMMED	BELITTLE s	BEREAVER s	BESTRIDE s
BEGETTER s	BELONGED	BERHYMED	BESTRODE
BEGIFTED	BELONGER s	BERIMING	BESTROWN
BEGILDED	BELOVING	BERINGED	BESUITED
BEGINNER s	BEMADDED	BEROBBED	BETAKING
BEGIRDED	BEMADDEN s	BEROUGED	BETATTER s
BEGIRDLE s	BEMAULED	BESCORCH	BETEEMED
BEGLAMOR s	BEMEANED	BESCRAWL s	BETHRALL s
BEGNAWED	BEMETING	BESCREEN s	BETHWACK s
BEGOTTEN	BEMINGLE s	BESEEING	BETIDING
BEGRIMED	BEMIRING	BESEEMED	BETIMING
BEGRUDGE s	BEMISTED	BESEEMLY	BETITLED

BETOILED	BEWAILED	BEWHORED	BEWORMED
BETOSSED	BEWAILER s	BEWIGGED	
BETOSSES	BEWARING	BEWILDER s	
BEUNCLED	BEWETTED	BEWINGED	

Words beginning with the prefix DE

An s shows that a word can take a valid –S hook.

Words are excluded that happen to take the prefix DE but are not genuine
DE- words. Thus words such as DELUGE, DESIRE, and DETOURED are
omitted.

Six-letter DE words

DEBARK s	DEFILE s	DELEAD s	DEPORT s
DEBASE s	DEFINE s	DELICE s	DEPOSE s
DEBATE s	DEFLEA s	DELIME s	DERAIL s
DEBEAK s	DEFLEX	DELINK s	DERATE s
DEBONE s	DEFOAM s	DELIST s	DERIDE s
DEBOSS	DEFORM s	DELOPE s	DERIVE s
DEBUNK s	DEFOUL s	DELUDE s	DESALT s
DEBURR s	DEFRAG s	DEMARK s	DESAND s
DECAFF s	DEFRAY s	DEMAST s	DESEED s
DECAMP s	DEFUEL s	DEMEAN s	DESORB s
DECARB s	DEFUND s	DEMISE s	DESPOT s
DECLAW s	DEFUSE s	DEMIST s	DETICK s
DECODE s	DEFUZE s	DEMODE	DETUNE s
DECOKE s	DEGERM s	DEMOTE s	DEVEIN s
DECREW s	DEGOUT s	DENOTE s	DEVEST s
DEDUCE s	DEGUST s	DENUDE s	DEVOID
DEDUCT s	DEHAIR s	DEPART s	DEVOTE s
DEFACE s	DEHORN s	DEPEND s	DEWOOL s
DEFAME s	DEICED	DEPERM s	DEWORM s
DEFANG s	DEICER s	DEPLOY s	DEZINC s
DEFEAT s	DELATE s	DEPONE s	

Seven-letter DE words

DEAIRED	DEBASER s	DEBRIEF s	DECLAIM s
DEALATE s	DEBATED	DEBUSED	DECLASS
DEALIGN s	DEBEARD s	DEBUSES	DECLINE s
DEASHED	DEBONED	DECEASE s	DECODED
DEASHES	DEBONER s	DECIDED	DECODER s
DEBASED	DEBRIDE s	DECIDER s	DECOKED

DECOLOR s
DECOYED
DECOYER s
DECREED
DECRIED
DECRIER s
DECRIES
DECROWN s
DECRYPT s
DECURVE s
DEFACED
DEFACER s
DEFAMED
DEFAULT s
DEFENCE s
DEFILED
DEFILER s
DEFINED
DEFINER s
DEFOCUS
DEFORCE s
DEFRAUD s
DEFROCK s

DEFROST s
DEFROZE
DEFUSED
DEFUZED
DEGASES
DEGAUSS
DEGLAZE s
DEGRADE s
DEICING
DEINDEX
DELAPSE s
DELATED
DELAYED
DELAYER s
DELEAVE s
DELIMED
DELIMIT s
DELIVER s
DELOPED
DELOUSE s
DEMERGE s
DEMERIT s
DEMERSE s

DEMINER s
DEMOTED
DEMOUNT s
DENOTED
DENUDER s
DEORBIT s
DEPAINT s
DEPLANE s
DEPLUME s
DEPOSED
DEPOSER s
DEPOSIT s
DEPRESS
DEQUEUE s
DERANGE s
DERATED
DERAYED
DERIDER s
DERIVED
DERIVER s
DESCALE s
DESEXED
DESEXES

DESKILL s
DESNOOD s
DESPITE s
DESPOIL s
DESTAIN s
DESTOCK s
DESTROY s
DESUGAR s
DETRACT s
DETRAIN s
DETUNED
DEVALUE s
DEVISED
DEVISOR s
DEVOICE s
DEVOLVE s
DEVOTED
DEWATER s
DEWAXED
DEWAXES

Eight-letter DE words

DEAERATE s
DEAIRING
DEALATED
DEASHING
DEBAGGED
DEBARKED
DEBARKER s
DEBARRED
DEBASING
DEBATING s
DEBEAKED
DEBONING
DEBOSSED
DEBOSSES
DEBRIDED
DEBRUISE s
DEBUDDED
DEBUGGED
DEBUGGER s

DEBUNKED
DEBUNKER s
DEBURRED
DEBUSING
DEBUSSED
DEBUSSES
DECAMPED
DECEASED s
DECENTER s
DECENTRE s
DECIPHER s
DECLAWED
DECLUTCH
DECODING s
DECOKING
DECOLOUR s
DECOMMIT s
DECOUPLE s
DECOYING

DECREASE s
DECREWED
DECRYING
DECURVED
DEDUCTED
DEFACING
DEFAMING s
DEFANGED
DEFATTED
DEFEATED
DEFEATER s
DEFENCED
DEFENDED
DEFENDER s
DEFIANCE s
DEFILING
DEFINING
DEFINITE s
DEFLEXED

DEFLEXES
DEFLOWER s
DEFLUENT
DEFOAMED
DEFOAMER s
DEFOGGED
DEFOGGER s
DEFORCED
DEFORCER s
DEFOREST s
DEFORMED
DEFORMER s
DEFOULED
DEFRAYED
DEFREEZE s
DEFRIEND s
DEFROZEN
DEFUELED
DEFUNDED

DEFUSING
DEFUZING
DEGASSED
DEGASSER s
DEGASSES
DEGENDER s
DEGERMED
DEGLAZED
DEGRADED
DEGRADER s
DEGREASE s
DEGUMMED
DEGUSTED
DEHAIRED
DEHORNED
DEHORNER s
DEIONISE s
DEIONIZE s
DELAPSED
DELAYING
DELEADED
DELEAVED
DELEGATE s
DELIBATE s
DELIMING
DELINKED
DELISTED
DELOPING
DELOUSED
DELOUSER s
DELUGING
DELUSTER s

DELUSTRE s
DEMANNED
DEMARKED
DEMARKET s
DEMASTED
DEMEANED
DEMERGED
DEMERGER s
DEMINING s
DEMISTED
DEMISTER s
DEMOBBED
DEMOTION s
DENATURE s
DENAZIFY
DENETTED
DENOTATE s
DENOTING
DEPARTED s
DEPARTER s
DEPEINCT s
DEPEOPLE s
DEPERMED
DEPLANED
DEPLOYED
DEPLUMED
DEPOLISH
DEPONENT s
DEPORTED
DEPORTER s
DEPOSING
DEQUEUED

DERAILED
DERAILER s
DERANGED
DERANGER s
DERATING s
DERATION s
DERATTED
DERAYING
DERIDING
DERIGGED
DERIVING
DESALTED
DESALTER s
DESANDED
DESCALED
DESCALER s
DESCHOOL s
DESCRIBE s
DESCRIED
DESCRIVE s
DESEEDED
DESEEDER s
DESELECT s
DESERVED
DESERVER s
DESEXING
DESIGNED
DESIGNEE s
DESIGNER s
DESILVER s
DESINING
DESIRING

DESISTED
DESOLATE s
DESORBED
DESTREAM s
DESTRESS
DESULFUR s
DETAILED
DETAILER s
DETANGLE s
DETASSEL s
DETESTED
DETESTER s
DETHATCH
DETHRONE s
DETICKED
DETICKER s
DETUNING
DEVALUED
DEVEINED
DEVESTED
DEVISING
DEVOICED
DEVOLVED
DEVOTING
DEWAXING
DEWITTED
DEWOOLED
DEWORMED
DEWORMER s
DEZINCED

Words beginning with the prefix DIS

An s shows that a word can take a valid –S hook.

Words are excluded that happen to take the prefix DIS but are not genuine
DIS- words. Thus words such as DISCOED (DISCO+ED) and DISODIUM
(DI+SODIUM) are omitted.

Six-letter DIS words

DISARM s	DISMAL s	DISOWN s	DISUSE s
DISBAR s	DISMAN s	DISPEL s	
DISBUD s	DISMAY s	DISTIL s	

Seven-letter DIS words

DISABLE s	DISGEST s	DISMAST s	DISRATE s
DISALLY	DISGOWN s	DISMISS	DISROBE s
DISAVOW s	DISGUST s	DISNEST s	DISROOT s
DISBAND s	DISHELM s	DISOBEY s	DISSAVE s
DISBARK s	DISHOME s	DISPACE s	DISSEAT s
DISCAGE s	DISHORN s	DISPARK s	DISSECT s
DISCANT s	DISJOIN s	DISPART s	DISTEND s
DISCARD s	DISKING	DISPEND s	DISTENT s
DISCASE s	DISLEAF s	DISPLAY s	DISTILL s
DISCIDE s	DISLEAL	DISPLED	DISTORT s
DISCORD s	DISLIKE s	DISPONE s	DISTUNE s
DISCURE s	DISLIMB s	DISPORT s	DISUSED
DISEASE s	DISLIMN s	DISPOSE s	DISYOKE s
DISEDGE s	DISLINK s	DISPOST s	
DISFAME s	DISLOAD s	DISPRAD	
DISFORM s	DISMASK s	DISRANK s	

Eight-letter DIS words

DISABLED	DISCIDED	DISGUISE s	DISORDER s
DISABLER s	DISCLAIM s	DISHABIT s	DISOWNED
DISABUSE s	DISCLOSE s	DISHABLE s	DISOWNER s
DISADORN s	DISCOLOR s	DISHOARD s	DISPACED
DISAGREE s	DISCOUNT s	DISHOMED	DISPATCH
DISALLOW s	DISCOVER s	DISHONOR s	DISPEACE s
DISANNEX	DISCROWN s	DISHORSE s	DISPENCE s
DISANNUL s	DISCURED	DISHOUSE s	DISPERSE s
DISAPPLY	DISEASED	DISINTER s	DISPLACE s
DISARMED	DISEDGED	DISINURE s	DISPLANT s
DISARMER s	DISENDOW s	DISJOINT s	DISPLING
DISARRAY s	DISENROL s	DISLEAVE s	DISPLUME s
DISBENCH	DISFAMED	DISLIKED	DISPOSED
DISBOSOM s	DISFAVOR s	DISLIKEN s	DISPOSER s
DISBOUND	DISFLESH	DISLIKER s	DISPRIZE s
DISBOWEL s	DISFROCK s	DISLODGE s	DISPROOF s
DISBURSE s	DISGAVEL s	DISLOYAL	DISPROVE s
DISCAGED	DISGORGE s	DISMAYED	DISPURSE s
DISCANDY	DISGRACE s	DISMOUNT s	DISQUIET s
DISCASED	DISGRADE s	DISORBED	DISRATED

DISROBED	DISSIGHTs	DISTRAIT	DISUSING
DISSAVED	DISSOLVEs	DISTRUSTs	DISVALUEs
DISSAVERs	DISTALLY	DISTUNED	DISVOUCH
DISSEISEs	DISTASTEs	DISUNIONs	DISYOKED
DISSEIZEs	DISTRACTs	DISUNITEs	
DISSERVEs	DISTRAILs	DISUNITY	
DISSEVERs	DISTRAINs	DISUSAGEs	

Words beginning with the prefix EM

An s shows that a word can take a valid –S hook.

Words are excluded that happen to take the prefix EM but are not genuine EM- words. Thus words such as EMAILED, EMIRATE, and EMPRESS are omitted.

Six-letter EM words

EMBAILs	EMBARKs	EMBOSS	EMPALEs
EMBALEs	EMBASEs	EMBUSY	EMPAREs
EMBALLs	EMBODY	EMMESH	EMPARTs
EMBALMs	EMBOILs	EMMEWS	EMPLOYs
EMBANKs	EMBOSKs	EMMOVEs	

Seven-letter EM words

EMBALED	EMBOWELs	EMBUSED	EMPIGHTs
EMBASED	EMBOWERs	EMBUSES	EMPLACEs
EMBASTE	EMBOXED	EMMEWED	EMPLANEs
EMBATHEs	EMBOXES	EMMOVED	EMPLOYEs
EMBAYED	EMBRACEs	EMPAIREs	EMPLUMEs
EMBLAZEs	EMBRAIDs	EMPALED	EMPOWERs
EMBLOOMs	EMBRAVEs	EMPALERs	EMPRISEs
EMBOGUEs	EMBREADs	EMPANELs	EMPRIZEs
EMBOSOMs	EMBROILs	EMPARED	
EMBOUNDs	EMBROWNs	EMPEACH	
EMBOWED	EMBRUTEs	EMPERCEs	

Eight-letter EM words

EMBAILED	EMBARKED	EMBEDDED	EMBODIED
EMBALING	EMBARRED	EMBEZZLEs	EMBODIES
EMBALLED	EMBASING	EMBITTERs	EMBOGGED
EMBALMED	EMBATHED	EMBLAZED	EMBOILED
EMBANKED	EMBATTLEs	EMBLAZERs	EMBOLDENs
EMBANKERs	EMBAYING	EMBLAZONs	EMBORDERs

EMBOSSED	EMBUSIES	EMPAIRED	EMPIERCE s
EMBOSSER s	EMBUSING	EMPALING	EMPLACED
EMBOSSES	EMBUSSED	EMPARING	EMPLANED
EMBOWING	EMBUSSES	EMPARLED	EMPLEACH
EMBOXING	EMMARBLE s	EMPARTED	EMPLONGE s
EMBRACED	EMMESHED	EMPATHIC	EMPLOYED
EMBRACER s	EMMESHES	EMPATRON s	EMPLUMED
EMBRAVED	EMMEWING	EMPEOPLE s	EMPOISON s
EMBRUTED	EMMOVING	EMPERCED	EMPOLDER s
EMBUSIED	EMPACKET s	EMPERISH	EMPURPLE s

Words beginning with the prefix EN

An s shows that a word can take a valid –S hook.

Words are excluded that happen to take the prefix EN but are not genuine EN- words. Thus words such as ENTRÉE, ENVIED, and ENTRIST are omitted.

Six-letter EN words

ENABLE s	ENFIRE s	ENLARD s	ENSERF s
ENARCH	ENFOLD s	ENLINK s	ENSIGN s
ENCAGE s	ENFORM s	ENLIST s	ENSILE s
ENCALM s	ENFREE s	ENLOCK s	ENSOUL s
ENCAMP s	ENGAGE s	ENMESH	ENSUED
ENCASE s	ENGAOL s	ENMEWS	ENSURE s
ENCASH	ENGILD s	ENMOVE s	ENTAIL s
ENCAVE s	ENGILT	ENRACE s	ENTAME s
ENCODE s	ENGIRD s	ENRAGE s	ENTICE s
ENCORE s	ENGIRT	ENRANK s	ENTIRE s
ENCYST s	ENGLUT s	ENRAPT	ENTOIL s
ENDART s	ENGORE s	ENRICH	ENTOMB s
ENDEAR s	ENGRAM s	ENRING s	ENTRAP s
ENDITE s	ENGULF s	ENROBE s	ENURNS
ENDIVE s	ENHALO s	ENROLL s	ENWALL s
ENDOSS	ENISLE s	ENROOT s	ENWIND s
ENDUED	ENJAMB s	ENSEAL s	ENWOMB s
ENDURE s	ENJOIN s	ENSEAM s	ENWRAP s
ENFACE s	ENLACE s	ENSEAR s	ENZONE s

Seven-letter EN words

ENABLED	ENACTOR s	ENCAGED	ENCHAFE s
ENABLER s	ENAMOUR s	ENCASED	ENCHAIN s
ENACTED	ENARMED	ENCAVED	ENCHANT s

ENCHARM s	ENFLAME s	ENLIGHT s	ENSTEEP s
ENCHASE s	ENFLESH	ENLIVEN s	ENSTYLE s
ENCHEER s	ENFORCE s	ENMEWED	ENSUING
ENCLASP s	ENFRAME s	ENMOVED	ENSURED
ENCLAVE s	ENFREED	ENNOBLE s	ENSURER s
ENCLOSE s	ENFROZE	ENPLANE s	ENSWEEP s
ENCLOUD s	ENGAGED	ENPRINT s	ENSWEPT
ENCODED	ENGAGER s	ENQUEUE s	ENTAMED
ENCODER s	ENGLOBE s	ENQUIRE s	ENTICED
ENCORED	ENGLOOM s	ENRACED	ENTITLE s
ENCRUST s	ENGORED	ENRAGED	ENTOPIC
ENCRYPT s	ENGORGE s	ENRANGE s	ENTRAIL s
ENDEWED	ENGRACE s	ENRHEUM s	ENTRAIN s
ENDITED	ENGRAFF s	ENRIVEN	ENTRANT s
ENDORSE s	ENGRAFT s	ENROBED	ENTREAT s
ENDOWED	ENGRAIL s	ENROUGH s	ENTRUST s
ENDOWER s	ENGRAIN s	ENROUND s	ENTWINE s
ENDUING	ENGRASP s	ENSEWED	ENTWIST s
ENDURED	ENGRAVE s	ENSHELL s	ENURNED
ENFACED	ENGROSS	ENSILED	ENVAULT s
ENFELON s	ENGUARD s	ENSKIED	ENVENOM s
ENFEOFF s	ENGULPH s	ENSKIES	ENWHEEL s
ENFEVER s	ENHANCE s	ENSKYED	ENWOUND
ENFILED	ENISLED	ENSLAVE s	ENZONED
ENFIRED	ENJOYED	ENSNARE s	ENZYMIC
ENFIXED	ENLACED	ENSNARL s	
ENFIXES	ENLARGE s	ENSTAMP s	

Eight-letter EN words

ENABLING	ENCASING	ENCREASE s	ENFACING
ENACTING	ENCAVING	ENCUMBER s	ENFEEBLE s
ENACTION s	ENCHAFED	ENCYCLIC s	ENFETTER s
ENACTIVE	ENCHARGE s	ENDAMAGE s	ENFIERCE s
ENACTURE s	ENCHASED	ENDANGER s	ENFIRING
ENARCHED	ENCHASER s	ENDARTED	ENFIXING
ENARCHES	ENCIPHER s	ENDEARED	ENFLAMED
ENARMING	ENCIRCLE s	ENDERMIC	ENFLOWER s
ENAUNTER	ENCLOSED	ENDEWING	ENFOLDED
ENCAGING	ENCLOSER s	ENDITING	ENFOLDER s
ENCALMED	ENCLOTHE s	ENDORSER s	ENFORCED
ENCAMPED	ENCODING s	ENDOSSED	ENFORCER s
ENCARPUS	ENCOLOUR s	ENDOSSES	ENFOREST s
ENCASHED	ENCORING	ENDOWING	ENFORMED
ENCASHES	ENCRADLE s	ENDURING	ENFRAMED

ENFREEZE s	ENLACING	ENRINGED	ENSWATHE s
ENFROZEN	ENLARDED	ENROBING	ENTAILED
ENGAGING	ENLARGEN s	ENROLLED	ENTAILER s
ENGAOLED	ENLARGER s	ENROLLER s	ENTAMING
ENGENDER s	ENLINKED	ENROOTED	ENTANGLE s
ENGILDED	ENLISTED	ENSAMPLE s	ENTENDER s
ENGIRDED	ENLISTEE s	ENSCONCE s	ENTHRALL s
ENGIRDLE s	ENLISTER s	ENSCROLL s	ENTHRONE s
ENGLOBED	ENLOCKED	ENSEALED	ENTICING s
ENGORGED	ENLUMINE s	ENSEAMED	ENTITLED
ENGORING	ENMESHED	ENSEARED	ENTOILED
ENGRACED	ENMESHES	ENSEMBLE s	ENTOMBED
ENGRAVED	ENMEWING	ENSEWING	ENTRANCE s
ENGRAVEN	ENMOSSED	ENSHEATH s	ENTREATY
ENGRAVER s	ENMOVING	ENSHIELD s	ENTRENCH
ENGRIEVE s	ENNOBLER s	ENSHRINE s	ENTROPIC
ENGROOVE s	ENPLANED	ENSHROUD s	ENTWINED
ENGULFED	ENQUEUED	ENSIGNED	ENURNING
ENHALOED	ENQUIRED	ENSILAGE s	ENVASSAL s
ENHALOES	ENRACING	ENSILING	ENVISAGE s
ENHEARSE s	ENRAGING	ENSKYING	ENVISION s
ENHUNGER s	ENRANGED	ENSLAVED	ENWALLED
ENISLING	ENRANKED	ENSLAVER s	ENWALLOW s
ENJAMBED	ENRAUNGE s	ENSNARED	ENWOMBED
ENJOINED	ENRAVISH	ENSNARER s	ENWREATH s
ENJOINER s	ENRICHED	ENSOULED	ENZONING
ENJOYING	ENRICHER s	ENSPHERE s	
ENKERNEL s	ENRICHES	ENSTYLED	
ENKINDLE s	ENRIDGED	ENSURING	

Words beginning with the prefix EX

An s shows that a word can take a valid –S hook.

Words are excluded that happen to take the prefix EX but are not genuine EX- words. Thus words such as EXAMEN and EXPERT are omitted.

Six-letter EX words

EXARCH s	EXPEND s	EXTENT s
EXCIDE s	EXPORT s	EXTERN s
EXCITE s	EXPOSE s	EXTOLD
EXHALE s	EXSECT s	EXTOLL s
EXPAND s	EXTEND s	EXTORT s

Seven-letter EX words

EXACTED	EXCITER s	EXPOSED	EXTERNE s
EXACTOR s	EXCLAIM s	EXPOSER s	EXTRACT s
EXALTER s	EXCLAVE s	EXPOSIT s	EXTRAIT s
EXAPTED	EXCURSE s	EXPOUND s	EXTREAT s
EXCHEAT s	EXHALED	EXPULSE s	EXURBAN
EXCIDED	EXOSMIC	EXPURGE s	EXURBIA s
EXCITED	EXPLANT s	EXTENSE s	

Eight-letter EX words

EXACTING	EXCURSUS	EXPORTED	EXTENSOR s
EXACTION s	EXFILLED	EXPORTER s	EXTERNAL s
EXANTHEM s	EXHALING	EXPOSING	EXTOLLED
EXCHANGE s	EXOSMOSE s	EXPULSED	EXTOLLER s
EXCIDING	EXPANDER s	EXPURGED	EXTUBATE s
EXCITING	EXPELLED	EXTENDED	
EXCURSED	EXPENDED	EXTENDER s	

Words beginning with the prefix FOR

An s shows that a word can take a valid –S hook.

Words are excluded that happen to take the prefix FOR but are not genuine FOR- words. Thus words such as FORAGE, FORMAT, and FORTUNE are omitted.

Six-letter FOR words

FORBAD	FORBYE	FORSAY s
FORBID s	FORDID	FORWHY

Seven-letter FOR words

FORBADE	FORFEND s	FORLENT	FORSOOK
FORBARE	FORGAVE	FORLORE	FORWARD s
FORBEAR s	FORGIVE s	FORLORN s	FORWARN s
FORBODE s	FORGOER s	FORPINE s	FORWENT
FORBORE	FORGOES	FORSAID	FORWORN
FORDOES	FORGONE	FORSAKE s	
FORDONE	FORHENT s	FORSLOE s	
FOREVER	FORLEND s	FORSLOW s	

Eight-letter FOR words

FORBODED	FORDOING	FORFAULT s	FORGIVER s
FORBORNE	FORDONNE	FORGIVEN	FORGOING

FORJUDGE s	FORSOOTH	FORSPOKE	FORSWORN
FORPINED	FORSPEAK s	FORSWEAR s	FORTHINK s
FORSAKER s	FORSPEND s	FORSWINK s	FORWASTE s
FORSLACK s	FORSPENT	FORSWORE	FORWEARY

Words beginning with the prefix FORE

An s shows that a word can take a valid –S hook.

Words are excluded that happen to take the prefix FORE but are not genuine FORE- words. Thus words such as FOREST and FORESTED are omitted.

Six-letter FORE words

FOREBY	FOREDO	FOREGO

Seven-letter FORE words

FOREARM s	FOREGUT s	FOREMEN	FORESAY s
FOREBAY s	FORELAY s	FOREPAW s	FORESEE s
FOREBYE	FORELEG s	FORERAN	FORETOP s
FORECAR s	FORELIE s	FORERUN s	
FOREDID	FOREMAN	FORESAW	

Eight-letter FORE words

FOREBEAR s	FOREHAND s	FOREMAST s	FORESIDE s
FOREBITT s	FOREHEAD s	FOREMEAN s	FORESKIN s
FOREBODE s	FOREHENT s	FOREMILK s	FORESLOW s
FOREBODY	FOREHOCK s	FOREMOST	FORESTAY s
FOREBOOM s	FOREHOOF s	FORENAME s	FORETELL s
FORECAST s	FOREKING s	FORENOON s	FORETIME s
FOREDATE s	FOREKING s	FOREPART s	FORETOLD
FOREDECK s	FOREKNEW	FOREPAST	FOREWARD s
FOREDOES	FOREKNOW s	FOREPEAK s	FOREWARN s
FOREDONE	FORELADY	FOREPLAN s	FOREWENT
FOREDOOM s	FORELAID	FOREPLAY s	FOREWIND s
FOREFACE s	FORELAIN	FORERANK s	FOREWING s
FOREFEEL s	FORELAIN	FOREREAD s	FOREWORD s
FOREFEET	FORELAND s	FORESAID	FOREWORN
FOREFELT	FORELAND s	FORESAIL s	FOREYARD s
FOREFEND s	FORELEND s	FORESEEN	
FOREFOOT	FORELENT	FORESEER s	
FOREGOER s	FORELIFT s	FORESHEW s	
FOREGOES	FORELIMB s	FORESHIP s	
FOREGONE	FORELOCK s	FORESHOW s	

Words beginning with the prefix IN

An s shows that a word can take a valid –S hook.

Words are excluded that happen to take the prefix IN but are not genuine IN- words. Thus words such as INJURY, INSECT, and INFANCY are omitted.

Six-letter IN words

INARCH	INDUCE s	INHAUL s	INSOUL s
INBENT	INDUCT s	INHERE s	INSPAN s
INBORN	INDUED	INHOOP s	INSTAR s
INBRED s	INFALL s	INISLE s	INSTEP s
INCAGE s	INFAME s	INLACE s	INSURE s
INCANT s	INFARE s	INLAID	INTAKE s
INCASE s	INFEED s	INLAND s	INTOMB s
INCAVE s	INFELT	INLIER s	INTONE s
INCEDE s	INFEST s	INLOCK s	INTORT s
INCENT s	INFILL s	INMATE s	INTURN s
INCITE s	INFIRM s	INMESH	INVEST s
INCLIP s	INFLOW s	INMOST	INWALL s
INCOME s	INFLUX	INPOUR s	INWARD s
INCULT	INFOLD s	INROAD s	INWICK s
INDART s	INFORM s	INRUSH	INWIND s
INDEED	INFUSE s	INSANE	INWITH
INDENT s	INGATE s	INSEAM s	INWORK s
INDICT s	INGEST s	INSEEM s	INWORN
INDITE s	INGRAM s	INSHIP s	INWOVE
INDOLE s	INGULF s	INSIDE s	INWRAP s
INDOOR s	INHALE s	INSOLE s	

Seven-letter IN words

INAPTLY	INCEDED	INDEWED	INFEOFF s
INARMED	INCENSE s	INDITED	INFIELD s
INBEING s	INCHASE s	INDORSE s	INFIGHT s
INBOARD s	INCITED	INDOWED	INFIXED
INBOUND s	INCITER s	INDRAFT s	INFIXES
INBREAK s	INCIVIL	INDRAWN	INFLAME s
INBREED s	INCLASP s	INDUING	INFORCE s
INBRING s	INCLINE s	INDWELL s	INFRACT s
INBUILT	INCLOSE s	INDWELT	INFUSED
INBURST s	INCOMER s	INEARTH s	INGLOBE s
INCAGED	INCROSS	INEXACT	INGOING s
INCASED	INCRUST s	INFAMED	INGRAFT s
INCAVED	INCURVE s	INFAUNA s	INGRAIN s

INGRATE s INORBED INSPIRE s INTRUST s
INGROSS INPHASE INSTALL s INTWINE s
INGROUP s INQUEST s INSTATE s INTWIST s
INGROWN INQUIET s INSTEAD INURNED
INGULPH s INQUIRE s INSTILL s INUTILE
INHABIT s INSANER INSURED s INVALID s
INHALED INSCAPE s INSURER s INVERSE s
INHALER s INSCULP s INSWEPT INVEXED
INHUMAN INSHELL s INSWING s INVITAL
INISLED INSHORE INTENSE INVOICE s
INJELLY INSIDER s INTERNE s INVOLVE s
INJOINT s INSIGHT s INTITLE s INWEAVE s
INLACED INSINEW s INTONED INWOUND
INLAYER s INSNARE s INTONER s INWOVEN
INLYING INSOOTH INTRANT s
INNERVE s INSPECT s INTREAT s

Eight-letter IN words

INACTION s INCUMBER s INFAMOUS INFRINGE s
INACTIVE INCURRED INFAUNAE INFRUGAL
INARABLE INCURVED INFAUNAL INFUSING
INARCHED INDARTED INFECUND INFUSION s
INARCHES INDEBTED INFERIAE INGATHER s
INARMING INDECENT INFESTER s INGLOBED
INAURATE s INDENTED INFILLED INGROOVE s
INCAGING INDEVOUT INFINITE s INGROUND s
INCANTED INDEWING INFIRMED INGROWTH s
INCASING INDICTED INFIRMER INGULFED
INCAVING INDIGEST s INFIRMLY INHALING
INCEDING INDIRECT INFIXING INHAULER s
INCENSED INDITING INFLAMED INHEARSE s
INCENSER s INDOCILE INFLAMER s INHOLDER s
INCENSOR s INDOLENT INFLATUS INHOOPED
INCENTER s INDORSER s INFLEXED INHUMANE
INCENTRE s INDOWING INFLIGHT INHUMATE s
INCHASED INDRENCH INFLUENT s INISLING
INCITING INDUCTED INFLUXES INLACING
INCIVISM s INEDIBLE INFOLDED INLANDER s
INCLOSED INEDITED INFOLDER s INLAYING s
INCLOSER s INEQUITY INFORCED INLOCKED
INCOMING s INERRANT INFORMAL INMESHED
INCORPSE s INESSIVE s INFORMED INMESHES
INCREASE s INEXPERT s INFORMER s INNATIVE
INCREATE INFAMING INFOUGHT INNERVED

INNOCENT s	INSEEMED	INTENDED s	INUSTION s
INNOVATE s	INSETTER s	INTENDER s	INVERITY
INORBING	INSHEATH s	INTENSER	INVERSED
INORNATE	INSHRINE s	INTERNAL s	INVERTED
INPOURED	INSNARED	INTERNED	INVESTED
INPUTTED	INSNARER s	INTHRALL s	INVIABLE
INPUTTER s	INSOULED	INTHRONE s	INVIABLY
INQUIRED	INSOURCE s	INTITLED	INVIRILE
INRUSHES	INSPHERE s	INTITULE s	INVISCID
INSANELY	INSPIRED	INTOMBED	INVOICED
INSANEST	INSPIRIT s	INTONING s	INVOLUTE s
INSANITY	INSTABLE	INTRENCH	INVOLVED
INSCIENT	INSTANCE s	INTREPID	INWALLED
INSCONCE s	INSTATED	INTUBATE s	INWEAVED
INSCRIBE s	INSTRESS	INTURNED	INWICKED
INSCROLL s	INSTROKE s	INTWINED	INWORKED
INSCULPT	INSUCKEN	INUNDATE s	
INSEAMED	INSURING	INURBANE	
INSECURE	INSWATHE s	INURNING	

Words beginning with the prefix MIS

An s shows that a word can take a valid –S hook.

Words are excluded that happen to take the prefix MIS but are not genuine MIS- words. Thus words such as MISERE, MISSILE, and MISOLOGY are omitted.

Six-letter MIS words

MISACT s	MISEAT s	MISLAY s	MISSAY s
MISADD s	MISFED	MISLED	MISSEE s
MISAIM s	MISFIT s	MISLIE s	MISSET s
MISATE	MISHAP s	MISLIT	MISUSE s
MISCUE s	MISHIT s	MISMET	
MISCUT s	MISKEN s	MISPEN s	
MISDID	MISKEY s	MISSAW	

Seven-letter MIS words

MISALLY	MISBORN	MISCOIN s	MISDEAL s
MISAVER s	MISCALL s	MISCOOK s	MISDEED s
MISBIAS	MISCAST s	MISCOPY	MISDEEM s
MISBILL s	MISCITE s	MISCUED	MISDIAL s
MISBIND s	MISCODE s	MISDATE s	MISDIET s

MISDOER s
MISDOES
MISDONE
MISDRAW s
MISDREW
MISEASE s
MISEDIT s
MISFALL s
MISFARE s
MISFEED s
MISFELL
MISFILE s
MISFIRE s
MISFORM s
MISGAVE
MISGIVE s
MISGOES
MISGONE
MISGREW
MISGROW s

MISHEAR s
MISJOIN s
MISKEEP s
MISKENT
MISKEPT
MISKICK s
MISKNEW
MISKNOW s
MISLAID
MISLAIN
MISLEAD s
MISLIKE s
MISLIVE s
MISLUCK s
MISMADE
MISMAKE s
MISMARK s
MISMATE s
MISMEET s
MISMOVE s

MISNAME s
MISPAGE s
MISPART s
MISPLAN s
MISPLAY s
MISPLED
MISRATE s
MISREAD s
MISRELY
MISRULE s
MISSAID
MISSEAT s
MISSEEM s
MISSEEN
MISSELL s
MISSEND s
MISSENT
MISSHOD
MISSOLD
MISSORT s

MISSTEP s
MISSTOP s
MISSUIT s
MISTAKE s
MISTELL s
MISTEND s
MISTERM s
MISTIME s
MISTOLD
MISTOOK
MISTUNE s
MISTYPE s
MISUSED
MISUSER s
MISWEEN s
MISWEND s
MISWENT
MISWORD s
MISWRIT
MISYOKE s

Eight-letter MIS words

MISACTED
MISADAPT s
MISADDED
MISAGENT s
MISAIMED
MISALIGN s
MISALLOT s
MISALTER s
MISAPPLY
MISARRAY s
MISASSAY s
MISATONE s
MISAWARD s
MISBEGAN
MISBEGIN s
MISBEGOT
MISBEGUN
MISBIRTH s
MISBOUND
MISBRAND s
MISBUILD s
MISBUILT

MISCARRY
MISCHIEF s
MISCHOSE
MISCITED
MISCLAIM s
MISCLASS
MISCODED
MISCOLOR s
MISCOUNT s
MISCREED s
MISCUING
MISDATED
MISDEALT
MISDEMPT
MISDIGHT s
MISDOING s
MISDONNE
MISDOUBT s
MISDRAWN
MISDREAD s
MISDRIVE s
MISDROVE

MISEATEN
MISENROL s
MISENTER s
MISENTRY
MISEVENT s
MISFAITH s
MISFARED
MISFEIGN s
MISFIELD s
MISFILED
MISFIRED
MISFOCUS
MISFRAME s
MISGAUGE s
MISGIVEN
MISGOING
MISGRADE s
MISGRAFF
MISGRAFT s
MISGROWN
MISGUESS
MISGUIDE s

MISHEARD
MISINFER s
MISINTER s
MISJUDGE s
MISKEYED
MISKNOWN
MISLABEL s
MISLABOR s
MISLAYER s
MISLEARN s
MISLIGHT s
MISLIKED
MISLIKER s
MISLIVED
MISLODGE s
MISLYING
MISMARRY
MISMATCH
MISMATED
MISMETRE s
MISMOVED
MISNAMED

MISORDER s	MISRAISE s	MISSTART s	MISTRIAL s
MISPAGED	MISRATED	MISSTATE s	MISTRUST s
MISPAINT s	MISREFER s	MISSTEER s	MISTRUTH s
MISPARSE s	MISROUTE s	MISSTYLE s	MISTRYST s
MISPATCH	MISRULED	MISTAKEN	MISTUNED
MISPLACE s	MISSENSE s	MISTAKER s	MISTUTOR s
MISPLANT s	MISSHAPE s	MISTEACH	MISTYPED
MISPLEAD s	MISSOUND s	MISTHINK s	MISUNION s
MISPOINT s	MISSPACE s	MISTHREW	MISUSAGE s
MISPOISE s	MISSPEAK s	MISTHROW s	MISUSING
MISPRICE s	MISSPELL s	MISTIMED	MISVALUE s
MISPRINT s	MISSPELT	MISTITLE s	MISWRITE s
MISPRISE s	MISSPEND s	MISTOUCH	MISWROTE
MISPRIZE s	MISSPENT	MISTRACE s	MISYOKED
MISPROUD	MISSPOKE	MISTRAIN s	
MISQUOTE s	MISSTAMP s	MISTREAT s	

Words beginning with the prefix NON

An s shows that a word can take a valid –S hook.

Words are excluded that happen to take the prefix NON but are not genuine NON- words. Thus words such as NONARY and NONAGON are omitted.

Six-letter NON words

NONAGE s	NONFAT	NONPAR	NONWAR s
NONART s	NONGAY s	NONRUN	
NONEGO s	NONMAN	NONTAX	
NONFAN s	NONMEN	NONUSE s	

Seven-letter NON words

NONACID s	NONFOOD s	NONORAL	NONSTOP s
NONAGED	NONFUEL s	NONPAID	NONSUCH
NONBANK s	NONGAME	NONPAST s	NONSUIT s
NONBODY	NONHEME	NONPEAK s	NONUSER s
NONBOOK s	NONHERO	NONPLAY s	NONWAGE
NONCASH	NONHOME	NONPLUS	NONWOOL
NONCOLA s	NONIRON	NONPOOR s	NONWORD s
NONCORE	NONJURY	NONPROS	NONWORK s
NONDRIP	NONLIFE	NONSELF	NONZERO
NONDRUG	NONMEAT s	NONSKED s	
NONFACT s	NONNEWS	NONSKID	
NONFARM	NONOILY	NONSLIP	

Eight-letter NON words

NONACTOR s	NONGREEN	NONMUSIC s	NONSTORY
NONADULT s	NONGUEST s	NONNASAL	NONSTYLE s
NONBASIC	NONGUILT s	NONNAVAL	NONSUGAR s
NONBEING s	NONHARDY	NONNOBLE	NONTAXES
NONBLACK s	NONHUMAN s	NONNOVEL s	NONTIDAL
NONBRAND	NONIDEAL	NONOBESE	NONTITLE
NONCLASS	NONIMAGE s	NONOHMIC	NONTONAL
NONCLING	NONINERT	NONOWNER s	NONTONIC
NONCOLOR s	NONIONIC	NONPAGAN s	NONTOXIC
NONCOUNT	NONISSUE s	NONPAPAL	NONTRUMP
NONCRIME s	NONJUROR s	NONPARTY	NONTRUTH s
NONDAIRY	NONLABOR	NONPOINT	NONUNION s
NONDANCE s	NONLEAFY	NONPOLAR	NONURBAN
NONELECT	NONLEGAL	NONPRINT	NONUSING
NONELITE	NONLEVEL	NONQUOTA	NONVALID
NONEMPTY	NONLIVES	NONRATED	NONVIRAL
NONENTRY	NONLOCAL s	NONRIGID	NONVITAL
NONEQUAL s	NONLOYAL	NONRIVAL s	NONVOCAL s
NONEVENT s	NONLYRIC	NONROYAL s	NONVOTER s
NONFATAL	NONMAJOR s	NONRURAL	NONWHITE s
NONFATTY	NONMETAL s	NONSENSE s	NONWOODY
NONFINAL	NONMETRO	NONSKIER s	NONWOVEN s
NONFLUID s	NONMODAL	NONSOLAR	
NONFOCAL	NONMONEY	NONSOLID s	
NONGLARE s	NONMORAL	NONSTICK	

Words beginning with the prefix OUT

An s shows that a word can take a valid –S hook.

Words are excluded that happen to take the prefix OUT but are not genuine
OUT- words. Thus words such as OUTHER, OUTNESS, and OUTROOP are
omitted.

Six-letter OUT words

OUTACT s	OUTBID s	OUTERS	OUTJET s
OUTADD s	OUTBOX	OUTFIT s	OUTJUT s
OUTAGE s	OUTBUY s	OUTFLY	OUTLAW s
OUTASK s	OUTBYE	OUTFOX	OUTLAY s
OUTATE	OUTCRY	OUTGAS	OUTLED
OUTBAR s	OUTDID	OUTGUN s	OUTLET s
OUTBEG s	OUTEAT s	OUTHIT s	OUTLIE s

OUTMAN s
OUTPUT s
OUTRAN
OUTRED s
OUTRIG s
OUTROW s

OUTRUN s
OUTSAT
OUTSAW
OUTSAY s
OUTSEE s
OUTSET s

OUTSIN s
OUTSIT s
OUTSUM s
OUTTOP s
OUTVIE s
OUTWAR s

OUTWIN s
OUTWIT s
OUTWON

Seven-letter OUT words

OUTBACK s
OUTBAKE s
OUTBARK s
OUTBAWL s
OUTBEAM s
OUTBRAG s
OUTBRED
OUTBULK s
OUTBURN s
OUTCALL s
OUTCAST s
OUTCHID
OUTCITY
OUTCOME s
OUTCOOK s
OUTCROP s
OUTCROW s
OUTDARE s
OUTDATE s
OUTDOER s
OUTDOES
OUTDONE
OUTDOOR s
OUTDRAG s
OUTDRAW s
OUTDREW
OUTDROP s
OUTDUEL s
OUTDURE s
OUTEARN s
OUTECHO
OUTEDGE s
OUTFACE s
OUTFALL s
OUTFAST s
OUTFAWN s

OUTFEEL s
OUTFELT
OUTFIND s
OUTFIRE s
OUTFISH
OUTFLEW
OUTFLOW s
OUTFOOL s
OUTFOOT s
OUTGAIN s
OUTGATE s
OUTGAVE
OUTGAZE s
OUTGIVE s
OUTGLOW s
OUTGNAW s
OUTGOER s
OUTGOES
OUTGONE
OUTGREW
OUTGRIN s
OUTGROW s
OUTGUSH
OUTHAUL s
OUTHEAR s
OUTHIRE s
OUTHOWL s
OUTHUNT s
OUTJEST s
OUTJINX
OUTJUMP s
OUTKEEP s
OUTKEPT
OUTKICK s
OUTKILL s
OUTKISS

OUTLAID
OUTLAIN
OUTLAND s
OUTLASH
OUTLAST s
OUTLEAD s
OUTLEAP s
OUTLIED
OUTLIER s
OUTLINE s
OUTLIVE s
OUTLOOK s
OUTLOVE s
OUTMODE s
OUTMOST
OUTMOVE s
OUTNAME s
OUTPACE s
OUTPART s
OUTPASS
OUTPEEP s
OUTPEER s
OUTPITY
OUTPLAN s
OUTPLAY s
OUTPLOD s
OUTPLOT s
OUTPOLL s
OUTPORT s
OUTPOST s
OUTPOUR s
OUTPRAY s
OUTPULL s
OUTPUSH
OUTRACE s
OUTRAGE s

OUTRANG
OUTRANK s
OUTRATE s
OUTRAVE s
OUTREAD s
OUTRIDE s
OUTRING s
OUTROAR s
OUTROCK s
OUTRODE
OUTROLL s
OUTROOT s
OUTRUNG
OUTRUSH
OUTSAID
OUTSAIL s
OUTSANG
OUTSEEN
OUTSELL s
OUTSHOT s
OUTSIDE s
OUTSING s
OUTSIZE s
OUTSOAR s
OUTSOLD
OUTSOLE s
OUTSPAN s
OUTSPED
OUTSTAY s
OUTSTEP s
OUTSULK s
OUTSUNG
OUTSWAM
OUTSWIM s
OUTSWUM
OUTTAKE s

OUTTALK s	OUTVOTE s	OUTWELL s	OUTWISH
OUTTASK s	OUTWAIT s	OUTWENT	OUTWITH
OUTTELL s	OUTWALK s	OUTWEPT	OUTWORE
OUTTOLD	OUTWARD s	OUTWICK s	OUTWORK s
OUTTOOK	OUTWASH	OUTWILE s	OUTWORN
OUTTROT s	OUTWEAR s	OUTWILL s	OUTWRIT
OUTTURN s	OUTWEED s	OUTWIND s	OUTYELL s
OUTVIED	OUTWEEP s	OUTWING s	OUTYELP s

Eight-letter OUT words

OUTACTED	OUTCHEAT s	OUTFENCE s	OUTLAUGH s
OUTADDED	OUTCHIDE s	OUTFIELD s	OUTLAWED
OUTARGUE s	OUTCLASS	OUTFIGHT s	OUTLEAPT
OUTASKED	OUTCLIMB s	OUTFIRED	OUTLEARN s
OUTBAKED	OUTCLOMB	OUTFLANK s	OUTLINED
OUTBITCH	OUTCOACH	OUTFLASH	OUTLINER s
OUTBLAZE s	OUTCOUNT s	OUTFLIES	OUTLIVED
OUTBLEAT s	OUTCRAWL s	OUTFLING s	OUTLIVER s
OUTBLESS	OUTCRIED	OUTFLOAT s	OUTLOVED
OUTBLOOM s	OUTCRIES	OUTFLOWN	OUTLYING
OUTBLUFF s	OUTCROSS	OUTFLUNG	OUTMARCH
OUTBLUSH	OUTCROWD s	OUTFLUSH	OUTMATCH
OUTBOARD s	OUTCURSE s	OUTFOUND	OUTMOVED
OUTBOAST s	OUTCURVE s	OUTFOXED	OUTNAMED
OUTBOUND s	OUTDANCE s	OUTFOXES	OUTNIGHT s
OUTBOXED	OUTDARED	OUTFROWN s	OUTPACED
OUTBOXES	OUTDATED	OUTGASES	OUTPAINT s
OUTBRAVE s	OUTDODGE s	OUTGAZED	OUTPITCH
OUTBRAWL s	OUTDOING	OUTGIVEN	OUTPLACE s
OUTBREAK s	OUTDRANK	OUTGLARE s	OUTPOINT s
OUTBREED s	OUTDRAWN	OUTGLEAM s	OUTPOWER s
OUTBRIBE s	OUTDREAM s	OUTGNAWN	OUTPREEN s
OUTBROKE	OUTDRESS	OUTGOING s	OUTPRESS
OUTBUILD s	OUTDRINK s	OUTGROSS	OUTPRICE s
OUTBUILT	OUTDRIVE s	OUTGROUP s	OUTPRIZE s
OUTBULGE s	OUTDROVE	OUTGROWN	OUTPSYCH s
OUTBULLY	OUTDRUNK	OUTGUARD s	OUTPUNCH
OUTBURNT	OUTDURED	OUTGUESS	OUTPUPIL s
OUTBURST s	OUTDWELL s	OUTGUIDE s	OUTQUOTE s
OUTCAPER s	OUTDWELT	OUTHEARD	OUTRACED
OUTCASTE s	OUTEATEN	OUTHIRED	OUTRAGED
OUTCATCH	OUTFABLE s	OUTHOMER s	OUTRAISE s
OUTCAVIL s	OUTFACED	OUTHOUSE s	OUTRANCE s
OUTCHARM s	OUTFEAST s	OUTHUMOR s	OUTRANGE s

OUTRATED	OUTSKATE s	OUTSTATE s	OUTTRADE s
OUTRAVED	OUTSKIRT s	OUTSTEER s	OUTTRICK s
OUTREACH	OUTSLEEP s	OUTSTOOD	OUTTRUMP s
OUTREIGN s	OUTSLEPT	OUTSTRIP s	OUTVALUE s
OUTRIDER s	OUTSLICK s	OUTSTUDY	OUTVAUNT s
OUTRIGHT	OUTSMART s	OUTSTUNT s	OUTVENOM s
OUTRIVAL s	OUTSMELL s	OUTSWARE	OUTVOICE s
OUTROWED	OUTSMELT	OUTSWEAR s	OUTVOTED
OUTSAVOR s	OUTSMILE s	OUTSWEEP s	OUTVOTER s
OUTSCOLD s	OUTSMOKE s	OUTSWELL s	OUTVYING
OUTSCOOP s	OUTSNORE s	OUTSWEPT	OUTWASTE s
OUTSCORE s	OUTSPEAK s	OUTSWING s	OUTWATCH
OUTSCORN s	OUTSPEED s	OUTSWORE	OUTWEARY
OUTSERVE s	OUTSPELL s	OUTSWORN	OUTWEIGH s
OUTSHAME s	OUTSPELT	OUTSWUNG	OUTWHIRL s
OUTSHINE s	OUTSPEND s	OUTTAKEN	OUTWILED
OUTSHONE	OUTSPENT	OUTTHANK s	OUTWORTH s
OUTSHOOT s	OUTSPOKE	OUTTHINK s	OUTWOUND
OUTSHOUT s	OUTSPORT s	OUTTHREW	OUTWREST s
OUTSIDER s	OUTSTAND s	OUTTHROB s	OUTWRITE s
OUTSIGHT s	OUTSTARE s	OUTTHROW s	OUTWROTE
OUTSIZED	OUTSTART s	OUTTOWER s	OUTYIELD s

Words beginning with the prefix OVER

An s shows that a word can take a valid –S hook.

Words are excluded that happen to take the prefix OVER but are not genuine OVER- words. There is only one such word and that is OVERED.

Six-letter OVER words

OVERBY	OVERDO	OVERGO

Seven-letter OVER words

OVERACT s	OVERBID s	OVERDUE	OVERFLY
OVERAGE s	OVERBIG	OVERDYE s	OVERGET s
OVERALL s	OVERBUY s	OVEREAT s	OVERGOT
OVERAPT	OVERCOY	OVEREGG s	OVERHIT s
OVERARM s	OVERCUT s	OVEREYE s	OVERHOT
OVERATE	OVERDID	OVERFAR	OVERING
OVERAWE s	OVERDOG s	OVERFAT	OVERJOY s
OVERBED	OVERDRY	OVERFED	OVERLAP s
OVERBET s	OVERDUB s	OVERFIT	OVERLAX

OVERLAY s	OVERNET s	OVERRUN s	OVERSOW s
OVERLET s	OVERNEW	OVERSAD	OVERSUP s
OVERLIE s	OVERPAY s	OVERSAW	OVERTAX
OVERLIT	OVERPLY	OVERSEA s	OVERTIP s
OVERMAN s	OVERRAN	OVERSEE s	OVERTOP s
OVERMEN	OVERRED s	OVERSET s	OVERUSE s
OVERMIX	OVERREN s	OVERSEW s	OVERWET s

Eight-letter OVER words

OVERABLE	OVERCRAM s	OVERFUND s	OVERHYPE s
OVERAGED	OVERCRAW s	OVERGALL s	OVERIDLE
OVERARCH	OVERCROP s	OVERGANG s	OVERJUMP s
OVERAWED	OVERCROW s	OVERGAVE	OVERJUST
OVERBAKE s	OVERCURE s	OVERGEAR s	OVERKEEN
OVERBANK s	OVERDARE s	OVERGILD s	OVERKEEP s
OVERBEAR s	OVERDEAR	OVERGILT	OVERKEPT
OVERBEAT s	OVERDECK s	OVERGIRD s	OVERKEST
OVERBILL s	OVERDOER s	OVERGIRT	OVERKILL s
OVERBITE s	OVERDOES	OVERGIVE s	OVERKIND
OVERBLEW	OVERDONE	OVERGLAD	OVERKING s
OVERBLOW s	OVERDOSE s	OVERGOAD s	OVERKNEE
OVERBOIL s	OVERDRAW s	OVERGOES	OVERLADE s
OVERBOLD	OVERDREW	OVERGONE	OVERLAID
OVERBOOK s	OVERDUST s	OVERGREW	OVERLAIN
OVERBOOT s	OVERDYED	OVERGROW s	OVERLAND s
OVERBORE	OVERDYER s	OVERHAIR s	OVERLARD s
OVERBORN	OVEREASY	OVERHALE s	OVERLATE
OVERBRED	OVEREDIT s	OVERHAND s	OVERLEAF
OVERBRIM s	OVEREYED	OVERHANG s	OVERLEAP s
OVERBROW s	OVERFALL s	OVERHARD	OVERLEND s
OVERBULK s	OVERFAST	OVERHATE s	OVERLENT
OVERBURN s	OVERFEAR s	OVERHAUL s	OVERLIER s
OVERBUSY	OVERFEED s	OVERHEAD s	OVERLIVE s
OVERCALL s	OVERFELL	OVERHEAP s	OVERLOAD s
OVERCAME	OVERFILL s	OVERHEAR s	OVERLOCK s
OVERCAST s	OVERFINE	OVERHEAT s	OVERLONG
OVERCLAD	OVERFISH	OVERHELD	OVERLOOK s
OVERCLOY s	OVERFLEW	OVERHENT s	OVERLORD s
OVERCLUB s	OVERFLOW s	OVERHIGH	OVERLOUD
OVERCOAT s	OVERFOLD s	OVERHOLD s	OVERLOVE s
OVERCOLD	OVERFOND	OVERHOLY	OVERLUSH
OVERCOME s	OVERFOUL	OVERHOPE s	OVERMANY
OVERCOOK s	OVERFREE	OVERHUNG	OVERMAST s
OVERCOOL s	OVERFULL	OVERHUNT s	

OVERMEEK	OVERRATE s	OVERSOFT	OVERTRIP s
OVERMELT s	OVERREAD s	OVERSOLD	OVERTURN s
OVERMILD	OVERRICH	OVERSOON	OVERTYPE s
OVERMILK s	OVERRIDE s	OVERSOUL s	OVERURGE s
OVERMINE s	OVERRIFE	OVERSOWN	OVERUSED
OVERMUCH	OVERRIPE	OVERSPIN s	OVERVEIL s
OVERNAME s	OVERRODE	OVERSTAY s	OVERVIEW s
OVERNEAR	OVERRUDE	OVERSTEP s	OVERVOTE s
OVERNEAT	OVERRUFF s	OVERSTIR s	OVERWARM s
OVERNICE	OVERRULE s	OVERSUDS	OVERWARY
OVERPACK s	OVERSAIL s	OVERSURE	OVERWASH
OVERPAGE	OVERSALE s	OVERSWAM	OVERWEAK
OVERPAID	OVERSALT s	OVERSWAY s	OVERWEAR s
OVERPART s	OVERSAVE s	OVERSWIM s	OVERWEEN s
OVERPASS	OVERSEED s	OVERSWUM	OVERWENT
OVERPAST	OVERSEEN	OVERTAKE s	OVERWIDE
OVERPEER s	OVERSEER s	OVERTALK s	OVERWILY
OVERPERT	OVERSELL s	OVERTAME	OVERWIND s
OVERPLAN s	OVERSEWN	OVERTART	OVERWING s
OVERPLAY s	OVERSHOE s	OVERTASK s	OVERWISE
OVERPLOT s	OVERSHOT s	OVERTEEM s	OVERWORD s
OVERPLUS	OVERSICK	OVERTHIN	OVERWORE
OVERPOST s	OVERSIDE s	OVERTIME s	OVERWORK s
OVERPUMP s	OVERSIZE s	OVERTIRE s	OVERWORN
OVERRACK s	OVERSKIP s	OVERTOIL s	OVERWRAP s
OVERRAKE s	OVERSLIP s	OVERTONE s	OVERYEAR s
OVERRANK s	OVERSLOW	OVERTOOK	OVERZEAL s
OVERRASH	OVERSOAK s	OVERTRIM s	

Words beginning with the prefix PRE

An s shows that a word can take a valid –S hook.

Words are excluded that happen to take the prefix PRE but are not genuine PRE- words. Thus words such as PRETOR, PRELACY, and PRESENT are omitted.

Six-letter PRE words

PREACT s	PRECUT s	PREMAN	PRESET s
PREAMP s	PREDRY	PREMED s	PRETAX
PREARM s	PREFAB s	PREMEN	PREWAR
PREBID s	PREFIX	PREMIX	
PREBUY s	PRELAW	PREPAY s	

Seven-letter PRE words

PREAGED	PREDIVE	PRENAME s	PRESONG
PREANAL	PREDOOM s	PRENEED	PRESORT s
PREAVER s	PREDUSK s	PRENOON	PRETAPE s
PREBADE	PREEDIT s	PREORAL	PRETEEN s
PREBAKE s	PREEMPT s	PREPACK s	PRETELL s
PREBEND s	PREFACE s	PREPAID	PRETERM s
PREBILL s	PREFADE s	PREPARE s	PRETEST s
PREBIND s	PREFILE s	PREPAVE s	PRETEXT s
PREBOIL s	PREFIRE s	PREPILL	PRETOLD
PREBOOK s	PREFORM s	PREPLAN s	PRETRIM s
PREBOOM	PREFUND s	PREPONE s	PRETYPE s
PREBORN	PREGAME s	PREPOSE s	PREVAIL s
PRECAST s	PREHEAT s	PREPUPA s	PREVERB s
PRECEDE s	PREHEND s	PRERACE	PREVIEW s
PRECENT s	PRELIFE	PRERIOT	PREVISE s
PRECODE s	PRELOAD s	PREROCK	PREWARM s
PRECOOK s	PREMADE	PRESALE s	PREWARN s
PRECOOL s	PREMEAL	PRESELL s	PREWASH
PRECOUP	PREMEET	PRESHIP s	PREWIRE s
PRECURE s	PREMIXT	PRESHOW s	PREWORK s
PREDATE s	PREMOLD s	PRESIFT s	PREWORN
PREDAWN s	PREMOLT	PRESOAK s	PREWRAP s
PREDICT s	PREMOVE s	PRESOLD	

Eight-letter PRE words

PREACTED	PREBUILD s	PREDRIES	PREFROZE
PREADAPT s	PREBUILT	PREDRILL s	PREGUIDE s
PREADMIT s	PRECEDED	PREDYING	PREHUMAN s
PREADOPT s	PRECHECK s	PREELECT s	PREJUDGE s
PREADULT s	PRECHILL s	PREENACT s	PRELEGAL
PREALLOT s	PRECHOSE	PREERECT s	PRELIMIT s
PREALTER s	PRECITED	PREEXIST s	PRELIVES
PREAMBLE s	PRECLEAN s	PREFACED	PRELOVED
PREAPPLY	PRECLEAR s	PREFACER s	PRELUNCH
PREARMED	PRECODED	PREFADED	PREMEDIC s
PREAUDIT s	PRECRASH	PREFIGHT	PREMIXED
PREAXIAL	PRECURED	PREFILED	PREMIXES
PREBAKED	PRECURSE s	PREFIRED	PREMOLAR s
PREBASAL	PRECYCLE s	PREFIXED	PREMORAL
PREBIRTH s	PREDATED	PREFIXES	PREMOULD s
PREBLESS	PREDEATH s	PREFLAME	PREMOULT
PREBOARD s	PREDRAFT s	PREFOCUS	PREMOVED
PREBOUND	PREDRIED	PREFRANK s	PRENASAL s

PRENATAL s	PREPUBIS	PRESIDER s	PRETRAIN s
PREORDER s	PREPUNCH	PRESLEEP	PRETREAT s
PREOWNED	PREPUPAE	PRESLICE s	PRETRIAL s
PREPASTE s	PREPUPAL	PRESOLVE s	PRETYPED
PREPAVED	PRERADIO	PRESPLIT	PREUNION s
PREPLACE s	PRERENAL	PRESTAMP s	PREUNITE s
PREPLANT	PRERINSE s	PRESTING	PREVALUE s
PREPOSED	PRESCORE s	PRESTORE s	PREVISED
PREPRESS	PRESERVE s	PRETAPED	PREVISIT s
PREPRICE s	PRESHAPE s	PRETASTE s	PREVISOR s
PREPRINT s	PRESHOWN	PRETENSE s	PREWEIGH s
PREPUBES	PRESIDED	PRETONIC	PREWIRED

Words beginning with the prefix PRO

An s shows that a word can take a valid –S hook.

Words are excluded that happen to take the prefix PRO but are not genuine
PRO- words. Thus words such as PROFIT, PRODUCT, PROVIDE, and
PROMISER are omitted.

Six-letter PRO words

PROGUN	PROLEG s	PROLOG s	PROWAR

Seven-letter PRO words

PROBALL	PROFANE s	PROPEND s	PROTEND s
PROCARP s	PROFUSE	PROPONE s	PROTEST s
PROCURE s	PROLATE s	PROPOSE s	
PRODRUG s	PROLONG s	PRORATE s	
PROFACE	PRONOUN s	PROSECT s	

Eight-letter PRO words

PROBATED	PROFOUND s	PROPHASE s	PROTRADE
PROCINCT s	PROGRADE s	PROPOUND s	PROUNION
PROCLAIM s	PROLABOR	PRORATED	PROVIRAL
PROCURED	PROLAPSE s	PROROGUE s	PROVIRUS
PROCURER s	PROLATED	PROSTYLE s	
PRODROME s	PROMETAL s	PROTRACT s	

Words beginning with the prefix RE

An s shows that a word can take a valid –S hook.

Words are excluded that happen to take the prefix RE but are not genuine RE- words. Thus words such as REGENT, REGALED, and REMEMBER are omitted.

Six-letter RE words

REAVOW s	RECOMB s	REFLAG s	RELAND s
REBACK s	RECOOK s	REFLEW	RELATE s
REBAIT s	RECOPY	REFLOW s	RELEND s
REBASE s	RECORK s	REFOLD s	RELENT s
REBATE s	RECOUP s	REFOOT s	RELINE s
REBILL s	RECURE s	REFORM s	RELINK s
REBIND s	REDATE s	REFUEL s	RELIST s
REBITE s	REDEAL s	REFUND s	RELIVE s
REBODY	REDEEM s	REFUSE s	RELOAD s
REBOIL s	REDEFY	REGAIN s	RELOAN s
REBOOK s	REDENY	REGAVE	RELOCK s
REBOOT s	REDIAL s	REGEAR s	RELOOK s
REBORE s	REDIPT	REGIFT s	REMADE s
REBORN	REDOCK s	REGILD s	REMAIL s
REBUFF s	REDOES	REGILT	REMAKE s
REBUKE s	REDONE	REGIVE s	REMAND s
REBURY	REDRAW s	REGLOW s	REMATE s
RECALL s	REDREW	REGLUE s	REMEET s
RECANE s	REDYED	REGREW	REMELT s
RECANT s	REEARN s	REGROW s	REMEND s
RECAPS	REECHO	REHANG s	REMIND s
RECAST s	REEDIT s	REHASH	REMINT s
RECEDE s	REEMIT s	REHEAR s	REMIXT
RECENT	REFACE s	REHEAT s	REMOLD s
RECHEW s	REFALL s	REHEEL s	REMOVE s
RECHIP s	REFEED s	REHEMS	RENAIL s
RECITE s	REFEEL s	REHIRE s	RENAME s
RECITS	REFELL	REHOME s	RENEST s
RECLAD s	REFELT	REHUNG	REOPEN s
RECOAL s	REFILE s	REJOIN s	REPACK s
RECOAT s	REFILL s	REKING	REPAID
RECOCK s	REFILM s	REKNIT s	REPARK s
RECODE s	REFIND s	REKNOT s	REPASS
RECOIL s	REFINE s	RELACE s	REPAST s
RECOIN s	REFIRE s	RELAID	REPAVE s

REPEAL s	RESEAL s	RESPOT s	REUSED
REPEAT s	RESEAT s	RESTEM s	REVAMP s
REPERK s	RESECT s	RETACK s	REVEAL s
REPLAN s	RESEED s	RETAIL s	REVERB s
REPLAY s	RESEEK s	RETAIN s	REVERT s
REPLED	RESEEN	RETAKE s	REVEST s
REPLOT s	RESELL s	RETAPE s	REVIEW s
REPLOW s	RESEND s	RETEAM s	REVISE s
REPOLL s	RESENT s	RETEAR s	REVIVE s
REPONE s	RESEWN	RETELL s	REVOLT s
REPORT s	RESHIP s	RETEST s	REVOTE s
REPOSE s	RESHOD	RETIED	REWAKE s
REPOST s	RESHOE s	RETILE s	REWARD s
REPOUR s	RESHOT	RETIME s	REWARM s
REPULP s	RESHOW s	RETINT s	REWASH
REPUMP s	RESIDE s	RETIRE s	REWEAR s
REPURE s	RESIFT s	RETOLD	REWELD s
RERACK s	RESIGN s	RETOOK	REWILD s
RERAIL s	RESILE s	RETOOL s	REWIND s
REREAD s	RESITE s	RETORE	REWIRE s
RERENT s	RESIZE s	RETORN	REWOKE
RERISE s	RESKEW s	RETORT s	REWORD s
REROLL s	RESKIN s	RETRIM s	REWORE
REROOF s	RESOAK s	RETROD	REWORK s
REROSE	RESOLD	RETUNE s	REWORN
RESAID	RESOLE s	RETURF s	REWOVE
RESAIL s	RESORB s	RETURN s	REWRAP s
RESALE s	RESORT s	RETYPE s	REZERO s
RESAWN	RESOWN	REURGE s	REZONE s

Seven-letter RE words

REACTED	REANNEX	REBEGIN s	REBUILT
REACTOR s	REAPPLY	REBEGUN	RECANED
READAPT s	REARGUE s	REBIRTH s	RECARRY
READDED	REARISE s	REBLEND s	RECATCH
READMIT s	REARMED	REBLENT	RECEDED
READOPT s	REAROSE	REBLOOM s	RECENSE s
READORN s	REAVAIL s	REBOARD s	RECHART s
REAFFIX	REAWAKE s	REBORED	RECHEAT s
REAGENT s	REAWOKE	REBOUND s	RECHECK s
REALIGN s	REBADGE s	REBRACE s	RECHOSE
REALLOT s	REBASED	REBRAND s	RECITAL s
REALTER s	REBATED	REBREED s	RECITED
REAMEND s	REBEGAN	REBUILD s	RECITER s

RECLAIM s REEXPEL s REINCUR s REPATCH
RECLAME s REFACED REINDEX REPAVED
RECLASP s REFENCE s REINKED REPINED
RECLEAN s REFIGHT s REINTER s REPLACE s
RECLIMB s REFILED REISSUE s REPLANT s
RECLINE s REFIRED REJUDGE s REPLATE s
RECLOSE s REFIXED REKEYED REPLEAD s
RECODED REFIXES RELABEL s REPLIED
RECOLOR s REFLIES RELACED REPLIER s
RECOUNT s REFLOAT s RELAPSE s REPLIES
RECOUPE s REFLOOD s RELATED REPLUMB s
RECOURE s REFLOWN RELATER s REPOINT s
RECOVER s REFOCUS RELAXER s REPOSIT s
RECOWER s REFORGE s RELAXES REPOWER s
RECRATE s REFOUND s RELAYED REPRESS
RECROWN s REFRACT s RELEARN s REPRICE s
RECURED REFRAME s RELEASE s REPRIME s
RECURVE s REFRESH RELIGHT s REPRINT s
RECYCLE s REFRIED RELINED REPRISE s
REDATED REFRIES RELIVED REPRIZE s
REDEALT REFRONT s RELIVER s REPROBE s
REDOING REFROZE REMAKER s REPROOF s
REDOUBT s REGAUGE s REMARRY REPROVE s
REDRAFT s REGIVEN REMATCH REPULSE s
REDRAWN REGLAZE s REMATED REPURED
REDREAM s REGLOSS REMERGE s REQUOTE s
REDRESS REGLUED REMIXED RERAISE s
REDRIED REGORGE s REMIXER s RERISEN
REDRIES REGRADE s REMIXES REROUTE s
REDRILL s REGRAFT s REMODEL s RESAWED
REDRIVE s REGRANT s REMOULD s RESCALE s
REDROVE REGRATE s REMOUNT s RESCORE s
REEDIFY REGREEN s REMOVED RESEIZE s
REEJECT s REGREET s REMOVER s RESEWED
REEKING REGRIND s RENAMED RESHAPE s
REELECT s REGROOM s RENEWED RESHAVE s
REENACT s REGROUP s RENEWER s RESHINE s
REENDOW s REGROWN REOCCUR s RESHOED
REENJOY s REHEARD REOFFER s RESHONE
REENTER s REHINGE s REOILED RESHOOT s
REENTRY REHIRED REORDER s RESHOWN
REEQUIP s REHOMED REPAINT s RESIGHT s
REERECT s REHOUSE s REPANEL s RESITED
REEVOKE s REIMAGE s REPAPER s RESIZED

RESKILL s
RESLATE s
RESMELT s
RESOLED
RESOLVE s
RESOUND s
RESOWED
RESPACE s
RESPADE s
RESPEAK s
RESPECT s
RESPELL s
RESPELT
RESPIRE s
RESPITE s
RESPLIT s
RESPOKE
RESPOOL s
RESPRAY s
RESTACK s
RESTAFF s
RESTAGE s
RESTAMP s
RESTART s

RESTATE s
RESTOCK s
RESTOKE s
RESTORE s
RESTUDY
RESTUFF s
RESTUMP s
RESTYLE s
RESUSES
RESURGE s
RETAKEN
RETAKER s
RETALLY
RETAPED
RETASTE s
RETAXED
RETAXES
RETEACH
RETHINK s
RETILED
RETIMED
RETIRED
RETITLE s
RETOTAL s

RETOUCH
RETRACE s
RETRACK s
RETRACT s
RETRAIN s
RETRAIT s
RETREAD s
RETREAT s
RETRIAL s
RETRIED
RETRIES
RETUNED
RETWEET s
RETWIST s
RETYING
RETYPED
REUNIFY
REUNION s
REUNITE s
REURGED
REUSING
REUTTER s
REVALUE s
REVERSE s

REVISED
REVISIT s
REVISOR s
REVIVER s
REVOICE s
REVOLVE s
REVOTED
REVYING
REWAKED
REWAKEN s
REWATER s
REWAXED
REWAXES
REWEAVE s
REWEIGH s
REWIDEN s
REWIRED
REWOKEN
REWOUND
REWOVEN
REWRAPT
REWRITE s
REWROTE
REZONED

Eight-letter RE words

REABSORB s
REACCEDE s
REACCENT s
REACCEPT s
REACCUSE s
REACTANT s
REACTING
REACTION s
REACTIVE
READDICT s
READDING
READJUST s
READVISE s
REAFFIRM s
REAGENCY
REALLIED
REANOINT s
REANSWER s

REAPPEAR s
REARGUED
REARISEN
REARMING
REAROUSE s
REARREST s
REASCEND s
REASCENT s
REASSAIL s
REASSERT s
REASSESS
REASSIGN s
REASSORT s
REASSUME s
REASSURE s
REATTACH
REATTACK s
REATTAIN s

REAVOWED
REAWAKED
REAWAKEN s
REAWOKEN
REBACKED
REBADGED
REBAITED
REBASING
REBATING
REBELLOW s
REBIDDEN
REBILLED
REBITING
REBITTEN
REBODIED
REBODIES
REBOILED
REBOOKED

REBOOTED
REBORING
REBORROW s
REBOTTLE s
REBOUGHT
REBRACED
REBRANCH
REBUFFED
REBURIAL s
REBURIED
REBURIES
REBUTTON s
REBUYING
RECALLED
RECALLER s
RECANING
RECANTED
RECANTER s

RECAPPED	RECROSS	REENLIST s	REFUSING
RECAPTOR s	RECURING	REENROLL s	REFUSION s
RECARPET s	RECURRED	REEVOKED	REGAINED
RECAUGHT	RECURVED	REEXPORT s	REGAINER s
RECEDING	RECYCLED	REEXPOSE s	REGATHER s
RECEMENT s	RECYCLER s	REFACING	REGAUGED
RECENSED	REDAMAGE s	REFALLEN	REGEARED
RECENSOR s	REDATING	REFASTEN s	REGELATE s
RECENTER	REDECIDE s	REFENCED	REGIFTED
RECENTRE s	REDEEMED	REFIGURE s	REGILDED
RECHANGE s	REDEFEAT s	REFILING	REGIVING
RECHARGE s	REDEFECT s	REFILLED	REGLAZED
RECHEWED	REDEFIED	REFILMED	REGLOWED
RECHOOSE s	REDEFIES	REFILTER s	REGLUING
RECHOSEN	REDEFINE s	REFINERY	REGORGED
RECIRCLE s	REDEMAND s	REFINING s	REGRADED
RECITING	REDENIED	REFINISH	REGRATED
RECLOSED	REDENIES	REFIRING	REGRATER s
RECLOTHE s	REDEPLOY s	REFITTED	REGROOVE s
RECOALED	REDESIGN s	REFIXING	REGROUND
RECOATED	REDIALED	REFLEXED	REGROWTH s
RECOCKED	REDIGEST s	REFLEXES	REHAMMER s
RECODIFY	REDIPPED	REFLOWED	REHANDLE s
RECODING	REDIRECT s	REFLOWER s	REHANGED
RECOILED	REDISTIL s	REFLUENT	REHARDEN s
RECOILER s	REDIVIDE s	REFLUXED	REHASHED
RECOINED	REDOCKED	REFLUXES	REHASHES
RECOLOUR s	REDOLENT	REFLYING	REHEARSE s
RECOMBED	REDOUBLE s	REFOLDED	REHEATED
RECOMMIT s	REDRAWER s	REFOOTED	REHEATER s
RECONFER s	REDREAMT	REFOREST s	REHEELED
RECONVEY s	REDRIVEN	REFORGED	REHEMMED
RECOOKED	REDRYING	REFORMAT s	REHINGED
RECOPIED	REDUBBED	REFORMED	REHIRING
RECOPIES	REDYEING	REFORMER s	REHOMING s
RECORDED	REEARNED	REFOUGHT	REHOUSED
RECORDER s	REECHOED	REFRAMED	REIGNITE s
RECORKED	REECHOES	REFREEZE s	REILLUME s
RECOUPED	REEDITED	REFRINGE s	REIMAGED
RECOUPLE s	REEMBARK s	REFROZEN	REIMPORT s
RECOURSE s	REEMBODY	REFRYING	REIMPOSE s
RECRATED	REEMERGE s	REFUELED	REINCITE s
RECREANT s	REEMPLOY s	REFUNDED	REINDICT s
RECREATE s	REENGAGE s	REFUNDER s	REINDUCE s

REINDUCT s	RELOCATE s	REORIENT s	REPULPED
REINFECT s	RELOCKED	REOUTFIT s	REPULSED
REINFORM s	RELOOKED	REPACIFY	REPULSER s
REINFUSE s	REMAILED	REPACKED	REPUMPED
REINJECT s	REMAILER s	REPAIRED	REPURIFY
REINJURE s	REMAINED	REPAIRER s	REPURING
REINJURY	REMAKING	REPARKED	REPURSUE s
REINKING	REMANNED	REPASSED	REQUOTED
REINSERT s	REMAPPED	REPASSES	RERACKED
REINSTAL s	REMARKED	REPASTED	RERAILED
REINSURE s	REMARKER s	REPAVING	RERAISED
REINVADE s	REMARKET s	REPAYING	RERECORD s
REINVENT s	REMASTER s	REPEALED	REREMIND s
REINVEST s	REMATING	REPEGGED	RERENTED
REINVITE s	REMELTED	REPEOPLE s	REREPEAT s
REINVOKE s	REMENDED	REPERKED	REREVIEW s
REISSUED	REMERGED	REPERUSE s	REREVISE s
REISSUER s	REMINDED	REPHRASE s	RERIGGED
REJACKET s	REMINDER s	REPINING s	RERISING
REJIGGED	REMINTED	REPINNED	REROLLED
REJIGGER s	REMIXING	REPIQUED	REROLLER s
REJOINED	REMODIFY	REPLACED	REROOFED
REJUDGED	REMOLDED	REPLACER s	REROUTED
REJUGGLE s	REMOTION s	REPLATED	RESADDLE s
REKEYING	REMOVING	REPLAYED	RESAILED
REKINDLE s	REMURMUR s	REPLEDGE s	RESALUTE s
RELACING	RENAILED	REPLOUGH s	RESAMPLE s
RELANDED	RENAMING	REPLOWED	RESAWING
RELAPSED	RENATURE s	REPLUNGE s	RESAYING
RELAPSER s	RENEGATE s	REPLYING	RESCALED
RELAUNCH	RENESTED	REPOLISH	RESCHOOL s
RELAYING	RENEWING s	REPOLLED	RESCORED
RELEARNT	RENOTIFY	REPORTED	RESCREEN s
RELEASED	RENOVATE s	REPORTER s	RESCRIPT s
RELEASER s	RENUMBER s	REPOSTED	RESCULPT s
RELETTER s	REOBJECT s	REPOTTED	RESEALED
RELIABLE s	REOBTAIN s	REPOURED	RESEARCH
RELINING	REOCCUPY	REPRICED	RESEASON s
RELINKED	REOFFEND s	REPRIMED	RESEATED
RELISTED	REOILING	REPRISED	RESECURE s
RELIVING	REOPENED	REPRIZED	RESEEDED
RELOADED	REOPENER s	REPROBED	RESEEING
RELOADER s	REOPPOSE s	REPROVED	RESEIZED
RELOANED	REORDAIN s	REPROVER s	RESELECT s

RESELLER s	RESPACED	RETAGGED	REVALUED
RESERVED	RESPADED	RETAILED	REVAMPED
RESERVER s	RESPIRED	RETAILER s	REVAMPER s
RESETTER s	RESPITED	RETAILOR s	REVERIFY
RESETTLE s	RESPLICE s	RETAKING s	REVETTED
RESEWING	RESPOKEN	RETAPING	REVIEWED
RESHAPED	RESPRANG	RETARGET s	REVIEWER s
RESHAPER s	RESPREAD s	RETASTED	REVISING
RESHAVED	RESPRING s	RETAUGHT	REVISION s
RESHAVEN	RESPROUT s	RETAXING	REVIVIFY
RESHINED	RESPRUNG	RETEAMED	REVOICED
RESHOWED	RESTAGED	RETELLER s	REVOLVED
RESHOWER s	RESTATED	RETEMPER s	REVOTING
RESIFTED	RESTITCH	RETESTED	REWAKING
RESIGNED	RESTOKED	RETHREAD s	REWARDED
RESIGNER s	RESTORED	RETIEING	REWARDER s
RESILVER s	RESTORER s	RETILING	REWARMED
RESITING	RESTRAIN s	RETIMING	REWASHED
RESIZING	RESTRESS	RETINTED	REWASHES
RESKETCH	RESTRICT s	RETITLED	REWAXING
RESKEWED	RESTRIKE s	RETOOLED	REWEAVED
RESLATED	RESTRING s	RETRACED	REWEDDED
RESMOOTH s	RESTRIVE s	RETRACER s	REWELDED
RESOAKED	RESTROVE	RETRENCH	REWETTED
RESODDED	RESTRUCK	RETRYING	REWILDED
RESOFTEN s	RESTRUNG	RETUNING	REWINDED
RESOLDER s	RESTYLED	RETURFED	REWINDER s
RESOLING	RESUBMIT s	RETURNED	REWIRING s
RESOLVED	RESUMMON s	RETURNER s	REWORDED
RESOLVER s	RESUPINE	RETYPING	REWORKED
RESORBED	RESUPPLY	REUNITED	REWRITER s
RESORTED	RESURGED	REUNITER s	REZEROED
RESORTER s	RESURVEY s	REUPTAKE s	REZEROES
RESOUGHT	RESUSSES	REUPTOOK	REZONING
RESOURCE s	RETACKED	REURGING	
RESOWING	RETACKLE s	REUSABLE s	

Words beginning with the prefix SUB

An s shows that a word can take a valid –S hook.

Words are excluded that happen to take the prefix SUB but are not genuine
SUB-words. Thus words such as SUBDUE, SUBLIME, and SUBLATE are omitted.

Six-letter SUB words

SUBACT s	SUBGUM s	SUBMEN	SUBSET s
SUBDEB s	SUBLET s	SUBNET s	SUBTIL
SUBFEU s	SUBLOT s	SUBPAR	SUBURB s
SUBFIX	SUBMAN	SUBSEA	SUBWAY s

Seven-letter SUB words

SUBACID	SUBDUCE s	SUBORAL	SUBTASK s
SUBALAR	SUBDUCT s	SUBOVAL	SUBTAXA
SUBAQUA	SUBECHO	SUBPART s	SUBTEEN s
SUBAREA s	SUBEDIT s	SUBPLOT s	SUBTEND s
SUBARID	SUBFILE s	SUBRACE s	SUBTEST s
SUBATOM s	SUBFUSC s	SUBRENT s	SUBTEXT s
SUBBASE s	SUBFUSK s	SUBRING s	SUBTILE
SUBBASS	SUBGOAL s	SUBRULE s	SUBTONE s
SUBCELL s	SUBHEAD s	SUBSALE s	SUBTYPE s
SUBCLAN s	SUBIDEA s	SUBSECT s	SUBUNIT s
SUBCODE s	SUBITEM s	SUBSIST s	SUBVERT s
SUBCOOL s	SUBJOIN s	SUBSITE s	SUBZERO
SUBCULT s	SUBLINE s	SUBSOIL s	SUBZONE s
SUBDEAN s	SUBMENU s	SUBSONG s	
SUBDUAL s	SUBMISS	SUBTACK s	

Eight-letter SUB words

SUBABBOT s	SUBCOSTA	SUBGRADE s	SUBORDER s
SUBACRID	SUBCRUST s	SUBGRAPH s	SUBOVATE
SUBACTED	SUBCUTES	SUBGROUP s	SUBOXIDE s
SUBACUTE	SUBCUTIS	SUBHUMAN s	SUBPANEL s
SUBADULT s	SUBDEPOT s	SUBHUMID	SUBPHASE s
SUBAGENT s	SUBDUPLE	SUBIMAGO s	SUBPHYLA
SUBAUDIO	SUBDURAL	SUBINDEX	SUBPOLAR
SUBAURAL	SUBDWARF s	SUBLEASE s	SUBPRIME s
SUBAXIAL	SUBENTRY	SUBLEVEL s	SUBPRIOR s
SUBBASAL	SUBEPOCH s	SUBLIMED	SUBPUBIC
SUBBASIN s	SUBEQUAL	SUBLIMIT s	SUBSCALE s
SUBBLOCK s	SUBERECT	SUBLUNAR	SUBSENSE s
SUBBREED s	SUBFEUED	SUBMENTA	SUBSERVE s
SUBCASTE s	SUBFIELD s	SUBMERGE s	SUBSHAFT s
SUBCAUSE s	SUBFIXES	SUBMERSE s	SUBSHELL s
SUBCHIEF s	SUBFLOOR s	SUBNASAL	SUBSHRUB s
SUBCHORD s	SUBFLUID	SUBNICHE s	SUBSIZAR s
SUBCLAIM s	SUBFRAME s	SUBNODAL	SUBSKILL s
SUBCLASS	SUBGENRE s	SUBOCEAN	SUBSOLAR
SUBCLERK s	SUBGENUS	SUBOPTIC	SUBSONIC

SUBSPACE s	SUBTIDAL	SUBTRIBE s	SUBVIRAL
SUBSTAGE s	SUBTITLE s	SUBTRIST	SUBVIRUS
SUBSTATE s	SUBTONIC s	SUBTUNIC s	SUBVOCAL
SUBSTYLE s	SUBTOPIC s	SUBURBAN s	SUBWAYED
SUBTALAR	SUBTOTAL s	SUBURBIA s	SUBWORLD s
SUBTAXON s	SUBTRACT s	SUBVERSE s	SUBZONAL
SUBTENSE s	SUBTRADE s	SUBVERST	
SUBTHEME s	SUBTREND s	SUBVICAR s	

Words beginning with the prefix UN

An s shows that a word can take a valid –S hook.

Words are excluded that happen to take the prefix UN but are not genuine UN- words. Thus words such as UNDINE, UNCLING (UNCLE is a verb), and UNDERATE are omitted.

Six-letter UN words

UNABLE	UNCAKE s	UNDEAR	UNFOOL s
UNAGED	UNCAPE s	UNDECK s	UNFORM s
UNAKIN	UNCART s	UNDOCK s	UNFREE s
UNAWED	UNCASE s	UNDOER s	UNFURL s
UNAXED	UNCAST s	UNDOES	UNGAIN
UNBALE s	UNCATE	UNDONE	UNGEAR s
UNBARE s	UNCHIC	UNDRAW s	UNGILD s
UNBARK s	UNCLAD	UNDREW	UNGILT
UNBEAR s	UNCLEW s	UNDULY	UNGIRD s
UNBEEN	UNCLIP s	UNDYED	UNGIRT
UNBELT s	UNCLOG s	UNEASE s	UNGLAD
UNBEND s	UNCOCK s	UNEASY	UNGLUE s
UNBENT	UNCOIL s	UNEATH	UNGOWN s
UNBIAS	UNCOLT s	UNEDGE s	UNGYVE s
UNBIND s	UNCOOL	UNEVEN	UNHAIR s
UNBITT s	UNCOPE s	UNEYED	UNHAND s
UNBOLT s	UNCORD s	UNFACT s	UNHANG s
UNBONE s	UNCORK s	UNFAIR s	UNHASP s
UNBOOT s	UNCOWL s	UNFEED	UNHATS
UNBORE	UNCUFF s	UNFELT	UNHEAD s
UNBORN	UNCURB s	UNFINE	UNHEAL s
UNBRED	UNCURL s	UNFIRM	UNHELE s
UNBURY	UNCUTE	UNFIXT	UNHELM s
UNBUSY	UNDEAD	UNFOLD s	UNHEWN
UNCAGE s	UNDEAF s	UNFOND	UNHIVE s

UNHOLY
UNHOOD s
UNHOOK s
UNHOOP s
UNHUNG
UNHURT
UNHUSK s
UNICED
UNJUST
UNKENT
UNKEPT
UNKIND
UNKING s
UNKINK s
UNKISS
UNKNIT s
UNKNOT s
UNLACE s
UNLADE s
UNLAID
UNLASH
UNLAST
UNLEAD s
UNLEAL
UNLIKE s
UNLIME s
UNLINE s
UNLINK s
UNLIVE s
UNLOAD s
UNLOCK s
UNLORD s
UNLOST
UNLOVE s
UNMADE
UNMAKE s
UNMARD
UNMASK s

UNMEEK
UNMEET
UNMESH
UNMIRY
UNMIXT
UNMOLD s
UNMOOR s
UNMOWN
UNNAIL s
UNNEST s
UNOPEN
UNOWED
UNPACK s
UNPAID
UNPENT
UNPICK s
UNPILE s
UNPLUG s
UNPOPE s
UNPRAY s
UNPROP s
UNPURE
UNRAKE s
UNREAD
UNREAL
UNREEL s
UNREIN s
UNRENT
UNREST s
UNRIPE
UNROBE s
UNROLL s
UNROOF s
UNROOT s
UNROPE s
UNROVE
UNRUDE
UNRULE s

UNRULY
UNSAFE
UNSAID
UNSAWN
UNSEAL s
UNSEAM s
UNSEAT s
UNSEEL s
UNSEEN s
UNSELF s
UNSELL s
UNSENT
UNSEWN
UNSEXY
UNSHED
UNSHIP s
UNSHOD
UNSHOE s
UNSHOT s
UNSHUT s
UNSNAG s
UNSNAP s
UNSOFT
UNSOLD
UNSOUL s
UNSOWN
UNSPAR s
UNSPED
UNSPUN
UNSTEP s
UNSTOP s
UNSTOW s
UNSUIT s
UNSUNG
UNSUNK
UNSURE
UNTACK s
UNTAME s

UNTEAM s
UNTENT s
UNTHAW s
UNTIDY
UNTIED
UNTILE s
UNTOLD
UNTOMB s
UNTORN
UNTRIM s
UNTROD
UNTRUE
UNTUCK s
UNTUNE s
UNTURF s
UNTURN s
UNUSED
UNVAIL s
UNVEIL s
UNVEXT
UNWARE s
UNWARY
UNWEAL s
UNWELL
UNWEPT
UNWILL s
UNWIND s
UNWIRE s
UNWISE
UNWISH
UNWIST
UNWIVE s
UNWONT
UNWORK s
UNWORN
UNWOVE
UNWRAP s
UNYOKE s

Seven-letter UN words

UNACTED
UNADDED
UNADEPT s
UNADULT

UNAGILE
UNAGING
UNAIDED
UNAIMED

UNAIRED
UNAKING
UNALIKE
UNALIVE

UNAPTLY
UNARMED
UNASKED
UNAWAKE

UNAWARE s	UNCHOKE s	UNFAITH s	UNHIRED
UNBAKED	UNCITED	UNFAKED	UNHITCH
UNBALED	UNCIVIL	UNFAMED	UNHIVED
UNBARED	UNCLAMP s	UNFANCY	UNHOARD s
UNBASED	UNCLASP s	UNFAZED	UNHOPED
UNBATED	UNCLEAN	UNFENCE s	UNHORSE s
UNBEGET s	UNCLEAR	UNFEUED	UNHOUSE s
UNBEGOT	UNCLEFT	UNFILED	UNHUMAN
UNBEGUN	UNCLIPT	UNFIRED	UNIDEAL
UNBEING s	UNCLOAK s	UNFITLY	UNJADED
UNBLENT	UNCLOSE s	UNFIXED	UNJOINT s
UNBLESS	UNCLOUD s	UNFIXES	UNKEMPT
UNBLEST	UNCODED	UNFLESH	UNKNOWN s
UNBLIND s	UNCOMFY	UNFLUSH	UNLACED
UNBLOCK s	UNCOMIC	UNFOUND	UNLADED
UNBLOWN	UNCOPED	UNFREED	UNLADEN
UNBONED	UNCOUTH	UNFROCK s	UNLATCH
UNBORNE	UNCOVER s	UNFROZE	UNLAWED
UNBOSOM s	UNCRATE s	UNFUMED	UNLEARN s
UNBOUND	UNCRAZY	UNFUNNY	UNLEASH
UNBOWED	UNCROSS	UNFUSED	UNLEVEL s
UNBOXED	UNCROWN s	UNFUSSY	UNLIKED
UNBOXES	UNCURED	UNGATED	UNLIMED
UNBRACE s	UNCURSE s	UNGAZED	UNLINED
UNBRAID s	UNDATED	UNGIRTH s	UNLIVED
UNBRAKE s	UNDEALT	UNGLOVE s	UNLOBED
UNBROKE	UNDEIFY	UNGLUED	UNLOOSE s
UNBUILD s	UNDIGHT s	UNGODLY	UNLOVED
UNBUILT	UNDOING s	UNGORED	UNLUCKY
UNBULKY	UNDRAPE s	UNGREEN	UNMACHO
UNBURNT	UNDRAWN	UNGROUP s	UNMAKER s
UNCAGED	UNDRESS	UNGROWN	UNMANLY
UNCAKED	UNDREST	UNGUARD s	UNMARRY
UNCANNY	UNDRIED	UNGYVED	UNMATED
UNCAPED	UNDRUNK	UNHABLE	UNMEANT
UNCARED	UNDYING	UNHANDY	UNMERRY
UNCASED	UNEAGER	UNHAPPY	UNMETED
UNCEDED	UNEARED	UNHARDY	UNMEWED
UNCHAIN s	UNEARTH s	UNHASTY	UNMINED
UNCHAIR s	UNEATEN	UNHEARD	UNMITER s
UNCHARM s	UNEDGED	UNHEART s	UNMITRE s
UNCHARY	UNENDED	UNHEEDY	UNMIXED
UNCHECK s	UNEQUAL s	UNHELED	UNMIXES
UNCHILD s	UNFADED	UNHINGE s	UNMORAL

UNMOULD s	UNRIVEN	UNSMOTE	UNTIMED
UNMOUNT s	UNRIVET s	UNSNARL s	UNTIRED
UNMOVED	UNROBED	UNSNECK s	UNTONED
UNNAMED	UNROOST s	UNSOBER s	UNTRACE s
UNNEATH	UNROPED	UNSOLID	UNTRACK s
UNNERVE s	UNROUGH	UNSONSY	UNTREAD s
UNNOBLE s	UNROUND s	UNSOOTE	UNTRIDE
UNNOISY	UNROVEN	UNSOUND	UNTRIED
UNNOTED	UNROYAL	UNSOWED	UNTRUER
UNOAKED	UNRUFFE	UNSPEAK s	UNTRULY
UNOFTEN	UNRULED	UNSPELL s	UNTRUSS
UNOILED	UNSAFER	UNSPENT	UNTRUST s
UNORDER s	UNSAINT s	UNSPIDE	UNTRUTH s
UNOWNED	UNSATED	UNSPIED	UNTUNED
UNPACED	UNSAVED	UNSPILT	UNTWINE s
UNPAGED	UNSAWED	UNSPLIT	UNTWIST s
UNPAINT s	UNSCALE s	UNSPOKE	UNTYING s
UNPANEL s	UNSCARY	UNSPOOL s	UNURGED
UNPAPER s	UNSCREW s	UNSTACK s	UNUSUAL
UNPARED	UNSENSE s	UNSTAID	UNVEXED
UNPAVED	UNSEWED	UNSTATE s	UNVISOR s
UNPERCH	UNSEXED	UNSTEEL s	UNVITAL
UNPILED	UNSEXES	UNSTICK s	UNVOCAL
UNPLACE s	UNSHALE s	UNSTOCK s	UNVOICE s
UNPLAIT s	UNSHAPE s	UNSTRAP s	UNWAGED
UNPLUMB s	UNSHARP	UNSTRIP s	UNWAKED
UNPLUME s	UNSHELL s	UNSTUCK	UNWATER s
UNPOSED	UNSHENT	UNSTUNG	UNWAXED
UNPURSE s	UNSHEWN	UNSUNNY	UNWAYED
UNQUEEN s	UNSHIFT s	UNSURED	UNWEARY
UNQUIET s	UNSHOED	UNSURER	UNWEAVE s
UNQUOTE s	UNSHOOT s	UNSWEAR s	UNWHIPT
UNRACED	UNSHORN	UNSWEET	UNWHITE
UNRAKED	UNSHOUT s	UNSWEPT	UNWIPED
UNRATED	UNSHOWN	UNSWORE	UNWIRED
UNRAVEL s	UNSHOWY	UNSWORN	UNWISER
UNRAZED	UNSIGHT s	UNTAKEN	UNWITCH
UNREADY	UNSINEW s	UNTAMED	UNWITTY
UNREAVE s	UNSIZED	UNTAXED	UNWIVED
UNREEVE s	UNSLAIN	UNTAXES	UNWOMAN s
UNRIGHT s	UNSLICK	UNTEACH	UNWOOED
UNRIMED	UNSLING s	UNTENTY	UNWORTH s
UNRIPER	UNSLUNG	UNTHINK s	UNWOUND
UNRISEN	UNSMART	UNTILED	UNWOVEN

UNWRITE s   UNWRUNG   UNYOUNG
UNWROTE   UNYOKED   UNZONED

Eight-letter UN words

UNABATED	UNBELTED	UNBURDEN s	UNCLEWED
UNABUSED	UNBENDED	UNBURIED	UNCLINCH
UNACHING	UNBENIGN	UNBURIES	UNCLOSED
UNACIDIC	UNBEREFT	UNBURNED	UNCLOTHE s
UNACTIVE s	UNBESEEM s	UNBURROW s	UNCLOUDY
UNADORED	UNBIASED	UNBUSIED	UNCLOVEN
UNAFRAID	UNBIASES	UNBUSIER	UNCLOYED
UNAGEING	UNBIDDEN	UNBUSIES	UNCLUTCH
UNAGREED	UNBILLED	UNBUSTED	UNCOATED
UNALLIED	UNBISHOP s	UNBUTTON s	UNCOCKED
UNAMAZED	UNBITTED	UNCAGING	UNCOFFIN s
UNAMUSED	UNBITTEN	UNCAKING	UNCOILED
UNANCHOR s	UNBITTER	UNCALLED	UNCOINED
UNANELED	UNBLAMED	UNCANDID	UNCOLTED
UNARCHED	UNBLOODY	UNCANNED	UNCOMBED
UNARGUED	UNBLOWED	UNCAPING	UNCOMELY
UNARISEN	UNBOBBED	UNCAPPED	UNCOMMON
UNARMING	UNBODIED	UNCARDED	UNCOOKED
UNARTFUL	UNBODING	UNCARING	UNCOOLED
UNATONED	UNBOILED	UNCARTED	UNCOPING
UNAVOWED	UNBOLTED	UNCARVED	UNCORDED
UNAWAKED	UNBONDED	UNCASHED	UNCORKED
UNBACKED	UNBONING	UNCASING	UNCOSTLY
UNBAGGED	UNBONNET s	UNCASKED	UNCOUPLE s
UNBAITED	UNBOOKED	UNCASTED	UNCOWLED
UNBALING	UNBOOTED	UNCATCHY	UNCRATED
UNBANDED	UNBOTTLE s	UNCAUGHT	UNCREATE s
UNBANKED	UNBOUGHT	UNCAUSED	UNCREWED
UNBANNED	UNBOUNCY	UNCHANCY	UNCUFFED
UNBARBED	UNBOWING	UNCHARGE s	UNCULLED
UNBARING	UNBOXING	UNCHASTE	UNCURBED
UNBARKED	UNBRACED	UNCHEWED	UNCURLED
UNBARRED	UNBRAKED	UNCHICLY	UNCURSED
UNBASTED	UNBREECH	UNCHOKED	UNCURVED
UNBATHED	UNBRIDLE s	UNCHOSEN	UNDAMMED
UNBEARED	UNBRIGHT	UNCHURCH	UNDAMNED
UNBEATEN	UNBROKEN	UNCIPHER s	UNDAMPED
UNBEDDED	UNBUCKLE s	UNCLASSY	UNDARING
UNBEGGED	UNBUDDED	UNCLAWED	UNDASHED
UNBELIEF s	UNBUNDLE s	UNCLENCH	UNDAZZLE s

UNDECENT	UNFADING	UNFROZEN	UNHARMED
UNDECKED	UNFAIRED	UNFUNDED	UNHASPED
UNDEEDED	UNFAIRER	UNFURLED	UNHATTED
UNDEFIED	UNFAIRLY	UNFURRED	UNHEADED
UNDELETE s	UNFAMOUS	UNGAGGED	UNHEALED
UNDENIED	UNFALLEN	UNGAINLY	UNHEALTH s
UNDENTED	UNFANNED	UNGALLED	UNHEARSE s
UNDESERT s	UNFASTEN s	UNGARBED	UNHEATED
UNDEVOUT	UNFAULTY	UNGAUGED	UNHEDGED
UNDIMMED	UNFEARED	UNGAZING	UNHEEDED
UNDINTED	UNFELLED	UNGEARED	UNHELING
UNDIPPED	UNFELTED	UNGELDED	UNHELMED
UNDIVINE	UNFENCED	UNGENIAL	UNHELPED
UNDOABLE	UNFETTER s	UNGENTLE	UNHEROIC
UNDOCILE	UNFEUDAL	UNGENTLY	UNHIDDEN
UNDOCKED	UNFILIAL	UNGIFTED	UNHINGED
UNDOOMED	UNFILLED	UNGILDED	UNHIPPER
UNDOTTED	UNFILMED	UNGIRDED	UNHIVING
UNDOUBLE s	UNFISHED	UNGIVING	UNHOLIER
UNDRAPED	UNFITTED	UNGLAZED	UNHOLILY
UNDREAMT	UNFITTER	UNGLOVED	UNHOLPEN
UNDRIVEN	UNFIXING	UNGLUING	UNHOMELY
UNDROSSY	UNFIXITY	UNGODDED	UNHONEST
UNDUBBED	UNFLASHY	UNGORGED	UNHOODED
UNDULLED	UNFLAWED	UNGOTTEN	UNHOOKED
UNEARNED	UNFLEXED	UNGOWNED	UNHOOPED
UNEASIER	UNFLUTED	UNGRACED	UNHORSED
UNEASILY	UNFOILED	UNGRADED	UNHOUSED
UNEDGING	UNFOLDED	UNGRAZED	UNHUNTED
UNEDIBLE	UNFOLDER s	UNGREEDY	UNHUSKED
UNEDITED	UNFOLLOW s	UNGROUND	UNIDEAED
UNELATED	UNFOOLED	UNGUIDED	UNIMBUED
UNENDING	UNFOOTED	UNGUILTY	UNINSTAL s
UNENVIED	UNFORBID	UNGUMMED	UNINURED
UNERASED	UNFORCED	UNGYVING	UNIRONED
UNEROTIC	UNFORGED	UNHACKED	UNIRONIC
UNERRING	UNFORGOT	UNHAILED	UNISSUED
UNESPIED	UNFORKED	UNHAIRED	UNJAMMED
UNEVADED	UNFORMAL	UNHALLOW s	UNJOINED
UNEVENER	UNFORMED	UNHALSED	UNJOYFUL
UNEVENLY	UNFOUGHT	UNHALVED	UNJOYOUS
UNEXOTIC	UNFRAMED	UNHANDED	UNJUDGED
UNEXPERT	UNFREEZE s	UNHANGED	UNJUSTER
UNFABLED	UNFRIEND s	UNHAPPEN s	UNJUSTLY

UNKEELED	UNLORDLY	UNNETTED	UNPRIMED
UNKENNED	UNLOVELY	UNOBEYED	UNPRISON s
UNKENNEL s	UNLOVING	UNOPENED	UNPRIZED
UNKINDER	UNMAILED	UNORNATE	UNPROBED
UNKINDLY	UNMAIMED	UNPACKED	UNPROPER
UNKINGED	UNMAKING s	UNPACKER s	UNPROVED
UNKINGLY	UNMANFUL	UNPADDED	UNPROVEN
UNKINKED	UNMANNED	UNPAINED	UNPRUNED
UNKISSED	UNMANTLE s	UNPAIRED	UNPUCKER s
UNKISSES	UNMAPPED	UNPANGED	UNPULLED
UNKNIGHT s	UNMARKED	UNPARTED	UNPURELY
UNKOSHER	UNMARRED	UNPATHED	UNPURGED
UNLACING	UNMASKED	UNPAYING	UNPURSED
UNLADING s	UNMASKER s	UNPEELED	UNPUZZLE s
UNLASHED	UNMATTED	UNPEERED	UNQUOTED
UNLASHES	UNMEETLY	UNPEGGED	UNRACKED
UNLAWFUL	UNMELLOW	UNPENNED	UNRAISED
UNLAWING	UNMELTED	UNPEOPLE s	UNRAKING
UNLAYING	UNMENDED	UNPERSON s	UNRANKED
UNLEADED s	UNMESHED	UNPICKED	UNREALLY
UNLEARNT	UNMESHES	UNPILING	UNREAPED
UNLEASED	UNMEWING	UNPINKED	UNREASON s
UNLETHAL	UNMILKED	UNPINNED	UNREAVED
UNLETTED	UNMILLED	UNPITIED	UNRECKED
UNLEVIED	UNMINDED	UNPITTED	UNREELED
UNLICKED	UNMINGLE s	UNPLACED	UNREELER s
UNLIDDED	UNMIRIER	UNPLAYED	UNREEVED
UNLIKELY	UNMISSED	UNPLIANT	UNREINED
UNLIMBER s	UNMITRED	UNPLOWED	UNRENTED
UNLIMING	UNMIXING	UNPLUMED	UNREPAID
UNLINEAL	UNMOANED	UNPOETIC	UNREPAIR s
UNLINING	UNMODISH	UNPOISED	UNRESTED
UNLINKED	UNMOLDED	UNPOISON s	UNRETIRE s
UNLISTED	UNMOLTEN	UNPOLISH	UNRHYMED
UNLIVELY	UNMONIED	UNPOLITE	UNRIBBED
UNLIVING	UNMOORED	UNPOLLED	UNRIDDEN
UNLOADED	UNMOVING	UNPOSTED	UNRIDDLE s
UNLOADER s	UNMUFFLE s	UNPOTTED	UNRIFLED
UNLOCKED	UNMUZZLE s	UNPRAISE s	UNRIGGED
UNLOOKED	UNNAILED	UNPRAYED	UNRINGED
UNLOOSED	UNNATIVE s	UNPREACH	UNRINSED
UNLOOSEN s	UNNEEDED	UNPRETTY	UNRIPELY
UNLOPPED	UNNERVED	UNPRICED	UNRIPEST
UNLORDED	UNNESTED	UNPRIEST s	UNRIPPED

UNROBING	UNSETTLE s	UNSPHERE s	UNTENANT s
UNROLLED	UNSEWING	UNSPOILT	UNTENDED
UNROOFED	UNSEXIER	UNSPOKEN	UNTENDER
UNROOTED	UNSEXING	UNSPRUNG	UNTENTED
UNROPING	UNSEXIST	UNSTABLE	UNTESTED
UNROTTED	UNSEXUAL	UNSTABLY	UNTETHER s
UNROTTEN	UNSHADED	UNSTARCH	UNTHATCH
UNROUGED	UNSHADOW s	UNSTARRY	UNTHAWED
UNROUSED	UNSHAKED	UNSTATED	UNTHREAD s
UNRUBBED	UNSHAKEN	UNSTAYED	UNTHRIFT s
UNRUFFLE s	UNSHALED	UNSTEADY	UNTHRONE s
UNRULIER	UNSHAMED	UNSTITCH	UNTIDIED
UNRUSHED	UNSHAPED	UNSTONED	UNTIDIER
UNRUSTED	UNSHAPEN	UNSTOWED	UNTIDIES
UNSADDLE s	UNSHARED	UNSTRESS	UNTIDILY
UNSAFELY	UNSHAVED	UNSTRING s	UNTIEING
UNSAFEST	UNSHAVEN	UNSTRUCK	UNTILING
UNSAFETY	UNSHROUD s	UNSTRUNG	UNTILLED
UNSAILED	UNSHRUNK	UNSTUFFY	UNTILTED
UNSAINED	UNSICKER	UNSUBTLE	UNTIMELY
UNSALTED	UNSIFTED	UNSUBTLY	UNTINGED
UNSAPPED	UNSIGNED	UNSUCKED	UNTINNED
UNSASHED	UNSILENT	UNSUITED	UNTIPPED
UNSATING	UNSINFUL	UNSUMMED	UNTIRING
UNSAVORY	UNSLAKED	UNSUNNED	UNTITLED
UNSAYING	UNSLICED	UNSUPPLE	UNTOMBED
UNSCALED	UNSLUICE s	UNSURELY	UNTOWARD
UNSEALED	UNSMOKED	UNSUREST	UNTRACED
UNSEAMED	UNSMOOTH s	UNSWATHE s	UNTRADED
UNSEARED	UNSOAKED	UNSWAYED	UNTRENDY
UNSEASON s	UNSOAPED	UNTACKED	UNTRUEST
UNSEATED	UNSOCIAL	UNTACKLE s	UNTRUISM s
UNSECRET s	UNSOCKET s	UNTAGGED	UNTRUSTY
UNSEEDED	UNSODDEN	UNTAILED	UNTUCKED
UNSEEING	UNSOILED	UNTAMING	UNTUFTED
UNSEELED	UNSOLDER s	UNTANGLE s	UNTUNING
UNSEELIE	UNSOLEMN	UNTANNED	UNTURBID
UNSEEMLY	UNSOLVED	UNTAPPED	UNTURFED
UNSEIZED	UNSONSIE	UNTARRED	UNTURNED
UNSELDOM	UNSORTED	UNTASTED	UNTWINED
UNSELFED	UNSOUGHT	UNTAUGHT	UNUNITED
UNSELVES	UNSOULED	UNTAXING	UNUSABLE
UNSENSED	UNSOURED	UNTEAMED	UNUSABLY
UNSERVED	UNSPARED	UNTEMPER s	UNUSEFUL

UNVAILED	UNWALLED	UNWEDDED	UNWISEST
UNVALUED	UNWANING	UNWEEDED	UNWISHED
UNVARIED	UNWANTED	UNWEENED	UNWISHES
UNVEILED	UNWARDED	UNWEIGHT s	UNWITTED
UNVEILER s	UNWARIER	UNWELDED	UNWIVING
UNVEINED	UNWARILY	UNWETTED	UNWONTED
UNVENTED	UNWARMED	UNWIELDY	UNWOODED
UNVERSED	UNWARNED	UNWIFELY	UNWORDED
UNVESTED	UNWARPED	UNWIGGED	UNWORKED
UNVETTED	UNWASHED s	UNWILFUL	UNWORMED
UNVIABLE	UNWASHEN	UNWILLED	UNWORTHY
UNVIEWED	UNWASTED	UNWINDER s	UNYEANED
UNVIRTUE s	UNWATERY	UNWINGED	UNYOKING
UNVIZARD s	UNWEANED	UNWIRING	UNZIPPED
UNVOICED	UNWEAPON s	UNWISDOM s	
UNVULGAR	UNWEBBED	UNWISELY	

Words beginning with the prefix UP

An s shows that a word can take a valid –S hook.

Words are excluded that happen to take the prefix UP but are not genuine UP- words. Thus words such as UPPISH and UPPITY are omitted.

Six-letter UP words

UPBEAR s	UPDRAW s	UPHEAP s	UPLOCK s
UPBEAT s	UPDREW	UPHELD	UPLOOK s
UPBIND s	UPFILL s	UPHILD	UPMAKE s
UPBLEW	UPFLOW s	UPHILL s	UPMOST
UPBLOW s	UPFOLD s	UPHOLD s	UPPILE s
UPBOIL s	UPFURL s	UPHOVE	UPPROP s
UPBORE	UPGANG s	UPHUNG	UPRATE s
UPBOWS	UPGAZE s	UPHURL s	UPREAR s
UPBRAY s	UPGIRD s	UPKEEP s	UPREST s
UPCAST s	UPGIRT	UPKNIT s	UPRISE s
UPCOIL s	UPGOES	UPLAID	UPROAR s
UPCOME s	UPGONE	UPLAND s	UPROLL s
UPCURL s	UPGREW	UPLEAD s	UPROOT s
UPDART s	UPGROW s	UPLEAN s	UPROSE
UPDATE s	UPGUSH	UPLEAP s	UPRUSH
UPDIVE s	UPHAND	UPLIFT s	UPSELL s
UPDOVE	UPHANG s	UPLINK s	UPSEND s
UPDRAG s	UPHAUD s	UPLOAD s	UPSENT

UPSHOT s	UPSWAY s	UPTIME s	UPWARD s
UPSIDE s	UPTAKE s	UPTOOK	UPWELL s
UPSIZE s	UPTALK s	UPTORE	UPWENT
UPSOAR s	UPTEAR s	UPTORN	UPWIND s
UPSOLD	UPTICK s	UPTOSS	UPWRAP s
UPSTAY s	UPTIED	UPTOWN s	
UPSTEP s	UPTIES	UPTURN s	
UPSTIR s	UPTILT s	UPWAFT s	

Seven-letter UP words

UPALONG s	UPDIVED	UPPILED	UPSTARE s
UPBLOWN	UPDRAFT s	UPRAISE s	UPSTART s
UPBORNE	UPDRAWN	UPRATED	UPSTATE s
UPBOUND	UPDRIED	UPREACH	UPSTOOD
UPBRAID s	UPDRIES	UPRIGHT s	UPSURGE s
UPBRAST	UPENDED	UPRISEN	UPSWARM s
UPBREAK s	UPFIELD	UPRISER s	UPSWEEP s
UPBRING s	UPFLING s	UPRIVER s	UPSWELL s
UPBROKE	UPFLUNG	UPROUSE s	UPSWEPT
UPBUILD s	UPFRONT	UPSCALE s	UPSWING s
UPBUILT	UPGAZED	UPSHIFT s	UPSWUNG
UPBURST s	UPGOING s	UPSHOOT s	UPTAKEN
UPCATCH	UPGRADE s	UPSIZED	UPTEMPO s
UPCHEER s	UPGROWN	UPSKILL s	UPTHREW
UPCHUCK s	UPHEAVE s	UPSKIRT	UPTHROW s
UPCLIMB s	UPHOARD s	UPSLOPE s	UPTIGHT
UPCLOSE s	UPHOIST s	UPSPAKE	UPTRAIN s
UPCOAST	UPHOORD s	UPSPEAK s	UPTREND s
UPCOURT	UPLEANT	UPSPEAR s	UPTYING
UPCURVE s	UPLEAPT	UPSPOKE	UPVALUE s
UPCYCLE s	UPLIGHT s	UPSTAGE s	UPWHIRL s
UPDATED	UPLYING	UPSTAIR s	UPWOUND
UPDATER s	UPMAKER s	UPSTAND s	

Eight-letter UP words

UPBEARER s	UPCURVED	UPFLOWED	UPGROWTH s
UPBOILED	UPCYCLED	UPFOLDED	UPGUSHED
UPBRAYED	UPDARTED	UPFOLLOW s	UPGUSHES
UPBROKEN	UPDATING	UPFURLED	UPHEAPED
UPCAUGHT	UPDIVING	UPGATHER s	UPHEAVED
UPCLOSED	UPDOMING s	UPGAZING	UPHEAVER s
UPCOILED	UPDRYING	UPGIRDED	UPHOLDER s
UPCOMING	UPENDING	UPGRADED	UPHUDDEN
UPCURLED	UPFILLED	UPGRADER s	UPHURLED

UPJETTED	UPRAISED	UPSIZING	UPSWAYED
UPLANDER s	UPRAISER s	UPSOARED	UPTAKING
UPLAYING	UPRATING	UPSPOKEN	UPTALKED
UPLEANED	UPREARED	UPSPRANG	UPTHROWN
UPLEAPED	UPRISING s	UPSPRING s	UPTHRUST s
UPLIFTED	UPROARED	UPSPRUNG	UPTILTED
UPLIFTER s	UPROLLED	UPSTAGED	UPTOSSED
UPLINKED	UPROOTED	UPSTAGER s	UPTOSSES
UPLOADED	UPROOTER s	UPSTARED	UPTURNED
UPLOCKED	UPROUSED	UPSTATER s	UPVALUED
UPLOOKED	UPRUSHED	UPSTAYED	UPWAFTED
UPMAKING s	UPRUSHES	UPSTREAM s	UPWELLED
UPMARKET s	UPSCALED	UPSTROKE s	
UPPILING	UPSETTER s	UPSURGED	

Suffixes

Suffixes are just as useful as prefixes for the same reasons, so it's a good idea to study the lists of the most commonly available suffixes to help you find those elusive bonus words. This list is also useful for studying which adjective stems also form adverbs, as a glance at the -LY list demonstrates.

As with the prefixes list, words which end in the suffix letters by coincidence rather than etymology are excluded. For example, ENCAGE is omitted from the AGE words, DEMOLISH is omitted from the ISH words. Example of words omitted, if any, are given at the start of each suffix list.

Unlike prefixes though, the root part of the word may not always be a stand-alone word because often the root is modified when the suffix is added (eg DUTIFUL, EQUABLE).

Words six to eight letters in length ending in the suffix ABLE

Some can be pluralized as shown by the s. The addition of -ABLY shows where valid adverbial forms are allowed.

Words that happen to end in ABLE but not as a suffix are excluded so words such as BISTABLE and OVERABLE are omitted.

Six-letter ABLE words

ARABLE s
DOABLE
DYABLE
LIABLE

SUABLE   −ABLY
USABLE   −ABLY
VIABLE   −ABLY

Seven-letter ABLE words

ACCABLE
ACTABLE
ADDABLE
AFFABLE   −ABLY
AMIABLE   −ABLY
BATABLE
BITABLE
BUYABLE s
CAPABLE   −ABLY
CITABLE
CODABLE
CURABLE   −ABLY
DATABLE
DOWABLE
DRYABLE
DUPABLE
DURABLE s   −ABLY
DYEABLE
EATABLE s
EFFABLE
EQUABLE   −ABLY
ERRABLE
EYEABLE
FADABLE
FAXABLE
FINABLE
FIXABLE
FLYABLE
FRIABLE
FRYABLE
GELABLE
GETABLE
GIVABLE
HATABLE
HEWABLE
HIDABLE
HIRABLE

LIKABLE   −ABLY
LINABLE
LIVABLE
LOSABLE
LOVABLE   −ABLY
MAKABLE
MINABLE
MIRABLE
MIXABLE
MOVABLE s   −ABLY
MUTABLE   −ABLY
NAMABLE
NOTABLE s   −ABLY
OWNABLE
PACABLE
PAPABLE   −ABLY
PARABLE s
PAYABLE s
PLIABLE   −ABLY
POKABLE
POSABLE
POTABLE s
RATABLE s   −ABLY
RETABLE s
RIDABLE
ROPABLE
ROWABLE
RULABLE
SALABLE   −ABLY
SAVABLE
SAYABLE
SEEABLE
SEWABLE
SIZABLE   −ABLY
SKIABLE
SOWABLE
SUEABLE

TAKABLE
TAMABLE
TAXABLE s   -ABLY
TENABLE   -ABLY
TOTABLE
TOWABLE
TRIABLE
TUNABLE   -ABLY
TYPABLE

USEABLE   -ABLY
VATABLE
VOCABLE s
VOLABLE
VOTABLE
WADABLE
WAXABLE
WIRABLE
WOOABLE

Seven-letter ABLE words

ABATABLE
ABUSABLE
ADORABLE   -ABLY
AGITABLE
ALLIABLE
AMENABLE   -ABLY
AMICABLE   -ABLY
AMUSABLE
ARGUABLE   -ABLY
ATONABLE
AVOWABLE   -ABLY
BAILABLE
BANKABLE
BANNABLE
BARRABLE
BEARABLE   -ABLY
BEATABLE
BEDDABLE
BENDABLE
BIDDABLE   -ABLY
BILLABLE
BINDABLE
BITEABLE
BLAMABLE   -ABLY
BOATABLE
BOILABLE
BOMBABLE
BONDABLE
BOOKABLE
BOOTABLE
BRIBABLE
BUFFABLE
BURNABLE s

CALLABLE
CARTABLE
CASCABLE s
CASHABLE
CASTABLE
CAUSABLE
CHEWABLE
CITEABLE
CLOSABLE
CLUBABLE
COINABLE
COOKABLE s
COPIABLE
COPYABLE
CUFFABLE
CULPABLE   -ABLY
CURBABLE
CUTTABLE
DAMNABLE   -ABLY
DATEABLE
DENIABLE   -ABLY
DIGGABLE
DIMMABLE
DIPPABLE
DRAPABLE
DRAWABLE
DRIVABLE
DUTIABLE
EDITABLE
EDUCABLE s
ENVIABLE   -ABLY
ERASABLE
ERODABLE

EVADABLE
EVITABLE
EVOCABLE
EXILABLE
EXORABLE
EXPIABLE
FACEABLE
FARMABLE
FEEDABLE
FELLABLE
FILEABLE
FILLABLE
FILMABLE
FINDABLE
FINEABLE
FIREABLE
FISHABLE
FITTABLE
FLOWABLE
FOAMABLE
FOILABLE
FOLDABLE
FORDABLE
FORMABLE   −ABLY
FRAMABLE
FUNDABLE
FURLABLE
GAGEABLE   −ABLY
GAINABLE
GETTABLE
GIFTABLE s
GIVEABLE
GNAWABLE
GRADABLE s
GRAZABLE
GROWABLE
GUIDABLE
GULLABLE   −ABLY
GUSTABLE s
HACKABLE
HANGABLE
HATEABLE
HEALABLE
HEARABLE

HEATABLE
HELPABLE
HIREABLE
HITTABLE
HOLDABLE
HUGGABLE
HUMMABLE
HUNTABLE
IMITABLE
INARABLE
INSTABLE
INVIABLE   −ABLY
ISOLABLE
ISSUABLE   −ABLY
JAILABLE
JAMMABLE
JOINABLE
JUMPABLE
KEEPABLE
KICKABLE
KILLABLE
KISSABLE   −ABLY
KNOWABLE
LAPSABLE
LAUDABLE   −ABLY
LEADABLE
LEASABLE
LENDABLE
LETTABLE
LEVIABLE
LIENABLE
LIFTABLE
LIKEABLE   −ABLY
LINEABLE
LINKABLE
LIQUABLE
LISTABLE
LIVEABLE
LOADABLE
LOANABLE
LOCKABLE
LOVEABLE   −ABLY
LUGGABLE s
MAILABLE

MAKEABLE		PROBABLE s	–ABLY
MAPPABLE		PROVABLE	–ABLY
MASKABLE		PRUNABLE	
MELTABLE		PUMPABLE	
MENDABLE		QUOTABLE	–ABLY
MILLABLE		RACEABLE	
MINEABLE		RADIABLE	
MISSABLE		RAISABLE	
MOCKABLE		RATEABLE s	–ABLY
MOLDABLE		READABLE	–ABLY
MOOTABLE		REAPABLE	
MOVEABLE s	–ABLY	REEFABLE	
NAMEABLE		REELABLE	
NESTABLE		RELIABLE s	–ABLY
NETTABLE		RENTABLE	
OATHABLE		RESTABLE s	
OBEYABLE		REUSABLE s	
OBVIABLE		RIDEABLE	
OPENABLE		RINSABLE	
OPERABLE	–ABLY	RIPPABLE	
OPINABLE		ROCKABLE	
OUTFABLE s		ROLLABLE	
OVENABLE		ROPEABLE	
OXIDABLE		ROUSABLE	
PACKABLE		RUINABLE	
PALPABLE	–ABLY	RUNNABLE	
PANTABLE s		RUSTABLE	
PARSABLE		SACKABLE	
PASSABLE	–ABLY	SAILABLE	
PAWNABLE		SALEABLE	–ABLY
PECCABLE		SALVABLE	–ABLY
PEELABLE		SANDABLE	
PETTABLE		SATIABLE	–ABLY
PICKABLE		SAVEABLE	
PINTABLE s		SCALABLE	–ABLY
PITIABLE	–ABLY	SEALABLE	
PLACABLE	–ABLY	SEISABLE	
PLAYABLE		SEIZABLE	
PLOWABLE		SELLABLE	
PORTABLE s	–ABLY	SENDABLE	
POSEABLE		SERVABLE	
POTTABLE		SHAKABLE	
POURABLE		SHAMABLE	–ABLY
PRIZABLE		SHAPABLE	

SHARABLE
SHAVABLE
SHEDABLE
SHOWABLE
SIGNABLE
SINGABLE
SINKABLE
SIPPABLE
SIZEABLE   -ABLY
SLAKABLE
SLAYABLE
SLIDABLE
SMOKABLE
SOCIABLE s -ABLY
SOLVABLE
SORBABLE
SORTABLE   -ABLY
SPARABLE s
STATABLE
STEWABLE
STONABLE
STORABLE s
STOWABLE
SUITABLE   -ABLY
SUMMABLE
SURFABLE
SWAYABLE
SYLLABLE s
TAKEABLE
TALKABLE
TAMEABLE
TANNABLE
TAPEABLE
TAPPABLE
TASTABLE
TEARABLE
TEASABLE
TELLABLE
TESTABLE

TILLABLE
TILTABLE
TIPPABLE
TITHABLE
TITRABLE
TOLLABLE
TOTEABLE
TRADABLE
TUBBABLE
TUNEABLE   -ABLY
TURNABLE
TYPEABLE
UNDOABLE
UNUSABLE   -ABLY
UNVIABLE
VALUABLE s -ABLY
VARIABLE s -ABLY
VENDABLE s
VIEWABLE
VIOLABLE   -ABLY
VITIABLE
VOIDABLE
VOTEABLE
WADEABLE
WALKABLE
WARHABLE
WASHABLE s
WASTABLE
WEARABLE s
WELDABLE
WETTABLE
WILLABLE
WINDABLE
WINNABLE
WIPEABLE
WORKABLE   -ABLY
WRITABLE
ZOOMABLE

Words six to eight letters in length ending in the suffix AGE

<u>All</u> of these words can have an –S hook added.

Those words that happen to end in AGE where it has no relation to the suffix in any form are excluded, so words such as DEGAGE and UNCAGE are omitted.

Six-letter AGE words

ACHAGE	FUMAGE	MILAGE	SAVAGE
ALNAGE	GALAGE	MIRAGE	SEWAGE
AMBAGE	GARAGE	MURAGE	SILAGE
ANLAGE	GAVAGE	NONAGE	SOCAGE
BOCAGE	HIDAGE	OARAGE	SORAGE
BORAGE	HIRAGE	OHMAGE	TIRAGE
CEPAGE	HOMAGE	OUTAGE	TOWAGE
COWAGE	INNAGE	PARAGE	TRIAGE
CUBAGE	LAVAGE	PAVAGE	TUBAGE
DAMAGE	LINAGE	PELAGE	ULLAGE
DOSAGE	LOVAGE	PIPAGE	VISAGE
DOTAGE	LYNAGE	POTAGE	VOYAGE
EATAGE	MANAGE	RAVAGE	
ENNAGE	MENAGE	RIVAGE	
FORAGE	METAGE	ROMAGE	

Seven-letter AGE words

ABUSAGE	BROKAGE	CRANAGE	GUNNAGE
ACREAGE	BULKAGE	CUTTAGE	HAULAGE
AJUTAGE	BUOYAGE	DOCKAGE	HAYLAGE
AMENAGE	BURGAGE	DRAYAGE	HEADAGE
APANAGE	CABBAGE	DUNNAGE	HERBAGE
ARRIAGE	CAKEAGE	ECOTAGE	HIREAGE
ASSUAGE	CARNAGE	ESCUAGE	HOSTAGE
ASSWAGE	CARTAGE	ETALAGE	KEELAGE
AULNAGE	CENTAGE	FALDAGE	KIPPAGE
AVERAGE	COINAGE	FARDAGE	LAIRAGE
BAGGAGE	COLLAGE	FLOTAGE	LASTAGE
BANDAGE	COMPAGE	FLOWAGE	LEAFAGE
BARRAGE	CORDAGE	FOGGAGE	LEAKAGE
BEERAGE	CORKAGE	FOLIAGE	LIGNAGE
BONDAGE	CORNAGE	FOOTAGE	LINEAGE
BOSCAGE	CORSAGE	FROMAGE	LINKAGE
BOSKAGE	COTTAGE	FULLAGE	LOCKAGE
BREWAGE	COURAGE	GARBAGE	LUGGAGE
BROCAGE	COWHAGE	GUIDAGE	MASSAGE

MELTAGE	PORTAGE	SEPTAGE	TUNNAGE
MESSAGE	POSTAGE	SERFAGE	UMBRAGE
MILEAGE	POTTAGE	SIGNAGE	UNITAGE
MILLAGE	PRESAGE	SINKAGE	VANTAGE
MINTAGE	PRIMAGE	SOAKAGE	VENDAGE
MOCKAGE	PRISAGE	SOCCAGE	VENTAGE
MONTAGE	PROPAGE	SOILAGE	VIDUAGE
MOORAGE	QUAYAGE	SONDAGE	VILLAGE
MOULAGE	RAILAGE	SPINAGE	VINTAGE
OUVRAGE	RAMPAGE	STORAGE	VITRAGE
PACKAGE	REIMAGE	STOWAGE	VOLTAGE
PANNAGE	REMUAGE	SULLAGE	VORLAGE
PASSAGE	RESTAGE	TALLAGE	WAFTAGE
PAWNAGE	RIFFAGE	TANKAGE	WAINAGE
PAYSAGE	ROOTAGE	TANNAGE	WANTAGE
PEERAGE	RUMMAGE	TEENAGE	WARPAGE
PEONAGE	SACKAGE	TENTAGE	WASTAGE
PIERAGE	SALVAGE	THANAGE	WATTAGE
PILLAGE	SAUSAGE	THENAGE	WEFTAGE
PIPEAGE	SCALAGE	TILLAGE	WINDAGE
PLUMAGE	SCAVAGE	TOLLAGE	WORDAGE
PLUSAGE	SCUTAGE	TONNAGE	YARDAGE
PONDAGE	SEEPAGE	TRUCAGE	
PONTAGE	SELVAGE	TUNEAGE	

Eight-letter AGE words

ACCORAGE	BROCKAGE	DRESSAGE	GRAINAGE
ACIERAGE	CABOTAGE	DRIFTAGE	GRAMMAGE
ADJUTAGE	CARRIAGE	ENALLAGE	GRILLAGE
AGIOTAGE	CARUCAGE	ENDAMAGE	GROUPAGE
ALIENAGE	CERCLAGE	ENSILAGE	GUARDAGE
ALTARAGE	CHANTAGE	ENVISAGE	HELOTAGE
AMPERAGE	CHUMMAGE	EQUIPAGE	HERITAGE
APPANAGE	CLEARAGE	FERRIAGE	LANGRAGE
BADINAGE	CLEAVAGE	FLOATAGE	LANGUAGE
BALAYAGE	CLOUDAGE	FLOORAGE	LAYERAGE
BARONAGE	COMANAGE	FRAPEAGE	LEVERAGE
BERTHAGE	COVERAGE	FRAUTAGE	LITREAGE
BEVERAGE	COZENAGE	FRONDAGE	MALAXAGE
BLINDAGE	CREEPAGE	FRONTAGE	MARITAGE
BLOCKAGE	CRIBBAGE	FROTTAGE	MARRIAGE
BRAKEAGE	DIALLAGE	FRUITAGE	MESSUAGE
BRASSAGE	DISUSAGE	FUSELAGE	METAYAGE
BREAKAGE	DRAINAGE	GRAFTAGE	METERAGE

MISUSAGE	SABOTAGE	STERNAGE	UMPIRAGE
MORTGAGE	SEWERAGE	STILLAGE	VAULTAGE
MUCILAGE	SHORTAGE	STOCKAGE	VAUNTAGE
PILOTAGE	SLIPPAGE	STOPPAGE	VERBIAGE
PINOTAGE	SMALLAGE	STRAVAGE	VICARAGE
PLANTAGE	SPILLAGE	STREWAGE	VICINAGE
PLOTTAGE	SPOILAGE	STUMPAGE	WAGONAGE
PLUSSAGE	SPOUSAGE	SUFFRAGE	WATERAGE
POUNDAGE	SQUIRAGE	THIRLAGE	WEIGHAGE
PROPHAGE	STAFFAGE	TRACKAGE	WHARFAGE
PUCELAGE	STALLAGE	TRUCKAGE	WRAPPAGE
PUPILAGE	STEALAGE	TRUQUAGE	WRECKAGE
REDAMAGE	STEARAGE	TUTELAGE	
ROUGHAGE	STEERAGE	TUTORAGE	

Words six to eight letters in length ending in the suffix ANCE

All of these words can have an –S hook added.

Those words that happen to end in ANCE where it has no relation to the suffix in any form are excluded, so words such as TRANCE, ENHANCE, and OUTDANCE are omitted.

Six-letter ANCE words

NUANCE	USANCE

Seven-letter ANCE words

ADVANCE	DURANCE	PENANCE	VACANCE
AIDANCE	FINANCE	ROMANCE	VALANCE
BALANCE	JOYANCE	SONANCE	
CREANCE	NOYANCE	SURANCE	

Eight-letter ANCE words

ABEYANCE	BROMANCE	FEASANCE	PASTANCE
ABIDANCE	BUOYANCE	GUIDANCE	PIQUANCE
ACUTANCE	CREPANCE	INSTANCE	PITTANCE
ADAMANCE	DEFIANCE	ISSUANCE	PORTANCE
AFFIANCE	DEVIANCE	ITERANCE	RADIANCE
ALLIANCE	DISTANCE	LAITANCE	RELIANCE
AMBIANCE	ELEGANCE	NUISANCE	RESIANCE
AMORANCE	ENTRANCE	ORDNANCE	RIDDANCE
BRISANCE	EXITANCE	PARLANCE	SORTANCE

TENDANCE	VARIANCE	VOIDANCE
VALIANCE	VIBRANCE	

Words six to eight letters in length ending in the suffix ENCE

<u>All</u> of these words can have an –S hook added.

Those words that happen to end in ENCE where it has no relation to the suffix in any form are excluded, so words such as REFENCE, FLORENCE, and SIXPENCE are omitted.

Six-letter ENCE words
EGENCE

Seven-letter ENCE words

ABSENCE	ESSENCE	LATENCE	REGENCE
CADENCE	FAIENCE	LUCENCE	SILENCE
COGENCE	FAYENCE	OFFENCE	URGENCE
DEFENCE	FLUENCE	POTENCE	VALENCE

Eight-letter ENCE words

AMBIENCE	EXIGENCE	PRESENCE	SEQUENCE
AUDIENCE	LENIENCE	PRETENCE	TANGENCE
CLARENCE	MERGENCE	PRUDENCE	TENDENCE
CREDENCE	NASCENCE	PUNGENCE	VERGENCE
EMINENCE	OPULENCE	SALIENCE	VIOLENCE
EVIDENCE	PATIENCE	SAPIENCE	

Words five to eight letters in length reflecting ER and EST forms of adjectives

Where these words can be treated as a noun, or happen to be a noun spelt as if a comparative form, they can be pluralized as shown by the s.

Those words that happen to end in ER and EST but are not comparative and superlative forms are excluded, so pairs such as EARNER, EARNEST and CONQUER, CONQUEST are omitted. There are a few examples where there is no valid ER form such as MOSTEST and ONLIEST. There is one example, UTTEREST, where there is no ER comparative form but UTTERER is shown because it is a valid noun.

Adjectival forms in ER and EST that are not IER and IEST

Five-and six-letter ER/EST words

ABLER	ABLEST	LITER s	LITEST
AIRER s	AIREST	LIVER s	LIVEST
APTER	APTEST	LOWER s	LOWEST
BARER	BAREST	LUXER	LUXEST
BASER	BASEST	MERER	MEREST
BLAER	BLAEST	MUTER	MUTEST
BLUER	BLUEST	NEWER	NEWEST
COYER	COYEST	NICER	NICEST
CUTER	CUTEST	NUDER	NUDEST
DIRER	DIREST	ODDER	ODDEST
DOPER s	DOPEST	OFTER	OFTEST
DREER	DREEST	OLDER	OLDEST
DRYER s	DRYEST	PALER	PALEST
	EFTEST	PUCER	PUCEST
ELDER s	ELDEST s	PURER	PUREST
FAVER	FAVEST	RARER	RAREST
FAYER	FAYEST	RAWER	RAWEST
FERER	FEREST	RIFER	RIFEST
FEWER	FEWEST	RIPER s	RIPEST
FEYER	FEYEST	RUDER	RUDEST
FINER s	FINEST s	SAFER	SAFEST
FLYER s	FLYEST	SAGER	SAGEST
FOUER	FOUEST	SANER	SANEST
FREER s	FREEST	SERER	SEREST
GAMER s	GAMEST	SHYER s	SHYEST
GAYER	GAYEST	SLEER	SLEEST
GEYER	GEYEST	SLYER	SLYEST
HALER s	HALEST	SORER	SOREST
HUGER	HUGEST	SURER	SUREST
IDLER s	IDLEST	TAMER s	TAMEST
ILLER	ILLEST	TRUER	TRUEST
JIVER s	JIVEST	TWEER s	TWEEST
LAMER	LAMEST	VILER	VILEST
LATER	LATEST s	WIDER	WIDEST
LAWER	LAWEST	WISER	WISEST
LAXER	LAXEST	WRYER	WRYEST
LIKER s	LIKEST	YARER	YAREST

Six-and seven-letter ER/EST words

ACIDER	ACIDEST	AGILER	AGILEST
ACUTER	ACUTEST	AMPLER	AMPLEST

ARCHER s	ARCHEST	DIMMER s	DIMMEST
ARIDER	ARIDEST	DINKER	DINKEST
AULDER	AULDEST	DOUCER	DOUCEST
AVIDER	AVIDEST	DOURER	DOUREST
AWARER	AWAREST	DROLER	DROLEST
BADDER	BADDEST	DUFFER s	DUFFEST
BALDER	BALDEST	DULLER	DULLEST
BASSER s	BASSEST	DUMBER	DUMBEST
BEIGER	BEIGEST	DUNNER	DUNNEST
BIGGER	BIGGEST	DUSKER	DUSKEST
BLAHER	BLAHEST	EVENER s	EVENEST
BLATER	BLATEST	EVILER	EVILEST
BOLDER	BOLDEST	FABBER	FABBEST
BOSSER	BOSSEST	FAINER	FAINEST
BRAVER s	BRAVEST	FAIRER	FAIREST
BRAWER	BRAWEST	FALSER s	FALSEST
BRUTER s	BRUTEST	FASTER s	FASTEST
BUFFER s	BUFFEST	FATTER	FATTEST
BUMMER s	BUMMEST	FAURER	FAUREST
CALMER	CALMEST	FEATER	FEATEST
CAMPER s	CAMPEST	FELLER s	FELLEST
CANTER s	CANTEST	FIRMER s	FIRMEST
CHICER	CHICEST	FITTER s	FITTEST
CLOSER s	CLOSEST	FONDER	FONDEST
COLDER	COLDEST	FOULER	FOULEST
COOLER s	COOLEST	FULLER s	FULLEST
CRUDER	CRUDEST	FUNNER	FUNNEST
CURTER	CURTEST	GAINER s	GAINEST
DAFTER	DAFTEST	GASHER	GASHEST
DAMNER s	DAMNEST s	GOLDER	GOLDEST
DAMPER s	DAMPEST	GOWDER	GOWDEST
DANKER	DANKEST	GRAVER s	GRAVEST
DARKER	DARKEST	GRAYER	GRAYEST
DARNER s	DARNEST s	GREYER	GREYEST
DEADER s	DEADEST	HARDER	HARDEST
DEAFER	DEAFEST	HAUTER	HAUTEST
DEARER	DEAREST s	HEPPER	HEPPEST
DEEDER	DEEDEST	HICKER	HICKEST
DEEPER	DEEPEST	HIGHER s	HIGHEST
DEFFER	DEFFEST	HIPPER	HIPPEST
DEFTER	DEFTEST	HOTTER s	HOTTEST
DEIDER	DEIDEST	ICKLER	ICKLEST
DEIFER	DEIFEST	INANER	INANEST
DENSER	DENSEST	IRATER	IRATEST

JIMPER	JIMPEST	NUMBER s	NUMBEST
JUSTER s	JUSTEST	OBESER	OBESEST
KEENER s	KEENEST	OPENER s	OPENEST
KEWLER	KEWLEST	OULDER	OULDEST
KINDER s	KINDEST	PAIRER	PAIREST
LANGER s	LANGEST	PATTER s	PATTEST
LANKER	LANKEST	PERTER	PERTEST
LARGER	LARGEST	PINKER s	PINKEST
LEALER	LEALEST	POORER	POOREST
LEANER s	LEANEST	POSHER	POSHEST
LEFTER	LEFTEST	PRONER	PRONEST
LENGER	LENGEST	PROWER	PROWEST
LEWDER	LEWDEST	PUIRER	PUIREST
LIEFER	LIEFEST	PUNKER s	PUNKEST
LIEVER	LIEVEST	QUARER	QUAREST
LIMPER s	LIMPEST	RADDER	RADDEST
LITHER	LITHEST	RADGER	RADGEST
LONGER s	LONGEST	RANKER s	RANKEST
LOOSER	LOOSEST	RASHER s	RASHEST
LOTHER	LOTHEST	RATHER	RATHEST
LOUDER	LOUDEST	REALER	REALEST
LOWSER	LOWSEST	REDDER s	REDDEST
LUSHER s	LUSHEST	RENKER	RENKEST
MADDER s	MADDEST	RICHER	RICHEST
MAINER	MAINEST	RUMMER s	RUMMEST
MAUVER	MAUVEST	SADDER	SADDEST
MEANER s	MEANEST	SAFTER	SAFTEST
MEEKER	MEEKEST	SAIRER	SAIREST
MEETER s	MEETEST	SALTER s	SALTEST
	MIDDEST	SEARER	SEAREST
MILDER	MILDEST	SEIKER	SEIKEST
MIMMER	MIMMEST	SICKER	SICKEST
MIRKER	MIRKEST	SKEWER s	SKEWEST
MOOTER s	MOOTEST	SLOWER	SLOWEST
	MOSTEST s	SNIDER	SNIDEST
MURKER	MURKEST	SOFTER	SOFTEST
NAFFER	NAFFEST	SOONER s	SOONEST
NAIFER	NAIFEST	SOURER	SOUREST
NAIVER	NAIVEST	SPARER s	SPAREST
NEARER	NEAREST	SPRYER	SPRYEST
NEATER	NEATEST	STALER	STALEST
NESHER	NESHEST	STEYER	STEYEST
NIGHER	NIGHEST	SUAVER	SUAVEST
NOBLER	NOBLEST	TALLER	TALLEST

TANNER s	TANNEST	WACKER s	WACKEST
TARTER	TARTEST	WANNER	WANNEST
TAUTER	TAUTEST	WARMER s	WARMEST
TENSER	TENSEST	WATTER	WATTEST
TERSER	TERSEST	WEAKER	WEAKEST
TOOMER	TOOMEST	WEETER	WEETEST
TRITER	TRITEST	WETTER s	WETTEST
UNCOER	UNCOEST	WHITER	WHITEST
VAGUER	VAGUEST	WILDER s	WILDEST
VAINER	VAINEST	WILLER s	WILLEST
VASTER	VASTEST	WOWFER	WOWFEST

Seven- and eight-letter ER/EST words

ACERBER	ACERBEST	CAULDER	CAULDEST
ACRIDER	ACRIDEST	CHASTER	CHASTEST
ADEPTER	ADEPTEST	CHEAPER	CHEAPEST
ALERTER	ALERTEST	CHIEFER	CHIEFEST
ASTUTER	ASTUTEST	CHILLER s	CHILLEST
BANALER	BANALEST	CHIRKER	CHIRKEST
BEAUTER	BEAUTEST	CHOICER	CHOICEST
BLACKER	BLACKEST	CHUFFER	CHUFFEST
BLANDER	BLANDEST	CLEANER s	CLEANEST
BLANKER	BLANKEST	CLEARER s	CLEAREST
BLEAKER	BLEAKEST	COARSER	COARSEST
BLEARER	BLEAREST	COUTHER	COUTHEST
BLINDER s	BLINDEST	CRANKER	CRANKEST
BLINGER	BLINGEST	CRASSER	CRASSEST
BLITHER s	BLITHEST	CRISPER s	CRISPEST
BLONDER	BLONDEST	CRONKER	CRONKEST
BLUFFER s	BLUFFEST	CROOKER	CROOKEST
BLUNTER	BLUNTEST	CROSSER s	CROSSEST
BONEYER	BONEYEST	CRUELER	CRUELEST
BRAGGER s	BRAGGEST	CRUMPER	CRUMPEST
BRAIDER s	BRAIDEST		DAMNDEST s
BRASHER	BRASHEST		DARNDEST s
BRENTER	BRENTEST	DEMURER	DEMUREST
BRIEFER s	BRIEFEST	DIVINER s	DIVINEST
BRILLER	BRILLEST	DOCILER	DOCILEST
BRISKER	BRISKEST	DOILTER	DOILTEST
BROADER	BROADEST	DOTTLER	DOTTLEST
BROWNER s	BROWNEST	DRABBER s	DRABBEST
BRUSKER	BRUSKEST	DREADER s	DREADEST
BUTCHER s	BUTCHEST	DREARER	DREAREST
BUXOMER	BUXOMEST	DROLLER	DROLLEST

DRUNKER	DRUNKEST	HOARSER	HOARSEST
	DURNDEST	HOLEYER	HOLEYEST
DWARFER	DWARFEST	HUMANER	HUMANEST
EAGERER	EAGEREST	HUMBLER s	HUMBLEST
EVILLER	EVILLEST	HUMIDER	HUMIDEST
EXACTER s	EXACTEST	IMPURER	IMPUREST
FAINTER s	FAINTEST	INEPTER	INEPTEST
FARTHER	FARTHEST	INERTER	INERTEST
FEEBLER	FEEBLEST	INSANER	INSANEST
FEINTER	FEINTEST	KITTLER	KITTLEST
FETIDER	FETIDEST	LAIGHER	LAIGHEST
FICKLER	FICKLEST	LEISHER	LEISHEST
FIERCER	FIERCEST	LICHTER	LICHTEST
FLASHER s	FLASHEST	LIGHTER s	LIGHTEST
FLATTER s	FLATTEST	LITTLER	LITTLEST
FLEETER	FLEETEST	LIVIDER	LIVIDEST
FLIPPER s	FLIPPEST	LOATHER s	LOATHEST
FLUSHER s	FLUSHEST	LOUCHER	LOUCHEST
FRAILER	FRAILEST	LOYALER	LOYALEST
FRANKER s	FRANKEST	LUCIDER	LUCIDEST
FRESHER s	FRESHEST	LURIDER	LURIDEST
FRONTER s	FRONTEST	MATURER s	MATUREST
FURTHER s	FURTHEST	MEAGRER	MEAGREST
FUTILER	FUTILEST	MICKLER	MICKLEST
GAUCHER s	GAUCHEST	MINUTER	MINUTEST
GAUNTER	GAUNTEST	MOISTER	MOISTEST
GELIDER	GELIDEST	MOROSER	MOROSEST
GENTLER	GENTLEST	NAKEDER	NAKEDEST
GLADDER	GLADDEST	NIMBLER	NIMBLEST
GLAMMER	GLAMMEST	OBTUSER	OBTUSEST
GLEGGER	GLEGGEST	OFTENER	OFTENEST
GLIBBER	GLIBBEST	OPAQUER	OPAQUEST
GLIDDER	GLIDDEST	ORANGER	ORANGEST
GLUMMER	GLUMMEST	ORNATER	ORNATEST
GRANDER	GRANDEST	PEARTER	PEARTEST
GREATER	GREATEST s	PHATTER	PHATTEST
GREENER s	GREENEST	PLAINER	PLAINEST
GRIMMER	GRIMMEST	PLUMMER	PLUMMEST
GRITTER s	GRITTEST	PLUMPER s	PLUMPEST
GROSSER s	GROSSEST	PLUSHER	PLUSHEST
GROUSER s	GROUSEST	POLITER	POLITEST
GRUFFER	GRUFFEST	PRIMMER s	PRIMMEST
GRUMMER	GRUMMEST	PROUDER	PROUDEST
HARSHER	HARSHEST	PURPLER	PURPLEST

QUEERER	QUEEREST	SPRUCER	SPRUCEST
QUICKER	QUICKEST	SQUARER s	SQUAREST
QUIETER s	QUIETEST	STABLER s	STABLEST
RABIDER	RABIDEST	STAIDER	STAIDEST
RAPIDER	RAPIDEST	STARKER s	STARKEST
RAUCLER	RAUCLEST	STEEPER s	STEEPEST
REMOTER	REMOTEST	STEEVER	STEEVEST
RICHTER	RICHTEST	STERNER	STERNEST
RIGHTER s	RIGHTEST	STIEVER	STIEVEST
RIGIDER	RIGIDEST	STIFFER	STIFFEST
ROUGHER s	ROUGHEST	STILLER s	STILLEST
ROUNDER s	ROUNDEST	STOUTER	STOUTEST
SAVAGER	SAVAGEST	SUBTLER	SUBTLEST
SCANTER	SCANTEST	SUPPLER	SUPPLEST
SCARCER	SCARCEST	SVELTER	SVELTEST
SECURER s	SECUREST	SWANKER S	SWANKEST
SEDATER	SEDATEST	SWEETER	SWEETEST
SEMPLER	SEMPLEST	SWEIRER	SWEIREST
SERENER	SERENEST	SWELLER s	SWELLEST
SEVERER	SEVEREST	SWIFTER s	SWIFTEST
SHARPER s	SHARPEST	SWISHER s	SWISHEST
SHEERER	SHEEREST	TEPIDER	TEPIDEST
SHOALER	SHOALEST	TEUCHER	TEUCHEST
SHORTER	SHORTEST	TEUGHER	TEUGHEST
SIMPLER s	SIMPLEST	THICKER	THICKEST
SKIEYER	SKIEYEST	THINNER S	THINNEST
SKINTER	SKINTEST	TIGHTER	TIGHTEST
SLACKER s	SLACKEST	TIMIDER	TIMIDEST
SLEEKER s	SLEEKEST	TIREDER	TIREDEST
SLICKER s	SLICKEST	TOUGHER	TOUGHEST
SLIMMER s	SLIMMEST	TRIFFER	TRIFFEST
SMALLER	SMALLEST	TRIGGER s	TRIGGEST
SMARTER	SMARTEST	TRIMMER s	TRIMMEST
SMUGGER	SMUGGEST	UNIQUER	UNIQUEST
SNELLER	SNELLEST	UNRIPER	UNRIPEST
SNODDER	SNODDEST	UNSAFER	UNSAFEST
SNUGGER	SNUGGEST	UNSURER	UNSUREST
SOBERER	SOBEREST	UNTRUER	UNTRUEST
SOLIDER	SOLIDEST	UNWISER	UNWISEST
SOMBRER	SOMBREST	URBANER	URBANEST
SOOTHER S	SOOTHEST	UTTERER s	UTTEREST
SOUNDER S	SOUNDEST	VALIDER	VALIDEST
SPARSER	SPARSEST	VAPIDER	VAPIDEST
SPICKER	SPICKEST	VIVIDER	VIVIDEST

WEIRDER	WEIRDEST	WRONGER s	WRONGEST
WERSHER	WERSHEST	YOUNGER s	YOUNGEST

Adjectival forms in IER and IEST derived from adjectives ending in Y, EY, or IE

Five- and six-letter IER/IEST words

DRIER s	DRIEST	SHIER s	SHIEST
FLIER s	FLIEST	SLIER	SLIEST
GOIER	GOIEST	WRIER	WRIEST
ICIER	ICIEST		

Six- and seven-letter IER/IEST words

ACHIER	ACHIEST	DYKIER	DYKIEST
AERIER	AERIEST	EASIER	EASIEST
AIRIER	AIRIEST	EDGIER	EDGIEST
ARSIER	ARSIEST	EELIER	EELIEST
ARTIER	ARTIEST	EERIER	EERIEST
ASHIER	ASHIEST	EGGIER	EGGIEST
AWNIER	AWNIEST	ELMIER	ELMIEST
BABIER	BABIEST	FADIER	FADIEST
BLUIER	BLUIEST	FAKIER	FAKIEST
BONIER	BONIEST	FIKIER	FIKIEST
BOXIER	BOXIEST	FLUIER	FLUIEST
BUSIER	BUSIEST	FOXIER	FOXIEST
CAGIER	CAGIEST	FOZIER	FOZIEST
CAKIER	CAKIEST	FUMIER	FUMIEST
CANIER	CANIEST	GAMIER	GAMIEST
CLUIER	CLUIEST	GAPIER	GAPIEST
COKIER	COKIEST	GAZIER	GAZIEST
COSIER s	COSIEST	GLUIER	GLUIEST
COWIER	COWIEST	GOOIER	GOOIEST
COXIER	COXIEST	GORIER	GORIEST
COZIER s	COZIEST	HAYIER	HAYIEST
DEWIER	DEWIEST	HAZIER	HAZIEST
DICIER	DICIEST	HOKIER	HOKIEST
DIKIER	DIKIEST	HOLIER	HOLIEST
DOMIER	DOMIEST	HOMIER	HOMIEST
DOPIER	DOPIEST	ICKIER	ICKIEST
DOTIER	DOTIEST	IFFIER	IFFIEST
DOVIER	DOVIEST	INKIER	INKIEST
DOWIER	DOWIEST	JIVIER	JIVIEST
DOZIER	DOZIEST	JOKIER	JOKIEST

LACIER	LACIEST	RILIER	RILIEST
LAKIER	LAKIEST	RIMIER	RIMIEST
LAZIER	LAZIEST	ROKIER	ROKIEST
LIMIER	LIMIEST	ROPIER	ROPIEST
LINIER	LINIEST	RORIER	RORIEST
LOGIER	LOGIEST	ROSIER s	ROSIEST
LOVIER	LOVIEST	RUBIER	RUBIEST
LUNIER	LUNIEST	RULIER	RULIEST
MATIER	MATIEST	SAGIER	SAGIEST
MAZIER	MAZIEST	SAMIER	SAMIEST
MINIER	MINIEST	SEXIER	SEXIEST
MIRIER	MIRIEST	SIZIER	SIZIEST
MITIER	MITIEST	SKYIER	SKYIEST
MIXIER	MIXIEST	SPRIER	SPRIEST
MOPIER	MOPIEST	TAKIER	TAKIEST
MOTIER	MOTIEST	TAWIER	TAWIEST
NOSIER	NOSIEST	TEDIER	TEDIEST
OAKIER	OAKIEST	TIDIER s	TIDIEST
OARIER	OARIEST	TINIER	TINIEST
OATIER	OATIEST	TOEIER	TOEIEST
OILIER	OILIEST	TONIER	TONIEST
	ONLIEST	TOWIER	TOWIEST
OOFIER	OOFIEST	TUNIER	TUNIEST
OORIER	OORIEST	TYPIER	TYPIEST
OOSIER	OOSIEST	UGLIER	UGLIEST
OOZIER	OOZIEST	VERIER	VERIEST
ORBIER	ORBIEST	VIBIER	VIBIEST
OURIER	OURIEST	VINIER	VINIEST
OWLIER	OWLIEST	VOGIER	VOGIEST
OWRIER	OWRIEST	WALIER	WALIEST
PACIER	PACIEST	WANIER	WANIEST
PALIER	PALIEST	WARIER	WARIEST
PINIER	PINIEST	WAVIER	WAVIEST
PIPIER	PIPIEST	WAXIER	WAXIEST
POKIER	POKIEST	WILIER	WILIEST
PORIER	PORIEST	WINIER	WINIEST
POSIER	POSIEST	WIRIER	WIRIEST
POXIER	POXIEST	YAWIER	YAWIEST
PUKIER	PUKIEST	YUKIER	YUKIEST
PULIER	PULIEST	ZANIER	ZANIEST
PUNIER	PUNIEST	ZOOIER	ZOOIEST
RACIER	RACIEST		
RAVIER	RAVIEST		
RICIER	RICIEST		

Six- and seven-letter IER/IEST words

ACIDIER	ACIDIEST	BOPPIER	BOPPIEST
ANGRIER	ANGRIEST	BORTIER	BORTIEST
ANTSIER	ANTSIEST	BOSKIER	BOSKIEST
APPLIERs	APPLIEST	BOSSIER	BOSSIEST
ARTSIER	ARTSIEST	BOUSIER	BOUSIEST
BAGGIER	BAGGIEST	BOYSIER	BOYSIEST
BALDIER	BALDIEST	BRAKIER	BRAKIEST
BALKIER	BALKIEST	BRINIER	BRINIEST
BALMIER	BALMIEST	BROSIER	BROSIEST
BANDIER	BANDIEST	BUDDIER	BUDDIEST
BARDIER	BARDIEST	BUFFIER	BUFFIEST
BARKIER	BARKIEST	BUGGIER	BUGGIEST
BARMIER	BARMIEST	BULGIER	BULGIEST
BARNIER	BARNIEST	BULKIER	BULKIEST
BARRIERs	BARRIEST	BULLIER	BULLIEST
BASSIER	BASSIEST	BUMPIER	BUMPIEST
BATTIER	BATTIEST	BUNTIER	BUNTIEST
BAWDIER	BAWDIEST	BURLIER	BURLIEST
BEADIER	BEADIEST	BURRIER	BURRIEST
BEAKIER	BEAKIEST	BUSHIER	BUSHIEST
BEAMIER	BEAMIEST	BUSTIERs	BUSTIEST
BEATIER	BEATIEST	BUZZIER	BUZZIEST
BEEFIER	BEEFIEST	CACKIER	CACKIEST
BEERIER	BEERIEST	CADGIER	CADGIEST
BEIGIER	BEIGIEST	CALMIER	CALMIEST
BENDIER	BENDIEST	CAMPIER	CAMPIEST
BENTIER	BENTIEST	CANNIER	CANNIEST
BILGIER	BILGIEST	CANTIER	CANTIEST
BIRKIER	BIRKIEST	CARNIER	CARNIEST
BIRSIER	BIRSIEST	CASKIER	CASKIEST
BITSIER	BITSIEST	CATTIER	CATTIEST
BITTIER	BITTIEST	CHARIER	CHARIEST
BLADIER	BLADIEST	CHEWIER	CHEWIEST
BLOKIER	BLOKIEST	CHOKIER	CHOKIEST
BLOWIER	BLOWIEST	CISSIER	CISSIEST
BLUDIER	BLUDIEST	CLAYIER	CLAYIEST
BODGIER	BODGIEST	COALIER	COALIEST
BOGGIER	BOGGIEST	COBBIER	COBBIEST
BONNIER	BONNIEST	COCKIER	COCKIEST
BOOFIER	BOOFIEST	COMBIER	COMBIEST
BOOKIER	BOOKIEST	COMFIER	COMFIEST
BOOMIER	BOOMIEST	CONKIER	CONKIEST
BOOZIER	BOOZIEST	COOMIER	COOMIEST

COPSIER	COPSIEST	DOOMIER	DOOMIEST
CORKIER	CORKIEST	DORKIER	DORKIEST
CORNIER	CORNIEST	DORTIER	DORTIEST
CRAPIER	CRAPIEST	DOTTIER	DOTTIEST
CRAZIER	CRAZIEST	DOWDIER	DOWDIEST
CREPIER	CREPIEST	DOWLIER	DOWLIEST
CRUDIER	CRUDIEST	DOWNIER	DOWNIEST
CUBBIER	CUBBIEST	DRAPIERs	DRAPIEST
CULTIER	CULTIEST	DRONIER	DRONIEST
CUPPIER	CUPPIEST	DRUSIER	DRUSIEST
CURDIER	CURDIEST	DRUXIER	DRUXIEST
CURLIER	CURLIEST	DUCKIER	DUCKIEST
CURNIER	CURNIEST	DUDDIER	DUDDIEST
CURVIER	CURVIEST	DULLIER	DULLIEST
CUSHIER	CUSHIEST	DUMMIER	DUMMIEST
CUSPIER	CUSPIEST	DUMPIER	DUMPIEST
CUTTIER	CUTTIEST	DUNGIER	DUNGIEST
DAFFIER	DAFFIEST	DUNNIER	DUNNIEST
DAGGIER	DAGGIEST	DURGIER	DURGIEST
DAMPIER	DAMPIEST	DUSKIER	DUSKIEST
DANCIER	DANCIEST	DUSTIER	DUSTIEST
DANDIER	DANDIEST	EARLIER	EARLIEST
DASHIER	DASHIEST	ECHOIER	ECHOIEST
DAUBIER	DAUBIEST	EENSIER	EENSIEST
DEBBIER	DEBBIEST	EMPTIERs	EMPTIEST
DEEDIER	DEEDIEST	FABBIER	FABBIEST
DELLIER	DELLIEST	FADDIER	FADDIEST
DICKIER	DICKIEST	FAFFIER	FAFFIEST
DICTIER	DICTIEST	FAGGIER	FAGGIEST
DIDDIER	DIDDIEST	FAIRIER	FAIRIEST
DILLIER	DILLIEST	FANCIERs	FANCIEST
DINGIER	DINGIEST	FATTIER	FATTIEST
DINKIER	DINKIEST	FAWNIER	FAWNIEST
DIPPIER	DIPPIEST	FEIRIER	FEIRIEST
DIRTIER	DIRTIEST	FELTIER	FELTIEST
DISHIER	DISHIEST	FEMMIER	FEMMIEST
DITSIER	DITSIEST	FENDIER	FENDIEST
DITZIER	DITZIEST	FENNIER	FENNIEST
DIVVIER	DIVVIEST	FERLIER	FERLIEST
DIZZIER	DIZZIEST	FERNIER	FERNIEST
DODDIER	DODDIEST	FESTIER	FESTIEST
DODGIER	DODGIEST	FIERIER	FIERIEST
DOGGIER	DOGGIEST	FILMIER	FILMIEST
DONSIER	DONSIEST	FINNIER	FINNIEST

FIRRIER	FIRRIEST	GAWKIER	GAWKIEST
FISHIER	FISHIEST	GAWSIER	GAWSIEST
FISTIER	FISTIEST	GEEKIER	GEEKIEST
FITLIER	FITLIEST	GEMMIER	GEMMIEST
FIZZIER	FIZZIEST	GENTIER	GENTIEST
FLAKIER	FLAKIEST	GERMIER	GERMIEST
FLAMIER	FLAMIEST	GIDDIER	GIDDIEST
FLARIER	FLARIEST	GIMPIER	GIMPIEST
FLAWIER	FLAWIEST	GINNIER	GINNIEST
FLAXIER	FLAXIEST	GIRLIER	GIRLIEST
FLORIER	FLORIEST	GIRNIER	GIRNIEST
FLUKIER	FLUKIEST	GLADIER	GLADIEST
FLUTIER	FLUTIEST	GLARIER	GLARIEST
FOAMIER	FOAMIEST	GLAZIER s	GLAZIEST
FOGGIER	FOGGIEST	GLEBIER	GLEBIEST
FOLKIER	FOLKIEST	GLOBIER	GLOBIEST
FOOTIER	FOOTIEST	GOATIER	GOATIEST
FORKIER	FORKIEST	GOBBIER	GOBBIEST
FROWIER	FROWIEST	GODLIER	GODLIEST
FUBBIER	FUBBIEST	GOLDIER	GOLDIEST
FUBSIER	FUBSIEST	GOODIER	GOODIEST
FUDDIER	FUDDIEST	GOOFIER	GOOFIEST
FUDGIER	FUDGIEST	GOOKIER	GOOKIEST
FUFFIER	FUFFIEST	GOONIER	GOONIEST
FUGGIER	FUGGIEST	GOOPIER	GOOPIEST
FUGLIER	FUGLIEST	GOOSIER	GOOSIEST
FUNKIER	FUNKIEST	GORMIER	GORMIEST
FUNNIER	FUNNIEST	GORSIER	GORSIEST
FURRIER s	FURRIEST	GOTHIER	GOTHIEST
FURZIER	FURZIEST	GOUTIER	GOUTIEST
FUSSIER	FUSSIEST	GRAPIER	GRAPIEST
FUSTIER	FUSTIEST	GRIMIER	GRIMIEST
FUZZIER	FUZZIEST	GRIPIER	GRIPIEST
GABBIER	GABBIEST	GRODIER	GRODIEST
GALLIER	GALLIEST	GROVIER	GROVIEST
GAMMIER	GAMMIEST	GUCKIER	GUCKIEST
GAPPIER	GAPPIEST	GULFIER	GULFIEST
GASPIER	GASPIEST	GULPIER	GULPIEST
GASSIER	GASSIEST	GUMMIER	GUMMIEST
GAUCIER	GAUCIEST	GUNGIER	GUNGIEST
GAUDIER	GAUDIEST	GUNKIER	GUNKIEST
GAUMIER	GAUMIEST	GURLIER	GURLIEST
GAUZIER	GAUZIEST	GUSHIER	GUSHIEST
GAWCIER	GAWCIEST	GUSTIER	GUSTIEST

GUTSIER	GUTSIEST	JANTIER	JANTIEST
GUTTIER	GUTTIEST	JAZZIER	JAZZIEST
HAILIER	HAILIEST	JEMMIER	JEMMIEST
HAIRIER	HAIRIEST	JERKIER	JERKIEST
HAMMIER	HAMMIEST	JETTIER	JETTIEST
HANDIER	HANDIEST	JIGGIER	JIGGIEST
HAPPIER	HAPPIEST	JIMPIER	JIMPIEST
HARDIER	HARDIEST	JOCKIER	JOCKIEST
HASHIER	HASHIEST	JOLLIERs	JOLLIEST
HASTIER	HASTIEST	JOLTIER	JOLTIEST
HEADIER	HEADIEST	JOTTIER	JOTTIEST
HEAPIER	HEAPIEST	JOWLIER	JOWLIEST
HEAVIER	HEAVIEST	JUICIER	JUICIEST
HEDGIER	HEDGIEST	JUMPIER	JUMPIEST
HEEDIER	HEEDIEST	JUNKIER	JUNKIEST
HEFTIER	HEFTIEST	JUTTIER	JUTTIEST
HEMPIER	HEMPIEST	KEDGIER	KEDGIEST
HENNIER	HENNIEST	KEMPIER	KEMPIEST
HERBIER	HERBIEST	KERKIER	KERKIEST
HILLIER	HILLIEST	KICKIER	KICKIEST
HINKIER	HINKIEST	KIDGIER	KIDGIEST
HIPPIER	HIPPIEST	KINKIER	KINKIEST
HISSIER	HISSIEST	KISSIER	KISSIEST
HOARIER	HOARIEST	KOOKIER	KOOKIEST
HOODIER	HOODIEST	LADDIER	LADDIEST
HOOKIER	HOOKIEST	LAIRIER	LAIRIEST
HOOLIER	HOOLIEST	LAMBIER	LAMBIEST
HOOTIER	HOOTIEST	LANKIER	LANKIEST
HOPPIER	HOPPIEST	LARDIER	LARDIEST
HORNIER	HORNIEST	LARKIER	LARKIEST
HORSIER	HORSIEST	LARNIER	LARNIEST
HOUSIER	HOUSIEST	LATHIER	LATHIEST
HUFFIER	HUFFIEST	LAWNIER	LAWNIEST
HUGGIER	HUGGIEST	LEADIER	LEADIEST
HULKIER	HULKIEST	LEAFIER	LEAFIEST
HULLIER	HULLIEST	LEAKIER	LEAKIEST
HUMPIER	HUMPIEST	LEARIER	LEARIEST
HUNKIER	HUNKIEST	LEAVIER	LEAVIEST
HUSHIER	HUSHIEST	LEDGIER	LEDGIEST
HUSKIER	HUSKIEST	LEERIER	LEERIEST
IRONIER	IRONIEST	LEGGIER	LEGGIEST
ITCHIER	ITCHIEST	LIMBIER	LIMBIEST
JAGGIER	JAGGIEST	LINGIER	LINGIEST
JAMMIER	JAMMIEST	LINKIER	LINKIEST

LINTIER	LINTIEST	MINGIER	MINGIEST
LIPPIER	LIPPIEST	MINTIER	MINTIEST
LOAMIER	LOAMIEST	MIRKIER	MIRKIEST
LOFTIER	LOFTIEST	MIRLIER	MIRLIEST
LOGGIER	LOGGIEST	MISSIER	MISSIEST
LOOBIER	LOOBIEST	MISTIER	MISTIEST
LOONIER	LOONIEST	MOCHIER	MOCHIEST
LOOPIER	LOOPIEST	MOLDIER	MOLDIEST
LOPPIER	LOPPIEST	MOODIER	MOODIEST
LOSSIER	LOSSIEST	MOONTER	MOONIEST
LOURIER	LOURIEST	MOORIER	MOORIEST
LOUSIER	LOUSIEST	MOPPIER	MOPPIEST
LOWLIER	LOWLIEST	MOSSIER	MOSSIEST
LUCKIER	LUCKIEST	MOTHIER	MOTHIEST
LUMMIER	LUMMIEST	MOTLIER	MOTLIEST
LUMPIER	LUMPIEST	MOTTIER	MOTTIEST
LUSHIER	LUSHIEST	MOUSIER	MOUSIEST
LUSTIER	LUSTIEST	MUCKIER	MUCKIEST
MALMIER	MALMIEST	MUDDIER	MUDDIEST
MALTIER	MALTIEST	MUGGIER	MUGGIEST
MANGIER	MANGIEST	MUMSIER	MUMSIEST
MANKIER	MANKIEST	MURKIER	MURKIEST
MANLIER	MANLIEST	MURLIER	MURLIEST
MARDIER	MARDIEST	MUSHIER	MUSHIEST
MARLIER	MARLIEST	MUSKIER	MUSKIEST
MARVIER	MARVIEST	MUSSIER	MUSSIEST
MASHIER	MASHIEST	MUSTIER	MUSTIEST
MASSIER	MASSIEST	MUZZIER	MUZZIEST
MASTIER	MASTIEST	MYTHIER	MYTHIEST
MAUSIER	MAUSIEST	NAGGIER	NAGGIEST
MAUZIER	MAUZIEST	NAPPIER	NAPPIEST
MAWKIER	MAWKIEST	NARKIER	NARKIEST
MEALIER	MEALIEST	NASTIER	NASTIEST
MEATIER	MEATIEST	NATTIER	NATTIEST
MELTIER	MELTIEST	NEDDIER	NEDDIEST
MERRIER	MERRIEST	NEEDIER	NEEDIEST
MESHIER	MESHIEST	NERDIER	NERDIEST
MESSIER	MESSIEST	NERVIER	NERVIEST
MIDGIER	MIDGIEST	NETTIER	NETTIEST
MIFFIER	MIFFIEST	NEWSIER	NEWSIEST
MILKIER	MILKIEST	NIFFIER	NIFFIEST
MILTIER	MILTIEST	NIFTIER	NIFTIEST
MIMSIER	MIMSIEST	NIPPIER	NIPPIEST
MINCIER	MINCIEST	NIRLIER	NIRLIEST

NITTIER	NITTIEST	PODGIER	PODGIEST
NOBBIER	NOBBIEST	PONCIER	PONCIEST
NODDIER	NODDIEST	PONGIER	PONGIEST
NOILIER	NOILIEST	POOFIER	POOFIEST
NOISIER	NOISIEST	POOPIER	POOPIEST
NOOKIER	NOOKIEST	POOVIER	POOVIEST
NOUNIER	NOUNIEST	POPPIER	POPPIEST
NOWTIER	NOWTIEST	PORKIER	PORKIEST
NUBBIER	NUBBIEST	PORNIER	PORNIEST
NUMMIER	NUMMIEST	PORTIER	PORTIEST
NURDIER	NURDIEST	POTTIER	POTTIEST
NUTSIER	NUTSIEST	POUTIER	POUTIEST
NUTTIER	NUTTIEST	PRICIER	PRICIEST
ONERIER	ONERIEST	PRIVIER	PRIVIEST
OUNDIER	OUNDIEST	PROSIER	PROSIEST
PALLIER	PALLIEST	PRUNIER	PRUNIEST
PALMIERs	PALMIEST	PUDDIER	PUDDIEST
PALSIER	PALSIEST	PUDGIER	PUDGIEST
PAPPIER	PAPPIEST	PUDSIER	PUDSIEST
PARKIER	PARKIEST	PUFFIER	PUFFIEST
PASTIER	PASTIEST	PUGGIER	PUGGIEST
PAWKIER	PAWKIEST	PULPIER	PULPIEST
PEAKIER	PEAKIEST	PUNKIER	PUNKIEST
PEATIER	PEATIEST	PUNNIER	PUNNIEST
PECKIER	PECKIEST	PURSIER	PURSIEST
PEERIER	PEERIEST	PURTIER	PURTIEST
PEGGIER	PEGGIEST	PUSHIER	PUSHIEST
PEPPIER	PEPPIEST	PUSSIER	PUSSIEST
PERKIER	PERKIEST	QUAKIER	QUAKIEST
PERVIER	PERVIEST	RAGGIER	RAGGIEST
PESKIER	PESKIEST	RAINIER	RAINIEST
PESTIER	PESTIEST	RAMMIER	RAMMIEST
PETTIER	PETTIEST	RANDIER	RANDIEST
PHONIER	PHONIEST	RANGIER	RANGIEST
PICKIER	PICKIEST	RASPIER	RASPIEST
PIGGIER	PIGGIEST	RATTIER	RATTIEST
PINKIER	PINKIEST	READIER	READIEST
PIPPIER	PIPPIEST	REAMIER	REAMIEST
PISSIER	PISSIEST	REDDIER	REDDIEST
PITHIER	PITHIEST	REEDIER	REEDIEST
PLATIER	PLATIEST	REEFIER	REEFIEST
PLUMIER	PLUMIEST	REEKIER	REEKIEST
POCKIER	POCKIEST	RESTIER	RESTIEST
PODDIER	PODDIEST	RIBBIER	RIBBIEST

RIDGIER	RIDGIEST	SHOWIER	SHOWIEST
RIFTIER	RIFTIEST	SILKIER	SILKIEST
RINDIER	RINDIEST	SILLIER	SILLIEST
RISKIER	RISKIEST	SILTIER	SILTIEST
RITZIER	RITZIEST	SINKIER	SINKIEST
ROARIER	ROARIEST	SISSIER	SISSIEST
ROCKIER s	ROCKIEST	SKIVIER	SKIVIEST
ROILIER	ROILIEST	SLATIER	SLATIEST
ROOFIER	ROOFIEST	SLIMIER	SLIMIEST
ROOKIER	ROOKIEST	SLOPIER	SLOPIEST
ROOMIER	ROOMIEST	SMILIER	SMILIEST
ROOPIER	ROOPIEST	SMOKIER	SMOKIEST
ROOTIER	ROOTIEST	SNAKIER	SNAKIEST
RORTIER	RORTIEST	SNARIER	SNARIEST
ROUPIER	ROUPIEST	SNIDIER	SNIDIEST
ROWDIER	ROWDIEST	SNIPIER	SNIPIEST
RUDDIER	RUDDIEST	SNOWIER	SNOWIEST
RUGGIER	RUGGIEST	SOAPIER	SOAPIEST
RUMMIER	RUMMIEST	SODDIER	SODDIEST
RUNNIER	RUNNIEST	SOGGIER	SOGGIEST
RUNTIER	RUNTIEST	SOILIER	SOILIEST
RUSHIER	RUSHIEST	SONSIER	SONSIEST
RUSTIER	RUSTIEST	SOOTIER	SOOTIEST
RUTTIER	RUTTIEST	SOPPIER	SOPPIEST
SAGGIER	SAGGIEST	SORRIER	SORRIEST
SALTIER s	SALTIEST	SOUPIER	SOUPIEST
SANDIER	SANDIEST	SPACIER	SPACIEST
SAPPIER	SAPPIEST	SPEWIER	SPEWIEST
SARKIER	SARKIEST	SPICIER	SPICIEST
SASSIER	SASSIEST	SPIKIER	SPIKIEST
SAUCIER s	SAUCIEST	SPINIER	SPINIEST
SAVVIER	SAVVIEST	SPIRIER	SPIRIEST
SCALIER	SCALIEST	SPUMIER	SPUMIEST
SCARIER	SCARIEST	STAGIER	STAGIEST
SCODIER	SCODIEST	STEWIER	STEWIEST
SEAMIER	SEAMIEST	STIVIER	STIVIEST
SEDGIER	SEDGIEST	STONIER	STONIEST
SEEDIER	SEEDIEST	STYLIER	STYLIEST
SEELIER	SEELIEST	SUCKIER	SUCKIEST
SEEPIER	SEEPIEST	SUDSIER	SUDSIEST
SHADIER	SHADIEST	SUETIER	SUETIEST
SHAKIER	SHAKIEST	SULKIER	SULKIEST
SHALIER	SHALIEST	SUNNIER	SUNNIEST
SHINIER	SHINIEST	SURFIER	SURFIEST

SURGIER	SURGIEST	TUBBIER	TUBBIEST
SURLIER	SURLIEST	TUFTIER	TUFTIEST
SWALIER	SWALIEST	TUMPIER	TUMPIEST
SWIPIER	SWIPIEST	TURFIER	TURFIEST
TACKIER	TACKIEST	TUSKIER	TUSKIEST
TAGGIER	TAGGIEST	TWINIER	TWINIEST
TALCIER	TALCIEST	VAIRIER	VAIRIEST
TALKIER	TALKIEST	VAMPIER	VAMPIEST
TANGIER	TANGIEST	VASTIER	VASTIEST
TARDIER	TARDIEST	VEALIER	VEALIEST
TARRIER s	TARRIEST	VEILIER	VEILIEST
TARTIER	TARTIEST	VEINIER	VEINIEST
TASTIER	TASTIEST	VIEWIER	VIEWIEST
TATTIER	TATTIEST	VOGUIER	VOGUIEST
TAWNIER	TAWNIEST	VUGGIER	VUGGIEST
TAWTIER	TAWTIEST	VUGHIER	VUGHIEST
TEARIER	TEARIEST	VUTTIER	VUTTIEST
TECHIER	TECHIEST	WACKIER	WACKIEST
TEENIER	TEENIEST	WALLIER	WALLIEST
TENTIER	TENTIEST	WALTIER	WALTIEST
TESTIER	TESTIEST	WANKIER	WANKIEST
THAWIER	THAWIEST	WARBIER	WARBIEST
THEWIER	THEWIEST	WARTIER	WARTIEST
THYMIER	THYMIEST	WASHIER	WASHIEST
TICHIER	TICHIEST	WASPIER	WASPIEST
TIDDIER	TIDDIEST	WEARIER	WEARIEST
TILLIER	TILLIEST	WEBBIER	WEBBIEST
TINNIER	TINNIEST	WEDGIER	WEDGIEST
TINTIER	TINTIEST	WEEDIER	WEEDIEST
TIPPIER	TIPPIEST	WEENIER	WEENIEST
TIPSIER	TIPSIEST	WEEPIER	WEEPIEST
TOCKIER	TOCKIEST	WENNIER	WENNIEST
TOFFIER	TOFFIEST	WHEYIER	WHEYIEST
TOPPIER	TOPPIEST	WHINIER	WHINIEST
TOSHIER	TOSHIEST	WHITIER	WHITIEST
TOSSIER	TOSSIEST	WIFTIER	WIFTIEST
TOTTIER	TOTTIEST	WIGGIER	WIGGIEST
TOUSIER	TOUSIEST	WIMPIER	WIMPIEST
TOUTIER	TOUTIEST	WINDIER	WINDIEST
TOUZIER	TOUZIEST	WINGIER	WINGIEST
TOWNIER	TOWNIEST	WISPIER	WISPIEST
TOWSIER	TOWSIEST	WITHIER	WITHIEST
TOWZIER	TOWZIEST	WITTIER	WITTIEST
TRIPIER	TRIPIEST	WOMBIER	WOMBIEST

WONKIER	WONKIEST	YOBBIER	YOBBIEST
WOODIER	WOODIEST	YOLKIER	YOLKIEST
WOOFIER	WOOFIEST	YUCKIER	YUCKIEST
WOOLIER	WOOLIEST	YUKKIER	YUKKIEST
WOOZIER	WOOZIEST	YUMMIER	YUMMIEST
WORDIER	WORDIEST	ZAPPIER	ZAPPIEST
WORMIER	WORMIEST	ZESTIER	ZESTIEST
WUSSIER	WUSSIEST	ZINCIER	ZINCIEST
YAPPIER	YAPPIEST	ZINGIER	ZINGIEST
YAWNIER	YAWNIEST	ZINKIER	ZINKIEST
YECHIER	YECHIEST	ZIPPIER	ZIPPIEST
YEUKIER	YEUKIEST	ZOOTIER	ZOOTIEST

Words six to eight letters in length ending in the suffix FUL

Some of these words are nouns and can have an –S hook added as shown.

Six-letter FUL words

AIDFUL	DINFUL	LAWFUL	TINFUL s
AIMFUL	DUEFUL	MANFUL	TOPFUL
ARMFUL s	EARFUL s	MUGFUL s	TUBFUL s
ARTFUL	EYEFUL s	NETFUL s	URNFUL s
BAGFUL s	FITFUL	PANFUL s	USEFUL s
BARFUL	GUTFUL s	PENFUL s	VATFUL s
BIBFUL s	HATFUL s	PEPFUL	WAEFUL
BOXFUL s	IREFUL	POTFUL s	WILFUL
CANFUL s	JARFUL s	RUEFUL	WOEFUL
CAPFUL s	JOYFUL	SAPFUL	
CARFUL s	JUGFUL s	SINFUL	
CUPFUL s	LAPFUL s	SOBFUL	

Seven-letter FUL words

ARMSFUL	CANSFUL	DOOMFUL	FORMFUL
BAGSFUL	CAREFUL	DUREFUL	FRETFUL
BALEFUL	CARTFUL s	DUTIFUL	GAINFUL
BANEFUL	CROPFUL s	EASEFUL	GASHFUL
BASHFUL	CUPSFUL	FACTFUL	GAZEFUL
BOATFUL s	DAREFUL	FATEFUL	GLADFUL
BODEFUL	DEEDFUL	FEARFUL	GLEEFUL
BOOKFUL s	DERNFUL	FISHFUL	GUSTFUL
BOWLFUL s	DIREFUL	FISTFUL s	GUTSFUL s
BRIMFUL	DISHFUL s	FOODFUL	HANDFUL s
CAGEFUL s	DOLEFUL	FORKFUL s	HARMFUL

HATEFUL	MINDFUL	RACKFUL s	TEARFUL
HATSFUL	MISTFUL	RAGEFUL	TEEMFUL
HEADFUL s	MOANFUL	RESTFUL	TEENFUL
HEEDFUL	MUSEFUL	RISKFUL	TENTFUL s
HELPFUL	NEEDFUL s	ROOMFUL s	TOILFUL
HOPEFUL s	NESTFUL s	RUTHFUL	TRAYFUL s
HORNFUL s	ODORFUL	SACKFUL s	TUBEFUL s
HURTFUL	PAGEFUL s	SHEDFUL s	TUNEFUL
HUSHFUL	PAILFUL s	SHIPFUL s	VASEFUL s
JARSFUL	PAINFUL	SHOPFUL s	VIALFUL s
JESTFUL	PALMFUL s	SIGHFUL	WAILFUL
JUGSFUL	PESTFUL	SINKFUL s	WAKEFUL
KISTFUL s	PIPEFUL s	SKEPFUL s	WAMEFUL s
LIFEFUL	PITHFUL	SKILFUL	WILEFUL
LISTFUL	PITIFUL	SKINFUL s	WILLFUL
LOCKFUL s	PLAYFUL	SONGFUL	WISHFUL
LOOFFUL s	PLOTFUL	SOULFUL	WISTFUL
LUNGFUL s	POKEFUL s	SWAYFUL	WORKFUL
LUSTFUL	POUTFUL	TACTFUL	ZEALFUL
MASTFUL	PREYFUL	TALEFUL	ZESTFUL
MAZEFUL	PUSHFUL	TANKFUL s	

Eight-letter FUL words

APRONFUL s	DREAMFUL	GROANFUL	PAILSFUL
AVAILFUL	EVENTFUL	GUILEFUL	PAUSEFUL
BASINFUL s	FAITHFUL s	HANDSFUL	PEACEFUL
BELLYFUL s	FANCIFUL	HASTEFUL	PLAINFUL
BLAMEFUL	FAULTFUL	HONEYFUL	PLATEFUL s
BLISSFUL	FEASTFUL	HOUSEFUL s	POUCHFUL s
BLUSHFUL	FORCEFUL	HUMORFUL	POWERFUL
BOASTFUL	FORKSFUL	LADLEFUL s	PRANKFUL
CHARMFUL	FOUNTFUL	LAUGHFUL	PRESSFUL s
CHEEKFUL s	FRAUDFUL	LIGHTFUL	PRIDEFUL
CHEERFUL	FREAKFUL	LOATHFUL	PROUDFUL
CHESTFUL s	FRISKFUL	MENSEFUL	PURSEFUL s
CHOCKFUL	FRUITFUL	MERCIFUL	RIGHTFUL
COLORFUL	GHASTFUL	MIGHTFUL	ROOMSFUL
CRATEFUL s	GLASSFUL s	MIRTHFUL	SACKSFUL
CRIMEFUL	GLOOMFUL	MOISTFUL	SCENTFUL
DEARNFUL	GODAWFUL	MOURNFUL	SCOOPFUL s
DEATHFUL	GOURDFUL s	MOUTHFUL s	SCORNFUL
DIRGEFUL	GRACEFUL	NIEVEFUL s	SENSEFUL
DOUBTFUL s	GRATEFUL	NOISEFUL	SHAMEFUL
DREADFUL s	GRIEFFUL	ODOURFUL	SHEENFUL

SHELFFUL s	SPORTFUL	TROUTFUL	VENGEFUL
SHELLFUL s	STAGEFUL s	TRUCKFUL s	VOICEFUL
SKILLFUL	STARTFUL	TRUNKFUL s	WAGONFUL s
SLOTHFUL	STICKFUL s	TRUSTFUL	WASTEFUL
SMILEFUL	STORMFUL	TRUTHFUL	WATCHFUL
SNEERFUL	SURGEFUL	UDDERFUL	WEARIFUL
SNOOTFUL s	TABLEFUL s	UNARTFUL	WORTHFUL
SOOTHFUL	TASTEFUL	UNJOYFUL	WRACKFUL
SPADEFUL s	THANKFUL	UNLAWFUL	WRATHFUL
SPEEDFUL	TOOTHFUL s	UNMANFUL	WREAKFUL
SPELLFUL	TRADEFUL	UNSINFUL	WRECKFUL
SPITEFUL	TRAINFUL s	UNUSEFUL	WRONGFUL
SPOILFUL	TRISTFUL	UNWILFUL	WROTHFUL
SPOONFUL s	TROTHFUL	VAUNTFUL	YOUTHFUL

Words six to eight letters in length ending in the suffix IBLE

Some of these words are nouns and can have an –S hook added as shown.
The addition of -IBLY shows where valid adverbial forms are allowed.

Those words that happen to end in IBLE where it has no relation to the suffix
are excluded, so words such as FAIBLE and THURIBLE are omitted.

Six-letter IBLE words

ALIBLE	EDIBLE s

Seven-letter IBLE words

ADDIBLE		MIXIBLE	
AUDIBLE s	–IBLY	PATIBLE	
DELIBLE		RIBIBLE s	
DOCIBLE		RISIBLE s	–IBLY
FUSIBLE	–IBLY	VISIBLE s	–IBLY
LEGIBLE	–IBLY		

Eight-letter IBLE words

CREDIBLE	–IBLY	EVADIBLE	
CRUCIBLE s		EVASIBLE	
EDUCIBLE		EXIGIBLE	
ELIDIBLE		FALLIBLE	–IBLY
ELIGIBLE s	–IBLY	FEASIBLE	–IBLY
ELUDIBLE		FENCIBLE s	
ERODIBLE		FLEXIBLE	–IBLY
EROSIBLE		FORCIBLE	–IBLY

```
FUNGIBLEs                          RINSIBLE
GULLIBLE    -IBLY                  RUNCIBLE
HORRIBLEs   -IBLY                  SENSIBLEs  -IBLY
INEDIBLE    -IBLY                  SUASIBLE
LAPSIBLE                           TANGIBLEs  -IBLY
MANDIBLEs                          TENSIBLE   -IBLY
MISCIBLE                           TERRIBLEs  -IBLY
PARTIBLE                           UNEDIBLE
PASSIBLE    -IBLY                  VENDIBLEs  -IBLY
POSSIBLEs   -IBLY                  VINCIBLE   -IBLY
RENDIBLE
```

Words six to eight letters in length ending in the suffix IFY

Six-letter IFY words

AERIFY	LADIFY	OSSIFY	TONIFY
AURIFY	LENIFY	PACIFY	TYPIFY
BASIFY	MINIFY	PURIFY	UGLIFY
CITIFY	MODIFY	RAMIFY	VERIFY
CODIFY	MUNIFY	RARIFY	VILIFY
GAMIFY	NAZIFY	RATIFY	VINIFY
GASIFY	NIDIFY	RUBIFY	VIVIFY
HUMIFY	NOTIFY	SALIFY	WEBIFY
IGNIFY	OMNIFY	SANIFY	

Seven-letter IFY words

ACETIFY	DANDIFY	LIGNIFY	PETRIFY
ACIDIFY	DENSIFY	LIQUIFY	PLEBIFY
AMPLIFY	DIGNIFY	LITHIFY	PONTIFY
ANGLIFY	DULCIFY	MAGNIFY	PROSIFY
BEATIFY	FALSIFY	MATTIFY	PULPIFY
BRUTIFY	FANCIFY	MERCIFY	QUALIFY
CALCIFY	FARCIFY	METRIFY	RECTIFY
CAPRIFY	FISHIFY	MICRIFY	REEDIFY
CARNIFY	FORTIFY	MOLLIFY	REUNIFY
CERTIFY	FRUTIFY	MORTIFY	RUSSIFY
CHYLIFY	GLORIFY	MUMMIFY	SACRIFY
CHYMIFY	GRATIFY	MUNDIFY	SALSIFY
CLARIFY	HORRIFY	MYSTIFY	SCARIFY
COALIFY	ICONIFY	NIGRIFY	SCORIFY
CORNIFY	JELLIFY	NITRIFY	SIGNIFY
CRUCIFY	JOLLIFY	NULLIFY	SPECIFY
DAMNIFY	JUSTIFY	OPACIFY	TACKIFY
```
```

TERRIFY	TORRIFY	VITRIFY	ZOMBIFY
TESTIFY	UNDEIFY	YUPPIFY	
THURIFY	VERBIFY	ZINCIFY	
TIPSIFY	VERSIFY	ZINKIFY	

Eight-letter IFY words

ALKALIFY	ETHERIFY	PRETTIFY	RIGIDIFY
AMMONIFY	FLINTIFY	QUANTIFY	SANCTIFY
BEAUTIFY	FLUIDIFY	QUIZZIFY	SANGUIFY
BRONZIFY	FRUCTIFY	REAEDIFY	SAPONIFY
CLASSIFY	GENTRIFY	RECODIFY	SILICIFY
COCKNIFY	GLASSIFY	REMODIFY	SIMPLIFY
COPURIFY	HUMIDIFY	RENOTIFY	SOLIDIFY
DENAZIFY	IDENTIFY	REPACIFY	STELLIFY
DETOXIFY	KARSTIFY	REPURIFY	STRATIFY
DIVINIFY	LAPIDIFY	RESINIFY	STULTIFY
EMULSIFY	MOISTIFY	REVERIFY	TRENDIFY
ESTERIFY	OPSONIFY	REVIVIFY	ZINCKIFY

Words six to eight letters in length ending in INGS

An * indicates that there is no valid singular form in ING.

Single syllabic words ending in INGS are excluded, so words such as THINGS and SPRINGS are omitted.

Six-letter INGS words

AGINGS	DYINGS	LYINGS	TOINGS
BEINGS	GOINGS	RUINGS	VYINGS
DOINGS	ICINGS	SUINGS	

Seven-letter INGS words

ABLINGS	AWNINGS	BOOINGS	CAWINGS
ACHINGS	BAAINGS	BORINGS	CODINGS
ACTINGS	BAKINGS	BOWINGS	COKINGS
ADDINGS	BALINGS	BOXINGS	COMINGS
AGEINGS	BESINGS	BUSINGS	COOINGS
AIRINGS	BIDINGS	BUYINGS	COPINGS
ANTINGS	BIKINGS	CAKINGS	COVINGS
ARCINGS	BITINGS	CANINGS	CRYINGS
ARMINGS	BLUINGS	CARINGS	CUEINGS
ASKINGS	BODINGS	CASINGS	CURINGS
AUDINGS	BONINGS	CAVINGS	DARINGS

DATINGS	HOLINGS	OUTINGS	SPYINGS
DICINGS	HOMINGS	PACINGS	TAKINGS
DININGS	HYPINGS	PAGINGS	TAMINGS
DIVINGS	IMPINGS	PALINGS	TAPINGS
DONINGS	INNINGS	PARINGS	TARINGS
DOPINGS	JAPINGS	PAVINGS	TAWINGS
DOTINGS	JAWINGS	PAYINGS	TAXINGS
DOZINGS	JOKINGS	PIEINGS	TIDINGS
DRYINGS	KEYINGS	PIKINGS	TILINGS
DUPINGS	KITINGS	PILINGS	TIMINGS
DYEINGS	LACINGS	PIPINGS	TIRINGS
EARINGS	LADINGS	POLINGS	TOLINGS
EASINGS	LAKINGS	POSINGS	TONINGS
EATINGS	LASINGS	PRYINGS	TOWINGS
EDGINGS	LAWINGS	PULINGS	TOYINGS
EFFINGS	LAYINGS	RACINGS	TRYINGS
ELDINGS	LIKINGS	RAGINGS	TUBINGS
ENDINGS	LIMINGS	RAKINGS	TUNINGS
ENRINGS	LININGS	RATINGS	TYPINGS
ERRINGS	LIVINGS	RAVINGS	ULLINGS
FACINGS	LOBINGS	RAWINGS	UNKINGS
FADINGS	LORINGS	RIDINGS	UPPINGS
FENINGS	LOSINGS	RISINGS	URGINGS
FILINGS	LOVINGS	ROBINGS	URNINGS
FININGS	LOWINGS	RODINGS	VAPINGS
FIRINGS	LUGINGS	ROPINGS	VEXINGS
FIXINGS	LURINGS	ROVINGS	VIKINGS
FLYINGS	LUTINGS	ROWINGS	VOTINGS
FOXINGS	MAKINGS	RUEINGS	WADINGS
FROINGS	MATINGS	RULINGS	WAKINGS
FRYINGS	MAYINGS	SAVINGS	WANINGS
GAMINGS	MERINGS	SAWINGS	WAVINGS
GAPINGS	MILINGS	SAYINGS	WAXINGS
GATINGS	MININGS	SEEINGS	WIPINGS
GAZINGS	MIXINGS	SEWINGS	WIRINGS
GIVINGS	MOWINGS	SEXINGS	WONINGS
GORINGS	MUSINGS	SIDINGS	WOOINGS
HAVINGS	NAMINGS	SIRINGS	YOKINGS
HAYINGS	NIDINGS	SITINGS	ZONINGS
HAZINGS	NOSINGS	SIZINGS	
HEWINGS	OFFINGS	SKIINGS	
HEXINGS	OGLINGS	SORINGS	
HIDINGS	ONDINGS	SOWINGS	
HIRINGS	OOHINGS	SPAINGS	

Eight-letter INGS words

ABIDINGS	BLADINGS	CARDINGS	CYMLINGS
AISLINGS	BLOWINGS	CARLINGS	DAFFINGS
AMBLINGS	BLUEINGS	CARPINGS	DAGGINGS
ANGLINGS	BOATINGS	CARVINGS	DAMPINGS
ARCHINGS	BOILINGS	CASTINGS	DANCINGS
ARCKINGS	BOLTINGS	CATLINGS	DARLINGS
AWAKINGS	BOMBINGS	CEASINGS	DARNINGS
BACKINGS	BONDINGS	CEILINGS	DAUBINGS
BAGGINGS	BONKINGS	CELLINGS	DAWNINGS
BAITINGS	BOOKINGS	CHASINGS	DEALINGS
BALKINGS	BOOMINGS	CHIDINGS	DECKINGS
BALLINGS	BOOZINGS	CIELINGS	DESKINGS
BANDINGS	BORKINGS	CISSINGS	DEVLINGS
BANKINGS	BOSSINGS	CLONINGS	DIALINGS
BANNINGS	BOWLINGS	CLOSINGS	DICKINGS
BANTINGS	BRACINGS	COAMINGS	DIETINGS
BARRINGS	BRAKINGS	COATINGS	DIGGINGS
BASHINGS	BREWINGS	COAXINGS	DILLINGS
BASTINGS	BRIMINGS	CODLINGS	DIMMINGS
BATHINGS	BROKINGS	COGGINGS	DIPPINGS
BATTINGS	BRUTINGS	COININGS	DISHINGS
BAWLINGS	BUCKINGS	COLLINGS	DOATINGS
BEADINGS	BUDDINGS	COMBINGS	DOCKINGS
BEALINGS	BUFFINGS	COMPINGS	DODGINGS
BEAMINGS	BUGGINGS	CONNINGS	DOGGINGS
BEARINGS	BULKINGS	COOKINGS	DOPPINGS
BEATINGS	BULLINGS	COOLINGS	DOWSINGS
BEDDINGS	BUMPINGS	COPYINGS	DRAWINGS
BEGGINGS	BUNTINGS	CORDINGS	DRIVINGS
BELLINGS	BURNINGS	COSTINGS	DROVINGS
BELTINGS	BUSHINGS	COWLINGS	DUBBINGS
BENDINGS	BUSKINGS	CRAVINGS	DUCKINGS
BETTINGS	BUSSINGS	CRAZINGS	DUCTINGS
BIASINGS	BUSTINGS	CROWINGS	DUELINGS
BIBBINGS	BUZZINGS	CUBBINGS	DUFFINGS
BIDDINGS	CABLINGS	CULLINGS	DUMPINGS
BIGGINGS	CALKINGS	CUNNINGS	DUNKINGS
BILLINGS	CALLINGS	CUPPINGS	DUNNINGS
BINDINGS	CALMINGS	CURBINGS	DUSTINGS
BINGINGS	CAMPINGS	CURLINGS	EANLINGS
BIRDINGS	CANNINGS	CURSINGS	EARNINGS
BIRLINGS	CANTINGS	CUTTINGS	EARRINGS
BITTINGS	CAPPINGS	CYCLINGS	EASTINGS

EBAYINGS	FOOTINGS	GROWINGS	HOUSINGS
EDITINGS	FOPLINGS	GUIDINGS	HOUTINGS
EEVNINGS	FORGINGS	GUISINGS	HOWLINGS
EILDINGS	FORMINGS	GUMMINGS	HUFFINGS
EMPTINGS	FOULINGS	GUNNINGS	HUMMINGS
ENVYINGS	FOWLINGS	HACKINGS	HUNTINGS
ERLKINGS	FRAMINGS	HAININGS	HURLINGS
ETCHINGS	FRAYINGS	HALLINGS	HUSKINGS
EVENINGS	FUCKINGS	HALTINGS	HUSTINGS*
FABLINGS	FUNDINGS	HALVINGS	HUTTINGS
FAGGINGS	FURRINGS	HANGINGS	HYLDINGS
FAILINGS	GADLINGS	HARLINGS	IMAGINGS
FAIRINGS	GAFFINGS	HARPINGS	INBEINGS
FALLINGS	GAININGS	HASHINGS	INBRINGS
FANNINGS	GANGINGS	HASTINGS	INGOINGS
FARCINGS	GAPPINGS	HATTINGS	INKLINGS
FARDINGS	GASKINGS	HAULINGS	INSWINGS
FARMINGS	GASPINGS	HAWKINGS	IRONINGS
FASTINGS	GASSINGS	HEADINGS	ITCHINGS
FATLINGS	GAUGINGS	HEALINGS	JACKINGS
FAWNINGS	GAYWINGS*	HEARINGS	JAMMINGS
FEEDINGS	GEARINGS	HEATINGS	JARRINGS
FEELINGS	GELDINGS	HEAVINGS	JEERINGS
FEERINGS	GETTINGS	HEDGINGS	JEGGINGS*
FELLINGS	GIFTINGS	HEELINGS	JERKINGS
FELTINGS	GILDINGS	HELPINGS	JESTINGS
FENCINGS	GINNINGS	HERDINGS	JIBBINGS
FERNINGS	GIRDINGS	HERLINGS	JIGGINGS
FEUDINGS	GLAZINGS	HERRINGS	JOBBINGS
FILLINGS	GLEYINGS	HIDLINGS	JOGGINGS
FINDINGS	GLIDINGS	HILDINGS	JOININGS
FIRRINGS	GLOVINGS	HILLINGS	JOLTINGS
FISHINGS	GLOZINGS	HINTINGS	JOSHINGS
FISTINGS	GNAWINGS	HIPPINGS	JOTTINGS
FITTINGS	GODLINGS	HIRLINGS	JUDGINGS
FIZZINGS	GOLFINGS	HISSINGS	JUGGINGS
FLUTINGS	GOSLINGS	HOGGINGS	JUMPINGS
FLYTINGS	GRADINGS	HOLDINGS	KARTINGS
FOALINGS	GRATINGS	HOOKINGS	KAYOINGS
FOAMINGS	GRAVINGS	HOPPINGS	KEELINGS
FOGGINGS	GRAZINGS	HORNINGS	KEENINGS
FOILINGS	GREYINGS	HORSINGS	KEEPINGS
FOLDINGS	GRICINGS	HOSTINGS	KEGLINGS
FOOLINGS	GRIPINGS	HOTTINGS	KEMPINGS

KENNINGS	LOADINGS	MODDINGS	PASTINGS
KERBINGS	LOAFINGS	MOLDINGS	PAUSINGS
KERNINGS	LOANINGS	MOORINGS	PEAKINGS
KEYRINGS	LOCKINGS	MOOTINGS	PECKINGS
KICKINGS	LODGINGS	MORLINGS	PEELINGS
KIDDINGS	LOGGINGS	MORNINGS	PEENINGS
KIDLINGS	LONGINGS	MOSHINGS	PEGGINGS
KILLINGS	LOONINGS	MOSLINGS*	PELTINGS
KILTINGS	LOOPINGS	MOUSINGS	PERFINGS
KIRKINGS	LOOSINGS	MUGGINGS	PETTINGS
KISSINGS	LOOTINGS	MUMMINGS	PHASINGS
KITLINGS	LOPPINGS	MUNTINGS	PICKINGS
KNIFINGS	LORDINGS	MUSHINGS	PIECINGS
KNOWINGS	LOURINGS	NAGGINGS	PIGGINGS
LAGGINGS	LOUSINGS	NAILINGS	PIGLINGS
LALLINGS	LUGEINGS	NECKINGS	PILLINGS
LAMBINGS	LURKINGS	NERVINGS	PIMPINGS
LAMMINGS	MADLINGS	NESTINGS	PINKINGS
LAMPINGS	MAILINGS	NETTINGS	PINNINGS
LANDINGS	MAIMINGS	NITHINGS	PIONINGS
LAPPINGS	MALLINGS	NODDINGS	PITTINGS
LAPWINGS	MALTINGS	NOGGINGS	PLACINGS
LASHINGS	MAPPINGS	NOONINGS	PLATINGS
LASTINGS	MARKINGS	NOTHINGS	PLAYINGS
LATHINGS	MARLINGS	NUBBINGS	PLOWINGS
LEADINGS	MASHINGS	NULLINGS	POLLINGS
LEANINGS	MASKINGS	NURSINGS	POSTINGS
LEASINGS	MATTINGS	NUTTINGS	POURINGS
LEAVINGS	MAULINGS	OAKLINGS	POUTINGS
LEERINGS	MEANINGS	ONGOINGS	PRATINGS
LEGGINGS	MEETINGS	OPENINGS	PRAYINGS
LEKKINGS	MELTINGS	OUTRINGS	PRICINGS
LEMMINGS	MENDINGS	OUTSINGS	PRIMINGS
LENDINGS	MERGINGS	OUTWINGS	PROBINGS
LENSINGS	MERLINGS	PACKINGS	PROSINGS
LETTINGS	MESHINGS	PADDINGS	PROVINGS
LICKINGS	MICHINGS	PAIRINGS	PRUNINGS
LIDDINGS	MILKINGS	PANNINGS	PUBBINGS
LIGGINGS	MILLINGS	PANTINGS	PUDDINGS
LIMPINGS	MINDINGS	PARGINGS	PUFFINGS
LINTINGS	MISTINGS	PARKINGS	PUGGINGS
LIPPINGS	MOANINGS	PARSINGS	PULPINGS
LISPINGS	MOBBINGS	PARTINGS	PUMPINGS
LISTINGS	MOCKINGS	PASSINGS	PUNNINGS

PURGINGS	RIOTINGS	SEEWINGS	SOGGINGS
PURLINGS	RIPPINGS	SEININGS	SOILINGS
PURRINGS	RISPINGS	SEISINGS	SOOPINGS
PUTTINGS	ROADINGS	SEIZINGS	SOOTINGS
PYONINGS*	ROAMINGS	SELFINGS	SOPPINGS
QUAKINGS	ROARINGS	SELLINGS	SORNINGS
QUEUINGS	ROCKINGS	SENDINGS	SORTINGS
RACKINGS	RODDINGS	SENSINGS	SOSSINGS
RAFTINGS	ROLFINGS	SERGINGS	SOTTINGS
RAGGINGS	ROLLINGS	SERVINGS	SOUMINGS
RAIDINGS	ROOFINGS	SETTINGS	SOURINGS
RAILINGS	ROOTINGS	SEXTINGS	SOUSINGS
RAISINGS	RORTINGS	SHADINGS	SPACINGS
RAMPINGS	ROUMINGS	SHAKINGS	SPAEINGS
RANGINGS	ROUTINGS	SHAPINGS	SPILINGS
RANKINGS	RUBBINGS	SHARINGS	STAGINGS
RANTINGS	RUCHINGS	SHAVINGS	STARINGS
RAPPINGS	RUGGINGS	SHOEINGS	STEWINGS
RASPINGS	RUININGS	SHORINGS	STONINGS
RATLINGS	RUNNINGS	SHOVINGS	STOPINGS
RATTINGS	RUSHINGS	SHOWINGS	STOVINGS
RAZZINGS	RUSTINGS	SIBLINGS	STOWINGS
READINGS	RUTTINGS	SIFTINGS	STYLINGS
REAPINGS	SABBINGS	SIGHINGS	SUBBINGS
REARINGS	SACKINGS	SIGNINGS	SUBRINGS
REDDINGS	SACRINGS	SINDINGS	SUCKINGS
REDWINGS	SAGGINGS	SINGINGS	SUGGINGS
REEDINGS	SAILINGS	SINKINGS	SUITINGS
REEFINGS	SALTINGS	SITTINGS	SUMMINGS
REELINGS	SALVINGS	SKATINGS	SURFINGS
REFFINGS	SANDINGS	SKIVINGS	SURGINGS
REIVINGS	SAPLINGS	SLATINGS	SWALINGS
RENNINGS	SAPPINGS	SLAYINGS	SWAYINGS
RENTINGS	SARKINGS	SLICINGS	SWILINGS
REPPINGS	SCALINGS	SLIDINGS	SYNDINGS
RESTINGS	SCORINGS	SLOWINGS	TABBINGS
RIBBINGS	SCRYINGS	SMILINGS	TABLINGS
RIDGINGS	SEALINGS	SMOKINGS	TACKINGS
RIFLINGS	SEAMINGS	SNARINGS	TAGGINGS
RIGGINGS	SEARINGS	SNIPINGS	TAILINGS
RIGLINGS	SEATINGS	SNORINGS	TALKINGS
RIMMINGS	SEEDINGS	SOAKINGS	TAMPINGS
RINGINGS	SEELINGS	SOARINGS	TANKINGS
RINSINGS	SEEMINGS	SOBBINGS	TANLINGS

TANNINGS	TUBBINGS	VISHINGS	WETTINGS
TAPPINGS	TUCKINGS	VOGUINGS	WHALINGS
TARRINGS	TUFTINGS	VOICINGS	WHININGS
TASKINGS	TUGGINGS	VOIDINGS	WHITINGS
TASTINGS	TUNNINGS	WADDINGS	WHORINGS
TATTINGS	TUPPINGS	WAFTINGS	WICKINGS
TEAMINGS	TURFINGS	WAILINGS	WIGGINGS
TEASINGS	TURNINGS	WAITINGS	WILDINGS
TELLINGS	TUSKINGS	WALKINGS	WINCINGS
TEMPINGS	TUTTINGS	WALLINGS	WINDINGS
TENTINGS	TWININGS	WARDINGS	WINKINGS
TESTINGS	UNBEINGS	WARLINGS	WINNINGS
TEXTINGS	UNDOINGS	WARMINGS	WISHINGS
THAWINGS	UNITINGS	WARNINGS	WITLINGS
TICKINGS	UNSLINGS	WARPINGS	WITTINGS
TIFFINGS	UNTYINGS	WASHINGS	WOLFINGS
TILLINGS	UPBRINGS	WASTINGS	WOLVINGS
TILTINGS	UPFLINGS	WAULINGS	WONNINGS
TINNINGS	UPGOINGS	WAWLINGS	WORDINGS
TINTINGS	UPSWINGS	WAXWINGS	WORKINGS
TIPPINGS	VAMPINGS	WEANINGS	WRITINGS
TITHINGS	VANNINGS	WEARINGS	YAPPINGS
TITLINGS	VARYINGS	WEAVINGS	YARDINGS
TOILINGS	VEERINGS	WEBBINGS	YAWNINGS
TOLLINGS	VEILINGS	WEBRINGS	YAWPINGS
TOOLINGS	VEININGS	WEDDINGS	YEALINGS
TOPPINGS	VENDINGS	WEDGINGS	YELLINGS
TOSSINGS	VENTINGS	WEEDINGS	YELPINGS
TOTTINGS	VERBINGS	WEEPINGS	YORLINGS
TOURINGS	VERSINGS	WELDINGS	YOWLINGS
TOUSINGS	VESTINGS	WELLINGS	ZORBINGS
TRACINGS	VETTINGS	WELTINGS	
TRADINGS	VIEWINGS	WESTINGS	

Words six to eight letters in length ending in the suffix ISE

<u>All</u> of these words can also be spelt with IZE and all can have an −S hook added.

Unless they can also be spelt with IZE (eg AGNISE, COGNISE) those words that happen to end in ISE where it has no relation to the suffix are excluded, so words such as COTISE, BRANDISE, EDGEWISE, and TELEVISE are omitted.

Six-letter ISE words

AGNISE	AGUISE	IODISE
AGRISE	DORISE	IONISE

Seven-letter ISE words

ADONISE	COGNISE	GRECISE	ODORISE
AGATISE	CYANISE	HEROISE	OXIDISE
AGENISE	CYCLISE	ICONISE	OZONISE
AGONISE	DIARISE	IDOLISE	PECTISE
ANODISE	DOCKISE	IRIDISE	PEPTISE
APPRISE	DUALISE	IRONISE	POETISE
ARABISE	EBONISE	ITEMISE	REALISE
ATHEISE	ECHOISE	KYANISE	REPRISE
ATOMISE	EGOTISE	LAICISE	RIOTISE
AZOTISE	ELEGISE	LAIRISE	STYLISE
BAPTISE	EMPRISE	LIONISE	UNITISE
BROMISE	EROTISE	MYTHISE	UTILISE
COALISE	GALLISE	OBELISE	

Eight-letter ISE words

ACTIVISE	COMPRISE	FABULISE	LYRICISE
ALBITISE	CREOLISE	FARADISE	MACARISE
ALKALISE	CURARISE	FEMINISE	MADERISE
AMORTISE	CUTINISE	FIBERISE	MAXIMISE
ANNALISE	DEIONISE	FINALISE	MELANISE
ANTICISE	DEMONISE	FLUIDISE	MELODISE
APHETISE	DEPUTISE	FOCALISE	MEMORISE
APHORISE	DIGITISE	FRANCISE	MESPRISE
APPETISE	DIMERISE	GRAECISE	METALISE
ARBORISE	DISSEISE	HEBRAISE	MINIMISE
ARCHAISE	DIVINISE	HEPATISE	MISPRISE
ATHETISE	DYNAMISE	HOMINISE	MOBILISE
ATTICISE	EBIONISE	HUMANISE	MONETISE
AVIANISE	EMBOLISE	IDEALISE	MORALISE
BANALISE	EMPERISE	IMMUNISE	MOTORISE
BOTANISE	ENERGISE	INFAMISE	NASALISE
CALORISE	EQUALISE	JAPANISE	NEBULISE
CANALISE	ERGOTISE	JAROVISE	NODALISE
CANONISE	ETERNISE	JUMBOISE	NOMADISE
CAPONISE	ETHERISE	LATERISE	NOTARISE
CHROMISE	ETHICISE	LATINISE	NOVELISE
CIVILISE	EULOGISE	LEGALISE	OPSONISE
COLONISE	EUPHUISE	LOCALISE	OPTIMISE
COLORISE	EXORCISE	LOGICISE	ORGANISE

PAGANISE	RESINISE	SIRENISE	TUTORISE
PAPALISE	RIGIDISE	SIRONISE	UNIONISE
PATINISE	RIVALISE	SOBERISE	URBANISE
PENALISE	ROBOTISE	SODOMISE	VALORISE
POLARISE	ROMANISE	SOLARISE	VAPORISE
POLEMISE	ROYALISE	SOLECISE	VELARISE
POLONISE	RURALISE	SORORISE	VIRILISE
PTYALISE	SALINISE	SUBERISE	VITALISE
PYRITISE	SANITISE	SUBITISE	VOCALISE
PYROLISE	SATIRISE	SURPRISE	VOLUMISE
QUANTISE	SIMILISE	TETANISE	VOWELISE
RACEMISE	SIMONISE	THEORISE	WOMANISE
REGULISE	SINICISE	TOTALISE	

Words six to eight letters in length ending in the suffix ISH

Those words that happen to end in ISH where it has no relation to the suffix are excluded, so words such as FAMISH, POLISH, RELISH, BATFISH, DEMOLISH, and GOLDFISH are omitted.

Six-letter ISH words

AGUISH	ELFISH	MODISH	POPISH
ASPISH	ELVISH	MOPISH	RAKISH
BANISH	FIKISH	MORISH	RAWISH
BARISH	FLUISH	MULISH	RUDISH
BLUISH	GARISH	NEWISH	SHYISH
BOYISH	GLUISH	NICISH	SIXISH
COWISH	GOYISH	OAFISH	SKYISH
COYISH	HARISH	ODDISH	SLYISH
DANISH	IMPISH	OFFISH	TONISH
DAWISH	JADISH	OGRISH	TOYISH
DOTISH	LAKISH	OLDISH	TYKISH
DOVISH	LAMISH	OWLISH	UPPISH
DRYISH	LATISH	PALISH	WIDISH
DUDISH	LOWISH	PAPISH	WINISH

Seven-letter ISH words

ALUMISH	BEAUISH	BOGGISH	BRUTISH
BABYISH	BIGGISH	BOOBISH	BUCKISH
BADDISH	BLOKISH	BOOKISH	BULLISH
BALDISH	BLUEISH	BOORISH	CADDISH
BEAMISH	BOARISH	BOPPISH	CARLISH
BEARISH	BOBBISH	BRINISH	CATTISH

CHAVISH	GIRLISH	MAIDISH	RATTISH
CLAYISH	GLUEISH	MANNISH	REDDISH
COCKISH	GNOMISH	MAWKISH	RIGGISH
COLDISH	GOATISH	MILDISH	ROGUISH
COLTISH	GOLDISH	MINXISH	ROINISH
COOLISH	GOODISH	MISSISH	ROMPISH
CRONISH	GRAYISH	MOBBISH	ROOKISH
CUBBISH	GREYISH	MONKISH	ROYNISH
CULTISH	GULLISH	MOONISH	RUMMISH
CURRISH	HAGGISH	MOORISH	RUNTISH
DAMPISH	HAIMISH	MOREISH	RUTTISH
DANKISH	HARDISH	MUFFISH	SADDISH
DARKISH	HAWKISH	MUGGISH	SALTISH
DEAFISH	HEIMISH	MUMPISH	SELFISH
DIMMISH	HELLISH	MURKISH	SERFISH
DOGGISH	HENNISH	NEARISH	SICKISH
DOLLISH	HICKISH	NEDDISH	SLAVISH
DOLTISH	HIGHISH	NERDISH	SLOWISH
DONNISH	HIPPISH	NICEISH	SNAKISH
DORKISH	HOBBISH	NOIRISH	SNOWISH
DOVEISH	HOGGISH	NUNNISH	SOFTISH
DRONISH	HORNISH	NURDISH	SOONISH
DUCKISH	HOTTISH	OGREISH	SOTTISH
DULLISH	HUFFISH	PARKISH	SOURISH
DUMPISH	HUNNISH	PEAKISH	STONISH
DUNCISH	JIGGISH	PECKISH	STYLISH
DUNNISH	JOCKISH	PEEVISH	SWINISH
DUSKISH	KERNISH	PERKISH	TALLISH
FADDISH	KIDDISH	PETTISH	TANNISH
FAIRISH	KNAVISH	PIGGISH	TARTISH
FALSISH	LADDISH	PINKISH	TIGRISH
FASTISH	LADYISH	PIXYISH	TITTISH
FATTISH	LARGISH	PLANISH	TOADISH
FENNISH	LARKISH	PLENISH	TOFFISH
FILMISH	LAZYISH	POORISH	TONNISH
FINEISH	LEFTISH	POPPISH	TOWNISH
FOGYISH	LOGGISH	PRUDISH	TUBBISH
FOLKISH	LOMPISH	PUCKISH	VAGUISH
FOOLISH	LONGISH	PUGGISH	VAMPISH
FOPPISH	LOUDISH	PUNKISH	VOGUISH
FULLISH	LOUTISH	RAFFISH	WAGGISH
GAMPISH	LUMPISH	RAMMISH	WAIFISH
GAWKISH	LUSKISH	RANKISH	WAMPISH
GEEKISH	MADDISH	RASPISH	WANNISH

WARMISH WETTISH WIMPISH WONKISH
WASPISH WHEYISH WISPISH WORDISH
WEAKISH WHITISH WOGGISH WORMISH
WEARISH WHORISH WOLFISH YOBBISH
WENNISH WILDISH WOLVISH ZANYISH

Eight-letter ISH words

ACTORISH DANDYISH IDIOTISH SAINTISH
BABELISH DEVILISH JINGOISH SANDYISH
BAIRNISH DOWDYISH KNACKISH SCAMPISH
BLACKISH DRABBISH LEMONISH SHARKISH
BLANDISH DRAFFISH LIGHTISH SHARPISH
BLEAKISH DRECKISH LITTLISH SHEEPISH
BLIMPISH DREGGISH LIVERISH SHORTISH
BLOCKISH DREKKISH NABOBISH SHREWISH
BLOKEISH DROLLISH NANNYISH SISSYISH
BLONDISH DROOGISH NINNYISH SIXTYISH
BLUNTISH DRUNKISH NOHOWISH SKITTISH
BOOBYISH DWARFISH NOVELISH SLANGISH
BRACKISH DWEEBISH NYMPHISH SLIMMISH
BRAINISH ESSAYISH OCHERISH SLOBBISH
BRASSISH ETHERISH ORANGISH SLUGGISH
BRATTISH FAINTISH PAGANISH SLUTTISH
BRISKISH FEEBLISH PIXIEISH SMALLISH
BROADISH FEVERISH PLAINISH SMARTISH
BROGUISH FIENDISH PLUMPISH SNAPPISH
BROWNISH FIFTYISH POKERISH SNEAKISH
CAMELISH FLATTISH POSERISH SNIFFISH
CEORLISH FLIRTISH PRANKISH SNOBBISH
CHEAPISH FOGEYISH PRIGGISH SNOUTISH
CHILDISH FORTYISH PROUDISH SNUBBISH
CHURLISH FRAILISH PSEUDISH SOLIDISH
CLANNISH FREAKISH PUPPYISH SORRYISH
CLEANISH FRESHISH PURPLISH SPARKISH
CLERKISH FRUMPISH PYGMYISH SPIVVISH
CLIQUISH GHOULISH QUACKISH SPOFFISH
CLODDISH GIPSYISH QUALMISH SPOOKISH
CLOTTISH GLUMPISH QUEERISH SQUARISH
CLOWNISH GREENISH QUIPPISH SQUIRISH
CLUBBISH GRUFFISH QUIRKISH STARTISH
CLUMPISH GRUMPISH RIGHTISH STEEPISH
COARSISH GYPSYISH ROUGHISH STIFFISH
CRANKISH HEAVYISH ROUNDISH STILTISH
CROSSISH HIPPYISH ROWDYISH STOCKISH

STOUTISH	THIEVISH	TOUGHISH	VIPERISH
SUMPHISH	THINNISH	TRAMPISH	VIXENISH
SWAINISH	THUGGISH	TRICKISH	WATERISH
SWAMPISH	TICKLISH	TROLLISH	WOMANISH
SWEETISH	TIGERISH	TWITTISH	YOKELISH
SWELLISH	TIGHTISH	UNMODISH	YOUNGISH
SYLPHISH	TINGLISH	VAGARISH	
THICKISH	TOADYISH	VAPORISH	

Words six to eight letters in length ending in the suffix ISM

All of these words can have an –S hook added.

Six-letter ISM words

AGEISM	HYLISM	NANISM	SADISM
AUTISM	IODISM	NOMISM	SCHISM
BONISM	LAXISM	NUDISM	SEXISM
CIVISM	LYRISM	OBEISM	SIZISM
CUBISM	MAGISM	OBIISM	THEISM
DUDISM	MALISM	OGRISM	TRUISM
EGOISM	MERISM	PAPISM	VERISM
EONISM	MOMISM	PORISM	YOGISM
FAVISM	MONISM	PURISM	
HOLISM	MUTISM	RACISM	

Seven-letter ISM words

ABLEISM	BRUXISM	ECHOISM	GEEKISM
AGONISM	CAMBISM	EGOTISM	GURUISM
AMORISM	CHARISM	ELITISM	HANDISM
ANIMISM	CHEMISM	ENTRISM	HEROISM
ASTEISM	CHORISM	EPICISM	HEURISM
ATAVISM	CLADISM	EROTISM	HOBOISM
ATHEISM	CLONISM	ETACISM	IDOLISM
ATOMISM	COPYISM	ETATISM	IMAGISM
BAALISM	COSMISM	EXOTISM	ITACISM
BABUISM	CRETISM	FADDISM	JUJUISM
BAPTISM	CULTISM	FALSISM	KARAISM
BARDISM	CZARISM	FASCISM	LADDISM
BIPRISM	DADAISM	FATTISM	LADYISM
BOGYISM	DIORISM	FAUVISM	LAICISM
BOSSISM	DODOISM	FIDEISM	LEFTISM
BROMISM	DONNISM	FOGYISM	LEGGISM
BRUTISM	DUALISM	FOODISM	LIONISM

LOCOISM	ONANISM	REALISM	TROPISM
LOOKISM	ORALISM	SELFISM	TSARISM
MAIDISM	ORPHISM	SENSISM	TYCHISM
MOBBISM	PEONISM	SIZEISM	TZARISM
MYALISM	PHAEISM	SLUMISM	URANISM
MYTHISM	PHOBISM	SOPHISM	UTOPISM
NARCISM	PHOTISM	STATISM	WHOLISM
NEURISM	PIANISM	TACHISM	YOBBISM
OBELISM	PIETISM	TACTISM	ZANYISM
ODYLISM	PLENISM	TEXTISM	
OGREISM	RANKISM	TOURISM	

Eight-letter ISM words

ACOSMISM	CENTRISM	ETHERISM	JIHADISM
ACROTISM	CHARTISM	ETHICISM	JINGOISM
ACTINISM	CIVICISM	EUGENISM	KABALISM
ACTIVISM	CLASSISM	EUMERISM	LABORISM
ALARMISM	CLIQUISM	EUPHUISM	LACONISM
ALBINISM	CLUBBISM	EXORCISM	LEGALISM
ALGORISM	COLORISM	FABULISM	LOBBYISM
ALIENISM	CRONYISM	FAIRYISM	LOCALISM
ALLELISM	CULLYISM	FAKIRISM	LOGICISM
ALPINISM	CYNICISM	FAMILISM	LOOKSISM
ALTRUISM	DANDYISM	FARADISM	LOYALISM
ANEURISM	DEMONISM	FATALISM	LUMINISM
APHORISM	DEVILISM	FEMINISM	LYRICISM
APTERISM	DIMERISM	FINALISM	MACARISM
ARCHAISM	DIOECISM	FINITISM	MACHOISM
ASTERISM	DIRIGISM	FOGEYISM	MELANISM
ATROPISM	DITHEISM	FUTURISM	MERYCISM
ATTICISM	DONATISM	GIANTISM	METOPISM
AUTECISM	DOWDYISM	GIPSYISM	MINIMISM
BABELISM	DRUDGISM	GYPSYISM	MODALISM
BATHMISM	DRUIDISM	HEDONISM	MONADISM
BETACISM	DWARFISM	HELOTISM	MORALISM
BINARISM	DYNAMISM	HOBBYISM	MORONISM
BOGEYISM	EBIONISM	HUMANISM	NABOBISM
BOOBYISM	EMBOLISM	HYLICISM	NASALISM
BOTULISM	ENDEMISM	IDEALISM	NATIVISM
BOYARISM	ENTRYISM	IDIOTISM	NATURISM
BULLYISM	EPIZOISM	INCIVISM	NAVALISM
CABALISM	ERETHISM	INTIMISM	NEGROISM
CAFFEISM	ERGOTISM	IOTACISM	NEPHRISM
CASTEISM	ESCAPISM	JEHADISM	NEPOTISM

NIHILISM	POPULISM	SAPPHISM	TOKENISM
NIMBYISM	PRIAPISM	SATANISM	TOTALISM
NOMADISM	PRIGGISM	SAVAGISM	TOTEMISM
NOVELISM	PROSAISM	SCIOLISM	TRIADISM
OBEAHISM	PSELLISM	SCRIBISM	TRIALISM
OCKERISM	PSEPHISM	SEISMISM	TROILISM
OPIUMISM	PSYCHISM	SIMPLISM	TUTORISM
OPTIMISM	PTYALISM	SINAPISM	ULTRAISM
ORGANISM	PUGILISM	SNOBBISM	UNDINISM
PACIFISM	PUPPYISM	SOLARISM	UNIONISM
PAEANISM	PYGMYISM	SOLECISM	UNTRUISM
PAGANISM	QABALISM	SOLIDISM	URBANISM
PALUDISM	QUACKISM	SOMATISM	VEGANISM
PAPALISM	QUIETISM	STOICISM	VIRILISM
PARECISM	RACEMISM	STRABISM	VITALISM
PARTYISM	REGALISM	SWINGISM	VOCALISM
PELORISM	RIGHTISM	SYBOTISM	VOLTAISM
PETALISM	RIGORISM	TANTRISM	WOMANISM
PEYOTISM	ROBOTISM	TERATISM	XANTHISM
PHALLISM	ROWDYISM	THUGGISM	YAHOOISM
PHRENISM	ROYALISM	TIGERISM	ZOMBIISM
PLUMBISM	RURALISM	TITANISM	
POLONISM	SAINTISM	TOADYISM	

Words six to eight letters in length ending in the suffix IST

Note that there are a few IST words that cannot take an –S hook as indicated by the absence of an s against the word.

Those words that happen to end in IST where it has no relation to the suffix are excluded, so words such as DEMIST, ENLIST, ATTRIST, and SUBSIST are omitted.

Six-letter IST words

AGEIST s	HOLIST s	OBOIST s	SEXIST s
AORIST s	HYLIST s	OECIST s	SIZIST s
ARTIST s	JURIST s	OIKIST s	TANIST s
AURIST s	LAXIST s	PAPIST s	TAPIST s
AUTIST s	LEGIST s	PURIST s	THEIST s
BONIST s	LUTIST s	RACIST s	TIMIST s
CODIST s	LYRIST s	RAPIST s	TUBIST s
CUBIST s	MODIST s	RUDIST s	TYPIST s
CUEIST s	MONIST s	SADIST s	VERIST s
EGOIST s	NUDIST s	SAXIST s	VIBIST s

Seven-letter IST words

ABLEIST s	DIARIST s	HYGEIST s	POLLIST s
AGONIST s	DIETIST s	HYLOIST s	POLOIST s
ALTOIST s	DUALIST s	HYMNIST s	QUERIST s
AMORIST s	DUELIST s	IAMBIST s	RANKIST s
ANGLIST s	DUMAIST s	IDOLIST s	REALIST s
ANIMIST s	EBONIST s	IDYLIST s	REVUIST s
ATAVIST s	ECHOIST s	IMAGIST s	RHYMIST s
ATHEIST s	EGOTIST s	IRONIST s	SACRIST s
ATOMIST s	ELEGIST s	IVORIST s	SELFIST s
BAPTIST s	ELITIST s	JUDOIST s	SENSIST s
BASSIST s	ELOGIST s	JUJUIST s	SIZEIST s
BIBLIST s	ENTRIST s	LEFTIST s	SOLOIST s
BUNDIST s	EPEEIST s	LOOKIST s	SOPHIST s
CAMBIST s	EPICIST s	MAPPIST s	STATIST s
CASUIST s	ETATIST	METRIST s	STYLIST s
CELLIST s	EXODIST s	MYALIST s	SUMMIST s
CHEKIST s	FADDIST s	MYTHIST s	SUMOIST s
CHEMIST s	FASCIST s	NAIVIST	TACHIST s
CHORIST s	FATTIST s	NARCIST s	TENNIST s
CHUTIST s	FAUNIST s	OCULIST s	TITLIST s
CHYMIST s	FAUVIST s	OLIGIST s	TOURIST s
CLADIST s	FEUDIST s	OLOGIST s	TROPIST s
COOLIST s	FIDEIST s	ONANIST s	TSARIST s
COPYIST s	FLORIST s	ORALIST s	TUBAIST s
CORNIST s	FLUTIST s	PALMIST s	TZARIST s
COSMIST s	FOILIST s	PANNIST s	UNALIST s
CULTIST s	FUGUIST s	PHOBIST s	UTOPIST s
CYCLIST s	GAMBIST s	PIANIST s	VACUIST s
CZARIST s	GNOMIST s	PIARIST s	VIOLIST s
DADAIST s	HARPIST s	PIETIST s	WARMIST s
DENTIST s	HERBIST s	PLENIST s	WHOLIST s
DIALIST s	HORNIST s	PLUMIST s	

Eight-letter IST words

ACOSMIST s	AQUARIST s	AVIARIST s	CANOEIST s
ACTIVIST s	ARBALIST s	BANJOIST s	CANONIST s
ALARMIST s	ARBORIST s	BIGAMIST s	CENTOIST s
ALIENIST s	ARCANIST s	BLURBIST s	CENTRIST s
ALPINIST s	ARCHAIST s	BONGOIST s	CERAMIST s
ALTRUIST s	ARMORIST s	BOTANIST s	CHARTIST s
ANNALIST s	ARSONIST s	BURINIST s	CIVILIST s
APHORIST s	ATTICIST s	CABALIST s	CLASSIST s
APIARIST s	AVANTIST s	CALORIST s	CLUBBIST s

COLONIST s	HOBBYIST s	MODELIST s	SAFARIST s
COLORIST s	HOMILIST s	MONODIST s	SAPPHIST s
COMEDIST s	HUMANIST s	MORALIST s	SARODIST s
CONTRIST s	HUMORIST s	MOTORIST s	SATANIST s
CREOLIST s	HYGIEIST s	MURALIST s	SATIRIST s
DEMONIST s	HYLICIST s	NATIVIST s	SCIOLIST s
DEMOTIST s	HYPOCIST s	NATURIST s	SEMITIST s
DIALLIST s	IDEALIST s	NEPOTIST s	SHOOTIST s
DIGAMIST s	IDYLLIST s	NIELLIST s	SILURIST s
DITHEIST s	INTIMIST s	NIHILIST s	SIMONIST s
DRUGGIST s	JEHADIST s	NOVELIST s	SIMPLIST s
DUELLIST s	JIHADIST s	ODONTIST s	SITARIST s
DUETTIST s	JINGOIST s	OGHAMIST s	SODALIST s
DYNAMIST s	JUNGLIST s	OOLOGIST s	SODOMIST s
ENTRYIST s	KABALIST s	OPTICIST s	SOLARIST s
ERRORIST s	KENDOIST s	OPTIMIST s	SOLECIST s
ESCAPIST s	LABORIST s	ORGANIST s	SOLIDIST s
ESSAYIST s	LAPIDIST s	PACIFIST s	SOMATIST s
ETHERIST s	LEGALIST s	PAGANIST s	STOCKIST s
ETHICIST s	LIBELIST s	PANELIST s	TANGOIST s
EUGENIST s	LINGUIST s	PAPALIST s	TANTRIST s
EULOGIST s	LOBBYIST s	PARODIST s	TENORIST s
EUPHUIST s	LOCALIST s	PEYOTIST s	THEORIST s
EXORCIST s	LOGICIST s	PHALLIST s	TOTALIST s
FABULIST s	LONGLIST s	POLEMIST s	TOTEMIST s
FAMILIST	LOYALIST s	POPULIST s	TRIADIST s
FATALIST s	LUMINIST s	PROSAIST s	TRIALIST s
FEMINIST s	LUNARIST s	PSALMIST s	TROILIST s
FIGURIST s	LUTANIST s	PSYCHIST s	ULTRAIST s
FINALIST s	LUTENIST s	PUGILIST s	UNIONIST s
FINITIST s	LUXURIST s	QABALIST s	URBANIST s
FLAUTIST s	LYRICIST s	QUIETIST s	VEGETIST s
FUTURIST s	MAXIMIST s	RALLYIST s	VISAGIST s
GARAGIST s	MEDALIST s	REGALIST s	VITALIST s
GLOSSIST s	MELANIST s	REVERIST s	VOCALIST s
GROUPIST s	MELODIST s	RIGHTIST s	VOLUMIST s
HAGADIST s	METALIST s	RIGORIST s	VOTARIST s
HALAKIST s	MINIMIST s	ROYALIST s	WOMANIST s
HEDONIST s	MODALIST s	RURALIST s	

Words six to eight letters in length ending in the suffix ITY

Those words that happen to end in ITY where it has no relation to the suffix
are excluded, so words such as BEPITY, DACOITY, RABBITY, ANTICITY, and
BISCUITY are omitted.

Six-letter ITY words

ACUITY	ENTITY	NOVITY	SANITY
ASEITY	EQUITY	NUDITY	UPPITY
CAVITY	FERITY	ODDITY	VANITY
CECITY	FIXITY	ORBITY	VERITY
COMITY	LAXITY	PARITY	VOMITY
DIMITY	LENITY	POLITY	
EGOITY	LEVITY	PURITY	
ENMITY	MOYITY	RARITY	

Seven-letter ITY words

ABILITY	CRUDITY	LAICITY	REALITY
ACIDITY	CURVITY	NULLITY	SICCITY
AGILITY	DENSITY	OBESITY	SPIRITY
AMENITY	DIGNITY	OMNEITY	SUAVITY
AMINITY	DUALITY	OPACITY	SURDITY
ANALITY	EDACITY	ORALITY	TENSITY
ANILITY	EGALITY	OVALITY	TENUITY
ANNUITY	EXILITY	PANEITY	TRINITY
ARIDITY	FALSITY	PAUCITY	UTILITY
AUREITY	FATUITY	PIOSITY	VACUITY
AVIDITY	FURMITY	PRAVITY	VARSITY
BIGGITY	GASEITY	PRIVITY	VASTITY
BREVITY	GRAVITY	PROBITY	VIDUITY
CHARITY	INANITY	QUALITY	
CLARITY	JOLLITY	RAUCITY	

Eight-letter ITY words

ACERBITY	ATROCITY	CALIDITY	DEBILITY
ACRIDITY	AUDACITY	CANINITY	DICACITY
ACTIVITY	AURALITY	CAPACITY	DISUNITY
ADUNCITY	AXIALITY	CELERITY	DIVINITY
AFFINITY	BANALITY	CHASTITY	DOCILITY
ALACRITY	BASICITY	CIRCUITY	DUMOSITY
ALGIDITY	BIFIDITY	CIVILITY	ENORMITY
ALTERITY	BOVINITY	CONICITY	EQUALITY
ASPERITY	CADUCITY	CUBICITY	EQUINITY
ASTUCITY	CALAMITY	CUPIDITY	ETERNITY

EXIGUITY	INTIMITY	OTIOSITY	SORORITY
FACILITY	INVERITY	PENALITY	SPARSITY
FATALITY	IONICITY	PERSEITY	TELICITY
FELICITY	JEJUNITY	PILOSITY	TEMERITY
FELINITY	JOCOSITY	POLARITY	TENACITY
FEMALITY	LABILITY	POROSITY	TEPIDITY
FEMINITY	LANOSITY	PRIORITY	TIMIDITY
FERACITY	LATINITY	PUDICITY	TONALITY
FEROCITY	LEGALITY	QUANTITY	TONICITY
FETIDITY	LEGERITY	QUEERITY	TOROSITY
FIDELITY	LIVIDITY	QUIDDITY	TOTALITY
FINALITY	LOCALITY	RABIDITY	TOXICITY
FLUIDITY	LUCIDITY	RAMOSITY	TRIALITY
FORTUITY	MAJORITY	RAPACITY	TRIUNITY
FUGACITY	MATURITY	RAPIDITY	TUMIDITY
FUMOSITY	MEGACITY	REGALITY	UBIQUITY
FURACITY	MINACITY	RIGIDITY	UNFIXITY
FUTILITY	MINORITY	RIMOSITY	URBANITY
FUTURITY	MOBILITY	RIVALITY	VAGILITY
GELIDITY	MODALITY	RUGOSITY	VALIDITY
GRATUITY	MOLALITY	RURALITY	VAPIDITY
GULOSITY	MOLARITY	SAGACITY	VELLEITY
HELICITY	MORALITY	SALACITY	VELOCITY
HEREDITY	MORONITY	SALINITY	VENALITY
HILARITY	MOROSITY	SANCTITY	VENOSITY
HUMANITY	MOTILITY	SAPIDITY	VERACITY
HUMIDITY	MOTIVITY	SATANITY	VICINITY
HUMILITY	MUCIDITY	SCANTITY	VINOSITY
IDEALITY	MUCOSITY	SCARCITY	VIRALITY
IDENTITY	MULTEITY	SECURITY	VIRIDITY
IDONEITY	NASALITY	SEDULITY	VIRILITY
IMMANITY	NATALITY	SENILITY	VITALITY
IMMUNITY	NATIVITY	SERENITY	VIVACITY
IMPARITY	NIHILITY	SEROSITY	VIVIDITY
IMPUNITY	NOBILITY	SEVERITY	VOCALITY
IMPURITY	NODALITY	SODALITY	VORACITY
INEQUITY	NODOSITY	SODICITY	ZYGOSITY
INFINITY	NUBILITY	SOLICITY	
INIQUITY	OBTUSITY	SOLIDITY	
INSANITY	ORGANITY	SONORITY	

Words six to eight letters in length ending in the suffix LESS

Those words that happen to end in LESS where it has no relation to the suffix are excluded, so words such as UNBLESS and DEVILESS are omitted.

Six-letter LESS words
AWLESS

Seven-letter LESS words

AGELESS	ENDLESS	JOBLESS	SINLESS
AIDLESS	EYELESS	JOYLESS	SKYLESS
AIMLESS	FATLESS	KEYLESS	SONLESS
AIRLESS	FEELESS	KINLESS	SUMLESS
ARMLESS	FINLESS	LAWLESS	SUNLESS
ARTLESS	FLYLESS	LEGLESS	TAGLESS
ASHLESS	FOGLESS	LIDLESS	TAPLESS
AWELESS	FURLESS	LIPLESS	TAXLESS
AWNLESS	GAPLESS	MANLESS	TIELESS
BAGLESS	GASLESS	MAPLESS	TIPLESS
BARLESS	GODLESS	MATLESS	TOELESS
BEDLESS	GUMLESS	NAPLESS	TOPLESS
BIBLESS	GUNLESS	NETLESS	TOYLESS
BITLESS	GUTLESS	OARLESS	TUGLESS
BOWLESS	HAPLESS	ORBLESS	USELESS
BRALESS	HATLESS	PEGLESS	VOWLESS
BUDLESS	HIPLESS	PINLESS	WARLESS
CAPLESS	HITLESS	PIPLESS	WAYLESS
CARLESS	HUBLESS	RAYLESS	WEBLESS
COXLESS	HUELESS	RIBLESS	WIGLESS
CUBLESS	ICELESS	RIMLESS	WINLESS
DEWLESS	INKLESS	RODLESS	WITLESS
EARLESS	INNLESS	RUNLESS	ZIPLESS
EBBLESS	IRELESS	SACLESS	
EGGLESS	JAGLESS	SAPLESS	
EGOLESS	JAWLESS	SEXLESS	

Eight-letter LESS words

BACKLESS	BEAKLESS	BOLTLESS	BROWLESS
BARBLESS	BEAMLESS	BONDLESS	BUSHLESS
BARKLESS	BEATLESS	BONELESS	CALFLESS
BASELESS	BEEFLESS	BOOKLESS	CARELESS
BASHLESS	BELTLESS	BOONLESS	CASHLESS
BATELESS	BLOTLESS	BOOTLESS	CHADLESS
BATHLESS	BODILESS	BRIMLESS	CHAPLESS

CHINLESS	FIRELESS	HIVELESS	LUNGLESS
CLAWLESS	FIRMLESS	HOLELESS	LUSTLESS
CLOYLESS	FISHLESS	HOMELESS	MAIDLESS
CLUELESS	FLAGLESS	HOODLESS	MAILLESS
COALLESS	FLAPLESS	HOOFLESS	MAKELESS
COATLESS	FLAWLESS	HOOKLESS	MANELESS
CODELESS	FOAMLESS	HOOPLESS	MASSLESS
COMBLESS	FOODLESS	HOPELESS	MASTLESS
COOKLESS	FOOTLESS	HORNLESS	MATELESS
CORDLESS	FORDLESS	HOSTLESS	MEALLESS
CORELESS	FORKLESS	HUMPLESS	MEATLESS
COSTLESS	FORMLESS	HURTLESS	MILKLESS
CREWLESS	FRETLESS	HYMNLESS	MINDLESS
CROPLESS	FUMELESS	IDEALESS	MOONLESS
CUFFLESS	FUNDLESS	IRONLESS	MOVELESS
CURBLESS	FUSELESS	ISLELESS	NAILLESS
CURELESS	FUZELESS	JAILLESS	NAMELESS
DATELESS	GAINLESS	JURYLESS	NATHLESS
DEBTLESS	GAOLLESS	KEELLESS	NECKLESS
DECKLESS	GARBLESS	KINDLESS	NEEDLESS
DEEDLESS	GATELESS	KINGLESS	NEWSLESS
DINTLESS	GAUMLESS	KNOTLESS	NORMLESS
DISCLESS	GEARLESS	LACELESS	NOSELESS
DISKLESS	GIFTLESS	LAMPLESS	NOTELESS
DOORLESS	GOALLESS	LANDLESS	NOUNLESS
DOWNLESS	GOLDLESS	LASHLESS	ODORLESS
DRIPLESS	GORMLESS	LEADLESS	PAINLESS
DRUGLESS	GRITLESS	LEAFLESS	PANELESS
DUCTLESS	GUSTLESS	LEAKLESS	PANGLESS
DUSTLESS	HAIRLESS	LENSLESS	PASSLESS
EASELESS	HALTLESS	LIFELESS	PASTLESS
ECHOLESS	HANDLESS	LIMBLESS	PATHLESS
EDGELESS	HARMLESS	LIMELESS	PEAKLESS
EXITLESS	HATELESS	LINELESS	PEERLESS
FACELESS	HEADLESS	LINTLESS	PELTLESS
FADELESS	HEATLESS	LISTLESS	PILELESS
FAMELESS	HEEDLESS	LOAMLESS	PIPELESS
FANGLESS	HEELLESS	LOBELESS	PITHLESS
FEARLESS	HEIRLESS	LOCKLESS	PITILESS
FECKLESS	HELMLESS	LOFTLESS	PLANLESS
FEETLESS	HELPLESS	LORDLESS	PLAYLESS
FERNLESS	HERBLESS	LOSSLESS	PLOTLESS
FILMLESS	HIDELESS	LOVELESS	PLUGLESS
FINELESS	HILTLESS	LUCKLESS	POETLESS

POLELESS	SEATLESS	SUCKLESS	VENTLESS
POPELESS	SEEDLESS	SUDSLESS	VERBLESS
PORTLESS	SEEMLESS	TACKLESS	VESTLESS
PULPLESS	SELFLESS	TACTLESS	VETOLESS
PUMPLESS	SHIPLESS	TAILLESS	VICELESS
RAILLESS	SHITLESS	TAMELESS	VIEWLESS
RAINLESS	SHOELESS	TANKLESS	VINELESS
RANKLESS	SHOPLESS	TAPELESS	VOTELESS
RECKLESS	SHUNLESS	TASKLESS	WAGELESS
REDELESS	SIDELESS	TEARLESS	WAKELESS
REINLESS	SIGHLESS	TEEMLESS	WARDLESS
RESTLESS	SIGNLESS	TENTLESS	WARELESS
RIFTLESS	SKILLESS	TERMLESS	WARTLESS
RIMELESS	SKINLESS	TEXTLESS	WATTLESS
RINDLESS	SLIPLESS	THAWLESS	WAVELESS
RINGLESS	SLITLESS	THEWLESS	WEEDLESS
RISKLESS	SMOGLESS	THOWLESS	WEETLESS
RITELESS	SNAPLESS	TIDELESS	WELDLESS
ROADLESS	SNOWLESS	TIMELESS	WHIPLESS
ROCKLESS	SOAPLESS	TINTLESS	WICKLESS
ROOFLESS	SOCKLESS	TIRELESS	WIFELESS
ROOTLESS	SODALESS	TOADLESS	WINDLESS
ROSELESS	SOILLESS	TOILLESS	WINELESS
RULELESS	SOLELESS	TOMBLESS	WINGLESS
RUMPLESS	SONGLESS	TONELESS	WIRELESS
RUNGLESS	SOOTLESS	TOOLLESS	WISHLESS
RUSTLESS	SOULLESS	TOWNLESS	WITELESS
RUTHLESS	SOUPLESS	TRAMLESS	WONTLESS
SACKLESS	SPANLESS	TREELESS	WOODLESS
SAIKLESS	SPINLESS	TUBELESS	WORDLESS
SAILLESS	SPOTLESS	TUNELESS	WORKLESS
SALTLESS	SPURLESS	TURFLESS	YOKELESS
SANDLESS	STARLESS	TUSKLESS	YOLKLESS
SASHLESS	STAYLESS	TWIGLESS	ZEALLESS
SATELESS	STEMLESS	TYRELESS	ZESTLESS
SCARLESS	STEPLESS	VANELESS	ZONELESS
SCUMLESS	STIRLESS	VEILLESS	
SEAMLESS	STOPLESS	VEINLESS	

Words six to eight letters in length ending in the suffix LIKE

Those words that happen to end in LIKE where it has no relation to the suffix are excluded, so BELIKE, UNLIKE, DISLIKE, and UNALIKE are omitted.

Six-letter LIKE words

AXLIKE	OXLIKE

Seven-letter LIKE words

AIRLIKE	FANLIKE	KIDLIKE	RAYLIKE
ANTLIKE	FATLIKE	LAWLIKE	RIBLIKE
APELIKE	FINLIKE	LEGLIKE	RODLIKE
ARMLIKE	FOXLIKE	LIPLIKE	RUGLIKE
ASSLIKE	GEMLIKE	MANLIKE	SACLIKE
AXELIKE	GODLIKE	MAPLIKE	SAWLIKE
BAGLIKE	GUMLIKE	MISLIKE s	SICLIKE
BATLIKE	GUTLIKE	NETLIKE	SKYLIKE
BEDLIKE	HAGLIKE	NIBLIKE	SONLIKE
BEELIKE	HATLIKE	NUNLIKE	SUNLIKE
BIBLIKE	HENLIKE	NUTLIKE	TAGLIKE
BOWLIKE	HIPLIKE	OAKLIKE	TEALIKE
BOXLIKE	HOBLIKE	OARLIKE	TINLIKE
BUDLIKE	HOELIKE	OATLIKE	TOELIKE
CATLIKE	HOGLIKE	OWLLIKE	TOYLIKE
COWLIKE	HUTLIKE	PANLIKE	TUBLIKE
CUPLIKE	ICELIKE	PEALIKE	URNLIKE
DOGLIKE	INKLIKE	PEGLIKE	WARLIKE
EARLIKE	IVYLIKE	PIGLIKE	WAXLIKE
EELLIKE	JAMLIKE	PODLIKE	WEBLIKE
ELFLIKE	JAWLIKE	POTLIKE	WIGLIKE
EYELIKE	JETLIKE	PUSLIKE	
FADLIKE	JIGLIKE	RATLIKE	

Eight-letter LIKE words

AGUELIKE	BIRDLIKE	CLAYLIKE	DEERLIKE
AUNTLIKE	BOATLIKE	COCKLIKE	DISCLIKE
BABYLIKE	BOLTLIKE	COKELIKE	DISHLIKE
BALMLIKE	BOWLLIKE	COMBLIKE	DISKLIKE
BARNLIKE	BUSHLIKE	CORDLIKE	DOMELIKE
BEADLIKE	CAGELIKE	CORKLIKE	DOVELIKE
BEAKLIKE	CALFLIKE	CORMLIKE	DOWNLIKE
BEAMLIKE	CAVELIKE	CRABLIKE	DRUMLIKE
BEANLIKE	CLAMLIKE	CULTLIKE	DUNELIKE
BEARLIKE	CLAWLIKE	DAWNLIKE	DUSTLIKE

EPICLIKE	HYMNLIKE	PITHLIKE	STEPLIKE
FANGLIKE	IRONLIKE	PLAYLIKE	SUCHLIKE
FAUNLIKE	JADELIKE	PLUMLIKE	SUITLIKE
FAWNLIKE	JAZZLIKE	POETLIKE	SURFLIKE
FELTLIKE	JUTELIKE	POPELIKE	SWANLIKE
FERNLIKE	KILTLIKE	PUMPLIKE	TAILLIKE
FILMLIKE	KINGLIKE	PUSSLIKE	TANKLIKE
FISHLIKE	KITELIKE	QUAYLIKE	TAPELIKE
FOAMLIKE	KNOBLIKE	RASHLIKE	TEARLIKE
FOLKLIKE	KNOTLIKE	REEDLIKE	TENTLIKE
FOOTLIKE	LACELIKE	RINGLIKE	TIDELIKE
FORKLIKE	LADYLIKE	ROCKLIKE	TILELIKE
FROGLIKE	LAKELIKE	ROOFLIKE	TOADLIKE
FUMELIKE	LAMBLIKE	ROOTLIKE	TOMBLIKE
FUSELIKE	LARDLIKE	ROPELIKE	TRAPLIKE
GAMELIKE	LATHLIKE	ROSELIKE	TREELIKE
GATELIKE	LAVALIKE	RUBYLIKE	TUBELIKE
GERMLIKE	LEAFLIKE	RUFFLIKE	TURFLIKE
GLENLIKE	LIFELIKE	RUNELIKE	TUSKLIKE
GLUELIKE	LILYLIKE	RUSHLIKE	TWIGLIKE
GNATLIKE	LINELIKE	SACKLIKE	VASELIKE
GOADLIKE	LIONLIKE	SALTLIKE	VEILLIKE
GOATLIKE	LOFTLIKE	SANDLIKE	VEINLIKE
GONGLIKE	LORDLIKE	SCABLIKE	VESTLIKE
GULFLIKE	LYNXLIKE	SCUMLIKE	VICELIKE
HAIRLIKE	MASKLIKE	SEALLIKE	VINELIKE
HALOLIKE	MASTLIKE	SEAMLIKE	VISELIKE
HANDLIKE	MAZELIKE	SEEDLIKE	WAIFLIKE
HARELIKE	MILKLIKE	SERFLIKE	WANDLIKE
HAWKLIKE	MOATLIKE	SHEDLIKE	WARTLIKE
HEADLIKE	MOONLIKE	SIGHLIKE	WASPLIKE
HEMPLIKE	MOSSLIKE	SILKLIKE	WAVELIKE
HERBLIKE	MOTHLIKE	SKINLIKE	WEEDLIKE
HERDLIKE	NECKLIKE	SLABLIKE	WHEYLIKE
HIVELIKE	NESTLIKE	SLITLIKE	WHIPLIKE
HOMELIKE	NOOKLIKE	SNAGLIKE	WIFELIKE
HOODLIKE	NOSELIKE	SNOWLIKE	WINGLIKE
HOOFLIKE	NOVALIKE	SOAPLIKE	WIRELIKE
HOOKLIKE	OVENLIKE	SONGLIKE	WISPLIKE
HOOPLIKE	PALMLIKE	SOULLIKE	WOLFLIKE
HORNLIKE	PARKLIKE	SOUPLIKE	WOMBLIKE
HOSELIKE	PEAKLIKE	SPARLIKE	WOOLLIKE
HUMPLIKE	PINELIKE	STARLIKE	WORMLIKE
HUSKLIKE	PIPELIKE	STEMLIKE	

Words six to eight letters in length ending in the suffix LY

Those words that happen to end in LY where it has no relation to the LY
adjective and adverb forms are excluded, so words such as FAMILY, MAYFLY,
ANOMALY, and DISALLY are omitted.

Adverbs ending in ILY

Six-letter ILY words

AERILY	EDGILY	JOKILY	ROPILY
AIRILY	EERILY	LACILY	ROSILY
ARTILY	FOXILY	LAZILY	SEXILY
BODILY	GAMILY	LOGILY	TIDILY
BOXILY	GLUILY	MATILY	TINILY
BUSILY	GOOILY	MAZILY	UGLILY
CAGILY	GORILY	MOPILY	VERILY
COSILY	HAZILY	NOSILY	WARILY
COZILY	HOKILY	OILILY	WAVILY
DEWILY	HOLILY	OOZILY	WAXILY
DOPILY	HOMILY	POKILY	WILILY
DOZILY	ICKILY	PUNILY	WIRILY
EASILY	IFFILY	RACILY	ZANILY

Seven-letter ILY words

ANGRILY	CAMPILY	DOTTILY	FUNKILY
BAGGILY	CANNILY	DOWDILY	FUNNILY
BALKILY	CANTILY	DOWNILY	FURRILY
BALMILY	CATTILY	DUMPILY	FUSSILY
BARMILY	CHARILY	DUSKILY	FUSTILY
BATTILY	COCKILY	DUSTILY	FUZZILY
BAWDILY	COMFILY	EMPTILY	GASSILY
BEADILY	CORNILY	FAIRILY	GAUDILY
BEAMILY	CRAZILY	FANCILY	GAUZILY
BEEFILY	CRUSILY	FATTILY	GAWKILY
BEERILY	CURLILY	FIERILY	GEMMILY
BITTILY	CUSHILY	FILMILY	GIDDILY
BONNILY	DAFFILY	FISHILY	GLAZILY
BOOZILY	DANDILY	FIZZILY	GODLILY
BOSSILY	DEEDILY	FLAKILY	GOOFILY
BULKILY	DINGILY	FLUKILY	GOUTILY
BUMPILY	DIRTILY	FOAMILY	GRIMILY
BURLILY	DIZZILY	FOGGILY	GUMMILY
BUSHILY	DOOMILY	FUGGILY	GUSHILY

GUSTILY
GUTSILY
HAIRILY
HAMMILY
HANDILY
HAPPILY
HARDILY
HASTILY
HEADILY
HEAVILY
HEFTILY
HOARILY
HORNILY
HORSILY
HUFFILY
HUSKILY
ITCHILY
JAZZILY
JERKILY
JOLLILY
JOLTILY
JUICILY
JUMPILY
KINKILY
KOOKILY
LANKILY
LEAKILY
LEERILY
LOFTILY
LOOBILY
LOONILY
LOOPILY
LOUSILY
LOWLILY
LUCKILY
LUMPILY
LUSTILY
MANGILY
MANLILY
MEATILY
MERRILY

MESSILY
MIFFILY
MILKILY
MINGILY
MIRKILY
MISTILY
MOODILY
MOONILY
MOUSILY
MUCKILY
MUDDILY
MUGGILY
MURKILY
MUSHILY
MUSKILY
MUSSILY
MUSTILY
MUZZILY
NASTILY
NATTILY
NEEDILY
NERVILY
NIFTILY
NIPPILY
NOBBILY
NOISILY
NUTTILY
PASTILY
PAWKILY
PEPPILY
PERKILY
PESKILY
PETTILY
PHONILY
PICKILY
PITHILY
POCKILY
PODGILY
PRICILY
PRIVILY
PROSILY

PUDGILY
PUFFILY
PULPILY
PURSILY
PUSHILY
QUAKILY
RAINILY
RANDILY
RANGILY
RATTILY
READILY
REEDILY
RISKILY
RITZILY
ROCKILY
ROOMILY
ROUPILY
ROWDILY
RUDDILY
RUMMILY
RUSTILY
RUTTILY
SALTILY
SAPPILY
SARKILY
SASSILY
SAUCILY
SAVVILY
SCARILY
SEEDILY
SHADILY
SHAKILY
SHINILY
SHOWILY
SILKILY
SILLILY
SLIMILY
SMOKILY
SNAKILY
SNOWILY
SOAPILY

SOGGILY
SOOTILY
SOPPILY
SORRILY
SOUPILY
SPICILY
SPIKILY
STAGILY
STONILY
SULKILY
SUNNILY
SURLILY
TACKILY
TARDILY
TARTILY
TASTILY
TATTILY
TAWNILY
TEARILY
TECHILY
TESTILY
TINNILY
TIPSILY
TOSSILY
TUFTILY
WACKILY
WASHILY
WASPILY
WEARILY
WEEDILY
WEEPILY
WINDILY
WISPILY
WITTILY
WONKILY
WOOZILY
WORDILY
ZESTILY
ZIPPILY

Eight-letter ILY words

BAULKILY	CREAMILY	GRASSILY	SHIFTILY
BEASTILY	CREEPILY	GREASILY	SHIRTILY
BITCHILY	CRISPILY	GREEDILY	SHITTILY
BLEARILY	CROAKILY	GRITTILY	SHODDILY
BLOODILY	CROUPILY	GROGGILY	SICKLILY
BLOUSILY	CRUMMILY	GROOVILY	SKIMPILY
BLOWSILY	CRUSTILY	GRUBBILY	SLANGILY
BLOWZILY	DAINTILY	GRUFFILY	SLEAZILY
BLURRILY	DRAFTILY	GRUMPILY	SLEEPILY
BOTCHILY	DREAMILY	GUILTILY	SLINKILY
BOUNCILY	DREARILY	HEARTILY	SLIPPILY
BRAINILY	DRESSILY	HITCHILY	SLOPPILY
BRASSILY	DRIPPILY	HOMELILY	SLUSHILY
BRAWNILY	DROOPILY	HUNGRILY	SLUTTILY
BREEZILY	DROWSILY	JAUNTILY	SMALMILY
BROODILY	EARTHILY	KINDLILY	SMARMILY
BUNCHILY	FAULTILY	KNOTTILY	SMEARILY
CATCHILY	FEISTILY	LIVELILY	SMIRKILY
CHANCILY	FILTHILY	LONELILY	SMUDGILY
CHATTILY	FLABBILY	LOVELILY	SMUTTILY
CHEEKILY	FLASHILY	MIGHTILY	SNAPPILY
CHEERILY	FLEECILY	MOUTHILY	SNARKILY
CHEESILY	FLESHILY	PALTRILY	SNAZZILY
CHESTILY	FLIMSILY	PATCHILY	SNEAKILY
CHILLILY	FLINTILY	PEACHILY	SNIFFILY
CHIRPILY	FLOPPILY	PITCHILY	SNIPPILY
CHOOSILY	FLOSSILY	PLAGUILY	SNOBBILY
CHOPPILY	FLUFFILY	PLUCKILY	SNOOPILY
CHUBBILY	FOLKSILY	PLUSHILY	SNOOTILY
CHUMMILY	FREAKILY	PREPPILY	SNOTTILY
CHUNKILY	FRENZILY	PRETTILY	SNUFFILY
CLAMMILY	FRISKILY	PRISSILY	SPARKILY
CLASSILY	FRIZZILY	PUNCHILY	SPEEDILY
CLOGGILY	FROSTILY	QUEASILY	SPIFFILY
CLOUDILY	FROTHILY	QUIRKILY	SPONGILY
CLUBBILY	FROWZILY	SAVORILY	SPOOKILY
CLUMSILY	FRUITILY	SCABBILY	SPOONILY
COMELILY	FRUMPILY	SCANTILY	SPORTILY
CRABBILY	GLASSILY	SCATTILY	SPOTTILY
CRAFTILY	GLITZILY	SCUMMILY	SPUNKILY
CRAGGILY	GLOOMILY	SCURVILY	STALKILY
CRANKILY	GLOSSILY	SHABBILY	STARRILY
CREAKILY	GLUMPILY	SHAGGILY	STEADILY

STEAMILY	SULTRILY	TRASHILY	WHEEZILY
STICKILY	SUNDRILY	TRENDILY	WHIMSILY
STINGILY	SWANKILY	TRICKILY	WINTRILY
STOCKILY	SWEATILY	TRUSTILY	WOOLLILY
STODGILY	SWIMMILY	TWEEDILY	WORTHILY
STORMILY	TAWDRILY	UNEASILY	WOUNDILY
STUBBILY	TETCHILY	UNHOLILY	WRATHILY
STUFFILY	THORNILY	UNTIDILY	YEASTILY
STUMPILY	TOOTHILY	UNWARILY	
STURDILY	TOUCHILY	WATERILY	

Adverbs ending in LY

A few have comparative and superlative forms or plural forms as shown.

Six-letter LY adverbs

ACIDLY	–LIEST	FIRMLY	LATELY
AGEDLY	DEAFLY	FLATLY	LEALLY
ANALLY	DEARLY	FONDLY	LEANLY
ANERLY	DEEPLY	FOULLY	LEWDLY
ARCHLY	DEFFLY	FREELY	LIEFLY
ARIDLY	DEFTLY	GAMELY	LIMPLY
AVIDLY	DERNLY	GENTLY	LONGLY
BALDLY	DIRELY	GLADLY	LOUDLY
BARELY	DOUBLY	–LIER	–LIER
BASELY	DOURLY	–LIEST	–LIEST
BASSLY	DRABLY	GLEGLY	LUSHLY
BLUELY	DROLLY	GLIBLY	MAINLY
BOLDLY	DUALLY	GLUMLY	MEANLY
BRAGLY	–LIES	GRAYLY	MEEKLY
CALMLY	DUMBLY	GREYLY	MEETLY
CAMPLY	DUSKLY	GRIMLY	MERELY
CHICLY	EATHLY	GRUMLY	MILDLY
CLODLY	EGALLY	HARDLY	MOSTLY
COLDLY	EVENLY	HIGHLY	MUCHLY
COOLLY	EVILLY	HUGELY	MURKLY
CURTLY	FAINLY	HUMBLY	MUTELY
CUTELY	FAIRLY	JIMPLY	NAFFLY
DAFTLY	FASTLY	JUSTLY	NAIFLY
DAMPLY	FECKLY	KEENLY	NAMELY
DANKLY	FEEBLY	LAMELY	NEARLY
DARKLY	FICKLY	LANKLY	–LIER
–LIER	FINELY	LASTLY	–LIEST

NEATLY	RAGULY	SMUGLY	TRIMLY
NEXTLY	RANKLY	SNUGLY	TRIPLY
NICELY	RAPTLY	SOFTLY	-LIES
NIGHLY	RARELY	SOLELY	TWEELY
NIMBLY	RASHLY	SORELY	UNDULY
NUDELY	REALLY	SOURLY	VAINLY
NUMBLY	REARLY	SPRYLY	VASTLY
OPENLY	RICHLY	STABLY	VILDLY
ORALLY	RIFELY	SUBTLY	VILELY
OVALLY	RIPELY	SUPPLY	VIVELY
OVERLY	RUDELY	SURELY	WARMLY
PACKLY	SAFELY	SUTTLY	WHOLLY
PALELY	SAGELY	TAMELY	WIDELY
PARTLY	SALTLY	TARTLY	WILDLY
PERTLY	SAMELY	TAUTLY	WISELY
PINKLY	SANELY	THINLY	-LIER
POSHLY	SIMPLY	THUSLY	-LIEST
PRIMLY	SINGLY	TITELY	WISTLY
PROLLY	SLIMLY	TREBLY	YARELY
PURELY	SLOWLY	TRIGLY	

Seven-letter LY adverbs

ACRIDLY	BLEAKLY	CRASSLY	FALSELY
ACUTELY	BLINDLY	CRISPLY	FATALLY
ADDEDLY	BLUFFLY	CROSSLY	FETIDLY
ADEPTLY	BLUNTLY	CRUDELY	FIFTHLY
ADULTLY	BOGUSLY	CRUELLY	FINALLY
AGILELY	BRASHLY	CUBICLY	FIRSTLY
ALERTLY	BRAVELY	DATEDLY	FIXEDLY
ALIENLY	BRIEFLY	DAZEDLY	FLEETLY
ALONELY	BRISKLY	DEARNLY	FLUIDLY
ALOOFLY	BRITTLY	DENSELY	FOCALLY
ANTICLY	BROADLY	DOUCELY	FRAILLY
APISHLY	BRUTELY	DREADLY	FRANKLY
AREALLY	BUXOMLY	DUCALLY	FRESHLY
AURALLY	CECALLY	DYINGLY	FUGALLY
AWFULLY	CHEAPLY	EAGERLY	GAUNTLY
AXIALLY	CHEERLY	ELDERLY	GELIDLY
BANALLY	CHIEFLY	EQUALLY	GRANDLY
BASALLY	CIVILLY	ERECTLY	GRAVELY
BIFIDLY	CLEARLY	EROSELY	GREATLY
BLACKLY	CLOSELY	EXACTLY	GREENLY
BLANDLY	COWEDLY	FADEDLY	GROSSLY
BLANKLY	CRANKLY	FAINTLY	GRUFFLY

GYRALLY	MODALLY	ROYALLY	TERSELY
HARSHLY	MOISTLY	RURALLY	TEUGHLY
HARTELY	MORALLY	SCANTLY	THICKLY
HEARTLY	MUTEDLY	SHARPLY	THIRDLY
HUMANLY	NAIVELY	SHEERLY	TIDALLY
HUMIDLY	NAKEDLY	SHORTLY	TIGHTLY
IDEALLY	NASALLY	SIDEDLY	TIMIDLY
IGNOBLY	NAVALLY	SIXTHLY	TIREDLY
INANELY	NIGHTLY	SLACKLY	TONALLY
INAPTLY	NINTHLY	SLANTLY	TOTALLY
INEPTLY	NODALLY	SLEEKLY	TOUGHLY
INERTLY	NOTEDLY	SLICKLY	TRITELY
INNERLY	NOVELLY	SMARTLY	TUMIDLY
IRATELY	OBESELY	SMICKLY	UNAPTLY
JADEDLY	OVATELY	SNIDELY	UNFITLY
JOINTLY	OVERTLY	SNIVELY	UNTRULY
JURALLY	PAPALLY	SOBERLY	USUALLY
LAITHLY	PEARTLY	SOLIDLY	UTTERLY
LARGELY	PENALLY	SOLUBLY	VAGALLY
LEGALLY	PIOUSLY	SOOTHLY	VAGUELY
LEVELLY	PLAINLY	SOUNDLY	VALIDLY
LICHTLY	PLUMPLY	SPARELY	VAPIDLY
–LIES	PLUSHLY	SQUATLY	VENALLY
LICITLY	PRIMELY	STAIDLY	VEXEDLY
LIGHTLY	PRIORLY	STALELY	VIRALLY
–LIES	PRONELY	STARKLY	VITALLY
LITHELY	PROUDLY	STARTLY	VIVIDLY
LIVIDLY	QUEERLY	STEEPLY	VOCALLY
LOATHLY	QUICKLY	STERNLY	VOLUBLY
LOCALLY	QUIETLY	STIFFLY	VYINGLY
LOOSELY	RABIDLY	STOUTLY	WEIRDLY
LOYALLY	RAPIDLY	SUAVELY	WHITELY
LUCIDLY	RAVELLY	SWEETLY	WIGHTLY
LURIDLY	REGALLY	SWIFTLY	WOFULLY
LYINGLY	RIANTLY	SWITHLY	WRONGLY
MAJORLY	RIGHTLY	TACITLY	YOUNGLY
MAZEDLY	RIGIDLY	TENSELY	ZONALLY
MESALLY	ROUGHLY	TENTHLY	
MIXEDLY	ROUNDLY	TEPIDLY	

Eight-letter LY adverbs

ABASEDLY	ABRUPTLY	ACHINGLY	ADROITLY
ABJECTLY	ABSENTLY	ACTIVELY	AERIALLY
ABORALLY	ABSURDLY	ACTUALLY	AFFINELY

AGUISHLY	CALLOWLY	DIVINELY	FRIGIDLY
AIMFULLY	CANDIDLY	DOCILELY	FROZENLY
ALPINELY	CARINGLY	DOCTORLY	FRUGALLY
AMAZEDLY	CARNALLY	DOGGEDLY	FUMINGLY
AMORALLY	CASUALLY	DORSALLY	FUTILELY
AMUSEDLY	CAUDALLY	DOTARDLY	GAPINGLY
ANIMALLY	CAUSALLY	DOTINGLY	GARISHLY
ANNUALLY	CHASTELY	DUDISHLY	GAUCHELY
ANODALLY	CHOICELY	DULCETLY	GENIALLY
APICALLY	CHORALLY	EFFETELY	GIBINGLY
ARCANELY	CLEVERLY	EIGHTHLY	GIFTEDLY
ARDENTLY	CLINALLY	ELATEDLY	GINGERLY
ARGUTELY	CLONALLY	ELFISHLY	GLOBALLY
ARRANTLY	COARSELY	ELVISHLY	GOLDENLY
ARTFULLY	COEVALLY	ENTIRELY	GORGEDLY
ASTRALLY	COGENTLY	EPICALLY	GRAITHLY
ASTUTELY	COITALLY	EQUINELY	GRAVELLY
ATONALLY	COMMONLY	ERRANTLY	GRAVIDLY
AUGUSTLY	CONVEXLY	ERRINGLY	HEATEDLY
AVERSELY	COOINGLY	EXPERTLY	HECTICLY
AVOWEDLY	COSTALLY	FACETELY	HECTORLY
BADGERLY	COVERTLY	FACIALLY	HEROICLY
BANKERLY	COYISHLY	FACILELY	HIDDENLY
BARRENLY	CRAVENLY	FAMOUSLY	HOARSELY
BEGGARLY	CROUSELY	FAUNALLY	HOLLOWLY
BEHOVELY	CRYINGLY	FELINELY	HONESTLY
BENIGNLY	CURSEDLY	FELLOWLY	HONIEDLY
BIASEDLY	CURVEDLY	FERVIDLY	HOPINGLY
BINATELY	CUSSEDLY	FESTALLY	HORRIDLY
BITINGLY	CYCLICLY	FEUDALLY	HUMANELY
BITTERLY	CYMOSELY	FIERCELY	HUNGERLY
BLITHELY	DAPPERLY	FILIALLY	HUNTEDLY
BODINGLY	DARINGLY	FINITELY	HUSHEDLY
BORINGLY	DATIVELY	FISCALLY	IMMANELY
BOVINELY	DECENTLY	FITFULLY	IMPISHLY
BOWINGLY	DEMISSLY	FLORALLY	IMPURELY
BOYISHLY	DEMURELY	FLORIDLY	INDIGNLY
BRAZENLY	DENTALLY	FLUENTLY	INFIRMLY
BRIDALLY	DEUCEDLY	FOETIDLY	INNATELY
BRIGHTLY	DEVOUTLY	FORCEDLY	INSANELY
BROKENLY	DIRECTLY	FORKEDLY	INTACTLY
BRUTALLY	DISMALLY	FORMALLY	INTENTLY
BUCCALLY	DISTALLY	FORMERLY	INWARDLY
CAECALLY	DIVERSLY	FOURTHLY	IREFULLY

JADISHLY	MASSEDLY	OGRISHLY	RECTALLY
JAGGEDLY	MATTEDLY	ONWARDLY	REFLEXLY
JAPINGLY	MATURELY	OPAQUELY	REMISSLY
JEJUNELY	MEAGERLY	ORNATELY	REMOTELY
JIBINGLY	MEAGRELY	OTIOSELY	REPANDLY
JOCOSELY	MEDIALLY	OWLISHLY	RETRALLY
JOCUNDLY	MEDIANLY	PALLIDLY	RIBALDLY
JOKINGLY	MELLOWLY	PATENTLY	RIMOSELY
JOVIALLY	MENIALLY	PEDATELY	RITUALLY
JOYFULLY	MENTALLY	PETTEDLY	ROBUSTLY
JOYOUSLY	MESIALLY	PIPINGLY	ROOTEDLY
LABIALLY	MINDEDLY	PLACIDLY	ROTTENLY
LAICALLY	MINUTELY	PLIANTLY	ROTUNDLY
LATENTLY	MODERNLY	PLURALLY	ROVINGLY
LATTERLY	MODESTLY	PLYINGLY	RUEFULLY
LAVISHLY	MODISHLY	POLITELY	RUGGEDLY
LAWFULLY	MOLTENLY	POPISHLY	RUGOSELY
LEADENLY	MOMENTLY	POROUSLY	RUSTICLY
LETHALLY	MOPINGLY	PORTERLY	SACREDLY
LIMBERLY	MOPISHLY	POSINGLY	SALLOWLY
LIMPIDLY	MORBIDLY	POSTALLY	SAVAGELY
LINEALLY	MOROSELY	POTENTLY	SAVINGLY
LINEARLY	MORTALLY	PRIMALLY	SAVOURLY
LIQUIDLY	MOVINGLY	PROLIXLY	SCARCELY
LISSOMLY	MULISHLY	PROMPTLY	SCRIMPLY
LITHERLY	MUSINGLY	PROPERLY	SECANTLY
LIVINGLY	MUTUALLY	PROVENLY	SECONDLY
LOBATELY	MYSTICLY	PRYINGLY	SECRETLY
LOPINGLY	NARROWLY	PUBLICLY	SECUNDLY
LOSINGLY	NATANTLY	PULINGLY	SECURELY
LOUCHELY	NATIVELY	PULPALLY	SEDATELY
LOVINGLY	NEURALLY	PUTRIDLY	SELDOMLY
LUBBERLY	NEWISHLY	QUAINTLY	SELECTLY
LUCENTLY	NOCENTLY	RACIALLY	SENILELY
LUMBERLY	NORMALLY	RADIALLY	SERENELY
LUMPENLY	NOUNALLY	RAGGEDLY	SERIALLY
LUNATELY	OAFISHLY	RAGINGLY	SEVERELY
LURINGLY	OBLATELY	RAKISHLY	SEXUALLY
LYRATELY	OBLONGLY	RAMOSELY	SHREWDLY
MALIGNLY	OBTUSELY	RAMOUSLY	SICKERLY
MANFULLY	OCCULTLY	RANCIDLY	SIGNALLY
MANNERLY	OCULARLY	RANDOMLY	SILENTLY
MANUALLY	ODIOUSLY	RAVINGLY	SILVERLY
MARKEDLY	OFFISHLY	RECENTLY	SINFULLY

SLIGHTLY	SULLENLY	UNEVENLY	VEILEDLY
SMOOTHLY	SUPERBLY	UNFAIRLY	VENIALLY
SOCIALLY	SUPINELY	UNGENTLY	VENOUSLY
SODDENLY	SUPPLELY	UNGRAVLY	VERBALLY
SOLEMNLY	SVELTELY	UNIQUELY	VERNALLY
SOMBERLY	TAKINGLY	UNITEDLY	VESTALLY
SOMBRELY	TARNALLY	UNJUSTLY	VEXINGLY
SORDIDLY	TARTARLY	UNMEETLY	VINOUSLY
SOTTEDLY	TAXINGLY	UNPURELY	VIRILELY
SOVRANLY	TENDERLY	UNREALLY	VISCIDLY
SPARSELY	THRAWNLY	UNRIPELY	VISUALLY
SPINALLY	THWARTLY	UNSAFELY	VOTIVELY
SPIRALLY	TIMOUSLY	UNSUBTLY	VULGARLY
SPRUCELY	TONISHLY	UNSURELY	WANTONLY
SQUARELY	TORPIDLY	UNWARELY	WICKEDLY
STANCHLY	TORRIDLY	UNWISELY	WILFULLY
STATEDLY	TOWARDLY	UPPISHLY	WINGEDLY
STEEVELY	TOYISHLY	UPWARDLY	WOEFULLY
STIEVELY	TRIBALLY	URBANELY	WONTEDLY
STOLIDLY	TRUANTLY	URGENTLY	WOODENLY
STRAITLY	TRYINGLY	URGINGLY	WOOINGLY
STRICTLY	TURBIDLY	USEFULLY	YELLOWLY
STRONGLY	TURGIDLY	UVULARLY	YONDERLY
STUPIDLY	UNCHICLY	VACANTLY	
SUDDENLY	UNCIALLY	VARIEDLY	

Adverbs ending ABLY

Six-letter ABLY words

SUABLY	USABLY	VIABLY

Seven-letter ABLY words

AFFABLY	LIKABLY	PLIABLY	TUNABLY
AMIABLY	LOVABLY	RATABLY	USEABLY
CAPABLY	MOVABLY	SALABLY	VOCABLY
CURABLY	MUTABLY	SIZABLY	
DURABLY	NOTABLY	TAXABLY	
EQUABLY	PAYABLY	TENABLY	

Eight-letter ABLY words

ADORABLY	ARGUABLY	BIDDABLY	DAMNABLY
AMENABLY	AVOWABLY	BLAMABLY	DENIABLY
AMICABLY	BEARABLY	CULPABLY	ENVIABLY

FORMABLY	OPERABLY	READABLY	SUITABLY
GAGEABLY	PALPABLY	RELIABLY	TUNEABLY
GULLABLY	PASSABLY	SALEABLY	UNSTABLY
INVIABLY	PITIABLY	SALVABLY	UNUSABLY
ISSUABLY	PLACABLY	SATIABLY	VALUABLY
KISSABLY	PORTABLY	SCALABLY	VARIABLY
LAUDABLY	PROBABLY	SHAMABLY	VIOLABLY
LIKEABLY	PROVABLY	SIZEABLY	WORKABLY
LOVEABLY	QUOTABLY	SOCIABLY	
MOVEABLY	RATEABLY	SORTABLY	

Adverbs ending IBLY

Seven-letter IBLY words

AUDIBLY	LEGIBLY	VISIBLY
FUSIBLY	RISIBLY	

Eight-letter IBLY words

CREDIBLY	FORCIBLY	POSSIBLY	VENDIBLY
ELIGIBLY	GULLIBLY	SENSIBLY	VINCIBLY
FALLIBLY	HORRIBLY	TANGIBLY	
FEASIBLY	INEDIBLY	TENSIBLY	
FLEXIBLY	PASSIBLY	TERRIBLY	

Adjectives ending LY

Valid comparative and superlative forms are shown where applicable. Some are also nouns so the -LIES forms are shown for these. For completeness, and because there are so many, this list includes adjectives that happen to end in LY where the Y is just the suffix.

Six-letter LY adjectives

AUNTLY	-LIER/-LIEST	COMELY	-LIER/-LIEST
BABBLY	-LIER/-LIEST	COSTLY	-LIER/-LIEST
BOBBLY	-LIER/-LIEST	CRAWLY	-LIER/-LIEST
BRAWLY	-LIER/-LIEST	CUDDLY	-LIER/-LIEST
BUBBLY	-LIER/-LIEST	DANGLY	-LIER/-LIEST
	-LIES	DEADLY	-LIER/-LIEST
BURBLY	-LIER/-LIEST	DIMPLY	-LIER/-LIEST
CHILLY	-LIER/-LIEST	DINKLY	-LIER/-LIEST
	-LIES	DRAWLY	-LIER/-LIEST
COGGLY	-LIER/-LIEST	DROOLY	-LIER/-LIEST

DRUMLY	-LIER/-LIEST	MARBLY	-LIER/-LIEST
FEATLY	-LIER/-LIEST	MEASLY	-LIER/-LIEST
FIDDLY	-LIER/-LIEST	MIZZLY	-LIER/-LIEST
FRILLY	-LIER/-LIEST	MUDDLY	-LIER/-LIEST
	-LIES	MUMBLY	-LIER/-LIEST
GAINLY	-LIER/-LIEST	MUSCLY	-LIER/-LIEST
GANGLY	-LIER/-LIEST	NEBULY	
GASHLY	-LIER/-LIEST	NEEDLY	-LIER/-LIEST
GIGGLY	-LIER/-LIEST	NETTLY	-LIER/-LIEST
GNARLY	-LIER/-LIEST	NIBBLY	-LIES
GOGGLY	-LIER/-LIEST	NIGGLY	-LIER/-LIEST
GOODLY	-LIER/-LIEST	NUBBLY	-LIER/-LIEST
GRISLY	-LIER/-LIEST	OUGHLY	-LIES
	-LIES	PARKLY	
GROOLY	-LIER/-LIEST	PEARLY	-LIER/-LIEST
GROWLY	-LIER/-LIEST		-LIES
GURGLY	-LIER/-LIEST	PEBBLY	-LIER/-LIEST
HACKLY	-LIER/-LIEST	PIDDLY	-LIER/-LIEST
HOMELY	-LIER/-LIEST	PIMPLY	-LIER/-LIEST
HOSTLY		POORLY	-LIER/-LIEST
HOURLY	-LIES	POPPLY	-LIER/-LIEST
HUBBLY	-LIER/-LIEST	PORTLY	-LIER/-LIEST
JANGLY	-LIER/-LIEST	PUDDLY	-LIER/-LIEST
JEESLY		PURFLY	
JEEZLY		PURPLY	-LIER/-LIEST
JIGGLY	-LIER/-LIEST	RATTLY	-LIER/-LIEST
JINGLY	-LIER/-LIEST	RICKLY	-LIER/-LIEST
JUMBLY	-LIER/-LIEST	RIPPLY	-LIER/-LIEST
JUNGLY	-LIER/-LIEST	RUBBLY	-LIER/-LIEST
KINDLY	-LIER/-LIEST	RUFFLY	-LIER/-LIEST
KINGLY	-LIER/-LIEST	RUMBLY	-LIER/-LIEST
KITTLY	-LIER/-LIEST	RUMPLY	-LIER/-LIEST
KNARLY	-LIER/-LIEST	SEEMLY	-LIER/-LIEST
KNOLLY	-LIER/-LIEST	SHELLY	-LIER/-LIEST
KNURLY	-LIER/-LIEST	SHOALY	-LIER/-LIEST
LAIDLY	-LIER/-LIEST	SICKLY	-LIER/-LIEST
LANELY			-LIES
LIKELY	-LIER/-LIEST	SKEELY	-LIER/-LIEST
LIONLY		SKELLY	-LIER/-LIEST
LIVELY	-LIER/-LIEST		-LIES
LONELY	-LIER/-LIEST	SKILLY	-LIER/-LIEST
LORDLY	-LIER/-LIEST	SMELLY	-LIER/-LIEST
LOVELY	-LIER/-LIEST		-LIES
	-LIES	SNAILY	-LIER/-LIEST

SNARLY	-LIER/-LIEST	WABBLY	-LIER/-LIEST
SNELLY		WADDLY	-LIER/-LIEST
SOZZLY	-LIER/-LIEST	WAFFLY	-LIER/-LIEST
STEELY	-LIER/-LIEST	WAGGLY	-LIER/-LIEST
	-LIES	WAMBLY	-LIER/-LIEST
STILLY	-LIER/-LIEST	WARBLY	-LIER/-LIEST
STUDLY	-LIER/-LIEST	WEAKLY	
SWIRLY	-LIER/-LIEST	WEEKLY	-LIES
TANGLY	-LIER/-LIEST	WHALLY	
TERMLY	-LIES	WHEELY	-LIER/-LIEST
TICKLY	-LIER/-LIEST		-LIES
TIDDLY	-LIER/-LIEST	WHIRLY	-LIER/-LIEST
	-LIES		-LIES
TIMELY	-LIER/-LIEST	WIFELY	-LIER/-LIEST
TINGLY	-LIER/-LIEST	WIGGLY	-LIER/-LIEST
TINKLY	-LIER/-LIEST	WOBBLY	-LIER/-LIEST
TOWNLY	-LIER/-LIEST		-LIES
TWIRLY	-LIER/-LIEST	WOOLLY	-LIER/-LIEST
UNHOLY	-LIER/-LIEST		-LIES
UNRULY	-LIER/-LIEST	YEARLY	-LIES
VIEWLY			

Seven-letter LY adjectives

ACTORLY			-LIES
ANGERLY		FLESHLY	-LIER/-LIEST
BAIRNLY	-LIER/-LIEST	FRECKLY	-LIER/-LIEST
BEASTLY	-LIER/-LIEST	FRIARLY	
BRAMBLY	-LIER/-LIEST	FRIZZLY	-LIER/-LIEST
BRISTLY	-LIER/-LIEST	GHASTLY	-LIER/-LIEST
BUIRDLY	-LIER/-LIEST	GHOSTLY	-LIER/-BUIRDLY
CHILDLY	-LIER/-LIEST	GIANTLY	-LIER/-LIEST
CLEANLY	-LIER/-LIEST	GRADELY	-LIER/-LIEST
CLERKLY	-LIER/-LIEST	GREISLY	
COURTLY	-LIER/-LIEST	GRIESLY	
CRACKLY	-LIER/-LIEST	GRISELY	
CRINKLY	-LIER/-LIEST	GRISTLY	-LIER/-LIEST
	-LIES	GRIZZLY	-LIER/-LIEST
CRUMBLY	-LIER/-LIEST		-LIES
	-LIES	GRUMBLY	-LIER/-LIEST
CRUMPLY	-LIER/-LIEST	GRYSELY	
DEATHLY	-LIER/-LIEST	HAZELLY	
DRIBBLY	-LIER/-LIEST	JEEZELY	
DRIZZLY	-LIER/-LIEST	KNOBBLY	-LIER/-LIEST
EARTHLY	-LIER/-LIEST	KNUBBLY	-LIER/-LIEST

KNUCKLY	-LIER/-LIEST	SPRAWLY	-LIER/-LIEST
LAIRDLY	-LIER/-LIEST	SQUALLY	-LIER/-LIEST
LOVERLY		STATELY	-LIER/-LIEST
MASCULY		STUBBLY	-LIER/-LIEST
METALLY		STUMBLY	-LIER/-LIEST
MISERLY	-LIER/-LIEST	THEGNLY	
MONTHLY	-LIES	THISTLY	-LIER/-LIEST
NYMPHLY		THRILLY	-LIER/-LIEST
ORDERLY	-LIES	TIGERLY	
PRICKLY	-LIER/-LIEST	TINSELY	
QUEENLY	-LIER/-LIEST	TREACLY	-LIER/-LIEST
SAINTLY	-LIER/-LIEST	TREMBLY	-LIER/-LIEST
SCRAWLY	-LIER/-LIEST	TRICKLY	-LIER/-LIEST
SHAMBLY	-LIER/-LIEST	TWADDLY	-LIER/-LIEST
SHAPELY	-LIER/-LIEST	TWIDDLY	-LIER/-LIEST
SHINGLY	-LIER/-LIEST	TWINKLY	-LIER/-LIEST
SHOGGLY	-LIER/-LIEST	UNGODLY	-LIER/-LIEST
SHOOGLY	-LIER/-LIEST	UNMANLY	-LIER/-LIEST
SHRILLY	-LIER/-LIEST	VICARLY	
SIGHTLY	-LIER/-LIEST	VIXENLY	
SNIFFLY	-LIER/-LIEST	VOWELLY	
SNUFFLY	-LIER/-LIEST	WEASELY	
SNUGGLY	-LIER/-LIEST	WOMANLY	-LIER/-LIEST
SPANGLY	-LIER/-LIEST	WORLDLY	-LIER/-LIEST
SPARKLY	-LIER/-LIEST	WRIGGLY	-LIER/-LIEST
	-LIES	WRINKLY	-LIER/-LIEST
SPINDLY	-LIER/-LIEST		-LIES
SPITTLY	-LIER/-LIEST	YOUTHLY	

Eight-letter LY adjectives

BESEEMLY	-LIER/-LIEST	KNIGHTLY	-LIER/-LIEST
BIHOURLY		LAWYERLY	-LIER/-LIEST
BIWEEKLY	-LIES	MAIDENLY	
BIYEARLY		MARTYRLY	
CHURCHLY	-LIER/-LIEST	MASTERLY	
COUSINLY		MATRONLY	
COWARDLY		MOTHERLY	
EASTERLY	-LIES	OVERHOLY	
FATHERLY		PANDERLY	
FRIENDLY	-LIER/-LIEST	PASTORLY	
	-LIES	PATRONLY	
GOSPELLY		PRIESTLY	-LIER/-LIEST
HEAVENLY	-LIER/-LIEST	PRINCELY	-LIER/-LIEST
KERNELLY		RASCALLY	-LIER/-LIEST

READERLY		UNGAINLY	-LIER/-LIEST
SAILORLY		UNHOMELY	-LIER/-LIEST
SCRABBLY	-LIER/-LIEST	UNKINDLY	-LIER/-LIEST
SCRAGGLY	-LIER/-LIEST	UNKINGLY	-LIER/-LIEST
SCRIBBLY	-LIER/-LIEST	UNLIKELY	-LIER/-LIEST
SCRIGGLY	-LIER/-LIEST	UNLIVELY	-LIER/-LIEST
SEAMANLY		UNLORDLY	-LIER/-LIEST
SHAUCHLY	-LIER/-LIEST	UNLOVELY	-LIER/-LIEST
SISTERLY		UNSEEMLY	-LIER/-LIEST
SLOVENLY	-LIER/-LIEST	UNTIMELY	-LIER/-LIEST
SNIVELLY		UNWIFELY	-LIER/-LIEST
SOUTERLY		VIRGINLY	
SPRITELY	-LIER/-LIEST	WEASELLY	
SQUIGGLY	-LIER/-LIEST	WEEVILLY	
SQUIRELY		WESTERLY	-LIES
STRAGGLY	-LIER/-LIEST	WINTERLY	-LIER/-LIEST
SUMMERLY		WITTOLLY	-LIER/-LIEST
TASSELLY		WIZARDLY	-LIER/-LIEST
TINSELLY		WRITERLY	-LIER/-LIEST
UNCOMELY	-LIER/-LIEST	YEOMANLY	-LIER/-LIEST
UNCOSTLY	-LIER/-LIEST		

Words six to eight letters in length ending in the suffix MAN

A few of these MAN words can take an –S plural where shown, as well as the standard –MEN plural. There is one example, HILLMEN, where there is no MAN singular form.

Those words that happen to end in MAN where it has no relation to the suffix are excluded, so words such as CAYMAN, ADWOMAN, INHUMAN, and TALISMAN are omitted.

Six-letter MAN and MEN words

AIDMAN	-MEN	BINMAN	-MEN
AIRMAN	-MEN	BOGMAN	-MEN
APEMAN	-MEN	BOWMAN	-MEN
ASHMAN	-MEN	BUSMAN	-MEN
AXEMAN	-MEN	CABMAN	-MEN
BADMAN	-MEN	CARMAN	-MEN
BAGMAN	-MEN	CONMAN	-MEN
BARMAN	-MEN	COWMAN	-MEN
BATMAN	-MEN	CUPMAN	-MEN
BAYMAN	-MEN	DOGMAN	-MEN

FENMAN	-MEN		PIEMAN	-MEN
FLYMAN	-MEN		PIGMAN	-MEN
FOEMAN	-MEN		PITMAN s	-MEN
FOGMAN	-MEN		POTMAN	-MEN
GADMAN	-MEN		PREMAN	-MEN
GAGMAN	-MEN		RAGMAN s	-MEN
GASMAN	-MEN		RODMAN	-MEN
GEMMAN	-MEN		SAXMAN	-MEN
GIGMAN	-MEN		SEAMAN	-MEN
GUNMAN	-MEN		SKYMAN	-MEN
HETMAN s	-MEN		SOCMAN	-MEN
HITMAN	-MEN		SUBMAN	-MEN
HODMAN	-MEN		TAXMAN	-MEN
ICEMAN	-MEN		TINMAN	-MEN
LAWMAN	-MEN		TITMAN	-MEN
LAYMAN	-MEN		TOPMAN	-MEN
LEGMAN	-MEN		TOYMAN	-MEN
MADMAN	-MEN		TUTMAN	-MEN
MERMAN	-MEN		VANMAN	-MEN
NONMAN	-MEN		VATMAN	-MEN
OILMAN	-MEN		WARMAN	-MEN
PENMAN	-MEN		YEOMAN	-MEN

Seven-letter MAN and MEN words

ALMSMAN	-MEN		CASEMAN	-MEN
ANTIMAN	-MEN		CAVEMAN	-MEN
ARTSMAN	-MEN		CHAPMAN	-MEN
AUTOMAN	-MEN		CLUBMAN	-MEN
BASEMAN	-MEN		COALMAN	-MEN
BATSMAN	-MEN		CREWMAN	-MEN
BEADMAN	-MEN		DAYSMAN	-MEN
BEDEMAN	-MEN		DEADMAN	-MEN
BELLMAN	-MEN		DESKMAN	-MEN
BELTMAN	-MEN		DOORMAN	-MEN
BILLMAN	-MEN		DORYMAN	-MEN
BIRDMAN	-MEN		DRAYMAN	-MEN
BOATMAN	-MEN		DUSTMAN	-MEN
BODYMAN	-MEN		FACEMAN	-MEN
BOGYMAN	-MEN		FIREMAN	-MEN
BONDMAN	-MEN		FLAGMAN	-MEN
BOOKMAN	-MEN		FOOTMAN	-MEN
BOWSMAN	-MEN		FOREMAN	-MEN
BUSHMAN	-MEN		FREEMAN	-MEN
BYREMAN	-MEN		FROGMAN	-MEN

GADSMAN	-MEN	MOORMAN	-MEN
GATEMAN	-MEN	MOOTMAN	-MEN
GLEEMAN	-MEN	NEWSMAN	-MEN
GOODMAN	-MEN	OARSMAN	-MEN
GOWNMAN	-MEN	ODDSMAN	-MEN
GRIPMAN	-MEN	ORRAMAN	-MEN
GUDEMAN	-MEN	OVERMAN s	-MEN
HACKMAN	-MEN	PACEMAN	-MEN
HANGMAN	-MEN	PACKMAN	-MEN
HARDMAN	-MEN	PASSMAN	-MEN
HEADMAN	-MEN	PEATMAN	-MEN
HELIMAN	-MEN	PIKEMAN	-MEN
HERDMAN	-MEN	PLOWMAN	-MEN
HIGHMAN	-MEN	POLLMAN	-MEN
	HILLMEN	PORTMAN	-MEN
HOODMAN	-MEN	POSTMAN	-MEN
HOSEMAN	-MEN	PROPMAN	-MEN
IRONMAN	-MEN	RAFTMAN	-MEN
ISLEMAN	-MEN	RAILMAN	-MEN
JACKMAN	-MEN	REEDMAN	-MEN
JARKMAN	-MEN	REELMAN	-MEN
JAZZMAN	-MEN	REPOMAN	-MEN
JUNKMAN	-MEN	RINGMAN	-MEN
JURYMAN	-MEN	ROADMAN	-MEN
KEELMAN	-MEN	RODSMAN	-MEN
KINSMAN	-MEN	RUCKMAN	-MEN
KIRKMAN	-MEN	SAGAMAN	-MEN
LANDMAN	-MEN	SANDMAN	-MEN
LEADMAN	-MEN	SEEDMAN	-MEN
LENSMAN	-MEN	SHIPMAN	-MEN
LIFTMAN	-MEN	SHOPMAN	-MEN
LINEMAN	-MEN	SHOWMAN	-MEN
LINKMAN	-MEN	SIDEMAN	-MEN
LOCKMAN	-MEN	SNOWMAN	-MEN
LOCOMAN	-MEN	SOCKMAN	-MEN
MAGSMAN	-MEN	SOKEMAN	-MEN
MAILMAN	-MEN	SONGMAN	-MEN
MALTMAN	-MEN	SPAEMAN	-MEN
MARKMAN	-MEN	SURFMAN	-MEN
MASHMAN	-MEN	SWAGMAN	-MEN
MEATMAN	-MEN	TAPSMAN	-MEN
MESSMAN	-MEN	TAXIMAN	-MEN
MILKMAN	-MEN	TELEMAN	-MEN
MOBSMAN	-MEN	TOLLMAN	-MEN

TONGMAN	-MEN	WINGMAN	-MEN
TOOLMAN	-MEN	WIREMAN	-MEN
TOPSMAN	-MEN	WOODMAN	-MEN
TRIPMAN	-MEN	WOOLMAN	-MEN
TRUEMAN	-MEN	WORKMAN	-MEN
TURFMAN	-MEN	YARDMAN	-MEN
WAKEMAN	-MEN	YEGGMAN	-MEN

Eight-letter MAN and MEN words

ALDERMAN	-MEN	DALESMAN	-MEN
BAILSMAN	-MEN	DOOMSMAN	-MEN
BANDSMAN	-MEN	DOORSMAN	-MEN
BANDYMAN	-MEN	DRAGOMAN s	-MEN
BANKSMAN	-MEN	DRAGSMAN	-MEN
BARGEMAN	-MEN	DUTCHMAN	-MEN
BEADSMAN	-MEN	EARTHMAN	-MEN
BEDESMAN	-MEN	EVERYMAN	-MEN
BLUESMAN	-MEN	FERRYMAN	-MEN
BOARDMAN	-MEN	FOILSMAN	-MEN
BOATSMAN	-MEN	FORGEMAN	-MEN
BOGEYMAN	-MEN	FREEDMAN	-MEN
BONDSMAN	-MEN	FRESHMAN	-MEN
BOOGYMAN	-MEN	FRONTMAN	-MEN
BOTHYMAN	-MEN	FUGLEMAN	-MEN
BRAKEMAN	-MEN	FUNNYMAN	-MEN
BRIDEMAN	-MEN	GAMESMAN	-MEN
BRINKMAN	-MEN	GANGSMAN	-MEN
BUTTYMAN	-MEN	GAVELMAN	-MEN
CANDYMAN	-MEN	GILDSMAN	-MEN
CANOEMAN	-MEN	GLASSMAN	-MEN
CHAINMAN	-MEN	GOADSMAN	-MEN
CHAIRMAN s	-MEN	GOWNSMAN	-MEN
CHESSMAN	-MEN	HANDYMAN	-MEN
CHINAMAN	-MEN	HEADSMAN	-MEN
CHOIRMAN	-MEN	HELMSMAN	-MEN
CHOREMAN	-MEN	HENCHMAN	-MEN
CLANSMAN	-MEN	HERDSMAN	-MEN
CLASSMAN	-MEN	HOASTMAN	-MEN
COACHMAN	-MEN	HOISTMAN	-MEN
COCKSMAN	-MEN	HORSEMAN	-MEN
COLORMAN	-MEN	HOTELMAN	-MEN
CORPSMAN	-MEN	HOUSEMAN	-MEN
CRAGSMAN	-MEN	HUNTSMAN	-MEN
DAIRYMAN	-MEN	ISLESMAN	-MEN

KNIFEMAN	-MEN	SHEEPMAN	-MEN
LANDSMAN	-MEN	SHIREMAN	-MEN
LEADSMAN	-MEN	SHOREMAN	-MEN
LIEGEMAN	-MEN	SIDESMAN	-MEN
LINESMAN	-MEN	SONARMAN	-MEN
LINKSMAN	-MEN	SOUNDMAN	-MEN
LOCKSMAN	-MEN	SPACEMAN	-MEN
LODESMAN	-MEN	SPADEMAN	-MEN
LOFTSMAN	-MEN	SPEARMAN	-MEN
MARCHMAN	-MEN	SQUAWMAN	-MEN
MARKSMAN	-MEN	STAFFMAN	-MEN
MERESMAN	-MEN	STALLMAN	-MEN
MERRYMAN	-MEN	STEELMAN	-MEN
MONEYMAN	-MEN	STICKMAN	-MEN
MOTORMAN	-MEN	STILLMAN	-MEN
NOBLEMAN	-MEN	STOCKMAN	-MEN
OVERSMAN	-MEN	STOREMAN	-MEN
PETERMAN	-MEN	STUNTMAN	-MEN
PILOTMAN	-MEN	SUPERMAN	-MEN
PITCHMAN	-MEN	SWAGSMAN	-MEN
PIVOTMAN	-MEN	SWEETMAN	-MEN
PLACEMAN	-MEN	SWINGMAN	-MEN
PLAIDMAN	-MEN	SWORDMAN	-MEN
PLATEMAN	-MEN	TACKSMAN	-MEN
POINTMAN	-MEN	TALESMAN	-MEN
PRESSMAN	-MEN	TALLYMAN	-MEN
PRIZEMAN	-MEN	TENORMAN	-MEN
PROSEMAN	-MEN	TIDESMAN	-MEN
PUNTSMAN	-MEN	TOWNSMAN	-MEN
QUILLMAN	-MEN	TRACKMAN	-MEN
RADIOMAN	-MEN	TRAINMAN	-MEN
RAFTSMAN	-MEN	TRASHMAN	-MEN
RAMPSMAN	-MEN	TREWSMAN	-MEN
RANCHMAN	-MEN	TRUCHMAN s	-MEN
REINSMAN	-MEN	TRUCKMAN	-MEN
RIFLEMAN	-MEN	UNDERMAN s	-MEN
RIVERMAN	-MEN	VERSEMAN	-MEN
ROADSMAN	-MEN	WATCHMAN	-MEN
ROUTEMAN	-MEN	WATERMAN	-MEN
SALESMAN	-MEN	WEALSMAN	-MEN
SCENEMAN	-MEN	WEIGHMAN	-MEN
SEEDSMAN	-MEN	WHALEMAN	-MEN
SHAREMAN	-MEN	WHEELMAN	-MEN
SHEARMAN	-MEN	WIDOWMAN	-MEN

WINCHMAN	–MEN	YACHTMAN	–MEN
WOODSMAN	–MEN	YARRAMAN s	–MEN

Words six to eight letters in length ending in the suffix NESS

Those words that happen to end in NESS where it has no relation to the suffix are excluded, so words such as HARNESS and LIONESS are omitted.

Seven-letter NESS words

ALLNESS	FEWNESS	NEWNESS	SHINESS
APTNESS	FEYNESS	NOWNESS	SHYNESS
BADNESS	FITNESS	ODDNESS	SLYNESS
BIGNESS	FULNESS	OLDNESS	TWONESS
COYNESS	GAYNESS	ONENESS	WAENESS
DIMNESS	HIPNESS	OUTNESS	WANNESS
DRYNESS	HOTNESS	PATNESS	WETNESS
DUENESS	ICINESS	RAWNESS	WITNESS
DULNESS	ILLNESS	REDNESS	WOENESS
DUNNESS	LAXNESS	RUMNESS	WRYNESS
FARNESS	LOWNESS	SADNESS	
FATNESS	MADNESS	SETNESS	

Eight-letter NESS words

ACHINESS	BOXINESS	DEADNESS	EVENNESS
ACIDNESS	BUSINESS	DEAFNESS	EVILNESS
AGEDNESS	BUSYNESS	DEARNESS	EYEDNESS
AIRINESS	CAGINESS	DEEPNESS	FAINNESS
ALBINESS	CAGYNESS	DEFTNESS	FAIRNESS
ARCHNESS	CAKINESS	DEWINESS	FASTNESS
ARIDNESS	CALMNESS	DIRENESS	FELLNESS
ARTINESS	CAMPNESS	DONENESS	FINENESS
ASHINESS	CHICNESS	DOPINESS	FIRMNESS
AVIDNESS	COLDNESS	DOURNESS	FLATNESS
AWAYNESS	COOLNESS	DOWFNESS	FONDNESS
BALDNESS	COSINESS	DOZINESS	FOULNESS
BARENESS	COXINESS	DRABNESS	FOXINESS
BASENESS	COZINESS	DUDENESS	FOZINESS
BASSNESS	CURTNESS	DULLNESS	FREENESS
BEINNESS	CUTENESS	DUMBNESS	FULLNESS
BIASNESS	DAFTNESS	DUSKNESS	GAMENESS
BLUENESS	DAMPNESS	EASINESS	GAMINESS
BOLDNESS	DANKNESS	EDGINESS	GAMYNESS
BONINESS	DARKNESS	EERINESS	GASTNESS

GLADNESS	LITENESS	PERTNESS	SORENESS
GLEGNESS	LIVENESS	PIEDNESS	SOURNESS
GLIBNESS	LOGINESS	PINKNESS	SPRYNESS
GLUINESS	LONENESS	PIPINESS	SUCHNESS
GLUMNESS	LONGNESS	PIXINESS	SURENESS
GONENESS	LORNNESS	POKINESS	TALLNESS
GOODNESS	LOSTNESS	POORNESS	TAMENESS
GOOINESS	LOTHNESS	PORINESS	TARTNESS
GORINESS	LOUDNESS	POSHNESS	TAUTNESS
GRAYNESS	LUNTNESS	PRIMNESS	THATNESS
GREYNESS	LUSHNESS	PUNINESS	THINNESS
GRIMNESS	MALENESS	PURENESS	THISNESS
GRUMNESS	MATINESS	RACINESS	THUSNESS
HALENESS	MAZINESS	RANKNESS	TIDINESS
HALFNESS	MEANNESS	RAPTNESS	TININESS
HARDNESS	MEEKNESS	RARENESS	TRIGNESS
HAZINESS	MEETNESS	RASHNESS	TRIMNESS
HERENESS	MILDNESS	REALNESS	TRUENESS
HIGHNESS	MIRINESS	RICHNESS	TWEENESS
HOKINESS	MOOTNESS	RIFENESS	UGLINESS
HOLINESS	MOPINESS	RIMINESS	VAINNESS
HOMINESS	MORENESS	RIPENESS	VASTNESS
HUGENESS	MUCHNESS	ROPINESS	VILDNESS
ICKINESS	MUTENESS	ROSINESS	VILENESS
IDLENESS	NAFFNESS	RUDENESS	VOIDNESS
IFFINESS	NAIFNESS	SAFENESS	WARINESS
INKINESS	NEARNESS	SAGENESS	WARMNESS
IRONNESS	NEATNESS	SALTNESS	WASTNESS
JIMPNESS	NESHNESS	SAMENESS	WAVINESS
JOKINESS	NEXTNESS	SANENESS	WAXINESS
JUSTNESS	NICENESS	SEARNESS	WEAKNESS
KEENNESS	NIGHNESS	SEEDNESS	WELLNESS
KINDNESS	NOSINESS	SELFNESS	WHATNESS
LACINESS	NUDENESS	SEXINESS	WIDENESS
LADYNESS	NULLNESS	SICKNESS	WILDNESS
LAMENESS	NUMBNESS	SIZINESS	WILINESS
LANKNESS	OAKINESS	SKEWNESS	WIRINESS
LATENESS	OILINESS	SLIMNESS	WISENESS
LAZINESS	OOZINESS	SLOWNESS	WOODNESS
LEANNESS	OPENNESS	SMUGNESS	WORNNESS
LEWDNESS	OVALNESS	SNUBNESS	ZANINESS
LIKENESS	PACKNESS	SNUGNESS	
LIMINESS	PALENESS	SOFTNESS	
LIMPNESS	PASTNESS	SOLENESS	

Words six to eight letters in length ending in the suffix OID

Some of these words are nouns and can have an –S hook added as shown.

There is one word ending OID that has no relation to the suffix (DEVOID) so that is omitted.

Six-letter OID words

ALGOID	GANOID s	MELOID s	VIROID s
CEBOID s	HALOID s	MUCOID s	XYLOID
CONOID s	HEMOID	MYXOID	ZONOID s
CUBOID s	HYPOID s	NEVOID	ZYGOID
CYMOID	KELOID s	OPIOID s	ZYMOID
CYTOID	LAROID	PELOID s	
FUCOID s	LIPOID s	TOROID s	
GADOID s	LUPOID	TOXOID s	

Seven-letter OID words

ACAROID	CTENOID	HYPNOID	SARCOID s
ADENOID s	CYCLOID s	LABROID s	SAUROID s
AGAMOID s	CYSTOID s	LENTOID s	SIALOID
AGATOID	DELTOID s	LIANOID	SIGMOID s
AMBROID s	DENTOID	LITHOID	SIMIOID
AMEBOID	DERMOID s	MASTOID s	SPAROID s
AMYLOID s	DESMOID s	MATTOID s	SPIROID
ANDROID s	DIPLOID s	MUSCOID s	SPOROID
ANEROID s	DISCOID s	MYELOID	STEROID s
ANTHOID	EMEROID s	NAEVOID	STYLOID s
ARCTOID	ERICOID	NEGROID s	TABLOID s
ASTROID s	ETHMOID s	NEUROID s	TENIOID
BYSSOID	EUPLOID s	OBOVOID	THEROID
CACTOID	FACTOID s	OCELOID	THYROID s
CESTOID s	FIBROID s	OCHROID	TIGROID
CHELOID s	FUNGOID s	OIDIOID	TURDOID
CHOROID s	GLENOID s	OSTEOID s	TYPHOID s
CIRSOID	GLOBOID s	PERCOID s	VALGOID
CISSOID s	GOBIOID s	PHACOID	VESPOID
COCCOID s	HAEMOID	PHYTOID	VISCOID
COLLOID s	HAPLOID s	PIGMOID s	XIPHOID s
CORMOID	HELCOID	PLACOID s	ZEBROID
COSMOID	HISTOID	PLUTOID s	ZINCOID
COTTOID	HYALOID s	PYGMOID s	
CRICOID s	HYDROID s	QUINOID s	
CRINOID s	HYENOID	RHIZOID s	

Eight-letter OID words

ACTINOID s	EMBRYOID s	NUCLEOID s	SESAMOID s
ALKALOID s	EMULSOID s	OCHEROID	SILUROID s
AMBEROID s	ERGATOID s	OCTOPOID	SINUSOID s
AMMONOID s	GABBROID	ODONTOID s	SISTROID
AMOEBOID	GALENOID	OMOHYOID s	SLEAZOID s
ANCONOID	GEOMYOID	ONISCOID	SOLENOID s
ARILLOID	GROUPOID s	PARANOID s	SORICOID
ASCONOID	GYNECOID	PAROTOID s	SPHENOID s
ASTEROID s	HELICOID s	PETALOID	SPHEROID s
ATHETOID	HEMATOID	PEZIZOID	SPONGOID
AUTACOID s	HISTIOID	PHALLOID	SQUALOID
AUTOCOID s	HOMALOID s	PHELLOID	STURNOID
BLASTOID s	HOMINOID s	PHYLLOID s	SYCONOID
BOTRYOID	HUMANOID s	PINACOID s	TAENIOID
CALYCOID	HYDATOID	PINAKOID s	TAPIROID s
CAMELOID s	HYRACOID s	PITYROID	TARSIOID s
CANCROID s	INDIGOID s	PLASMOID s	TECHNOID s
CARDIOID s	ISTHMOID	POLYPOID	TERATOID
CATENOID s	KERATOID	PRISMOID s	TETANOID
CENTROID s	LAMBDOID	PSYCHOID s	THALLOID
CERATOID	LEMUROID s	PYRANOID	THYREOID s
CHOREOID	LIGULOID	PYRENOID s	THYRSOID
CHORIOID s	LIMULOID s	RACEMOID	TRENDOID s
CICHLOID	LYMPHOID	RESINOID s	TRICHOID
CLUPEOID s	MANATOID	RETINOID s	TRIPLOID s
CONCHOID s	MEDUSOID s	RHABDOID s	TROCHOID s
CORACOID s	MELANOID s	RHOMBOID s	TUBEROID s
CORONOID	MUCINOID	SCAPHOID s	VARICOID
COTYLOID s	MYCELOID	SCHIZOID s	VIBRIOID
DENDROID s	MYTILOID	SCINCOID s	VIRUSOID s
DORIDOID s	NEMATOID	SCIUROID	VOLUTOID
ECHINOID s	NEPHROID	SCLEROID	YPSILOID
ELYTROID	NOCTUOID s	SEPALOID	

Words six to eight letters in length ending in the suffix OUS

Those words that happen to end in OUS where it has no relation to the suffix in any form are excluded, so words such as COUSCOUS and plurals of words ending in OU such as BINIOUS and ROUCOUS are omitted.

Six-letter OUS words

ALMOUS	FUMOUS	NOYOUS	SEROUS
AUROUS	GYROUS	ODIOUS	SETOUS
AWMOUS	HAMOUS	OSMOUS	TIMOUS
CEROUS	HUMOUS	PAROUS	TOROUS
COMOUS	IODOUS	PILOUS	UVEOUS
CYMOUS	JOYOUS	POROUS	VENOUS
DUMOUS	LIMOUS	RAMOUS	VINOUS
FAMOUS	LUPOUS	RIMOUS	VIROUS
FAVOUS	MUCOUS	RUFOUS	
FUCOUS	NODOUS	RUGOUS	

Seven-letter OUS words

ACEROUS	CALLOUS	FOLIOUS	LIMBOUS
ACETOUS	CARIOUS	FULVOUS	LUTEOUS
ACINOUS	CASEOUS	FUNGOUS	NACROUS
ADIPOUS	CEREOUS	FURIOUS	NERVOUS
AENEOUS	CESIOUS	FUSCOUS	NIMIOUS
AGAMOUS	CHYLOUS	GALLOUS	NIOBOUS
AMOROUS	CHYMOUS	GASEOUS	NITROUS
ANUROUS	CIRROUS	GEALOUS	NIVEOUS
ANXIOUS	CITROUS	GIBBOUS	NOCUOUS
APODOUS	COCCOUS	GLEBOUS	NOXIOUS
AQUEOUS	COPIOUS	GLOBOUS	OBVIOUS
ARDUOUS	CORIOUS	GRUMOUS	OCHROUS
ARENOUS	CORMOUS	GUMMOUS	ODOROUS
ATHEOUS	CUPROUS	HEINOUS	OMINOUS
ATOKOUS	CURIOUS	HERBOUS	ONEROUS
AZOTOUS	DEVIOUS	HIDEOUS	ONYMOUS
AZYGOUS	DUBIOUS	HOUMOUS	OPACOUS
AZYMOUS	DUTEOUS	HUGEOUS	OSMIOUS
BADIOUS	EMULOUS	HYDROUS	OSSEOUS
BILIOUS	ENVIOUS	IGNEOUS	OZONOUS
BIVIOUS	ESTROUS	IMPIOUS	PAPPOUS
BRUMOUS	FATUOUS	INVIOUS	PARLOUS
BULBOUS	FEATOUS	JEALOUS	PERLOUS
BULLOUS	FERROUS	LENTOUS	PETROUS
BURNOUS	FIBROUS	LEPROUS	PICEOUS

PILEOUS	RUBIOUS	TALCOUS	VALGOUS
PITEOUS	RUINOUS	TEDIOUS	VARIOUS
PLUMOUS	SANIOUS	TENUOUS	VEINOUS
POMPOUS	SARCOUS	TIMEOUS	VICIOUS
PORTOUS	SERIOUS	TYPHOUS	VIDUOUS
PULPOUS	SIMIOUS	UBEROUS	VILLOUS
RAMEOUS	SINUOUS	UMBROUS	VISCOUS
RAUCOUS	SOUKOUS	URANOUS	VITIOUS
RHODOUS	SPINOUS	URINOUS	ZEALOUS
RIOTOUS	SPUMOUS	USUROUS	ZINCOUS
ROUTOUS	SUCCOUS	VACUOUS	

Eight-letter OUS words

ACARPOUS	CAPTIOUS	EDACIOUS	GRACIOUS
ACAULOUS	CARNEOUS	ELYTROUS	GRIEVOUS
ACOELOUS	CAUTIOUS	ENGINOUS	GRISEOUS
ADUNCOUS	CERNUOUS	ENORMOUS	GYPSEOUS
AMBEROUS	CHLOROUS	EPIGEOUS	HALITOUS
ANGINOUS	CHROMOUS	EUROKOUS	HAMULOUS
ANGULOUS	CITREOUS	EXIGUOUS	HUMOROUS
ANOUROUS	CORNEOUS	EXIMIOUS	ICHOROUS
ANSEROUS	COVETOUS	FABULOUS	IDONEOUS
ANTICOUS	COVINOUS	FACTIOUS	IMPOROUS
APHONOUS	CRANKOUS	FASHIOUS	INCUBOUS
APHTHOUS	CRIBROUS	FASTUOUS	INERMOUS
APTEROUS	CROCEOUS	FEATEOUS	INFAMOUS
ARACEOUS	CROUPOUS	FEATUOUS	LACTEOUS
ARANEOUS	CUMBROUS	FELONOUS	LAMINOUS
ARBOROUS	CUMULOUS	FERREOUS	LEAPROUS
ARSENOUS	CUPREOUS	FEVEROUS	LIBELOUS
ARSONOUS	DARTROUS	FIDDIOUS	LIGNEOUS
ASPEROUS	DECOROUS	FLATUOUS	LUMINOUS
ASTOMOUS	DESIROUS	FLEXUOUS	LUSCIOUS
ATROPOUS	DEXTROUS	FRABJOUS	LUSTROUS
BIBULOUS	DIDYMOUS	FRONDOUS	LYMPHOUS
BIGAMOUS	DIECIOUS	GEMINOUS	MELANOUS
BIJUGOUS	DIGAMOUS	GEMMEOUS	MIASMOUS
BIMANOUS	DIGYNOUS	GENEROUS	MUCINOUS
BIPAROUS	DIMEROUS	GLABROUS	MUTICOUS
BIRAMOUS	DIOICOUS	GLAREOUS	MUTINOUS
BUTYROUS	DIPNOOUS	GLAUCOUS	NACREOUS
CADUCOUS	DITOKOUS	GLORIOUS	NAUSEOUS
CAESIOUS	DIZYGOUS	GOITROUS	NEBULOUS
CANOROUS	DOLOROUS	GORGEOUS	NEMOROUS

NIDOROUS	PRECIOUS	SOMBROUS	TUMULOUS
NITREOUS	PREVIOUS	SONOROUS	ULCEROUS
NODULOUS	PYRITOUS	SOPOROUS	UNCTUOUS
NUBILOUS	PYRRHOUS	SPACIOUS	UNDULOUS
NUMEROUS	RACEMOUS	SPECIOUS	UNFAMOUS
NUMINOUS	RAMULOUS	SPERMOUS	UNJOYOUS
OCHEROUS	RAVENOUS	SPURIOUS	USURIOUS
OCHREOUS	RESINOUS	SQUAMOUS	UXORIOUS
OESTROUS	RIGOROUS	STANNOUS	VALOROUS
OOGAMOUS	ROSINOUS	STOCIOUS	VANADOUS
ORAGIOUS	RUCTIOUS	STOTIOUS	VAPOROUS
ORDUROUS	RUMOROUS	STRATOUS	VENOMOUS
ORGULOUS	SABULOUS	STRUMOUS	VENTROUS
OVARIOUS	SAPOROUS	STUDIOUS	VENULOUS
PABULOUS	SAVOROUS	SUBEROUS	VERTUOUS
PALUDOUS	SCABIOUS	SUDOROUS	VIGOROUS
PAPULOUS	SCABROUS	TEMEROUS	VIPEROUS
PATULOUS	SCARIOUS	TENUIOUS	VIRTUOUS
PERILOUS	SCIOLOUS	THALLOUS	VITREOUS
PERVIOUS	SCLEROUS	TIMOROUS	VOMITOUS
PETALOUS	SCORIOUS	TITANOUS	WAVEROUS
PLUMBOUS	SEDULOUS	TORTIOUS	WONDROUS
PLUVIOUS	SELENOUS	TORTUOUS	WRONGOUS
POACEOUS	SENSUOUS	TRAPPOUS	XANTHOUS
POLYPOUS	SEPALOUS	TUBEROUS	YTTRIOUS
POPULOUS	SETULOUS	TUBULOUS	
PORTEOUS	SIBILOUS	TUMOROUS	

Words six to eight letters in length ending in the suffix TION

<u>All</u> of these words can have an –S hook added.

Six-letter TION words

ACTION	LOTION	NOTION	RATION
CATION	MOTION	OPTION	ULTION
KATION	NATION	POTION	USTION

Seven-letter TION words

ALATION	CANTION	DICTION	EMPTION
AMATION	CAPTION	EDITION	ENATION
AMOTION	CAUTION	ELATION	FACTION
AUCTION	COCTION	ELUTION	FICTION
BASTION	COITION	EMOTION	LECTION

MENTION	OVATION	RUCTION	TACTION
MICTION	PACTION	SECTION	TUITION
MIXTION	PORTION	STATION	UNCTION
ORATION	RECTION	SUCTION	UNITION

Eight-letter TION words

ABLATION	EDUCTION	IODATION	PETITION
ABLUTION	EGESTION	JOBATION	POSITION
ABORTION	EJECTION	JUNCTION	POTATION
ADAPTION	ELECTION	LAVATION	PUNITION
ADDITION	EMICTION	LAXATION	PUPATION
ADNATION	ENACTION	LEGATION	QUESTION
ADOPTION	EQUATION	LENITION	REACTION
AERATION	ERECTION	LIBATION	RELATION
AGNATION	ERUPTION	LIGATION	REMOTION
AMBITION	EVECTION	LIMATION	ROGATION
AUDITION	EVICTION	LOBATION	ROTATION
AVIATION	EXACTION	LOCATION	SANCTION
BIBATION	EXERTION	LOCUTION	SCONTION
CIBATION	FETATION	LUNATION	SEDATION
CITATION	FIXATION	LUXATION	SEDITION
COACTION	FLECTION	MONITION	SOLATION
CONATION	FRACTION	MUNITION	SOLUTION
COOPTION	FRICTION	MUTATION	SORPTION
CREATION	FRUITION	NATATION	STICTION
CURATION	FUNCTION	NEGATION	SUDATION
DELATION	GELATION	NIDATION	SWAPTION
DELETION	GUMPTION	NIVATION	TAXATION
DEMOTION	GYRATION	NODATION	TRACTION
DERATION	HALATION	NOLITION	VACATION
DEVOTION	HIMATION	NOTATION	VENATION
DILATION	IDEATION	NOVATION	VEXATION
DILUTION	IGNITION	NUDATION	VOCATION
DONATION	ILLATION	NUTATION	VOLITION
DOTATION	INACTION	OBLATION	VOLUTION
DURATION	INUSTION	PACATION	ZONATION

Vowel endings

E aside, it can be difficult to think of words that end in the vowels. But these words can be very useful. A, I, O and U represent almost a third of the tiles in the game, and there are a great many two-letter words that begin or end with vowels other than E. Moreover, if you have an E you may well want to keep it on your rack and use the more awkward vowels. It may be that the vowel you need to end with for a double- or triple-word score is already on the board. The lists in this section detail all words from two letters to six in length, ending in A, I, O, or U.

Words that end with A

Two-letter words

AA	EA	JA	MA	TA
BA	FA	KA	NA	YA
DA	HA	LA	PA	ZA

Three-letter words

ABA	BOA	KOA	OVA	SPA
AGA	BRA	LEA	PEA	TEA
AHA	CAA	MAA	PIA	TWA
AIA	CHA	MNA	POA	UTA
AKA	ERA	MOA	PYA	UVA
ALA	ETA	OBA	QUA	VIA
AMA	FAA	OCA	RIA	WHA
ANA	FRA	ODA	RYA	YEA
AUA	GOA	OKA	SEA	ZEA
AVA	HOA	OMA	SHA	ZOA
AWA	ITA	OPA	SKA	
BAA	KEA	ORA	SMA	

Four-letter words

ABBA	ANSA	BIGA	CASA	DITA
ACCA	ANTA	BIMA	CAVA	DIVA
ACTA	AQUA	BOBA	CECA	DIYA
AGHA	ARBA	BOLA	CHIA	DONA
AGMA	AREA	BOMA	COCA	DOPA
AIDA	ARIA	BONA	CODA	DOSA
AIGA	ARNA	BORA	COLA	DUKA
ALBA	ARPA	BOTA	COMA	DUMA
ALFA	ASEA	BUBA	COXA	DURA
ALGA	ATMA	BUDA	CRIA	EGMA
ALMA	ATUA	BUNA	CYMA	EINA
AMIA	AULA	BURA	DADA	EKKA
AMLA	AURA	CABA	DATA	EMMA
ANGA	BABA	CACA	DEVA	EPHA
ANNA	BEMA	CAMA	DIKA	ETNA
ANOA	BETA	CAPA	DISA	EYRA

FAVA	JURA	MICA	PICA	SOCA
FETA	KAKA	MIHA	PIKA	SODA
FILA	KAMA	MINA	PILA	SOFA
FLEA	KANA	MOLA	PIMA	SOJA
FORA	KAPA	MONA	PINA	SOLA
GAGA	KARA	MORA	PIPA	SOMA
GALA	KATA	MOWA	PITA	SORA
GAMA	KAVA	MOXA	PLEA	SOYA
GENA	KAWA	MOYA	PROA	STOA
GETA	KETA	MURA	PUHA	SUBA
GIGA	KINA	MYNA	PUJA	SURA
GILA	KIVA	NADA	PUKA	TAHA
GLIA	KOHA	NAGA	PULA	TAKA
GORA	KOKA	NALA	PUMA	TALA
GUGA	KOLA	NANA	PUNA	TANA
GULA	KORA	NAPA	PUPA	TAPA
HAHA	KUIA	NEMA	RACA	TARA
HAKA	KULA	NIPA	RAGA	TAVA
HILA	KUNA	NOMA	RAIA	TAWA
HIYA	KUTA	NONA	RAJA	TAXA
HOHA	LAMA	NOTA	RANA	TELA
HOKA	LANA	NOVA	RATA	TEPA
HOMA	LAVA	OBIA	RAYA	TIKA
HORA	LEVA	OCTA	RHEA	TINA
HOYA	LIMA	ODEA	RIBA	TOEA
HUIA	LIPA	OFFA	RIMA	TOGA
HULA	LIRA	OHIA	RIVA	TOLA
HUMA	LOCA	OKRA	RIZA	TORA
HYLA	LOMA	OKTA	ROMA	TOSA
IDEA	LOTA	OLEA	ROTA	TUBA
ILEA	LUMA	OLLA	RUGA	TUFA
ILIA	LUNA	ORCA	RUSA	TUNA
ILKA	LYRA	ORRA	SAGA	ULNA
INIA	MAHA	OSSA	SAMA	ULVA
IOTA	MALA	OUMA	SENA	UMMA
ISBA	MAMA	OUPA	SERA	UMRA
ISNA	MANA	OUTA	SETA	UPTA
IXIA	MARA	PACA	SHEA	UREA
JAFA	MASA	PAPA	SHWA	URSA
JAGA	MAYA	PARA	SIDA	URVA
JAVA	MEGA	PAUA	SIKA	UVEA
JOTA	MELA	PAWA	SIMA	VARA
JUBA	MESA	PEBA	SKUA	VASA
JUGA	META	PELA	SOBA	VEGA

VELA	VITA	WENA	YUGA	ZUPA
VENA	VIVA	WETA	ZEDA	ZYGA
VERA	VOLA	WHOA	ZETA	
VIGA	WAKA	YABA	ZILA	
VINA	WAWA	YOGA	ZOEA	
VISA	WEKA	YUCA	ZONA	

Five-letter words

ABACA	ARABA	BONZA	CILIA	DOLMA
ABAKA	ARECA	BORNA	CIRCA	DONGA
ABAYA	ARENA	BOXLA	CNIDA	DONNA
ABOMA	AREPA	BOYLA	COALA	DOONA
ABUNA	AROBA	BRAVA	COBIA	DORBA
ACETA	AROHA	BRAZA	COBRA	DORSA
ADYTA	AROMA	BUBBA	COBZA	DOSHA
AECIA	ASANA	BUFFA	COCOA	DOULA
AFARA	ASURA	BULLA	COLZA	DOUMA
AGAMA	ASYLA	BUNIA	COMMA	DOURA
AGILA	ATRIA	BUNYA	CONGA	DOWNA
AGITA	AYAYA	BURKA	CONIA	DRAMA
AGORA	BABKA	BURQA	COPRA	DUKKA
AGRIA	BACCA	BURSA	CORIA	DULIA
AGUNA	BACHA	BWANA	COSTA	DUMKA
AINGA	BAISA	CAECA	COTTA	DURRA
AJIVA	BAIZA	CALLA	COUTA	EDEMA
AJUGA	BAJRA	CALPA	CRENA	ENEMA
AKELA	BAKRA	CANNA	CRURA	ENTIA
AKITA	BALSA	CARTA	CULPA	ERBIA
ALAPA	BANDA	CAUDA	CUPPA	ERICA
ALDEA	BANIA	CAUSA	CURIA	ETYMA
ALIYA	BANYA	CEIBA	DABBA	EXTRA
ALOHA	BARCA	CELLA	DACHA	FACIA
ALPHA	BARRA	CERIA	DAGGA	FACTA
ALULA	BASTA	CESTA	DARGA	FAENA
AMEBA	BATTA	CHANA	DELTA	FANGA
AMIGA	BELGA	CHARA	DERMA	FATWA
AMNIA	BENGA	CHAYA	DICTA	FAUNA
ANANA	BETTA	CHEKA	DINNA	FELLA
ANATA	BHUNA	CHELA	DIOTA	FERIA
ANIMA	BIGHA	CHICA	DIVNA	FESTA
ANTRA	BIOTA	CHINA	DOBLA	FETTA
ANURA	BIVIA	CHOLA	DOBRA	FETWA
AORTA	BOCCA	CHOTA	DOGMA	FINCA
APNEA	BOHEA	CHUFA	DOLIA	FITNA

FLAVA	HANSA	KEEMA	LOUMA	MOOLA
FLORA	HAOMA	KEHUA	LUBRA	MORIA
FLOTA	HASTA	KERMA	LUFFA	MORRA
FOLIA	HATHA	KHAYA	LUTEA	MOTZA
FONDA	HEJRA	KHEDA	LYCEA	MOWRA
FORZA	HENNA	KHOJA	LYCRA	MUDRA
FOSSA	HERMA	KIBLA	LYSSA	MUGGA
FOVEA	HEVEA	KINDA	LYTTA	MULGA
FRENA	HIJRA	KIPPA	MAFIA	MULLA
FURCA	HODJA	KOALA	MAGMA	MUNGA
GABBA	HOLLA	KOFTA	MAHUA	MURRA
GAITA	HONDA	KOKRA	MAHWA	MURVA
GALEA	HOOKA	KOPPA	MALVA	MUSCA
GAMBA	HOSTA	KORMA	MALWA	MUSHA
GAMMA	HOVEA	KOURA	MAMBA	MUTHA
GANJA	HUDNA	KRONA	MAMMA	MYOMA
GARDA	HURRA	KURTA	MANGA	NABLA
GEMMA	HUTIA	KWELA	MANIA	NAIRA
GENOA	HUZZA	LABDA	MANNA	NAKFA
GENUA	HYDRA	LABIA	MANTA	NALLA
GLEBA	HYENA	LABRA	MARIA	NAMMA
GOGGA	HYPHA	LAIKA	MARKA	NANNA
GOMPA	IDOLA	LAKSA	MARRA	NANUA
GONIA	INDIA	LAMIA	MASSA	NAPPA
GONNA	INFRA	LARVA	MATZA	NERKA
GOTTA	INTRA	LAURA	MBIRA	NGANA
GOURA	INULA	LAVRA	MECCA	NGOMA
GRAMA	IXORA	LEHUA	MEDIA	NINJA
GRANA	JAFFA	LEMMA	MEKKA	NORIA
GROMA	JAGRA	LEPRA	MELBA	NORMA
GUANA	JARTA	LEPTA	MENSA	NUBIA
GUAVA	JHALA	LEZZA	MENTA	NUCHA
GUMMA	JIBBA	LIANA	MICRA	NULLA
GUSLA	JIRGA	LIBRA	MIKRA	NYALA
GUTTA	JNANA	LIMBA	MIKVA	NYSSA
GYOZA	JUNTA	LIMMA	MILIA	OCREA
HAIKA	KAAMA	LIMPA	MILPA	OIDIA
HAKEA	KACHA	LINGA	MIRZA	OMASA
HALFA	KAIKA	LLAMA	MISSA	OMEGA
HALMA	KALPA	LOGIA	MOCHA	OPERA
HALVA	KANGA	LONGA	MOHUA	ORGIA
HALWA	KAPPA	LOOFA	MOIRA	ORIXA
HAMBA	KARMA	LOTSA	MOLLA	OSSIA
HAMZA	KASHA	LOTTA	MOMMA	OSTIA

OUIJA	PORTA	SADZA	SOPRA	TERRA
OUTTA	PRANA	SAIGA	SORDA	TESLA
PACHA	PRESA	SAKIA	SORRA	TESTA
PACTA	PRIMA	SALPA	SORTA	TETRA
PADMA	PRUTA	SALSA	SPAZA	THANA
PAISA	PSORA	SAMBA	SPICA	THECA
PAKKA	PUCKA	SANGA	SPINA	THEMA
PALEA	PUFFA	SANSA	SPUTA	THETA
PALLA	PUKKA	SAOLA	STELA	THUJA
PALSA	PULKA	SAUBA	STIPA	THUYA
PAMPA	PUNGA	SAUNA	STOMA	TIARA
PANDA	PUNKA	SCALA	STRIA	TIBIA
PANGA	PURDA	SCAPA	STUPA	TICCA
PARKA	QIBLA	SCENA	SUBHA	TIKKA
PARRA	QORMA	SCHWA	SULFA	TINEA
PASHA	QUENA	SCOPA	SUMMA	TOMIA
PASKA	QUINA	SCUBA	SUNNA	TONGA
PASTA	QUOTA	SCUTA	SUPRA	TONKA
PATKA	RAGGA	SEIZA	SURRA	TORTA
PELMA	RAITA	SELLA	SUTRA	TREFA
PELTA	RAKIA	SELVA	SUTTA	TREMA
PENNA	RANGA	SENNA	SYLVA	TRONA
PEPLA	RASTA	SENSA	TAATA	TRYMA
PEREA	RATHA	SENZA	TABLA	TSUBA
PHOCA	REATA	SEPIA	TAFIA	TUGRA
PHYLA	RECTA	SEPTA	TAGMA	TUINA
PICRA	REDIA	SERRA	TAIGA	TULPA
PIETA	REGMA	SESSA	TAIRA	ULAMA
PILEA	REGNA	SHAMA	TALEA	ULEMA
PINNA	RENGA	SHAYA	TALMA	ULTRA
PINTA	REPLA	SHEVA	TALPA	UMBRA
PITTA	RETIA	SHIVA	TANGA	UNCIA
PIZZA	RHYTA	SHOLA	TANKA	UNICA
PLAYA	RIATA	SHURA	TANNA	URBIA
PLAZA	RIOJA	SIDHA	TAPPA	URENA
PLENA	ROOSA	SIGLA	TARGA	USNEA
PLICA	RUANA	SIGMA	TASSA	UVULA
POAKA	RUEDA	SIGNA	TAYRA	VACUA
PODIA	RUMBA	SILVA	TAZZA	VANDA
POLKA	RUPIA	SIMBA	TECTA	VARIA
PONGA	RUSMA	SIRRA	TEGUA	VARNA
POOJA	SABHA	SISTA	TELIA	VEENA
POOKA	SABRA	SITKA	TENIA	VERRA
POPPA	SACRA	SOFTA	TERGA	VESPA

VESTA	VOILA	WILJA	YAKKA	ZEBRA
VIFDA	VOLTA	WINNA	YARFA	ZERDA
VIGIA	VOLVA	WIRRA	YARTA	ZILLA
VILLA	VULVA	WISHA	YENTA	ZOAEA
VINCA	WAGGA	WOKKA	YERBA	ZONDA
VIOLA	WALLA	WONGA	YUCCA	ZOOEA
VIRGA	WANNA	WUXIA	YURTA	ZOPPA
VISTA	WHATA	XENIA	ZABRA	ZUPPA
VITTA	WHYDA	XOANA	ZAIDA	
VIVDA	WICCA	YABBA	ZAMIA	
VODKA	WIGGA	YACCA	ZANJA	
VOEMA	WILGA	YACKA	ZANZA	

Six-letter words

ABASIA	AMOEBA	ARROBA	BHAJIA	CALIMA
ABELIA	AMRITA	ASRAMA	BHAKTA	CALTHA
ABOLLA	AMUSIA	ASTHMA	BHOONA	CAMBIA
ABULIA	ANANDA	ATAATA	BIFIDA	CAMERA
ACACIA	ANATTA	ATAXIA	BILBOA	CAMISA
ACEDIA	ANCORA	ATOCIA	BOCCIA	CANADA
ADNEXA	ANEMIA	ATONIA	BODEGA	CANCHA
AFTOSA	ANGINA	AUCUBA	BONITA	CANOLA
AGENDA	ANGOLA	AURORA	BOONGA	CANULA
AGGADA	ANGORA	AVRUGA	BOORKA	CAPITA
AGOUTA	ANICCA	AXILLA	BOSHTA	CARDIA
AHIMSA	ANNONA	AZALEA	BRAATA	CARINA
AIKONA	ANOPIA	AZOLLA	BRAHMA	CASABA
AKATEA	ANOXIA	BACKRA	BREGMA	CASAVA
AKEBIA	ANTARA	BACULA	BROLGA	CASITA
AKHARA	ANTLIA	BAHADA	BROTHA	CASSIA
ALALIA	ANURIA	BAJADA	BUCKRA	CATENA
ALASKA	APHTHA	BALATA	BUDDHA	CEDULA
ALBATA	APNOEA	BALBOA	BUGSHA	CEMBRA
ALEXIA	APORIA	BANANA	BUNNIA	CENTRA
ALISMA	ARAARA	BARAZA	BUQSHA	CESURA
ALODIA	ARALIA	BARYTA	BURKHA	CHACMA
ALOGIA	ARCANA	BATATA	BUSERA	CHAETA
ALPACA	AREOLA	BAUERA	BUSHWA	CHAKRA
ALTEZA	ARGALA	BEFANA	CABALA	CHALLA
ALTHEA	ARISTA	BEFLEA	CABANA	CHANGA
ALUMNA	ARMADA	BELUGA	CADAGA	CHAPKA
AMARNA	ARNICA	BEMATA	CAEOMA	CHARKA
AMELIA	AROLLA	BERTHA	CAFILA	CHARTA
AMENTA	ARRIBA	BETCHA	CALESA	CHATTA

CHICHA	CUESTA	EUREKA	GORGIA	ISTANA
CHIGGA	CUMBIA	EXACTA	GOTCHA	JACANA
CHIMLA	CUPOLA	EXEDRA	GRAMMA	JARINA
CHOANA	CUPULA	EXUVIA	GRAMPA	JATAKA
CHOKRA	CURARA	FACULA	GRAPPA	JEJUNA
CHOLLA	CUTCHA	FAJITA	GRINGA	JEMIMA
CHORDA	CZAPKA	FANEGA	GUINEA	JERBOA
CHOREA	DAGABA	FARINA	GYTTJA	JHATKA
CHORIA	DAGOBA	FASCIA	HALALA	JICAMA
CHROMA	DAHLIA	FATSIA	HALLOA	JOANNA
CHUKKA	DATCHA	FAVELA	HAMADA	JOJOBA
CHUPPA	DATURA	FECULA	HANIWA	JUDOKA
CICADA	DEFLEA	FEDORA	HAPUKA	JUGULA
CICALA	DHAMMA	FEIJOA	HARIRA	KABAKA
CICUTA	DHARMA	FEMORA	HAWALA	KABALA
CINEMA	DHARNA	FERULA	HEBONA	KABAYA
CITOLA	DHOORA	FIBULA	HEDERA	KACCHA
CLIVIA	DHURNA	FIESTA	HEGIRA	KAFILA
CLOACA	DHURRA	FLAUTA	HEJIRA	KAHUNA
CLUSIA	DHYANA	FOOTRA	HEMINA	KAINGA
COAITA	DJIBBA	FOUSSA	HERNIA	KALMIA
COBAEA	DOLINA	FOUTRA	HILLOA	KAMALA
CODEIA	DOOSRA	FRAENA	HOLLOA	KAMELA
CONCHA	DUENNA	FRISKA	HOLMIA	KAMILA
CONIMA	DUHKHA	FRUSTA	HOODIA	KANAKA
CONTRA	DUKKHA	FULCRA	HOOPLA	KANGHA
COPITA	DUMELA	FUNKIA	HRYVNA	KANTHA
COPPRA	ECZEMA	FUSUMA	HULLOA	KANUKA
COPULA	EGESTA	GALENA	HUTZPA	KAPUKA
CORNEA	EIDOLA	GAMBIA	HYAENA	KARAKA
CORNUA	EJECTA	GARRYA	HYDRIA	KATANA
CORONA	ELODEA	GARUDA	IDEATA	KEMBLA
CORREA	ELUVIA	GEISHA	IGUANA	KENTIA
CORYZA	ELYTRA	GELADA	IMPALA	KERRIA
COSMEA	EMPUSA	GENERA	INANGA	KETMIA
COWPEA	ENCINA	GENEVA	INDABA	KGOTLA
CRACKA	ENIGMA	GITANA	INDUNA	KHANDA
CRANIA	ENTERA	GLIOMA	INFIMA	KHANGA
CRESTA	EPEIRA	GLORIA	INFULA	KHODJA
CRISSA	EPIZOA	GLOSSA	INJERA	KHURTA
CRISTA	EPOCHA	GNAMMA	INSULA	KINARA
CROWEA	ERRATA	GOANNA	INTIMA	KINEMA
CRUSTA	ESPADA	GOONDA	INYALA	KIRANA
CUBICA	EUPNEA	GOPURA	ISCHIA	KISHKA

KOCHIA	MANAIA	MUTUCA	PARERA	PULKHA
KORORA	MANANA	MYOPIA	PARURA	PUNCTA
KORUNA	MANAWA	MYRICA	PASELA	PURANA
KUBASA	MANILA	MYXOMA	PASHKA	PYEMIA
KUCCHA	MANTRA	NAGANA	PASKHA	PYJAMA
KUMARA	MANTUA	NATURA	PATACA	PYROLA
KUMERA	MANUKA	NAUSEA	PATAKA	PYURIA
KUTCHA	MARACA	NEBULA	PATERA	QABALA
KWACHA	MARINA	NEPETA	PATINA	QASIDA
KWANZA	MARKKA	NOCTUA	PAYOLA	QUAGGA
LABARA	MASALA	NOMINA	PELOTA	QUALIA
LACUNA	MASHUA	NOVENA	PENNIA	QUANTA
LAGENA	MASULA	NUMINA	PEPITA	QUELEA
LAGUNA	MATATA	NUTRIA	PERAEA	QUINOA
LAMBDA	MAUNNA	NYANZA	PEREIA	QUINTA
LAMINA	MAXIMA	NYMPHA	PESETA	QUOKKA
LATINA	MAZUMA	OBELIA	PESEWA	QUOTHA
LATRIA	MEDAKA	OCHREA	PESHWA	RADULA
LEIPOA	MEDINA	OEDEMA	PETARA	RAFFIA
LESULA	MEDUSA	OMENTA	PHARMA	RAKIJA
LEXICA	MEGARA	OMERTA	PHOBIA	RAMADA
LIGULA	MELENA	ONYCHA	PIAZZA	RAMBLA
LIKUTA	MESETA	OPTIMA	PICARA	RAMONA
LIMINA	METEPA	ORARIA	PILULA	RANULA
LINGUA	MEZUZA	ORBITA	PINATA	RAPHIA
LIPOMA	MGANGA	ORGANA	PINETA	RAZZIA
LITHIA	MIASMA	ORISHA	PIRANA	REALIA
LOBOLA	MIBUNA	OSCULA	PIRAYA	REDOWA
LOCHIA	MIMOSA	OSETRA	PITARA	REGINA
LOGGIA	MINIMA	OTTAVA	PITAYA	REGULA
LOMATA	MIZUNA	OUGIYA	PLANTA	RELATA
LORCHA	MODENA	OZAENA	PLASMA	REMORA
LORICA	MODICA	PAELLA	PLEURA	REMUDA
LUCUMA	MOKSHA	PAGODA	PNEUMA	RESEDA
LUMINA	MONERA	PAJAMA	POISHA	RETAMA
LUMPIA	MOORVA	PAKEHA	POPERA	RETINA
LUNULA	MORCHA	PAKORA	PORINA	RHANJA
LUSTRA	MORULA	PALAMA	POSADA	RHUMBA
MABELA	MOTUCA	PALAPA	PRAJNA	RISTRA
MACOYA	MUCOSA	PALLIA	PREMIA	ROBATA
MACULA	MULETA	PANADA	PROTEA	ROSTRA
MAFFIA	MUMMIA	PANAMA	PRUINA	ROSULA
MAKUTA	MURENA	PAPAYA	PSYLLA	ROTULA
MALTHA	MURRHA	PAPULA	PTERIA	RUCOLA

RUGOLA	SHEILA	STOMIA	TIPUNA	VIZSLA
RUGOSA	SHELTA	STRATA	TORANA	VOMICA
RUMINA	SHERIA	STRIGA	TORULA	WAIATA
RUSSIA	SHERPA	STROMA	TOTARA	WAIRUA
SABKHA	SHIKRA	STRUMA	TRAUMA	WATCHA
SAHIBA	SHIKSA	SUBSEA	TREIFA	WHATNA
SALINA	SHIRRA	SULPHA	TREYFA	WHENUA
SALIVA	SHISHA	SUNDRA	TRIVIA	WILTJA
SALVIA	SHOORA	SYLVIA	TROIKA	WOMERA
SAMARA	SIDDHA	SYNURA	TSAMBA	WOTCHA
SAMOSA	SIENNA	TABULA	TUATUA	XEROMA
SANCTA	SIERRA	TAENIA	TUGHRA	XYLOMA
SANGHA	SIESTA	TAFFIA	TUNDRA	YAKUZA
SAPOTA	SIFAKA	TAHINA	TUNICA	YANTRA
SASTRA	SILICA	TAIAHA	TUPUNA	YAQONA
SATARA	SIMCHA	TAIHOA	UJAMAA	YARPHA
SATYRA	SISTRA	TALUKA	ULTIMA	YAUTIA
SCARPA	SITULA	TAMARA	UNGULA	YOJANA
SCHEMA	SKOLIA	TANKIA	URANIA	YTTRIA
SCILLA	SMEGMA	TANTRA	UREDIA	YUKATA
SCLERA	SOLERA	TAONGA	UREMIA	ZABETA
SCOLIA	SOMATA	TAPETA	URTICA	ZANANA
SCORIA	SONATA	TARAMA	UTOPIA	ZAPATA
SCOTIA	SPIREA	TARSIA	VAGINA	ZAREBA
SCOZZA	SQUAMA	TEGULA	VAHANA	ZARIBA
SCROTA	SRADHA	TELEGA	VALETA	ZENANA
SECULA	STADDA	TEPHRA	VALUTA	ZEREBA
SEMEIA	STADIA	TERATA	VARROA	ZERIBA
SEMINA	STANZA	TERBIA	VEDUTA	ZEUGMA
SENECA	STATUA	TEREFA	VELETA	ZINNIA
SENEGA	STELLA	TERTIA	VESICA	ZIPOLA
SENORA	STEMMA	THANNA	VICUNA	ZOARIA
SEROSA	STERNA	THORIA	VIENNA	ZOECIA
SHAMBA	STEVIA	THULIA	VIHARA	ZONULA
SHARIA	STIGMA	TINAJA	VIMANA	ZOYSIA
SHASTA	STIRRA	TIPULA	VIMINA	ZYGOMA

Words that end with I

Two-letter words

AI	GI	LI	PI	TI
BI	HI	MI	QI	XI
DI	KI	OI	SI	

Three-letter words

AHI	DUI	KHI	PSI	SUI
AJI	GHI	KOI	RAI	TAI
AMI	HOI	LEI	REI	TUI
ANI	HUI	MOI	SAI	UNI
BOI	IWI	OBI	SEI	WAI
CHI	JAI	PHI	SKI	
DEI	KAI	POI	SRI	

Four-letter words

ABRI	FOCI	LATI	NORI	SORI
ACAI	FUCI	LIRI	PADI	SUMI
ANTI	FUJI	LOBI	PALI	SUNI
ARTI	GADI	LOCI	PENI	SYLI
ASCI	GARI	LOTI	PERI	TABI
BANI	GLEI	LWEI	PFUI	TAKI
BENI	GOBI	MAGI	PIKI	TALI
BHAI	GOJI	MAKI	PILI	TAXI
BIDI	GORI	MALI	PIPI	TIKI
BREI	GYRI	MANI	PTUI	TIPI
BUDI	HAJI	MAXI	PULI	TITI
CADI	HILI	MERI	PURI	TOPI
CAMI	HIOI	MIDI	QADI	TORI
CAPI	HOKI	MIHI	QUAI	UNAI
CEDI	HORI	MINI	RABI	UNCI
CHAI	IMPI	MIRI	RAGI	VAGI
CONI	INTI	MOAI	RAKI	VALI
DALI	JEDI	MODI	RAMI	VLEI
DARI	KADI	MOKI	RANI	WADI
DEFI	KAKI	MOMI	REFI	WALI
DELI	KALI	MOOI	ROJI	WIKI
DENI	KAMI	MOTI	ROTI	WILI
DESI	KATI	MUNI	RUDI	YAGI
DEVI	KAZI	MUTI	SADI	YETI
DIVI	KEPI	NAOI	SAKI	YOGI
DIXI	KIWI	NAZI	SARI	YONI
DUCI	KOJI	NEVI	SATI	ZARI
ELHI	KRAI	NGAI	SEMI	ZATI
ETUI	KUFI	NIDI	SHRI	ZITI
EUOI	KURI	NISI	SIMI	ZORI
FENI	KUTI	NODI	SIRI	
FINI	LARI	NONI	SOLI	

Five-letter words

AALII	BUFFI	DURZI	KHADI	NIMBI
AARTI	BURFI	ELCHI	KHAKI	NISEI
ABACI	BUSTI	ELEMI	KHAZI	NKOSI
ACARI	BWAZI	EMOJI	KIBBI	NOMOI
ACINI	BYSSI	ENNUI	KIBEI	OBELI
ADUKI	CACTI	ENOKI	KIKOI	OBOLI
AGAMI	CAMPI	ENVOI	KIRRI	OCULI
AGGRI	CAPRI	FARCI	KOORI	OKAPI
AGUTI	CARDI	FASCI	KORAI	ORIBI
AIDOI	CARPI	FASTI	KRUBI	OVOLI
AIOLI	CAURI	FERMI	KUKRI	OZEKI
ALIBI	CEILI	FILII	KULFI	PADRI
AMICI	CELLI	FILMI	LAARI	PAGRI
ANIMI	CERCI	FRATI	LANAI	PALKI
APPUI	CESTI	FUNDI	LASSI	PALPI
ARCHI	CHILI	FUNGI	LATHI	PAOLI
ARDRI	CHOLI	GADDI	LAZZI	PAPPI
ARIKI	CIPPI	GARNI	LENTI	PARDI
ASKOI	CIRRI	GENII	LIBRI	PARKI
ASSAI	CLAVI	GHAZI	LICHI	PARTI
ATIGI	COATI	GIBLI	LIMBI	PENNI
AULOI	COCCI	GLOBI	LITAI	PEPSI
AUREI	COMBI	GOBBI	LOGOI	PERAI
AZUKI	COQUI	GUMMI	LUMBI	PETRI
BAJRI	CORGI	GUSLI	LUNGI	PETTI
BALTI	CORNI	HADJI	LURGI	PIANI
BAMBI	CROCI	HAJJI	MACHI	PILEI
BARFI	CULTI	HANGI	MANDI	PIRAI
BASSI	CUNEI	HAPPI	MAQUI	POORI
BASTI	CURLI	HIKOI	MARRI	PRIMI
BEEDI	CURSI	HONGI	MATAI	PSOAI
BENNI	DARZI	HOURI	MAURI	PULLI
BESTI	DASHI	IAMBI	MEDII	PUNJI
BHAJI	DEMOI	IMARI	MOCHI	PUTTI
BIALI	DESHI	IMSHI	MODII	QUASI
BINDI	DHOBI	INDRI	MOOLI	RABBI
BLINI	DHOTI	ISSEI	MUFTI	RADII
BOCCI	DHUTI	JINNI	MURRI	RAHUI
BODHI	DILLI	KADAI	MURTI	RANGI
BOOAI	DISCI	KANJI	MYTHI	RECTI
BRAAI	DOLCI	KARRI	NAEVI	REIKI
BRAVI	DOSAI	KATTI	NASHI	RISHI
BRIKI	DUOMI	KAURI	NGATI	ROSHI

ROSTI	SENSI	SULCI	THALI	UMAMI
RUBAI	SENTI	SUSHI	THOLI	URAEI
RUBLI	SERAI	SWAMI	THYMI	URALI
SAKAI	SHCHI	TAKHI	TONDI	URARI
SAKTI	SHIAI	TANGI	TOPHI	UTERI
SALMI	SHOGI	TANTI	TOPOI	VILLI
SAMPI	SHOJI	TARSI	TORII	VOLTI
SATAI	SOLDI	TAWAI	TORSI	WONGI
SCAPI	SOLEI	TELOI	TRAGI	XYSTI
SCUDI	SPAHI	TEMPI	TSADI	ZIMBI
SEGNI	STOAI	TERAI	TULSI	ZOMBI
SEHRI	STYLI	TETRI	TUTTI	
SENGI	SUCCI	THAGI	UGALI	

Six-letter words

ACULEI	BOLETI	CURARI	GHARRI	KABUKI
ADSUKI	BONACI	CYATHI	GHIBLI	KAIKAI
ADZUKI	BONSAI	CYTISI	GILGAI	KALUKI
AGAPAI	BOOHAI	DALASI	GLUTEI	KAMAHI
AGOUTI	BORZOI	DECANI	GOMUTI	KARAHI
ALFAKI	BUIBUI	DEGAMI	GRIGRI	KAWAII
ALKALI	BUKSHI	DENARI	GUANXI	KIMCHI
ALUMNI	BURITI	DEWANI	GURAMI	KOKIRI
AMAUTI	BUZUKI	DHIMMI	HAIKAI	KONAKI
AMBARI	CADAGI	DHOOTI	HAKARI	KONINI
ANELLI	CALAMI	DJINNI	HAMULI	KORARI
ANNULI	CANTHI	DROMOI	HEGARI	KOUROI
ARCHEI	CAROLI	DUELLI	HEISHI	KOWHAI
ARGALI	CASINI	DUETTI	HERMAI	KROONI
ARGULI	CENTAI	ECHINI	HUMERI	KULAKI
ARILLI	CESTOI	ELTCHI	ILLUPI	KUMARI
ARIOSI	CESTUI	EMBOLI	INCAVI	LAOGAI
ARTIGI	CHADRI	EPHEBI	INCUBI	LAZULI
ASKARI	CHATTI	EPHORI	INKOSI	LIMULI
AVANTI	CHICHI	EQUALI	ISTHMI	LITCHI
BAILLI	CHILLI	EURIPI	JALEBI	LOBULI
BANZAI	CHOKRI	EXODOI	JAWARI	LOCULI
BHAKTI	CHOWRI	FAMULI	JEHADI	LUNGYI
BHINDI	CLYPEI	FLOCCI	JIHADI	MALLEI
BHISTI	COLOBI	FRACTI	JOWARI	MALOTI
BIKINI	COLONI	FUMULI	JUDOGI	MANATI
BIMINI	CONGII	GARDAI	JUNGLI	MARABI
BINDHI	CUBITI	GELATI	JUPATI	MARARI
BINGHI	CUMULI	GEMINI	KABIKI	MAULVI

MAZHBI	OUREBI	RENVOI	SIDDHI	TIRITI
MEHNDI	PACZKI	RHOMBI	SIFREI	TITOKI
MEISHI	PAKAHI	ROESTI	SIGLOI	TITULI
MILADI	PAKIHI	ROMAJI	SILENI	TOITOI
MIRCHI	PALAGI	ROTINI	SIMPAI	TORULI
MIRITI	PANINI	RUBATI	SMALTI	TROCHI
MISHMI	PAPYRI	RUMAKI	SMRITI	TROPHI
MODULI	PATIKI	SACCOI	SOLIDI	TSOTSI
MOIRAI	PERITI	SAFARI	SOMONI	TUFOLI
MOKIHI	PEROGI	SAIKEI	SONERI	TULADI
MOOLVI	PETSAI	SAKKOI	SOUARI	TUMULI
MOPANI	PHALLI	SALAMI	STELAI	TZADDI
MUESLI	PIROGI	SALUKI	STRATI	UAKARI
MUNSHI	PITHOI	SAMITI	SUNDRI	UMFAZI
MYTHOI	PITURI	SANCAI	SURIMI	UNCINI
NAGARI	PLUTEI	SANDHI	TABULI	URACHI
NEINEI	POHIRI	SANSEI	TAHINI	WAKIKI
NEROLI	POLYPI	SATORI	TAMARI	WAPITI
NIELLI	PRIAPI	SBIRRI	TANUKI	WARAGI
NIGIRI	PROTEI	SCAMPI	TAPETI	WASABI
NILGAI	PUJARI	SCYPHI	TATAMI	XYSTOI
NOSTOI	PUNANI	SENITI	TATSOI	YANQUI
NUCLEI	PURIRI	SENSEI	TAUIWI	YIDAKI
OCELLI	PUTELI	SESELI	TAWHAI	YOGINI
OCTOPI	PYLORI	SHALLI	TENESI	ZAIKAI
OCTROI	RAGINI	SHANTI	TENUTI	ZUFOLI
ONAGRI	RAMULI	SHENAI	THALLI	
OORALI	RAPINI	SHTCHI	THOLOI	
OURALI	REGULI	SHUFTI	THYRSI	
OURARI	REISHI	SHUMAI	TIFOSI	

Words that end with O

Two-letter words

BO	HO	KO	NO	SO	YO
DO	IO	LO	OO	TO	ZO
GO	JO	MO	PO	WO	

Three-letter words

ABO	AVO	BRO	DUO	EMO
ADO	AZO	COO	DZO	EVO
AGO	BIO	DOO	ECO	EXO
APO	BOO	DSO	EGO	FOO

FRO	LOO	OXO	SHO	UPO
GEO	MHO	PHO	TAO	WHO
GIO	MOO	POO	THO	WOO
GOO	NOO	PRO	TOO	YGO
HAO	OBO	REO	TWO	ZHO
HOO	OHO	RHO	UDO	ZOO
ISO	ONO	ROO	UFO	

Four-letter words

ACRO	CHAO	FINO	KINO	MOZO
AERO	CIAO	GAJO	KOBO	MUSO
AFRO	CITO	GAPO	KOLO	MYXO
AGIO	COCO	GIRO	KORO	NANO
AGRO	COHO	GOBO	KOTO	NOLO
ALCO	DADO	GOGO	KUDO	ODSO
ALKO	DAGO	GYNO	KYBO	OLEO
ALOO	DATO	GYPO	LAZO	OLIO
ALSO	DECO	GYRO	LENO	ONTO
ALTO	DEFO	HALO	LEVO	OPPO
AMBO	DELO	HARO	LIDO	ORDO
AMMO	DEMO	HELO	LILO	ORZO
ANNO	DERO	HERO	LIMO	OTTO
APSO	DEVO	HOBO	LINO	OUZO
ARCO	DIDO	HOLO	LIPO	PACO
ARVO	DINO	HOMO	LOBO	PEPO
AUTO	DIVO	HUSO	LOCO	PESO
BEGO	DOCO	HYPO	LOGO	PISO
BIRO	DODO	INFO	LOTO	POCO
BITO	DOJO	INGO	LUDO	POGO
BOBO	DURO	INRO	MAKO	POLO
BOHO	DZHO	INTO	MANO	POMO
BOKO	ECCO	JATO	MAYO	PRAO
BOLO	ECHO	JIAO	MEMO	PROO
BOYO	EDDO	JOCO	MENO	PYRO
BOZO	ERGO	JOMO	MICO	RATO
BRIO	EURO	JUCO	MILO	REDO
BROO	EXPO	JUDO	MINO	REGO
BUBO	FADO	KAGO	MIRO	RENO
BUDO	FANO	KARO	MISO	REPO
BUFO	FARO	KAYO	MOFO	RIVO
CALO	FICO	KENO	MOHO	ROTO
CAMO	FIDO	KERO	MOJO	SADO
CAPO	FIGO	KETO	MOKO	SAGO
CERO	FILO	KILO	MONO	SECO

SEGO	SUGO	TOHO	UMBO	VINO
SHMO	SUMO	TOKO	UNCO	VIVO
SHOO	SYBO	TOMO	UNDO	WERO
SIJO	TACO	TOPO	UNTO	WHIO
SILO	TARO	TORO	UPDO	WINO
SKEO	THIO	TOYO	UPGO	YEBO
SKIO	THRO	TRIO	URAO	YUKO
SOHO	TIRO	TYPO	VEGO	ZERO
SOLO	TOCO	TYRO	VETO	ZOBO

Five-letter words

ABMHO	BEANO	CHADO	DECKO	FUERO
ACHOO	BENTO	CHEMO	DEFFO	FUGIO
ADDIO	BERKO	CHIAO	DEKKO	FUNGO
ADOBO	BIFFO	CHICO	DERRO	GADJO
AGGRO	BILBO	CHIMO	DIAZO	GADSO
AGLOO	BIMBO	CHINO	DILDO	GALVO
ALAMO	BINGO	CHIRO	DIMBO	GAMBO
ALTHO	BIZZO	CHOCO	DINGO	GARBO
AMIDO	BOFFO	CHOKO	DIPSO	GAZOO
AMIGO	BOMBO	CHOLO	DISCO	GECKO
AMINO	BONGO	CISCO	DITTO	GENRO
AMNIO	BORGO	CLARO	DOBRO	GESSO
ANCHO	BRAVO	COCCO	DOGGO	GINZO
ANDRO	BROMO	COMBO	DOHYO	GIPPO
ANGLO	BUCKO	COMMO	DONKO	GISMO
APPRO	BUFFO	COMPO	DRACO	GIZMO
ASPRO	BUMBO	CONDO	DSOBO	GOBBO
AUDIO	BUNCO	CONGO	DSOMO	GODSO
AVISO	BUNKO	CONTO	DUBBO	GOMBO
AWATO	BUROO	CONVO	DUMBO	GONZO
AWETO	BURRO	CORNO	DUNNO	GREBO
AZIDO	BUTEO	CORSO	DUOMO	GREGO
BABOO	CACAO	CREDO	EJIDO	GUACO
BACCO	CAMEO	CRUDO	ERUGO	GUANO
BALOO	CAMPO	CUFFO	ESTRO	GUIRO
BANCO	CANSO	CURIO	FANGO	GUMBO
BANJO	CANTO	CUSSO	FATSO	GUSTO
BARDO	CARBO	CUTTO	FIBRO	GYPPO
BARRO	CARGO	CYANO	FILLO	HALLO
BASHO	CASCO	CYCLO	FLEXO	HELIO
BASSO	CELLO	DAIKO	FOLIO	HELLO
BASTO	CENTO	DANIO	FORDO	HILLO
BAZOO	CHACO	DATTO	FORGO	HIMBO

HIPPO	MAIKO	PASEO	RESTO	TANGO
HOLLO	MAMBO	PATIO	RETRO	TANTO
HOWSO	MANGO	PEDRO	RHINO	TARDO
HULLO	MANTO	PENGO	RODEO	TASSO
HYDRO	MATLO	PERVO	ROMEO	TELCO
IGAPO	MATZO	PESTO	RONDO	TEMPO
IGLOO	MENTO	PETTO	RONEO	TENNO
IMAGO	MESTO	PHONO	RUMBO	THORO
IMIDO	METHO	PHOTO	RUMPO	TIMBO
IMINO	METRO	PIANO	SADDO	TONDO
IMPRO	MEZZO	PIEZO	SALTO	TORSO
INTRO	MICRO	PILAO	SALVO	TRIGO
IROKO	MILKO	PINGO	SAMBO	TRUGO
JAMBO	MIMEO	PINKO	SANGO	TSUBO
JELLO	MISDO	PINTO	SANKO	TURBO
JINGO	MISGO	PISCO	SANTO	TYPTO
JOCKO	MOLTO	POLIO	SARGO	UREDO
JUMBO	MONDO	PONGO	SCHMO	VERSO
JUNCO	MONGO	PORNO	SCUDO	VIDEO
JUNTO	MORRO	POSHO	SECCO	VIREO
KAROO	MOSSO	POTOO	SEGNO	VISTO
KAZOO	MOTTO	POTTO	SERVO	VULGO
KEENO	MUCHO	PRIMO	SEXTO	WACKO
KEMBO	MUCRO	PROMO	SHAKO	WAHOO
KENDO	MUNGO	PROSO	SHERO	WALDO
KIDDO	NACHO	PROTO	SHISO	WAZOO
KIMBO	NAPOO	PUBCO	SHOJO	WHAMO
KONDO	NARCO	PULAO	SICKO	WHOSO
KUSSO	NEGRO	PULMO	SIXMO	WILCO
LAEVO	NGAIO	PUNTO	SKIMO	YAHOO
LARGO	NITRO	PUTTO	SLOMO	YARCO
LASSO	NUTSO	QUINO	SMOKO	YARTO
LAZZO	ORTHO	QUIPO	SOCKO	YOBBO
LEGGO	OUTDO	RADIO	SOLDO	YUCKO
LENTO	OUTGO	RATIO	SORBO	YUMMO
LESBO	OUTRO	RATOO	SORDO	ZAMBO
LEUCO	OVOLO	RAUPO	SORGO	ZENDO
LIMBO	PAEDO	RAZOO	SPADO	ZHOMO
LINGO	PANKO	REALO	STENO	ZINCO
LITHO	PANTO	RECCO	STYLO	ZIPPO
LLANO	PAOLO	RECTO	SULFO	ZOCCO
LOTTO	PAREO	REFFO	TABOO	ZOPPO
MACHO	PARGO	REGGO	TACHO	ZORRO
MACRO	PARVO	REPRO	TAIKO	

Six-letter words

ABRAZO	BOOCOO	DOPPIO	GORGIO	LIBIDO
ADAGIO	BOOHOO	DORADO	GREEBO	LIVEDO
ADJIGO	BOOKOO	DRONGO	GRINGO	LOBOLO
AERUGO	BRASCO	DUELLO	GROTTO	LOLIGO
AHCHOO	BRILLO	DUETTO	GUANGO	LUCUMO
AIKIDO	BROCHO	DYNAMO	HAIRDO	MACACO
AKIMBO	BRONCO	EMBRYO	HALLOO	MADURO
ALBEDO	BUMALO	ENDURO	HERETO	MAMAKO
ALBINO	BURGOO	ENHALO	HETERO	MANITO
ALBUGO	CABRIO	ENVIRO	HOLLOO	MANOAO
ALNICO	CALICO	ERINGO	HONCHO	MAOMAO
AMMINO	CALIGO	ERYNGO	HOODOO	MARERO
AMMONO	CAMSHO	ESCUDO	HOOPOO	MATICO
ANATTO	CARDIO	FASCIO	HOOROO	MATIPO
ANGICO	CASHOO	FIASCO	HULLOO	MEDICO
ANTHRO	CASINO	FINITO	HUPIRO	MELANO
APOLLO	CATALO	FINSKO	IGNARO	MENUDO
ARIOSO	CHARRO	FOREDO	IMBIZO	MERINO
ARISTO	CHEAPO	FOREGO	INCAVO	MIKADO
ARROYO	CHEERO	FORHOO	INDIGO	MIOMBO
ARSENO	CHOCHO	FRANCO	JAZZBO	MODULO
ARSINO	CHOCKO	FRESCO	JINGKO	MOJITO
ASIAGO	CHROMO	FUGATO	JOURNO	MOKORO
AUSUBO	CHURRO	FUMADO	KAKAPO	MONOAO
AWHATO	CICERO	GABBRO	KAKURO	MOOLOO
AWHETO	COGITO	GALAGO	KARORO	MORPHO
BABACO	COLUGO	GANGBO	KARROO	NANDOO
BAGNIO	COMEDO	GAUCHO	KATIPO	NARDOO
BAGUIO	COMODO	GAZABO	KEKENO	NIELLO
BAMBOO	CONCHO	GAZEBO	KIMONO	NOCEBO
BAROLO	COOCOO	GELATO	KLEPTO	NONEGO
BARRIO	COROZO	GENTOO	KOKAKO	NOSTRO
BASUCO	CRAMBO	GHERAO	KOODOO	NUNCIO
BAYAMO	CRYPTO	GHETTO	KORERO	NYMPHO
BEENTO	CUATRO	GIGOLO	KOUSSO	OBENTO
BILLYO	CUCKOO	GINGKO	KWAITO	OCTAVO
BISTRO	DAIMIO	GINKGO	LADINO	OLINGO
BLANCO	DAIMYO	GITANO	LANUGO	OVERDO
BLOTTO	DAYGLO	GIUSTO	LATIGO	OVERGO
BOLERO	DEXTRO	GOMBRO	LATINO	PAKOKO
BONITO	DINERO	GOMUTO	LAVABO	PALOLO
BONOBO	DOMINO	GONGYO	LEGATO	PANINO
BOOBOO	DOODOO	GOOROO	LIBERO	PARAMO

PEDALO	QUARTO	SCAMTO	STUCCO	VELCRO
PEEPBO	RABATO	SCHIZO	STUDIO	VIBRIO
PEPINO	RACINO	SCRUTO	SUBITO	VIGORO
PERNIO	RANCHO	SHACKO	TAPALO	VIRAGO
PEROXO	REBATO	SHEEPO	TATTOO	VIRINO
PHYLLO	REBOZO	SHIPPO	TECHNO	VOMITO
PHYSIO	REECHO	SHIVOO	TENUTO	VOODOO
PICARO	REGULO	SHYPOO	TERCIO	VORAGO
PIOPIO	REZERO	SISSOO	TEREDO	VOSTRO
PLONKO	RIALTO	SKIDOO	THICKO	WANDOO
POMATO	RIGHTO	SLEAZO	THUGGO	WEIRDO
POMELO	ROADEO	SMALTO	TIFOSO	WHACKO
PONCHO	ROBALO	SOLANO	TOLEDO	WHAMMO
POTATO	ROCOCO	SOLITO	TOMATO	WHATSO
PRESTO	ROMANO	SORGHO	TORERO	WHIZZO
PRONTO	ROTOLO	SPEEDO	TRILLO	WHOMSO
PSEUDO	RUBATO	SPINTO	TROPPO	WOOHOO
PSYCHO	RUBIGO	STALKO	TUKTOO	ZELOSO
PUEBLO	SAMFOO	STANZO	TUPELO	ZOCALO
PUKEKO	SANCHO	STATTO	TURACO	ZOOZOO
PUMELO	SANPRO	STEREO	TUXEDO	ZORINO
PUNCTO	SAPEGO	STINGO	ULTIMO	ZUFOLO
QUANGO	SBIRRO	STINKO	VAUDOO	ZYDECO

Words that end with U

Two-letter words

GU	NU	XU
MU	OU	YU

Three-letter words

ALU	EMU	JEU	PLU	UTU
AMU	FEU	KYU	RYU	VAU
AYU	FLU	LEU	SAU	YOU
BRU	FOU	LOU	SOU	
CRU	GAU	MEU	TAU	
EAU	GJU	MOU	ULU	
ECU	GNU	PIU	UMU	

Four-letter words

AGLU	BAHU	BAPU	BUBU	DEGU
AITU	BAJU	BEAU	CHOU	DOCU
BABU	BALU	BEDU	CLOU	ECRU

EMEU	KAGU	MASU	RAKU	TOLU
ERHU	KAPU	MENU	RATU	TROU
FRAU	KORU	MEOU	RIMU	TUTU
FUGU	KUDU	MOTU	RURU	UNAU
GENU	KUKU	MUMU	SOJU	VATU
GURU	KURU	NAMU	SULU	VROU
HABU	KUTU	OMBU	SUSU	WUDU
HAKU	KUZU	PATU	TABU	YUZU
HAPU	LATU	PRAU	TAPU	ZEBU
HUHU	LEKU	PUDU	TATU	ZOBU
IGLU	LIEU	PUKU	TEGU	ZULU
JEHU	LITU	PULU	THOU	
JUJU	LUAU	PUPU	THRU	
JUKU	LULU	RAGU	TOFU	

Five-letter words

ADIEU	CORNU	KONBU	PERDU	TENDU
AHURU	COYAU	KUDZU	PIKAU	TUKTU
BANTU	COYPU	LASSU	PILAU	UHURU
BATTU	FICHU	MAPAU	POILU	URUBU
BAYOU	FOGOU	MIAOU	PONZU	VENDU
BIJOU	FONDU	MUNTU	POYOU	VERTU
BITOU	HAIKU	NAIRU	PRAHU	VIRTU
BOYAU	HINAU	NANDU	QUIPU	VODOU
BUCHU	HOKKU	NIKAU	SADHU	VOULU
BUCKU	JAMBU	NOYAU	SAJOU	WAGYU
BUNDU	KANZU	OTAKU	SAMFU	WUSHU
BUSSU	KAURU	PAREU	SHOYU	
CENTU	KAWAU	PELAU	SNAFU	
CHIRU	KOMBU	PENDU	TATOU	

Six-letter words

ABATTU	CADEAU	HAPUKU	MALIBU	ORIHOU
ACAJOU	CALALU	INGENU	MAMAKU	ORMOLU
ALLYOU	CONGOU	JABIRU	MANATU	PILLAU
AMADOU	COTEAU	KARAMU	MANITU	PISTOU
APERCU	COYPOU	KERERU	MATATU	PIUPIU
BABACU	DETENU	KIKUYU	MEVROU	QUIPPU
BATEAU	EPERDU	KOKOPU	MILIEU	RAWARU
BHIKHU	GAGAKU	KOTUKU	MUUMUU	RESEAU
BINIOU	GATEAU	LANDAU	MZUNGU	ROUCOU
BOUBOU	GOMOKU	MADAFU	NHANDU	SABICU
BUREAU	GRUGRU	MAHEWU	NILGAU	SADDHU
CACHOU	HALERU	MAKUTU	NOGAKU	SAMSHU

SENRYU	SHOCHU	TAMANU	UBUNTU	YNAMBU
SHINJU	SUBFEU	TAUHOU	VOUDOU	
SHITZU	SUDOKU	TELEDU	WHANAU	

Unique beginnings and endings

Here are some fascinating words with unique beginnings and endings to impress your opponents with, some perhaps more useful in Scrabble than others. Note that in some cases with beginnings there are other forms of the same word or its plural form that also begin with the same two letters (eg ZLOTE, ZLOTYS, ZLOTIES, and ZLOTYCH are valid as well as ZLOTY, but it is still worthy of being considered a word with a unique beginning). An additional list of words with a rare J or Q ending has also been included.

Words with unique first two letters

BD :	BDELLIUM	African or Asian tree yielding gum resin
CS :	CSARDAS	Hungarian folk dance
CT :	CTENE	comblike swimming organ
GM :	GMELINITE	zeolitic mineral
HM :	HMM	interjection expressing doubt
HR :	HRYVNA	monetary unit of Ukraine
IH :	IHRAM	white robes worn by Muslim pilgrims to Mecca
IJ :	IJTIHAD	effort deriving a legal ruling from the Koran
IU :	IURE	by right or by law
IW :	IWI	any Maori tribe
JN :	JNANA	type of yoga
KB :	KBAR	unit of atmospheric pressure
KG :	KGOTLA	assembly of tribal elders in Botswana
KS :	KSAR	old form of tsar
LH :	LHERZOLITE	olivine mineral
LW :	LWEI	monetary unit of Angola
MG :	MGANGA	witch doctor
MM :	MMM	expressing enjoyment of taste or smell
MP :	MPRET	former Albanian ruler
MR :	MRIDANG	drum used in Indian music
MV :	MVULE	tropical African tree
NH :	NHANDU	South American ostrich
NK :	NKOSI	South African address to a superior
OJ :	OJIME	Japanese bead used to secure cords
OQ :	OQUASSA	North American trout
PN :	PNEUMA	a person's breath, spirit or soul
PW :	PWN	to humiliate an opponent in online gaming

PZ : PZAZZ	pizzazz, attractive energy and style
QW : QWERTY	type of standard English keyboard
SB : SBIRRO	Italian police officer
SG : SGRAFFITI	ceramic decoration technique
TJ : TJANTING	tool used for applying wax in batik
TM : TMESES	interpolation of a word within a compound word
UA : UAKARI	South American monkey
UC : UCKERS	form of ludo played in the Royal Navy
UE : UEY	U-turn (Australian)
UJ : UJAMAA	communally organized Tanzanian village
UX : UXORIAL	of or relating to wife
VY : VYING	verb form of vie, to compete or contend
XO : XOANON	primitive religious statue
XR : XRAY	radio codeword for the letter X
YF : YFERE	together; an associate
YN : YNAMBU	large South American bird
ZL : ZLOTY	monetary unit of Poland
ZZ : ZZZ	representing sleep

Note

There are some noteworthy examples of near misses to the above list such as BW (BWANA and BWAZI), MW (MWAH and MWALIMU) and VL (VLEI, VLOG, and VLY).

Words with unique last two letters

BD : UNSHRUBD	without shrubs (poetic)
BK : NABK	type of shrub or its edible berry
DJ : HADJ	Muslim pilgrimage to Mecca
EJ : BASEEJ	militia volunteer in Iran
IJ : BASIJ	variant of baseej
JD : SLOJD	system of using woodwork to teach manual skills
JJ : HAJJ	variant of hadj
JY : BUNJY	bungee, a strong elastic rope or cable
KF : WAKF	endowment in Muslim law
KR : DHIKR	Sufi religious ceremony
MD : FREMD	alien or strange person or thing
MH : OLLAMH	old Irish term for a wise man
MT : DREAMT	a past tense of dream
NF : CONF	online discussion forum
NJ : BENJ	preparation of Indian hemp as a narcotic
PF : DUMMKOPF	stupid person
QA : BURQA	garment worn by Muslim women

QF	WAQF	variant of wakf
QH	FIQH	Islamic jurisprudence
SD	PAYSD	poised
SN	HISN	belonging to him (dialect)
UU	MUUMUU	loose dress worn by Hawaiian women
VD	YRIVD	archaic past tense of rive, to tear apart
VN	EEVN	archaic or poetic spelling of even or evening
WU	MAHEWU	type of South African porridge
XL	CACOMIXL	carnivorous mammal like a raccoon
YK	BASHLYK	Russian hood with long ends
ZS	ZZZS	sleeps

> ## *Note*
> There are some noteworthy examples of near misses to the above list such as GD (PLONGD and SMARAGD) and NQ (CINQ and TRANQ).

The rarest single-letter endings are Q (ten words) and J (12 words):

CINQ	number of five in card or dice games
KAMOTIQ	type of Inuit sled
QAJAQ	Inuit kayak
QULLIQ	Inuit oil lamp
SUQ	marketplace in Muslim countries
TALAQ	Muslim form of divorce
TRANQ	tranquilliser
TSADDIQ	Hasidic Jewish leader
TZADDIQ	variant of tsaddiq
UMIAQ	Inuit board made of skins
AFLAJ	the plural of FALAJ (see below)
BASEEJ	militia volunteer in Iran
BASIJ	variant of baseej
BENJ	preparation of Indian hemp as a narcotic
FALAJ	irrigation canal in ancient Oman
HADJ	Muslim pilgrimage to Mecca
HAJ	variant of hadj
HAJJ	variant of hadj
RAJ	rule or government in India
SVARAJ	self-government in former British India
SWARAJ	variant of svaraj
TAJ	crown; a dervish's tall conical cap

VOWEL AND CONSONANT THEMES

- This section deals with words that will help solve problems with too many vowels, too many consonants, or awkward combinations such as a W and U together.

- There are lists of words with multiples of the same vowels, helpfully arranged according to the pattern of the vowels.

- There are lists of words termed 'light words' that have an abundance of vowels in them. Newer players will find the shorter words in these lists extremely useful.

- Conversely, there are lists of words termed 'heavy words' to help offload a rack full of consonants.

- If you find yourself with duplicates of the same higher-scoring consonant (3pts or more) then there are specific lists of short words that enable both of them to be used.

Awkward vowel combinations

A problem every Scrabble player faces is an unpromising combination of letters. With the exception of E, drawing duplicates of any vowel can be awkward. In this respect duplicate As and Os are manageable but duplicate Is and Us can make things very awkward. If you find yourself with three or more of a particular vowel on your rack, it's a good idea to try to offload the excess ones. With three Is on your rack, you should try to play a word with two of them. And because I is one of the most common letters in the game, if you don't get rid of both Is in a single turn, you are highly likely to end up with the same problem on your next turn. It's a good idea, therefore, to have a cache of words that use duplicate vowels so that you can deal with the problem as soon as it arises, allowing you to clear out the excess vowels on your rack without having to change letters and fall behind on the score.

The lists in this section provide words with multiple As, Es, Is, Os and Us arranged according to the pattern of the vowels which makes it easier to learn them as small groups of similar words. Words with two As, two Es and two Os are excluded because generally it is not difficult to deal with those duplicates and, anyway, you may well be wise to keep an A or E on the rack if there are not many left in the bag.

Words with three [A]s

Five-letter words
Pattern A _ A _ A

ABACA	ANANA
ABAKA	ANATA
ABAYA	ARABA
AFARA	ASANA
AGAMA	AYAYA
ALAPA	

> **Note**
> ANANA contains the valid words
> ANAN NANA ANA NAN AN NA

Other patterns

ALAAP	KAAMA	TAATA

Six-letter words
Pattern A _ A _ A _

ANABAS	ATABAL	ATAMAN	AVATAR

Pattern A _ A _ _ A

ALASKA	ANANDA
AMARNA	ANATTA

Pattern A _ _ A _ A

AGGADA	ALPACA	ARGALA
AKHARA	ANTARA	ARMADA
ALBATA	ARCANA	ASRAMA

Pattern _ A _ A _ A

BAHADA	CASAVA
BAJADA	DAGABA
BALATA	HALALA
BANANA	HAMADA
BARAZA	HAWALA
BATATA	JACANA
CABALA	JATAKA
CABANA	KABAKA
CADAGA	KABALA
CANADA	KABAYA
CASABA	KAMALA

> ## *Note*
> Words with two Ks in will need a blank as one of the Ks.

KANAKA	PANAMA
KARAKA	PAPAYA
KATANA	PATACA
LABARA	PATAKA
MANANA	QABALA
MANAWA	RAMADA
MARACA	SAMARA
MASALA	SATARA
MATATA	TAMARA
NAGANA	TARAMA
PAJAMA	VAHANA
PALAMA	ZANANA
PALAPA	ZAPATA
PANADA	

> ## *Note*
> Although proper nouns are not allowed in Scrabble, some have alternative meanings spelt without a capital, thus ALASKA (type of dessert) and CANADA (small narrow canyon) are allowed.

Pattern _ A _ A A _

BAZAAR	JAMAAT	SAMAAN
HARAAM	SALAAM	

Other patterns

BRAATA

Words with three or more Es

Four-letter words

EEEW	EPEE

Five-letter words
Pattern E _ _ E E

ELPEE	EMCEE	ETWEE

Pattern _ E _ E E

BELEE	LEVEE	RESEE
BESEE	MELEE	SEMEE
GELEE	PEWEE	TEPEE

Pattern _ E E _ E

DEERE	JEEZE	NEEZE	TEENE
DEEVE	KEEVE	PEECE	WEEKE
FEESE	LEESE	PEEPE	WEETE
FEEZE	LEEZE	PEEVE	
GEESE	NEELE	REEDE	
HEEZE	NEESE	REEVE	

Other patterns

EEVEN	EXEME	EMEER
		EXEEM

Six-letter words
Pattern _ E E _ E E

BEEBEE	TEEPEE	VEEPEE
PEEWEE	TEEVEE	WEEWEE

Words with two or more ⏹ s

Four-letter words
Pattern I _ I _

IBIS	IRIS
ILIA	ISIT
IMID	IWIS
INIA	IXIA
IRID	

> ## Note
> For this set, it is deemed worthwhile including the few with other vowels apart from the Is.

Pattern I _ _ I

IMPI	INTI

Pattern _ I _ I

BIDI	LIRI	PIKI	TITI
DIVI	MIDI	PILI	WIKI
DIXI	MIHI	PIPI	WILI
FINI	MINI	SIMI	ZITI
HILI	MIRI	SIRI	
HIOI	NIDI	TIKI	
KIWI	NISI	TIPI	

Words with three Is
FILII

Pattern I _ I _ I _
IMIDIC   IRITIC
IRIDIC   IRITIS

> ## *Note*
> FILII is the plural of FILIUS which is
> listed in the source dictionary as
> Latin for 'son' and used in genealogy.

Pattern _ I _ I _ I
BIKINI   MIRITI   TIRITI
BIMINI   NIGIRI

Words with three or more O s

Words with three Os
Five-letter words
OVOLO   POTOO

Six-letter words
Pattern _ O _ O _ O
BONOBO   COROZO   MOKORO   ROTOLO
COMODO   LOBOLO   ROCOCO

Pattern _ O O _ O _
DOOCOT   DOOWOP   GOOGOL

Other patterns
COCOON   FORHOO   OOLOGY
                HOLLOO   OOLONG

Words with four Os
Pattern _OO_OO with repeated parts
BOOBOO   COOCOO   DOODOO   ZOOZOO

Others with pattern _OO_OO
BOOCOO   HOOPOO   WOOHOO
BOOHOO   HOOROO
BOOKOO   KOODOO
GOOROO   MOOLOO
HOODOO   VOODOO

Words with two or more U s

Four-letter words with two Us
Pattern _ U _ U with repeated parts

BUBU	MUMU
HUHU	PUPU
JUJU	RURU
KUKU	SUSU
LULU	TUTU

> ***Note***
> For this set, it is deemed worthwhile including the few with other vowels apart from the Us.

Others with pattern _ U _ U

FUGU	PUDU
GURU	PUKU
JUKU	PULU
KUDU	SULU
KURU	WUDU
KUTU	YUZU
KUZU	ZULU
LUAU	

> ***Note***
> Quite a few of these words are worth noting as hooks of three-letter words, eg HUH(U), (K)UTU, (L)ULU, (M)UMU or MUM(U).

Other patterns

UNAU	URUS

Five-letter words with three Us

UHURU	URUBU

Six-letter words with three or more Us

MUTUUM	MUUMUU

> ***Note***
> MUUMUU is one of the most unlikely six-letter words in Scrabble, requiring all the Ms and Us from the set on the rack at the same time, or at least five of them and one available on the board.

Light words

While duplicate vowels on your rack can be a real pain, having too many vowels in general can be frustrating. For this reason, it's helpful to have a number of 'light' words up your sleeve – words that contain a high proportion of vowels. The lists of light words include words from three to six letters, excluding –S plurals, where more than half the letters are vowels. In addition, there are lists of vowel-heavy seven- and eight-letter bonus words. In this case they include –S plurals. The sevens and eights are those with five or more vowels. Seven-letter words with four vowels are in abundance and not considered especially vowel heavy.

Two-letter words with only vowels AEIOU

AA	EA	OE	OU
AE	EE	OI	
AI	IO	OO	

Three-letter words with only vowels AEIOU

AIA	AUA	AUE	EAU

Four-letter words with three or more of AEIOU

ACAI	CIAO	LUAU	OUMA
AEON	EALE	MEOU	OUPA
AERO	EASE	MOAI	OUTA
AGEE	EAUX	MOOI	OUZO
AGIO	EAVE	MOUE	PAUA
AGUE	EEEW	NAOI	QUAI
AIDA	EIDE	OBIA	RAIA
AIDE	EINA	OBOE	ROUE
AIGA	EINE	ODEA	TOEA
AINE	EMEU	OGEE	UNAI
AITU	EOAN	OHIA	UNAU
AJEE	EPEE	OLEA	URAO
AKEE	ETUI	OLEO	UREA
ALAE	EUGE	OLIO	UVAE
ALEE	EUOI	ONIE	UVEA
ALOE	EURO	OOSE	VIAE
ALOO	EVOE	OOZE	ZOEA
AMIA	HIOI		
AMIE	HUIA		
ANOA	IDEA		
AQUA	IDEE		
AREA	ILEA		
ARIA	ILIA		
ASEA	INIA		
ATUA	IOTA		
AULA	IURE		
AUNE	IXIA		
AURA	JIAO		
AUTO	KAIE		
AWEE	KUIA		
BEAU	LIEU		

Note

The interjection EUOI, expressing Bacchic frenzy, gets a special mention as the only way to dump four vowels in a four-letter word. This is one of the regularly played vowel-heavy words at clubs and tournaments, often using a vowel on the board.

Five-letter words with four of the vowels AEIOU

AALII	AQUAE	EERIE	QUEUE
ADIEU	AREAE	LOOIE	URAEI
AECIA	AUDIO	LOUIE	ZOAEA
AERIE	AULOI	MIAOU	ZOEAE
AIDOI	AURAE	OIDIA	ZOOEA
AINEE	AUREI	OORIE	
AIOLI	BOOAI	OUIJA	
AIYEE	COOEE	OURIE	

Six-letter words with four or more of AEIOU

ABASIA	AKATEA	ARIOSO	BEANIE
ABELIA	AKEAKE	AROUSE	BEEBEE
ABULIA	AKEBIA	ASIAGO	BEEDIE
ACACIA	ALALIA	ATAATA	BINIOU
ACAJOU	ALEXIA	ATAXIA	BLOOIE
ACEDIA	ALODIA	ATOCIA	BOATIE
ACUATE	ALOGIA	ATONIA	BOOBIE
ACULEI	ALULAE	AUBADE	BOOBOO
ADAGIO	AMADOU	AUCUBA	BOOCOO
ADIEUX	AMAUTI	AUDIAL	BOODIE
AECIAL	AMEBAE	AUDILE	BOOGIE
AECIUM	AMELIA	AUGITE	BOOHAI
AEDILE	AMOEBA	AUMAIL	BOOHOO
AEDINE	AMOOVE	AUNTIE	BOOKIE
AEMULE	AMUSIA	AURATE	BOOKOO
AENEUS	ANEMIA	AUREUS	BOOTEE
AEONIC	ANOMIE	AURORA	BOOTIE
AERATE	ANOPIA	AUROUS	BOUBOU
AERIAL	ANOXIA	AUSUBO	BOUGIE
AERIED	ANURIA	AUTEUR	BUIBUI
AERIER	AORTAE	AUTOED	BUREAU
AEROBE	AOUDAD	AVAILE	CADEAU
AERUGO	APIECE	AVENUE	CAEOMA
AGAPAE	APNOEA	AVIATE	CAIQUE
AGAPAI	APOGEE	AVOURE	CAUDAE
AGORAE	APORIA	AZALEA	CAUSAE
AGOUTA	ARAARA	AZIONE	COAITA
AGOUTI	ARAISE	BAGUIO	COATEE
AGUISE	ARALIA	BAILEE	COBAEA
AGUIZE	AREOLA	BAILIE	CODEIA
AIKIDO	AREOLE	BATEAU	COOCOO
AIKONA	ARIOSE	BAUBEE	COOEED
AIRIER	ARIOSI	BAUERA	COOKIE

COOLIE	EMEUTE	FERIAE	IODIZE
COORIE	EOCENE	FLOOIE	IODOUS
COOTIE	EOLIAN	FOEFIE	IOLITE
COTEAU	EONIAN	FOODIE	IONISE
COULEE	EOSINE	FOOTIE	IONIUM
COUPEE	EPAULE	FOULIE	IONIZE
COURIE	EPEIRA	FOVEAE	IONONE
CURIAE	EPIZOA	GALEAE	JEELIE
DAIMIO	EPOPEE	GATEAU	KAIKAI
DAUTIE	EPUISE	GAUCIE	KAWAII
DEARIE	EQUALI	GIAOUR	KEAVIE
DEAWIE	EQUATE	GOALIE	KEELIE
DEEPIE	EQUINE	GOATEE	KIEKIE
DOOBIE	EQUIPE	GOODIE	KIERIE
DOODOO	ETOILE	GOOIER	KOODOO
DOOLEE	EUCAIN	GOOLIE	KOOKIE
DOOLIE	EUOUAE	GOONIE	KOUROI
DOOZIE	EUPNEA	GOORIE	LAESIE
DOUANE	EUREKA	GOOROO	LAMIAE
EASIED	EURIPI	GUAIAC	LAOGAI
EASIER	EVOLUE	GUINEA	LAURAE
EASIES	EVOVAE	HAIKAI	LEAGUE
EATAGE	EXODOI	HAIQUE	LEIPOA
ECURIE	EXUVIA	HEALEE	LIAISE
EELIER	FACIAE	HEARIE	LIENEE
EERIER	FAERIE	HEAUME	LOANEE
EIDOLA	FAUNAE	HEEZIE	LOERIE
EKUELE	FEAGUE	HEINIE	LOOKIE
ELODEA	FEERIE	HOAGIE	LOONIE
ELUATE	FEIJOA	HOODIA	LOOSIE
ELUVIA	FEIRIE	HOODIE	LOURIE
		HOODOO	MANAIA
		HOOLIE	MANOAO
		HOOPOE	MAOMAO
		HOOPOO	MEALIE
		HOOROO	MEANIE
		IDEAED	MEDIAE
		IDEATA	MEEMIE
		IDEATE	MEINIE
		IGUANA	MEOUED
		IODATE	MIELIE
		IODIDE	MILIEU
		IODINE	MOIRAI
		IODISE	MONOAO

Note

The word EUOUAE, a Gregorian chant, gets a special mention as a way of dumping five (using one on the board) or six vowels in one word. The way to remember the spelling is to imagine the Us as Vs and pronounce it as in the alternative spelling of EVOVAE, which is also on this list.

MOOLOO
MOUSIE
MUUMUU
NAUSEA
NEINEI
NOOGIE
NOOKIE
OAKIER
OAKIES
OARAGE
OARIER
OATIER
OBELIA
OCREAE
ODIOUS
OEDEMA
OEUVRE
OIDIUM
OILIER
OLEATE
OLEINE
ONESIE
OOFIER
OOIDAL
OOLITE
OOMIAC
OOMIAK
OORALI
OORIAL
OORIER
OOSIER
OOZIER
OPAQUE

OPIATE
OPIOID
ORARIA
OREIDE
ORIHOU
ORIOLE
OROIDE
OTIOSE
OUBAAS
OUGIYA
OUGLIE
OURALI
OURARI
OUREBI
OURIER
OUTAGE
OUTATE
OUTEAT
OUTLIE
OUTSEE
OUTVIE
OZAENA
PALEAE
PEERIE
PEEWEE
PERAEA
PEREIA
PIOPIO
PIUPIU
POURIE
QUAERE
QUALIA
QUELEA

Note

QUEUED and QUEUER are two common six-letter words with four vowels in a row. Another common example is GOOIER. Other less common sixes with that attribute in this list are BLOOIE, COOEED, FLOOIE, GIAOUR, GUAIAC, MEOUED, TOEIER, ZOAEAE, ZOOEAE, ZOOEAL, and ZOOIER.

QUEUED
QUEUER
QUINIE
QUINOA
QUOOKE
REALIA
REDIAE
REEKIE
RESEAU
ROADEO
ROADIE
ROARIE
ROOFIE
ROOKIE
ROOMIE
ROUCOU
SAIKEI
SAIQUE
SAULIE
SEELIE
SEMEIA
SOAPIE
SOIREE
SOOGEE
SOOGIE
SOUARI
SOUTIE
TAENIA
TAIAHA
TAIHOA
TALEAE

TAUHOU
TAUIWI
TAUPIE
TEEPEE
TEEVEE
TENIAE
TIBIAE
TOEBIE
TOEIER
TOETOE
TOITOI
TOOLIE
TOONIE
TOORIE
TOUPEE
TOUPIE
TOURIE
TOUTIE
TUATUA
UAKARI
UBIQUE
UJAMAA
UNCIAE
UNEASE
UNIQUE
URAEUS
URANIA
UREASE
UREDIA
UREIDE
UREMIA

Note

One way to remember the spelling of TAUIWI, a Māori word for anyone in New Zealand who is not Māori, is to break it down into the two valid three-letter words TAU and IWI. This trick also works for such words as TAIAHA.

UTOPIA	VOUDOU	WOODIE	ZOARIA
UVEOUS	WAIATA	WOOHOO	ZOECIA
UVULAE	WAIRUA	WOOLIE	ZOOEAE
VAUDOO	WEENIE	WOOPIE	ZOOEAL
VEEPEE	WEEPIE	YAUTIA	ZOOIER
VOIDEE	WEEWEE	ZAIKAI	ZOOZOO
VOODOO	WIENIE	ZOAEAE	ZOUAVE

Seven-letter bonus words with five or more vowels, including –S plurals

ABOULIA	AURORAE	EVACUEE	OUAKARI
ACEQUIA	AUTOCUE	EXUVIAE	OUGUIYA
AECIDIA	CAMAIEU	IPOMOEA	QUEENIE
AENEOUS	COUTEAU	KOEKOEA	RAOULIA
AEOLIAN	DEQUEUE	MIAOUED	ROULEAU
AEONIAN	DIANOIA	MOINEAU	SAOUARI
AERADIO	DOULEIA	NOUVEAU	SEQUOIA
AEROBIA	EATERIE	OIDIOID	TAENIAE
AGEUSIA	ENQUEUE	OLEARIA	URAEMIA
AIERIES	EPINAOI	OOGONIA	ZOOECIA
ALIENEE	EPUISEE	OUABAIN	
AMOEBAE	EQUINIA		
ANAEMIA	ETAERIO		
AQUARIA	EUCAINE		
AQUEOUS	EUGARIE		
AREOLAE	EUGENIA		
AUDITEE	EULOGIA		
AUREATE	EUOUAES		
AURELIA	EUPNOEA		
AUREOLA	EUTAXIA		
AUREOLE	EUTEXIA		

> ## *Note*
> MIAOUED is an aesthetically pleasing vowel-heavy bonus word containing all of the vowels AEIOU together in the middle, and the only seven to have five vowels in a row apart from the plural of EUOUAE shown above.

Eight-letter bonus words with five or more vowels, including –S plurals

ABOIDEAU	ACIDURIA	AECIDIUM	AEROFOIL
ABOITEAU	ACIERAGE	AEDICULE	AEROLITE
ABOULIAS	ACIERATE	AEGIRINE	AERONAUT
ACADEMIA	ACOELOUS	AEGIRITE	AEROTONE
ACAUDATE	ACOEMETI	AEGLOGUE	AGACERIE
ACAULINE	ACQUIREE	AENEUSES	AGENESIA
ACAULOSE	ACTINIAE	AEQUORIN	AGEUSIAS
ACAULOUS	ACUITIES	AERADIOS	AGIOTAGE
ACEQUIAS	ACULEATE	AERATION	AGOUTIES
ACHAENIA	ADEQUATE	AERIFIED	AGUACATE
ACICULAE	ADULARIA	AERIFIES	AGUELIKE
ACIDEMIA	AECIDIAL	AEROBIUM	AGUEWEED

AIGUILLE	ASSEGAAI	AZOTURIA	DETAINEE
AKINESIA	ATARAXIA	BAHOOKIE	DIALOGUE
ALEHOUSE	AUBRETIA	BANLIEUE	DIANOIAS
ALEURONE	AUBRIETA	BAUHINIA	DIAPAUSE
ALIENAGE	AUDIENCE	BEAUCOUP	DIECIOUS
ALIENATE	AUDITEES	BEAUTIED	DIOECIES
ALIENEES	AUDITION	BEAUTIES	DIOICOUS
ALLELUIA	AUDITIVE	BEAUXITE	DOUANIER
ALOCASIA	AUGURIES	BIUNIQUE	DOULEIAS
ALOPECIA	AULARIAN	BOISERIE	DOUPIONI
AMEERATE	AUMAILED	BOOGALOO	DUOLOGUE
AMEIOSES	AURELIAN	BOOHOOED	EARPIECE
AMEIOSIS	AURELIAS	BOUDERIE	EATERIES
AMOEBEAN	AUREOLAE	BOUSOUKI	EBIONISE
AMOEBOID	AUREOLAS	BOUTIQUE	EBIONIZE
ANABAENA	AUREOLED	BOUZOUKI	ECAUDATE
ANAEMIAS	AUREOLES	CAESIOUS	ECOTOPIA
ANAEROBE	AURICULA	CAESURAE	EDACIOUS
ANALOGUE	AURIFIED	CAMAIEUX	EGOITIES
ANIRIDIA	AURIFIES	CAPOEIRA	EGOMANIA
ANOOPSIA	AUROREAN	CARIACOU	ELUVIATE
ANOREXIA	AUTACOID	CAUSERIE	EMACIATE
ANOUROUS	AUTOCADE	CAUTIOUS	EMEERATE
ANOXEMIA	AUTOCOID	CAVIARIE	EMERAUDE
APIARIAN	AUTOCUES	COENOBIA	EMERITAE
APIARIES	AUTODIAL	COEQUATE	ENCAENIA
APIMANIA	AUTOGIRO	COOEEING	ENQUEUED
APOGAEIC	AUTOLOAD	COUMAROU	ENQUEUES
APOLOGIA	AUTOMATA	COUTEAUX	EOLIENNE
APOLOGUE	AUTOMATE	DAIQUIRI	EOLIPILE
APOSITIA	AUTOPSIA	DEAERATE	EOLOPILE
AQUACADE	AUTOSAVE	DECIDUAE	EPICEDIA
AQUANAUT	AUTOSOME	DEIONISE	EPIFAUNA
AQUARIAL	AUTOTUNE	DEIONIZE	EPIGAEAL
AQUARIAN	AUTUNITE	DEQUEUED	EPIGAEAN
AQUARIUM	AUXILIAR	DEQUEUES	EPIGEOUS
AQUATONE	AVIANISE		
AQUILINE	AVIANIZE		
ARACEOUS	AVIARIES		
ARANEOUS	AVIATION		
ARAPAIMA	AVIFAUNA		
AREOLATE	AVOISION		
ARIARIES	AWEARIED		
ASEITIES	AZOTEMIA		

Note

COOEEING, and MIAOUING and QUEUEING shown later, are the only eight-letter vowel-heavy bonus words to have five vowels in a row.

EPILOGUE	EUTAXIES	IDEATIVE	MOIETIES
EPIZOITE	EUTAXITE	IDIOCIES	MOINEAUS
EPOPOEIA	EUTEXIAS	IDONEOUS	MONILIAE
EQUALISE	EUXENITE	IGUANIAN	MOVIEOKE
EQUALIZE	EVACUATE	INAURATE	MOVIEOLA
EQUATION	EVACUEES	INDUCIAE	NAUSEATE
EQUATIVE	EVALUATE	INDUVIAE	NAUSEOUS
EQUINIAS	EXAMINEE	INERTIAE	NEURULAE
EQUIPAGE	EXEQUIAL	INFAUNAE	NIRAMIAI
EQUISETA	EXEQUIES	INFERIAE	NOTITIAE
EQUITIES	EXIGUOUS	INITIATE	NOUVEAUX
EQUIVOKE	EXIMIOUS	IODATION	OBSEQUIE
ERADIATE	EXONUMIA	IODINATE	OCEANAUT
ERIONITE	EXUVIATE	IOPANOIC	ODALIQUE
ETAERIOS	EYEPIECE	IPOMOEAS	OEDEMATA
ETIOLATE	FACETIAE	ISOLOGUE	OEDIPEAN
ETOUFFEE	FAUNULAE	JALOUSIE	OEILLADE
ETOURDIE	FAUTEUIL	JEALOUSE	OILERIES
EUCAINES	FEATEOUS	KABLOOIE	OITICICA
EUDAEMON	FEATUOUS	KALOOKIE	OLEARIAS
EUDAIMON	FEIJOADA	KAMAAINA	OLIGEMIA
EUGARIES	FILARIAE	KAREAREA	OLIGURIA
EUGENIAS	FILIOQUE	KAUMATUA	ONIONIER
EULOGIAE	FOEDARIE	KOEKOEAS	OOGAMETE
EULOGIAS	FORHOOIE	LACINIAE	OOGAMIES
EULOGIES	FOVEOLAE	LAUREATE	OOGAMOUS
EULOGISE	GAIETIES	LEUCEMIA	OOGENIES
EULOGIUM	GUAIACOL	LEUKEMIA	OOGONIAL
EULOGIZE	GUAIACUM	LIPAEMIA	OOGONIUM
EUPEPSIA	GUAIOCUM	MAIASAUR	OOLOGIES
EUPHOBIA	HAEREMAI	MAIEUTIC	OOTHECAE
EUPHONIA	HEMIOLIA	MAIOLICA	OPTIONEE
EUPHORIA	HEMIOPIA	MAIREHAU	ORAGIOUS
EUPHUISE	HETAERAE	MAUSOLEA	ORATORIO
EUPHUIZE	HETAIRAI	MAUVAISE	OSIERIES
EUPNOEAS	HETAIRIA	MAUVEINE	OUABAINS
EUPNOEIC	HONOUREE	MAZAEDIA	OUAKARIS
EUROKIES	HOODOOED	MEIONITE	OUBAASES
EUROKOUS	HUAQUERO	METAIRIE	OUGUIYAS
EURONOTE	IBOGAINE	METANOIA	OUISTITI
EUROPIUM	ICEHOUSE	MEUNIERE	OUTARGUE
EUROZONE	IDEALISE	MIAOUING	OUTASITE
EUSOCIAL	IDEALIZE	MILIARIA	OUTEATEN
EUTAXIAS	IDEATION	MINUTIAE	OUTGUIDE

OUTHOUSE	POULAINE	SAPUCAIA	UNIONIZE
OUTQUOTE	PRIEDIEU	SAUTOIRE	UNSEELIE
OUTRAISE	QUAALUDE	SEAPIECE	URAEMIAS
OUTVALUE	QUEASIER	SEAQUAKE	URAEUSES
OUTVOICE	QUEAZIER	SEQUELAE	UREDINIA
OUVRIERE	QUEENIER	SEQUOIAS	URINEMIA
OVARIOLE	QUEENIES	SILIQUAE	USQUABAE
OVARIOUS	QUEENITE	SQUEEGEE	USQUEBAE
PAENULAE	QUEUEING	SUBAUDIO	USURIOUS
PAEONIES	QUIETIVE	TAENIATE	UXORIOUS
PAHAUTEA	QUIETUDE	TAENIOID	VIRAEMIA
PAHOEHOE	QUILLAIA	TAQUERIA	VOODOOED
PARANOEA	QUINIELA	TEAHOUSE	VOUDOUED
PARANOIA	RADIALIA	TENUIOUS	WEIGELIA
PAROEMIA	RAOULIAS	THIOUREA	ZABAIONE
PAROUSIA	REAROUSE	TOEPIECE	ZOIATRIA
PATOOTIE	RELEASEE	TOXAEMIA	ZOOECIUM
PAURAQUE	RENEAGUE	UBIETIES	ZOOGLEAE
PEEKABOO	RETIARII	UINTAITE	ZOOGLOEA
PEEKAPOO	ROULEAUS	UNEASIER	ZOOMANIA
PERIAGUA	ROULEAUX	UNIAXIAL	ZOONOMIA
PIHOIHOI	ROUSSEAU	UNIDEAED	
POACEOUS	SAOUARIS	UNIONISE	

Consonant doubles

The higher-scoring consonants can be just as awkward as vowels when they show up more than one at a time on your rack. The following lists give all the words with doubles of the three- and four-point letters (B, C, F, H, M, P, V, W and Y), excluding words containing other consonants – but note that there are no three-letter words with two Cs.

Words with duplicate B C F H M P V W Y and no other consonants

Two Bs	Two Cs
ABB	ACCA
BIB	CACA
BOB	CECA
BUB	COCA
EBB	COCO
ABBA	ECCE
ABBE	ECCO
BABA	CACAO
BABE	CAECA
BABU	COCOA
BIBE	ACACIA
BOAB	COOCOO
BOBA	
BOBO	
BOOB	
BUBA	
BUBO	
BUBU	
BABOO	
BAUBEE	
BEEBEE	
BOOBIE	
BOOBOO	
BOUBOU	
BUIBUI	

> ## *Note*
>
> Although words with more than two Cs have been excluded because they require blanks, it is nevertheless interesting to mention the unique COCCIC (pertaining to spherical bacterium) with four Cs.

Two Fs

EFF
IFF
OFF
FIEF
FIFE
OFFA
OFFIE
FOEFIE

Two Hs

HEH
HOH
HUH
HAHA
HOHA
HUHU

Note

Although words with more than two Fs have been excluded because they require blanks, FEOFFEE (one to whom a feudal state is granted) is an interesting seven-letter word.

Two Ms

MAM
MEM
MIM
MOM
MUM
UMM
AMMO
EMMA
IMAM
MAIM
MAMA
MEME
MEMO
MIME
MOME
MOMI
MUMU
UMMA
IMAUM
MAMEE
MAMIE
MIMEO
UMAMI
MAOMAO
MEEMIE
MUUMUU

Two Ps

APP
PAP
PEP
PIP
POP
PUP
OPPO
PAPA
PAPE
PEEP
PEPO
PIPA
PIPE
PIPI
POEP
POOP
POPE
PUPA
PUPU
APOOP
APPUI
OPEPE
PEEPE
POUPE
PUPAE
EPOPEE
PIOPIO
PIUPIU
EPOPOEIA

Two Vs

VAV
VIVA
VIVE
VIVO
EVOVAE

> ### Note
> EVOVAE (a Gregorian chant) has
> an alternative spelling EUOUAE,
> the latter being easily
> remembered by imagining the Us
> as Vs.

Two Ws

WAW
WOW
WAWA
WAWE
WOWEE
WEEWEE

Two Ys

YAY
AYAYA

> ### Note
> EPOPOEIA means the same as
> EPOPEE (an epic poem) and is also
> noteworthy as being one of only
> five eights with six vowels.

The awkward W and U combination

Having a U and W on the rack at the same time can be very awkward to deal with. Neither letter is worth retaining, yet there are relatively few words that contain both. So, although the words don't fit a vowel-heavy or a consonant-heavy theme, this is the best place for such a list in this book.

Three- to five-letter words containing a U and W

WUD	UNWET
WUS	UNWIT
WUZ	UNWON
	UPBOW
SWUM	VROUW
WAUK	WAGYU
WAUL	WAMUS
WAUR	WAUFF
WHUP	WAUGH
WUDU	WAULK
WULL	WHAUP
	WHAUR
AWFUL	WHUMP
DWAUM	WOFUL
KAWAU	WOJUS
SQUAW	WOULD
SWOUN	WOUND
SWUNG	WRUNG
UNLAW	WURST
UNMEW	WUSHU
UNSEW	WUSSY
UNWED	WUXIA

Heavy words

In contrast to light words, 'heavy' words have a high proportion of consonants. Arranged by word-length, these lists contain words with no vowels (and no Ys), words with Y as the only vowel, and six-letter words with only one vowel (AEIOUY). Plurals ending in S have not been included in these lists. Even if you have a rack of seven consonants you may only need an appropriate vowel on the board to use four or five of them.

Words with none of AEIOUY

CH	TSK
HM	TWP
MM	ZZZ
SH	BRRR
ST	GRRL
BRR	HMMM
CWM	PFFT
GRR	PSST
HMM	SHHH
MMM	CRWTH
NTH	CWTCH
PHT	GRRRL
PST	PHPHT
PWN	TSKTSK
SHH	

> ## 𝒩ote
> Words such as MMM, HMMM, and TSKTSK are unlikely to be valuable because they would need a blank to be played, and ZZZ even more so as it requires both blanks. And you are unlikely to want to waste two Ss in PSST. A word like CRWTH is much more useful with five different letters.

Words with only a Y as a vowel

BY	PRY	WYN	SPRY
FY	PYX	BYRL	SYNC
KY	RHY	CYST	SYND
MY	SHY	FYRD	SYPH
NY	SKY	GYMP	TRYP
CLY	SLY	HWYL	TYMP
CRY	SNY	HYMN	TYND
DRY	SPY	JYNX	TYPP
FLY	STY	KYND	WYCH
FRY	SWY	LYCH	WYND
GYM	SYN	LYNX	WYNN
GYP	THY	MYTH	XYST
HYP	TRY	RYND	YMPT
LYM	TYG	SCRY	CHYND
MYC	VLY	SKRY	CRYPT
NYM	WHY	SKYF	GHYLL
PLY	WRY	SKYR	GLYPH

GRYPT	MYRRH	SYNCH	RHYTHM
KYDST	NYMPH	SYNTH	SPHYNX
LYMPH	PSYCH	TRYST	
LYNCH	SYLPH	FLYSCH	

Words with two or more Ys as vowels

GYNY	HYPHY
TYPY	MYTHY
DRYLY	PYGMY
FLYBY	SHYLY
GYNNY	SLYLY
GYPPY	STYMY
GYPSY	THYMY

> ***Note***
> The plural of FLYBY is unusual in that it takes a straight –S for FLYBYS. You might like to note other similar words in this list: BYS, DRYS, NYS, PRYS, and WHYS – although NYS and PRYS are different words and not plurals of NY and PRY.

> ***Note***
> The plurals GLYCYLS and RHYTHMS, the verb form TSKTSKS, and the adverb NYMPHLY are the only sevens without any of AEIOU.

WRYLY	SPRYLY
XYLYL	SYLPHY
GLYCYL	SYZYGY
MYRRHY	

Six-letter words with one of AEIOU

BLANCH	CLENCH	FLITCH	KNIGHT
BLENCH	CLINCH	FRATCH	KNITCH
BLIGHT	CLUNCH	FRENCH	KRANTZ
BLINTZ	CLUTCH	FRICHT	KVETCH
BLOTCH	CRANCH	FRIGHT	LENGTH
BORSCH	CRANTS	FROWST	MENSCH
BORSHT	CRATCH	GLITCH	MONGST
BRANCH	CROTCH	GLUMPS	PHLEGM
BRICHT	CRUNCH	GLUNCH	PLANCH
BRIGHT	CRUTCH	GLUTCH	PLENCH
BROWST	CULTCH	GRINCH	PLIGHT
BRUNCH	DIRNDL	GROWTH	PLINTH
CATCHT	DRACHM	GRUMPH	PLONGD
CHINCH	DRENCH	GRUTCH	PRANCK
CHINTS	DROWND	HIGHTH	PROMPT
CHINTZ	FLANCH	KIRSCH	PUTSCH
CHRISM	FLENCH	KITSCH	PWNING
CHURCH	FLETCH	KLATCH	SCARPH
CLASPT	FLIGHT	KLEPHT	SCARTH
CLATCH	FLINCH	KNICKS	SCATCH

SCHELM	SHMUCK	SPLASH	STROMB
SCHISM	SHNAPS	SPLENT	STROND
SCHIST	SHRANK	SPLIFF	STRONG
SCHLEP	SHREWD	SPLINT	STROWN
SCHLUB	SHRIFT	SPLISH	STRUCK
SCHNOZ	SHRILL	SPLOSH	STRUNG
SCHORL	SHRIMP	SPLURT	STRUNT
SCHRIK	SHRINK	SPRACK	SWARTH
SCHROD	SHROFF	SPRANG	SWATCH
SCHTIK	SHROWD	SPRAWL	SWITCH
SCHTUM	SHRUNK	SPREDD	SWOWND
SCHTUP	SHTCHI	SPRENT	TCHICK
SCHULN	SHTETL	SPRING	THATCH
SCHUSS	SHTICK	SPRINT	THETCH
SCHWAG	SHTUCK	SPRITZ	THIRST
SCLAFF	SHTUMM	SPRONG	THRALL
SCLIFF	SHVITZ	SPRUNG	THRANG
SCORCH	SKARTH	SPRUSH	THRASH
SCOTCH	SKETCH	STANCH	THRAWN
SCOWTH	SKITCH	STANCK	THRESH
SCRAMB	SKLENT	STARCH	THRIFT
SCRAWB	SKLIFF	STENCH	THRILL
SCRAWL	SKRIMP	STITCH	THRIST
SCRAWM	SKRONK	STOWND	THRONG
SCRAWP	SKRUMP	STRACK	THROWN
SCRIMP	SLATCH	STRAFF	THRUSH
SCRIPT	SLIGHT	STRAMP	THRUST
SCROLL	SLUTCH	STRAND	THWACK
SCRORP	SMATCH	STRANG	THWART
SCROWL	SMIGHT	STRASS	TRENCH
SCRUFF	SMIRCH	STRATH	TROGGS
SCRUMP	SMUTCH	STRAWN	TROWTH
SCRUNT	SNATCH	STRESS	TSKING
SCULCH	SNITCH	STREWN	TWIGHT
SCULPT	SPARTH	STRICH	TWITCH
SCUTCH	SPELTZ	STRICK	WARMTH
SHLEPP	SPERST	STRICT	WHILST
SHLOCK	SPETCH	STRIFT	WHISHT
SHLONG	SPHINX	STRING	WRENCH
SHLUMP	SPIGHT	STRIPT	WRETCH
SHMOCK	SPILTH	STROLL	WRIGHT

SECTION 6

BONUS WORDS

....

- Using all of your letters in a single turn is usually the best way to really boost your score, especially using the lower-scoring letters.

- The 50-point bonus that you get for using all the letters on your rack is likely to exceed any other score except that from an exceptionally high-scoring word with a power tile (JQXZ) reaping the points from a combination of premium squares.

- For this reason, any serious Scrabble player should devote serious effort to mastering 'bonus words' – words of seven or eight letters that will allow you to empty your rack in one go.

- This section presents the most likely bonus words in a way that will make them easy to learn and recall, by grouping them together according to common sets of letters (stems).

- There are also lists of the top 1000 most likely seven-letter words and most likely eight-letter words which, by definition, you are more likely to get given the Scrabble letter pool. These lists neatly complement the bonus word sets for a well-rounded bonus word vocabulary.

- Finally, all of the possible seven-letter anagram couplets are provided because it is often easier to recall a pair of anagrams than it is a singleton. Familiarity with these will also prompt unusual anagrams of common words such as FEATHER and TEREFAH.

Stems and mnemonics

Knowing whether the letters on your rack can be used to form a word that will use up all your tiles gives you a great advantage in a game. If you know that there is a seven- or eight-letter word that fits your letters, then it's simply a matter of finding the right word from the letters. If, on the other hand, you know that there isn't a valid word that you can fit on the board, you won't need to waste time looking for one. One invaluable way of knowing whether your rack can furnish you with a bonus word is to be aware of 'stems'. Stems are groups of six and seven letters which combine with one more letter to form a valid word. This can be a daunting task, but it's made much easier if you concentrate only on the stems that are both likely and rewarding (ie those that are most common, and which will combine with many letters). In the following lists, the top 50 six-letter stems and the top 20 seven-letter stems have been determined for you, based on an algorithm of the likelihood of the stem occurring and the probability of that stem yielding a bonus word.

One way to help you remember which letters combine with which stems is through the use of 'mnemonics'. To create a mnemonic, identify the letters that combine with a given stem, and arrange those letters into a short phrase or sentence. It doesn't matter if you have to repeat some of the letters. Then find a common or easy-to-spot word that can be made from the letters of the stem that could possibly be connected to the phrase or sentence. In other words, establish a link between the stem and the phrase. For example, the six-letter stem **AEINRT** goes with **B C D E F G H I J K L M N O P R S T U W**. A common word that can be made from the letters of the AEINRT stem is RETAIN. So for the sentence, you might come up with: Keep light brown ducks from Jim, the link being RETAIN and KEEP.

   RETAIN - Keep light brown ducks from Jim

Many veteran Scrabble players will have their own mnemonics, but a suggested mnemonic phrase has been provided for each six-letter stem in this book to save you the effort. However, it can be fun compiling your own, and the more personal a phrase is, the more likely you are to remember it.

Six-letter stems

The 50 stems given here are derived using an algorithm which was originally developed by American Mike Baron to assess the usefulness of each stem for Scrabble play. It is based on the probability of the six-letter stem being drawn and the probability of any seventh letter being drawn that yields a seven-letter word, given the letter distribution of the set. The first list here shows the rankings of usefulness: the most useful stem is AEINRT, followed by AEINST, and so on. Against each stem is shown a suggested mnemonic word that can be made from the letters of the stem as a keyword prompt.

The subsequent pages show each of the six-letter stems arranged in two subsections:

Part one: The 30 stems where eight-letter words have also been given for combinations where there are no seven-letter words yielded.

Part two: The 20 stems without any associated eight-letter words being shown. This is because there are too many such eights for these sets and, anyway, most of the relevant ones will be listed among the 20 seven-letter stems.

In both cases, the sets are shown in alphabetical order of the stem, along with their ranking of usefulness, the letters which can be added to the stem, and the seven-letter words which can be formed. There will be seven-letter words that appear in more than one set but that can only serve to reinforce the learning.

The 50 six-letter stems in order of ranking

A mnemonic keyword is given for each set which is either a valid word or, if in brackets, a made-up word that best serves as a keyword even if there might be valid words possible. Those that also have associated eight-letter words shown, and are therefore listed in part one, are indicated.

1	AEINRT	RETAIN	plus eights
2	AEINST	(SATINE)	plus eights
3	AEEIRT	(EATIER)	
4	AEIRST	SATIRE	plus eights
5	EIORST	(TORIES)	plus eights
6	ADEINR	RAINED	plus eights
7	EINORS	SENIOR	plus eights
8	AEILNR	NAILER	plus eights
9	AEORST	ORATES	
10	AEINRS	SARNIE	
11	AENORT	ORNATE	
12	EEINRT	ENTIRE	
13	EINOST	TONIES	
14	AENRST	(ANTERS)	plus eights
15	EINORT	TONIER	
16	AEILRT	RETAIL	
17	AEGINR	REGAIN	plus eights
18	AEEINT	(NEATIE)	plus eights
19	AEILNT	ENTAIL	
20	ADEIRT	TIRADE	
21	AEIORT	OATIER	
22	ADEIRS	RAISED	plus eights
23	EILNOR	(INROLE)	plus eights
24	ENORST	TONERS	plus eights
25	AEINOT	(ATONIE)	
26	AENORS	REASON	plus eights
27	AEIOST	(OATIES)	plus eights
28	DEINOR	IRONED	plus eights
29	EINRST	INTERS	
30	ADEILR	RAILED	plus eights
31	AEILRS	(AILERS)	
32	EILORT	LOITER	plus eights
33	AINORT	RATION	
34	EEIRST	RESITE	
35	AEINOR	(AIRONE)	
36	AEERST	EATERS	plus eights
37	AEILNS	ALINES	plus eights

38	AEINOS	(ANOSIE)	plus eights
39	EILOST	(ELIOTS)	plus eights
40	ADEINS	(SANDIE)	plus eights
41	EILNOS	(NOLIES)	plus eights
42	AENOST	ATONES	plus eights
43	EILNOT	(NOLITE)	plus eights
44	DEIORS	DORISE	plus eights
45	AEILST	SALTIE	
46	ADEIST	SAITED	
47	EINRTU	UNITER	plus eights
48	ADEILS	LADIES	plus eights
49	ADEORS	ADORES	
50	AELORT	LORATE	plus eights

ADEILR: The DERAIL seven-letter set
(Ranked No.30)

A
RADIALE

B
BALDIER
BEDRAIL
BLADIER
BRAILED
RAILBED
RIDABLE

C
DECRIAL
RADICEL
RADICLE

D
DIEDRAL
DRAILED
LADDIER

E
LEADIER

G
GLADIER
GLAIRED

DERAIL

I
DELIRIA
IRIDEAL

L
DALLIER
DIALLER
RALLIED

O
DARIOLE

P
LIPREAD
PEDRAIL
PREDIAL

R
LARDIER

S
DERAILS
DIALERS
REDIALS
SIDERAL

T
DILATER
REDTAIL
TRAILED
TRIALED

U
UREDIAL

V
RIVALED
VALIDER

Y
READILY

Note

A mnemonic to help remember which letters DERAIL combines with is:
SO PRODUCTIVITY GETS DISABLED
Note the association of the keyword DERAIL with disabling productivity. The SO is arguably superfluous because S and O are used elsewhere but it creates a stronger link.

The DERAIL eights where there are no sevens.

These are the eights to watch out for when you have DERAIL and a seventh
letter that doesn't yield a seven.

F

+A FAIRLEAD
+C FILECARD
    FRICADEL
+I AIRFIELD
+N FILANDER
+O FORELAID

H

+A HEADRAIL
    RAILHEAD
+C HERALDIC
+D DIHEDRAL
+N HARDLINE

J

NONE

K

+L LARDLIKE
+R DARKLIER

M

+E REMAILED
    REMEDIAL
+P IMPARLED
+S DISMALER
+Y DREAMILY

N

+B BILANDER
+E RENAILED
+F FILANDER
+G DANGLIER
    DEARLING
    DRAGLINE
+H HARDLINE
+N INLANDER
+S ISLANDER

Q

NONE

W

+D WADDLIER
+R DRAWLIER

X

+O EXORDIAL

Z

+E REALIZED
+I LAIRIZED
+Y DIALYZER

ADEILS: The LADIES seven-letter set
(Ranked No.48)

A
ALIASED

H
HALIDES

N
DENIALS
SNAILED

R
DERAILS
DIALERS
REDIALS
SIDERAL

B
BALDIES
DIABLES
DISABLE

I
DAILIES
LIAISED
SEDILIA

O
DEASOIL
ISOLEAD

S
AIDLESS
DEASILS

C
SCAILED

K
SKAILED

T
DETAILS
DILATES

D
DAIDLES
LADDIES

L **A** **D** **I** **E** **S**

U
AUDILES
DEASIUL
DUALISE

E
AEDILES
DEISEAL

L
DALLIES
DISLEAL
LALDIES
SALLIED

P
ALIPEDS
ELAPIDS
LAIPSED
LAPIDES
PAIDLES
PALSIED
PLEIADS

V
DEVISAL

F
DISLEAF

Y
DIALYSE
EYLIADS

G
SILAGED

M
MAELIDS
MEDIALS
MISDEAL
MISLEAD

Note
A mnemonic to help remember which letters LADIES combines with is:
CURVY GIRLS TAKE PART IN BOND FILM SHOOT
Note the association of the keyword LADIES with GIRLS and BOND FILM.

The LADIES eights where there are no sevens.

These are the eights to watch out for when you have LADIES and a seventh letter that doesn't yield a seven.

J

NONE

Q

+U   SQUAILED

W

+H   WHAISLED
+K   SIDEWALK
+L   SIDEWALL
+Y   SLIDEWAY

X

+Y   DYSLEXIA

Z

+O   DIAZOLES
     SLEAZOID
+U   DUALIZES
+Y   DIALYZES

ADEINR: The RAINED seven-letter set
(Ranked No.6)

A
ARANEID

B
BANDIER
BRAINED

C
CAIRNED
CARNIED
DANCIER

D
DANDIER
DRAINED

F
FRIANDE

G
AREDING
DEARING
DERAIGN
EARDING
GRADINE
GRAINED
READING

H
HANDIER

I
DENARII

M
ADERMIN
INARMED

N
NARDINE

R A I N E D

O
ANEROID

P
PARDINE

R
DRAINER
RANDIER

S
RANDIES
SANDIER
SARDINE

T
ANTIRED
DETRAIN
TRAINED

U
UNAIRED
URANIDE

V
INVADER
RAVINED

Note

A mnemonic to help remember which letters RAINED combines with is:
STORM GIVING BAD FA CUP MATCH
Note the association of the keyword RAINED with STORM.

The RAINED eights where there are no sevens.

These are the eights to watch out for when you have RAINED and a seventh letter that doesn't yield a seven.

E

+C	DERACINE
+F	FREDAINE
+G	REGAINED
+L	RENAILED
+M	REMAINED
+P	PINDAREE
+S	ARSENIDE
	DENARIES
	DRAISENE
	NEARSIDE
+T	DETAINER
	RETAINED
+V	REINVADE

J

NONE

K

+G	DAKERING
+P	KIDNAPER

L

+B	BILANDER
+E	RENAILED
+F	FILANDER
+G	DANGLIER
	DEARLING
	DRAGLINE
+H	HARDLINE
+N	INLANDER
+S	ISLANDER

Q

NONE

W

NONE

X

NONE

Y

+G	DERAYING
	READYING
	YEARDING
+M	DAIRYMEN
+S	SYNEDRIA
+V	VINEYARD

Z

+M	ZEMINDAR
+N	RENDZINA
+O	ANODIZER

ADEINS: The SANDIE seven-letter set
(Ranked No.40)

A
NAIADES

B
BANDIES
BASINED

C
CANDIES
INCASED

D
DANDIES
SDAINED

E
ANISEED

F
FADEINS

G
AGNISED

K
KANDIES

L
DENIALS
SNAILED

S A N D I E

M
DEMAINS
MAIDENS
MEDIANS
MEDINAS
SIDEMAN

N
DANNIES

O
ADONISE
ANODISE
SODAINE

P
PANDIES
PANSIED
SPAINED

R
RANDIES
SANDIER
SARDINE

S
SDAINES

T
DESTAIN
DETAINS
INSTEAD
NIDATES
SAINTED
SATINED
STAINED

V
INVADES

W
DEWANIS

Note

A mnemonic to help remember which letters SANDIE combines with is:
SANDY GRAVEL KEEPS MY WET FEET COMFORTABLE
Note the association of the keyword SANDIE with SANDY.

The SANDIE eights where there are no sevens.

These are the eights to watch out for when you have SANDIE and a seventh letter that doesn't yield a seven.

H

+B	BANISHED
+C	ECHIDNAS
	INCHASED
+G	DEASHING
	HEADINGS
	SHEADING
+K	SKINHEAD
+O	ADHESION
+P	DEANSHIP
	HEADPINS
	PINHEADS
+S	DANISHES
	SHANDIES
+T	HANDIEST
+V	VANISHED

I

+C	SCIAENID
+F	SANIFIED
+M	AMIDINES
	DIAMINES
+N	SANIDINE
+R	DRAISINE
+T	ADENITIS
	DAINTIES
+Z	DIAZINES.

J

NONE

Q

NONE

U

+B	UNBIASED
+L	UNSAILED
+M	MAUNDIES
+N	UNSAINED
+R	DENARIUS
	UNRAISED
	URANIDES
+T	AUDIENTS
	SINUATED

X

+N	DISANNEX
+O	DIOXANES

Y

+C	CYANIDES
	CYANISED
+K	KYANISED
+M	DYNAMISE
+R	SYNEDRIA
+T	DESYATIN

Z

+A	ZENAIDAS
+I	DIAZINES
+O	ADONIZES
	ANODIZES

ADEIRS: The RAISED seven-letter set
(Ranked No.22)

A.
ARAISED

B.
ABIDERS
BARDIES
BRAISED
DARBIES
SEABIRD
SIDEBAR

C.
CARDIES
DARCIES
RADICES
SIDECAR

E.
DEARIES
READIES

F.
FARSIDE
FRAISED

G.
AGRISED

H.
AIRSHED
DASHIER
DEHAIRS
HARDIES
SHADIER

I.
AIRSIDE
DAIRIES
DIARIES
DIARISE

K.
DAIKERS
DARKIES

L.
DERAILS
DIALERS
REDIALS
SIDERAL

M.
ADMIRES
MARDIES
MISREAD
SEDARIM
SIDEARM

N.
RANDIES
SANDIER
SARDINE

R A I S E D

O.
RADIOES
ROADIES
SOREDIA

P.
ASPIRED
DESPAIR
DIAPERS
PRAISED

R.
ARRIDES
RAIDERS

T.
ARIDEST
ASTERID
ASTRIDE
DIASTER
DISRATE
STAIDER
STAIRED
TARDIES
TIRADES

U.
RESIDUA

V.
ADVISER
VARDIES

X.
RADIXES

Note

A mnemonic to help remember which letters RAISED combines with is:
MORE FOR BLOCKING UP TAX HAVEN
Note the keyword RAISED becomes part of the phrase in this case: RAISED
MORE FOR...

The RAISED eights where there are no sevens.

These are the eights to watch out for when you have RAISED and a seventh letter that doesn't yield a seven.

D

+G	DISGRADE
+H	DIEHARDS
+I	DIARISED
+L	DIEDRALS
+M	DISARMED
	MISDREAD
+N	SARDINED
+O	ROADSIDE
	SIDEROAD
+P	DISPREAD
+T	DISRATED
+U	RADIUSED
+W	SIDEWARD

J

+E	JADERIES
+M	JEMIDARS

Q

+U	QUERIDAS

S

+B	SEABIRDS
	SIDEBARS
+C	SIDECARS
+F	FARSIDES
+H	AIRSHEDS
	RADISHES
+I	AIRSIDES
	DIARISES
+M	MISREADS
	SIDEARMS
+N	ARIDNESS
	SARDINES
+P	DESPAIRS
+T	ASTERIDS
	DIASTERS
	DISASTER
	DISRATES
+U	RADIUSES
	SUDARIES
+V	ADVISERS
	DISSAVER

W

+B	BAWDRIES
	DAWBRIES
+D	SIDEWARD
+H	DISHWARE
	RAWHIDES
+P	RIPSAWED
+R	SWARDIER
+T	TAWDRIES

Y

+H	HAYRIDES
+L	DIALYSER
+M	MIDYEARS
+N	SYNEDRIA

Z

+I	DIARIZES

AEEINT: The NEATIE seven-letter set
(Ranked No.18)

A
TAENIAE

L
LINEATE

R
ARENITE
RETINAE
TRAINEE

T
TAENITE

B
BETAINE

V
NAIVETE

K
KETAINE

N E A T I E

M
ETAMINE
MATINEE

S
ETESIAN

Note

A mnemonic to help remember which letters NEATIE combines with is:
SMART TV TASKBAR ALARM
Note the association of the keyword NEATIE (NEAT) with SMART.

The NEATIE eights where there are no sevens.

These are the eights to watch out for when you have NEATIE and a seventh letter that doesn't yield a seven.

C

+G	AGENETIC
+H	ECHINATE
+P	PATIENCE
+R	CENTIARE
	CREATINE
	INCREATE
	ITERANCE
+S	CINEASTE
+V	ENACTIVE
+X	EXITANCE

D

+D	DETAINED
+E	DETAINEE
+L	DATELINE
	ENTAILED
	LINEATED
+M	DEMENTIA
+P	DIAPENTE
+R	DETAINER
	RETAINED
+S	ANDESITE
+W	ANTIWEED

E

+D	DETAINEE

F

NONE

G

+C	AGENETIC
+L	GALENITE
	GELATINE
	LEGATINE
+M	GEMINATE
+N	ANTIGENE
+R	ENARGITE
	GRATINEE
	INTERAGE
+S	SAGENITE
+V	AGENTIVE
	NEGATIVE
+X	EXIGEANT

H

+B	THEBAINE
+C	ECHINATE
+M	HEMATEIN
	HEMATINE
+R	ATHERINE
	HERNIATE

I

+R	INERTIAE

J

NONE

N

+G	ANTIGENE
+V	VENETIAN

O

NONE

P

+C	PATIENCE
+D	DIAPENTE
+L	PETALINE
	TAPELINE
+R	APERIENT
+T	PIANETTE

Q

NONE

U

NONE

W

+D	ANTIWEED

X

+C	EXITANCE
+G	EXIGEANT

Y

+B	AYENBITE

Z

+T	TETANIZE

AEERST: The EATERS seven-letter set
(Ranked No.36)

A
AERATES

B
BEATERS
BERATES
REBATES

C
CERATES
CREATES
ECARTES
SECRETA

D
DEAREST
DERATES
ESTRADE
REASTED
REDATES
SEDATER
STEARED
TASERED

F
AFREETS
FEASTER

G
ERGATES
RESTAGE

H
AETHERS
HEATERS
REHEATS

I
AERIEST
SERIATE

E A T E R S

K
RETAKES
SAKERET

L
ELATERS
REALEST
RELATES
RESLATE
STEALER

M
REMATES
RETEAMS
STEAMER
TEAMERS

N
EARNEST
EASTERN
NEAREST
RATEENS
STERANE

O
ROSEATE

P
EPATERS
REPEATS
RETAPES

R
RETEARS
SERRATE
TEARERS

S
EASTERS
RESEATS
SAETERS
SEAREST
SEATERS
STEARES
TEASERS
TESSERA

T
ESTREAT
RESTATE
RETASTE

U
AUSTERE

W
SWEATER

X
RETAXES

𝒩ote
A mnemonic to help remember which letters EATERS combines with is:
SAMPLING BOXFUL OF DUCK WITH FRUIT
Note the association of the keyword EATERS with food items.

The EATERS eights where there are no sevens.

These are the eights to watch out for when you have EATERS and a seventh letter that doesn't yield a seven.

E

+D RESEATED
+G EAGEREST
    ETAGERES
    STEERAGE
+I EATERIES
+L TEASELER
+N SERENATE
+R ARRESTEE
+S ESTERASE
    TESSERAE

J

+N SERJEANT

Q

NONE

V

+H THREAVES
+I EVIRATES
+N AVENTRES
    VETERANS
+O OVEREATS
+R AVERTERS
    TRAVERSE

Y

+D ESTRAYED
+I YEASTIER
+L EASTERLY
+M METAYERS

Z

+P TRAPEZES
+S ERSATZES

AEGINR: The REGAIN seven-letter set
(Ranked No.17)

A
ANERGIA

H
HEARING

N
AGINNER
EARNING
ENGRAIN
GRANNIE
NEARING

S
ANGRIES
EARINGS
ERASING
GAINERS
GRAINES
REAGINS
REGAINS
REGINAS
SEARING
SERINGA

B
BEARING

K
REAKING

C
ANERGIC
GRECIAN

R E G A I N

D
AREDING
DEARING
DERAIGN
EARDING
GRADINE
GRAINED
READING

L
ALIGNER
ENGRAIL
LAERING
LEARING
NARGILE
REALIGN
REGINAL

O
ORIGANE

P
REAPING

T
GRANITE
GRATINE
INGRATE
TANGIER
TEARING

E
REGINAE

M
GERMAIN
GERMINA
MANGIER
MEARING
REAMING

R
ANGRIER
EARRING
GRAINER
RANGIER
REARING

V
REAVING
VINEGAR

F
FEARING

W
WEARING

G
GEARING
NAGGIER

Z
ZINGARE

𝒩ote

A mnemonic to help remember which letters REGAIN combines with is:
GET BACK A DOZEN WOLVES FROM SHOP
Note the association of the keyword REGAIN with GET BACK.

The REGAIN eights where there are no sevens.

These are the eights to watch out for when you have REGAIN and a seventh letter that doesn't yield a seven.

[I]

+C	REAGINIC
+D	DEAIRING
+E	AEGIRINE
+L	GAINLIER
+M	IMAGINER
	MIGRAINE
+N	ARGININE
+R	GRAINIER

[J]

| +L | JANGLIER |

[Q]

NONE

[U]

| +M | GERANIUM |
| | MAUNGIER |

[X]

+L	RELAXING
+T	RETAXING
+W	REWAXING

[Y]

+B	BERAYING
+D	DERAYING
	READYING
	YEARDING
+F	AREFYING
+L	LAYERING
	RELAYING
	YEARLING
+N	RENAYING
	YEARNING
+P	REPAYING
+S	RESAYING
	SYNERGIA
+V	VINEGARY
+W	WEARYING

AEILNR: The NAILER seven-letter set
(Ranked No.8)

C
CARLINE

E
ALIENER

G
ALIGNER
ENGRAIL
LAERING
LEARING
NARGILE
REALIGN
REGINAL

H
HERNIAL
INHALER

I
AIRLINE

K
LANKIER

L
RALLINE

N A I L E R

M
MANLIER
MARLINE
MINERAL
RAILMEN

O
AILERON
ALERION
ALIENOR

P
PEARLIN
PLAINER
PRALINE

R
LARNIER

S
ALINERS
NAILERS
RENAILS

T
ENTRAIL
LATRINE
RATLINE
RELIANT
RETINAL
TRENAIL

V
RAVELIN

W
LAWNIER

X
RELAXIN

Y
INLAYER
NAILERY

𝒩ote

A mnemonic to help remember which letters NAILER combines with is:
STRIKES PEG WITH VERY COMPLEX HIT
Note the association of the keyword NAILER with striking something.

The NAILER eights where there are no sevens.

These are the eights to watch out for when you have NAILER and a seventh letter that doesn't yield a seven.

A

+B	INARABLE
+G	GERANIAL
	REGALIAN
+P	AIRPLANE
+U	AURELIAN
+V	VALERIAN

B

+A	INARABLE
+D	BILANDER
+G	BLEARING
+H	HIBERNAL
+I	BILINEAR
+K	BARNLIKE
+S	RINSABLE
+U	RUINABLE

D

+B	BILANDER
+E	RENAILED
+F	FILANDER
+G	DANGLIER
	DEARLING
	DRAGLINE
+H	HARDLINE
+N	INLANDER
+S	ISLANDER

F

+D	FILANDER
+E	FLANERIE
+G	FINAGLER
+M	INFLAMER
	RIFLEMAN
+N	INFERNAL
+O	FORELAIN
+T	INFLATER
+U	FRAULEIN

J

+G	JANGLIER

N

+C	ENCRINAL
+D	INLANDER
+F	INFERNAL
+G	LEARNING
+T	INTERNAL

Q

NONE

U

+A	AURELIAN
+B	RUINABLE
+F	FRAULEIN
+H	INHAULER
+M	LEMURIAN
+S	LUNARIES
+T	AUNTLIER
	RETINULA
	TENURIAL

Z

NONE

AEILNS: The ALINES seven-letter set
(Ranked No.37)

B
LESBIAN

H
INHALES

P
ALPINES
PINEALS
SPANIEL
SPLENIA

T
EASTLIN
ELASTIN
ENTAILS
NAILSET
SALIENT
SALTINE
SLAINTE
STANIEL
TENAILS

C
INLACES
SANICLE
SCALENI

K
ALKINES

L
AINSELL

R
ALINERS
NAILERS
RENAILS

D
DENIALS
SNAILED

E
SEALINE

A L I N E S

U
INSULAE
INULASE

V
ALEVINS
VALINES

F
FINALES

M
ISLEMAN
MALINES
MENIALS
SEMINAL

S
SALINES
SILANES

G
LEASING
LINAGES
SEALING

O
ANISOLE

W
LAWINES

X
ALEXINS

Y
ELYSIAN

Note

A mnemonic to help remember which letters ALINES combines with is:
PUTS ROWS OF FOXGLOVES BY MY DUCKHOUSE
Note the association of the keyword ALINES with putting in rows.

The ALINES eights where there are no sevens.

These are the eights to watch out for when you have ALINES and a seventh letter that doesn't yield a seven.

A

+B	BANALISE
+C	CANALISE
+N	ALANINES
	ANNALISE
+S	NASALISE
+Z	NASALIZE

I

+C	SALICINE
+F	FINALISE
+M	ALIENISM
	MILESIAN
+N	ANILINES
+R	AIRLINES
	SNAILIER
+S	SALINISE
+T	ALIENIST
	LATINISE
	LITANIES
+Z	SALINIZE

J

+V	JAVELINS
+W	JAWLINES

N

+A	ALANINES
	ANNALISE
+D	ANNELIDS
	LINDANES
+E	SELENIAN
+F	FLANNIES
+G	EANLINGS
	LEANINGS
+I	ANILINES
+L	NAINSELL
+M	LINESMAN
	MELANINS
+O	SOLANINE
+Y	INSANELY

Q

NONE

Z

+A	NASALIZE
+G	SLEAZING
+I	SALINIZE
+S	LAZINESS

AEINOS: The ANOSIE seven-letter set
(Ranked No.38)

C
ACINOSE

L
ANISOLE

P
EPINAOS
SENOPIA

S
ANOESIS

D
ADONISE
ANODISE
SODAINE

A N O S I E

T
ATONIES

V
EVASION

G
AGONIES
AGONISE

M
ANOMIES

R
ERASION

Z
AZIONES

Note
As there are no vowels among the combining letters it is not possible to create a mnemonic.

The ANOSIE eights where there are no sevens.

These are the eights to watch out for when you have ANOSIE and a seventh letter that doesn't yield a seven.

A

NONE

B

+D BEDSONIA
+G BEGONIAS
+N BESONIAN
+R BARONIES
   SEAROBIN
+T BOTANIES
   BOTANISE
   NIOBATES
   OBEISANT

E

+P PAEONIES

F

+R FARINOSE

H

+D ADHESION
+P APHONIES

I

NONE

J

NONE

K

+L KAOLINES
+S OAKINESS

N

+B BESONIAN
+C CANONISE
+G ANGINOSE
   GANOINES
+L SOLANINE
+P SAPONINE
+R NONARIES
   RAISONNE
+T ENATIONS
   SONATINE

O

NONE

Q

NONE

U

+M MOINEAUS

W

+M WOMANISE

X

+D DIOXANES
+L SILOXANE
+S SAXONIES
+T SAXONITE
+Z OXAZINES

Y

NONE

AEINRT: The RETAIN seven-letter set
(Ranked No.1)

B.
ATEBRIN

C.
CANTIER
CERATIN
CERTAIN
CREATIN
CRINATE
NACRITE
TACRINE

D.
ANTIRED
DETRAIN
TRAINED

E.
ARENITE
RETINAE
TRAINEE

F.
FAINTER
FENITAR

G.
GRANITE
GRATINE
INGRATE
TANGIER
TEARING

H.
HAIRNET
INEARTH
THERIAN

I.
INERTIA

R E T A I N

J.
JANTIER
NARTJIE

K.
KERATIN

L.
ENTRAIL
LATRINE
RATLINE
RELIANT
RETINAL
TRENAIL

M.
MERANTI
MINARET
RAIMENT

N.
ENTRAIN
TRANNIE

O.
NOTAIRE
OTARINE

P.
PAINTER
PERTAIN
REPAINT

R.
RETRAIN
TERRAIN
TRAINER

S.
ANESTRI
ANTSIER
NASTIER
RATINES
RESIANT
RETAINS
RETINAS
RETSINA
STAINER
STARNIE
STEARIN

T.
INTREAT
ITERANT
NATTIER
NITRATE
TARTINE
TERTIAN

U.
RUINATE
TAURINE
URANITE
URINATE

W.
TAWNIER
TINWARE

Note

A mnemonic to help remember which letters RETAIN combines with is:
KEEP LIGHT BROWN DUCKS FROM JIM
Note the association of the keyword RETAIN with KEEP.

The RETAIN eights where there are no sevens.

These are the eights to watch out for when you have RETAIN and a seventh letter that doesn't yield a seven.

A		**Q**		**X**	
+B	ATABRINE	+U	ANTIQUER	+C	XERANTIC
	RABATINE		QUAINTER	+G	RETAXING
+C	CARINATE			+P	EXPIRANT
	CRANIATE	**V**			
+D	DENTARIA	+C	NAVICERT	**Y**	
	RAINDATE	+G	AVERTING	+L	INTERLAY
+G	AERATING		GRIEVANT	+M	TYRAMINE
+J	NAARTJIE		TAVERING		
+M	ANIMATER		VINTAGER	**Z**	
	MARINATE	+L	INTERVAL	+A	ATRAZINE
+O	AERATION	+R	VERATRIN	+I	TRIAZINE
+P	ANTIRAPE	+U	VAUNTIER	+O	NOTARIZE
+S	ANTISERA	+W	VAWNTIER		
	ARTESIAN				
	RATANIES				
	RESINATA				
	SANTERIA				
	SEATRAIN				
+T	ATTAINER				
	REATTAIN				
+U	INAURATE				
+W	ANTIWEAR				
+Z	ATRAZINE				

AEINST: The SATINE seven-letter set
(Ranked No.2)

A

ENTASIA
TAENIAS

B

BANTIES
BASINET
BESAINT
BESTAIN

C

ACETINS
CANIEST
CINEAST

D

DESTAIN
DETAINS
INSTEAD
NIDATES
SAINTED
SATINED
STAINED

E

ETESIAN

F

FAINEST
FANSITE
NAIFEST

G

EASTING
EATINGS
GAINEST
GENISTA
INGATES
INGESTA
SEATING
TAGINES
TANGIES
TEASING
TSIGANE

S A T I N E

H

SHEITAN
STHENIA

I

ISATINE

J

JANTIES
TAJINES

K

INTAKES
KENTIAS
TANKIES

L

EASTLIN
ELASTIN
ENTAILS
NAILSET
SALIENT
SALTINE
SLAINTE
STANIEL
TENAILS

M

ETAMINS
INMATES
MAINEST
MANTIES
TAMEINS
TAMINES

N

INANEST
NANITES
STANINE
TANNIES

O

ATONIES

P

PANTIES
PATINES
SAPIENT
SPINATE

R

ANESTRI
ANTSIER
NASTIER
RATINES
RESIANT
RETAINS
RETINAS
RETSINA
STAINER
STARNIE
STEARIN

S

ENTASIS
NASTIES
SEITANS
SESTINA
TANSIES
TISANES

T

INSTATE
SATINET

U

AUNTIES
SINUATE

V

NAIVEST
NATIVES
VAINEST

W

AWNIEST
TAWNIES
WANIEST
WANTIES

X

ANTISEX
SEXTAIN

Z

ZANIEST
ZEATINS

Note

A mnemonic to help remember which letters SATINE combines with is best geared to the two letters that it does not combine with, thus: **NOT Your Q**. That reminds you that it goes with everything but not Y Q.

The SATINE eights where there are no sevens.

These are the eights to watch out for when you have SATINE and a seventh letter that doesn't yield a seven.

+U	ANTIQUES	+C	CYANITES
	QUANTISE	+D	DESYATIN
		+G	YEASTING
		+K	KYANITES
		+P	EPINASTY
		+W	YAWNIEST

AEIOST: The OATIES seven-letter set
(Ranked No.27)

B
BOATIES

K
OAKIEST

N
ATONIES

S
SOSATIE

C
SOCIATE

L
ISOLATE

P
ATOPIES
OPIATES

T
OATIEST
OSTIATE
TOASTIE

D
IODATES
TOADIES

O A T I E S

Z
AZOTISE

G
GOATIES

M
AMOSITE
ATOMIES
ATOMISE
OSMIATE

R
OARIEST
OTARIES
ROASTIE

Note

As there are no vowels among the combining letters it is not possible to create a mnemonic.

The OATIES eights where there are no sevens.

These are the eights to watch out for when you have OATIES and a seventh letter that doesn't yield a seven.

A
NONE

E
+R ETAERIOS

F
+L FOLIATES
+M FOAMIEST

H
+C ACHIOTES
    TOISEACH
+L HALIOTES
+R HOARIEST

I
NONE

J
+R JAROSITE

O
NONE

Q
NONE

U
+G AGOUTIES
+R OUTRAISE
    SAUTOIRE
+T OUTASITE

V
+B OBVIATES
+L VIOLATES
+N STOVAINE
+R TRAVOISE
    VIATORES
    VOTARIES

W
+B BIOWASTE

X
+D OXIDATES
+G GEOTAXIS
+M TOXEMIAS
+N SAXONITE

Y
NONE

AEIRST: The SATIRE seven-letter set
(Ranked No.4)

A
ARISTAE
ASTERIA
ATRESIA

B
BAITERS
BARITES
REBAITS
TERBIAS

C
ATRESIC
CRISTAE
RACIEST
STEARIC

D
ARIDEST
ASTERID
ASTRIDE
DIASTER
DISRATE
STAIDER
STAIRED
TARDIES
TIRADES

E
AERIEST
SERIATE

F
FAIREST

G
AGISTER
AIGRETS
GAITERS
SEAGIRT
STAGIER
STRIGAE
TIRAGES
TRIAGES

S A T I R E

H
HASTIER
SHERIAT

I
AIRIEST
IRISATE

K
ARKITES
KARITES

L
REALIST
RETAILS
SALTIER
SALTIRE
SLATIER
TAILERS

M
IMARETS
MAESTRI
MAISTER
MASTIER
MISRATE
SEMITAR
SMARTIE

N
ANESTRI
ANTSIER
NASTIER
RATINES
RESIANT
RETAINS
RETINAS
RETSINA
STAINER
STARNIE
STEARIN

O
OARIEST
OTARIES
ROASTIE

P
PAIREST
PARTIES
PASTIER
PIASTER
PIASTRE
PIRATES
PRATIES
TRAIPSE

R
ARTSIER
SERRATI
TARRIES
TARSIER

S
ARSIEST
ARTSIES
SAIREST
SATIRES
TIRASSE

T
ARTIEST
ARTISTE
ATTIRES
IRATEST
RATITES
STRIATE
TASTIER
TERTIAS

V
RAVIEST
TAIVERS
VASTIER
VERITAS

W
WAISTER
WAITERS
WARIEST
WASTRIE

> ### Note
> A mnemonic to help remember which letters SATIRE combines with is:
> **DEVELOPING CRAFTSMANSHIP OF WIT FOR BOOK**
> Note the association of the keyword SATIRE with WIT.

The SATIRE eights where there are no sevens.

These are the eights to watch out for when you have SATIRE and a seventh letter that doesn't yield a seven.

J.

+N NARTJIES
+O JAROSITE

Q.

NONE

U.

+C SURICATE
+H THESAURI
+L URALITES
+M MURIATES
    SEMITAUR
+N RUINATES
    TAURINES
    URANITES
    URINATES
+O OUTRAISE
    SAUTOIRE
+Z AZURITES

X.

+I SEXTARII
+M MATRIXES
+T EXTRAITS

Y.

+B BESTIARY
    SYBARITE
+E YEASTIER
+H HYSTERIA
+M SYMITARE
+P ASPERITY
+V VESTIARY

Z.

+C CRAZIEST
+I SATIRIZE
+T TRISTEZA
+U AZURITES

AELORT: The LORATE seven-letter set
(Ranked No.50)

B,
BLOATER
RETABLO

G,
GLOATER
LEGATOR

R,
REALTOR
RELATOR

U,
ROTULAE
TORULAE

C,
LOCATER
CROTALE

H,
LOATHER
RATHOLE

S,
OESTRAL
OLESTRA

V,
LEVATOR

D,
DELATOR
LEOTARD

Y,
ROYALET

L O R A T E

Z,
ZELATOR

F,
FLOATER
FLOREAT
REFLOAT

L,
REALLOT

T,
RETOTAL

P,
PROLATE

Note

As there is only a U as a combining vowel it is not possible to create a meaningful mnemonic.

The LORATE eights where there are no sevens.

These are the eights to watch out for when you have LORATE and a seventh letter that doesn't yield a seven.

A

| +E | AREOLATE |
| +Y | ALEATORY |

E

+A	AREOLATE
+C	CORELATE
	RELOCATE
+I	AEROLITE
+N	REALTONE
+T	TOLERATE
+S	OLEASTER
+V	ELEVATOR
	OVERLATE
+W	TOLEWARE

I

+B	LABORITE
+C	EROTICAL
	LORICATE
+D	IDOLATER
	TAILORED
+E	AEROLITE
+F	FLOATIER
+H	AEROLITH
+M	AMITROLE
	ROLAMITE
+N	OREINTAL
	RELATION
	TAILERON
+P	EPILATOR
	PETIOLAR
+R	RETAILOR
+S	SOTERIAL
+T	LITERATO
+V	VIOLATER
+Z	TRIAZOLE

J

| +V | TOLARJEV |

K

| +P | LAKEPORT |
| +V | OVERTALK |

M

+I	AMITROLE
	ROLAMITE
+L	MARTELLO
+P	PROMETAL
	TEMPORAL
+Z	METRAZOL

N

+E	REALTONE
+F	FLOREANT
+I	ORIENTAL
	RELATION
	TAILERON
+T	TETRONAL
	TOLERANT
+U	OUTLEARN
+Y	ORNATELY

O

| +W | WATERLOO |
| +Z | ZOOLATER |

Q

NONE

W

+D	LEADWORT
+E	TOLEWARE
+F	FLEAWORT
+G	WATERLOG
+O	WATERLOO

X

NONE

AENORS: The REASON seven-letter set
(Ranked No.26)

B.
BORANES

H.
HOARSEN
SENHORA

M.
ENAMORS
MOANERS
OARSMEN

S.
REASONS
SENORAS

C.
CANOERS
CARNOSE
COARSEN
CORNEAS
EARCONS
NARCOSE

I.
ERASION

P.
PERSONA

T.
ATONERS
SANTERO
SENATOR
TREASON

E.
ARENOSE

R. E. A. S. O. N.

U.
ARENOUS

G.
ONAGERS
ORANGES

L.
LOANERS
ORLEANS
RELOANS

R.
SERRANO

Note
A mnemonic to help remember which letters REASON combines with is:
PREMISE MIGHT BE THE CLUE
Note the association of the keyword REASON with PREMISE.

The REASON eights where there are no sevens.

These are the eights to watch out for when you have REASON and a seventh letter that doesn't yield a seven.

A

+M	AMARONES
+T	ANOESTRA
+U	ARANEOUS

D

+B	BANDORES
	BROADENS
+C	DRACONES
	ENDOSARC
+E	REASONED
+H	HARDNOSE
+I	ANEROIDS
	ANODISER
	DONARIES
+L	LADRONES
	SOLANDER
+M	MADRONES
	RANSOMED
	ROADSMEN
+P	OPERANDS
	PADRONES
	PANDORES
+R	ADORNERS
	READORNS
+T	TORNADES

F

+I	FARINOSE
+K	FORSAKEN
+L	FARNESOL
+M	FORAMENS
+P	PROFANES
+T	SEAFRONT
+U	FURANOSE

J

+Z	ZANJEROS

K

+F	FORSAKEN
+G	KARENGOS

N

+B	BARONNES
+I	NONARIES
	RAISONNE
+M	MONERANS
	SONARMEN
+T	NORTENAS
	RESONANT
+U	UNREASON
+Y	ANNOYERS

O

+G	OREGANOS

Q

NONE

V

+I	AVERSION
+L	VERONALS
+M	OVERMANS
	OVERSMAN
+T	VENATORS
+U	RAVENOUS

W

+G	WAGONERS
+T	STONERAW
+Z	WARZONES

X

NONE

Y

+M	ROMNEYAS
+N	ANNOYERS
+P	PYRANOSE

Z

+B	ZEBRANOS
+J	ZANJEROS
+W	WARZONES

AENOST: The ATONES seven-letter set
(Ranked No.42)

B ONBEATS

C COSTEAN OCTANES

D ASTONED DONATES ONSTEAD

G ONSTAGE TANGOES

I ATONIES

L ETALONS TOLANES

M MANTOES

P TEOPANS

R ATONERS SANTERO SENATOR TREASON

A T O N E S

S ASTONES

T ATTONES NOTATES

U SOUTANE

V NOVATES

Note

A mnemonic to help remember which letters ATONES combines with is:
VICTIM'S DRUG BLIP
Note the association of the keyword ATONES with a victim.

The ATONES eights where there are no sevens.

These are the eights to watch out for when you have ATONES and a seventh letter that doesn't yield a seven.

A

+R   ANOESTRA
+S   ASSONATE

E

+C   ACETONES
     NOTECASE
+D   ENDOSTEA
+N   NEONATES
+R   EARSTONE
     RESONATE

F

+R   SEAFRONT

H

+L   ANETHOLS
     ETHANOLS
+M   HOASTMEN
+P   PHAETONS
     PHONATES
     STANHOPE

J

+C   JACONETS

K

NONE

N

+E   NEONATES
+G   NEGATONS
     TONNAGES
+I   ENATIONS
     SONATINE
+M   MONTANES
     NONMEATS
+P   PENTOSAN
+R   NORTENAS
     RESONANT
+U   TONNEAUS
+X   NONTAXES

O

+D   ODONATES
+P   TEASPOON
+Z   OZONATES

Q

NONE

W

+R   STONERAW

X

+I   SAXONITE
+N   NONTAXES

Y

+B   BAYONETS
+L   ANOLYTES

Z

+O   OZONATES
+S   STANZOES

AENRST: The ANTERS seven-letter set
(Ranked No.14)

A

ANESTRA
SANTERA

B

BANTERS
BARNETS

C

CANTERS
CARNETS
NECTARS
RECANTS
SCANTER
TANRECS
TRANCES

D

DARNEST
ENDARTS
STANDER
STARNED

E

EARNEST
EASTERN
NEAREST
RATEENS
STERANE

G

ARGENTS
GARNETS
STRANGE

H

ANTHERS
HARTENS
THENARS

I

ANESTRI
ANTSIER
NASTIER
RATINES
RESIANT
RETAINS
RETINAS
RETSINA
STAINER
STARNIE
STEARIN

A N T E R S

K

RANKEST
STARKEN
TANKERS

L

ANTLERS
RENTALS
SALTERN
SLANTER
STERNAL

M

ARTSMEN
MARTENS
SARMENT
SMARTEN

N

TANNERS

O

ATONERS
SANTERO
SENATOR
TREASON

P

ARPENTS
ENTRAPS
PANTERS
PARENTS
PASTERN
PERSANT
TREPANS

R

ERRANTS
RANTERS

S

SARSNET
TRANSES

T

NATTERS
RATTENS

U

AUNTERS
NATURES
SAUNTER

V

SERVANT
TAVERNS
VERSANT

W

STRAWEN
WANTERS

Y

TRAYNES

Note

A mnemonic to help remember which letters ANTERS combines with is best used for the letters it doesn't go with: **Forget JQXZ** which tells you that F and JQXZ are not allowed.

The ANTERS eights where there are no sevens.

These are the eights to watch out for when you have ANTER and a seventh letter that doesn't yield a seven.

F

+C	CANTREFS
+E	FASTENER
	FENESTRA
	REFASTEN
+G	ENGRAFTS
+I	FAINTERS
	FENITARS
+K	FRANKEST
+M	RAFTSMEN
+O	SEAFRONT
+R	TRANSFER
+U	AFTERSUN

J

+A	NAARTJES
+E	SERJEANT
+I	NARTJIES

Q

NONE

X

+D	DEXTRANS

Z

+K	KRANTZES

DEINOR: The IRONED seven-letter set
(Ranked No.28)

A.
ANEROID

H.
HORDEIN

P.
POINDER
PROINED

U.
DOURINE
NEUROID
OUNDIER

B.
INORBED

J.
JOINDER

R.
DRONIER

D.
NODDIER

W.
DOWNIER
WINDORE

I. R. O. N. E. D.

E.
ORDINEE

G.
ERODING
GROINED
IGNORED
NEGROID
REDOING

M.
MINORED

N.
ENDIRON

S.
DINEROS
DONSIER
INDORSE
ORDINES
ROSINED
SORDINE

Note

A mnemonic to help remember which letters IRONED combines with is:
HUSBAND DAMAGED NEW JUMPER
Note the association of the keyword IRONED with a husband not being able to iron properly!

The IRONED eights where there are no sevens.

These are the eights to watch out for when you have IRONED and a seventh letter that doesn't yield a seven.

C

+C	CORNICED
+E	RECOINED
+F	CONFIDER
	INFORCED
+G	RECODING
+R	CORDINER
+S	CONSIDER
+T	CENTROID
	DOCTRINE
+U	DECURION
+V	CODRIVEN

F

+C	CONFIDER
	INFORCED
+L	INFOLDER
+M	INFORMED
+P	FORPINED
+W	FOREWIND

I

+S	DERISION
	IRONISED
	IRONSIDE
	RESINOID
+T	RETINOID
+Z	IRONIZED

K

+B	BRODEKIN
+N	DONNIKER
+V	OVERKIND
+W	INWORKED

L

+F	INFOLDER
+H	INHOLDER
+S	DISENROL

O

+G	RODEOING

Q

NONE

T

+A	AROINTED
	DERATION
	ORDINATE
	RATIONED
+C	CENTROID
	DOCTRINE
+D	TRENDOID
+E	ORIENTED
+I	RETINOID
+M	DORMIENT
+N	INDENTOR
+P	DIPTERON
+S	DRONIEST
+T	INTORTED

V

+C	CODRIVEN
+G	DOVERING
	RINGDOVE
+B	OVENBIRD
+K	OVERKIND
+W	OVERWIND
+P	PROVINED

X

NONE

Y

+P	PYRENOID

Z

+A	ANODIZER
+I	IRONIZED

DEIORS: The DORISE seven-letter set
(Ranked No.44)

A,

RADIOES
ROADIES
SOREDIA

B,

BORIDES
DISROBE

C,

DISCOER
SCODIER

D,

DORISED
SODDIER

E,

OREIDES
OSIERED

H,

RHODIES

I,

IODISER

D, O, R, I, S, E,

L,

SOLDIER
SOLIDER

M,

MISDOER
MOIDERS

N,

DINEROS
DONSIER
INDORSE
ORDINES
ROSINED
SORDINE

O,

ODORISE
OROIDES

P,

PERIODS

S,

DORISES
DOSSIER

T,

EDITORS
ROISTED
ROSITED
SORTIED
STEROID
STORIED
TRIODES

V,

DEVISOR
DEVOIRS
VISORED
VOIDERS

W,

DOWRIES
ROWDIES
WEIRDOS

Z,

DORIZES

Note

A mnemonic to help remember which letters DORISE combines with is:
LEAVE BED TO CHAMPION SHOWBIZ
Note the association of the keyword DORISE (DO RISE) with getting out of bed and rising to fame in showbiz.

The DORISE eights where there are no sevens.

These are the eights to watch out for when you have DORISE and a seventh letter that doesn't yield a seven.

F.

+A	FORESAID
+B	FIBROSED
+E	FORESIDE
+F	OFFSIDER
+G	FIREDOGS
+U	FOUDRIES

G.

+F	FIREDOGS
+G	DISGORGE
+N	NEGROIDS
+O	GOODSIRE
+T	DIGESTOR
	GRODIEST
	STODGIER

J.

+N	JOINDERS
+Y	JOYRIDES

K.

+O	SKIDOOER
+S	DROSKIES
+T	DORKIEST

Q.

NONE

R.

+B	BROIDERS
	DISROBER
+D	DISORDER
	SORDIDER
+M	MISORDER
	MORRISED
+N	INDORSER
+O	ODORISER
+S	DROSSIER
+W	DROWSIER
+Y	DERISORY

U.

+C	DISCOURE
+F	FOUDRIES
+L	SOULDIER
+M	DIMEROUS
	ERODIUMS
	SOREDIUM
+N	DOURINES
	NEUROIDS
	SOURDINE
+S	DESIROUS
+T	IODURETS
	OUTRIDES
	OUTSIDER
	SUITORED

X.

+I	OXIDISER
+P	PEROXIDS

Y.

+C	DECISORY
+J	JOYRIDES
+L	SOLDIERY
+R	DERISORY

EILNOR: The INROLE seven-letter set
(Ranked No.23)

A
AILERON
ALERION
ALIENOR

I
NOILIER

O
LOONIER

R
LORINER

I N R O L E

S
LIENORS
NEROLIS

E
ELOINER

N
ONLINER

P
PLERION
PROLINE

T
RETINOL

Note

A mnemonic to help remember which letters INROLE combines with is:
PRESENTATION
Note there is a loose association with someone in a key role (IN ROLE)
having to make a PRESENTATION.

The INROLE eights where there are no sevens.

These are the eights to watch out for when you have NOILER and a seventh letter that doesn't yield a seven.

B
+M	BROMELIN
+G	IGNOBLER

C
+A	ACROLEIN
	COLINEAR
	CREOLIAN
	LONICERA
+C	CORNICLE
+H	CHLORINE
+K	CLONKIER
+P	PERCOLIN
	REPLICON
+S	INCLOSER
	LICENSOR

D
+F	INFOLDER
+H	INHOLDER
+S	DISENROL

F
+A	FORELAIN
+D	INFOLDER
+G	FLORIGEN
+O	ROOFLINE
+U	FLUORINE

G
+A	GERANIOL
	REGIONAL
+B	IGNOBLER
+E	ELOIGNER
+F	FLORIGEN
+I	LIGROINE
	RELIGION
	REOILING
+S	RESOLING
+U	LOUNGIER
+W	LOWERING
	ROWELING

H
+C	CHLORINE
+D	INHOLDER
+K	HORNLIKE
+T	HOTLINER
+U	UNHOLIER

J
NONE

K
+C	CLONKIER
+H	HORNLIKE
+I	IRONLIKE
+L	KNOLLIER
+O	OERLIKON
+P	PLONKIER

L
+A	ALLERION
+E	LONELIER
+K	KNOLLIER

M
+B	BROMELIN
+E	LEMONIER
+S	MISENROL

Q
NONE

U
+F	FLUORINE
+G	LOUNGIER
+H	UNHOLIER
+P	NEUROPIL
+T	OUTLINER

V
+A	OVERLAIN
+V	INVOLVER

W
+G	LOWERING
	ROWELING
+T	TOWNLIER

X
NONE

Y
NONE

Z
+I	LIONIZER

EILNOS: The NOLIES seven-letter set
(Ranked No.41)

A.
ANISOLE

B.
BOLINES

C.
CINEOLS
CONSEIL
INCLOSE

D.
DOLINES
INDOLES
SONDELI

E.
OLEINES

F.
OLEFINS

N O L I E S

G.
ELOIGNS
LEGIONS
LIGNOSE
LINGOES
LONGIES

I.
ELISION
ISOLINE
LIONISE
NOILIES

K.
SONLIKE

L.
LIONELS
NIELLOS

M.
LOMEINS
MOLINES

O.
LOONIES

P.
EPSILON
PINOLES

R.
LIENORS
NEROLIS

S.
ESLOINS
INSOLES
LESIONS
LIONESS

T.
ENTOILS
LIONETS
ONLIEST

U.
ELUSION

Note

A mnemonic to help remember which letters NOLIES combines with is:
IT'S TRUE, PM BACKED GOLF
Note the association of the keyword NOLIES (NO LIES) with TRUE.

The NOLIES eights where there are no sevens.

These are the eights to watch out for when you have NOLIES and a seventh letter that doesn't yield a seven.

H

+C	CHOLINES
	HELICONS
+K	SINKHOLE
+L	HELLIONS
+M	LEMONISH
+P	PINHOLES
+S	HOLINESS
+T	HOLSTEIN
	HOTLINES
	NEOLITHS
+V	NOVELISH

J

NONE

N

+A	SOLANINE
+R	ONLINERS
+T	INSOLENT
+V	NONLIVES
+W	SNOWLINE

Q

NONE

V

+E	NOVELISE
+H	NOVELISH
+I	OLIVINES
+M	NOVELISM
+N	NONLIVES
+O	VIOLONES
+T	NOVELIST
	VIOLENTS
+U	EVULSION
+V	INVOLVES

W

+B	BOWLINES
+G	LONGWISE
+K	SNOWLIKE
+N	SNOWLINE
+S	LEWISSON
+T	TOWLINES

X

+A	SILOXANE
+C	LEXICONS
+F	FLEXIONS

Y

NONE

Z

+I	LIONIZES

EILNOT: The NOLITE seven-letter set
(Ranked No.43)

A₁

ELATION
TOENAIL

H₄

HOTLINE
NEOLITH

P₃

POINTEL
PONTILE
POTLINE
TOPLINE

S₁

ENTOILS
LIONETS
ONLIEST

C₃

LECTION

U₁

ELUTION
OUTLINE

D₂

LENTOID

N₁ O₁ L₁ I₁ T₁ E₁

V₄

VIOLENT

G₂

LENTIGO

I₁

ETIOLIN

R₁

RETINOL

W₄

TOWLINE

M₃

MOLINET

Note

A mnemonic to help remember which letters NOLITE combines with is:
CHURCH VICAR'S CIGAR WAS DAMP
Note the association of the keyword NOLITE (sounds like NO LIGHT) with damp cigar.

The NOLITE eights where there are no sevens.

These are the eights to watch out for when you have NOLITE and a seventh letter that doesn't yield a seven.

B
+A   TAILBONE

E
+C   COTELINE
      ELECTION
+D   DELETION
      ENTOILED
+N   NONELITE
+S   NOSELITE

F
+A   OLEFIANT
+C   FLECTION

J
      NONE

K
+K   KNOTLIKE

L
+P   PLOTLINE
+S   STELLION
+U   LUTEOLIN

N
+C   CONTLINE
+D   INDOLENT
+E   NONELITE
+I   LENITION
+S   INSOLENT
+T   NONTITLE
+V   VINOLENT

O
+S   LOONIEST
      OILSTONE

Q
      NONE

T
+A   TONALITE
+I   TOILINET
+N   NONTITLE
+R   TROTLINE

X
+H   XENOLITH
+Y   XYLONITE

Y
+M   MYLONITE
+P   LINOTYPE
+X   XYLONITE
+Z   ZYLONITE

Z
+Y   ZYLONITE

EILORT: The LOITER seven-letter set
(Ranked No.32)

B.
TRILOBE

J.
JOLTIER

O.
TROOLIE

T.
TORTILE
TRIOLET

C.
CORTILE

L O I T E R

U.
OUTLIER

D.
DOILTER

M.
MOTLIER

P.
POITREL
POLITER

V.
OVERLIT

E.
TROELIE

N.
RETINOL

F.
LOFTIER
TREFOIL

S.
ESTRIOL
LOITERS
TOILERS

Note

A mnemonic to help remember which letters LOITER combines with is:
PUT OFF SECOND MOVE DUE TO JOB CUTS
Note the association of the keyword LOITER with not moving.

The LOITER eights where there are no sevens.

These are the eights to watch out for when you have LOITER and a seventh letter that doesn't yield a seven.

A

+B	LABORITE
+C	EROTICAL
	LORICATE
+D	IDOLATER
	TAILORED
+E	AEROLITE
+F	FLOATIER
+H	AEROLITH
+M	AMITROLE
	ROLAMITE
+N	ORIENTAL
	RELATION
	TAILERON
+P	EPILATOR
	PETIOLAR
+R	RETAILOR
+S	SOTERIAL
+T	LITERATO
+V	VIOLATER
+Z	TRIAZOLE

G

+H	REGOLITH
+V	OVERGILT
+Y	GYROLITE

H

+A	AEROLITH
+C	CHLORITE
	CLOTHIER
+E	HOTELIER
+G	REGOLITH
+N	HOTLINER
+P	HELIPORT
+Y	RHYOLITE

I

+C	ELICITOR
+N	TRIOLEIN
+S	ROILIEST
+T	TROILITE

K

+E	LORIKEET
+O	ROOTLIKE
+Y	KRYOLITE

L

+T	TORTELLI
+S	TRILLOES
	TROLLIES
+D	TROLLIED

Q

NONE

R

+A	RETAILOR
+E	LOITERER
+N	RITORNEL
+P	PORTLIER
+U	ULTERIOR

W

+N	TOWNLIER
+P	PILEWORT

X

NONE

Y

+C	CRYOLITE
+D	ELYTROID
+G	GYROLITE
+H	RHYOLITE
+K	KRYOLITE
+T	TOILETRY

Z

+A	TRIAZOLE

EILOST: The ELIOTS seven-letter set
(Ranked No.39)

A,
ISOLATE

I,
IOLITES
OILIEST

O,
OOLITES
OSTIOLE
STOOLIE
TOOLIES

U,
OUTLIES

B,
BETOILS

V,
LOVIEST
OLIVETS
VIOLETS

C,
CITOLES

E L I O T S

W,
OWLIEST

E,
ESTOILE
ETOILES

L,
OILLETS
STELLIO
TOLLIES

P,
PIOLETS
PISTOLE

Z,
ZLOTIES

G,
ELOGIST
LOGIEST

M,
MOTILES

R,
ESTRIOL
LOITERS
TOILERS

H,
EOLITHS
HOLIEST
HOSTILE
LITHOES

N,
ENTOILS
LIONETS
ONLIEST

T,
LITOTES
TOILETS

Note

A mnemonic to help remember which letters ELIOTS combines with is:
POET WHIZ GAVE MUCH BRILLIANCE
Note the association of the keyword ELIOTS (T S ELIOT the poet) with
brilliant poet.

The ELIOTS eights where there are no sevens.

These are the eights to watch out for when you have ELIOTS and a seventh letter that doesn't yield a seven.

D

+A	DIASTOLE
	ISOLATED
	SODALITE
	SOLIDATE
+C	DOCILEST
+D	DELTOIDS
+G	GODLIEST
	GOLDIEST
+M	MELODIST
	MODELIST
	MOLDIEST
+N	LENTOIDS
+P	PISTOLED
	POSTILED
+R	STOLIDER
+S	SOLIDEST
+T	DOILTEST
+U	SOLITUDE
	TOLUIDES
+W	DOWLIEST

F

+A	FOLIATES
+B	BOTFLIES
+J	JETFOILS
+K	FOLKIEST
+M	FILEMOTS
+R	FLORIEST
	TREFOILS
+T	LOFTIEST
+U	OUTFLIES

J

+F	JETFOILS
+L	JOLLIEST
+T	JOLTIEST
+W	JOWLIEST

K

+A	KEITLOAS
+B	BLOKIEST
+F	FOLKIEST
+Y	YOLKIEST

Q

NONE

S

+A	ISOLATES
+C	SOLECIST
	SOLSTICE
+D	SOLIDEST
+E	ESTOILES
+G	ELOGISTS
+H	HOSTILES
+I	SOILIEST
+L	TOILLESS
+O	OSTIOLES
	STOOLIES
+P	PISTOLES
	PTILOSES
	SLOPIEST
+R	ESTRIOLS
+S	LOSSIEST
+U	LOUSIEST

X

+P	EXPLOITS

Y

+O	OTIOSELY
+K	YOLKIEST

EINORS: The SENIOR seven-letter set
(Ranked No.7)

A
ERASION

C
COINERS
CRINOSE
CRONIES
ORCEINS
ORCINES
RECOINS
SERICON

D
DINEROS
DONSIER
INDORSE
ORDINES
ROSINED
SORDINE

G
ERINGOS
IGNORES
REGIONS
SIGNORE

H
HEROINS
INSHORE

I
IONISER
IRONIES
IRONISE
NOISIER

S E N I O R

J
JOINERS
REJOINS

L
LIENORS
NEROLIS

M
MERINOS
MERSION

N
RONNIES

O
EROSION

P
ORPINES
PIONERS
PROINES

R
IRONERS
ROSINER

S
ORNISES
SENIORS
SONERIS
SONSIER

T
NORITES
OESTRIN
ORIENTS
STONIER
TERSION
TRIONES

U
URINOSE

V
ENVIROS
RENVOIS
VERSION

W
SNOWIER

X
OREXINS

Note

A mnemonic to help remember which letters SENIOR combines with is:
OLD JIM HAD GRUMPS WITH TAX ON SAVING CASH
Note the association of the keyword SENIOR with OLD JIM.

The SENIOR eights where there are no sevens.

These are the eights to watch out for when you have SENIOR and a seventh letter that doesn't yield a seven.

B

+A	BARONIES
	SEAROBIN
+B	SNOBBIER
+C	BICORNES
+F	BONFIRES
+G	SOBERING
+I	BRIONIES
+M	BROMINES
+T	BORNITES
	RIBSTONE
+W	BROWNIES
+Y	BRYONIES

E

+D	INDORSEE
	ORDINEES
+G	ERINGOES
+H	HEROINES
	NOSHERIE
+K	KEROSINE
+L	ELOINERS
+M	EMERSION
+P	ISOPRENE
	PEREIONS
	PIONEERS
+S	ESSOINER
+T	ONERIEST
	SEROTINE
+V	EVERSION

F

+A	FARINOSE
+B	BONFIRES
+C	COINFERS
	CONIFERS
	FORENSIC
	FORINSEC
	FORNICES
	INFORCES
+K	FORESKIN
+M	ENSIFORM
	FERMIONS
+N	INFERNOS
+P	FORPINES
+U	REFUSION

K

+E	KEROSINE
+F	FORESKIN
+H	SHONKIER
+M	MONIKERS
+N	EINKORNS
	NONSKIER
+O	ROOINEKS
+T	INSTROKE
+V	INVOKERS

Q

NONE

Y

+B	BRYONIES
+G	SEIGNORY
+T	SEROTINY
	TYROSINE

Z

+I	IONIZERS
	IRONIZES
	SIRONIZE
+O	OZONISER
	SNOOZIER
+T	TRIZONES

EINRTU: The UNITER seven-letter set
(Ranked No.47)

A
RUINATE
TAURINE
URANITE
URINATE

E
NEURITE
RETINUE
REUNITE
UTERINE

O
ROUTINE

T
NUTTIER

P
REPUNIT

V
UNRIVET
VENTURI

B
BUNTIER
TRIBUNE
TURBINE

G
TRUEING

R
RUNTIER

W
UNWRITE

D
INTRUDE
TURDINE
UNTIRED
UNTRIDE
UNTRIED

U N I T E R

M
MINUTER
MUNTRIE
UNMITER
UNMITRE

S
NUTSIER
TRIUNES
UNITERS

Note

A mnemonic to help remember which letters UNITER combines with is:
GAVE BAD TEAM PROWESS
Note the association of the keyword UNITER with bringing a team
together for success.

The UNITER eights where there are no sevens.

These are the eights to watch out for when you have UNITER and a seventh letter that doesn't yield a seven.

C

+A	ANURETIC
+C	CINCTURE
+D	REINDUCT
+E	CEINTURE
	ENURETIC
+G	ERUCTING
+H	RUTHENIC
+I	NEURITIC
+L	LINCTURE
+O	NEUROTIC
	UNEROTIC
+S	CURNIEST
+T	INTERCUT
	TINCTURE

F

+G	FEUTRING
	REFUTING
+T	UNFITTER

H

+C	RUTHENIC
+U	HAURIENT

I

+C	NEURITIC
+D	UNTIDIER
+G	INTRIGUE
+S	NEURITIS
	UNITISER
+Z	UNITIZER

J

+A	JAUNTIER
+O	JOINTURE

K

+P	TURNPIKE
+R	RETURNIK

L

+A	AUNTLIER
	RETINULA
	TENURIAL
+C	LINCTURE
+D	UNDERLIT
+S	INSULTER
	LUSTRINE
+U	OUTLINER
+V	VIRULENT

N

+D	INTURNED
+G	RETUNING
	TENURING
+O	NEUTRINO
+S	RUNNIEST
	STURNINE
+T	NUTRIENT

Q

+A	ANTIQUER
	QUAINTER
+O	REQUINTO
+S	SQUINTER
+T	QUITRENT

U

+V	UNVIRTUE

X

NONE

Y

NONE

Z

+I	UNITIZER

EIORST: The TORIES seven-letter set
(Ranked No.5)

A₁

OARIEST
OTARIES
ROASTIE

B₃

ORBIEST
SORBITE

C₃

CORSITE
EROTICS
TERCIOS

D₂

EDITORS
ROISTED
ROSITED
SORTIED
STEROID
STORIED
TRIODES

E₁

EROTISE

F₄

FOISTER
FORTIES

G₂

GOITERS
GOITRES
GORIEST

H₄

HERIOTS
HOISTER
SHORTIE
TOSHIER

I₁

RIOTISE

T₁O₁R₁I₁E₁S₁

K₅

ROKIEST

L₁

ESTRIOL
LOITERS
TOILERS

M₃

EROTISM
MOISTER
MORTISE
TRISOME

N₁

NORITES
OESTRIN
ORIENTS
STONIER
TERSION
TRIONES

O₁

OORIEST
ROOTIES
SOOTIER
TOORIES

P₃

PERIOST
PORIEST
PROSTIE
REPOSIT
RIPOSTE
ROPIEST

R₁

RIOTERS
ROISTER
RORIEST

S₁

ROESTIS
ROSIEST
SIROSET
SORITES
SORTIES
STORIES
TOSSIER
TRIOSES

T₁

STOITER
TORTIES

U₁

OURIEST
STOURIE
TOURIES
TOUSIER

V₄

TORSIVE

W₄

OWRIEST
TOWSIER

Note

A mnemonic to help remember which letters TORIES combines with is:
IF VOTING SLUMPS THIS WILL BE A DRAWBACK
Note the association of the keyword TORIES with VOTING.

The TORIES eights where there are no sevens.

These are the eights to watch out for when you have TORIES and a seventh letter that doesn't yield a seven.

J

+A	JAROSITE
+N	JOINTERS

Q

+U	QUOITERS

X

+C	EXCITORS
	EXORCIST
+N	NITROXES

Y

+B	SOBRIETY
+G	OYSTRIGE
+M	ISOMETRY
+N	SEROTINY
	TYROSINE
+S	SEROSITY

Z

+E	EROTIZES
+G	ZORGITES
+I	RIOTIZES
+N	TRIZONES

ENORST: The TONERS seven-letter set
(Ranked No.24)

A.
ATONERS
SANTERO
SENATOR
TREASON

B.
BRETONS
SORBENT

C.
CONSTER
CORNETS
CRESTON
CRETONS
CRONETS

D.
RODENTS
SNORTED

E.
ESTRONE

F.
FRONTES

G.
TONGERS

H.
HORNETS
SHORTEN
THRENOS
THRONES

T O N E R S

I.
NORITES
OESTRIN
ORIENTS
STONIER
TERSION
TRIONES

K.
REKNOTS
STONKER
STROKEN
TONKERS

L.
LENTORS

M.
MENTORS
MONSTER
MONTRES

N.
STONERN
TONNERS

O.
ENROOTS

P.
POSTERN
PRONEST

R.
SNORTER

S.
NESTORS
STONERS
TENSORS

T.
ROTTENS
SNOTTER
STENTOR

U.
TENOURS
TONSURE

Y.
TYRONES

Note

A mnemonic to help remember which letters TONERS combines with is:
THEY ADD COLOURED INK BEFORE PUBLISHING FILM
Note the association of the keyword TONERS with adding colour.

The TONERS eights where there are no sevens.

These are the eights to watch out for when you have TONERS and a seventh letter that doesn't yield a seven.

J

+I   JOINTERS

Q

NONE

V

+A   VENATORS
+C   CONVERTS
+E   OVERNETS
+I   INVESTOR
+U   VENTROUS

W

+A   STONERAW
+B   BESTROWN
        BROWNEST
+C   CROWNETS
+G   WRONGEST
+K   NETWORKS

X

+E   EXTENSOR
+I   NITROXES

Z

+I   TRIZONES

ADEIRT: The TIRADE seven-letter set
(Ranked No.20)

A
AIRDATE
RADIATE
TIARAED

B
REDBAIT
TRIBADE

D
TARDIED

G
TRIAGED

H
AIRTHED

K
TRAIKED

L
DILATER
REDTAIL
TRAILED
TRIALED

M
READMIT

T I R A D E

N
ANTIRED
DETRAIN
TRAINED

P
DIPTERA
PARTIED
PIRATED

R
TARDIER
TARRIED

S
ARIDEST
ASTERID
ASTRIDE
DIASTER
DISRATE
STAIDER
STAIRED
TARDIES
TIRADES

T
ATTIRED

V
TARDIVE

Y
DIETARY

Note

A mnemonic to help remember which letters TIRADE combines with is:
ANGRY MAN HAD RANT AT BLANK PLASMA TV
Note the association of the keyword TIRADE with an angry man having a rant.

ADEIST: The SAITED seven-letter set
(Ranked No.46)

B₃
BASTIDE

C₃
ACIDEST
DACITES

D₂
TADDIES

E₁
IDEATES

F₄
DAFTIES
FADIEST

G₂
AGISTED

L₁
DETAILS
DILATES

M₃
DIASTEM
MISDATE

N₁
DESTAIN
DETAINS
INSTEAD
NIDATES
SAINTED
SATINED
STAINED

S₁ A₁ I₁ T₁ E₁ D₂

O₁
IODATES
TOADIES

R₁
ARIDEST
ASTERID
ASTRIDE
DIASTER
DISRATE
STAIDER
STAIRED
TARDIES
TIRADES

S₁
DISSEAT
SAIDEST

U₁
DAUTIES

V₄
AVIDEST
DATIVES
VISTAED

W₄
DAWTIES
WAISTED

Note
A mnemonic to help remember which letters SAITED combines with is:
WOLVES CONSUMED BEEFBURGER
Note the association of the keyword SAITED (sounds like SATED) with consuming food.

ADEORS: The ADORES seven-letter set
(Ranked No.49)

C
SARCODE

L
LOADERS
ORDEALS
RELOADS

S
SARODES

D
DEODARS

M
RADOMES

T
DOATERS
ROASTED
TORSADE
TROADES

E
OREADES

A D O R E S

F
FEDORAS

U
AROUSED

G
DOGEARS

O
ROADEOS

V
OVERSAD
SAVORED

I
RADIOES
ROADIES
SOREDIA

R
ADORERS
DROSERA

W
REDOWAS

Note
A mnemonic to help remember which letters ADORES combines with is:
MULTI-CURVED MODEL WIFE'S LEGS
Note the association of the keyword ADORES with MODEL WIFE.

AEEIRT: The EATIER seven-letter set
(Ranked No.3)

B
BEATIER
EBRIATE

N
ARENITE
RETINAE
TRAINEE

R
TEARIER

S
AERIEST
SERIATE

E
EATERIE

E A T I E R

T
ARIETTE
ITERATE

L
ATELIER
REALTIE

O
ETAERIO

M
EMERITA
EMIRATE
MEATIER

P
PEATIER

V
EVIRATE

A mnemonic to help remember which letters EATIER combines with is:
MORE LOBSTER OVEN POTS
Note the association of the keyword EATIER (more to eat perhaps) with
MORE LOBSTER.

AEILNT: The ENTAIL seven-letter set
(Ranked No.19)

A

ANTLIAE

E

LINEATE

F

INFLATE

G

ATINGLE
ELATING
GELATIN
GENITAL
TAGLINE

K

ANTLIKE

M

AILMENT
ALIMENT

O

ELATION
TOENAIL

P

PANTILE

ENTAIL

R

ENTRAIL
LATRINE
RATLINE
RELIANT
RETINAL
TRENAIL

S

EASTLIN
ELASTIN
ENTAILS
NAILSET
SALIENT
SALTINE
SLAINTE
STANIEL
TENAILS

U

ALUNITE

V

VENTAIL

Note

A mnemonic to help remember which letters ENTAIL combines with is:
MAKEOVER FOR PUG'S REAR
Note the association of the TAIL part of the keyword ENTAIL with
PUG'S REAR.

AEILRS: The AILERS seven-letter set
(Ranked No.31)

A,
AERIALS

B,
BAILERS

C,
CLARIES
ECLAIRS
SCALIER

D,
DERAILS
DIALERS
REDIALS
SIDERAL

E,
EARLIES
REALISE

G,
GLAIRES
GRAILES

H,
HAILERS
HALIERS
SHALIER

I,
LAIRISE

J,
JAILERS

K,
LAIKERS
SERKALI

A, I, L, E, R, S,

L,
RALLIES
SALLIER

M,
MAILERS
REALISM
REMAILS

N,
ALINERS
NAILERS
RENAILS

P,
PALSIER
PARLIES

R,
RAILERS
RERAILS

S,
AIRLESS
RESAILS
SAILERS
SERAILS
SERIALS

T,
REALIST
RETAILS
SALTIER
SALTIRE
SLATIER
TAILERS

V,
REVISAL

W,
SWALIER
WAILERS

Note
A mnemonic to help remember which letters AILERS combines with is:
MEN WITH BLACKDEATH GET PRIVATE JABS
Note the association of the keyword AILERS with sick men.

AEILRT: The RETAIL seven-letter set
(Ranked No.16)

B
LIBRATE
TABLIER
TRIABLE

C
ARTICLE
RECITAL
TALCIER

D
DILATER
REDTAIL
TRAILED
TRIALED

E
ATELIER
REALTIE

H
LATHIER

K
RATLIKE
TALKIER

L
LITERAL
TALLIER
TRIELLA

M
LAMITER
MALTIER
MARLITE

R E T A I L

N
ENTRAIL
LATRINE
RATLINE
RELIANT
RETINAL
TRENAIL

P
PLATTER
PLATIER

R
RETIRAL
RETRIAL
TRAILER

S
REALIST
RETAILS
SALTIER
SALTIRE
SLATIER
TAILERS

T
TERTIAL

U
URALITE

W
WALTIER

Y
IRATELY
REALITY
TEARILY

Note

A mnemonic to help remember which letters RETAIL combines with is:
SPEND THE WEEKLY CRUMBS
Note the association of the keyword RETAIL with spending.

AEILST: The SALTIE seven-letter set
(Ranked No.45)

B
ABLEIST
ALBITES
ASTILBE
BASTILE
BESTIAL
BLASTIE
LIBATES
STABILE

C
ASTELIC
ELASTIC
LACIEST
LATICES
SALICET

D
DETAILS
DILATES

F
FETIALS
SEALIFT

G
AGILEST
AIGLETS
GELATIS
LIGATES
TAIGLES

H
HALITES
HELIAST

I
LAITIES

K
LAKIEST
TALKIES

L
SITELLA
TAILLES
TALLIES

S A L T I E

N
EASTLIN
ELASTIN
ENTAILS
NAILSET
SALIENT
SALTINE
SLAINTE
STANIEL
TENAILS

O
ISOLATE

P
APLITES
PALIEST
PLATIES
TALIPES

R
REALIST
RETAILS
SALTIER
SALTIRE
SLATIER
TAILERS

S
SALTIES

U
SITULAE

V
ESTIVAL

W
WALIEST

Y
TAILYES

Z
LAZIEST

Note

A mnemonic to help remember which letters SALTIE combines with is:
PROVIDING RISKY FOUL SHOWBIZ LUNCH
Note the association of the keyword SALTIE (salty) with a foul lunch.

AEINOR: The AIRONE seven-letter set
(Ranked No.35)

D ANEROID

G ORIGANE

L
AILERON
ALERION
ALIENOR

A I R O N E

M
MORAINE
ROMAINE

S ERASION

T
NOTAIRE
OTARINE

Note

As there are no vowels among the combining letters it is not possible to create a mnemonic but you only have six letters to remember anyway.

AEINOT: The ATONIE seven-letter set
(Ranked No.25)

B

NIOBATE

M

AMNIOTE

R

NOTAIRE
OTARINE

C

ACONITE
ANOETIC

A T O N I E

S

ATONIES

L

ELATION
TOENAIL

N

ENATION

Note

As there are no vowels among the combining letters it is not possible to create a mnemonic but you only have seven letters to remember anyway.

AEINRS: The SARNIE seven-letter set
(Ranked No.10)

C
ARCSINE
ARSENIC
CARNIES
CERASIN

D
RANDIES
SANDIER
SARDINE

F
INFARES
SERAFIN

G
ANGRIES
EARINGS
ERASING
GAINERS
GRAINES
REAGINS
REGAINS
REGINAS
SEARING
SERINGA

H
ARSHINE
HERNIAS
NEARISH

I
SENARII

J
INJERAS

K
SNAKIER

S A R N I E

L
ALINERS
NAILERS
RENAILS

M
MARINES
REMAINS
SEMINAR
SIRNAME

N
INSANER
INSNARE

O
ERASION

P
PANIERS
RAPINES

R
SIERRAN
SNARIER

S
ARSINES
SARNIES

T
ANESTRI
ANTSIER
NASTIER
RATINES
RESIANT
RETAINS
RETINAS
RETSINA
STAINER
STARNIE
STEARIN

V
AVENIRS
RAVINES

Note

A mnemonic to help remember which letters SARNIE combines with is:
GIVING JOSH MILD PORK FLITCH
Note the association of the keyword SARNIE with PORK as something that might be in a sarnie.

AEIORT: The OATIER seven-letter set
(Ranked No.21)

C EROTICA

E ETAERIO

G GOATIER

O A T I E R

N
NOTAIRE
OTARINE

S
OARIEST
OTARIES
ROASTIE

Note

A mnemonic to help remember which letters OATIER combines with is:
EGG ESSENCE
Note with so few letters to combine with it's not possible to come up with a mnemonic that relates to the keyword.

AENORT: The ORNATE seven-letter set
(Ranked No.11)

B₃
BARONET
REBOANT

C₃
ENACTOR

D₂
TORNADE

G₂
NEGATOR

H₄
ANOTHER

I₁
NOTAIRE
OTARINE

M₃
TONEARM

N₁
NORTENA

O₁ R₁ N₁ A₁ T₁ E₁

P₃
OPERANT
PRONATE
PROTEAN

R₁
ORNATER

S₁
ATONERS
SANTERO
SENATOR
TREASON

U₁
OUTEARN

V₄
VENATOR

> ## Note
>
> A mnemonic to help remember which letters ORNATE combines with is:
> **CURVING BUMPS IN DISH**
> Note the loose association of the keyword ORNATE with CURVING.

AEORST: The ORATES seven-letter set
(Ranked No.9)

A.
AEROSAT

B.
BOASTER
BOATERS
BORATES
REBATOS
SORBATE

C.
COASTER
COATERS
RECOATS

D.
DOATERS
ROASTED
TORSADE
TROADES

E.
ROSEATE

G.
GAROTES
ORGEATS
STORAGE
TOERAGS

ORATES

H.
ASTHORE
EARSHOT
HAROSET

I.
OARIEST
OTARIES
ROASTIE

K.
KOTARES

L.
OESTRAL
OLESTRA

M.
AMORETS
MAESTRO
OMERTAS

N.
ATONERS
SANTERO
SENATOR
TREASON

P.
ESPARTO
PROTEAS
SEAPORT

R.
ROASTER

S.
OSETRAS
OSSETRA

T.
ROTATES
TOASTER

Note

A mnemonic to help remember which letters ORATES combines with is:
SPEAKS AT HIS ADMIRING PUBLIC
Note the association of the keyword ORATES with public speaking, but you have to remember it is speaking AT and not TO.

AINORT: The RATION seven-letter set
(Ranked No.33)

B.
TABORIN

H.
ORTHIAN

P.
ATROPIN

C.
CAROTIN
CORTINA

J.
JANITOR

S.
AROINTS
RATIONS

D.
DIATRON

R A T I O N

U.
RAINOUT

E.
NOTAIRE
OTARINE

M.
TORMINA

W.
WAITRON

G.
ORATING
ROATING

O.
ORATION

X.
TRIAXON

Note
A mnemonic to help remember which letters RATION combines with is:
SO JUDGE CHEWED EXPOSED GUMBO
Note the association of the keyword RATION with having to make do with
chewing gumbo.

EEINRT: The ENTIRE seven-letter set
(Ranked No.12)

A
ARENITE
RETINAE
TRAINEE

B
BENTIER

C
ENTERIC
ENTICER

E
TEENIER

F
FEINTER

G
GENTIER
INTEGER
TEERING
TREEING

H
NEITHER
THEREIN

I
ERINITE
NITERIE

E N T I R E

K
KERNITE

N
INTERNE

P
INEPTER

R
INERTER
REINTER
RENTIER
TERRINE

S
ENTIRES
ENTRIES
NERITES
RETINES
TRENISE
TRIENES

T
NETTIER
TENTIER

U
NEURITE
RETINUE
REUNITE
UTERINE

Note

A mnemonic to help remember which letters ENTIRE combines with is:
ENTIRE PUB HATES FRACKING
Note the Keyword ENTIRE is also part of the phrase here.

EEIRST: The RESITE seven-letter set
(Ranked No.34)

A
AERIEST
SERIATE

B
REBITES

C
CERITES
RECITES
TIERCES

D
DIESTER
DIETERS
REEDITS
REISTED
RESITED

E
EERIEST

F
FESTIER

H
HEISTER

K
KEISTER
KIESTER

L
LEISTER
RETILES
STERILE

M
MEISTER
METIERS
REEMITS
RETIMES
TREMIES
TRISEME

R E S I T E

N
ENTIRES
ENTRIES
NERITES
RETINES
TRENISE
TRIENES

O
EROTISE

P
PESTIER
RESPITE

R
ETRIERS
REITERS
RESTIER
RETIRES
RETRIES
TERRIES

S
RESITES

T
TESTIER

U
SUETIER

V
RESTIVE
SIEVERT
STIEVER
VERIEST
VERITES

W
STEWIER

Z
ZESTIER

Note
A mnemonic to help remember which letters RESITE combines with is:
STAFF MOVED HUMPBACK WHALE TO NEW ZOO
Note the association of the keyword RESITE with moving to somewhere new.

EINORT: The TONIER seven-letter set
(Ranked No.15)

A

NOTAIRE
OTARINE

B

BORNITE

C

COINTER
NOTICER
RECTION

G

GENITOR

J

JOINTER

L

RETINOL

N

INTONER
NOINTER
TERNION

T O N I E R

P

POINTER
PROTEIN
PTERION
REPOINT
TROPINE

S

NORITES
OESTRIN
ORIENTS
STONIER
TERSION
TRIONES

T

TRITONE

U

ROUTINE

W

NOWTIER
TOWNIER

Z

TRIZONE

Note

A mnemonic to help remember which letters TONIER combines with is:
TWANG AT PUB JAZZ CLASS
Note the association of the keyword TONIER with music.

EINOST: The TONIES seven-letter set
(Ranked No.13)

A
ATONIES

B
BONIEST
EBONIST

C
NOTICES
SECTION

D
DITONES
STONIED

H
ETHIONS
HISTONE

I
INOSITE

J
JONTIES

L
ENTOILS
LIONETS
ONLIEST

M
MESTINO
MOISTEN
MONTIES
SENTIMO

T O N I E S

N
INTONES
TENSION

O
ISOTONE
TOONIES

P
PINTOES
POINTES
PONTIES

R
NORITES
OESTRIN
ORIENTS
STONIER
TERSION
TRIONES

S
NOSIEST
SONTIES
STONIES

T
SNOTTIE
TONIEST
TONITES

W
TOWNIES
TWONIES

X
TOXINES

Note
A mnemonic to help remember which letters TONIES combines with is:
SIX BAD ACTORS PLAN MAJOR AWARD SHOW
Note the association of the keyword TONIES with The TONYs (US theatre award show).

EINRST: The INTERS seven-letter set
(Ranked No.29)

A.

ANESTRI
ANTSIER
NASTIER
RATINES
RESIANT
RETAINS
RETINAS
RETSINA
STAINER
STARNIE
STEARIN

C.

CISTERN
CRETINS

D.

SNIRTED
TINDERS

E.

ENTIRES
ENTRIES
NERITES
RETINES
TRENISE
TRIENES

F.

SNIFTER

G.

RESTING
STINGER

H.

HINTERS
NITHERS

K.

REKNITS
SKINTER
STINKER
TINKERS

I N T E R S

L.

LINTERS
SLINTER
SNIRTLE

M.

ENTRISM
MINSTER
MINTERS
REMINTS

N.

INTERNS
TINNERS

O.

NORITES
OESTRIN
ORIENTS
STONIER
TERSION
TRIONES

P.

NIPTERS
PTERINS

S.

ESTRINS
INSERTS
SINTERS
STRINES

T.

ENTRIST
RETINTS
STINTER
TINTERS

U.

NUTSIER
TRIUNES
UNITERS

V.

INVERTS
STRIVEN

W.

TWINERS
WINTERS

Y.

SINTERY

Note

A mnemonic to help remember which letters INTERS combines with is:
GOOFY VAMP STUCK DOWN HOLE
Note the loose association of the keyword INTERS with possibly being
buried in a hole.

Seven-letter stems

The 20 seven-letter stems listed here are high-probability ones that you are likely to find on your rack, thus showing the words you may be able to make using an available letter on the board. Of course, they also serve to help you learn likely eight-letter words to play if you have any of the seven letters within the eight-letter words. The stems are shown below in order of ranking together with a suggested keyword (with brackets if it is not a real word).

```
1    AEINORT OTARINE
2    AEINRST RETAINS
3    EINORST STONIER
4    AEIORST OTARIES
5    AENORST TREASON
6    ADEINRT TRAINED
7    AEILNRT ENTRAIL
8    ADEINOT [ADONITE]
9    ADEINRS SARDINE
10   AEEIRST SERIATE
11   AEEINRT TRAINEE
12   EEINRST ENTRIES
13   AEILRST RETAILS
14   AEEILRT REALTIE
15   AEINORS ERASION
16   ADEIRST TIRADES
17   ADEIORT [TOADIER]
18   AEILNRS NAILERS
19   AEINOST ATONIES
20   AEENRST EASTERN
```

Any of the seven-letter stems that have already appeared alongside the six-letter stems have been excluded. As with the six-letter stems there is some overlap of eight-letter words among the lists but this can only serve to reinforce the learning.

The individual stems are shown in alphabetical order of the stem together with the words that can be formed by combining them with another letter.

ADEINOT: The ADONITE seven-letter set
(Ranked No.8)

B

OBTAINED

C

ACTIONED
CATENOID

I

IDEATION
IODINATE
TAENIOID

L

DELATION

M

DOMINATE
NEMATOID

N

ANOINTED
ANTINODE

$$\boxed{A}\boxed{D}\boxed{O}\boxed{N}\boxed{I}\boxed{T}\boxed{E}$$

P

ANTIPODE

R

AROINTED
DERATION
ORDINATE
RATIONED

S

ASTONIED
SEDATION

T

ANTIDOTE
TETANOID

V

DONATIVE

ADEINRS: The SARDINE seven-letter set
(Ranked No.9)

A
ARANEIDS

B
BRANDIES
BRANDISE

D
SARDINED

E
ARSENIDE
DENARIES
DRAISENE
NEARSIDE

F
FRIANDES

G
DERAIGNS
GRADINES
READINGS

I
DRAISINE

L
ISLANDER

M
ADERMINS
SIRNAMED

S A R D I N E

N
INSNARED

O
ANEROIDS
ANODISER
DONARIES

P
SPRAINED

R
DRAINERS
SERRANID

S
ARIDNESS
SARDINES

T
DETRAINS
RANDIEST
STRAINED

U
DENARIUS
UNRAISED
URANIDES

V
INVADERS
SANDIVER

Y
SYNEDRIA

ADEINRT: The TRAINED seven-letter set
(Ranked No.6)

A

DENTARIA
RAINDATE

C

CRINATED
DICENTRA

D

INDARTED

E

DETAINER
RETAINED

G

DERATING
GRADIENT
REDATING
TREADING

H

ANTHERID

I

DAINTIER

T R A I N E D

O

AROINTED
DERATION
ORDINATE
RATIONED

P

DIPTERAN

S

DETRAINS
RANDIEST
STRAINED

T

NITRATED

U

DATURINE
INDURATE
RUINATED
URINATED

ADEIORT: The TOADIER seven-letter set
(Ranked No.17)

C₃
CERATOID

G₂
ERGATOID

K₅
KERATOID

L₁
IDOLATER
TAILORED

M₃
MEDIATOR

T₁ O₁ A₁ D₂ I₁ E₁ R₁

N₁
AROINTED
DERATION
ORDINATE
RATIONED

R₁
ADROITER

S₁
ASTEROID

T₁
TERATOID

V₄
DEVIATOR

ADEIRST: The TIRADES seven-letter set
(Ranked No.16)

A
AIRDATES
DATARIES
RADIATES

B
BARDIEST
BRAIDEST
RABIDEST
REDBAITS
TRIBADES

C
ACRIDEST

D
DISRATED

E
READIEST
SERIATED
SIDERATE
STEADIER

H
HAIRSTED
HARDIEST

I
IRISATED

K
STRAIKED

T I R A D E S

L
DILATERS
LARDIEST
REDTAILS

M
MARDIEST
MISRATED
READMITS

N
DETRAINS
RANDIEST
STRAINED

O
ASTEROID

P
DIPTERAS
DRAPIEST
RAPIDEST
SPIRATED
TARSIPED
TRAIPSED

S
ASTERIDS
DIASTERS
DISASTER
DISRATES

T
STRAITED
STRIATED
TARDIEST

W
TAWDRIES

AEEILRT: The REALTIE seven-letter set
(Ranked No.14)

B
LIBERATE

D
DETAILER
ELATERID
RETAILED

F
FEATLIER
FRAILTEE

G
LITREAGE

H
ETHERIAL

K
TEARLIKE

L
LAETRILE

M
EREMITAL
MATERIEL
REALTIME

N
ELATERIN
ENTAILER
TREENAIL

R E A L T I E

O
AEROLITE

P
PEARLITE

R
RETAILER

S
ATELIERS
EARLIEST
LATERISE
LEARIEST
REALTIES

T
LATERITE
LITERATE

V
LEVIRATE
RELATIVE

Z
LATERIZE

AEEINRT: The TRAINEE seven-letter set
(Ranked No.11)

C

CENTIARE
CREATINE
INCREATE
ITERANCE

D

DETAINER
RETAINED

G

ENARGITE
GRATINEE
INTERAGE

H

ATHERINE
HERNIATE

I

INERTIAE

K

ANKERITE
KREATINE

T R A I N E E

L

ELATERIN
ENTAILER
TREENAIL

M

ANTIMERE

P

APERIENT

R

RETAINER

S

ARENITES
ARSENITE
RESINATE
STEARINE
TRAINEES

AEEIRST: The SERIATE seven-letter set
(Ranked No.10)

D₂
READIEST
SERIATED
SIDERATE
STEADIER

E₁
EATERIES

H₄
HEARTIES

L₁
ATELIERS
EARLIEST
LATERISE
LEARIEST
REALTIES

M₃
EMERITAS
EMIRATES
REAMIEST
STEAMIER

N₁
ARENITES
ARSENITE
RESINATE
STEARINE
TRAINEES

O₁
ETAERIOS

S₁ **E**₁ **R**₁ **I**₁ **A**₁ **T**₁ **E**₁

P₃
PARIETES
PETARIES

R₁
ARTERIES
REASTIER

S₁
SERIATES

T₁
ARIETTES
ITERATES
TEARIEST
TREATIES
TREATISE

V₄
EVIRATES

W₄
SWEATIER
TAWERIES
WASTERIE
WEARIEST

Y₄
YEASTIER

AEENRST: The EASTERN seven-letter set
(Ranked No.20)

A
ARSENATE
SERENATA

B
ABSENTER

C
CENTARES
ENCASTRE
REASCENT
REENACTS
SARCENET

E
SERENATE

F
FASTENER
FENESTRA
REFASTEN

G
ESTRANGE
GRANTEES
GREATENS
NEGATERS
REAGENTS
SEGREANT
SERGEANT
STERNAGE

H
HASTENER
HEARTENS

I
ARENITES
ARSENITE
RESINATE
STEARINE
TRAINEES

E A S T E R N

J
SERJEANT

L
ALTERNES
ETERNALS
TELERANS

M
REMANETS

O
EARSTONE
RESONATE

R
TERRANES

S
ASSENTER
EARNESTS
SARSENET
STERANES

T
ENTREATS
RATTEENS

U
SAUTERNE

V
AVENTRES
VETERANS

AEILNRS: The NAILERS seven-letter set
(Ranked No.18)

B

RINSABLE

C

CARLINES
LANCIERS

D

ISLANDER

E

ALIENERS

G

ALIGNERS
ENGRAILS
LASERING
NARGILES
REALIGNS
SALERING
SANGLIER
SIGNALER
SLANGIER

H

INHALERS

I

AIRLINES
SNAILIER

M

MARLINES
MINERALS
MISLEARN

N A I L E R S

O

AILERONS
ALERIONS
ALIENORS

P

PEARLINS
PRALINES

R

SNARLIER

S

RAINLESS

T

ENTRAILS
LARNIEST
LATRINES
RATLINES
REINSTAL
RETINALS
SLANTIER
TRENAILS

U

LUNARIES

V

RAVELINS

X

RELAXINS

Y

INLAYERS
SNAILERY

AEILNRT: The ENTRAIL seven-letter set
(Ranked No.7)

C
CLARINET

E
ELATERIN
ENTAILER
TREENAIL

F
INFLATER

G
ALERTING
ALTERING
INTEGRAL
RELATING
TANGLIER
TERAGLIN
TRIANGLE

I
INERTIAL

M
TERMINAL
TRAMLINE

N
INTERNAL

E N T R A I L

O
ORIENTAL
RELATION
TAILERON

P
INTERLAP
TRAPLINE
TRIPLANE

S
ENTRAILS
LARNIEST
LATRINES
RATLINES
REINSTAL
RETINALS
SLANTIER
TRENAILS

T
RATTLINE

U
AUNTLIER
RETINULA
TENURIAL

V
INTERVAL

Y
INTERLAY

AEILRST: The RETAILS seven-letter set
(Ranked No.13)

B

BLASTIER
LIBRATES
TABLIERS

C

ALTRICES
ARTICLES
RECITALS
SELICTAR
STERICAL

D

DILATERS
LARDIEST
REDTAILS

E

ATELIERS
EARLIEST
LATERISE
LEARIEST
REALTIES

F

FLARIEST
FRAILEST

G

GLARIEST
REGALIST

I

LAIRIEST
LISTERIA

K

LARKIEST
STALKIER
STARLIKE

R E T A I L S

L

LITERALS
TALLIERS
TRIELLAS

M

LAMISTER
LAMITERS
MARLIEST
MARLITES
MISALTER

N

ENTRAILS
LARNIEST
LATRINES
RATLINES
REINSTAL
RETINALS
SLANTIER
TRENAILS

O

SOTERIAL

P

PILASTER
PLAISTER
PLAITERS

R

RETIRALS
RETRIALS
TRAILERS

S

REALISTS
SALTIERS
SALTIRES
SLAISTER

T

TERTIALS

U

URALITES

AEINORS: The ERASION seven-letter set
(Ranked No.15)

B

BARONIES
SEAROBIN

C

SCENARIO

D

ANEROIDS
ANODISER
DONARIES

F

FARINOSE

G

IGNAROES
ORGANISE
ORIGANES

L

AILERONS
ALERIONS
ALIENORS

E R A S I O N

M

MORAINES
ROMAINES
ROMANISE

N

NONARIES
RAISONNE

S

ERASIONS
SENSORIA

T

ANOESTRI
ARSONITE
NOTAIRES
NOTARIES
NOTARISE
ROSINATE
SENORITA

V

AVERSION

AEINORT: The OTARINE seven-letter set
(Ranked No.1)

A
AERATION

H
ANTIHERO

R
ANTERIOR

B
BARITONE
OBTAINER
REOBTAIN
TABORINE

L
ORIENTAL
RELATION
TAILERON

S
ANOESTRI
ARSONITE
NOTAIRES
NOTARIES
NOTARISE
ROSINATE
SENORITA

C
ACTIONER
ANORETIC
CREATION
REACTION

O T A R I N E

T
TENTORIA

N
ANOINTER
INORNATE
REANOINT

D
AROINTED
DERATION
ORDINATE
RATIONED

Z
NOTARIZE

P
ATROPINE

AEINOST: The ATONIES seven-letter set
(Ranked No.19)

B

BOTANIES
BOTANISE
NIOBATES
OBEISANT

C

ACONITES
CANOEIST
SONICATE

D

ASTONIED
SEDATION

L

ELATIONS
INSOLATE
TOENAILS

M

AMNIOTES
MASONITE
MISATONE
SOMNIATE

A T O N I E S

N

ENATIONS
SONATINE

P

SAPONITE

R

ANOESTRI
ARSONITE
NOTAIRES
NOTARIES
NOTARISE
ROSINATE
SENORITA

S

ASSIENTO
ASTONIES

V

STOVAINE

X

SAXONITE

AEINRST: The RETAINS seven-letter set
(Ranked No.2)

A

ANTISERA
ARTESIAN
RATANIES
RESINATA
SANTERIA
SEATRAIN

B

ATEBRINS
BANISTER
BARNIEST

C

CANISTER
CARNIEST
CERATINS
CISTERNA
CREATINS
NACRITES
SCANTIER
TACRINES

D

DETRAINS
RANDIEST
STRAINED

E

ARENITES
ARSENITE
RESINATE
STEARINE
TRAINEES

F

FAINTERS
FENITARS

G

ANGRIEST
ANGSTIER
ASTRINGE
GANISTER
GANTRIES
GRANITES
INGRATES
RANGIEST
REASTING
STEARING
TASERING

H

HAIRNETS
INEARTHS
THERIANS

I

INERTIAS
RAINIEST

J

NARTJIES

K

KERATINS
NARKIEST

L

ENTRAILS
LARNIEST
LATRINES
RATLINES
REINSTAL
RETINALS
SLANTIER
TRENAILS

R E T A I N S

M

MERANTIS
MINARETS
RAIMENTS

N

ENTRAINS
TRANNIES

O

ANOESTRI
ARSONITE
NOTAIRES
NOTARIES
NOTARISE
ROSINATE
SENORITA

P

PAINTERS
PANTRIES
PERTAINS
PINASTER
PRISTANE
REPAINTS

R

RESTRAIN
RETRAINS
STRAINER
TERRAINS
TRAINERS
TRANSIRE

S

ARTINESS
RESIANTS
RETSINAS
SNARIEST
STAINERS
STARNIES
STEARINS

T

INTREATS
NITRATES
STRAITEN
TARTINES
TERTIANS

U

RUINATES
TAURINES
URANITES
URINATES

W

TINWARES

AEIORST: The OTARIES seven-letter set
(Ranked No.4)

B
SABOTIER

C
EROTICAS

D
ASTEROID

E
ETAERIOS

H
HOARIEST

J
JAROSITE

L
SOTERIAL

M
AMORTISE
ATOMISER

N
ANOESTRI
ARSONITE
NOTAIRES
NOTARIES
NOTARISE
ROSINATE
SENORITA

O T A R I E S

P
SEPTORIA

R
ROARIEST
ROTARIES

S
ROASTIES

T
TOASTIER

U
OUTRAISE
SAUTOIRE

V
TRAVOISE
VIATORES
VOTARIES

AENORST: The TREASON seven-letter set
(Ranked No.5)

A

ANOESTRA

B

BARONETS

C

ANCESTOR
ENACTORS
SARCONET
SORTANCE

D

TORNADES

E

EARSTONE
RESONATE

F

SEAFRONT

G

ESTRAGON
NEGATORS
ORANGEST
RAGSTONE
STONERAG

I

ANOESTRI
ARSONITE
NOTAIRES
NOTARIES
NOTARISE
ROSINATE
SENORITA

M

MONSTERA
ONSTREAM
STOREMAN
TONEARMS

T R E A S O N

N

NORTENAS
RESONANT

P

OPERANTS
PRONATES
PROTEANS

R

ANTRORSE

S

ASSENTOR
SANTEROS
SENATORS
STARNOSE
TREASONS

T

ORNATEST

U

OUTEARNS

V

VENATORS

W

STONERAW

EEINRST: The ENTRIES seven-letter set
(Ranked No.12)

A.

ARENITES
ARSENITE
RESINATE
STEARINE
TRAINEES

C.

CENTRIES
ENTERICS
ENTICERS
SCIENTER
SECRETIN

D.

INSERTED
NERDIEST
RESIDENT
SINTERED
TRENDIES

E.

ETERNISE
TEENSIER

F.

FERNIEST
INFESTER

G.

GENTRIES
INTEGERS
REESTING
STEERING
STREIGNE

I.

ERINITES
NITERIES

K.

KERNITES

L.

ENLISTER
LISTENER
REENLIST
SILENTER

E N T R I E S

M.

MISENTER

N.

INTENSER
INTERNES

O.

ONERIEST
SEROTINE

R.

INSERTER
REINSERT
REINTERS
RENTIERS
TERRINES

S.

INTERESS
SENTRIES
TRENISES

T.

INERTEST
INSETTER
INTEREST
STERNITE
TRIENTES

U.

ESURIENT
NEURITES
RETINUES
REUNITES

V.

NERVIEST
REINVEST
SERVIENT
SIRVENTE

X.

INTERSEX

Y.

SERENITY

EINORST: The STONIER seven-letter set
(Ranked No.3)

A

ANOESTRI
ARSONITE
NOTAIRES
NOTARIES
NOTARISE
ROSINATE
SENORITA

B

BORNITES
RIBSTONE

C

COINTERS
CORNIEST
NOTICERS
RECTIONS

D

DRONIEST

E

ONERIEST
SEROTINE

G

GENITORS
ROSETING

H

HORNIEST
ORNITHES

I

IRONIEST

J

JOINTERS

K

INSTROKE

L

RETINOLS

S T O N I E R

N

INTONERS
NOINTERS
TERNIONS

O

SNOOTIER

P

POINTERS
PORNIEST
PROTEINS
REPOINTS
TROPINES

R

INTRORSE
SNORTIER

S

OESTRINS
TERSIONS

T

SNOTTIER
TENORIST
TRITONES

U

NITREOUS
ROUTINES
SNOUTIER

V

INVESTOR

X

NITROXES

Y

SEROTINY
TYROSINE

Z

TRIZONES

Top 1000 most likely seven-letter words

These 1000 seven-letter words, arranged in anagram form, represent the most likely ones that will occur given the distribution of letters in the Scrabble set. This list is largely complementary to the seven-letter words listed in the bonus word sets but there are some words appearing in both.

AABEIOR	AEROBIA	**AAEIRTW**	AWAITER		REBOANT
AACEINR	ACARINE	**AAELORS**	AREOLAS	**ACDEINO**	CODEINA
	CARINAE	**AAELORU**	AUREOLA		OCEANID
AADEENR	ANEARED	**AAENRST**	ANESTRA	**ACDEINR**	CAIRNED
AADEERT	AERATED		SANTERA		CARNIED
AADEILR	RADIALE	**AAENRTU**	NATURAE		DANCIER
AADEINR	ARANEID		TAUREAN	**ACEEINR**	CINEREA
AADEINS	NAIADES	**AAEORRT**	AERATOR	**ACEENOR**	CORNEAE
AADEIOR	AERADIO	**AAEORST**	AEROSAT	**ACEENOT**	ACETONE
AADEIRS	ARAISED	**AAIINRT**	ANTIAIR	**ACEEORT**	OCREATE
AADEIRT	AIRDATE	**AAILNOT**	AILANTO	**ACEGINO**	COINAGE
	RADIATE		ALATION	**ACEILNR**	CARLINE
	TIARAED	**AAINOST**	ATONIAS	**ACEILOR**	CALORIE
AAEEINT	TAENIAE	**AAINRST**	ANTIARS		CARIOLE
AAEELOR	AREOLAE		ARTISAN		COALIER
AAEELRT	LAETARE		TSARINA		LORICAE
AAEERST	AERATES	**ABDEINR**	BANDIER	**ACEILOT**	ALOETIC
AAEERTU	AUREATE		BRAINED	**ACEILRT**	ARTICLE
AAEGINR	ANERGIA	**ABEEINT**	BETAINE		RECITAL
AAEGIST	AGATISE	**ABEEIRT**	BEATIER		TALCIER
AAEILNO	AEOLIAN		EBRIATE	**ACEINOS**	ACINOSE
AAEILNT	ANTLIAE	**ABEEORT**	ABORTEE	**ACEINOT**	ACONITE
AAEILOR	OLEARIA	**ABEGINO**	BEGONIA		ANOETIC
AAEILRS	AERIALS	**ABEIINT**	BAINITE	**ACEINRS**	ARCSINE
AAEILRU	AURELIA	**ABEINOT**	NIOBATE		ARSENIC
AAEIMNT	AMENTIA	**ABEINRT**	ATEBRIN		CARNIES
	ANIMATE	**ABEINST**	BANTIES		CERASIN
AAEIMRT	AMIRATE		BASINET	**ACEINRT**	CANTIER
AAEINNO	AEONIAN		BESAINT		CERATIN
AAEINST	ENTASIA		BESTAIN		CERTAIN
	TAENIAS	**ABEIORS**	ISOBARE		CREATIN
AAEIPRT	APTERIA	**ABEIOST**	BOATIES		CRINATE
AAEIRRT	TARAIRE	**ABEIRST**	BAITERS		NACRITE
AAEIRST	ARISTAE		BARITES		TACRINE
	ASTERIA		REBAITS	**ACEINST**	ACETINS
	ATRESIA		TERBIAS		CANIEST
AAEIRTT	ARIETTA	**ABENORT**	BARONET		CINEAST

ACEIORS	CARIOSE		ESTRADE		SNAILED
	ORACIES		REASTED	**ADEILNU**	ALIUNDE
	SCORIAE		REDATES		UNIDEAL
ACEIORT	EROTICA		SEDATER	**ADEILOR**	DARIOLE
ACEIOST	SOCIATE		STEARED	**ADEILOS**	DEASOIL
ACEIRST	ATRESIC		TASERED		ISOLEAD
	CRISTAE	**ADEFINR**	FRIANDE	**ADEILOU**	DOULEIA
	RACIEST	**ADEFINT**	DEFIANT	**ADEILRS**	DERAILS
	STEARIC		FAINTED		DIALERS
ACENORT	ENACTOR	**ADEGILN**	ALIGNED		REDIALS
ACINORT	CAROTIN		DEALIGN		SIDERAL
	CORTINA		DEALING	**ADEILRT**	DILATER
ADDEINO	ADENOID		LEADING		REDTAIL
ADEEGOT	DOGEATE	**ADEGILO**	GEOIDAL		TRAILED
	GOATEED	**ADEGILR**	GLADIER		TRIALED
ADEEILN	ALIENED		GLAIRED	**ADEILRU**	UREDIAL
	DELAINE	**ADEGINR**	AREDING	**ADEILST**	DETAILS
ADEEILR	LEADIER		DEARING		DILATES
ADEEILS	AEDILES		DERAIGN	**ADEIMNO**	AMIDONE
	DEISEAL		EARDING		DOMAINE
ADEEINN	ADENINE		GRADINE	**ADEIMNR**	ADERMIN
ADEEINS	ANISEED		GRAINED		INARMED
ADEEIRR	READIER		READING	**ADEINNR**	NARDINE
ADEEIRS	DEARIES	**ADEGINS**	AGNISED	**ADEINOR**	ANEROID
	READIES	**ADEGIOT**	GODETIA	**ADEINOS**	ADONISE
ADEEIST	IDEATES	**ADEGIRS**	AGRISED		ANODISE
ADEEITU	AUDITEE	**ADEGIRT**	TRIAGED		SODAINE
ADEELNR	LEARNED	**ADEGIRU**	GAUDIER	**ADEINOV**	NAEVOID
ADEELNT	EDENTAL	**ADEGIST**	AGISTED	**ADEINPT**	DEPAINT
	LATENED	**ADEGNOR**	GROANED		PAINTED
ADEELOS	ELODEAS	**ADEGNOT**	TANGOED		PATINED
ADEELRT	ALERTED	**ADEGNRT**	DRAGNET	**ADEINRR**	DRAINER
	ALTERED		GRANTED		RANDIER
	REDEALT	**ADEGORT**	GAROTED	**ADEINRS**	RANDIES
	RELATED	**ADEHIRT**	AIRTHED		SANDIER
	TREADLE	**ADEIILR**	DELIRIA		SARDINE
ADEENRS	DEANERS		IRIDEAL	**ADEINRT**	ANTIRED
	ENDEARS	**ADEIINR**	DENARII		DETRAIN
ADEENRU	UNEARED	**ADEIINT**	INEDITA		TRAINED
ADEENST	STANDEE	**ADEIIRS**	AIRSIDE	**ADEINRU**	UNAIRED
	STEANED		DAIRIES		URANIDE
ADEEORS	OREADES		DIARIES	**ADEINST**	DESTAIN
ADEERST	DEAREST		DIARISE		DETAINS
	DERATES	**ADEILNS**	DENIALS		INSTEAD

	NIDATES	**ADELOTU**	OUTLEAD	**ADIORTU**	AUDITOR
	SAINTED	**ADENOOT**	ODONATE	**AEEEILN**	ALIENEE
	SATINED	**ADENORR**	ADORNER	**AEEEIRT**	EATERIE
	STAINED		READORN	**AEEGILN**	LINEAGE
ADEINTT	TAINTED	**ADENORT**	TORNADE	**AEEGILT**	EGALITE
ADEINTU	AUDIENT	**ADENORU**	RONDEAU	**AEEGINR**	REGINAE
ADEINTV	DEVIANT	**ADENOST**	ASTONED	**AEEGINS**	AGENISE
ADEIOPT	OPIATED		DONATES	**AEEGINU**	EUGENIA
ADEIORS	RADIOES		ONSTEAD	**AEEGIRU**	EUGARIE
	ROADIES	**ADENOSU**	DOUANES	**AEEGLOR**	AEROGEL
	SOREDIA	**ADENOTT**	ATTONED	**AEEGNRT**	GRANTEE
ADEIORV	AVODIRE		NOTATED		GREATEN
	AVOIDER	**ADENRST**	DARNEST		NEGATER
ADEIOST	IODATES		ENDARTS		REAGENT
	TOADIES		STANDER	**AEEGOST**	GOATEES
ADEIPRT	DIPTERA		STARNED	**AEEHINR**	HERNIAE
	PARTIED	**ADENRTU**	DAUNTER	**AEEIIRS**	AIERIES
	PIRATED		NATURED	**AEEILNR**	ALIENER
ADEIRRT	TARDIER		UNRATED	**AEEILNS**	SEALINE
	TARRIED		UNTREAD	**AEEILNT**	LINEATE
ADEIRST	ARIDEST	**ADEOORS**	ROADEOS	**AEEILRR**	EARLIER
	ASTERID	**ADEOORT**	ODORATE		LEARIER
	ASTRIDE	**ADEORST**	DOATERS	**AEEILRS**	EARLIES
	DIASTER		ROASTED		REALISE
	DISRATE		TORSADE	**AEEILRT**	ATELIER
	STAIDER		TROADES		REALTIE
	STAIRED	**ADEORSU**	AROUSED	**AEEILTT**	AILETTE
	TARDIES	**ADEORTT**	ROTATED	**AEEIMNR**	REMANIE
	TIRADES		TROATED	**AEEIMNT**	ETAMINE
ADEIRSU	RESIDUA	**ADEORTU**	OUTDARE		MATINEE
ADEIRTT	ATTIRED		OUTREAD	**AEEIMRT**	EMERITA
ADEIRTY	DIETARY		READOUT		EMIRATE
ADEISTU	DAUTIES	**ADGINOR**	ADORING		MEATIER
ADELNOR	LADRONE		GRADINO	**AEEINPR**	PERINEA
ADELNOS	LOADENS		ROADING	**AEEINRT**	ARENITE
ADELNOT	TALONED	**ADGINOT**	DOATING		RETINAE
ADELORS	LOADERS	**ADILNOR**	ORDINAL		TRAINEE
	ORDEALS	**ADILORT**	DILATOR	**AEEINST**	ETESIAN
	RELOADS	**ADINORS**	DONAIRS	**AEEINTT**	TAENITE
ADELORT	DELATOR		INROADS	**AEEINTV**	NAIVETE
	LEOTARD		ORDAINS	**AEEIORT**	ETAERIO
ADELORU	ROULADE		SADIRON	**AEEIPRT**	PEATIER
ADELOST	SALTOED	**ADINORT**	DIATRON	**AEEIRRS**	REARISE
	SOLATED	**ADIORST**	ASTROID		RERAISE

AEEIRRT	TEARIER	**AEFILOT**	FOLIATE		TANGIER
AEEIRST	AERIEST	**AEFINRT**	FAINTER		TEARING
	SERIATE		FENITAR	**AEGINST**	EASTING
AEEIRTT	ARIETTE	**AEFINST**	FAINEST		EATINGS
	ITERATE		FANSITE		GAINEST
AEEIRTV	EVIRATE		NAIFEST		GENISTA
AEELNOS	ENOLASE	**AEFIRST**	FAIREST		INGATES
	LOANEES	**AEGILNR**	ALIGNER		INGESTA
AEELNRS	LEANERS		ENGRAIL		SEATING
AEELNRT	ALTERNE		LAERING		TAGINES
	ENTERAL		LEARING		TANGIES
	ETERNAL		NARGILE		TEASING
	TELERAN		REALIGN		TSIGANE
AEELNST	ELANETS		REGINAL	**AEGINTU**	UNITAGE
	LATEENS	**AEGILNT**	ATINGLE	**AEGIORT**	GOATIER
	LEANEST		ELATING	**AEGIOST**	GOATIES
AEELORS	AREOLES		GELATIN	**AEGIRST**	AGISTER
AEELORU	AUREOLE		GENITAL		AIGRETS
AEELOST	OLEATES		TAGLINE		GAITERS
AEELRST	ELATERS	**AEGILOS**	GOALIES		SEAGIRT
	REALEST		SOILAGE		STAGIER
	RELATES	**AEGILOU**	EULOGIA		STRIGAE
	RESLATE	**AEGILST**	AGILEST		TIRAGES
	STEALER		AIGLETS		TRIAGES
AEEMORT	EROTEMA		GELATIS	**AEGISTU**	AUGITES
AEENNOT	NEONATE		LIGATES	**AEGLNOT**	TANGELO
AEENOPR	PERAEON		TAIGLES	**AEGLORT**	GLOATER
AEENORS	ARENOSE	**AEGINNO**	GANOINE		LEGATOR
AEENOSU	AENEOUS	**AEGINOR**	ORIGANE	**AEGNOOR**	OREGANO
AEENRRT	TERRANE	**AEGINOS**	AGONIES	**AEGNORS**	ONAGERS
AEENRST	EARNEST		AGONISE		ORANGES
	EASTERN	**AEGINRS**	ANGRIES	**AEGNORT**	NEGATOR
	NEAREST		EARINGS	**AEGNOST**	ONSTAGE
	RATEENS		ERASING		TANGOES
	STERANE		GAINERS	**AEGNRST**	ARGENTS
AEENRTT	ENTREAT		GRAINES		GARNETS
	RATTEEN		REAGINS		STRANGE
	TERNATE		REGAINS	**AEGNRTU**	GAUNTER
AEEOPRT	OPERATE		REGINAS	**AEGOORT**	ROOTAGE
AEEORRS	REAROSE		SEARING	**AEGORST**	GAROTES
AEEORST	ROSEATE		SERINGA		ORGEATS
AEEORTV	OVERATE	**AEGINRT**	GRANITE		STORAGE
	OVEREAT		GRATINE		TOERAGS
AEERSTU	AUSTERE		INGRATE	**AEGORTU**	OUTRAGE

AEHILOR	AIRHOLE		SALIENT	**AEINNRS**	INSANER
AEHINRS	ARSHINE		SALTINE		INSNARE
	HERNIAS		SLAINTE	**AEINNRT**	ENTRAIN
	NEARISH		STANIEL		TRANNIE
AEHINRT	HAIRNET		TENAILS	**AEINNRU**	ANEURIN
	INEARTH	**AEILNSU**	INSULAE	**AEINNST**	INANEST
	THERIAN		INULASE		NANITES
AEHNORT	ANOTHER	**AEILNTU**	ALUNITE		STANINE
AEIILNR	AIRLINE	**AEILOPR**	PELORIA		TANNIES
AEIILRS	LAIRISE	**AEILORV**	VARIOLE	**AEINOPS**	EPINAOS
AEIILST	LAITIES	**AEILOST**	ISOLATE		SENOPIA
AEIIMRT	AIRTIME	**AEILOTV**	VIOLATE	**AEINORS**	ERASION
AEIINOP	EPINAOI	**AEILRRT**	RETIRAL	**AEINORT**	NOTAIRE
AEIINRR	RAINIER		RETRIAL		OTARINE
AEIINRS	SENARII		TRAILER	**AEINOSS**	ANOESIS
AEIINRT	INERTIA	**AEILRST**	REALIST	**AEINOST**	ATONIES
AEIINST	ISATINE		RETAILS	**AEINOSV**	EVASION
AEIIRST	AIRIEST		SALTIER	**AEINPRT**	PAINTER
	IRISATE		SALTIRE		PERTAIN
AEILMNO	MINEOLA		SLATIER		REPAINT
AEILMNT	AILMENT		TAILERS	**AEINRRS**	SIERRAN
	ALIMENT	**AEILRTT**	TERTIAL		SNARIER
AEILMOR	LOAMIER	**AEILRTU**	URALITE	**AEINRRT**	RETRAIN
AEILNOP	OPALINE	**AEILSTU**	SITULAE		TERRAIN
AEILNOR	AILERON	**AEIMNOR**	MORAINE		TRAINER
	ALERION		ROMAINE	**AEINRST**	ANESTRI
	ALIENOR	**AEIMNOS**	ANOMIES		ANTSIER
AEILNOS	ANISOLE	**AEIMNOT**	AMNIOTE		NASTIER
AEILNOT	ELATION	**AEIMNOU**	MOINEAU		RATINES
	TOENAIL	**AEIMNRT**	MERANTI		RESIANT
AEILNRR	LARNIER		MINARET		RETAINS
AEILNRS	ALINERS		RAIMENT		RETINAS
	NAILERS	**AEIMNST**	ETAMINS		RETSINA
	RENAILS		INMATES		STAINER
AEILNRT	ENTRAIL		MAINEST		STARNIE
	LATRINE		MANTIES		STEARIN
	RATLINE		TAMEINS	**AEINRSV**	AVENIRS
	RELIANT		TAMINES		RAVINES
	RETINAL	**AEIMORS**	AIRSOME	**AEINRTT**	INTREAT
	TRENAIL	**AEIMOST**	AMOSITE		ITERANT
AEILNST	EASTLIN		ATOMIES		NATTIER
	ELASTIN		ATOMISE		NITRATE
	ENTAILS		OSMIATE		TARTINE
	NAILSET	**AEINNOT**	ENATION		TERTIAN

AEINRTU	RUINATE	**AELNRST**	ANTLERS	**AGINOST**	AGONIST
	TAURINE		RENTALS		GITANOS
	URANITE		SALTERN	**AGINOTU**	AUTOING
	URINATE		SLANTER		OUTGAIN
AEINRTW	TAWNIER		STERNAL	**AGIORST**	AGISTOR
AEINSTT	TINWARE	**AELNRTU**	NEUTRAL		ORGIAST
AEINSTU	INSTATE	**AELOORS**	AEROSOL	**AILNOST**	LATINOS
	SATINET		ROSEOLA		TALIONS
	AUNTIES	**AELORRT**	REALTOR	**AILNOTU**	OUTLAIN
	SINUATE		RELATOR	**AILORST**	ORALIST
AEINSTW	AWNIEST	**AELORST**	OESTRAL		RIALTOS
	TAWNIES		OLESTRA		SLIOTAR
	WANIEST	**AELORTT**	RETOTAL		TAILORS
	WANTIES	**AELORTU**	ROTULAE	**AINOORT**	ORATION
AEIOPRS	SOAPIER		TORULAE	**AINOPRT**	ATROPIN
AEIOPST	ATOPIES	**AEMNORT**	TONEARM	**AINORST**	AROINTS
	OPIATES	**AENNORT**	NORTENA		RATIONS
AEIORST	OARIEST	**AENNOTU**	TONNEAU	**AINORTU**	RAINOUT
	OTARIES	**AENOPRT**	OPERANT	**AIORSTU**	SAUTOIR
	ROASTIE		PRONATE	**BEEINOT**	EBONITE
AEIORSV	OVARIES		PROTEAN	**BEINORT**	BORNITE
AEIOSTT	OATIEST	**AENORRS**	SERRANO	**CEEIORT**	COTERIE
	OSTIATE	**AENORRT**	ORNATER	**CEINORT**	COINTER
	TOASTIE	**AENORST**	ATONERS		NOTICER
AEIRRST	ARTSIER		SANTERO		RECTION
	SERRATI		SENATOR	**DEEEINR**	NEEDIER
	TARRIES		TREASON	**DEEIINT**	DIETINE
	TARSIER	**AENORSU**	ARENOUS	**DEEILNO**	ELOINED
AEIRSTT	ARTIEST	**AENORTU**	OUTEARN	**DEEILNR**	REDLINE
	ARTISTE	**AENORTV**	VENATOR		RELINED
	ATTIRES	**AENOSTT**	ATTONES	**DEEILNT**	LENITED
	IRATEST		NOTATES	**DEEILOR**	REOILED
	RATITES	**AENOSTU**	SOUTANE	**DEEILOS**	OILSEED
	STRIATE	**AENRSTU**	AUNTERS	**DEEILRT**	RETILED
	TASTIER		NATURES	**DEEINOR**	ORDINEE
	TERTIAS		SAUNTER	**DEEINRS**	DENIERS
AEIRTUY	AUREITY	**AEORRST**	ROASTER		NEREIDS
AELNOOS	ALSOONE	**AEORRTU**	ORATURE		RESINED
AELNORS	LOANERS	**AEORSTT**	ROTATES	**DEEINRU**	UREDINE
	ORLEANS		TOASTER	**DEEINST**	DESTINE
	RELOANS	**AEORTTU**	OUTRATE		ENDITES
AELNORU	ALEURON	**AGILNOT**	ANTILOG		STEINED
AELNOST	ETALONS	**AGINORT**	ORATING	**DEEINTU**	DETINUE
	TOLANES		ROATING	**DEEIORS**	OREIDES

	OSIERED		NOINTED	**EEGINOS**	GENOISE
DEEIRST	DIESTER	**DEINORR**	DRONIER		SOIGNEE
	DIETERS	**DEINORS**	DINEROS	**EEGINRT**	GENTIER
	REEDITS		DONSIER		INTEGER
	REISTED		INDORSE		TEERING
	RESITED		ORDINES		TREEING
DEEIRTU	ERUDITE		ROSINED	**EEGIOST**	EGOTISE
DEELNOT	DOLENTE		SORDINE		GOETIES
DEENORS	ENDORSE	**DEINORU**	DOURINE	**EEHINOR**	HEROINE
DEENORT	ERODENT		NEUROID	**EEIINRT**	ERINITE
DEENOST	DENOTES		OUNDIER		NITERIE
DEEORST	OERSTED	**DEINOST**	DITONES	**EEIINST**	SIENITE
	ROSETED		STONIED	**EEILNNO**	LEONINE
	TEREDOS	**DEINRST**	SNIRTED	**EEILNOR**	ELOINER
DEGINOR	ERODING		TINDERS	**EEILNOS**	OLEINES
	GROINED	**DEINRTU**	INTRUDE	**EEILNRS**	LIERNES
	IGNORED		TURDINE		RELINES
	NEGROID		UNTIRED	**EEILNST**	LENITES
	REDOING		UNTRIDE		LISENTE
DEGINOT	INGOTED		UNTRIED		SETLINE
DEGIORT	GOITRED	**DEIOORS**	ODORISE		TENSILE
DEIINOS	IODINES		OROIDES	**EEILORS**	LOERIES
	IONISED	**DEIOOST**	OSTEOID	**EEILORT**	TROELIE
DEIINOT	EDITION	**DEIORRT**	DORTIER	**EEILOST**	ESTOILE
	TENIOID	**DEIORST**	EDITORS		ETOILES
DEIINRT	INDITER		ROISTED	**EEILRST**	LEISTER
	NITRIDE		ROSITED		RETILES
DEIIORS	IODISER		SORTIED		STERILE
DEIIORT	DIORITE		STEROID	**EEIMNOT**	ONETIME
DEILNOO	EIDOLON		STORIED	**EEINNRT**	INTERNE
DEILNOS	DOLINES		TRIODES	**EEINOPR**	PEREION
	INDOLES	**DEIORTT**	DOTTIER		PIONEER
	SONDELI	**DEIORTU**	ETOURDI	**EEINORR**	ONERIER
DEILNOT	LENTOID		IODURET	**EEINRRT**	INERTER
DEILNOU	UNOILED		OUTRIDE		REINTER
DEILNRT	TENDRIL	**DEIOSTU**	OUTSIDE		RENTIER
	TRINDLE		TEDIOUS		TERRINE
DEILORS	SOLDIER	**DELNORT**	ENTROLD	**EEINRST**	ENTIRES
	SOLIDER	**DENORST**	RODENTS		ENTRIES
DEILORT	DOILTER		SNORTED		NERITES
DEILOTU	OUTLIED	**EEEINRS**	EENSIER		RETINES
	TOLUIDE		ESERINE		TRENISE
DEINNOR	ENDIRON	**EEEINRT**	TEENIER		TRIENES
DEINNOT	INTONED	**EEEIRST**	EERIEST	**EEINRTT**	NETTIER

	TENTIER	**EIIORST**	RIOTISE	**EINOPRT**	POINTER
EEINRTU	NEURITE	**EILNNOR**	ONLINER		PROTEIN
	RETINUE	**EILNOOR**	LOONIER		PTERION
	REUNITE	**EILNOOS**	LOONIES		REPOINT
	UTERINE	**EILNORR**	LORINER		TROPINE
EEINSTU	ENSUITE	**EILNORS**	LIENORS	**EINORRS**	IRONERS
EEIORRS	ROSIERE		NEROLIS		ROSINER
EEIORST	EROTISE	**EILNORT**	RETINOL	**EINORST**	NORITES
EEIOSTT	TOEIEST	**EILNOST**	ENTOILS		OESTRIN
EEIRSTU	SUETIER		LIONETS		ORIENTS
EELNOTU	TOLUENE		ONLIEST		STONIER
EELORST	SOLERET	**EILNOSU**	ELUSION		TERSION
EENNORT	ENTERON	**EILNOTU**	ELUTION		TRIONES
	TENONER		OUTLINE	**EINORSU**	URINOSE
EENORST	ESTRONE	**EILNRST**	LINTERS	**EINORTT**	TRITONE
EENOSTU	OUTSEEN		SLINTER	**EINORTU**	ROUTINE
EGILNOT	LENTIGO		SNIRTLE	**EINORTW**	NOWTIER
EGINOOR	GOONIER	**EILOORS**	ORIOLES		TOWNIER
EGINORS	ERINGOS	**EILOORT**	TROOLIE	**EINOSTT**	SNOTTIE
	IGNORES	**EILOOST**	OOLITES		TONIEST
	REGIONS		OSTIOLE		TONITES
	SIGNORE		STOOLIE	**EINRSTU**	NUTSIER
EGINORT	GENITOR		TOOLIES		TRIUNES
EGIORST	GOITERS	**EILORST**	ESTRIOL		UNITERS
	GOITRES		LOITERS	**EIOORST**	OORIEST
	GORIEST		TOILERS		ROOTIES
EGIORTU	GOUTIER	**EILORSU**	LOURIES		SOOTIER
EIILNOR	NOILIER		LOUSIER		TOORIES
EIILNOS	ELISION		SOILURE	**EIORRST**	RIOTERS
	ISOLINE	**EILORTT**	TORTILE		ROISTER
	LIONISE		TRIOLET		RORIEST
	NOILIES	**EILORTU**	OUTLIER	**EIORSTT**	STOITER
EIILNOT	ETIOLIN	**EILOSTU**	OUTLIES		TORTIES
EIILNRT	LINTIER	**EINNORS**	RONNIES	**EIORSTU**	OURIEST
	NITRILE	**EINNORT**	INTONER		STOURIE
EIILORS	SOILIER		NOINTER		TOURIES
EIILOST	IOLITES		TERNION		TOUSIER
	OILIEST	**EINNORU**	NOUNIER	**EIORTTU**	TOUTIER
EIINORR	IRONIER		REUNION	**ELNORST**	LENTORS
EIINORS	IONISER	**EINNOST**	INTONES	**ENOORST**	ENROOTS
	IRONIES		TENSION	**ENORSTU**	TENOURS
	IRONISE	**EINOORS**	EROSION		TONSURE
	NOISIER	**EINOOST**	ISOTONE		
EIINOST	INOSITE		TOONIES		

Top 1000 most likely eight-letter words

These 1000 eight-letter words, arranged in anagram form, represent the most likely ones that will occur given the distribution of letters in the Scrabble set and the likelihood of common letters being available to play through on the board. This list is largely complementary to the eight-letter words listed in the bonus word sets but there are some words appearing in both.

AABEINRT	ATABRINE	**AAEGINRS**	ANERGIAS
	RABATINE		ANGARIES
AABEIOTU	ABOITEAU		ARGINASE
AACEEIRT	ACIERATE	**AAEGINRT**	AERATING
AACEINRT	CARINATE	**AAEGINST**	SAGINATE
	CRANIATE	**AAEILNRU**	AURELIAN
AADEEIRT	ERADIATE	**AAEILORS**	OLEARIAS
AADEGINR	AREADING	**AAEILRSU**	AURELIAS
	DRAINAGE	**AAEIMNOT**	METANOIA
	GARDENIA	**AAEIMNRT**	ANIMATER
AADEGINT	INDAGATE		MARINATE
AADEILNT	DENTALIA	**AAEINORT**	AERATION
AADEILRS	SALARIED	**AAEINPRT**	ANTIRAPE
AADEILRT	LARIATED	**AAEINRST**	ANTISERA
AADEINRS	ARANEIDS		ARTESIAN
AADEINRT	DENTARIA		RATANIES
	RAINDATE		RESINATA
AADEIORS	AERADIOS		SANTERIA
AADEIRST	AIRDATES		SEATRAIN
	DATARIES	**AAEINRTT**	ATTAINER
	RADIATES		REATTAIN
AADILNOR	ORDALIAN	**AAEINRTU**	INAURATE
AADINORT	ANTIDORA	**AAEINRTW**	ANTIWEAR
AAEEGILN	ALIENAGE	**AAELNRST**	ASTERNAL
AAEEGINS	AGENESIA	**AAEMNORT**	EMANATOR
AAEEGNRT	TAGAREEN	**AAENORST**	ANOESTRA
AAEEILNT	ALIENATE	**AAENORSU**	ARANEOUS
AAEEINTT	TAENIATE	**AAENORTU**	AERONAUT
AAEELORT	AREOLATE	**AAILNORS**	ORINASAL
AAEELORU	AUREOLAE	**AAILNORT**	NOTARIAL
AAEENRST	ARSENATE		RATIONAL
	SERENATA	**AAILNOST**	AILANTOS
AAEGILNR	GERANIAL		ALATIONS
	REGALIAN	**ABDEEIRT**	EBRIATED
AAEGILNT	AGENTIAL		REBAITED
	ALGINATE	**ABDEINOR**	DEBONAIR

ABDEINOS	BEDSONIA		CREATINE
ABDEINOT	OBTAINED		INCREATE
ABEEILRT	LIBERATE		ITERANCE
ABEEINST	BETAINES	**ACEEINST**	CINEASTE
ABEGINOR	ABORIGEN	**ACEENORT**	CAROTENE
ABEILNOT	TAILBONE	**ACEIINRT**	ARENITIC
ABEILORS	BOREALIS	**ACEILNOR**	ACROLEIN
ABEILORT	LABORITE		COLINEAR
ABEINORS	BARONIES		CREOLIAN
	SEAROBIN		LONICERA
	BARITONE	**ACEILNRT**	CLARINET
ABEINORT	OBTAINER	**ACEILORS**	CALORIES
	REOBTAIN		CALORISE
	TABORINE		CARIOLES
ABEINOST	BOTANIES	**ACEILORT**	EROTICAL
	BOTANISE		LORICATE
	NIOBATES	**ACEILOST**	ALOETICS
	OBEISANT		COALIEST
ABEINRST	ATEBRINS		SOCIETAL
	BANISTER	**ACEINORS**	SCENARIO
	BARNIEST	**ACEINORT**	ACTIONER
ABEINRTU	BRAUNITE		ANORETIC
	URBANITE		CREATION
ABEIORST	SABOTIER		REACTION
ABENORST	BARONETS	**ACEINOST**	ACONITES
ACDEEINR	DERACINE		CANOEIST
ACDEINOS	CODEINAS		SONICATE
	DIOCESAN	**ACEINRST**	CANISTER
	OCEANIDS		CARNIEST
ACDEINOT	ACTIONED		CERATINS
	CATENOID		CISTERNA
ACDEINRT	CRINATED		CREATINS
	DICENTRA		NACRITES
ACDEIORS	IDOCRASE		SCANTIER
ACDEIORT	CERATOID		TACRINES
ACDENORT	CARTONED	**ACEINRTU**	ANURETIC
	NOTECARD	**ACEIORST**	EROTICAS
ACEEILNR	CARELINE	**ACENORST**	ANCESTOR
	CINEREAL		ENACTORS
	RELIANCE		SARCONET
ACEEINRS	CINEREAS		SORTANCE
	INCREASE	**ACENORTU**	COURANTE
	RESIANCE		OUTRANCE
ACEEINRT	CENTIARE	**ADDEINOR**	ORDAINED

ADEEEINT	DETAINEE	**ADEEIRTV**	DERIVATE
ADEEFINR	FREDAINE		EVIRATED
ADEEFIOR	FOEDARIE		TAIVERED
ADEEGINR	REGAINED	**ADEEIRTW**	WAITERED
ADEEGINS	AGENISED	**ADEEISTU**	AUDITEES
ADEEGIRS	DISAGREE	**ADEELNOR**	OLEANDER
ADEEGIRT	GAITERED		RELOANED
ADEEGNOR	RENEGADO	**ADEELNRT**	ANTLERED
ADEEGORT	DEROGATE	**ADEELORU**	AUREOLED
ADEEHIRT	DEATHIER	**ADEELOST**	DESOLATE
ADEEILNR	RENAILED	**ADEENORS**	REASONED
ADEEILNS	DELAINES	**ADEENOST**	ENDOSTEA
ADEEILNT	DATELINE	**ADEENOTT**	DENOTATE
	ENTAILED		DETONATE
	LINEATED	**ADEENRTU**	DENATURE
ADEEILRS	REALISED		UNDERATE
	RESAILED		UNDEREAT
	SIDEREAL	**ADEFILOR**	FORELAID
ADEEILRT	DETAILER	**ADEFILOT**	FOLIATED
	ELATERID	**ADEFIORS**	FORESAID
	RETAILED	**ADEGIINR**	DEAIRING
ADEEILST	LEADIEST	**ADEGIINT**	IDEATING
ADEEIMNR	REMAINED	**ADEGIIRT**	DIGERATI
ADEEIMNT	DEMENTIA	**ADEGILNO**	GALENOID
ADEEIMRT	DIAMETER	**ADEGILNR**	DANGLIER
	DIATREME		DEARLING
	REMEDIAT		DRAGLINE
ADEEINOP	OEDIPEAN	**ADEGILNT**	DELATING
ADEEINPR	PINDAREE	**ADEGILOR**	DIALOGER
ADEEINPT	DIAPENTE	**ADEGILOS**	GOLIASED
ADEEINRS	ARSENIDE	**ADEGILOU**	DIALOGUE
	DENARIES	**ADEGINOR**	ORGANDIE
	DRAISENE	**ADEGINOS**	AGONISED
	NEARSIDE		DIAGNOSE
ADEEINRT	DETAINER	**ADEGINRS**	DERAIGNS
	RETAINED		GRADINES
ADEEINRV	REINVADE		READINGS
ADEEINST	ANDESITE	**ADEGINRT**	DERATING
ADEEINTW	ANTIWEED		GRADIENT
ADEEIRST	READIEST		REDATING
	SERIATED		TREADING
	SIDERATE	**ADEGINST**	SEDATING
	STEADIER		STEADING
ADEEIRTT	ITERATED	**ADEGIORT**	ERGATOID

ADEGIOST	GODETIAS		REDTAILS
ADEGNORT	DRAGONET	**ADEILRSU**	RESIDUAL
ADEGORST	GOADSTER	**ADEIMNOR**	RADIOMEN
ADEGORTU	OUTRAGED	**ADEIMNOS**	AMIDONES
	RAGOUTED		DAIMONES
ADEHILNO	LIONHEAD		DOMAINES
ADEHINOS	ADHESION		NOMADIES
ADEHINRT	ANTHERID		NOMADISE
ADEIILRS	LAIRISED	**ADEIMNOT**	DOMINATE
ADEIILST	IDEALIST		NEMATOID
ADEIINOT	IDEATION	**ADEIMNOU**	EUDAIMON
	IODINATE	**ADEIMORT**	MEDIATOR
	TAENIOID	**ADEIMOST**	ATOMISED
ADEIINRS	DRAISINE	**ADEINNOT**	ANOINTED
ADEIINRT	DAINTIER		ANTINODE
ADEIINRU	UREDINIA	**ADEINOPT**	ANTIPODE
ADEIINST	ADENITIS	**ADEINORR**	ORDAINER
	DAINTIES		REORDAIN
ADEIIRST	IRISATED	**ADEINORS**	ANEROIDS
ADEILMNO	MELANOID		ANODISER
ADEILNNO	NONIDEAL		DONARIES
ADEILNOP	PALINODE	**ADEINORT**	AROINTED
ADEILNOS	NODALISE		DERATION
ADEILNOT	DELATION		ORDINATE
ADEILNRS	ISLANDER		RATIONED
ADEILNSU	UNSAILED	**ADEINORU**	DOUANIER
ADEILNTU	UNTAILED	**ADEINOST**	ASTONIED
ADEILOPT	PETALOID		SEDATION
ADEILORS	DARIOLES	**ADEINOTT**	ANTIDOTE
	SOLIDARE		TETANOID
	SOREDIAL	**ADEINOTV**	DONATIVE
ADEILORT	IDOLATER	**ADEINPRT**	DIPTERAN
	TAILORED	**ADEINRST**	DETRAINS
ADEILORV	OVERLAID		RANDIEST
ADEILOST	DIASTOLE		STRAINED
	ISOLATED	**ADEINRSU**	DENARIUS
	SODALITE		UNRAISED
	SOLIDATE		URANIDES
ADEILOSU	DOULEIAS	**ADEINRTT**	NITRATED
ADEILOTT	DATOLITE	**ADEINRTU**	DATURINE
ADEILOTV	DOVETAIL		INDURATE
	VIOLATED		RUINATED
ADEILRST	DILATERS		URINATED
	LARDIEST	**ADEINSTU**	AUDIENTS

	SINUATED	**ADINORSU**	DINOSAUR
ADEIOPRS	DIASPORE	**ADINORTU**	DURATION
	PARODIES	**ADINOSTU**	SUDATION
ADEIOPST	DIOPTASE	**ADIORSTU**	AUDITORS
ADEIORRT	ADROITER	**AEEEILNS**	ALIENEES
ADEIORST	ASTEROID	**AEEEIRST**	EATERIES
ADEIORSV	AVODIRES	**AEEELNRT**	LATEENER
	AVOIDERS	**AEEENRST**	SERENATE
ADEIORTT	TERATOID	**AEEFIINR**	INFERIAE
ADEIORTV	DEVIATOR	**AEEFILNR**	FLANERIE
ADELNORS	LADRONES	**AEEFILRT**	FEATLIER
	SOLANDER		FRAILTEE
ADELNORU	EUROLAND	**AEEGIINR**	AEGIRINE
	UNLOADER	**AEEGIIRT**	AEGIRITE
	URODELAN	**AEEGIIST**	GAIETIES
ADELNRTU	DENTURAL	**AEEGILNR**	ALGERINE
ADELORST	DELATORS	**AEEGILNS**	ENSILAGE
	LEOTARDS		LINEAGES
	LODESTAR	**AEEGILNT**	GALENITE
ADENNORT	NONRATED		GELATINE
ADENOORT	RATOONED		LEGATINE
ADENOOST	ODONATES	**AEEGILOU**	EULOGIAE
ADENOPRT	PRONATED	**AEEGILRS**	GASELIER
ADENORST	TORNADES	**AEEGILRT**	LITREAGE
ADENORTT	ATTORNED	**AEEGILST**	EGALITES
ADENORTW	DANEWORT		ELEGIAST
	DOWNRATE	**AEEGINRS**	ANERGIES
	TEARDOWN		GESNERIA
ADENORTY	AROYNTED	**AEEGINRT**	ENARGITE
ADENRSTU	DAUNTERS		GRATINEE
	TRANSUDE		INTERAGE
	UNTREADS	**AEEGINST**	SAGENITE
ADEORSTU	OUTDARES	**AEEGINSU**	EUGENIAS
	OUTREADS	**AEEGIRSU**	EUGARIES
	READOUTS	**AEEGLNOT**	ELONGATE
ADIILNOT	DILATION	**AEEGLNRT**	REGENTAL
ADIINOTU	AUDITION	**AEEGNRST**	ESTRANGE
ADIIORST	TARSIOID		GRANTEES
ADILNORS	ORDINALS		GREATENS
ADILNORT	TRINODAL		NEGATERS
ADILORST	DILATORS		REAGENTS
ADINOORT	TANDOORI		SEGREANT
ADINORST	DIATRONS		SERGEANT
	INTRADOS		STERNAGE

AEEGNRTU	GAUNTREE		REAMIEST
AEEHILRT	ETHERIAL		STEAMIER
AEEHINRS	INHEARSE	**AEEINNRS**	ANSERINE
AEEHINRT	ATHERINE	**AEEINOPS**	PAEONIES
	HERNIATE	**AEEINPRS**	NAPERIES
AEEHIRST	HEARTIES	**AEEINPRT**	APERIENT
AEEIIMRT	METAIRIE	**AEEINRRS**	REARISEN
AEEIINRT	INERTIAE	**AEEINRRT**	RETAINER
AEEILMNT	LINEMATE	**AEEINRST**	ARENITES
	MELANITE		ARSENITE
AEEILMRT	EREMITAL		RESINATE
	MATERIEL		STEARINE
	REALTIME		TRAINEES
AEEILNPR	PERINEAL	**AEEINRSU**	UNEASIER
AEEILNPT	PETALINE	**AEEINSTT**	ANISETTE
	TAPELINE		TAENITES
AEEILNRR	NEARLIER		TETANIES
AEEILNRS	ALIENERS		TETANISE
AEEILNRT	ELATERIN	**AEEINSTV**	NAIVETES
	ENTAILER	**AEEIORST**	ETAERIOS
	TREENAIL	**AEEIPRST**	PARIETES
AEEILNTV	ELVANITE		PETARIES
	VENTAILE	**AEEIRRST**	ARTERIES
AEEILORT	AEROLITE		REASTIER
AEEILOTT	ETIOLATE	**AEEIRSTT**	ARIETTES
AEEILPRT	PEARLITE		ITERATES
AEEILRRT	RETAILER		TEARIEST
AEEILRST	ATELIERS		TREATIES
	EARLIEST		TREATISE
	LATERISE	**AEEIRSTV**	EVIRATES
	LEARIEST	**AEEIRSTW**	SWEATIER
	REALTIES		TAWERIES
AEEILRTT	LATERITE		WASTERIE
	LITERATE		WEARIEST
AEEILRTV	LEVIRATE	**AEEIRSTY**	YEASTIER
	RELATIVE	**AEELNORT**	REALTONE
AEEIMNRS	REMANIES	**AEELNORU**	ALEURONE
AEEIMNRT	ANTIMERE	**AEELNRST**	ALTERNES
AEEIMNST	ETAMINES		ETERNALS
	MATINEES		TELERANS
	MISEATEN	**AEELORST**	OLEASTER
	SEMINATE	**AEELORSU**	AUREOLES
AEEIMRST	EMERITAS	**AEELORTT**	TOLERATE
	EMIRATES	**AEENNOST**	NEONATES

AEENOORT	AEROTONE
AEENORRS	REASONER
AEENORST	EARSTONE
	RESONATE
AEENORTV	OVERNEAT
	RENOVATE
AEENOTTU	OUTEATEN
AEENRSTU	SAUTERNE
AEFIINRT	FAINTIER
AEFILNOR	FORELAIN
AEFILNOT	OLEFIANT
AEFILNRT	INFLATER
AEFILORS	FORESAIL
AEFILORT	FLOATIER
AEFILOST	FOLIATES
AEFINORS	FARINOSE
AEFINRST	FAINTERS
	FENITARS
AEFLNORT	FLOREANT
AEFNORST	SEAFRONT
AEGIILNR	GAINLIER
AEGILNOR	GERANIOL
	REGIONAL
AEGILNOS	GASOLINE
AEGILNOT	GELATION
	LEGATION
AEGILNRS	ALIGNERS
	ENGRAILS
	LASERING
	NARGILES
	REALIGNS
	SALERING
	SANGLIER
	SIGNALER
	SLANGIER
AEGILNRT	ALERTING
	ALTERING
	INTEGRAL
	RELATING
	TANGLIER
	TERAGLIN
	TRIANGLE
AEGILNST	EASTLING
	GELATINS

	GENITALS
	STEALING
	TAGLINES
AEGILORS	GASOLIER
	GIRASOLE
	SERAGLIO
AEGILOST	LATIGOES
	OTALGIES
AEGILOSU	EULOGIAS
AEGILRST	GLARIEST
	REGALIST
AEGILRTU	LIGATURE
AEGINNOT	NEGATION
AEGINOPT	PINOTAGE
AEGINORR	ORANGIER
AEGINORS	IGNAROES
	ORGANISE
	ORIGANES
AEGINRST	ANGRIEST
	ANGSTIER
	ASTRINGE
	GANISTER
	GANTRIES
	GRANITES
	INGRATES
	RANGIEST
	REASTING
	STEARING
	TASERING
AEGINRTT	ARETTING
	GNATTIER
	TREATING
AEGINSTU	SAUTEING
	UNITAGES
AEGIORTV	RAVIGOTE
AEGIOSTU	AGOUTIES
AEGLNOST	TANGELOS
AEGLORST	GLOATERS
	LEGATORS
AEGLORTU	OUTGLARE
AEGNORST	ESTRAGON
	NEGATORS
	ORANGEST
	RAGSTONE

	STONERAG	AEILNORS	AILERONS
AEGNORTU	OUTRANGE		ALERIONS
AEGORSTU	OUTRAGES		ALIENORS
AEHILORS	AIRHOLES	AEILNORT	ORIENTAL
	SHOALIER		RELATION
AEHILORT	AEROLITH		TAILERON
AEHILOST	HALIOTES	AEILNORV	OVERLAIN
AEHINORT	ANTIHERO	AEILNOST	ELATIONS
AEHINRST	HAIRNETS		INSOLATE
	INEARTHS		TOENAILS
	THERIANS	AEILNOTT	TONALITE
AEHINRTU	HAURIENT	AEILNPRT	INTERLAP
AEHIORST	HOARIEST		TRAPLINE
AEHIORTU	THIOUREA		TRIPLANE
AEIILMNO	MONILIAE	AEILNRST	ENTRAILS
AEIILNRS	AIRLINES		LARNIEST
	SNAILIER		LATRINES
AEIILNRT	INERTIAL		RATLINES
AEIILNST	ALIENIST		REINSTAL
	LATINISE		RETINALS
	LITANIES		SLANTIER
AEIILRST	LAIRIEST		TRENAILS
	LISTERIA	AEILNRSU	LUNARIES
AEIINNRT	TRIENNIA	AEILNRTT	RATTLINE
AEIINOTT	NOTITIAE	AEILNRTU	AUNTLIER
AEIINPRT	PAINTIER		RETINULA
AEIINRST	INERTIAS		TENURIAL
	RAINIEST	AEILNRTV	INTERVAL
AEILLNOR	ALLERION	AEILNRTY	INTERLAY
AEILMNOS	LAMINOSE	AEILNSTU	ALUNITES
	MINEOLAS		INSULATE
	SEMOLINA	AEILOPRS	PELORIAS
AEILMNRT	TERMINAL		POLARISE
	TRAMLINE	AEILOPRT	EPILATOR
AEILMORS	MORALISE		PETIOLAR
AEILMORT	AMITROLE	AEILOPST	SPOLIATE
	ROLAMITE	AEILORRT	RETAILOR
AEILMOST	LOAMIEST	AEILORST	SOTERIAL
AEILNNOS	SOLANINE	AEILORSV	OVERSAIL
AEILNNRT	INTERNAL		VALORISE
AEILNOPR	PELORIAN		VARIOLES
AEILNOPS	OPALINES		VOLARIES
AEILNOPT	ANTIPOLE	AEILORSY	ROYALISE
AEILNOPU	POULAINE	AEILORTT	LITERATO

AEILORTV	VIOLATER	**AEINOSTV**	STOVAINE
AEILOSTT	TOTALISE	**AEINPRST**	PAINTERS
AEILRSTU	URALITES		PANTRIES
AEIMNORS	MORAINES		PERTAINS
	ROMAINES		PINASTER
	ROMANISE		PRISTANE
AEIMNOST	AMNIOTES		REPAINTS
	MASONITE	**AEINPRTU**	PAINTURE
	MISATONE	**AEINRRST**	RESTRAIN
	SOMNIATE		RETRAINS
AEIMNOSU	MOINEAUS		STRAINER
AEIMNRST	MERANTIS		TERRAINS
	MINARETS		TRAINERS
	RAIMENTS		TRANSIRE
AEIMNRTU	RUMINATE	**AEINRSTT**	INTREATS
AEIMORST	AMORTISE		NITRATES
	ATOMISER		STRAITEN
AEINNORS	NONARIES		TARTINES
	RAISONNE		TERTIANS
AEINNORT	ANOINTER	**AEINRSTU**	RUINATES
	INORNATE		TAURINES
	REANOINT		URANITES
AEINNOST	ENATIONS		URINATES
	SONATINE	**AEINRSTW**	TINWARES
AEINNOTT	INTONATE	**AEINRTTU**	TAINTURE
AEINNRST	ENTRAINS	**AEINRTUV**	VAUNTIER
	TRANNIES	**AEIOPRST**	SEPTORIA
AEINOPRT	ATROPINE	**AEIORRST**	ROARIEST
AEINOPST	SAPONITE		ROTARIES
AEINORRT	ANTERIOR	**AEIORSST**	ROASTIES
AEINORSS	ERASIONS	**AEIORSTT**	TOASTIER
	SENSORIA	**AEIORSTU**	OUTRAISE
AEINORST	ANOESTRI		SAUTOIRE
	ARSONITE	**AEIORSTV**	TRAVOISE
	NOTAIRES		VIATORES
	NOTARIES		VOTARIES
	NOTARISE	**AEIOSTTU**	OUTASITE
	ROSINATE	**AELNORSU**	ALEURONS
	SENORITA		NEUROSAL
AEINORSV	AVERSION	**AELNORTT**	TETRONAL
AEINORTT	TENTORIA		TOLERANT
AEINORTZ	NOTARIZE	**AELNORTU**	OUTLEARN
AEINOSST	ASSIENTO	**AELNORTY**	ORNATELY
	ASTONIES	**AELNRSTU**	NEUTRALS

AELORSTU	OESTRUAL		LESIONED
	ROSULATE	**DEEILNOT**	DELETION
AEMNORST	MONSTERA		ENTOILED
	ONSTREAM	**DEEILORT**	DOLERITE
	STOREMAN		LOITERED
	TONEARMS	**DEEINORS**	INDORSEE
AEMNORTU	ROUTEMAN		ORDINEES
AENNORST	NORTENAS	**DEEINORT**	ORIENTED
	RESONANT	**DEEINOST**	SIDENOTE
AENNORTU	UNORNATE	**DEEINRST**	INSERTED
AENOORRT	RATOONER		NERDIEST
AENOPRST	OPERANTS		RESIDENT
	PRONATES		SINTERED
	PROTEANS		TRENDIES
AENORRST	ANTRORSE	**DEEINRTU**	RETINUED
AENORSTT	ORNATEST		REUNITED
AENORSTU	OUTEARNS	**DEEIORST**	EROTISED
AENORSTW	STONERAW	**DEEIORTU**	ETOURDIE
AGIINORT	RIGATONI	**DEELNORT**	REDOLENT
AGILNORT	TRIGONAL		RONDELET
AGINORST	ORGANIST	**DEENOORT**	ENROOTED
	ROASTING	**DEENORST**	ERODENTS
AILNORST	TONSILAR	**DEENORTU**	DEUTERON
AILORSTU	SUTORIAL	**DEGINORS**	NEGROIDS
AINOORST	ORATIONS	**DEGINORU**	GUERIDON
AINORSTU	RAINOUTS	**DEGIORST**	DIGESTOR
	SUTORIAN		GRODIEST
BEEINORT	TENEBRIO		STODGIER
BEINORST	BORNITES	**DEIILNOT**	TOLIDINE
	RIBSTONE	**DEIINORS**	DERISION
CDEINORT	CENTROID		IRONISED
	DOCTRINE		IRONSIDE
CEEINORT	ERECTION		RESINOID
	NEOTERIC	**DEIINORT**	RETINOID
CEIINORT	RETINOIC	**DEIINOST**	EDITIONS
CEINORST	COINTERS		SEDITION
	CORNIEST	**DEIINRST**	DISINTER
	NOTICERS		INDITERS
	RECTIONS		NITRIDES
CEINORTU	NEUROTIC		RINDIEST
	UNEROTIC	**DEIINRTU**	UNTIDIER
DEEGIORT	GOITERED	**DEIIORST**	DIORITES
DEEIINOS	DEIONISE	**DEILNORS**	DISENROL
DEEILNOS	ESLOINED	**DEILNOST**	LENTOIDS

DEILNOTU	OUTLINED	EEILNORS	ELOINERS
DEILNRST	SNIRTLED	EEILNOST	NOSELITE
	TENDRILS	EEILNRST	ENLISTER
	TRINDLES		LISTENER
DEILNRTU	UNDERLIT		REENLIST
DEILORST	STOLIDER		SILENTER
DEIMNORT	DORMIENT	EEILORRT	LOITERER
DEINNORT	INDENTOR	EEILORST	LITEROSE
DEINOPRT	DIPTERON		TROELIES
DEINORST	DRONIEST	EEIMNORT	TIMONEER
DEINORSU	DOURINES	EEINORRT	ORTENTER
	NEUROIDS		REORIENT
	SOURDINE	EEINORST	ONERIEST
DEINORTT	INTORTED		SEROTINE
DEINOSTU	OUNDIEST	EEINORTT	TENORITE
DEINRSTU	INTRUDES	EEINOSTT	NOISETTE
	NURDIEST		TEOSINTE
DEIORSTU	IODURETS	EEINRSTU	ESURIENT
	OUTRIDES		NEURITES
	OUTSIDER		RETINUES
	SUITORED		REUNITES
EEEILNRT	TREELINE	EELNORST	ENTRESOL
EEEINRST	ETERNISE	EENOORST	OESTRONE
	TEENSIER		ROESTONE
EEGIINRT	REIGNITE	EENOORTU	EURONOTE
	RETIEING	EFIINORT	NOTIFIER
EEGILNOR	ELOIGNER	EGIILNOR	LIGROINE
EEGILNRT	GREENLIT		RELIGION
EEGINORS	ERINGOES		REOILING
EEGINOST	EGESTION	EGIINORS	SEIGNIOR
EEGINRST	GENTRIES	EGILNORS	RESOLING
	INTEGERS	EGILNORU	LOUNGIER
	REESTING	EGINORST	GENITORS
	STEERING		ROSETING
	STREIGNE	EGINORTU	OUTREIGN
EEGINRTU	GENITURE		ROUTEING
EEGIORST	ERGOTISE	EGIORSTU	GOUSTIER
EEHINORT	ETHERION	EHILNORT	HOTLINER
	HEREINTO	EHINORST	HORNIEST
EEIILORS	OILERIES		ORNITHES
EEIINORT	ERIONITE	EIILNORS	LIONISER
EEIINRST	ERINITES	EIILNORT	TRIOLEIN
	NITERIES	EIILNOST	ETIOLINS
EEILNNOT	NONELITE		NOILIEST

EIILNRST	NIRLIEST		OUTLIERS
	NITRILES	EINNOORT	TENORINO
EIILORST	ROILIEST	EINNORST	INTONERS
EIINNORT	TENORINI		NOINTERS
EIINOPRT	POINTIER		TERNIONS
	POITRINE	EINNORTU	NEUTRINO
EIINORRT	INTERIOR	EINOORST	SNOOTIER
EIINORST	IRONIEST	EINOPRST	POINTERS
EIINRSTU	NEURITIS		PORNIEST
	UNITISER		PROTEINS
EILNOOST	LOONIEST		REPOINTS
	OILSTONE		TROPINES
EILNOPRT	TERPINOL	EINOPRTU	ERUPTION
	TOPLINER	EINORRST	INTRORSE
EILNORRT	RITORNEL		SNORTIER
EILNORST	RETINOLS	EINORSTT	SNOTTIER
EILNORTT	TROTLINE		TENORIST
EILNORTU	OUTLINER		TRITONES
EILNORTW	TOWNLIER	EINORSTU	NITREOUS
EILNOSTU	ELUTIONS		ROUTINES
	OUTLINES		SNOUTIER
EILNRSTU	INSULTER	EINORSTV	INVESTOR
	LUSTRINE	EINORSTY	SEROTINY
EILOORST	OESTRIOL		TYROSINE
	TROOLIES	EINORTTU	RITENUTO
EILORSTU	LOURIEST		

Couplets

Couplets are anagram pairs. It is often easier to recall these than it is a singleton solution for a set of seven-letters. These are especially useful where one word is common and the other more unusual. So if you discover the common word on your rack it might immediately prompt its more unusual anagram. While it may also be useful to list other multiple anagram sets such as triples, quadruplets and so on, space limitation has necessitated a focus just on couplets, which are also considered the most useful to focus on.

ABACTOR	ABDUCES	ABIDDEN	ABLATED	ABLUENT
ACROBAT	SCUBAED	BANDIED	DATABLE	TUNABLE
ABATERS	ABETTER	ABIOSES	ABLATES	ABOUNDS
ABREAST	BERETTA	ISOBASE	ASTABLE	BAUSOND

ABRAIDS	ACEROUS	ACROGEN	ADOPTER	AFFYING
BAIDARS	CAROUSE	CORNAGE	READOPT	YAFFING
ABRASAX	ACETALS	ACTINGS	ADORERS	AFREETS
ABRAXAS	LACTASE	CASTING	DROSERA	FEASTER
ABRIDGE	ACETOSE	ACUATED	ADORNER	AGAMETE
BRIGADE	COATEES	CAUDATE	READORN	AGEMATE
ABSENTS	ACETOUS	ACUTEST	ADUSTED	AGAROSE
BASNETS	COTEAUS	SCUTATE	SUDATED	OARAGES
ABYEING	ACETYLS	ADAPTER	ADVENED	AGEINGS
EBAYING	SCYTALE	READAPT	DAVENED	SIGNAGE
ABYSMAL	ACHARNE	ADDICTS	ADVERSE	AGEISTS
BALSAMY	ARCHEAN	DIDACTS	EVADERS	SAGIEST
ACANTHI	ACHENES	ADDINGS	ADVERTS	AGELESS
TACHINA	ENCHASE	SADDING	STARVED	ALGESES
ACARINE	ACHIEST	ADDREST	ADVISER	AGENDUM
CARINAE	AITCHES	RADDEST	VARDIES	GUDEMAN
ACATERS	ACHIRAL	ADDUCES	ADVISES	AGGADAH
CARATES	RACHIAL	SCAUDED	DISSAVE	HAGGADA
ACATOUR	ACIDEST	ADELGID	ADWARES	AGGRADE
AUTOCAR	DACITES	GLADDIE	SEAWARD	GARAGED
ACCITES	ACIFORM	ADERMIN	ADWOMEN	AGISTOR
ASCETIC	FORMICA	INARMED	WOMANED	ORGIAST
ACCOILS	ACNODAL	ADHARMA	AEDILES	AGNAMED
CALICOS	CALANDO	HARAMDA	DEISEAL	MANAGED
ACCOMPT	ACNODES	ADHERED	AEGISES	AGNIZES
COMPACT	DEACONS	REDHEAD	ASSIEGE	SEAZING
ACCOYLD	ACOLYTE	ADHERER	AERIEST	AGNOMEN
CACODYL	COTYLAE	REHEARD	SERIATE	NONGAME
ACCRUAL	ACONITE	ADIPSIA	AEROSOL	AGNOSIC
CARACUL	ANOETIC	ASPIDIA	ROSEOLA	ANGICOS
ACCRUED	ACORNED	ADMIRAL	AETATIS	AGONIES
CARDECU	DRACONE	AMILDAR	SATIATE	AGONISE
ACCUSED	ACQUIST	ADMIRED	AFFAIRS	AGONIST
SUCCADE	ACQUITS	MARDIED	RAFFIAS	GITANOS
ACERBIC	ACRIDER	ADONIZE	AFFIXER	AGRISES
BRECCIA	CARRIED	ANODIZE	REAFFIX	GASSIER

AGUISED	ALEMBIC	ALLONGE	AMARANT	AMMETER
GAUDIES	CEMBALI	GALLEON	MARANTA	METAMER
AIBLINS	ALEPINE	ALLOVER	AMATION	AMMINES
BILIANS	ELAPINE	OVERALL	ANIMATO	MISNAME
AIDLESS	ALETHIC	ALLUDED	AMBARIS	AMNESIA
DEASILS	ETHICAL	DUALLED	MARABIS	ANEMIAS
AILANTO	ALEVINS	ALLUDES	AMBOINA	AMNESIC
ALATION	VALINES	ALUDELS	BONAMIA	CINEMAS
AILMENT	ALEYING	ALLURED	AMBONES	AMOOVES
ALIMENT	YEALING	UDALLER	BEMOANS	VAMOOSE
AIRBALL	ALFAKIS	ALLURES	AMEARST	AMORCES
BARILLA	KAFILAS	LAURELS	RETAMAS	SCREAMO
AIRBASE	ALIENED	ALMANAC	AMELIAS	AMPERES
ARABISE	DELAINE	MANCALA	MALAISE	EMPARES
AIRIEST	ALINING	ALMONDS	AMENDED	AMRITAS
IRISATE	NAILING	DOLMANS	DEADMEN	TAMARIS
AIRPORT	ALISMAS	ALMONER	AMENING	AMULETS
PARITOR	SALAMIS	NEMORAL	MEANING	MULETAS
AIRTING	ALISONS	ALMUCES	AMENITY	AMYLOSE
RAITING	SIALONS	MACULES	ANYTIME	SOYMEAL
AIRVACS	ALIUNDE	ALMUDES	AMENTIA	ANADEMS
CAVIARS	UNIDEAL	MEDUSAL	ANIMATE	MAENADS
ALANYLS	ALKALIS	ALNICOS	AMERCER	ANAPEST
NASALLY	ALLIAKS	OILCANS	CREAMER	PEASANT
ALBUGOS	ALKANET	ALOGIAS	AMIDASE	ANCILIA
SUBGOAL	KANTELA	LAOGAIS	SEAMAID	LACINIA
ALCADES	ALLAYER	ALPEENS	AMIDINE	ANCONES
SCALADE	AREALLY	SPELEAN	DIAMINE	SONANCE
ALCAICS	ALLEDGE	ALSIKES	AMIDINS	ANCRESS
CICALAS	ALLEGED	ASSLIKE	DIAMINS	CASERNS
ALCOVES	ALLICES	ALYSSUM	AMIDONE	ANDVILE
COEVALS	CAILLES	ASYLUMS	DOMAINE	ANVILED
ALDOSES	ALLISES	AMABILE	AMISSES	ANERGIC
LASSOED	SALLIES	AMIABLE	MESSIAS	GRECIAN
ALEGARS	ALLODIA	AMANDLA	AMITIES	ANESTRA
LAAGERS	ALODIAL	MANDALA	ATIMIES	SANTERA

ANETHOL	ANTISEX	APOSTIL	ARCMINS	ARRIVES
ETHANOL	SEXTAIN	TOPSAIL	NARCISM	VARIERS
ANGARIA	ANTRUMS	APPENDS	ARCTOID	ARROBAS
NIAGARA	UNSMART	SNAPPED	CAROTID	RASBORA
ANGINAS	ANUROUS	APPLIES	AREFIED	ARSHINS
INANGAS	URANOUS	LAPPIES	FEDARIE	SHAIRNS
ANGLIFY	ANYMORE	APPOSED	ARETTED	ARSINES
FLAYING	ROMNEYA	PEAPODS	TREATED	SARNIES
ANGUINE	APEDOMS	APPOSER	ARGALIS	ARTSMAN
GUANINE	POMADES	POPERAS	GARIALS	MANTRAS
ANGUISH	APELIKE	APPRESS	ARGHANS	ARUGULA
HAUSING	PEALIKE	SAPPERS	HANGARS	AUGURAL
ANICUTS	APERCUS	APPRISE	ARGLING	ASCESIS
NAUTICS	SCAUPER	SAPPIER	GLARING	CASSIES
ANKLING	APERIES	APPRIZE	ARGONON	ASCIDIA
LANKING	EPEIRAS	ZAPPIER	ORGANON	DIASCIA
ANNELID	APHESES	APTOTES	ARGUERS	ASCITES
LINDANE	SPAHEES	TEAPOTS	SUGARER	ECTASIS
ANNOYED	APHETIC	ARAYSED	ARGYLES	ASCITIC
ANODYNE	HEPATIC	DARESAY	GRAYLES	SCIATIC
ANSWERS	APHIDES	ARAYSES	ARIETTE	ASEPSIS
RAWNESS	DIPHASE	ASSAYER	ITERATE	ASPISES
ANTHEMS	APICALS	ARBITER	ARISTAS	ASININE
HETMANS	SPACIAL	RAREBIT	TARSIAS	INSANIE
ANTIBUG	APIEZON	ARBORES	ARKITES	ASKINGS
TABUING	EPIZOAN	BRASERO	KARITES	GASKINS
ANTICLY	APLENTY	ARCADES	ARMLOCK	ASPERGE
CANTILY	PENALTY	ASCARED	LOCKRAM	PRESAGE
ANTIFLU	APNOEAS	ARCHERS	ARMREST	ASPIRIN
FLUTINA	PAESANO	CRASHER	SMARTER	RAPINIS
ANTIMEN	APNOEIC	ARCHILS	AROINTS	ASPORTS
MANNITE	PAEONIC	CARLISH	RATIONS	PASTORS
ANTINGS	APOLLOS	ARCHINE	ARRIDES	ASPREAD
STANING	PALOLOS	CHAINER	RAIDERS	PARADES
ANTIQUE	APOMICT	ARCHLET	ARRIERO	ASQUINT
QUINATE	POTAMIC	TRACHLE	ROARIER	QUINTAS

ASSARTS	ATABEGS	AUTOING	AWESOME	BAGWASH
SASTRAS	TEABAGS	OUTGAIN	WAESOME	WASHBAG
ASSENTS	ATELIER	AUTOPSY	AWMRIES	BAKINGS
SNASTES	REALTIE	PAYOUTS	SEMIRAW	BASKING
ASSERTS	ATHAMES	AVAILED	BABBLED	BALDING
TRASSES	HAMATES	VEDALIA	BLABBED	BLADING
ASSIGNS	ATHEIST	AVALING	BABIEST	BALEENS
SASSING	STAITHE	VAGINAL	TABBIES	ENABLES
ASSUAGE	ATLATLS	AVARICE	BABOOSH	BALKILY
SAUSAGE	TALLATS	CAVIARE	HABOOBS	LIKABLY
ASSUMED	ATMOSES	AVENGED	BACCIES	BALLAST
MEDUSAS	OSMATES	VENDAGE	SEBACIC	BALLATS
ASSURED	ATOCIAS	AVENGER	BACKERS	BALLUTE
RUDASES	COAITAS	ENGRAVE	REBACKS	BULLATE
ASSURER	ATOPIES	AVENGES	BACKFAT	BALSAMS
RASURES	OPIATES	GENEVAS	FATBACK	SAMBALS
ASSURES	ATRIUMS	AVENIRS	BACKOUT	BAMPOTS
SARUSES	MATSURI	RAVINES	OUTBACK	SPAMBOT
ASSWIPE	ATTONED	AVERTED	BAETYLS	BANDARS
WASPIES	NOTATED	TAVERED	BEASTLY	SANDBAR
ASTARTS	ATTONES	AVGASES	BAFFLED	BANDIER
STRATAS	NOTATES	SAVAGES	BLAFFED	BRAINED
ASTHENY	ATTRIST	AVIATIC	BAGARRE	BANDIES
SHANTEY	ATTRITS	VIATICA	BARRAGE	BASINED
ASTHMAS	AUCTION	AVIETTE	BAGASSE	BANDORE
MATSAHS	CAUTION	EVITATE	SEABAGS	BROADEN
ASTRALS	AUGMENT	AVISING	BAGELED	BANGERS
TARSALS	MUTAGEN	VISAING	BEAGLED	GRABENS
ASTRAND	AULDEST	AVOCETS	BAGFULS	BANKERS
TARANDS	SALUTED	OCTAVES	BAGSFUL	BARKENS
ASTRICT	AULNAGE	AVODIRE	BAGGERS	BANTAMS
TRIACTS	LEGUAAN	AVOIDER	BEGGARS	BATSMAN
ASTUTER	AUNTIES	AWAKENS	BAGNIOS	BANTERS
STATURE	SINUATE	WAKANES	GABIONS	BARNETS
ASTYLAR	AUTOCUE	AWELESS	BAGUETS	BAPTISM
SATYRAL	COUTEAU	WEASELS	TUBAGES	BITMAPS

BARAZAS	BASHERS	BEARERS	BEENTOS	BEMUSED
BAZAARS	BRASHES	BREARES	BONESET	EMBUSED
BARBIES	BASHLIK	BEATIER	BEETING	BEMUSES
RABBIES	KIBLAHS	EBRIATE	BEIGNET	EMBUSES
BARCODE	BASSERS	BECALMS	BEEYARD	BENDIER
BROCADE	BRASSES	SCAMBLE	BERAYED	INBREED
BARDING	BASSEST	BECRUST	BEEZERS	BENISON
BRIGAND	BASSETS	BECURST	BREEZES	BONNIES
BAREFIT	BASTLES	BEDERAL	BEFANAS	BENTHIC
FIBRATE	STABLES	BLEARED	FANBASE	BITCHEN
BARGING	BATBOYS	BEDEWED	BEFLUMS	BERDASH
GARBING	BOBSTAY	WEEDBED	FUMBLES	BRASHED
BARISTA	BATCHER	BEDIGHT	BEGIRDS	BERGAMA
BARTSIA	BRACHET	BIGHTED	BRIDGES	MEGABAR
BARKEEP	BATFISH	BEDLAMS	BEGUINS	BERRIED
PREBAKE	BIFTAHS	BELDAMS	BUNGIES	BRIERED
BARKIER	BATTERS	BEDLESS	BEINING	BERTHES
BRAKIER	TABRETS	BLESSED	INBEING	SHERBET
BARKING	BATTLED	BEDRALS	BELACED	BESCOUR
BRAKING	BLATTED	BLADERS	DEBACLE	OBSCURE
BARLESS	BAUBLES	BEDRAPE	BELATED	BESINGS
BRALESS	BUBALES	PREBADE	BLEATED	BIGNESS
BAROLOS	BAUERAS	BEDROCK	BELAYED	BESLIME
ROBALOS	SUBAREA	BROCKED	DYEABLE	BESMILE
BARONET	BAWBLES	BEDTIME	BELGARD	BESPAKE
REBOANT	WABBLES	BETIMED	GARBLED	BESPEAK
BARONGS	BAWLERS	BEDUINS	BELTERS	BESTIES
BROGANS	WARBLES	BUNDIES	TREBLES	BETISES
BARRETS	BAWLEYS	BEDUSTS	BELTMAN	BESTILL
BARTERS	BYELAWS	BESTUDS	LAMBENT	BILLETS
BARRIES	BAWLING	BEECHES	BELUGAS	BESTORM
BRASIER	BLAWING	BESEECH	BLAGUES	MOBSTER
BARYTES	BEADIER	BEEFIER	BEMETES	BESTREW
BETRAYS	BEARDIE	FREEBIE	BETEEMS	WEBSTER
BASALLY	BEAKERS	BEEGAHS	BEMIRED	BESTRID
SALABLY	BERAKES	BHAGEES	BERIMED	BISTRED

BESTUCK	BIOPICS	BLINDER	BLUBBED	BOMBING
BUCKETS	BIOPSIC	BRINDLE	BUBBLED	MOBBING
BETIDED	BIPEDAL	BLOATED	BLUBBER	BONDAGE
DEBITED	PIEBALD	LOBATED	BUBBLER	DOGBANE
BHAKTAS	BIPOLAR	BLOATER	BLUDGER	BONIEST
SABKHAT	PARBOIL	RETABLO	BURGLED	EBONIST
BHINDIS	BIRDIES	BLOBBED	BLUEING	BONXIES
BINDHIS	BRIDIES	BOBBLED	BULGINE	INBOXES
BICOLOR	BIRDING	BLOGGED	BLUEISH	BOODIES
BROCOLI	BRIDING	BOGGLED	HELIBUS	DOOBIES
BICORNS	BIRSIER	BLOGGER	BLUIEST	BOOGERS
BICRONS	RIBIERS	BOGGLER	SUBTILE	GOOBERS
BIFIDUS	BIRSLED	BLONDES	BLUNDER	BOOGIES
FIDIBUS	BRIDLES	BOLDENS	BUNDLER	GOOBIES
BIFTERS	BIRSLES	BLOODED	BLUNGED	BOOHING
FIBSTER	RIBLESS	BOODLED	BUNGLED	HOBOING
BILBOES	BIRTHER	BLOOMER	BLUNGER	BOOINGS
LOBBIES	REBIRTH	REBLOOM	BUNGLER	BOOSING
BILLERS	BISTORT	BLOTTED	BLUNGES	BOOKERS
REBILLS	BITTORS	BOTTLED	BUNGLES	REBOOKS
BILOBED	BITTURS	BLOTTER	BLUSHER	BOOKIER
LOBBIED	TURBITS	BOTTLER	BURHELS	BROOKIE
RILTONG	BIZARRE	BLOUSED	BOASTED	BOOKIES
BOLTING	BRAZIER	DOUBLES	SABOTED	BOOKSIE
BIMBOES	BLATHER	BLOUSES	BOATELS	BOONGAS
MOBBIES	HALBERT	BOLUSES	OBLATES	GABOONS
BINGLED	BLATING	BLOWERS	BOBSLED	BOOSTER
BLINGED	TABLING	BOWLERS	SLOBBED	REBOOTS
BINGOED	BLEARER	BLOWFLY	BOCAGES	BOOZERS
BOINGED	ERRABLE	FLYBLOW	BOSCAGE	REBOZOS
BINGOES	BLEATER	BLOWING	BODICES	BOPEEPS
BIOGENS	RETABLE	BOWLING	CEBOIDS	PEEPBOS
BIOGENY	BLENDER	BLOWSES	BOGLING	BORACIC
OBEYING	REBLEND	BOWLESS	GLOBING	BRACCIO
BIONTIC	BLETHER	BLOWUPS	BOMBERS	BORDURE
BITCOIN	HERBLET	UPBLOWS	MOBBERS	BOURDER

BOREENS	BOUTONS	BRASSED	BROUZES	BULLOUS
ENROBES	UNBOOTS	SERDABS	SUBZERO	LOBULUS
BORIDES	BOWELED	BRAWEST	BRUCKLE	BUMMLED
DISROBE	ELBOWED	WABSTER	BUCKLER	MUMBLED
BORKING	BOWINGS	BRAWLED	BRUISED	BUNDIST
BROKING	BOWSING	WARBLED	BURDIES	DUSTBIN
BORSCHT	BOWLDER	BRAWLER	BRUMOUS	BUNTALS
BORTSCH	LOWBRED	WARBLER	UMBROUS	TULBANS
BORTIER	BOWLEGS	BRAWLIE	BRUSHES	BURDASH
ORBITER	WEBLOGS	WIRABLE	BUSHERS	RHABDUS
BOSHTER	BOWSERS	BREAKUP	BRUSKER	BURIALS
BOTHERS	BROWSES	UPBREAK	BURKERS	RAILBUS
BOSSEST	BOWSMEN	BREDIES	BRUTELY	BURKHAS
BOSSETS	ENWOMBS	DERBIES	BUTLERY	KURBASH
BOSSIER	BOXIEST	BRETONS	BRUTERS	BURLERS
RIBOSES	BOXTIES	SORBENT	BURSTER	BURRELS
BOUCHES	BOXWOOD	BREWING	BRUTEST	BURNOUT
SUBECHO	WOODBOX	WEBRING	BUTTERS	OUTBURN
BOUGETS	BOYARDS	BRIBERS	BUCKSAW	BURPING
OUTBEGS	BYROADS	RIBBERS	SAWBUCK	UPBRING
BOULDER	BRADOON	BRIBING	BUDDERS	BURSERA
DOUBLER	ONBOARD	RIBBING	REDBUDS	SABREUR
BOULTED	BRAHMAS	BRICOLE	BUFFERS	BURYING
DOUBLET	SAMBHAR	CORBEIL	REBUFFS	RUBYING
BOULTER	BRAILLE	BRIGUES	BUFFEST	BUSBIES
TROUBLE	LIBERAL	RUGBIES	BUFFETS	SUBBIES
BOUNCED	BRAIRDS	BRINING	BUGLING	BUSIEST
BUNCOED	BRIARDS	INBRING	BULGING	SUBSITE
BOUNCES	BRAIZES	BRISTLY	BUILDUP	BUSINGS
BUNCOES	ZERIBAS	TRILBYS	UPBUILD	BUSSING
BOUNDEN	BRANDER	BRISTOL	BUISTED	BUSTICS
UNBONED	REBRAND	STROBIL	SUBEDIT	CUBISTS
BOURDED	BRANLES	BROMINS	BULGHUR	BUSTIER
OBDURED	BRANSLE	MISBORN	BURGHUL	RUBIEST
BOUSIER	BRASHER	BROOSES	BULKERS	BUSTING
OUREBIS	HERBARS	SORBOSE	BURLESK	TUBINGS

BUSTLES	CALDERA	CALYCLE	CANULAR	CARDIOS
SUBLETS	CRAALED	CECALLY	LACUNAR	SARCOID
BUSYING	CALENDS	CALYPSO	CANULAS	CAREERS
BUYINGS	CANDLES	COSPLAY	LACUNAS	CREASER
BUTANES	CALIBER	CAMARON	CANYONS	CARGOED
SUNBEAT	CALIBRE	NARCOMA	SONANCY	CORDAGE
BUTENES	CALICES	CAMBREL	CAPABLE	CARHOPS
SUBTEEN	CELIACS	CLAMBER	PACABLE	COPRAHS
BUYOUTS	CALICHE	CAMOTES	CAPEESH	CARIOUS
OUTBUYS	CHALICE	COMATES	PEACHES	CURIOSA
BYREMAN	CALIMAS	CAMPERS	CAPERER	CARNEYS
MYRBANE	CAMAILS	SCAMPER	PRERACE	SCENARY
CACHETS	CALIPER	CAMPLED	CAPITAL	CAROCHE
CATCHES	REPLICA	CLAMPED	PLACITA	COACHER
CACHING	CALKING	CANDIES	CAPITAN	CAROLED
CHACING	LACKING	INCASED	CAPTAIN	ORACLED
CACKIER	CALLOPS	CANDIRU	CAPIZES	CAROTIN
CRACKIE	SCALLOP	IRACUND	CAPSIZE	CORTINA
CACKLED	CALLOSE	CANDOUR	CAPLETS	CARPING
CLACKED	LOCALES	CAUDRON	PLACETS	CRAPING
CACTOID	CALLOUT	CANFULS	CAPLINS	CARRIES
OCTADIC	OUTCALL	CANSFUL	INCLASP	SCARIER
CADRANS	CALLUNA	CANGLES	CAPORAL	CARROTS
CANARDS	LACUNAL	GLANCES	CRAPOLA	TROCARS
CAESTUS	CALMANT	CANGUES	CAPOUCH	CARSEYS
CUESTAS	CLAMANT	UNCAGES	PACHUCO	SCRAYES
CAIMANS	CALMEST	CANKLES	CAPTION	CARTOON
MANIACS	CAMLETS	SLACKEN	PACTION	CORANTO
CAITIVE	CALQUES	CANNERS	CARACKS	CARVERS
VICIATE	CLAQUES	SCANNER	CRACKAS	CRAVERS
CAKIEST	CALTROP	CANNIER	CARBEEN	CARVING
TACKIES	PROCTAL	NARCEIN	CARBENE	CRAVING
CALALUS	CALVARY	CANTRED	CARBONS	CASABAS
CLAUSAL	CAVALRY	TRANCED	CORBANS	CASSABA
CALAMUS	CALYCES	CANULAE	CARDERS	CASAVAS
MACULAS	CYCLASE	LACUNAE	SCARRED	CASSAVA

CASCADE	CATTILY	CERIUMS	CHAMISO	CHEAPED
SACCADE	TACITLY	MURICES	CHAMOIS	PEACHED
CASKIER	CAUDLES	CEROTIC	CHANCER	CHEAPER
EIRACKS	CEDULAS	ORECTIC	CHANCRE	PEACHER
CASQUES	CAULOME	CERRADO	CHANGED	CHECKER
SACQUES	LEUCOMA	CORRADE	GANCHED	RECHECK
CASSOCK	CAUSEYS	CERTIFY	CHANGES	CHEEPED
COSSACK	CAYUSES	RECTIFY	GANCHES	DEPECHE
CASTLED	CAUSING	CERVIDS	CHANSON	CHEERED
SCLATED	SAUCING	SCRIVED	NONCASH	REECHED
CASTLES	CAUSTIC	CESIUMS	CHANTER	CHEERIO
SCLATES	CICUTAS	MISCUES	TRANCHE	ECHOIER
CASTOFF	CAUTELS	CESSERS	CHAPKAS	CHEERLY
OFFCAST	SULCATE	CRESSES	PACHAKS	LECHERY
CASTORS	CAVEATS	CESSPIT	CHARIOT	CHEKIST
COSTARS	VACATES	SEPTICS	HARICOT	HICKEST
CASUALS	CAVERNS	CESTODE	CHARMED	CHELOID
CAUSALS	CRAVENS	ESCOTED	MARCHED	HELCOID
CATALOS	CAWKERS	CETANES	CHARMER	CHELONE
COASTAL	WACKERS	TENACES	MARCHER	ECHELON
CATCHER	CEASING	CHACHKA	CHARNEL	CHEMISE
RECATCH	INCAGES	KACHCHA	LARCHEN	SCHEMIE
CATCHUP	CEILING	CHACOES	CHARPAI	CHEMIST
UPCATCH	CIELING	COACHES	HAIRCAP	MITCHES
CATELOG	CELESTA	CHAINED	CHARTED	CHENARS
GELCOAT	SELECTA	ECHIDNA	RATCHED	RANCHES
CATFLAP	CELOSIA	CHAINES	CHARTER	CHENETS
FLATCAP	COALISE	INCHASE	RECHART	TENCHES
CATHOLE	CENSING	CHAKRAS	CHASTEN	CHERISH
CHOLATE	SCENING	CHARKAS	NATCHES	SHRIECH
CATLING	CENTILE	CHALKED	CHATTEL	CHESILS
TALCING	LICENTE	HACKLED	LATCHET	CHISELS
CATLINS	CENTRED	CHALLIE	CHATTER	CHETAHS
TINCALS	CREDENT	HELICAL	RATCHET	HATCHES
CATSUPS	CERAMIC	CHAMISA	CHAWING	CHEVETS
UPCASTS	RACEMIC	CHIASMA	CHINWAG	VETCHES

CHEVIES	CHOLINE	CHYPRES	CLASHES	CLOCKER
SEVICHE	HELICON	CYPHERS	SEALCHS	COCKLER
CHEWERS	CHOOSER	CIDARIS	CLASPED	CLODDED
RECHEWS	SOROCHE	SCIARID	SCALPED	CODDLED
CHICEST	CHOPINE	CILICES	CLASSED	CLOGGED
HECTICS	PHOCINE	ICICLES	DECLASS	COGGLED
CHICLES	CHOPINS	CINGULA	CLASSES	CLOISON
CLICHES	PHONICS	GLUCINA	SACLESS	SCOLION
CHICONS	CHORDAE	CINQUES	CLAVIES	CLOKING
COCHINS	ROACHED	QUINCES	VESICAL	LOCKING
CHIDERS	CHORDAL	CIPOLIN	CLEANER	CLONERS
HERDICS	DORLACH	PICOLIN	RECLEAN	CORNELS
CHIELDS	CHORING	CIRCARS	CLEANUP	CLOSEST
CHILDES	OCHRING	RICRACS	UNPLACE	CLOSETS
CHIGRES	CHORISM	CIRCLES	CLEFTED	CLOSURE
SCREIGH	CHRISOM	CLERICS	DEFLECT	COLURES
CHIKORS	CHORIST	CIRRATE	CLEUCHS	CLOTTER
CHOKRIS	OSTRICH	ERRATIC	CULCHES	CROTTLE
CHIMERS	CHOROID	CISTERN	CLEUGHS	CLOVERS
MICHERS	OCHROID	CRETINS	GULCHES	VELCROS
CHIMING	CHORTEN	CITATOR	CLIMATE	CLOWING
MICHING	NOTCHER	RICOTTA	METICAL	COWLING
CHIPSET	CHOUSES	CITHERN	CLIMBER	CLUEING
PITCHES	HOCUSES	CITHREN	RECLIMB	LUCIGEN
CHIVIES	CHOWDER	CITIZEN	CLINGER	CLUMBER
VICHIES	COWHERD	ZINCITE	CRINGLE	CRUMBLE
CHOICER	CHOWSED	CITOLAS	CLINKED	CLUMPER
CHOREIC	COWSHED	STOICAL	NICKLED	CRUMPLE
CHOKEYS	CHROMAS	CLADDER	CLINKER	CLUNKER
HOCKEYS	MORCHAS	CRADLED	CRINKLE	CRUNKLE
CHOKING	CHUNDER	CLANGER	CLIPPER	CNEMIAL
HOCKING	CHURNED	GLANCER	CRIPPLE	MELANIC
CHOLENT	CHYLOUS	CLAQUER	CLOBBER	COADIES
NOTCHEL	SLOUCHY	LACQUER	COBBLER	CODEIAS
CHOLERS	CHYMIST	CLARINO	CLOCKED	COAGENT
ORCHELS	TYCHISM	CLARION	COCKLED	COGNATE

COATING	COLITIS	CONDORS	COOKOUT	CORKING
COTINGA	SOLICIT	CORDONS	OUTCOOK	ROCKING
COCAINE	COLLOPS	CONDUIT	COOLANT	CORNERS
OCEANIC	SCOLLOP	NOCTUID	OCTANOL	SCORNER
COCKERS	COLLUDE	CONGAED	COOLERS	CORNILY
RECOCKS	LOCULED	DECAGON	CREOSOL	LYRICON
COCKILY	COLOBUS	CONGIUS	COOLEST	CORNUAL
COLICKY	SUBCOOL	SOUCING	OCELOTS	COURLAN
CODDLES	COLONES	CONICAL	COOLING	CORONAS
SCOLDED	CONSOLE	LACONIC	LOCOING	RACOONS
CODEINA	COLORER	CONIINE	COOLIST	CORONER
OCEANID	RECOLOR	INCONIE	SCIOLTO	CROONER
CODLING	COMARBS	CONINES	COOPERS	CORPSES
LINGCOD	CRAMBOS	CONNIES	SCOOPER	PROCESS
CODRIVE	COMBERS	CONIUMS	COOSERS	CORSIVE
DIVORCE	RECOMBS	UNICOMS	ROSCOES	VOICERS
CODROVE	COMBIER	CONKERS	COOTERS	COSIERS
VOCODER	MICROBE	RECKONS	SCOOTER	CRIOSES
COENURI	COMICES	CONKING	COPITAS	COSMIST
NOURICE	MOCCIES	NOCKING	PSOATIC	SITCOMS
COFFERS	COMPARE	CONSENT	COPOUTS	COSTEAN
SCOFFER	COMPEAR	NOCENTS	OCTOPUS	OCTANES
COGENER	COMPEER	CONSIST	COPTERS	COSTING
CONGREE	COMPERE	TOCSINS	PROSECT	GNOSTIC
COGNISE	COMPILE	CONSORT	COPULAR	COTTISE
COIGNES	POLEMIC	CROTONS	CUPOLAR	SCOTTIE
COHEIRS	COMPOST	CONSULT	CORCASS	COUGHED
HEROICS	COMPOTS	UNCOLTS	CORSACS	GOUCHED
COIFFES	COMUSES	CONSUME	CORDATE	COUPLET
OFFICES	MUSCOSE	MUSCONE	REDCOAT	OCTUPLE
COILERS	CONARIA	CONURES	CORDERS	COUPONS
RECOILS	OCARINA	ROUNCES	RECORDS	SOUPCON
COKINGS	CONCENT	CONVEYS	CORELLA	COURIES
SOCKING	CONNECT	COVYNES	OCELLAR	SCOURIE
COLEADS	CONDOES	COOKERS	CORKIER	COURTED
SOLACED	SECONDO	RECOOKS	ROCKIER	EDUCTOR

COUTILS	CREMONA	CRUELTY	CURACAO	DABSTER
OCULIST	ROMANCE	CUTLERY	CURACOA	TABERDS
COUZINS	CREMSIN	CRUISED	CURAGHS	DADDLES
ZINCOUS	MINCERS	DISCURE	SCRAUGH	SADDLED
COVERER	CREOLES	CRUIVES	CURATED	DAFTIES
RECOVER	RECLOSE	CURSIVE	TRADUCE	FADIEST
COVINES	CREPING	CRUNKED	CURDLES	DAGGLES
NOVICES	PERCING	DRUCKEN	SCUDLER	SLAGGED
COWRIES	CRETISM	CRUSADE	CURINGS	DAIDLES
SCOWRIE	METRICS	SCAURED	CURSING	LADDIES
COYOTES	CRIMINA	CRUSTAL	CURNIER	DAIKERS
OOCYTES	MINICAR	CURTALS	REINCUR	DARKIES
CRAFTED	CRIMSON	CRYINGS	CURPELS	DALLIED
FRACTED	MICRONS	SCRYING	SCRUPLE	DIALLED
CRAFTER	CRISPER	CUDDLES	CURTAIL	DALTONS
REFRACT	PRICERS	SCUDDLE	TRUCIAL	SANDLOT
CRAMPIT	CROQUET	CUFFLES	CURTAIN	DAMAGER
PTARMIC	ROCQUET	SCUFFLE	TURACIN	MEGARAD
CRANING	CROSSED	CUISHES	CURTESY	DAMMERS
RANCING	SCORSED	CUSHIES	CURTSEY	SMARMED
CRANIUM	CROSSES	CULTIER	CUSPATE	DAMNEST
CUMARIN	SCORSES	UTRICLE	TEACUPS	TANDEMS
CRAPPIE	CROTALE	CUMBERS	CUSSING	DAMPEST
EPICARP	LOCATER	SCUMBER	SCUSING	STAMPED
CRASHED	CROUPED	CUMMERS	CUTOFFS	DAMPISH
ECHARDS	PRODUCE	SCUMMER	OFFCUTS	PHASMID
CREASES	CROUPER	CUNNERS	CYCLISE	DANDIER
SEARCES	PROCURE	SCUNNER	CYLICES	DRAINED
CRECHES	CROWERS	CUPELED	CYLIKES	DANDIES
SCREECH	SCOWRER	DECUPLE	KYLICES	SDAINED
CREDITS	CROWNED	CUPFULS	CYSTEIN	DANGLED
DIRECTS	DECROWN	CUPSFUL	CYSTINE	GLADDEN
CREEPED	CROWNER	CUPPERS	CYTASES	DANGLER
PRECEDE	RECROWN	SCUPPER	ECSTASY	GNARLED
CREMATE	CRUDEST	CUPRITE	DABBLES	DANKEST
MEERCAT	CRUSTED	PICTURE	SLABBED	STANKED

DANTONS	DEASOIL	DECTETS	DEFUSER	DEMETON
DONNATS	ISOLEAD	DETECTS	REFUSED	TEENDOM
DARINGS	DEAVING	DEDIMUS	DEHORTS	DEMINER
GRADINS	EVADING	MUDDIES	SHORTED	ERMINED
DARKNET	DEAWING	DEDUCES	DEIDEST	DEMISED
TRANKED	WINDAGE	SEDUCED	TEDDIES	MISDEED
DARLING	DEBASES	DEEDEST	DEIFIED	DEMOING
LARDING	SEABEDS	STEEDED	EDIFIED	MENDIGO
DARSHAN	DEBTORS	DEEDILY	DEIFIES	DEMONRY
DHARNAS	STROBED	YIELDED	EDIFIES	DORYMEN
DARTING	DECAFFS	DEEDING	DEINDEX	DEMOUNT
TRADING	SCAFFED	DEIGNED	INDEXED	MOUNTED
DARTLES	DECAMPS	DEEPEST	DEISTIC	DEMURES
SLARTED	SCAMPED	STEEPED	DICIEST	RESUMED
DASHERS	DECANES	DEFACER	DEKARES	DENDRON
SHADERS	ENCASED	REFACED	SKEARED	DONNERD
DASHING	DECERNS	DEFAULT	DELATES	DENGUES
SHADING	SCERNED	FAULTED	STEALED	UNEDGES
DATARIA	DECIDER	DEFIANT	DELATOR	DENIALS
RADIATA	DECRIED	FAINTED	LEOTARD	SNAILED
DAUNTED	DECILES	DEFIERS	DELENDA	DENNETS
UNDATED	DELICES	SERIFED	LADENED	STENNED
DAWDING	DECKELS	DEFILED	DELIGHT	DENSITY
WADDING	DECKLES	FIELDED	LIGHTED	DESTINY
DAWDLED	DECKOED	DEFINES	DELIMIT	DENTALS
WADDLED	DECOKED	INFEEDS	LIMITED	SLANTED
DAWTIES	DECODER	DEFOCUS	DELIRIA	DENTELS
WAISTED	RECODED	FOCUSED	IRIDEAL	NESTLED
DAYWORK	DECREED	DEFORMS	DELVING	DENTING
WORKDAY	RECEDED	SERFDOM	DEVLING	TENDING
DEAIRED	DECREET	DEFOULS	DEMANDS	DENUDER
READIED	ERECTED	FLOUSED	MADDENS	ENDURED
DEANERS	DECREWS	DEFROCK	DEMERGE	DEPERMS
ENDEARS	SCREWED	FROCKED	EMERGED	PREMEDS
DEARIES	DECRIES	DEFROST	DEMESNE	DEPICTS
READIES	DEICERS	FROSTED	SEEDMEN	DISCEPT

DEPLANE	DESMANS	DEWITTS	DIEOFFS	DIOXIDS
PANELED	MADNESS	TWISTED	OFFSIDE	IXODIDS
DEPLOYS	DESMINE	DEWLAPS	DIGESTS	DIPHONE
PODLEYS	SIDEMEN	SPAWLED	DISGEST	PHONIED
DEPONES	DESNOOD	DHANSAK	DIGNITY	DIPNETS
SPONDEE	SNOODED	KHANDAS	TIDYING	STIPEND
DEPOSAL	DESPISE	DHIMMIS	DIGONAL	DIPNOAN
PEDALOS	PEDESIS	DIMMISH	LOADING	NONPAID
DEPOSED	DESUGAR	DHURRIE	DIKASTS	DIRHAMS
SEEDPOD	SUGARED	HURRIED	TSADIKS	MIDRASH
DEPOSER	DESYNES	DIALYSE	DILUENT	DIRTIED
REPOSED	ENDYSES	EYLIADS	UNTILED	TIDDIER
DEPOSES	DETAILS	DIASTEM	DILUTES	DISCOER
SPEEDOS	DILATES	MISDATE	DUELIST	SCODIER
DERAYED	DETENTE	DIATOMS	DIMNESS	DISEASE
YEARDED	NEDETTE	MASTOID	MISSEND	SEASIDE
DERHAMS	DETENTS	DIAXONS	DINDLES	DISEURS
MARSHED	STENTED	DIOXANS	SLIDDEN	SUDSIER
DERNIER	DETENUS	DIAZINS	DINGERS	DISGOWN
NERDIER	DETUNES	DIZAINS	ENGIRDS	DOWSING
DERVISH	DETERGE	DIBBLER	DINGEYS	DISHORN
SHRIVED	GREETED	DRIBBLE	DYEINGS	DRONISH
DESANDS	DETICKS	DICHTED	DINKEST	DISMAYD
SADDENS	STICKED	DITCHED	KINDEST	MIDDAYS
DESCEND	DETORTS	DICINGS	DINKEYS	DISMAYL
SCENDED	DOTTERS	DISCING	KIDNEYS	LADYISM
DESCENT	DETRACT	DICKENS	DINKIES	DISPELS
SCENTED	TRACTED	SNICKED	KINDIES	DISPLES
DESERVE	DEUCING	DICKERS	DINKING	DISPLED
SEVERED	EDUCING	SCRIKED	KINDING	PIDDLES
DESIGNS	DEUTONS	DICTIER	DINNERS	DISPONE
SDEIGNS	SNOUTED	ICTERID	ENDRINS	SPINODE
DESIRES	DEVEINS	DIDDLER	DINNLES	DISROOT
RESIDES	ENDIVES	RIDDLED	LINDENS	TOROIDS
DESKILL	DEVOLVE	DIEHARD	DINTING	DISSEAT
SKILLED	EVOLVED	DIHEDRA	TINDING	SAIDEST

DISSERT	DOGLIKE	DOORMEN	DRAFTER	DROICHS
STRIDES	GODLIKE	MORENDO	REDRAFT	ORCHIDS
DISSING	DOGRELS	DOPINGS	DRAGEES	DROOMES
SIDINGS	LODGERS	PONGIDS	GREASED	SMOORED
DISTUNE	DOGSHIP	DORISED	DRAGNET	DROPLET
DUNITES	GODSHIP	SODDIER	GRANTED	PRETOLD
DITCHES	DOILIES	DORISES	DRAGOON	DROPOUT
SICHTED	IDOLISE	DOSSIER	GADROON	OUTDROP
DITHERS	DOLINAS	DORMANT	DRAINER	DROWSED
SHIRTED	LADINOS	MORDANT	RANDIER	SWORDED
DITHIOL	DONATED	DORMINS	DRAPERS	DRUGGED
LITHOID	NODATED	NIMRODS	SPARRED	GRUDGED
DITONES	DONGLES	DORTERS	DRAPPIE	DRUGGER
STONIED	GOLDENS	RODSTER	PREPAID	GRUDGER
DIURONS	DONGOLA	DOSAGES	DRAWEES	DRUMBLE
DURIONS	GONDOLA	SEADOGS	RESAWED	RUMBLED
DIVERGE	DONINGS	DOSSERS	DRAWING	DRUPELS
GRIEVED	ONDINGS	DROSSES	WARDING	SLURPED
DIVISOR	DONNERT	DOTCOMS	DRAYAGE	DRUSIER
VIROIDS	TENDRON	TOMCODS	YARDAGE	DURRIES
DIVVIER	DONNIES	DOTIEST	DRAYING	DRYSUIT
VIVIDER	ONDINES	STOITED	YARDING	SURDITY
DOCKERS	DOOBREY	DOTTLER	DRAYMAN	DUALINS
REDOCKS	OREBODY	DOTTREL	YARDMAN	SUNDIAL
DODGERS	DOODLER	DOUSING	DRAYMEN	DUALIST
GORSEDD	DROOLED	GUIDONS	YARDMEN	TULADIS
DODGING	DOOFERS	DOWAGER	DREADED	DUCTILE
GODDING	FORDOES	WORDAGE	READDED	DULCITE
DODMANS	DOOKETS	DOWLIER	DREADLY	DUDDIER
ODDSMAN	STOOKED	WORLDIE	LADDERY	RUDDIED
DOGATES	DOOLANS	DOWNERS	DRESSER	DUDETTE
DOTAGES	ONLOADS	WONDERS	REDRESS	DUETTED
DOGEATE	DOOMILY	DOWNIER	DRILLER	DUELERS
GOATEED	MOODILY	WINDORE	REDRILL	ELUDERS
DOGLEGS	DOORMAN	DOWNLOW	DROGUET	DUETTOS
SLOGGED	MADRONO	LOWDOWN	GROUTED	TESTUDO

DUFFEST	DUNTING	EBAYERS	ELATION	EMITTER
STUFFED	TUNDING	EYEBARS	TOENAIL	TERMITE
DUGITES	DUOTONE	EBONIES	ELCHEES	EMONGES
GIUSTED	OUTDONE	EBONISE	LEECHES	GENOMES
DUGONGS	DUPIONS	ECHOIST	ELECTOR	EMOTING
GUNDOGS	UNIPODS	TOISECH	ELECTRO	MITOGEN
DUIKERS	DURIANS	ECOMAPS	ELEGIES	EMPALER
DUSKIER	SUNDARI	POMACES	ELEGISE	PREMEAL
DUKKAHS	DURMAST	ECONOMY	ELEGIST	EMPANEL
DUKKHAS	MUSTARD	MONOECY	ELEGITS	EMPLANE
DULCIAN	DUSTERS	EDENTAL	ELEMENT	EMPARED
INCUDAL	TRUSSED	LATENED	TELEMEN	PREMADE
DULOSIS	DWARVES	EDGINGS	ELOGIST	EMPORIA
SOLIDUS	SWARVED	SNIGGED	LOGIEST	MEROPIA
DUMAIST	DWINDLE	EDITION	ELOPERS	EMPTIES
STADIUM	WINDLED	TENIOID	LEPROSE	SEPTIME
DUMMIER	DWINING	EELIEST	ELUATES	EMPTINS
IMMURED	WINDING	STEELIE	SETUALE	PIMENTS
DUMMIES	DYELINE	EENSIER	ELUENTS	EMPTION
MEDIUMS	NEEDILY	ESERINE	UNSTEEL	PIMENTO
DUMPIER	EARFLAP	EEVNING	ELUTION	EMULGES
UMPIRED	PARAFLE	EVENING	OUTLINE	LEGUMES
DUMPIES	EARLIER	EFTSOON	EMAILED	EMUNGED
MUDPIES	LEARIER	FESTOON	LIMEADE	GUDEMEN
DUMPLES	EARLIES	EGGLERS	EMAILER	ENAMELS
SLUMPED	REALISE	LEGGERS	MEALIER	MELENAS
DUNGING	EARLIKE	EGOISMS	EMBLICS	ENAMOUR
NUDGING	LEAKIER	MISGOES	LIMBECS	NEUROMA
DUNNEST	EARNERS	EGOISTS	EMBRUED	ENCAVED
STUNNED	REEARNS	STOGIES	UMBERED	VENDACE
DUNNIER	EARTHED	EGOTISE	EMENDER	ENCHARM
INURNED	HEARTED	GOETIES	REEDMEN	MARCHEN
DUNNIES	EARTHEN	EILDING	EMERGES	ENCLASP
UNDINES	HEARTEN	ELIDING	MERGEES	SPANCEL
DUNSHES	EARWIGS	EISWEIN	EMICANT	ENCLAVE
SNUSHED	GAWSIER	WIENIES	NEMATIC	VALENCE

ENCODER	ENGORES	ENSOULS	EPARCHY	ERISTIC
ENCORED	NEGROES	NOUSLES	PREACHY	RICIEST
ENCODES	ENGUARD	ENSTAMP	EPEIRIC	ERRANTS
SECONDE	RAUNGED	TAPSMEN	EPICIER	RANTERS
ENCORES	ENJOYER	ENSTEEP	EPHEBOS	ERRATUM
NECROSE	REENJOY	STEEPEN	PHOEBES	MATURER
ENDARCH	ENLIGHT	ENSTYLE	EPIGRAM	ERUPTED
RANCHED	LIGHTEN	TENSELY	PRIMAGE	REPUTED
ENDINGS	ENLOCKS	ENTAMES	EPILATE	ERYNGOS
SENDING	SLOCKEN	MEANEST	PILEATE	GROYNES
ENDITED	ENMOVED	ENTASIA	EPIMERE	ESCROCS
TEINDED	VENOMED	TAENIAS	PREEMIE	SOCCERS
ENDNOTE	ENOLASE	ENTERIC	EPINAOS	ESPADAS
TENONED	LOANEES	ENTICER	SENOPIA	PASSADE
ENDOWER	ENOLOGY	ENTERON	EPISODE	ESPANOL
REENDOW	NEOLOGY	TENONER	POESIED	NOPALES
ENDURES	ENQUIRE	ENTOPIC	EPISTLE	ESPIERS
ENSURED	INQUERE	NEPOTIC	PELITES	PRESSIE
ENDWISE	ENRACED	ENTOTIC	EPOXIDE	ESPOUSE
SINEWED	RECANED	TONETIC	EPOXIED	POSEUSE
ENDZONE	ENRINGS	ENTOZOA	EPSILON	ESQUIRE
ENZONED	GINNERS	OZONATE	PINOLES	QUERIES
ENEWING	ENROUGH	ENTRAIN	EQUATOR	ESSENCE
WEENING	ROUGHEN	TRANNIE	QUORATE	SENESCE
ENFOLDS	ENSIGNS	ENTRUST	EQUINAL	ESSOYNE
FONDLES	SENSING	NUTTERS	QUINELA	NOYESES
ENFRAME	ENSKIED	ENTWIST	ERATHEM	ESTEEMS
FREEMAN	SKEINED	TWINSET	THERMAE	MESTEES
ENGINED	ENSKIES	ENWOUND	ERECTER	ESTHETE
NEEDING	KINESES	UNOWNED	REERECT	TEETHES
ENGINER	ENSLAVE	EOSINES	EREPSIN	ESTOILE
INGENER	LEAVENS	ONESIES	REPINES	ETOILES
ENGLISH	ENSNARE	EPACRID	ERGATES	ESTREPE
SHINGLE	RENNASE	PERACID	RESTAGE	STEEPER
ENGLUTS	ENSNARL	EPARCHS	ERINITE	ESTRUAL
GLUTENS	LANNERS	PARCHES	NITERIE	SALUTER

ETALAGE	EXCIDES	FALCONS	FARMOST	FEODARY
GALEATE	EXCISED	FLACONS	FORMATS	FORAYED
ETALONS	EXCITOR	FALLERS	FARSIDE	FERNIER
TOLANES	XEROTIC	REFALLS	FRAISED	REFINER
ETAMINE	EXCURSE	FALLOUT	FASTENS	FERROUS
MATINEE	EXCUSER	OUTFALL	FATNESS	FURORES
ETATIST	EXPANDS	FALSERS	FASTERS	FETIALS
TATTIES	SPANDEX	FLASERS	STRAFES	SEALIFT
ETCHERS	EXPERTS	FALSIES	FASTEST	FETICHE
RETCHES	SEXPERT	FILASSE	SAFTEST	FITCHEE
ETHIONS	EXPIRES	FAMINES	FATSOES	FETTLES
HISTONE	PREXIES	INFAMES	FOSSATE	LEFTEST
ETHIOPS	EXPOSED	FANGIRL	FAUTORS	FEUTRED
OPHITES	PODEXES	FLARING	FOUTRAS	REFUTED
ETHNICS	EXPOSIT	FANGLED	FAVORER	FEUTRES
STHENIC	POXIEST	FLANGED	OVERFAR	REFUTES
ETTLING	EXTINES	FANGLES	FEATHER	FICKLED
LETTING	SIXTEEN	FLANGES	TEREFAH	FLICKED
EUMONGS	EYELIDS	FANKLED	FECHTER	FICKLER
MUNGOES	SEEDILY	FLANKED	FETCHER	FLICKER
EVANISH	EYESPOT	FANNELL	FEEDERS	FICTORS
VAHINES	PEYOTES	FLANNEL	REFEEDS	FRICOTS
EVENTER	FACTEND	FANTAIL	FEEDING	FIGURED
EVERNET	FANCIED	TAILFAN	FEIGNED	FUDGIER
EVOKERS	FACTORS	FARCERS	FEELERS	FILAREE
REVOKES	FORCATS	SCARFER	REFEELS	LEAFIER
EVOLUTE	FACTURE	FARCIES	FEELING	FILLERS
VELOUTE	FURCATE	FIACRES	FLEEING	REFILLS
EVOLVER	FAIENCE	FARDENS	FELCHES	FILMERS
REVOLVE	FIANCEE	SNARFED	FLECHES	REFILMS
EXACTER	FAINNES	FARFELS	FELLATE	FILMSET
EXCRETA	FANNIES	RAFFLES	LEAFLET	LEFTISM
EXAMPLE	FAINTER	FARMERS	FELTIER	FINALIS
EXEMPLA	FENITAR	FRAMERS	FERTILE	FINIALS
EXCEPTS	FAIRISH	FARMING	FEMINAL	FINGERS
EXPECTS	HAIRIFS	FRAMING	INFLAME	FRINGES

FINITES	FLETTON	FOCUSES	FRESHER	GABELLE
NIFTIES	FONTLET	FUCOSES	REFRESH	GELABLE
FINKING	FLIRTED	FOISTER	FRESHET	GABNASH
KNIFING	TRIFLED	FORTIES	HEFTERS	NASHGAB
FIRELIT	FLIRTER	FOLDERS	FRESHIE	GADGETS
FITLIER	TRIFLER	REFOLDS	HEIFERS	STAGGED
FIREPOT	FLITING	FOLDUPS	FRETFUL	GAHNITE
PIEFORT	LIFTING	UPFOLDS	TRUFFLE	HEATING
FIRLOTS	FLOORER	FONDLER	FRETSAW	GALERES
FLORIST	FORLORE	FORLEND	WAFTERS	REGALES
FIRMEST	FLOOSIE	FONDUED	FRONTER	GALLEIN
FREMITS	FOLIOSE	FOUNDED	REFRONT	NIGELLA
FISTING	FLORETS	FORAMEN	FUGLIER	GALLICA
SIFTING	LOFTERS	FOREMAN	GULFIER	GLACIAL
FITTERS	FLOTING	FORBARE	FUGLING	GALLIES
TITFERS	LOFTING	FORBEAR	GULFING	GALLISE
FITTING	FLOURED	FORESTS	FULNESS	GALLING
TIFTING	FOULDER	FOSTERS	UNSELFS	GINGALL
FIZZERS	FLUATES	FORETOP	FUNDERS	GALLNUT
FRIZZES	SULFATE	POOFTER	REFUNDS	NUTGALL
FLARIER	FLUERIC	FORFEIT	FUNDIES	GALLONS
FRAILER	LUCIFER	TOFFIER	INFUSED	GOLLANS
FLASHED	FLUIEST	FORMERS	FUNFAIR	GALORES
FLEADHS	SULFITE	REFORMS	RUFFIAN	GAOLERS
FLATCAR	FLUSHED	FORRAYS	FUNSTER	GAMBIST
FRACTAL	SHEDFUL	ORFRAYS	NETSURF	GAMBITS
FLECKER	FLUTIER	FORWARD	FURANES	GAMBLER
FRECKLE	FUTILER	FROWARD	UNSAFER	GAMBREL
FLEMISH	FLUVIAL	FOUNDER	FUROLES	GAMETES
HIMSELF	VIALFUL	REFOUND	OURSELF	METAGES
FLENSER	FLYOVER	FOUTERS	FUSIBLE	GAMIEST
FRESNEL	OVERFLY	FOUTRES	SUBFILE	SIGMATE
FLESHED	FOALING	FRANGER	FUSTIER	GAMMERS
SHELFED	LOAFING	GRANFER	SURFEIT	GRAMMES
FLESHER	FOCUSER	FRENUMS	GABBLER	GAMONES
HERSELF	REFOCUS	SURFMEN	GRABBLE	MANGOES

GANGBOS	GELDING	GINGELY	GLADIER	GLOWERS
GOBANGS	NIGGLED	GLEYING	GLAIRED	REGLOWS
GANGING	GEMMATE	GINGKOS	GLAIKET	GLOWING
NAGGING	TAGMEME	GINKGOS	TAGLIKE	GOWLING
GANSEYS	GENOISE	GINNELS	GLAIRES	GLUEING
GAYNESS	SOIGNEE	LENSING	GRAILES	LUGEING
GANTING	GENTLED	GINNERY	GLEAVES	GLUGGED
TANGING	GLENTED	RENYING	SELVAGE	GUGGLED
GAOLING	GENTLES	GINNIER	GLEEING	GLUIEST
GOALING	LENGEST	REINING	NEGLIGE	UGLIEST
GARNERS	GENUINE	GINSHOP	GLEEMAN	GLUTTED
RANGERS	INGENUE	POSHING	MELANGE	GUTTLED
GASLESS	GENUSES	GIPPERS	GLIBBER	GNARRED
GLASSES	NEGUSES	GRIPPES	GRIBBLE	GRANDER
GASPERS	GERENTS	GIRAFFE	GLIMPSE	GNASHED
SPARGES	REGENTS	RIFFAGE	MEGILPS	HAGDENS
GASSERS	GERMING	GIRASOL	GLINTED	GOALIES
GRASSES	MERGING	GLORIAS	TINGLED	SOILAGE
GASTERS	GESTATE	GIRDERS	GLISTER	GODDENS
STAGERS	TAGETES	RIDGERS	GRISTLE	GODSEND
GASTRIC	GETOUTS	GIRLOND	GLOATER	GODLING
TRAGICS	GOUTTES	LORDING	LEGATOR	LODGING
GATCHER	GHRELIN	GIRNING	GLOBIER	GOLOSHE
GERTCHA	HERLING	RINGING	OBLIGER	SHOOGLE
GATEWAY	GIBBONS	GIRONNY	GLOIRES	GONGING
GETAWAY	SOBBING	ROYNING	GLORIES	NOGGING
GAUDGIE	GILDING	GIRSHES	GLOMERA	GONIFFS
GUIDAGE	GLIDING	SIGHERS	GOMERAL	OFFINGS
GAUFERS	GILLERS	GIRTHED	GLONOIN	GOODIES
GAUFRES	GRILLES	RIGHTED	LOONING	SOOGIED
GAUNTED	GILLNET	GIRTING	GLOSSED	GOOLIES
UNGATED	TELLING	RINGGIT	GODLESS	OLOGIES
GEARING	GIMMERS	GITTERN	GLOSSER	GOONERY
NAGGIER	MEGRIMS	RETTING	REGLOSS	OROGENY
GELATOS	GINGALS	GLACIER	GLOVERS	GOORIES
LEGATOS	LAGGINS	GRACILE	GROVELS	GOOSIER

GOOSIES	GRAVURE	GROUSER	GUNSHIP	HAEMINS
SOOGIES	VERRUGA	ROGUERS	PUSHING	HEMINAS
GORGETS	GREASER	GROWERS	GURGING	HAGBORN
TOGGERS	REGEARS	REGROWS	RUGGING	HORNBAG
GORINGS	GREATER	GROWNUP	GURRIES	HAGDONS
GRINGOS	REGRATE	UPGROWN	SURGIER	SANDHOG
GOSLING	GREENED	GRUEING	GURSHES	HAGRIDE
OGLINGS	RENEGED	GUNGIER	GUSHERS	HEADRIG
GOWANED	GREETER	GRUMOSE	GUSHING	HAILING
WAGONED	REGREET	MORGUES	SUGHING	NILGHAI
GRADDAN	GREMIAL	GRUMOUS	GUSTIER	HAIQUES
GRANDAD	LAMIGER	SOURGUM	GUTSIER	QUASHIE
GRADERS	GRIEVES	GRUNGES	GUSTILY	HALAKAH
REGARDS	REGIVES	SNUGGER	GUTSILY	HALAKHA
GRADING	GRIFFIN	GRUNTED	GUSTING	HALITES
NIGGARD	RIFFING	TRUDGEN	GUTSING	HELIAST
GRADINI	GRINDED	GRUSHIE	GUTLESS	HALITUS
RAIDING	REDDING	GUSHIER	TUGLESS	THULIAS
GRAFTER	GRINDER	GRUTTEN	GUTROTS	HALLANS
REGRAFT	REGRIND	TURGENT	ROTGUTS	NALLAHS
GRAHAMS	GRIPMAN	GUBBINS	GUTTIER	HALLOED
GRAMASH	RAMPING	SUBBING	TURGITE	HOLLAED
GRANDAM	GROANER	GUDDLES	GUYLING	HALLOOS
GRANDMA	ORANGER	SLUDGED	UGLYING	HOLLOAS
GRANTER	GROOMER	GUIDERS	GYMNAST	HALLOWS
REGRANT	REGROOM	GURDIES	SYNTAGM	SHALLOW
GRAPING	GROOVED	GUINEPS	GYMPIES	HALTERE
PARGING	OVERDOG	SPUEING	PYGMIES	LEATHER
GRAPLIN	GROSERS	GULLIES	GYRATED	HALTING
PARLING	GROSSER	LIGULES	TRAGEDY	LATHING
GRASPER	GROSSED	GULPERS	HACKLES	HAMATSA
SPARGER	SODGERS	SPLURGE	SHACKLE	TAMASHA
GRATING	GROUPER	GUNDIES	HACKSAW	HAMBLES
TARGING	REGROUP	SUEDING	KWACHAS	SHAMBLE
GRAVELS	GROUPIE	GUNLESS	HADARIM	HAMMERS
VERGLAS	PIROGUE	GUNSELS	HARAMDI	SHAMMER

HANDERS	HASSOCK	HELLERS	HILLERS	HOEDOWN
HARDENS	SHACKOS	SHELLER	RELLISH	WOODHEN
HANDLES	HASTIER	HEMPIES	HILLOES	HOLDUPS
HANDSEL	SHERIAT	IMPHEES	HOLLIES	UPHOLDS
HANDOFF	HASTING	HEPCATS	HILTING	HOLINGS
OFFHAND	TASHING	PATCHES	LITHING	LONGISH
HANGUPS	HATFULS	HEPTADS	HINDGUT	HOLSTER
UPHANGS	HATSFUL	SPATHED	UNDIGHT	HOSTLER
HANJARS	HATTING	HERMITS	HINGING	HOMAGES
RHANJAS	TATHING	MITHERS	NIGHING	OHMAGES
HANKERS	HAULING	HERNIAL	HINTERS	HOMERED
HARKENS	NILGHAU	INHALER	NITHERS	REHOMED
HANTING	HAULOUT	HEROINS	HINTING	HONGIES
TANGHIN	OUTHAUL	INSHORE	NITHING	SHOEING
HAPLESS	HAVINGS	HEROISM	HIPBONE	HOODMAN
PLASHES	SHAVING	MOREISH	HOPBINE	MANHOOD
HAPLONT	HAWKIES	HERRIED	HIPPENS	HOOPING
NAPHTOL	WEAKISH	REHIRED	SHIPPEN	POOHING
HARDASS	HAYRIDE	HERRIES	HIPPIES	HOPPERS
SRADHAS	HYDRIAE	REHIRES	SHIPPIE	SHOPPER
HARDIER	HAZMATS	HERSHIP	HIRINGS	HORMONE
HARRIED	MATZAHS	PHISHER	SHIRING	MOORHEN
HARDMEN	HEADPIN	HESPING	HIRSELS	HORRENT
HERDMAN	PINHEAD	PHESING	HIRSLES	NORTHER
HAREEMS	HEAVERS	HESSIAN	HISSELF	HORSIES
MAHSEER	RESHAVE	SHENAIS	SELFISH	HOSIERS
HARELDS	HEEDING	HEURISM	HISSIER	HORSING
HERALDS	NEIGHED	MUSHIER	REISHIS	SHORING
HARISSA	HEELERS	HICATEE	HITLESS	HORSTES
SHARIAS	REHEELS	TEACHIE	TEHSILS	TOSHERS
HARPIES	HEIRESS	HIDLING	HITTING	HOSTING
SHARPIE	HERISSE	HILDING	TITHING	TOSHING
HARVEST	HELIMEN	HIELAND	HOARSEN	HOTCHES
THRAVES	HEMLINE	INHALED	SENHORA	SHOCHET
HASSLED	HELLERI	HIGHTED	HODDENS	HOTLINE
SLASHED	HELLIER	THIGHED	SHODDEN	NEOLITH

HOTTERS	HYDROUS	IMPALES	INCESTS	INLIERS
TOTHERS	SHROUDY	PALMIES	INSECTS	RESILIN
HOTTING	HYLISTS	IMPANEL	INCISED	INNAGES
TONIGHT	STYLISH	MANIPLE	INDICES	SEANING
HOUTING	ICELESS	IMPASSE	INCLUDE	INNINGS
THOUING	SIECLES	PESSIMA	NUCLIDE	SINNING
HOWEVER	ICHNITE	IMPASTE	INDEWED	INQUEST
WHOEVER	NITCHIE	PASTIME	WIDENED	QUINTES
HOWLETS	ICINESS	IMPASTO	INDEXER	INSANER
THOWELS	INCISES	MATIPOS	REINDEX	INSNARE
HUDDLER	IDEATUM	IMPEDES	INDITER	INSCAPE
HURDLED	TAEDIUM	SEMIPED	NITRIDE	PINCASE
HUMECTS	IDENTIC	IMPLATE	INDITES	INSIDER
MUTCHES	INCITED	PALMIET	TINEIDS	SNIDIER
HUMIDOR	IGNITOR	IMPONES	INDOORS	INSTATE
RHODIUM	RIOTING	PEONISM	SORDINO	SATINET
HUMITES	IGNOBLE	IMPORTS	INDRAWN	INSTEPS
TUMSHIE	INGLOBE	TROPISM	WINNARD	SPINETS
HUNGANS	ILLAPSE	IMPOSES	INDUSIA	INSULAE
UNHANGS	PALLIES	MOPSIES	SUIDIAN	INULASE
HURLIES	ILLICIT	IMPOSTS	INDWELT	INSULAR
LUSHIER	ILLITIC	MISSTOP	WINTLED	URINALS
HURRIES	ILLIPES	IMPRESA	INFARES	INSULIN
RUSHIER	PILLIES	SAMPIRE	SERAFIN	INULINS
HURTFUL	ILLUDES	IMPREST	INFEFTS	INSULSE
RUTHFUL	SULLIED	PERMITS	STIFFEN	SILENUS
HURTLES	IMBOSOM	IMPUGNS	INFIDEL	INSURER
HUSTLER	MIOMBOS	SPUMING	INFIELD	RUINERS
HUSHERS	IMBOWER	IMPURER	INHUMER	INSURES
SHUSHER	WOMBIER	PRIMEUR	RHENIUM	SUNRISE
HYACINE	IMBRUTE	IMPUTER	INISLED	INTAGLI
HYAENIC	TERBIUM	TUMPIER	LINDIES	TAILING
HYALINS	IMPAINT	INAPTLY	INKPOTS	INTENTS
LINHAYS	TIMPANI	PTYALIN	INKSPOT	TENNIST
HYDRATE	IMPALED	INCANTS	INLAYER	INTERNS
THREADY	IMPLEAD	STANNIC	NAILERY	TINNERS

INTIMAE	IONIUMS	JACKMAN	JOURNOS	KEENEST
MINIATE	NIMIOUS	MANJACK	SOJOURN	KETENES
INTINES	IONIZER	JALOUSE	JOYPOPS	KEENING
TINNIES	IRONIZE	JEALOUS	POPJOYS	KNEEING
INTONED	IONOMER	JAMBOKS	JUGFULS	KEEPING
NOINTED	MOONIER	SJAMBOK	JUGSFUL	PEEKING
INTONES	IRELESS	JAMBONE	JUJITSU	KEESTER
TENSION	RESILES	JOBNAME	JUJUIST	SKEETER
INTORTS	IRISING	JAMBULS	JUMARED	KEGGERS
TRITONS	NIGIRIS	JUMBALS	MUDEJAR	SKEGGER
INTRADA	IRKSOME	JAMMIES	KAISERS	KEIRINS
RADIANT	SMOKIER	JEMIMAS	KARSIES	SINKIER
INTWIST	IRONERS	JANTIER	KALMIAS	KEISTER
NITWITS	ROSINER	NARTJIE	KAMILAS	KIESTER
INVADED	IRONING	JANTIES	KAMOTIK	KEITLOA
VIDENDA	ROINING	TAJINES	KOMATIK	OATLIKE
INVADER	IRONIST	JARFULS	KANGHAS	KEKENOS
RAVINED	ROTINIS	JARSFUL	KHANGAS	KONEKES
INVERTS	IRRUPTS	JAWINGS	KANTING	KELLIES
STRIVEN	STIRRUP	JIGSAWN	TANKING	SKELLIE
INVITER	ISOSPIN	JAYVEES	KARAMUS	KELSONS
VITRINE	SINOPIS	VEEJAYS	KUMARAS	SLOKENS
INVITES	ISOTONE	JERBILS	KARYONS	KELTIES
VINIEST	TOONIES	JIRBLES	RYOKANS	SLEEKIT
INWRAPS	ISSUANT	JERKINS	KASBAHS	KENOTIC
RIPSAWN	SUSTAIN	JINKERS	SABKHAS	KETONIC
IODATED	ISSUERS	JITTERS	KASHERS	KEPHIRS
TOADIED	RISUSES	TRIJETS	SHAKERS	PERKISH
IODATES	ITCHIER	JOINERS	KASHMIR	KERRIAS
TOADIES	TICHIER	REJOINS	KHIMARS	SARKIER
IODIDES	IVORIST	JOLLITY	KATSINA	KETMIAS
IODISED	VISITOR	JOLTILY	TANKIAS	MISTAKE
IODINES	IVRESSE	JOLTERS	KAYOING	KEYINGS
IONISED	REVISES	JOSTLER	OKAYING	YESKING
IOLITES	JACKIES	JOUNCES	KEELERS	KEYRING
OILIEST	JACKSIE	JUNCOES	SLEEKER	YERKING

KICKOUT	KNEIDEL	LADRONS	LASINGS	LEAVING
OUTKICK	LIKENED	LARDONS	SIGNALS	VEALING
KIDDERS	KNITTER	LADYISH	LASKETS	LECHAIM
SKIDDER	TRINKET	SHADILY	SKLATES	MICHAEL
KILLERS	KNURLED	LAGERED	LASQUES	LECHWES
RESKILL	RUNKLED	REGALED	SQUEALS	WELCHES
KILTING	KOOKUMS	LAIKERS	LATINOS	LEEPING
KITLING	SKOOKUM	SERKALI	TALIONS	PEELING
KIMMERS	KOORIES	LAISSES	LATTICE	LEERING
SKIMMER	ROOKIES	LASSIES	TACTILE	REELTNG
KIMONOS	KRAKENS	LAKIEST	LAUNCED	LEESING
MONOSKI	SKANKER	TALKIES	UNLACED	SEELING
KINARAS	KREESED	LAKINGS	LAVAGES	LEEWAYS
KIRANAS	SKEERED	SLAKING	SALVAGE	WEASELY
KINGCUP	KUMARIS	LAMINAL	LAWINGS	LEGGISM
PUCKING	RUMAKIS	MANILLA	SWALING	MIGGLES
KINGPIN	KUMISES	LAMINAR	LAYINGS	LEIGERS
PINKING	MUSKIES	RAILMAN	SLAYING	LIEGERS
KINSHIP	KUMITES	LAMMIES	LAYOUTS	LEIRING
PINKISH	MISTEUK	MELISMA	OUTLAYS	LINGIER
KIPPERS	KURSAAL	LAMPING	LAYOVER	LEISLER
SKIPPER	RUSALKA	PALMING	OVERLAY	RELLIES
KIRNING	KYANISE	LANCERS	LAYTIME	LEMURES
RINKING	YANKIES	RANCELS	MEATILY	RELUMES
KIRPANS	KYLIKES	LANGARS	LEACHER	LENGTHY
PARKINS	SKYLIKE	RAGLANS	RELACHE	THEGNLY
KIRTANS	LABELER	LANGUID	LEAGUER	LENTISK
RANKIST	RELABEL	LAUDING	REGULAE	TINKLES
KISSING	LABOURS	LANIARD	LEAKING	LESSONS
SKIINGS	SUBORAL	NADIRAL	LINKAGE	SONLESS
KISTFUL	LABRUMS	LAPPING	LEARNER	LETOUTS
LUTFISK	LUMBARS	PALPING	RELEARN	OUTLETS
KITSCHY	LACINGS	LARIATS	LEASHED	LETTERN
SHTICKY	SCALING	LATRIAS	SHEALED	NETTLER
KNEADER	LADINGS	LARMIER	LEAVIER	LEVERED
NAKEDER	LIGANDS	MARLIER	VEALIER	REVELED

LEWDEST	LIMITER	LITTLIE	LOMEINS	LOWERED
SWELTED	MILTIER	TILLITE	MOLINES	ROWELED
LEXISES	LIMMERS	LIVINGS	LOMENTS	LOWPING
SILEXES	SLIMMER	SLIVING	MELTONS	PLOWING
LIAISES	LIMNERS	LIVYERS	LOMPISH	LOWSEST
SILESIA	MERLINS	SILVERY	PHLOMIS	SLOWEST
LIASSIC	LIMPEST	LOACHES	LOOKERS	LOXYGEN
SILICAS	LIMPETS	OSCHEAL	RELOOKS	XYLOGEN
LICHENS	LINCHET	LOAFERS	LOOKOUT	LUCUMOS
LINCHES	TINCHEL	SAFROLE	OUTLOOK	OSCULUM
LIENORS	LINEMAN	LOATHER	LOOKUPS	LUDSHIP
NEROLIS	MELANIN	RATHOLE	UPLOOKS	SULPHID
LIERNES	LINGAMS	LOATHLY	LOOMING	LUMINED
RELINES	MALIGNS	TALLYHO	MOOLING	UNLIMED
LIGATED	LINGUAE	LOBBERS	LOOPING	LUMPENS
TAIGLED	UNAGILE	SLOBBER	POOLING	PLENUMS
LIGHTER	LINGUAL	LOCHIAS	LOOSEST	LUMPERS
RELIGHT	LINGULA	SCHOLIA	LOTOSES	RUMPLES
LIGNANS	LINIEST	LOCKERS	LOOTING	LUMPIER
LINSANG	LINTIES	RELOCKS	TOOLING	PLUMIER
LIGNINS	LINSEYS	LOCKETS	LOPPERS	LUMPING
LININGS	LYSINES	LOCKSET	PROPELS	PLUMING
LIGROIN	LINTIER	LOCKUPS	LORDOMA	LUNATED
ROILING	NITRILE	UPLOCKS	MALODOR	UNDEALT
LIGULAS	LIONELS	LOCOMEN	LOTHEST	LUNGIES
LUGSAIL	NIELLOS	MONOCLE	SHOTTLE	SLUEING
LIKINGS	LIPPENS	LOCULES	LOTIONS	LUNKERS
SILKING	NIPPLES	OCELLUS	SOLITON	RUNKLES
LILTING	LIQUATE	LOCUSTA	LOUNDED	LURINGS
TILLING	TEQUILA	TALCOUS	NODULED	RULINGS
LIMACEL	LISTERS	LOESSIC	LOUVARS	LURRIES
MICELLA	RELISTS	OSSICLE	VALOURS	SURLIER
LIMACES	LITOTES	LOFTIER	LOVABLE	LUSHING
MALICES	TOILETS	TREFOIL	VOLABLE	SHULING
LIMACON	LITTERY	LOGGERS	LOVINGS	LUSKING
MALONIC	TRITELY	SLOGGER	SOLVING	SULKING

LUTITES	MANEGES	MARGATE	MASSIER	MEANIES
TITULES	MENAGES	REGMATA	SARMIES	NEMESIA
LYCEUMS	MANGELS	MARITAL	MASSIVE	MEDAKAS
MUSCLEY	MANGLES	MARTIAL	MAVISES	SMAAKED
LYCHEES	MANIHOC	MARKERS	MASTERS	MEDALET
SLEECHY	MOHICAN	REMARKS	STREAMS	METALED
LYDDITE	MANIKIN	MARMITE	MASTICH	MEDICOS
TIDDLEY	MANKINI	TRAMMIE	TACHISM	MISCODE
MACABER	MANITOS	MAROONS	MATCHER	MEDUSAN
MACABRE	STAMNOI	ROMANOS	REMATCH	SUDAMEN
MADRONE	MANITOU	MARQUES	MATLESS	MEERING
ROADMEN	TINAMOU	MASQUER	SAMLETS	REGIMEN
MAGIANS	MANKIER	MARRANO	MATRONS	MEETING
SIAMANG	RAMEKIN	ORRAMAN	TRANSOM	TEEMING
MAGNONS	MANPACK	MARRIES	MATROSS	MEGASSE
SONGMAN	PACKMAN	SIMARRE	STROAMS	MESSAGE
MAGPIES	MANRENT	MARRUMS	MATTERS	MEGILLA
MISPAGE	REMNANT	MURRAMS	SMATTER	MILLAGE
MAIMERS	MANROPE	MARTIAN	MATURES	MEINEYS
RAMMIES	REPOMAN	TAMARIN	STRUMAE	MENYIES
MAISTRY	MANTEEL	MARTING	MAUGRES	MELICKS
SYMITAR	TELEMAN	MIGRANT	MURAGES	MICKLES
MAKEUPS	MANTRAP	MASALAS	MAULERS	MELLAYS
UPMAKES	RAMPANT	SALAAMS	SERUMAL	MESALLY
MAKINGS	MAORMOR	MASHIER	MAUMETS	MENDERS
MASKING	MORMAOR	MISHEAR	SUMMATE	REMENDS
MALANGA	MAPLESS	MASHIES	MAUSIER	MERCERY
NAGMAAL	SAMPLES	MESSIAH	UREMIAS	REMERCY
MALICHO	MARBLED	MASHING	MAUVEIN	MERELLS
MOCHILA	RAMBLED	SHAMING	MAUVINE	SMELLER
MANATIS	MARBLER	MASHUPS	MAXIMIN	MERINOS
STAMINA	RAMBLER	SMASHUP	MINIMAX	MERSION
MANDOLA	MARCONI	MASONRY	MAZIEST	MERISIS
MONADAL	MINORCA	MORNAYS	MESTIZA	MISSIER
MANDRIL	MARENGO	MASQUES	MEANERS	MERISMS
RIMLAND	MEGARON	SQUAMES	RENAMES	SIMMERS

MERLOTS	MIREXES	MODULES	MOPPIER	MUCOIDS
MOLTERS	REMIXES	MOUSLED	POMPIER	MUSCOID
MESEEMS	MISDOER	MOITHER	MORAINE	MUDGERS
SEMEMES	MOIDERS	MOTHIER	ROMAINE	SMUDGER
MESETAS	MISEASE	MOLLAHS	MORONIC	MUGGERS
SEAMSET	SIAMESE	OLLAMHS	OMICRON	SMUGGER
MESPILS	MISERLY	MOMENTO	MOROSER	MUGGLES
SIMPLES	MISRELY	MOOTMEN	ROOMERS	SMUGGLE
MESTERS	MISHAPS	MOMENTS	MORSALS	MUISTED
RESTEMS	PASHIMS	MONTEMS	SAMLORS	TEDIUMS
METRING	MISPLAN	MOMUSES	MORTALS	MUNDANE
TERMING	PLASMIN	MOUSMES	STROMAL	UNNAMED
METTLES	MISSEES	MONARCH	MOSCATO	MURDERS
STEMLET	SEMISES	NOMARCH	SCOTOMA	SMURRED
MIDTERM	MISSOUT	MONAULS	MOTIVED	MURLAIN
TRIMMED	SUMOIST	SOLANUM	VOMITED	RUMINAL
MIGRATE	MISTERS	MONGERS	MOTTIER	MURREES
RAGTIME	SMITERS	MORGENS	OMITTER	RESUMER
MIKRONS	MISTERY	MONISMS	MOULDER	MUSIMON
MORKINS	SMYTRIE	NOMISMS	REMOULD	OMNIUMS
MILDEST	MISTLES	MONITOR	MOUSERS	MUSINGS
MISTLED	SMILETS	TROMINO	SMOUSER	MUSSING
MILLETS	MISTRAL	MONOMER	MOUSING	MUSKLES
MISTELL	RAMTILS	MOORMEN	SOUMING	SKELUMS
MIMESES	MITERER	MONTANE	MOUSSED	MUSMONS
MISSEEM	TRIREME	NONMEAT	SMOUSED	SUMMONS
MINCEUR	MITISES	MOONLET	MOUSSES	MUSSELS
NUMERIC	STIMIES	TOOLMEN	SMOUSES	SUMLESS
MINDERS	MITOSES	MOORIER	MOUSTED	MUTANDA
REMINDS	SOMITES	ROOMIER	SMOUTED	TAMANDU
MINDSET	MITTENS	MOORING	MOUTERS	MUTUALS
MISTEND	SMITTEN	ROOMING	OESTRUM	UMLAUTS
MINIMUS	MODELER	MOORVAS	MOWINGS	MUTUELS
MINIUMS	REMODEL	VAROOMS	SOWMING	MUTULES
MINUEND	MODERNS	MOOTING	MUCHELS	MUTULAR
UNMINED	RODSMEN	TOOMING	MULCHES	TUMULAR

MYOSOTE	NETTIER	NORITIC	NUTBARS	OMELETS
TOYSOME	TENTIER	TIRONIC	TURBANS	TELOMES
MYTHIER	NETTING	NOSHERS	NUTPICK	OMNEITY
THYMIER	TENTING	SENHORS	PINTUCK	OMNIETY
NANDINE	NETTLES	NOSTOCS	NUZZLES	ONAGERS
NANNIED	TELNETS	ONCOSTS	SNUZZLE	ORANGES
NAPPIES	NEURONS	NOTAIRE	OARSMAN	ONEYERS
PINESAP	NONUSER	OTARINE	RAMONAS	ONEYRES
NARKING	NEXUSES	NOTCHES	OBDURES	ONSTAGE
RANKING	UNSEXES	TECHNOS	ROSEBUD	TANGOES
NASTILY	NHANDUS	NOTEPAD	ODDNESS	OOHINGS
SAINTLY	UNHANDS	TONEPAD	SODDENS	SHOOING
NASUTES	NICKERS	NOTICES	ODORISE	OOMPAHS
UNSEATS	SNICKER	SECTION	OROIDES	SHAMPOO
NATRONS	NICTATE	NOUGATS	OESTRAL	OORALIS
NONARTS	TETANIC	OUTSANG	OLESTRA	OORIALS
NATTERS	NIFFERS	NOUNIER	OEUVRES	OOZIEST
RATTENS	SNIFFER	REUNION	OVERUSE	ZOOIEST
NATURAE	NIPPERS	NOVALIA	OFFENDS	OPCODES
TAUREAN	SNIPPER	VALONIA	SENDOFF	SCOOPED
NAVARIN	NIPTERS	NOWCAST	OFFERER	OPINING
NIRVANA	PTERINS	SNOWCAT	REOFFER	PIONING
NEAPING	NITROUS	NOWHERE	OFFPUTS	OPPRESS
PEANING	TURIONS	WHEREON	PUTOFFS	PORPESS
NEBULAS	NOIRISH	NOWTIER	OFFSETS	OPPUGNS
UNBALES	ROINISH	TOWNIER	SETOFFS	POPGUNS
NEGATES	NONETTI	NUCLEUS	OFFTAKE	OPSONIC
SANGEET	TONTINE	NUCULES	TAKEOFF	POCOSIN
NEGATON	NONPAST	NURDLED	OGRISMS	OPUNTIA
TONNAGE	PANTONS	RUNDLED	SIMORGS	UTOPIAN
NEITHER	NONSTOP	NURSING	OILCUPS	ORATING
THEREIN	PONTONS	URNINGS	UPCOILS	ROATING
NEOSOUL	NOODLES	NURSLES	OILNUTS	ORBIEST
UNLOOSE	SNOOLED	RUNLESS	ULTIONS	SORBITE
NESTLES	NOOKIER	NURTURE	OLIVERS	ORDERER
NETLESS	ROOINEK	UNTRUER	VIOLERS	REORDER

OREIDES	OUTLIED	OUTWASH	PADRONA	PARKIES
OSIERED	TOLUIDE	WASHOUT	PANDORA	SPARKIE
ORGONES	OUTNESS	OUTWITH	PADRONI	PARODIC
OROGENS	TONUSES	WITHOUT	PONIARD	PICADOR
ORPHISM	OUTPASS	OUTWORK	PAINIMS	PAROLES
ROMPISH	PASSOUT	WORKOUT	PIANISM	REPOSAL
ORRISES	OUTPOST	OVARIAL	PALETTE	PARPING
ROSIERS	OUTTOPS	VARIOLA	PELTATE	RAPPING
OSETRAS	OUTPULL	OVERATE	PALLIER	PARROTS
OSSETRA	PULLOUT	OVEREAT	PERILLA	RAPTORS
OSPREYS	OUTPUTS	OVERLIE	PALLONE	PARROTY
PYROSES	PUTOUTS	RELIEVO	PLEONAL	PORTRAY
OSSELET	OUTRIGS	OVERMEN	PALMARY	PARSONS
TOELESS	RIGOUTS	VENOMER	PALMYRA	SANPROS
OSSETER	OUTROLL	OVERNEW	PALSHIP	PARTERS
STEREOS	ROLLOUT	REWOVEN	SHIPLAP	PRATERS
OSSUARY	OUTRUNS	OVERPLY	PALSIER	PARTIAL
SUASORY	RUNOUTS	PLOVERY	PARLIES	PATRIAL
OTTERED	OUTSELL	OVERRED	PANDITS	PARTURE
TETRODE	SELLOUT	REDROVE	SANDPIT	RAPTURE
OUGHTED	OUTSETS	OVERRUN	PANGENS	PARTYER
TOUGHED	SETOUTS	RUNOVER	PENANGS	PETRARY
OUTACTS	OUTSIDE	OVERSAD	PANIERS	PARURES
OUTCAST	TEDIOUS	SAVORED	RAPINES	UPREARS
OUTDOER	OUTSINS	OVERTIP	PANNERS	PARVISE
OUTRODE	USTIONS	PIVOTER	SPANNER	PAVISER
OUTDRAW	OUTSPED	OWRIEST	PANNIST	PASEARS
OUTWARD	SPOUTED	TOWSIER	SNAPTIN	SARAPES
OUTGUNS	OUTSTEP	OXTERED	PANTINE	PASHKAS
OUTSUNG	TOUPETS	RETOXED	PINNATE	PASKHAS
OUTHIRE	OUTTAKE	OYSTERS	PARETIC	PASSADO
ROUTHIE	TAKEOUT	STOREYS	PICRATE	POSADAS
OUTJEST	OUTTURN	PACKERS	PARIAHS	PASSELS
OUTJETS	TURNOUT	REPACKS	RAPHIAS	SAPLESS
OUTLAID	OUTWALK	PADANGS	PARIANS	PASSING
TOULADI	WALKOUT	PADNAGS	PIRANAS	SPAINGS

PASSMAN	PEACODS	PENSIVE	PERTUSE	PICKETS
SAMPANS	PEASCOD	VESPINE	REPUTES	SKEPTIC
PASTEUP	PEANUTS	PEPPIER	PERUSER	PICKLER
PUPATES	PESAUNT	PREPPIE	REPURES	PRICKLE
PASTILS	PEARTER	PEPTISE	PERVIER	PIGNORA
SPITALS	TAPERER	TIPPEES	REPRIVE	PORANGI
PASTILY	PECKIER	PERCALE	PERVING	PIGNUTS
PAYLIST	PICKEER	REPLACE	PREVING	STUPING
PASTING	PEDALED	PERCENT	PESTERS	PILEUPS
TAPINGS	PLEADED	PRECENT	PRESETS	UPPILES
PATENTS	PEDANTS	PERCEPT	PESTIER	PILLAUS
PATTENS	PENTADS	PRECEPT	RESPITE	PILULAS
PATRICK	PEDDERS	PERCUSS	PETALED	PILULES
TRIPACK	SPREDDE	SPRUCES	PLEATED	PULLIES
PATROLS	PEDDLES	PERDURE	PETASOS	PINANGS
PORTALS	SPELDED	REPURED	SAPOTES	SPANING
PATROON	PEDICEL	PEREION	PETITES	PINCHES
PRONOTA	PEDICLE	PIONEER	PETTIES	SPHENIC
PATTERN	PEDLERS	PERFECT	PETROLS	PINDARI
REPTANT	SPELDER	PREFECT	REPLOTS	PRIDIAN
PATTIES	PEERIES	PERFORM	PHAETON	PINGLED
TAPETIS	SEEPIER	PREFORM	PHONATE	PLINGED
PATTLES	PEERING	PERILED	PHENOME	PINGLES
PELTAST	PREEING	REPLIED	PHONEME	SPIGNEL
PAULINS	PEEVERS	PERITUS	PHENOMS	PINIONS
SPINULA	PREEVES	PUIREST	SHOPMEN	SPINONI
PAUNCES	PELORIC	PERJINK	PHILTER	PINNERS
UNCAPES	POLICER	PREJINK	PHILTRE	SPINNER
PAUPERS	PENCILS	PERKINS	PHRASED	PINOCLE
UPSPEAR	SPLENIC	PINKERS	SHARPED	PLEONIC
PAVINGS	PENNATE	PERLITE	PHYTOID	PINSPOT
VAPINGS	PENTANE	REPTILE	TYPHOID	TOPSPIN
PAYINGS	PENNIES	PERORAL	PICAROS	PIOLETS
SPAYING	PINENES	PREORAL	PROSAIC	PISTOLE
PAYSLIP	PENSELS	PERSUES	PICENES	PIONIES
SAPPILY	SPLEENS	PERUSES	PIECENS	SINOPIE

PIOUSLY	PLANETS	PLUNGES	PORTAGE	POURERS
SOUPILY	PLATENS	PUNGLES	POTAGER	REPOURS
PIPINGS	PLASHER	PLUSSES	PORTEND	POURIES
SIPPING	SPHERAL	PUSSELS	PROTEND	SOUPIER
PIPLESS	PLASMIC	PLUTEUS	PORTICO	POURSUE
SIPPLES	PSALMIC	PUSTULE	PROOTIC	UPROUSE
PISHEOG	PLECTRE	PLUTONS	PORTING	POUSSES
PISHOGE	PRELECT	PULTONS	TROPING	SPOUSES
PISMIRE	PLERION	POCOSEN	PORTOUS	POUSSIN
PRIMSIE	PROLINE	POONCES	UPROOTS	SPINOUS
PISSANT	PLEROMA	PODIUMS	POSINGS	POWNIES
PTISANS	RAMPOLE	SPODIUM	POSSING	WINESOP
PISSERS	PLOATED	POGONIP	POSNETS	POWTERS
PRISSES	TADPOLE	POOPING	STEPSON	PROWEST
PISTOLS	PLODDED	POINDER	POSSERS	PRAETOR
POSTILS	PODDLED	PROINED	PROSSES	PRORATE
PITEOUS	PLODGES	POISONS	POSTBOY	PRAWNED
TOUPIES	SPLODGE	POISSON	POTBOYS	PREDAWN
PITIERS	PLOPPED	POITREL	POSTERN	PRAWNER
TIPSIER	POPPLED	POLITER	PRONEST	PREWARN
PITSAWS	PLOTFUL	POLDERS	POSTING	PREARMS
SAWPITS	TOPFULL	PRESOLD	STOPING	RAMPERS
PLACITS	PLOUTER	POLINGS	POSTMEN	PREDOOM
PLASTIC	POULTER	SLOPING	TOPSMEN	PROMOED
PLACOID	PLOWERS	POLLERS	POTASSA	PREEDIT
PODALIC	REPLOWS	REPOLLS	SAPOTAS	TEPIDER
PLAGUES	PLUGGED	POLOIST	POTLUCK	PREENED
PLUSAGE	PUGGLED	TOPSOIL	PUTLOCK	PRENEED
PLAICES	PLUMBER	POODLES	POUDERS	PREFILE
SPECIAL	REPLUMB	SPOOLED	POUDRES	PRELIFE
PLAITED	PLUMBIC	POPERIN	POULPES	PREIFES
TALIPED	UPCLIMB	PROPINE	UPSLOPE	PRIEFES
PLAITER	PLUMOSE	PORKERS	POUNCED	PREMIER
PLATIER	PUMELOS	PROKERS	UNCOPED	REPRIME
PLANERS	PLUNGED	PORKING	POUNDER	PRENTED
REPLANS	PUNGLED	PROKING	UNROPED	PRETEND

PREPAYS	PROPERS	PUNKIES	QUESTER	RATOONS
YAPPERS	PROSPER	SPUNKIE	REQUEST	SANTOOR
PREPONE	PROTIST	PUNNETS	QUIETER	RATTILY
PROPENE	TROPIST	UNSPENT	REQUITE	TARTILY
PRESHIP	PROTORE	PUNSTER	QUINNAT	RATTING
SHIPPER	TROOPER	PUNTERS	QUINTAN	TARTING
PRESONG	PRUNERS	PURITAN	RABATTE	RAUNCHY
SPONGER	SPURNER	UPTRAIN	TABARET	UNCHARY
PRESSES	PRUNIER	PURLERS	RACISTS	RAUNGES
SPERSES	UNRIPER	SLURPER	SACRIST	UNGEARS
PRESSOR	PRUSIKS	PURSIER	RACKERS	RAVAGES
PROSERS	SPRUIKS	UPRISER	RERACKS	SAVAGER
PRESUME	PSALMED	PURSUER	RAGGIES	RAWHEAD
SUPREME	SAMPLED	USURPER	SAGGIER	WARHEAD
PRETEEN	PSEUDOS	PUTTERS	RAGTAGS	RAYLESS
TERPENE	SPOUSED	SPUTTER	TAGRAGS	SLAYERS
PREVISE	PUDDERS	PUTTIED	RAGWEED	RAYLETS
PRIEVES	SPUDDER	TITUPED	WAGERED	SALTERY
PREWRAP	PUDDIER	PUZZELS	RAILERS	REALTOR
WRAPPER	UPDRIED	PUZZLES	RERAILS	RELATOR
PRINTER	PUDDLES	PYEMIAS	RAKINGS	REAMERS
REPRINT	SPUDDLE	YAMPIES	SARKING	SMEARER
PRISONS	PUDSIES	PYRALID	RALLIES	REAMIER
SPINORS	UPSIDES	RAPIDLY	SALLIER	REREMAI
PRISSED	PUISNES	PYRITES	RAMSONS	REAPERS
SPIDERS	SUPINES	STRIPEY	RANSOMS	SPEARER
PROETTE	PULSANT	PYROPES	RAMSTAM	REARISE
TREETOP	PULTANS	YOPPERS	TAMMARS	RERAISE
PROGENY	PULSION	QUEERER	RANDOMS	REASONS
PYROGEN	UPSILON	REQUERE	RODSMAN	SENORAS
PROLLED	PUMPERS	QUELEAS	RASHERS	REAVAIL
REDPOLL	REPUMPS	SEQUELA	SHARERS	VELARIA
PRONAOS	PUNCHER	QUERIER	RASSLED	REAVING
SOPRANO	UNPERCH	REQUIRE	SARDELS	VINEGAR
PROOFER	PUNIEST	QUERIST	RATLIKE	REBORES
REPROOF	PUNTIES	REQUITS	TALKIER	SOBERER

REBUSES	RELEVES	RESIDUE	RETREES	REWORDS
SUBSERE	SLEEVER	UREIDES	STEERER	SWORDER
RECITED	RELIVER	RESIGHT	RETRIMS	REWORKS
TIERCED	REVILER	SIGHTER	TRIMERS	WORKERS
RECLUSE	REMEIDS	RESISTS	RETUNDS	REWOUND
RECULES	REMISED	SISTERS	UNDREST	WOUNDER
RECULED	REMORSE	RESIZES	RETURNS	REWRAPS
ULCERED	ROEMERS	SEIZERS	TURNERS	WARPERS
RECURED	RENAGUE	RESKEWS	RETWEET	RHUMBAS
REDUCER	UNEAGER	SKEWERS	TWEETER	SAMBHUR
REDACTS	RENNETS	RESKINS	REUTTER	RIBAUDS
SCARTED	TENNERS	SINKERS	UTTERER	SUBARID
REDBAIT	RENOWNS	RESTIFF	REVAMPS	RIBBIES
TRIBADE	WONNERS	STIFFER	VAMPERS	RIBIBES
REDDEST	REORGED	RESTING	REVENUE	RIBBONS
TEDDERS	ROGERED	STINGER	UNREEVE	ROBBINS
REDDLES	REPINED	RESTYLE	REVIEWS	RICKEYS
SLEDDER	RIPENED	TERSELY	VIEWERS	YICKERS
REDLINE	REPINER	RESURGE	REWAKED	RIDGIER
RELINED	RIPENER	REURGES	WREAKED	RIGIDER
REDWING	REPLIES	RETAKES	REWAKEN	RIKISHA
WRINGED	SPIELER	SAKERET	WAKENER	SHIKARI
REEDILY	RERISEN	RETELLS	REWATER	RILIEST
YIELDER	RESINER	TELLERS	WATERER	SILTIER
REESTED	REROLLS	RETHINK	REWEIGH	RIMLESS
STEERED	ROLLERS	THINKER	WEIGHER	SMILERS
REFUTAL	REROOFS	RETICLE	REWELDS	RIPTIDE
TEARFUL	ROOFERS	TIERCEL	WELDERS	TIDERIP
REGRESS	RESEEDS	RETIRER	REWIDEN	RISINGS
SERGERS	SEEDERS	TERRIER	WIDENER	SIRINGS
REGROWN	RESELLS	RETOXES	REWINDS	RISTRAS
WRONGER	SELLERS	XEROTES	WINDERS	STIRRAS
REISSUE	RESHOES	RETRACK	REWIRED	RITTERS
SEISURE	SHEROES	TRACKER	WEIRDER	TERRITS
REIVING	RESHOWS	RETREAD	REWIRES	RITUALS
RIEVING	SHOWERS	TREADER	SWEIRER	TRISULA

RIVALED	ROTCHIE	SACKBUT	SANNIES	SAWLIKE
VALIDER	THEORIC	SUBTACK	SIENNAS	WALKIES
RIVERET	ROTULAE	SACKERS	SANNUPS	SAWYERS
RIVETER	TORULAE	SCREAKS	UNSNAPS	SWAYERS
RIVETED	ROTULAS	SACRIFY	SANSEIS	SAXTUBA
VERDITE	TORULAS	SCARIFY	SASINES	SUBTAXA
RIVIERA	ROUSANT	SADDISH	SANTOLS	SCAMPIS
VAIRIER	SANTOUR	SIDDHAS	STANOLS	SPASMIC
RODENTS	ROUSING	SAGENES	SANTONS	SCEDULE
SNORTED	SOURING	SENEGAS	SONANTS	SECLUDE
RODINGS	ROWDILY	SAIMINS	SANTURS	SCHOUTS
SORDING	WORDILY	SIMIANS	SUNSTAR	SCOUTHS
RODNEYS	ROWINGS	SALADES	SAPOURS	SCHTICK
YONDERS	WORSING	SALSAED	UPSOARS	TCHICKS
ROGUING	ROWTING	SALFERN	SARCOUS	SCHTIKS
ROUGING	TROWING	SNARFLE	SOUCARS	SHTICKS
ROLLTOP	ROYSTER	SALINES	SAROSES	SCOURGE
TROLLOP	STROYER	SILANES	SEROSAS	SCROUGE
ROLLUPS	RUBACES	SALOONS	SARSNET	SCOWING
UPROLLS	SUBRACE	SOLANOS	TRANSES	SOWCING
ROOTLET	RUBELLA	SALTANT	SATANGS	SCOWLER
TOOTLER	RULABLE	TALANTS	SATSANG	SCROWLE
RORTERS	RUINOUS	SALTISH	SATNAVS	SCREAKY
TERRORS	URINOUS	TAHSILS	SAVANTS	YACKERS
RORTIER	RUNDLET	SALTOED	SAUCIER	SCREICH
TERROIR	TRUNDLE	SOLATED	URICASE	SCRIECH
ROSALIA	RUNNETS	SALUTES	SAUNTED	SCRIEVE
SOLARIA	STUNNER	TALUSES	UNSATED	SERVICE
ROSETTE	RUSTRES	SAMOYED	SAVINES	SCULKED
TETROSE	TRUSSER	SOMEDAY	VINASSE	SUCKLED
ROSYING	SABELLA	SANDERS	SAVIOUR	SDEIGNE
SIGNORY	SALABLE	SARSDEN	VARIOUS	SEEDING
ROTATED	SACBUTS	SANGERS	SAVORER	SEAMIER
TROATED	SUBACTS	SERANGS	SEROVAR	SERIEMA
ROTATES	SACHETS	SANIOUS	SAWDERS	SEAWORM
TOASTER	SCATHES	SUASION	SWEARDS	WOMERAS

SECKELS	SERVLET	SHIRRAS	SILVERS	SLOPIER
SECKLES	SVELTER	SIRRAHS	SLIVERS	SPOILER
SEEKING	SESELIS	SHIVERS	SINKFUL	SMOKILY
SKEEING	SESSILE	SHRIVES	SKINFUL	SOYMILK
SEETHED	SESTETS	SHLOCKY	SIPHONS	SMOODGE
SHEETED	TSETSES	SHYLOCK	SONSHIP	SMOOGED
SEETHER	SETTEES	SHOOTIE	SIPPLED	SNAFUED
SHEETER	TESTEES	TOOSHIE	SLIPPED	UNDEAFS
SEEWING	SETTING	SHOUTED	SISTING	SNEAPED
SWEEING	TESTING	SOUTHED	SITINGS	SPEANED
SEITENS	SEWINGS	SHOUTER	SITTINE	SNICKET
SESTINE	SWINGES	SOUTHER	TINIEST	TICKENS
SELFIST	SHAITAN	SHOVERS	SITUSES	SNIRTED
STIFLES	TAHINAS	SHROVES	TISSUES	TINDERS
SELSYNS	SHAPEUP	SHYSTER	SIZEIST	SNIVELY
SLYNESS	UPHEAPS	THYRSES	SIZIEST	SYLVINE
SEMMITS	SHAWLIE	SICKLED	SKATOLS	SNOOPED
TSIMMES	WHAISLE	SLICKED	STALKOS	SPOONED
SENNITS	SHEIKHS	SIDEWAY	SKIVING	SNOOTED
SINNETS	SHIKSEH	WAYSIDE	VIKINGS	STOODEN
SENSUAL	SHEITAN	SIDLERS	SKLATED	SNORERS
UNSEALS	STHENIA	SLIDERS	STALKED	SORNERS
SEPHENS	SHEITEL	SIDLING	SKREIGH	SNORING
SPHENES	SHELTIE	SLIDING	SKRIEGH	SORNING
SEPTATE	SHEWELS	SIERRAN	SKRYING	SNOWING
SPATTEE	WELSHES	SNARIER	SKYRING	WONINGS
SERENER	SHIATSU	SIESTAS	SLAMMED	SOLANDS
SNEERER	THIASUS	TASSIES	SMALMED	SOLDANS
SERRANS	SHICKER	SIEVING	SLEEPRY	SOLDIER
SNARERS	SKRIECH	VISEING	YELPERS	SOLIDER
SERVERS	SHIKARS	SIGNARY	SLEWING	SOLLERS
VERSERS	SHIKRAS	SYRINGA	SWINGLE	SORELLS
SERVEWE	SHINERS	SIGNING	SLIPWAY	SOMBERS
WEEVERS	SHRINES	SINGING	WASPILY	SOMBRES
SERVING	SHIRKED	SILOING	SLITTED	SOREXES
VERSING	SHRIKED	SOILING	STILTED	XEROSES

SOULDAN	STARDOM	STIRING	STREETY	SULLENS
UNLOADS	TSARDOM	TIRINGS	SYRETTE	UNSELLS
SOURSES	STARTED	STIRRED	STRETTE	SULPHUR
SOUSERS	TETRADS	STRIDER	TETTERS	UPHURLS
SOVIETS	STARTUP	STODGER	STREWED	SUMATRA
STOVIES	UPSTART	TODGERS	WRESTED	TRAUMAS
SOWARRY	STATELY	STOITER	STREWER	SUNCARE
YARROWS	STYLATE	TORTIES	WRESTER	SURANCE
SOWINGS	STATING	STOKERS	STROWED	SUNDECK
SOWSING	TASTING	STROKES	WORSTED	UNDECKS
SPALTED	STATINS	STOMPER	STUDDIE	SUNDERS
STAPLED	TANISTS	TROMPES	STUDIED	UNDRESS
SPEEDER	STATUTE	STONERN	STUDENT	SUNLIKE
SPEERED	TAUTEST	TONNERS	STUNTED	UNLIKES
SPINARS	STAYING	STONILY	STUDIES	SUNROOF
SPRAINS	STYGIAN	TYLOSIN	TISSUED	UNROOFS
SPIRANT	STEEVES	STONNED	STUMBLE	SUNROOM
SPRAINT	VESTEES	TENDONS	TUMBLES	UNMOORS
SPIRITS	STELLAR	STOOKER	STURNUS	SUNSPOT
TRIPSIS	TELLARS	STROOKE	UNTRUSS	UNSTOPS
SPIRTED	STEMING	STOTTIE	STURTED	SUNSUIT
STRIPED	TEMSING	TOTTIES	TRUSTED	UNSUITS
SPURIAE	STERVED	STOUTEN	STUSHIE	SUNTRAP
UPRAISE	VERDETS	TENUTOS	TUSHIES	UNSTRAP
SPUTNIK	STEWERS	STOVERS	STYLITE	SUNWARD
UPKNITS	WESTERS	VOTRESS	TESTILY	UNDRAWS
SPYWARE	STICKUP	STOVING	STYLIZE	SUPPING
YAWPERS	UPTICKS	VOTINGS	ZESTILY	UPPINGS
STABBED	STIDDIE	STOWAGE	STYRENE	SURAMIN
TEBBADS	TIDDIES	TOWAGES	YESTERN	URANISM
STACKET	STINGOS	STRAINT	SUBDEAN	SURGING
TACKETS	TOSSING	TRANSIT	UNBASED	URGINGS
STALKER	STIPELS	STRAWEN	SUEABLE	SWADDIE
TALKERS	TIPLESS	WANTERS	USEABLE	WADDIES
STANDEE	STIPPLE	STREELS	SUITORS	SWAGGER
STEANED	TIPPLES	TRESSEL	TSOURIS	WAGGERS

SWALIER	SWOONED	TARDIER	THIRSTY	TRIDUAN
WAILERS	WOODENS	TARRIED	THRISTY	UNITARD
SWALLOW	SWOOPED	TARTLET	THRAWED	TRISHAW
WALLOWS	WOOPSED	TATTLER	WRATHED	WRAITHS
SWANKER	SWOUNED	TATUING	TICKLER	TRIVIAL
WANKERS	UNSOWED	TAUTING	TRICKLE	VITRAIL
SWAPPER	TABLEAU	TAWIEST	TILTING	TROWELS
WAPPERS	TABULAE	TWAITES	TITLING	WORTLES
SWARDED	TACKIER	TAWNIER	TITANIS	TUBULIN
WADDERS	TRACKIE	TINWARE	TITIANS	UNBUILT
SWATTED	TACKLED	TAXWISE	TOADLET	TUFTIER
WADSETT	TALCKED	WAXIEST	TOTALED	TURFITE
SWATTER	TACTICS	TEABOWL	TOOLSET	TUILZIE
TEWARTS	TICTACS	TOWABLE	TOOTLES	UTILIZE
SWEEPER	TAKEUPS	TEAZELS	TOPWORK	TULCHAN
WEEPERS	UPTAKES	TEAZLES	WORKTOP	UNLATCH
SWIGGER	TALLEST	TEAZING	TORPEDO	TUMBLER
WIGGERS	TALLETS	TZIGANE	TROOPED	TUMBREL
SWILLER	TALLOWY	TEETERS	TORTILE	TURKIES
WILLERS	TOLLWAY	TERETES	TRIOLET	TUSKIER
SWINDGE	TAMARAS	TEMENOS	TORTIVE	TURNIPS
SWINGED	TARAMAS	TONEMES	VIRETOT	UNSTRIP
SWINDLE	TAMPANS	TEMPLAR	TORTURE	TURNUPS
WINDLES	TAPSMAN	TRAMPLE	TROUTER	UPTURNS
SWINGER	TANGLER	TENDRIL	TOSSILY	TURPSES
WINGERS	TRANGLE	TRINDLE	TYLOSIS	UPRESTS
SWINKER	TANGRAM	TENOURS	TOWBARS	TWEEDLE
WINKERS	TRANGAM	TONSURE	WARBOTS	TWEELED
SWIPIER	TANNAHS	TENSIVE	TOWNIES	TWINERS
WISPIER	THANNAS	VENITES	TWONIES	WINTERS
SWISHED	TANNERY	TESTOON	TOWTING	TWIRING
WHISSED	TYRANNE	TOSTONE	WOTTING	WRITING
SWISHER	TANNEST	TEXTURE	TRAVOIS	ULICONS
WISHERS	TENANTS	URTEXTE	VIATORS	UNCOILS
SWISHES	TANTARA	THIRSTS	TREVETS	UNAIRED
WHISSES	TARTANA	THRISTS	VETTERS	URANIDE

UNALIVE	UNRAVEL	UPSWELL	WARNERS	WHITRET
UNVAILE	VENULAR	UPWELLS	WARRENS	WHITTER
UNBARES	UNRIVET	UPWINDS	WASHIER	WHOSESO
UNBEARS	VENTURI	WINDUPS	WEARISH	WOOSHES
UNCAPED	UNROOST	VAILING	WEIRING	WIGGLER
UNPACED	UNROOTS	VIALING	WINGIER	WRIGGLE
UNCASES	UNSEENS	VALETED	WELKINS	WILLEST
USANCES	UNSENSE	VELATED	WINKLES	WILLETS
UNDRAPE	UNSPILT	VALISES	WELTING	WILTING
UNPARED	UNSPLIT	VESSAIL	WINGLET	WITLING
UNFILDE	UNSTACK	VAMPIER	WENCHES	WINKLER
UNFILED	UNTACKS	VAMPIRE	WHENCES	WRINKLE
UNFURLS	UNSTUCK	VENTERS	WESANDS	WISENTS
URNFULS	UNTUCKS	VENTRES	WESSAND	WITNESS
UNGLUED	UNSWEAR	VENTOSE	WESKITS	WRISTER
UNGULED	UNWARES	VOTEENS	WISKETS	WRITERS
UNITIES	UNTAMES	VIRGATE	WESTLIN	ZAFFERS
UNITISE	UNTEAMS	VITRAGE	WINTLES	ZAFFRES
UNLADES	UNWIRES	VIRINOS	WETHERS	ZANIEST
UNLEADS	UNWISER	VIRIONS	WRETHES	ZEATINS
UNLIVES	UPDATER	VIRTUAL	WHEEDLE	
UNVEILS	UPRATED	VITULAR	WHEELED	
UNMATED	UPDRAWS	VODOUNS	WHITIER	
UNTAMED	UPWARDS	VOUDONS	WITHIER	
UNNAILS	UPSPAKE	VOLATIC	WHITIES	
UNSLAIN	UPSPEAK	VOLTAIC	WITHIES	
UNNOTED	UPSWARM	WANGLER	WHITING	
UNTONED	WARMUPS	WRANGLE	WITHING	

SECTION 7

VARIANTS

....

- One of the confusing things about the English language is the number of variant spellings that exist. But to a Scrabble player, variant spellings can be a great opportunity.

- If you know that a word can end in -EY as well as -Y, for example, then you have an extra possibility for playing it, maybe using up a surplus E. If you know a word can be spelt -EI- or -IE- it will save you fretting about the spelling.

- There is a selection of the most common variants in the list below; the words are listed in alphabetical order. Excluded from this section are the most obvious set of variants – verbs that end in -IZE or -ISE. There are simply far too many of these to include. See the -ISE suffix list in Section 4 for these.

-EI/-IE

BEIN – BIEN
CEIL – CIEL
CEILED – CIELED
CEILING – CIELING
DEID – DIED
DEIL – DIEL
DREIGH – DRIEGH
FEINT – FIENT
FEIRIER – FIERIER
FEIRIEST – FIERIEST
FEIST – FIEST
GREISLY – GRIESLY
HEID – HIED
KEIR – KIER
KEISTER – KIESTER
LEIGER – LIEGER
LEIR – LIER
MEIN – MIEN
NEIF – NIEF
NEIVE – NIEVE
OMNEITY – OMNIETY
PREIF – PRIEF
PREIFE – PRIEFE

REIVE – RIEVE
REIVER – RIEVER
REIVING – RIEVING
SCREICH – SCRIECH
SCREICHED – SCRIECHED
SCREICHING – SCRIECHING
SHEILING – SHIELING
SHREIK – SHRIEK
SHREIKED – SHRIEKED
SHREIKING – SHRIEKING
SKREIGH – SKRIEGH
SKREIGHED – SKRIEGHED
SKREIGHING – SKRIEGHING
SPEIL – SPIEL
SPEILED – SPIELED
SPEILING – SPIELING
SPEILS – SPIELS
SPEIR – SPIER
SPEIRED – SPIERED
SPEIRING – SPIERING
WEIL – WIEL
WEINER – WIENER

-EN/-IN

ENACTION – INACTION
ENACTIVE – INACTIVE
ENARCH – INARCH
ENARCHED – INARCHED
ENARCHING – INARCHING
ENARM – INARM
ENARMED – INARMED
ENARMING – INARMING
ENCAGE – INCAGE
ENCAGED – INCAGED
ENCAGING – INCAGING
ENCASE – INCASE
ENCASED – INCASED
ENCASING – INCASING
ENCAVE – INCAVE
ENCAVED – INCAVED
ENCAVING – INCAVING

ENCHASE – INCHASE
ENCHASED – INCHASED
ENCHASING – INCHASING
ENCLASP – INCLASP
ENCLASPED – INCLASPED
ENCLOSE – INCLOSE
ENCLOSED – INCLOSED
ENCLOSER – INCLOSER
ENCLOSES – INCLOSES
ENCLOSING – INCLOSING
ENCLOSURE – INCLOSURE
ENCREASE – INCREASE
ENCREASED – INCREASED
ENCRUST – INCRUST
ENCRUSTED – INCRUSTED
ENCUMBER – INCUMBER
ENDART – INDART

ENDARTED – INDARTED
ENDARTING – INDARTING
ENDEW – INDEW
ENDEWED – INDEWED
ENDEWING – INDEWING
ENDITE – INDITE
ENDITED – INDITED
ENDITING – INDITING
ENDORSE – INDORSE
ENDORSED – INDORSED
ENDORSEE – INDORSEE
ENDORSER – INDORSER
ENDORSING – INDORSING
ENDORSOR – INDORSOR
ENDOW – INDOW
ENDOWED – INDOWED
ENDOWING – INDOWING
ENDUE – INDUE
ENDUED – INDUED
ENDUING – INDUING
ENFANT – INFANT
ENFEOFF – INFEOFF
ENFEOFFED – INFEOFFED
ENFESTED – INFESTED
ENFIX – INFIX
ENFIXED – INFIXED
ENFIXING – INFIXING
ENFLAME – INFLAME
ENFLAMED – INFLAMED
ENFLAMING – INFLAMING
ENFOLD – INFOLD
ENFOLDED – INFOLDED
ENFOLDER – INFOLDER
ENFOLDING – INFOLDING
ENFORCE – INFORCE
ENFORCED – INFORCED
ENFORCING – INFORCING
ENFORM – INFORM
ENFORMED – INFORMED
ENFORMING – INFORMING
ENGINE – INGINE
ENGLOBE – INGLOBE
ENGLOBED – INGLOBED
ENGLOBING – INGLOBING

ENGRAFT – INGRAFT
ENGRAFTED – INGRAFTED
ENGRAIN – INGRAIN
ENGRAINED – INGRAINED
ENGRAINER – INGRAINER
ENGRAM – INGRAM
ENGROOVE – INGROOVE
ENGROOVED – INGROOVED
ENGROSS – INGROSS
ENGROSSED – INGROSSED
ENGULF – INGULF
ENGULFED – INGULFED
ENGULFING – INGULFING
ENGULPH – INGULPH
ENGULPHED – INGULPHED
ENHEARSE – INHEARSE
ENHEARSED – INHEARSED
ENISLE – INISLE
ENISLED – INISLED
ENISLING – INISLING
ENLACE – INLACE
ENLACED – INLACED
ENLACING – INLACING
ENLOCK – INLOCK
ENLOCKED – INLOCKED
ENLOCKING – INLOCKING
ENMESH – INMESH
ENMESHED – INMESHED
ENMESHING – INMESHING
ENNAGE – INNAGE
ENQUIRE – INQUIRE
ENQUIRED – INQUIRED
ENQUIRER – INQUIRER
ENQUIRING – INQUIRING
ENQUIRY – INQUIRY
ENSCONCE – INSCONCE
ENSCONCED – INSCONCED
ENSCROLL – INSCROLL
ENSEAM – INSEAM
ENSEAMED – INSEAMED
ENSEAMING – INSEAMING
ENSHEATH – INSHEATH
ENSHEATHE – INSHEATHE
ENSHELL – INSHELL

ENSHELLED – INSHELLED
ENSHELTER – INSHELTER
ENSHRINE – INSHRINE
ENSHRINED – INSHRINED
ENSNARE – INSNARE
ENSNARED – INSNARED
ENSNARER – INSNARER
ENSNARING – INSNARING
ENSOUL – INSOUL
ENSOULED – INSOULED
ENSOULING – INSOULING
ENSPHERE – INSPHERE
ENSPHERED – INSPHERED
ENSURE – INSURE
ENSURED – INSURED
ENSURER – INSURER
ENSURING – INSURING
ENSWATHE – INSWATHE
ENSWATHED – INSWATHED
ENSWEPT – INSWEPT
ENTENDER – INTENDER
ENTHRAL – INTHRAL
ENTHRALL – INTHRALL
ENTHRONE – INTHRONE
ENTHRONED – INTHRONED
ENTIRE – INTIRE
ENTITLE – INTITLE
ENTITLED – INTITLED
ENTITLING – INTITLING
ENTOMB – INTOMB
ENTOMBED – INTOMBED

ENTOMBING – INTOMBING
ENTRANT – INTRANT
ENTREAT – INTREAT
ENTREATED – INTREATED
ENTRENCH – INTRENCH
ENTROLD – INTROLD
ENTRUST – INTRUST
ENTRUSTED – INTRUSTED
ENTWINE – INTWINE
ENTWINED – INTWINED
ENTWINING – INTWINING
ENTWIST – INTWIST
ENTWISTED – INTWISTED
ENURE – INURE
ENURED – INURED
ENUREMENT – INUREMENT
ENURING – INURING
ENVEIGLE – INVEIGLE
ENVEIGLED – INVEIGLED
ENVIABLE – INVIABLE
ENVIABLY – INVIABLY
ENVIOUS – INVIOUS
ENWALL – INWALL
ENWALLED – INWALLED
ENWALLING – INWALLING
ENWIND – INWIND
ENWINDING – INWINDING
ENWOUND – INWOUND
ENWRAP – INWRAP
ENWRAPPED – INWRAPPED
ENWREATHE – INWREATHE

-ER/-OR

ABATER – ABATOR
ABETTER – ABETTOR
ACCEPTER – ACCEPTOR
ADAPTER – ADAPTOR
ADDRESSER – ADDRESSOR
ADJURER – ADJUROR
ADJUSTER – ADJUSTOR
ADVISER – ADVISOR
AGISTER – AGISTOR
ALIENER – ALIENOR

ANIMATER – ANIMATOR
APPOINTER – APPOINTOR
ARRESTER – ARRESTOR
ASPERSER – ASPERSOR
ASSENTER – ASSENTOR
ASSERTER – ASSERTOR
ASSIGNER – ASSIGNOR
ASSISTER – ASSISTOR
ASSURER – ASSUROR
ATTESTER – ATTESTOR

ATTRACTER – ATTRACTOR
AUGMENTER – AUGMENTOR
BAILER – BAILOR
BARRATER – BARRATOR
BETTER – BETTOR
BEVER – BEVOR
BITTER – BITTOR
CANTER – CANTOR
CASTER – CASTOR
CENSER – CENSOR
CHANTER – CHANTOR
CLANGER – CLANGOR
COHABITER – COHABITOR
COMMENTER – COMMENTOR
COMPACTER – COMPACTOR
COMPANDER – COMPANDOR
CONCOCTER – CONCOCTOR
CONDEMNER – CONDEMNOR
CONDER – CONDOR
CONFIRMER – CONFIRMOR
CONJURER – CONJUROR
CONNECTER – CONNECTOR
CONNER – CONNOR
CONSIGNER – CONSIGNOR
CONSULTER – CONSULTOR
CONTEMNER – CONTEMNOR
CONVENER – CONVENOR
CONVERTER – CONVERTOR
CONVEYER – CONVEYOR
CORRECTER – CORRECTOR
CORRUPTER – CORRUPTOR
CURSER – CURSOR
DEFLATER – DEFLATOR
DEPICTER – DEPICTOR
DESOLATER – DESOLATOR
DETECTER – DETECTOR
DEVISER – DEVISOR
DIFFUSER – DIFFUSOR
DIGESTER – DIGESTOR
DILATER – DILATOR
DILUTER – DILUTOR
DIRECTER – DIRECTOR
DISRUPTER – DISRUPTOR
EFFECTER – EFFECTOR

ENDORSER – ENDORSOR
ERECTER – ERECTOR
EXACTER – EXACTOR
EXCERPTER – EXCERPTOR
EXCITER – EXCITOR
EXECUTER – EXECUTOR
EXHIBITER – EXHIBITOR
EXPANDER – EXPANDOR
EXPEDITER – EXPEDITOR
FEOFFER – FEOFFOR
FERMENTER – FERMENTOR
GARNISHER – GARNISHOR
GIMMER – GIMMOR
GRANTER – GRANTOR
HESITATER – HESITATOR
HUMIDER – HUMIDOR
HUNDREDER – HUNDREDOR
IDOLATER – IDOLATOR
IGNITER – IGNITOR
IMPACTER – IMPACTOR
IMPEDER – IMPEDOR
IMPELLER – IMPELLOR
IMPOSTER – IMPOSTOR
INCENSER – INCENSOR
INDENTER – INDENTOR
INDICTER – INDICTOR
INDORSER – INDORSOR
INFECTER – INFECTOR
INFLATER – INFLATOR
INFLICTER – INFLICTOR
INHABITER – INHABITOR
INHIBITER – INHIBITOR
INVENTER – INVENTOR
INVERTER – INVERTOR
JAILER – JAILOR
KRONER – KRONOR
LESSER – LESSOR
LICENSER – LICENSOR
LOCATER – LOCATOR
MACERATER – MACERATOR
MORTGAGER – MORTGAGOR
NARRATER – NARRATOR
NEGATER – NEGATOR
NEGLECTER – NEGLECTOR

NESTER – NESTOR
OBLIGER – OBLIGOR
OFFERER – OFFEROR
PASTER – PASTOR
PAWNER – PAWNOR
PAYER – PAYOR
PERFECTER – PERFECTOR
PLEDGER – PLEDGOR
PREDICTER – PREDICTOR
PRESSER – PRESSOR
PROMISER – PROMISOR
PROMOTER – PROMOTOR
PROPELLER – PROPELLOR
PROTESTER – PROTESTOR
PROVIDER – PROVIDOR
QUESTER – QUESTOR
QUITTER – QUITTOR
REALTER – REALTOR
RECOVERER – RECOVEROR
REDRESSER – REDRESSOR
REFLECTER – REFLECTOR
REGRATER – REGRATOR
REJECTER – REJECTOR
RELATER – RELATOR
RELEASER – RELEASOR
REMITTER – REMITTOR
REPRESSER – REPRESSOR
REQUESTER – REQUESTOR
RESISTER – RESISTOR
RESPONSER – RESPONSOR
RETAILER – RETAILOR
REVISER – REVISOR
REVIVER – REVIVOR

RIZZER – RIZZOR
SAILER – SAILOR
SALVER – SALVOR
SATURATER – SATURATOR
SECRETER – SECRETOR
SEISER – SEISOR
SEIZER – SEIZOR
SETTLER – SETTLOR
SIGNER – SIGNOR
STATER – STATOR
STRIDER – STRIDOR
SUITER – SUITOR
SURVIVER – SURVIVOR
SUSPENSER – SUSPENSOR
TABER – TABOR
TAILER – TAILOR
TAXER – TAXOR
TELEVISER – TELEVISOR
TENSER – TENSOR
TERMER – TERMOR
THRUSTER – THRUSTOR
TORMENTER – TORMENTOR
TREMBLER – TREMBLOR
TRIER – TRIOR
TRUSTER – TRUSTOR
TUSSER – TUSSOR
TWISTER – TWISTOR
VENDER – VENDOR
VERDERER – VERDEROR
VIOLATER – VIOLATOR
VISITER – VISITOR
WARRANTER – WARRANTOR
WELDER – WELDOR

-EY/-Y/-IE

AGLEY – AGLY
ALLEY – ALLY
APPLEY – APPLY
ARSEY – ARSY
BAILEY – BAILIE
BARNEY – BARNY
BINGEY – BINGY
BLIMEY – BLIMY

BLOOEY – BLOOIE
BOGEY – BOGY – BOGIE
BONEY – BONY – BONIE
BOOGEY – BOOGY – BOOGIE
BOOZEY – BOOZY
BUNGEY – BUNGY – BUNGIE
BURLEY – BURLY
CAGEY – CAGY

CAKEY – CAKY	GINGELEY – GINGELY
CARNEY – CARNY – CARNIE	GOOLEY – GOOLY – GOOLIE
CHANCEY – CHANCY	GOONEY – GOONY – GOONIE
CHANTEY – CHANTY – CHANTIE	GOOSEY – GOOSY
CHARLEY – CHARLIE	GORBLIMEY – GORBLIMY
CHIMBLEY – CHIMBLY	GRAPEY – GRAPY
CHOKEY – CHOKY	GRIPEY – GRIPY
CHOOSEY – CHOOSY	GULLEY – GULLY
CLIQUEY – CLIQUY	GYNNEY – GYNNY
COLEY – COLY	HAWKEY – HAWKIE
CONEY – CONY	HEADACHEY – HEADACHY
COOKEY – COOKY – COOKIE	HICKEY – HICKIE
COREY – CORY	HOLEY – HOLY
COSEY – COSY – COSIE	HOMEY – HOMY – HOMIE
COZEY – COSY – COZIE	HONKEY – HONKY – HONKIE
CREPEY – CREPY	HOOKEY – HOOKY
CRICKEY – CRICKY	HOOLEY – HOOLY – HOOLIE
CURNEY – CURNY	HORSEY – HORSY – HORSIE
CURTSEY – CURTSY	HURLEY – HURLY
CURVEY – CURVY	JARVEY – JARVIE
CUTEY – CUTIE	JASEY – JASY
DANCEY – DANCY	JIVEY – JIVY
DARKEY – DARKY – DARKIE	JOCKEY – JOCKY
DICKEY – DICKY – DICKIE	JOKEY – JOKY
DIDDLEY – DIDDLY	JOLLEY – JOLLY
DINGEY – DINGY	KARSEY – KARSY
DINKEY – DINKY – DINKIE	LACEY – LACY
DOGEY – DOGY – DOGIE	LIMEY – LIMY
DOPEY – DOPY	LIMPSEY – LIMPSY
DOVEKEY – DOVEKIE	LINEY – LINY
DOYLEY – DOYLY	LINNEY – LINNY
FAKEY – FAKIE	LOOEY – LOOIE
FIDDLEY – FIDDLY	LOONEY – LOONY – LOONIE
FLAKEY – FLAKY	LOVEY – LOVIE
FLOOEY – FLOOIE	MALARKEY – MALARKY
FLUKEY – FLUKY	MAMEY – MAMIE
FLUNKEY – FLUNKY – FLUNKIE	MAMMEY – MAMMY – MAMMIE
FLUTEY – FLUTY	MANGABEY – MANGABY
FOGEY – FOGY – FOGIE	MANGEY – MANGY
FOLEY – FOLIE – FOLIE	MATEY – MATY
GALLEY – GALLY	MAZEY – MAZY
GAMEY – GAMY	MEINEY – MEINY – MEINIE
GARVEY – GARVIE	MICKEY – MICKY
GILPEY – GILPY	MIMSEY – MIMSY

MONEY – MONY – MONIE
MOOLEY – MOOLY
MOPEY – MOPY
MOUSEY – MOUSY – MOUSIE
MULEY – MULIE
MURREY – MURRY
NOSEY – NOSY
OCHREY – OCHRY
ORANGEY – ORANGY
PACEY – PACY
PARLEY – PARLY
PEAVEY – PEAVY
PHONEY – PHONY
PIGSNEY – PIGSNEY – PIGSNIE
PINEY – PINY
PINKEY – PINKIE – PINKY
PIONEY – PIONY
PLAGUEY – PLAGUY
POGEY – POGY
POKEY – POKY – POKIE
POLEY – POLY
PONCEY – PONCY
PONEY – PONY
POSEY – POSY
POWNEY – POWNY – POWNIE
PRICEY – PRICY
PUDSEY – PUDSY
PULLEY – PULLY
PUNKEY – PUNKY – PUNKIE
PUSSLEY – PUSSLY
RENEY – RENY
RICEY – RICY
ROPEY – ROPY
SARNEY – SARNIE
SAVVEY – SAVVY
SCAREY – SCARY
SHALEY – SHALY
SHANTEY – SHANTY
SHAWLEY – SHAWLIE
SHEENEY – SHEENY – SHEENIE
SHIMMEY – SHIMMY
SHINNEY – SHINNY

SLATEY – SLATY
SMOKEY – SMOKY – SMOKIE
SNAKEY – SNAKY
SPACEY – SPACY
SPICEY – SPICY
SPIKEY – SPIKY
SPINNEY – SPINNY
SPOONEY – SPOONY
SPURREY – SPURRY
STAGEY – STAGY
STOGEY – STOGY – STOGIE
STONEY – STONY
STOREY – STORY
STRIPEY – STRIPY
SWANKEY – SWANKY – SWANKIE
SWEENEY – SWEENY
TACKEY – TACKY
TAWNEY – TAWNY
THYMEY – THYMY
TICKEY – TICKY
TIDDLEY – TIDDLY
TONEY – TONY
TRIPEY – TRIPY
TROLLEY – TROLLY
TYPEY – TYPY
UPSEY – UPSY
VERREY – VERRY
WANEY – WANY
WAVEY – WAVY
WHIMSEY – WHIMSY
WHINEY – WHINY
WHISKEY – WHISKY
WHITEY – WHITY
WILLEY – WILLY – WILLIE
WINEY – WINY
WURLEY – WURLIE
YAWEY – YAWY

-OUR/-OR

ARBOUR – ARBOR
ARDOUR – ARDOR
ARMOUR – ARMOR
BEGLAMOUR – BEGLAMOR
BEHAVIOUR – BEHAVIOR
BELABOUR – BELABOR
BICOLOUR – BICOLOR
BITTOUR – BITTOR
CANDOUR – CANDOR
CLAMOUR – CLAMOR
CLANGOUR – CLANGOR
COLOUR – COLOR
DECOLOUR – DECOLOR
DEMEANOUR – DEMEANOR
DISCOLOUR – DISCOLOR
DISFAVOUR – DISFAVOR
DISHONOUR – DISHONOR
DOLOUR – DOLOR
ENAMOUR – ENAMOR
ENDEAVOUR – ENDEAVOR
FAITOUR – FAITOR
FAVOUR – FAVOR
FERVOUR – FERVOR
FLAVOUR – FLAVOR
FULGOUR – FULGOR
GLAMOUR – GLAMOR
HARBOUR – HARBOR
HAVIOUR – HAVIOR
HONOUR – HONOR

HUMOUR – HUMOR
LABOUR – LABOR
MAINOUR – MAINOR
MALODOUR – MALODOR
MISCOLOUR – MISCOLOR
NEIGHBOUR – NEIGHBOR
ODOUR – ODOR
PARLOUR – PARLOR
PAVIOUR – PAVIOR
PROLABOUR – PROLABOR
RANCOUR – RANCOR
RECOLOUR – RECOLOR
RIGOUR – RIGOR
RUMOUR – RUMOR
SAPOUR – SAPOR
SAVIOUR – SAVIOR
SAVOUR – SAVOR
SPLENDOUR – SPLENDOR
STENTOUR – STENTOR
SUCCOUR – SUCCOR
TABOUR – TABOR
TENOUR – TENOR
TRICOLOUR – TRICOLOR
TUMOUR – TUMOR
UNICOLOUR – UNICOLOR
VALOUR – VALOR
VAPOUR – VAPOR
VAVASOUR – VAVASOR
VIGOUR – VIGOR

SECTION 8

HOOKS

....

- Hooks are single letters that can be added before or after a word to form another valid word. Such words are sometimes called hook words.

- These extensions enable you to play a word at right-angles to an existing word by extending that word and reaping the points value of that word in the process.

- Hooks that form valid words with a letter added to their beginning are known as front hooks; those that take a letter at the end are, naturally enough, end hooks.

- This section is organised by length of root word, up to six letters, then alphabetical within that. The root word itself is shown in **bold** and the words formed by hooking shown after each hook word. If a root word has no hooks it does not appear on the list, so FLY, for example, is not listed in the three-letter word hook list. Five- and Six-letter root words that only take an end –S hook are excluded because there are so many of them and they will detract from the benefit of the list.

- At the end of the main hook lists are some related lists of 'unexpected –S hooks'. These are words that look like they can't be extended but which can have an –S hook. For example, HANDLES can become HANDLESS and MARRIED can become MARRIEDS.

Root words

Two-letter root words

AA	ADO	DAH	ALS	AND
BAA	ADS	FAH	ALT	ANE
CAA	ADZ	HAH	ALU	ANI
FAA	**AE**	LAH	**AM**	ANN
MAA	DAE	NAH	BAM	ANS
AAH	FAE	PAH	CAM	ANT
AAL	GAE	RAH	DAM	ANY
AAS	HAE	YAH	GAM	**AR**
AB	KAE	AHA	HAM	BAR
CAB	MAE	AHI	JAM	CAR
DAB	NAE	AHS	KAM	EAR
FAB	SAE	**AI**	LAM	FAR
GAB	TAE	JAI	MAM	GAR
JAB	VAE	KAI	NAM	JAR
KAB	WAE	RAI	PAM	LAR
LAB	YAE	SAI	RAM	MAR
NAB	**AG**	TAI	SAM	OAR
SAB	BAG	WAI	TAM	PAR
TAB	CAG	AIA	YAM	SAR
WAB	DAG	AID	AMA	TAR
ABA	FAG	AIL	AME	VAR
ABB	GAG	AIM	AMI	WAR
ABO	HAG	AIN	AMP	YAR
ABS	JAG	AIR	AMU	ARB
ABY	LAG	AIS	**AN**	ARC
AD	MAG	AIT	BAN	ARD
BAD	NAG	**AL**	CAN	ARE
CAD	RAG	AAL	DAN	ARF
DAD	SAG	BAL	EAN	ARK
FAD	TAG	CAL	FAN	ARM
GAD	VAG	DAL	GAN	ARS
HAD	WAG	GAL	HAN	ART
LAD	YAG	MAL	MAN	ARY
MAD	ZAG	PAL	NAN	**AS**
PAD	AGA	SAL	PAN	AAS
RAD	AGE	ALA	RAN	BAS
SAD	AGO	ALB	SAN	DAS
TAD	AGS	ALE	TAN	EAS
WAD	**AH**	ALF	VAN	FAS
YAD	AAH	ALL	WAN	GAS
ADD	BAH	ALP	ANA	HAS

KAS	KAW	YAY	BOA	IDE
LAS	LAW	AYE	BOB	ODE
MAS	MAW	AYS	BOD	DEB
NAS	NAW	AYU	BOG	DEE
PAS	PAW	**BA**	BOH	DEF
RAS	RAW	ABA	BOI	DEG
TAS	SAW	OBA	BOK	DEI
VAS	TAW	BAA	BON	DEL
WAS	VAW	BAC	BOO	DEN
YAS	WAW	BAD	BOP	DEP
ZAS	YAW	BAG	BOR	DEV
ASH	AWA	BAH	BOS	DEW
ASK	AWE	BAL	BOT	DEX
ASP	AWK	BAM	BOW	DEY
ASS	AWL	BAN	BOX	**DI**
AT	AWN	BAP	BOY	DIB
BAT	**AX**	BAR	**BY**	DID
CAT	FAX	BAS	ABY	DIE
EAT	LAX	BAT	BYE	DIF
FAT	MAX	BAY	BYS	DIG
GAT	PAX	**BE**	**CH**	DIM
HAT	RAX	OBE	ACH	DIN
KAT	SAX	BED	ECH	DIP
LAT	TAX	BEE	ICH	DIS
MAT	WAX	BEG	OCH	DIT
NAT	ZAX	BEL	CHA	DIV
OAT	AXE	BEN	CHE	**DO**
PAT	**AY**	BES	CHI	ADO
QAT	BAY	BET	**DA**	UDO
RAT	CAY	BEY	ODA	DOB
SAT	DAY	BEZ	DAB	DOC
TAT	FAY	**BI**	DAD	DOD
VAT	GAY	OBI	DAE	DOE
WAT	HAY	BIB	DAG	DOF
ATE	JAY	BID	DAH	DOG
ATS	KAY	BIG	DAK	DOH
ATT	LAY	BIN	DAL	DOL
AW	MAY	BIO	DAM	DOM
CAW	NAY	BIS	DAN	DON
DAW	PAY	BIT	DAP	DOO
FAW	RAY	BIZ	DAS	DOP
GAW	SAY	**BO**	DAW	DOR
HAW	TAY	ABO	DAY	DOS
JAW	WAY	OBO	**DE**	DOT

DOW	SEE	**EM**	ERR	YEX
DOY	TEE	FEM	ERS	ZEX
EA	VEE	GEM	**ES**	EXO
KEA	WEE	HEM	BES	**FA**
LEA	ZEE	MEM	FES	FAA
PEA	EEK	REM	HES	FAB
SEA	EEL	WEM	LES	FAD
TEA	EEN	EME	MES	FAE
YEA	EEW	EMO	OES	FAG
ZEA	**EF**	EMS	PES	FAH
EAN	DEF	EMU	RES	FAN
EAR	KEF	**EN**	TES	FAP
EAS	NEF	BEN	YES	FAR
EAT	REF	DEN	ESS	FAS
EAU	TEF	EEN	EST	FAT
ED	EFF	FEN	**ET**	FAW
BED	EFS	GEN	BET	FAX
FED	EFT	HEN	FET	FAY
GED	**EH**	KEN	GET	**FE**
KED	FEH	MEN	HET	FED
LED	HEH	PEN	JET	FEE
MED	MEH	REN	KET	FEG
NED	PEH	SEN	LET	FEH
PED	REH	TEN	MET	FEM
RED	YEH	WEN	NET	FEN
SED	EHS	YEN	PET	FER
TED	**EL**	END	RET	FES
WED	BEL	ENE	SET	FET
XED	CEL	ENG	TET	FEU
ZED	DEL	ENS	VET	FEW
EDH	EEL	**ER**	WET	FEY
EDS	GEL	FER	YET	FEZ
EE	MEL	GER	ETA	**GI**
BEE	PEL	HER	ETH	GIB
CEE	SEL	PER	**EX**	GID
DEE	TEL	SER	DEX	GIE
FEE	ZEL	YER	HEX	GIF
GEE	ELD	ERA	KEX	GIG
JEE	ELF	ERE	LEX	GIN
LEE	ELK	ERF	REX	GIO
MEE	ELL	ERG	SEX	GIP
NEE	ELM	ERK	TEX	GIS
PEE	ELS	ERM	VEX	GIT
REE	ELT	ERN	WEX	**GO**

AGO	HAY	HOD	FIN	ISM
EGO	**HE**	HOE	GIN	ISO
YGO	CHE	HOG	HIN	**IT**
GOA	SHE	HOH	JIN	AIT
GOB	THE	HOI	KIN	BIT
GOD	HEH	HOM	LIN	CIT
GOE	HEM	HON	PIN	DIT
GON	HEN	HOO	QIN	FIT
GOO	HEP	HOP	RIN	GIT
GOR	HER	HOS	SIN	HIT
GOS	HES	HOT	TIN	KIT
GOT	HET	HOW	VIN	LIT
GOV	HEW	HOX	WIN	NIT
GOX	HEX	HOY	YIN	PIT
GOY	HEY	**ID**	ZIN	RIT
GU	**HI**	AID	ING	SIT
GUB	AHI	BID	INK	TIT
GUE	CHI	CID	INN	WIT
GUL	GHI	DID	INS	ZIT
GUM	KHI	FID	**IO**	ITA
GUN	PHI	GID	BIO	ITS
GUP	HIC	HID	GIO	**JA**
GUR	HID	KID	ION	JAB
GUS	HIE	LID	IOS	JAG
GUT	HIM	MID	**IS**	JAI
GUV	HIN	NID	AIS	JAK
GUY	HIP	RID	BIS	JAM
HA	HIS	TID	CIS	JAP
AHA	HIT	VID	DIS	JAR
CHA	**HM**	YID	GIS	JAW
SHA	OHM	IDE	HIS	JAY
WHA	HMM	IDS	KIS	**JO**
HAD	**HO**	**IF**	LIS	JOB
HAE	MHO	DIF	MIS	JOE
HAG	OHO	GIF	NIS	JOG
HAH	PHO	KIF	OIS	JOL
HAJ	RHO	RIF	PIS	JOR
HAM	SHO	SIF	QIS	JOT
HAN	THO	IFF	SIS	JOW
HAO	WHO	IFS	TIS	JOY
HAP	ZHO	**IN**	VIS	**KA**
HAS	HOA	AIN	WIS	AKA
HAT	HOB	BIN	XIS	OKA
HAW	HOC	DIN	ISH	SKA

KAB	LAV	MAX	MON	NEE
KAE	LAW	MAY	MOO	NEF
KAF	LAX	**ME**	MOP	NEG
KAI	LAY	AME	MOR	NEK
KAK	**LI**	EME	MOS	NEP
KAM	LIB	MED	MOT	NET
KAS	LID	MEE	MOU	NEW
KAT	LIE	MEG	MOW	**NO**
KAW	LIG	MEH	MOY	ONO
KAY	LIN	MEL	MOZ	NOB
KI	LIP	MEM	**MU**	NOD
SKI	LIS	MEN	AMU	NOG
KID	LIT	MES	EMU	NOH
KIF	**LO**	MET	UMU	NOM
KIN	LOB	MEU	MUD	NON
KIP	LOD	MEW	MUG	NOO
KIR	LOG	**MI**	MUM	NOR
KIS	LOO	AMI	MUN	NOS
KIT	LOP	MIB	MUS	NOT
KO	LOR	MIC	MUT	NOW
KOA	LOS	MID	MUX	NOX
KOB	LOT	MIG	**MY**	NOY
KOI	LOU	MIL	MYC	**NU**
KON	LOW	MIM	**NA**	GNU
KOP	LOX	MIR	ANA	NUB
KOR	LOY	MIS	MNA	NUG
KOS	**MA**	MIX	NAB	NUN
KOW	AMA	MIZ	NAE	NUR
KY	OMA	**MM**	NAG	NUS
SKY	SMA	HMM	NAH	NUT
KYE	MAA	MMM	NAM	**NY**
KYU	MAC	UMM	NAN	ANY
LA	MAD	MMM	NAP	ONY
ALA	MAE	**MO**	NAS	SNY
LAB	MAG	EMO	NAT	NYE
LAC	MAK	MOA	NAV	NYM
LAD	MAL	MOB	NAW	NYS
LAG	MAM	MOC	NAY	**OB**
LAH	MAN	MOD	**NE**	BOB
LAM	MAP	MOE	ANE	COB
LAP	MAR	MOG	ENE	DOB
LAR	MAS	MOI	ONE	FOB
LAS	MAT	MOL	NEB	GOB
LAT	MAW	MOM	NED	HOB

JOB	DOF	EON	FOP	KOS
KOB	OOF	FON	HOP	LOS
LOB	WOF	GON	KOP	MOS
MOB	OFF	HON	LOP	NOS
NOB	OFT	ION	MOP	OOS
ROB	**OH**	KON	OOP	POS
SOB	BOH	MON	POP	SOS
YOB	DOH	NON	SOP	WOS
OBA	FOH	OON	TOP	ZOS
OBE	HOH	SON	WOP	OSE
OBI	NOH	TON	OPA	**OU**
OBO	OOH	WON	OPE	FOU
OBS	POH	YON	OPS	LOU
OD	SOH	ONE	OPT	MOU
BOD	OHM	ONO	**OR**	SOU
COD	OHO	ONS	BOR	YOU
DOD	OHS	ONY	COR	OUD
GOD	**OI**	**OO**	DOR	OUK
HOD	BOI	BOO	FOR	OUP
LOD	HOI	COO	GOR	OUR
MOD	KOI	DOO	JOR	OUS
NOD	MOI	FOO	KOR	OUT
POD	POI	GOO	LOR	**OW**
ROD	OIK	HOO	MOR	BOW
SOD	OIL	LOO	NOR	COW
TOD	OIS	MOO	OOR	DOW
YOD	**OM**	NOO	TOR	HOW
ODA	DOM	POO	VOR	JOW
ODD	HOM	ROO	ORA	KOW
ODE	MOM	TOO	ORB	LOW
ODS	NOM	WOO	ORC	MOW
OE	OOM	ZOO	ORD	NOW
DOE	POM	OOF	ORE	POW
FOE	ROM	OOH	ORF	ROW
GOE	SOM	OOM	ORG	SOW
HOE	TOM	OON	ORS	TOW
JOE	VOM	OOP	ORT	VOW
MOE	YOM	OOR	**OS**	WOW
ROE	OMA	OOS	BOS	YOW
TOE	OMS	OOT	COS	OWE
VOE	**ON**	**OP**	DOS	OWL
WOE	BON	BOP	GOS	OWN
OES	CON	COP	HOS	OWT
OF	DON	DOP	IOS	**OX**

BOX	PAX	POX	SIK	TAN
COX	PAY	POZ	SIM	TAO
FOX	**PE**	**QI**	SIN	TAP
GOX	APE	QIN	SIP	TAR
HOX	OPE	QIS	SIR	TAS
LOX	PEA	**RE**	SIS	TAT
NOX	PEC	ARE	SIT	TAU
POX	PED	ERE	SIX	TAV
SOX	PEE	IRE	**SO**	TAW
VOX	PEG	ORE	DSO	TAX
WOX	PEH	PRE	ISO	TAY
OXO	PEL	URE	SOB	**TE**
OXY	PEN	REB	SOC	ATE
OY	PEP	REC	SOD	UTE
BOY	PER	RED	SOG	TEA
COY	PES	REE	SOH	TEC
DOY	PET	REF	SOL	TED
FOY	PEW	REG	SOM	TEE
GOY	**PI**	REH	SON	TEF
HOY	PIA	REI	SOP	TEG
JOY	PIC	REM	SOS	TEL
LOY	PIE	REN	SOT	TEN
MOY	PIG	REO	SOU	TES
NOY	PIN	REP	SOV	TET
SOY	PIP	RES	SOW	TEW
TOY	PIR	RET	SOX	TEX
OYE	PIS	REV	SOY	**TI**
OYS	PIT	REW	SOZ	TIC
PA	PIU	REX	**ST**	TID
OPA	PIX	REZ	EST	TIE
SPA	**PO**	**SH**	PST	TIG
PAC	APO	ASH	STY	TIK
PAD	UPO	ISH	**TA**	TIL
PAH	POA	SHA	ETA	TIN
PAK	POD	SHE	ITA	TIP
PAL	POH	SHH	UTA	TIS
PAM	POI	SHO	TAB	TIT
PAN	POL	SHY	TAD	TIX
PAP	POM	**SI**	TAE	TIZ
PAR	POO	PSI	TAG	**TO**
PAS	POP	SIB	TAI	TOC
PAT	POS	SIC	TAJ	TOD
PAV	POT	SIF	TAK	TOE
PAW	POW	SIG	TAM	TOG

TOM	UMM	URD	WEY	TYE
TON	UMP	URE	**WO**	WYE
TOO	UMS	URN	TWO	YEA
TOP	UMU	URP	WOE	YEH
TOR	**UN**	**US**	WOF	YEN
TOT	BUN	BUS	WOG	YEP
TOW	DUN	GUS	WOK	YER
TOY	FUN	JUS	WON	YES
UG	GUN	MUS	WOO	YET
BUG	HUN	NUS	WOP	YEW
DUG	JUN	OUS	WOS	YEX
FUG	LUN	PUS	WOT	YEZ
HUG	MUN	SUS	WOW	**YO**
JUG	NUN	WUS	WOX	YOB
LUG	PUN	YUS	**XI**	YOD
MUG	RUN	USE	XIS	YOK
NUG	SUN	**UT**	**YA**	YOM
PUG	TUN	BUT	PYA	YON
RUG	UNI	CUT	RYA	YOU
SUG	UNS	GUT	YAD	YOW
TUG	**UP**	HUT	YAE	**YU**
VUG	CUP	JUT	YAG	AYU
YUG	DUP	MUT	YAH	KYU
UGH	GUP	NUT	YAK	RYU
UGS	HUP	OUT	YAM	YUG
UH	OUP	PUT	YAP	YUK
DUH	PUP	RUT	YAR	YUM
HUH	SUP	TUT	YAS	YUP
PUH	TUP	UTA	YAW	YUS
UM	YUP	UTE	YAY	**ZA**
BUM	UPO	UTS	**YE**	ZAG
CUM	UPS	UTU	AYE	ZAP
DUM	**UR**	**WE**	BYE	ZAS
FUM	BUR	AWE	DYE	ZAX
GUM	CUR	EWE	EYE	**ZO**
HUM	FUR	OWE	HYE	AZO
LUM	GUR	WEB	KYE	DZO
MUM	LUR	WED	LYE	ZOA
RUM	NUR	WEE	NYE	ZOL
SUM	OUR	WEM	OYE	ZOO
TUM	PUR	WEN	PYE	ZOS
VUM	SUR	WET	RYE	
YUM	URB	WEX	SYE	

Three-letter root words

AAH	ABYE	GADS	MAGE	DAHS
WAAH	ABYS	HADS	PAGE	FAHS
AAHS	**ACE**	LADS	RAGE	HAHS
AAL	DACE	MADS	SAGE	LAHS
BAAL	FACE	NADS	WAGE	PAHS
DAAL	LACE	PADS	YAGE	RAHS
KAAL	MACE	RADS	AGED	YAHS
PAAL	PACE	SADS	AGEE	**AIA**
TAAL	RACE	TADS	AGEN	RAIA
AALS	TACE	WADS	AGER	AIAS
AAS	ACED	YADS	AGES	**AID**
BAAS	ACER	**ADZ**	**AGO**	CAID
CAAS	ACES	ADZE	DAGO	GAID
FAAS	**ACH**	**AFF**	KAGO	KAID
KAAS	BACH	BAFF	SAGO	LAID
MAAS	EACH	CAFF	AGOG	MAID
ABA	GACH	DAFF	AGON	PAID
BABA	MACH	FAFF	**AGS**	QAID
CABA	NACH	GAFF	BAGS	RAID
YABA	RACH	HAFF	CAGS	SAID
ABAC	TACH	NAFF	DAGS	WAID
ABAS	ACHE	RAFF	FAGS	AIDA
ABB	ACHY	WAFF	GAGS	AIDE
ABBA	**ACT**	YAFF	HAGS	AIDS
ABBE	FACT	AFFY	JAGS	**AIL**
ABBS	PACT	**AFT**	LAGS	BAIL
ABO	TACT	BAFT	MAGS	FAIL
ABOS	ACTA	DAFT	NAGS	HAIL
ABS	ACTS	HAFT	RAGS	JAIL
CABS	**ADD**	RAFT	SAGS	KAIL
DABS	WADD	SAFT	TAGS	MAIL
FABS	ADDS	WAFT	VAGS	NAIL
GABS	ADDY	**AGA**	WAGS	PAIL
JABS	**ADO**	GAGA	YAGS	RAIL
KABS	DADO	JAGA	ZAGS	SAIL
LABS	FADO	NAGA	**AHA**	TAIL
NABS	SADO	RAGA	HAHA	VAIL
SABS	ADOS	SAGA	MAHA	WAIL
TABS	**ADS**	AGAR	TAHA	AILS
WABS	BADS	AGAS	**AHI**	**AIM**
ABY	CADS	**AGE**	AHIS	KAIM
BABY	DADS	CAGE	**AHS**	MAIM
GABY	FADS	GAGE	AAHS	SAIM

AIMS	TAIT	BALE	AALS	KAMI
AIN	WAIT	DALE	BALS	RAMI
CAIN	AITS	EALE	DALS	AMIA
FAIN	AITU	GALE	GALS	AMID
GAIN	**AJI**	HALE	MALS	AMIE
HAIN	HAJI	KALE	PALS	AMIN
KAIN	AJIS	MALE	SALS	AMIR
LAIN	**AKA**	PALE	ALSO	AMIS
MAIN	HAKA	RALE	**ALT**	**AMP**
NAIN	KAKA	SALE	DALT	CAMP
PAIN	TAKA	TALE	HALT	DAMP
RAIN	WAKA	VALE	MALT	GAMP
SAIN	AKAS	WALE	SALT	LAMP
TAIN	**AKE**	YALE	ALTO	RAMP
VAIN	BAKE	ALEC	ALTS	SAMP
WAIN	CAKE	ALEE	**ALU**	TAMP
AINE	FAKE	ALEF	BALU	VAMP
AINS	HAKE	ALES	ALUM	AMPS
AIR	JAKE	ALEW	ALUS	**AMU**
FAIR	LAKE	**ALF**	**AMA**	NAMU
GAIR	MAKE	CALF	CAMA	AMUS
HAIR	RAKE	HALF	GAMA	**ANA**
LAIR	SAKE	ALFA	KAMA	KANA
MAIR	TAKE	ALFS	LAMA	LANA
PAIR	WAKE	**ALL**	MAMA	MANA
SAIR	AKED	BALL	SAMA	NANA
VAIR	AKEE	CALL	AMAH	RANA
WAIR	AKES	FALL	AMAS	TANA
AIRN	**ALA**	GALL	**AME**	ANAL
AIRS	GALA	HALL	CAME	ANAN
AIRT	MALA	LALL	DAME	ANAS
AIRY	NALA	MALL	FAME	**AND**
AIS	TALA	PALL	GAME	BAND
DAIS	ALAE	SALL	HAME	FAND
KAIS	ALAN	TALL	KAME	HAND
PAIS	ALAP	WALL	LAME	LAND
RAIS	ALAR	ALLS	NAME	MAND
SAIS	ALAS	ALLY	SAME	PAND
TAIS	ALAY	**ALP**	TAME	RAND
WAIS	**ALB**	CALP	WAME	SAND
AIT	ALBA	PALP	AMEN	WAND
BAIT	ALBE	SALP	AMES	ANDS
GAIT	ALBS	ALPS	**AMI**	**ANE**
RAIT	**ALE**	**ALS**	CAMI	BANE

CANE	BANT	APTS	YARE	OARS
FANE	CANT	**ARB**	AREA	PARS
GANE	DANT	BARB	ARED	SARS
JANE	GANT	CARB	AREG	TARS
KANE	HANT	DARB	ARES	VARS
LANE	KANT	GARB	ARET	WARS
MANE	LANT	WARB	AREW	ARSE
NANE	PANT	ARBA	**ARF**	ARSY
PANE	RANT	ARBS	BARF	**ART**
SANE	SANT	**ARC**	ZARF	CART
TANE	VANT	MARC	ARFS	DART
VANE	WANT	NARC	**ARK**	FART
WANE	ANTA	ARCH	BARK	GART
ANES	ANTE	ARCO	CARK	HART
ANEW	ANTI	ARCS	DARK	KART
ANI	ANTS	**ARD**	HARK	MART
BANI	**ANY**	BARD	JARK	PART
MANI	CANY	CARD	KARK	TART
RANI	MANY	EARD	LARK	WART
ANIL	WANY	FARD	MARK	ARTI
ANIS	ZANY	HARD	NARK	ARTS
ANN	**APE**	LARD	PARK	ARTY
CANN	CAPE	MARD	RARK	**ARY**
JANN	GAPE	NARD	SARK	MARY
ANNA	JAPE	PARD	WARK	NARY
ANNO	NAPE	SARD	YARK	OARY
ANNS	PAPE	WARD	ARKS	VARY
ANS	RAPE	YARD	**ARM**	WARY
BANS	TAPE	ARDS	BARM	ARYL
CANS	VAPE	**ARE**	FARM	**ASH**
DANS	APED	BARE	HARM	BASH
EANS	APER	CARE	MARM	CASH
FANS	APES	DARE	WARM	DASH
GANS	APEX	FARE	ARMS	FASH
KANS	**APO**	GARE	ARMY	GASH
MANS	CAPO	HARE	**ARS**	HASH
NANS	GAPO	LARE	BARS	LASH
PANS	APOD	MARE	CARS	MASH
SANS	APOS	NARE	EARS	PASH
TANS	**APP**	PARE	FARS	RASH
VANS	YAPP	RARE	GARS	SASH
WANS	APPS	TARE	JARS	TASH
ANSA	**APT**	VARE	LARS	WASH
ANT	RAPT	WARE	MARS	ASHY

ASK	GATS	FAVE	DAWN	**BAC**
BASK	HATS	GAVE	FAWN	ABAC
CASK	KATS	HAVE	LAWN	BACH
HASK	LATS	LAVE	MAWN	BACK
MASK	MATS	NAVE	PAWN	BACS
TASK	NATS	PAVE	RAWN	**BAD**
ASKS	OATS	RAVE	SAWN	BADE
ASP	PATS	SAVE	YAWN	BADS
GASP	QATS	WAVE	AWNS	**BAG**
HASP	RATS	AVEL	AWNY	BAGH
JASP	TATS	AVER	**AXE**	BAGS
RASP	VATS	AVES	SAXE	**BAH**
WASP	WATS	**AVO**	AXED	BAHT
ASPS	**ATT**	AVOS	AXEL	BAHU
ASS	BATT	AVOW	AXES	**BAL**
BASS	MATT	**AWA**	**AYE**	BALD
HASS	TATT	KAWA	BAYE	BALE
JASS	WATT	PAWA	AYES	BALK
LASS	**AUA**	TAWA	**AYS**	BALL
MASS	PAUA	WAWA	BAYS	BALM
PASS	AUAS	AWAY	CAYS	BALS
SASS	**AUF**	**AWE**	DAYS	BALU
TASS	CAUF	WAWE	FAYS	**BAM**
ATE	HAUF	AWED	GAYS	BAMS
BATE	LAUF	AWEE	HAYS	**BAN**
CATE	AUFS	AWES	JAYS	BANC
DATE	**AUK**	**AWK**	KAYS	BAND
FATE	BAUK	BAWK	LAYS	BANE
GATE	CAUK	CAWK	MAYS	BANG
HATE	JAUK	DAWK	NAYS	BANI
LATE	WAUK	GAWK	PAYS	BANK
MATE	AUKS	HAWK	RAYS	BANS
PATE	**AVA**	LAWK	SAYS	BANT
RATE	CAVA	MAWK	TAYS	**BAP**
SATE	FAVA	PAWK	WAYS	BAPS
TATE	JAVA	AWKS	YAYS	BAPU
WATE	KAVA	**AWL**	**AYU**	**BAR**
YATE	LAVA	BAWL	AYUS	KBAR
ATES	TAVA	PAWL	**AZO**	BARB
ATS	AVAL	WAWL	LAZO	BARD
BATS	AVAS	YAWL	AZON	BARE
CATS	**AVE**	AWLS	**BAA**	BARF
EATS	CAVE	**AWN**	BAAL	BARK
FATS	EAVE	BAWN	BAAS	BARM

BARN	BENS	BIST	**BOO**	**BRA**
BARP	BENT	**BIT**	BOOB	BRAD
BARS	**BES**	OBIT	BOOH	BRAE
BAS	OBES	BITE	BOOK	BRAG
ABAS	BEST	BITO	BOOL	BRAK
OBAS	**BET**	BITS	BOOM	BRAN
BASE	ABET	BITT	BOON	BRAP
BASH	YBET	**BIZ**	BOOR	BRAS
BASK	BETA	BIZE	BOOS	BRAT
BASS	BETE	**BOA**	BOOT	BRAW
BAST	BETH	BOAB	**BOP**	BRAY
BAT	BETS	BOAK	BOPS	**BRO**
BATE	**BEY**	BOAR	**BOR**	BROD
BATH	OBEY	BOAS	BORA	BROG
BATS	BEYS	BOAT	BORD	BROO
BATT	**BIB**	**BOB**	BORE	BROS
BAY	BIBB	BOBA	BORK	BROW
BAYE	BIBE	BOBO	BORM	**BRR**
BAYS	BIBS	BOBS	BORN	BRRR
BAYT	**BID**	**BOD**	BORS	**BRU**
BED	ABID	BODE	BORT	BRUS
ABED	BIDE	BODS	**BOS**	BRUT
BEDE	BIDI	BODY	ABOS	BRUX
BEDS	BIDS	**BOG**	OBOS	**BUB**
BEDU	**BIG**	BOGS	BOSH	BUBA
BEE	BIGA	BOGY	BOSK	BURO
BEEF	BIGG	**BOH**	BOSS	BUBS
BEEN	BIGS	BOHO	**BOT**	BUBU
BEEP	**BIN**	BOHS	BOTA	**BUD**
BEER	BIND	**BOI**	BOTE	BUDA
BEES	BINE	BOIL	BOTH	BUDI
BEET	BING	BOIS	BOTS	BUDO
BEG	BINK	**BOK**	BOTT	BUDS
BEGO	BINS	BOKE	**BOW**	**BUG**
BEGS	BINT	BOKO	BOWL	BUGS
BEL	**BIO**	BOKS	BOWR	**BUM**
BELL	BIOG	**BON**	BOWS	BUMF
BELS	BIOS	EBON	**BOX**	BUMP
BELT	**BIS**	BONA	BOXY	BUMS
BEN	IBIS	BOND	**BOY**	**BUN**
BEND	OBIS	BONE	BOYF	BUNA
BENE	BISE	BONG	BOYG	BUND
BENI	BISH	BONK	BOYO	BUNG
BENJ	BISK	BONY	BOYS	BUNK

BUNN	CADS	CARD	ACHE	**COL**
BUNS	**CAF**	CARE	ECHE	COLA
BUNT	CAFE	CARK	OCHE	COLD
BUR	CAFF	CARL	CHEF	COLE
BURA	CAFS	CARN	CHEM	COLL
BURB	**CAG**	CARP	CHER	COLS
BURD	SCAG	CARR	CHEW	COLT
BURG	CAGE	CARS	CHEZ	COLY
BURK	CAGS	CART	**CHI**	**CON**
BURL	CAGY	**CAT**	CHIA	ICON
BURN	**CAL**	SCAT	CHIB	COND
BURP	CALF	CATE	CHIC	CONE
BURR	CALK	CATS	CHID	CONF
BURS	CALL	**CAW**	CHIK	CONI
BURY	CALM	SCAW	CHIN	CONK
BUS	CALO	CAWK	CHIP	CONN
BUSH	CALP	CAWS	CHIS	CONS
BUSK	CALX	**CAY**	CHIT	CONY
BUSS	**CAM**	CAYS	CHIV	**COO**
BUST	SCAM	**CAZ**	CHIZ	COOF
BUSY	CAMA	CAZH	**CID**	COOK
BUT	CAME	**CEE**	ACID	COOL
ABUT	CAMI	CEES	CIDE	COOM
BUTE	CAMO	**CEL**	CIDS	COON
BUTS	CAMP	CELL	**CIG**	COOP
BUTT	CAMS	CELS	CIGS	COOS
BUY	**CAN**	CELT	**CIS**	COOT
BUYS	SCAN	**CEP**	CIST	**COP**
BYE	CANE	CEPE	**CIT**	SCOP
ABYE	CANG	CEPS	CITE	COPE
BYES	CANN	**CHA**	CITO	COPS
BYS	CANS	CHAD	CITS	COPY
ABYS	CANT	CHAI	CITY	**COR**
CAA	CANY	CHAL	**COB**	CORD
CAAS	**CAP**	CHAM	COBB	CORE
CAB	CAPA	CHAO	COBS	CORF
SCAB	CAPE	CHAP	**COD**	CORK
CABA	CAPH	CHAR	ECOD	CORM
CABS	CAPI	CHAS	CODA	CORN
CAD	CAPO	CHAT	CODE	CORS
ECAD	CAPS	CHAV	CODS	CORY
SCAD	**CAR**	CHAW	**COG**	**COS**
CADE	SCAR	CHAY	SCOG	ECOS
CADI	CARB	**CHE**	COGS	COSE

COSH	CUMS	DALT	DEFY	DIEL
COSS	**CUP**	**DAM**	**DEG**	DIES
COST	SCUP	DAME	DEGS	DIET
COSY	CUPS	DAMN	DEGU	**DIF**
COT	**CUR**	DAMP	**DEI**	DIFF
SCOT	SCUR	DAMS	DEID	DIFS
COTE	CURB	**DAN**	DEIF	**DIG**
COTH	CURD	DANG	DEIL	DIGS
COTS	CURE	DANK	**DEL**	**DIM**
COTT	CURF	DANS	DELE	DIME
COW	CURL	DANT	DELF	DIMP
SCOW	CURN	**DAP**	DELI	DIMS
COWK	CURR	DAPS	DELL	**DIN**
COWL	CURS	**DAS**	DELO	DINE
COWP	CURT	ODAS	DELS	DING
COWS	**CUT**	DASH	DELT	DINK
COWY	SCUT	**DAW**	**DEN**	DINO
COX	CUTE	ADAW	DENE	DINS
COXA	CUTS	DAWD	DENI	DINT
COXY	**CWM**	DAWK	DENS	**DIP**
COY	CWMS	DAWN	DENT	DIPS
COYS	**DAB**	DAWS	DENY	DIPT
COZ	DABS	DAWT	**DEP**	**DIS**
COZE	**DAD**	**DAY**	DEPS	DISA
COZY	DADA	DAYS	**DEV**	DISC
CRU	DADO	**DEB**	DEVA	DISH
ECRU	DADS	DEBE	DEVI	DISK
CRUD	**DAE**	DEBS	DEVO	DISS
CRUE	DAES	DEBT	DEVS	**DIT**
CRUS	**DAG**	**DEE**	**DEW**	ADIT
CRUX	DAGO	IDEE	DEWS	EDIT
CRY	DAGS	DEED	DEWY	DITA
SCRY	**DAH**	DEEK	**DEX**	DITE
CUB	ODAH	DEEM	DEXY	DITS
CUBE	DAHL	DEEN	**DEY**	DITT
CUBS	DAHS	DEEP	DEYS	DITZ
CUD	**DAK**	DEER	**DIB**	**DIV**
SCUD	DAKS	DEES	DIBS	DIVA
CUDS	**DAL**	DEET	**DID**	DIVE
CUE	ODAL	DEEV	DIDO	DIVI
CUED	UDAL	**DEF**	DIDY	DIVO
CUES	DALE	DEFI	**DIE**	DIVS
CUM	DALI	DEFO	DIEB	**DOB**
SCUM	DALS	DEFT	DIED	DOBE

DOBS	DOON	DRYS	LEAN	LEAT
DOBY	DOOR	**DSO**	MEAN	MEAT
DOC	DOOS	ODSO	PEAN	NEAT
DOCK	**DOP**	DSOS	REAN	PEAT
DOCO	DOPA	**DUB**	SEAN	SEAT
DOCS	DOPE	DUBS	WEAN	TEAT
DOCU	DOPS	**DUD**	YEAN	EATH
DOD	DOPY	DUDE	EANS	EATS
DODO	**DOR**	DUDS	**EAR**	**EAU**
DODS	ODOR	**DUE**	BEAR	BEAU
DOE	DORB	DUED	DEAR	EAUS
DOEK	DORE	DUEL	FEAR	EAUX
DOEN	DORK	DUES	GEAR	**EBB**
DOER	DORM	DUET	HEAR	EBBS
DOES	DORP	**DUG**	LEAR	**ECH**
DOF	DORR	DUGS	NEAR	EECH
DOFF	DORS	**DUI**	PEAR	HECH
DOG	DORT	DUIT	REAR	LECH
DOGE	DORY	**DUM**	SEAR	MECH
DOGS	**DOS**	DUMA	TEAR	PECH
DOGY	ADOS	DUMB	WEAR	SECH
DOH	UDOS	DUMP	YEAR	TECH
DOHS	DOSA	**DUN**	EARD	YECH
DOL	DOSE	DUNE	EARL	ECHE
IDOL	DOSH	DUNG	EARN	ECHO
DOLE	DOSS	DUNK	EARS	ECHT
DOLL	DOST	DUNS	**EAS**	**ECO**
DOLS	**DOT**	DUNT	CEAS	DECO
DOLT	DOTE	**DUO**	KEAS	SECO
DOM	DOTH	DUOS	LEAS	ECOD
DOME	DOTS	**DUP**	PEAS	ECOS
DOMS	DOTY	DUPE	SEAS	**ECU**
DOMY	**DOW**	DUPS	TEAS	ECUS
DON	DOWD	**DYE**	YEAS	**EDH**
UDON	DOWF	DYED	ZEAS	EDHS
DONA	DOWL	DYER	EASE	**EDS**
DONE	DOWN	DYES	EAST	BEDS
DONG	DOWP	**DZO**	EASY	FEDS
DONS	DOWS	DZOS	**EAT**	GEDS
DOO	DOWT	**EAN**	BEAT	KEDS
DOOB	**DOY**	BEAN	FEAT	MEDS
DOOK	DOYS	DEAN	GEAT	NEDS
DOOL	**DRY**	GEAN	HEAT	PEDS
DOOM	ADRY	JEAN	JEAT	REDS

TEDS	KEFS	VELD	WELS	LEND
WEDS	NEFS	WELD	ZELS	MEND
ZEDS	REFS	YELD	ELSE	PEND
EEK	TEFS	ELDS	**ELT**	REND
DEEK	**EFT**	**ELF**	BELT	SEND
GEEK	DEFT	DELF	CELT	TEND
KEEK	HEFT	PELF	DELT	VEND
LEEK	LEFT	SELF	FELT	WEND
MEEK	REFT	ELFS	GELT	ENDS
PEEK	WEFT	**ELK**	KELT	**ENE**
REEK	EFTS	WELK	MELT	BENE
SEEK	**EGG**	YELK	PELT	DENE
TEEK	TEGG	ELKS	TELT	GENE
WEEK	YEGG	**ELL**	WELT	MENE
EEL	EGGS	BELL	YELT	NENE
FEEL	EGGY	CELL	ELTS	PENE
HEEL	**EGO**	DELL	**EME**	SENE
JEEL	BEGO	FELL	DEME	TENE
KEEL	REGO	HELL	FEME	ENES
PEEL	SEGO	JELL	HEME	ENEW
REEL	VEGO	KELL	LEME	**ENG**
SEEL	EGOS	MELL	MEME	LENG
TEEL	**EHS**	PELL	SEME	MENG
WEEL	FEHS	SELL	TEME	ENGS
EELS	HEHS	TELL	EMES	**ENS**
EELY	PEHS	VELL	EMEU	BENS
EEN	REHS	WELL	**EMO**	CENS
BEEN	**EIK**	YELL	DEMO	DENS
DEEN	REIK	ELLS	MEMO	FENS
FEEN	SEIK	**ELM**	EMOS	GENS
KEEN	EIKS	HELM	**EMS**	HENS
PEEN	**EKE**	YELM	FEMS	KENS
REEN	DEKE	ELMS	GEMS	LENS
SEEN	LEKE	ELMY	HEMS	PENS
TEEN	PEKE	**ELS**	MEMS	RENS
WEEN	REKE	BELS	REMS	SENS
EEW	EKED	CELS	TEMS	TENS
EEEW	EKES	DELS	WEMS	WENS
EFF	**ELD**	EELS	**EMU**	YENS
JEFF	GELD	GELS	EMUS	**EON**
MEFF	HELD	MELS	**END**	AEON
TEFF	MELD	PELS	BEND	JEON
EFFS	SELD	SELS	FEND	NEON
EFS	TELD	TELS	HEND	PEON

EONS	PERM	ZEST	NEWT	FATS
ERA	TERM	ESTS	EWTS	**FAW**
SERA	**ERN**	**ETA**	**EXO**	FAWN
VERA	DERN	BETA	EXON	FAWS
ERAS	FERN	FETA	**EYE**	**FAY**
ERE	HERN	GETA	EYED	OFAY
BERE	KERN	KETA	EYEN	FAYS
CERE	PERN	META	EYER	**FED**
DERE	TERN	SETA	EYES	FEDS
FERE	ERNE	WETA	**FAA**	**FEE**
GERE	ERNS	ZETA	FAAN	FEEB
HERE	**ERR**	ETAS	FAAS	FEED
LERE	SERR	ETAT	**FAB**	FEEL
MERE	ERRS	**ETH**	FABS	FEEN
PERE	**ERS**	BETH	**FAD**	FEER
SERE	GERS	HETH	FADE	FEES
WERE	HERS	METH	FADO	FEET
ERED	SERS	TETH	FADS	**FEG**
ERES	VERS	ETHE	FADY	FEGS
EREV	ERST	ETHS	**FAG**	**FEH**
ERF	**ESS**	**EUK**	FAGS	FEHM
KERF	CESS	NEUK	**FAH**	FEHS
SERF	FESS	YEUK	FAHS	**FEM**
TERF	JESS	EUKS	**FAN**	FEME
ERG	LESS	**EVE**	FAND	FEMS
BERG	MESS	LEVE	FANE	**FEN**
ERGO	NESS	MEVE	FANG	FEND
ERGS	SESS	NEVE	FANK	FENI
ERK	ESSE	YEVE	FANO	FENS
BERK	**EST**	EVEN	FANS	FENT
JERK	BEST	EVER	**FAR**	**FER**
MERK	FEST	EVES	AFAR	FERE
NERK	GEST	EVET	FARD	FERM
PERK	HEST	**EVO**	FARE	FERN
SERK	JEST	DEVO	FARL	**FES**
YERK	KEST	LEVO	FARM	FESS
ZERK	LEST	EVOE	FARO	FEST
ERKS	NEST	EVOS	FARS	**FET**
ERM	PEST	**EWE**	FART	FETA
BERM	REST	EWER	**FAS**	FETE
DERM	TEST	EWES	FASH	FETS
FERM	VEST	**EWK**	FAST	FETT
GERM	WEST	EWKS	**FAT**	**FEU**
HERM	YEST	**EWT**	FATE	FEUD

FEUS	**FLU**	**FRA**	GADI	AGAS
FEW	FLUB	FRAB	GADS	GASH
FEWS	FLUE	FRAE	**GAE**	GASP
FEY	FLUS	FRAG	GAED	GAST
FEYS	FLUX	FRAP	GAEN	**GAT**
FIB	**FOB**	FRAS	GAES	GATE
FIBS	FOBS	FRAT	**GAG**	GATH
FID	**FOE**	FRAU	GAGA	GATS
FIDO	FOEN	FRAY	GAGE	**GAU**
FIDS	FOES	**FRO**	GAGS	GAUD
FIE	**FOG**	AFRO	**GAK**	GAUM
FIEF	FOGS	FROE	GAKS	GAUN
FIER	FOGY	FROG	**GAL**	GAUP
FIG	**FOH**	FROM	EGAL	GAUR
FIGO	FOHN	FROS	GALA	GAUS
FIGS	**FON**	FROW	GALE	**GAW**
FIL	FOND	**FUB**	GALL	GAWD
FILA	FONE	FUBS	GALS	GAWK
FILE	FONS	**FUD**	**GAM**	GAWP
FILK	FONT	FUDS	OGAM	GAWS
FILL	**FOO**	**FUG**	GAMA	**GAY**
FILM	FOOD	FUGS	GAMB	GAYS
FILO	FOOL	FUGU	GAME	**GED**
FILS	FOOS	**FUM**	GAMP	AGED
FIN	FOOT	FUME	GAMS	GEDS
FIND	**FOP**	FUMS	GAMY	**GEE**
FINE	FOPS	FUMY	**GAN**	AGEE
FINI	**FOR**	**FUN**	GANE	OGEE
FINK	FORA	FUND	GANG	GEED
FINO	FORB	FUNG	GANS	GEEK
FINS	FORD	FUNK	GANT	GEEP
FIR	FORE	FUNS	**GAP**	GEES
FIRE	FORK	**FUR**	GAPE	GEEZ
FIRK	FORM	FURL	GAPO	**GEL**
FIRM	FORT	FURR	GAPS	GELD
FIRN	**FOU**	FURS	GAPY	GELS
FIRS	FOUD	FURY	**GAR**	GELT
FIT	FOUL	**GAB**	AGAR	**GEM**
FITS	FOUR	GABS	GARB	GEMS
FITT	FOUS	GABY	GARE	**GEN**
FIX	**FOX**	**GAD**	GARI	AGEN
FIXT	FOXY	EGAD	GARS	GENA
FIZ	**FOY**	IGAD	GART	GENE
FIZZ	FOYS	GADE	**GAS**	GENS

GENT	GISM	**GOR**	GURN	CHAM
GENU	GIST	GORA	GURS	SHAM
GEO	**GIT**	GORE	GURU	WHAM
GEOS	GITE	GORI	**GUS**	HAME
GER	GITS	GORM	GUSH	HAMS
AGER	**GJU**	GORP	GUST	**HAN**
EGER	GJUS	GORS	**GUT**	KHAN
GERE	**GNU**	GORY	GUTS	SHAN
GERM	GNUS	**GOS**	**GUV**	THAN
GERS	**GOA**	EGOS	GUVS	HAND
GERT	GOAD	GOSH	**GUY**	HANG
GET	GOAF	GOSS	GUYS	HANK
GETA	GOAL	**GOT**	**GYM**	HANT
GETS	GOAS	GOTH	GYMP	**HAO**
GHI	GOAT	**GOV**	GYMS	CHAO
GHIS	**GOB**	GOVS	**GYP**	HAOS
GIB	GOBI	**GOY**	GYPO	**HAP**
GIBE	GOBO	GOYS	GYPS	CHAP
GIBS	GOBS	**GRR**	**HAD**	WHAP
GID	GOBY	GRRL	CHAD	HAPS
GIDS	**GOD**	**GUB**	SHAD	HAPU
GIE	GODS	GUBS	HADE	**HAS**
GIED	**GOE**	**GUE**	HADJ	CHAS
GIEN	YGOE	AGUE	HADS	HASH
GIES	GOEL	GUES	**HAE**	HASK
GIF	GOER	**GUL**	THAE	HASP
GIFS	GOES	GULA	WHAE	HASS
GIFT	GOEY	GULE	HAED	HAST
GIG	**GON**	GULF	HAEM	**HAT**
GIGA	AGON	GULL	HAEN	BHAT
GIGS	GONE	GULP	HAES	CHAT
GIN	GONG	GULS	HAET	GHAT
AGIN	GONK	GULY	**HAG**	KHAT
GING	GONS	**GUM**	SHAG	PHAT
GINK	**GOO**	GUMP	HAGG	SHAT
GINN	GOOD	GUMS	HAGS	THAT
GINS	GOOF	**GUN**	**HAH**	WHAT
GIO	GOOG	GUNG	SHAH	HATE
AGIO	GOOK	GUNK	HAHA	HATH
GIOS	GOOL	GUNS	HAHS	HATS
GIP	GOON	**GUP**	**HAJ**	**HAW**
GIPS	GOOP	GUPS	HAJI	CHAW
GIS	GOOR	**GUR**	HAJJ	SHAW
EGIS	GOOS	GURL	**HAM**	THAW

HAWK	WHET	HIPT	**HOH**	HOSS
HAWM	HETE	**HIS**	PHOH	HOST
HAWS	HETH	AHIS	HOHA	**HOT**
HAY	HETS	CHIS	HOHS	PHOT
CHAY	**HEW**	GHIS	**HOI**	SHOT
SHAY	CHEW	KHIS	HOIK	WHOT
HAYS	PHEW	PHIS	HOIS	HOTE
HEH	SHEW	THIS	**HOM**	HOTS
HEHS	THEW	HISH	WHOM	**HOW**
HEM	WHEW	HISN	HOMA	CHOW
AHEM	HEWN	HISS	HOME	DHOW
CHEM	HEWS	HIST	HOMO	SHOW
THEM	**HEY**	**HIT**	HOMS	WHOW
HEME	THEY	CHIT	HOMY	HOWE
HEMP	WHEY	SHIT	**HON**	HOWF
HEMS	HEYS	WHIT	CHON	HOWK
HEN	**HIC**	HITS	PHON	HOWL
SHEN	CHIC	**HMM**	THON	HOWS
THEN	HICK	HMMM	HOND	**HOY**
WHEN	**HID**	**HOA**	HONE	AHOY
HEND	CHID	WHOA	HONG	HOYA
HENS	WHID	HOAR	HONK	HOYS
HENT	HIDE	HOAS	HONS	**HUB**
HEP	**HIE**	HOAX	**HOO**	CHUB
HEPS	HIED	**HOB**	SHOO	HUBS
HEPT	HIES	HOBO	HOOD	**HUE**
HER	**HIM**	HOBS	HOOF	HUED
CHER	SHIM	**HOC**	HOOK	HUER
HERB	WHIM	CHOC	HOON	HUES
HERD	HIMS	HOCK	HOOP	**HUG**
HERE	**HIN**	**HOD**	HOOR	CHUG
HERL	CHIN	SHOD	HOOT	THUG
HERM	SHIN	HODS	**HOP**	HUGE
HERN	THIN	**HOE**	CHOP	HUGS
HERO	WHIN	SHOE	SHOP	HUGY
HERS	HIND	HOED	WHOP	**HUH**
HERY	HING	HOER	HOPE	HUHU
HES	HINS	HOES	HOPS	**HUI**
SHES	HINT	**HOG**	**HOS**	HUIA
HESP	**HIP**	CHOG	MHOS	HUIC
HEST	CHIP	SHOG	PHOS	HUIS
HET	SHIP	HOGG	RHOS	**HUM**
KHET	WHIP	HOGH	ZHOS	CHUM
SHET	HIPS	HOGS	HOSE	HUMA

HUMF	DICH	FIDS	GILL	BINK
HUMP	LICH	GIDS	HILL	DINK
HUMS	MICH	KIDS	JILL	FINK
HUN	RICH	LIDS	KILL	GINK
SHUN	SICH	MIDS	LILL	JINK
HUNG	TICH	NIDS	MILL	KINK
HUNH	WICH	RIDS	NILL	LINK
HUNK	ICHS	TIDS	PILL	MINK
HUNS	**ICK**	VIDS	RILL	OINK
HUNT	DICK	YIDS	SILL	PINK
HUP	H1CK	**IFF**	TILL	RINK
WHUP	KICK	BIFF	VILL	SINK
HUPS	LICK	DIFF	WILL	TINK
HUT	MICK	JIFF	YILL	WINK
BHUT	NICK	KIFF	ZILL	INKS
CHUT	PICK	MIFF	ILLS	INKY
PHUT	RICK	NIFF	ILLY	**INN**
SHUT	SICK	RIFF	**IMP**	GINN
HUTS	TICK	TIFF	DIMP	JINN
HYE	WICK	VIFF	GIMP	LINN
HYED	ICKS	ZIFF	JIMP	WINN
HYEN	ICKY	**IFFY**	LIMP	INNS
HYES	**ICY**	**IFS**	PIMP	**INS**
HYP	RICY	DIFS	SIMP	AINS
HYPE	**IDE**	GIFS	WIMP	BINS
HYPO	AIDE	KIFS	IMPI	DINS
HYPS	BIDE	RIFS	IMPS	FINS
ICE	CIDE	**IGG**	**ING**	GINS
BICE	EIDE	BIGG	BING	HINS
DICE	HIDE	MIGG	DING	JINS
FICE	NIDE	RIGG	GING	KINS
LICE	RIDE	IGGS	HING	LINS
MICE	SIDE	**ILK**	KING	PINS
NICE	TIDE	BILK	LING	QINS
PICE	VIDE	FILK	MING	RINS
RICE	WIDE	MILK	PING	SINS
SICE	IDEA	SILK	RING	TINS
TICE	IDEE	ILKA	SING	VINS
VICE	IDEM	ILKS	TING	WINS
WICE	IDES	**ILL**	WING	YINS
ICED	**IDS**	BILL	ZING	ZINS
ICER	AIDS	CILL	INGO	**ION**
ICES	BIDS	DILL	INGS	CION
ICH	CIDS	FILL	**INK**	LION

PION	ISOS	JAPE	**JOE**	KAID
IONS	**ITA**	JAPS	SJOE	KAIE
IOS	DITA	**JAR**	JOES	KAIF
BIOS	PITA	AJAR	JOEY	KAIK
GIOS	VITA	JARK	**JOG**	KAIL
IRE	ITAS	JARL	JOGS	KAIM
CIRE	**ITS**	JARP	**JOL**	KAIN
DIRE	AITS	JARS	JOLE	KAIS
FIRE	BITS	**JAW**	JOLL	**KAK**
HIRE	CITS	JAWS	JOLS	KAKA
LIRE	DITS	**JAY**	JOLT	KAKI
MIRE	FITS	JAYS	**JOR**	KAKS
SIRE	GITS	**JEE**	JORS	**KAM**
TIRE	HITS	AJEE	**JOT**	KAMA
VIRE	KITS	JEED	JOTA	KAME
WIRE	LITS	JEEL	JOTS	KAMI
IRED	NITS	JEEP	**JOW**	**KAS**
IRES	PITS	JEER	JOWL	AKAS
IRK	RITS	JEES	JOWS	OKAS
BIRK	SITS	JEEZ	**JOY**	SKAS
DIRK	TITS	**JET**	JOYS	**KAT**
FIRK	WITS	JETE	**JUD**	IKAT
KIRK	ZITS	JETS	JUDO	SKAT
LIRK	**IVY**	**JEU**	JUDS	KATA
MIRK	JIVY	JEUX	JUDY	KATI
YIRK	TIVY	**JEW**	**JUG**	KATS
IRKS	**IWI**	JEWS	JUGA	**KAW**
ISH	KIWI	**JIB**	JUGS	SKAW
BISH	IWIS	JIBB	**JUN**	KAWA
DISH	**JAB**	JIBE	JUNK	KAWS
EISH	JABS	JIBS	**JUS**	**KAY**
FISH	**JAG**	**JIG**	GJUS	OKAY
HISH	JAGA	JIGS	JUST	KAYO
KISH	JAGG	**JIN**	**JUT**	KAYS
NISH	JAGS	DJIN	JUTE	**KEA**
PISH	**JAI**	JINK	JUTS	KEAS
WISH	JAIL	JINN	**KAB**	**KEB**
ISM	**JAK**	JINS	KABS	KEBS
GISM	JAKE	JINX	**KAE**	**KED**
JISM	JAKS	**JIZ**	KAED	AKED
ISMS	**JAM**	JIZZ	KAES	EKED
ISO	JAMB	**JOB**	**KAF**	SKED
MISO	JAMS	JOBE	KAFS	KEDS
PISO	**JAP**	JOBS	**KAI**	**KEF**

KEFS	KIPS	KUES	CLAP	FLAX
KEG	**KIR**	**KYE**	FLAP	**LAY**
SKEG	KIRK	KYES	KLAP	ALAY
KEGS	KIRN	**KYU**	PLAP	BLAY
KEN	KIRS	KYUS	SLAP	CLAY
SKEN	**KIS**	**LAB**	LAPS	FLAY
KENO	SKIS	BLAB	**LAR**	PLAY
KENS	KISH	FLAB	ALAR	SLAY
KENT	KISS	SLAB	LARD	LAYS
KEP	KIST	LABS	LARE	**LEA**
SKEP	**KIT**	**LAC**	LARI	FLEA
KEPI	SKIT	LACE	LARK	ILEA
KEPS	KITE	LACK	LARN	OLEA
KEPT	KITH	LACS	LARS	PLEA
KET	KITS	LACY	**LAS**	LEAD
SKET	**KOA**	**LAD**	ALAS	LEAF
KETA	KOAN	BLAD	LASE	LEAK
KETE	KOAP	CLAD	LASH	LEAL
KETO	KOAS	GLAD	LASS	LEAM
KETS	**KOB**	LADE	LAST	LEAN
KEY	KOBO	LADS	**LAT**	LEAP
KEYS	KOBS	LADY	BLAT	LEAR
KHI	**KOI**	**LAG**	CLAT	LEAS
KHIS	KOIS	BLAG	FLAT	LEAT
KID	**KON**	CLAG	PLAT	**LED**
SKID	IKON	FLAG	SLAT	BLED
KIDS	KOND	SLAG	LATE	FLED
KIF	KONK	LAGS	LATH	GLED
KIFF	KONS	**LAH**	LATI	PLED
KIFS	**KOP**	BLAH	LATS	SLED
KIN	KOPH	LAHS	LATU	LEDE
AKIN	KOPS	**LAM**	**LAV**	**LEE**
SKIN	**KOR**	BLAM	LAVA	ALEE
KINA	KORA	CLAM	LAVE	BLEE
KIND	KORE	FLAM	LAVS	FLEE
KINE	KORO	GLAM	**LAW**	GLEE
KING	KORS	SLAM	BLAW	SLEE
KINK	KORU	LAMA	CLAW	LEED
KINO	**KOS**	LAMB	FLAW	LEEK
KINS	KOSS	LAME	SLAW	LEEP
KIP	**KOW**	LAMP	LAWK	LEER
SKIP	KOWS	LAMS	LAWN	LEES
KIPE	**KUE**	**LAP**	LAWS	LEET
KIPP	KUEH	ALAP	**LAX**	**LEG**

CLEG	PLEX	SLIP	LOGY	LOUN
FLEG	ULEX	LIPA	**LOO**	LOUP
GLEG	**LEY**	LIPE	ALOO	LOUR
LEGS	BLEY	LIPO	LOOF	LOUS
LEI	FLEY	LIPS	LOOK	LOUT
GLEI	GLEY	**LIS**	LOOM	**LOW**
VLEI	SLEY	LISK	LOON	ALOW
LEIR	LEYS	LISP	LOOP	BLOW
LEIS	**LEZ**	LIST	LOOR	CLOW
LEK	LEZZ	**LIT**	LOOS	FLOW
LEKE	**LIB**	ALIT	LOOT	GLOW
LEKS	GLIB	BLIT	**LOP**	PLOW
LEKU	LIBS	CLIT	CLOP	SLOW
LEP	**LID**	FLIT	FLOP	LOWE
LEPS	GLID	GLIT	GLOP	LOWN
LEPT	OLID	SLIT	PLOP	LOWP
LES	SLID	LITE	SLOP	LOWS
ALES	LIDO	LITH	LOPE	LOWT
OLES	LIDS	LITS	LOPS	**LOX**
ULES	**LIE**	LITU	**LOR**	FLOX
LESS	PLIE	**LOB**	FLOR	**LOY**
LEST	LIED	BLOB	LORD	CLOY
LET	LIEF	FLOB	LORE	PLOY
BLET	LIEN	GLOB	LORN	LOYS
LETS	LIER	SLOB	LORY	**LUD**
LEU	LIES	LOBE	**LOS**	LUDE
LEUD	LIEU	LOBI	LOSE	LUDO
LEV	**LIG**	LOBO	LOSH	LUDS
LEVA	LIGS	LOBS	LOSS	**LUG**
LEVE	**LIN**	**LOD**	LOST	GLUG
LEVO	BLIN	ALOD	**LOT**	PLUG
LEVS	LIND	CLOD	BLOT	SLUG
LEVY	LINE	PLOD	CLOT	LUGE
LEW	LING	LODE	PLOT	LUGS
ALEW	LINK	LODS	SLOT	**LUM**
BLEW	LINN	**LOG**	LOTA	ALUM
CLEW	LINO	BLOG	LOTE	GLUM
FLEW	LINS	CLOG	LOTH	PLUM
PLEW	LINT	FLOG	LOTI	SLUM
SLEW	LINY	SLOG	LOTO	LUMA
LEWD	**LIP**	VLOG	LOTS	LUMP
LEX	BLIP	LOGE	**LOU**	LUMS
FLEX	CLIP	LOGO	CLOU	**LUN**
ILEX	FLIP	LOGS	LOUD	LUNA

LUNE	MAKS	MAST	MEND	MIGS
LUNG	**MAL**	MASU	MENE	**MIL**
LUNK	MALA	**MAT**	MENG	MILD
LUNS	MALE	MATE	MENO	MILE
LUNT	MALI	MATH	MENT	MILF
LUNY	MALL	MATS	MENU	MILK
LUR	MALM	MATT	**MES**	MILL
BLUR	MALS	MATY	AMES	MILO
SLUR	MALT	**MAW**	EMES	MILS
LURE	**MAM**	MAWK	MESA	MILT
LURK	IMAM	MAWN	MESE	**MIM**
LURS	MAMA	MAWR	MESH	MIME
LUV	MAMS	MAWS	MESS	**MIR**
LUVS	**MAN**	**MAX**	**MET**	AMIR
LUX	MANA	MAXI	META	EMIR
FLUX	MAND	**MAY**	METE	SMIR
LUXE	MANE	MAYA	METH	MIRE
LYE	MANG	MAYO	METS	MIRI
LYES	MANI	MAYS	`**MEU**	MIRK
LYM	MANO	**MED**	EMEU	MIRO
LYME	MANS	MEDS	MEUS	MIRS
LYMS	MANY	**MEE**	**MEW**	MIRV
MAA	**MAP**	SMEE	SMEW	MIRY
MAAR	MAPS	MEED	MEWL	**MIS**
MAAS	**MAR**	MEEK	MEWS	AMIS
MAC	MARA	MEER	**MHO**	MISE
MACE	MARC	MEES	MHOS	MISO
MACH	MARD	MEET	**MIB**	MISS
MACK	MARE	MEG	MIBS	MIST
MACS	MARG	**MEG**	**MIC**	**MIX**
MAD	MARK	MEGA	EMIC	MIXT
MADE	MARL	MEGS	MICA	MIXY
MADS	MARM	**MEL**	MICE	**MIZ**
MAE	MARS	MELA	MICH	MIZZ
MAES	MART	MELD	MICK	**MMM**
MAG	MARY	MELL	MICO	HMMM
MAGE	**MAS**	MELS	MICS	**MNA**
MAGG	AMAS	MELT	**MID**	MNAS
MAGI	OMAS	**MEM**	AMID	**MOA**
MAGS	MASA	MEME	IMID	MOAI
MAK	MASE	MEMO	MIDI	MOAN
MAKE	MASH	MEMS	MIDS	MOAS
MAKI	MASK	**MEN**	**MIG**	MOAT
MAKO	MASS	AMEN	MIGG	**MOB**

MOBE	MOON	MOZZ	SNAG	NEED
MOBS	MOOP	**MUD**	NAGA	NEEM
MOBY	MOOR	MUDS	NAGS	NEEP
MOC	MOOS	**MUG**	**NAM**	**NEF**
MOCH	MOOT	SMUG	NAME	NEFS
MOCK	**MOP**	MUGG	NAMS	**NEG**
MOCS	MOPE	MUGS	NAMU	NEGS
MOD	MOPS	**MUM**	**NAN**	**NEK**
MODE	MOPY	MUMM	ANAN	NEKS
MODI	**MOR**	MUMP	NANA	**NEP**
MODS	MORA	MUMS	NANE	NEPS
MOE	MORE	MUMU	NANG	**NET**
MOER	MORN	**MUN**	NANO	NETE
MOES	MORS	MUNG	NANS	NETS
MOG	MORT	MUNI	**NAP**	NETT
SMOG	**MOS**	MUNS	KNAP	**NEW**
MOGS	EMOS	MUNT	SNAP	ANEW
MOI	MOSE	**MUS**	NAPA	ENEW
MOIL	MOSH	AMUS	NAPE	KNEW
MOIT	MOSK	EMUS	NAPS	NEWB
MOL	MOSS	UMUS	**NAS**	NEWS
MOLA	MOST	MUSE	ANAS	NEWT
MOLD	**MOT**	MUSH	MNAS	**NIB**
MOLE	MOTE	MUSK	**NAT**	SNIB
MOLL	MOTH	MUSO	GNAT	NIBS
MOLS	MOTI	MUSS	NATS	**NID**
MOLT	MOTS	MUST	**NAV**	NIDE
MOLY	MOTT	**MUT**	NAVE	NIDI
MOM	MOTU	SMUT	NAVS	NIDS
MOME	**MOU**	MUTE	NAVY	**NIE**
MOMI	MOUE	MUTI	**NAW**	ONIE
MOMS	MOUP	MUTS	GNAW	NIED
MON	MOUS	MUTT	SNAW	NIEF
MONA	**MOW**	**MYC**	**NAY**	NIES
MONG	MOWA	MYCS	NAYS	**NIL**
MONK	MOWN	**NAB**	**NEB**	ANIL
MONO	MOWS	SNAB	SNEB	NILL
MONS	**MOY**	NABE	NEBS	NILS
MONY	MOYA	NABK	**NED**	**NIM**
MOO	MOYL	NABS	SNED	NIMB
MOOD	MOYS	**NAE**	NEDS	NIMS
MOOI	**MOZ**	NAES	**NEE**	**NIP**
MOOK	MOZE	**NAG**	KNEE	SNIP
MOOL	MOZO	KNAG	SNEE	NIPA

NIPS	NORI	GNUS	ROBE	OCHE
NIS	NORK	ONUS	OBES	**ODA**
ANIS	NORM	**NUT**	OBEY	CODA
UNIS	**NOS**	KNUT	**OBI**	SODA
NISH	ONOS	NUTS	GOBI	ODAH
NISI	NOSE	**NYE**	LOBI	ODAL
NIT	NOSH	SNYE	OBIA	ODAS
KNIT	NOSY	NYED	OBIS	**ODD**
SNIT	**NOT**	NYES	OBIT	ODDS
UNIT	KNOT	**OAF**	**OBO**	**ODE**
NITE	SNOT	GOAF	BOBO	BODE
NITS	NOTA	LOAF	GOBO	CODE
NIX	NOTE	OAFS	HOBO	LODE
NIXE	NOTT	**OAK**	KOBO	MODE
NIXY	**NOW**	BOAK	LOBO	NODE
NOB	ANOW	SOAK	ZOBO	RODE
KNOB	ENOW	OAKS	OBOE	YODE
SNOB	GNOW	OAKY	OBOL	ODEA
NOBS	KNOW	**OAR**	OBOS	ODES
NOD	SNOW	BOAR	**OBS**	**ODS**
SNOD	NOWL	HOAR	BOBS	BODS
NODE	NOWN	ROAR	COBS	CODS
NODI	NOWS	SOAR	DOBS	DODS
NODS	NOWT	VOAR	FOBS	GODS
NOG	NOWY	OARS	GOBS	HODS
SNOG	**NOY**	OARY	HOBS	LODS
NOGG	NOYS	**OAT**	JOBS	MODS
NOGS	**NUB**	BOAT	KOBS	NODS
NOM	KNUB	COAT	LOBS	PODS
NOMA	SNUB	DOAT	MOBS	RODS
NOME	NUBS	GOAT	NOBS	SODS
NOMS	**NUG**	MOAT	ROBS	TODS
NON	SNUG	OATH	SOBS	YODS
ANON	NUGS	OATS	YOBS	ODSO
NONA	**NUN**	OATY	**OCA**	**OES**
NONE	NUNS	**OBA**	COCA	DOES
NONG	**NUR**	BOBA	LOCA	FOES
NONI	KNUR	SOBA	SOCA	GOES
NOO	NURD	OBAS	OCAS	HOES
NOOB	NURL	**OBE**	**OCH**	JOES
NOOK	NURR	DOBE	COCH	MOES
NOON	NURS	JOBE	LOCH	NOES
NOOP	**NUS**	LOBE	MOCH	ROES
NOR	ANUS	MOBE	ROCH	TOES

VOES	OILS	DOLE	HONE	YOOF
WOES	OILY	GOLE	LONE	OOFS
OFF	**OIS**	HOLE	NONE	OOFY
BOFF	BOIS	JOLE	PONE	**OOH**
COFF	HOIS	MOLE	RONE	BOOH
DOFF	KOIS	NOLE	SONE	POOH
GOFF	POIS	POLE	TONE	OOHS
KOFF	**OKA**	ROLE	ZONE	**OOM**
TOFF	HOKA	SOLE	ONER	BOOM
OFFA	KOKA	TOLE	ONES	COOM
OFFS	OKAS	VOLE	**ONO**	DOOM
OFFY	OKAY	OLEA	MONO	LOOM
OFT	**OKE**	OLEO	ONOS	ROOM
COFT	BOKE	OLES	**ONS**	SOOM
LOFT	COKE	**OLM**	CONS	TOOM
SOFT	HOKE	HOLM	DONS	ZOOM
TOFT	JOKE	OLMS	EONS	OOMS
OHM	LOKE	**OMA**	FONS	**OON**
OHMS	MOKE	BOMA	GONS	BOON
OHO	POKE	COMA	HONS	COON
BOHO	ROKE	HOMA	IONS	DOON
COHO	SOKE	LOMA	KONS	GOON
MOHO	TOKE	NOMA	MONS	HOON
SOHO	WOKE	ROMA	OONS	LOON
TOHO	YOKE	SOMA	PONS	MOON
OHS	OKEH	OMAS	SONS	NOON
BOHS	OKES	**OMS**	TONS	POON
DOHS	**OLD**	COMS	WONS	ROON
HOHS	BOLD	DOMS	ONST	SOON
OOHS	COLD	HOMS	**ONY**	TOON
POHS	FOLD	MOMS	BONY	WOON
SOHS	GOLD	NOMS	CONY	ZOON
OIK	HOLD	OOMS	MONY	OONS
HOIK	MOLD	POMS	PONY	OONT
OIKS	SOLD	ROMS	TONY	**OOP**
OIL	TOLD	SOMS	ONYX	COOP
BOIL	WOLD	TOMS	**OOF**	GOOP
COIL	YOLD	VOMS	COOF	HOOP
FOIL	OLDE	**ONE**	GOOF	LOOP
MOIL	OLDS	BONE	HOOF	MOOP
NOIL	OLDY	CONE	LOOF	NOOP
ROIL	**OLE**	DONE	POOF	POOP
SOIL	BOLE	FONE	ROOF	ROOP
TOIL	COLE	GONE	WOOF	SOOP

YOOP	COPE	ORBY	JORS	COUP
OOPS	DOPE	**ORC**	KORS	DOUP
OOR	HOPE	TORC	MORS	LOUP
BOOR	LOPE	ORCA	TORS	MOUP
DOOR	MOPE	ORCS	VORS	NOUP
GOOR	NOPE	**ORD**	**ORT**	ROUP
HOOR	POPE	BORD	BORT	SOUP
LOOR	ROPE	CORD	DORT	OUPA
MOOR	TOPE	FORD	FORT	OUPH
POOR	OPED	LORD	MORT	OUPS
OOS	OPEN	SORD	PORT	**OUR**
BOOS	OPES	WORD	RORT	COUR
COOS	**OPS**	ORDO	SORT	DOUR
DOOS	BOPS	ORDS	TORT	FOUR
FOOS	COPS	**ORE**	WORT	HOUR
GOOS	DOPS	BORE	ORTS	JOUR
LOOS	FOPS	CORE	**OSE**	LOUR
MOOS	HOPS	DORE	COSE	POUR
POOS	KOPS	FORE	DOSE	SOUR
ROOS	LOPS	GORE	HOSE	TOUR
WOOS	MOPS	HORE	LOSE	YOUR
ZOOS	OOPS	KORE	MOSE	OURN
OOSE	POPS	LORE	NOSE	OURS
OOSY	SOPS	MORE	OOSE	**OUS**
OOT	TOPS	PORE	POSE	FOUS
BOOT	WOPS	RORE	ROSE	LOUS
COOT	**OPT**	SORE	TOSE	MOUS
FOOT	OPTS	TORE	OSES	NOUS
HOOT	**ORA**	WORE	**OUD**	SOUS
LOOT	BORA	YORE	FOUD	YOUS
MOOT	FORA	ORES	LOUD	OUST
POOT	GORA	**ORF**	OUDS	**OUT**
ROOT	HORA	CORF	**OUK**	BOUT
SOOT	KORA	ORFE	BOUK	DOUT
TOOT	MORA	ORFS	DOUK	GOUT
WOOT	SORA	**ORG**	GOUK	HOUT
ZOOT	TORA	ORGS	JOUK	LOUT
OOTS	ORAD	ORGY	POUK	NOUT
OPA	ORAL	**ORS**	SOUK	POUT
DOPA	**ORB**	BORS	TOUK	ROUT
OPAH	DORB	CORS	YOUK	SOUT
OPAL	FORB	DORS	ZOUK	TOUT
OPAS	SORB	GORS	OUKS	OUTA
OPE	ORBS	HORS	**OUP**	OUTS

OVA	FOXY	**PAM**	PAWA	PELF
NOVA	POXY	SPAM	PAWK	PELL
OVAL	**OYE**	PAMS	PAWL	PELS
OWE	OYER	**PAN**	PAWN	PELT
HOWE	OYES	SPAN	PAWS	**PEN**
LOWE	OYEZ	PAND	**PAY**	OPEN
YOWE	**OYS**	PANE	APAY	PEND
OWED	BOYS	PANG	SPAY	PENE
OWER	COYS	PANS	PAYS	PENI
OWES	DOYS	PANT	**PEA**	PENK
OWL	FOYS	**PAP**	PEAG	PENS
BOWL	GOYS	PAPA	PEAK	PENT
COWL	HOYS	PAPE	PEAL	**PEP**
DOWL	JOYS	PAPS	PEAN	PEPO
FOWL	LOYS	**PAR**	PEAR	PEPS
GOWL	MOYS	SPAR	PEAS	**PER**
HOWL	NOYS	PARA	PEAT	APER
JOWL	SOYS	PARD	**PEC**	PERC
NOWL	TOYS	PARE	SPEC	PERE
SOWL	**PAC**	PARK	PECH	PERI
YOWL	PACA	PARP	PECK	PERK
OWLS	PACE	PARR	PECS	PERM
OWLY	PACK	PARS	**PED**	PERN
OWN	PACO	PART	APED	PERP
DOWN	PACS	**PAS**	OPED	PERT
GOWN	PACT	OPAS	SPED	PERV
LOWN	PACY	SPAS	PEDS	**PES**
MOWN	**PAD**	UPAS	**PEE**	APES
NOWN	PADI	PASE	EPEE	OPES
POWN	PADS	PASH	PEED	PESO
SOWN	**PAH**	PASS	PEEK	PEST
TOWN	OPAH	PAST	PEEL	**PET**
OWNS	PAHS	**PAT**	PEEN	SPET
OWT	**PAK**	SPAT	PEEP	PETS
DOWT	PAKS	PATE	PEER	**PEW**
LOWT	**PAL**	PATH	PEES	SPEW
NOWT	OPAL	PATS	**PEG**	PEWS
ROWT	PALE	PATU	PEGH	**PHI**
TOWT	PALI	PATY	PEGS	PHIS
OWTS	PALL	**PAV**	**PEH**	PHIZ
OXY	PALM	PAVE	PEHS	**PHO**
BOXY	PALP	PAVS	**PEL**	PHOH
COXY	PALS	**PAW**	PELA	PHON
DOXY	PALY	SPAW	PELE	PHOS

PHOT	**PIT**	POON	PROS	PURE
PIA	SPIT	POOP	PROW	PURI
PIAL	PITA	POOR	**PRY**	PURL
PIAN	PITH	POOS	SPRY	PURR
PIAS	PITS	POOT	PRYS	PURS
PIC	PITY	**POP**	**PSI**	**PUS**
EPIC	**PIU**	POPE	PSIS	OPUS
SPIC	PIUM	POPS	**PUB**	PUSH
PICA	**PIX**	**POS**	PUBE	PUSS
PICE	PIXY	APOS	PUBS	**PUT**
PICK	**PLU**	EPOS	**PUD**	PUTS
PICS	PLUE	POSE	SPUD	PUTT
PIE	PLUG	POSH	PUDS	PUTZ
SPIE	PLUM	POSS	PUDU	**PUY**
PIED	PLUS	POST	**PUG**	PUYS
PIER	**POA**	POSY	SPUG	**PWN**
PIES	POAS	**POT**	PUGH	PWNS
PIET	**POD**	SPOT	PUGS	**PYA**
PIG	APOD	POTE	**PUH**	PYAS
PIGS	SPOD	POTS	PUHA	PYAT
PIN	PODS	POTT	**PUL**	**PYE**
SPIN	**POH**	**POW**	PULA	PYES
PINA	POHS	POWN	PULE	PYET
PINE	**POI**	POWS	PULI	**QAT**
PING	POIS	**POX**	PULK	QATS
PINK	**POL**	POXY	PULL	**QIN**
PINS	POLE	**POZ**	PULP	QINS
PINT	POLK	POZZ	PULS	**QUA**
PINY	POLL	**PRE**	PULU	AQUA
PIP	POLO	PREE	PULY	QUAD
PIPA	POLS	PREM	**PUN**	QUAG
PIPE	POLT	PREP	SPUN	QUAI
PIPI	POLY	PREX	PUNA	QUAT
PIPS	**POM**	PREY	PUNG	QUAY
PIPY	POME	PREZ	PUNK	**RAD**
PIR	POMO	**PRO**	PUNS	BRAD
PIRL	POMP	PROA	PUNT	DRAD
PIRN	POMS	PROB	PUNY	GRAD
PIRS	**POO**	PROD	**PUP**	ORAD
PIS	POOD	PROF	PUPA	PRAD
PISE	POOF	PROG	PUPS	TRAD
PISH	POOH	PROM	PUPU	RADE
PISO	POOK	PROO	**PUR**	RADS
PISS	POOL	PROP	SPUR	**RAG**

BRAG	CRAP	GRAY	REGO	TRET
CRAG	DRAP	KRAY	REGS	RETE
DRAG	FRAP	PRAY	**REH**	RETS
FRAG	TRAP	TRAY	REHS	**REV**
RAGA	WRAP	XRAY	**REI**	EREV
RAGE	RAPE	RAYA	BREI	REVS
RAGG	RAPS	RAYS	REIF	**REW**
RAGI	RAPT	**REB**	REIK	AREW
RAGS	**RAS**	REBS	REIN	BREW
RAGU	BRAS	**REC**	REIS	CREW
RAH	ERAS	RECK	**REM**	DREW
RAHS	FRAS	RECS	CREM	GREW
RAI	RASE	**RED**	PREM	TREW
KRAI	RASH	ARED	TREM	REWS
RAIA	RASP	BRED	REMS	**REX**
RAID	RAST	CRED	**REN**	GREX
RAIK	**RAT**	ERED	BREN	PREX
RAIL	BRAT	IRED	GREN	**REZ**
RAIN	DRAT	REDD	WREN	PREZ
RAIS	FRAT	REDE	REND	TREZ
RAIT	GRAT	REDO	RENK	**RHO**
RAJ	PRAT	REDS	RENO	RHOS
RAJA	TRAT	**REE**	RENS	**RIA**
RAM	RATA	BREE	RENT	ARIA
CRAM	RATE	CREE	RENY	CRIA
DRAM	RATH	DREE	**REO**	RIAD
GRAM	RATO	FREE	REOS	RIAL
PRAM	RATS	GREE	**REP**	RIAS
TRAM	RATU	PREE	PREP	**RIB**
RAMI	**RAV**	TREE	REPO	CRIB
RAMP	GRAV	REED	REPP	DRIB
RAMS	RAVE	REEF	REPS	FRIB
RAN	RAVS	REEK	**RES**	RIBA
BRAN	**RAW**	REEL	ARES	RIBS
CRAN	BRAW	REEN	ERES	**RID**
GRAN	CRAW	REES	IRES	ARID
RANA	DRAW	**REF**	ORES	GRID
RAND	RAWN	TREF	TRES	IRID
RANG	RAWS	REFI	URES	RIDE
RANI	**RAY**	REFS	RESH	RIDS
RANK	BRAY	REFT	REST	**RIF**
RANT	CRAY	**REG**	**RET**	RIFE
RAP	DRAY	AREG	ARET	RIFF
BRAP	FRAY	DREG	FRET	RIFS

RIFT	RITE	ROOM	CRUE	SADE
RIG	RITS	ROON	GRUE	SADI
BRIG	RITT	ROOP	TRUE	SADO
FRIG	RITZ	ROOS	RUED	SADS
GRIG	**RIZ**	ROOT	RUER	**SAG**
PRIG	FRIZ	**ROT**	RUES	SAGA
TRIG	GRIZ	GROT	**RUG**	SAGE
RIGG	RIZA	TROT	DRUG	SAGO
RIGS	**ROB**	VROT	FRUG	SAGS
RIM	PROB	ROTA	TRUG	SAGY
BRIM	ROBE	ROTE	RUGA	**SAI**
CRIM	ROBS	ROTI	RUGS	SAIC
GRIM	**ROC**	ROTL	**RUM**	SAID
PRIM	CROC	ROTO	ARUM	SAIL
TRIM	ROCH	ROTS	DRUM	SAIM
RIMA	ROCK	**ROW**	GRUM	SAIN
RIME	ROCS	AROW	RUME	SAIR
RIMS	**ROD**	BROW	RUMP	SAIS
RIMU	BROD	CROW	RUMS	**SAL**
RIMY	PROD	DROW	**RUN**	SALE
RIN	TROD	FROW	RUND	SALL
BRIN	RODE	GROW	RUNE	SALP
GRIN	RODS	PROW	RUNG	SALS
TRIN	**ROE**	TROW	RUNS	SALT
RIND	FROE	VROW	RUNT	**SAM**
RINE	ROED	ROWS	**RUT**	SAMA
RING	ROES	ROWT	BRUT	SAME
RINK	**ROK**	**RUB**	RUTH	SAMP
RINS	GROK	DRUB	RUTS	SAMS
RIP	ROKE	GRUB	**RYA**	**SAN**
CRIP	ROKS	RUBE	RYAL	SAND
DRIP	ROKY	RUBS	RYAS	SANE
GRIP	**ROM**	RUBY	**RYE**	SANG
TRIP	FROM	**RUC**	TRYE	SANK
RIPE	PROM	RUCK	RYES	SANS
RIPP	ROMA	RUCS	**RYU**	SANT
RIPS	ROMP	**RUD**	RYUS	**SAP**
RIPT	ROMS	CRUD	**SAB**	SAPS
RIT	**ROO**	RUDD	SABE	**SAR**
BRIT	BROO	RUDE	SABS	ASAR
CRIT	PROO	RUDI	**SAC**	KSAR
FRIT	ROOD	RUDS	SACK	OSAR
GRIT	ROOF	RUDY	SACS	TSAR
WRIT	ROOK	**RUE**	**SAD**	SARD

SARI	SEGO	SHAG	SIMA	SKYR
SARK	SEGS	SHAH	SIMI	**SNY**
SARS	**SEI**	SHAM	SIMP	SNYE
SAT	SEIF	SHAN	SIMS	**SOB**
SATE	SEIK	SHAT	**SIN**	SOBA
SATI	SEIL	SHAW	SIND	SOBS
SAU	SEIR	SHAY	SINE	**SOC**
SAUL	SEIS	**SHE**	SING	SOCA
SAUT	**SEL**	SHEA	SINH	SOCK
SAV	SELD	SHED	SINK	SOCS
SAVE	SELE	SHEN	SINS	**SOD**
SAVS	SELF	SHES	**SIP**	SODA
SAW	SELL	SHET	SIPE	SODS
SAWN	SELS	SHEW	SIPS	**SOG**
SAWS	**SEN**	**SHH**	**SIR**	SOGS
SAX	SENA	SHHH	SIRE	**SOH**
SAXE	SEND	**SHO**	SIRI	SOHO
SAY	SENE	SHOD	SIRS	SOHS
SAYS	SENS	SHOE	**SIS**	**SOL**
SEA	SENT	SHOG	PSIS	SOLA
ASEA	**SER**	SHOO	SISS	SOLD
SEAL	USER	SHOP	SIST	SOLE
SEAM	SERA	SHOT	**SIT**	SOLI
SEAN	SERE	SHOW	ISIT	SOLO
SEAR	SERF	**SHY**	SITE	SOLS
SEAS	SERK	ASHY	SITH	**SOM**
SEAT	SERR	**SIB**	SITS	SOMA
SEC	SERS	SIBB	SITZ	SOME
SECH	**SET**	SIBS	**SKA**	SOMS
SECO	SETA	**SIC**	SKAG	SOMY
SECS	SETS	SICE	SKAS	**SON**
SECT	SETT	SICH	SKAT	SONE
SED	**SEV**	SICK	SKAW	SONG
USED	SEVS	SICS	**SKI**	SONS
SEE	**SEW**	**SIF**	SKID	**SOP**
SEED	SEWN	SIFT	SKIM	SOPH
SEEK	SEWS	**SIG**	SKIN	SOPS
SEEL	**SEX**	SIGH	SKIO	**SOS**
SEEM	SEXT	SIGN	SKIP	DSOS
SEEN	SEXY	SIGS	SKIS	ISOS
SEEP	**SEY**	**SIK**	SKIT	SOSS
SEER	SEYS	SIKA	**SKY**	**SOT**
SEES	**SHA**	SIKE	ESKY	SOTH
SEG	SHAD	**SIM**	SKYF	SOTS

SOU	SUED	SYNC	STAP	**TAY**
SOUK	SUER	SYND	TAPA	STAY
SOUL	SUES	SYNE	TAPE	TAYS
SOUM	SUET	**TAB**	TAPS	**TEA**
SOUP	**SUG**	STAB	TAPU	TEAD
SOUR	SUGH	TABI	**TAR**	TEAK
SOUS	SUGO	TABS	STAR	TEAL
SOUT	SUGS	TABU	TARA	TEAM
SOV	**SUI**	**TAD**	TARE	TEAR
SOVS	SUID	TADS	TARN	TEAS
SOW	SUIT	**TAE**	TARO	TEAT
SOWF	**SUK**	TAED	TARP	**TEC**
SOWL	SUKH	TAEL	TARS	TECH
SOWM	SUKS	TAES	TART	TECS
SOWN	**SUM**	**TAG**	**TAS**	**TED**
SOWP	SUMI	STAG	ETAS	STED
SOWS	SUMO	TAGS	ITAS	TEDS
SOY	SUMP	**TAI**	UTAS	TEDY
SOYA	SUMS	TAIG	TASE	**TEE**
SOYS	SUMY	TAIL	TASH	TEED
SPA	**SUN**	TAIN	TASK	TEEK
SPAE	SUNG	TAIS	TASS	TEEL
SPAG	SUNI	TAIT	**TAT**	TEEM
SPAM	SUNK	**TAK**	ETAT	TEEN
SPAN	SUNN	TAKA	STAT	TEER
SPAR	SUNS	TAKE	TATE	TEES
SPAS	**SUP**	TAKI	TATH	**TEF**
SPAT	SUPE	TAKS	TATS	TEFF
SPAW	SUPS	TAKY	TATT	TEFS
SPAY	**SUQ**	**TAM**	TATU	**TEG**
SPAZ	SUQS	TAME	**TAU**	TEGG
SPY	**SUR**	TAMP	TAUS	TEGS
ESPY	SURA	TAMS	TAUT	TEGU
SRI	SURD	**TAN**	**TAV**	**TEL**
SRIS	SURE	TANA	TAVA	TELA
STY	SURF	TANE	TAVS	TELD
STYE	**SUS**	TANG	**TAW**	TELE
SUB	SUSS	TANH	STAW	TELL
SUBA	SUSU	TANK	TAWA	TELS
SUBS	**SYE**	TANS	TAWS	TELT
SUD	SYED	**TAO**	TAWT	**TEN**
SUDD	SYEN	TAOS	**TAX**	ETEN
SUDS	SYES	**TAP**	TAXA	STEN
SUE	**SYN**	ATAP	TAXI	TEND

TENE	TIGE	TOES	STOT	TUTU
TENS	TIGS	TOEY	TOTE	**TWA**
TENT	**TIK**	**TOG**	TOTS	TWAE
TES	TIKA	TOGA	**TOW**	TWAL
ATES	TIKE	TOGE	STOW	TWAS
UTES	TIKI	TOGS	TOWN	TWAT
TEST	TIKS	**TOM**	TOWS	TWAY
TET	**TIL**	ATOM	TOWT	**TWO**
STET	TILE	TOMB	TOWY	TWOS
TETE	TILL	TOME	**TOY**	**TYE**
TETH	TILS	TOMO	TOYO	STYE
TETS	TILT	TOMS	TOYS	TYED
TEW	**TIN**	**TON**	**TRY**	TYEE
STEW	TINA	TONE	TRYE	TYER
TEWS	TIND	TONG	TRYP	TYES
TEX	TINE	TONK	**TSK**	**TYG**
TEXT	TING	TONS	TSKS	TYGS
THE	TINK	TONY	**TUB**	**UDO**
ETHE	TINS	**TOO**	STUB	BUDO
THEE	TINT	TOOK	TUBA	JUDO
THEM	TINY	TOOL	TUBE	KUDO
THEN	**TIP**	TOOM	TUBS	LUDO
THEW	TIPI	TOON	**TUG**	UDON
THEY	TIPS	TOOT	TUGS	UDOS
THO	TIPT	**TOP**	**TUI**	**UDS**
THON	**TIS**	ATOP	ETUI	BUDS
THOU	UTIS	STOP	PTUI	CUDS
TIC	**TIT**	TOPE	TUIS	DUDS
ETIC	TITE	TOPH	**TUM**	DUDS
OTIC	TITI	TOPI	STUM	FUDS
TICE	TITS	TOPO	TUMP	JUDS
TICH	**TIZ**	TOPS	TUMS	LUDS
TICK	TIZZ	**TOR**	**TUN**	MUDS
TICS	**TOC**	TORA	STUN	OUDS
TID	ATOC	TORC	TUNA	PUDS
TIDE	TOCK	TORE	TUND	RUDS
TIDS	TOCO	TORI	TUNE	SUDS
TIDY	TOCS	TORN	TUNG	WUDS
TIE	**TOD**	TORO	TUNS	**UEY**
STIE	TODS	TORR	TUNY	QUEY
TIED	TODY	TORS	**TUP**	UEYS
TIER	**TOE**	TORT	TUPS	**UFO**
TIES	TOEA	TORY	**TUT**	BUFO
TIG	TOED	**TOT**	TUTS	UFOS
				UGH

AUGH	PULU	BUNS	MURE	PUTS
EUGH	SULU	DUNS	PURE	RUTS
PUGH	ZULU	FUNS	SURE	TUTS
SUGH	ULUS	GUNS	UREA	**UTU**
VUGH	**UMM**	HUNS	URES	KUTU
UGHS	MUMM	LUNS	**URN**	TUTU
UGS	UMMA	MUNS	BURN	UTUS
BUGS	**UMP**	NUNS	CURN	**UVA**
DUGS	BUMP	PUNS	DURN	UVAE
FUGS	DUMP	RUNS	GURN	UVAS
HUGS	GUMP	SUNS	OURN	**VAC**
JUGS	HUMP	TUNS	TURN	VACS
LUGS	JUMP	**UPO**	URNS	**VAE**
MUGS	LUMP	UPON	**URP**	UVAE
NUGS	MUMP	**UPS**	BURP	VAES
PUGS	PUMP	CUPS	RURP	**VAG**
RUGS	RUMP	DUPS	URPS	VAGI
SUGS	SUMP	GUPS	**USE**	VAGS
TUGS	TUMP	HUPS	FUSE	**VAN**
VUGS	YUMP	OUPS	MUSE	VANE
YUGS	UMPH	PUPS	RUSE	VANG
UKE	UMPS	SUPS	USED	VANS
BUKE	UMPY	TUPS	USER	VANT
CUKE	**UMS**	YUPS	USES	**VAR**
DUKE	BUMS	UPSY	**UTA**	VARA
JUKE	CUMS	**URB**	KUTA	VARE
LUKE	FUMS	BURB	OUTA	VARS
NUKE	GUMS	CURB	UTAS	VARY
PUKE	HUMS	URBS	**UTE**	**VAS**
YUKE	LUMS	**URD**	BUTE	AVAS
UKES	MUMS	BURD	CUTE	KVAS
ULE	RUMS	CURD	JUTE	UVAS
DULE	SUMS	NURD	LUTE	VASA
GULE	TUMS	SURD	MUTE	VASE
HULE	VUMS	TURD	UTES	VAST
MULE	**UMU**	URDE	**UTS**	**VAT**
PULE	MUMU	URDS	BUTS	VATS
RULE	UMUS	URDY	CUTS	VATU
TULE	**UNI**	**URE**	GUTS	**VAU**
YULE	MUNI	CURE	HUTS	VAUS
ULES	SUNI	DURE	JUTS	VAUT
ULEX	UNIS	IURE	MUTS	**VAV**
ULU	UNIT	JURE	NUTS	VAVS
LULU	**UNS**	LURE	OUTS	**VAW**

VAWS	VOES	WAIL	WAWE	**WEY**
VEE	**VOG**	WAIN	WAWL	SWEY
VEEP	**VOGS**	WAIR	WAWS	WEYS
VEER	**VOL**	WAIS	**WAX**	**WHA**
VEES	VOLA	WAIT	WAXY	WHAE
VEG	VOLE	**WAN**	**WAY**	WHAM
VEGA	VOLK	HWAN	AWAY	WHAP
VEGO	VOLS	SWAN	SWAY	WHAT
VET	VOLT	WAND	TWAY	**WHO**
EVET	**VOM**	WANE	WAYS	WHOA
VETO	VOMS	WANG	**WAZ**	WHOM
VETS	**VOR**	WANK	WAZZ	WHOP
VEX	VORS	WANS	**WEB**	WHOT
VEXT	**VOW**	WANT	WEBS	WHOW
VIA	AVOW	WANY	**WED**	**WHY**
VIAE	VOWS	**WAP**	AWED	WHYS
VIAL	**VUG**	SWAP	OWED	**WIG**
VIAS	VUGG	WAPS	WEDS	SWIG
VID	VUGH	**WAR**	**WEE**	TWIG
AVID	VUGS	WARB	AWEE	WIGS
VIDE	**VUM**	WARD	SWEE	**WIN**
VIDS	OVUM	WARE	TWEE	TWIN
VIE	VUMS	WARK	WEED	WIND
VIED	**WAB**	WARM	WEEK	WINE
VIER	SWAB	WARN	WEEL	WING
VIES	WABS	WARP	WEEM	WINK
VIEW	**WAD**	WARS	WEEN	WINN
VIG	SWAD	WART	WEEP	WINO
VIGA	WADD	WARY	WEER	WINS
VIGS	WADE	**WAS**	WEES	WINY
VIM	WADI	TWAS	WEET	**WIS**
VIMS	WADS	WASE	**WEM**	IWIS
VIN	WADT	WASH	WEMB	YWIS
VINA	WADY	WASM	WEMS	WISE
VINE	**WAE**	WASP	**WEN**	WISH
VINO	TWAE	WAST	WENA	WISP
VINS	WAES	**WAT**	WEND	WISS
VINT	**WAG**	SWAT	WENS	WIST
VINY	SWAG	TWAT	WENT	**WIT**
VIS	WAGE	WATE	**WET**	TWIT
VISA	WAGS	WATS	WETA	WITE
VISE	**WAI**	WATT	WETS	WITH
VOE	WAID	**WAW**	**WEX**	WITS
EVOE	WAIF	WAWA	WEXE	**WIZ**

SWIZ	WYNN	YAWY	**YEW**	YUKO
WOE	WYNS	**YAY**	YEWS	YUKS
WOES	**XED**	YAYS	**YEZ**	YUKY
WOF	AXED	**YEA**	OYEZ	**YUM**
WOFS	EXED	YEAD	**YGO**	YUMP
WOG	**XIS**	YEAH	YGOE	**YUP**
WOGS	AXIS	YEAN	**YID**	YUPS
WOK	**YAD**	YEAR	YIDS	**YUS**
WOKE	DYAD	YEAS	**YIN**	AYUS
WOKS	YADS	**YEN**	AYIN	KYUS
WON	**YAG**	EYEN	PYIN	RYUS
WONK	YAGE	HYEN	TYIN	**ZAG**
WONS	YAGI	SYEN	YINS	ZAGS
WONT	YAGS	YENS	**YIP**	**ZAP**
WOO	**YAH**	**YEP**	YIPE	ZAPS
WOOD	AYAH	YEPS	YIPS	**ZEA**
WOOF	NYAH	**YER**	**YOB**	ZEAL
WOOL	YAHS	DYER	YOBS	ZEAS
WOON	**YAK**	EYER	**YOD**	**ZED**
WOOS	KYAK	OYER	YODE	ZEDA
WOOT	YAKS	TYER	YODH	ZEDS
WOP	**YAM**	YERD	YODS	**ZEE**
SWOP	LYAM	YERK	**YOK**	MZEE
WOPS	YAMS	**YES**	YOKE	ZEES
WOS	**YAP**	AYES	YOKS	**ZEK**
TWOS	YAPP	BYES	**YOM**	ZEKS
WOST	YAPS	DYES	YOMP	**ZEL**
WOT	**YAR**	EYES	**YON**	ZELS
SWOT	KYAR	HYES	YOND	**ZEP**
WOTS	YARD	KYES	YONI	ZEPS
WOW	YARE	LYES	YONT	**ZHO**
WOWF	YARK	NYES	**YOU**	DZHO
WOWS	YARN	OYES	YOUK	ZHOS
WRY	YARR	PYES	YOUR	**ZIG**
AWRY	**YAS**	RYES	YOUS	ZIGS
WUD	EYAS	SYES	**YOW**	**ZIN**
WUDS	NYAS	TYES	YOWE	ZINC
WUDU	PYAS	WYES	YOWL	ZINE
WUS	RYAS	YESK	YOWS	ZING
WUSS	**YAW**	YEST	**YUG**	ZINS
WYE	YAWL	**YET**	YUGA	**ZIP**
WYES	YAWN	PYET	YUGS	ZIPS
WYN	YAWP	YETI	**YUK**	**ZIT**
WYND	YAWS	YETT	YUKE	ZITE

ZITI	ZIZZ	**ZOO**	ZOOS	DZOS
ZITS	**ZOL**	ZOOM	ZOOT	**ZZZ**
ZIZ	ZOLS	ZOON	**ZOS**	ZZZS

Four-letter root words

AALS	**ABLE**	RACER	PACTS	TAFFY
BAALS	CABLE	ACERB	TACTS	**AFRO**
DAALS	FABLE	ACERS	**ACYL**	AFROS
PAALS	GABLE	**ACES**	ACYLS	**AGAR**
TAALS	HABLE	DACES	**ADAW**	AGARS
ABAC	SABLE	FACES	ADAWS	**AGAS**
ABACA	TABLE	LACES	**ADDS**	JAGAS
ABACI	ABLED	MACES	WADDS	NAGAS
ABACK	ABLER	PACES	**ADDY**	RAGAS
ABACS	ABLES	RACES	BADDY	SAGAS
ABAS	ABLET	TACES	CADDY	AGAST
BABAS	**ABRI**	**ACHE**	DADDY	**AGED**
CABAS	ABRIM	CACHE	FADDY	CAGED
YABAS	ABRIN	MACHE	LADDY	GAGED
ABASE	ABRIS	NACHE	PADDY	PAGED
ABASH	**ABUT**	RACHE	WADDY	RAGED
ABASK	ABUTS	TACHE	**ADIT**	WAGED
ABBA	**ABYE**	ACHED	ADITS	**AGEE**
DABBA	ABYES	ACHES	**ADOS**	RAGEE
GABBA	**ABYS**	**ACID**	DADOS	**AGEN**
YABBA	ABYSM	ACIDS	FADOS	AGENE
ABBAS	ABYSS	ACIDY	SADOS	AGENT
ABBE	**ACAI**	**ACME**	**ADZE**	**AGER**
ABBED	ACAIS	ACMES	ADZED	CAGER
ABBES	**ACCA**	**ACNE**	ADZES	EAGER
ABBEY	BACCA	ACNED	**AEON**	GAGER
ABED	YACCA	ACNES	PAEON	JAGER
SABED	ACCAS	**ACRE**	AEONS	LAGER
ABER	**ACED**	NACRE	**AERO**	PAGER
CABER	FACED	ACRED	AEROS	RAGER
SABER	LACED	ACRES	**AERY**	SAGER
TABER	MACED	**ACRO**	FAERY	WAGER
ABERS	PACED	MACRO	**AFAR**	YAGER
ABET	RACED	ACROS	AFARA	AGERS
ABETS	**ACER**	**ACTA**	AFARS	**AGES**
ABID	FACER	FACTA	**AFFY**	CAGES
RABID	LACER	PACTA	BAFFY	GAGES
TABID	MACER	**ACTS**	DAFFY	MAGES
ABIDE	PACER	FACTS	FAFFY	PAGES

RAGES	CAIDS	RAINS	BAKED	GALAS
SAGES	GAIDS	SAINS	CAKED	MALAS
WAGES	KAIDS	TAINS	FAKED	NALAS
YAGES	LAIDS	WAINS	LAKED	PALAS
AGHA	MAIDS	**AIRN**	NAKED	TALAS
AGHAS	QAIDS	BAIRN	OAKED	**ALAY**
AGIN	RAIDS	CAIRN	RAKED	PALAY
FAGIN	SAIDS	AIRNS	WAKED	ALAYS
AGING	**AIGA**	**AIRS**	**AKEE**	**ALBA**
AGIO	SAIGA	FAIRS	RAKEE	ALBAS
AGIOS	TAIGA	GAIRS	AKEES	**ALBE**
AGLU	AIGAS	HAIRS	**AKES**	ALBEE
AGLUS	**AILS**	LAIRS	BAKES	**ALCO**
AGMA	BAILS	MAIRS	CAKES	ALCOS
MAGMA	FAILS	PAIRS	FAKES	**ALEC**
TAGMA	HAILS	SAIRS	HAKES	ALECK
AGMAS	JAILS	VAIRS	JAKES	ALECS
AGOG	KAILS	WAIRS	LAKES	**ALEF**
AGOGE	MAILS	**AIRT**	MAKES	ALEFS
AGON	NAILS	AIRTH	RAKES	ALEFT
WAGON	PAILS	AIRTS	SAKES	**ALES**
AGONE	RAILS	**AIRY**	TAKES	BALES
AGONS	SAILS	DAIRY	WAKES	DALES
AGONY	TAILS	FAIRY	**AKIN**	EALES
AGRO	VAILS	HAIRY	LAKIN	GALES
AGROS	WAILS	LAIRY	TAKIN	HALES
AGUE	**AIMS**	VAIRY	AKING	KALES
VAGUE	KAIMS	**AITS**	**ALAN**	MALES
AGUED	MAIMS	BAITS	ALAND	PALES
AGUES	SAIMS	GAITS	ALANE	RALES
AHED	**AINE**	RAITS	ALANG	SALES
AAHED	DAINE	TAITS	ALANS	TALES
RAHED	FAINE	WAITS	ALANT	VALES
AIAS	RAINE	**AITU**	**ALAP**	WALES
RAIAS	SAINE	AITUS	JALAP	YALES
AIDA	AINEE	**AJIS**	ALAPA	**ALEW**
ZAIDA	**AINS**	HAJIS	ALAPS	ALEWS
AIDAS	CAINS	**AKAS**	**ALAR**	**ALFA**
AIDE	FAINS	HAKAS	MALAR	HALFA
WAIDE	GAINS	KAKAS	TALAR	ALFAS
AIDED	HAINS	TAKAS	ALARM	**ALFS**
AIDER	KAINS	VAKAS	ALARY	CALFS
AIDES	MAINS	WAKAS	**ALAS**	HALFS
AIDS	PAINS	**AKED**	BALAS	**ALGA**

ALGAE	BALMS	**AMBO**	AMINE	MANAS
ALGAL	CALMS	GAMBO	AMINO	NANAS
ALGAS	HALMS	JAMBO	AMINS	RANAS
ALIF	MALMS	MAMBO	**AMIR**	TANAS
CALIF	PALMS	SAMBO	AMIRS	**ANCE**
KALIF	**ALOD**	ZAMBO	**AMIS**	DANCE
ALIFS	ALODS	AMBOS	CAMIS	HANCE
ALKO	**ALOE**	**AMEN**	KAMIS	LANCE
ALKOS	ALOED	RAMEN	RAMIS	NANCE
ALKY	ALOES	SAMEN	TAMIS	PANCE
BALKY	**ALOO**	YAMEN	AMISS	RANCE
TALKY	BALOO	AMEND	**AMLA**	**ANDS**
ALKYD	ALOOF	AMENE	AMLAS	BANDS
ALKYL	ALOOS	AMENS	**AMMO**	FANDS
ALLS	**ALOW**	AMENT	AMMON	HANDS
BALLS	ALOWE	**AMES**	AMMOS	LANDS
CALLS	**ALPS**	CAMES	**AMOK**	PANDS
FALLS	CALPS	DAMES	AMOKS	RANDS
GALLS	PALPS	FAMES	**AMPS**	SANDS
HALLS	SALPS	GAMES	CAMPS	WANDS
LALLS	**ALTO**	HAMES	DAMPS	**ANES**
MALLS	SALTO	JAMES	GAMPS	BANES
PALLS	ALTOS	KAMES	LAMPS	CANES
TALLS	**ALTS**	LAMES	RAMPS	FANES
WALLS	DALTS	NAMES	SAMPS	JANES
ALLY	HALTS	SAMES	TAMPS	KANES
BALLY	MALTS	TAMES	VAMPS	LANES
DALLY	SALTS	WAMES	**AMUS**	MANES
GALLY	**ALUM**	**AMIA**	CAMUS	PANES
PALLY	ALUMS	LAMIA	NAMUS	SANES
RALLY	**ALUS**	ZAMIA	RAMUS	VANES
SALLY	BALUS	AMIAS	WAMUS	WANES
TALLY	MALUS	**AMID**	AMUSE	**ANGA**
WALLY	TALUS	AMIDE	**AMYL**	FANGA
ALLYL	**AMAH**	AMIDO	AMYLS	KANGA
ALMA	AMAHS	AMIDS	**ANAL**	MANGA
HALMA	**AMAS**	**AMIE**	BANAL	PANGA
TALMA	CAMAS	MAMIE	CANAL	RANGA
ALMAH	GAMAS	RAMIE	FANAL	SANGA
ALMAS	KAMAS	AMIES	**ANAN**	TANGA
ALME	LAMAS	**AMIN**	ANANA	ANGAS
ALMEH	MAMAS	GAMIN	**ANAS**	**ANIL**
ALMES	SAMAS	RAMIN	KANAS	ANILE
ALMS	AMASS	TAMIN	LANAS	ANILS

ANIS	BANTS	TAPES	NARCS	PARES
MANIS	CANTS	VAPES	**ARDS**	RARES
RANIS	DANTS	**APEX**	BARDS	TARES
ANISE	GANTS	CAPEX	CARDS	VARES
ANKH	HANTS	**APOD**	EARDS	WARES
ANKHS	KANTS	APODE	FARDS	**ARET**
ANNA	LANTS	APODS	HARDS	CARET
CANNA	PANTS	**APOS**	LARDS	ARETE
MANNA	RANTS	CAPOS	NARDS	ARETS
NANNA	SANTS	GAPOS	PARDS	ARETT
TANNA	VANTS	**APPS**	SARDS	**ARFS**
WANNA	WANTS	YAPPS	WARDS	BARFS
ANNAL	ANTSY	**APSE**	YARDS	ZARFS
ANNAS	**ANUS**	LAPSE	**AREA**	**ARGH**
ANNAT	MANUS	APSES	AREAD	AARGH
ANNO	**APAY**	**APSO**	AREAE	**ARIA**
ANNOY	APAYD	APSOS	AREAL	MARIA
ANNS	APAYS	**AQUA**	AREAR	VARIA
BANNS	**APED**	AQUAE	AREAS	ARIAS
CANNS	CAPED	AQUAS	**ARED**	**ARID**
JANNS	GAPED	**ARAK**	BARED	MARID
ANOA	JAPED	YARAK	CARED	**ARIL**
ANOAS	NAPED	ARAKS	DARED	ARILS
ANON	RAPED	**ARAR**	EARED	**ARIS**
CANON	TAPED	ARARS	FARED	DARIS
FANON	VAPED	**ARBA**	HARED	GARIS
ANSA	**APER**	ARBAS	OARED	LARIS
HANSA	CAPER	**ARBS**	PARED	NARIS
SANSA	GAPER	BARBS	RARED	PARIS
ANSAE	JAPER	CARBS	SARED	SARIS
ANTA	PAPER	DARBS	TARED	ZARIS
MANTA	RAPER	GARBS	WARED	ARISE
ANTAE	TAPER	WARBS	AREDD	ARISH
ANTAR	VAPER	**ARCH**	AREDE	**ARKS**
ANTAS	APERS	LARCH	**ARES**	BARKS
ANTE	APERT	MARCH	BARES	CARKS
ZANTE	APERY	PARCH	CARES	DARKS
ANTED	**APES**	ARCHI	DARES	HARKS
ANTES	CAPES	**ARCO**	FARES	JARKS
ANTI	GAPES	NARCO	GARES	KARKS
TANTI	JAPES	YARCO	HARES	LARKS
ANTIC	NAPES	ARCOS	LARES	MARKS
ANTIS	PAPES	**ARCS**	MARES	NARKS
ANTS	RAPES	MARCS	NARES	PARKS

RARKS	HARTS	**ATES**	CAUKS	**AVEL**
SARKS	KARTS	BATES	JAUKS	CAVEL
WARKS	MARTS	CATES	WAUKS	FAVEL
YARKS	PARTS	DATES	**AULA**	GAVEL
ARLE	TARTS	FATES	AULAS	JAVEL
CARLE	WARTS	GATES	**AULD**	NAVEL
FARLE	ARTSY	HATES	CAULD	RAVEL
MARLE	**ARTY**	MATES	FAULD	AVELS
PARLE	PARTY	NATES	HAULD	**AVER**
ARLED	TARTY	PATES	TAULD	CAVER
ARLES	WARTY	RATES	YAULD	FAVER
ARMS	**ARUM**	SATES	**AUNE**	HAVER
BARMS	GARUM	TATES	AUNES	LAVER
FARMS	LARUM	YATES	**AUNT**	PAVER
GARMS	ARUMS	**ATMA**	DAUNT	RAVER
HARMS	**ARVO**	ATMAN	GAUNT	SAVER
MARMS	PARVO	ATMAS	HAUNT	TAVER
WARMS	ARVOS	**ATOC**	JAUNT	WAVER
ARMY	**ARYL**	ATOCS	NAUNT	AVERS
BARMY	ARYLS	**ATOK**	SAUNT	AVERT
ARNA	**ASAR**	ATOKE	TAUNT	**AVES**
VARNA	TASAR	ATOKS	VAUNT	CAVES
ARNAS	**ASCI**	**ATOM**	AUNTS	EAVES
ARPA	FASCI	ATOMS	AUNTY	FAVES
ARPAS	**ASHY**	ATOMY	**AURA**	HAVES
ARSE	DASHY	**ATOP**	LAURA	LAVES
CARSE	HASHY	ATOPY	AURAE	NAVES
FARSE	MASHY	**ATUA**	AURAL	OAVES
MARSE	WASHY	ATUAS	AURAR	PAVES
PARSE	**ASKS**	**AUAS**	AURAS	RAVES
ARSED	BASKS	PAUAS	**AUTO**	SAVES
ARSES	CASKS	**AUFS**	AUTOS	WAVES
ARSEY	HASKS	HAUFS	**AVAL**	**AVID**
ARSY	MASKS	LAUFS	KAVAL	PAVID
KARSY	TASKS	**AUGH**	NAVAL	**AVOW**
ARTI	**ASPS**	FAUGH	AVALE	AVOWS
AARTI	GASPS	HAUGH	**AVAS**	**AWAY**
PARTI	HASPS	KAUGH	CAVAS	AWAYS
ARTIC	JASPS	LAUGH	FAVAS	**AWDL**
ARTIS	RASPS	SAUGH	JAVAS	AWDLS
ARTS	WASPS	WAUGH	KAVAS	**AWED**
CARTS	**ATAP**	AUGHT	LAVAS	CAWED
DARTS	WATAP	**AUKS**	TAVAS	DAWED
FARTS	ATAPS	BAUKS	AVAST	HAWED

JAWED	MAXED	AZANS	BAITS	**BANI**
KAWED	RAXED	**AZON**	**BAJU**	BANIA
LAWED	TAXED	GAZON	BAJUS	**BANK**
MAWED	WAXED	AZONS	**BAKE**	BANKS
PAWED	**AXEL**	**AZYM**	BAKED	**BANT**
SAWED	AXELS	AZYME	BAKEN	BANTS
TAWED	**AXES**	AZYMS	BAKER	BANTU
YAWED	FAXES	**BAAL**	BAKES	BANTY
AWEE	LAXES	BAALS	**BALD**	**BAPU**
AWEEL	MAXES	**BABA**	BALDS	BAPUS
AWES	PAXES	BABAS	BALDY	**BARB**
WAWES	RAXES	**BABE**	**BALE**	BARBE
AWKS	SAXES	BABEL	BALED	BARBS
BAWKS	TAXES	BABES	BALER	BARBY
CAWKS	WAXES	**BABU**	BALES	**BARD**
DAWKS	ZAXES	BABUL	**BALK**	BARDE
GAWKS	**AXIL**	BABUS	BALKS	BARDO
HAWKS	AXILE	**BACH**	BALKY	BARDS
LAWKS	AXILS	BACHA	**BALL**	BARDY
MAWKS	**AXIS**	BACHS	BALLS	**BARE**
PAWKS	MAXIS	**BACK**	BALLY	BARED
AWLS	TAXIS	ABACK	**BALM**	BARER
BAWLS	**AXLE**	BACKS	BALMS	BARES
PAWLS	AXLED	**BACS**	BALMY	**BARF**
WAWLS	AXLES	ABACS	**BALS**	BARFI
YAWLS	**AXON**	**BAEL**	BALSA	BARFS
AWNS	CAXON	BAELS	**BALU**	**BARK**
BAWNS	TAXON	**BAFF**	BALUN	BARKS
DAWNS	AXONE	BAFFS	BALUS	BARKY
FAWNS	AXONS	BAFFY	**BANC**	**BARM**
LAWNS	**AYAH**	**BAFT**	BANCO	BARMS
MAWNS	RAYAH	ABAFT	BANCS	BARMY
PAWNS	AYAHS	BAFTS	**BAND**	**BARN**
RAWNS	**AYES**	**BAGH**	ABAND	BARNS
YAWNS	BAYES	BAGHS	BANDA	BARNY
AWNY	**AYIN**	**BAHT**	BANDH	**BARP**
FAWNY	LAYIN	BAHTS	BANDS	BARPS
LAWNY	ZAYIN	**BAHU**	BANDY	**BARS**
TAWNY	AYINS	BAHUS	**BANE**	KBARS
YAWNY	**AYRE**	BAHUT	BANED	**BASE**
AWOL	FAYRE	**BAIL**	BANES	ABASE
AWOLS	AYRES	BAILS	**BANG**	BASED
AXED	**AZAN**	**BAIT**	OBANG	BASEN
FAXED	HAZAN	BAITH	BANGS	BASER

BASES	BAWNS	**BEEF**	**BERM**	BIFFO
BASH	**BAWR**	BEEFS	BERME	BIFFS
ABASH	BAWRS	BEEFY	BERMS	BIFFY
BASHO	**BAYE**	**BEEP**	**BEST**	**BIGA**
BASK	BAYED	BEEPS	BESTI	BIGAE
ABASK	BAYES	**BEER**	BESTS	**BIGG**
BASKS	**BAYT**	BEERS	**BETA**	BIGGS
BASS	BAYTS	BEERY	BETAS	BIGGY
BASSE	**BEAD**	**BEET**	BETE	**BIKE**
BASSI	BEADS	BEETS	BETED	BIKED
BASSO	BEADY	**BEGO**	BETEL	BIKER
BASSY	**BEAK**	BEGOT	BETES	BIKES
BAST	BEAKS	**BEIN**	**BETH**	**BILE**
BASTA	BEAKY	BEING	BETHS	BILED
BASTE	**BEAL**	BEINS	**BETS**	BILES
BASTI	BEALS	**BELL**	ABETS	**BILK**
BASTO	**BEAM**	BELLE	**BEYS**	BILKS
BASTS	ABEAM	BELLS	OBEYS	**BILL**
BATE	BEAMS	BELLY	**BHAI**	BILLS
ABATE	BEAMY	**BELT**	BHAIS	BILLY
BATED	**BEAN**	BELTS	**BHEL**	**BIMA**
BATES	BEANO	**BEMA**	BHELS	BIMAH
BATH	BEANS	BEMAD	**BHUT**	BIMAS
BATHE	BEANY	BEMAS	BHUTS	**BIND**
BATHS	**BEAR**	**BEND**	**BIAS**	BINDI
BATT	ABEAR	BENDS	OBIAS	BINDS
BATTA	BEARD	BENDY	**BIBB**	**BINE**
BATTS	BEARE	**BENE**	BIBBS	BINER
BATTU	BEARS	BENES	**BIBE**	BINES
BATTY	**BEAT**	BENET	BIBES	**BING**
BAUD	BEATH	**BENI**	**BICE**	BINGE
BAUDS	BEATS	BENIS	BICEP	BINGO
BAUK	BEATY	**BENT**	BICES	BINGS
BAUKS	**BEAU**	BENTO	**BIDE**	BINGY
BAUR	BEAUS	BENTS	ABIDE	**BINK**
BAURS	BEAUT	BENTY	BIDED	BINKS
BAWD	BEAUX	**BERE**	BIDER	**BINT**
BAWDS	**BECK**	BERES	BIDES	BINTS
BAWDY	BECKE	BERET	BIDET	**BIOG**
BAWK	BECKS	**BERG**	**BIDI**	BIOGS
BAWKS	**BEDE**	BERGS	BIDIS	**BIRD**
BAWL	BEDEL	**BERK**	**BIER**	BIRDS
BAWLS	BEDES	BERKO	BIERS	**BIRK**
BAWN	BEDEW	BERKS	**BIFF**	BIRKS

BIRL	BLATS	BLOWN	**BOFF**	**BONK**
BIRLE	BLATT	BLOWS	BOFFO	BONKS
BIRLS	**BLAW**	BLOWY	BOFFS	**BONY**
BIRO	BLAWN	**BLUB**	**BOHO**	EBONY
BIROS	BLAWS	BLUBS	BOHOS	**BOOB**
BIRR	**BLAY**	**BLUE**	**BOIL**	BOOBS
BIRRS	BLAYS	BLUED	ABOIL	BOOBY
BISE	**BLEB**	BLUER	BOILS	**BOOH**
BISES	BLEBS	BLUES	**BOKE**	BOOHS
BISK	**BLED**	BLUET	BOKED	**BOOK**
BISKS	ABLED	BLUEY	BOKES	EBOOK
BITE	**BLEE**	**BLUR**	**BOKO**	BOOKS
BITER	BLEED	BLURB	BOKOS	BOOKY
BITES	BLEEP	BLURS	**BOLA**	**BOOL**
BITO	BLEES	BLURT	BOLAR	BOOLS
BITOS	**BLET**	**BOAB**	BOLAS	**BOOM**
BITOU	ABLET	BOABS	**BOLD**	BOOMS
BITS	BLETS	**BOAK**	BOLDS	BOOMY
OBITS	**BLEY**	BOAKS	**BOLE**	**BOON**
BITSY	BLEYS	**BOAR**	OBOLE	ABOON
BITT	**BLIN**	BOARD	BOLES	BOONG
BITTE	BLIND	BOARS	**BOLL**	BOONS
BITTS	BLING	BOART	BOLLS	**BOOR**
BITTY	BLINI	**BOAS**	**BOLO**	BOORD
BIZE	BLINK	BOAST	BOLOS	BOORS
BIZES	BLINS	**BOAT**	**BOLT**	**BOOS**
BLAB	BLINY	BOATS	BOLTS	BOOSE
BLABS	**BLIP**	**BOBA**	**BOMA**	BOOST
BLAD	BLIPS	BOBAC	ABOMA	**BOOT**
BLADE	**BLIT**	BOBAK	BOMAS	BOOTH
BLADS	BLITE	BOBAS	**BOMB**	BOOTS
BLADY	BLITS	**BOBO**	BOMBE	BOOTY
BLAE	BLITZ	BOBOL	BOMBO	**BORA**
BLAER	**BLOB**	BOBOS	BOMBS	BORAK
BLAES	BLOBS	**BOCK**	**BOND**	BORAL
BLAG	**BLOC**	BOCKS	BONDS	BORAS
BLAGS	BLOCK	**BODE**	**BONE**	BORAX
BLAH	BLOCS	ABODE	BONED	**BORD**
BLAHS	**BLOG**	BODED	BONER	ABORD
BLAM	BLOGS	BODES	BONES	BORDE
BLAME	**BLOT**	**BOEP**	BONEY	BORDS
BLAMS	BLOTS	BOEPS	**BONG**	**BORE**
BLAT	**BLOW**	**BOET**	BONGO	ABORE
BLATE	ABLOW	BOETS	BONGS	YBORE

BORED	BOWRS	BREDS	BRISK	BUDIS
BOREE	**BOWS**	**BREE**	BRISS	**BUDO**
BOREL	BOWSE	BREED	**BRIT**	BUDOS
BORER	**BOYF**	BREEM	BRITH	**BUFF**
BORES	BOYFS	BREER	BRITS	BUFFA
BORK	**BOYG**	BREES	BRITT	BUFFE
BORKS	BOYGS	**BREI**	**BROD**	BUFFI
BORM	**BOYO**	BREID	BRODS	BUFFO
BORMS	BOYOS	BREIS	**BROG**	BUFFS
BORN	**BOYS**	**BREN**	BROGH	BUFFY
BORNA	BOYSY	BRENS	BROGS	**BUFO**
BORNE	**BOZO**	BRENT	**BROO**	BUFOS
BORT	BOZOS	**BRER**	BROOD	**BUHL**
ABORT	**BRAD**	BRERE	BROOK	BUHLS
BORTS	BRADS	BRERS	BROOL	**BUHR**
BORTY	**BRAE**	**BREW**	BROOM	BUHRS
BORTZ	BRAES	BREWS	BROOS	**BUIK**
BOSK	**BRAG**	**BREY**	**BROS**	BUIKS
BOSKS	BRAGS	BREYS	BROSE	**BUKE**
BOSKY	**BRAK**	**BRIE**	BROSY	BUKES
BOSS	BRAKE	BRIEF	**BROW**	**BULB**
BOSSY	BRAKS	BRIER	BROWN	BULBS
BOTA	BRAKY	BRIES	BROWS	**BULK**
BOTAS	**BRAN**	**BRIG**	**BRUS**	BULKS
BOTE	BRAND	BRIGS	BRUSH	BULKY
BOTEL	BRANE	**BRIK**	BRUSK	**BULL**
BOTES	BRANK	IBRIK	BRUST	BULLA
BOTH	BRANS	BRIKI	**BRUT**	BULLS
BOTHY	BRANT	BRIKS	BRUTE	BULLY
BOTT	**BRAS**	**BRIM**	BRUTS	**BUMF**
BOTTE	BRASH	ABRIM	**BUAT**	BUMFS
BOTTS	BRASS	BRIMS	BUATS	**BUMP**
BOTTY	BRAST	**BRIN**	**BUBA**	BUMPH
BOUK	**BRAT**	ABRIN	BUBAL	BUMPS
BOUKS	BRATS	BRINE	BUBAS	BUMPY
BOUN	**BRAW**	BRING	**BUBU**	**BUNA**
BOUND	BRAWL	BRINK	BUBUS	ABUNA
BOUNS	BRAWN	BRINS	**BUCK**	BUNAS
BOUT	BRAWS	BRINY	BUCKO	**BUND**
ABOUT	**BRAY**	**BRIO**	BUCKS	BUNDE
BOUTS	ABRAY	BRIOS	BUCKU	BUNDH
BOWL	BRAYS	**BRIS**	**BUDA**	BUNDS
BOWLS	**BRED**	ABRIS	BUDAS	BUNDT
BOWR	BREDE	BRISE	**BUDI**	BUNDU

BUNDY	BURST	CACAO	CALMS	CANTO
BUNG	BUSH	CACAS	CALMY	CANTS
BUNGS	BUSHY	CACK	CALO	CANTY
BUNGY	BUSK	CACKS	CALOS	CAPA
BUNK	BUSKS	CACKY	CALP	SCAPA
BUNKO	BUSKY	CADE	SCALP	CAPAS
BUNKS	BUSS	CADEE	CALPA	CAPE
BUNN	BUSSU	CADES	CALPS	SCAPE
BUNNS	BUST	CADET	CAMA	CAPED
BUNNY	BUSTI	CADI	CAMAN	CAPER
BUNT	BUSTS	CADIE	CAMAS	CAPES
BUNTS	BUSTY	CADIS	CAME	CAPEX
BUNTY	BUTE	CADS	CAMEL	CAPH
BUOY	BUTEO	ECADS	CAMEO	CAPHS
BUOYS	BUTES	SCADS	CAMES	CAPI
BURA	BUTS	CAFE	CAMI	SCAPI
BURAN	ABUTS	CAFES	CAMIS	CAPIZ
BURAS	BUTT	CAFF	CAMO	CAPO
BURB	BUTTE	SCAFF	CAMOS	CAPON
BURBS	BUTTS	CAFFS	CAMP	CAPOS
BURD	BUTTY	CAGE	SCAMP	CAPOT
BURDS	BUZZ	CAGED	CAMPI	CARB
BURG	ABUZZ	CAGER	CAMPO	CARBO
BURGH	BUZZY	CAGES	CAMPS	CARBS
BURGS	BYDE	CAGEY	CAMPY	CARBY
BURK	BYDED	CAGS	CAMS	CARD
BURKA	BYDES	SCAGS	SCAMS	CARDI
BURKE	BYES	CAID	CANE	CARDS
BURKS	ABYES	CAIDS	CANED	CARDY
BURL	BYKE	CAIN	CANEH	CARE
BURLS	BYKED	CAINS	CANER	SCARE
BURLY	BYKES	CAKE	CANES	CARED
BURN	BYRE	CAKED	CANG	CARER
BURNS	BYRES	CAKES	CANGS	CARES
BURNT	BYRL	CAKEY	CANN	CARET
BURP	BYRLS	CALF	CANNA	CAREX
BURPS	BYTE	CALFS	CANNS	CARK
BURR	BYTES	CALK	CANNY	CARKS
BURRO	CABA	CALKS	CANS	CARL
BURRS	CABAL	CALL	SCANS	CARLE
BURRY	CABAS	SCALL	CANSO	CARLS
BURS	CABS	CALLA	CANST	CARN
BURSA	SCABS	CALLS	CANT	CARNS
BURSE	CACA	CALM	SCANT	CARNY

CARP	**CAVE**	CERTS	CHAVS	CHITS
SCARP	CAVED	CERTY	**CHAW**	**CHIV**
CARPI	CAVEL	**CESS**	CHAWK	CHIVE
CARPS	CAVER	CESSE	CHAWS	CHIVS
CARR	CAVES	**CETE**	**CHAY**	CHIVY
CARRS	**CAWK**	CETES	CHAYA	**CHIZ**
CARRY	CAWKS	**CHAD**	CHAYS	CHIZZ
CARS	**CAWS**	CHADO	**CHEF**	**CHOC**
SCARS	SCAWS	CHADS	CHEFS	CHOCK
CARSE	**CEAS**	**CHAI**	**CHEM**	CHOCO
CART	CEASE	CHAIN	CHEMO	CHOCS
SCART	**CECA**	CHAIR	CHEMS	**CHOG**
CARTA	CECAL	CHAIS	**CHER**	CHOGS
CARTE	**CEDE**	**CHAL**	OCHER	**CHON**
CARTS	CEDED	CHALK	CHERE	CHONS
CASA	CEDER	CHALS	CHERT	**CHOP**
CASAS	CEDES	**CHAM**	**CHEW**	CHOPS
CASE	**CEDI**	CHAMP	CHEWS	**CHOU**
CASED	CEDIS	CHAMS	CHEWY	CHOUT
CASES	**CEIL**	**CHAO**	**CHIA**	CHOUX
CASK	CEILI	CHAOS	CHIAO	**CHOW**
CASKS	CEILS	**CHAP**	CHIAS	CHOWK
CASKY	**CELL**	CHAPE	**CHIB**	CHOWS
CAST	CELLA	CHAPS	CHIBS	**CHUB**
CASTE	CELLI	CHAPT	**CHIC**	CHUBS
CASTS	CELLO	**CHAR**	CHICA	**CHUG**
CATE	CELLS	ACHAR	CHICH	CHUGS
CATER	**CELT**	CHARA	CHICK	**CHUM**
CATES	CELTS	CHARD	CHICO	CHUMP
CATS	**CENS**	CHARE	CHICS	CHUMS
SCATS	CENSE	CHARK	**CHID**	**CHUR**
CAUK	**CENT**	CHARM	CHIDE	CHURL
CAUKS	SCENT	CHARR	**CHIK**	CHURN
CAUL	CENTO	CHARS	CHIKS	CHURR
CAULD	CENTS	CHART	**CHIN**	**CHUT**
CAULK	CENTU	CHARY	CHINA	CHUTE
CAULS	**CEPE**	**CHAS**	CHINE	CHUTS
CAUM	CEPES	CHASE	CHING	**CIDE**
CAUMS	**CERE**	CHASM	CHINK	CIDED
CAUP	CERED	**CHAT**	CHINO	CIDER
SCAUP	CERES	CHATS	CHINS	CIDES
CAUPS	**CERO**	**CHAV**	**CHIP**	**CIDS**
CAVA	CEROS	SCHAV	CHIPS	ACIDS
CAVAS	**CERT**	CHAVE	**CHIT**	**CIEL**

CIELS	CLAWS	CLUBS	COHOS	COMMA
CILL	**CLAY**	**CLUE**	**COIF**	COMMO
CILLS	CLAYS	CLUED	COIFS	COMMS
CINE	**CLEF**	CLUES	**COIL**	COMMY
CINES	CLEFS	CLUEY	COILS	**COMP**
CINQ	CLEFT	**COAL**	**COIN**	COMPO
CINQS	**CLEG**	COALA	COINS	COMPS
CION	CLEGS	COALS	**COIR**	COMPT
SCION	**CLEM**	COALY	COIRS	**COND**
CIONS	CLEMS	**COAT**	**COIT**	YCOND
CIRE	**CLEW**	COATE	COITS	CONDO
CIRES	CLEWS	COATI	**COKE**	**CONE**
CIRL	**CLIP**	COATS	COKED	SCONE
CIRLS	CLIPE	**COBB**	COKES	CONED
CIST	CLIPS	COBBS	**COLA**	CONES
CISTS	CLIPT	COBBY	COLAS	CONEY
CITE	**CLIT**	**COCA**	**COLD**	**CONF**
CITED	CLITS	COCAS	ACOLD	CONFS
CITER	**CLOD**	**COCK**	SCOLD	**CONI**
CITES	CLODS	ACOCK	COLDS	CONIA
CIVE	**CLOG**	COCKS	**COLE**	CONIC
CIVES	CLOGS	COCKY	COLED	CONIN
CIVET	**CLON**	**COCO**	COLES	**CONK**
CLAD	CLONE	COCOA	COLEY	CONKS
YCLAD	CLONK	COCOS	**COLL**	CONKY
CLADE	CLONS	**CODA**	COLLS	**CONN**
CLADS	**CLOP**	CODAS	COLLY	CONNE
CLAG	CLOPS	**CODE**	**COLT**	CONNS
CLAGS	**CLOT**	CODEC	COLTS	**CONS**
CLAM	CLOTE	CODED	**COMA**	ICONS
CLAME	CLOTH	CODEN	COMAE	**COOF**
CLAMP	CLOTS	CODER	COMAL	COOFS
CLAMS	**CLOU**	CODES	COMAS	**COOK**
CLAN	CLOUD	CODEX	**COMB**	COOKS
CLANG	CLOUR	**COED**	COMBE	COOKY
CLANK	CLOUS	COEDS	COMBI	**COOL**
CLANS	CLOUT	**COFF**	COMBO	COOLS
CLAP	**CLOW**	SCOFF	COMBS	COOLY
CLAPS	CLOWN	COFFS	COMBY	**COOM**
CLAPT	CLOWS	**COGS**	**COME**	COOMB
CLAT	**CLOY**	SCOGS	COMER	COOMS
ECLAT	CLOYE	**COHO**	COMES	COOMY
CLATS	CLOYS	COHOE	COMET	**COON**
CLAW	**CLUB**	COHOG	**COMM**	COONS

COOP	COSEC	COWPS	SCREE	**CROP**
SCOOP	COSED	**COWS**	CREED	CROPS
COOPS	COSES	SCOWS	CREEK	**CROW**
COOPT	COSET	**COXA**	CREEL	SCROW
COOS	COSEY	COXAE	CREEP	CROWD
COOST	**COST**	COXAL	CREES	CROWN
COOT	COSTA	**COZE**	**CREM**	CROWS
SCOOT	COSTE	COZED	CREME	**CRUD**
COOTS	COSTS	COZEN	CREMS	CRUDE
COPE	**COTE**	COZES	**CREW**	CRUDO
SCOPE	COTED	COZEY	SCREW	CRUDS
COPED	COTES	**CRAB**	CREWE	CRUDY
COPEN	**COTH**	SCRAB	CREWS	**CRUE**
COPER	COTHS	CRABS	**CRIA**	CRUEL
COPES	**COTS**	**CRAG**	CRIAS	CRUES
COPS	SCOTS	SCRAG	**CRIB**	CRUET
SCOPS	**COTT**	CRAGS	CRIBS	**CRUS**
COPSE	COTTA	**CRAM**	**CRIM**	ECRUS
COPSY	COTTS	SCRAM	SCRIM	CRUSE
CORD	**COUP**	CRAME	CRIME	CRUSH
CORDS	SCOUP	CRAMP	CRIMP	CRUST
CORE	COUPE	CRAMS	CRIMS	CRUSY
SCORE	COUPS	**CRAN**	**CRIP**	**CUBE**
CORED	**COUR**	SCRAN	SCRIP	CUBEB
CORER	SCOUR	CRANE	CRIPE	CUBED
CORES	COURB	CRANK	CRIPS	CUBER
COREY	COURD	CRANS	**CRIS**	CUBES
CORK	COURE	**CRAP**	CRISE	**CUDS**
CORKS	COURS	SCRAP	CRISP	SCUDS
CORKY	COURT	CRAPE	**CRIT**	**CUFF**
CORM	**COVE**	CRAPS	CRITH	SCUFF
CORMS	COVED	CRAPY	CRITS	CUFFO
CORN	COVEN	**CRAW**	**CROC**	CUFFS
ACORN	COVER	SCRAW	CROCI	**CUIF**
SCORN	COVES	CRAWL	CROCK	CUIFS
CORNI	COVET	CRAWS	CROCS	**CUIT**
CORNO	COVEY	**CRAY**	**CROG**	CUITS
CORNS	**COWK**	SCRAY	SCROG	**CUKE**
CORNU	COWKS	CRAYS	CROGS	CUKES
CORNY	**COWL**	**CRED**	**CRON**	**CULL**
CORS	SCOWL	ACRED	CRONE	SCULL
CORSE	COWLS	CREDO	CRONK	CULLS
CORSO	**COWP**	CREDS	CRONS	CULLY
COSE	SCOWP	**CREE**	CRONY	**CULM**

CULMS	CUSPS	DAHLS	**DARN**	IDEAL
CULT	CUSPY	**DAHS**	DARNS	DEALS
CULTI	**CUSS**	ODAHS	**DART**	DEALT
CULTS	CUSSO	**DAIS**	DARTS	**DEAN**
CULTY	**CUTE**	DAISY	**DASH**	DEANS
CUMS	ACUTE	**DALE**	DASHI	**DEAR**
SCUMS	SCUTE	DALED	DASHY	DEARE
CUNT	CUTER	DALES	**DATA**	DEARN
CUNTS	CUTES	**DALI**	DATAL	DEARS
CUPS	CUTEY	DALIS	**DATE**	DEARY
SCUPS	**CUTS**	**DALS**	DATED	**DEAW**
CURB	SCUTS	ODALS	DATER	DEAWS
CURBS	**CYAN**	UDALS	DATES	DEAWY
CURD	CYANO	**DALT**	**DATO**	**DEBE**
CURDS	CYANS	DALTS	DATOS	DEBEL
CURDY	**CYMA**	**DAME**	**DAUB**	DEBES
CURE	CYMAE	DAMES	DAUBE	**DEBT**
CURED	CYMAR	**DAMN**	DAUBS	DEBTS
CURER	CYMAS	DAMNS	DAUBY	**DECK**
CURES	**CYME**	**DAMP**	**DAUD**	DECKO
CURET	CYMES	DAMPS	DAUDS	DECKS
CURF	**CYST**	DAMPY	**DAUR**	**DECO**
SCURF	CYSTS	**DANG**	DAURS	DECOR
CURFS	**CYTE**	DANGS	**DAUT**	DECOS
CURL	CYTES	**DANK**	DAUTS	DECOY
CURLI	**CZAR**	DANKS	**DAWD**	**DEED**
CURLS	CZARS	**DANT**	DAWDS	DEEDS
CURLY	**DAAL**	IDANT	**DAWK**	DEEDY
CURN	DAALS	DANTS	DAWKS	**DEEM**
CURNS	**DACE**	**DARB**	**DAWN**	ADEEM
CURNY	DACES	DARBS	DAWNS	DEEMS
CURR	**DACK**	**DARE**	**DAWS**	**DEEN**
CURRS	DACKS	DARED	ADAWS	DEENS
CURRY	**DADA**	DARER	**DAWT**	**DEEP**
CURS	DADAH	DARES	DAWTS	DEEPS
SCURS	DADAS	**DARG**	**DAYS**	**DEER**
CURSE	**DADO**	DARGA	ADAYS	DEERE
CURSI	DADOS	DARGS	**DAZE**	DEERS
CURST	**DAFF**	**DARI**	DAZED	**DEES**
CUSH	DAFFS	DARIC	DAZER	IDEES
CUSHY	DAFFY	DARIS	DAZES	**DEET**
CUSK	**DAGO**	**DARK**	**DEAD**	DEETS
CUSKS	DAGOS	DARKS	DEADS	**DEEV**
CUSP	**DAHL**	DARKY	**DEAL**	DEEVE

DEEVS	DENIM	**DICE**	DINES	ADITS
DEFI	DENIS	DICED	**DING**	EDITS
DEFIS	**DENS**	DICER	DINGE	DITSY
DEFO	DENSE	DICES	DINGO	**DITT**
DEFOG	**DENT**	DICEY	DINGS	DITTO
DEGU	IDENT	**DICH**	DINGY	DITTS
DEGUM	DENTS	DICHT	**DINK**	DITTY
DEGUS	**DERE**	**DICK**	DINKS	**DITZ**
DEID	DERED	DICKS	DINKY	DITZY
DEIDS	DERES	DICKY	**DINO**	**DIVA**
DEIF	**DERM**	**DICT**	DINOS	DIVAN
DEIFY	DERMA	EDICT	**DINT**	DIVAS
DEIL	DERMS	DICTA	DINTS	**DIVE**
DEILS	**DERN**	DICTS	**DIOL**	DIVED
DEKE	DERNS	DICTY	DIOLS	DIVER
DEKED	**DERO**	**DIDO**	**DIPS**	DIVES
DEKES	DEROS	DIDOS	DIPSO	**DIVI**
DELE	**DERV**	**DIEB**	**DIRE**	DIVIS
DELED	DERVS	DIEBS	DIRER	**DIVO**
DELES	**DESI**	**DIEL**	**DIRK**	DIVOS
DELF	DESIS	DIELS	DIRKE	DIVOT
DELFS	**DESK**	**DIET**	DIRKS	**DIXI**
DELFT	DESKS	DIETS	**DIRL**	DIXIE
DELI	**DEVA**	**DIFF**	DIRLS	DIXIT
DELIS	DEVAS	DIFFS	**DIRT**	**DIYA**
DELL	**DEVI**	**DIKA**	DIRTS	DIYAS
DELLS	DEVIL	DIKAS	DIRTY	**DJIN**
DELLY	DEVIS	**DIKE**	**DISA**	DJINN
DELO	**DEVO**	DIKED	DISAS	DJINS
DELOS	DEVON	DIKER	**DISC**	**DOAB**
DELT	DEVOS	DIKES	DISCI	DOABS
DELTA	DEVOT	DIKEY	DISCO	**DOAT**
DELTS	**DHAK**	**DILL**	DISCS	DOATS
DEME	DHAKS	DILLI	**DISH**	**DOBE**
DEMES	**DHAL**	DILLS	DISHY	ADOBE
DEMO	DHALS	DILLY	**DISK**	DOBES
DEMOB	**DHOL**	**DIME**	DISKS	**DOCK**
DEMOI	DHOLE	DIMER	**DITA**	DOCKS
DEMON	DHOLL	DIMES	DITAL	**DOCO**
DEMOS	DHOLS	**DIMP**	DITAS	DOCOS
DENE	**DHOW**	DIMPS	**DITE**	**DOCU**
DENES	DHOWS	**DINE**	DITED	DOCUS
DENET	**DIAL**	DINED	DITES	**DODO**
DENI	DIALS	DINER	**DITS**	DODOS

DOEK	**DOOL**	DOSAI	DOWNY	DREKS
DOEKS	DOOLE	DOSAS	**DOWP**	**DREY**
DOER	DOOLS	**DOSE**	DOWPS	DREYS
DOERS	DOOLY	DOSED	**DOWS**	**DRIB**
DOES	**DOOM**	DOSEH	DOWSE	DRIBS
DOEST	DOOMS	DOSER	**DOWT**	**DRIP**
DOFF	DOOMY	DOSES	DOWTS	DRIPS
DOFFS	**DOON**	**DOSH**	**DOZE**	DRIPT
DOGE	DOONA	DOSHA	ADOZE	**DROP**
DOGES	**DOOR**	**DOTE**	DOZED	DROPS
DOGEY	DOORN	DOTED	DOZEN	DROPT
DOIT	DOORS	DOTER	DOZER	**DROW**
DOITS	**DOPA**	DOTES	DOZES	DROWN
DOJO	DOPAS	**DOUC**	**DRAB**	DROWS
DOJOS	**DOPE**	DOUCE	DRABS	**DRUB**
DOLE	DOPED	DOUCS	**DRAC**	DRUBS
DOLED	DOPER	**DOUK**	DRACK	**DRUG**
DOLES	DOPES	DOUKS	DRACO	DRUGS
DOLL	DOPEY	**DOUM**	**DRAD**	**DRUM**
DOLLS	**DORB**	DOUMA	ADRAD	DRUMS
DOLLY	DORBA	DOUMS	YDRAD	**DUAD**
DOLS	DORBS	**DOUP**	**DRAG**	DUADS
IDOLS	**DORE**	DOUPS	DRAGS	**DUAL**
DOLT	ADORE	**DOUR**	**DRAM**	DUALS
DOLTS	DOREE	ODOUR	DRAMA	**DUAN**
DOME	DORES	DOURA	DRAMS	DUANS
DOMED	**DORK**	**DOUT**	**DRAP**	**DUAR**
DOMES	DORKS	DOUTS	DRAPE	DUARS
DONA	DORKY	**DOVE**	DRAPS	**DUCE**
DONAH	**DORM**	DOVED	**DRAT**	EDUCE
DONAS	DORMS	DOVEN	DRATS	DUCES
DONE	DORMY	DOVER	**DRAW**	**DUCK**
DONEE	**DORP**	DOVES	DRAWL	DUCKS
DONER	DORPS	**DOWD**	DRAWN	DUCKY
DONG	**DORR**	DOWDS	DRAWS	**DUCT**
DONGA	DORRS	DOWDY	**DRAY**	EDUCT
DONGS	**DORS**	**DOWL**	DRAYS	DUCTS
DONS	ODORS	DOWLE	**DREE**	**DUDE**
UDONS	DORSA	DOWLS	DREED	DUDED
DONSY	DORSE	DOWLY	DREER	DUDES
DOOB	**DORT**	**DOWN**	DREES	**DUEL**
DOOBS	DORTS	ADOWN	**DREG**	DUELS
DOOK	DORTY	DOWNA	DREGS	**DUET**
DOOKS	**DOSA**	DOWNS	**DREK**	DUETS

DUETT	**DURN**	DEANS	PEASE	EAVED
DUFF	DURNS	GEANS	SEASE	EAVES
DUFFS	**DURO**	JEANS	TEASE	**EBON**
DUIT	DUROC	LEANS	EASED	EBONS
DUITS	DUROS	MEANS	EASEL	EBONY
DUKA	DUROY	PEANS	EASER	**ECAD**
DUKAS	**DURR**	REANS	EASES	DECAD
DUKE	DURRA	SEANS	**EAST**	ECADS
DUKED	DURRS	WEANS	BEAST	**ECCE**
DUKES	DURRY	YEANS	FEAST	RECCE
DULE	**DUSK**	**EARD**	HEAST	**ECCO**
DULES	DUSKS	BEARD	LEAST	RECCO
DULL	DUSKY	HEARD	REAST	SECCO
DULLS	**DUST**	YEARD	YEAST	**ECHE**
DULLY	ADUST	EARDS	EASTS	ECHED
DUMA	DUSTS	**EARL**	**EATH**	ECHES
DUMAS	DUSTY	PEARL	BEATH	**ECHO**
DUMB	**DWAM**	EARLS	DEATH	ECHOS
DUMBO	DWAMS	EARLY	HEATH	**ECHT**
DUMBS	**DYAD**	**EARN**	MEATH	FECHT
DUMP	DYADS	DEARN	NEATH	HECHT
DUMPS	**DYER**	LEARN	EATHE	WECHT
DUMPY	DYERS	YEARN	**EATS**	**ECOS**
DUNE	**DYKE**	EARNS	BEATS	DECOS
DUNES	DYKED	**EARS**	FEATS	**ECRU**
DUNG	DYKES	BEARS	GEATS	ECRUS
DUNGS	DYKEY	DEARS	HEATS	**EDDY**
DUNGY	**DYNE**	FEARS	JEATS	NEDDY
DUNK	DYNEL	GEARS	LEATS	REDDY
DUNKS	DYNES	HEARS	MEATS	TEDDY
DUNS	**DZHO**	LEARS	NEATS	**EDGE**
DUNSH	DZHOS	NEARS	PEATS	HEDGE
DUNT	**EACH**	PEARS	SEATS	KEDGE
DUNTS	BEACH	REARS	TEATS	LEDGE
DUPE	LEACH	SEARS	**EAUS**	SEDGE
DUPED	PEACH	TEARS	BEAUS	WEDGE
DUPER	REACH	WEARS	**EAUX**	EDGED
DUPES	TEACH	YEARS	BEAUX	EDGER
DURA	**EALE**	EARST	**EAVE**	EDGES
DURAL	VEALE	**EASE**	DEAVE	**EDGY**
DURAS	EALED	CEASE	HEAVE	HEDGY
DURE	EALES	FEASE	LEAVE	KEDGY
DURED	**EANS**	LEASE	REAVE	LEDGY
DURES	BEANS	MEASE	WEAVE	SEDGY

WEDGY	LEGER	WELDS	TEMES	TENDS
EDIT	EGERS	**ELFS**	**EMEU**	VENDS
EDITS	**EGGS**	DELFS	EMEUS	WENDS
EECH	TEGGS	PELFS	**EMIC**	**ENES**
BEECH	YEGGS	SELFS	DEMIC	BENES
KEECH	**EGGY**	**ELKS**	HEMIC	DENES
LEECH	LEGGY	WELKS	EMICS	GENES
REECH	PEGGY	YELKS	**EMIR**	LENES
EELS	**EGIS**	**ELLS**	EMIRS	MENES
FEELS	AEGIS	BELLS	**EMIT**	NENES
HEELS	**EGMA**	CELLS	DEMIT	PENES
JEELS	REGMA	DELLS	REMIT	SENES
KEELS	EGMAS	FELLS	EMITS	TENES
PEELS	**EGOS**	HELLS	**EMMA**	**ENEW**
REELS	REGOS	JELLS	GEMMA	RENEW
SEELS	SEGOS	KELLS	LEMMA	ENEWS
TEELS	VEGOS	MELLS	EMMAS	**ENGS**
WEELS	**EIDE**	PELLS	**EMMY**	LENGS
EELY	EIDER	SELLS	FEMMY	MENGS
DEELY	**EIKS**	TELLS	GEMMY	**ENOL**
JEELY	REIKS	VELLS	JEMMY	ENOLS
SEELY	**EILD**	WELLS	EMMYS	**ENOW**
EERY	EILDS	YELLS	**EMOS**	ENOWS
BEERY	**EINE**	**ELMS**	DEMOS	**ENTS**
LEERY	SEINE	HELMS	MEMOS	BENTS
PEERY	**EISH**	YELMS	**EMPT**	CENTS
VEERY	LEISH	**ELTS**	DEMPT	DENTS
EEVN	**EKED**	BELTS	KEMPT	FENTS
EEVNS	DEKED	CELTS	NEMPT	GENTS
EFFS	REKED	DELTS	TEMPT	HENTS
JEFFS	**EKES**	FELTS	EMPTS	KENTS
MEFFS	DEKES	GELTS	EMPTY	PENTS
TEFFS	PEKES	KELTS	**EMYD**	RENTS
EFTS	REKES	MELTS	EMYDE	SENTS
HEFTS	**EKKA**	PELTS	EMYDS	TENTS
LEFTS	MEKKA	WELTS	**ENDS**	VENTS
WEFTS	EKKAS	YELTS	BENDS	WENTS
EGAD	**ELAN**	**EMES**	FENDS	**ENVY**
BEGAD	ELAND	DEMES	HENDS	SENVY
EGADS	ELANS	FEMES	LENDS	**EONS**
EGAL	**ELDS**	HEMES	MENDS	AEONS
LEGAL	GELDS	LEMES	PENDS	JEONS
REGAL	MELDS	MEMES	RENDS	NEONS
EGER	VELDS	SEMES	SENDS	PEONS

EORL	**ERHU**	PERST	ZETAS	FEVER
CEORL	ERHUS	VERST	**ETAT**	LEVER
EORLS	**ERIC**	**ERUV**	ETATS	NEVER
EPEE	CERIC	ERUVS	**ETCH**	SEVER
TEPEE	SERIC	**ESES**	FETCH	EVERT
EPEES	XERIC	BESES	KETCH	EVERY
EPHA	ERICA	LESES	LETCH	**EVES**
EPHAH	ERICK	MESES	RETCH	LEVES
EPHAS	ERICS	RESES	VETCH	MEVES
EPIC	**ERKS**	YESES	**ETEN**	NEVES
SEPIC	BERKS	**ESKY**	ETENS	YEVES
EPICS	JERKS	PESKY	**ETHE**	**EVET**
EPOS	MERKS	**ESNE**	LETHE	REVET
PEPOS	NERKS	MESNE	ETHER	EVETS
REPOS	PERKS	ESNES	**ETHS**	**EVIL**
ERAS	SERKS	**ESSE**	BETHS	DEVIL
TERAS	YERKS	CESSE	HETHS	KEVIL
ERASE	ZERKS	DESSE	METHS	EVILS
ERED	**ERNE**	FESSE	TETHS	**EVOS**
CERED	CERNE	GESSE	**ETIC**	DEVOS
DERED	GERNE	JESSE	METIC	**EWER**
LERED	KERNE	ESSES	ETICS	FEWER
MERED	TERNE	**ESTS**	**ETNA**	HEWER
SERED	ERNED	BESTS	ETNAS	NEWER
ERES	ERNES	FESTS	**ETUI**	SEWER
BERES	**ERNS**	GESTS	ETUIS	EWERS
CERES	DERNS	HESTS	**EUGH**	**EWES**
DERES	FERNS	JESTS	HEUGH	EWEST
FERES	HERNS	KESTS	LEUGH	**EWTS**
GERES	KERNS	LESTS	TEUGH	NEWTS
HERES	PERNS	NESTS	EUGHS	**EXAM**
LERES	TERNS	PESTS	**EUKS**	EXAMS
MERES	**EROS**	RESTS	NEUKS	**EXEC**
PERES	AEROS	TESTS	YEUKS	EXECS
SERES	CEROS	VESTS	**EURO**	**EXED**
TERES	DEROS	WESTS	EUROS	HEXED
EREV	HEROS	YESTS	**EVEN**	SEXED
EREVS	KEROS	ZESTS	EEVEN	VEXED
ERGO	WEROS	**ETAS**	SEVEN	WEXED
ERGON	ZEROS	BETAS	YEVEN	YEXED
ERGOS	EROSE	FETAS	EVENS	**EXES**
ERGOT	**ERRS**	GETAS	EVENT	DEXES
ERGS	SERRS	KETAS	**EVER**	HEXES
BERGS	**ERST**	WETAS	BEVER	KEXES

LEXES	**FADE**	FARDS	FAZED	FENTS
REXES	FADED	**FARE**	FAZES	**FEOD**
SEXES	FADER	FARED	**FEAL**	FEODS
TEXES	FADES	FARER	FEALS	**FERE**
VEXES	**FADO**	FARES	**FEAR**	YFERE
WEXES	FADOS	**FARL**	AFEAR	FERER
YEXES	**FAFF**	FARLE	FEARE	FERES
ZEXES	FAFFS	FARLS	FEARS	**FERM**
EXIT	FAFFY	**FARM**	FEART	FERMI
EXITS	**FAIK**	FARMS	**FEAT**	FERMS
EXON	FAIKS	**FARO**	FEATS	**FERN**
EXONS	**FAIL**	FAROS	**FECK**	FERNS
EXPO	FAILS	**FARS**	FECKS	FERNY
EXPOS	**FAIN**	AFARS	**FEEB**	**FESS**
EXUL	FAINE	FARSE	FEEBS	FESSE
EXULS	FAINS	**FART**	**FEED**	**FEST**
EXULT	FAINT	FARTS	FEEDS	FESTA
EYAS	**FAIR**	**FAST**	**FEEL**	FESTS
EYASS	FAIRS	FASTI	FEELS	FESTY
EYED	FAIRY	FASTS	**FEEN**	**FETA**
FEYED	**FAKE**	**FATE**	FEENS	FETAL
HEYED	FAKED	FATED	**FEER**	FETAS
KEYED	FAKER	FATES	FEERS	**FETE**
EYEN	FAKES	**FATS**	**FEES**	FETED
SEYEN	FAKEY	FATSO	FEESE	FETES
EYER	**FALL**	**FAUN**	**FEHM**	**FETT**
FEYER	FALLS	FAUNA	FEHME	FETTA
GEYER	**FAME**	FAUNS	**FEIS**	FETTS
KEYER	FAMED	**FAUR**	FEIST	**FEUD**
EYERS	FAMES	FAURD	**FELL**	FEUDS
EYOT	**FAND**	FAUT	FELLA	**FIAR**
EYOTS	FANDS	FAUTS	FELLS	FIARS
EYRA	**FANE**	**FAVA**	FELLY	**FIAT**
EYRAS	FANES	FAVAS	**FELT**	FIATS
EYRE	**FANG**	**FAVE**	FELTS	**FICE**
EYRES	FANGA	FAVEL	FELTY	FICES
FACE	FANGO	FAVER	**FEME**	**FICO**
FACED	FANGS	FAVES	FEMES	FICOS
FACER	**FANK**	**FAWN**	**FEND**	**FIDO**
FACES	FANKS	FAWNS	FENDS	FIDOS
FACET	**FANO**	FAWNY	FENDY	**FIEF**
FACT	FANON	**FAYS**	FENI	FIEFS
FACTA	FANOS	OFAYS	FENIS	**FIER**
FACTS	**FARD**	**FAZE**	FENT	FIERE

FIERS	FIQHS	FLAMY	FLITE	**FOLK**
FIERY	**FIRE**	**FLAN**	FLITS	FOLKS
FIFE	AFIRE	FLANE	FLITT	FOLKY
FIFED	FIRED	FLANK	**FLOB**	**FOND**
FIFER	FIRER	FLANS	FLOBS	FONDA
FIFES	FIRES	**FLAP**	**FLOC**	FONDS
FIGO	**FIRK**	FLAPS	FLOCK	FONDU
FIGOS	FIRKS	**FLAT**	FLOCS	**FONT**
FIKE	**FIRM**	FLATS	**FLOE**	FONTS
FIKED	FIRMS	**FLAW**	FLOES	**FOOD**
FIKES	**FIRN**	FLAWN	**FLOG**	FOODS
FILA	FIRNS	FLAWS	FLOGS	FOODY
FILAR	**FIRS**	FLAWY	**FLOP**	**FOOL**
FILE	FIRST	**FLAX**	FLOPS	FOOLS
FILED	**FISC**	FLAXY	**FLOR**	**FOOT**
FILER	FISCS	**FLAY**	FLORA	AFOOT
FILES	**FISH**	FLAYS	FLORS	FOOTS
FILET	FISHY	**FLEA**	FLORY	FOOTY
FILK	**FISK**	FLEAM	**FLOW**	**FORA**
FILKS	FISKS	FLEAS	FLOWN	FORAM
FILL	**FIST**	**FLEE**	FLOWS	FORAY
FILLE	FISTS	FLEER	**FLUB**	**FORB**
FILLO	FISTY	FLEES	FLUBS	FORBS
FILLS	**FITT**	FLEET	**FLUE**	FORBY
FILLY	FITTE	**FLEG**	FLUED	**FORD**
FILM	FITTS	FLEGS	FLUES	FORDO
FILMI	**FIVE**	**FLEW**	FLUEY	FORDS
FILMS	FIVER	FLEWS	**FLUS**	**FORE**
FILMY	FIVES	**FLEX**	FLUSH	AFORE
FILO	**FIZZ**	FLEXO	**FOAL**	FOREL
FILOS	FIZZY	**FLEY**	FOALS	FORES
FIND	**FLAB**	FLEYS	**FOAM**	FOREX
FINDS	FLABS	**FLIC**	FOAMS	**FORK**
FINE	**FLAG**	FLICK	FOAMY	FORKS
FINED	OFLAG	FLICS	**FOHN**	FORKY
FINER	FLAGS	**FLIM**	FOHNS	**FORM**
FINES	**FLAK**	FLIMP	**FOID**	FORME
FINI	FLAKE	FLIMS	FOIDS	FORMS
FINIS	FLAKS	**FLIP**	**FOIL**	**FORT**
FINK	FLAKY	FLIPS	FOILS	FORTE
FINKS	**FLAM**	**FLIR**	**FOIN**	FORTH
FINO	FLAME	FLIRS	FOINS	FORTS
FINOS	FLAMM	FLIRT	**FOLD**	FORTY
FIQH	FLAMS	**FLIT**	FOLDS	**FOSS**

FOSSA	FRIST	FUMES	FYRDS	**GAMB**
FOSSE	**FRIT**	FUMET	**GADE**	GAMBA
FOUD	AFRIT	**FUND**	GADES	GAMBE
FOUDS	FRITH	FUNDI	**GADI**	GAMBO
FOUL	FRITS	FUNDS	GADID	GAMBS
AFOUL	FRITT	FUNDY	GADIS	**GAME**
FOULE	FRITZ	**FUNG**	**GADS**	GAMED
FOULS	**FRIZ**	FUNGI	EGADS	GAMER
FOUR	FRIZE	FUNGO	GADSO	GAMES
FOURS	FRIZZ	FUNGS	**GAFF**	GAMEY
FOWL	**FROE**	**FUNK**	GAFFE	**GAMP**
FOWLS	FROES	FUNKS	GAFFS	GAMPS
FRAB	**FROG**	FUNKY	**GAGE**	**GAMS**
FRABS	FROGS	**FURL**	GAGED	OGAMS
FRAG	**FROS**	FURLS	GAGER	**GANE**
FRAGS	AFROS	**FURR**	GAGES	GANEF
FRAP	FROSH	FURRS	**GAID**	GANEV
FRAPE	FROST	FURRY	GAIDS	**GANG**
FRAPS	**FROW**	**FUSE**	**GAIN**	GANGS
FRAS	FROWN	FUSED	AGAIN	**GANT**
FRASS	FROWS	FUSEE	GAINS	GANTS
FRAT	FROWY	FUSEL	**GAIR**	**GAOL**
FRATE	**FRUG**	FUSES	GAIRS	GAOLS
FRATI	FRUGS	**FUSK**	**GAIT**	**GAPE**
FRATS	**FUBS**	FUSKS	GAITA	AGAPE
FRAU	FUBSY	**FUSS**	GAITS	GAPED
FRAUD	**FUCK**	FUSSY	GAITT	GAPER
FRAUS	FUCKS	**FUST**	**GAJO**	GAPES
FRAY	**FUEL**	FUSTS	GAJOS	**GAPO**
FRAYS	FUELS	FUSTY	**GALA**	IGAPO
FREE	**FUFF**	**FUZE**	GALAH	GAPOS
FREED	FUFFS	FUZED	GALAS	**GARB**
FREER	FUFFY	FUZEE	GALAX	GARBE
FREES	**FUGU**	FUZES	**GALE**	GARBO
FREET	FUGUE	**FUZZ**	GALEA	GARBS
FRET	FUGUS	FUZZY	GALED	**GARE**
FRETS	**FUJI**	**FYCE**	GALES	GARES
FRIB	FUJIS	FYCES	**GALL**	**GARI**
FRIBS	**FULL**	**FYKE**	GALLS	GARIS
FRIG	FULLS	FYKED	GALLY	**GARS**
FRIGS	FULLY	FYKES	**GAMA**	AGARS
FRIS	**FUME**	**FYLE**	AGAMA	**GART**
FRISE	FUMED	FYLES	GAMAS	GARTH
FRISK	FUMER	**FYRD**	GAMAY	**GASP**

GASPS	GEALS	**GERM**	**GINK**	**GLED**
GASPY	**GEAN**	GERMS	GINKS	OGLED
GAST	GEANS	GERMY	**GINN**	GLEDE
AGAST	**GEAR**	**GERS**	GINNY	GLEDS
GASTS	GEARE	AGERS	**GIOS**	**GLEE**
GATE	GEARS	EGERS	AGIOS	AGLEE
AGATE	**GEAT**	**GEST**	**GIPS**	GLEED
GATED	GEATS	EGEST	GIPSY	GLEEK
GATER	**GECK**	GESTE	**GIRD**	GLEES
GATES	GECKO	GESTS	GIRDS	GLEET
GATH	GECKS	**GETA**	**GIRL**	**GLEI**
GATHS	**GEED**	GETAS	GIRLS	GLEIS
GAUD	OGEED	**GEUM**	GIRLY	**GLEN**
GAUDS	**GEEK**	GEUMS	**GIRN**	GLENS
GAUDY	GEEKS	**GHAT**	GIRNS	GLENT
GAUM	GEEKY	GHATS	**GIRO**	**GLEY**
GAUMS	**GEEP**	**GHEE**	GIRON	AGLEY
GAUMY	GEEPS	GHEES	GIROS	GLEYS
GAUN	**GEES**	**GIBE**	**GIRR**	**GLIA**
GAUNT	OGEES	GIBED	GIRRS	GLIAL
GAUP	GEESE	GIBEL	**GIRT**	GLIAS
GAUPS	GEEST	GIBER	GIRTH	**GLIB**
GAUR	**GEIT**	GIBES	GIRTS	GLIBS
GAURS	GEITS	**GIFT**	**GISM**	**GLID**
GAUS	**GELD**	GIFTS	AGISM	GLIDE
GAUSS	GELDS	**GIGA**	GISMO	**GLIM**
GAVE	**GELT**	GIGAS	GISMS	GLIME
AGAVE	GELTS	**GILA**	**GIST**	GLIMS
GAVEL	**GENA**	AGILA	AGIST	**GLIT**
GAWD	GENAL	GILAS	GISTS	GLITS
GAWDS	GENAS	**GILD**	**GITE**	GLITZ
GAWK	**GENE**	GILDS	GITES	**GLOB**
GAWKS	AGENE	**GILL**	**GIVE**	GLOBE
GAWKY	GENES	GILLS	OGIVE	GLOBI
GAWP	GENET	GILLY	GIVED	GLOBS
GAWPS	**GENT**	**GILT**	GIVEN	GLOBY
GAWS	AGENT	GILTS	GIVER	**GLOM**
GAWSY	GENTS	**GIMP**	GIVES	GLOMS
GAZE	GENTY	GIMPS	**GLAD**	**GLOP**
AGAZE	**GENU**	GIMPY	GLADE	GLOPS
GAZED	GENUA	**GING**	GLADS	**GLOW**
GAZER	GENUS	AGING	GLADY	AGLOW
GAZES	**GERE**	GINGE	**GLAM**	GLOWS
GEAL	GERES	GINGS	GLAMS	**GLUE**

GLUED	**GOFF**	GOONS	**GOWK**	GRIDS
GLUER	GOFFS	GOONY	GOWKS	**GRIG**
GLUES	**GOGO**	**GOOP**	**GOWL**	GRIGS
GLUEY	GOGOS	GOOPS	GOWLS	**GRIM**
GLUG	**GOJI**	GOOPY	**GOWN**	GRIME
GLUGS	GOJIS	**GOOR**	GOWNS	GRIMY
GLUM	**GOLD**	GOORS	**GRAB**	**GRIN**
GLUME	GOLDS	GOORY	GRABS	AGRIN
GLUMS	GOLDY	**GOOS**	**GRAD**	GRIND
GLUT	**GOLE**	GOOSE	GRADE	GRINS
GLUTE	GOLEM	GOOSY	GRADS	**GRIP**
GLUTS	GOLES	**GORA**	**GRAM**	GRIPE
GNAR	**GOLF**	AGORA	GRAMA	GRIPS
GNARL	GOLFS	GORAL	GRAME	GRIPT
GNARR	**GOLP**	GORAS	GRAMP	GRIPY
GNARS	GOLPE	**GORE**	GRAMS	**GRIS**
GNAT	GOLPS	GORED	**GRAN**	GRISE
GNATS	**GONE**	GORES	GRANA	GRIST
GNAW	AGONE	**GORI**	GRAND	GRISY
GNAWN	GONEF	GORIS	GRANS	**GRIT**
GNAWS	GONER	**GORM**	GRANT	GRITH
GNOW	**GONG**	GORMS	**GRAT**	GRITS
GNOWS	GONGS	GORMY	GRATE	**GRIZ**
GOAD	**GONK**	**GORP**	**GRAV**	GRIZE
GOADS	GONKS	GORPS	GRAVE	**GROG**
GOAF	**GONS**	**GORS**	GRAVS	GROGS
GOAFS	AGONS	GORSE	GRAVY	**GROK**
GOAL	**GOOD**	GORSY	**GRAY**	GROKS
GOALS	AGOOD	**GOSH**	GRAYS	**GROT**
GOAT	GOODS	GOSHT	**GREE**	GROTS
GOATS	GOODY	**GOSS**	AGREE	**GROW**
GOATY	**GOOF**	GOSSE	GREED	GROWL
GOBI	GOOFS	**GOTH**	GREEK	GROWN
GOBIS	GOOFY	GOTHS	GREEN	GROWS
GOBO	**GOOG**	GOTHY	GREES	**GRRL**
GOBOS	GOOGS	**GOUK**	GREET	GRRLS
GODS	**GOOK**	GOUKS	**GREN**	**GRUB**
GODSO	GOOKS	**GOUT**	GRENS	GRUBS
GOEL	GOOKY	GOUTS	**GREW**	**GRUE**
GOELS	**GOOL**	GOUTY	GREWS	GRUED
GOER	GOOLD	**GOWD**	**GREY**	GRUEL
GOERS	GOOLS	GOWDS	GREYS	GRUES
GOES	GOOLY	**GOWF**	**GRID**	**GRUM**
GOEST	**GOON**	GOWFS	GRIDE	GRUME

GRUMP	GUNGE	GYTES	SHAHS	**HALM**
GUAN	GUNGY	**GYVE**	**HAIK**	SHALM
GUANA	**GUNK**	GYVED	HAIKA	HALMA
GUANO	GUNKS	GYVES	HAIKS	HALMS
GUANS	GUNKY	**HAAF**	HAIKU	**HALO**
GUAR	**GURL**	HAAFS	**HAIL**	HALON
GUARD	GURLS	**HAAR**	HAILS	HALOS
GUARS	GURLY	HAARS	HAILY	**HALT**
GUCK	**GURN**	**HABU**	**HAIN**	SHALT
GUCKS	GURNS	HABUS	CHAIN	HALTS
GUCKY	**GURS**	**HACK**	HAINS	**HAME**
GUDE	GURSH	CHACK	HAINT	SHAME
GUDES	**GURU**	SHACK	**HAIR**	HAMED
GUES	GURUS	THACK	CHAIR	HAMES
AGUES	**GUSH**	WHACK	HAIRS	**HAMS**
GUESS	GUSHY	HACKS	HAIRY	CHAMS
GUEST	**GUST**	**HADE**	**HAJI**	SHAMS
GUFF	GUSTO	SHADE	BHAJI	WHAMS
GUFFS	GUSTS	HADED	HAJIS	**HAND**
GUGA	GUSTY	HADES	**HAJJ**	SHAND
GUGAS	**GUTS**	**HADJ**	HAJJI	HANDS
GUID	GUTSY	HADJI	**HAKA**	HANDY
GUIDE	**GUYS**	**HADS**	HAKAM	**HANG**
GUIDS	GUYSE	CHADS	HAKAS	BHANG
GULA	**GYAL**	SHADS	**HAKE**	CHANG
GULAG	GYALS	HADST	SHAKE	PHANG
GULAR	**GYBE**	**HAEM**	HAKEA	THANG
GULAS	GYBED	HAEMS	HAKES	WHANG
GULE	GYBES	**HAET**	**HAKU**	HANGI
GULES	**GYMP**	HAETS	HAKUS	HANGS
GULET	GYMPS	**HAFF**	**HALE**	**HANK**
GULF	**GYNO**	CHAFF	SHALE	CHANK
GULFS	GYNOS	HAFFS	THALE	SHANK
GULFY	**GYPO**	**HAFT**	WHALE	THANK
GULL	GYPOS	CHAFT	HALED	HANKS
GULLS	**GYPS**	SHAFT	HALER	HANKY
GULLY	GYPSY	HAFTS	HALES	**HANT**
GULP	**GYRE**	**HAGG**	**HALF**	CHANT
GULPH	GYRED	HAGGS	HALFA	HANTS
GULPS	GYRES	**HAGS**	HALFS	**HAOS**
GULPY	**GYRO**	SHAGS	**HALL**	CHAOS
GUMP	GYRON	**HAHA**	SHALL	**HAPS**
GUMPS	GYROS	HAHAS	HALLO	CHAPS
GUNG	**GYTE**	**HAHS**	HALLS	SHAPS

WHAPS	**HASP**	SHAWM	HEBES	**HEME**
HAPU	HASPS	HAWMS	**HECH**	RHEME
HAPUS	**HAST**	**HAWS**	HECHT	THEME
HARD	GHAST	CHAWS	**HECK**	HEMES
CHARD	HASTA	SHAWS	CHECK	**HEMP**
SHARD	HASTE	THAWS	HECKS	HEMPS
HARDS	HASTY	HAWSE	**HEED**	HEMPY
HARDY	**HATE**	**HAYS**	THEED	**HEMS**
HARE	HATED	CHAYS	HEEDS	CHEMS
CHARE	HATER	SHAYS	HEEDY	**HEND**
PHARE	HATES	**HAZE**	**HEEL**	SHEND
SHARE	**HATH**	HAZED	HEEL	HENDS
WHARE	HATHA	HAZEL	SHEEL	**HENS**
HARED	**HATS**	HAZER	WHEEL	THENS
HAREM	CHATS	HAZES	HEELS	WHENS
HARES	GHATS	**HEAD**	**HEFT**	**HENT**
HARK	KHATS	AHEAD	THEFT	AHENT
CHARK	WHATS	HEADS	WHEFT	SHENT
SHARK	**HAUD**	HEADY	HEFTE	HENTS
HARKS	HAUDS	**HEAL**	HEFTS	**HERB**
HARL	**HAUF**	SHEAL	HEFTY	HERBS
HARLS	HAUFS	WHEAL	**HEID**	HERBY
HARM	**HAUL**	HEALD	HEIDS	**HERD**
CHARM	SHAUL	HEALS	**HEIL**	SHERD
PHARM	HAULD	**HEAP**	HEILS	HERDS
THARM	HAULM	AHEAP	**HEIR**	**HERE**
HARMS	HAULS	CHEAP	THEIR	CHERE
HARN	HAULT	HEAPS	HEIRS	SHERE
SHARN	**HAUN**	HEAPY	**HELE**	THERE
HARNS	HAUNS	**HEAR**	HELED	WHERE
HARO	HAUNT	SHEAR	HELES	HERES
HAROS	**HAUT**	WHEAR	**HELL**	**HERL**
HARP	GHAUT	HEARD	SHELL	HERLS
SHARP	HAUTE	HEARE	HELLO	**HERM**
HARPS	**HAVE**	HEARS	HELLS	THERM
HARPY	CHAVE	HEART	**HELM**	HERMA
HART	SHAVE	**HEAT**	WHELM	HERMS
CHART	HAVEN	CHEAT	HELMS	**HERN**
HARTS	HAVER	WHEAT	**HELO**	HERNS
HASH	HAVES	HEATH	HELOS	**HERO**
SHASH	**HAWK**	HEATS	HELOT	SHERO
HASHY	CHAWK	**HEBE**	**HELP**	HERON
HASK	HAWKS	THEBE	CHELP	HEROS
HASKS	**HAWM**	HEBEN	WHELP	**HERS**

HERSE	**HIGH**	AHINT	HOARY	HOLED
HERY	AHIGH	HINTS	**HOAS**	HOLES
HERYE	THIGH	**HIOI**	HOAST	HOLEY
HESP	HIGHS	HIOIS	**HOBO**	**HOLK**
THESP	HIGHT	**HIPS**	HOBOS	HOLKS
HESPS	**HIKE**	CHIPS	**HOCK**	**HOLM**
HEST	HIKED	SHIPS	CHOCK	HOLME
CHEST	HIKER	WHIPS	SHOCK	HOLMS
GHEST	HIKES	**HIPT**	HOCKS	**HOLO**
HESTS	**HILA**	WHIPT	**HOED**	CHOLO
HETE	HILAR	**HIRE**	**HOER**	HOLON
THETE	**HILD**	SHIRE	SHOER	HOLOS
HETES	CHILD	HIRED	HOERS	**HOLS**
HETH	**HILI**	HIREE	**HOES**	DHOLS
CHETH	CHILI	HIRER	SHOES	**HOLT**
KHETH	**HILL**	HIRES	**HOGG**	HOLTS
HETHS	CHILL	**HISH**	HOGGS	**HOMA**
HETS	SHILL	PHISH	**HOGH**	HOMAS
KHETS	THILL	SHISH	HOGHS	**HOME**
SHETS	HILLO	WHISH	**HOGS**	HOMED
WHETS	HILLS	**HISS**	CHOGS	HOMER
HEWN	HILLY	WHISS	SHOGS	HOMES
SHEWN	**HILT**	HISSY	**HOIK**	HOMEY
HEWS	HILTS	**HIST**	HOIKS	**HOMO**
CHEWS	**HIMS**	SHIST	**HOIS**	ZHOMO
SHEWS	SHIMS	WHIST	**HOISE**	HOMOS
THEWS	WHIMS	HISTS	HOISE	**HOND**
WHEWS	**HIND**	**HITS**	HOIST	HONDA
HEYS	AHIND	CHITS	**HOKA**	HONDS
WHEYS	HINDS	SHITS	HOKAS	**HONE**
HICK	**HING**	WHITS	**HOKE**	OHONE
CHICK	AHING	**HIVE**	CHOKE	PHONE
THICK	CHING	CHIVE	HOKED	RHONE
HICKS	EHING	SHIVE	HOKES	SHONE
HIDE	OHING	HIVED	HOKEY	HONED
CHIDE	THING	HIVER	**HOKI**	HONER
HIDED	HINGE	HIVES	HOKIS	HONES
HIDER	HINGS	**HIZZ**	**HOLD**	HONEY
HIDES	**HINS**	CHIZZ	AHOLD	**HONG**
HIED	CHINS	PHIZZ	HOLDS	THONG
SHIED	SHINS	WHIZZ	**HOLE**	HONGI
HIES	THINS	**HOAR**	DHOLE	HONGS
RHIES	WHINS	HOARD	THOLE	**HONK**
SHIES	**HINT**	HOARS	WHOLE	HONKS

HONKY	HORAL	**HOUR**	HUFFS	SHUNS
HONS	HORAS	HOURI	HUFFY	**HUNT**
CHONS	**HORE**	HOURS	**HUGE**	SHUNT
PHONS	CHORE	**HOUT**	HUGER	HUNTS
HOOD	SHORE	CHOUT	**HUGS**	**HUPS**
HOODS	WHORE	SHOUT	CHUGS	WHUPS
HOODY	**HORI**	HOUTS	THUGS	**HURL**
HOOF	HORIS	**HOVE**	**HUHU**	CHURL
CHOOF	**HORK**	SHOVE	HUHUS	THURL
WHOOF	HORKS	HOVEA	**HUIA**	HURLS
HOOFS	**HORN**	HOVED	HUIAS	HURLY
HOOK	SHORN	HOVEL	**HULA**	**HURT**
CHOOK	THORN	HOVEN	HULAS	HURTS
SHOOK	HORNS	HOVER	**HULE**	**HUSH**
HOOKA	HORNY	HOVES	SHULE	SHUSH
HOOKS	**HORS**	**HOWE**	HULES	HUSHY
HOOKY	KHORS	HOWES	**HULK**	**HUSK**
HOON	HORSE	**HOWF**	HULKS	HUSKS
CHOON	HORST	HOWFF	HULKY	HUSKY
SHOON	HORSY	HOWFS	**HULL**	**HUSO**
HOONS	**HOSE**	**HOWK**	AHULL	HUSOS
HOOP	CHOSE	CHOWK	HULLO	**HUSS**
WHOOP	THOSE	HOWKS	HULLS	HUSSY
HOOPS	WHOSE	**HOWL**	HULLY	**HUTS**
HOOR	HOSED	THOWL	**HUMA**	BHUTS
HOORD	HOSEL	HOWLS	HUMAN	CHUTS
HOORS	HOSEN	**HOWS**	HUMAS	PHUTS
HOOT	HOSER	CHOWS	**HUMF**	SHUTS
BHOOT	HOSES	DHOWS	HUMFS	**HWYL**
SHOOT	HOSEY	SHOWS	**HUMP**	HWYLS
WHOOT	**HOST**	WHOWS	CHUMP	**HYEN**
HOOTS	GHOST	HOWSO	THUMP	HYENA
HOOTY	HOSTA	**HOYA**	WHUMP	HYENS
HOPE	HOSTS	HOYAS	HUMPH	**HYKE**
SHOPE	**HOTE**	**HUBS**	HUMPS	HYKES
HOPED	SHOTE	CHUBS	HUMPY	**HYLA**
HOPER	HOTEL	**HUCK**	**HUMS**	PHYLA
HOPES	HOTEN	CHUCK	CHUMS	HYLAS
HOPS	**HOTS**	SHUCK	**HUNK**	**HYLE**
CHOPS	PHOTS	HUCKS	CHUNK	CHYLE
SHOPS	SHOTS	**HUER**	THUNK	PHYLE
WHOPS	**HOUF**	HUERS	HUNKS	HYLEG
HORA	HOUFF	**HUFF**	HUNKY	HYLES
HORAH	HOUFS	CHUFF	**HUNS**	**HYMN**

HYMNS	KICKY	**IGLU**	YILLS	DINGO
HYPE	MICKY	IGLUS	ZILLS	JINGO
HYPED	PICKY	**IKAN**	**ILLY**	LINGO
HYPER	SICKY	IKANS	BILLY	PINGO
HYPES	TICKY	**IKAT**	DILLY	INGOT
HYPO	WICKY	IKATS	FILLY	**INGS**
HYPOS	**ICON**	**IKON**	GILLY	BINGS
IAMB	ICONS	EIKON	HILLY	DINGS
IAMBI	**IDEA**	IKONS	SILLY	GINGS
IAMBS	IDEAL	**ILEA**	TILLY	HINGS
IBEX	IDEAS	PILEA	WILLY	KINGS
VIBEX	**IDEE**	ILEAC	**IMAM**	LINGS
ICED	IDEES	ILEAL	IMAMS	MINGS
DICED	**IDES**	**ILEX**	**IMID**	PINGS
RICED	AIDES	SILEX	TIMID	RINGS
TICED	BIDES	**ILIA**	IMIDE	SINGS
VICED	CIDES	CILIA	IMIDO	TINGS
ICER	FIDES	MILIA	IMIDS	WINGS
DICER	HIDES	ILIAC	**IMMY**	ZINGS
NICER	NIDES	ILIAD	JIMMY	**INKS**
RICER	RIDES	ILIAL	**IMPI**	BINKS
ICERS	SIDES	**ILKS**	IMPIS	DINKS
ICES	TIDES	BILKS	**IMPS**	FINKS
BICES	WIDES	FILKS	DIMPS	GINKS
DICES	**IDLE**	MILKS	GIMPS	JINKS
FICES	SIDLE	SILKS	LIMPS	KINKS
RICES	IDLED	**ILLS**	NIMPS	LINKS
SICES	IDLER	BILLS	PIMPS	**MINKS**
TICES	IDLES	CILLS	SIMPS	OINKS
VICES	**IDOL**	DILLS	TIMPS	PINKS
ICKS	IDOLA	FILLS	WIMPS	RINKS
DICKS	IDOLS	GILLS	**INBY**	SINKS
HICKS	**IDYL**	HILLS	INBYE	TINKS
KICKS	IDYLL	JILLS	**INCH**	WINKS
LICKS	IDYLS	KILLS	CINCH	**INKY**
MICKS	**IFFY**	LILLS	FINCH	DINKY
NICKS	BIFFY	MILLS	GINCH	HINKY
PICKS	JIFFY	NILLS	LINCH	KINKY
RICKS	MIFFY	PILLS	PINCH	LINKY
SICKS	NIFFY	RILLS	WINCH	PINKY
TICKS	**IGGS**	SILLS	**INFO**	SINKY
WICKS	BIGGS	TILLS	INFOS	ZINKY
ICKY	MIGGS	VILLS	**INGO**	**INNS**
DICKY	RIGGS	WILLS	BINGO	JINNS

LINNS	LIRKS	ITEMS	JARKS	JEONS
WINNS	MIRKS	**IWIS**	**JARL**	**JERK**
INTI	YIRKS	KIWIS	JARLS	JERKS
INTIL	**IRON**	**IXIA**	JARP	JERKY
INTIS	GIRON	IXIAS	JARPS	**JESS**
INTO	IRONE	**IZAR**	**JASP**	JESSE
PINTO	IRONS	SIZAR	JASPE	**JEST**
IONS	IRONY	IZARD	JASPS	JESTS
CIONS	**ISBA**	IZARS	**JATO**	**JETE**
LIONS	ISBAS	**JAAP**	JATOS	JETES
PIONS	**ISIT**	JAAPS	**JAUK**	**JIAO**
IOTA	VISIT	**JACK**	JAUKS	JIAOS
BIOTA	**ISLE**	JACKS	**JAUP**	**JIBB**
DIOTA	AISLE	JACKY	JAUPS	JIBBA
IOTAS	LISLE	**JADE**	**JAVA**	JIBBS
IRED	ISLED	JADED	JAVAS	**JIBE**
AIRED	ISLES	JADES	**JAZZ**	JIBED
FIRED	ISLET	**JAFA**	JAZZY	JIBER
HIRED	**ISMS**	JAFAS	**JEAN**	JIBES
MIRED	GISMS	**JAGA**	JEANS	**JIFF**
SIRED	JISMS	JAGAS	**JEAT**	JIFFS
TIRED	**ISNA**	**JAGG**	JEATS	JIFFY
VIRED	ISNAE	JAGGS	**JEDI**	**JILL**
WIRED	**ISOS**	JAGGY	JEDIS	JILLS
IRES	MISOS	**JAIL**	**JEEL**	**JILT**
CIRES	PISOS	JAILS	JEELS	JILTS
FIRES	**ITAS**	**JAKE**	JEELY	**JIMP**
HIRES	DITAS	JAKES	**JEEP**	JIMPY
MIRES	LITAS	JAKEY	JEEPS	**JINK**
SIRES	PITAS	**JAMB**	**JEER**	JINKS
TIRES	VITAS	JAMBE	JEERS	**JINN**
VIRES	**ITCH**	JAMBO	**JEEZ**	DJINN
WIRES	AITCH	JAMBS	JEEZE	JINNE
IRID	BITCH	JAMBU	**JEFE**	JINNI
MIRID	DITCH	**JANE**	JEFES	JINNS
VIRID	FITCH	JANES	**JEFF**	**JINS**
IRIDS	GITCH	**JANN**	JEFFS	DJINS
IRIS	HITCH	JANNS	**JEHU**	**JIRD**
SIRIS	MITCH	JANNY	JEHUS	JIRDS
IRKS	PITCH	**JAPE**	**JELL**	**JISM**
BIRKS	TITCH	JAPED	JELLO	JISMS
DIRKS	WITCH	JAPER	JELLS	**JIVE**
FIRKS	ITCHY	JAPES	JELLY	JIVED
KIRKS	**ITEM**	**JARK**	**JEON**	JIVER

JIVES	JOURS	**KADE**	**KANE**	KAWAS
JIVEY	**JOWL**	KADES	KANEH	KAWAU
JOBE	JOWLS	**KADI**	KANES	**KAWS**
JOBED	JOWLY	KADIS	**KANG**	SKAWS
JOBES	**JUBA**	**KAGO**	KANGA	**KAYO**
JOCK	JUBAS	KAGOS	KANGS	KAYOS
JOCKO	**JUBE**	**KAGU**	**KANS**	**KAYS**
JOCKS	JUBES	KAGUS	IKANS	OKAYS
JOCKY	**JUCO**	**KAID**	**KANT**	**KAZI**
JOCO	JUCOS	KAIDS	KANTS	KAZIS
JOCOS	**JUDO**	**KAIE**	**KAON**	**KBAR**
JOEY	JUDOS	KAIES	KAONS	KBARS
JOEYS	**JUGA**	**KAIF**	**KAPA**	**KECK**
JOHN	AJUGA	KAIFS	KAPAS	KECKS
JOHNS	JUGAL	**KAIK**	**KAPH**	**KEDS**
JOIN	**JUJU**	KAIKA	KAPHS	SKEDS
JOINS	JUJUS	KAIKS	**KAPU**	**KEEF**
JOINT	**JUKE**	**KAIL**	KAPUS	SKEEF
JOKE	JUKED	SKAIL	KAPUT	KEEFS
JOKED	JUKES	KAILS	**KARA**	**KEEK**
JOKER	**JUKU**	**KAIM**	KARAS	KEEKS
JOKES	JUKUS	KAIMS	KARAT	**KEEL**
JOKEY	**JUMP**	**KAIN**	**KARK**	KEELS
JOLE	JUMPS	KAING	KARKS	**KEEN**
JOLED	JUMPY	KAINS	**KARN**	SKEEN
JOLES	**JUNK**	**KAKA**	KARNS	KEENO
JOLL	JUNKS	KAKAS	**KARO**	KEENS
JOLLS	JUNKY	**KAKI**	KAROO	**KEEP**
JOLLY	**JUPE**	KAKIS	KAROS	KEEPS
JOLT	JUPES	**KALE**	**KART**	**KEET**
JOLTS	**JURA**	KALES	SKART	SKEET
JOLTY	JURAL	**KALI**	KARTS	KEETS
JOMO	JURAT	KALIF	**KATA**	**KEGS**
JOMON	**JURE**	KALIS	KATAL	SKEGS
JOMOS	JUREL	**KAMA**	KATAS	**KEIR**
JONG	JURES	KAMAS	**KATI**	KEIRS
JONGS	**JUST**	**KAME**	KATIS	**KELL**
JOOK	JUSTS	KAMES	**KATS**	SKELL
JOOKS	**JUTE**	**KAMI**	IKATS	KELLS
JOTA	JUTES	KAMIK	SKATS	KELLY
JOTAS	**JUVE**	KAMIS	**KAVA**	**KELP**
JOUK	JUVES	**KANA**	KAVAL	SKELP
JOUKS	**KACK**	KANAE	KAVAS	KELPS
JOUR	KACKS	KANAS	**KAWA**	KELPY

KELT	**KHAT**	KINDA	**KIWI**	KOELS
KELTS	KHATS	KINDS	KIWIS	**KOFF**
KELTY	**KHET**	KINDY	**KLAP**	SKOFF
KEMB	KHETH	**KINE**	KLAPS	KOFFS
KEMBO	KHETS	KINES	**KLIK**	**KOHA**
KEMBS	**KHOR**	**KING**	KLIKS	KOHAS
KEMP	KHORS	AKING	**KNAG**	**KOHL**
KEMPS	**KHUD**	EKING	KNAGS	KOHLS
KEMPT	KHUDS	KINGS	**KNAP**	**KOJI**
KEMPY	**KIBE**	**KINK**	KNAPS	KOJIS
KENO	KIBEI	SKINK	**KNAR**	**KOKA**
KENOS	KIBES	KINKS	KNARL	KOKAM
KENS	**KICK**	KINKY	KNARS	KOKAS
SKENS	KICKS	**KINO**	**KNEE**	**KOLA**
KENT	KICKY	KINOS	KNEED	KOLAS
KENTE	**KIDS**	**KINS**	KNEEL	**KOLO**
KENTS	SKIDS	SKINS	KNEES	KOLOS
KEPI	**KIEF**	**KIPE**	**KNIT**	**KOND**
KEPIS	KIEFS	KIPES	KNITS	KONDO
KEPS	**KIER**	**KIPP**	**KNOB**	**KONK**
SKEPS	SKIER	KIPPA	KNOBS	KONKS
KERB	KIERS	KIPPS	**KNOP**	**KONS**
KERBS	**KIEV**	**KIPS**	KNOPS	IKONS
KERF	KIEVE	SKIPS	**KNOT**	**KOOK**
KERFS	KIEVS	**KIRK**	KNOTS	KOOKS
KERN	**KIFF**	KIRKS	**KNOW**	KOOKY
KERNE	SKIFF	**KIRN**	KNOWE	**KOPH**
KERNS	**KIKE**	KIRNS	KNOWN	KOPHS
KERO	KIKES	**KISS**	KNOWS	**KORA**
KEROS	**KILL**	KISSY	**KNUB**	KORAI
KEST	SKILL	**KIST**	KNUBS	KORAS
KESTS	KILLS	KISTS	**KNUR**	KORAT
KETA	**KILN**	**KITE**	KNURL	**KORE**
KETAS	KILNS	SKITE	KNURR	KORES
KETE	**KILO**	KITED	KNURS	**KORO**
KETES	KILOS	KITER	**KNUT**	KOROS
KETO	**KILP**	KITES	KNUTS	**KORU**
KETOL	KILPS	**KITH**	**KOAN**	KORUN
KETS	**KILT**	KITHE	KOANS	KORUS
SKETS	KILTS	KITHS	**KOAP**	**KOTO**
KHAF	KILTY	**KITS**	KOAPS	KOTOS
KHAFS	**KINA**	SKITS	**KOBO**	KOTOW
KHAN	**KIND**	**KIVA**	KOBOS	**KRAB**
KHANS	KIND	KIVAS	**KOEL**	KRABS

KRAI	KYLES	GLADY	LALLS	SLANG
KRAIS	**KYND**	**LAER**	**LAMA**	**LANK**
KRAIT	KYNDE	BLAER	LLAMA	BLANK
KRAY	KYNDS	LAERS	ULAMA	CLANK
KRAYS	**KYPE**	**LAGS**	LAMAS	FLANK
KSAR	KYPES	BLAGS	**LAMB**	PLANK
KSARS	**KYTE**	CLAGS	LAMBS	SLANK
KUDO	SKYTE	FLAGS	LAMBY	LANKS
KUDOS	KYTES	SLAGS	**LAME**	LANKY
KUDU	**LABS**	**LAHS**	BLAME	**LANT**
KUDUS	BLABS	BLAHS	CLAME	ALANT
KUFI	FLABS	**LAIC**	FLAME	PLANT
KUFIS	SLABS	LAICH	LAMED	SLANT
KUIA	**LACE**	LAICS	LAMER	LANTS
KUIAS	GLACE	**LAID**	LAMES	**LAPS**
KUKU	PLACE	PLAID	**LAMP**	ALAPS
KUKUS	LACED	SLAID	CLAMP	CLAPS
KULA	LACER	LAIDS	LAMPS	FLAPS
KULAK	LACES	**LAIK**	**LAMS**	KLAPS
KULAN	LACET	GLAIK	BLAMS	PLAPS
KULAS	LACEY	LAIKA	CLAMS	SLAPS
KURI	**LACK**	LAIKS	FLAMS	LAPSE
KURIS	ALACK	**LAIN**	GLAMS	**LARD**
KURU	BLACK	BLAIN	SLAMS	LARDS
KURUS	CLACK	ELAIN	**LANA**	LARDY
KUTA	FLACK	PLAIN	LANAI	**LARE**
KUTAS	PLACK	SLAIN	LANAS	BLARE
KUTI	SLACK	**LAIR**	**LAND**	FLARE
KUTIS	LACKS	FLAIR	ALAND	GLARE
KUTU	**LADE**	GLAIR	BLAND	LAREE
KUTUS	BLADE	LAIRD	ELAND	LARES
KUZU	CLADE	LAIRS	GLAND	**LARI**
KUZUS	GLADE	LAIRY	LANDE	LARIS
KVAS	SLADE	**LAKE**	LANDS	**LARK**
KVASS	LADED	FLAKE	**LANE**	LARKS
KYAK	LADEN	SLAKE	ALANE	LARKY
KYAKS	LADER	LAKED	FLANE	**LARN**
KYAR	LADES	LAKER	PLANE	LARNS
KYARS	**LADS**	LAKES	SLANE	LARNT
KYAT	BLADS	**LAKH**	LANES	**LASE**
KYATS	CLADS	LAKHS	**LANG**	BLASE
KYBO	GLADS	**LAKY**	ALANG	LASED
KYBOS	**LADY**	FLAKY	CLANG	LASER
KYLE	BLADY	**LALL**	KLANG	LASES

LASH	**LAUF**	LEAFS	**LEED**	LEISH
BLASH	LAUFS	LEAFY	BLEED	**LEME**
CLASH	**LAVA**	**LEAK**	GLEED	FLEME
FLASH	FLAVA	BLEAK	**LEEK**	LEMED
PLASH	LAVAS	LEAKS	CLEEK	LEMEL
SLASH	**LAVE**	LEAKY	GLEEK	LEMES
LASS	CLAVE	**LEAL**	SLEEK	**LEND**
CLASS	SLAVE	ILEAL	LEEKS	BLEND
GLASS	LAVED	**LEAM**	**LEEP**	LENDS
LASSI	LAVER	FLEAM	BLEEP	**LENG**
LASSO	LAVES	GLEAM	CLEEP	LENGS
LASSU	**LAWK**	LEAMS	SLEEP	**LENO**
LASSY	LAWKS	**LEAN**	LEEPS	LENOS
LAST	**LAWN**	CLEAN	**LEER**	**LENS**
BLAST	BLAWN	GLEAN	FLEER	GLENS
CLAST	FLAWN	LEANS	SLEER	LENSE
PLAST	LAWNS	LEANT	LEERS	**LENT**
LASTS	LAWNY	LEANY	LEERY	BLENT
LATE	**LAWS**	**LEAP**	**LEES**	GLENT
ALATE	BLAWS	LEAPS	BLEES	OLENT
BLATE	CLAWS	LEAPT	FLEES	LENTI
ELATE	FLAWS	**LEAR**	GLEES	LENTO
PLATE	SLAWS	BLEAR	LEESE	**LEPT**
SLATE	**LAYS**	CLEAR	**LEET**	CLEPT
LATED	ALAYS	LEARE	FLEET	SLEPT
LATEN	BLAYS	LEARN	GLEET	LEPTA
LATER	CLAYS	LEARS	SLEET	**LERE**
LATEX	FLAYS	LEARY	LEETS	LERED
LATH	PLAYS	**LEAS**	**LEFT**	LERES
LATHE	SLAYS	FLEAS	ALEFT	**LERP**
LATHI	**LAZE**	PLEAS	CLEFT	LERPS
LATHS	BLAZE	LEASE	LEFTE	**LESS**
LATHY	GLAZE	LEASH	LEFTS	BLESS
LATS	LAZED	LEAST	LEFTY	**LEST**
BLATS	LAZES	**LEAT**	**LEGS**	BLEST
CLATS	**LAZO**	BLEAT	CLEGS	LESTS
FLATS	LAZOS	CLEAT	FLEGS	**LETS**
PLATS	**LAZY**	PLEAT	**LEHR**	BLETS
SLATS	GLAZY	LEATS	LEHRS	**LEUD**
LATU	**LEAD**	**LECH**	**LEIR**	LEUDS
LATUS	PLEAD	BLECH	LEIRS	**LEVA**
LAUD	LEADS	**LEDE**	**LEIS**	LEVAS
BLAUD	LEADY	GLEDE	GLEIS	**LEVE**
LAUDS	**LEAF**	LEDES	VLEIS	CLEVE

LEVEE	FLIER	LIMBY	BLINK	LISKS
LEVEL	PLIER	**LIME**	CLINK	**LISP**
LEVER	SLIER	CLIME	PLINK	LISPS
LEVES	LIERS	GLIME	SLINK	**LIST**
LEYS	**LIES**	SLIME	LINKS	ALIST
BLEYS	CLIES	LIMED	LINKY	BLIST
FLEYS	FLIES	LIMEN	**LINN**	LISTS
GLEYS	PLIES	LIMES	LINNS	**LITE**
SLEYS	VLIES	LIMEY	LINNY	BLITE
LEZZ	**LIEU**	**LIMN**	**LINO**	ELITE
LEZZA	LIEUS	LIMNS	LINOS	FLITE
LEZZY	**LIFE**	**LIMO**	**LINS**	LITED
LIAR	LIFER	LIMOS	BLINS	LITER
LIARD	LIFES	**LIMP**	**LINT**	LITES
LIARS	**LIFT**	BLIMP	CLINT	**LITH**
LIART	CLIFT	FLIMP	ELINT	LITHE
LIAS	GLIFT	LIMPA	FLINT	LITHO
ALIAS	LIFTS	LIMPS	GLINT	LITHS
GLIAS	**LIKE**	**LIMY**	LINTS	**LITS**
LIBS	ALIKE	BLIMY	LINTY	BLITS
GLIBS	GLIKE	SLIMY	**LINY**	CLITS
LICE	YLIKE	**LIND**	BLINY	FLITS
SLICE	LIKED	BLIND	**LION**	GLITS
LICH	LIKEN	LINDS	LIONS	SLITS
LICHI	LIKER	LINDY	**LIPA**	**LIVE**
LICHT	LIKES	**LINE**	LIPAS	ALIVE
LICK	**LILL**	ALINE	**LIPE**	BLIVE
CLICK	LILLS	CLINE	CLIPE	OLIVE
FLICK	**LILO**	LINED	SLIPE	SLIVE
KLICK	LILOS	LINEN	LIPES	LIVED
SLICK	**LILT**	LINER	**LIPO**	LIVEN
LICKS	LILTS	LINES	LIPOS	LIVER
LIDO	**LILY**	LINEY	**LIPS**	LIVES
LIDOS	SLILY	**LING**	BLIPS	**LOAD**
LIED	**LIMA**	BLING	CLIPS	LOADS
CLIED	LIMAN	CLING	FLIPS	**LOAF**
FLIED	LIMAS	FLING	SLIPS	LOAFS
PLIED	LIMAX	PLING	**LIRA**	**LOAM**
LIEF	**LIMB**	SLING	LIRAS	CLOAM
LIEFS	CLIMB	LINGA	**LIRK**	GLOAM
LIEN	LIMBA	LINGO	LIRKS	LOAMS
ALIEN	LIMBI	LINGS	**LISK**	LOAMY
LIENS	LIMBO	LINGY	FLISK	**LOAN**
LIER	LIMBS	**LINK**	GLISK	SLOAN

LOANS	**LOGO**	LONGE	CLOPS	**LOTI**
LOBE	LOGOI	LONGS	ELOPS	LOTIC
GLOBE	LOGON	**LOOF**	FLOPS	**LOTO**
LOBED	LOGOS	ALOOF	GLOPS	LOTOS
LOBES	**LOGS**	KLOOF	PLOPS	**LOTS**
LOBI	BLOGS	LOOFA	SLOPS	BLOTS
GLOBI	CLOGS	LOOFS	**LORD**	CLOTS
LOBO	FLOGS	**LOOK**	LORDS	PLOTS
LOBOS	SLOGS	BLOOK	LORDY	SLOTS
LOBS	VLOGS	PLOOK	**LORE**	LOTSA
BLOBS	**LOGY**	LOOKS	BLORE	**LOUD**
FLOBS	ELOGY	LOOKY	LOREL	ALOUD
GLOBS	OLOGY	**LOOM**	LORES	CLOUD
SLOBS	**LOID**	BLOOM	**LORY**	**LOUN**
LOCA	SLOID	GLOOM	FLORY	LOUND
LOCAL	LOIDS	SLOOM	GLORY	LOUNS
LOCH	**LOIN**	LOOMS	**LOSE**	**LOUP**
LOCHE	ALOIN	**LOON**	CLOSE	LOUPE
LOCHS	ELOIN	LOONS	LOSED	LOUPS
LOCI	LOINS	LOONY	LOSEL	**LOUR**
LOCIE	**LOIR**	**LOOP**	LOSEN	CLOUR
LOCIS	LOIRS	BLOOP	LOSER	FLOUR
LOCK	**LOKE**	CLOOP	LOSES	LOURE
BLOCK	BLOKE	GLOOP	**LOSH**	LOURS
CLOCK	CLOKE	SLOOP	FLOSH	LOURY
FLOCK	LOKES	LOOPS	SLOSH	**LOUS**
LOCKS	**LOLL**	LOOPY	**LOSS**	CLOUS
LOCO	LOLLS	**LOOR**	FLOSS	LOUSE
LOCOS	LOLLY	FLOOR	GLOSS	LOUSY
LODE	**LOMA**	LOORD	LOSSY	**LOUT**
GLODE	LOMAS	**LOOS**	**LOST**	CLOUT
LODEN	**LOME**	ALOOS	GLOST	FLOUT
LODES	LOMED	LOOSE	**LOTA**	GLOUT
LODS	LOMES	**LOOT**	FLOTA	LOUTS
ALODS	**LONE**	CLOOT	LOTAH	**LOVE**
CLODS	ALONE	SLOOT	LOTAS	CLOVE
PLODS	CLONE	LOOTS	**LOTE**	GLOVE
LOFT	LONER	**LOPE**	CLOTE	SLOVE
ALOFT	**LONG**	ELOPE	FLOTE	LOVED
LOFTS	ALONG	SLOPE	ZLOTE	LOVER
LOFTY	FLONG	LOPED	LOTES	LOVES
LOGE	KLONG	LOPER	**LOTH**	LOVEY
ELOGE	PLONG	LOPES	CLOTH	**LOWE**
LOGES	LONGA	**LOPS**	SLOTH	ALOWE

LOWED	BLUES	**LUNA**	LUSTY	MACHO
LOWER	CLUES	LUNAR	**LUTE**	MACHS
LOWES	FLUES	LUNAS	ELUTE	**MACK**
LOWN	GLUES	**LUNE**	FLUTE	SMACK
BLOWN	PLUES	LUNES	GLUTE	MACKS
CLOWN	SLUES	LUNET	LUTEA	**MACS**
FLOWN	**LUFF**	**LUNG**	LUTED	EMACS
LOWND	BLUFF	CLUNG	LUTER	**MAGE**
LOWNE	FLUFF	FLUNG	LUTES	IMAGE
LOWNS	PLUFF	SLUNG	**LUTZ**	MAGES
LOWP	SLUFF	LUNGE	KLUTZ	**MAGG**
LOWPS	LUFFA	LUNGI	**LUXE**	MAGGS
LOWS	LUFFS	LUNGS	LUXED	**MAGI**
BLOWS	**LUGE**	**LUNK**	LUXER	MAGIC
CLOWS	KLUGE	BLUNK	LUXES	**MAID**
FLOWS	LUGED	CLUNK	**LWEI**	MAIDS
GLOWS	LUGER	FLUNK	LWEIS	**MAIK**
PLOWS	LUGES	PLUNK	**LYAM**	SMAIK
SLOWS	**LUGS**	SLUNK	LYAMS	MAIKO
LOWSE	GLUGS	LUNKS	**LYME**	MAIKS
LOWT	PLUGS	**LUNT**	LYMES	**MAIL**
LOWTS	SLUGS	BLUNT	**LYNE**	EMAIL
LOYS	**LUIT**	LUNTS	LYNES	MAILE
CLOYS	SLUIT	**LURE**	**LYRE**	MAILL
PLOYS	**LUKE**	ALURE	LYRES	MAILS
LUAU	FLUKE	LURED	**LYSE**	**MAIM**
LUAUS	**LULL**	LURER	LYSED	MAIMS
LUBE	LULLS	LURES	LYSES	**MAIN**
LUBED	**LULU**	LUREX	**LYTE**	AMAIN
LUBES	LULUS	**LURK**	FLYTE	MAINS
LUCE	**LUMA**	LURKS	LYTED	**MAIR**
LUCES	LUMAS	**LURS**	LYTES	MAIRE
LUCK	**LUMP**	BLURS	**MAAR**	MAIRS
CLUCK	CLUMP	SLURS	MAARE	**MAKE**
PLUCK	FLUMP	**LUSH**	MAARS	MAKER
LUCKS	PLUMP	BLUSH	**MABE**	MAKES
LUCKY	SLUMP	FLUSH	MABES	**MAKI**
LUDE	LUMPS	PLUSH	**MACE**	MAKIS
BLUDE	LUMPY	SLUSH	MACED	**MAKO**
ELUDE	**LUMS**	LUSHY	MACER	MAKOS
LUDES	ALUMS	**LUSK**	MACES	**MALA**
LUDO	GLUMS	LUSKS	**MACH**	MALAM
LUDOS	PLUMS	**LUST**	MACHE	MALAR
LUES	SLUMS	LUSTS	MACHI	MALAS

MALAX	MANOR	**MASK**	MAYAS	MEFFS
MALE	MANOS	MASKS	**MAYO**	**MEGA**
MALES	**MANS**	**MASS**	MAYOR	OMEGA
MALI	MANSE	AMASS	MAYOS	**MEIN**
MALIC	**MARA**	MASSA	**MAYS**	MEINS
MALIK	MARAE	MASSE	MAYST	MEINT
MALIS	MARAH	MASSY	**MAZE**	MEINY
MALL	MARAS	**MAST**	AMAZE	**MELA**
SMALL	**MARC**	MASTS	SMAZE	MELAS
MALLS	MARCH	MASTY	MAZED	**MELD**
MALM	MARCS	**MASU**	MAZER	MELDS
SMALM	**MARD**	MASUS	MAZES	**MELL**
MALMS	MARDY	**MATE**	MAZEY	SMELL
MALMY	**MARE**	AMATE	**MEAD**	MELLS
MALT	MARES	MATED	MEADS	**MELT**
SMALT	**MARG**	MATER	**MEAL**	SMELT
MALTS	MARGE	MATES	MEALS	MELTS
MALTY	MARGS	MATEY	MEALY	MELTY
MAMA	**MARK**	**MATH**	**MEAN**	**MEME**
MAMAS	MARKA	MATHS	MEANE	MEMES
MAMS	MARKS	**MATT**	MEANS	**MEMO**
IMAMS	**MARL**	MATTE	MEANT	MEMOS
MANA	MARLE	MATTS	MEANY	**MEND**
MANAS	MARLS	**MAUD**	**MEAT**	AMEND
MANAT	MARLY	MAUDS	MEATH	EMEND
MAND	**MARM**	**MAUL**	MEATS	MENDS
MANDI	SMARM	MAULS	MEATY	**MENE**
MANE	MARMS	**MAUN**	**MECH**	AMENE
MANEB	**MARS**	MAUND	MECHS	MENED
MANED	MARSE	**MAUT**	**MECK**	MENES
MANEH	MARSH	AMAUT	MECKS	**MENG**
MANES	**MART**	MAUTS	**MEED**	MENGE
MANET	SMART	**MAWK**	MEEDS	MENGS
MANG	MARTS	MAWKS	**MEEK**	**MENT**
MANGA	**MASA**	MAWKY	SMEEK	AMENT
MANGE	OMASA	**MAWN**	**MEER**	MENTA
MANGO	MASAS	MAWNS	AMEER	MENTO
MANGS	**MASE**	**MAWR**	EMEER	**MENU**
MANGY	MASED	MAWRS	MEERS	MENUS
MANI	MASER	**MAXI**	**MEES**	**MEOU**
MANIA	MASES	MAXIM	SMEES	MEOUS
MANIC	**MASH**	MAXIS	**MEET**	**MEOW**
MANIS	SMASH	**MAYA**	MEETS	MEOWS
MANO	MASHY	MAYAN	**MEFF**	**MERC**

MERCH	MEWLS	**MILE**	**MINK**	MITER
MERCS	**MEWS**	SMILE	MINKE	MITES
MERCY	SMEWS	MILER	MINKS	**MITT**
MERE	**MEZE**	MILES	**MINO**	MITTS
MERED	MEZES	**MILF**	AMINO	**MITY**
MEREL	**MEZZ**	MILFS	IMINO	AMITY
MERER	MEZZE	**MILK**	MINOR	**MIXT**
MERES	MEZZO	MILKO	MINOS	MIXTE
MERI	**MICA**	MILKS	**MINT**	**MIZZ**
MERIL	MICAS	MILKY	MINTS	MIZZY
MERIS	**MICE**	**MILL**	MINTY	**MOAN**
MERIT	AMICE	MILLE	**MIRE**	MOANS
MERK	**MICH**	MILLS	MIRED	**MOAT**
SMERK	MICHE	**MILO**	MIRES	MOATS
MERKS	MICHT	MILOR	MIREX	**MOBE**
MERL	**MICK**	MILOS	**MIRI**	MOBES
MERLE	MICKS	**MILT**	MIRID	MOBEY
MERLS	MICKY	MILTS	MIRIN	**MOCH**
MESA	**MICO**	MILTY	**MIRK**	MOCHA
MESAL	MICOS	MILTZ	SMIRK	MOCHI
MESAS	**MICS**	**MIME**	MIRKS	MOCHS
MESE	EMICS	MIMED	MIRKY	MOCHY
MESEL	**MIDI**	MIMEO	**MIRO**	**MOCK**
MESES	MIDIS	MIMER	MIROS	SMOCK
MESH	**MIDS**	MIMES	**MIRS**	MOCKS
MESHY	AMIDS	**MINA**	AMIRS	**MODE**
MESS	IMIDS	MINAE	EMIRS	MODEL
MESSY	MIDST	MINAR	SMIRS	MODEM
META	**MIEN**	MINAS	**MIRV**	MODER
METAL	MIENS	**MIND**	MIRVS	MODES
METE	**MIFF**	MINDS	**MISE**	**MODI**
METED	MIFFS	**MINE**	MISER	MODII
METER	MIFFY	AMINE	MISES	**MOER**
METES	**MIGG**	IMINE	**MISO**	MOERS
METH	MIGGS	MINED	MISOS	**MOFO**
METHO	**MIHA**	MINER	**MISS**	MOFOS
METHS	MIHAS	MINES	AMISS	**MOGS**
MEUS	**MIHI**	**MING**	MISSA	SMOGS
EMEUS	MIHIS	MINGE	MISSY	**MOHO**
MEUSE	**MIKE**	MINGS	**MIST**	MOHOS
MEVE	MIKED	MINGY	MISTS	**MOHR**
MEVED	MIKES	**MINI**	MISTY	MOHRS
MEVES	**MILD**	MINIM	**MITE**	**MOIL**
MEWL	MILDS	MINIS	SMITE	MOILE

MOILS	MONGO	**MORE**	**MOTU**	**MUID**
MOIT	MONGS	SMORE	MOTUS	MUIDS
MOITS	**MONK**	MOREL	**MOUE**	**MUIL**
MOJO	MONKS	MORES	MOUES	MUILS
MOJOS	**MONO**	**MORN**	**MOUP**	**MUIR**
MOKE	MONOS	MORNE	MOUPS	MUIRS
SMOKE	**MOOD**	MORNS	**MOUS**	**MULE**
MOKES	MOODS	**MORS**	MOUSE	EMULE
MOKI	MOODY	MORSE	MOUST	MULED
MOKIS	**MOOK**	**MORT**	MOUSY	MULES
MOKO	MOOKS	AMORT	**MOVE**	MULEY
SMOKO	**MOOL**	MORTS	AMOVE	**MULL**
MOKOS	MOOLA	**MOSE**	EMOVE	MULLA
MOLA	MOOLI	MOSED	MOVED	MULLS
MOLAL	MOOLS	MOSES	MOVER	**MUMM**
MOLAR	MOOLY	MOSEY	MOVES	MUMMS
MOLAS	**MOON**	**MOSK**	**MOWA**	MUMMY
MOLD	MOONG	MOSKS	MOWAS	**MUMP**
MOLDS	MOONS	**MOSS**	**MOXA**	MUMPS
MOLDY	MOONY	MOSSO	MOXAS	**MUMS**
MOLE	**MOOP**	MOSSY	**MOYA**	MUMSY
AMOLE	MOOPS	**MOST**	MOYAS	**MUMU**
MOLED	**MOOR**	MOSTE	**MOYL**	MUMUS
MOLES	SMOOR	MOSTS	MOYLE	**MUNG**
MOLL	MOORS	**MOTE**	MOYLS	MUNGA
MOLLA	MOORY	EMOTE	**MOZE**	MUNGE
MOLLS	**MOOS**	SMOTE	MOZED	MUNGO
MOLLY	MOOSE	MOTED	MOZES	MUNGS
MOLT	**MOOT**	MOTEL	**MOZO**	**MUNI**
SMOLT	SMOOT	MOTEN	MOZOS	MUNIS
YMOLT	MOOTS	MOTES	**MUCH**	**MUNT**
MOLTO	**MOPE**	MOTET	MUCHO	MUNTS
MOLTS	MOPED	MOTEY	**MUCK**	MUNTU
MOLY	MOPER	**MOTH**	AMUCK	**MUON**
MOLYS	MOPES	MOTHS	MUCKS	MUONS
MOME	MOPEY	MOTHY	MUCKY	**MURA**
MOMES	**MOPS**	**MOTI**	**MUFF**	MURAL
MONA	MOPSY	MOTIF	MUFFS	MURAS
MONAD	**MORA**	MOTIS	**MUGG**	**MURE**
MONAL	MORAE	**MOTT**	MUGGA	EMURE
MONAS	MORAL	MOTTE	MUGGS	MURED
MONG	MORAS	MOTTO	MUGGY	MURES
AMONG	MORAT	MOTTS	**MUGS**	MUREX
EMONG	MORAY	MOTTY	SMUGS	**MURK**

MURKS	MUZZY	NALAS	NAVEW	NEONS
MURKY	**MYAL**	**NAME**	**NAZE**	**NERD**
MURL	MYALL	NAMED	NAZES	NERDS
MURLS	**MYNA**	NAMER	**NAZI**	NERDY
MURLY	MYNAH	NAMES	NAZIR	**NERK**
MURR	MYNAS	**NAMU**	NAZIS	NERKA
MURRA	**MYTH**	NAMUS	**NEAL**	NERKS
MURRE	MYTHI	**NANA**	NEALS	**NEST**
MURRI	MYTHS	ANANA	**NEAP**	NESTS
MURRS	**MYTHY**	JNANA	SNEAP	**NETE**
MURRY	**MYXO**	NANAS	NEAPS	NETES
MUSE	MYXOS	**NANE**	**NEAR**	**NETT**
AMUSE	**MZEE**	INANE	ANEAR	NETTS
MUSED	MZEES	**NANO**	NEARS	NETTY
MUSER	**NAAM**	NANOS	**NEAT**	**NEUK**
MUSES	NAAMS	**NAPA**	NEATH	NEUKS
MUSET	**NAAN**	NAPAS	NEATS	**NEUM**
MUSH	NAANS	**NAPE**	**NEBS**	NEUME
SMUSH	**NABE**	NAPED	SNEBS	NEUMS
MUSHA	NABES	NAPES	**NECK**	**NEVE**
MUSHY	**NABK**	**NAPS**	SNECK	NEVEL
MUSK	NABKS	KNAPS	NECKS	NEVER
MUSKS	**NABS**	SNAPS	**NEDS**	NEVES
MUSKY	SNABS	**NARC**	SNEDS	**NEWB**
MUSO	**NACH**	NARCO	**NEED**	NEWBS
MUSOS	NACHE	NARCS	KNEED	**NEWS**
MUSS	NACHO	**NARD**	SNEED	ENEWS
MUSSE	**NADA**	NARDS	NEEDS	NEWSY
MUSSY	NADAS	**NARE**	NEEDY	**NEWT**
MUST	**NAFF**	SNARE	**NEEM**	NEWTS
MUSTH	NAFFS	NARES	NEEMB	**NEXT**
MUSTS	**NAGA**	**NARK**	NEEMS	NEXTS
MUSTY	NAGAS	SNARK	**NEEP**	**NGAI**
MUTE	**NAGS**	NARKS	NEEPS	NGAIO
MUTED	KNAGS	NARKY	**NEIF**	**NIBS**
MUTER	SNAGS	**NARY**	NEIFS	SNIBS
MUTES	**NAIF**	SNARY	**NEMA**	**NICE**
MUTI	NAIFS	UNARY	ENEMA	NICER
MUTIS	**NAIK**	**NATS**	NEMAS	**NICK**
MUTS	NAIKS	GNATS	**NEMN**	SNICK
SMUTS	**NAIL**	**NAVE**	NEMNS	NICKS
MUTT	SNAIL	KNAVE	**NENE**	**NIDE**
MUTTS	NAILS	NAVEL	NENES	SNIDE
MUZZ	**NALA**	NAVES	**NEON**	NIDED

NIDES	NIXED	**NONE**	NOUNY	NURDY
NIEF	NIXER	NONES	**NOUP**	**NURL**
NIEFS	NIXES	NONET	NOUPS	KNURL
NIES	**NOAH**	**NONG**	**NOUT**	NURLS
SNIES	NOAHS	NONGS	KNOUT	**NURR**
NIFE	**NOBS**	**NONI**	SNOUT	KNURR
KNIFE	KNOBS	NONIS	**NOVA**	NURRS
NIFES	SNOBS	**NOOB**	NOVAE	**NURS**
NIFF	**NOCK**	NOOBS	NOVAS	KNURS
SNIFF	KNOCK	**NOOK**	**NOWL**	NURSE
NIFFS	NOCKS	SNOOK	NOWLS	**NUTS**
NIFFY	**NODE**	NOOKS	**NOWN**	KNUTS
NIGH	ANODE	NOOKY	KNOWN	NUTSO
ANIGH	NODES	**NOON**	**NOWS**	NUTSY
NIGHS	**NODS**	NOONS	ENOWS	**NYES**
NIGHT	SNODS	**NOOP**	GNOWS	SNYES
NILL	**NOEL**	SNOOP	KNOWS	**OAFS**
NILLS	NOELS	NOOPS	SNOWS	GOAFS
NILS	**NOGG**	**NORI**	**NOWT**	LOAFS
ANILS	NOGGS	NORIA	NOWTS	**OAKS**
NIMB	**NOGS**	NORIS	NOWTY	BOAKS
NIMBI	SNOGS	**NORK**	**NOWY**	SOAKS
NIMBS	**NOIL**	NORKS	SNOWY	**OARS**
NINE	NOILS	**NORM**	**NUBS**	BOARS
NINER	NOILY	ENORM	KNUBS	HOARS
NINES	**NOIR**	NORMA	SNUBS	ROARS
NIPA	NOIRS	NORMS	**NUDE**	SOARS
NIPAS	**NOLE**	**NOSE**	NUDER	VOARS
NIPS	ANOLE	NOSED	NUDES	**OARY**
SNIPS	NOLES	NOSER	**NUFF**	GOARY
NIRL	**NOLL**	NOSES	SNUFF	HOARY
NIRLS	KNOLL	NOSEY	NUFFS	ROARY
NIRLY	NOLLS	**NOTA**	**NUGS**	**OAST**
NISH	**NOLO**	NOTAL	SNUGS	BOAST
KNISH	NOLOS	**NOTE**	**NUKE**	COAST
NITE	**NOMA**	NOTED	NUKED	HOAST
UNITE	NOMAD	NOTER	NUKES	LOAST
NITER	NOMAS	NOTES	**NULL**	ROAST
NITES	**NOME**	**NOUL**	NULLA	TOAST
NITS	GNOME	NOULD	NULLS	OASTS
KNITS	NOMEN	NOULE	**NUMB**	**OATH**
SNITS	NOMES	NOULS	NUMBS	LOATH
UNITS	**NONA**	**NOUN**	**NURD**	OATHS
NIXE	NONAS	NOUNS	NURDS	**OATS**

BOATS	SOCAS	COFFS	BOINK	WOLDS
COATS	**OCHE**	DOFFS	OINKS	**OLDY**
DOATS	BOCHE	GOFFS	**OINT**	GOLDY
GOATS	LOCHE	KOFFS	JOINT	MOLDY
MOATS	OCHER	TOFFS	NOINT	**OLEO**
OATY	OCHES	**OFFY**	POINT	OLEOS
GOATY	**OCTA**	TOFFY	OINTS	**OLES**
OBAS	OCTAD	**OGAM**	**OKAS**	BOLES
BOBAS	OCTAL	OGAMS	HOKAS	COLES
SOBAS	OCTAN	**OGEE**	KOKAS	DOLES
OBES	OCTAS	YOGEE	**OKAY**	GOLES
DOBES	**ODAH**	OGEED	TOKAY	HOLES
JOBES	ODAHS	OGEES	OKAYS	JOLES
LOBES	**ODAL**	**OGLE**	**OKEH**	MOLES
MOBES	MODAL	BOGLE	OKEHS	NOLES
ROBES	NODAL	FOGLE	**OKES**	POLES
OBESE	PODAL	OGLED	BOKES	ROLES
OBEY	ODALS	OGLER	COKES	SOLES
MOBEY	**ODAS**	OGLES	HOKES	TOLES
OBEYS	CODAS	**OGRE**	JOKES	VOLES
OBIA	SODAS	OGRES	LOKES	**OLID**
COBIA	**ODES**	**OHED**	MOKES	SOLID
OBIAS	BODES	HOHED	POKES	**OLIO**
OBIS	CODES	OOHED	ROKES	FOLIO
GOBIS	LODES	POHED	SOKES	POLIO
OBIT	MODES	**OHIA**	TOKES	OLIOS
OOBIT	NODES	OHIAS	YOKES	**OLLA**
OBITS	RODES	**OIKS**	**OKRA**	HOLLA
OBOE	**ODIC**	HOIKS	KOKRA	MOLLA
OBOES	IODIC	**OILS**	OKRAS	OLLAS
OBOL	SODIC	BOILS	**OKTA**	OLLAV
BOBOL	**ODOR**	COILS	OKTAS	**OLMS**
OBOLE	ODORS	FOILS	**OLDE**	HOLMS
OBOLI	**ODSO**	MOILS	SOLDE	**OLPE**
OBOLS	GODSO	NOILS	OLDEN	GOLPE
OBOS	**ODYL**	ROILS	OLDER	OLPES
BOBOS	ODYLE	SOILS	**OLDS**	**OMAS**
GOBOS	ODYLS	TOILS	BOLDS	BOMAS
HOBOS	**OFAY**	**OILY**	COLDS	COMAS
KOBOS	OFAYS	DOILY	FOLDS	HOMAS
LOBOS	**OFFA**	NOILY	GOLDS	LOMAS
ZOBOS	OFFAL	ROILY	HOLDS	NOMAS
OCAS	**OFFS**	SOILY	MOLDS	SOMAS
COCAS	BOFFS	**OINK**	SOLDS	OMASA

OMBU	RONES	ZOOMS	LOOTS	**OPPO**
KOMBU	SONES	**OONS**	MOOTS	ZOPPO
OMBUS	TONES	BOONS	POOTS	OPPOS
OMEN	ZONES	COONS	ROOTS	**OPUS**
NOMEN	**ONIE**	GOONS	SOOTS	MOPUS
WOMEN	BONIE	HOONS	TOOTS	**ORAD**
OMENS	MONIE	LOONS	**OOZE**	DORAD
OMER	**ONLY**	MOONS	BOOZE	**ORAL**
COMER	FONLY	NOONS	COOZE	BORAL
GOMER	SONLY	POONS	OOZED	CORAL
HOMER	**ONOS**	ROONS	OOZES	GORAL
VOMER	MONOS	TOONS	**OOZY**	HORAL
OMERS	**ONTO**	WOONS	BOOZY	LORAL
OMIT	CONTO	ZOONS	DOOZY	MORAL
VOMIT	**ONUS**	**OONT**	WOOZY	PORAL
OMITS	BONUS	OONTS	**OPAH**	RORAL
OMOV	CONUS	**OOPS**	OPAHS	SORAL
OMOVS	TONUS	COOPS	**OPAL**	ORALS
ONCE	**OOFS**	GOOPS	COPAL	**ORBS**
BONCE	COOFS	HOOPS	NOPAL	DORBS
NONCE	GOOFS	LOOPS	OPALS	FORBS
PONCE	HOOFS	MOOPS	**OPAS**	SORBS
SONCE	LOOFS	NOOPS	DOPAS	**ORBY**
ONCER	POOFS	POOPS	**OPED**	CORBY
ONCES	ROOFS	ROOPS	COPED	FORBY
ONCET	WOOFS	SOOPS	DOPED	**ORCA**
ONER	YOOFS	WOOPS	HOPED	ORCAS
BONER	**OOFY**	YOOPS	LOPED	**ORCS**
DONER	BOOFY	**OOSE**	MOPED	TORCS
GONER	GOOFY	BOOSE	OOPED	**ORDO**
HONER	POOFY	GOOSE	ROPED	FORDO
LONER	ROOFY	LOOSE	TOPED	SORDO
MONER	WOOFY	MOOSE	**OPEN**	ORDOS
TONER	**OOHS**	NOOSE	COPEN	**ORDS**
ZONER	BOOHS	ROOSE	OPENS	BORDS
ONERS	POOHS	WOOSE	**OPES**	CORDS
ONERY	**OOMS**	OOSES	COPES	FORDS
ONES	BOOMS	**OOSY**	DOPES	LORDS
BONES	COOMS	GOOSY	HOPES	SORDS
CONES	DOOMS	**OOTS**	LOPES	WORDS
HONES	LOOMS	BOOTS	MOPES	**ORES**
JONES	ROOMS	COOTS	POPES	BORES
NONES	SOOMS	FOOTS	ROPES	CORES
PONES	TOOMS	HOOTS	TOPES	DORES

FORES	FOSSA	**OUPS**	HOVEL	TOWER
GORES	**OTIC**	COUPS	NOVEL	VOWER
KORES	LOTIC	DOUPS	OVELS	**OWES**
LORES	**OTTO**	LOUPS	**OVEN**	BOWES
MORES	LOTTO	MOUPS	COVEN	HOWES
PORES	MOTTO	NOUPS	DOVEN	LOWES
RORES	POTTO	ROUPS	HOVEN	YOWES
SORES	OTTOS	SOUPS	ROVEN	**OWLS**
TORES	**OUCH**	**OURN**	WOVEN	BOWLS
YORES	COUCH	BOURN	OVENS	COWLS
ORFE	GOUCH	MOURN	**OVER**	DOWLS
ORFES	MOUCH	YOURN	COVER	FOWLS
ORGY	POUCH	**OURS**	DOVER	GOWLS
PORGY	TOUCH	COURS	HOVER	HOWLS
ORLE	VOUCH	FOURS	LOVER	JOWLS
ORLES	OUCHT	HOURS	MOVER	NOWLS
ORRA	**OUDS**	JOURS	ROVER	SOWLS
MORRA	FOUDS	LOURS	OVERS	YOWLS
SORRA	**OUKS**	POURS	OVERT	**OWLY**
ORTS	BOUKS	SOURS	**OVUM**	DOWLY
BORTS	DOUKS	TOURS	NOVUM	JOWLY
DORTS	GOUKS	YOURS	**OWED**	LOWLY
FORTS	JOUKS	**OUST**	BOWED	**OWNS**
MORTS	POUKS	JOUST	COWED	DOWNS
PORTS	SOUKS	MOUST	DOWED	GOWNS
RORTS	TOUKS	ROUST	JOWED	LOWNS
SORTS	YOUKS	OUSTS	LOWED	POWNS
TORTS	ZOUKS	**OUTA**	MOWED	TOWNS
WORTS	**OULD**	COUTA	NOWED	**OWRE**
ORZO	COULD	**OUTS**	ROWED	HOWRE
ORZOS	MOULD	BOUTS	SOWED	POWRE
OSES	NOULD	DOUTS	TOWED	OWRES
COSES	WOULD	GOUTS	VOWED	**OWSE**
DOSES	**OULK**	HOUTS	WOWED	BOWSE
HOSES	OULKS	LOUTS	YOWED	DOWSE
KOSES	**OUMA**	POUTS	**OWER**	LOWSE
LOSES	DOUMA	ROUTS	BOWER	SOWSE
MOSES	LOUMA	SOUTS	COWER	TOWSE
NOSES	OUMAS	TOUTS	DOWER	OWSEN
OOSES	**OUPA**	**OUZO**	LOWER	**OWTS**
POSES	OUPAS	OUZOS	MOWER	DOWTS
ROSES	**OUPH**	**OVAL**	POWER	LOWTS
TOSES	OUPHE	OVALS	ROWER	NOWTS
OSSA	OUPHS	**OVEL**	SOWER	ROWTS

TOWTS	**PACK**	PALIS	PAPES	PASHM
OXEN	PACKS	**PALL**	**PARA**	**PASS**
BOXEN	**PACO**	SPALL	PARAE	PASSE
WOXEN	PACOS	PALLA	PARAS	**PAST**
OXER	**PACT**	PALLS	**PARD**	PASTA
BOXER	EPACT	PALLY	SPARD	PASTE
OXERS	PACTA	**PALM**	PARDI	PASTS
OXES	PACTS	PALMS	PARDS	PASTY
BOXES	**PACY**	PALMY	PARDY	**PATE**
COXES	SPACY	**PALP**	**PARE**	SPATE
FOXES	**PADI**	PALPI	SPARE	PATED
GOXES	PADIS	PALPS	PARED	PATEN
HOXES	**PAGE**	**PALS**	PAREN	PATER
LOXES	APAGE	OPALS	PAREO	PATES
NOXES	PAGED	PALSA	PARER	**PATH**
POXES	PAGER	PALSY	PARES	PATHS
OXIC	PAGES	**PAMS**	PAREU	**PATS**
TOXIC	**PAHS**	SPAMS	PAREV	SPATS
OXID	OPAHS	**PAND**	**PARK**	PATSY
OXIDE	**PAID**	PANDA	SPARK	**PATU**
OXIDS	APAID	PANDS	PARKA	PATUS
OXIM	**PAIK**	PANDY	PARKI	**PAUA**
OXIME	PAIKS	**PANE**	PARKS	PAUAS
OXIMS	**PAIL**	SPANE	PARKY	**PAUL**
OYER	SPAIL	PANED	**PARP**	SPAUL
COYER	PAILS	PANEL	PARPS	PAULS
FOYER	**PAIN**	PANES	**PARR**	**PAVE**
TOYER	SPAIN	**PANG**	PARRA	PAVED
OYERS	PAINS	SPANG	PARRS	PAVEN
OYES	PAINT	PANGA	PARRY	PAVER
NOYES	**PAIR**	PANGS	**PARS**	PAVES
PAAL	PAIRE	**PANS**	SPARS	**PAWA**
PAALS	PAIRS	SPANS	PARSE	PAWAS
PAAN	**PAIS**	PANSY	**PART**	PAWAW
PAANS	PAISA	**PANT**	APART	**PAWK**
PACA	PAISE	PANTO	SPART	PAWKS
PACAS	**PALE**	PANTS	PARTI	PAWKY
PACE	SPALE	PANTY	PARTS	**PAWL**
APACE	PALEA	**PAPA**	PARTY	SPAWL
SPACE	PALED	PAPAL	**PASE**	PAWLS
PACED	PALER	PAPAS	PASEO	**PAWN**
PACER	PALES	PAPAW	PASES	SPAWN
PACES	PALET	**PAPE**	**PASH**	PAWNS
PACEY	**PALI**	PAPER	PASHA	**PAWS**

SPAWS	**PEEK**	PENES	PERVS	**PICS**
PAYS	APEEK	**PENI**	PERVY	EPICS
APAYS	PEEKS	PENIE	**PESO**	SPICS
SPAYS	**PEEL**	PENIS	PESOS	**PIED**
PAYSD	SPEEL	**PENK**	**PEST**	SPIED
PEAG	PEELS	PENKS	PESTO	**PIER**
PEAGE	**PEEN**	**PENS**	PESTS	SPIER
PEAGS	PEENS	OPENS	PESTY	PIERS
PEAK	**PEEP**	**PENT**	**PETS**	PIERT
APEAK	PEEPE	SPENT	SPETS	**PIES**
SPEAK	PEEPS	PENTS	**PEWS**	SPIES
PEAKS	**PEER**	**PEON**	SPEWS	**PIET**
PEAKY	SPEER	PEONS	**PHIS**	PIETA
PEAL	PEERS	PEONY	APHIS	PIETS
SPEAL	PEERY	**PEPO**	PHISH	PIETY
PEALS	**PEES**	PEPOS	**PHIZ**	**PIKA**
PEAN	EPEES	**PEPS**	PHIZZ	PIKAS
SPEAN	**PEGH**	PEPSI	**PHON**	PIKAU
PEANS	PEGHS	**PERC**	PHONE	**PIKE**
PEAR	**PEIN**	PERCE	PHONO	SPIKE
SPEAR	PEINS	PERCH	PHONS	PIKED
PEARE	**PEKE**	PERCS	PHONY	PIKER
PEARL	PEKES	**PERE**	**PHOT**	PIKES
PEARS	**PELA**	PEREA	PHOTO	PIKEY
PEART	PELAS	PERES	PHOTS	**PIKI**
PEAS	PELAU	**PERI**	**PHUT**	PIKIS
PEASE	**PELE**	PERIL	PHUTS	**PILA**
PEAT	PELES	PERIS	**PIAL**	PILAE
SPEAT	**PELF**	**PERK**	SPIAL	PILAF
PEATS	PELFS	PERKS	**PIAN**	PILAO
PEATY	**PELL**	PERKY	APIAN	PILAR
PEBA	SPELL	**PERM**	PIANI	PILAU
PEBAS	PELLS	SPERM	PIANO	PILAW
PECH	**PELT**	PERMS	PIANS	**PILE**
PECHS	SPELT	**PERN**	**PICA**	SPILE
PECK	PELTA	PERNS	SPICA	PILEA
SPECK	PELTS	**PERP**	PICAL	PILED
PECKE	**PEND**	PERPS	PICAS	PILEI
PECKS	SPEND	**PERT**	**PICE**	PILER
PECKY	UPEND	APERT	SPICE	PILES
PECS	PENDS	PERTS	**PICK**	**PILI**
SPECS	PENDU	**PERV**	SPICK	PILIS
PEED	**PENE**	PERVE	PICKS	**PILL**
SPEED	PENED	PERVO	PICKY	SPILL

PILLS	PIPES	SPLAY	PLUSH	POMOS
PIMA	PIPET	UPLAY	**POCK**	**POMP**
PIMAS	**PIPI**	PLAYA	POCKS	POMPS
PIMP	PIPIS	PLAYS	POCKY	**POND**
PIMPS	PIPIT	**PLEA**	**PODS**	PONDS
PINA	**PIRL**	PLEAD	APODS	**PONE**
SPINA	PIRLS	PLEAS	SPODS	PONES
PINAS	**PIRN**	PLEAT	**POEM**	PONEY
PINE	PIRNS	**PLEB**	POEMS	**PONG**
OPINE	**PISE**	PLEBE	**POEP**	PONGA
SPINE	PISES	PLEBS	POEPS	PONGO
PINED	**PISH**	**PLED**	**POET**	PONGS
PINES	APISH	UPLED	POETS	PONGY
PINEY	**PISO**	**PLEW**	**POGO**	**PONK**
PING	PISOS	PLEWS	POGOS	PONKS
APING	**PISS**	**PLIE**	**POIS**	**PONT**
OPING	PISSY	PLIED	POISE	PONTS
PINGO	**PITA**	PLIER	**POKE**	PONTY
PINGS	PITAS	PLIES	SPOKE	**POOD**
PINK	**PITH**	**PLIM**	POKED	POODS
SPINK	PITHS	PLIMS	POKER	**POOF**
PINKO	PITHY	**PLOD**	POKES	SPOOF
PINKS	**PITS**	PLODS	POKEY	POOFS
PINKY	SPITS	**PLOP**	**POLE**	POOFY
PINS	**PIUM**	PLOPS	POLED	**POOH**
SPINS	OPIUM	**PLOT**	POLER	POOHS
PINT	PIUMS	PLOTS	POLES	**POOK**
PINTA	**PIZE**	PLOTZ	POLEY	SPOOK
PINTO	PIZED	**PLOW**	**POLK**	POOKA
PINTS	PIZES	PLOWS	POLKA	POOKS
PINY	**PLAN**	**PLOY**	POLKS	**POOL**
SPINY	PLANE	PLOYE	**POLL**	SPOOL
PION	PLANK	PLOYS	POLLS	POOLS
PIONS	PLANS	**PLUE**	POLLY	**POON**
PIONY	PLANT	PLUES	**POLO**	SPOON
PIOY	**PLAP**	**PLUG**	POLOS	POONS
PIOYE	PLAPS	PLUGS	**POLT**	**POOP**
PIOYS	**PLAT**	**PLUM**	POLTS	APOOP
PIPA	SPLAT	PLUMB	**POLY**	POOPS
PIPAL	PLATE	PLUME	POLYP	POOPY
PIPAS	PLATS	PLUMP	POLYS	**POOR**
PIPE	PLATT	PLUMS	**POME**	SPOOR
PIPED	PLATY	PLUMY	POMES	POORI
PIPER	**PLAY**	**PLUS**	**POMO**	POORT

POOT	**POTT**	PREED	PROSE	PUKES
SPOOT	POTTO	PREEN	PROSO	PUKEY
POOTS	POTTS	PREES	PROSS	**PUKU**
POPE	POTTY	**PREM**	PROST	PUKUS
POPES	**POUF**	PREMS	PROSY	**PULA**
POPS	POUFF	PREMY	**PROW**	PULAO
POPSY	POUFS	**PREP**	PROWL	PULAS
PORE	**POUK**	PREPS	PROWS	**PULE**
SPORE	POUKE	**PREX**	**PRYS**	SPULE
PORED	POUKS	PREXY	PRYSE	PULED
PORER	**POUR**	**PREY**	**PSIS**	PULER
PORES	POURS	PREYS	APSIS	PULES
PORK	**POUT**	**PRIG**	**PUBE**	**PULI**
SPORK	SPOUT	SPRIG	PUBES	PULIK
PORKS	POUTS	PRIGS	**PUCE**	PULIS
PORKY	POUTY	**PRIM**	PUCER	**PULK**
PORN	**POWN**	PRIMA	PUCES	PULKA
PORNO	POWND	PRIME	**PUCK**	PULKS
PORNS	POWNS	PRIMI	PUCKA	**PULL**
PORNY	POWNY	PRIMO	PUCKS	PULLI
PORT	**POXY**	PRIMP	**PUDS**	PULLS
APORT	EPOXY	PRIMS	SPUDS	PULLY
SPORT	**POZZ**	PRIMY	PUDSY	**PULP**
PORTA	POZZY	**PROA**	**PUDU**	PULPS
PORTS	**PRAD**	PROAS	PUDUS	PULPY
PORTY	SPRAD	**PROB**	**PUER**	**PULS**
POSE	PRADS	PROBE	SPUER	PULSE
POSED	**PRAM**	PROBS	PUERS	**PULU**
POSER	PRAMS	**PROD**	**PUFF**	PULUS
POSES	**PRAO**	SPROD	PUFFA	**PUMA**
POSEY	PRAOS	PRODS	PUFFS	PUMAS
POSH	**PRAT**	**PROF**	PUFFY	**PUMP**
SPOSH	SPRAT	PROFS	**PUGS**	PUMPS
POSHO	PRATE	**PROG**	SPUGS	**PUMY**
POSS	PRATS	SPROG	**PUHA**	SPUMY
POSSE	PRATT	PROGS	PUHAS	**PUNA**
POST	PRATY	**PROM**	**PUJA**	PUNAS
POSTS	**PRAU**	PROMO	PUJAH	**PUNG**
POTE	PRAUS	PROMS	PUJAS	PUNGA
POTED	**PRAY**	**PROO**	**PUKA**	PUNGS
POTES	SPRAY	PROOF	PUKAS	**PUNK**
POTS	PRAYS	**PROP**	**PUKE**	SPUNK
SPOTS	**PREE**	PROPS	PUKED	PUNKA
POTSY	SPREE	**PROS**	PUKER	PUNKS

PUNKY	PYNES	QUINS	IRADE	TRAIK
PUNT	**PYOT**	QUINT	TRADE	RAIKS
PUNTO	PYOTS	**QUIP**	**RADS**	**RAIL**
PUNTS	**PYRE**	EQUIP	BRADS	BRAIL
PUNTY	SPYRE	QUIPO	GRADS	DRAIL
PUPA	PYRES	QUIPS	PRADS	FRAIL
PUPAE	PYREX	QUIPU	TRADS	GRAIL
PUPAL	**PYRO**	**QUIT**	**RAFF**	TRAIL
PUPAS	PYROS	SQUIT	DRAFF	RAILE
PUPU	**QADI**	QUITE	GRAFF	RAILS
PUPUS	QADIS	QUITS	**RAFFS**	**RAIN**
PURE	**QAID**	**QUIZ**	**RAFT**	BRAIN
PURED	QAIDS	SQUIZ	CRAFT	DRAIN
PUREE	**QOPH**	**QUOD**	DRAFT	GRAIN
PURER	QOPHS	QUODS	GRAFT	TRAIN
PURES	**QUAD**	**QUOP**	KRAFT	RAINE
PURI	SQUAD	QUOPS	**RAFTS**	RAINS
PURIN	QUADS	**RABI**	**RAGA**	RAINY
PURIS	**QUAG**	RABIC	RAGAS	**RAIS**
PURL	QUAGS	RABID	**RAGE**	KRAIS
PURLS	**QUAI**	RABIS	RAGED	RAISE
PURR	QUAIL	**RACE**	RAGEE	**RAIT**
PURRS	QUAIR	BRACE	RAGER	KRAIT
PURS	QUAIS	GRACE	RAGES	TRAIT
SPURS	**QUAT**	TRACE	**RAGG**	RAITA
PURSE	SQUAT	RACED	RAGGA	RAITS
PURSY	QUATE	RACER	RAGGS	**RAJA**
PUSH	QUATS	RACES	RAGGY	RAJAH
PUSHY	**QUAY**	**RACH**	**RAGI**	RAJAS
PUSS	QUAYD	BRACH	TRAGI	**RAKE**
PUSSY	QUAYS	ORACH	RAGIS	BRAKE
PUTT	**QUEY**	RACHE	**RAGS**	CRAKE
PUTTI	QUEYN	**RACK**	BRAGS	DRAKE
PUTTO	QUEYS	BRACK	CRAGS	RAKED
PUTTS	**QUID**	CRACK	DRAGS	RAKEE
PUTTY	EQUID	DRACK	FRAGS	RAKER
PYAT	SQUID	FRACK	**RAGU**	RAKES
PYATS	QUIDS	TRACK	RAGUS	**RAKI**
PYET	**QUIM**	WRACK	**RAIA**	RAKIA
PYETS	QUIMS	RACKS	RAIAS	RAKIS
PYIN	**QUIN**	**RACY**	**RAID**	**RAKU**
PYINS	QUINA	ORACY	BRAID	RAKUS
PYNE	QUINE	**RADE**	RAIDS	**RALE**
PYNED	QUINO	GRADE	**RAIK**	RALES

RAMI	RANKE	**RASH**	RATUS	RAZEE
RAMIE	RANKS	BRASH	**RAUN**	RAZER
RAMIN	**RANT**	CRASH	RAUNS	RAZES
RAMIS	BRANT	TRASH	**RAVE**	**READ**
RAMP	DRANT	**RASP**	BRAVE	AREAD
CRAMP	GRANT	GRASP	CRAVE	BREAD
GRAMP	ORANT	RASPS	DRAVE	DREAD
TRAMP	TRANT	RASPY	GRAVE	OREAD
RAMPS	RANTS	**RAST**	TRAVE	TREAD
RAMS	**RAPE**	BRAST	RAVED	READD
CRAMS	CRAPE	WRAST	RAVEL	READS
DRAMS	DRAPE	RASTA	RAVEN	READY
GRAMS	FRAPE	**RATA**	RAVER	**REAK**
PRAMS	GRAPE	RATAL	RAVES	BREAK
TRAMS	TRAPE	RATAN	RAVEY	CREAK
RANA	RAPED	RATAS	**RAVS**	FREAK
GRANA	RAPER	**RATE**	GRAVS	WREAK
PRANA	RAPES	CRATE	**RAWN**	REAKS
RANAS	**RAPS**	FRATE	BRAWN	**REAL**
RAND	CRAPS	GRATE	DRAWN	AREAL
BRAND	DRAPS	IRATE	PRAWN	UREAL
GRAND	FRAPS	ORATE	RAWNS	REALM
RANDS	TRAPS	PRATE	**RAWS**	REALO
RANDY	WRAPS	URATE	BRAWS	REALS
RANG	**RAPT**	WRATE	CRAWS	**REAM**
KRANG	TRAPT	RATED	DRAWS	BREAM
ORANG	WRAPT	RATEL	**RAYA**	CREAM
PRANG	YRAPT	RATER	RAYAH	DREAM
WRANG	**RARE**	RATES	RAYAS	REAME
RANGA	CRARE	**RATH**	**RAYS**	REAMS
RANGE	URARE	WRATH	BRAYS	REAMY
RANGI	RARED	RATHA	CRAYS	**REAN**
RANGS	RAREE	RATHE	DRAYS	REANS
RANGY	RARER	RATHS	FRAYS	**REAP**
RANI	RARES	**RATO**	GRAYS	REAPS
RANID	**RARK**	RATOO	KRAYS	**REAR**
RANIS	RARKS	RATOS	PRAYS	AREAR
RANK	**RASE**	**RATS**	TRAYS	DREAR
BRANK	ERASE	BRATS	XRAYS	REARM
CRANK	PRASE	DRATS	**RAZE**	REARS
DRANK	URASE	FRATS	BRAZE	**RECK**
FRANK	RASED	PRATS	CRAZE	DRECK
PRANK	RASER	TRATS	GRAZE	TRECK
TRANK	RASES	**RATU**	RAZED	WRECK

RECKS	TREEN	TREND	**REWS**	RICKS
REDD	REENS	RENDS	BREWS	**RICY**
AREDD	**REES**	**RENO**	CREWS	PRICY
REDDS	BREES	RENOS	GREWS	**RIDE**
REDDY	CREES	**RENS**	TREWS	BRIDE
REDE	DREES	BRENS	**RHEA**	GRIDE
AREDE	FREES	GRENS	RHEAS	PRIDE
BREDE	GREES	WRENS	**RHUS**	TRIDE
REDED	PREES	**RENT**	ERHUS	RIDER
REDES	TREES	BRENT	**RIAD**	RIDES
REDO	REEST	DRENT	TRIAD	**RIDS**
CREDO	**REFI**	PRENT	RIADS	GRIDS
UREDO	REFIS	URENT	**RIAL**	IRIDS
REDON	REFIT	YRENT	PRIAL	**RIEL**
REDOS	REFIX	RENTE	TRIAL	ARIEL
REDOX	**REGO**	RENTS	URIAL	ORIEL
REDS	GREGO	**REPO**	RIALS	RIELS
BREDS	REGOS	REPOS	**RIAS**	**RIEM**
CREDS	**REGS**	REPOT	ARIAS	RIEMS
REED	DREGS	**REPP**	CRIAS	**RIFE**
BREED	**REIF**	REPPS	**RIBA**	RIFER
CREED	PREIF	**REPS**	RIBAS	**RIFF**
DREED	TREIF	CREPS	**RIBS**	GRIFF
FREED	REIFS	PREPS	CRIBS	TRIFF
GREED	REIFY	**RESH**	DRIBS	RIFFS
PREED	**REIK**	FRESH	FRIBS	**RIFT**
TREED	REIKI	**REST**	**RICE**	DRIFT
REEDE	REIKS	CREST	DRICE	GRIFT
REEDS	**REIN**	DREST	GRICE	RIFTE
REEDY	GREIN	PREST	PRICE	RIFTS
REEF	REINK	TREST	TRICE	RIFTY
REEFS	REINS	WREST	RICED	**RIGG**
REEFY	**REIS**	RESTO	RICER	RIGGS
REEK	BREIS	RESTS	RICES	**RIGS**
CREEK	REIST	RESTY	RICEY	BRIGS
GREEK	**REKE**	**RETE**	**RICH**	FRIGS
REEKS	REKED	ARETE	RICHT	GRIGS
REEKY	REKES	RETEM	**RICK**	PRIGS
REEL	REKEY	**RETS**	BRICK	TRIGS
CREEL	**REMS**	ARETS	CRICK	**RILE**
REELS	CREMS	FRETS	ERICK	RILED
REEN	PREMS	TRETS	PRICK	RILES
GREEN	TREMS	**REVS**	TRICK	RILEY
PREEN	**REND**	EREVS	WRICK	**RILL**

BRILL	RINGS	BRISK	**ROAN**	GROIN
DRILL	**RINK**	FRISK	GROAN	PROIN
FRILL	BRINK	RISKS	ROANS	ROINS
GRILL	DRINK	RISKY	**ROAR**	**ROJI**
KRILL	PRINK	**RISP**	ROARS	ROJIS
PRILL	RINKS	CRISP	ROARY	**ROKE**
TRILL	**RINS**	RISPS	**ROBE**	BROKE
RILLE	BRINS	**RITE**	PROBE	DROKE
RILLS	GRINS	TRITE	ROBED	PROKE
RIMA	TRINS	URITE	ROBES	TROKE
PRIMA	RINSE	WRITE	**ROBS**	WROKE
RIMAE	**RIOT**	RITES	PROBS	ROKED
RIME	ARIOT	**RITS**	**ROCH**	ROKER
CRIME	GRIOT	BRITS	BROCH	ROKES
GRIME	RIOTS	CRITS	**ROCK**	**ROKS**
PRIME	**RIPE**	FRITS	BROCK	GROKS
RIMED	CRIPE	GRITS	CROCK	**ROLE**
RIMER	GRIPE	WRITS	FROCK	DROLE
RIMES	TRIPE	**RITT**	TROCK	PROLE
RIMS	RIPED	BRITT	ROCKS	ROLES
BRIMS	RIPEN	FRITT	ROCKY	**ROLF**
CRIMS	RIPER	RITTS	**ROCS**	ROLFS
PRIMS	RIPES	**RITZ**	CROCS	**ROLL**
TRIMS	**RIPP**	FRITZ	**RODE**	DROLL
RIMU	RIPPS	RITZY	ERODE	PROLL
RIMUS	**RIPS**	**RIVA**	TRODE	TROLL
RIMY	CRIPS	RIVAL	RODED	ROLLS
GRIMY	DRIPS	RIVAS	RODEO	**ROMA**
PRIMY	GRIPS	**RIVE**	RODES	AROMA
RIND	TRIPS	DRIVE	**RODS**	GROMA
GRIND	**RIPT**	RIVED	BRODS	ROMAL
RINDS	DRIPT	RIVEL	PRODS	ROMAN
RINDY	GRIPT	RIVEN	TRODS	**ROMP**
RINE	**RISE**	RIVER	**ROES**	TROMP
BRINE	ARISE	RIVES	FROES	ROMPS
CRINE	BRISE	RIVET	**ROID**	**ROMS**
TRINE	CRISE	**RIZA**	AROID	PROMS
URINE	FRISE	RIZAS	DROID	**RONE**
RINES	GRISE	**ROAD**	**ROIL**	CRONE
RING	PRISE	BROAD	BROIL	DRONE
BRING	RISEN	TROAD	DROIL	GRONE
ERING	RISER	ROADS	ROILS	IRONE
IRING	RISES	**ROAM**	ROILY	KRONE
WRING	**RISK**	ROAMS	**ROIN**	PRONE

TRONE	**ROOT**	ROTED	**ROWS**	**RUES**
RONEO	WROOT	ROTES	BROWS	CRUES
RONES	ROOTS	**ROTI**	CROWS	GRUES
RONG	ROOTY	ROTIS	DROWS	TRUES
PRONG	**ROPE**	**ROTL**	FROWS	**RUFF**
WRONG	GROPE	ROTLS	GROWS	GRUFF
RONT	TROPE	**ROTO**	PROWS	RUFFE
FRONT	ROPED	PROTO	TROWS	RUFFS
RONTE	ROPER	ROTON	VROWS	**RUGA**
RONTS	ROPES	ROTOR	**ROWT**	RUGAE
ROOD	ROPEY	ROTOS	ROWTH	RUGAL
BROOD	**RORE**	**ROTS**	ROWTS	**RUGS**
ROODS	CRORE	GROTS	**RUBE**	DRUGS
ROOF	FRORE	TROTS	RUBEL	FRUGS
GROOF	PRORE	**ROUE**	RUBES	TRUGS
PROOF	RORES	ROUEN	**RUBS**	**RUIN**
ROOFS	**RORT**	ROUES	DRUBS	BRUIN
ROOFY	RORTS	**ROUL**	GRUBS	RUING
ROOK	RORTY	PROUL	**RUCK**	RUINS
BROOK	**RORY**	ROULE	CRUCK	**RUKH**
CROOK	FRORY	ROULS	TRUCK	RUKHS
DROOK	**ROSE**	**ROUM**	RUCKS	**RULE**
ROOKS	AROSE	ROUMS	**RUDD**	BRULE
ROOKY	BROSE	**ROUP**	RUDDS	RULED
ROOM	EROSE	CROUP	RUDDY	RULER
BROOM	PROSE	GROUP	**RUDE**	RULES
GROOM	ROSED	ROUPS	CRUDE	**RULY**
VROOM	ROSES	ROUPY	PRUDE	TRULY
ROOMS	ROSET	**ROUT**	RUDER	**RUME**
ROOMY	**ROST**	CROUT	RUDES	BRUME
ROON	CROST	GROUT	**RUDI**	GRUME
CROON	FROST	TROUT	RUDIE	RUMEN
KROON	PROST	ROUTE	RUDIS	RUMES
ROONS	ROSTI	ROUTH	**RUDS**	**RUMP**
ROOP	ROSTS	ROUTS	CRUDS	CRUMP
DROOP	**ROSY**	**ROVE**	**RUDY**	FRUMP
TROOP	BROSY	DROVE	CRUDY	GRUMP
ROOPS	PROSY	GROVE	**RUED**	TRUMP
ROOPY	**ROTA**	PROVE	GRUED	RUMPO
ROOS	ROTAL	TROVE	TRUED	RUMPS
BROOS	ROTAN	ROVED	RUEDA	RUMPY
ROOSA	ROTAS	ROVEN	**RUER**	**RUMS**
ROOSE	**ROTE**	ROVER	TRUER	ARUMS
ROOST	WROTE	ROVES	RUERS	DRUMS

RUND	RUTHS	SAGES	**SAMA**	SASSE
GRUND	**RUTS**	**SAGO**	SAMAN	SASSY
RUNDS	BRUTS	SAGOS	SAMAS	**SATE**
RUNE	**RYAL**	**SAIC**	**SAME**	SATED
PRUNE	RYALS	SAICE	YSAME	SATEM
RUNED	**RYAS**	SAICK	SAMEK	SATES
RUNES	DRYAS	SAICS	SAMEL	**SATI**
RUNG	**RYKE**	**SAID**	SAMEN	SATIN
BRUNG	GRYKE	SAIDS	SAMES	SATIS
WRUNG	TRYKE	**SAIL**	SAMEY	**SAUL**
RUNGS	RYKED	SAILS	**SAMP**	SAULS
RUNT	RYKES	**SAIM**	SAMPI	SAULT
BRUNT	**RYND**	SAIMS	SAMPS	**SAUT**
GRUNT	RYNDS	**SAIN**	**SAND**	SAUTE
PRUNT	**RYOT**	SAINE	SANDS	SAUTS
RUNTS	RYOTS	SAINS	SANDY	**SAVE**
RUNTY	**RYPE**	SAINT	**SANE**	SAVED
RURP	GRYPE	**SAIR**	SANED	SAVER
RURPS	RYPER	SAIRS	SANER	SAVES
RURU	**SAAG**	**SAIS**	SANES	SAVEY
RURUS	SAAGS	SAIST	**SANG**	**SAXE**
RUSA	**SABE**	**SAKE**	SANGA	SAXES
RUSAS	SABED	SAKER	SANGH	**SAYS**
RUSE	SABER	SAKES	SANGO	SAYST
CRUSE	SABES	**SAKI**	SANGS	**SCAB**
DRUSE	**SACK**	SAKIA	**SANK**	SCABS
RUSES	SACKS	SAKIS	SANKO	**SCAD**
RUSH	**SADE**	**SALE**	**SANS**	SCADS
BRUSH	TSADE	SALEP	SANSA	**SCAG**
CRUSH	SADES	SALES	**SANT**	SCAGS
FRUSH	**SADI**	SALET	SANTO	**SCAM**
RUSHY	TSADI	**SALL**	SANTS	SCAMP
RUSK	SADIS	SALLE	**SARD**	SCAMS
BRUSK	**SADO**	SALLY	SARDS	**SCAN**
RUSKS	SADOS	**SALP**	**SARI**	SCAND
RUST	**SAFE**	SALPA	SARIN	SCANS
BRUST	SAFED	SALPS	SARIS	SCANT
CRUST	SAFER	**SALS**	**SARK**	**SCAR**
FRUST	SAFES	SALSA	SARKS	ESCAR
TRUST	**SAGA**	SALSE	SARKY	OSCAR
RUSTS	SAGAS	**SALT**	**SARS**	SCARE
RUSTY	**SAGE**	SALTO	KSARS	SCARF
RUTH	USAGE	SALTS	TSARS	SCARP
TRUTH	SAGER	SALTY	**SASS**	SCARS

SCART	**SCYE**	**SEIR**	SERED	SHAWL
SCARY	SCYES	SEIRS	SERER	SHAWM
SCAT	**SEAL**	**SEIS**	SERES	SHAWN
SCATH	SEALS	SEISE	**SERF**	SHAWS
SCATS	**SEAM**	SEISM	SERFS	**SHAY**
SCATT	SEAME	**SEKT**	**SERK**	SHAYA
SCAW	SEAMS	SEKTS	SERKS	SHAYS
SCAWS	SEAMY	**SELE**	**SERR**	**SHEA**
SCOG	**SEAN**	SELES	SERRA	SHEAF
SCOGS	SEANS	**SELF**	SERRE	SHEAL
SCOP	**SEAR**	SELFS	SERRS	SHEAR
SCOPA	SEARE	**SELL**	SERRY	SHEAS
SCOPE	SEARS	SELLA	**SERS**	**SHED**
SCOPS	**SEAS**	SELLE	USERS	ASHED
SCOT	SEASE	SELLS	**SESE**	SHEDS
ASCOT	**SEAT**	**SEME**	SESEY	**SHEN**
ESCOT	SEATS	SEMEE	**SESS**	ASHEN
SCOTS	**SECH**	SEMEN	SESSA	SHEND
SCOW	SECHS	SEMES	**SETA**	SHENT
SCOWL	**SECT**	**SEMI**	SETAE	**SHES**
SCOWP	SECTS	SEMIE	SETAL	ASHES
SCOWS	**SEED**	SEMIS	**SETT**	ISHES
SCUD	SEEDS	**SENA**	SETTS	**SHET**
SCUDI	SEEDY	SENAS	**SEXT**	ASHET
SCUDO	**SEEK**	**SEND**	SEXTO	SHETS
SCUDS	SEEKS	SENDS	SEXTS	**SHEW**
SCUG	**SEEL**	SENE	SHAD	SHEWN
SCUGS	SEELD	SENES	SHADE	SHEWS
SCUL	SEELS	**SENS**	SHADS	**SHIM**
SCULK	SEELY	SENSA	SHADY	SHIMS
SCULL	**SEEM**	SENSE	**SHAG**	**SHIN**
SCULP	SEEMS	SENSI	SHAGS	SHINE
SCULS	**SEEP**	**SENT**	**SHAH**	SHINS
SCUM	SEEPS	SENTE	SHAHS	SHINY
SCUMS	SEEPY	SENTI	**SHAM**	**SHIP**
SCUP	**SEER**	SENTS	SHAMA	SHIPS
SCUPS	SEERS	**SEPT**	SHAME	**SHIR**
SCUR	**SEGO**	SEPTA	SHAMS	SHIRE
SCURF	SEGOL	SEPTS	**SHAN**	SHIRK
SCURS	SEGOS	**SERA**	SHAND	SHIRR
SCUT	**SEIF**	SERAC	SHANK	SHIRS
SCUTA	SEIFS	SERAI	SHANS	SHIRT
SCUTE	**SEIL**	SERAL	**SHAW**	**SHIT**
SCUTS	SEILS	**SERE**	PSHAW	SHITE

SHITS	**SHWA**	**SILE**	SIRED	**SKEN**
SHIV	SHWAS	ESILE	SIREE	SKENE
SHIVA	**SIAL**	SILED	SIREN	SKENS
SHIVE	SIALS	SILEN	SIRES	**SKEO**
SHIVS	**SIBB**	SILER	**SIRI**	SKEOS
SHMO	SIBBS	SILES	SIRIH	**SKEP**
SHMOE	**SICE**	SILEX	SIRIS	SKEPS
SHOE	SICES	**SILK**	**SISS**	**SKER**
SHOED	**SICH**	SILKS	SISSY	ASKER
SHOER	SICHT	SILKY	**SIST**	ESKER
SHOES	**SICK**	**SILL**	SISTA	SKERS
SHOG	SICKO	SILLS	SISTS	**SKET**
SHOGI	SICKS	SILLY	**SITE**	SKETS
SHOGS	SICKY	**SILO**	SITED	**SKEW**
SHOO	**SIDA**	SILOS	SITES	ASKEW
SHOOK	SIDAS	**SILT**	**SITH**	SKEWS
SHOOL	**SIDE**	SILTS	SITHE	**SKID**
SHOON	ASIDE	SILTY	**SIZE**	SKIDS
SHOOS	SIDED	**SIMA**	SIZED	**SKIM**
SHOOT	SIDER	SIMAR	SIZEL	SKIMO
SHOP	SIDES	SIMAS	SIZER	SKIMP
SHOPE	**SIDH**	**SIMI**	SIZES	SKIMS
SHOPS	SIDHA	SIMIS	**SKAG**	**SKIN**
SHOT	SIDHE	**SIMP**	SKAGS	SKINK
SHOTE	**SIEN**	SIMPS	**SKAT**	SKINS
SHOTS	SIENS	**SIND**	SKATE	SKINT
SHOTT	SIENT	SINDS	SKATS	**SKIO**
SHOW	**SIFT**	**SINE**	SKATT	SKIOS
SHOWD	SIFTS	SINED	**SKAW**	**SKIP**
SHOWN	**SIGH**	SINES	SKAWS	SKIPS
SHOWS	SIGHS	SINEW	**SKED**	**SKIT**
SHOWY	SIGHT	**SING**	ASKED	SKITE
SHRI	**SIGN**	USING	TSKED	SKITS
SHRIS	SIGNA	SINGE	SKEDS	**SKOG**
SHUL	SIGNS	SINGS	**SKEE**	SKOGS
SHULE	**SIJO**	**SINH**	SKEED	**SKOL**
SHULN	SIJOS	SINHS	SKEEF	SKOLS
SHULS	**SIKA**	**SINK**	SKEEN	**SKUA**
SHUN	SIKAS	SINKS	SKEER	SKUAS
SHUNS	**SIKE**	SINKY	SKEES	**SKUG**
SHUNT	SIKER	**SIPE**	SKEET	SKUGS
SHUT	SIKES	SIPED	**SKEG**	**SKYF**
SHUTE	**SILD**	SIPES	SKEGG	SKYFS
SHUTS	SILDS	**SIRE**	SKEGS	**SKYR**

SKYRE	**SLIT**	SMITE	**SNOB**	SOILY
SKYRS	SLITS	SMITH	SNOBS	**SOJA**
SLAB	**SLOB**	SMITS	**SNOD**	SOJAS
SLABS	SLOBS	**SMOG**	SNODS	**SOJU**
SLAE	**SLOE**	SMOGS	**SNOG**	SOJUS
SLAES	SLOES	**SMUG**	SNOGS	**SOKE**
SLAG	**SLOG**	SMUGS	**SNOT**	SOKEN
SLAGS	SLOGS	**SMUR**	SNOTS	SOKES
SLAM	**SLOP**	SMURS	**SNOW**	**SOLA**
SLAMS	SLOPE	**SMUT**	SNOWK	SOLAH
SLAP	SLOPS	SMUTS	SNOWS	SOLAN
SLAPS	SLOPY	**SNAB**	SNOWY	SOLAR
SLAT	**SLOT**	SNABS	**SNUB**	SOLAS
SLATE	SLOTH	**SNAG**	SNUBS	**SOLD**
SLATS	SLOTS	SNAGS	**SNUG**	SOLDE
SLATY	**SLOW**	**SNAP**	SNUGS	SOLDI
SLAW	SLOWS	SNAPS	**SNYE**	SOLDO
SLAWS	**SLUB**	**SNAR**	SNYES	SOLDS
SLAY	SLUBB	SNARE	**SOAK**	**SOLE**
SLAYS	SLUBS	SNARF	SOAKS	SOLED
SLEB	**SLUE**	SNARK	**SOAP**	SOLEI
SLEBS	SLUED	SNARL	SOAPS	SOLER
SLED	SLUES	SNARS	SOAPY	SOLES
ISLED	**SLUG**	SNARY	**SOAR**	**SOLI**
SLEDS	SLUGS	**SNAW**	SOARE	SOLID
SLEE	**SLUM**	SNAWS	SOARS	**SOLO**
SLEEK	SLUMP	**SNEB**	**SOBA**	SOLON
SLEEP	SLUMS	SNEBS	SOBAS	SOLOS
SLEER	**SLUR**	**SNED**	**SOCA**	**SOMA**
SLEET	SLURB	SNEDS	SOCAS	SOMAN
SLEW	SLURP	**SNEE**	**SOCK**	SOMAS
SLEWS	SLURS	SNEED	SOCKO	**SONE**
SLEY	**SLUT**	SNEER	SOCKS	SONES
SLEYS	SLUTS	SNEES	**SODA**	**SONG**
SLID	**SMEE**	**SNIB**	SODAS	SONGS
SLIDE	SMEEK	SNIBS	**SOFA**	**SONS**
SLIM	SMEES	**SNIG**	SOFAR	SONSE
SLIME	**SMEW**	SNIGS	SOFAS	SONSY
SLIMS	SMEWS	**SNIP**	**SOFT**	**SOOK**
SLIMY	**SMIR**	SNIPE	SOFTA	SOOKS
SLIP	SMIRK	SNIPS	SOFTS	**SOOL**
SLIPE	SMIRR	SNIPY	SOFTY	SOOLE
SLIPS	SMIRS	**SNIT**	**SOIL**	SOOLS
SLIPT	**SMIT**	SNITS	SOILS	**SOOM**

SOOMS	SOUPY	**SPAS**	SPIKY	STARE
SOOP	**SOUR**	SPASM	**SPIM**	STARK
SOOPS	SOURS	**SPAT**	SPIMS	STARN
SOOT	**SOUS**	SPATE	**SPIN**	STARR
SOOTE	SOUSE	SPATS	SPINA	STARS
SOOTH	**SOUT**	**SPAW**	SPINE	START
SOOTS	SOUTH	SPAWL	SPINK	**STAT**
SOOTY	SOUTS	SPAWN	SPINS	STATE
SOPH	**SOWF**	SPAWS	SPINY	STATS
SOPHS	SOWFF	**SPAY**	**SPIT**	**STAW**
SOPHY	SOWFS	SPAYD	SPITE	STAWS
SORA	**SOWL**	SPAYS	SPITS	**STAY**
PSORA	SOWLE	**SPAZ**	SPITZ	STAYS
SORAL	SOWLS	SPAZA	**SPIV**	**STED**
SORAS	**SOWM**	SPAZZ	SPIVS	STEDD
SORB	SOWMS	**SPEC**	**SPOD**	STEDE
SORBO	**SOWN**	SPECK	SPODE	STEDS
SORBS	SOWND	SPECS	SPODS	**STEM**
SORD	SOWNE	SPECT	**SPOT**	STEME
SORDA	**SOWP**	**SPEK**	SPOTS	STEMS
SORDO	SOWPS	SPEKS	**SPUD**	**STEN**
SORDS	**SOWS**	**SPET**	SPUDS	STEND
SORE	SOWSE	SPETS	**SPUE**	STENO
SORED	**SOYA**	**SPEW**	SPUED	STENS
SOREE	SOYAS	SPEWS	SPUER	STENT
SOREL	**SPAE**	SPEWY	SPUES	**STEP**
SORER	SPAED	**SPIC**	**SPUG**	STEPS
SORES	SPAER	ASPIC	SPUGS	STEPT
SOREX	SPAES	SPICA	**SPUN**	**STET**
SORN	**SPAG**	SPICE	SPUNK	STETS
SORNS	SPAGS	SPICK	**SPUR**	**STEW**
SORT	**SPAM**	SPICS	SPURN	STEWS
SORTA	SPAMS	SPICY	SPURS	STEWY
SORTS	**SPAN**	**SPIE**	SPURT	**STEY**
SOTH	SPANE	SPIED	**STAB**	STEYS
SOTHS	SPANG	SPIEL	STABS	**STIE**
SOUK	SPANK	SPIER	**STAG**	STIED
SOUKS	SPANS	SPIES	STAGE	STIES
SOUL	**SPAR**	**SPIF**	STAGS	**STIM**
SOULS	SPARD	SPIFF	STAGY	STIME
SOUM	SPARE	SPIFS	**STAP**	STIMS
SOUMS	SPARK	**SPIK**	STAPH	STIMY
SOUP	SPARS	SPIKE	STAPS	**STIR**
SOUPS	SPART	SPIKS	**STAR**	ASTIR

STIRE	SUBAH	**SUNN**	SWATH	SYNCS
STIRK	SUBAS	SUNNA	SWATS	**SYND**
STIRP	**SUCK**	SUNNS	**SWAY**	SYNDS
STIRS	SUCKS	SUNNY	ASWAY	**SYNE**
STOA	SUCKY	**SUPE**	SWAYL	SYNED
STOAE	**SUDD**	SUPER	SWAYS	SYNES
STOAI	SUDDS	SUPES	**SWEE**	**SYPE**
STOAS	**SUDS**	**SURA**	SWEED	SYPED
STOAT	SUDSY	ASURA	SWEEL	SYPES
STOB	**SUED**	SURAH	SWEEP	**SYPH**
STOBS	SUEDE	SURAL	SWEER	SYPHS
STOP	**SUER**	SURAS	SWEES	**TAAL**
ESTOP	SUERS	SURAT	SWEET	TAALS
STOPE	**SUET**	**SURD**	**SWEY**	**TABI**
STOPS	SUETE	SURDS	SWEYS	TABID
STOPT	SUETS	**SURE**	**SWIG**	TABIS
STOT	SUETY	USURE	SWIGS	**TABS**
STOTS	**SUGH**	SURED	**SWIM**	STABS
STOTT	SUGHS	SURER	ASWIM	**TABU**
STOW	**SUGO**	SURES	SWIMS	TABUN
STOWN	SUGOS	**SURF**	**SWIZ**	TABUS
STOWP	**SUID**	SURFS	SWIZZ	**TACE**
STOWS	SUIDS	SURFY	**SWOB**	TACES
STUB	**SUIT**	**SUSU**	SWOBS	TACET
STUBS	SUITE	SUSUS	**SWOP**	**TACH**
STUD	SUITS	**SWAB**	SWOPS	TACHE
STUDE	**SUKH**	SWABS	SWOPT	TACHO
STUDS	SUKHS	**SWAD**	**SWOT**	TACHS
STUDY	**SULK**	SWADS	SWOTS	**TACK**
STUM	SULKS	**SWAG**	**SYBO**	STACK
STUMM	SULKY	SWAGE	SYBOE	TACKS
STUMP	**SULU**	SWAGS	SYBOW	TACKY
STUMS	SULUS	**SWAM**	**SYCE**	**TACO**
STUN	**SUMI**	SWAMI	SYCEE	TACOS
ASTUN	SUMIS	SWAMP	SYCES	**TACT**
STUNG	**SUMO**	SWAMY	**SYEN**	TACTS
STUNK	SUMOS	**SWAN**	SYENS	**TAEL**
STUNS	**SUMP**	SWANG	**SYKE**	TAELS
STUNT	SUMPH	SWANK	SYKER	**TAGS**
STYE	SUMPS	SWANS	SYKES	STAGS
STYED	**SUNI**	**SWAP**	**SYLI**	**TAHA**
STYES	SUNIS	SWAPS	SYLIS	TAHAS
SUBA	**SUNK**	SWAPT	**SYNC**	**TAHR**
TSUBA	SUNKS	**SWAT**	SYNCH	TAHRS

TAIG	TALLY	**TARE**	TATTY	**TEDS**
STAIG	**TAME**	STARE	**TATU**	STEDS
TAIGA	TAMED	TARED	TATUS	**TEED**
TAIGS	TAMER	TARES	**TAUT**	STEED
TAIL	TAMES	**TARN**	TAUTS	**TEEK**
TAILS	**TAMP**	STARN	**TAVA**	STEEK
TAIN	STAMP	TARNS	TAVAH	**TEEL**
STAIN	TAMPS	**TARO**	TAVAS	STEEL
TAINS	**TANA**	TAROC	**TAWA**	TEELS
TAINT	TANAS	TAROK	TAWAI	**TEEM**
TAIS	**TANE**	TAROS	TAWAS	STEEM
TAISH	STANE	TAROT	**TAWS**	TEEMS
TAIT	**TANG**	**TARP**	STAWS	**TEEN**
TAITS	STANG	TARPS	TAWSE	STEEN
TAKA	TANGA	**TARS**	**TAWT**	TEEND
TAKAS	TANGI	STARS	TAWTS	TEENE
TAKE	TANGO	TARSI	**TAXI**	TEENS
STAKE	TANGS	**TART**	TAXIS	TEENY
TAKEN	TANGY	START	**TAYS**	**TEER**
TAKER	**TANH**	TARTS	STAYS	STEER
TAKES	TANHS	TARTY	**TEAD**	TEERS
TAKI	**TANK**	**TASE**	STEAD	**TEFF**
TAKIN	STANK	TASED	TEADE	TEFFS
TAKIS	TANKA	TASER	TEADS	**TEGG**
TALA	TANKS	TASES	**TEAK**	TEGGS
TALAK	TANKY	**TASH**	STEAK	**TEGU**
TALAQ	**TANS**	STASH	TEAKS	TEGUA
TALAR	TANSY	**TASK**	**TEAL**	TEGUS
TALAS	**TAPA**	TASKS	STEAL	**TEHR**
TALC	TAPAS	**TASS**	TEALS	TEHRS
TALCS	**TAPE**	TASSA	**TEAM**	**TEIL**
TALCY	ETAPE	TASSE	STEAM	STEIL
TALE	TAPED	TASSO	TEAMS	TEILS
STALE	TAPEN	**TATE**	**TEAR**	**TEIN**
TALEA	TAPER	STATE	STEAR	STEIN
TALER	TAPES	TATER	TEARS	TEIND
TALES	TAPET	TATES	TEARY	TEINS
TALK	**TAPS**	**TATH**	**TEAS**	**TELA**
STALK	ATAPS	TATHS	TEASE	STELA
TALKS	STAPS	**TATS**	**TEAT**	TELAE
TALKY	**TAPU**	ETATS	TEATS	**TELE**
TALL	TAPUS	STATS	**TECH**	STELE
STALL	**TARA**	**TATT**	TECHS	TELES
TALLS	TARAS	TATTS	TECHY	TELEX

TELL	TERNE	THIGS	TIDES	TINDS
STELL	TERNS	**THIN**	**TIED**	**TINE**
TELLS	**TEST**	THINE	STIED	TINEA
TELLY	TESTA	THING	**TIER**	TINED
TEME	TESTE	THINK	TIERS	TINES
STEME	TESTS	THINS	**TIES**	**TING**
TEMED	TESTY	**THIO**	STIES	STING
TEMES	**TETE**	THIOL	**TIFF**	TINGE
TEMP	TETES	**THIR**	STIFF	TINGS
TEMPI	**TETH**	THIRD	TIFFS	**TINK**
TEMPO	TETHS	THIRL	**TIFT**	STINK
TEMPS	**TETS**	**THON**	TIFTS	TINKS
TEMPT	STETS	THONG	**TIGE**	**TINT**
TEMS	**TEWS**	**THOU**	TIGER	STINT
ITEMS	STEWS	THOUS	TIGES	TINTS
STEMS	**TEXT**	**THRO**	**TIKA**	TINTY
TEMSE	TEXTS	THROB	TIKAS	**TIPI**
TEND	**THAN**	THROE	**TIKE**	TIPIS
STEND	THANA	THROW	TIKES	**TIPS**
TENDS	THANE	**THRU**	**TIKI**	TIPSY
TENDU	THANG	THRUM	TIKIS	**TIRE**
TENE	THANK	**THUD**	**TILE**	STIRE
CTENE	THANS	THUDS	STILE	TIRED
TENES	THANX	**THUG**	UTILE	TIRES
TENET	**THAR**	THUGS	TILED	**TIRL**
TENS	THARM	**TIAN**	TILER	TIRLS
ETENS	THARS	TIANS	TILES	**TIRO**
STENS	**THAW**	**TIAR**	**TILL**	TIROS
TENSE	THAWS	TIARA	STILL	**TIRR**
TENT	THAWY	TIARS	TILLS	TIRRS
STENT	**THEE**	**TICE**	TILLY	**TITE**
TENTH	THEED	TICED	**TILT**	TITER
TENTS	THEEK	TICES	ATILT	**TITI**
TENTY	THEES	**TICH**	STILT	TITIS
TEPA	**THEM**	STICH	TILTH	**TIVY**
TEPAL	THEMA	TICHY	TILTS	STIVY
TEPAS	THEME	**TICK**	**TIME**	**TIYN**
TERF	**THEN**	STICK	STIME	TIYNS
TERFE	THENS	TICKS	TIMED	**TIZZ**
TERFS	**THEW**	TICKY	TIMER	TIZZY
TERM	THEWS	**TICS**	TIMES	**TOAD**
TERMS	THEWY	ETICS	**TINA**	TOADS
TERN	**THIG**	**TIDE**	TINAS	TOADY
STERN	THIGH	TIDED	**TIND**	**TOCK**

STOCK	TOLES	**TOOT**	TORSO	TOWSY
TOCKS	**TOLL**	TOOTH	**TORT**	**TOWT**
TOCKY	ATOLL	TOOTS	TORTA	TOWTS
TOCO	TOLLS	**TOPE**	TORTE	**TOYO**
TOCOS	TOLLY	STOPE	TORTS	TOYON
TOCS	**TOLT**	TOPED	**TORY**	TOYOS
ATOCS	TOLTS	TOPEE	STORY	**TOZE**
TOEA	**TOLU**	TOPEK	**TOSA**	TOZED
TOEAS	TOLUS	TOPER	TOSAS	TOZES
TOFF	**TOMB**	TOPES	**TOSE**	**TRAD**
TOFFS	TOMBS	**TOPH**	TOSED	STRAD
TOFFY	**TOME**	TOPHE	TOSES	TRADE
TOFT	TOMES	TOPHI	**TOSH**	TRADS
TOFTS	**TOMO**	TOPHS	TOSHY	**TRAM**
TOFU	TOMOS	**TOPI**	**TOSS**	TRAMP
TOFUS	**TOMS**	TOPIC	STOSS	TRAMS
TOGA	ATOMS	TOPIS	TOSSY	**TRAP**
TOGAE	**TONE**	**TOPO**	**TOST**	STRAP
TOGAS	ATONE	TOPOI	YTOST	TRAPE
TOGE	STONE	TOPOS	**TOTE**	TRAPS
TOGED	TONED	**TOPS**	TOTED	TRAPT
TOGES	TONER	STOPS	TOTEM	**TRAT**
TOIL	TONES	**TORA**	TOTER	TRATS
TOILE	TONEY	TORAH	TOTES	TRATT
TOILS	**TONG**	TORAN	**TOTS**	**TRAY**
TOIT	STONG	TORAS	STOTS	STRAY
STOIT	TONGA	**TORC**	**TOUK**	TRAYF
TOITS	TONGS	TORCH	TOUKS	TRAYS
TOKE	**TONK**	TORCS	**TOUN**	**TREE**
ATOKE	STONK	**TORE**	STOUN	TREED
STOKE	TONKA	STORE	TOUNS	TREEN
TOKED	TONKS	TORES	**TOUR**	TREES
TOKEN	**TONY**	**TORI**	STOUR	**TREF**
TOKER	ATONY	TORIC	TOURS	TREFA
TOKES	STONY	TORII	**TOUT**	**TREK**
TOKO	**TOOK**	**TORO**	STOUT	TREKS
TOKOS	STOOK	TOROS	TOUTS	**TREM**
TOLA	**TOOL**	TOROT	**TOWN**	TREMA
TOLAN	STOOL	**TORR**	STOWN	TREMS
TOLAR	TOOLS	TORRS	TOWNS	**TRES**
TOLAS	**TOOM**	**TORS**	TOWNY	TRESS
TOLE	TOOMS	TORSE	**TOWS**	TREST
STOLE	**TOON**	TORSI	STOWS	**TRET**
TOLED	TOONS	TORSK	TOWSE	TRETS

TREW	**TROT**	TUFFE	TUSHY	**TYMP**
STREW	TROTH	TUFFS	**TUSK**	TYMPS
TREWS	TROTS	**TUFT**	TUSKS	**TYND**
TREY	**TROU**	TUFTS	TUSKY	TYNDE
TREYF	TROUT	TUFTY	**TUTU**	**TYNE**
TREYS	**TROW**	**TUIS**	TUTUS	TYNED
TRIE	STROW	ETUIS	**TWAE**	TYNES
TRIED	TROWS	TUISM	TWAES	**TYPE**
TRIER	**TROY**	**TULE**	**TWAL**	TYPED
TRIES	STROY	TULES	TWALS	TYPES
TRIG	TROYS	**TUMP**	**TWAT**	TYPEY
STRIG	**TRUE**	STUMP	TWATS	**TYPO**
TRIGO	TRUED	TUMPS	**TWAY**	TYPOS
TRIGS	TRUER	TUMPY	TWAYS	**TYPP**
TRIM	TRUES	**TUMS**	**TWEE**	TYPPS
STRIM	**TRUG**	STUMS	ETWEE	**TYRE**
TRIMS	TRUGO	**TUNA**	TWEED	STYRE
TRIN	TRUGS	TUNAS	TWEEL	TYRED
TRINE	**TRYE**	**TUND**	TWEEN	TYRES
TRINS	TRYER	TUNDS	TWEEP	**TYRO**
TRIO	**TRYP**	**TUNE**	TWEER	TYROS
TRIOL	TRYPS	TUNED	TWEET	**TYTE**
TRIOR	**TSAR**	TUNER	**TWIG**	STYTE
TRIOS	TSARS	TUNES	TWIGS	**TZAR**
TRIP	**TUAN**	**TUNG**	**TWIN**	TZARS
ATRIP	TUANS	STUNG	TWINE	**UDAL**
STRIP	**TUBA**	TUNGS	TWINK	UDALS
TRIPE	TUBAE	**TUNS**	TWINS	**UDON**
TRIPS	TUBAL	STUNS	TWINY	UDONS
TRIPY	TUBAR	**TURD**	**TWIT**	**UDOS**
TROD	TUBAS	TURDS	TWITE	BUDOS
TRODE	**TUBE**	**TURF**	TWITS	JUDOS
TRODS	TUBED	TURFS	**TYED**	KUDOS
TROG	TUBER	TURFY	STYED	LUDOS
TROGS	TUBES	**TURK**	**TYEE**	**UEYS**
TRON	**TUBS**	TURKS	TYEES	QUEYS
TRONA	STUBS	**TURM**	**TYER**	**UFOS**
TRONC	**TUCK**	TURME	TYERS	BUFOS
TRONE	STUCK	TURMS	**TYES**	**UGHS**
TRONK	TUCKS	**TURN**	STYES	EUGHS
TRONS	**TUFA**	TURNS	**TYIN**	SUGHS
TROP	TUFAS	**TURR**	TYING	VUGHS
STROP	**TUFF**	TURRS	**TYKE**	**UGLY**
TROPE	STUFF	**TUSH**	TYKES	FUGLY

UKES	GUMMA	DUNCE	YUPON	CURNS
BUKES	SUMMA	OUNCE	**UPTA**	DURNS
CUKES	UMMAH	PUNCE	UPTAK	GURNS
DUKES	UMMAS	UNCES	**URAO**	TURNS
JUKES	**UMPH**	**UNCI**	URAOS	**URPS**
NUKES	BUMPH	UNCIA	**URBS**	BURPS
PUKES	HUMPH	**UNCO**	BURBS	RURPS
YUKES	SUMPH	BUNCO	CURBS	TURPS
ULAN	UMPHS	JUNCO	**URDE**	**URSA**
KULAN	**UMPS**	UNCOS	URDEE	BURSA
YULAN	BUMPS	UNCOY	**URDS**	URSAE
ULANS	DUMPS	**UNDE**	BURDS	**URUS**
ULES	GUMPS	BUNDE	CURDS	GURUS
DULES	HUMPS	UNDEE	HURDS	KURUS
GULES	JUMPS	UNDER	NURDS	RURUS
HULES	LUMPS	**UNDO**	SURDS	**URVA**
MULES	MUMPS	UNDOS	TURDS	MURVA
PULES	PUMPS	**UNDY**	**URDY**	URVAS
RULES	RUMPS	BUNDY	CURDY	**USED**
TULES	SUMPS	CUNDY	GURDY	BUSED
YULES	TUMPS	FUNDY	NURDY	FUSED
ULEX	YUMPS	GUNDY	**UREA**	MUSED
CULEX	**UMPY**	OUNDY	UREAL	SUSED
ULNA	BUMPY	**UNIS**	UREAS	**USER**
ULNAD	DUMPY	MUNIS	**URES**	LUSER
ULNAE	HUMPY	SUNIS	AURES	MUSER
ULNAR	JUMPY	**UNIT**	CURES	USERS
ULNAS	LUMPY	CUNIT	DURES	**USES**
ULUS	RUMPY	UNITE	JURES	BUSES
LULUS	TUMPY	UNITS	LURES	FUSES
PULUS	**UMRA**	UNITY	MURES	MUSES
SULUS	UMRAH	**UNTO**	PURES	PUSES
ZULUS	UMRAS	JUNTO	SURES	RUSES
ULVA	**UMUS**	PUNTO	**URGE**	SUSES
VULVA	HUMUS	**UPAS**	GURGE	WUSES
ULVAS	MUMUS	OUPAS	PURGE	**UTAS**
UMBO	**UNAI**	PUPAS	SURGE	KUTAS
BUMBO	UNAIS	ZUPAS	URGED	**UTES**
DUMBO	**UNAU**	**UPBY**	URGER	BUTES
GUMBO	UNAUS	UPBYE	URGES	CUTES
JUMBO	**UNBE**	**UPDO**	**URIC**	JUTES
RUMBO	UNBED	UPDOS	AURIC	LUTES
UMBOS	**UNCE**	**UPON**	**URNS**	MUTES
UMMA	BUNCE	JUPON	BURNS	**UTIS**

CUTIS	VARAS	**VELD**	**VICE**	VIOLD
KUTIS	**VARE**	VELDS	VICED	VIOLS
MUTIS	VAREC	VELDT	VICES	**VIRE**
UTUS	VARES	**VELE**	**VIDE**	VIRED
KUTUS	**VARY**	VELES	VIDEO	VIREO
TUTUS	OVARY	**VELL**	**VIED**	VIRES
UVEA	**VASA**	KVELL	IVIED	**VIRL**
UVEAL	VASAL	VELLS	**VIER**	VIRLS
UVEAS	**VASE**	**VENA**	VIERS	**VISA**
VADE	VASES	VENAE	**VIES**	VISAS
EVADE	**VAST**	VENAL	IVIES	**VISE**
VADED	AVAST	**VEND**	**VIEW**	AVISE
VADES	VASTS	VENDS	VIEWS	VISED
VAIL	VASTY	VENDU	VIEWY	VISES
AVAIL	**VATU**	**VENT**	**VIFF**	**VITA**
VAILS	VATUS	EVENT	VIFFS	VITAE
VAIR	**VAUT**	VENTS	**VIGA**	VITAL
VAIRE	VAUTE	**VERB**	VIGAS	VITAS
VAIRS	VAUTS	VERBS	**VILD**	**VITE**
VAIRY	**VEAL**	**VERS**	VILDE	EVITE
VALE	UVEAL	AVERS	**VILE**	VITEX
AVALE	VEALE	OVERS	VILER	**VIVA**
VALES	VEALS	VERSE	**VILL**	VIVAS
VALET	VEALY	VERSO	VILLA	VIVAT
VALI	**VEEP**	VERST	VILLI	**VIVE**
VALID	VEEPS	**VERT**	VILLS	VIVER
VALIS	**VEER**	AVERT	**VINA**	VIVES
VAMP	VEERS	EVERT	VINAL	**VLEI**
VAMPS	VEERY	OVERT	VINAS	VLEIS
VAMPY	**VEGA**	VERTS	**VINE**	**VLOG**
VANE	VEGAN	VERTU	AVINE	VLOGS
VANED	VEGAS	**VERY**	OVINE	**VOAR**
VANES	**VEGO**	EVERY	VINED	VOARS
VANG	VEGOS	**VEST**	VINER	**VOID**
VANGS	**VEHM**	VESTA	VINES	AVOID
VANT	VEHME	VESTS	VINEW	OVOID
AVANT	**VEIL**	**VETS**	**VINO**	VOIDS
VANTS	VEILS	EVETS	VINOS	**VOIP**
VAPE	VEILY	**VIAL**	**VINT**	VOIPS
VAPED	**VEIN**	VIALS	VINTS	**VOLA**
VAPER	VEINS	**VIBE**	**VINY**	VOLAE
VAPES	VEINY	VIBES	VINYL	VOLAR
VARA	**VELA**	VIBEX	**VIOL**	**VOLE**
VARAN	VELAR	VIBEY	VIOLA	VOLED

VOLES	WADED	**WAKE**	WANKS	SWASH
VOLET	WADER	AWAKE	WANKY	WASHY
VOLK	WADES	WAKED	**WANS**	**WASM**
VOLKS	**WADI**	WAKEN	SWANS	WASMS
VOLT	WADIS	WAKER	**WANT**	**WASP**
VOLTA	**WADS**	WAKES	WANTS	WASPS
VOLTE	SWADS	**WAKF**	WANTY	WASPY
VOLTI	**WADT**	WAKFS	**WAPS**	**WAST**
VOLTS	WADTS	**WALD**	SWAPS	WASTE
VOTE	**WAES**	WALDO	**WAQF**	WASTS
VOTED	TWAES	WALDS	WAQFS	**WATE**
VOTER	**WAFF**	**WALE**	**WARB**	WATER
VOTES	WAFFS	DWALE	WARBS	**WATS**
VOWS	**WAFT**	SWALE	WARBY	SWATS
AVOWS	WAFTS	WALED	**WARD**	TWATS
VRIL	**WAGE**	WALER	AWARD	**WATT**
VRILS	SWAGE	WALES	SWARD	WATTS
VROU	WAGED	**WALI**	WARDS	**WAUK**
VROUS	WAGER	WALIS	**WARE**	WAUKS
VROUW	WAGES	**WALK**	AWARE	**WAUL**
VROW	**WAGS**	WALKS	SWARE	WAULK
VROWS	SWAGS	**WALL**	WARED	WAULS
VUGG	**WAID**	WALLA	WARES	**WAUR**
VUGGS	WAIDE	WALLS	WAREZ	WAURS
VUGGY	**WAIF**	WALLY	**WARK**	**WAVE**
VUGH	WAIFS	**WALY**	WARKS	AWAVE
VUGHS	WAIFT	SWALY	**WARM**	WAVED
VUGHY	**WAIL**	**WAME**	SWARM	WAVER
VULN	SWAIL	WAMED	WARMS	WAVES
VULNS	WAILS	WAMES	**WARN**	WAVEY
WAAC	**WAIN**	**WAND**	AWARN	**WAWA**
WAACS	SWAIN	WANDS	WARNS	WAWAS
WABS	TWAIN	**WANE**	**WARP**	**WAWE**
SWABS	WAINS	WANED	WARPS	WAWES
WACK	**WAIR**	WANES	**WARS**	**WAWL**
SWACK	WAIRS	WANEY	WARST	WAWLS
WACKE	**WAIS**	**WANG**	**WART**	**WAYS**
WACKO	WAIST	DWANG	SWART	AWAYS
WACKS	**WAIT**	SWANG	WARTS	SWAYS
WACKY	AWAIT	TWANG	WARTY	TWAYS
WADD	WAITE	WANGS	**WASE**	**WEAK**
WADDS	WAITS	**WANK**	WASES	TWEAK
WADDY	**WAKA**	SWANK	**WASH**	**WEAL**
WADE	WAKAS	TWANK	AWASH	SWEAL

WEALD	WEFTE	**WEXE**	**WHIT**	WILIS
WEALS	WEFTS	WEXED	WHITE	**WILL**
WEAN	**WEID**	WEXES	WHITS	SWILL
WEANS	WEIDS	**WEYS**	WHITY	TWILL
WEAR	**WEIL**	SWEYS	**WHIZ**	WILLS
SWEAR	WEILS	**WHAM**	WHIZZ	WILLY
WEARS	**WEIR**	WHAMO	**WHOM**	**WILT**
WEARY	SWEIR	WHAMS	WHOMP	TWILT
WEED	WEIRD	**WHAP**	**WHOP**	WILTS
SWEED	WEIRS	WHAPS	WHOPS	**WIMP**
TWEED	**WEKA**	**WHAT**	**WHOW**	WIMPS
WEEDS	WEKAS	WHATA	EWHOW	WIMPY
WEEDY	**WELD**	WHATS	WHOWS	**WIND**
WEEK	WELDS	**WHEE**	**WHUP**	WINDS
WEEKE	**WELK**	WHEEL	WHUPS	WINDY
WEEKS	WELKE	WHEEN	**WICE**	**WINE**
WEEL	WELKS	WHEEP	TWICE	DWINE
AWEEL	WELKT	**WHEN**	**WICK**	GWINE
SWEEL	**WELL**	WHENS	WICKS	SWINE
TWEEL	DWELL	**WHET**	WICKY	TWINE
WEELS	SWELL	WHETS	**WIDE**	WINED
WEEM	WELLS	**WHEW**	WIDEN	WINES
WEEMS	WELLY	WHEWS	WIDER	WINEY
WEEN	**WELS**	**WHEY**	WIDES	**WING**
TWEEN	WELSH	WHEYS	**WIEL**	AWING
WEENS	**WELT**	**WHID**	WIELD	OWING
WEENY	DWELT	WHIDS	WIELS	SWING
WEEP	SWELT	**WHIG**	**WIFE**	WINGE
SWEEP	WELTS	WHIGS	WIFED	WINGS
TWEEP	**WEMB**	**WHIM**	WIFES	WINGY
WEEPS	WEMBS	WHIMS	WIFEY	**WINK**
WEEPY	**WEND**	**WHIN**	**WIGS**	SWINK
WEER	WENDS	WHINE	SWIGS	TWINK
SWEER	**WENT**	WHINS	TWIGS	WINKS
TWEER	WENTS	WHINY	**WIKI**	**WINN**
WEES	**WEPT**	**WHIO**	WIKIS	WINNA
SWEES	SWEPT	WHIOS	**WILD**	WINNS
WEEST	**WERO**	**WHIP**	WILDS	**WINO**
WEET	WEROS	WHIPS	**WILE**	WINOS
SWEET	**WEST**	WHIPT	DWILE	**WINS**
TWEET	EWEST	**WHIR**	SWILE	TWINS
WEETE	WESTS	WHIRL	WILED	**WINY**
WEETS	**WETA**	WHIRR	WILES	TWINY
WEFT	WETAS	WHIRS	**WILI**	**WIPE**

SWIPE	WOADS	**WORK**	**YAAR**	YARRS
WIPED	**WOCK**	AWORK	YAARS	**YATE**
WIPER	WOCKS	WORKS	**YABA**	YATES
WIPES	**WOKE**	**WORM**	YABAS	**YAUD**
WIRE	AWOKE	WORMS	**YACK**	YAUDS
SWIRE	WOKEN	WORMY	KYACK	**YAUP**
TWIRE	**WOLD**	**WORN**	YACKA	YAUPS
WIRED	WOLDS	SWORN	YACKS	**YAWL**
WIRER	**WOLF**	**WORT**	**YADS**	YAWLS
WIRES	WOLFS	WORTH	DYADS	**YAWN**
WISE	**WOMB**	WORTS	**YAFF**	YAWNS
WISED	WOMBS	**WOTS**	NYAFF	YAWNY
WISER	WOMBY	SWOTS	YAFFS	**YAWP**
WISES	**WONK**	**WOVE**	**YAGE**	YAWPS
WISH	WONKS	WOVEN	YAGER	**YEAD**
SWISH	WONKY	**WRAP**	YAGES	YEADS
WISHA	**WONT**	WRAPS	**YAGI**	**YEAH**
WISHT	WONTS	WRAPT	YAGIS	YEAHS
WISP	**WOOD**	**WREN**	**YAHS**	**YEAN**
WISPS	WOODS	WRENS	AYAHS	YEANS
WISPY	WOODY	**WRIT**	**YAKS**	**YEAR**
WISS	**WOOF**	WRITE	KYAKS	YEARD
SWISS	WOOFS	WRITS	**YALE**	YEARN
WIST	WOOFY	**WUDU**	YALES	YEARS
TWIST	**WOOL**	WUDUS	**YAMS**	**YEAS**
WISTS	WOOLD	**WULL**	LYAMS	YEAST
WITE	WOOLS	WULLS	**YANG**	**YECH**
TWITE	WOOLY	**WUSS**	KYANG	YECHS
WITED	**WOON**	WUSSY	YANGS	YECHY
WITES	SWOON	**WYLE**	**YANK**	**YEDE**
WITH	WOONS	WYLED	YANKS	YEDES
SWITH	**WOOS**	WYLES	**YAPP**	**YEED**
WITHE	WOOSE	**WYND**	YAPPS	YEEDS
WITHS	WOOSH	WYNDS	YAPPY	**YEGG**
WITHY	**WOOT**	**WYNN**	**YARD**	YEGGS
WITS	WOOTZ	WYNNS	LYARD	**YELD**
SWITS	**WOPS**	**WYTE**	YARDS	GYELD
TWITS	SWOPS	WYTED	**YARE**	**YELK**
WIVE	**WORD**	WYTES	YARER	YELKS
SWIVE	SWORD	**XRAY**	**YARK**	**YELL**
WIVED	WORDS	XRAYS	YARKS	YELLS
WIVER	WORDY	**XYST**	**YARN**	**YELM**
WIVES	**WORE**	XYSTI	YARNS	YELMS
WOAD	SWORE	XYSTS	**YARR**	**YELP**

AYELP	YLEM	YORP	ZARFS	AZINE
YELPS	XYLEM	YORPS	ZARI	EZINE
YELT	YLEMS	YOUK	ZARIS	ZINEB
YELTS	YLKE	YOUKS	ZATI	ZINES
YENS	YLKES	YOUR	ZATIS	ZING
HYENS	YMPE	YOURN	ZEAL	ZINGS
SYENS	YMPES	YOURS	ZEALS	ZINGY
YERD	YOCK	YOURT	ZEBU	ZITI
YERDS	YOCKS	YOUS	ZEBUB	ZITIS
YERK	YODE	YOUSE	ZEBUS	ZOBO
YERKS	YODEL	YOWE	ZEDA	ZOBOS
YESK	YODH	YOWED	ZEDAS	ZOBU
YESKS	YODHS	YOWES	ZEES	ZOBUS
YEST	YOGA	YOWL	MZEES	ZOEA
YESTS	YOGAS	YOWLS	ZEIN	ZOEAE
YESTY	YOGH	YUAN	ZEINS	ZOEAL
YETI	YOGHS	YUANS	ZERK	ZOEAS
YETIS	YOGI	YUCA	ZERKS	ZOIC
YETT	YOGIC	YUCAS	ZERO	AZOIC
YETTS	YOGIN	YUCK	ZEROS	ZONA
YEUK	YOGIS	YUCKO	ZEST	ZONAE
YEUKS	YOKE	YUCKS	ZESTS	ZONAL
YEUKY	YOKED	YUCKY	ZESTY	ZONE
YEVE	YOKEL	YUFT	ZETA	OZONE
YEVEN	YOKER	YUFTS	ZETAS	ZONED
YEVES	YOKES	YUGA	ZEZE	ZONER
YIKE	YOLK	YUGAS	ZEZES	ZONES
YIKED	YOLKS	YUKE	ZHOS	ZONK
YIKES	YOLKY	YUKED	DZHOS	ZONKS
YILL	YOMP	YUKES	ZIFF	ZOOM
YILLS	YOMPS	YUKO	ZIFFS	ZOOMS
YINS	YONI	YUKOS	ZILA	ZOON
AYINS	YONIC	YULE	ZILAS	ZOONS
PYINS	YONIS	YULES	ZILL	ZOOT
YIPE	YONT	YUMP	ZILLA	ZOOTY
YIPES	AYONT	YUMPS	ZILLS	ZORI
YIRD	YOOF	YURT	ZIMB	ZORIL
YIRDS	YOOFS	YURTA	ZIMBI	ZORIS
YIRK	YOOP	YURTS	ZIMBS	ZOUK
YIRKS	YOOPS	YUZU	ZINC	ZOUKS
YIRR	YORE	YUZUS	ZINCO	ZULU
YIRRS	YORES	ZACK	ZINCS	ZULUS
YITE	YORK	ZACKS	ZINCY	ZUPA
YITES	YORKS	ZARF	ZINE	ZUPAN

ZUPAS	ZURFS	ZYGAL	AZYME	
ZURF	**ZYGA**	**ZYME**	ZYMES	

Five-letter root words

ABAKA	GABIES	FACERS	TACKER	DADDLE
KABAKA	RABIES	LACERS	WACKER	FADDLE
ABAKAS	**ABLED**	MACERS	YACKER	PADDLE
ABASE	CABLED	PACERS	ACKERS	RADDLE
ABASED	FABLED	RACERS	**ACRED**	SADDLE
ABASER	GABLED	**ACETA**	NACRED	WADDLE
ABASES	SABLED	ACETAL	SACRED	ADDLED
ABATE	TABLED	**ACHED**	**ACRES**	ADDLES
ABATED	**ABLER**	BACHED	NACRES	**ADIEU**
ABATER	CABLER	CACHED	**ACROS**	ADIEUS
ABATES	FABLER	GACHED	MACROS	ADIEUX
ABAYA	**ABLES**	**ACHES**	ACROSS	**ADIOS**
KABAYA	CABLES	BACHES	**ACTIN**	RADIOS
ABAYAS	FABLES	CACHES	ACTING	**ADMAN**
ABBAS	GABLES	GACHES	ACTINS	BADMAN
DABBAS	SABLES	LACHES	**ACTOR**	GADMAN
GABBAS	TABLES	MACHES	FACTOR	MADMAN
YABBAS	ABLEST	NACHES	ACTORS	**ADMEN**
ABBED	**ABLET**	RACHES	**ACUTE**	BADMEN
CABBED	CABLET	TACHES	ACUTER	GADMEN
DABBED	FABLET	**ACING**	ACUTES	MADMEN
GABBED	GABLET	FACING	**ADDED**	**ADMIX**
JABBED	TABLET	LACING	DADDED	ADMIXT
NABBED	ABLETS	MACING	GADDED	**ADORE**
SABBED	**ABODE**	PACING	MADDED	ADORED
TABBED	ABODED	RACING	PADDED	ADORER
ABELE	ABODES	**ACINI**	RADDED	ADORES
KABELE	**ABOON**	ACINIC	SADDED	**AECIA**
ABELES	BABOON	**ACKEE**	WADDED	AECIAL
ABERS	GABOON	HACKEE	**ADDER**	**AEONS**
CABERS	**ABUSE**	ACKEES	BADDER	PAEONS
JABERS	ABUSED	**ACKER**	GADDER	**AERIE**
SABERS	ABUSER	BACKER	LADDER	FAERIE
TABERS	ABUSES	DACKER	MADDER	AERIED
ABIDE	**ACARI**	HACKER	PADDER	AERIER
ABIDED	ACARID	JACKER	RADDER	AERIES
ABIDER	**ACCAS**	LACKER	SADDER	**AFEAR**
ABIDES	BACCAS	PACKER	WADDER	AFEARD
ABIES	YACCAS	RACKER	ADDERS	AFEARS
BABIES	**ACERS**	SACKER	**ADDLE**	**AFTER**

DAFTER	VAGILE	AIDERS	TAIVER	**ALFAS**
HAFTER	AGILER	**AIGAS**	WAIVER	HALFAS
RAFTER	**AGING**	SAIGAS	AIVERS	**ALIFS**
SAFTER	CAGING	TAIGAS	**AKEES**	CALIFS
WAFTER	GAGING	**AILED**	RAKEES	KALIFS
AFTERS	PAGING	BAILED	**AKING**	**ALIGN**
AGAMI	RAGING	FAILED	BAKING	MALIGN
AGAMIC	WAGING	HAILED	CAKING	ALIGNS
AGAMID	AGINGS	JAILED	FAKING	**ALINE**
AGAMIS	**AGISM**	MAILED	LAKING	MALINE
AGAZE	MAGISM	NAILED	MAKING	SALINE
AGAZED	AGISMS	RAILED	RAKING	VALINE
AGENE	**AGLET**	SAILED	TAKING	ALINED
SAGENE	EAGLET	TAILED	WAKING	ALINER
AGENES	HAGLET	VAILED	**AKKAS**	ALINES
AGERS	AGLETS	WAILED	YAKKAS	**ALIST**
CAGERS	**AGMAS**	**AIMED**	**ALANG**	MALIST
EAGERS	MAGMAS	MAIMED	LALANG	**ALIYA**
GAGERS	**AGONS**	**AIMER**	ALANGS	ALIYAH
JAGERS	WAGONS	MAIMER	**ALANT**	ALIYAS
LAGERS	**AGORA**	AIMERS	GALANT	**ALKIE**
PAGERS	AGORAE	**AINGA**	TALANT	TALKIE
RAGERS	AGORAS	KAINGA	ALANTS	ALKIES
WAGERS	**AGREE**	AINGAS	**ALAPA**	**ALLEE**
YAGERS	AGREED	**AIRED**	PALAPA	CALLEE
AGGER	AGREES	FAIRED	ALAPAS	MALLEE
BAGGER	**AGUED**	HAIRED	**ALAPS**	SALLEE
DAGGER	VAGUED	LAIRED	JALAPS	ALLEES
GAGGER	**AGUES**	PAIRED	**ALARY**	**ALLEL**
JAGGER	VAGUES	SAIRED	SALARY	HALLEL
LAGGER	**AGUNA**	WAIRED	**ALATE**	ALLELE
NAGGER	LAGUNA	**AIRER**	MALATE	ALLELS
SAGGER	AGUNAH	FAIRER	PALATE	**ALLEY**
TAGGER	**AHING**	PAIRER	ALATED	GALLEY
WAGGER	AAHING	SAIRER	ALATES	VALLEY
YAGGER	RAHING	AIRERS	**ALAYS**	WALLEY
AGGERS	**AIDAS**	**AIRNS**	PALAYS	ALLEYS
AGGIE	ZAIDAS	BAIRNS	**ALDER**	**ALLIS**
BAGGIE	**AIDED**	CAIRNS	BALDER	TALLIS
MAGGIE	LAIDED	**AISLE**	ALDERN	**ALLOT**
AGGIES	MAIDED	AISLED	ALDERS	BALLOT
AGHAS	RAIDED	AISLES	**ALEYE**	HALLOT
AGHAST	**AIDER**	**AIVER**	ALEYED	TALLOT
AGILE	RAIDER	NAIVER	ALEYES	ALLOTS

ALLOW	**AMATE**	RAMENS	CAMPLE	**ANGER**
BALLOW	HAMATE	YAMENS	SAMPLE	BANGER
CALLOW	RAMATE	**AMENT**	AMPLER	DANGER
FALLOW	AMATED	LAMENT	**AMPLY**	GANGER
GALLOW	AMATES	AMENTA	CAMPLY	HANGER
HALLOW	**AMAUT**	AMENTS	DAMPLY	LANGER
MALLOW	AMAUTI	**AMIAS**	**AMPUL**	MANGER
SALLOW	AMAUTS	LAMIAS	AMPULE	RANGER
TALLOW	**AMAZE**	ZAMIAS	AMPULS	SANGER
WALLOW	AMAZED	**AMIDO**	**AMRIT**	ANGERS
ALLOWS	AMAZES	AMIDOL	AMRITA	**ANGLE**
ALMAS	**AMBER**	**AMIDS**	AMRITS	BANGLE
HALMAS	CAMBER	AMIDST	**AMUSE**	CANGLE
TALMAS	JAMBER	**AMIES**	AMUSED	DANGLE
ALMUD	LAMBER	MAMIES	AMUSER	FANGLE
TALMUD	TAMBER	RAMIES	AMUSES	GANGLE
ALMUDE	AMBERS	**AMINE**	**ANANA**	JANGLE
ALMUDS	AMBERY	FAMINE	BANANA	MANGLE
ALOED	**AMBIT**	GAMINE	MANANA	TANGLE
HALOED	GAMBIT	TAMINE	ZANANA	WANGLE
ALOES	AMBITS	AMINES	ANANAS	ANGLED
HALOES	**AMBLE**	**AMINS**	**ANCHO**	ANGLER
ALONG	GAMBLE	GAMINS	RANCHO	ANGLES
KALONG	HAMBLE	RAMINS	SANCHO	**ANGRY**
ALOOS	RAMBLE	TAMINS	ANCHOR	HANGRY
BALOOS	WAMBLE	**AMMON**	ANCHOS	**ANGST**
ALTER	AMBLED	GAMMON	**ANCON**	ANGSTS
FALTER	AMBLER	MAMMON	ANCONE	ANGSTY
HALTER	AMBLES	AMMONO	**ANELE**	**ANIGH**
PALTER	**AMBOS**	AMMONS	ANELED	ANIGHT
SALTER	GAMBOS	**AMNIO**	ANELES	**ANIMA**
ALTERN	MAMBOS	AMNION	**ANENT**	ANIMAL
ALTERS	SAMBOS	AMNIOS	MANENT	ANIMAS
ALTOS	ZAMBOS	**AMOVE**	**ANGAS**	**ANION**
SALTOS	**AMEBA**	AMOVED	FANGAS	FANION
ALULA	AMEBAE	AMOVES	KANGAS	WANION
ALULAE	AMEBAN	**AMPED**	MANGAS	ANIONS
ALULAR	AMEBAS	CAMPED	PANGAS	**ANKER**
ALULAS	**AMEND**	DAMPED	RANGAS	BANKER
ALVAR	AMENDE	LAMPED	SANGAS	CANKER
VALVAR	AMENDS	RAMPED	TANGAS	DANKER
ALVARS	**AMENE**	TAMPED	**ANGEL**	HANKER
AMASS	AMENED	VAMPED	MANGEL	JANKER
CAMASS	**AMENS**	**AMPLE**	ANGELS	LANKER

RANKER	WANTED	CAPING	FARCED	CARKED
TANKER	**ANTES**	GAPING	**ARCHI**	DARKED
WANKER	MANTES	JAPING	ARCHIL	HARKED
YANKER	ZANTES	NAPING	**ARCOS**	KARKED
ANKERS	**ANTIC**	RAPING	NARCOS	LARKED
ANKLE	CANTIC	TAPING	YARCOS	MARKED
CANKLE	MANTIC	VAPING	**AREFY**	NARKED
FANKLE	ANTICK	**APISH**	RAREFY	PARKED
RANKLE	ANTICS	PAPISH	**ARETS**	RARKED
WANKLE	**ANTIS**	**APISM**	CARETS	WARKED
ANKLED	MANTIS	PAPISM	**ARGAL**	YARKED
ANKLES	**ANTRA**	APISMS	ARGALA	**ARLED**
ANKLET	MANTRA	**APNEA**	ARGALI	HARLED
ANKUS	TANTRA	APNEAL	ARGALS	MARLED
ANKUSH	YANTRA	APNEAS	**ARGAN**	PARLED
ANNAS	ANTRAL	**APPAL**	ARGAND	**ARLES**
CANNAS	**ANURA**	APPALL	ARGANS	CARLES
MANNAS	ANURAL	APPALS	**ARGLE**	FARLES
NANNAS	ANURAN	**APPAY**	DARGLE	MARLES
TANNAS	**ANYON**	APPAYD	GARGLE	PARLES
ANNEX	CANYON	APPAYS	ARGLED	**ARMED**
ANNEXE	ANYONE	**APPEL**	ARGLES	FARMED
ANNOY	ANYONS	LAPPEL	**ARGON**	HARMED
TANNOY	**AORTA**	RAPPEL	JARGON	WARMED
ANNOYS	AORTAE	APPELS	ARGONS	**ARMER**
ANNUL	AORTAL	**APPLE**	**ARGUE**	FARMER
ANNULI	AORTAS	DAPPLE	ARGUED	HARMER
ANNULS	**APEEK**	SAPPLE	ARGUER	WARMER
ANTAR	KAPEEK	APPLES	ARGUES	ARMERS
CANTAR	**APERS**	APPLET	**ARGUS**	**ARMOR**
KANTAR	CAPERS	APPLEY	SARGUS	ARMORS
ANTARA	GAPERS	**APRON**	**ARIAS**	ARMORY
ANTARS	JAPERS	NAPRON	VARIAS	**ARNAS**
ANTAS	PAPERS	APRONS	**ARISE**	VARNAS
MANTAS	RAPERS	**APSES**	ARISEN	**AROID**
ANTED	TAPERS	LAPSES	ARISES	LAROID
BANTED	VAPERS	**APTLY**	**ARISH**	AROIDS
CANTED	**APERY**	RAPTLY	BARISH	**ARPEN**
DANTED	JAPERY	**ARAKS**	GARISH	PARPEN
GANTED	NAPERY	YARAKS	HARISH	ARPENS
HANTED	PAPERY	**ARBOR**	MARISH	ARPENT
KANTED	**APHIS**	HARBOR	PARISH	**ARRAH**
PANTED	RAPHIS	ARBORS	**ARKED**	JARRAH
RANTED	**APING**	**ARCED**	BARKED	**ARRAS**

BARRAS	MARTEL	MASHES	ASSETS	**AUGHT**
MARRAS	ARTELS	PASHES	**ASSOT**	CAUGHT
NARRAS	**ARTIS**	RASHES	ASSOTS	HAUGHT
PARRAS	AARTIS	SASHES	ASSOTT	NAUGHT
TARRAS	PARTIS	TASHES	**ASTER**	RAUGHT
ARRAY	ARTIST	WASHES	BASTER	TAUGHT
WARRAY	**ARUMS**	**ASKED**	CASTER	WAUGHT
ARRAYS	GARUMS	BASKED	EASTER	AUGHTS
ARRET	LARUMS	CASKED	FASTER	**AUGUR**
BARRET	**ARVAL**	MASKED	GASTER	AUGURS
GARRET	LARVAL	TASKED	LASTER	AUGURY
ARRETS	**ARVOS**	**ASKER**	MASTER	**AUNTS**
ARRIS	PARVOS	MASKER	PASTER	DAUNTS
KARRIS	**ASCON**	TASKER	RASTER	GAUNTS
MARRIS	GASCON	ASKERS	TASTER	HAUNTS
ARRISH	MASCON	**ASPER**	VASTER	JAUNTS
ARROW	ASCONS	GASPER	WASTER	NAUNTS
BARROW	**ASCOT**	JASPER	ASTERN	SAUNTS
FARROW	MASCOT	RASPER	ASTERS	TAUNTS
HARROW	ASCOTS	ASPERS	ASTERT	VAUNTS
MARROW	**ASHED**	**ASPIC**	**ATAPS**	**AUNTY**
NARROW	BASHED	ASPICK	WATAPS	JAUNTY
TARROW	CASHED	ASPICS	**ATMAN**	VAUNTY
YARROW	DASHED	**ASPIS**	BATMAN	**AURAE**
ARROWS	FASHED	JASPIS	VATMAN	LAURAE
ARROWY	GASHED	ASPISH	ATMANS	**AURAS**
ARSED	HASHED	**ASSAI**	**ATOKE**	LAURAS
FARSED	LASHED	ASSAIL	MATOKE	**AURIC**
PARSED	MASHED	ASSAIS	ATOKES	LAURIC
ARSES	PASHED	**ASSES**	**ATONE**	TAURIC
CARSES	RASHED	BASSES	ATONED	**AURIS**
FARSES	SASHED	GASSES	ATONER	CAURIS
MARSES	TASHED	HASSES	ATONES	KAURIS
PARSES	WASHED	JASSES	**ATRIA**	MAURIS
ARSEY	**ASHEN**	LASSES	LATRIA	AURIST
CARSEY	WASHEN	MASSES	ATRIAL	**AVAIL**
KARSEY	**ASHES**	PASSES	**AUDAD**	AVAILE
ARSON	BASHES	RASSES	CAUDAD	AVAILS
PARSON	CASHES	SASSES	AUDADS	**AVALE**
ARSONS	DASHES	TASSES	**AUGER**	AVALED
ARTAL	FASHES	ASSESS	GAUGER	AVALES
HARTAL	GASHES	**ASSET**	MAUGER	**AVANT**
ARTEL	HASHES	BASSET	SAUGER	SAVANT
CARTEL	LASHES	TASSET	AUGERS	AVANTI

AVELS	VAWARD	TAXMAN	BALSAM	BARRES
CAVELS	AWARDS	**AXMEN**	BALSAS	BARRET
FAVELS	**AWARE**	SAXMEN	**BALTI**	**BARRO**
GAVELS	AWARER	TAXMEN	BALTIC	BARROW
JAVELS	**AWFUL**	**AXONS**	BALTIS	**BASAL**
NAVELS	LAWFUL	CAXONS	**BANDA**	BASALT
RAVELS	**AWING**	TAXONS	BANDAR	**BASAN**
AVENS	CAWING	**AYAHS**	BANDAS	BASANS
DAVENS	DAWING	RAYAHS	**BANDS**	BASANT
HAVENS	HAWING	**AYINS**	ABANDS	**BASED**
MAVENS	JAWING	LAYINS	**BANGS**	ABASED
PAVENS	KAWING	ZAYINS	OBANGS	**BASER**
RAVENS	LAWING	**AYRES**	**BANIA**	ABASER
AVERS	MAWING	FAYRES	BANIAN	**BASES**
CAVERS	PAWING	**AZANS**	BANIAS	ABASES
HAVERS	RAWING	HAZANS	**BANYA**	BASEST
LAVERS	SAWING	**AZONS**	BANYAN	**BASIN**
PAVERS	TAWING	GAZONS	BANYAS	BASING
RAVERS	YAWING	**AZOTE**	**BARBE**	BASINS
SAVERS	**AWNED**	AZOTED	BARBED	**BASSE**
TAVERS	DAWNED	AZOTES	BARBEL	BASSED
WAVERS	FAWNED	**AZURE**	BARBER	BASSER
AVERSE	LAWNED	RAZURE	BARBES	BASSES
AVERT	PAWNED	AZURES	BARBET	BASSET
TAVERT	YAWNED	**BABOO**	**BARDE**	**BASTE**
AVERTS	**AWNER**	BABOOL	BARDED	BASTED
AVINE	DAWNER	BABOON	BARDES	BASTER
RAVINE	FAWNER	BABOOS	**BARES**	BASTES
SAVINE	PAWNER	**BACCA**	BAREST	**BATED**
AVISE	YAWNER	BACCAE	**BARGE**	ABATED
PAVISE	AWNERS	BACCAS	BARGED	**BATES**
AVISED	**AWOKE**	**BADGE**	BARGEE	ABATES
AVISES	AWOKEN	BADGED	BARGES	**BATHE**
AVIZE	**AXING**	BADGER	**BARON**	BATHED
AVIZED	FAXING	BADGES	BARONG	BATHER
AVIZES	MAXING	**BAIZE**	BARONS	BATHES
AVYZE	RAXING	BAIZED	BARONY	**BATTU**
AVYZED	TAXING	BAIZES	**BARRA**	ABATTU
AVYZES	WAXING	**BAKER**	BARRAS	BATTUE
AWAKE	**AXITE**	BAKERS	BARRAT	**BAULK**
AWAKED	TAXITE	BAKERY	**BARRE**	BAULKS
AWAKEN	AXITES	**BALLS**	BARRED	BAULKY
AWAKES	**AXMAN**	BALLSY	BARREL	**BAZOO**
AWARD	SAXMAN	**BALSA**	BARREN	BAZOOM

BAZOOS	BELLED	BIDERS	BLADES	ABLETS
BEACH	BELLES	**BIDES**	**BLAES**	**BLING**
BEACHY	**BELON**	ABIDES	BLAEST	ABLING
BEARD	BELONG	**BIELD**	**BLAME**	BLINGS
BEARDS	BELONS	BIELDS	BLAMED	BLINGY
BEARDY	**BEMIX**	BIELDY	BLAMER	**BLINS**
BEARE	BEMIXT	**BIFID**	BLAMES	ABLINS
BEARED	**BENCH**	BIFIDA	**BLANK**	**BLOCK**
BEARER	BENCHY	**BIJOU**	BLANKS	BLOCKS
BEARES	**BENNE**	BIJOUS	BLANKY	BLOCKY
BEARS	BENNES	BIJOUX	**BLARE**	**BLOKE**
ABEARS	BENNET	**BILBO**	BLARED	BLOKES
BEAUT	**BENTO**	BILBOA	BLARES	BLOKEY
BEAUTS	OBENTO	BILBOS	**BLASH**	**BLOND**
BEAUTY	BENTOS	**BILGE**	BLASHY	BLONDE
BECKE	**BERME**	BILGED	**BLAST**	BLONDS
BECKED	BERMED	BILGES	OBLAST	**BLOOD**
BECKES	BERMES	**BILLY**	BLASTS	BLOODS
BECKET	**BERTH**	BILLYO	BLASTY	BLOODY
BEDEL	BERTHA	**BINGE**	**BLATE**	**BLOOM**
BEDELL	BERTHE	BINGED	ABLATE	ABLOOM
BEDELS	BERTHS	BINGER	OBLATE	BLOOMS
BEDYE	**BESEE**	BINGES	BLATED	BLOOMY
BEDYED	BESEEM	**BIRLE**	BLATER	**BLOOP**
BEDYES	BESEEN	BIRLED	BLATES	BLOOPS
BEECH	BESEES	BIRLER	**BLAZE**	BLOOPY
BEECHY	**BESTI**	BIRLES	ABLAZE	**BLOWS**
BEEDI	BESTIE	**BIRSE**	BLAZED	BLOWSE
BEEDIE	BESTIR	BIRSED	BLAZER	BLOWSY
BEGUN	BESTIS	BIRSES	BLAZES	**BLUES**
BEGUNK	**BETID**	**BISES**	**BLEAK**	BLUEST
BEIGE	BETIDE	IBISES	BLEAKS	BLUESY
BEIGEL	**BETON**	**BITCH**	BLEAKY	**BLUID**
BEIGER	BETONS	BITCHY	**BLEAR**	BLUIDS
BEIGES	BETONY	**BITER**	BLEARS	BLUIDY
BELEE	**BHAJI**	OBITER	BLEARY	**BLUME**
BELEED	BHAJIA	BITERS	**BLEND**	BLUMED
BELEES	BHAJIS	**BITTE**	BLENDE	BLUMES
BELIE	**BICES**	BITTED	BLENDS	**BLUSH**
BELIED	IBICES	BITTEN	**BLENT**	ABLUSH
BELIEF	**BIDED**	BITTER	YBLENT	**BOARD**
BELIER	ABIDED	**BLADE**	**BLEST**	ABOARD
BELIES	**BIDER**	BLADED	ABLEST	BOARDS
BELLE	ABIDER	BLADER	**BLETS**	**BOCCI**

BOCCIA	**BOOSE**	BOURNE	BRASHY	BRIBER
BOCCIE	BOOSED	BOURNS	**BRASS**	BRIBES
BOCCIS	BOOSES	**BOUSE**	BRASSY	**BRICK**
BODED	**BOOZE**	BOUSED	**BRAVE**	BRICKS
ABODED	BOOZED	BOUSES	BRAVED	BRICKY
BODES	BOOZER	**BOUTS**	BRAVER	**BRIDE**
ABODES	BOOZES	ABOUTS	BRAVES	BRIDED
BODGE	BOOZEY	**BOWER**	**BRAWL**	BRIDES
BODGED	**BORAL**	BOWERS	BRAWLS	**BRIER**
BODGER	ABORAL	BOWERY	BRAWLY	BRIERS
BODGES	BORALS	**BOWNE**	**BRAWN**	BRIERY
BOGIE	**BORDE**	BOWNED	BRAWNS	**BRIKS**
BOGIED	BORDEL	BOWNES	BRAWNY	IBRIKS
BOGIES	BORDER	**BOWSE**	**BRAYS**	**BRILL**
BOGLE	BORDES	BOWSED	ABRAYS	BRILLO
BOGLED	**BORDS**	BOWSER	**BRAZE**	BRILLS
BOGLES	ABORDS	BOWSES	BRAZED	**BRINE**
BOLES	**BOREE**	BOWSEY	BRAZEN	BRINED
OBOLES	BOREEN	**BOYAR**	BRAZER	BRINER
BOLUS	BOREES	BOYARD	BRAZES	BRINES
OBOLUS	**BORNE**	BOYARS	**BREAD**	**BRINS**
BOMAS	ABORNE	**BOYAU**	BREADS	ABRINS
ABOMAS	**BORTS**	BOYAUX	BREADY	**BRISK**
BOMBE	ABORTS	**BRACE**	**BREDE**	BRISKS
BOMBED	**BOSOM**	BRACED	BREDED	BRISKY
BOMBER	BOSOMS	BRACER	BREDES	**BROAD**
BOMBES	BOSOMY	BRACES	**BREES**	ABROAD
BONIE	**BOTCH**	**BRAID**	BREESE	BROADS
BONIER	BOTCHY	ABRAID	BREEST	**BROCH**
BONNE	**BOTTE**	BRAIDE	**BREIS**	BROCHE
BONNES	BOTTED	BRAIDS	BREIST	BROCHO
BONNET	BOTTES	**BRAIN**	**BRENT**	BROCHS
BONZE	**BOUGE**	BRAINS	YBRENT	**BROKE**
BONZER	BOUGED	BRAINY	BRENTS	BROKED
BONZES	BOUGES	**BRAKE**	**BREVE**	BROKEN
BOOKS	BOUGET	BRAKED	BREVES	BROKER
EBOOKS	**BOUGH**	BRAKES	BREVET	BROKES
BOOKSY	BOUGHS	**BRAND**	**BRIAR**	**BRONC**
BOONG	BOUGHT	BRANDS	BRIARD	BRONCO
BOONGA	**BOUND**	BRANDY	BRIARS	BRONCS
BOONGS	ABOUND	**BRANK**	BRIARY	**BROOD**
BOORD	YBOUND	BRANKS	**BRIBE**	BROODS
BOORDE	BOUNDS	BRANKY	BRIBED	BROODY
BOORDS	**BOURN**	**BRASH**	BRIBEE	**BROOM**

BROOMS	BULLAE	BUTTED	CAMASS	**CARAT**
BROOMY	**BUMBO**	BUTTER	**CAMEL**	CARATE
BROOS	BUMBOS	BUTTES	SCAMEL	CARATS
BROOSE	BUMBOY	**CABAL**	CAMELS	**CARBO**
BROTH	**BUNAS**	CABALA	**CAMES**	CARBON
BROTHA	ABUNAS	CABALS	CAMESE	CARBOS
BROTHS	**BUNCE**	**CABBY**	**CAMIS**	CARBOY
BROTHY	BUNCED	SCABBY	CAMISA	**CARDI**
BROWN	**BUNCES**	**CABLE**	CAMISE	CARDIA
BROWNS	**BUNCH**	CABLED	**CAMPI**	CARDIE
BROWNY	BUNCHY	CABLER	SCAMPI	CARDIO
BROWS	**BUNDE**	CABLES	**CAMPS**	CARDIS
BROWSE	BUNDED	CABLET	SCAMPS	**CARED**
BROWST	**BUNJE**	**CACHE**	**CANNA**	SCARED
BROWSY	BUNJEE	CACHED	CANNAE	**CARER**
BRUSH	BUNJES	CACHES	CANNAS	SCARER
BRUSHY	**BURKE**	CACHET	**CANOE**	CARERS
BRUTE	BURKED	**CADGE**	CANOED	**CARES**
BRUTED	BURKER	CADGED	CANOER	SCARES
BRUTER	BURKES	CADGER	CANOES	CARESS
BRUTES	**BURRO**	CADGES	**CANTO**	**CARNY**
BUBAL	BURROS	**CAECA**	CANTON	CARNYX
BUBALE	BURROW	CAECAL	CANTOR	**CAROL**
BUBALS	**BURSA**	**CAFFS**	CANTOS	CAROLI
BUDGE	BURSAE	SCAFFS	**CANTS**	CAROLS
BUDGED	BURSAL	**CAIRN**	SCANTS	**CARPS**
BUDGER	BURSAR	CAIRNS	**CANTY**	SCARPS
BUDGES	BURSAS	CATRNY	SCANTY	**CARRY**
BUDGET	**BURST**	**CALLA**	**CAPAS**	SCARRY
BUFFE	ABURST	CALLAN	SCAPAS	**CARSE**
BUFFED	BURSTS	CALLAS	**CAPED**	CARSES
BUFFEL	BURSTY	**CALLS**	SCAPED	CARSEY
BUFFER	**BUSED**	SCALLS	**CAPES**	**CARTE**
BUFFET	ABUSED	**CALPA**	SCAPES	ECARTE
BUGLE	**BUSES**	CALPAC	**CAPLE**	CARTED
BUGLED	ABUSES	CALPAS	CAPLES	CARTEL
BUGLER	**BUSTI**	**CALPS**	CAPLET	CARTER
BUGLES	BUSTIC	SCALPS	**CAPOT**	CARTES
BUGLET	BUSTIS	**CALVE**	CAPOTE	**CARTS**
BULGE	**BUTLE**	CALVED	CAPOTS	SCARTS
BULGED	BUTLED	CALVER	**CAPRI**	**CARVE**
BULGER	BUTLER	CALVES	CAPRIC	CARVED
BULGES	BUTLES	**CAMAS**	CAPRID	CARVEL
BULLA	**BUTTE**	CAMASH	CAPRIS	CARVEN

CARVER	**CEDAR**	**CHAIS**	**CHAVS**	**CHILD**
CARVES	CEDARN	CHAISE	SCHAVS	CHILDE
CASTE	CEDARS	**CHALK**	**CHEAP**	CHILDS
CASTED	CEDARY	CHALKS	CHEAPO	**CHILL**
CASTER	**CELLA**	CHALKY	CHEAPS	CHILLI
CASTES	CELLAE	**CHAMP**	CHEAPY	CHILLS
CATCH	CELLAR	CHAMPS	**CHECK**	CHILLY
SCATCH	**CELLI**	CHAMPY	CHECKS	**CHIME**
CATCHT	OCELLI	**CHANG**	CHECKY	CHIMED
CATCHY	**CENSE**	CHANGA	**CHEEK**	CHIMER
CATER	CENSED	CHANGE	CHEEKS	CHIMES
ACATER	CENSER	CHANGS	CHEEKY	**CHINA**
CATERS	CENSES	**CHANT**	**CHEER**	CHINAR
CATES	**CENTS**	CHANTS	CHEERO	CHINAS
ACATES	SCENTS	CHANTY	CHEERS	**CHINE**
CATTY	**CENTU**	**CHAPE**	CHEERY	CHINED
SCATTY	CENTUM	CHAPEL	**CHELA**	CHINES
CAUDA	**CERNE**	CHAPES	CHELAE	**CHING**
CAUDAD	SCERNE	**CHARD**	CHELAS	ACHING
CAUDAE	CERNED	ECHARD	**CHERT**	ECHING
CAUDAL	CERNES	CHARDS	CHERTS	ICHING
CAUPS	**CESSE**	**CHARE**	CHERTY	CHINGS
SCAUPS	CESSED	CHARED	**CHEST**	**CHINK**
CAUSA	CESSER	CHARES	CHESTS	CHINKS
CAUSAE	CESSES	CHARET	CHESTY	CHINKY
CAUSAL	**CETYL**	**CHARK**	**CHIAS**	**CHINS**
CAUSE	ACETYL	CHARKA	CHIASM	CHINSE
CAUSED	CETYLS	CHARKS	**CHICH**	**CHIRP**
CAUSEN	**CHACE**	**CHARR**	CHICHA	CHIRPS
CAUSER	CHACED	CHARRO	CHICHI	CHIRPY
CAUSES	CHACES	CHARRS	**CHICK**	**CHIRR**
CAUSEY	**CHADO**	CHARRY	TCHICK	CHIRRE
CAVER	CHADOR	**CHARS**	CHICKS	CHIRRS
CAVERN	CHADOS	ACHARS	**CHICO**	**CHIVE**
CAVERS	**CHAFE**	**CHART**	CHICON	CHIVED
CAVIE	CHAFED	CHARTA	CHICOS	CHIVES
CAVIER	CHAFER	CHARTS	CHICOT	**CHOCK**
CAVIES	CHAFES	**CHASE**	**CHIDE**	CHOCKO
CEASE	**CHAFF**	CHASED	CHIDED	CHOCKS
CEASED	CHAFFS	CHASER	CHIDER	**CHOKE**
CEASES	CHAFFY	CHASES	CHIDES	CHOKED
CEAZE	**CHAIN**	**CHASM**	**CHIEL**	CHOKER
CEAZED	CHAINE	CHASMS	CHIELD	CHOKES
CEAZES	CHAINS	CHASMY	CHIELS	CHOKEY

CHOLI	CIRCAR	CLIPES	CNIDAE	COMMOT
CHOLIC	**CLANK**	**CLOKE**	**COACH**	**COMPO**
CHOLIS	CLANKS	CLOKED	COACHY	COMPOS
CHORD	CLANKY	CLOKES	**COATE**	COMPOT
CHORDA	**CLART**	**CLONE**	COATED	**CONCH**
CHORDS	CLARTS	CLONED	COATEE	CONCHA
CHORE	CLARTY	CLONER	COATER	CONCHE
CHOREA	**CLASP**	CLONES	COATES	CONCHO
CHORED	CLASPS	**CLONK**	**COCCI**	CONCHS
CHOREE	CLASPT	CLONKS	COCCIC	CONCHY
CHORES	**CLASS**	CLONKY	COCCID	**CONDO**
CHOSE	CLASSY	**CLOSE**	**COCKS**	CONDOM
CHOSEN	**CLATS**	ECLOSE	COCKSY	CONDOR
CHOSES	ECLATS	CLOSED	**COFFS**	CONDOS
CHOUT	**CLAVE**	CLOSER	SCOFFS	**CONES**
SCHOUT	SCLAVE	CLOSES	**COHOS**	ICONES
CHOUTS	CLAVER	CLOSET	COHOSH	SCONES
CHOWS	CLAVES	**CLOTH**	COHOST	**CONGE**
CHOWSE	**CLAVI**	CLOTHE	**COIGN**	CONGED
CHUCK	CLAVIE	CLOTHS	COIGNE	CONGEE
CHUCKS	CLAVIS	**CLOUD**	COIGNS	CONGER
CHUCKY	**CLECK**	CLOUDS	**COLDS**	CONGES
CHUFF	CLECKS	CLOUDY	SCOLDS	**CONGO**
CHUFFS	CLECKY	**CLOVE**	**COLON**	CONGOS
CHUFFY	**CLEPE**	CLOVEN	COLONE	CONGOU
CHUNK	CLEPED	CLOVER	COLONI	**CONIC**
CHUNKS	CLEPES	CLOVES	COLONS	ICONIC
CHUNKY	**CLEPT**	**CLOYE**	COLONY	CONICS
CHURR	YCLEPT	CLOYED	**COLOR**	**CONIN**
CHURRO	**CLEVE**	CLOYES	COLORS	CONINE
CHURRS	CLEVER	**CLUCK**	COLORY	CONING
CHUSE	CLEVES	CLUCKS	**COMBE**	CONINS
CHUSED	**CLIFF**	CLUCKY	COMBED	**CONNE**
CHUSES	SCLIFF	**CLUMP**	COMBER	CONNED
CHUTE	CLIFFS	CLUMPS	COMBES	CONNER
CHUTED	CLIFFY	CLUMPY	**COMET**	CONNES
CHUTES	**CLIFT**	**CLUNK**	COMETH	**CONVO**
CIDER	CLIFTS	CLUNKS	COMETS	CONVOS
ACIDER	CLIFTY	CLUNKY	**COMIC**	CONVOY
CIDERS	**CLING**	**CLYPE**	COMICE	**COOCH**
CIDERY	CLINGS	CLYPED	COMICS	SCOOCH
CIONS	CLINGY	CLYPEI	**COMMO**	**COOEE**
SCIONS	**CLIPE**	CLYPES	COMMON	COOEED
CIRCA	CLIPED	**CNIDA**	COMMOS	COOEES

COOMB	CORSEY	COVENT	SCRANS	CREEPY
COOMBE	**COSEC**	**COVER**	**CRAPE**	**CREES**
COOMBS	COSECH	COVERS	SCRAPE	SCREES
COOPS	COSECS	COVERT	CRAPED	CREESE
SCOOPS	**COSIE**	**COVIN**	CRAPES	CREESH
COOTS	COSIED	COVINE	**CRAPS**	**CREPE**
SCOOTS	COSIER	COVING	SCRAPS	CREPED
COPAL	COSIES	COVINS	**CRATE**	CREPES
COPALM	**COSTA**	**COWED**	CRATED	CREPEY
COPALS	COSTAE	SCOWED	CRATER	**CRESS**
COPED	COSTAL	**COWLS**	CRATES	CRESSY
SCOPED	COSTAR	SCOWLS	**CRAVE**	**CREST**
COPES	**COSTE**	**COWPS**	CRAVED	CRESTA
SCOPES	COSTED	SCOWPS	CRAVEN	CRESTS
COPRA	COSTER	**COZIE**	CRAVER	**CREWE**
COPRAH	COSTES	COZIED	CRAVES	CREWED
COPRAS	**COTTA**	COZIER	**CRAWL**	CREWEL
COPSE	COTTAE	COZIES	ACRAWL	CREWES
COPSED	COTTAR	**CRABS**	SCRAWL	**CREWS**
COPSES	COTTAS	SCRABS	CRAWLS	SCREWS
CORBE	**COUCH**	**CRACK**	CRAWLY	**CRICK**
CORBEL	COUCHE	CRACKA	**CRAWS**	CRICKS
CORBES	**COUNT**	CRACKS	SCRAWS	CRICKY
CORED	COUNTS	CRACKY	**CRAYS**	**CRIED**
SCORED	COUNTY	**CRAFT**	SCRAYS	SCRIED
CORER	**COUPE**	CRAFTS	**CRAZE**	**CRIES**
SCORER	COUPED	CRAFTY	CRAZED	SCRIES
CORERS	COUPEE	**CRAGS**	CRAZES	**CRIME**
CORES	COUPER	SCRAGS	**CREAK**	CRIMED
SCORES	COUPES	**CRAKE**	SCREAK	CRIMEN
CORIA	**COUPS**	CRAKED	CREAKS	CRIMES
SCORIA	SCOUPS	CRAKES	CREAKY	**CRIMP**
CORNS	**COURE**	**CRAMP**	**CREAM**	SCRIMP
ACORNS	COURED	CRAMPS	SCREAM	CRIMPS
SCORNS	COURES	CRAMPY	CREAMS	CRIMPY
CORNU	**COURS**	**CRAMS**	CREAMY	**CRIMS**
CORNUA	SCOURS	SCRAMS	**CREED**	SCRIMS
CORNUS	COURSE	**CRANE**	SCREED	**CRINE**
CORPS	**COUTH**	CRANED	CREEDS	SCRINE
CORPSE	SCOUTH	CRANES	**CREEK**	CRINED
CORSE	COUTHS	**CRANK**	CREEKS	CRINES
SCORSE	COUTHY	CRANKS	CREEKY	**CRIPS**
CORSES	**COVEN**	CRANKY	**CREEP**	SCRIPS
CORSET	COVENS	**CRANS**	CREEPS	**CRISP**

CRISPS	CRUMPY	CURIET	DAMMED	DECAFS
CRISPY	**CRURA**	**CURRY**	DAMMER	**DECAN**
CROAK	CRURAL	SCURRY	**DANCE**	DECANE
CROAKS	**CRUSE**	**CURSE**	DANCED	DECANI
CROAKY	CRUSES	CURSED	DANCER	DECANS
CROGS	CRUSET	CURSER	DANCES	DECANT
SCROGS	**CRUST**	CURSES	DANCEY	**DEEMS**
CROME	CRUSTA	**CURVE**	**DANTS**	ADEEMS
SCROME	CRUSTS	CURVED	IDANTS	**DEEVE**
CROMED	**CRUSTY**	CURVES	**DARGA**	DEEVED
CROMES	**CRYER**	CURVET	DARGAH	DEEVES
CRONE	SCRYER	CURVEY	DARGAS	**DEGUS**
CRONES	CRYERS	**CURVY**	**DARRE**	DEGUST
CRONET	**CRYPT**	SCURVY	DARRED	**DEICE**
CROON	CRYPTO	**CUTCH**	DARRES	DEICED
CROONS	CRYPTS	SCUTCH	**DAUBE**	DEICER
CROONY	**CUBIC**	CUTCHA	DAUBED	DEICES
CROSS	CUBICA	**CUTER**	DAUBER	**DEIGN**
ACROSS	CUBICS	ACUTER	DAUBES	SDEIGN
CROSSE	**CUBIT**	**CUTES**	**DAWED**	DEIGNS
CROUP	CUBITI	ACUTES	ADAWED	**DELIS**
CROUPE	CUBITS	SCUTES	**DEALS**	DELISH
CROUPS	**CUFFS**	CUTEST	IDEALS	DELIST
CROUPY	SCUFFS	CUTESY	**DEARE**	**DELVE**
CROUT	**CULCH**	**CUTTO**	DEARED	DELVED
CROUTE	SCULCH	CUTTOE	DEARER	DELVER
CROUTS	**CULLS**	**CYCLE**	DEARES	DELVES
CROWD	SCULLS	CYCLED	**DEATH**	**DEMAN**
CROWDS	**CULPA**	CYCLER	DEATHS	DEMAND
CROWDY	CULPAE	CYCLES	DEATHY	DEMANS
CROWS	**CULTI**	**DAIKO**	**DEAVE**	**DEMUR**
SCROWS	CULTIC	DAIKON	DEAVED	DEMURE
CROZE	**CURAT**	DAIKOS	DEAVES	DEMURS
CROZER	CURATE	**DAINE**	**DEBAR**	**DENAR**
CROZES	CURATS	SDAINE	DEBARK	DENARI
CRUDE	**CURFS**	DAINED	DEBARS	DENARS
CRUDER	SCURFS	DAINES	**DEBUR**	DENARY
CRUDES	**CURIA**	**DAINT**	DEBURR	**DENSE**
CRUMB	CURIAE	DAINTS	DEBURS	DENSER
CRUMBS	CURIAL	DAINTY	**DECAD**	**DENTS**
CRUMBY	CURIAS	**DALED**	DECADE	IDENTS
CRUMP	**CURIE**	DALEDH	DECADS	**DERAT**
SCRUMP	ECURIE	DALEDS	**DECAF**	DERATE
CRUMPS	CURIES	**DAMME**	DECAFF	DERATS

DERMA	DIVEST	DORSAL	DRAWLS	**DROOL**
DERMAL	**DJINN**	**DORSE**	DRAWLY	DROOLS
DERMAS	DJINNI	DORSEL	**DREAD**	DROOLY
DESIS	DJINNS	DORSER	ADREAD	**DROOP**
DESIST	DJINNY	DORSES	DREADS	DROOPS
DEUCE	**DOBES**	**DOUCE**	**DREAM**	DROOPY
DEUCED	ADOBES	DOUCER	DREAMS	**DROPS**
DEUCES	**DODGE**	DOUCET	DREAMT	DROPSY
DEVIS	DODGED	**DOUGH**	DREAMY	**DROSS**
DEVISE	DODGEM	DOUGHS	**DREAR**	DROSSY
DEVOT	DODGER	DOUGHT	DREARE	**DROVE**
DEVOTE	DODGES	DOUGHY	DREARS	DROVED
DEVOTS	**DOGMA**	**DOURA**	DREARY	DROVER
DEWAN	DOGMAN	DOURAH	**DRECK**	DROVES
DEWANI	DOGMAS	DOURAS	DRECKS	**DROWN**
DEWANS	**DOLMA**	**DOUSE**	DRECKY	DROWND
DICTS	DOLMAN	DOUSED	**DREES**	DROWNS
EDICTS	DOLMAS	DOUSER	DREEST	**DROWS**
DIKAS	**DONNA**	DOUSES	**DRESS**	DROWSE
DIKAST	DONNAS	**DOVIE**	DRESSY	DROWSY
DILDO	DONNAT	DOVIER	**DRIES**	**DRUPE**
DILDOE	**DONNE**	**DOWER**	DRIEST	DRUPEL
DILDOS	DONNED	DOWERS	**DRIFT**	DRUPES
DIMPS	DONNEE	DOWERY	ADRIFT	**DRUSE**
DIMPSY	DONNES	**DOWIE**	DRIFTS	DRUSEN
DINER	**DOOCE**	DOWIER	DRIFTY	DRUSES
DINERO	DOOCED	**DOWSE**	**DRIVE**	**DUCES**
DINERS	DOOCES	DOWSED	DRIVEL	EDUCES
DINGE	**DOOLE**	DOWSER	DRIVEN	**DUCTS**
DINGED	DOOLEE	DOWSES	DRIVER	EDUCTS
DINGER	DOOLES	DOWSET	DRIVES	**DUETT**
DINGES	**DOORS**	**DRAFF**	**DROIT**	DUETTI
DINGEY	ADOORS	DRAFFS	ADROIT	DUETTO
DINNA	**DOPES**	DRAFFY	DROITS	DUETTS
DINNAE	DOPEST	**DRAFT**	**DROLE**	**DUKKA**
DIRKE	**DORAD**	DRAFTS	DROLER	DUKKAH
DIRKED	DORADO	DRAFTY	DROLES	DUKKAS
DIRKES	DORADS	**DRAPE**	**DROLL**	**DULCE**
DITED	**DORES**	DRAPED	DROLLS	DULCES
EDITED	ADORES	DRAPER	DROLLY	DULCET
DIVER	**DORIS**	DRAPES	**DRONE**	**DUPER**
DIVERS	DORISE	DRAPET	DRONED	DUPERS
DIVERT	**DORSA**	DRAPEY	DRONER	DUPERY
DIVES	DORSAD	**DRAWL**	DRONES	**DUPLE**

DUPLET	**EARDS**	WEASEL	DEAVES	SEDILE
DUPLEX	BEARDS	EASELS	HEAVES	EDILES
DUSTS	HEARDS	**EASER**	LEAVES	**EDUCE**
ADUSTS	YEARDS	LEASER	REAVES	DEDUCE
DWEEB	**EARED**	TEASER	WEAVES	REDUCE
DWEEBS	BEARED	EASERS	**EBBED**	SEDUCE
DWEEBY	DEARED	**EASES**	KEBBED	EDUCED
DWINE	FEARED	CEASES	NEBBED	EDUCES
DWINED	GEARED	FEASES	WEBBED	**EDUCT**
DWINES	LEARED	LEASES	**EBOOK**	DEDUCT
EAGER	NEARED	MEASES	REBOOK	EDUCTS
MEAGER	REARED	PEASES	EBOOKS	**EENSY**
EAGERS	SEARED	SEASES	**ECADS**	TEENSY
EAGLE	TEARED	TEASES	DECADS	WEENSY
BEAGLE	WEARED	**EASLE**	**ECHED**	**EERIE**
TEAGLE	**EARLS**	MEASLE	EECHED	FEERIE
EAGLED	PEARLS	EASLES	LECHED	PEERIE
EAGLES	**EARLY**	**EASTS**	PECHED	EERIER
EAGLET	DEARLY	BEASTS	TECHED	**EFFED**
EAGRE	NEARLY	FEASTS	**ECHES**	JEFFED
MEAGRE	PEARLY	HEASTS	EECHES	REFFED
EAGRES	REARLY	LEASTS	LECHES	**EGERS**
EALED	YEARLY	REASTS	**EDEMA**	LEGERS
FEALED	**EARNS**	YEASTS	OEDEMA	**EGEST**
GEALED	DEARNS	**EATEN**	EDEMAS	REGEST
HEALED	LEARNS	BEATEN	**EDGED**	EGESTA
MEALED	YEARNS	NEATEN	HEDGED	EGESTS
NEALED	**EARST**	**EATER**	KEDGED	**EGGAR**
PEALED	PEARST	BEATER	LEDGED	BEGGAR
SEALED	**EARTH**	FEATER	SEDGED	SEGGAR
VEALED	DEARTH	HEATER	WEDGED	EGGARS
EALES	HEARTH	NEATER	**EDGER**	**EGGED**
REALES	EARTHS	SEATER	HEDGER	BEGGED
VEALES	EARTHY	EATERS	KEDGER	DEGGED
EANED	**EASED**	EATERY	LEDGER	KEGGED
BEANED	CEASED	**EATHE**	EDGERS	LEGGED
DEANED	FEASED	MEATHE	**EDGES**	PEGGED
JEANED	LEASED	**EAVED**	HEDGES	VEGGED
LEANED	MEASED	DEAVED	KEDGES	**EGGER**
MEANED	PEASED	HEAVED	LEDGES	KEGGER
PEANED	SEASED	LEAVED	SEDGES	LEGGER
SEANED	TEASED	REAVED	WEDGES	EGGERS
WEANED	**EASEL**	WEAVED	**EDILE**	EGGERY
YEANED	TEASEL	**EAVES**	AEDILE	**EGRET**

REGRET	**ELDIN**	EMBARS	**EMURE**	TENTER
EGRETS	ELDING	**EMBED**	DEMURE	VENTER
EIDER	ELDINS	KEMBED	EMURED	ENTERA
DEIDER	**ELECT**	EMBEDS	EMURES	ENTERS
EIDERS	SELECT	**EMBER**	**ENATE**	**ENTIA**
EIGHT	ELECTS	MEMBER	SENATE	KENTIA
HEIGHT	**ELFED**	EMBERS	ENATES	**ENTRY**
KEIGHT	SELFED	**EMBUS**	**ENDED**	CENTRY
WEIGHT	**ELFIN**	EMBUSY	BENDED	GENTRY
EIGHTH	ELFING	**EMCEE**	FENDED	SENTRY
EIGHTS	ELFINS	EMCEED	HENDED	**ENURE**
EIGHTY	**ELIDE**	EMCEES	MENDED	TENURE
EIGNE	RELIDE	**EMEND**	PENDED	ENURED
BEIGNE	ELIDED	REMEND	RENDED	ENURES
EISEL	ELIDES	EMENDS	SENDED	**ENVOI**
EISELL	**ELITE**	**EMERG**	TENDED	RENVOI
EISELS	PELITE	EMERGE	VENDED	ENVOIS
EJECT	ELITES	EMERGS	WENDED	**ENVOY**
DEJECT	**ELOPE**	**EMITS**	**ENDER**	LENVOY
REJECT	DELOPE	DEMITS	BENDER	RENVOY
EJECTA	ELOPED	REMITS	FENDER	ENVOYS
EJECTS	ELOPER	**EMMAS**	GENDER	**ENZYM**
EKING	ELOPES	LEMMAS	LENDER	ENZYME
DEKING	**ELUDE**	**EMMER**	MENDER	ENZYMS
REKING	DELUDE	HEMMER	RENDER	**EORLS**
EKKAS	ELUDED	YEMMER	SENDER	CEORLS
MEKKAS	ELUDER	EMMERS	TENDER	**EOSIN**
ELAND	ELUDES	**EMOTE**	VENDER	EOSINE
RELAND	**ELUTE**	DEMOTE	ENDERS	EOSINS
ELANDS	ELUTED	GEMOTE	**ENDUE**	**EPEES**
ELATE	ELUTES	REMOTE	VENDUE	TEPEES
BELATE	**ELVER**	EMOTED	ENDUED	**EPHOR**
DELATE	DELVER	EMOTER	ENDUES	EPHORI
GELATE	ELVERS	EMOTES	**ENEWS**	EPHORS
RELATE	**ELVES**	**EMOVE**	RENEWS	**EPOCH**
VELATE	DELVES	REMOVE	**ENROL**	EPOCHA
ELATED	HELVES	EMOVED	ENROLL	EPOCHS
ELATER	PELVES	EMOVES	ENROLS	**EPRIS**
ELATES	SELVES	**EMPTS**	**ENSUE**	EPRISE
ELDER	**EMAIL**	TEMPTS	ENSUED	**EQUAL**
GELDER	REMAIL	**EMULE**	ENSUES	EQUALI
MELDER	EMAILS	AEMULE	**ENTER**	EQUALS
WELDER	**EMBAR**	EMULED	CENTER	**EQUIP**
ELDERS	EMBARK	EMULES	RENTER	EQUIPE

EQUIPS	AERUGO	**ETHER**	DEVILS	EXPOSE
ERASE	ERUGOS	AETHER	KEVILS	**EXTOL**
ERASED	**ERVEN**	HETHER	**EVITE**	EXTOLD
ERASER	VERVEN	NETHER	LEVITE	EXTOLL
ERASES	**ESCAR**	PETHER	EVITED	EXTOLS
ERBIA	ESCARP	TETHER	EVITES	**EXUDE**
TERBIA	ESCARS	WETHER	**EVOKE**	EXUDED
ERBIAS	**ESILE**	ETHERS	REVOKE	EXUDES
ERING	RESILE	**ETHOS**	EVOKED	**EYERS**
CERING	ESILES	METHOS	EVOKER	KEYERS
DERING	**ESNES**	**ETHYL**	EVOKES	**EYING**
LERING	MESNES	METHYL	**EWERS**	FEYING
MERING	**ESSES**	ETHYLS	HEWERS	HEYING
SERING	CESSES	**ETICS**	SEWERS	KEYING
ERINGO	DESSES	METICS	**EWEST**	**FABLE**
ERNED	FESSES	**ETTLE**	FEWEST	FABLED
CERNED	GESSES	FETTLE	NEWEST	FABLER
DERNED	JESSES	KETTLE	**EXACT**	FABLES
GERNED	LESSES	METTLE	HEXACT	FABLET
KERNED	MESSES	NETTLE	EXACTA	**FACET**
PERNED	NESSES	PETTLE	EXACTS	FACETE
TERNED	SESSES	SETTLE	**EXEME**	FACETS
ERNES	YESSES	ETTLED	LEXEME	**FACIA**
CERNES	**ESTER**	ETTLES	EXEMED	FACIAE
GERNES	FESTER	**EUGHS**	EXEMES	FACIAL
KERNES	JESTER	HEUGHS	**EXIES**	FACIAS
TERNES	MESTER	**EUKED**	DEXIES	**FADGE**
ERODE	NESTER	YEUKED	**EXILE**	FADGED
ERODED	PESTER	**EVADE**	EXILED	FADGES
ERODES	RESTER	EVADED	EXILER	**FAINE**
EROSE	TESTER	EVADER	EXILES	FAINED
REROSE	WESTER	EVADES	**EXINE**	FAINER
EROSES	YESTER	**EVENS**	REXINE	FAINES
ERRED	ZESTER	EEVENS	EXINES	**FAINT**
SERRED	ESTERS	SEVENS	**EXING**	FAINTS
ERROR	**ETAGE**	**EVERT**	HEXING	FAINTY
TERROR	METAGE	REVERT	SEXING	**FAKER**
ERRORS	ETAGES	EVERTS	VEXING	FAKERS
ERSES	**ETAPE**	**EVERY**	WEXING	FAKERY
HERSES	RETAPE	REVERY	YEXING	**FAKIE**
MERSES	ETAPES	SEVERY	**EXIST**	FAKIER
PERSES	**ETHAL**	**EVETS**	SEXIST	FAKIES
VERSES	LETHAL	REVETS	EXISTS	**FALSE**
ERUGO	ETHALS	**EVILS**	**EXPOS**	FALSED

FALSER	FEASED	FIDGED	FLAKED	FLISKY
FALSES	FEASES	FIDGES	FLAKER	**FLITE**
FARCE	**FEAZE**	FIDGET	FLAKES	FLITED
FARCED	FEAZED	**FIELD**	FLAKEY	FLITES
FARCER	FEAZES	AFIELD	**FLAME**	**FLOAT**
FARCES	**FEESE**	FIELDS	AFLAME	AFLOAT
FARCI	FEESED	**FIEST**	FLAMED	FLOATS
FARCIE	FEESES	FIESTA	FLAMEN	FLOATY
FARCIN	**FEEZE**	**FILLE**	FLAMER	**FLOCK**
FARSE	FEEZED	FILLED	FLAMES	FLOCKS
FARSED	FEEZES	FILLER	**FLANE**	FLOCKY
FARSES	**FEIST**	FILLES	FLANED	**FLORA**
FASCI	FEISTS	FILLET	FLANES	FLORAE
FASCIA	FEISTY	**FILMI**	**FLARE**	FLORAL
FASCIO	**FELLA**	FILMIC	FLARED	FLORAS
FASCIS	FELLAH	FILMIS	FLARES	**FLOSS**
FASTI	FELLAS	**FILOS**	**FLASH**	FLOSSY
FASTIE	**FELON**	FILOSE	FLASHY	**FLOTE**
FATWA	FELONS	**FILTH**	**FLECK**	FLOTED
FATWAH	FELONY	FILTHS	FLECKS	FLOTEL
FATWAS	**FEMAL**	FILTHY	FLECKY	FLOTES
FAULT	FEMALE	**FINAL**	**FLEME**	**FLOUR**
FAULTS	FEMALS	FINALE	FLEMED	FLOURS
FAULTY	**FENCE**	FINALS	FLEMES	FLOURY
FAUNA	FENCED	**FINER**	**FLESH**	**FLUFF**
FAUNAE	FENCER	FINERS	FLESHY	FLUFFS
FAUNAL	FENCES	FINERY	**FLEUR**	FLUFFY
FAUNAS	**FERES**	**FINES**	FLEURS	**FLUKE**
FAVEL	YFERES	FINEST	FLEURY	FLUKED
FAVELA	FEREST	**FINIS**	**FLEXO**	FLUKES
FAVELL	**FERIA**	FINISH	FLEXOR	FLUKEY
FAVELS	FERIAE	**FITCH**	FLEXOS	**FLUME**
FAVES	FERIAL	FITCHE	**FLIES**	FLUMED
FAVEST	FERIAS	FITCHY	FLIEST	FLUMES
FAYNE	**FESSE**	**FITTE**	**FLIMS**	**FLUNK**
FAYNED	FESSED	FITTED	FLIMSY	FLUNKS
FAYNES	FESSES	FITTER	**FLINT**	FLUNKY
FEARE	**FESTA**	FITTES	FLINTS	**FLURR**
FEARED	FESTAL	**FIXIT**	FLINTY	FLURRS
FEARER	FESTAS	FIXITS	**FLIRT**	FLURRY
FEARES	**FIBRE**	FIXITY	FLIRTS	**FLUSH**
FEARS	FIBRED	**FLAGS**	FLIRTY	FLUSHY
AFEARS	FIBRES	OFLAGS	**FLISK**	**FLUTE**
FEASE	**FIDGE**	**FLAKE**	FLISKS	FLUTED

FLUTER	FORTHY	**FREET**	FROWST	GABLED
FLUTES	**FOSSA**	AFREET	FROWSY	GABLES
FLUTEY	FOSSAE	FREETS	**FROZE**	GABLET
FLYPE	FOSSAS	FREETY	FROZEN	**GADGE**
FLYPED	**FOSSE**	**FREIT**	**FRUIT**	GADGES
FLYPES	FOSSED	FREITS	FRUITS	GADGET
FLYTE	FOSSES	FREITY	FRUITY	**GAFFE**
FLYTED	**FOULE**	**FRESH**	**FRUMP**	GAFFED
FLYTES	FOULED	AFRESH	FRUMPS	GAFFER
FOCAL	FOULER	**FRIAR**	FRUMPY	GAFFES
AFOCAL	FOULES	FRIARS	**FRUST**	**GAINS**
FOLIA	**FOVEA**	FRIARY	FRUSTA	GAINST
FOLIAR	FOVEAE	**FRILL**	FRUSTS	**GALAX**
FOLKS	FOVEAL	FRILLS	**FUDGE**	GALAXY
FOLKSY	FOVEAS	FRILLY	FUDGED	**GALEA**
FONDU	**FOXIE**	**FRISE**	FUDGES	GALEAE
FONDUE	FOXIER	FRISEE	**FUGLE**	GALEAS
FONDUS	FOXIES	FRISES	FUGLED	**GALLY**
FOOTS	**FOYLE**	**FRISK**	FUGLES	EGALLY
FOOTSY	FOYLED	FRISKA	**FUGUE**	**GALUT**
FORBY	FOYLES	FRISKS	FUGUED	GALUTH
FORBYE	**FOYNE**	FRISKY	FUGUES	GALUTS
FORCE	FOYNED	**FRITS**	**FUNDI**	**GAMAS**
FORCED	FOYNES	AFRITS	FUNDIC	AGAMAS
FORCER	**FRACT**	**FRIZE**	FUNDIE	GAMASH
FORCES	FRACTI	FRIZED	FUNDIS	**GAMBE**
FORES	FRACTS	FRIZER	**FUNGI**	GAMBES
FOREST	**FRAME**	FRIZES	FUNGIC	GAMBET
FORGE	FRAMED	**FRIZZ**	**FURAN**	**GAMBO**
FORGED	FRAMER	FRIZZY	FURANE	GAMBOL
FORGER	FRAMES	**FRONT**	FURANS	GAMBOS
FORGES	**FRANC**	AFRONT	**FURCA**	**GAMES**
FORGET	FRANCO	FRONTS	FURCAE	GAMEST
FORGO	FRANCS	**FRORE**	FURCAL	GAMESY
FORGOT	**FRAPE**	FROREN	**FUROL**	**GAMIC**
FORME	FRAPED	**FRORN**	FUROLE	AGAMIC
FORMED	FRAPES	FRORNE	FUROLS	OGAMIC
FORMEE	**FRATE**	**FROST**	**FUROR**	**GAMIN**
FORMER	FRATER	FROSTS	FURORE	GAMINE
FORMES	**FREAK**	FROSTY	FURORS	GAMING
FORTE	FREAKS	**FROTH**	**FUSIL**	GAMINS
FORTED	FREAKY	FROTHS	FUSILE	**GAMMA**
FORTES	**FREES**	FROTHY	FUSILS	GAMMAS
FORTH	FREEST	**FROWS**	**GABLE**	GAMMAT

GAMME	**GEMMA**	**GIVES**	**GLOBE**	GOOSEY
GAMMED	GEMMAE	OGIVES	GLOBED	**GORAS**
GAMMER	GEMMAN	**GLACE**	GLOBES	AGORAS
GAMMES	**GEMOT**	GLACED	**GLOBI**	**GORGE**
GANJA	GEMOTE	GLACES	GLOBIN	GORGED
GANJAH	GEMOTS	**GLAIR**	**GLOOM**	GORGER
GANJAS	**GENES**	GLAIRE	GLOOMS	GORGES
GAPES	AGENES	GLAIRS	GLOOMY	GORGET
AGAPES	**GENOM**	GLAIRY	**GLOOP**	**GOSSE**
GAPOS	GENOME	**GLARE**	GLOOPS	GOSSED
IGAPOS	GENOMS	AGLARE	GLOOPY	GOSSES
GARBE	**GENTS**	GLARED	**GLOSS**	**GOTCH**
GARBED	AGENTS	GLARES	GLOSSA	GOTCHA
GARBES	**GERNE**	**GLASS**	GLOSSY	**GOUGE**
GARDA	GERNED	GLASSY	**GLOVE**	GOUGED
GARDAI	GERNES	**GLAUR**	GLOVED	GOUGER
GARIS	**GESSE**	GLAURS	GLOVER	GOUGES
GARISH	GESSED	GLAURY	GLOVES	**GOURD**
GARRE	GESSES	**GLAZE**	**GLOZE**	GOURDE
GARRED	**GESTS**	GLAZED	GLOZED	GOURDS
GARRES	EGESTS	GLAZEN	GLOZES	GOURDY
GARRET	**GHAST**	GLAZER	**GLUTE**	**GOUTY**
GASTS	AGHAST	GLAZES	GLUTEI	AGOUTY
AGASTS	GHASTS	**GLEAM**	GLUTEN	**GOWAN**
GATES	**GHOST**	AGLEAM	GLUTES	GOWANS
AGATES	GHOSTS	GLEAMS	**GNARL**	GOWANY
GAUCH	GHOSTY	GLEAMY	GNARLS	**GRACE**
GAUCHE	**GILAS**	**GLEBA**	GNARLY	GRACED
GAUCHO	AGILAS	GLEBAE	**GOATS**	GRACES
GAUGE	**GIMME**	**GLEET**	GOATSE	**GRADE**
GAUGED	GIMMER	GLEETS	**GOBAN**	GRADED
GAUGER	GIMMES	GLEETY	GOBANG	GRADER
GAUGES	**GINGE**	**GLIDE**	GOBANS	GRADES
GAZED	GINGER	GLIDED	**GODSO**	**GRAIL**
AGAZED	GINGES	GLIDER	GODSON	GRAILE
GAZOO	**GINGS**	GLIDES	**GOING**	GRAILS
GAZOON	AGINGS	**GLIME**	AGOING	**GRAIN**
GAZOOS	**GISMS**	GLIMED	GOINGS	GRAINE
GEARE	AGISMS	GLIMES	**GONIF**	GRAINS
GEARED	**GISTS**	**GLINT**	GONIFF	GRAINY
GEARES	AGISTS	GLINTS	GONIFS	**GRAMP**
GEIST	**GIUST**	GLINTY	**GOOSE**	GRAMPA
AGEIST	GIUSTO	**GLITZ**	GOOSED	GRAMPS
GEISTS	GIUSTS	GLITZY	GOOSES	GRAMPY

GRAND	**GRIDE**	GROVEL	GURGES	**HALER**
GRANDE	GRIDED	GROVES	**GUSLA**	THALER
GRANDS	GRIDES	GROVET	GUSLAR	WHALER
GRAPE	**GRIFF**	**GROWL**	GUSLAS	HALERS
GRAPED	GRIFFE	GROWLS	**GUTTA**	HALERU
GRAPES	GRIFFS	GROWLY	GUTTAE	**HALES**
GRAPEY	**GRILL**	**GRUFF**	GUTTAS	SHALES
GRASS	GRILLE	GRUFFS	**GUYLE**	WHALES
GRASSY	GRILLS	GRUFFY	GUYLED	HALEST
GRATE	**GRIME**	**GRUMP**	GUYLER	**HALID**
GRATED	GRIMED	GRUMPH	GUYLES	HALIDE
GRATER	GRIMES	GRUMPS	**GYROS**	HALIDS
GRATES	**GRINS**	GRUMPY	GYROSE	**HALLO**
GRAVE	AGRINS	**GRYDE**	**HACKS**	HALLOA
GRAVED	**GRIPE**	GRYDED	CHACKS	HALLOO
GRAVEL	GRIPED	GRYDES	SHACKS	HALLOS
GRAVEN	GRIPER	**GUANA**	THACKS	HALLOT
GRAVER	GRIPES	IGUANA	WHACKS	HALLOW
GRAVES	GRIPEY	GUANAS	**HADED**	**HALMS**
GRAZE	**GRISE**	GUANAY	SHADED	SHALMS
GRAZED	AGRISE	**GUIDE**	**HADES**	**HALSE**
GRAZER	GRISED	GUIDED	SHADES	HALSED
GRAZES	GRISES	GUIDER	**HAFFS**	HALSER
GREED	**GRIZE**	GUIDES	CHAFFS	HALSES
AGREED	AGRIZE	**GUILE**	**HAFTS**	**HALVA**
GREEDS	GRIZES	GUILED	CHAFTS	HALVAH
GREEDY	**GRONE**	GUILER	SHAFTS	HALVAS
GREEN	GRONED	GUILES	**HAIKA**	**HALVE**
GREENS	GRONES	**GUILT**	HAIKAI	HALVED
GREENY	**GROPE**	GUILTS	**HAINS**	HALVER
GREES	GROPED	GUILTY	CHAINS	HALVES
AGREES	GROPER	**GUIMP**	**HAIRS**	**HAMAL**
GREESE	GROPES	GUIMPE	CHAIRS	SHAMAL
GREET	**GROSZ**	GUIMPS	HAIRST	HAMALS
GREETE	GROSZE	**GUISE**	**HAJIS**	**HAMBA**
GREETS	GROSZY	AGUISE	BHAJIS	SHAMBA
GREGE	**GROUP**	GUISED	**HAKES**	**HAMED**
AGREGE	GROUPS	GUISER	SHAKES	SHAMED
GREGED	GROUPY	GUISES	**HALAL**	**HAMES**
GREGES	**GROUT**	**GUNGE**	HALALA	SHAMES
GRICE	GROUTS	GUNGED	HALALS	**HAMMY**
GRICED	GROUTY	GUNGES	**HALED**	CHAMMY
GRICER	**GROVE**	**GURGE**	SHALED	SHAMMY
GRICES	GROVED	GURGED	WHALED	WHAMMY

HAMZA	THARMS	HAVENS	HEASTE	**HEIRS**
HAMZAH	**HARNS**	**HAVER**	HEASTS	THEIRS
HAMZAS	SHARNS	SHAVER	**HEATH**	**HEIST**
HANCE	**HAROS**	HAVERS	SHEATH	THEIST
CHANCE	PHAROS	**HAVES**	HEATHS	HEISTS
HANCES	**HARPS**	SHAVES	HEATHY	**HELLS**
HANDS	SHARPS	**HAWED**	**HEATS**	SHELLS
SHANDS	**HARPY**	CHAWED	CHEATS	**HELMS**
HANDY	SHARPY	SHAWED	WHEATS	WHELMS
SHANDY	**HARRY**	THAWED	**HEAVE**	**HELPS**
HANGS	CHARRY	**HAWKS**	SHEAVE	CHELPS
BHANGS	GHARRY	CHAWKS	THEAVE	WHELPS
CHANGS	**HARTS**	**HAWMS**	HEAVED	**HELVE**
PHANGS	CHARTS	SHAWMS	HEAVEN	SHELVE
THANGS	**HASTA**	**HAWSE**	HEAVER	HELVED
WHANGS	SHASTA	HAWSED	HEAVES	HELVES
HANKS	**HASTE**	HAWSER	**HEBES**	**HEMES**
CHANKS	CHASTE	HAWSES	THEBES	RHEMES
SHANKS	HASTED	**HAZAN**	**HECKS**	THEMES
THANKS	HASTEN	CHAZAN	CHECKS	**HEMIC**
HANSE	HASTES	HAZANS	**HEDER**	CHEMIC
HANSEL	**HATCH**	**HAZEL**	CHEDER	**HEMIN**
HANSES	THATCH	GHAZEL	HEDERA	HEMINA
HANTS	**HAUGH**	HAZELS	HEDERS	HEMINS
CHANTS	SHAUGH	**HEALS**	**HEDGE**	**HENCE**
HAPPY	HAUGHS	SHEALS	HEDGED	THENCE
CHAPPY	HAUGHT	WHEALS	HEDGER	WHENCE
HARDS	**HAULM**	**HEAPS**	HEDGES	**HENDS**
CHARDS	HAULMS	CHEAPS	**HEELS**	SHENDS
SHARDS	HAULMY	**HEAPY**	SHEELS	**HERDS**
HARED	**HAULS**	CHEAPY	WHEELS	SHERDS
CHARED	SHAULS	**HEARE**	**HEEZE**	**HERES**
SHARED	HAULST	WHEARE	PHEEZE	THERES
HARES	**HAUNT**	HEARER	WHEEZE	WHERES
CHARES	CHAUNT	HEARES	HEEZED	HERESY
PHARES	HAUNTS	**HEARS**	HEEZES	**HERMA**
SHARES	**HAUSE**	SHEARS	**HEFTE**	HERMAE
WHARES	HAUSED	HEARSE	HEFTED	HERMAI
HARKS	HAUSEN	HEARSY	HEFTER	**HERMS**
CHARKS	HAUSES	**HEART**	**HEFTS**	THERMS
SHARKS	**HAUTE**	HEARTH	THEFTS	**HERRY**
HARMS	HAUTER	HEARTS	WHEFTS	CHERRY
CHARMS	**HAVEN**	HEARTY	**HEIGH**	SHERRY
PHARMS	SHAVEN	**HEAST**	HEIGHT	WHERRY

HERSE	**HIDES**	SHIRES	**HOLLA**	CHOOKS
HERSED	CHIDES	**HISTS**	CHOLLA	SHOOKS
HERSES	**HIGHS**	SHISTS	HOLLAS	**HOOLY**
HERYE	THIGHS	WHISTS	**HOLLO**	DHOOLY
HERYED	**HIGHT**	**HITCH**	HOLLOA	**HOONS**
HERYES	HIGHTH	HITCHY	HOLLOO	CHOONS
HESPS	HIGHTS	**HITHE**	HOLLOS	**HOOPS**
THESPS	**HIJRA**	HITHER	HOLLOW	WHOOPS
HESTS	HIJRAH	HITHES	**HOLLY**	**HOOSH**
CHESTS	HIJRAS	**HIVED**	WHOLLY	SHOOSH
HETES	**HILLO**	CHIVED	**HOLOS**	WHOOSH
THETES	HILLOA	**HIVER**	CHOLOS	ZHOOSH
HETHS	HILLOS	SHIVER	THOLOS	**HOOTS**
CHETHS	**HILLS**	HIVERS	**HOMIE**	BHOOTS
KHETHS	CHILLS	**HIVES**	HOMIER	SHOOTS
HEUCH	SHILLS	CHIVES	HOMIES	WHOOTS
SHEUCH	THILLS	SHIVES	**HOMOS**	**HOOVE**
HEUCHS	**HILLY**	**HOARS**	ZHOMOS	HOOVED
HEUGH	CHILLY	HOARSE	**HONED**	HOOVEN
SHEUGH	WHILLY	**HOCKS**	PHONED	HOOVER
WHEUGH	**HINGE**	CHOCKS	**HONER**	HOOVES
HEUGHS	WHINGE	SHOCKS	PHONER	**HOPPY**
HEWED	HINGED	**HODJA**	HONERS	CHOPPY
CHEWED	HINGER	KHODJA	**HONES**	SHOPPY
SHEWED	HINGES	HODJAS	PHONES	**HORAL**
THEWED	**HINGS**	**HOERS**	RHONES	CHORAL
WHEWED	CHINGS	SHOERS	HONEST	**HORDE**
HEWER	THINGS	**HOISE**	**HONEY**	HORDED
CHEWER	**HINKY**	HOISED	PHONEY	HORDES
SHEWER	CHINKY	HOISES	HONEYS	**HORNS**
HEWERS	**HINNY**	**HOKED**	**HONGS**	THORNS
HEXAD	SHINNY	CHOKED	THONGS	**HORNY**
HEXADE	WHINNY	**HOKES**	**HONKY**	THORNY
HEXADS	**HINTS**	CHOKES	SHONKY	**HORSE**
HEXES	CHINTS	**HOKEY**	**HOOEY**	AHORSE
RHEXES	**HIPPO**	CHOKEY	PHOOEY	HORSED
HICKS	SHIPPO	**HOLDS**	HOOEYS	HORSES
CHICKS	HIPPOS	AHOLDS	**HOOFS**	HORSEY
THICKS	**HIPPY**	**HOLED**	CHOOFS	**HORST**
HIDED	CHIPPY	THOLED	WHOOFS	HORSTE
CHIDED	WHIPPY	**HOLES**	**HOOKA**	HORSTS
HIDER	**HIRED**	DHOLES	HOOKAH	**HOSEN**
CHIDER	SHIRED	THOLES	HOOKAS	CHOSEN
HIDERS	**HIRES**	WHOLES	**HOOKS**	HOSES

CHOSES	**HULES**	HYPHAL	NICKLE	EIKONS
HOSTS	SHULES	**IAMBI**	PICKLE	**ILEUM**
GHOSTS	**HULLO**	IAMBIC	RICKLE	PILEUM
HOUGH	HULLOA	**ICERS**	SICKLE	**ILEUS**
CHOUGH	HULLOO	DICERS	TICKLE	PILEUS
SHOUGH	HULLOS	RICERS	ICKLER	**ILIAL**
THOUGH	**HUMAN**	**ICHED**	**ICTAL**	FILIAL
HOUGHS	HUMANE	MICHED	RICTAL	**ILIUM**
HOUSE	HUMANS	NICHED	**ICTUS**	CILIUM
CHOUSE	**HUMPS**	RICHED	RICTUS	MILIUM
SHOUSE	CHUMPS	**ICHES**	**IDANT**	**ILLER**
HOUSED	THUMPS	FICHES	AIDANT	BILLER
HOUSEL	WHUMPS	LICHES	**IDANTS**	FILLER
HOUSER	**HUMUS**	MICHES	**IDENT**	GILLER
HOUSES	HUMUSY	NICHES	BIDENT	HILLER
HOUSEY	**HUNKS**	RICHES	EIDENT	KILLER
HOUTS	CHUNKS	TICHES	RIDENT	MILLER
CHOUTS	THUNKS	WICHES	**IDENTS**	SILLER
SHOUTS	**HUNKY**	**ICIER**	**IDIOT**	TILLER
HOVED	CHUNKY	DICIER	VIDIOT	WILLER
SHOVED	**HUNTS**	RICIER	**IDIOTS**	**IMAGE**
HOVEL	SHUNTS	**ICING**	**IDLED**	IMAGED
SHOVEL	**HURLS**	DICING	SIDLED	IMAGER
HOVELS	CHURLS	RICING	**IDLER**	IMAGES
HOVER	THURLS	TICING	SIDLER	**IMBAR**
SHOVER	**HURRA**	VICING	IDLERS	MIMBAR
HOVERS	DHURRA	**ICINGS**	**IDLES**	IMBARK
HOVES	HURRAH	**ICKER**	SIDLES	IMBARS
SHOVES	HURRAS	BICKER	IDLEST	**IMBED**
HOWKS	HURRAY	DICKER	**IDOLA**	LIMBED
CHOWKS	**HUZZA**	HICKER	EIDOLA	NIMBED
HOWLS	HUZZAH	KICKER	**IGGED**	IMBEDS
THOWLS	HUZZAS	LICKER	BIGGED	**IMBUE**
HUBBY	**HYDRA**	NICKER	DIGGED	IMBUED
CHUBBY	HYDRAE	PICKER	FIGGED	IMBUES
HUCKS	HYDRAS	RICKER	GIGGED	**IMPED**
CHUCKS	**HYING**	SICKER	JIGGED	GIMPED
SHUCKS	SHYING	TICKER	LIGGED	LIMPED
HUFFS	**HYLES**	WICKER	PIGGED	PIMPED
CHUFFS	CHYLES	YICKER	RIGGED	WIMPED
HUFFY	**HYLIC**	**ICKERS**	TIGGED	IMPEDE
CHUFFY	PHYLIC	**ICKLE**	WIGGED	**IMPIS**
HUGGY	**HYPHA**	FICKLE	ZIGGED	IMPISH
SHUGGY	HYPHAE	MICKLE	**IKONS**	**IMPLY**

DIMPLY	**INGOT**	**INNER**	TIRADE	TISSUE
JIMPLY	LINGOT	DINNER	IRADES	ISSUED
LIMPLY	INGOTS	FINNER	**IRATE**	ISSUER
PIMPLY	**INION**	GINNER	PIRATE	ISSUES
SIMPLY	MINION	PINNER	IRATER	**ISTLE**
IMPRO	PINION	SINNER	**IRIDS**	MISTLE
IMPROS	INIONS	TINNER	MIRIDS	ISTLES
IMPROV	**INKED**	WINNER	**IRING**	**TTCHY**
INANE	DINKED	INNERS	AIRING	BITCHY
INANER	FINKED	**INTEL**	FIRING	FITCHY
INANES	JINKED	LINTEL	HIRING	HITCHY
INCUS	KINKED	INTELS	MIRING	PITCHY
INCUSE	LINKED	**INTER**	SIRING	TITCHY
INDIE	OINKED	HINTER	TIRING	WITCHY
KINDIE	PINKED	LINTER	VIRING	**ITHER**
YINDIE	RINKED	MINTER	WIRING	CITHER
INDIES	TINKED	SINTER	**IRKED**	DITHER
INDOL	WINKED	TINTER	DIRKED	EITHER
INDOLE	ZINKED	WINTER	FIRKED	HITHER
INDOLS	**INKER**	INTERN	KIRKED	LITHER
INDOW	DINKER	INTERS	LIRKED	MITHER
WINDOW	JINKER	**INTRO**	YIRKED	NITHER
INDOWS	LINKER	INTRON	**IRONE**	TITHER
INDUE	PINKER	INTROS	IRONED	WITHER
INDUED	SINKER	**INURE**	IRONER	ZITHER
INDUES	TINKER	INURED	IRONES	**IVIED**
INFER	WINKER	INURES	**IRONS**	DIVIED
INFERE	INKERS	**INWIT**	GIRONS	**IVIES**
INFERS	**INKLE**	INWITH	**ISHES**	CIVIES
INGAN	KINKLE	INWITS	BISHES	**IZARD**
FINGAN	TINKLE	**IODID**	DISHES	LIZARD
INGANS	WINKLE	IODIDE	FISHES	RIZARD
INGLE	INKLED	IODIDS	HISHES	VIZARD
BINGLE	INKLES	**IODIN**	KISHES	WIZARD
DINGLE	**INNED**	IODINE	NISHES	IZARDS
GINGLE	BINNED	IODINS	PISHES	**IZARS**
JINGLE	DINNED	**IONIC**	WISHES	SIZARS
KINGLE	FINNED	BIONIC	**ISLED**	**JACKS**
LINGLE	GINNED	PIONIC	AISLED	JACKSY
MINGLE	LINNED	IONICS	MISLED	**JALOP**
PINGLE	PINNED	**IOTAS**	**ISLES**	JALOPS
SINGLE	SINNED	BIOTAS	AISLES	JALOPY
TINGLE	TINNED	DIOTAS	LISLES	**JAMBE**
INGLES	WINNED	**IRADE**	**ISSUE**	JAMBED

JAMBEE	JIVEST	KEDGED	SKILLS	KNOWES
JAMBER	**JOCOS**	KEDGER	**KIMBO**	**KNURL**
JAMBES	JOCOSE	KEDGES	AKIMBO	KNURLS
JAMBO	**JOTUN**	**KEENS**	KIMBOS	KNURLY
JAMBOK	JOTUNN	SKEENS	**KINAS**	**KOBAN**
JAMBU	JOTUNS	**KEETS**	KINASE	KOBANG
JAMBUL	**JOULE**	SKEETS	**KINKS**	KOBANS
JAMBUS	JOULED	**KELLS**	SKINKS	**KOFFS**
JAPER	JOULES	SKELLS	**KIPPA**	SKOFFS
JAPERS	**JOWAR**	**KELLY**	KIPPAH	**KORUN**
JAPERY	JOWARI	SKELLY	KIPPAS	KORUNA
JASPE	JOWARS	**KELPS**	**KITED**	KORUNY
JASPER	**JUDGE**	SKELPS	SKITED	**KRANS**
JASPES	JUDGED	**KENTE**	**KITES**	SKRANS
JAUNT	JUDGER	KENTED	SKITES	**KRONE**
JAUNTS	JUDGES	KENTES	**KITHE**	KRONEN
JAUNTY	**JUICE**	**KERNE**	KITHED	KRONER
JEBEL	JUICED	KERNED	KITHES	**KROON**
DJEBEL	JUICER	KERNEL	**KLUGE**	KROONI
JEBELS	JUICES	KERNES	KLUGED	KROONS
JEHAD	**JUMAR**	**KERRY**	KLUGES	**KULAK**
JEHADI	JUMARS	SKERRY	**KLUTZ**	KULAKI
JEHADS	JUMART	**KERVE**	KLUTZY	KULAKS
JEMBE	**KAIKA**	KERVED	**KNACK**	**KURUS**
DJEMBE	KAIKAI	KERVES	KNACKS	KURUSH
JEMBES	KAIKAS	**KETCH**	KNACKY	**KUTCH**
JESSE	**KAILS**	SKETCH	**KNARL**	KUTCHA
JESSED	SKAILS	**KHAYA**	KNARLS	**KYBOS**
JESSES	**KAING**	KHAYAL	KNARLY	KYBOSH
JIBBA	KAINGA	KHAYAS	**KNAWE**	**KYNDE**
DJIBBA	**KALPA**	**KHEDA**	KNAWEL	KYNDED
JIBBAH	KALPAC	KHEDAH	KNAWES	KYNDES
JIBBAS	KALPAK	KHEDAS	**KNIFE**	**KYTES**
JIHAD	KALPAS	**KIBBE**	KNIFED	SKYTES
JIHADI	**KAPUT**	KIBBEH	KNIFER	**KYTHE**
JIHADS	KAPUTT	KIBBES	KNIFES	KYTHED
JINNE	**KARAT**	**KIBLA**	**KNIVE**	KYTHES
JINNEE	KARATE	KIBLAH	KNIVED	**LABIA**
JINNI	KARATS	KIBLAS	KNIVES	LABIAL
DJINNI	**KARTS**	**KIDDY**	**KNOLL**	**LABRA**
JINNIS	SKARTS	SKIDDY	KNOLLS	LABRAL
JINNS	**KECKS**	**KIERS**	KNOLLY	**LACED**
DJINNS	KECKSY	SKIERS	**KNOWE**	GLACED
JIVES	**KEDGE**	**KILLS**	KNOWER	PLACED

LACER	SLAKED	FLANCH	LARVAE	**LATUS**
PLACER	**LAKER**	PLANCH	LARVAL	FLATUS
LACERS	FLAKER	**LANDE**	LARVAS	**LAUDS**
LACES	SLAKER	LANDED	**LASER**	BLAUDS
GLACES	LAKERS	LANDER	FLASER	**LAUGH**
PLACES	**LAKES**	LANDES	LASERS	LAUGHS
LACET	FLAKES	**LANDS**	**LASSI**	LAUGHY
PLACET	SLAKES	ALANDS	LASSTE	**LAURA**
LACETS	**LAKIN**	BLANDS	LASSIS	LAURAE
LACKS	LAKING	ELANDS	**LASSY**	LAURAS
BLACKS	LAKINS	GLANDS	CLASSY	**LAVAS**
CLACKS	**LAMAS**	**LANES**	GLASSY	FLAVAS
FLACKS	LLAMAS	FLANES	**LASTS**	LAVASH
PLACKS	ULAMAS	PLANES	BLASTS	**LAVED**
SLACKS	**LAMED**	SLANES	CLASTS	SLAVED
LADED	BLAMED	**LANKS**	**LATCH**	**LAVER**
BLADED	FLAMED	BLANKS	CLATCH	CLAVER
LADER	LAMEDH	CLANKS	KLATCH	SLAVER
BLADER	LAMEDS	FLANKS	SLATCH	LAVERS
LADERS	**LAMER**	PLANKS	**LATED**	**LAVES**
LADES	BLAMER	**LANKY**	ALATED	CLAVES
BLADES	FLAMER	BLANKY	BLATED	SLAVES
CLADES	**LAMES**	CLANKY	ELATED	**LAWED**
GLADES	BLAMES	**LANTS**	PLATED	BLAWED
SLADES	CLAMES	ALANTS	SLATED	CLAWED
LADLE	FLAMES	PLANTS	**LATEN**	FLAWED
LADLED	LAMEST	SLANTS	PLATEN	**LAWER**
LADLER	**LAMIA**	**LAPSE**	LATENS	CLAWER
LADLES	LAMIAE	ELAPSE	LATENT	**LAWIN**
LAHAL	LAMIAS	LAPSED	**LATER**	LAWINE
SLAHAL	**LAMMY**	LAPSER	BLATER	LAWING
LAHALS	CLAMMY	LAPSES	ELATER	LAWINS
LAIDS	GLAMMY	**LARES**	PLATER	**LAWNS**
PLAIDS	**LAMPS**	BLARES	SLATER	FLAWNS
SLAIDS	CLAMPS	FLARES	**LATHE**	**LAXES**
LAIKS	**LANCE**	GLARES	LATHED	FLAXES
GLAIKS	ELANCE	**LARGE**	LATHEE	LAXEST
LAIRS	GLANCE	LARGEN	LATHEN	**LAYED**
FLAIRS	LANCED	LARGER	LATHER	ALAYED
GLAIRS	LANCER	LARGES	LATHES	CLAYED
LAIRY	LANCES	**LARUM**	**LATTE**	FLAYED
GLAIRY	LANCET	ALARUM	LATTEN	PLAYED
LAKED	**LANCH**	LARUMS	LATTER	SLAYED
FLAKED	BLANCH	**LARVA**	LATTES	**LAYER**

FLAYER	PLEASE	**LEETS**	LEUCON	SLIEVE
PLAYER	LEASED	FLEETS	**LEUGH**	LIEVER
SLAYER	LEASER	GLEETS	CLEUGH	LIEVES
LAYERS	LEASES	SLEETS	PLEUGH	**LIFTS**
LAYIN	**LEATS**	**LEFTE**	**LEVEE**	CLIFTS
LAYING	BLEATS	LEFTER	LEVEED	GLIFTS
LAYINS	CLEATS	**LEFTS**	LEVEES	**LIGAN**
LAZAR	PLEATS	CLEFTS	**LEVER**	LIGAND
BLAZAR	**LEAVE**	**LEGGE**	CLEVER	LIGANS
LAZARS	CLEAVE	ALEGGE	LEVERS	**LIGGE**
LAZED	GLEAVE	LEGGED	**LEVES**	LIGGED
BLAZED	SLEAVE	LEGGER	CLEVES	LIGGER
GLAZED	LEAVED	LEGGES	**LEVIN**	LIGGES
LAZES	LEAVEN	**LEGIT**	ALEVIN	**LIGHT**
BLAZES	LEAVER	ELEGIT	LEVINS	ALIGHT
GLAZES	LEAVES	LEGITS	**LEVIS**	BLIGHT
LEACH	**LEAZE**	**LEMED**	CLEVIS	FLIGHT
BLEACH	SLEAZE	FLEMED	**LEXES**	PLIGHT
PLEACH	LEAZES	**LEMES**	FLEXES	SLIGHT
LEACHY	**LEDES**	FLEMES	ILEXES	LIGHTS
LEADS	GLEDES	**LEMON**	PLEXES	**LIKES**
PLEADS	**LEDGE**	LEMONS	ULEXES	GLIKES
LEAKS	FLEDGE	LEMONY	**LIBER**	LIKEST
BLEAKS	GLEDGE	**LENDS**	LIBERO	**LIKIN**
LEAKY	PLEDGE	BLENDS	LIBERS	LIKING
BLEAKY	SLEDGE	**LENSE**	**LIBRA**	LIKINS
LEAMS	LEDGED	FLENSE	LIBRAE	**LIMAX**
FLEAMS	LEDGER	LENSED	LIBRAS	CLIMAX
GLEAMS	LEDGES	LENSES	**LICIT**	**LIMBI**
LEANS	**LEDGY**	**LENTI**	ELICIT	LIMBIC
CLEANS	FLEDGY	LENTIC	**LICKS**	**LIMBS**
GLEANS	**LEECH**	LENTIL	CLICKS	CLIMBS
LEARE	FLEECH	**LENTO**	FLICKS	**LIMED**
LEARED	SLEECH	LENTOR	KLICKS	GLIMED
LEARES	**LEEKS**	LENTOS	SLICKS	SLIMED
LEARN	CLEEKS	**LETCH**	**LIEGE**	**LIMES**
LEARNS	GLEEKS	FLETCH	LIEGER	CLIMES
LEARNT	SLEEKS	**LETHE**	LIEGES	GLIMES
LEARS	**LEEPS**	LETHEE	**LIENS**	SLIMES
BLEARS	BLEEPS	LETHES	ALIENS	**LIMEY**
CLEARS	CLEEPS	**LEUCH**	**LIERS**	BLIMEY
LEARY	SLEEPS	CLEUCH	FLIERS	LIMEYS
BLEARY	**LEERS**	PLEUCH	PLIERS	**LIMPS**
LEASE	FLEERS	**LEUCO**	**LIEVE**	BLIMPS

FLIMPS	SLINKY	OLIVER	PLODGE	LOOEYS
LIMPSY	**LINTS**	SLIVER	LODGED	**LOOFA**
LINCH	CLINTS	LIVERS	LODGER	LOOFAH
CLINCH	ELINTS	LIVERY	LODGES	LOOFAS
FLINCH	FLINTS	**LIVES**	**LOGAN**	**LOOFS**
LINDS	GLINTS	OLIVES	SLOGAN	KLOOFS
BLINDS	**LINTY**	SLIVES	LOGANS	**LOOIE**
LINED	FLINTY	LIVEST	**LOGES**	BLOOIE
ALINED	GLINTY	**LOAMS**	ELOGES	FLOOIE
LINEN	**LIPAS**	CLOAMS	**LOGGY**	LOOIES
LINENS	LIPASE	GLOAMS	CLOGGY	**LOOKS**
LINENY	**LIPES**	**LOANS**	**LOGIA**	BLOOKS
LINER	CLIPES	SLOANS	ALOGIA	PLOOKS
ALINER	SLIPES	**LOATH**	**LOGIE**	**LOOKY**
LINERS	**LIPID**	LOATHE	LOGIER	PLOOKY
LINES	LIPIDE	LOATHY	LOGIES	**LOOMS**
ALINES	LIPIDS	**LOAVE**	**LOIDS**	BLOOMS
CLINES	**LIPPY**	LOAVED	SLOIDS	GLOOMS
LINGA	FLIPPY	LOAVES	**LOINS**	SLOOMS
LINGAM	SLIPPY	**LOBBY**	ALOINS	**LOOPS**
LINGAS	**LIROT**	BLOBBY	ELOINS	BLOOPS
LINGO	LIROTH	GLOBBY	**LOIPE**	CLOOPS
OLINGO	**LISKS**	SLOBBY	LOIPEN	GLOOPS
LINGOS	FLISKS	**LOBED**	**LOKES**	SLOOPS
LINGOT	GLISKS	GLOBED	BLOKES	**LOOPY**
LINGS	**LITED**	**LOBES**	CLOKES	BLOOPY
BLINGS	FLITED	GLOBES	**LONER**	GLOOPY
CLINGS	**LITES**	**LOBOS**	CLONER	**LOOSE**
FLINGS	BLITES	LOBOSE	LONERS	LOOSED
PLINGS	ELITES	**LOBUS**	**LONGA**	LOOSEN
SLINGS	FLITES	GLOBUS	LONGAN	LOOSER
LINGY	LITEST	**LOCAL**	LONGAS	LOOSES
BLINGY	**LITHE**	LOCALE	**LONGE**	**LOOTS**
CLINGY	BLITHE	LOCALS	PLONGE	CLOOTS
LININ	LITHED	**LOCHE**	LONGED	SLOOTS
LINING	LITHER	CLOCHE	LONGER	**LOPED**
LININS	LITHES	LOCHES	LONGES	ELOPED
LINKS	**LIVED**	**LOCKS**	**LONGS**	SLOPED
BLINKS	SLIVED	BLOCKS	FLONGS	**LOPER**
CLINKS	LIVEDO	CLOCKS	KLONGS	ELOPER
PLINKS	**LIVEN**	FLOCKS	PLONGS	SLOPER
SLINKS	SLIVEN	**LOCUS**	**LOOEY**	LOPERS
LINKY	LIVENS	LOCUST	BLOOEY	**LOPES**
PLINKY	**LIVER**	**LODGE**	FLOOEY	ELOPES

SLOPES	**LOURE**	PLOWER	SLUMPS	PLUSHY
LOPPY	LOURED	SLOWER	**LUMPY**	SLUSHY
FLOPPY	LOURES	LOWERS	CLUMPY	**LUTEA**
GLOPPY	**LOURS**	LOWERY	GLUMPY	LUTEAL
SLOPPY	CLOURS	**LOWES**	PLUMPY	**LUTED**
LORAL	FLOURS	LOWEST	SLUMPY	ELUTED
FLORAL	**LOURY**	**LOWLY**	**LUNAR**	FLUTED
LORES	FLOURY	SLOWLY	LUNARS	**LUTER**
BLORES	**LOUSE**	**LOWNE**	LUNARY	FLUTER
LORIC	BLOUSE	LOWNED	**LUNCH**	LUTERS
LORICA	FLOUSE	LOWNES	CLUNCH	**LUTES**
LORICS	LOUSED	**LOWNS**	GLUNCH	ELUTES
LOSED	LOUSER	CLOWNS	**LUNGE**	FLUTES
CLOSED	LOUSES	**LOWSE**	BLUNGE	GLUTES
LOSER	**LOUSY**	BLOWSE	PLUNGE	**LUXED**
CLOSER	BLOUSY	LOWSED	LUNGED	FLUXED
LOSERS	**LOUTS**	LOWSER	LUNGEE	**LUXES**
LOSES	CLOUTS	LOWSES	LUNGER	FLUXES
CLOSES	FLOUTS	**LUCKS**	LUNGES	LUXEST
ULOSES	GLOUTS	CLUCKS	**LUNGI**	**LYING**
LOSSY	**LOVED**	PLUCKS	LUNGIE	CLYING
FLOSSY	GLOVED	**LUCKY**	LUNGIS	FLYING
GLOSSY	**LOVER**	CLUCKY	**LUNKS**	PLYING
LOTAS	CLOVER	PLUCKY	BLUNKS	LYINGS
FLOTAS	GLOVER	**LUDES**	CLUNKS	**LYSIN**
LOTES	PLOVER	BLUDES	FLUNKS	LYSINE
CLOTES	LOVERS	ELUDES	PLUNKS	LYSING
FLOTES	**LOVES**	**LUFFS**	**LUNTS**	LYSINS
LOTTE	CLOVES	BLUFFS	BLUNTS	**LYTED**
LOTTED	GLOVES	FLUFFS	**LUPIN**	FLYTED
LOTTER	**LOVIE**	PLUFFS	LUPINE	**LYTES**
LOTTES	LOVIER	SLUFFS	LUPINS	FLYTES
LOTTO	LOVIES	**LUGED**	**LURES**	**LYTTA**
BLOTTO	**LOWED**	KLUGED	ALURES	LYTTAE
LOTTOS	BLOWED	**LUGES**	**LURRY**	LYTTAS
LOUGH	CLOWED	KLUGES	BLURRY	**MACHE**
CLOUGH	FLOWED	**LUMMY**	FLURRY	MACHER
PLOUGH	GLOWED	PLUMMY	PLURRY	MACHES
SLOUGH	PLOWED	SLUMMY	SLURRY	**MACKS**
LOUGHS	SLOWED	**LUMPS**	**LURVE**	SMACKS
LOUPE	**LOWER**	CLUMPS	SLURVE	**MACLE**
LOUPED	BLOWER	FLUMPS	LURVES	MACLED
LOUPEN	FLOWER	GLUMPS	**LUSHY**	MACLES
LOUPES	GLOWER	PLUMPS	FLUSHY	**MACRO**

MACRON	MANGEL	**MATZO**	MEDLEY	EMERGE
MACROS	MANGER	MATZOH	**MEERS**	MERGED
MADAM	MANGES	MATZOS	AMEERS	MERGEE
MADAME	MANGEY	MATZOT	EMEERS	MERGER
MADAMS	**MANIA**	**MAUND**	**MELIC**	MERGES
MAGES	MANIAC	MAUNDS	MELICK	**MERIS**
IMAGES	MANIAS	MAUNDY	MELICS	MERISM
MAIKS	**MANNA**	**MAUTS**	**MELLS**	**MERKS**
SMAIKS	MANNAN	AMAUTS	SMELLS	SMERKS
MAILE	MANNAS	**MAUVE**	**MELON**	**MERSE**
MAILED	**MARLE**	MAUVER	MELONS	EMERSE
MAILER	MARLED	MAUVES	MELONY	MERSES
MAILES	MARLES	**MAXIM**	**MELTS**	**MESES**
MAILS	**MARMS**	MAXIMA	SMELTS	EMESES
EMAILS	SMARMS	MAXIMS	**MENDS**	TMESES
MALIC	**MARRA**	**MAZED**	AMENDS	**MESTO**
MALICE	MARRAM	AMAZED	EMENDS	MESTOM
MALIS	MARRAS	**MAZES**	**MENED**	**METHO**
MALISM	**MARSH**	AMAZES	AMENED	METHOD
MALIST	MARSHY	SMAZES	OMENED	METHOS
MALLS	**MARTS**	**MEANE**	**MENGE**	**METIC**
SMALLS	SMARTS	MEANED	MENGED	EMETIC
MALMS	**MASSE**	MEANER	MENGES	METICS
SMALMS	MASSED	MEANES	**MENSA**	**METRE**
MALMY	MASSES	**MEASE**	MENSAE	METRED
SMALMY	**MATCH**	MEASED	MENSAL	METRES
MALTS	SMATCH	MEASES	MENSAS	**MEUSE**
SMALTS	**MATED**	**MEATH**	**MENSE**	SMEUSE
MAMMA	AMATED	SMEATH	MENSED	MEUSED
MAMMAE	**MATES**	MEATHE	MENSES	MEUSES
MAMMAL	AMATES	MEATHS	**MENTA**	**MIASM**
MAMMAS	**MATIN**	**MEDIA**	AMENTA	MIASMA
MANAT	MATING	MEDIAD	OMENTA	MIASMS
MANATI	MATINS	MEDIAE	MENTAL	**MICHE**
MANATS	**MATLO**	MEDIAL	**MENTO**	MICHED
MANATU	MATLOS	MEDIAN	MENTOR	MICHER
MANDI	MATLOW	MEDIAS	MENTOS	MICHES
MANDIR	**MATTE**	**MEDIC**	**MEREL**	**MICRO**
MANDIS	MATTED	MEDICK	MERELL	MICRON
MANGA	MATTER	MEDICO	MERELS	MICROS
MANGAL	MATTES	MEDICS	MERELY	**MIDDY**
MANGAS	**MATZA**	**MEDLE**	**MERES**	SMIDDY
MANGE	MATZAH	MEDLED	MEREST	**MIDGE**
MANGED	MATZAS	MEDLES	**MERGE**	SMIDGE

MIDGES	**MINOS**	**MOGGY**	**MOOTS**	AMOUNT
MIDGET	AMINOS	SMOGGY	SMOOTS	MOUNTS
MIDST	**MIRIN**	**MOILE**	**MOOVE**	**MOUSE**
AMIDST	MIRING	SMOILE	AMOOVE	SMOUSE
MIDSTS	MIRINS	MOILED	MOOVED	MOUSED
MIEVE	**MIRKS**	MOILER	MOOVES	MOUSER
MIEVED	SMIRKS	MOILES	**MOPER**	MOUSES
MIEVES	**MIRKY**	**MOIRA**	MOPERS	MOUSEY
MIGHT	SMIRKY	MOIRAI	MOPERY	**MOUTH**
SMIGHT	**MISER**	**MOKES**	**MORAL**	MOUTHS
MIGHTS	MISERE	SMOKES	AMORAL	MOUTHY
MIGHTY	MISERS	**MOKOS**	MORALE	**MOVED**
MIKVA	MISERY	SMOKOS	MORALL	AMOVED
MIKVAH	**MISES**	**MOLES**	MORALS	EMOVED
MIKVAS	AMISES	AMOLES	**MORES**	**MOVES**
MILER	**MISSA**	MOLEST	SMORES	AMOVES
SMILER	MISSAE	**MOLLA**	**MORNE**	EMOVES
MILERS	MISSAL	MOLLAH	MORNED	**MOYLE**
MILES	MISSAW	MOLLAS	MORNES	SMOYLE
SMILES	MISSAY	**MOLTS**	**MORPH**	MOYLED
MILLE	**MITER**	SMOLTS	MORPHO	MOYLES
MILLED	SMITER	**MONER**	MORPHS	**MUCKS**
MILLER	MITERS	MONERA	**MORRO**	AMUCKS
MILLES	**MITES**	**MONGO**	MORROS	**MUDGE**
MILLET	SMITES	MONGOE	MORROW	SMUDGE
MILOR	**MITRE**	MONGOL	**MORSE**	MUDGED
MILORD	MITRED	MONGOS	MORSEL	MUDGER
MILORS	MITRES	**MONGS**	MORSES	MUDGES
MINCE	**MOBLE**	MONGST	**MOTED**	**MUGGA**
MINCED	MOBLED	**MONIE**	EMOTED	MUGGAR
MINCER	MOBLES	MONIED	**MOTES**	MUGGAS
MINCES	**MOCHI**	MONIES	EMOTES	**MULED**
MINES	MOCHIE	**MONOS**	**MOTET**	EMULED
AMINES	MOCHIS	MONOSY	MOTETS	**MULES**
IMINES	**MOCKS**	**MONTE**	MOTETT	EMULES
MINGE	SMOCKS	MONTEM	**MOTOR**	**MULLA**
MINGED	**MODER**	MONTES	MOTORS	MULLAH
MINGER	MODERN	**MOOCH**	MOTORY	MULLAS
MINGES	MODERS	SMOOCH	**MOUCH**	**MUNCH**
MINIM	**MODES**	**MOOLA**	SMOUCH	MUNCHY
MINIMA	MODEST	MOOLAH	**MOULD**	**MUNGE**
MINIMS	**MODGE**	MOOLAS	MOULDS	EMUNGE
MINIS	MODGED	**MOORS**	MOULDY	MUNGED
MINISH	MODGES	SMOORS	**MOUNT**	MUNGES

MURED	MUZAKY	GNATTY	KNICKS	KNOCKS
EMURED	**MYRRH**	**NAVES**	SNICKS	**NODAL**
MURES	MYRRHS	KNAVES	**NIDED**	ANODAL
EMURES	MYRRHY	**NEAPS**	SNIDED	ENODAL
MURRA	**MYTHI**	SNEAPS	**NIDES**	**NODES**
MURRAM	MYTHIC	**NEARS**	SNIDES	ANODES
MURRAS	**NACRE**	ANEARS	**NIFES**	**NOINT**
MURRAY	NACRED	**NEATH**	KNIFES	ANOINT
MURRE	NACRES	ANEATH	**NIFFS**	NOINTS
MURREE	**NAGGY**	SNEATH	SNIFFS	**NOISE**
MURREN	KNAGGY	UNEATH	**NIFFY**	NOISED
MURRES	SNAGGY	**NECKS**	SNIFFY	NOISES
MURREY	**NAILS**	SNECKS	**NIFTY**	**NOLES**
MURRI	SNAILS	**NEESE**	SNIFTY	ANOLES
MURRIN	**NAIVE**	NEESED	**NIGHT**	**NOLLS**
MURRIS	NAIVER	NEESES	ANIGHT	KNOLLS
MURRY	NAIVES	**NEEZE**	KNIGHT	**NOMAD**
SMURRY	**NAKED**	SNEEZE	NIGHTS	NOMADE
MUSCA	SNAKED	NEEZED	NIGHTY	NOMADS
MUSCAE	**NALLA**	NEEZES	**NIPPY**	NOMADY
MUSCAT	NALLAH	**NELLY**	SNIPPY	**NOMES**
MUSED	NALLAS	SNELLY	**NITER**	GNOMES
AMUSED	**NAMMA**	**NEMAS**	UNITER	**NOMIC**
MUSER	GNAMMA	ENEMAS	NITERS	ANOMIC
AMUSER	**NANAS**	**NEROL**	NITERY	GNOMIC
MUSERS	ANANAS	NEROLI	**NITES**	**NOOKS**
MUSES	JNANAS	NEROLS	UNITES	SNOOKS
AMUSES	**NAPPE**	**NERTS**	**NITRO**	**NOOPS**
MUSIC	NAPPED	INERTS	NITROS	SNOOPS
AMUSIC	NAPPER	**NERVE**	NITROX	**NOOSE**
MUSICK	NAPPES	ENERVE	**NITRY**	SNOOSE
MUSICS	**NAPPY**	NERVED	NITRYL	NOOSED
MUSSE	SNAPPY	NERVER	**NITTY**	NOOSER
MUSSED	**NARES**	NERVES	SNITTY	NOOSES
MUSSEL	SNARES	**NEWED**	**NKOSI**	**NORMA**
MUSSES	**NARKS**	ENEWED	INKOSI	NORMAL
MUTCH	SNARKS	**NEWEL**	NKOSIS	NORMAN
SMUTCH	**NARKY**	NEWELL	**NOBBY**	NORMAS
MUTES	SNARKY	NEWELS	KNOBBY	**NOSES**
MUTEST	**NATCH**	**NICHE**	SNOBBY	ENOSES
MUTIS	SNATCH	NICHED	**NOBLE**	GNOSES
MUTISM	**NATES**	NICHER	NOBLER	**NOTCH**
MUZAK	ENATES	NICHES	NOBLES	NOTCHY
MUZAKS	**NATTY**	**NICKS**	**NOCKS**	**NOULD**

NOULDE	SOAKEN	**OCCAM**	NODDER	POHING
NOWED	**OAKER**	OCCAMS	**ODISM**	**OILED**
SNOWED	SOAKER	OCCAMY	IODISM	BOILED
UNOWED	OAKERS	**OCHER**	ODISMS	COILED
NOYAU	**OARED**	TOCHER	**ODIST**	DOILED
NOYAUS	HOARED	OCHERS	CODIST	FOILED
NOYAUX	ROARED	OCHERY	MODIST	MOILED
NUBBY	SOARED	**OCHES**	ODISTS	ROILED
KNUBBY	**OASTS**	BOCHES	**ODIUM**	SOILED
SNUBBY	BOASTS	COCHES	PODIUM	TOILED
NUCHA	COASTS	LOCHES	SODIUM	**OILER**
NUCHAE	HOASTS	ROCHES	ODIUMS	BOILER
NUCHAL	ROASTS	**OCHRE**	**OFFED**	COILER
NUDES	TOASTS	OCHREA	BOFFED	MOILER
NUDEST	**OATER**	OCHRED	COFFED	TOILER
NUDGE	BOATER	OCHRES	DOFFED	OILERS
SNUDGE	COATER	OCHREY	GOFFED	OILERY
NUDGED	DOATER	**OCKER**	**OFFER**	**OINKS**
NUDGER	OATERS	COCKER	COFFER	BOINKS
NUDGES	**OAVES**	DOCKER	DOFFER	**OINTS**
NUFFS	LOAVES	HOCKER	GOFFER	JOINTS
SNUFFS	SOAVES	LOCKER	OFFERS	NOINTS
NULLA	**OBANG**	MOCKER	**OFFIE**	POINTS
NULLAH	GOBANG	ROCKER	MOFFIE	**OKAYS**
NULLAS	KOBANG	OCKERS	OFFIES	TOKAYS
NURLS	OBANGS	**OCREA**	**OFTEN**	**OKRAS**
KNURLS	**OBELI**	OCREAE	SOFTEN	KOKRAS
NURRS	OBELIA	OCREAS	**OFTER**	**OLDEN**
KNURRS	**OBESE**	**OCTAN**	LOFTER	BOLDEN
NURSE	OBESER	OCTANE	SOFTER	GOLDEN
NURSED	**OBEYS**	OCTANS	**OGEES**	HOLDEN
NURSER	MOBEYS	OCTANT	YOGEES	OLDENS
NURSES	**OBIAS**	**OCTET**	**OGGIN**	**OLDER**
NYALA	COBIAS	OCTETS	HOGGIN	BOLDER
INYALA	**OBITS**	OCTETT	NOGGIN	COLDER
NYALAS	OOBITS	**OCULI**	OGGINS	FOLDER
NYMPH	**OBOES**	LOCULI	**OGLED**	GOLDER
NYMPHA	GOBOES	**ODALS**	BOGLED	HOLDER
NYMPHO	HOBOES	MODALS	**OGLES**	MOLDER
NYMPHS	**OBOLE**	**ODDER**	BOGLES	POLDER
OAKED	SOBOLE	CODDER	FOGLES	SOLDER
BOAKED	OBOLES	DODDER	**OHING**	**OLDIE**
SOAKED	**OBOLS**	FODDER	HOHING	COLDIE
OAKEN	BOBOLS	MODDER	OOHING	OLDIES

OLEIN	OMBERS	WONNED	COPING	ORDERS
SOLEIN	**OMBRE**	**ONTIC**	DOPING	**ORGAN**
OLEINE	HOMBRE	PONTIC	HOPING	MORGAN
OLEINS	SOMBRE	**OOHED**	LOPING	ORGANA
OLENT	OMBRES	BOOHED	MOPING	ORGANS
DOLENT	**OMBUS**	POOHED	OOPING	**ORGIA**
OLIOS	KOMBUS	**OOPED**	ROPING	GORGIA
FOLIOS	**OMENS**	COOPED	TOPING	ORGIAC
POLIOS	NOMENS	GOOPED	**OPPOS**	ORGIAS
OLIVE	**OMERS**	HOOPED	OPPOSE	**ORGUE**
SOLIVE	COMERS	LOOPED	**OPTER**	MORGUE
OLIVER	GOMERS	MOOPED	COPTER	ORGUES
OLIVES	HOMERS	POOPED	OPTERS	**ORMER**
OLIVET	VOMERS	ROOPED	**ORACH**	DORMER
OLLAS	**OMITS**	SOOPED	ORACHE	FORMER
HOLLAS	VOMITS	**OORIE**	**ORALS**	WORMER
MOLLAS	**ONCES**	COORIE	BORALS	ORMERS
OLLER	BONCES	GOORIE	CORALS	**ORPIN**
GOLLER	NONCES	TOORIE	GORALS	ORPINE
HOLLER	PONCES	OORIER	MORALS	ORPINS
JOLLER	SONCES	**OOSES**	**ORANG**	**ORRIS**
LOLLER	**ONELY**	BOOSES	ORANGE	MORRIS
POLLER	LONELY	GOOSES	ORANGS	**OSIER**
ROLLER	**ONERS**	LOOSES	ORANGY	COSIER
SOLLER	BONERS	NOOSES	**ORANT**	HOSIER
TOLLER	GONERS	ROOSES	VORANT	NOSIER
OLLERS	HONERS	WOOSES	ORANTS	OOSIER
OLLIE	LONERS	**OOZED**	**ORATE**	POSIER
COLLIE	TONERS	BOOZED	BORATE	ROSIER
MOLLIE	ZONERS	**OOZES**	LORATE	OSIERS
ROLLIE	**ONION**	BOOZES	ORATED	OSIERY
TOLLIE	GONION	COOZES	ORATES	**OSMIC**
OLLIED	RONION	**OPALS**	**ORBED**	COSMIC
OLLIES	ONIONS	COPALS	SORBED	OSMICS
OLOGY	ONIONY	NOPALS	**ORBIT**	**OSMOL**
OOLOGY	**ONIUM**	**OPENS**	ORBITA	OSMOLE
OLPES	CONIUM	COPENS	ORBITS	OSMOLS
GOLPES	GONIUM	**OPERA**	ORBITY	**OSTIA**
OMASA	IONIUM	POPERA	**ORCIN**	OSTIAL
OMASAL	ONIUMS	OPERAS	ORCINE	**OTARY**
OMBER	**ONNED**	**OPINE**	ORCINS	NOTARY
BOMBER	CONNED	OPINED	**ORDER**	ROTARY
COMBER	DONNED	OPINES	BORDER	VOTARY
SOMBER	FONNED	**OPING**	CORDER	**OTHER**

BOTHER	BOUNCE	TOUTER	TOWING	MOXIES
FOTHER	JOUNCE	OUTERS	VOWING	**OYERS**
LOTHER	POUNCE	**OUTRE**	WOWING	FOYERS
MOTHER	ROUNCE	FOUTRE	YOWING	TOYERS
NOTHER	OUNCES	OUTRED	**OWLED**	**OZZIE**
POTHER	**OUNDY**	**OUTRO**	BOWLED	COZZIE
ROTHER	WOUNDY	OUTROS	COWLED	MOZZIE
TOTHER	**OUPED**	OUTROW	FOWLED	OZZIES
OTHERS	COUPED	**OVARY**	GOWLED	**PACED**
OTTAR	LOUPED	COVARY	HOWLED	SPACED
COTTAR	MOUPED	**OVATE**	JOWLED	**PACER**
OTTARS	POUPED	BOVATE	SOWLED	SPACER
OTTER	ROUPED	NOVATE	YOWLED	PACERS
COTTER	SOUPED	OVATED	**OWLER**	**PACES**
DOTTER	**OURIE**	OVATES	BOWLER	SPACES
HOTTER	COURIE	**OVELS**	FOWLER	**PACEY**
JOTTER	LOURIE	HOVELS	HOWLER	SPACEY
LOTTER	POURIE	NOVELS	JOWLER	**PACHA**
POTTER	TOURIE	**OVENS**	YOWLER	PACHAK
ROTTER	OURIER	COVENS	OWLERS	PACHAS
TOTTER	**OUSEL**	DOVENS	OWLERY	**PACTS**
OTTERS	HOUSEL	WOVENS	**OWLET**	EPACTS
OTTOS	OUSELS	**OVERS**	HOWLET	**PAEON**
LOTTOS	**OUSTS**	COVERS	OWLETS	PAEONS
MOTTOS	JOUSTS	DOVERS	**OWNED**	PAEONY
POTTOS	MOUSTS	HOVERS	BOWNED	**PAGOD**
OUBIT	ROUSTS	LOVERS	DOWNED	PAGODA
WOUBIT	**OUTBY**	MOVERS	GOWNED	PAGODS
OUBITS	OUTBYE	ROVERS	LOWNED	**PAILS**
OUENS	**OUTED**	**OVERT**	**OWNER**	SPAILS
ROUENS	DOUTED	COVERT	DOWNER	**PAINS**
OUGHT	HOUTED	**OVINE**	OWNERS	SPAINS
BOUGHT	LOUTED	BOVINE	**OWRES**	**PAINT**
DOUGHT	POUTED	COVINE	HOWRES	PAINTS
FOUGHT	ROUTED	OVINES	POWRES	PAINTY
MOUGHT	TOUTED	**OWING**	**OWRIE**	**PAIRE**
NOUGHT	**OUTER**	BOWING	COWRIE	PAIRED
ROUGHT	COUTER	COWING	LOWRIE	PAIRER
SOUGHT	DOUTER	DOWING	OWRIER	PAIRES
OUGHTS	FOUTER	JOWING	**OXERS**	**PAISA**
OUMAS	MOUTER	LOWING	BOXERS	PAISAN
DOUMAS	POUTER	MOWING	**OXIES**	PAISAS
LOUMAS	ROUTER	ROWING	DOXIES	**PALEA**
OUNCE	SOUTER	SOWING	FOXIES	PALEAE

PALEAL	PARENT	PARTIS	PAVANE	**PECKS**
PALED	**PARER**	**PARTS**	PAVANS	SPECKS
OPALED	SPARER	SPARTS	**PAVIN**	**PECKY**
PALES	PARERA	**PASES**	SPAVIN	SPECKY
SPALES	PARERS	UPASES	PAVING	**PEDAL**
PALEST	**PARES**	**PASSE**	PAVINS	PEDALO
PALIS	SPARES	PASSED	**PAVIS**	PEDALS
PALISH	**PAREV**	PASSEE	PAVISE	**PEELS**
PALLA	PAREVE	PASSEL	**PAWLS**	SPEELS
PALLAE	**PARGE**	PASSER	SPAWLS	**PEEPE**
PALLAH	SPARGE	PASSES	**PAWNS**	PEEPED
PALLS	PARGED	**PASTE**	SPAWNS	PEEPER
SPALLS	PARGES	PASTED	**PAYED**	PEEPES
PANDA	PARGET	PASTEL	SPAYED	**PEERS**
PANDAN	**PARIS**	PASTER	**PEACE**	SPEERS
PANDAR	PARISH	PASTES	PEACED	**PEEVE**
PANDAS	**PARKI**	**PATCH**	PEACES	PEEVED
PANED	PARKIE	PATCHY	**PEACH**	PEEVER
SPANED	PARKIN	**PATEN**	PEACHY	PEEVES
PANES	PARKIS	PATENS	**PEAKS**	**PEISE**
SPANES	**PARKS**	PATENT	SPEAKS	SPEISE
PANGS	SPARKS	**PATER**	**PEALS**	PEISED
SPANGS	**PARKY**	EPATER	SPEALS	PEISES
PANIC	SPARKY	PATERA	**PEANS**	**PEIZE**
PANICK	**PARLE**	PATERS	SPEANS	PEIZED
PANICS	PARLED	**PATES**	**PEARL**	PEIZES
PANNE	PARLES	SPATES	PEARLS	**PELLS**
PANNED	PARLEY	**PATIN**	PEARLY	SPELLS
PANNER	**PAROL**	PATINA	**PEARS**	**PELTA**
PANNES	PAROLE	PATINE	SPEARS	PELTAE
PANTO	PAROLS	PATINS	PEARST	PELTAS
PANTON	**PARRA**	**PATTE**	**PEASE**	**PELTS**
PANTOS	PARRAL	PATTED	PEASED	SPELTS
PAPER	PARRAS	PATTEE	PEASEN	**PENCE**
PAPERS	**PARRY**	PATTEN	PEASES	SPENCE
PAPERY	SPARRY	PATTER	**PEATS**	PENCEL
PARCH	**PARSE**	PATTES	SPEATS	PENCES
EPARCH	SPARSE	**PAULS**	**PEAZE**	**PENDS**
PARDI	PARSEC	SPAULS	PEAZED	SPENDS
PARDIE	PARSED	**PAUSE**	PEAZES	UPENDS
PARED	PARSER	PAUSED	**PECKE**	**PENED**
SPARED	PARSES	PAUSER	PECKED	OPENED
PAREN	**PARTI**	PAUSES	PECKER	**PENNA**
PARENS	PARTIM	**PAVAN**	PECKES	PENNAE

PENNAL	PETRES	PIANIC	SPINAS	PLAINT
PENNE	**PEYSE**	**PICAL**	**PINED**	**PLANE**
PENNED	PEYSED	APICAL	OPINED	PLANED
PENNER	PEYSES	EPICAL	SPINED	PLANER
PENNES	**PHANG**	**PICAS**	**PINES**	PLANES
PENNI	UPHANG	SPICAS	OPINES	PLANET
PENNIA	PHANGS	**PICKS**	SPINES	**PLANT**
PENNIS	**PHARM**	SPICKS	**PINKS**	PLANTA
PEPSI	PHARMA	**PICOT**	SPINKS	PLANTS
PEPSIN	PHARMS	PICOTE	**PINNA**	**PLASH**
PEPSIS	**PHASE**	PICOTS	PINNAE	SPLASH
PERCE	PHASED	**PIECE**	PINNAL	PLASHY
PERCED	PHASER	APIECE	PINNAS	**PLASM**
PERCEN	PHASES	PIECED	**PINNY**	PLASMA
PERCES	**PHEER**	PIECEN	SPINNY	PLASMS
PERDU	PHEERE	PIECER	**PINTO**	**PLAST**
EPERDU	PHEERS	PIECES	SPINTO	YPLAST
PERDUE	**PHENE**	**PIERS**	PINTOS	PLASTE
PERDUS	SPHENE	SPIERS	**PIQUE**	**PLATE**
PERIS	PHENES	PIERST	PIQUED	PLATED
PERISH	**PHESE**	**PIGHT**	PIQUES	PLATEN
PERMS	PHESED	SPIGHT	PIQUET	PLATER
SPERMS	PHESES	YPIGHT	**PIROG**	PLATES
PEROG	**PHOCA**	PIGHTS	PIROGI	**PLATS**
PEROGI	PHOCAE	**PIKED**	**PISTE**	SPLATS
PEROGS	PHOCAS	SPIKED	PISTED	**PLAYS**
PEROGY	**PHONE**	**PIKER**	PISTES	SPLAYS
PERSE	PHONED	SPIKER	**PITCH**	UPLAYS
SPERSE	PHONER	PIKERS	PITCHY	**PLEAD**
PERSES	PHONES	**PIKES**	**PIUMS**	UPLEAD
PERST	PHONEY	SPIKES	OPIUMS	PLEADS
SPERST	**PHONO**	**PIKEY**	**PIZZA**	**PLEAS**
PERVE	PHONON	SPIKEY	PIZZAS	PLEASE
PERVED	PHONOS	PIKEYS	PIZZAZ	**PLICA**
PERVES	**PHONY**	**PILAF**	**PLACE**	PLICAE
PETAR	APHONY	PILAFF	PLACED	PLICAL
PETARA	**PHOTO**	PILAFS	PLACER	PLICAS
PETARD	PHOTOG	**PILED**	PLACES	**PLINK**
PETARS	PHOTON	SPILED	PLACET	UPLINK
PETARY	PHOTOS	**PILES**	**PLAID**	PLINKS
PETIT	**PHYLA**	SPILES	UPLAID	PLINKY
PETITE	PHYLAE	**PILLS**	PLAIDS	**PLONG**
PETRE	PHYLAR	SPILLS	**PLAIN**	PLONGD
PETREL	**PIANI**	**PINAS**	PLAINS	PLONGE

PLONGS	**POISE**	**PORAL**	POULPS	**PREST**
PLONK	POISED	SPORAL	**POUPE**	UPREST
PLONKO	POISER	**PORED**	POUPED	PRESTO
PLONKS	POISES	SPORED	POUPES	PRESTS
PLONKY	**POKED**	**PORES**	**POUTS**	**PREVE**
PLOOK	SPOKED	SPORES	SPOUTS	PREVED
UPLOOK	**POKES**	**PORGE**	**POUTY**	PREVES
PLOOKS	SPOKES	PORGED	SPOUTY	**PRICE**
PLOOKY	**POKIE**	PORGES	**POWRE**	PRICED
PLOUK	POKIER	**PORIN**	POWRED	PRICER
PLOUKS	POKIES	PORINA	POWRES	PRICES
PLOUKY	**POLEY**	PORING	**POYSE**	PRICEY
PLOYE	POLEYN	PORINS	POYSED	**PRICK**
PLOYED	POLEYS	**PORKS**	POYSES	PRICKS
PLOYES	**POLIS**	SPORKS	**PRANG**	PRICKY
PLUCK	POLISH	**PORTA**	SPRANG	**PRIDE**
PLUCKS	**POLYP**	PORTAL	PRANGS	PRIDED
PLUCKY	POLYPE	PORTAS	**PRANK**	PRIDES
PLUFF	POLYPI	**PORTS**	PRANKS	**PRIEF**
PLUFFS	POLYPS	SPORTS	PRANKY	PRIEFE
PLUFFY	**PONCE**	**PORTY**	**PRATE**	PRIEFS
PLUME	PONCED	SPORTY	UPRATE	**PRIER**
PLUMED	PONCES	**POSES**	PRATED	SPRIER
PLUMES	PONCEY	EPOSES	PRATER	PRIERS
PLUMP	**PONGA**	**POSSE**	PRATES	**PRIES**
PLUMPS	PONGAL	POSSED	**PRATS**	PRIEST
PLUMPY	PONGAS	POSSER	SPRATS	**PRIGS**
PLUNK	**PONGY**	POSSES	**PRAYS**	SPRIGS
PLUNKS	SPONGY	POSSET	SPRAYS	**PRIMA**
PLUNKY	**POOFS**	POTCH	**PREED**	PRIMAL
PLUSH	SPOOFS	POTCHE	SPREED	PRIMAS
PLUSHY	**POOFY**	**POTIN**	**PREES**	**PRIME**
POACH	SPOOFY	POTING	SPREES	PRIMED
POACHY	**POOJA**	POTINS	**PREIF**	PRIMER
PODAL	POOJAH	**POTTY**	PREIFE	PRIMES
APODAL	POOJAS	SPOTTY	PREIFS	**PRINT**
PODDY	**POOKS**	**POUCH**	**PRENT**	SPRINT
SPODDY	SPOOKS	POUCHY	SPRENT	PRINTS
PODIA	**POOLS**	**POUFF**	PRENTS	**PRIOR**
PODIAL	SPOOLS	POUFFE	**PRESE**	PRIORS
POINT	**POONS**	POUFFS	PRESES	PRIORY
POINTE	SPOONS	POUFFY	PRESET	**PRISE**
POINTS	**POOTS**	**POULP**	**PRESS**	EPRISE
POINTY	SPOOTS	POULPE	PRESSY	UPRISE

PRISED	PROSED	SPULES	PURSES	**QUATE**
PRISER	PROSER	**PULIS**	PURSEW	EQUATE
PRISES	PROSES	EPULIS	**PUSES**	QUATES
PRISM	**PROTO**	**PULSE**	OPUSES	**QUATS**
PRISMS	PROTON	PULSED	**PUSLE**	SQUATS
PRISMY	**PROVE**	PULSER	PUSLED	**QUEEN**
PRISS	PROVED	PULSES	PUSLES	QUEENS
PRISSY	PROVEN	**PULUS**	PUSLEY	QUEENY
PRIZE	PROVER	OPULUS	**PUTTI**	**QUEME**
PRIZED	PROVES	**PUNCE**	PUTTIE	QUEMED
PRIZER	**PROYN**	PUNCED	**PYRES**	QUEMES
PRIZES	PROYNE	PUNCES	SPYRES	**QUEUE**
PROBE	PROYNS	**PUNCH**	**QUACK**	QUEUED
PROBED	**PRUNE**	PUNCHY	QUACKS	QUEUER
PROBER	PRUNED	**PUNKA**	QUACKY	QUEUES
PROBES	PRUNER	PUNKAH	**QUADS**	**QUICH**
PRODS	PRUNES	PUNKAS	SQUADS	QUICHE
SPRODS	PRUNEY	**PUNKS**	**QUAIL**	**QUICK**
PROGS	**PRUTA**	SPUNKS	SQUAIL	QUICKS
SPROGS	PRUTAH	**PUNKY**	QUAILS	QUICKY
PROIN	**PRYER**	SPUNKY	**QUAKE**	**QUIDS**
PROINE	SPRYER	**PURDA**	QUAKED	EQUIDS
PROINS	PRYERS	PURDAH	QUAKER	SQUIDS
PROKE	**PRYSE**	PURDAS	QUAKES	**QUIFF**
PROKED	PRYSED	**PUREE**	**QUALM**	SQUIFF
PROKER	PRYSES	PUREED	QUALMS	QUIFFS
PROKES	**PSEUD**	PUREES	QUALMY	**QUILL**
PROLE	PSEUDO	**PURES**	**QUANT**	SQUILL
PROLED	PSEUDS	PUREST	EQUANT	QUILLS
PROLEG	**PSYCH**	**PURGE**	QUANTA	**QUINE**
PROLER	PSYCHE	SPURGE	QUANTS	EQUINE
PROLES	PSYCHO	PURGED	**QUARE**	QUINES
PROLL	PSYCHS	PURGER	SQUARE	**QUINO**
UPROLL	**PUCES**	PURGES	QUARER	QUINOA
PROLLS	PUCEST	**PURIN**	**QUARK**	QUINOL
PROLLY	**PUDDY**	PURINE	SQUARK	QUINOS
PRONE	SPUDDY	PURING	QUARKS	**QUINS**
PRONER	**PUERS**	PURINS	**QUART**	QUINSY
PRONES	SPUERS	**PURIS**	QUARTE	**QUINT**
PRONG	**PUGGY**	PURISM	QUARTO	SQUINT
SPRONG	SPUGGY	PURIST	QUARTS	QUINTA
PRONGS	**PUKKA**	**PURSE**	QUARTZ	QUINTE
PROSE	PUKKAH	PURSED	**QUASH**	QUINTS
UPROSE	**PULES**	PURSER	SQUASH	**QUIPS**

EQUIPS	**RACES**	BRAILS	ORALLY	PRANKS
QUIRE	BRACES	DRAILS	RALLYE	TRANKS
SQUIRE	GRACES	FRAILS	**RAMPS**	**RANTS**
QUIRED	TRACES	GRAILS	CRAMPS	BRANTS
QUIRES	**RACHE**	TRAILS	GRAMPS	CRANTS
QUIRK	ORACHE	**RAINE**	TRAMPS	DRANTS
QUIRKS	RACHES	GRAINE	**RANAS**	GRANTS
QUIRKY	RACHET	RAINED	PRANAS	ORANTS
QUIRT	**RACKS**	RAINES	**RANCE**	TRANTS
SQUIRT	BRACKS	**RAINS**	PRANCE	**RAPED**
QUIRTS	CRACKS	BRAINS	TRANCE	CRAPED
QUITE	FRACKS	DRAINS	RANCED	DRAPED
QUITED	TRACKS	GRAINS	RANCEL	FRAPED
QUITES	WRACKS	TRAINS	RANCES	GRAPED
QUITS	**RADGE**	**RAINY**	**RANCH**	TRAPED
SQUITS	RADGER	BRAINY	BRANCH	**RAPER**
QUOTE	RADGES	GRAINY	CRANCH	DRAPER
QUOTED	**RAFFS**	**RAIRD**	RANCHO	RAPERS
QUOTER	DRAFFS	BRAIRD	**RANDS**	**RAPES**
QUOTES	GRAFFS	RAIRDS	BRANDS	CRAPES
QUOTH	**RAFTS**	**RAISE**	GRANDS	DRAPES
QUOTHA	CRAFTS	ARAISE	**RANDY**	FRAPES
QUYTE	DRAFTS	BRAISE	BRANDY	GRAPES
QUYTED	GRAFTS	FRAISE	**RANGE**	TRAPES
QUYTES	KRAFTS	PRAISE	GRANGE	**RAPPE**
RABAT	**RAGEE**	RAISED	ORANGE	FRAPPE
RABATO	DRAGEE	RAISER	RANGED	RAPPED
RABATS	RAGEES	RAISES	RANGER	RAPPEE
RABBI	**RAGGY**	**RAITS**	RANGES	RAPPEL
RABBIN	BRAGGY	KRAITS	**RANGS**	RAPPEN
RABBIS	CRAGGY	TRAITS	KRANGS	RAPPER
RABBIT	DRAGGY	**RAKED**	ORANGS	RAPPES
RABIC	**RAGUS**	BRAKED	PRANGS	**RARES**
ARABIC	TRAGUS	CRAKED	WRANGS	CRARES
RABIS	**RAIDS**	**RAKER**	**RANGY**	URARES
ARABIS	BRAIDS	RAKERS	ORANGY	RAREST
RACED	**RAIKS**	RAKERY	**RANKE**	**RASED**
BRACED	TRAIKS	**RAKES**	RANKED	ERASED
GRACED	**RAILE**	BRAKES	RANKER	**RASER**
TRACED	GRAILE	CRAKES	RANKES	ERASER
RACER	RAILED	DRAKES	**RANKS**	RASERS
BRACER	RAILER	**RAKIS**	BRANKS	**RASES**
TRACER	RAILES	RAKISH	CRANKS	BRASES
RACERS	**RAILS**	**RALLY**	FRANKS	CRASES

ERASES	BRATTY	DRAYED	**READY**	**REBUY**
PRASES	**RAVED**	FRAYED	BREADY	PREBUY
URASES	BRAVED	GRAYED	**REAKS**	REBUYS
RASPS	CRAVED	PRAYED	BREAKS	**RECAL**
GRASPS	GRAVED	**RAYLE**	CREAKS	RECALL
RASSE	**RAVEL**	GRAYLE	FREAKS	RECALS
WRASSE	GRAVEL	RAYLED	WREAKS	**RECCE**
RASSES	TRAVEL	RAYLES	**REAME**	RECCED
RATAN	RAVELS	RAYLET	REAMED	RECCES
RATANS	**RAVEN**	**RAYNE**	REAMER	**RECIT**
RATANY	CRAVEN	TRAYNE	REAMES	RECITE
RATCH	GRAVEN	RAYNES	**REAMS**	RECITS
CRATCH	RAVENS	**RAYON**	BREAMS	**RECKS**
FRATCH	**RAVER**	CRAYON	CREAMS	DRECKS
RATED	BRAVER	RAYONS	DREAMS	TRECKS
CRATED	CRAVER	**RAZED**	**REAMY**	WRECKS
GRATED	GRAVER	BRAZED	CREAMY	**RECTA**
ORATED	RAVERS	CRAZED	DREAMY	RECTAL
PRATED	**RAVES**	GRAZED	**REARM**	**RECTO**
RATER	BRAVES	**RAZEE**	PREARM	RECTOR
CRATER	CRAVES	RAZEED	REARMS	RECTOS
FRATER	GRAVES	RAZEES	**REARS**	**RECUR**
GRATER	TRAVES	**RAZER**	AREARS	RECURE
IRATER	**RAVIN**	BRAZER	DREARS	RECURS
KRATER	RAVINE	GRAZER	**REAST**	**RECUT**
PRATER	RAVING	RAZERS	BREAST	PRECUT
RATERS	RAVINS	**RAZES**	REASTS	RECUTS
RATES	**RAWER**	BRAZES	REASTY	**REDED**
CRATES	BRAWER	CRAZES	**REATE**	BREDED
GRATES	DRAWER	GRAZES	CREATE	**REDES**
ORATES	**RAWIN**	**REACH**	REATES	AREDES
PRATES	RAWING	AREACH	**REAVE**	BREDES
URATES	RAWINS	BREACH	GREAVE	**REDIA**
RATHE	**RAWLY**	CREACH	REAVED	UREDIA
RATHER	BRAWLY	PREACH	REAVER	REDIAE
RATHS	CRAWLY	**REACT**	REAVES	REDIAL
WRATHS	DRAWLY	PREACT	**REBEC**	REDIAS
RATIO	**RAWNS**	REACTS	REBECK	**REDIP**
RATION	BRAWNS	**READS**	REBECS	REDIPS
RATIOS	PRAWNS	AREADS	**REBID**	REDIPT
RATOO	**RAXES**	BREADS	PREBID	**REDON**
RATOON	PRAXES	DREADS	REBIDS	REDONE
RATOOS	**RAYED**	OREADS	**REBIT**	REDONS
RATTY	BRAYED	TREADS	REBITE	**REDOS**

CREDOS	REFELL	RELIES	RESAWS	RETIES
UREDOS	REFELS	**REMAN**	**RESEE**	**RETRO**
REDRY	REFELT	PREMAN	RESEED	RETROD
PREDRY	**REFER**	REMAND	RESEEK	RETROS
REDYE	PREFER	REMANS	RESEEN	**REUSE**
REDYED	REFERS	**REMEN**	RESEES	REUSED
REDYES	**REFIX**	PREMEN	**RESES**	REUSES
REECH	PREFIX	REMEND	GRESES	**REVET**
BREECH	**REGAL**	REMENS	PRESES	BREVET
REECHO	REGALE	**REMIT**	URESES	TREVET
REECHY	REGALS	FREMIT	**RESET**	REVETS
REEDE	**REGAR**	REMITS	PRESET	**REVIE**
REEDED	REGARD	**REMIX**	RESETS	REVIED
REEDEN	REGARS	PREMIX	**RESEW**	REVIES
REEDER	**REGES**	REMIXT	RESEWN	REVIEW
REEDES	GREGES	**RENDS**	RESEWS	**REVUE**
REEDS	REGEST	TRENDS	**RESID**	PREVUE
BREEDS	**REGMA**	**RENNE**	RESIDE	REVUES
CREEDS	BREGMA	BRENNE	RESIDS	**REWED**
GREEDS	**REGNA**	FRENNE	**RESIN**	BREWED
REEDY	REGNAL	RENNED	RESINS	CREWED
GREEDY	**REGOS**	RENNES	RESINY	GREWED
REEKS	GREGOS	RENNET	**RESIT**	REWEDS
BREEKS	**REHAB**	**RENTE**	RESITE	**REWIN**
CREEKS	PREHAB	RENTED	RESITS	REWIND
REEKY	REHABS	RENTER	**RESOW**	REWINS
CREEKY	**REIFS**	RENTES	RESOWN	**REXES**
REELS	PREIFS	**RENTS**	RESOWS	GREXES
CREELS	**REINS**	BRENTS	**RESTO**	PREXES
REENS	GREINS	PRENTS	PRESTO	**REZES**
GREENS	**REIST**	**REPAY**	RESTOS	PREZES
PREENS	BREIST	PREPAY	**RESTS**	TREZES
TREENS	REISTS	REPAYS	CRESTS	**RHEUM**
REEST	**REIVE**	**REPIN**	PRESTS	RHEUMS
BREEST	REIVED	REPINE	TRESTS	RHEUMY
DREEST	REIVER	REPINS	WRESTS	**RHOMB**
FREEST	REIVES	**REPLA**	**RETAX**	RHOMBI
REESTS	**RELIC**	REPLAN	PRETAX	RHOMBS
REESTY	RELICS	REPLAY	**RETCH**	**RHUMB**
REEVE	RELICT	**REPOS**	WRETCH	RHUMBA
PREEVE	**RELIE**	REPOSE	**RETIA**	RHUMBS
REEVED	RELIED	REPOST	RETIAL	**RHYME**
REEVES	RELIEF	**RESAW**	**RETIE**	RHYMED
REFEL	RELIER	RESAWN	RETIED	RHYMER

RHYMES	**RIDES**	**RIGID**	WRINGS	FRITES
RIADS	BRIDES	FRIGID	**RINKS**	TRITES
TRIADS	GRIDES	RIGIDS	BRINKS	URITES
RIALS	IRIDES	**RIGOL**	DRINKS	WRITES
PRIALS	PRIDES	RIGOLL	PRINKS	**RITTS**
TRIALS	**RIDGE**	RIGOLS	**RINSE**	BRITTS
URIALS	BRIDGE	**RILED**	RINSED	FRITTS
RIANT	FRIDGE	ARILED	RINSER	**RIVEL**
CRIANT	RIDGED	**RILLE**	RINSES	DRIVEL
RIBES	RIDGEL	GRILLE	**RIOTS**	RIVELS
BRIBES	RIDGER	RILLED	GRIOTS	**RIVEN**
TRIBES	RIDGES	RILLES	**RIPED**	DRIVEN
RICED	**RIDIC**	RILLET	GRIPED	**RIVER**
GRICED	IRIDIC	**RILLS**	**RIPER**	DRIVER
PRICED	**RIELS**	BRILLS	GRIPER	RIVERS
TRICED	ARIELS	DRILLS	RIPERS	RIVERY
RICER	ORIELS	FRILLS	**RIPES**	**RIVES**
GRICER	**RIEVE**	GRILLS	CRIPES	DRIVES
PRICER	GRIEVE	KRILLS	GRIPES	**RIVET**
RICERS	PRIEVE	PRILLS	TRIPES	GRIVET
RICES	RIEVER	TRILLS	RIPEST	PRIVET
DRICES	RIEVES	**RIMED**	**RISEN**	TRIVET
GRICES	**RIFFS**	CRIMED	ARISEN	RIVETS
PRICES	GRIFFS	GRIMED	**RISER**	**ROACH**
TRICES	**RIFLE**	PRIMED	PRISER	BROACH
RICEY	TRIFLE	**RIMER**	RISERS	**ROADS**
PRICEY	RIFLED	PRIMER	**RISES**	BROADS
RICHT	RIFLER	TRIMER	ARISES	TROADS
BRICHT	RIFLES	RIMERS	BRISES	**ROANS**
FRICHT	**RIFTE**	**RIMES**	CRISES	GROANS
RICHTS	RIFTED	CRIMES	FRISES	**ROAST**
RICIN	**RIFTS**	GRIMES	GRISES	BROAST
RICING	DRIFTS	PRIMES	IRISES	ROASTS
RICINS	GRIFTS	**RIMUS**	KRISES	**ROATE**
RICKS	**RIFTY**	PRIMUS	PRISES	ROATED
BRICKS	DRIFTY	**RINDS**	**RISKS**	ROATES
CRICKS	**RIGHT**	GRINDS	BRISKS	**ROBED**
ERICKS	ARIGHT	**RINES**	FRISKS	PROBED
PRICKS	BRIGHT	BRINES	**RISKY**	**ROBES**
TRICKS	FRIGHT	CRINES	BRISKY	PROBES
WRICKS	WRIGHT	TRINES	FRISKY	**ROBIN**
RIDER	RIGHTO	URINES	**RISPS**	ROBING
ARIDER	RIGHTS	**RINGS**	CRISPS	ROBINS
RIDERS	RIGHTY	BRINGS	**RITES**	**ROCKS**

BROCKS	TROLLS	**ROOPY**	**ROSIT**	**ROUSE**
CROCKS	**ROMAL**	DROOPY	PROSIT	AROUSE
FROCKS	BROMAL	**ROOSE**	ROSITS	CROUSE
TROCKS	ROMALS	BROOSE	**ROSTS**	GROUSE
RODED	**ROMAN**	ROOSED	FROSTS	TROUSE
ERODED	ROMANO	ROOSER	**ROTAL**	ROUSED
RODES	ROMANS	ROOSES	CROTAL	ROUSER
ERODES	**ROMPS**	**ROOTS**	**ROTCH**	ROUSES
TRODES	TROMPS	WROOTS	CROTCH	**ROUTE**
ROGER	**RONDE**	ROOTSY	ROTCHE	CROUTE
DROGER	RONDEL	**ROPED**	**ROTON**	ROUTED
ROGERS	RONDES	GROPED	CROTON	ROUTER
ROGUE	**RONES**	TROPED	PROTON	ROUTES
BROGUE	CRONES	**ROPER**	ROTONS	**ROUTH**
DROGUE	DRONES	GROPER	**ROTTE**	DROUTH
ROGUED	GRONES	PROPER	ROTTED	ROUTHS
ROGUER	IRONES	ROPERS	ROTTEN	**ROUTS**
ROGUES	PRONES	ROPERY	ROTTER	CROUTS
ROILS	TRONES	**ROPES**	ROTTES	GROUTS
BROILS	**RONNE**	GROPES	**ROUGE**	TROUTS
DROILS	RONNEL	TROPES	ROUGED	**ROVED**
ROINS	**RONTS**	**ROQUE**	ROUGES	DROVED
GROINS	FRONTS	ROQUES	**ROUGH**	GROVED
PROINS	**ROODS**	ROQUET	BROUGH	PROVED
ROKED	BROODS	**RORES**	GROUGH	**ROVEN**
BROKED	**ROOFS**	CRORES	TROUGH	PROVEN
GROKED	GROOFS	PRORES	ROUGHS	**ROVER**
PROKED	PROOFS	**RORIE**	ROUGHT	DROVER
TROKED	**ROOKS**	RORIER	ROUGHY	PROVER
ROKER	BROOKS	**ROSED**	**ROULE**	TROVER
BROKER	CROOKS	PROSED	TROULE	ROVERS
PROKER	DROOKS	**ROSES**	ROULES	**ROVES**
ROKERS	**ROOMS**	BROSES	**ROULS**	DROVES
ROKES	BROOMS	EROSES	PROULS	GROVES
BROKES	GROOMS	PROSES	**ROUND**	PROVES
DROKES	VROOMS	UROSES	AROUND	TROVES
PROKES	**ROOMY**	**ROSET**	GROUND	**ROWDY**
TROKES	BROOMY	GROSET	ROUNDS	CROWDY
ROLES	**ROONS**	ROSETS	**ROUPS**	**ROWED**
DROLES	CROONS	ROSETY	CROUPS	BROWED
PROLES	KROONS	**ROSIN**	GROUPS	CROWED
ROLLS	**ROOPS**	ROSING	**ROUPY**	TROWED
DROLLS	DROOPS	ROSINS	CROUPY	**ROWEL**
PROLLS	TROOPS	ROSINY	GROUPY	TROWEL

ROWELS	RUDISH	CRUMPY	RYMMES	SALPAE
ROWER	RUDIST	FRUMPY	**SABIN**	SALPAS
CROWER	**RUFFE**	GRUMPY	SABINE	**SALUE**
GROWER	TRUFFE	**RUNCH**	SABINS	SALUED
PROWER	RUFFED	BRUNCH	**SABLE**	SALUES
ROWERS	RUFFES	CRUNCH	USABLE	**SALUT**
ROWIE	**RUFFS**	**RUNED**	SABLED	SALUTE
FROWIE	GRUFFS	PRUNED	SABLES	**SALVE**
ROWIES	**RUGAL**	**RUNES**	**SABRE**	SALVED
ROWND	FRUGAL	PRUNES	SABRED	SALVER
DROWND	**RUGGY**	**RUNTS**	SABRES	SALVES
ROWNDS	DRUGGY	BRUNTS	**SACRA**	**SALVO**
ROWTH	**RUING**	GRUNTS	SACRAL	SALVOR
GROWTH	GRUING	PRUNTS	**SADES**	SALVOS
TROWTH	TRUING	**RUPIA**	TSADES	**SAMBA**
ROWTHS	RUINGS	RUPIAH	**SADIS**	TSAMBA
ROYNE	**RUINS**	RUPIAS	TSADIS	SAMBAL
GROYNE	BRUINS	**RURAL**	SADISM	SAMBAR
PROYNE	**RULES**	CRURAL	SADIST	SAMBAS
ROYNED	BRULES	RURALS	**SAFES**	**SAMEK**
ROYNES	**RUMAL**	**RUSES**	SAFEST	SAMEKH
RUBBY	BRUMAL	CRUSES	**SAGER**	SAMEKS
GRUBBY	RUMALS	DRUSES	USAGER	**SAMEL**
RUBIN	**RUMEN**	URUSES	**SAGES**	SAMELY
RUBINE	CRUMEN	**RUSHY**	USAGES	**SANES**
RUBINS	RUMENS	BRUSHY	SAGEST	SANEST
RUBUS	**RUMES**	**RUSSE**	**SAHIB**	**SANGA**
URUBUS	BRUMES	RUSSEL	SAHIBA	SANGAR
RUCHE	GRUMES	RUSSET	SAHIBS	SANGAS
RUCHED	**RUMLY**	**RUSTS**	**SAIDS**	**SANGH**
RUCHES	DRUMLY	BRUSTS	SAIDST	SANGHA
RUCKS	GRUMLY	CRUSTS	**SAINE**	SANGHS
CRUCKS	**RUMMY**	FRUSTS	SAINED	**SANSA**
TRUCKS	CRUMMY	TRUSTS	**SAITH**	SANSAR
RUDDY	DRUMMY	**RUSTY**	SAITHE	SANSAS
CRUDDY	**RUMPO**	CRUSTY	SAITHS	**SANTO**
RUDER	RUMPOS	TRUSTY	**SALAD**	SANTOL
CRUDER	RUMPOT	**RUTHS**	SALADE	SANTON
RUDERY	**RUMPS**	TRUTHS	SALADS	SANTOS
RUDES	CRUMPS	**RYKES**	**SALLE**	**SARIN**
CRUDES	FRUMPS	GRYKES	SALLEE	SARING
PRUDES	GRUMPS	TRYKES	SALLES	SARINS
RUDEST	TRUMPS	**RYMME**	SALLET	**SAROD**
RUDIS	**RUMPY**	RYMMED	**SALPA**	SARODE

SARODS	SCALLS	SCENES	**SCREE**	SEAMEN
SASIN	SCALLY	**SCENT**	SCREED	SEAMER
SASINE	**SCAMP**	ASCENT	SCREEN	SEAMES
SASINS	SCAMPI	SCENTS	SCREES	**SEARE**
SASSE	SCAMPS	**SCHMO**	SCREET	SEARED
SASSED	**SCANT**	SCHMOE	**SCREW**	SEARER
SASSES	SCANTS	SCHMOS	SCREWS	**SEASE**
SATIN	SCANTY	**SCHUL**	SCREWY	SEASED
ISATIN	**SCAPE**	SCHULN	**SCRIM**	SEASES
SATING	ESCAPE	SCHULS	SCRIMP	**SEAZE**
SATINS	SCAPED	**SCHWA**	SCRIMS	SEAZED
SATINY	SCAPES	SCHWAG	**SCRIP**	SEAZES
SATYR	**SCARE**	SCHWAS	SCRIPS	**SEDGE**
SATYRA	SCARED	**SCOPA**	SCRIPT	SEDGED
SATYRE	SCARER	SCOPAE	**SCROB**	SEDGES
SATYRS	SCARES	SCOPAS	SCROBE	**SEGUE**
SAUCE	SCAREY	**SCOPE**	SCROBS	SEGUED
SAUCED	**SCARP**	SCOPED	**SCROW**	SEGUES
SAUCER	ESCARP	SCOPES	ESCROW	**SEINE**
SAUCES	SCARPA	**SCORE**	SCROWL	SEINED
SAUGH	SCARPH	SCORED	SCROWS	SEINER
SAUGHS	SCARPS	SCORER	**SCRUM**	SEINES
SAUGHY	**SCARS**	SCORES	SCRUMP	**SEISE**
SAUTE	ESCARS	**SCOTS**	SCRUMS	SEISED
SAUTED	OSCARS	ASCOTS	**SCUDO**	SEISER
SAUTES	**SCART**	ESCOTS	ESCUDO	SEISES
SAVIN	SCARTH	**SCOUT**	**SCULL**	**SEITY**
SAVINE	SCARTS	SCOUTH	SCULLE	ASEITY
SAVING	**SCATH**	SCOUTS	SCULLS	**SEIZE**
SAVINS	SCATHE	**SCRAM**	**SCULP**	SEIZED
SAVOR	SCATHS	SCRAMB	SCULPS	SEIZER
SAVORS	**SCATT**	SCRAMS	SCULPT	SEIZES
SAVORY	SCATTS	**SCRAP**	**SCURF**	**SELLA**
SCAFF	SCATTY	SCRAPE	SCURFS	SELLAE
SCAFFS	**SCAUR**	SCRAPS	SCURFY	SELLAS
SCAFFY	SCAURS	**SCRAW**	**SCUSE**	**SELLE**
SCALA	SCAURY	SCRAWB	SCUSED	SELLER
SCALAE	**SCEAT**	SCRAWL	SCUSES	SELLES
SCALAR	SCEATT	SCRAWM	**SCUTA**	**SEMEE**
SCALE	**SCEND**	SCRAWP	SCUTAL	SEMEED
SCALED	ASCEND	SCRAWS	**SCUZZ**	**SENOR**
SCALER	SCENDS	**SCRAY**	SCUZZY	SENORA
SCALES	**SCENE**	SCRAYE	**SEAME**	SENORS
SCALL	SCENED	SCRAYS	SEAMED	**SENSE**

SENSED	SHACKY	**SHAVE**	SHIFTS	SHORTS
SENSEI	**SHADE**	SHAVED	SHIFTY	SHORTY
SENSES	SHADED	SHAVEN	**SHINE**	**SHOTT**
SENTE	SHADER	SHAVER	ASHINE	SHOTTE
SENTED	SHADES	SHAVES	SHINED	SHOTTS
SEPTA	**SHAKE**	**SHAWS**	SHINER	**SHOUT**
SEPTAL	ASHAKE	PSHAWS	SHINES	SHOUTS
SERAI	SHAKED	**SHEAF**	**SHIRE**	SHOUTY
SERAIL	SHAKEN	SHEAFS	SHIRED	**SHOVE**
SERAIS	SHAKER	SHEAFY	SHIRES	SHOVED
SERES	SHAKES	**SHEEN**	**SHIRR**	SHOVEL
SEREST	**SHALE**	SHEENS	SHIRRA	SHOVER
SERGE	SHALED	SHEENY	SHIRRS	SHOVES
SERGED	SHALES	**SHEEP**	**SHIRT**	**SHREW**
SERGER	SHALEY	SHEEPO	SHIRTS	SHREWD
SERGES	**SHALL**	SHEEPY	SHIRTY	SHREWS
SERIN	SHALLI	**SHEET**	**SHISH**	**SHROW**
SERINE	**SHAMA**	SHEETS	SHISHA	SHROWD
SERING	SHAMAL	SHEETY	**SHITE**	SHROWS
SERINS	SHAMAN	**SHEIK**	SHITED	**SHTUM**
SERRA	SHAMAS	SHEIKH	SHITES	SHTUMM
SERRAE	**SHAME**	SHEIKS	**SHIVA**	**SHULE**
SERRAN	ASHAME	**SHELF**	SHIVAH	SHULED
SERRAS	SHAMED	SHELFS	SHIVAS	SHULES
SERRE	SHAMER	SHELFY	**SHIVE**	**SHUTE**
SERRED	SHAMES	**SHELL**	SHIVER	SHUTED
SERRES	**SHAND**	SHELLS	SHIVES	SHUTES
SERVE	SHANDS	SHELLY	**SHLEP**	**SIDES**
SERVED	SHANDY	**SHEND**	SHLEPP	ASIDES
SERVER	**SHAPE**	YSHEND	SHLEPS	**SIDLE**
SERVES	SHAPED	SHENDS	**SHOAL**	SIDLED
SEVER	SHAPEN	**SHENT**	SHOALS	SIDLER
SEVERE	SHAPER	YSHENT	SHOALY	SIDLES
SEVERS	SHAPES	**SHETS**	**SHOOL**	**SIEGE**
SEVERY	**SHARE**	ASHETS	SHOOLE	SIEGED
SEWIN	SHARED	**SHIEL**	SHOOLS	SIEGER
SEWING	SHARER	SHIELD	**SHOOS**	SIEGES
SEWINS	SHARES	SHIELS	SHOOSH	**SIEVE**
SEXTO	**SHARN**	**SHIER**	**SHORE**	SIEVED
SEXTON	SHARNS	ASHIER	ASHORE	SIEVES
SEXTOS	SHARNY	SHIERS	SHORED	**SIGNA**
SHACK	**SHARP**	**SHIES**	SHORER	SIGNAL
SHACKO	SHARPS	SHIEST	SHORES	**SILEN**
SHACKS	SHARPY	**SHIFT**	**SHORT**	SILENE

SILENI	SKEERS	ASLANT	SLIPES	ASMEAR
SILENS	SKEERY	SLANTS	**SLIVE**	SMEARS
SILENT	**SKELL**	SLANTY	SLIVED	SMEARY
SILES	SKELLS	**SLATE**	SLIVEN	**SMEKE**
ESILES	SKELLY	SLATED	SLIVER	SMEKED
SILVA	**SKERS**	SLATER	SLIVES	SMEKES
SILVAE	ASKERS	SLATES	**SLOOM**	**SMELL**
SILVAN	ESKERS	SLATEY	SLOOMS	SMELLS
SILVAS	**SKIES**	**SLAVE**	SLOOMY	SMELLY
SINEW	ESKIES	SLAVED	**SLOPE**	**SMILE**
SINEWS	**SKILL**	SLAVER	ASLOPE	SMILED
SINEWY	SKILLS	SLAVES	SLOPED	SMILER
SINGE	SKILLY	SLAVEY	SLOPER	SMILES
SINGED	**SKIMP**	**SLEEK**	SLOPES	SMILET
SINGER	SKIMPS	SLEEKS	**SLOSH**	SMILEY
SINGES	SKIMPY	SLEEKY	ASLOSH	**SMIRK**
SIRRA	**SKITE**	**SLEEP**	SLOSHY	SMIRKS
SIRRAH	SKITED	ASLEEP	**SLOVE**	SMIRKY
SIRRAS	SKITES	SLEEPS	SLOVEN	**SMIRR**
SIRUP	**SKIVE**	SLEEPY	**SLUBB**	SMIRRS
SIRUPS	SKIVED	**SLEET**	SLUBBS	SMIRRY
SIRUPY	SKIVER	SLEETS	SLUBBY	**SMITE**
SITHE	SKIVES	SLEETY	**SLUMP**	SMITER
SITHED	**SKRIK**	**SLICE**	SLUMPS	SMITES
SITHEE	SKRIKE	SLICED	SLUMPY	**SMITH**
SITHEN	SKRIKS	SLICER	**SLURP**	SMITHS
SITHES	**SKUNK**	SLICES	SLURPS	SMITHY
SKANK	SKUNKS	**SLIDE**	SLURPY	**SMOKE**
SKANKS	SKUNKY	SLIDED	**SLUSH**	SMOKED
SKANKY	**SKYRE**	SLIDER	SLUSHY	SMOKER
SKART	SKYRED	SLIDES	**SMALM**	SMOKES
SKARTH	SKYRES	**SLIME**	SMALMS	SMOKEY
SKARTS	**SKYTE**	SLIMED	SMALMY	**SMOOT**
SKATE	SKYTED	SLIMES	**SMALT**	SMOOTH
SKATED	SKYTES	**SLIMS**	SMALTI	SMOOTS
SKATER	**SLAKE**	SLIMSY	SMALTO	**SMORE**
SKATES	ASLAKE	**SLING**	SMALTS	SMORED
SKEAN	SLAKED	ISLING	**SMARM**	SMORES
SKEANE	SLAKER	SLINGS	SMARMS	**SNACK**
SKEANS	SLAKES	**SLINK**	SMARMY	SNACKS
SKEAR	**SLANG**	SLINKS	**SMART**	SNACKY
SKEARS	SLANGS	SLINKY	SMARTS	**SNAIL**
SKEARY	SLANGY	**SLIPE**	SMARTY	SNAILS
SKEER	**SLANT**	SLIPED	**SMEAR**	SNAILY

SNAKE	SNOKED	SOLVED	**SOWCE**	SPARTH
SNAKED	SNOKES	SOLVER	SOWCED	SPARTS
SNAKES	**SNOOP**	SOLVES	SOWCES	**SPAUL**
SNAKEY	SNOOPS	**SONDE**	**SOWLE**	SPAULD
SNARE	SNOOPY	SONDER	SOWLED	SPAULS
SNARED	**SNOOT**	SONDES	SOWLES	**SPAWN**
SNARER	SNOOTS	**SONNE**	**SOWSE**	SPAWNS
SNARES	SNOOTY	SONNES	SOWSED	SPAWNY
SNARK	**SNORE**	SONNET	SOWSES	**SPEAR**
SNARKS	SNORED	**SOOLE**	**SOYLE**	SPEARS
SNARKY	SNORER	SOOLED	SOYLED	SPEARY
SNARL	SNORES	SOOLER	SOYLES	**SPECK**
SNARLS	**SNORT**	SOOLES	**SOZIN**	SPECKS
SNARLY	SNORTS	**SOOTE**	SOZINE	SPECKY
SNATH	SNORTY	SOOTED	SOZINS	**SPECT**
SNATHE	**SNOUT**	SOOTES	**SPACE**	ASPECT
SNATHS	SNOUTS	**SOOTH**	SPACED	SPECTS
SNEAK	SNOUTY	SOOTHE	SPACER	**SPEED**
SNEAKS	**SNUFF**	SOOTHS	SPACES	SPEEDO
SNEAKY	SNUFFS	**SORAS**	SPACEY	SPEEDS
SNEER	SNUFFY	PSORAS	**SPADE**	SPEEDY
SNEERS	**SOARE**	**SORDO**	SPADED	**SPELT**
SNEERY	SOARED	SORDOR	SPADER	SPELTS
SNEES	SOARER	**SOREL**	SPADES	SPELTZ
SNEESH	SOARES	SORELL	**SPAIN**	**SPEND**
SNELL	**SODOM**	SORELS	SPAING	SPENDS
SNELLS	SODOMS	SORELY	SPAINS	SPENDY
SNELLY	SODOMY	**SORES**	**SPALL**	**SPIAL**
SNIDE	**SOLAN**	TSORES	SPALLE	ESPIAL
SNIDED	SOLAND	SOREST	SPALLS	SPIALS
SNIDER	SOLANO	**SORTA**	**SPANE**	**SPICA**
SNIDES	SOLANS	SORTAL	SPANED	SPICAE
SNIDEY	**SOLDE**	**SOUCE**	SPANES	SPICAS
SNIFF	SOLDER	SOUCED	**SPARE**	**SPICE**
SNIFFS	SOLDES	SOUCES	SPARED	SPICED
SNIFFY	**SOLEI**	**SOUGH**	SPARER	SPICER
SNIFT	SOLEIN	SOUGHS	SPARES	SPICES
SNIFTS	**SOLER**	SOUGHT	**SPARK**	SPICEY
SNIFTY	SOLERA	**SOURS**	SPARKE	**SPICK**
SNIPE	SOLERS	SOURSE	SPARKS	ASPICK
SNIPED	**SOLID**	**SOUSE**	SPARKY	SPICKS
SNIPER	SOLIDI	SOUSED	**SPARS**	**SPICS**
SNIPES	SOLIDS	SOUSER	SPARSE	ASPICS
SNOKE	**SOLVE**	SOUSES	**SPART**	**SPIDE**

SPIDER	SPOILT	**SPURN**	STATES	STEERY
SPIDES	**SPOKE**	SPURNE	**STAVE**	**STELA**
SPIED	SPOKED	SPURNS	STAVED	STELAE
ESPIED	SPOKEN	**SQUAT**	STAVES	STELAI
SPIER	SPOKES	ASQUAT	**STEAD**	STELAR
ESPIER	**SPOOF**	SQUATS	STEADS	**STELL**
SPIERS	SPOOFS	**SQUAW**	STEADY	STELLA
SPIES	SPOOFY	SQUAWK	**STEAL**	STELLS
ESPIES	**SPOOK**	SQUAWS	OSTEAL	**STEME**
SPIFF	SPOOKS	**STAGE**	STEALE	STEMED
SPIFFS	SPOOKY	STAGED	STEALS	STEMES
SPIFFY	**SPOON**	STAGER	STEALT	**STENT**
SPIKE	SPOONS	STAGES	**STEAM**	OSTENT
SPIKED	SPOONY	STAGEY	STEAMS	STENTS
SPIKER	**SPORE**	**STAKE**	STEAMY	**STERE**
SPIKES	SPORED	STAKED	**STEAN**	STEREO
SPIKEY	SPORES	STAKER	STEANE	STERES
SPILE	**SPORT**	STAKES	STEANS	**STERN**
SPILED	ASPORT	**STALE**	**STEAR**	ASTERN
SPILES	SPORTS	STALED	STEARD	STERNA
SPILT	SPORTY	STALER	STEARE	STERNS
SPILTH	**SPOSH**	STALES	STEARS	**STICK**
SPINA	SPOSHY	**STALK**	**STEDD**	STICKS
SPINAE	**SPOUT**	STALKO	STEDDE	STICKY
SPINAL	ASPOUT	STALKS	STEDDS	**STIFF**
SPINAR	SPOUTS	STALKY	STEDDY	STIFFS
SPINAS	SPOUTY	**STANE**	**STEDE**	STIFFY
SPINE	**SPRED**	STANED	STEDED	**STILE**
ASPINE	SPREDD	STANES	STEDES	STILED
SPINED	SPREDS	**STARE**	**STEED**	STILES
SPINEL	**SPREE**	ASTARE	STEEDS	STILET
SPINES	SPREED	STARED	STEEDY	**STILL**
SPINET	SPREES	STARER	**STEEL**	STILLS
SPIRE	**SPRIT**	STARES	STEELD	STILLY
ASPIRE	ESPRIT	**STARR**	STEELS	**STILT**
SPIREA	SPRITE	STARRS	STEELY	STILTS
SPIRED	SPRITS	STARRY	**STEEM**	STILTY
SPIREM	SPRITZ	**START**	ESTEEM	**STIME**
SPIRES	**SPUME**	ASTART	STEEMS	STIMED
SPITE	SPUMED	STARTS	**STEEP**	STIMES
SPITED	SPUMES	**STATE**	STEEPS	**STING**
SPITES	**SPUNK**	ESTATE	STEEPY	STINGE
SPOIL	SPUNKS	STATED	**STEER**	STINGO
SPOILS	SPUNKY	STATER	STEERS	STINGS

STINGY	STONNE	**STRAK**	**STYLE**	SUNNAS
STINK	STONNS	STRAKE	STYLED	**SUPER**
STINKO	**STONY**	**STRAW**	STYLEE	SUPERB
STINKS	ASTONY	STRAWN	STYLER	SUPERS
STINKY	**STOOL**	STRAWS	STYLES	**SURAS**
STINT	STOOLS	STRAWY	STYLET	ASURAS
STINTS	STOOLY	**STRAY**	**STYLI**	**SURED**
STINTY	**STOOP**	ASTRAY	STYLIE	USURED
STIPE	ASTOOP	ESTRAY	**STYME**	**SURER**
STIPED	STOOPE	STRAYS	STYMED	USURER
STIPEL	STOOPS	**STREW**	STYMES	**SURES**
STIPES	**STOPE**	STREWN	**STYRE**	USURES
STIRE	STOPED	STREWS	STYRED	SUREST
STIRED	STOPER	**STRIA**	STYRES	**SURGE**
STIRES	STOPES	STRIAE	**STYTE**	SURGED
STIVE	**STOPS**	**STRIG**	STYTED	SURGER
STIVED	ESTOPS	STRIGA	STYTES	SURGES
STIVER	**STORE**	STRIGS	**SUAVE**	**SWAGE**
STIVES	STORED	**STRIP**	SUAVER	SWAGED
STOCK	STORER	STRIPE	**SUBAS**	SWAGER
STOCKS	STORES	STRIPS	TSUBAS	SWAGES
STOCKY	STOREY	STRIPT	**SUEDE**	**SWALE**
STOKE	**STORM**	STRIPY	SUEDED	SWALED
STOKED	STORMS	**STROW**	SUEDES	SWALES
STOKER	STORMY	STROWN	**SUGAR**	**SWAMP**
STOKES	**STOTT**	STROWS	SUGARS	SWAMPS
STOLE	STOTTS	**STRUM**	SUGARY	SWAMPY
STOLED	STOTTY	ESTRUM	**SUITE**	**SWANK**
STOLEN	**STOUN**	STRUMA	SUITED	SWANKS
STOLES	STOUND	STRUMS	SUITER	SWANKY
STOMA	STOUNS	**STRUT**	SUITES	**SWARD**
STOMAL	**STOUR**	ASTRUT	**SULPH**	USWARD
STOMAS	STOURE	STRUTS	SULPHA	SWARDS
STOMP	STOURS	**STUFF**	SULPHS	SWARDY
STOMPS	STOURY	STUFFS	**SUMAC**	**SWARM**
STOMPY	**STOUT**	STUFFY	SUMACH	ASWARM
STONE	STOUTH	**STUMP**	SUMACS	SWARMS
ASTONE	STOUTS	STUMPS	**SUMMA**	**SWART**
STONED	**STOVE**	STUMPY	SUMMAE	SWARTH
STONEN	STOVED	**STUNS**	SUMMAR	SWARTY
STONER	STOVER	ASTUNS	SUMMAS	**SWASH**
STONES	STOVES	**STUPE**	SUMMAT	SWASHY
STONEY	**STOWN**	STUPED	**SUNNA**	**SWATH**
STONN	STOWND	STUPES	SUNNAH	SWATHE

SWATHS	SWITHE	**TAINS**	**TAMPS**	TASSEL
SWATHY	**SWIVE**	STAINS	STAMPS	TASSES
SWEAR	SWIVED	**TAKER**	**TANGI**	TASSET
SWEARD	SWIVEL	STAKER	TANGIE	**TASTE**
SWEARS	SWIVES	TAKERS	TANGIS	TASTED
SWEARY	SWIVET	**TAKES**	**TANGS**	TASTER
SWEAT	**SWOON**	STAKES	STANGS	TASTES
SWEATS	ASWOON	**TAKIN**	**TANKS**	**TATER**
SWEATY	SWOONS	TAKING	STANKS	STATER
SWEEP	SWOONY	TAKINS	**TANNA**	TATERS
SWEEPS	**SWOOP**	**TALEA**	TANNAH	**TATES**
SWEEPY	SWOOPS	TALEAE	TANNAS	STATES
SWEER	SWOOPY	**TALER**	**TAPES**	**TATUS**
SWEERS	**SWOUN**	STALER	ETAPES	STATUS
SWEERT	SWOUND	TALERS	STAPES	**TAVER**
SWEET	SWOUNE	**TALES**	**TAPET**	TAVERN
SWEETS	SWOUNS	STALES	TAPETA	TAVERS
SWEETY	**SYLPH**	**TALKS**	TAPETI	TAVERT
SWEIR	SYLPHS	STALKS	TAPETS	**TAWED**
SWEIRS	SYLPHY	**TALKY**	**TAPIS**	STAWED
SWEIRT	**SYLVA**	STALKY	TAPIST	**TAWER**
SWIFT	SYLVAE	**TALLS**	**TARED**	TAWERS
SWIFTS	SYLVAN	STALLS	STARED	TAWERY
SWIFTY	SYLVAS	**TALON**	**TARES**	**TAWIE**
SWILE	**SYRUP**	ETALON	STARES	TAWIER
SWILER	SYRUPS	TALONS	**TARGE**	**TAWSE**
SWILES	SYRUPY	**TALPA**	TARGED	TAWSED
SWING	**TAATA**	TALPAE	TARGES	TAWSES
ASWING	ATAATA	TALPAS	**TARGET**	**TEADS**
SWINGE	TAATAS	**TALUK**	**TARNS**	STEADS
SWINGS	**TABER**	TALUKA	STARNS	**TEAKS**
SWINGY	TABERD	TALUKS	**TARRE**	STEAKS
SWIPE	TABERS	**TAMAL**	TARRED	**TEALS**
SWIPED	**TABLE**	TAMALE	TARRES	STEALS
SWIPER	STABLE	TAMALS	**TARRY**	**TEAMS**
SWIPES	TABLED	**TAMES**	STARRY	STEAMS
SWIPEY	TABLES	TAMEST	**TARSI**	**TEARS**
SWIRL	TABLET	**TAMIN**	TARSIA	STEARS
ASWIRL	**TACKS**	ETAMIN	**TARTS**	**TEASE**
SWIRLS	STACKS	TAMINE	STARTS	TEASED
SWIRLY	**TAGGY**	TAMING	**TASES**	TEASEL
SWISH	STAGGY	TAMINS	STASES	TEASER
SWISHY	**TAIGS**	**TAMIS**	UTASES	TEASES
SWITH	STAIGS	TAMISE	**TASSE**	**TEAZE**

TEAZED	TEMSED	TESTEE	**THORO**	**TILER**
TEAZEL	TEMSES	TESTER	THORON	TILERS
TEAZES	**TENCH**	TESTES	**THORP**	TILERY
TECTA	STENCH	**TETRA**	THORPE	**TILES**
TECTAL	**TENDS**	TETRAD	THORPS	STILES
TEDDY	STENDS	TETRAS	**THRAW**	UTILES
STEDDY	**TENES**	**TEWED**	THRAWN	**TILLS**
TEELS	CTENES	STEWED	THRAWS	STILLS
STEELS	TENESI	**THALE**	**THREE**	**TILLY**
TEEMS	**TENIA**	THALER	THREEP	STILLY
STEEMS	TENIAE	**THANA**	THREES	**TILTS**
TEENE	TENIAS	THANAH	**THROB**	STILTS
TEENED	**TENNE**	THANAS	ATHROB	**TIMED**
TEENER	TENNER	**THANE**	THROBS	STIMED
TEENES	TENNES	ETHANE	**THROE**	**TIMES**
TEENS	**TENSE**	THANES	THROED	STIMES
STEENS	TENSED	**THECA**	THROES	**TINEA**
TEENSY	TENSER	THECAE	**THROW**	TINEAL
TEERS	TENSES	THECAL	THROWE	TINEAS
STEERS	**TENTS**	**THEIN**	THROWN	**TINGE**
TEETH	STENTS	THEINE	THROWS	STINGE
TEETHE	**TERCE**	THEINS	**THUMB**	TINGED
TEILS	TERCEL	**THEME**	THUMBS	TINGES
STEILS	TERCES	THEMED	THUMBY	**TINGS**
TEINS	TERCET	THEMES	**THYME**	STINGS
STEINS	**TERES**	**THERM**	THYMES	**TINKS**
TELAE	STERES	THERME	THYMEY	STINKS
STELAE	**TERGA**	THERMS	**THYMI**	**TINTS**
TELES	TERGAL	**THICK**	THYMIC	STINTS
STELES	**TERNE**	THICKO	**TIBIA**	**TINTY**
TELESM	ETERNE	THICKS	TIBIAE	STINTY
TELIA	TERNED	THICKY	TIBIAL	**TIRED**
TELIAL	TERNES	**THING**	TIBIAS	STIRED
TELIC	**TERNS**	THINGS	**TICKS**	**TIRES**
ATELIC	STERNS	THINGY	STICKS	STIRES
STELIC	**TERRA**	**THOLE**	**TICKY**	**TITCH**
TELLS	TERRAE	THOLED	STICKY	STITCH
STELLS	TERRAS	THOLES	**TIFFS**	TITCHY
TEMED	**TERSE**	**THONG**	STIFFS	**TITHE**
ITEMED	TERSER	THONGS	**TIGER**	TITHED
STEMED	**TESTA**	THONGY	TIGERS	TITHER
TEMES	TESTAE	**THORN**	TIGERY	TITHES
STEMES	**TESTE**	THORNS	**TILED**	**TITIS**
TEMSE	TESTED	THORNY	STILED	OTITIS

TITLE	**TOLES**	**TOPIC**	TOUZED	TRAITS
TITLED	STOLES	ATOPIC	TOUZES	**TRAMP**
TITLER	**TOLLS**	TOPICS	**TOWED**	STRAMP
TITLES	ATOLLS	**TOQUE**	STOWED	TRAMPS
TITUP	**TOMIA**	TOQUES	**TOWER**	TRAMPY
TITUPS	STOMIA	TOQUET	STOWER	**TRANS**
TITUPY	TOMIAL	**TORAN**	TOWERS	TRANSE
TOAST	**TONAL**	TORANA	TOWERY	**TRAPE**
TOASTS	ATONAL	TORANS	**TOWIE**	TRAPED
TOASTY	**TONED**	**TORCH**	TOWIER	TRAPES
TOAZE	ATONED	TORCHY	TOWIES	**TRAPS**
TOAZED	STONED	**TORES**	**TOWSE**	STRAPS
TOAZES	**TONER**	STORES	TOWSED	TRAPSE
TOCKS	ATONER	**TOROS**	TOWSER	**TRASH**
STOCKS	STONER	TOROSE	TOWSES	TRASHY
TOCKY	TONERS	**TOROT**	**TOWZE**	**TRASS**
STOCKY	**TONES**	TOROTH	TOWZED	STRASS
TODDE	ATONES	**TORSE**	TOWZES	**TRAVE**
TODDED	STONES	TORSEL	**TOXIN**	TRAVEL
TODDES	**TONEY**	TORSES	TOXINE	TRAVES
TOGAE	STONEY	**TORTE**	TOXINS	**TRAYS**
TOGAED	**TONIC**	TORTEN	**TRACE**	STRAYS
TOILE	ATONIC	TORTES	TRACED	**TREAT**
ETOILE	TONICS	**TOSES**	TRACER	TREATS
TOILED	**TONKS**	PTOSES	TRACES	TREATY
TOILER	STONKS	**TOTTY**	**TRACK**	**TREFA**
TOILES	**TONNE**	STOTTY	STRACK	TREFAH
TOILET	STONNE	**TOUCH**	TRACKS	**TREIF**
TOITS	TONNER	TOUCHE	**TRADE**	TREIFA
STOITS	TONNES	TOUCHY	TRADED	**TREND**
TOKED	**TOOLS**	**TOUGH**	TRADER	TRENDS
STOKED	STOOLS	TOUGHS	TRADES	TRENDY
TOKER	**TOOTH**	TOUGHY	**TRADS**	**TRESS**
STOKER	TOOTHS	**TOUNS**	STRADS	STRESS
TOKERS	TOOTHY	STOUNS	**TRAGI**	TRESSY
TOKES	**TOOTS**	**TOURS**	TRAGIC	**TREWS**
ATOKES	TOOTSY	STOURS	**TRAIK**	STREWS
STOKES	**TOPED**	**TOUSE**	STRAIK	**TREYF**
TOLAN	STOPED	TOUSED	TRAIKS	TREYFA
TOLANE	**TOPER**	TOUSER	**TRAIN**	**TRIAC**
TOLANS	STOPER	TOUSES	STRAIN	TRIACS
TOLED	TOPERS	**TOUTS**	TRAINS	TRIACT
STOLED	**TOPES**	STOUTS	**TRAIT**	**TRIAL**
TOLEDO	STOPES	**TOUZE**	STRAIT	ATRIAL

TRIALS	TRITER	TRUSTY	**TWEED**	STYING
TRICE	TRITES	**TRUTH**	TWEEDS	**TYLER**
TRICED	**TROAD**	TRUTHS	TWEEDY	STYLER
TRICEP	TROADE	TRUTHY	**TWEEL**	TYLERS
TRICES	TROADS	**TRYST**	ATWEEL	**TYPIC**
TRICK	**TRODE**	TRYSTE	TWEELS	ATYPIC
STRICK	STRODE	TRYSTS	TWEELY	ETYPIC
TRICKS	TRODES	**TSADI**	**TWEEN**	**TYRAN**
TRICKY	**TROKE**	TSADIK	ATWEEN	TYRANS
TRIDE	STROKE	TSADIS	TWEENS	TYRANT
STRIDE	TROKED	**TUBBY**	TWEENY	**TYRED**
TRIER	TROKES	STUBBY	**TWERP**	STYRED
ETRIER	**TROLL**	**TUCKS**	TWERPS	**TYRES**
TRIERS	STROLL	STUCKS	TWERPY	STYRES
TRIGO	TROLLS	**TUFFE**	**TWICE**	**TYTHE**
TRIGON	TROLLY	TUFFES	TWICER	TYTHED
TRIGOS	**TROMP**	TUFFET	**TWILL**	TYTHES
TRIGS	TROMPE	**TUFFS**	TWILLS	**UDDER**
STRIGS	TROMPS	STUFFS	TWILLY	BUDDER
TRIKE	**TROPE**	**TUMPS**	**TWINE**	DUDDER
STRIKE	TROPED	STUMPS	TWINED	JUDDER
TRIKES	TROPES	**TUMPY**	TWINER	MUDDER
TRILL	**TROUT**	STUMPY	TWINES	PUDDER
TRILLO	STROUT	**TUNIC**	**TWINK**	RUDDER
TRILLS	TROUTS	TUNICA	TWINKS	SUDDER
TRIMS	TROUTY	TUNICS	TWINKY	UDDERS
STRIMS	**TROVE**	**TURBO**	**TWIRE**	**UGGED**
TRINE	STROVE	TURBOS	TWIRED	BUGGED
STRINE	TROVER	TURBOT	TWIRES	FUGGED
TRINED	TROVES	**TUYER**	**TWIRL**	HUGGED
TRINES	**TROWS**	TUYERE	TWIRLS	JUGGED
TRIOS	STROWS	TUYERS	TWIRLY	LUGGED
TRIOSE	**TROYS**	**TWAIN**	**TWIRP**	MUGGED
TRIPE	STROYS	ATWAIN	TWIRPS	PUGGED
STRIPE	**TRUCE**	TWAINS	TWIRPY	RUGGED
TRIPES	TRUCED	**TWANG**	**TWIST**	SUGGED
TRIPEY	TRUCES	TWANGS	TWISTS	TUGGED
TRIPS	**TRUCK**	TWANGY	TWISTY	**ULANS**
STRIPS	STRUCK	**TWANK**	**TWIXT**	KULANS
TRIPY	TRUCKS	TWANKS	ATWIXT	YULANS
STRIPY	**TRUES**	TWANKY	**TWYER**	**ULNAR**
TRIST	TRUEST	**TWEAK**	TWYERE	ULNARE
TRISTE	**TRUST**	TWEAKS	TWYERS	**ULVAS**
TRITE	TRUSTS	TWEAKY	**TYING**	VULVAS

UMBER	BUMPED	UNCLES	TUNKET	PUPPED
CUMBER	DUMPED	UNCLEW	**UNLET**	SUPPED
DUMBER	GUMPED	**UNCOS**	RUNLET	TUPPED
LUMBER	HUMPED	BUNCOS	**UNLIT**	**UPPER**
NUMBER	JUMPED	JUNCOS	SUNLIT	CUPPER
UMBERS	LUMPED	**UNCUS**	**UNMAN**	SUPPER
UMBERY	MUMPED	JUNCUS	GUNMAN	UPPERS
UMBLE	PUMPED	**UNCUT**	UNMANS	**UPTAK**
BUMBLE	RUMPED	UNCUTE	**UNMIX**	UPTAKE
FUMBLE	TUMPED	**UNDER**	UNMIXT	UPTAKS
HUMBLE	YUMPED	DUNDER	**UNPEN**	**UPTIE**
JUMBLE	**UMPHS**	FUNDER	UNPENS	UPTIED
MUMBLE	BUMPHS	SUNDER	UNPENT	UPTIES
RUMBLE	HUMPHS	UNDERN	**UNRED**	**URALI**
TUMBLE	SUMPHS	**UNFIX**	UNREDY	OURALI
UMBLES	**UMPIE**	UNFIXT	**UNRIG**	URALIS
UMBOS	YUMPIE	**UNHAT**	RUNRIG	**URARE**
BUMBOS	UMPIES	SUNHAT	UNRIGS	CURARE
DUMBOS	**UMPTY**	UNHATS	**UNRIP**	URARES
GUMBOS	HUMPTY	**UNICA**	UNRIPE	**URARI**
JUMBOS	NUMPTY	TUNICA	UNRIPS	CURARI
RUMBOS	**UNARY**	**UNIFY**	**UNSET**	OURARI
UMBRA	LUNARY	MUNIFY	SUNSET	URARIS
UMBRAE	**UNBAR**	**UNION**	UNSETS	**URATE**
UMBRAL	UNBARE	BUNION	**UNSEW**	AURATE
UMBRAS	UNBARK	UNIONS	UNSEWN	CURATE
UMBRE	UNBARS	**UNITE**	UNSEWS	URATES
UMBREL	**UNBED**	DUNITE	**UNSEX**	**URBAN**
UMBRES	SUNBED	GUNITE	UNSEXY	RURBAN
UMIAC	UNBEDS	MUNITE	**UNTIE**	TURBAN
UMIACK	**UNCAP**	UNITED	AUNTIE	URBANE
UMIACS	UNCAPE	UNITER	UNTIED	**UREAS**
UMMAS	UNCAPS	UNITES	UNTIES	UREASE
GUMMAS	**UNCES**	**UNITS**	**UNTIL**	**URENA**
SUMMAS	BUNCES	CUNITS	UNTILE	MURENA
UMMED	DUNCES	**UNKED**	UNTIN	URENAS
BUMMED	OUNCES	BUNKED	MUNTIN	**URGED**
CUMMED	PUNCES	DUNKED	UNTINS	GURGED
GUMMED	**UNCIA**	FUNKED	**UNWON**	PURGED
HUMMED	UNCIAE	GUNKED	UNWONT	SURGED
MUMMED	UNCIAL	JUNKED	**UPPED**	**URGER**
SUMMED	**UNCLE**	**UNKET**	CUPPED	BURGER
VUMMED	NUNCLE	JUNKET	DUPPED	PURGER
UMPED	UNCLED	SUNKET	HUPPED	SURGER

URGERS	BUSING	**VALSE**	**VENDU**	KVETCH
URGES	FUSING	VALSED	VENDUE	VETCHY
GURGES	MUSING	VALSES	VENDUS	**VICAR**
PURGES	SUSING	**VALUE**	**VENGE**	VICARS
SURGES	**USURE**	VALUED	AVENGE	VICARY
URIAL	USURED	VALUER	VENGED	**VIGOR**
BURIAL	USURER	VALUES	VENGER	VIGORO
CURIAL	USURES	**VALVE**	VENGES	VIGORS
URIALS	**UTILE**	VALVED	**VENIN**	**VILER**
URINE	FUTILE	VALVES	VENINE	EVILER
MURINE	RUTILE	**VANDA**	VENINS	**VILLA**
PURINE	SUTILE	VANDAL	**VENTS**	VILLAE
URINED	UTILES	VANDAS	EVENTS	VILLAN
URINES	**UTTER**	**VAPOR**	**VENUE**	VILLAR
URITE	BUTTER	VAPORS	AVENUE	VILLAS
CURITE	CUTTER	VAPORY	VENUES	**VINER**
URITES	GUTTER	**VAREC**	**VERGE**	VINERS
URNED	MUTTER	VARECH	VERGED	VINERY
BURNED	NUTTER	VARECS	VERGER	**VINES**
DURNED	PUTTER	**VARVE**	VERGES	OVINES
GURNED	RUTTER	VARVED	**VERSE**	**VIRGA**
TURNED	UTTERS	VARVEL	AVERSE	VIRGAE
URPED	**UVULA**	VARVES	VERSED	VIRGAS
BURPED	UVULAE	**VASES**	VERSER	**VIRGE**
URSAE	UVULAR	KVASES	VERSES	VIRGER
BURSAE	UVULAS	**VAULT**	VERSET	VIRGES
URVAS	**VADED**	VAULTS	**VERST**	**VIRTU**
MURVAS	EVADED	VAULTY	VERSTE	VIRTUE
USAGE	**VADES**	**VAUNT**	VERSTS	VIRTUS
USAGER	EVADES	AVAUNT	**VERTS**	**VISED**
USAGES	**VAGUE**	VAUNTS	AVERTS	AVISED
USERS	VAGUED	VAUNTY	EVERTS	**VISES**
LUSERS	VAGUER	**VAUTE**	**VERTU**	AVISES
MUSERS	VAGUES	VAUTED	VERTUE	**VISIE**
USHER	**VAILS**	VAUTES	VERTUS	VISIED
BUSHER	AVAILS	**VAWTE**	**VERVE**	VISIER
GUSHER	**VALES**	VAWTED	VERVEL	VISIES
HUSHER	AVALES	VAWTES	VERVEN	**VISIT**
LUSHER	**VALET**	**VEALE**	VERVES	VISITE
MUSHER	VALETA	VEALED	VERVET	VISITS
PUSHER	VALETE	VEALER	**VESTA**	**VISTA**
RUSHER	VALETS	VEALES	VESTAL	VISTAL
USHERS	**VALIS**	**VELLS**	VESTAS	VISTAS
USING	VALISE	KVELLS	**VETCH**	**VITAL**

AVITAL	**VULVA**	AWAKEN	WASTED	TWEEDY
VITALS	VULVAE	WAKENS	WASTEL	**WEELS**
VITTA	VULVAL	**WAKES**	WASTER	SWEELS
VITTAE	VULVAR	AWAKES	WASTES	TWEELS
VODOU	VULVAS	**WALED**	**WATAP**	**WEENS**
VODOUN	**WACKE**	SWALED	WATAPE	TWEENS
VODOUS	WACKED	**WALES**	WATAPS	WEENSY
VOGIE	WACKER	DWALES	**WATCH**	**WEENY**
VOGIER	WACKES	SWALES	AWATCH	SWEENY
VOGUE	**WACKS**	**WALIS**	SWATCH	TWEENY
VOGUED	SWACKS	WALISE	WATCHA	**WEEPS**
VOGUER	**WADDY**	**WALLA**	**WATER**	SWEEPS
VOGUES	SWADDY	WALLAH	WATERS	TWEEPS
VOGUEY	**WAFER**	WALLAS	WATERY	**WEEPY**
VOICE	WAFERS	**WALLY**	**WAUGH**	SWEEPY
VOICED	WAFERY	SWALLY	WAUGHS	**WEEST**
VOICER	**WAGED**	**WANGS**	WAUGHT	TWEEST
VOICES	SWAGED	DWANGS	**WAURS**	**WEETE**
VOIDS	**WAGER**	TWANGS	WAURST	WEETED
AVOIDS	SWAGER	**WANKS**	**WAVER**	WEETEN
OVOIDS	WAGERS	SWANKS	WAVERS	WEETER
VOLAR	**WAGES**	TWANKS	WAVERY	**WEETS**
VOLARY	SWAGES	**WANKY**	**WAYED**	SWEETS
VOLTE	**WAILS**	SWANKY	SWAYED	TWEETS
VOLTED	SWAILS	TWANKY	**WEALS**	**WEFTE**
VOLTES	**WAINS**	**WANZE**	SWEALS	WEFTED
VOLVA	SWAINS	WANZED	**WEARS**	WEFTES
VOLVAE	TWAINS	WANZES	SWEARS	**WEIGH**
VOLVAS	**WATRS**	**WARDS**	**WEARY**	AWEIGH
VOLVE	WAIRSH	AWARDS	AWEARY	WEIGHS
EVOLVE	**WAITE**	SWARDS	SWEARY	WEIGHT
VOLVED	TWAITE	**WARMS**	**WEAVE**	**WEIRD**
VOLVES	WAITED	SWARMS	WEAVED	WEIRDO
VOMIT	WAITER	**WARNS**	WEAVER	WEIRDS
VOMITO	WAITES	AWARNS	WEAVES	WEIRDY
VOMITS	**WAITS**	**WARRE**	**WEDEL**	**WEIRS**
VOMITY	AWAITS	WARRED	WEDELN	SWEIRS
VOUCH	**WAIVE**	WARREN	WEDELS	**WEISE**
AVOUCH	WAIVED	WARREY	**WEDGE**	WEISED
VOWED	WAIVER	**WARTY**	WEDGED	WEISES
AVOWED	WAIVES	SWARTY	WEDGES	**WEIZE**
VOWER	**WAKED**	**WASHY**	**WEEDS**	WEIZED
AVOWER	AWAKED	SWASHY	TWEEDS	WEIZES
VOWERS	**WAKEN**	**WASTE**	**WEEDY**	**WELKE**

WELKED	AWHIRL	**WILLS**	**WIRRA**	SWORDS
WELKES	WHIRLS	SWILLS	WIRRAH	**WORSE**
WELLS	WHIRLY	TWILLS	**WISES**	WORSED
DWELLS	**WHIRR**	**WILLY**	WISEST	WORSEN
SWELLS	WHIRRS	TWILLY	**WISTS**	WORSER
WELTS	WHIRRY	**WILTS**	TWISTS	WORSES
SWELTS	**WHISH**	TWILTS	**WITCH**	WORSET
WHACK	WHISHT	**WINCE**	SWITCH	**WORTH**
WHACKO	**WHISK**	WINCED	TWITCH	WORTHS
WHACKS	WHISKS	WINCER	WITCHY	WORTHY
WHACKY	WHISKY	WINCES	**WITES**	**WOUND**
WHALE	**WHITE**	WINCEY	TWITES	SWOUND
WHALED	WHITED	**WINED**	**WITHE**	WOUNDS
WHALER	WHITEN	DWINED	SWITHE	WOUNDY
WHALES	WHITER	TWINED	WITHED	**WRACK**
WHATS	WHITES	**WINES**	WITHER	AWRACK
WHATSO	WHITEY	DWINES	WITHES	WRACKS
WHEAR	**WHIZZ**	SWINES	**WIVED**	**WRATH**
WHEARE	WHIZZO	TWINES	SWIVED	WRATHS
WHEAT	WHIZZY	**WINGE**	**WIVER**	WRATHY
WHEATS	**WHORE**	SWINGE	WIVERN	**WRIER**
WHEATY	WHORED	TWINGE	WIVERS	OWRIER
WHEEL	WHORES	WINGED	**WIVES**	**WRIES**
AWHEEL	**WHYDA**	WINGER	SWIVES	WRIEST
WHEELS	WHYDAH	WINGES	**WOKEN**	**WRIST**
WHEELY	WHYDAS	**WINGS**	AWOKEN	WRISTS
WHELK	**WICCA**	SWINGS	**WOLVE**	WRISTY
WHELKS	WICCAN	**WINGY**	WOLVED	**WRITE**
WHELKY	WICCAS	SWINGY	WOLVER	WRITER
WHIFF	**WIDES**	**WINKS**	WOLVES	WRITES
WHIFFS	WIDEST	SWINKS	**WOODS**	**WROKE**
WHIFFY	**WIELD**	TWINKS	WOODSY	YWROKE
WHILE	WIELDS	**WIPED**	**WOONS**	WROKEN
AWHILE	WIELDY	SWIPED	SWOONS	**WRONG**
WHILED	**WIFTY**	**WIPER**	**WOOPS**	AWRONG
WHILES	SWIFTY	SWIPER	SWOOPS	WRONGS
WHIMS	**WIGGY**	WIPERS	**WOOPY**	**XENIA**
WHIMSY	TWIGGY	**WIPES**	SWOOPY	XENIAL
WHINE	**WIGHT**	SWIPES	**WOOSE**	XENIAS
WHINED	TWIGHT	**WIRED**	WOOSEL	**XENIC**
WHINER	WIGHTS	TWIRED	WOOSES	AXENIC
WHINES	**WILES**	**WIRES**	**WOOSH**	**YACKS**
WHINEY	DWILES	SWIRES	SWOOSH	KYACKS
WHIRL	SWILES	TWIRES	**WORDS**	**YAFFS**

NYAFFS	**YODLE**	YOUTHS	ZILLAS	ZOMBIE
YANGS	YODLED	YOUTHY	**ZINES**	ZOMBIS
KYANGS	YODLER	**ZAMAN**	AZINES	**ZONAL**
YCLED	YODLES	ZAMANG	EZINES	AZONAL
CYCLED	**YOGIN**	ZAMANS	**ZINKE**	**ZONES**
YEAST	YOGINI	**ZEBEC**	ZINKED	OZONES
YEASTS	YOGINS	ZEBECK	ZINKES	**ZOOEA**
YEASTY	**YOGIS**	ZEBECS	**ZIZIT**	ZOOEAE
YESES	YOGISM	**ZIBET**	ZIZITH	ZOOEAL
CYESES	**YOJAN**	ZIBETH	**ZOAEA**	ZOOEAS
OYESES	YOJANA	ZIBETS	ZOAEAE	**ZYMES**
YLEMS	YOJANS	**ZILLA**	ZOAEAS	AZYMES
XYLEMS	**YOUTH**	ZILLAH	**ZOMBI**	

Six-letter root words

AARRGH	CABLETS	**ACCEDE**	SACKERS	**ACTURE**
AARRGHH	FABLETS	ACCEDED	TACKERS	FACTURE
ABACUS	GABLETS	ACCEDER	WACKERS	ACTURES
BABACUS	TABLETS	ACCEDES	YACKERS	**ACUATE**
ABAKAS	**ABLING**	**ACCITE**	**ACKNOW**	VACUATE
KABAKAS	CABLING	ACCITED	ACKNOWN	ACUATED
ABAYAS	FABLING	ACCITES	ACKNOWS	ACUATES
KABAYAS	GABLING	**ACCRUE**	**ACNODE**	**ACUITY**
ABDABS	SABLING	ACCRUED	TACNODE	VACUITY
HABDABS	TABLING	ACCRUES	ACNODES	**ACUMEN**
ABDUCE	ABLINGS	**ACCUSE**	**ACQUIS**	CACUMEN
ABDUCED	**ABOLLA**	ACCUSED	ACQUIST	ACUMENS
ABDUCES	ABOLLAE	ACCUSER	**ACQUIT**	**ACUTES**
ABELES	ABOLLAS	ACCUSES	ACQUITE	ACUTEST
KABELES	**ABOMAS**	**ACHING**	ACQUITS	**ADDEND**
ABELIA	ABOMASA	BACHING	**ACTION**	ADDENDA
ABELIAN	ABOMASI	CACHING	FACTION	ADDENDS
ABELIAS	**ABRADE**	GACHING	PACTION	**ADDERS**
ABIDER	ABRADED	ACHINGS	TACTION	GADDERS
RABIDER	ABRADER	**ACKEES**	ACTIONS	LADDERS
ABIDERS	ABRADES	HACKEES	**ACTIVE**	MADDERS
ABJURE	**ABYING**	**ACKERS**	FACTIVE	PADDERS
ABJURED	BABYING	BACKERS	ACTIVES	WADDERS
ABJURER	**ACANTH**	DACKERS	**ACTORS**	**ADDIES**
ABJURES	ACANTHA	HACKERS	FACTORS	BADDIES
ABLATE	ACANTHI	JACKERS	**ACTUAL**	CADDIES
ABLATED	ACANTHS	LACKERS	FACTUAL	DADDIES
ABLATES	**ACATES**	PACKERS	TACTUAL	HADDIES
ABLETS	VACATES	RACKERS	ACTUALS	LADDIES

PADDIES	BADLAND	**AFFINE**	MAGNATE	TAILING
SADDIES	ADLANDS	AFFINED	AGNATES	VAILING
TADDIES	**ADMIRE**	AFFINES	**AGNISE**	WAILING
WADDIES	ADMIRED	**AFGHAN**	AGNISED	**AIMERS**
ADDING	ADMIRER	AFGHANI	AGNISES	MAIMERS
DADDING	ADMIRES	AFGHANS	**AGNIZE**	**AIMING**
GADDING	**ADNEXA**	**AFTERS**	AGNIZED	MAIMING
HADDING	ADNEXAL	HAFTERS	AGNIZES	**AINGAS**
MADDING	**ADONIS**	RAFTERS	**AGOROT**	KAINGAS
PADDING	ADONISE	WAFTERS	AGOROTH	**AIREST**
RADDING	**ADVENE**	**AGENES**	**AGRISE**	FAIREST
SADDING	ADVENED	SAGENES	AGRISED	PAIREST
WADDING	ADVENES	**AGGADA**	AGRISES	SAIREST
ADDINGS	**ADVISE**	HAGGADA	**AGRIZE**	**AIRIER**
ADDLED	ADVISED	AGGADAH	AGRIZED	FAIRIER
DADDLED	ADVISEE	AGGADAS	AGRIZES	HAIRIER
FADDLED	ADVISER	**AGGERS**	**AGRYZE**	LAIRIER
PADDLED	ADVISES	BAGGERS	AGRYZED	VAIRIER
RADDLED	**ADWARE**	DAGGERS	AGRYZES	**AIRILY**
SADDLED	BADWARE	GAGGERS	**AGUISE**	FAIRILY
WADDLED	ADWARES	JAGGERS	AGUISED	HAIRILY
ADDLES	**AEMULE**	LAGGERS	AGUISES	**AIRING**
DADDLES	AEMULED	NAGGERS	**AGUISH**	FAIRING
FADDLES	AEMULES	SAGGERS	VAGUISH	HAIRING
PADDLES	**AEONIC**	TAGGERS	**AGUIZE**	LAIRING
RADDLES	PAEONIC	WAGGERS	AGUIZED	PAIRING
SADDLES	**AERATE**	YAGGERS	AGUIZES	SAIRING
WADDLES	AERATED	**AGGIES**	**AGUNOT**	WAIRING
ADDUCE	AERATES	BAGGIES	AGUNOTH	AIRINGS
ADDUCED	**AERIES**	JAGGIES	**AIDERS**	**AIRNED**
ADDUCER	FAERIES	MAGGIES	RAIDERS	CAIRNED
ADDUCES	AERIEST	RAGGIES	**AIDING**	**AIRWAY**
ADHERE	**AFFAIR**	**AGINGS**	LAIDING	FAIRWAY
ADHERED	AFFAIRE	PAGINGS	MAIDING	AIRWAYS
ADHERER	AFFAIRS	RAGINGS	RAIDING	**AIVERS**
ADHERES	**AFFEAR**	**AGISMS**	**AILING**	TAIVERS
ADJOIN	AFFEARD	MAGISMS	BAILING	WAIVERS
ADJOINS	AFFEARE	**AGLETS**	FAILING	**ALANGS**
ADJOINT	AFFEARS	EAGLETS	HAILING	LALANGS
ADJURE	**AFFIES**	HAGLETS	JAILING	**ALANIN**
ADJURED	BAFFIES	**AGNAME**	MAILING	ALANINE
ADJURER	DAFFIES	AGNAMED	NAILING	ALANINS
ADJURES	TAFFIES	AGNAMES	RAILING	**ALANTS**
ADLAND	WAFFIES	**AGNATE**	SAILING	TALANTS

ALAPAS	ALKALIS	GALLONS	ALUMINS	AMERCES
PALAPAS	**ALKANE**	**ALLOTS**	**ALUMNA**	**AMIDIN**
ALATED	ALKANES	BALLOTS	ALUMNAE	AMIDINE
PALATED	ALKANET	TALLOTS	**AMATES**	AMIDINS
ALATES	**ALKIES**	**ALLOWS**	HAMATES	**AMINES**
MALATES	TALKIES	BALLOWS	**AMAUTI**	FAMINES
PALATES	WALKIES	CALLOWS	AMAUTIK	GAMINES
ALBERT	**ALLEES**	FALLOWS	AMAUTIS	TAMINES
HALBERT	CALLEES	GALLOWS	**AMBERS**	**AMISES**
ALBERTS	MALLEES	HALLOWS	CAMBERS	CAMISES
ALCADE	SALLEES	MALLOWS	JAMBERS	KAMISES
FALCADE	**ALLEGE**	SALLOWS	LAMBERS	TAMISES
ALCADES	ALLEGED	TALLOWS	TAMBERS	**AMMONS**
ALCOVE	ALLEGER	WALLOWS	**AMBITS**	GAMMONS
ALCOVED	ALLEGES	**ALLUDE**	GAMBITS	MAMMONS
ALCOVES	**ALLELS**	ALLUDED	**AMBLED**	**AMOEBA**
ALEGGE	HALLELS	ALLUDES	GAMBLED	AMOEBAE
ALEGGED	**ALLEYS**	**ALLURE**	HAMBLED	AMOEBAN
ALEGGES	GALLEYS	ALLURED	RAMBLED	AMOEBAS
ALEXIN	VALLEYS	ALLURER	WAMBLED	**AMOOVE**
ALEXINE	WALLEYS	ALLURES	**AMBLER**	AMOOVED
ALEXINS	**ALLIED**	**ALMOND**	GAMBLER	AMOOVES
ALGOID	DALLIED	ALMONDS	RAMBLER	**AMPING**
VALGOID	GALLIED	ALMONDY	AMBLERS	CAMPING
ALIDAD	PALLIED	**ALMUDS**	**AMBLES**	DAMPING
ALIDADE	RALLIED	TALMUDS	GAMBLES	LAMPING
ALIDADS	SALLIED	**ALNAGE**	HAMBLES	RAMPING
ALIGNS	TALLIED	ALNAGER	RAMBLES	TAMPING
MALIGNS	**ALLIES**	ALNAGES	WAMBLES	VAMPING
ALINES	BALLIES	**ALODIA**	**AMELIA**	**AMPLER**
MALINES	DALLIES	ALODIAL	CAMELIA	SAMPLER
SALINES	GALLIES	**ALSOON**	AMELIAS	**AMTRAC**
VALINES	PALLIES	ALSOONE	**AMENDE**	AMTRACK
ALIPED	RALLIES	**ALTERN**	AMENDED	AMTRACS
TALIPED	SALLIES	SALTERN	AMENDER	**AMUSES**
ALIPEDS	TALLIES	ALTERNE	AMENDES	CAMUSES
ALISON	WALLIES	**ALTERS**	**AMENTA**	WAMUSES
MALISON	**ALLIUM**	FALTERS	RAMENTA	**ANALLY**
ALISONS	BALLIUM	HALTERS	AMENTAL	BANALLY
ALIYOT	GALLIUM	PALTERS	**AMENTS**	**ANALOG**
ALIYOTH	PALLIUM	SALTERS	LAMENTS	ANALOGA
ALKALI	ALLIUMS	**ALUMIN**	**AMERCE**	ANALOGS
ALKALIC	**ALLONS**	ALUMINA	AMERCED	ANALOGY
ALKALIN	BALLONS	ALUMINE	AMERCER	**ANANAS**

BANANAS	**ANGLES**	TANNOYS	**APISMS**	**ARAYSE**
MANANAS	BANGLES	**ANONYM**	PAPISMS	ARAYSED
ZANANAS	CANGLES	ANONYMA	**APLITE**	ARAYSES
ANARCH	DANGLES	ANONYMS	HAPLITE	**ARBORS**
ANARCHS	FANGLES	**ANSATE**	APLITES	HARBORS
ANARCHY	GANGLES	ANSATED	**APNOEA**	**ARBOUR**
ANATAS	JANGLES	**ANTARA**	APNOEAL	HARBOUR
ANATASE	MANGLES	TANTARA	APNOEAS	ARBOURS
ANCHOS	TANGLES	ANTARAS	**APOLOG**	**ARCADE**
RANCHOS	WANGLES	**ANTARS**	APOLOGS	ARCADED
SANCHOS	**ANILIN**	CANTARS	APOLOGY	ARCADES
ANELED	ANILINE	KANTARS	**APPELS**	**ARCHED**
PANELED	ANILINS	**ANTHER**	LAPPELS	MARCHED
ANGELS	**ANIMIS**	PANTHER	RAPPELS	PARCHED
MANGELS	ANIMISM	ANTHERS	**APPEND**	**ARCHER**
ANGERS	ANIMIST	**ANTICK**	WAPPEND	MARCHER
BANGERS	**ANIONS**	ANTICKE	APPENDS	ARCHERS
DANGERS	FANIONS	ANTICKS	**APPLES**	ARCHERY
GANGERS	WANIONS	**ANTING**	DAPPLES	**ARCHES**
HANGERS	**ANISES**	BANTING	SAPPLES	LARCHES
LANGERS	MANISES	CANTING	**APPORT**	MARCHES
MANGERS	**ANKERS**	DANTING	RAPPORT	PARCHES
RANGERS	BANKERS	GANTING	APPORTS	ARCHEST
SANGERS	CANKERS	HANTING	**APPOSE**	**ARCING**
ANGINA	HANKERS	KANTING	PAPPOSE	FARCING
ANGINAL	JANKERS	PANTING	APPOSED	ARCINGS
ANGINAS	RANKERS	RANTING	APPOSER	**AREOLA**
ANGLED	TANKERS	WANTING	APPOSES	AREOLAE
BANGLED	WANKERS	ANTINGS	**APRONS**	AREOLAR
CANGLED	YANKERS	**ANTLER**	NAPRONS	AREOLAS
DANGLED	**ANKLED**	PANTLER	**ARABIC**	**ARGENT**
FANGLED	FANKLED	ANTLERS	ARABICA	MARGENT
GANGLED	RANKLED	**ANTLIA**	**ARABIN**	ARGENTS
JANGLED	**ANKLES**	ANTLIAE	CARABIN	**ARGLED**
MANGLED	CANKLES	**ANTRUM**	ARABINS	GARGLED
TANGLED	FANKLES	TANTRUM	**ARABIS**	**ARGLES**
WANGLED	RANKLES	ANTRUMS	MARABIS	DARGLES
ANGLER	**ANLAGE**	**ANYONS**	ARABISE	GARGLES
DANGLER	ANLAGEN	CANYONS	**ARABLE**	**ARGONS**
JANGLER	ANLAGES	**APEXES**	PARABLE	JARGONS
MANGLER	**ANNEXE**	CAPEXES	ARABLES	**ARIOSE**
TANGLER	ANNEXED	**APHTHA**	**ARAISE**	CARIOSE
WANGLER	ANNEXES	NAPHTHA	ARAISED	**ARISES**
ANGLERS	**ANNOYS**	APHTHAE	ARAISES	PARISES

ARISTA	AROUSED	**ARSING**	HASHIER	ASPIRER
BARISTA	AROUSER	FARSING	MASHIER	ASPIRES
ARISTAE	AROUSES	PARSING	WASHIER	**ASPISH**
ARISTAS	**ARPENS**	**ARSONS**	**ASHING**	RASPISH
ARKING	PARPENS	PARSONS	BASHING	WASPISH
BARKING	**ARPENT**	**ARTELS**	CASHING	**ASSAIL**
CARKING	PARPENT	CARTELS	DASHING	VASSAIL
DARKING	ARPENTS	MARTELS	FASHING	WASSAIL
HARKING	**ARRACK**	**ARTFUL**	GASHING	ASSAILS
KARKING	BARRACK	CARTFUL	HASHING	**ASSETS**
LARKING	CARRACK	**ARTIER**	LASHING	BASSETS
MARKING	ARRACKS	PARTIER	MASHING	TASSETS
NARKING	**ARRANT**	TARTIER	PASHING	**ASSIST**
PARKING	FARRANT	WARTIER	RASHING	BASSIST
RARKING	WARRANT	**ARTIES**	SASHING	ASSISTS
SARKING	**ARRAYS**	PARTIES	TASHING	**ASSIZE**
WARKING	WARRAYS	ARTIEST	WASHING	ASSIZED
YARKING	**ARRECT**	**ARTILY**	**ASHMAN**	ASSIZER
ARLING	CARRECT	TARTILY	MASHMAN	ASSIZES
CARLING	**ARRETS**	**ARTIST**	**ASHMEN**	**ASSUME**
DARLING	BARRETS	ARTISTE	MASHMEN	ASSUMED
HARLING	GARRETS	ARTISTS	**ASHRAM**	ASSUMER
MARLING	**ARRIDE**	**ARTSIE**	ASHRAMA	ASSUMES
PARLING	ARRIDED	ARTSIER	ASHRAMS	**ASSURE**
WARLING	ARRIDES	ARTSIES	**ASKERS**	ASSURED
ARMERS	**ARRIVE**	**ASCENT**	MASKERS	ASSURER
FARMERS	ARRIVED	NASCENT	TASKERS	ASSURES
HARMERS	ARRIVER	ASCENTS	**ASKING**	**ASTERN**
WARMERS	ARRIVES	**ASCONS**	BASKING	EASTERN
ARMFUL	**ARROWS**	GASCONS	CASKING	PASTERN
HARMFUL	BARROWS	MASCONS	GASKING	**ASTERS**
ARMFULS	FARROWS	**ASCOTS**	MASKING	BASTERS
ARMIES	HARROWS	MASCOTS	TASKING	CASTERS
SARMIES	MARROWS	**ASEITY**	ASKINGS	EASTERS
ARMING	NARROWS	GASEITY	**ASLAKE**	FASTERS
FARMING	TARROWS	**ASHAME**	ASLAKED	GASTERS
HARMING	YARROWS	ASHAMED	ASLAKES	LASTERS
WARMING	**ARROWY**	ASHAMES	**ASPERS**	MASTERS
ARMINGS	MARROWY	**ASHERY**	GASPERS	PASTERS
ARMOUR	**ARSHIN**	FASHERY	JASPERS	RASTERS
ARMOURS	ARSHINE	WASHERY	RASPERS	TASTERS
ARMOURY	ARSHINS	**ASHIER**	ASPERSE	WASTERS
AROUSE	**ARSIER**	CASHIER	**ASPIRE**	**ASTONE**
CAROUSE	TARSIER	DASHIER	ASPIRED	ASTONED

ASTONES	**AUDING**	**AVAILE**	AXILLAR	BALSAMY
ASTRAL	DAUDING	AVAILED	AXILLAS	**BANDAR**
CASTRAL	GAUDING	AVAILES	**AXISES**	BANDARI
GASTRAL	HAUDING	**AVENGE**	TAXISES	BANDARS
ASTRALS	LAUDING	AVENGED	**AXITES**	**BANDED**
ASTUTE	AUDINGS	AVENGER	TAXITES	ABANDED
ASTUTER	**AUGERS**	AVENGES	**AXLIKE**	**BANDIT**
ATOKES	GAUGERS	**AVIATE**	WAXLIKE	BANDITO
MATOKES	SAUGERS	AVIATED	**AYWORD**	BANDITS
ATONED	**AUGHTS**	AVIATES	NAYWORD	**BANGLE**
BATONED	NAUGHTS	**AVISES**	AYWORDS	BANGLED
ATRIAL	WAUGHTS	MAVISES	**AZURES**	BANGLES
PATRIAL	**AUGUST**	PAVISES	RAZURES	**BARBEL**
ATRIUM	AUGUSTE	**AVULSE**	**BABBLE**	BARBELL
NATRIUM	AUGUSTS	AVULSED	BABBLED	BARBELS
ATRIUMS	**AULDER**	AVULSES	BABBLER	**BARDIE**
ATTACH	CAULDER	**AWARDS**	BABBLES	BARDIER
ATTACHE	**AUNTER**	VAWARDS	**BABIES**	BARDIES
ATTAIN	DAUNTER	**AWHAPE**	BABIEST	**BARGES**
ATTAINS	GAUNTER	AWHAPED	**BABOOS**	BARGEST
ATTAINT	HAUNTER	AWHAPES	BABOOSH	**BARMIE**
ATTASK	SAUNTER	**AWLESS**	**BAFFLE**	BARMIER
ATTASKS	TAUNTER	JAWLESS	BAFFLED	**BARRIE**
ATTASKT	VAUNTER	LAWLESS	BAFFLER	BARRIER
ATTEST	AUNTERS	**AWNERS**	BAFFLES	BARRIES
FATTEST	**AUNTIE**	DAWNERS	**BAGASS**	**BASHED**
PATTEST	JAUNTIE	FAWNERS	BAGASSE	ABASHED
WATTEST	VAUNTIE	PAWNERS	**BAGGIE**	**BASHES**
ATTESTS	AUNTIES	YAWNERS	BAGGIER	ABASHES
ATTIRE	**AUNTLY**	**AWNIER**	BAGGIES	**BASING**
ATTIRED	GAUNTLY	FAWNIER	**BAILLI**	ABASING
ATTIRES	**AURATE**	LAWNIER	BAILLIE	**BASQUE**
ATTONE	AURATED	TAWNIER	BAILLIS	BASQUED
ATTONED	AURATES	YAWNIER	**BALDIE**	BASQUES
ATTONES	**AURORA**	**AWNING**	BALDIER	**BASSES**
ATTRAP	AURORAE	DAWNING	BALDIES	BASSEST
RATTRAP	AURORAL	FAWNING	**BALLAD**	**BASSET**
ATTRAPS	AURORAS	LAWNING	BALLADE	BASSETS
ATTRIT	**AUTEUR**	PAWNING	BALLADS	BASSETT
ATTRITE	HAUTEUR	YAWNING	**BALLAN**	**BATEAU**
ATTRITS	AUTEURS	AWNINGS	BALLANS	BATEAUX
ATTUNE	**AUTUMN**	**AXILLA**	BALLANT	**BATING**
ATTUNED	AUTUMNS	MAXILLA	**BALSAM**	ABATING
ATTUNES	AUTUMNY	AXILLAE	BALSAMS	**BATTER**

BATTERO	BEHAVES	**BENZIN**	ABETTOR	BINGLES
BATTERS	**BEHOVE**	BENZINE	BETTORS	**BIOGEN**
BATTERY	BEHOVED	BENZINS	**BEWARE**	BIOGENS
BATTLE	BEHOVES	**BENZOL**	BEWARED	BIOGENY
BATTLED	**BEIGES**	BENZOLE	BEWARES	**BIOTIC**
BATTLER	BEIGEST	BENZOLS	**BEWRAP**	ABIOTIC
BATTLES	**BEIGNE**	**BERAKE**	BEWRAPS	BIOTICS
BAYING	BEIGNES	BERAKED	BEWRAPT	**BIRDIE**
EBAYING	BEIGNET	BERAKES	BEZZLE	BIRDIED
BEAGLE	**BEJADE**	**BERATE**	BEZZLED	BIRDIES
BEAGLED	BEJADED	BERATED	BEZZLES	**BIRKIE**
BEAGLER	BEJADES	BERATES	**BHISTI**	BIRKIER
BEAGLES	**BELACE**	**BERBER**	BHISTIE	BIRKIES
BEAVER	BELACED	BERBERE	BHISTIS	**BIRSLE**
BEAVERS	BELACES	BERBERS	**BIBBER**	BIRSLED
BEAVERY	**BELATE**	**BERIME**	BIBBERS	BIRSLES
BEDAZE	BELATED	BERIMED	BIBBERY	**BISTRE**
BEDAZED	BELATES	BERIMES	**BICORN**	BISTRED
BEDAZES	**BELDAM**	**BERLIN**	BICORNE	BISTRES
BEDLAM	BELDAME	BERLINE	BICORNS	**BITTER**
BEDLAMP	BELDAMS	BERLINS	**BIDDEN**	BITTERN
BEDLAMS	**BELEAP**	**BERTHE**	ABIDDEN	BITTERS
BEDROP	BELEAPS	BERTHED	**BIDERS**	**BITTIE**
BEDROPS	BELEAPT	BERTHES	ABIDERS	BITTIER
BEDROPT	**BELOVE**	**BESPAT**	**BIDING**	BITTIES
BEETLE	BELOVED	BESPATE	ABIDING	**BLAGUE**
BEETLED	BELOVES	**BETAKE**	BIDINGS	BLAGUER
BEETLER	**BEMEAN**	BETAKEN	**BIFFIN**	BLAGUES
BEETLES	BEMEANS	BETAKES	BIFFING	**BLASTS**
BEGAZE	BEMEANT	**BETEEM**	BIFFINS	OBLASTS
BEGAZED	**BEMETE**	BETEEME	**BIGGIN**	**BLATED**
BEGAZES	BEMETED	BETEEMS	BIGGING	ABLATED
BEGGAR	BEMETES	**BETIDE**	BIGGINS	**BLATES**
BEGGARS	**BEMIRE**	BETIDED	**BILLOW**	ABLATES
BEGGARY	BEMIRED	BETIDES	BILLOWS	OBLATES
BEGRIM	BEMIRES	**BETIME**	BILLOWY	BLATEST
BEGRIME	**BEMUSE**	BETIMED	**BILLYO**	**BLENDE**
BEGRIMS	BEMUSED	BETIMES	BILLYOH	BLENDED
BEGUIN	BEMUSES	**BETTED**	BILLYOS	BLENDER
BEGUINE	**BENAME**	ABETTED	**BINDER**	BLENDES
BEGUINS	BENAMED	**BETTER**	BINDERS	**BLIGHT**
BEHAVE	BENAMES	ABETTER	BINDERY	BLIGHTS
BEHAVED	**BENTOS**	BETTERS	**BINGLE**	BLIGHTY
BEHAVER	OBENTOS	**BETTOR**	BINGLED	**BLINGS**

ABLINGS	BODGIER	BORSCHT	**BRANCH**	BROCHED
BLINTZ	BODGIES	**BOSQUE**	BRANCHY	BROCHES
BLINTZE	**BODING**	BOSQUES	**BRAVER**	**BROKER**
BLITHE	ABODING	BOSQUET	BRAVERS	BROKERS
BLITHER	BODINGS	**BOSSES**	BRAVERY	BROKERY
BLONDE	**BOFFIN**	BOSSEST	**BRAVES**	**BROMID**
BLONDER	BOFFING	**BOTONE**	BRAVEST	BROMIDE
BLONDES	BOFFINS	BOTONEE	**BRAYED**	BROMIDS
BLOTCH	BOFFINY	**BOTTLE**	ABRAYED	**BROMIN**
BLOTCHY	**BOGGLE**	BOTTLED	**BREAST**	BROMINE
BLOUSE	BOGGLED	BOTTLER	ABREAST	BROMINS
BLOUSED	BOGGLER	BOTTLES	BREASTS	**BRONZE**
BLOUSES	BOGGLES	**BOUCHE**	**BREATH**	BRONZED
BLOWIE	**BOILER**	BOUCHEE	BREATHE	BRONZEN
BLOWIER	BOILERS	BOUCHES	BREATHS	BRONZER
BLOWIES	BOILERY	**BOUCLE**	BREATHY	BRONZES
BLOWSE	**BONIST**	BOUCLEE	**BREEZE**	**BROUGH**
BLOWSED	EBONIST	BOUCLES	BREEZED	BROUGHS
BLOWSES	BONISTS	**BOUGHT**	BREEZES	BROUGHT
BLOWZE	**BONNIE**	ABOUGHT	**BREVET**	**BROWSE**
BLOWZED	BONNIER	BOUGHTS	BREVETE	BROWSED
BLOWZES	BONNIES	**BOUNCE**	BREVETS	BROWSER
BLUDGE	**BOOBOO**	BOUNCED	**BREWER**	BROWSES
BLUDGED	BOOBOOK	BOUNCER	BREWERS	**BRUCIN**
BLUDGER	BOOBOOS	BOUNCES	BREWERY	BRUCINE
BLUDGES	**BOODIE**	**BOUNDS**	**BRIBER**	BRUCINS
BLUDIE	BOODIED	ABOUNDS	BRIBERS	**BRUISE**
BLUDIER	BOODIES	**BOVATE**	BRIBERY	BRUISED
BLUNGE	**BOODLE**	OBOVATE	**BRIDGE**	BRUISER
BLUNGED	BOODLED	BOVATES	ABRIDGE	BRUISES
BLUNGER	BOODLER	**BRACER**	BRIDGED	**BRUTES**
BLUNGES	BOODLES	BRACERO	BRIDGES	BRUTEST
BOBBER	**BOOGIE**	BRACERS	**BRIDLE**	**BUBBLE**
BOBBERS	BOOGIED	**BRAHMA**	BRIDLED	ABUBBLE
BOBBERY	BOOGIES	BRAHMAN	BRIDLER	BUBBLED
BOBBIN	**BOOKIE**	BRAHMAS	BRIDLES	BUBBLER
BOBBING	BOOKIER	**BRAIDE**	**BRIGUE**	BUBBLES
BOBBINS	BOOKIES	BRAIDED	BRIGUED	**BUCKLE**
BOBBLE	**BORATE**	BRAIDER	BRIGUES	BUCKLED
BOBBLED	BORATED	**BRAIDS**	**BROACH**	BUCKLER
BOBBLES	BORATES	ABRAIDS	ABROACH	BUCKLES
BOCKED	**BORREL**	**BRAISE**	**BROADS**	**BUCKRA**
BOCKEDY	BORRELL	BRAISED	ABROADS	BUCKRAM
BODGIE	**BORSCH**	BRAISES	**BROCHE**	BUCKRAS

BUDDLE	BURSARS	**CABBED**	CAMERAS	**CANTHI**
BUDDLED	BURSARY	SCABBED	**CAMMED**	ACANTHI
BUDDLES	**BUSHIE**	**CACKLE**	SCAMMED	CANTHIC
BUDGER	BUSHIER	CACKLED	**CAMPED**	**CANTIC**
BUDGERO	BUSHIES	CACKLER	SCAMPED	CANTICO
BUDGERS	**BUSHWA**	CACKLES	**CAMPER**	**CANTLE**
BUGGAN	BUSHWAH	**CADDIE**	SCAMPER	SCANTLE
BUGGANE	BUSHWAS	CADDIED	CAMPERS	CANTLED
BUGGANS	**BUSIES**	CADDIES	CAMPERY	CANTLES
BUGGER	BUSIEST	**CADDIS**	**CAMPLE**	CANTLET
BUGGERS	**BUSING**	CADDISH	CAMPLED	**CANULA**
BUGGERY	ABUSING	**CADEAU**	CAMPLES	CANULAE
BUGGIN	BUSINGS	CADEAUX	**CANDID**	CANULAR
BUGGING	**BUSKIN**	**CAGOUL**	CANDIDA	CANULAS
BUGGINS	BUSKING	CAGOULE	CANDIDS	**CAPING**
BUMBLE	BUSKINS	CAGOULS	**CANDIE**	SCAPING
BUMBLED	**BUSTLE**	**CAJOLE**	CANDIED	**CAPITA**
BUMBLER	BUSTLED	CAJOLED	CANDIES	CAPITAL
BUMBLES	BUSTLER	CAJOLER	**CANDLE**	CAPITAN
BUMMLE	BUSTLES	CAJOLES	CANDLED	**CAPRIC**
BUMMLED	**BUTLER**	**CALKIN**	CANDLER	CAPRICE
BUMMLES	BUTLERS	CALKING	CANDLES	**CARDIA**
BUNDLE	BUTLERY	CALKINS	**CANGLE**	CARDIAC
BUNDLED	**BUTTED**	**CALLAN**	CANGLED	CARDIAE
BUNDLER	ABUTTED	CALLANS	CANGLES	CARDIAS
BUNDLES	**BUTTER**	CALLANT	**CANKER**	**CARERS**
BUNGLE	ABUTTER	**CALLED**	CANKERS	SCARERS
BUNGLED	BUTTERS	SCALLED	CANKERY	**CARINA**
BUNGLER	BUTTERY	**CALLOP**	**CANNED**	OCARINA
BUNGLES	**BUTTLE**	SCALLOP	SCANNED	CARINAE
BURBLE	BUTTLED	CALLOPS	**CANNER**	CARINAL
BURBLED	BUTTLES	**CALPAC**	SCANNER	CARINAS
BURBLER	**BUTTON**	CALPACK	CANNERS	**CARING**
BURBLES	BUTTONS	CALPACS	CANNERY	SCARING
BUREAU	BUTTONY	**CALQUE**	**CANNIE**	CARINGS
BUREAUS	**BUZUKI**	CALQUED	CANNIER	**CARLIN**
BUREAUX	BUZUKIA	CALQUES	**CANTAL**	CARLINE
BURGLE	BUZUKIS	**CAMBIA**	CANTALA	CARLING
BURGLED	**BYLINE**	CAMBIAL	CANTALS	CARLINS
BURGLES	BYLINED	**CAMELS**	**CANTED**	**CARNIE**
BURREL	BYLINER	SCAMELS	SCANTED	CARNIED
BURRELL	BYLINES	**CAMERA**	**CANTER**	CARNIER
BURRELS	**BYSSAL**	CAMERAE	SCANTER	CARNIES
BURSAR	ABYSSAL	CAMERAL	CANTERS	**CAROCH**

CAROCHE	**CATERS**	**CESTOI**	CHAUFED	CHIRREN
CARPAL	ACATERS	CESTOID	CHAUFER	CHIRRES
CARPALE	**CATLIN**	**CESURA**	CHAUFES	**CHOANA**
CARPALS	CATLING	CESURAE	**CHEESE**	CHOANAE
CARPED	CATLINS	CESURAL	CHEESED	**CHOICE**
SCARPED	**CATTED**	CESURAS	CHEESES	CHOICER
CARPER	SCATTED	**CETYLS**	**CHEQUE**	CHOICES
SCARPER	**CATTIE**	ACETYLS	CHEQUER	**CHOLER**
CARPERS	CATTIER	**CHAETA**	CHEQUES	CHOLERA
CARREL	CATTIES	CHAETAE	**CHEVRE**	CHOLERS
CARRELL	**CAUDAL**	CHAETAL	CHEVRES	**CHOOSE**
CARRELS	ACAUDAL	**CHAINE**	CHEVRET	CHOOSER
CARROT	**CAUDLE**	CHAINED	**CHEWIE**	CHOOSES
CARROTS	CAUDLED	CHAINER	CHEWIER	CHOOSEY
CARROTY	CAUDLES	CHAINES	CHEWIES	**CHOPIN**
CARTED	**CAUTER**	**CHALLA**	**CHIASM**	CHOPINE
SCARTED	CAUTERS	CHALLAH	CHIASMA	CHOPINS
CARTES	CAUTERY	CHALLAN	CHIASMI	**CHORAL**
ECARTES	**CAVIAR**	CHALLAS	CHIASMS	CHORALE
CARVED	CAVIARE	**CHALOT**	**CHICKS**	CHORALS
SCARVED	CAVIARS	CHALOTH	TCHICKS	**CHORDA**
CARVER	**CELLAR**	**CHANCE**	**CHILDE**	CHORDAE
CARVERS	OCELLAR	CHANCED	CHILDED	CHORDAL
CARVERY	CELLARS	CHANCEL	CHILDER	**CHOREA**
CARVES	**CELLOS**	CHANCER	CHILDES	CHOREAL
SCARVES	CELLOSE	CHANCES	**CHIMER**	CHOREAS
CASERN	**CEMENT**	CHANCEY	CHIMERA	**CHORIA**
CASERNE	CEMENTA	**CHANGE**	CHIMERE	CHORIAL
CASERNS	CEMENTS	CHANGED	CHIMERS	**CHOUSE**
CASQUE	**CENTRA**	CHANGER	**CHINCH**	CHOUSED
CASQUED	CENTRAL	CHANGES	CHINCHY	CHOUSER
CASQUES	**CENTRE**	**CHARDS**	**CHINES**	CHOUSES
CASTLE	CENTRED	ECHARDS	CHINESE	**CHOUTS**
CASTLED	CENTRES	**CHARGE**	**CHINGS**	SCHOUTS
CASTLES	**CERATE**	CHARGED	ACHINGS	**CHOWSE**
CASTOR	ACERATE	CHARGER	**CHINSE**	CHOWSED
CASTORS	CERATED	CHARGES	CHINSED	CHOWSES
CASTORY	CERATES	**CHASSE**	CHINSES	**CHRISM**
CATALO	**CERNED**	CHASSED	**CHINTZ**	CHRISMA
CATALOG	SCERNED	CHASSES	CHINTZY	CHRISMS
CATALOS	**CERNES**	**CHASTE**	**CHIRAL**	**CHROME**
CATENA	SCERNES	CHASTEN	ACHIRAL	CHROMED
CATENAE	**CEROUS**	CHASTER	**CHIRRE**	CHROMEL
CATENAS	ACEROUS	**CHAUFE**	CHIRRED	CHROMES

CHROMY	**CLEANS**	**COCAIN**	COHERES	COMPAST
CHROMYL	CLEANSE	COCAINE	**COIFFE**	**COMPER**
CHUKKA	**CLEAVE**	COCAINS	COIFFED	COMPERE
CHUKKAR	CLEAVED	**COCKLE**	COIFFES	COMPERS
CHUKKAS	CLEAVER	COCKLED	**COIGNE**	**COMPOS**
CHUPPA	CLEAVES	COCKLER	COIGNED	COMPOSE
CHUPPAH	**CLEPED**	COCKLES	COIGNES	COMPOST
CHUPPAS	YCLEPED	**CODDLE**	**COLDER**	**COMPOT**
CHURCH	**CLICHE**	CODDLED	SCOLDER	COMPOTE
CHURCHY	CLICHED	CODDLER	**COLLAR**	COMPOTS
CICADA	CLICHES	CODDLES	COLLARD	**CONCHA**
CICADAE	**CLIFFS**	**CODEIN**	COLLARS	CONCHAE
CICADAS	SCLIFFS	CODEINA	**COLLIE**	CONCHAL
CINDER	**CLINIC**	CODEINE	COLLIED	CONCHAS
CINDERS	ACLINIC	CODEINS	COLLIER	**CONCHE**
CINDERY	CLINICS	**CODLIN**	COLLIES	CONCHED
CINEOL	**CLIQUE**	CODLING	**COLLOP**	CONCHES
CINEOLE	CLIQUED	CODLINS	SCOLLOP	**CONGEE**
CINEOLS	CLIQUES	**COELOM**	COLLOPS	CONGEED
CIRCLE	CLIQUEY	COELOME	**COLOBI**	CONGEES
CIRCLED	**CLOACA**	COELOMS	COLOBID	**CONGES**
CIRCLER	CLOACAE	**COERCE**	**COLONE**	CONGEST
CIRCLES	CLOACAL	COERCED	COLONEL	**CONJEE**
CIRCLET	CLOACAS	COERCER	COLONES	CONJEED
CIRCUS	**CLOSED**	COERCES	**COLONI**	CONJEES
CIRCUSY	ECLOSED	**COFFED**	COLONIC	**CONSOL**
CITHER	**CLOSES**	SCOFFED	**COLOUR**	CONSOLE
CITHERN	ECLOSES	**COFFER**	COLOURS	CONSOLS
CITHERS	CLOSEST	SCOFFER	COLOURY	**CONSUL**
CITRIN	**CLOTHE**	COFFERS	**COMAKE**	CONSULS
CITRINE	CLOTHED	**COFFIN**	COMAKER	CONSULT
CITRINS	CLOTHES	COFFING	COMAKES	**CONTES**
CITRUS	**CLOVER**	COFFINS	**COMMER**	CONTEST
CITRUSY	CLOVERS	**COFFLE**	COMMERE	**CONTRA**
CLAMBE	CLOVERY	COFFLED	COMMERS	CONTRAS
CLAMBER	**CLUTCH**	COFFLES	**COMMIS**	CONTRAT
CLAQUE	CLUTCHY	**COGGED**	COMMISH	**COOKER**
CLAQUER	**COARSE**	SCOGGED	**COMMIX**	COOKERS
CLAQUES	COARSEN	**COGGLE**	COMMIXT	COOKERY
CLAVES	COARSER	COGGLED	**COMMOT**	**COOPED**
SCLAVES	**COBBLE**	COGGLES	COMMOTE	SCOOPED
CLAVIE	COBBLED	**COHERE**	COMMOTS	**COOPER**
CLAVIER	COBBLER	COHERED	**COMPAS**	SCOOPER
CLAVIES	COBBLES	COHERER	COMPASS	COOPERS

COOPERY	CORONAL	SCOUPED	**CRANIA**	**CRIMPS**
COORIE	CORONAS	**COUPLE**	CRANIAL	SCRIMPS
COORIED	**CORPSE**	COUPLED	**CRANNY**	**CRIMPY**
COORIES	CORPSED	COUPLER	SCRANNY	SCRIMPY
COOTCH	CORPSES	COUPLES	**CRAPED**	**CRINES**
SCOOTCH	**CORSES**	COUPLET	SCRAPED	SCRINES
COOTER	SCORSES	**COURED**	**CRAPES**	**CRINGE**
SCOOTER	**CORTIN**	SCOURED	SCRAPES	CRINGED
COOTERS	CORTINA	**COURIE**	**CRAPPY**	CRINGER
COPING	CORTINS	SCOURIE	SCRAPPY	CRINGES
SCOPING	**CORYZA**	COURIED	**CRATCH**	**CRISSA**
COPINGS	CORYZAL	COURIER	SCRATCH	CRISSAL
COPPER	CORYZAS	COURIES	**CRAVAT**	**CRISTA**
COPPERS	**COSHER**	**COURSE**	CRAVATE	CRISTAE
COPPERY	COSHERS	SCOURSE	CRAVATS	**CROCHE**
COPPIN	COSHERY	COURSED	**CRAWLS**	CROCHES
COPPING	**COSIES**	COURSER	SCRAWLS	CROCHET
COPPINS	COSIEST	COURSES	**CRAWLY**	**CROGGY**
COPULA	**COSMIN**	**COUTER**	SCRAWLY	SCROGGY
SCOPULA	COSMINE	SCOUTER	**CREAKS**	**CROMED**
COPULAE	COSMINS	COUTERS	SCREAKS	SCROMED
COPULAR	**COSTAR**	**COUTHS**	**CREAKY**	**CROMES**
COPULAS	COSTARD	SCOUTHS	SCREAKY	SCROMES
CORERS	COSTARS	**COWING**	**CREAMS**	**CROSSE**
SCORERS	**COTEAU**	SCOWING	SCREAMS	CROSSED
CORING	COTEAUS	**COWLED**	**CREASE**	CROSSER
SCORING	COTEAUX	SCOWLED	CREASED	CROSSES
CORNEA	**COTING**	**COWPED**	CREASER	**CROTAL**
CORNEAE	COTINGA	SCOWPED	CREASES	SCROTAL
CORNEAL	**COTISE**	**COWRIE**	**CREATE**	CROTALA
CORNEAS	COTISED	SCOWRIE	OCREATE	CROTALE
CORNED	COTISES	COWRIES	CREATED	CROTALS
ACORNED	**COTTON**	**COZIES**	CREATES	**CROUPE**
SCORNED	COTTONS	COZIEST	**CREEDS**	CROUPED
CORNER	COTTONY	**CRADLE**	SCREEDS	CROUPER
SCORNER	**COTYPE**	CRADLED	**CREESE**	CROUPES
CORNERS	ECOTYPE	CRADLER	CREESED	**CRUDES**
CORNET	COTYPES	CRADLES	CREESES	CRUDEST
CORNETS	**COUCHE**	**CRAGGY**	**CREESH**	**CRUISE**
CORNETT	COUCHED	SCRAGGY	CREESHY	CRUISED
CORNUA	COUCHEE	**CRAMES**	**CRESTA**	CRUISER
CORNUAL	COUCHER	CRAMESY	CRESTAL	CRUISES
CORONA	COUCHES	**CRANCH**	**CREWED**	CRUISEY
CORONAE	**COUPED**	SCRANCH	SCREWED	**CRUMMY**

SCRUMMY	CULLERS	SCURRED	CYMBALO	**DAPPLE**
CRUMPS	**CULTCH**	**CURRIE**	CYMBALS	DAPPLED
SCRUMPS	SCULTCH	CURRIED	**CYMLIN**	DAPPLES
CRUMPY	**CULVER**	CURRIER	CYMLING	**DARKLE**
SCRUMPY	CULVERS	CURRIES	CYMLINS	DARKLED
CRUNCH	CULVERT	**CURSOR**	**DABBLE**	DARKLES
SCRUNCH	**CUMBER**	CURSORS	DABBLED	**DARTLE**
CRUNCHY	SCUMBER	CURSORY	DABBLER	DARTLED
CRUSTA	CUMBERS	**CUSHIE**	DABBLES	DARTLES
CRUSTAE	**CUMMED**	CUSHIER	**DACOIT**	**DAUBER**
CRUSTAL	SCUMMED	CUSHIES	DACOITS	DAUBERS
CRUSTAS	**CUMMER**	**CUTELY**	DACOITY	DAUBERY
CRYERS	SCUMMER	ACUTELY	**DACTYL**	**DAWDLE**
SCRYERS	CUMMERS	**CUTEST**	DACTYLI	DAWDLED
CRYING	**CUMMIN**	ACUTEST	DACTYLS	DAWDLER
SCRYING	CUMMING	**CUTLER**	**DADDLE**	DAWDLES
CRYINGS	CUMMINS	CUTLERS	DADDLED	**DAWING**
CRYPTO	**CUNNER**	CUTLERY	DADDLES	ADAWING
CRYPTON	SCUNNER	**CUTTER**	**DAGGLE**	**DAYGLO**
CRYPTOS	CUNNERS	SCUTTER	DAGGLED	DAYGLOW
CUBICA	**CUPOLA**	CUTTERS	DAGGLES	**DAZZLE**
CUBICAL	CUPOLAR	**CUTTLE**	**DAIDLE**	DAZZLED
CUBICAS	CUPOLAS	SCUTTLE	DAIDLED	DAZZLER
CUDDLE	**CUPPER**	CUTTLED	DAIDLES	DAZZLES
SCUDDLE	SCUPPER	CUTTLES	**DAINED**	**DEANER**
CUDDLED	CUPPERS	**CUZZES**	SDAINED	DEANERS
CUDDLER	**CUPULA**	SCUZZES	**DAINES**	DEANERY
CUDDLES	CUPULAE	**CYANID**	SDAINES	**DEARES**
CUFFED	CUPULAR	CYANIDE	**DAKOIT**	DEAREST
SCUFFED	**CURATE**	CYANIDS	DAKOITI	**DEBASE**
CUFFIN	CURATED	**CYANIN**	DAKOITS	DEBASED
CUFFING	CURATES	CYANINE	DAKOITY	DEBASER
CUFFINS	**CURDLE**	CYANINS	**DAMAGE**	DEBASES
CUFFLE	CURDLED	**CYATHI**	DAMAGED	**DEBATE**
SCUFFLE	CURDLER	CYATHIA	DAMAGER	DEBATED
CUFFLED	CURDLES	**CYCLER**	DAMAGES	DEBATER
CUFFLES	**CURIES**	CYCLERS	**DANDLE**	DEBATES
CUISSE	ECURIES	CYCLERY	DANDLED	**DEBONE**
CUISSER	**CURIOS**	**CYCLIC**	DANDLER	DEBONED
CUISSES	CURIOSA	ACYCLIC	DANDLES	DEBONER
CULLED	**CURRAN**	**CYCLIN**	**DANGLE**	DEBONES
SCULLED	CURRANS	CYCLING	DANGLED	**DECIDE**
CULLER	CURRANT	CYCLINS	DANGLER	DECIDED
SCULLER	**CURRED**	**CYMBAL**	DANGLES	DECIDER

DECIDES	DEFUZED	DEMOTED	DERIVER	**DIAZIN**
DECKLE	DEFUZES	DEMOTES	DERIVES	DIAZINE
DECKLED	**DEGREE**	**DEMURE**	**DESINE**	DIAZINS
DECKLES	DEGREED	DEMURED	DESINED	**DIBBLE**
DECODE	DEGREES	DEMURER	DESINES	DIBBLED
DECODED	**DEIGNS**	DEMURES	**DESIRE**	DIBBLER
DECODER	SDEIGNS	**DENARI**	DESIRED	DIBBLES
DECODES	**DEJECT**	DENARII	DESIRER	**DICKIE**
DECOKE	DEJECTA	**DENOTE**	DESIRES	DICKIER
DECOKED	DEJECTS	DENOTED	**DESYNE**	DICKIES
DECOKES	**DELATE**	DENOTES	DESYNED	**DIDDLE**
DECREE	DELATED	**DENTAL**	DESYNES	DIDDLED
DECREED	DELATES	EDENTAL	**DETENT**	DIDDLER
DECREER	**DELETE**	DENTALS	DETENTE	DIDDLES
DECREES	DELETED	**DENTIN**	DETENTS	DIDDLEY
DECREET	DELETES	DENTINE	**DETENU**	**DILATE**
DEDUCE	**DELIME**	DENTING	DETENUE	DILATED
DEDUCED	DELIMED	DENTINS	DETENUS	DILATER
DEDUCES	DELIMES	**DENUDE**	**DETUNE**	DILATES
DEEMED	**DELOPE**	DENUDED	DETUNED	**DILUTE**
ADEEMED	DELOPED	DENUDER	DETUNES	DILUTED
DEFACE	DELOPES	DENUDES	**DEVISE**	DILUTEE
DEFACED	**DELUDE**	**DEODAR**	DEVISED	DILUTER
DEFACER	DELUDED	DEODARA	DEVISEE	DILUTES
DEFACES	DELUDER	DEODARS	DEVISER	**DIMPLE**
DEFAME	DELUDES	**DEPONE**	DEVISES	DIMPLED
DEFAMED	**DELUGE**	DEPONED	**DEVOTE**	DIMPLES
DEFAMER	DELUGED	DEPONES	DEVOTED	**DINDLE**
DEFAMES	DELUGES	**DEPOSE**	DEVOTEE	DINDLED
DEFAST	**DEMAIN**	DEPOSED	DEVOTES	DINDLES
DEFASTE	DEMAINE	DEPOSER	**DEWLAP**	**DINKIE**
DEFILE	DEMAINS	DEPOSES	DEWLAPS	DINKIER
DEFILED	**DEMEAN**	**DEPUTE**	DEWLAPT	DINKIES
DEFILER	DEMEANE	DEPUTED	**DHARMA**	**DINNLE**
DEFILES	DEMEANS	DEPUTES	ADHARMA	DINNLED
DEFINE	**DEMENT**	**DERATE**	DHARMAS	DINNLES
DEFINED	DEMENTI	DERATED	**DHOOTI**	**DIOXAN**
DEFINER	DEMENTS	DERATES	DHOOTIE	DIOXANE
DEFINES	**DEMISE**	**DERIDE**	DHOOTIS	DIOXANS
DEFUSE	DEMISED	DERIDED	**DIAMIN**	**DIOXID**
DEFUSED	DEMISES	DERIDER	DIAMINE	DIOXIDE
DEFUSER	**DEMODE**	DERIDES	DIAMINS	DIOXIDS
DEFUSES	DEMODED	**DERIVE**	**DIARCH**	**DIPLON**
DEFUZE	**DEMOTE**	DERIVED	DIARCHY	DIPLONS

DIPLONT	DODGERS	DOUCHED	DUBBING	**EANING**
DISBAR	DODGERY	DOUCHES	DUBBINS	BEANING
DISBARK	**DOGGER**	**DOUGHT**	**DUCKIE**	DEANING
DISBARS	DOGGERS	DOUGHTY	DUCKIER	LEANING
DISMAY	DOGGERY	**DOWLNE**	DUCKIES	MEANING
DISMAYD	**DOGGIE**	DOWLNES	**DUDDER**	PEANING
DISMAYL	DOGGIER	DOWLNEY	DUDDERS	SEANING
DISMAYS	DOGGIES	**DRACHM**	DUDDERY	WEANING
DISPLE	**DOLENT**	DRACHMA	**DUDDIE**	YEANING
DISPLED	DOLENTE	DRACHMS	DUDDIER	**EARDED**
DISPLES	**DOMAIN**	**DRAPER**	DUDDIES	BEARDED
DISTIL	DOMAINE	DRAPERS	**DUMPLE**	YEARDED
DISTILL	DOMAINS	DRAPERY	DUMPLED	**EARFUL**
DISTILS	**DOMINE**	**DREADS**	DUMPLES	FEARFUL
DISUSE	DOMINEE	ADREADS	**DURESS**	TEARFUL
DISUSED	DOMINES	**DREARE**	DURESSE	EARFULS
DISUSES	**DONATE**	DREARER	**DUSTED**	**EARING**
DITHER	ODONATE	DREARES	ADUSTED	BEARING
DITHERS	DONATED	**DREDGE**	**DYNAST**	DEARING
DITHERY	DONATES	DREDGED	DYNASTS	FEARING
DITING	**DONSIE**	DREDGER	DYNASTY	GEARING
EDITING	DONSIER	DREDGES	**DYVOUR**	HEARING
DIVERS	**DOODLE**	**DROGUE**	DYVOURS	LEARING
DIVERSE	DOODLED	DROGUES	DYVOURY	MEARING
DIVIDE	DOODLER	DROGUET	**EAGLED**	NEARING
DIVIDED	DOODLES	**DROICH**	BEAGLED	REARING
DIVIDER	**DORISE**	DROICHS	TEAGLED	SEARING
DIVIDES	ODORISE	DROICHY	**EAGLES**	TEARING
DIVINE	DORISED	**DROLES**	BEAGLES	WEARING
DIVINED	DORISES	DROLEST	TEAGLES	EARINGS
DIVINER	**DORIZE**	**DROMON**	**EAGRES**	**EARNED**
DIVINES	ODORIZE	DROMOND	MEAGRES	DEARNED
DJIBBA	DORIZED	DROMONS	**EALING**	LEARNED
DJIBBAH	DORIZES	**DROUTH**	BEALING	YEARNED
DJIBBAS	**DOTTLE**	DROUTHS	DEALING	**EARNER**
DOBBIN	DOTTLED	DROUTHY	FEALING	LEARNER
DOBBING	DOTTLER	**DROWSE**	GEALING	YEARNER
DOBBINS	DOTTLES	DROWSED	HEALING	EARNERS
DOCILE	**DOUBLE**	DROWSES	MEALING	**EARTHS**
DOCILER	DOUBLED	**DRUDGE**	NEALING	DEARTHS
DODDER	DOUBLER	DRUDGED	PEALING	HEARTHS
DODDERS	DOUBLES	DRUDGER	SEALING	**EASELS**
DODDERY	DOUBLET	DRUDGES	VEALING	TEASELS
DODGER	**DOUCHE**	**DUBBIN**	YEALING	WEASELS

EASERS	REBOOKS	**EECHED**	**EGGARS**	DELAPSE
LEASERS	**ECHING**	LEECHED	BEGGARS	RELAPSE
TEASERS	EECHING	REECHED	SEGGARS	ELAPSED
EASIES	LECHING	**EECHES**	**EGGERS**	ELAPSES
EASIEST	PECHING	BEECHES	KEGGERS	**ELATED**
EASING	**ECLOSE**	KEECHES	LEGGERS	BELATED
CEASING	RECLOSE	LEECHES	**EGGIER**	DELATED
FEASING	ECLOSED	REECHES	LEGGIER	GELATED
LEASING	ECLOSES	**EELIER**	PEGGIER	RELATED
MEASING	**EDDIES**	SEELIER	**EGGING**	VELATED
PEASING	NEDDIES	**EERIER**	BEGGING	**ELATER**
SEASING	TEDDIES	BEERIER	DEGGING	RELATER
TEASING	**EDDISH**	LEERIER	KEGGING	ELATERS
EASINGS	NEDDISH	PEERIER	LEGGING	**ELATES**
EASLES	REDDISH	**EERILY**	PEGGING	BELATES
MEASLES	**EDEMAS**	BEERILY	VEGGING	DELATES
EASTED	OEDEMAS	LEERILY	**EGISES**	GELATES
BEASTED	**EDGERS**	**EFFACE**	AEGISES	RELATES
FEASTED	HEDGERS	EFFACED	**EGRESS**	**ELDERS**
REASTED	KEDGERS	EFFACER	NEGRESS	GELDERS
YEASTED	LEDGERS	EFFACES	REGRESS	MELDERS
EASTER	**EDGIER**	**EFFERE**	**EGRETS**	WELDERS
FEASTER	HEDGIER	EFFERED	REGRETS	**ELDING**
EASTERN	KEDGIER	EFFERES	**EIGHTH**	GELDING
EASTERS	LEDGIER	**EFFING**	HEIGHTH	MELDING
EATERS	SEDGIER	JEFFING	EIGHTHS	WELDING
BEATERS	WEDGIER	REFFING	**EIGHTS**	ELDINGS
HEATERS	**EDGING**	EFFINGS	HEIGHTS	**ELECTS**
SEATERS	HEDGING	**EFFUSE**	WEIGHTS	SELECTS
EATERY	KEDGING	EFFUSED	**EIGHTY**	**ELENCH**
PEATERY	WEDGING	EFFUSES	WEIGHTY	ELENCHI
EATHLY	EDGINGS	**EFTEST**	**EITHER**	ELENCHS
DEATHLY	**EDILES**	DEFTEST	NEITHER	**ELFING**
EATING	AEDILES	LEFTEST	**EJECTA**	SELFING
BEATING	**EDUCED**	**EGALLY**	DEJECTA	**ELFISH**
FEATING	DEDUCED	LEGALLY	**EJECTS**	SELFISH
HEATING	REDUCED	REGALLY	DEJECTS	**ELITES**
SEATING	SEDUCED	**EGENCE**	REJECTS	PELITES
EATINGS	**EDUCES**	REGENCE	**ELANCE**	VELITES
EBBING	DEDUCES	EGENCES	ELANCED	**ELOPED**
KEBBING	REDUCES	**EGENCY**	ELANCES	DELOPED
NEBBING	SEDUCES	REGENCY	**ELANDS**	**ELOPES**
WEBBING	**EDUCTS**	**EGESTS**	RELANDS	DELOPES
EBOOKS	DEDUCTS	REGESTS	**ELAPSE**	**ELUDED**

DELUDED	NEMESES	**EMULGE**	LENDERS	ENFREED
ELUDER	**EMESIS**	EMULGED	MENDERS	ENFREES
DELUDER	NEMESIS	EMULGES	RENDERS	**ENGAGE**
ELUDERS	**EMETIC**	**EMUNGE**	SENDERS	ENGAGED
ELUDES	MEMETIC	EMUNGED	TENDERS	ENGAGEE
DELUDES	EMETICS	EMUNGES	VENDERS	ENGAGER
ELUVIA	**EMETIN**	**EMURED**	**ENDING**	ENGAGES
ELUVIAL	EMETINE	DEMURED	BENDING	**ENGINE**
ELVERS	EMETINS	**EMURES**	FENDING	ENGINED
DELVERS	**EMMERS**	DEMURES	HENDING	ENGINER
ELYTRA	HEMMERS	LEMURES	LENDING	ENGINES
ELYTRAL	YEMMERS	**ENABLE**	MENDING	**ENGORE**
EMAILS	**EMMOVE**	TENABLE	PENDING	ENGORED
REMAILS	EMMOVED	ENABLED	RENDING	ENGORES
EMBALE	EMMOVES	ENABLER	SENDING	**ENISLE**
EMBALED	**EMOTED**	ENABLES	TENDING	ENISLED
EMBALES	DEMOTED	**ENATES**	VENDING	ENISLES
EMBASE	**EMOTER**	PENATES	WENDING	**ENLACE**
EMBASED	REMOTER	SENATES	ENDINGS	ENLACED
EMBASES	EMOTERS	**ENATIC**	**ENDITE**	ENLACES
EMBERS	**EMOTES**	VENATIC	ENDITED	**ENLOCK**
MEMBERS	DEMOTES	**ENCAGE**	ENDITES	GENLOCK
EMBLEM	GEMOTES	ENCAGED	**ENDUES**	ENLOCKS
EMBLEMA	REMOTES	ENCAGES	VENDUES	**ENMOVE**
EMBLEMS	**EMOVED**	**ENCASE**	**ENDURE**	ENMOVED
EMBOLI	REMOVED	ENCASED	ENDURED	ENMOVES
EMBOLIC	**EMOVES**	ENCASES	ENDURER	**ENNUYE**
EMBRUE	REMOVES	**ENCAVE**	ENDURES	ENNUYED
EMBRUED	**EMPALE**	ENCAVED	**ENERVE**	ENNUYEE
EMBRUES	EMPALED	ENCAVES	ENERVED	**ENOSES**
EMBRYO	EMPALER	**ENCINA**	ENERVES	KENOSES
EMBRYON	EMPALES	ENCINAL	**ENEWED**	**ENOSIS**
EMBRYOS	**EMPARE**	ENCINAS	RENEWED	KENOSIS
EMENDS	EMPARED	**ENCODE**	**ENFACE**	**ENRACE**
REMENDS	EMPARES	ENCODED	ENFACED	ENRACED
EMERGE	**EMPLOY**	ENCODER	ENFACES	ENRACES
DEMERGE	EMPLOYE	ENCODES	**ENFIRE**	**ENRAGE**
REMERGE	EMPLOYS	**ENCORE**	ENFIRED	ENRAGED
EMERGED	**EMPTED**	ENCORED	ENFIRES	ENRAGES
EMERGES	TEMPTED	ENCORES	**ENFOLD**	**ENROBE**
EMERSE	**EMULED**	**ENDERS**	PENFOLD	ENROBED
DEMERSE	AEMULED	BENDERS	TENFOLD	ENROBER
EMERSED	**EMULES**	FENDERS	ENFOLDS	ENROBES
EMESES	AEMULES	GENDERS	**ENFREE**	**ENSATE**

SENSATE	LENVOYS	REPRISE	ESCROLS	ETCHERS
ENSILE	RENVOYS	**EPUISE**	**ESILES**	**ETCHES**
PENSILE	**ENZONE**	EPUISEE	RESILES	FETCHES
SENSILE	ENZONED	**EQUATE**	**ESTATE**	KETCHES
TENSILE	ENZONES	EQUATED	GESTATE	LETCHES
ENSILED	**EOLIAN**	EQUATES	RESTATE	RETCHES
ENSILES	AEOLIAN	**ERBIAS**	TESTATE	VETCHES
ENSURE	**EOLITH**	TERBIAS	ESTATED	**ETHALS**
CENSURE	NEOLITH	**ERBIUM**	ESTATES	LETHALS
ENSURED	EOLITHS	TERBIUM	**ESTERS**	**ETHANE**
ENSURER	**EONIAN**	ERBIUMS	FESTERS	METHANE
ENSURES	AEONIAN	**ERMINE**	JESTERS	ETHANES
ENTAIL	**EONISM**	ERMINED	MESTERS	**ETHERS**
VENTAIL	PEONISM	ERMINES	NESTERS	AETHERS
ENTAILS	EONISMS	**ERNING**	PESTERS	PETHERS
ENTAME	**EPARCH**	CERNING	RESTERS	TETHERS
ENTAMED	EPARCHS	DERNING	TESTERS	WETHERS
ENTAMES	EPARCHY	FERNING	WESTERS	**ETHOXY**
ENTERA	**EPAULE**	GERNING	ZESTERS	METHOXY
ENTERAL	EPAULES	KERNING	**ESTRAL**	ETHOXYL
ENTERS	EPAULET	PERNING	OESTRAL	**ETHYLS**
CENTERS	**EPERDU**	TERNING	VESTRAL	METHYLS
RENTERS	EPERDUE	**EROSES**	**ESTRIN**	**ETTLED**
TENTERS	**EPHEBI**	XEROSES	OESTRIN	FETTLED
VENTERS	EPHEBIC	**EROTIC**	ESTRINS	KETTLED
ENTETE	**EPIGON**	CEROTIC	**ESTRUM**	METTLED
ENTETEE	EPIGONE	XEROTIC	OESTRUM	NETTLED
ENTICE	EPIGONI	EROTICA	ESTRUMS	PETTLED
PENTICE	EPIGONS	EROTICS	**ESTRUS**	SETTLED
ENTICED	**EPIMER**	**ERRING**	OESTRUS	**ETTLES**
ENTICER	EPIMERE	HERRING	**ETAGES**	FETTLES
ENTICES	EPIMERS	SERRING	METAGES	KETTLES
ENURED	**EPIZOA**	ERRINGS	**ETAMIN**	METTLES
TENURED	EPIZOAN	**ERRORS**	ETAMINE	NETTLES
ENURES	**EPOCHA**	TERRORS	ETAMINS	PETTLES
TENURES	EPOCHAL	**ERUGOS**	**ETAPES**	SETTLES
ENVIES	EPOCHAS	AERUGOS	RETAPES	**EUCAIN**
SENVIES	**EPONYM**	**ESCAPE**	**ETCHED**	EUCAINE
ENVIRO	EPONYMS	ESCAPED	FETCHED	EUCAINS
ENVIRON	EPONYMY	ESCAPEE	LETCHED	**EUCHRE**
ENVIROS	**EPOSES**	ESCAPER	RETCHED	EUCHRED
ENVOIS	DEPOSES	ESCAPES	TETCHED	EUCHRES
RENVOIS	REPOSES	**ESCROL**	**ETCHER**	**EUGHEN**
ENVOYS	**EPRISE**	ESCROLL	FETCHER	LEUGHEN

EUKING	EXCISES	**EXUVIA**	FASCIAS	FETTLER
YEUKING	**EXCITE**	EXUVIAE	**FASCIS**	FETTLES
EUPHON	EXCITED	EXUVIAL	FASCISM	**FEUTRE**
EUPHONS	EXCITER	**FACETE**	FASCIST	FEUTRED
EUPHONY	EXCITES	FACETED	**FAVELL**	FEUTRES
EUREKA	**EXCUSE**	**FACTOR**	FAVELLA	**FIANCE**
HEUREKA	EXCUSED	FACTORS	**FEAGUE**	FIANCEE
EUREKAS	EXCUSER	FACTORY	FEAGUED	FIANCES
EVERTS	EXCUSES	**FACULA**	FEAGUES	**FIBBER**
REVERTS	**EXEDRA**	FACULAE	**FEARED**	FIBBERS
EVILER	EXEDRAE	FACULAR	AFEARED	FIBBERY
REVILER	EXEDRAS	**FADDLE**	**FECKIN**	**FIBROS**
EVINCE	**EXEMES**	FADDLED	FECKING	FIBROSE
EVINCED	LEXEMES	FADDLES	**FECULA**	**FIBULA**
EVINCES	**EXHALE**	**FAGGOT**	FECULAE	FIBULAE
EVITES	EXHALED	FAGGOTS	FECULAS	FIBULAR
LEVITES	EXHALES	FAGGOTY	**FEEBLE**	FIBULAS
EVOKED	**EXHUME**	**FAINES**	FEEBLED	**FICKLE**
REVOKED	EXHUMED	FAINEST	FEEBLER	FICKLED
EVOKER	EXHUMER	**FAKIES**	FEEBLES	FICKLER
REVOKER	EXHUMES	FAKIEST	**FEERIN**	FICKLES
EVOKERS	**EXINES**	**FALSES**	FEERING	**FIDDLE**
EVOKES	REXINES	FALSEST	FEERINS	FIDDLED
REVOKES	**EXISTS**	**FANGLE**	**FEIRIE**	FIDDLER
EVOLVE	SEXISTS	FANGLED	FEIRIER	FIDDLES
DEVOLVE	**EXOTIC**	FANGLES	**FEMORA**	FIDDLEY
REVOLVE	EXOTICA	**FANKLE**	FEMORAL	**FIDGET**
EVOLVED	EXOTICS	FANKLED	**FERLIE**	FIDGETS
EVOLVER	**EXPERT**	FANKLES	FERLIED	FIDGETY
EVOLVES	SEXPERT	**FANNEL**	FERLIER	**FIERCE**
EVULSE	EXPERTS	FANNELL	FERLIES	FIERCER
EVULSED	**EXPIRE**	FANNELS	**FERRET**	**FIGURE**
EVULSES	EXPIRED	**FARCIE**	FERRETS	FIGURED
EXACTS	EXPIRER	FARCIED	FERRETY	FIGURER
HEXACTS	EXPIRES	FARCIES	**FERULA**	FIGURES
EXARCH	**EXPOSE**	**FARCIN**	FERULAE	**FILMIS**
HEXARCH	EXPOSED	FARCING	FERULAS	FILMISH
EXARCHS	EXPOSER	FARCINS	**FERULE**	**FINNAC**
EXARCHY	EXPOSES	**FARMER**	FERULED	FINNACK
EXCIDE	**EXTANT**	FARMERS	FERULES	FINNACS
EXCIDED	SEXTANT	FARMERY	**FETICH**	**FIRKIN**
EXCIDES	**EXTERN**	**FASCIA**	FETICHE	FIRKING
EXCISE	EXTERNE	FASCIAE	**FETTLE**	FIRKINS
EXCISED	EXTERNS	FASCIAL	FETTLED	**FISHER**

FISHERS	FLENSES	**FORMAT**	FRINGES	GALANTY
FISHERY	**FLIGHT**	FORMATE	**FROWIE**	**GALLET**
FISSLE	FLIGHTS	FORMATS	FROWIER	GALLETA
FISSLED	FLIGHTY	**FORMIC**	**FROWST**	GALLETS
FISSLES	**FLOUSE**	FORMICA	FROWSTS	**GALLIC**
FITCHE	FLOUSED	**FOUGHT**	FROWSTY	GALLICA
FITCHEE	FLOUSES	FOUGHTY	**FUDDLE**	**GALOSH**
FITCHES	**FLOWER**	**FOULES**	FUDDLED	GALOSHE
FITCHET	FLOWERS	FOULEST	FUDDLER	**GAMBLE**
FITCHEW	FLOWERY	**FOUTRE**	FUDDLES	GAMBLED
FITTES	**FOLIOS**	FOUTRED	**FULFIL**	GAMBLER
FITTEST	FOLIOSE	FOUTRES	FULFILL	GAMBLES
FIXATE	**FOLKIE**	**FOXIES**	FULFILS	**GAMETE**
FIXATED	FOLKIER	FOXIEST	**FULLER**	AGAMETE
FIXATES	FOLKIES	**FRAISE**	FULLERS	GAMETES
FIZZLE	**FONDLE**	FRAISED	FULLERY	**GANGLE**
FIZZLED	FONDLED	FRAISES	**FUMBLE**	GANGLED
FIZZLES	FONDLER	**FRAPPE**	FUMBLED	GANGLES
FLAMBE	FONDLES	FRAPPED	FUMBLER	**GANOIN**
FLAMBEE	**FONDUE**	FRAPPEE	FUMBLES	GANOINE
FLAMBES	FONDUED	FRAPPES	**FURROW**	GANOINS
FLANGE	FONDUES	**FRATCH**	FURROWS	**GARAGE**
FLANGED	**FOOTIE**	FRATCHY	FURROWY	GARAGED
FLANGER	FOOTIER	**FRATER**	**FUTILE**	GARAGES
FLANGES	FOOTIES	FRATERS	FUTILER	GARAGEY
FLAUNT	**FOOTLE**	FRATERY	**FUZZLE**	**GARBLE**
FLAUNTS	FOOTLED	**FREETS**	FUZZLED	GARBLED
FLAUNTY	FOOTLER	AFREETS	FUZZLES	GARBLER
FLAVIN	FOOTLES	**FREEZE**	**GABBLE**	GARBLES
FLAVINE	**FOOZLE**	FREEZER	GABBLED	**GARGET**
FLAVINS	FOOZLED	FREEZES	GABBLER	GARGETS
FLAVOR	FOOZLER	**FRIAND**	GABBLES	GARGETY
FLAVORS	FOOZLES	FRIANDE	**GADGET**	**GARGLE**
FLAVORY	**FORAGE**	FRIANDS	GADGETS	GARGLED
FLEDGE	FORAGED	**FRIDGE**	GADGETY	GARGLER
FLEDGED	FORAGER	FRIDGED	**GAGGER**	GARGLES
FLEDGES	FORAGES	FRIDGES	GAGGERS	**GAROTE**
FLEECE	**FORBAD**	**FRIEZE**	GAGGERY	GAROTED
FLEECED	FORBADE	FRIEZED	**GAGGLE**	GAROTES
FLEECER	**FOREBY**	FRIEZES	GAGGLED	**GARROT**
FLEECES	FOREBYE	**FRIJOL**	GAGGLES	GARROTE
FLENSE	**FORGER**	FRIJOLE	**GAINST**	GARROTS
FLENSED	FORGERS	**FRINGE**	AGAINST	**GASHES**
FLENSER	FORGERY	FRINGED	**GALANT**	GASHEST

GASKIN	GHESSED	GLITCHY	GOONIES	GRAVELY
GASKING	GHESSES	**GLOBIN**	**GOPURA**	**GRAVES**
GASKINS	**GIGGLE**	GLOBING	GOPURAM	GRAVEST
GASTED	GIGGLED	GLOBINS	GOPURAS	**GRAVID**
AGASTED	GIGGLER	**GLOSSA**	**GOSSIP**	GRAVIDA
GATEAU	GIGGLES	GLOSSAE	GOSSIPS	**GREASE**
GATEAUS	**GILLIE**	GLOSSAL	GOSSIPY	GREASED
GATEAUX	GILLIED	GLOSSAS	**GOUGER**	GREASER
GAUCHE	GILLIES	**GLYCIN**	GOUGERE	GREASES
GAUCHED	**GINGAL**	GLYCINE	GOUGERS	**GREAVE**
GAUCHER	GINGALL	GLYCINS	**GOWLAN**	GREAVED
GAUCHES	GINGALS	**GOATEE**	GOWLAND	GREAVES
GAUCIE	**GINGER**	GOATEED	GOWLANS	**GREETE**
GAUCIER	GINGERS	GOATEES	**GOYISH**	GREETED
GAWSIE	GINGERY	**GOBBLE**	GOYISHE	GREETER
GAWSIER	**GINNER**	GOBBLED	**GRADIN**	GREETES
GEISTS	AGINNER	GOBBLER	GRADINE	**GREGES**
AGEISTS	GINNERS	GOBBLES	GRADING	AGREGES
GELATE	GINNERY	**GODDAM**	GRADINI	**GRIECE**
GELATED	**GIRDLE**	GODDAMN	GRADINO	GRIECED
GELATES	GIRDLED	GODDAMS	GRADINS	GRIECES
GELATI	GIRDLER	**GOGGLE**	**GRAINE**	**GRIEVE**
GELATIN	GIRDLES	GOGGLED	GRAINED	GRIEVED
GELATIS	**GIRLIE**	GOGGLER	GRAINER	GRIEVER
GENERA	GIRLIER	GOGGLES	GRAINES	GRIEVES
GENERAL	GIRLIES	**GOITRE**	**GRAMAS**	**GRILLE**
GENTIL	**GIRNIE**	GOITRED	GRAMASH	GRILLED
GENTILE	GIRNIER	GOITRES	**GRAMMA**	GRILLER
GENTLE	**GITTIN**	**GOLLAN**	GRAMMAR	GRILLES
GENTLED	GITTING	GOLLAND	GRAMMAS	**GRIPPE**
GENTLER	**GLAIRE**	GOLLANS	**GRANDE**	GRIPPED
GENTLES	GLAIRED	**GOLOSH**	GRANDEE	GRIPPER
GENTRY	GLAIRES	GOLOSHE	GRANDER	GRIPPES
AGENTRY	**GLAIVE**	**GOODBY**	**GRANGE**	**GRISED**
GEODES	GLAIVED	GOODBYE	GRANGER	AGRISED
GEODESY	GLAIVES	GOODBYS	GRANGES	**GRISES**
GERMAN	**GLANCE**	**GOODIE**	**GRASTE**	AGRISES
GERMANE	GLANCED	GOODIER	AGRASTE	**GRIZES**
GERMANS	GLANCER	GOODIES	**GRATIN**	AGRIZES
GERMIN	GLANCES	**GOOGLE**	GRATINE	**GROCER**
GERMINA	**GLEDGE**	GOOGLED	GRATING	GROCERS
GERMING	GLEDGED	GOOGLES	GRATINS	GROCERY
GERMINS	GLEDGES	**GOONIE**	**GRAVEL**	**GROOVE**
GHESSE	**GLITCH**	GOONIER	GRAVELS	GROOVED

GROOVER	AGUISED	WHACKER	HALLALI	HANDLES
GROOVES	**GUISES**	HACKERS	HALLALS	**HANGED**
GROSER	AGUISES	HACKERY	**HALLAN**	CHANGED
GROSERS	**GULLER**	**HACKLE**	CHALLAN	PHANGED
GROSERT	GULLERS	SHACKLE	HALLANS	WHANGED
GROUCH	GULLERY	HACKLED	**HALLOT**	**HANGER**
GROUCHY	**GUNNER**	HACKLER	CHALLOT	CHANGER
GROUND	GUNNERA	HACKLES	SHALLOT	HANGERS
AGROUND	GUNNERS	HACKLET	HALLOTH	**HANJAR**
GROUNDS	GUNNERY	**HADING**	**HALLOW**	KHANJAR
GROUSE	**GURGLE**	SHADING	SHALLOW	HANJARS
GROUSED	GURGLED	**HAFTED**	HALLOWS	**HANKED**
GROUSER	GURGLES	SHAFTED	**HALTER**	SHANKED
GROUSES	GURGLET	**HAFTER**	HALTERE	THANKED
GROWTH	**GUSSIE**	SHAFTER	HALTERS	**HANKER**
GROWTHS	GUSSIED	HAFTERS	**HALUTZ**	THANKER
GROWTHY	GUSSIES	**HAGGED**	CHALUTZ	HANKERS
GRUDGE	**GUSTIE**	SHAGGED	**HAMALS**	**HANTED**
GRUDGED	GUSTIER	**HAGGIS**	SHAMALS	CHANTED
GRUDGER	**GUTTER**	HAGGISH	**HAMBLE**	**HAPPED**
GRUDGES	GUTTERS	**HAGGLE**	SHAMBLE	CHAPPED
GRUMPH	GUTTERY	HAGGLED	HAMBLED	WHAPPED
GRUMPHS	**GUTTLE**	HAGGLER	HAMBLES	**HAPTEN**
GRUMPHY	GUTTLED	HAGGLES	**HAMING**	HAPTENE
GRUNGE	GUTTLER	**HAINED**	SHAMING	HAPTENS
GRUNGER	GUTTLES	CHAINED	**HAMLET**	**HARING**
GRUNGES	**GUZZLE**	**HAIRED**	CHAMLET	CHARING
GRUNGEY	GUZZLED	CHAIRED	HAMLETS	SHARING
GUANAS	GUZZLER	**HALALA**	**HAMMED**	**HARKED**
IGUANAS	GUZZLES	HALALAH	SHAMMED	CHARKED
GUANASE	**GWEDUC**	HALALAS	WHAMMED	SHARKED
GUANIN	GWEDUCK	**HALERS**	**HAMMER**	**HARMED**
GUANINE	GWEDUCS	THALERS	SHAMMER	CHARMED
GUANINS	**GYRATE**	WHALERS	HAMMERS	PHARMED
GUDDLE	GYRATED	**HALIER**	**HAMPER**	**HARMER**
GUDDLED	GYRATES	SHALIER	CHAMPER	CHARMER
GUDDLES	**HACHIS**	HALIERS	HAMPERS	PHARMER
GUGGLE	RHACHIS	**HALING**	**HANCES**	HARMERS
GUGGLED	**HACKED**	SHALING	CHANCES	**HARMIN**
GUGGLES	CHACKED	WHALING	**HANDAX**	HARMINE
GUIMPE	SHACKED	**HALLAH**	HANDAXE	HARMING
GUIMPED	THACKED	CHALLAH	**HANDLE**	HARMINS
GUIMPES	WHACKED	HALLAHS	HANDLED	**HARPED**
GUISED	**HACKER**	**HALLAL**	HANDLER	SHARPED

HARPER	**HAZANS**	HEDDLES	**HENNER**	**HEUCHS**
SHARPER	CHAZANS	**HEDERA**	HENNERS	SHEUCHS
HARPERS	**HAZELS**	HEDERAL	HENNERY	**HEUGHS**
HARPIN	GHAZELS	HEDERAS	**HENNIN**	SHEUGHS
HARPING	**HAZZAN**	**HEDERS**	HENNING	WHEUGHS
HARPINS	CHAZZAN	CHEDERS	HENNINS	**HEWERS**
HASHED	HAZZANS	**HEELED**	**HERBAR**	CHEWERS
SHASHED	**HEALED**	SHEELED	HERBARS	SHEWERS
HASHES	SHEALED	WHEELED	HERBARY	**HEWING**
SHASHES	**HEALTH**	**HEELER**	**HEREAT**	CHEWING
HASSES	HEALTHS	WHEELER	THEREAT	SHEWING
CHASSES	HEALTHY	HEELERS	WHEREAT	WHEWING
HASSLE	**HEAPED**	**HEEZED**	**HEREBY**	HEWINGS
HASSLED	CHEAPED	PHEEZED	THEREBY	**HICCUP**
HASSLES	**HEAPER**	WHEEZED	WHEREBY	HICCUPS
HASTED	CHEAPER	**HEEZES**	**HEREIN**	HICCUPY
GHASTED	HEAPERS	PHEEZES	THEREIN	**HICKER**
HASTEN	**HEARER**	WHEEZES	WHEREIN	SHICKER
CHASTEN	SHEARER	**HEIGHT**	**HEREOF**	THICKER
HASTENS	HEARERS	AHEIGHT	THEREOF	WHICKER
HATTED	**HEARSE**	HEIGHTH	WHEREOF	**HICKIE**
CHATTED	HEARSED	HEIGHTS	**HEREON**	THICKIE
HATTER	HEARSES	**HEISTS**	THEREON	HICKIES
CHATTER	**HEATED**	THEISTS	WHEREON	**HIDDEN**
PHATTER	CHEATED	**HELLED**	**HERETO**	CHIDDEN
SHATTER	**HEATER**	SHELLED	THERETO	**HIDDER**
HATTERS	CHEATER	**HELLER**	WHERETO	SHIDDER
HAUGHS	THEATER	SHELLER	**HERMAE**	WHIDDER
SHAUGHS	HEATERS	HELLERI	THERMAE	HIDDERS
HAUGHT	**HEATHS**	HELLERS	**HERMIT**	**HIDERS**
HAUGHTY	SHEATHS	HELLERY	THERMIT	CHIDERS
HAULED	**HEATHY**	**HELMED**	HERMITS	**HIDING**
SHAULED	SHEATHY	WHELMED	**HERNIA**	CHIDING
HAUNTS	**HEAVED**	**HELPED**	HERNIAE	HIDINGS
CHAUNTS	SHEAVED	CHELPED	HERNIAL	**HIGGLE**
HAVERS	**HEAVES**	WHELPED	HERNIAS	HIGGLED
SHAVERS	SHEAVES	**HELVED**	**HEROES**	HIGGLER
HAVING	THEAVES	SHELVED	SHEROES	HIGGLES
SHAVING	**HECKLE**	**HELVES**	**HEROIN**	**HIGHED**
HAVINGS	HECKLED	SHELVES	HEROINE	THIGHED
HAWING	HECKLER	THELVES	HEROINS	**HILLED**
CHAWING	HECKLES	**HEMPIE**	**HETHER**	CHILLED
SHAWING	**HEDDLE**	HEMPIER	THETHER	SHILLED
THAWING	HEDDLED	HEMPIES	WHETHER	**HILLER**

CHILLER	PHISHED	CHOCKER	HOLISMS	WHOOPLA
THILLER	WHISHED	SHOCKER	**HOLIST**	HOOPLAS
HILLERS	**HISHES**	HOCKERS	WHOLIST	**HOOTED**
HINGED	PHISHES	**HOCKLE**	HOLISTS	WHOOTED
WHINGED	WHISHES	HOCKLED	**HOLLAS**	**HOOTER**
HINGER	**HISSED**	HOCKLES	CHOLLAS	SHOOTER
WHINGER	WHISSED	**HODDEN**	**HOMAGE**	HOOTERS
HINGERS	**HISSES**	SHODDEN	HOMAGED	**HOPPED**
HINGES	WHISSES	HODDENS	HOMAGER	CHOPPED
WHINGES	**HISTED**	**HODDIN**	HOMAGES	SHOPPED
HINNIE	WHISTED	HODDING	**HOMELY**	WHOPPED
HINNIED	**HISTIE**	HODDINS	HOMELYN	**HOPPER**
HINNIES	BHISTIE	**HODDLE**	**HOMIES**	CHOPPER
HIPPED	**HITHER**	HODDLED	HOMIEST	SHOPPER
CHIPPED	THITHER	HODDLES	**HONDLE**	WHOPPER
SHIPPED	WHITHER	**HODJAS**	HONDLED	HOPPERS
WHIPPED	HITHERS	KHODJAS	HONDLES	**HOPPLE**
HIPPEN	**HITTER**	**HOEING**	**HONERS**	HOPPLED
SHIPPEN	CHITTER	SHOEING	PHONERS	HOPPLER
HIPPENS	SHITTER	**HOGGED**	**HONEST**	HOPPLES
HIPPER	WHITTER	SHOGGED	HONESTY	**HORDED**
CHIPPER	HITTERS	**HOGGER**	**HONEYS**	CHORDED
SHIPPER	**HIVERS**	HOGGERS	PHONEYS	**HORNED**
WHIPPER	SHIVERS	HOGGERY	**HONIED**	THORNED
HIPPIE	**HIVING**	**HOGGIN**	PHONIED	**HORSIE**
CHIPPIE	CHIVING	HOGGING	**HONING**	HORSIER
SHIPPIE	**HIZZED**	HOGGINS	PHONING	HORSIES
HIPPIER	CHIZZED	**HOGTIE**	**HOODIE**	**HOSIER**
HIPPIES	WHIZZED	HOGTIED	HOODIER	HOSIERS
HIPPIN	**HIZZES**	HOGTIES	HOODIES	HOSIERY
HIPPING	CHIZZES	**HOISIN**	**HOOFED**	**HOSTED**
HIPPINS	PHIZZES	HOISING	CHOOFED	GHOSTED
HIPPOS	WHIZZES	HOISINS	WHOOFED	**HOSTLY**
SHIPPOS	**HOARSE**	**HOKIER**	**HOOKED**	GHOSTLY
HIRING	HOARSEN	CHOKIER	CHOOKED	**HOTTED**
SHIRING	HOARSER	**HOKING**	**HOOLIE**	SHOTTED
HIRINGS	**HOBBLE**	CHOKING	HOOLIER	**HOUGHS**
HIRPLE	HOBBLED	**HOLIES**	HOOLIES	CHOUGHS
HIRPLED	HOBBLER	HOLIEST	**HOOPED**	SHOUGHS
HIRPLES	HOBBLES	**HOLING**	WHOOPED	**HOUSED**
HIRSLE	**HOCKED**	THOLING	**HOOPER**	CHOUSED
HIRSLED	CHOCKED	HOLINGS	WHOOPER	**HOUSER**
HIRSLES	SHOCKED	**HOLISM**	HOOPERS	CHOUSER
HISHED	**HOCKER**	WHOLISM	**HOOPLA**	HOUSERS

HOUSES	WHUMMLE	HUSTLED	**ICKIER**	ZIGGING
CHOUSES	**HUMPED**	HUSTLER	DICKIER	**IGNIFY**
SHOUSES	CHUMPED	HUSTLES	KICKIER	DIGNIFY
HOUTED	THUMPED	**HUTTED**	PICKIER	LIGNIFY
SHOUTED	WHUMPED	PHUTTED	**ICKILY**	SIGNIFY
HOVELS	**HUMPER**	**HUTZPA**	PICKILY	**IGNITE**
SHOVELS	THUMPER	CHUTZPA	**ICKLER**	LIGNITE
HOVERS	HUMPERS	HUTZPAH	FICKLER	**IGNITED**
SHOVERS	**HUNGRY**	HUTZPAS	MICKLER	IGNITER
HOVING	AHUNGRY	**HYALIN**	PICKLER	IGNITES
SHOVING	**HUNKIE**	HYALINE	TICKLER	**IGNORE**
HOWDIE	HUNKIER	HYALINS	**IDANTS**	SIGNORE
HOWDIED	HUNKIES	**HYDRAS**	AIDANTS	IGNORED
HOWDIES	**HUNTED**	HYDRASE	**IDEATE**	IGNORER
HUCKED	SHUNTED	**HYDRIA**	IDEATED	IGNORES
CHUCKED	**HUNTER**	HYDRIAE	IDEATES	**ILEXES**
SHUCKED	CHUNTER	**HYDRID**	**IDENTS**	SILEXES
HUCKLE	SHUNTER	HYDRIDE	BIDENTS	**ILICES**
CHUCKLE	HUNTERS	HYDRIDS	**IDIOTS**	CILICES
HUCKLED	**HUPPAH**	**IBICES**	VIDIOTS	**ILLEST**
HUCKLES	CHUPPAH	VIBICES	**IDLERS**	WILLEST
HUDDLE	HUPPAHS	**ICHING**	SIDLERS	**ILLITE**
HUDDLED	**HUPPED**	MICHING	**IDLING**	TILLITE
HUDDLER	WHUPPED	NICHING	HIDLING	ILLITES
HUDDLES	**HUPPOT**	RICHING	KIDLING	**ILLUDE**
HUFFED	CHUPPOT	**ICICLE**	SIDLING	ILLUDED
CHUFFED	HUPPOTH	ICICLED	**IDOLON**	ILLUDES
HUFFER	**HURDLE**	ICICLES	EIDOLON	**ILLUME**
CHUFFER	HURDLED	**ICIEST**	**IFFIER**	ILLUMED
HUFFERS	HURDLER	DICIEST	MIFFIER	ILLUMES
HUGGED	HURDLES	RICIEST	NIFFIER	**IMAGER**
CHUGGED	**HURRAS**	**ICINGS**	**IFFILY**	IMAGERS
HUGGER	DHURRAS	DICINGS	MIFFILY	IMAGERY
CHUGGER	**HURTLE**	**ICKERS**	**IGGING**	**IMBARS**
HUGGERS	HURTLED	BICKERS	BIGGING	MIMBARS
HUMANE	HURTLES	DICKERS	DIGGING	**IMBASE**
HUMANER	**HUSHED**	KICKERS	FIGGING	IMBASED
HUMBLE	SHUSHED	LICKERS	GIGGING	IMBASES
HUMBLED	**HUSHER**	NICKERS	JIGGING	**IMBIBE**
HUMBLER	SHUSHER	PICKERS	LIGGING	IMBIBED
HUMBLES	HUSHERS	RICKERS	PIGGING	IMBIBER
HUMMED	**HUSHES**	TICKERS	RIGGING	IMBIBES
CHUMMED	SHUSHES	WICKERS	TIGGING	**IMBRUE**
HUMMLE	**HUSTLE**	YICKERS	WIGGING	IMBRUED

IMBRUES	IMPROVE	INCITED	INFUSED	**INISLE**
IMMIES	IMPROVS	INCITER	INFUSER	INISLED
GIMMIES	**IMPURE**	INCITES	INFUSES	INISLES
JIMMIES	IMPURER	**INCOME**	**INGANS**	**INJURE**
IMMURE	**IMPUTE**	INCOMER	FINGANS	INJURED
IMMURED	IMPUTED	INCOMES	**INGENU**	INJURER
IMMURES	IMPUTER	**INCUSE**	INGENUE	INJURES
IMPALE	IMPUTES	INCUSED	INGENUS	**INKERS**
IMPALED	**INANES**	INCUSES	**INGEST**	JINKERS
IMPALER	INANEST	**INDEED**	INGESTA	LINKERS
IMPALES	**INCAGE**	INDEEDY	INGESTS	PINKERS
IMPAVE	INCAGED	**INDIES**	**INGLES**	SINKERS
IMPAVED	INCAGES	KINDIES	BINGLES	TINKERS
IMPAVES	**INCASE**	LINDIES	DINGLES	WINKERS
IMPEDE	PINCASE	YINDIES	GINGLES	**INKIER**
IMPEDED	INCASED	**INDIGO**	JINGLES	DINKIER
IMPEDER	INCASES	WINDIGO	KINGLES	HINKIER
IMPEDES	**INCAVE**	INDIGOS	LINGLES	KINKIER
IMPING	INCAVED	**INDITE**	MINGLES	LINKIER
GIMPING	INCAVES	INDITED	PINGLES	PINKIER
LIMPING	**INCEDE**	INDITER	SINGLES	SINKIER
PIMPING	INCEDED	INDITES	TINGLES	ZINKIER
WIMPING	INCEDES	**INDOWS**	**INGOES**	**INKING**
IMPINGE	**INCHED**	WINDOWS	BINGOES	DINKING
IMPINGS	CINCHED	**INDUCE**	DINGOES	FINKING
IMPISH	FINCHED	INDUCED	JINGOES	JINKING
WIMPISH	PINCHED	INDUCER	LINGOES	KINKING
IMPLED	WINCHED	INDUCES	PINGOES	LINKING
DIMPLED	**INCHER**	**INFALL**	**INGOTS**	OINKING
PIMPLED	PINCHER	PINFALL	LINGOTS	PINKING
RIMPLED	WINCHER	INFALLS	**INHALE**	RINKING
SIMPLED	INCHERS	**INFAME**	INHALED	SINKING
WIMPLED	**INCHES**	INFAMED	INHALER	TINKING
IMPLEX	CINCHES	INFAMES	INHALES	WINKING
SIMPLEX	FINCHES	**INFANT**	**INHERE**	ZINKING
IMPONE	GINCHES	INFANTA	INHERED	**INKLED**
IMPONED	LINCHES	INFANTE	INHERES	TINKLED
IMPONES	PINCHES	INFANTS	**INHUME**	WINKLED
IMPOSE	WINCHES	**INFOLD**	INHUMED	**INKLES**
IMPOSED	**INCISE**	PINFOLD	INHUMER	KINKLES
IMPOSER	INCISED	INFOLDS	INHUMES	TINKLES
IMPOSES	INCISES	**INFULA**	**INIONS**	WINKLES
IMPOSEX	**INCITE**	INFULAE	MINIONS	INKLESS
IMPROV	ZINCITE	**INFUSE**	PINIONS	**INLACE**

INLACED	INSURES	IODATES	**ISCHIA**	WIZARDS
INLACES	**INTELS**	**IODISE**	ISCHIAL	**IZZARD**
INNATE	LINTELS	IODISED	**ISLING**	DIZZARD
PINNATE	**INTERN**	IODISER	AISLING	GIZZARD
INNERS	INTERNE	IODISES	**ISOBAR**	IZZARDS
DINNERS	INTERNS	**IODIZE**	ISOBARE	**JABBLE**
FINNERS	**INTERS**	IODIZED	ISOBARS	JABBLED
GINNERS	HINTERS	IODIZER	**ISOGON**	JABBLES
PINNERS	LINTERS	IODIZES	ISOGONE	**JAGGER**
SINNERS	MINTERS	**IONICS**	ISOGONS	JAGGERS
TINNERS	SINTERS	BIONICS	ISOGONY	JAGGERY
WINNERS	TINTERS	**IONISE**	**ISOMER**	**JAGHIR**
INNING	WINTERS	LIONISE	ISOMERE	JAGHIRE
BINNING	**INTIMA**	IONISED	ISOMERS	JAGHIRS
DINNING	INTIMAE	IONISER	**ISSUED**	**JAMBOK**
FINNING	INTIMAL	IONISES	TISSUED	SJAMBOK
GINNING	INTIMAS	**IONIZE**	**ISSUES**	JAMBOKS
LINNING	**INTONE**	LIONIZE	TISSUES	**JAMPAN**
PINNING	INTONED	IONIZED	**ISTHMI**	JAMPANI
RINNING	INTONER	IONIZER	ISTHMIC	JAMPANS
SINNING	INTONES	IONIZES	**ISTLES**	**JANGLE**
TINNING	**INULAS**	**IRADES**	MISTLES	JANGLED
WINNING	INULASE	TIRADES	**ITCHED**	JANGLER
INNINGS	**INVADE**	**IREFUL**	BITCHED	JANGLES
INSANE	INVADED	DIREFUL	DITCHED	**JARGON**
INSANER	INVADER	**IRENIC**	HITCHED	JARGONS
INSHIP	INVADES	EIRENIC	MITCHED	JARGONY
KINSHIP	**INVITE**	SIRENIC	PITCHED	**JASMIN**
INSHIPS	INVITED	IRENICS	WITCHED	JASMINE
INSIDE	INVITEE	**IRITIS**	**ITCHES**	JASMINS
INSIDER	INVITER	MIRITIS	AITCHES	**JASPER**
INSIDES	INVITES	TIRITIS	BITCHES	JASPERS
INSTAL	**INVOKE**	**IRKING**	DITCHES	JASPERY
INSTALL	INVOKED	DIRKING	FITCHES	**JAUNCE**
INSTALS	INVOKER	FIRKING	GITCHES	JAUNCED
INSTIL	INVOKES	KIRKING	HITCHES	JAUNCES
INSTILL	**INWORK**	LIRKING	MITCHES	**JAUNSE**
INSTILS	PINWORK	YIRKING	PITCHES	JAUNSED
INSULA	TINWORK	**IRONIC**	TITCHES	JAUNSES
INSULAE	INWORKS	GIRONIC	WITCHES	**JEBELS**
INSULAR	**INWOVE**	TIRONIC	**IZARDS**	DJEBELS
INSURE	INWOVEN	**ISATIN**	LIZARDS	**JEELIE**
INSURED	**IODATE**	ISATINE	RIZARDS	JEELIED
INSURER	IODATED	ISATINS	VIZARDS	JEELIES

JEJUNA	JOGGLER	KAOLINE	KIMMERS	**KOOKUM**
JEJUNAL	**JOGGLES**	KAOLINS	**KIMONO**	SKOOKUM
JEMBES	**JOINER**	**KECKLE**	OKIMONO	KOOKUMS
DJEMBES	JOINERS	KECKLED	KIMONOS	**KREESE**
JERKIN	JOINERY	KECKLES	**KINDLE**	KREESED
JERKING	**JOSTLE**	**KEGGER**	KINDLED	KREESES
JERKINS	JOSTLED	SKEGGER	KINDLER	**KVETCH**
JERQUE	JOSTLER	KEGGERS	KINDLES	KVETCHY
JERQUED	JOSTLES	**KELPED**	**KINGLE**	**LACERS**
JERQUER	**JOUNCE**	SKELPED	KINGLES	PLACERS
JERQUES	JOUNCED	**KELTER**	KINGLET	**LACETS**
JIBBAH	JOUNCES	SKELTER	**KINKED**	PLACETS
DJIBBAH	**JUBILE**	KELTERS	SKINKED	**LACHES**
JIBBAHS	JUBILEE	**KENNED**	**KIPPED**	CLACHES
JIBBAS	JUBILES	SKENNED	SKIPPED	**LACIER**
DJIBBAS	**JUDDER**	**KENNET**	**KIPPER**	GLACIER
JIGGLE	JUDDERS	KENNETS	SKIPPER	**LACING**
JIGGLED	JUDDERY	KENNETT	KIPPERS	PLACING
JIGGLES	**JUGGLE**	**KEPPED**	**KIRTLE**	LACINGS
JIGSAW	JUGGLED	SKEPPED	KIRTLED	**LACKED**
JIGSAWN	JUGGLER	**KETTLE**	KIRTLES	BLACKED
JIGSAWS	JUGGLES	KETTLED	**KITING**	CLACKED
JIMMIE	**JUGULA**	KETTLES	SKITING	FLACKED
JIMMIED	JUGULAR	**KHALIF**	KITINGS	SLACKED
JIMMIES	**JUMBLE**	KHALIFA	**KITSCH**	**LACKER**
JINGAL	JUMBLED	KHALIFS	KITSCHY	BLACKER
JINGALL	JUMBLER	**KIBBLE**	**KITTEN**	CLACKER
JINGALS	JUMBLES	KIBBLED	KITTENS	FLACKER
JINGLE	**JUNGLE**	KIBBLES	KITTENY	SLACKER
JINGLED	JUNGLED	**KIDDED**	**KITTLE**	LACKERS
JINGLER	JUNGLES	SKIDDED	SKITTLE	**LACUNA**
JINGLES	**JUNKIE**	**KIDDER**	KITTLED	LACUNAE
JINGLET	JUNKIER	SKIDDER	KITTLER	LACUNAL
JIRBLE	JUNKIES	KIDDERS	KITTLES	LACUNAR
JIRBLED	**JUSTLE**	**KIDDIE**	**KLUDGE**	LACUNAS
JIRBLES	JUSTLED	KIDDIED	KLUDGED	**LADDER**
JITTER	JUSTLES	KIDDIER	KLUDGES	BLADDER
JITTERS	**KAGOUL**	KIDDIES	KLUDGEY	CLADDER
JITTERY	KAGOULE	**KIDGIE**	**KOLHOZ**	GLADDER
JOBBER	KAGOULS	KIDGIER	KOLHOZY	LADDERS
JOBBERS	**KAINIT**	**KILLED**	**KOLKOZ**	LADDERY
JOBBERY	KAINITE	SKILLED	KOLKOZY	**LADDIE**
JOGGLE	KAINITS	**KIMMER**	**KOOKIE**	CLADDIE
JOGGLED	**KAOLIN**	SKIMMER	KOOKIER	GLADDIE

LADDIER	CLAMBER	BLANDED	**LARGES**	LASTERS
LADDIES	LAMBERS	**LANDER**	LARGESS	**LATENS**
LADERS	LAMBERT	BLANDER	LARGEST	PLATENS
BLADERS	**LAMBIE**	SLANDER	**LARNEY**	**LATEST**
LADING	LAMBIER	LANDERS	BLARNEY	BLATEST
BLADING	LAMBIES	**LANDES**	LARNEYS	LATESTS
LADINGS	**LAMINA**	GLANDES	**LARUMS**	**LATHER**
LADRON	LAMINAE	**LANGER**	ALARUMS	BLATHER
LADRONE	LAMINAL	CLANGER	**LASERS**	SLATHER
LADRONS	LAMINAR	FLANGER	FLASERS	LATHERS
LAGGED	LAMINAS	SLANGER	**LASHED**	LATHERY
BLAGGED	**LAMING**	LANGERS	BLASHED	**LATINA**
CLAGGED	BLAMING	**LANGUE**	CLASHED	PLATINA
FLAGGED	FLAMING	LANGUED	FLASHED	LATINAS
SLAGGED	**LAMMED**	LANGUES	PLASHED	**LATTEN**
LAGGER	BLAMMED	LANGUET	SLASHED	FLATTEN
BLAGGER	CLAMMED	**LANKED**	**LASHER**	LATTENS
FLAGGER	FLAMMED	BLANKED	CLASHER	**LATTER**
LAGGERS	GLAMMED	CLANKED	FLASHER	BLATTER
LAGGIN	SLAMMED	FLANKED	PLASHER	CLATTER
LAGGING	**LAMMER**	PLANKED	SLASHER	FLATTER
LAGGINS	CLAMMER	**LANKER**	LASHERS	PLATTER
LAHALS	GLAMMER	BLANKER	**LASHES**	SLATTER
SLAHALS	SLAMMER	FLANKER	BLASHES	LATTERS
LAIDED	LAMMERS	**LANKLY**	CLASHES	**LAUDED**
PLAIDED	**LAMPED**	BLANKLY	FLASHES	BLAUDED
LAIPSE	CLAMPED	**LANNER**	PLASHES	**LAUNCE**
LAIPSED	**LAMPER**	PLANNER	SLASHES	LAUNCED
LAIPSES	CLAMPER	LANNERS	**LASKET**	LAUNCES
LAIRED	LAMPERN	**LAPPED**	FLASKET	**LAUNCH**
GLAIRED	LAMPERS	CLAPPED	LASKETS	FLAUNCH
LAKERS	**LANATE**	FLAPPED	**LASSES**	**LAVERS**
FLAKERS	PLANATE	KLAPPED	CLASSES	CLAVERS
SLAKERS	LANATED	PLAPPED	GLASSES	SLAVERS
LAKIER	**LANCED**	SLAPPED	**LASSIE**	**LAVING**
FLAKIER	ELANCED	**LAPPER**	GLASSIE	SLAVING
LAKING	GLANCED	CLAPPER	LASSIES	**LAVISH**
FLAKING	**LANCER**	FLAPPER	**LASSIS**	SLAVISH
SLAKING	GLANCER	SLAPPER	CLASSIS	**LAVOLT**
LAKINGS	LANCERS	LAPPERS	**LASTED**	LAVOLTA
LALLAN	**LANCES**	**LAPSED**	BLASTED	LAVOLTS
LALLAND	ELANCES	ELAPSED	**LASTER**	**LAWING**
LALLANS	GLANCES	**LAPSES**	BLASTER	BLAWING
LAMBER	**LANDED**	ELAPSES	PLASTER	CLAWING

FLAWING	**LEANER**	**LEDGER**	FLEMING	LIBATES
LAWINGS	CLEANER	PLEDGER	**LENDER**	**LIBBED**
LAYERS	GLEANER	SLEDGER	BLENDER	GLIBBED
FLAYERS	LEANERS	LEDGERS	SLENDER	**LIBBER**
PLAYERS	**LEANLY**	**LEDGES**	LENDERS	GLIBBER
SLAYERS	CLEANLY	FLEDGES	**LENGTH**	LIBBERS
LAYING	**LEARED**	GLEDGES	ALENGTH	**LICHES**
ALAYING	BLEARED	PLEDGES	LENGTHS	CLICHES
CLAYING	CLEARED	SLEDGES	LENGTHY	ELICHES
FLAYING	**LEASED**	**LEEING**	**LENITE**	**LICKED**
PLAYING	PLEASED	FLEEING	LENITED	CLICKED
SLAYING	**LEASER**	GLEEING	LENITES	FLICKED
LAYINGS	PLEASER	**LEEPED**	**LENSED**	SLICKED
LAYOFF	LEASERS	BLEEPED	FLENSED	**LICKER**
PLAYOFF	**LEASES**	CLEEPED	**LENSES**	CLICKER
LAYOFFS	PLEASES	**LEERED**	FLENSES	FLICKER
LAZARS	**LEASOW**	FLEERED	**LESSER**	SLICKER
BLAZARS	LEASOWE	**LEGATE**	BLESSER	LICKERS
LAZIER	LEASOWS	LEGATED	**LESSES**	**LIENEE**
GLAZIER	**LEAVED**	LEGATEE	BLESSES	ALIENEE
LAZIES	CLEAVED	LEGATES	**LESSOR**	LIENEES
LAZIEST	SLEAVED	**LEGATO**	PLESSOR	**LIENOR**
LAZILY	**LEAVER**	LEGATOR	LESSORS	ALIENOR
GLAZILY	CLEAVER	LEGATOS	**LETTED**	LIENORS
LAZING	LEAVERS	**LEGGED**	BLETTED	**LIEVES**
BLAZING	**LEAVES**	ALEGGED	**LETTER**	SLIEVES
GLAZING	CLEAVES	FLEGGED	LETTERN	LIEVEST
LEADED	GLEAVES	**LEGGER**	LETTERS	**LIFTED**
PLEADED	SLEAVES	GLEGGER	**LEUCIN**	CLIFTED
LEADER	**LEAZES**	LEGGERS	LEUCINE	**LIGATE**
PLEADER	SLEAZES	**LEGGES**	LEUCINS	LIGATED
LEADERS	**LECHER**	ALEGGES	**LEVINS**	LIGATES
LEAGUE	LECHERS	**LEGGIE**	ALEVINS	**LIGHTS**
LEAGUED	LECHERY	LEGGIER	**LEXICA**	ALIGHTS
LEAGUER	**LECHES**	LEGGIES	LEXICAL	BLIGHTS
LEAGUES	FLECHES	**LEGGIN**	**LIABLE**	FLIGHTS
LEAKER	**LECTOR**	LEGGING	PLIABLE	PLIGHTS
BLEAKER	ELECTOR	LEGGINS	**LIAISE**	SLIGHTS
LEAKERS	LECTORS	**LEGIST**	LIAISED	**LIGULA**
LEAMED	**LEDGED**	ELEGIST	LIAISES	LIGULAE
GLEAMED	FLEDGED	LEGISTS	**LIASES**	LIGULAR
LEANED	GLEDGED	**LEGITS**	ALIASES	LIGULAS
CLEANED	PLEDGED	ELEGITS	**LIBATE**	**LIMBEC**
GLEANED	SLEDGED	**LEMING**	LIBATED	LIMBECK

LIMBECS	SLINKED	LISTENS	SLOBBER	VLOGGED
LIMBED	**LINKER**	**LISTER**	LOBBERS	**LOGGER**
CLIMBED	BLINKER	BLISTER	**LOBING**	BLOGGER
LIMBER	CLINKER	GLISTER	GLOBING	CLOGGER
CLIMBER	KLINKER	KLISTER	LOBINGS	FLOGGER
LIMBERS	PLINKER	LISTERS	**LOBOSE**	SLOGGER
LIMIER	SLINKER	**LITHER**	GLOBOSE	VLOGGER
SLIMIER	LINKERS	BLITHER	**LOBULE**	LOGGERS
LIMINA	**LINNED**	SLITHER	GLOBULE	**LOGGIE**
LIMINAL	BLINNED	**LITHES**	LOBULES	LOGGIER
LIMING	**LINTED**	LITHEST	**LOCATE**	**LOGIES**
GLIMING	FLINTED	**LITING**	LOCATED	ELOGIES
SLIMING	GLINTED	FLITING	LOCATER	OLOGIES
LIMINGS	**LINTER**	**LITTER**	LOCATES	LOGIEST
LIMMER	SLINTER	BLITTER	**LOCHES**	**LOLLOP**
GLIMMER	LINTERS	CLITTER	CLOCHES	LOLLOPS
SLIMMER	**LINTIE**	FLITTER	**LOCHIA**	LOLLOPY
LIMMERS	LINTIER	GLITTER	LOCHIAL	**LOMENT**
LIMPED	LINTIES	SLITTER	LOCHIAS	LOMENTA
BLIMPED	**LIPPED**	LITTERS	**LOCKED**	LOMENTS
FLIMPED	BLIPPED	LITTERY	BLOCKED	**LONELY**
LIMPSY	CLIPPED	**LITTLE**	CLOCKED	ALONELY
SLIMPSY	FLIPPED	LITTLER	FLOCKED	**LONERS**
LINERS	SLIPPED	LITTLES	**LOCKER**	CLONERS
ALINERS	**LIPPER**	**LIVERS**	BLOCKER	**LONGED**
LINGER	CLIPPER	CLIVERS	CLOCKER	PLONGED
BLINGER	FLIPPER	OLIVERS	LOCKERS	**LONGES**
CLINGER	SLIPPER	SLIVERS	**LOCULE**	PLONGES
FLINGER	LIPPERS	**LIVING**	LOCULED	LONGEST
SLINGER	**LIPPIE**	SLIVING	LOCULES	**LOOKIE**
LINGERS	CLIPPIE	LIVINGS	**LOCUST**	PLOOKIE
LINGOS	LIPPIER	**LOATHE**	LOCUSTA	**LOOMED**
OLINGOS	LIPPIES	LOATHED	LOCUSTS	BLOOMED
LINGUA	**LIQUID**	LOATHER	**LODGED**	GLOOMED
LINGUAE	LIQUIDS	LOATHES	PLODGED	SLOOMED
LINGUAL	LIQUIDY	**LOBATE**	**LODGES**	**LOONIE**
LINGUAS	**LISSES**	GLOBATE	PLODGES	LOONIER
LINING	BLISSES	LOBATED	**LOGANS**	LOONIES
ALINING	GLISSES	**LOBBED**	SLOGANS	**LOOPED**
LININGS	PLISSES	BLOBBED	**LOGGED**	BLOOPED
LINKED	**LISSOM**	FLOBBED	BLOGGED	GLOOPED
BLINKED	LISSOME	SLOBBED	CLOGGED	**LOOPER**
CLINKED	**LISTEN**	**LOBBER**	FLOGGED	BLOOPER
PLINKED	GLISTEN	CLOBBER	SLOGGED	LOOPERS

LOOSES	LOTTERY	BLOWERS	FLUFFED	BLUNGED
LOOSEST	**LOUCHE**	FLOWERS	PLUFFED	PLUNGED
LOOSIE	LOUCHER	GLOWERS	SLUFFED	**LUNGER**
FLOOSIE	**LOUGHS**	PLOWERS	**LUGGED**	BLUNGER
LOOSIES	CLOUGHS	**LOWERY**	GLUGGED	PLUNGER
LOPERS	PLOUGHS	FLOWERY	PLUGGED	LUNGERS
ELOPERS	SLOUGHS	**LOWEST**	SLUGGED	**LUNGES**
SLOPERS	**LOUNGE**	SLOWEST	**LUGGER**	BLUNGES
LOPING	LOUNGED	**LOWING**	PLUGGER	PLUNGES
ELOPING	LOUNGER	BLOWING	SLUGGER	**LUNIES**
SLOPING	LOUNGES	CLOWING	LUGGERS	LUNIEST
LOPPED	LOUNGEY	FLOWING	**LUGING**	**LUNKER**
CLOPPED	**LOURED**	GLOWING	KLUGING	BLUNKER
FLOPPED	CLOURED	PLOWING	LUGINGS	CLUNKER
GLOPPED	FLOURED	SLOWING	**LUMBER**	FLUNKER
PLOPPED	**LOURIE**	LOWINGS	CLUMBER	PLUNKER
SLOPPED	LOURIER	**LOWISH**	PLUMBER	LUNKERS
LOPPER	LOURIES	SLOWISH	SLUMBER	**LUNTED**
FLOPPER	**LOUSED**	**LOWNED**	LUMBERS	BLUNTED
LOPPERS	BLOUSED	CLOWNED	**LUMINA**	**LUNULA**
LORICA	FLOUSED	**LOWSED**	ALUMINA	LUNULAE
LORICAE	**LOUSES**	BLOWSED	LUMINAL	LUNULAR
LORICAS	BLOUSES	**LOWSES**	**LUMINE**	**LURDAN**
LORIES	FLOUSES	BLOWSES	ALUMINE	LURDANE
GLORIES	**LOUTED**	LOWSEST	LUMINED	LURDANS
LOSERS	CLOUTED	**LUBBER**	LUMINES	**LURVES**
CLOSERS	FLOUTED	BLUBBER	**LUMMOX**	SLURVES
LOSING	GLOUTED	CLUBBER	FLUMMOX	**LUSHED**
CLOSING	**LOUVRE**	FLUBBER	**LUMPED**	BLUSHED
LOSINGS	LOUVRED	SLUBBER	CLUMPED	FLUSHED
LOSSES	LOUVRES	LUBBERS	FLUMPED	PLUSHED
FLOSSES	**LOVERS**	**LUCERN**	PLUMPED	SLUSHED
GLOSSES	CLOVERS	LUCERNE	SLUMPED	**LUSHER**
LOTTED	GLOVERS	LUCERNS	**LUMPEN**	BLUSHER
BLOTTED	PLOVERS	**LUCHOT**	PLUMPEN	FLUSHER
CLOTTED	**LOVIES**	LUCHOTH	LUMPENS	PLUSHER
PLOTTED	LOVIEST	**LUCKED**	**LUMPER**	LUSHERS
SLOTTED	**LOVING**	CLUCKED	CLUMPER	**LUSHES**
LOTTER	GLOVING	PLUCKED	PLUMPER	BLUSHES
BLOTTER	LOVINGS	**LUCKIE**	LUMPERS	FLUSHES
CLOTTER	**LOWBOY**	LUCKIER	**LUNATE**	PLUSHES
PLOTTER	PLOWBOY	LUCKIES	LUNATED	SLUSHES
SLOTTER	LOWBOYS	**LUFFED**	LUNATES	LUSHEST
LOTTERS	**LOWERS**	BLUFFED	**LUNGED**	**LUSHLY**

PLUSHLY	MACULED	MANGLER	SMARTED	MATINGS
LUSTER	MACULES	MANGLES	**MARTEN**	**MATRIC**
BLUSTER	**MADAME**	**MANIOC**	SMARTEN	MATRICE
CLUSTER	MADAMED	MANIOCA	MARTENS	MATRICS
FLUSTER	MADAMES	MANIOCS	**MARTIN**	**MATTER**
LUSTERS	**MADRAS**	**MANITO**	MARTING	SMATTER
LUSTRA	MADRASA	MANITOS	MARTINI	MATTERS
LUSTRAL	**MAGGOT**	MANITOU	MARTINS	MATTERY
LUSTRE	MAGGOTS	**MANTLE**	**MARTYR**	**MATTIN**
LUSTRED	MAGGOTY	MANTLED	MARTYRS	MATTING
LUSTRES	**MAGISM**	MANTLES	MARTYRY	MATTINS
LUTEAL	IMAGISM	MANTLET	**MASCLE**	**MATURE**
GLUTEAL	MAGISMS	**MANTRA**	MASCLED	MATURED
PLUTEAL	**MAGNET**	MANTRAM	MASCLES	MATURER
LUTERS	MAGNETO	MANTRAP	**MASHED**	MATURES
FLUTERS	MAGNETS	MANTRAS	SMASHED	**MATZOT**
LUTING	**MAILED**	**MANURE**	**MASHER**	MATZOTH
ELUTING	EMAILED	MANURED	SMASHER	**MAUGRE**
FLUTING	**MAILER**	MANURER	MASHERS	MAUGRED
LUTINGS	EMAILER	MANURES	**MASHES**	MAUGRES
LUTIST	MAILERS	**MAPPER**	SMASHES	**MAUVES**
FLUTIST	**MALGRE**	MAPPERS	**MASHIE**	MAUVEST
LUTISTS	MALGRED	MAPPERY	MASHIER	**MAUVIN**
LUTZES	MALGRES	**MARBLE**	MASHIES	MAUVINE
KLUTZES	**MALICE**	MARBLED	**MASHUP**	MAUVINS
LUXATE	MALICED	MARBLER	SMASHUP	**MAXIMA**
LUXATED	MALICES	MARBLES	MASHUPS	MAXIMAL
LUXATES	**MALLED**	**MARINE**	**MASQUE**	**MAZING**
LUXING	SMALLED	MARINER	MASQUER	AMAZING
FLUXING	**MANAGE**	MARINES	MASQUES	**MEADOW**
LYINGS	MANAGED	**MARKKA**	**MASSED**	MEADOWS
FLYINGS	MANAGER	MARKKAA	AMASSED	MEADOWY
LYRATE	MANAGES	MARKKAS	**MASSES**	**MEAGRE**
LYRATED	**MANCHE**	**MARLIN**	AMASSES	MEAGRER
LYTING	MANCHES	MARLINE	**MASTER**	MEAGRES
FLYTING	MANCHET	MARLING	MASTERS	**MEALIE**
MACKLE	**MANDIR**	MARLINS	MASTERY	MEALIER
MACKLED	MANDIRA	**MARQUE**	**MASTIC**	MEALIES
MACKLES	MANDIRS	MARQUEE	MASTICH	**MEANES**
MACULA	**MANEGE**	MARQUES	MASTICS	MEANEST
MACULAE	MANEGED	**MARROW**	**MATIES**	**MEASLE**
MACULAR	MANEGES	MARROWS	MATIEST	MEASLED
MACULAS	**MANGLE**	MARROWY	**MATING**	MEASLES
MACULE	MANGLED	**MARTED**	AMATING	**MEATHS**

SMEATHS	MENDERS	**MICATE**	MILLIES	**MISUSE**
MEDDLE	**MENING**	EMICATE	**MIMOSA**	MISUSED
MEDDLED	AMENING	MICATED	MIMOSAE	MISUSER
MEDDLER	OMENING	MICATES	MIMOSAS	MISUSES
MEDDLES	**MENSCH**	**MICELL**	**MINGLE**	**MITERS**
MEDIAN	MENSCHY	MICELLA	MINGLED	SMITERS
MEDIANS	**MENTAL**	MICELLE	MINGLER	**MITTEN**
MEDIANT	AMENTAL	MICELLS	MINGLES	SMITTEN
MEDUSA	OMENTAL	**MICKLE**	**MINIMA**	MITTENS
MEDUSAE	**MENTUM**	MICKLER	MINIMAL	**MIZZLE**
MEDUSAL	AMENTUM	MICKLES	MINIMAX	MIZZLED
MEDUSAN	OMENTUM	**MICRON**	**MINUTE**	MIZZLES
MEDUSAS	**MERCER**	OMICRON	MINUTED	**MOBBLE**
MEGARA	AMERCER	MICRONS	MINUTER	MOBBLED
MEGARAD	MERCERS	**MIDDLE**	MINUTES	MOBBLES
MEGASS	MERCERY	MIDDLED	**MIRKER**	**MOCHIE**
MEGASSE	**MERCES**	MIDDLER	SMIRKER	MOCHIER
MEGILP	AMERCES	MIDDLES	**MISCUE**	**MOCKED**
MEGILPH	**MERGED**	**MIDGES**	MISCUED	SMOCKED
MEGILPS	EMERGED	SMIDGES	MISCUES	**MOCKER**
MELLED	**MERGES**	**MIDGIE**	**MISHAP**	MOCKERS
SMELLED	EMERGES	MIDGIER	MISHAPS	MOCKERY
MELLOW	**MERLIN**	MIDGIES	MISHAPT	**MODERN**
MELLOWS	MERLING	**MIGHTS**	**MISKEN**	MODERNE
MELLOWY	MERLINS	SMIGHTS	MISKENS	MODERNS
MELTED	**MERRIE**	MIGHTST	MISKENT	**MODEST**
SMELTED	MERRIER	**MIKRON**	**MISSEE**	MODESTY
MELTER	MERRIES	OMIKRON	MISSEEM	**MODIST**
SMELTER	**MESTOM**	MIKRONS	MISSEEN	MODISTE
MELTERS	MESTOME	**MIKVOT**	MISSEES	MODISTS
MENACE	MESTOMS	MIKVOTH	**MISSEL**	**MOILED**
MENACED	**METICS**	**MILDEW**	MISSELL	SMOILED
MENACER	EMETICS	MILDEWS	MISSELS	**MOILES**
MENACES	**METTLE**	MILDEWY	**MISSES**	SMOILES
MENAGE	METTLED	**MILERS**	AMISSES	**MOLDER**
AMENAGE	METTLES	SMILERS	**MISSIS**	SMOLDER
MENAGED	**MEUSES**	**MILIEU**	MISSISH	MOLDERS
MENAGES	SMEUSES	MILIEUS	**MISTER**	**MOLINE**
MENDED	**MEZUZA**	MILIEUX	MISTERM	MOLINES
AMENDED	MEZUZAH	**MILING**	MISTERS	MOLINET
EMENDED	MEZUZAS	SMILING	MISTERY	**MOLTEN**
MENDER	**MIASMA**	MILINGS	**MISTLE**	YMOLTEN
AMENDER	MIASMAL	**MILLIE**	MISTLED	**MOMENT**
EMENDER	MIASMAS	MILLIER	MISTLES	MOMENTA

MOMENTO	MOTHERY	MOZZLES	MUMMERS	**MUTTON**
MOMENTS	**MOTION**	**MUCHEL**	MUMMERY	MUTTONS
MONERA	AMOTION	MUCHELL	**MUNGED**	MUTTONY
MONERAN	EMOTION	MUCHELS	EMUNGED	**MUZZLE**
MONGER	MOTIONS	**MUCOSA**	**MUNGES**	MUZZLED
MONGERS	**MOTIVE**	MUCOSAE	EMUNGES	MUZZLER
MONGERY	EMOTIVE	MUCOSAL	**MUNITE**	MUZZLES
MONGST	MOTIVED	MUCOSAS	MUNITED	**MYELIN**
AMONGST	MOTIVES	**MUDDLE**	MUNITES	MYELINE
EMONGST	**MOTTLE**	MUDDLED	**MUNTIN**	MYELINS
MONTAN	MOTTLED	MUDDLER	MUNTING	**NAGGED**
MONTANE	MOTTLER	MUDDLES	MUNTINS	SNAGGED
MONTANT	MOTTLES	**MUDGED**	**MURING**	**NAGGER**
MOOLVI	**MOUNTS**	SMUDGED	EMURING	SNAGGER
MOOLVIE	AMOUNTS	**MUDGER**	**MURLIN**	NAGGERS
MOOLVIS	**MOUSED**	SMUDGER	MURLING	**NAILED**
MOORED	SMOUSED	MUDGERS	MURLINS	SNAILED
SMOORED	**MOUSER**	**MUDGES**	**MURRIN**	**NAILER**
MOOTED	SMQUSER	SMUDGES	MURRINE	NAILERS
SMOOTED	MOUSERS	**MUFFIN**	MURRINS	NAILERY
MOOVED	MOUSERY	MUFFING	**MUSCLE**	**NAIVES**
AMOOVED	**MOUSES**	MUFFINS	MUSCLED	NAIVEST
MOOVES	SMOUSES	**MUFFLE**	MUSCLES	**NANDIN**
AMOOVES	**MOUSIE**	MUFFLED	MUSCLEY	NANDINA
MORALL	MOUSIER	MUFFLER	**MUSERS**	NANDINE
MORALLS	MOUSIES	MUFFLES	AMUSERS	NANDINS
MORALLY	**MOUSLE**	**MUGGED**	**MUSHED**	**NANISM**
MORASS	MOUSLED	SMUGGED	SMUSHED	ONANISM
MORASSY	MOUSLES	**MUGGER**	**MUSHES**	NANISMS
MOROSE	**MOUSME**	SMUGGER	SMUSHES	**NANNIE**
MOROSER	MOUSMEE	MUGGERS	**MUSING**	NANNIED
MORTAR	MOUSMES	**MUGGLE**	AMUSING	NANNIES
MORTARS	**MOUSSE**	SMUGGLE	MUSINGS	**NANOBE**
MORTARY	MOUSSED	MUGGLES	**MUSIVE**	NANOBEE
MORULA	MOUSSES	**MULING**	AMUSIVE	NANOBES
MORULAE	**MOVING**	EMULING	**MUSKIE**	**NAPPED**
MORULAR	AMOVING	**MULMUL**	MUSKIER	KNAPPED
MORULAS	EMOVING	MULMULL	MUSKIES	SNAPPED
MOSSIE	**MOYLED**	MULMULS	**MUTATE**	**NAPPER**
MOSSIER	SMOYLED	**MUMBLE**	MUTATED	KNAPPER
MOSSIES	**MOYLES**	MUMBLED	MUTATES	SNAPPER
MOTHER	SMOYLES	MUMBLER	**MUTINE**	NAPPERS
SMOTHER	**MOZZLE**	MUMBLES	MUTINED	**NAPPIE**
MOTHERS	MOZZLED	**MUMMER**	MUTINES	NAPPIER

NAPPIES	SNEEZES	NIDATED	NITROSO	**NOODGE**
NARCOS	**NEGATE**	NIDATES	**NKOSIS**	NOODGED
NARCOSE	NEGATED	**NIDING**	INKOSIS	NOODGES
NATION	NEGATER	SNIDING	**NOBBLE**	**NOODLE**
ENATION	NEGATES	NIDINGS	KNOBBLE	NOODLED
NATIONS	**NERVED**	**NIFFED**	NOBBLED	NOODLES
NATTER	ENERVED	SNIFFED	NOBBLER	**NOOKIE**
NATTERS	**NERVES**	**NIFFER**	NOBBLES	NOOKIER
NATTERY	ENERVES	SNIFFER	**NOBLES**	NOOKIES
NATURA	**NESTLE**	NIFFERS	NOBLEST	**NOOSES**
NATURAE	NESTLED	**NIGGER**	**NOCKED**	SNOOSES
NATURAL	NESTLER	SNIGGER	KNOCKED	**NOSHER**
NATURE	NESTLES	NIGGERS	**NODDED**	NOSHERS
NATURED	**NETTIE**	NIGGERY	SNODDED	NOSHERY
NATURES	NETTIER	**NIGGLE**	**NODDER**	**NOSIES**
NAUGHT	NETTIES	SNIGGLE	SNODDER	NOSIEST
NAUGHTS	**NETTLE**	NIGGLED	NODDERS	**NOTATE**
NAUGHTY	NETTLED	NIGGLER	**NODDLE**	NOTATED
NEAPED	NETTLER	NIGGLES	NODDLED	NOTATES
SNEAPED	NETTLES	**NIGHTS**	NODDLES	**NOTHER**
NEARED	**NEURON**	KNIGHTS	**NODULE**	ANOTHER
ANEARED	NEURONE	**NIMBLE**	NODULED	**NOTICE**
UNEARED	NEURONS	NIMBLER	NODULES	NOTICED
NEATEN	**NEWING**	**NIPPED**	**NOESES**	NOTICER
UNEATEN	ENEWING	SNIPPED	ANOESES	NOTICES
NEATENS	**NEWSIE**	**NIPPER**	**NOESIS**	**NOUSLE**
NEBBED	NEWSIER	SNIPPER	ANOESIS	NOUSLED
SNEBBED	NEWSIES	NIPPERS	**NOETIC**	NOUSLES
NEBULA	**NIBBED**	**NIPPLE**	ANOETIC	**NOVATE**
NEBULAE	SNIBBED	NIPPLED	**NOGGED**	NOVATED
NEBULAR	**NIBBLE**	NIPPLES	SNOGGED	NOVATES
NEBULAS	NIBBLED	**NIRLIE**	**NOGGIN**	**NOVENA**
NECKED	NIBBLER	NIRLIER	NOGGING	NOVENAE
SNECKED	NIBBLES	**NISHES**	NOGGINS	NOVENAS
NECTAR	**NICKED**	KNISHES	**NOINTS**	**NUANCE**
NECTARS	SNICKED	**NITERS**	ANOINTS	NUANCED
NECTARY	**NICKER**	UNITERS	**NOMINA**	NUANCES
NEEDLE	KNICKER	**NITRID**	NOMINAL	**NUBBED**
NEEDLED	SNICKER	NITRIDE	**NONAGE**	SNUBBED
NEEDLER	NICKERS	NITRIDS	NONAGED	**NUBBIN**
NEEDLES	**NICKLE**	**NITRIL**	NONAGES	NUBBING
NEEZED	NICKLED	NITRILE	**NONUSE**	NUBBINS
SNEEZED	NICKLES	NITRILS	NONUSER	**NUBBLE**
NEEZES	**NIDATE**	**NITROS**	NONUSES	KNUBBLE

NUBBLED	OAKIEST	**OCHERS**	GOFFING	**OLDIES**
NUBBLES	**OARIER**	TOCHERS	OFFINGS	COLDIES
NUBBLY	HOARIER	**OCHREA**	**OFFISH**	GOLDIES
KNUBBLY	ROARIER	OCHREAE	TOFFISH	**OLDISH**
NUCLEI	**OARING**	OCHREAS	**OFTEST**	COLDISH
NUCLEIC	HOARING	**OCKERS**	SOFTEST	GOLDISH
NUCLEIN	ROARING	COCKERS	**OGGINS**	**OLEFIN**
NUDGED	SOARING	DOCKERS	HOGGINS	OLEFINE
SNUDGED	**OATERS**	HOCKERS	NOGGINS	OLEFINS
NUDGES	BOATERS	LOCKERS	**OGLING**	**OLIVES**
SNUDGES	COATERS	MOCKERS	BOGLING	SOLIVES
NUGGET	DOATERS	ROCKERS	OGLINGS	**OLLERS**
NUGGETS	**OATIER**	**OCTETT**	**OILERS**	GOLLERS
NUGGETY	GOATIER	OCTETTE	BOILERS	HOLLERS
NURDLE	**OBANGS**	OCTETTS	COILERS	JOLLERS
NURDLED	GOBANGS	**OCULAR**	MOILERS	LOLLERS
NURDLES	KOBANGS	JOCULAR	TOILERS	POLLERS
NURLED	**OBDURE**	LOCULAR	**OILERY**	ROLLERS
KNURLED	OBDURED	VOCULAR	BOILERY	SOLLERS
NURSER	OBDURES	OCULARS	**OILIER**	TOLLERS
NURSERS	**OBECHE**	**OCULUS**	NOILIER	**OLLIED**
NURSERY	BOBECHE	LOCULUS	ROILIER	COLLIED
NURSLE	OBECHES	**ODISMS**	SOILIER	DOLLIED
NURSLED	**OBELIA**	IODISMS	**OILING**	FOLLIED
NURSLES	LOBELIA	**ODISTS**	BOILING	GOLLIED
NUTATE	OBELIAS	CODISTS	COILING	JOLLIED
NUTATED	**OBJURE**	MODISTS	FOILING	**OLLIES**
NUTATES	OBJURED	**ODIUMS**	MOILING	COLLIES
NUTTER	OBJURES	PODIUMS	ROILING	DOLLIES
NUTTERS	**OBLAST**	SODIUMS	SOILING	FOLLIES
NUTTERY	OBLASTI	**OFFERS**	TOILING	GOLLIES
NUZZLE	OBLASTS	COFFERS	**OINKED**	HOLLIES
SNUZZLE	**OBLIGE**	DOFFERS	BOINKED	JOLLIES
NUZZLED	OBLIGED	GOFFERS	**OINTED**	LOLLIES
NUZZLER	OBLIGEE	**OFFICE**	JOINTED	MOLLIES
NUZZLES	OBLIGER	OFFICER	NOINTED	POLLIES
NYALAS	OBLIGES	OFFICES	POINTED	ROLLIES
INYALAS	**OBOLES**	**OFFIES**	**OLDENS**	TOLLIES
NYMPHA	SOBOLES	MOFFIES	BOLDENS	WOLLIES
NYMPHAE	**OBTUSE**	TOFFIES	GOLDENS	**OMBERS**
NYMPHAL	OBTUSER	**OFFING**	**OLDEST**	BOMBERS
OAKERS	**OCCIES**	BOFFING	BOLDEST	COMBERS
SOAKERS	BOCCIES	COFFING	COLDEST	SOMBERS
OAKIES	MOCCIES	DOFFING	GOLDEST	**OMBRES**

HOMBRES	ROOFIER	WOOZILY	**ORBITA**	**ORTHOS**
SOMBRES	WOOFIER	**OOZING**	ORBITAL	PORTHOS
OMENTA	**OOGAMY**	BOOZING	ORBITAS	**OSCULA**
LOMENTA	ZOOGAMY	**OPAQUE**	**ORCINE**	OSCULAR
MOMENTA	**OOGENY**	OPAQUED	PORCINE	**OSIERS**
TOMENTA	ZOOGENY	OPAQUER	ORCINES	COSIERS
OMENTAL	**OOHING**	OPAQUES	**ORDERS**	HOSIERS
ONDING	BOOHING	**OPERAS**	BORDERS	ROSIERS
BONDING	POOHING	POPERAS	CORDERS	**OSIERY**
FONDING	OOHINGS	**OPIATE**	**ORDURE**	HOSIERY
PONDING	**OOIDAL**	OPIATED	BORDURE	**OSMOSE**
ONDINGS	ZOOIDAL	OPIATES	ORDURES	OSMOSED
ONEYER	**OOLITE**	**OPPOSE**	**ORGANS**	OSMOSES
BONEYER	ZOOLITE	OPPOSED	MORGANS	**OSMUND**
MONEYER	OOLITES	OPPOSER	**ORGIAS**	OSMUNDA
ONEYERS	**OOLITH**	OPPOSES	GORGIAS	OSMUNDS
ONIONS	ZOOLITH	**OPTERS**	ORGIAST	**OSTLER**
RONIONS	OOLITHS	COPTERS	**ORGIES**	HOSTLER
ONIUMS	**OOLOGY**	**OPTIMA**	PORGIES	JOSTLER
CONIUMS	NOOLOGY	OPTIMAL	**ORGONE**	OSTLERS
IONIUMS	ZOOLOGY	**OPUSES**	FORGONE	**OTHERS**
ONLINE	**OOMIAC**	MOPUSES	ORGONES	BOTHERS
ONLINER	OOMIACK	**ORACLE**	**ORGUES**	FOTHERS
ONNING	OOMIACS	CORACLE	MORGUES	MOTHERS
CONNING	**OOPING**	ORACLED	**ORIGAN**	POTHERS
DONNING	COOPING	ORACLES	ORIGANE	ROTHERS
FONNING	HOOPING	**ORALLY**	ORIGANS	TOTHERS
KONNING	LOOPING	MORALLY	**ORMERS**	**OTTARS**
RONNING	MOOPING	**ORANGE**	DORMERS	COTTARS
WONNING	POOPING	ORANGER	FORMERS	**OTTERS**
ONUSES	ROOPING	ORANGES	WORMERS	COTTERS
BONUSES	SOOPING	ORANGEY	**ORNATE**	DOTTERS
NONUSES	**OORALI**	**ORARIA**	ORNATER	HOTTERS
TONUSES	WOORALI	ORARIAN	**OROGEN**	JOTTERS
OODLES	OORALIS	**ORATED**	OROGENS	LOTTERS
BOODLES	**OORIER**	BORATED	OROGENY	POTTERS
DOODLES	MOORIER	**ORATES**	**ORPHIC**	ROTTERS
NOODLES	**OOSIER**	BORATES	MORPHIC	TOTTERS
POODLES	GOOSIER	**ORATOR**	**ORPINE**	**OUBITS**
TOODLES	**OOZIER**	ORATORS	FORPINE	WOUBITS
OOFIER	BOOZIER	ORATORY	ORPINES	**OUCHED**
BOOFIER	WOOZIER	**ORBING**	**ORRICE**	COUCHED
GOOFIER	**OOZILY**	SORBING	MORRICE	DOUCHED
POOFIER	BOOZILY	ZORBING	ORRICES	GOUCHED

MOUCHED	**OURIER**	**OUTRAN**	LOVERED	**OXYGEN**
POUCHED	COURIER	OUTRANG	**OVERGO**	LOXYGEN
ROUCHED	LOURIER	OUTRANK	OVERGOT	OXYGENS
TOUCHED	**OUSELS**	**OUTRED**	**OVERLY**	**OYESES**
VOUCHED	HOUSELS	FOUTRED	LOVERLY	NOYESES
OUCHES	**OUSTED**	OUTREDS	**OVINES**	**OYSTER**
BOUCHES	JOUSTED	**OUTRUN**	BOVINES	ROYSTER
COUCHES	MOUSTED	OUTRUNG	COVINES	OYSTERS
DOUCHES	ROUSTED	OUTRUNS	**OVULAR**	**OZZIES**
GOUCHES	**OUSTER**	**OUTSEE**	OVULARY	COZZIES
MOUCHES	JOUSTER	OUTSEEN	**OWLERS**	MOZZIES
POUCHES	ROUSTER	OUTSEES	BOWLERS	POZZIES
ROUCHES	OUSTERS	**OUTSIN**	FOWLERS	**PACERS**
TOUCHES	**OUTBAR**	OUTSING	HOWLERS	SPACERS
VOUCHES	OUTBARK	OUTSINS	JOWLERS	**PACIER**
OUGHLY	OUTBARS	**OUTVIE**	YOWLERS	SPACIER
ROUGHLY	**OUTERS**	OUTVIED	**OWLETS**	**PACIFY**
TOUGHLY	COUTERS	OUTVIES	HOWLETS	OPACIFY
OUGHTS	DOUTERS	**OUTWAR**	**OWLIER**	**PACING**
BOUGHTS	FOUTERS	OUTWARD	DOWLIER	SPACING
NOUGHTS	MOUTERS	OUTWARS	JOWLIER	PACINGS
OUGLIE	POUTERS	**OUTWIN**	LOWLIER	**PADDLE**
OUGLIED	ROUTERS	OUTWIND	**OWLING**	PADDLED
OUGLIES	SOUTERS	OUTWING	BOWLING	PADDLER
OULDER	TOUTERS	OUTWINS	COWLING	PADDLES
BOULDER	**OUTFLY**	**OUTWIT**	FOWLING	**PAESAN**
FOULDER	GOUTFLY	OUTWITH	GOWLING	PAESANI
MOULDER	**OUTHER**	OUTWITS	HOWLING	PAESANO
POULDER	COUTHER	**OUVERT**	JOWLING	PAESANS
OUNCES	MOUTHER	COUVERT	SOWLING	**PAINED**
BOUNCES	POUTHER	OUVERTE	YOWLING	SPAINED
JOUNCES	SOUTHER	**OVATED**	**OWNERS**	**PAIOCK**
POUNCES	**OUTING**	NOVATED	DOWNERS	PAIOCKE
ROUNCES	DOUTING	**OVATES**	**OWNING**	PAIOCKS
OUPING	HOUTING	BOVATES	BOWNING	**PAIRES**
COUPING	LOUTING	NOVATES	DOWNING	PAIREST
LOUPING	POUTING	**OVENED**	GOWNING	**PAISAN**
MOUPING	ROUTING	DOVENED	LOWNING	PAISANA
POUPING	TOUTING	**OVERDO**	**OXLIKE**	PAISANO
ROUPING	OUTINGS	OVERDOG	BOXLIKE	PAISANS
SOUPING	**OUTLIE**	**OVERED**	FOXLIKE	**PAJOCK**
OURALI	OUTLIED	COVERED	**OXTAIL**	PAJOCKE
WOURALI	OUTLIER	DOVERED	FOXTAIL	PAJOCKS
OURALIS	OUTLIES	HOVERED	OXTAILS	**PALACE**

PALACED	PAPULAS	PARROTS	**PAUNCH**	**PEERED**
PALACES	**PARADE**	PARROTY	PAUNCHY	SPEERED
PALAMA	PARADED	**PARSER**	**PAVINS**	**PEERIE**
PALAMAE	PARADER	SPARSER	SPAVINS	PEERIER
PALATE	PARADES	PARSERS	**PAVISE**	PEERIES
PALATED	**PARDAL**	**PARTAN**	PAVISER	**PEISES**
PALATES	PARDALE	SPARTAN	PAVISES	SPEISES
PALLED	PARDALS	PARTANS	**PAWNED**	**PELLED**
SPALLED	**PARERS**	**PARVIS**	SPAWNED	SPELLED
PALLIA	SPARERS	PARVISE	**PAWNER**	**PELTAS**
PALLIAL	**PARGED**	**PASTER**	SPAWNER	PELTAST
PALMAR	SPARGED	PASTERN	PAWNERS	**PELTER**
PALMARY	**PARGES**	PASTERS	**PAYING**	SPELTER
PALMIE	SPARGES	**PASTIE**	APAYING	PELTERS
PALMIER	**PARING**	PASTIER	SPAYING	**PENCES**
PALMIES	SPARING	PASTIES	PAYINGS	SPENCES
PALMIET	PARINGS	**PASTIL**	**PEANED**	**PENDED**
PAMPER	**PARKED**	PASTILS	SPEANED	UPENDED
PAMPERO	SPARKED	PASTILY	**PEARCE**	**PENING**
PAMPERS	**PARKER**	**PATERA**	PEARCED	OPENING
PANDAN	SPARKER	PATERAE	PEARCES	**PENSIL**
PANDANI	PARKERS	**PATERS**	**PEBBLE**	PENSILE
PANDANS	**PARKIE**	EPATERS	PEBBLED	PENSILS
PANGED	SPARKIE	**PATHED**	PEBBLES	**PEOPLE**
SPANGED	PARKIER	SPATHED	**PECKED**	PEOPLED
PANGEN	PARKIES	**PATHIC**	SPECKED	PEOPLER
PANGENE	**PARKIN**	SPATHIC	**PEDDLE**	PEOPLES
PANGENS	PARKING	PATHICS	PEDDLED	**PEPPER**
PANICK	PARKINS	**PATINA**	PEDDLER	PEPPERS
PANICKS	**PARKIS**	PATINAE	PEDDLES	PEPPERY
PANICKY	PARKISH	PATINAS	**PEDLAR**	**PEPSIN**
PANING	**PARKLY**	**PATINE**	PEDLARS	PEPSINE
SPANING	SPARKLY	PATINED	PEDLARY	PEPSINS
PANNED	**PAROLE**	PATINES	**PEDLER**	**PEPTID**
SPANNED	PAROLED	**PATTED**	PEDLERS	PEPTIDE
PANNER	PAROLEE	SPATTED	PEDLERY	PEPTIDS
SPANNER	PAROLES	**PATTEE**	**PEELED**	**PERCEN**
PANNERS	**PARPEN**	SPATTEE	SPEELED	PERCENT
PAPAYA	PARPEND	**PATTER**	**PEELER**	**PERDUE**
PAPAYAN	PARPENS	SPATTER	SPEELER	EPERDUE
PAPAYAS	PARPENT	PATTERN	PEELERS	PERDUES
PAPULA	**PARRED**	PATTERS	**PEENGE**	**PERFIN**
PAPULAE	SPARRED	**PATTES**	PEENGED	PERFING
PAPULAR	**PARROT**	PATTEST	PEENGES	PERFINS

PERKIN	PHEEZED	**PICOTE**	**PILULA**	PIRATES
PERKING	PHEEZES	PICOTED	PILULAE	**PISTOL**
PERKINS	**PHENES**	PICOTEE	PILULAR	PISTOLE
PEROGI	SPHENES	**PIDDLE**	PILULAS	PISTOLS
PEROGIE	**PHENIC**	PIDDLED	**PIMENT**	**PITARA**
PEROGIS	SPHENIC	PIDDLER	PIMENTO	PITARAH
PERSES	**PHENOM**	PIDDLES	PIMENTS	PITARAS
SPERSES	PHENOME	**PIERCE**	**PIMPLE**	**PITTED**
PERSON	PHENOMS	PIERCED	PIMPLED	SPITTED
PERSONA	**PHESES**	PIERCER	PIMPLES	**PITTEN**
PERSONS	APHESES	PIERCES	**PINGLE**	SPITTEN
PERSUE	**PHLEGM**	**PIEROG**	PINGLED	**PITTER**
PERSUED	PHLEGMS	PIEROGI	PINGLER	SPITTER
PERSUES	PHLEGMY	PIEROGS	PINGLES	PITTERS
PERUKE	**PHONIC**	**PIFFLE**	PINIER	**PIZAZZ**
PERUKED	APHONIC	PIFFLED	SPINIER	PIZAZZY
PERUKES	PHONICS	PIFFLER	**PINIES**	**PIZZAZ**
PERUSE	**PHOTIC**	PIFFLES	PINIEST	PIZZAZZ
PERUSED	APHOTIC	**PIGGIE**	**PINING**	**PLACIT**
PERUSER	PHOTICS	PIGGIER	OPINING	PLACITA
PERUSES	**PHRASE**	PIGGIES	**PINION**	PLACITS
PESANT	PHRASED	**PIGGIN**	OPINION	**PLAGUE**
PESANTE	PHRASER	PIGGING	PINIONS	PLAGUED
PESANTS	PHRASES	PIGGINS	**PINKED**	PLAGUER
PESTLE	**PIAFFE**	**PIGHTS**	SPINKED	PLAGUES
PESTLED	PIAFFED	SPIGHTS	**PINKEY**	PLAGUEY
PESTLES	PIAFFER	**PIGMEN**	PINKEYE	**PLANCH**
PETTLE	PIAFFES	PIGMENT	PINKEYS	PLANCHE
PETTLED	**PICENE**	**PIKERS**	**PINKIE**	**PLANTA**
PETTLES	EPICENE	SPIKERS	PINKIER	PLANTAE
PEWTER	PICENES	**PIKING**	PINKIES	PLANTAR
PEWTERS	**PICKAX**	SPIKING	**PINNER**	PLANTAS
PEWTERY	PICKAXE	PIKINGS	SPINNER	**PLASHY**
PHALLI	**PICKER**	**PILFER**	PINNERS	SPLASHY
PHALLIC	SPICKER	PILFERS	**PINNET**	**PLASTE**
PHALLIN	PICKERS	PILFERY	SPINNET	PLASTER
PHANGS	PICKERY	**PILING**	PINNETS	**PLATAN**
UPHANGS	**PICKIN**	SPILING	**PINTOS**	PLATANE
PHASIC	PICKING	PILINGS	SPINTOS	PLATANS
APHASIC	PICKINS	**PILLED**	**PIPPIN**	**PLAYED**
PHEESE	**PICKLE**	SPILLED	PIPPING	SPLAYED
PHEESED	PICKLED	**PILLOW**	PIPPINS	**PLEADS**
PHEESES	PICKLER	PILLOWS	**PIRATE**	UPLEADS
PHEEZE	PICKLES	PILLOWY	PIRATED	**PLEASE**

PLEASED	PODDLES	POONCED	POTCHES	UPRATES
PLEASER	**PODIUM**	POONCES	**POTHER**	**PRAYED**
PLEASES	SPODIUM	**POORER**	POTHERB	SPRAYED
PLEDGE	PODIUMS	SPOORER	POTHERS	**PRAYER**
PLEDGED	**POINTE**	**POORIS**	POTHERY	SPRAYER
PLEDGEE	POINTED	POORISH	**POTTED**	PRAYERS
PLEDGER	POINTEL	**POOTLE**	SPOTTED	**PREACE**
PLEDGES	POINTER	POOTLED	**POTTER**	PREACED
PLEDGET	POINTES	POOTLES	SPOTTER	PREACES
PLENTY	**POKIES**	**POPPLE**	POTTERS	**PREACH**
APLENTY	POKIEST	POPPLED	POTTERY	UPREACH
PLEURA	**POKING**	POPPLES	**POUFFE**	PREACHY
PLEURAE	SPOKING	**PORING**	POUFFED	**PREASE**
PLEURAL	**POLEAX**	SPORING	POUFFES	PREASED
PLEURAS	POLEAXE	**PORTED**	**POUNCE**	PREASES
PLIGHT	**POLICE**	SPORTED	POUNCED	**PRECIP**
UPLIGHT	POLICED	**PORTER**	POUNCER	PRECIPE
YPLIGHT	POLICER	SPORTER	POUNCES	PRECIPS
PLIGHTS	POLICES	PORTERS	POUNCET	**PRECIS**
PLINKS	**POLITE**	**POSHES**	**POUTED**	PRECISE
UPLINKS	POLITER	SPOSHES	SPOUTED	**PREEVE**
PLODGE	**POLLEN**	POSHEST	**POUTER**	PREEVED
SPLODGE	POLLENS	**POSIES**	SPOUTER	PREEVES
PLODGED	POLLENT	POSIEST	POUTERS	**PREMIE**
PLODGES	**POLYPE**	**POSSUM**	**POWDER**	PREMIER
PLONGE	POLYPED	OPOSSUM	POWDERS	PREMIES
PLONGED	POLYPES	POSSUMS	POWDERY	**PREMIX**
PLONGES	**POMADE**	**POSTER**	**PRAISE**	PREMIXT
PLOOKS	POMADED	POSTERN	UPRAISE	**PRENTS**
UPLOOKS	POMADES	POSTERS	PRAISED	SPRENTS
PLOVER	**POMMEL**	**POSTIL**	PRAISER	**PRESTS**
PLOVERS	POMMELE	APOSTIL	PRAISES	UPRESTS
PLOVERY	POMMELS	POSTILS	**PRANCE**	**PREVUE**
PLUNGE	**PONGED**	**POSTIN**	PRANCED	PREVUED
PLUNGED	SPONGED	POSTING	PRANCER	PREVUES
PLUNGER	**PONTIL**	POSTINS	PRANCES	**PREWAR**
PLUNGES	PONTILE	**POTAGE**	**PRANCK**	PREWARM
PLYING	PONTILS	POTAGER	PRANCKE	PREWARN
UPLYING	**POOLED**	POTAGES	PRANCKS	**PRIAPI**
PODDIE	SPOOLED	**POTASS**	**PRANGS**	PRIAPIC
PODDIER	**POOLER**	POTASSA	SPRANGS	**PRIEST**
PODDIES	SPOOLER	**POTCHE**	**PRATED**	SPRIEST
PODDLE	POOLERS	POTCHED	UPRATED	PRIESTS
PODDLED	**POONCE**	POTCHER	**PRATES**	**PRIEVE**

PRIEVED	PROYNED	**PUNKIE**	QABALAH	**QUINTA**
PRIEVES	PROYNES	SPUNKIE	QABALAS	QUINTAL
PRIMER	**PRUTOT**	PUNKIER	**QAWWAL**	QUINTAN
PRIMERO	PRUTOTH	PUNKIES	QAWWALI	QUINTAR
PRIMERS	**PSYCHE**	**PUPATE**	QAWWALS	QUINTAS
PRINCE	PSYCHED	PUPATED	**QUAERE**	**QUINTE**
PRINCED	PSYCHES	PUPATES	QUAERED	QUINTES
PRINCES	**PTERIA**	**PURFLE**	QUAERES	QUINTET
PRINTS	APTERIA	PURFLED	**QUAILS**	**QUINTS**
SPRINTS	**PTOTIC**	PURFLER	SQUAILS	SQUINTS
PRISER	APTOTIC	PURFLES	**QUANTA**	**QUIRED**
UPRISER	**PUCKER**	**PURGES**	QUANTAL	SQUIRED
PRISERE	PUCKERS	SPURGES	**QUANTS**	**QUIRES**
PRISERS	PUCKERY	**PURLIN**	EQUANTS	SQUIRES
PRISES	**PUDDER**	PURLINE	**QUARER**	**QUIRTS**
UPRISES	SPUDDER	PURLING	SQUARER	SQUIRTS
PROBIT	PUDDERS	PURLINS	**QUARKS**	**QUITCH**
PROBITS	**PUDDLE**	**PURPLE**	SQUARKS	SQUITCH
PROBITY	SPUDDLE	PURPLED	**QUARTE**	**QUITES**
PROINE	PUDDLED	PURPLER	QUARTER	EQUITES
PROINED	PUDDLER	PURPLES	QUARTES	**QUIVER**
PROINES	PUDDLES	**PURRED**	QUARTET	AQUIVER
PROLLS	**PUFFER**	SPURRED	**QUARTZ**	QUIVERS
UPROLLS	PUFFERS	**PURSUE**	QUARTZY	QUIVERY
PRONES	PUFFERY	PURSUED	**QUATES**	**RABBET**
PRONEST	**PUFFIN**	PURSUER	EQUATES	DRABBET
PROPYL	PUFFING	PURSUES	**QUAVER**	RABBETS
PROPYLA	PUFFINS	**PUTTER**	QUAVERS	**RABBIT**
PROPYLS	**PUGGIE**	SPUTTER	QUAVERY	CRABBIT
PROTEA	PUGGIER	PUTTERS	**QUEACH**	FRABBIT
PROTEAN	PUGGIES	**PUTTIE**	QUEACHY	RABBITO
PROTEAS	**PUGGLE**	PUTTIED	**QUELCH**	RABBITS
PROTEI	PUGGLED	PUTTIER	SQUELCH	RABBITY
PROTEID	PUGGLES	PUTTIES	**QUICHE**	**RABBLE**
PROTEIN	**PUMICE**	**PUZZLE**	QUICHED	BRABBLE
PROTYL	PUMICED	PUZZLED	QUICHES	DRABBLE
PROTYLE	PUMICER	PUZZLER	**QUILLS**	GRABBLE
PROTYLS	PUMICES	PUZZLES	SQUILLS	PRABBLE
PROVEN	**PUMMEL**	**PYLORI**	**QUINES**	RABBLED
PROVEND	PUMMELO	PYLORIC	EQUINES	RABBLER
PROVER	PUMMELS	**PYRROL**	**QUININ**	RABBLES
PROVERB	**PUNGLE**	PYRROLE	QUININA	**RACEME**
PROVERS	PUNGLED	PYRROLS	QUININE	RACEMED
PROYNE	PUNGLES	**QABALA**	QUININS	RACEMES

RACERS	RADIALE	BRAILED	RAMBLER	FRANKED
BRACERS	RADIALS	DRAILED	RAMBLES	PRANKED
TRACERS	**RADIAN**	TRAILED	**RAMMED**	TRANKED
RACHES	RADIANS	**RAILER**	CRAMMED	**RANKER**
BRACHES	RADIANT	FRAILER	DRAMMED	CRANKER
ORACHES	**RADULA**	TRAILER	TRAMMED	FRANKER
RACHET	RADULAE	RAILERS	**RAMMEL**	RANKERS
BRACHET	RADULAR	**RAILES**	TRAMMEL	**RANKES**
RACHETS	RADULAS	GRAILES	RAMMELS	RANKEST
RACHIS	**RAFFLE**	**RAILLY**	**RAMMER**	**RANKLE**
ARACHIS	RAFFLED	FRAILLY	CRAMMER	CRANKLE
RACING	RAFFLER	**RAINED**	RAMMERS	PRANKLE
BRACING	RAFFLES	BRAINED	**RAMPED**	RANKLED
GRACING	**RAFTED**	DRAINED	CRAMPED	RANKLES
TRACING	CRAFTED	GRAINED	TRAMPED	**RANKLY**
RACINGS	DRAFTED	TRAINED	**RAMPER**	CRANKLY
RACKED	GRAFTED	**RAINES**	CRAMPER	FRANKLY
CRACKED	**RAFTER**	GRAINES	TRAMPER	**RANSOM**
FRACKED	CRAFTER	**RAIRDS**	RAMPERS	TRANSOM
TRACKED	DRAFTER	BRAIRDS	**RANCED**	RANSOMS
WRACKED	GRAFTER	**RAISED**	PRANCED	**RANTED**
RACKER	RAFTERS	ARAISED	TRANCED	DRANTED
CRACKER	**RAGEES**	BRAISED	**RANCES**	GRANTED
FRACKER	DRAGEES	FRAISED	PRANCES	TRANTED
TRACKER	**RAGGED**	PRAISED	TRANCES	**RANTER**
RACKERS	BRAGGED	**RAISER**	**RANDED**	GRANTER
RACKET	CRAGGED	PRAISER	BRANDED	TRANTER
BRACKET	DRAGGED	RAISERS	**RANDIE**	RANTERS
CRACKET	FRAGGED	**RAISES**	RANDIER	**RANULA**
RACKETS	RAGGEDY	ARAISES	RANDIES	RANULAR
RACKETT	**RAGGLE**	BRAISES	**RANGED**	RANULAS
RACKETY	DRAGGLE	FRAISES	PRANGED	**RAPERS**
RACKLE	RAGGLED	PRAISES	WRANGED	DRAPERS
CRACKLE	RAGGLES	**RAISIN**	**RANGER**	**RAPIER**
GRACKLE	**RAGMEN**	RAISING	FRANGER	CRAPIER
RACKLES	RAGMENT	RAISINS	GRANGER	DRAPIER
RADDED	**RAIDED**	RAISINY	ORANGER	GRAPIER
BRADDED	BRAIDED	**RAKING**	RANGERS	RAPIERS
RADDLE	**RAIDER**	BRAKING	**RANGES**	**RAPING**
RADDLED	BRAIDER	CRAKING	GRANGES	CRAPING
RADDLES	RAIDERS	RAKINGS	ORANGES	DRAPING
RADGES	**RAIKED**	**RAMBLE**	**RANKED**	FRAPING
RADGEST	TRAIKED	BRAMBLE	BRANKED	GRAPING
RADIAL	**RAILED**	RAMBLED	CRANKED	TRAPING

RAPPED	GRASSES	RATTLED	DRAYING	DREARER
CRAPPED	TRASSES	RATTLER	FRAYING	REARERS
DRAPPED	WRASSES	RATTLES	GRAYING	**REARMS**
FRAPPED	**RASSLE**	**RAUCLE**	PRAYING	PREARMS
TRAPPED	WRASSLE	RAUCLER	**RAYLES**	**REASON**
WRAPPED	RASSLED	**RAUGHT**	GRAYLES	TREASON
RAPPEE	RASSLER	DRAUGHT	RAYLESS	REASONS
FRAPPEE	RASSLES	FRAUGHT	**RAYNES**	**REASTS**
RAPPEES	**RASURE**	**RAUNCH**	TRAYNES	BREASTS
RAPPER	ERASURE	BRAUNCH	**RAYONS**	**REATES**
CRAPPER	RASURES	CRAUNCH	CRAYONS	CREATES
TRAPPER	**RATERS**	GRAUNCH	**RAZERS**	**REAVED**
WRAPPER	CRATERS	RAUNCHY	BRAZERS	GREAVED
RAPPERS	FRATERS	**RAUNGE**	GRAZERS	**REAVER**
RAPPES	GRATERS	RAUNGED	**RAZING**	PREAVER
FRAPPES	KRATERS	RAUNGES	BRAZING	REAVERS
RASERS	PRATERS	**RAVAGE**	CRAZING	**REAVES**
ERASERS	**RATIFY**	RAVAGED	GRAZING	GREAVES
RASHED	GRATIFY	RAVAGER	**RAZZLE**	**REBASE**
BRASHED	**RATINE**	RAVAGES	FRAZZLE	REBASED
CRASHED	GRATINE	**RAVELS**	RAZZLES	REBASES
TRASHED	RATINES	GRAVELS	**REACTS**	**REBATE**
RASHER	**RATING**	TRAVELS	PREACTS	REBATED
BRASHER	CRATING	**RAVENS**	**READER**	REBATER
CRASHER	GRATING	CRAVENS	DREADER	REBATES
TRASHER	ORATING	**RAVERS**	TREADER	**REBIDS**
RASHERS	PRATING	BRAVERS	READERS	PREBIDS
RASHES	RATINGS	CRAVERS	**REAKED**	**REBILL**
BRASHES	**RATION**	GRAVERS	CREAKED	PREBILL
CRASHES	ORATION	**RAVINE**	FREAKED	REBILLS
TRASHES	RATIONS	RAVINED	WREAKED	**REBIND**
RASHEST	**RATLIN**	RAVINES	**REALES**	PREBIND
RASHLY	RATLINE	**RAVING**	REALEST	REBINDS
BRASHLY	RATLING	BRAVING	**REALLY**	**REBODY**
RASING	RATLINS	CRAVING	AREALLY	OREBODY
ERASING	**RATTED**	GRAVING	**REAMED**	**REBOIL**
RASPED	DRATTED	RAVINGS	BREAMED	PREBOIL
GRASPED	PRATTED	**RAWEST**	CREAMED	REBOILS
RASPER	**RATTER**	BRAWEST	DREAMED	**REBOOK**
GRASPER	RATTERS	**RAWING**	**REAMER**	PREBOOK
RASPERS	RATTERY	DRAWING	CREAMER	REBOOKS
RASSES	**RATTLE**	RAWINGS	DREAMER	**REBORE**
BRASSES	BRATTLE	**RAYING**	REAMERS	REBORED
FRASSES	PRATTLE	BRAYING	**REARER**	REBORES

REBORN	RECOUPE	BREEDER	**REFUGE**	**REHEAT**
PREBORN	RECOUPS	REEDERS	REFUGED	PREHEAT
REBUKE	**RECTOR**	**REEDIT**	REFUGEE	REHEATS
REBUKED	ERECTOR	PREEDIT	REFUGES	**REHIRE**
REBUKER	RECTORS	REEDITS	**REFUND**	REHIRED
REBUKES	RECTORY	**REEKED**	PREFUND	REHIRES
REBUYS	**RECULE**	GREEKED	REFUNDS	**REHOME**
PREBUYS	RECULED	**REEKIE**	**REFUSE**	REHOMED
RECANE	RECULES	REEKIER	REFUSED	REHOMES
RECANED	**RECURE**	**REELED**	REFUSER	**REINED**
RECANES	PRECURE	CREELED	REFUSES	GREINED
RECAST	RECURED	**REESTS**	**REFUTE**	**REISTS**
PRECAST	RECURES	BREESTS	REFUTED	BREISTS
RECASTS	**RECUSE**	**REEVED**	REFUTER	**RELACE**
RECEDE	RECUSED	PREEVED	REFUTES	RELACED
PRECEDE	RECUSES	**REEVES**	**REGALE**	RELACES
RECEDED	**RECUTS**	PREEVES	GREGALE	**RELATE**
RECEDES	PRECUTS	**REFACE**	REGALED	PRELATE
RECENT	**REDATE**	PREFACE	REGALER	RELATED
PRECENT	PREDATE	REFACED	REGALES	RELATER
RECEPT	REDATED	REFACES	**REGIME**	RELATES
PRECEPT	REDATES	**REFECT**	REGIMEN	**RELINE**
RECEPTS	**REDDLE**	PREFECT	REGIMES	RELINED
RECESS	TREDDLE	REFECTS	**REGINA**	RELINES
PRECESS	REDDLED	**REFERS**	REGINAE	**RELIVE**
RECIPE	REDDLES	PREFERS	REGINAL	RELIVED
PRECIPE	**REDEAL**	**REFILE**	REGINAS	RELIVER
RECIPES	REDEALS	PREFILE	**REGIVE**	RELIVES
RECITE	REDEALT	REFILED	REGIVEN	**RELOAD**
RECITED	**REDIAL**	REFILES	REGIVES	PRELOAD
RECITER	PREDIAL	**REFINE**	**REGLUE**	RELOADS
RECITES	UREDIAL	REFINED	REGLUED	**RELUME**
RECKED	REDIALS	REFINER	REGLUES	RELUMED
TRECKED	**REDING**	REFINES	**REGROW**	RELUMES
WRECKED	AREDING	**REFIRE**	REGROWN	**REMADE**
RECODE	BREDING	PREFIRE	REGROWS	PREMADE
PRECODE	**REDRAW**	REFIRED	**REGULA**	REMADES
RECODED	REDRAWN	REFIRES	REGULAE	**REMAKE**
RECODES	REDRAWS	**REFLOW**	REGULAR	REMAKER
RECOOK	**REDUCE**	REFLOWN	**REHABS**	REMAKES
PRECOOK	REDUCED	REFLOWS	PREHABS	**REMATE**
RECOOKS	REDUCER	**REFORM**	**REHEAR**	CREMATE
RECOUP	REDUCES	PREFORM	REHEARD	REMATED
PRECOUP	**REEDER**	REFORMS	REHEARS	REMATES

REMBLE	**RENNED**	REPOSER	PRESHOW	**RESUME**
TREMBLE	GRENNED	REPOSES	RESHOWN	PRESUME
REMBLED	**RENNES**	**REPPED**	RESHOWS	RESUMED
REMBLES	BRENNES	PREPPED	**RESIDE**	RESUMER
REMEDE	FRENNES	**REPURE**	PRESIDE	RESUMES
REMEDED	**RENNIN**	REPURED	RESIDED	**RETAKE**
REMEDES	RENNING	REPURES	RESIDER	RETAKEN
REMEET	RENNINS	**REPUTE**	RESIDES	RETAKER
PREMEET	**RENTAL**	REPUTED	**RESIFT**	RETAKES
REMEETS	TRENTAL	REPUTES	PRESIFT	**RETAPE**
REMISE	RENTALS	**REQUIT**	RESIFTS	PRETAPE
PREMISE	**RENTED**	REQUITE	**RESILE**	RETAPED
REMISED	PRENTED	REQUITS	RESILED	RETAPES
REMISES	**RENTER**	**RERISE**	RESILES	**RETELL**
REMISS	BRENTER	RERISEN	**RESITE**	PRETELL
PREMISS	RENTERS	RERISES	RESITED	RETELLS
REMITS	**REPACK**	**RESALE**	RESITES	**RETEST**
FREMITS	PREPACK	PRESALE	**RESIZE**	PRETEST
REMIXT	REPACKS	RESALES	RESIZED	RETESTS
PREMIXT	**REPAID**	**RESCUE**	RESIZES	**RETILE**
REMOLD	PREPAID	RESCUED	**RESKUE**	RETILED
PREMOLD	**REPAVE**	RESCUEE	RESKUED	RETILES
REMOLDS	PREPAVE	RESCUER	RESKUES	**RETIME**
REMOTE	REPAVED	RESCUES	**RESOAK**	RETIMED
REMOTER	REPAVES	**RESEAU**	PRESOAK	RETIMES
REMOTES	**REPAYS**	RESEAUS	RESOAKS	**RETINA**
REMOVE	PREPAYS	RESEAUX	**RESOLD**	RETINAE
PREMOVE	**REPINE**	**RESELL**	PRESOLD	RETINAL
REMOVED	REPINED	PRESELL	**RESOLE**	RETINAS
REMOVER	REPINER	RESELLS	RESOLED	**RETIRE**
REMOVES	REPINES	**RESENT**	RESOLES	RETIRED
RENAIL	**REPLAN**	PRESENT	**RESORT**	RETIREE
TRENAIL	PREPLAN	RESENTS	PRESORT	RETIRER
RENAILS	REPLANS	**RESETS**	RESORTS	RETIRES
RENAME	REPLANT	PRESETS	**RESTED**	**RETOLD**
PRENAME	**REPLUM**	**RESHES**	CRESTED	PRETOLD
RENAMED	REPLUMB	FRESHES	PRESTED	**RETRIM**
RENAMES	**REPONE**	**RESHIP**	WRESTED	PRETRIM
RENDED	PREPONE	PRESHIP	**RESTER**	RETRIMS
TRENDED	REPONED	RESHIPS	PRESTER	**RETTED**
RENEGE	REPONES	**RESHOE**	WRESTER	ARETTED
RENEGED	**REPOSE**	RESHOED	RESTERS	FRETTED
RENEGER	PREPOSE	RESHOES	**RESTOS**	**RETUNE**
RENEGES	REPOSED	**RESHOW**	PRESTOS	RETUNED

RETUNES	REVOTES	**RIBBIE**	TRICKLE	**RIFLES**
RETYPE	**REVUES**	RIBBIER	RICKLES	TRIFLES
PRETYPE	PREVUES	RIBBIES	**RICKLY**	**RIFTED**
RETYPED	**REWAKE**	**RIBBON**	PRICKLY	DRIFTED
RETYPES	REWAKED	RIBBONS	TRICKLY	GRIFTED
REURGE	REWAKEN	RIBBONY	**RIDDED**	**RIGGED**
REURGED	REWAKES	**RIBLET**	GRIDDED	FRIGGED
REURGES	**REWARM**	DRIBLET	**RIDDER**	GRIGGED
REVERB	PREWARM	TRIBLET	GRIDDER	PRIGGED
PREVERB	REWARMS	RIBLETS	RIDDERS	TRIGGED
REVERBS	**REWASH**	**RICERS**	**RIDDLE**	**RIGGER**
REVERE	PREWASH	GRICERS	GRIDDLE	FRIGGER
REVERED	**REWIRE**	PRICERS	RIDDLED	PRIGGER
REVERER	PREWIRE	**RICHES**	RIDDLER	TRIGGER
REVERES	REWIRED	RICHEST	RIDDLES	RIGGERS
REVERS	REWIRES	**RICHTS**	**RIDENT**	**RIGHTS**
REVERSE	**REWOKE**	FRICHTS	TRIDENT	BRIGHTS
REVERSI	REWOKEN	**RICIER**	**RIDGED**	FRIGHTS
REVERSO	**REWORK**	PRICIER	BRIDGED	WRIGHTS
REVETS	PREWORK	**RICING**	FRIDGED	**RIGLIN**
BREVETS	REWORKS	GRICING	**RIDGES**	RIGLING
TREVETS	**REWORN**	PRICING	BRIDGES	RIGLINS
REVIEW	PREWORN	TRICING	FRIDGES	**RILLED**
PREVIEW	**REWOVE**	**RICKED**	**RIDING**	DRILLED
REVIEWS	REWOVEN	BRICKED	BRIDING	FRILLED
REVILE	**REWRAP**	CRICKED	GRIDING	GRILLED
REVILED	PREWRAP	PRICKED	PRIDING	PRILLED
REVILER	REWRAPS	TRICKED	RIDINGS	TRILLED
REVILES	REWRAPT	WRICKED	**RIEVER**	**RILLES**
REVISE	**REZONE**	**RICKER**	GRIEVER	GRILLES
PREVISE	REZONED	PRICKER	RIEVERS	**RIMERS**
REVISED	REZONES	TRICKER	**RIEVES**	PRIMERS
REVISER	**RHOMBI**	RICKERS	GRIEVES	TRIMERS
REVISES	RHOMBIC	**RICKET**	PRIEVES	**RIMIER**
REVIVE	**RHYTHM**	CRICKET	**RIFFLE**	GRIMIER
REVIVED	RHYTHMI	PRICKET	RIFFLED	**RIMING**
REVIVER	RHYTHMS	RICKETS	RIFFLER	BRIMING
REVIVES	**RIBBED**	RICKETY	RIFFLES	CRIMING
REVOKE	CRIBBED	**RICKEY**	**RIFLED**	GRIMING
REVOKED	DRIBBED	CRICKEY	TRIFLED	PRIMING
REVOKER	**RIBBER**	RICKEYS	**RIFLER**	**RIMMED**
REVOKES	CRIBBER	**RICKLE**	TRIFLER	BRIMMED
REVOTE	DRIBBER	BRICKLE	RIFLERS	PRIMMED
REVOTED	RIBBERS	PRICKLE	RIFLERY	TRIMMED

RIMMER	ARIPPLE	GRIVETS	**ROCKER**	PROLLER
BRIMMER	CRIPPLE	PRIVETS	ROCKERS	TROLLER
CRIMMER	GRIPPLE	TRIVETS	ROCKERY	ROLLERS
GRIMMER	TRIPPLE	**RIVING**	**ROCKET**	**ROMAGE**
KRIMMER	RIPPLED	DRIVING	BROCKET	FROMAGE
PRIMMER	RIPPLER	**RIZZAR**	CROCKET	ROMAGES
TRIMMER	RIPPLES	RIZZARS	ROCKETS	**ROMALS**
RIMMERS	RIPPLET	RIZZART	**RODDED**	BROMALS
RIMPLE	**RIPSAW**	**RIZZER**	BRODDED	**ROMPED**
CRIMPLE	RIPSAWN	FRIZZER	PRODDED	TROMPED
RIMPLED	RIPSAWS	RIZZERS	**RODENT**	**RONTES**
RIMPLES	**RISERS**	**ROARIE**	ERODENT	FRONTES
RINDED	PRISERS	ROARIER	RODENTS	**RONZER**
BRINDED	**RISING**	**ROASTS**	**RODING**	BRONZER
GRINDED	ARISING	BROASTS	ERODING	RONZERS
RINGED	GRISING	**ROATED**	RODINGS	**ROOFED**
CRINGED	IRISING	TROATED	**ROGERS**	PROOFED
FRINGED	KRISING	**ROBAND**	DROGERS	**ROOFER**
WRINGED	PRISING	PROBAND	**ROGUER**	PROOFER
RINGER	RISINGS	ROBANDS	ROGUERS	ROOFERS
BRINGER	**RISKED**	**ROBBER**	ROGUERY	**ROOFIE**
CRINGER	BRISKED	ROBBERS	**ROGUES**	ROOFIER
WRINGER	FRISKED	ROBBERY	BROGUES	ROOFIES
RINGERS	**RISKER**	**ROBBIN**	DROGUES	**ROOKED**
RINKED	BRISKER	ROBBING	**ROILED**	BROOKED
PRINKED	FRISKER	ROBBINS	BROILED	CROOKED
RIPERS	RISKERS	**ROBING**	DROILED	DROOKED
GRIPERS	**RISPED**	PROBING	**ROINED**	**ROOKIE**
RIPING	CRISPED	ROBINGS	GROINED	BROOKIE
GRIPING	**RITTED**	**ROBUST**	PROINED	ROOKIER
RIPOST	FRITTED	ROBUSTA	**ROKERS**	ROOKIES
RIPOSTE	GRITTED	**ROCHES**	BROKERS	**ROOMED**
RIPOSTS	**RITTER**	BROCHES	PROKERS	BROOMED
RIPPED	CRITTER	CROCHES	**ROKING**	GROOMED
DRIPPED	FRITTER	TROCHES	BROKING	VROOMED
GRIPPED	GRITTER	**ROCHET**	GROKING	**ROOMER**
TRIPPED	RITTERS	CROCHET	PROKING	GROOMER
RIPPER	**RITZES**	ROCHETS	TROKING	ROOMERS
DRIPPER	FRITZES	**ROCKED**	**ROLLED**	**ROOMIE**
FRIPPER	**RIVELS**	BROCKED	DROLLED	ROOMIER
GRIPPER	DRIVELS	CROCKED	PROLLED	ROOMIES
TRIPPER	**RIVERS**	FROCKED	TROLLED	**ROOPED**
RIPPERS	DRIVERS	GROCKED	**ROLLER**	DROOPED
RIPPLE	**RIVETS**	TROCKED	DROLLER	TROOPED

ROOSES	ROTATED	GROUNDS	ROWINGS	**RUDEST**
BROOSES	ROTATES	**ROUPED**	**ROWNDS**	CRUDEST
ROOTED	**ROTHER**	CROUPED	DROWNDS	**RUDISH**
WROOTED	BROTHER	GROUPED	**ROWTHS**	PRUDISH
ROOTLE	FROTHER	TROUPED	GROWTHS	**RUEING**
ROOTLED	ROTHERS	**ROUSED**	TROWTHS	GRUEING
ROOTLES	**ROTONS**	AROUSED	**ROYNED**	TRUEING
ROOTLET	CROTONS	GROUSED	PROYNED	RUEINGS
ROPERS	PROTONS	**ROUSER**	**ROYNES**	**RUFFED**
GROPERS	**ROTTED**	AROUSER	GROYNES	GRUFFED
PROPERS	TROTTED	GROUSER	PROYNES	**RUFFES**
ROPING	**ROTTER**	TROUSER	**RUBBED**	TRUFFES
GROPING	TROTTER	ROUSERS	DRUBBED	**RUFFIN**
TROPING	ROTTERS	**ROUSES**	GRUBBED	RUFFING
ROPINGS	**ROTULA**	AROUSES	**RUBBER**	RUFFINS
ROQUET	ROTULAE	GROUSES	DRUBBER	**RUFFLE**
CROQUET	ROTULAS	TROUSES	GRUBBER	TRUFFLE
ROQUETS	**ROTUND**	**ROUTED**	RUBBERS	RUFFLED
ROSACE	OROTUND	GROUTED	RUBBERY	RUFFLER
ROSACEA	ROTUNDA	**ROUTER**	**RUBBIT**	RUFFLES
ROSACES	ROTUNDS	GROUTER	RUBBITY	**RUFFLY**
ROSETS	**ROUBLE**	TROUTER	**RUBBLE**	GRUFFLY
GROSETS	TROUBLE	ROUTERS	GRUBBLE	**RUGGED**
ROSIER	ROUBLES	**ROUTES**	RUBBLED	DRUGGED
BROSIER	**ROUCHE**	CROUTES	RUBBLES	FRUGGED
CROSIER	ROUCHED	**ROUTHS**	**RUBIES**	**RUGGER**
PROSIER	ROUCHES	DROUTHS	RUBIEST	DRUGGER
ROSIERE	**ROUGHS**	**ROVERS**	**RUCKED**	RUGGERS
ROSIERS	BROUGHS	DROVERS	TRUCKED	**RUGOLA**
ROSIES	GROUGHS	PROVERS	**RUCKLE**	ARUGOLA
ROSIEST	TROUGHS	TROVERS	BRUCKLE	RUGOLAS
ROSILY	**ROUGHT**	**ROVING**	TRUCKLE	**RUMBLE**
PROSILY	BROUGHT	DROVING	RUCKLED	CRUMBLE
ROSING	DROUGHT	PROVING	RUCKLES	DRUMBLE
PROSING	WROUGHT	ROVINGS	**RUDDED**	GRUMBLE
ROSSER	**ROUGHY**	**ROWELS**	CRUDDED	RUMBLED
CROSSER	FROUGHY	TROWELS	**RUDDLE**	RUMBLER
GROSSER	**ROULES**	**ROWERS**	CRUDDLE	RUMBLES
ROSSERS	TROULES	CROWERS	RUDDLED	**RUMBLY**
ROSTED	**ROUNCE**	GROWERS	RUDDLES	CRUMBLY
FROSTED	FROUNCE	**ROWING**	**RUDELY**	GRUMBLY
ROSTRA	TROUNCE	CROWING	CRUDELY	**RUMENS**
ROSTRAL	ROUNCES	GROWING	**RUDERY**	CRUMENS
ROTATE	**ROUNDS**	TROWING	PRUDERY	**RUMINA**

RUMINAL	BRUSHES	SALLOWY	**SAVANT**	SCHNOZZ
RUMMER	CRUSHES	**SALMON**	SAVANTE	**SCHOOL**
BRUMMER	FRUSHES	SALMONS	SAVANTS	SCHOOLE
DRUMMER	**RUSSET**	SALMONY	**SAVOUR**	SCHOOLS
GRUMMER	RUSSETS	**SALTER**	SAVOURS	**SCLATE**
RUMMERS	RUSSETY	PSALTER	SAVOURY	SCLATED
RUMPED	**RUSTED**	SALTERN	**SCALAR**	SCLATES
CRUMPED	CRUSTED	SALTERS	SCALARE	**SCLERA**
FRUMPED	TRUSTED	SALTERY	SCALARS	SCLERAE
GRUMPED	**RUSTLE**	**SALTIE**	**SCAPED**	SCLERAL
TRUMPED	RUSTLED	SALTIER	ESCAPED	SCLERAS
RUMPLE	RUSTLER	SALTIES	**SCAPES**	**SCONCE**
CRUMPLE	RUSTLES	**SALUTE**	ESCAPES	ASCONCE
FRUMPLE	**RUSTRE**	SALUTED	**SCARCE**	SCONCED
RUMPLED	RUSTRED	SALUTER	SCARCER	SCONCES
RUMPLES	RUSTRES	SALUTES	**SCARED**	**SCORIA**
RUMPLY	**RUTHER**	**SAMBAS**	ASCARED	SCORIAC
CRUMPLY	DRUTHER	TSAMBAS	SCAREDY	SCORIAE
RUNDLE	TRUTHER	**SAMPLE**	**SCARPS**	**SCORSE**
GRUNDLE	**SABBAT**	SAMPLED	ESCARPS	SCORSED
TRUNDLE	SABBATH	SAMPLER	**SCARRE**	SCORSER
RUNDLED	SABBATS	SAMPLES	SCARRED	SCORSES
RUNDLES	**SABKHA**	**SANGHA**	SCARRES	**SCOURS**
RUNDLET	SABKHAH	SANGHAS	**SCATHE**	SCOURSE
RUNKLE	SABKHAS	SANGHAT	SCATHED	**SCOUSE**
CRUNKLE	SABKHAT	**SANTIM**	SCATHES	SCOUSER
RUNKLED	**SADDLE**	SANTIMI	**SCENDS**	SCOUSES
RUNKLES	SADDLED	SANTIMS	ASCENDS	**SCRAPE**
RUNNEL	SADDLER	SANTIMU	**SCENTS**	SCRAPED
TRUNNEL	SADDLES	**SAPPLE**	ASCENTS	SCRAPER
RUNNELS	**SAFROL**	SAPPLED	**SCERNE**	SCRAPES
RUNTED	SAFROLE	SAPPLES	SCERNED	**SCRAWL**
BRUNTED	SAFROLS	**SATINS**	SCERNES	SCRAWLS
GRUNTED	**SAGGAR**	ISATINS	**SCHEME**	SCRAWLY
PRUNTED	SAGGARD	**SATRAP**	SCHEMED	**SCREAK**
RUSHED	SAGGARS	SATRAPS	SCHEMER	SCREAKS
BRUSHED	**SAHIBA**	SATRAPY	SCHEMES	SCREAKY
CRUSHED	SAHIBAH	**SATYRA**	**SCHISM**	**SCREAM**
FRUSHED	SAHIBAS	SATYRAL	SCHISMA	SCREAMO
RUSHER	**SALIVA**	SATYRAS	SCHISMS	SCREAMS
BRUSHER	SALIVAL	**SAVAGE**	**SCHLEP**	**SCRIBE**
CRUSHER	SALIVAS	SAVAGED	SCHLEPP	ASCRIBE
RUSHERS	**SALLOW**	SAVAGER	SCHLEPS	ESCRIBE
RUSHES	SALLOWS	SAVAGES	**SCHNOZ**	SCRIBED

SCRIBER	SCYTHED	SEDUCES	SERENED	SHANTIH
SCRIBES	SCYTHER	**SEELIE**	SERENER	SHANTIS
SCRIKE	SCYTHES	SEELIER	SERENES	**SHARIA**
SCRIKED	**SDAINE**	**SEETHE**	**SERINE**	SHARIAH
SCRIKES	SDAINED	SEETHED	ESERINE	SHARIAS
SCRIMP	SDAINES	SEETHER	SERINES	SHARIAT
SCRIMPS	**SDEIGN**	SEETHES	**SERING**	**SHAWED**
SCRIMPY	SDEIGNE	**SEISIN**	SERINGA	PSHAWED
SCRIVE	SDEIGNS	SEISING	**SEROSA**	**SHEATH**
SCRIVED	**SEALER**	SEISINS	SEROSAE	SHEATHE
SCRIVES	SEALERS	**SEIZIN**	SEROSAL	SHEATHS
SCROLL	SEALERY	SEIZING	SEROSAS	SHEATHY
ESCROLL	**SEARCE**	SEIZINS	**SERRAN**	**SHEAVE**
SCROLLS	SEARCED	**SELECT**	SERRANO	SHEAVED
SCROME	SEARCES	SELECTA	SERRANS	SHEAVES
SCROMED	**SEAWAN**	SELECTS	**SERVER**	**SHEESH**
SCROMES	SEAWANS	**SEMBLE**	SERVERS	SHEESHA
SCROTA	SEAWANT	SEMBLED	SERVERY	**SHEIKH**
SCROTAL	**SECEDE**	SEMBLES	**SESTET**	SHEIKHA
SCROWL	SECEDED	**SEMINA**	SESTETS	SHEIKHS
SCROWLE	SECEDER	SEMINAL	SESTETT	**SHELVE**
SCROWLS	SECEDES	SEMINAR	**SETTLE**	SHELVED
SCROWS	**SECOND**	**SEMPLE**	SETTLED	SHELVER
ESCROWS	SECONDE	SEMPLER	SETTLER	SHELVES
SCRUFF	SECONDI	**SENHOR**	SETTLES	**SHENDS**
SCRUFFS	SECONDO	SENHORA	**SEVERE**	YSHENDS
SCRUFFY	SECONDS	SENHORS	SEVERED	**SHERIA**
SCRUMP	**SECRET**	**SENSIS**	SEVERER	SHERIAS
SCRUMPS	SECRETA	SENSISM	**SEXTAN**	SHERIAT
SCRUMPY	SECRETE	SENSIST	SEXTANS	**SHERIF**
SCRUNT	SECRETS	**SENSOR**	SEXTANT	SHERIFF
SCRUNTS	**SECULA**	SENSORS	**SEXTET**	SHERIFS
SCRUNTY	SECULAR	SENSORY	SEXTETS	**SHIEST**
SCRUZE	**SECURE**	**SEPSES**	SEXTETT	ASHIEST
SCRUZED	SECURED	ASEPSES	**SEXUAL**	**SHIKAR**
SCRUZES	SECURER	**SEPSIS**	ASEXUAL	SHIKARA
SCULLE	SECURES	ASEPSIS	**SHADOW**	SHIKARI
SCULLED	**SEDATE**	**SEPTIC**	SHADOWS	SHIKARS
SCULLER	SEDATED	ASEPTIC	SHADOWY	**SHIKSE**
SCULLES	SEDATER	SEPTICS	**SHAMED**	SHIKSEH
SCUNGE	SEDATES	**SEQUEL**	ASHAMED	SHIKSES
SCUNGED	**SEDUCE**	SEQUELA	**SHAMES**	**SHINNE**
SCUNGES	SEDUCED	SEQUELS	ASHAMES	SHINNED
SCYTHE	SEDUCER	**SERENE**	**SHANTI**	SHINNES

SHINNEY	SHRIMPS	SILVERY	**SLAKED**	**SMOILE**
SHIPPO	SHRIMPY	**SIMPLE**	ASLAKED	SMOILED
SHIPPON	**SHRINE**	SIMPLED	YSLAKED	SMOILES
SHIPPOS	SHRINED	SIMPLER	**SLAKES**	**SMOKIE**
SHIVER	SHRINES	SIMPLES	ASLAKES	SMOKIER
ASHIVER	**SHRIVE**	SIMPLEX	**SLAVER**	SMOKIES
SHIVERS	SHRIVED	**SIMURG**	SLAVERS	**SMOOCH**
SHIVERY	SHRIVEL	SIMURGH	SLAVERY	SMOOCHY
SHLEPP	SHRIVEN	SIMURGS	**SLEAVE**	**SMOOGE**
SHLEPPS	SHRIVER	**SINGLE**	SLEAVED	SMOOGED
SHLEPPY	SHRIVES	SINGLED	SLEAVES	SMOOGES
SHLOCK	**SHROUD**	SINGLES	**SLEAZE**	**SMOOTH**
SHLOCKS	SHROUDS	SINGLET	SLEAZED	SMOOTHE
SHLOCKY	SHROUDY	**SINTER**	SLEAZES	SMOOTHS
SHLUMP	**SHROVE**	SINTERS	**SLEDGE**	SMOOTHY
SHLUMPS	SHROVED	SINTERY	SLEDGED	**SMOUSE**
SHLUMPY	SHROVES	**SIPPLE**	SLEDGER	SMOUSED
SHMUCK	**SHTICK**	SIPPLED	SLEDGES	SMOUSER
SHMUCKS	SHTICKS	SIPPLES	**SLEECH**	SMOUSES
SHMUCKY	SHTICKY	**SITULA**	SLEECHY	**SMOYLE**
SHOOLE	**SICKLE**	SITULAE	**SLEEVE**	SMOYLED
SHOOLED	SICKLED	**SIXAIN**	SLEEVED	SMOYLES
SHOOLES	SICKLES	SIXAINE	SLEEVER	**SMUDGE**
SHOPPE	**SIERRA**	SIXAINS	SLEEVES	SMUDGED
SHOPPED	SIERRAN	**SIZZLE**	**SLEIGH**	SMUDGER
SHOPPER	SIERRAS	SIZZLED	SLEIGHS	SMUDGES
SHOPPES	**SIFFLE**	SIZZLER	SLEIGHT	**SMUTCH**
SHOTTE	SIFFLED	SIZZLES	**SLOUCH**	SMUTCHY
SHOTTED	SIFFLES	**SKATOL**	SLOUCHY	**SNATCH**
SHOTTEN	**SIGNOR**	SKATOLE	**SLOUGH**	SNATCHY
SHOTTES	SIGNORA	SKATOLS	SLOUGHI	**SNEBBE**
SHOWER	SIGNORE	**SKETCH**	SLOUGHS	SNEBBED
SHOWERS	SIGNORI	SKETCHY	SLOUGHY	SNEBBES
SHOWERY	SIGNORS	**SKIVIE**	**SLUDGE**	**SNEEZE**
SHRIEK	SIGNORY	SKIVIER	SLUDGED	SNEEZED
SHRIEKS	**SILAGE**	**SKLATE**	SLUDGES	SNEEZER
SHRIEKY	SILAGED	SKLATED	**SLUICE**	SNEEZES
SHRIKE	SILAGES	SKLATES	SLUICED	**SNIDES**
SHRIKED	**SILKIE**	**SKLENT**	SLUICES	SNIDEST
SHRIKES	SILKIER	ASKLENT	**SLUTCH**	**SNITCH**
SHRILL	SILKIES	SKLENTS	SLUTCHY	SNITCHY
SHRILLS	**SILVER**	**SKRIKE**	**SMIDGE**	**SNIVEL**
SHRILLY	SILVERN	SKRIKED	SMIDGEN	SNIVELS
SHRIMP	SILVERS	SKRIKES	SMIDGES	SNIVELY

SNOOZE	SOOGEED	SPARRES	ESPIERS	SPRAWLY
SNOOZED	SOOGEES	**SPARSE**	**SPIKER**	**SPREAD**
SNOOZER	**SOOGIE**	SPARSER	SPIKERS	ASPREAD
SNOOZES	SOOGIED	**SPARTH**	SPIKERY	SPREADS
SNUBBE	SOOGIES	SPARTHE	**SPINES**	**SPREDD**
SNUBBED	**SOOTHE**	SPARTHS	ASPINES	SPREDDE
SNUBBER	SOOTHED	**SPATHE**	**SPIRED**	SPREDDS
SNUBBES	SOOTHER	SPATHED	ASPIRED	**SPRING**
SNUDGE	SOOTHES	SPATHES	**SPIREM**	SPRINGE
SNUDGED	**SOPITE**	**SPAVIE**	SPIREME	SPRINGS
SNUDGES	SOPITED	SPAVIES	SPIREMS	SPRINGY
SOAPIE	SOPITES	SPAVIET	**SPIRES**	**SPRITS**
SOAPIER	**SORTIE**	**SPECTS**	ASPIRES	ESPRITS
SOAPIES	SORTIED	ASPECTS	**SPIRIT**	**SPRITZ**
SOCAGE	SORTIES	**SPENCE**	SPIRITS	SPRITZY
SOCAGER	**SOUPLE**	SPENCER	SPIRITY	**SPROUT**
SOCAGES	SOUPLED	SPENCES	**SPLASH**	ASPROUT
SOCIAL	SOUPLES	**SPERRE**	SPLASHY	SPROUTS
ASOCIAL	**SOURCE**	SPERRED	**SPLEEN**	**SPRUCE**
SOCIALS	SOURCED	SPERRES	SPLEENS	SPRUCED
SODAIN	SOURCES	**SPERSE**	SPLEENY	SPRUCER
SODAINE	**SOWSSE**	ASPERSE	**SPLICE**	SPRUCES
SODDIE	SOWSSED	SPERSED	SPLICED	**SPULYE**
SODDIER	SOWSSES	SPERSES	SPLICER	SPULYED
SODDIES	**SOZZLE**	**SPHAER**	SPLICES	SPULYES
SOIGNE	SOZZLED	SPHAERE	**SPLINE**	**SPURNE**
SOIGNEE	SOZZLES	SPHAERS	SPLINED	SPURNED
SOLACE	**SPALLE**	**SPHEAR**	SPLINES	SPURNER
SOLACED	SPALLED	SPHEARE	**SPONGE**	SPURNES
SOLACER	SPALLER	SPHEARS	SPONGED	**SPYING**
SOLACES	SPALLES	**SPHERE**	SPONGER	ESPYING
SOLATE	**SPARES**	SPHERED	SPONGES	SPYINGS
ISOLATE	SPAREST	SPHERES	**SPORTS**	**SQUALL**
SOLATED	**SPARGE**	**SPIALS**	ASPORTS	SQUALLS
SOLATES	SPARGED	ESPIALS	**SPOUSE**	SQUALLY
SOLITO	SPARGER	**SPICER**	ESPOUSE	**SQUAMA**
SOLITON	SPARGES	SPICERS	SPOUSED	SQUAMAE
SOMBRE	**SPARKE**	SPICERY	SPOUSES	**SQUARE**
SOMBRED	SPARKED	**SPICKS**	**SPRAIN**	SQUARED
SOMBRER	SPARKER	ASPICKS	SPRAINS	SQUARER
SOMBRES	SPARKES	**SPIDER**	SPRAINT	SQUARES
SONSIE	**SPARRE**	SPIDERS	**SPRAWL**	**SQUASH**
SONSIER	SPARRED	SPIDERY	ASPRAWL	SQUASHY
SOOGEE	SPARRER	**SPIERS**	SPRAWLS	**SQUAWK**

SQUAWKS	STARCHY	**STEEVE**	STIRRAS	STRAKED
SQUAWKY	**STARTS**	STEEVED	**STIRRE**	STRAKES
SQUEAK	ASTARTS	STEEVER	STIRRED	**STRAND**
SQUEAKS	STARTSY	STEEVES	STIRRER	ASTRAND
SQUEAKY	**STARVE**	**STELIC**	STIRRES	STRANDS
SQUIFF	STARVED	ASTELIC	**STODGE**	**STRANG**
SQUIFFY	STARVER	**STELLA**	STODGED	STRANGE
SQUILL	STARVES	STELLAR	STODGER	**STRATA**
SQUILLA	**STATED**	STELLAS	STODGES	STRATAL
SQUILLS	ESTATED	**STEMME**	**STONED**	STRATAS
SQUINT	**STATES**	STEMMED	ASTONED	**STRAYS**
ASQUINT	ESTATES	STEMMER	**STONER**	ESTRAYS
SQUINTS	**STATIC**	STEMMES	STONERN	**STREAK**
SQUINTY	ASTATIC	**STENCH**	STONERS	STREAKS
SQUIRE	STATICE	STENCHY	**STONES**	STREAKY
ESQUIRE	STATICS	**STENTS**	ASTONES	**STREAM**
SQUIRED	**STATIN**	OSTENTS	**STONNE**	STREAMS
SQUIRES	STATING	**STEPPE**	STONNED	STREAMY
SQUIRM	STATINS	STEPPED	STONNES	**STREET**
SQUIRMS	**STATUE**	STEPPER	**STOOGE**	STREETS
SQUIRMY	STATUED	STEPPES	STOOGED	STREETY
SQUISH	STATUES	**STERNA**	STOOGES	**STRESS**
SQUISHY	**STATUS**	STERNAL	**STOOPE**	STRESSY
STABLE	STATUSY	**STERVE**	STOOPED	**STRICH**
ASTABLE	**STAYNE**	STERVED	STOOPER	ESTRICH
STABLED	STAYNED	STERVES	STOOPES	OSTRICH
STABLER	STAYNES	**STIEVE**	**STOOZE**	**STRICT**
STABLES	**STEALE**	STIEVER	STOOZED	ASTRICT
STADIA	STEALED	**STIFLE**	STOOZER	**STRIDE**
STADIAL	STEALER	STIFLED	STOOZES	ASTRIDE
STADIAS	STEALES	STIFLER	**STOUND**	STRIDER
STAGER	**STEALT**	STIFLES	ASTOUND	STRIDES
STAGERS	STEALTH	**STIGMA**	STOUNDS	**STRIGA**
STAGERY	**STEANE**	STIGMAL	**STOVER**	STRIGAE
STAITH	STEANED	STIGMAS	ESTOVER	**STRIKE**
STAITHE	STEANES	**STIMIE**	STOVERS	STRIKER
STAITHS	**STEARE**	STIMIED	**STRAFE**	STRIKES
STALES	STEARED	STIMIES	STRAFED	**STRING**
STALEST	STEARES	**STINGE**	STRAFER	STRINGS
STAPLE	**STEDDE**	STINGED	STRAFES	STRINGY
STAPLED	STEDDED	STINGER	**STRAIN**	**STRIPE**
STAPLER	STEDDES	STINGES	STRAINS	STRIPED
STAPLES	**STEEMS**	**STIRRA**	STRAINT	STRIPER
STARCH	ESTEEMS	STIRRAH	**STRAKE**	STRIPES

STRIPEY	SUCCORY	**SURGER**	SYLVINE	TAIGLES
STRIVE	**SUCCOS**	SURGERS	SYLVINS	**TAIVER**
STRIVED	SUCCOSE	SURGERY	**SYMBOL**	TAIVERS
STRIVEN	**SUCCOT**	**SURING**	SYMBOLE	TAIVERT
STRIVER	SUCCOTH	USURING	SYMBOLS	**TAKERS**
STRIVES	**SUCKLE**	**SUTLER**	**SYNURA**	STAKERS
STROBE	SUCKLED	SUTLERS	SYNURAE	**TAKING**
STROBED	SUCKLER	SUTLERY	**TAATAS**	STAKING
STROBES	SUCKLES	**SUTTLE**	ATAATAS	TAKINGS
STROKE	**SUDATE**	SUTTLED	**TABBED**	**TALKED**
STROKED	SUDATED	SUTTLES	STABBED	STALKED
STROKEN	SUDATES	**SUTURE**	**TABLED**	**TALKER**
STROKER	**SUDDEN**	SUTURED	STABLED	STALKER
STROKES	ASUDDEN	SUTURES	**TABLES**	TALKERS
STROMA	SUDDENS	**SVELTE**	STABLES	**TALKIE**
STROMAL	**SUKKOT**	SVELTER	**TABULA**	TALKIER
STROOK	SUKKOTH	**SWARDS**	TABULAE	TALKIES
STROOKE	**SULFID**	USWARDS	TABULAR	**TALLIS**
STRUMA	SULFIDE	**SWARTH**	**TACKED**	TALLISH
STRUMAE	SULFIDS	SWARTHS	STACKED	**TALLIT**
STRUMAS	**SULFUR**	SWARTHY	**TACKER**	TALLITH
STRUMS	SULFURS	**SWARVE**	STACKER	TALLITS
ESTRUMS	SULFURY	SWARVED	**TACKERS**	**TALLOW**
STYLAR	**SULTAN**	SWARVES	**TACKET**	TALLOWS
ASTYLAR	SULTANA	**SWATHE**	STACKET	TALLOWY
STYLIE	SULTANS	SWATHED	TACKETS	**TALONS**
STYLIER	**SUMMAR**	SWATHER	TACKETY	ETALONS
STYMIE	SUMMARY	SWATHES	**TACKLE**	**TAMARA**
STYMIED	**SUMMAT**	**SWERVE**	TACKLED	TAMARAO
STYMIES	SUMMATE	SWERVED	TACKLER	TAMARAS
SUBDUE	SUMMATS	SWERVER	TACKLES	TAMARAU
SUBDUED	**SUMMER**	SWERVES	**TACTIC**	**TAMARI**
SUBDUER	SUMMERS	**SWINGE**	ATACTIC	TAMARIN
SUBDUES	SUMMERY	SWINGED	TACTICS	TAMARIS
SUBMEN	**SUNDER**	SWINGER	**TAENIA**	**TAMBUR**
SUBMENU	ASUNDER	SWINGES	TAENIAE	TAMBURA
SUBPAR	SUNDERS	**SWITCH**	TAENIAS	TAMBURS
SUBPART	**SUPPLE**	SWITCHY	**TAGGED**	**TAMINE**
SUBTIL	SUPPLED	**SWITHE**	STAGGED	ETAMINE
SUBTILE	SUPPLER	SWITHER	**TAGGER**	TAMINES
SUBTLE	SUPPLES	**SWOUNE**	STAGGER	**TAMINS**
SUBTLER	**SURFIE**	SWOUNED	TAGGERS	ETAMINS
SUCCOR	SURFIER	SWOUNES	**TAIGLE**	**TAMMIE**
SUCCORS	SURFIES	**SYLVIN**	TAIGLED	TAMMIED

TAMMIES	STARTER	**TEAZLE**	STENTED	**THIRST**
TAMPED	**TARTLY**	TEAZLED	**TENTIE**	ATHIRST
STAMPED	STARTLY	TEAZLES	TENTIER	THIRSTS
TAMPER	**TASHED**	**TECHIE**	**TENURE**	THIRSTY
STAMPER	STASHED	TECHIER	TENURED	**THOUGH**
TAMPERS	**TASHES**	TECHIES	TENURES	THOUGHT
TANGED	STASHES	**TEDDED**	**TEREFA**	**THRASH**
STANGED	**TASSEL**	STEDDED	TEREFAH	THRASHY
TANGIE	TASSELL	**TEEMED**	**TERNAL**	**THREAD**
TANGIER	TASSELS	STEEMED	ETERNAL	THREADS
TANGIES	**TATERS**	**TEENED**	STERNAL	THREADY
TANGLE	STATERS	STEENED	**TERNED**	**THRIFT**
TANGLED	**TATTER**	**TEERED**	STERNED	THRIFTS
TANGLER	TATTERS	STEERED	**TERTIA**	THRIFTY
TANGLES	TATTERY	**TEETHE**	TERTIAL	**THRILL**
TANKED	**TATTIE**	TEETHED	TERTIAN	ATHRILL
STANKED	TATTIER	TEETHER	TERTIAS	THRILLS
TANNER	TATTIES	TEETHES	**TESTER**	THRILLY
TANNERS	**TATTLE**	**TEGULA**	TESTERN	**THRIST**
TANNERY	TATTLED	TEGULAE	TESTERS	THRISTS
TANNIC	TATTLER	TEGULAR	**TEWING**	THRISTY
STANNIC	TATTLES	**TELLAR**	STEWING	**THRIVE**
TANNIN	**TATUED**	STELLAR	**THALLI**	THRIVED
TANNING	STATUED	TELLARS	THALLIC	THRIVEN
TANNINS	**TAVERN**	**TELLIN**	**THANES**	THRIVER
TAPETA	TAVERNA	TELLING	ETHANES	THRIVES
TAPETAL	TAVERNS	TELLINS	**THANNA**	**THROAT**
TAPPED	**TAWING**	**TEMPER**	THANNAH	THROATS
STAPPED	STAWING	TEMPERA	THANNAS	THROATY
TARING	TAWINGS	TEMPERS	**THATCH**	**THRONE**
STARING	**TAWTIE**	**TEMPLE**	THATCHT	THRONED
TARINGS	TAWTIER	STEMPLE	THATCHY	THRONES
TARRED	**TAXIES**	TEMPLED	**THEISM**	**THROWE**
STARRED	ATAXIES	TEMPLES	ATHEISM	THROWER
TARTAN	**TEAGLE**	TEMPLET	THEISMS	THROWES
TARTANA	TEAGLED	**TENDED**	**THEIST**	**THWART**
TARTANE	TEAGLES	STENDED	ATHEIST	ATHWART
TARTANS	**TEAMED**	**TENNES**	THEISTS	THWARTS
TARTAR	STEAMED	TENNESI	**THERME**	**TIBIAL**
TARTARE	**TEAMER**	**TENNIS**	THERMEL	STIBIAL
TARTARS	STEAMER	TENNIST	THERMES	**TICKED**
TARTED	TEAMERS	**TENSES**	**THIEVE**	STICKED
STARTED	**TEARED**	TENSEST	THIEVED	**TICKER**
TARTER	STEARED	**TENTED**	THIEVES	STICKER

TICKERS	TIMBERY	**TIPTOE**	STOKERS	**TOODLE**
TICKLE	**TIMBRE**	TIPTOED	**TOKING**	TOODLED
STICKLE	TIMBREL	TIPTOES	STOKING	TOODLES
TICKLED	TIMBRES	**TIRING**	**TOLUID**	**TOOLED**
TICKLER	**TIMING**	STIRING	TOLUIDE	STOOLED
TICKLES	STIMING	TIRINGS	TOLUIDS	**TOOLIE**
TIDDLE	TIMINGS	**TIRRED**	**TOLUOL**	STOOLIE
TIDDLED	**TINDER**	STIRRED	TOLUOLE	TOOLIES
TIDDLER	TINDERS	**TISSUE**	TOLUOLS	**TOOTLE**
TIDDLES	TINDERY	TISSUED	**TOMBAC**	TOOTLED
TIDDLEY	**TINGED**	TISSUES	TOMBACK	TOOTLER
TIDIES	STINGED	TISSUEY	TOMBACS	TOOTLES
TIDIEST	**TINGES**	**TITTLE**	**TOMIUM**	**TOPERS**
TIERCE	STINGES	TITTLED	STOMIUM	STOPERS
TIERCED	**TINGLE**	TITTLES	**TONERS**	**TOPFUL**
TIERCEL	ATINGLE	**TITTUP**	ATONERS	TOPFULL
TIERCES	TINGLED	TITTUPS	STONERS	**TOPING**
TIERCET	TINGLER	TITTUPY	**TONGUE**	STOPING
TIETAC	TINGLES	**TITULE**	TONGUED	**TOPPED**
TIETACK	**TINIES**	TITULED	TONGUES	STOPPED
TIETACS	TINIEST	TITULES	**TONICS**	**TOPPER**
TIFFED	**TINKER**	**TOCKED**	ATONICS	STOPPER
STIFFED	STINKER	STOCKED	**TONIER**	TOPPERS
TIFFIN	TINKERS	**TODDLE**	STONIER	**TOPPLE**
TIFFING	**TINKLE**	TODDLED	**TONIES**	STOPPLE
TIFFINS	TINKLED	TODDLER	ATONIES	TOPPLED
TILING	TINKLER	TODDLES	STONIES	TOPPLES
STILING	TINKLES	**TODGER**	TONIEST	**TORIES**
TILINGS	**TINNIE**	STODGER	**TONING**	STORIES
TILLED	TINNIER	TODGERS	ATONING	**TORQUE**
STILLED	TINNIES	**TOGATE**	STONING	TORQUED
TILLER	**TINSEL**	TOGATED	TONINGS	TORQUER
STILLER	TINSELS	**TOGGER**	**TONISH**	TORQUES
TILLERS	TINSELY	TOGGERS	STONISH	TORQUEY
TILTED	**TINTED**	TOGGERY	**TONKED**	**TORULA**
STILTED	STINTED	**TOGGLE**	STONKED	TORULAE
TILTER	**TINTER**	TOGGLED	**TONKER**	TORULAS
STILTER	STINTER	TOGGLER	STONKER	**TORULI**
TILTERS	TINTERS	TOGGLES	TONKERS	TORULIN
TIMBAL	**TIPPLE**	**TOILES**	**TONNAG**	**TOSSES**
TIMBALE	STIPPLE	ETOILES	TONNAGE	STOSSES
TIMBALS	TIPPLED	**TOITED**	TONNAGS	**TOTTED**
TIMBER	TIPPLER	STOITED	**TONNES**	STOTTED
TIMBERS	TIPPLES	**TOKERS**	STONNES	**TOTTER**

STOTTER	TOWNIES	TRIFLED	TROPHIC	**TURACO**
TOTTERS	**TRACER**	TRIFLER	**TROPHY**	TURACOS
TOTTERY	TRACERS	TRIFLES	ATROPHY	TURACOU
TOTTIE	TRACERY	**TRIKES**	**TROPIN**	**TURBAN**
STOTTIE	**TRAIKS**	STRIKES	ATROPIN	TURBAND
TOTTIER	STRAIKS	**TRINES**	TROPINE	TURBANS
TOTTIES	**TRAINS**	STRINES	TROPING	TURBANT
TOUCHE	STRAINS	**TRIPES**	TROPINS	**TURBIT**
TOUCHED	**TRAITS**	STRIPES	**TROULE**	TURBITH
TOUCHER	STRAITS	**TRIPEY**	TROULED	TURBITS
TOUCHES	**TRAMEL**	STRIPEY	TROULES	**TURNER**
TOUPEE	TRAMELL	**TRIPLE**	**TROUPE**	TURNERS
TOUPEED	TRAMELS	TRIPLED	TROUPED	TURNERY
TOUPEES	**TRAMPS**	TRIPLES	TROUPER	**TURNIP**
TOURIE	STRAMPS	TRIPLET	TROUPES	TURNIPS
STOURIE	**TRANCE**	TRIPLEX	**TROUSE**	TURNIPY
TOURIES	TRANCED	**TRIPOD**	TROUSER	**TURTLE**
TOUSLE	TRANCES	TRIPODS	TROUSES	TURTLED
TOUSLED	TRANCEY	TRIPODY	**TROUTS**	TURTLER
TOUSLES	**TRAPPY**	**TRISUL**	STROUTS	TURTLES
TOUTER	STRAPPY	TRISULA	**TROWED**	**TUSHIE**
STOUTER	**TRAPSE**	TRISULS	STROWED	STUSHIE
TOUTERS	TRAPSED	**TRITES**	**TRUDGE**	TUSHIES
TOUTIE	TRAPSES	TRITEST	TRUDGED	**TUSSLE**
TOUTIER	**TRAYNE**	**TRITON**	TRUDGEN	TUSSLED
TOUZLE	TRAYNED	TRITONE	TRUDGER	TUSSLES
TOUZLED	TRAYNES	TRITONS	TRUDGES	**TUSSOR**
TOUZLES	**TREBLE**	**TRIVIA**	**TRYSTE**	TUSSORE
TOWAGE	TREBLED	TRIVIAL	TRYSTED	TUSSORS
STOWAGE	TREBLES	**TROCHE**	TRYSTER	**TWEEZE**
TOWAGES	**TREPAN**	TROCHEE	TRYSTES	TWEEZED
TOWERS	TREPANG	TROCHES	**TUBBED**	TWEEZER
STOWERS	TREPANS	**TROCHI**	STUBBED	TWEEZES
TOWIES	**TRESSY**	TROCHIL	**TUMBLE**	**TWIBIL**
TOWIEST	STRESSY	**TROKED**	STUMBLE	TWIBILL
TOWING	**TRIAGE**	STROKED	TUMBLED	TWIBILS
STOWING	TRIAGED	**TROKES**	TUMBLER	**TWINGE**
TOWINGS	TRIAGES	STROKES	TUMBLES	TWINGED
TOWMON	**TRICKS**	**TROLLS**	**TUMPED**	TWINGES
TOWMOND	STRICKS	STROLLS	STUMPED	**TWITCH**
TOWMONS	TRICKSY	**TROMPE**	TUNICA	TWITCHY
TOWMONT	**TRIERS**	TROMPED	TUNICAE	**TYLERS**
TOWNIE	ETRIERS	TROMPES	**TUNNED**	STYLERS
TOWNIER	**TRIFLE**	**TROPHI**	STUNNED	**TYMPAN**

TYMPANA	SUGGING	MUMBLES	UNBALES	**UNDECK**
TYMPANI	TUGGING	NUMBLES	**UNBARE**	SUNDECK
TYMPANO	**UGLIED**	RUMBLES	UNBARED	UNDECKS
TYMPANS	OUGLIED	TUMBLES	UNBARES	**UNDIES**
TYMPANY	**UGLIER**	**UMBREL**	**UNBEDS**	BUNDIES
TYRING	FUGLIER	TUMBREL	SUNBEDS	CUNDIES
STYRING	**UGLIES**	UMBRELS	**UNBELT**	FUNDIES
TZADDI	OUGLIES	**UMBRIL**	SUNBELT	GUNDIES
TZADDIK	UGLIEST	TUMBRIL	UNBELTS	**UNDINE**
TZADDIQ	**ULEXES**	UMBRILS	**UNBONE**	NUNDINE
TZADDIS	CULEXES	**UMMING**	UNBONED	UNDINES
UAKARI	**ULICES**	BUMMING	UNBONES	**UNDRAW**
OUAKARI	CULICES	CUMMING	**UNBORN**	UNDRAWN
UAKARIS	**ULLAGE**	GUMMING	UNBORNE	UNDRAWS
UBERTY	FULLAGE	HUMMING	**UNBURY**	**UNEDGE**
PUBERTY	SULLAGE	MUMMING	BUNBURY	UNEDGED
UBIETY	ULLAGED	SUMMING	**UNCAGE**	UNEDGES
DUBIETY	ULLAGES	VUMMING	UNCAGED	**UNFAIR**
UCKERS	**ULLING**	**UMPIES**	UNCAGES	FUNFAIR
BUCKERS	BULLING	DUMPIES	**UNCAKE**	UNFAIRS
DUCKERS	CULLING	HUMPIES	UNCAKED	**UNFREE**
FUCKERS	DULLING	RUMPIES	UNCAKES	UNFREED
MUCKERS	FULLING	YUMPIES	**UNCAPE**	UNFREES
PUCKERS	GULLING	**UMPING**	UNCAPED	**UNGIRT**
SUCKERS	HULLING	BUMPING	UNCAPES	UNGIRTH
TUCKERS	LULLING	DUMPING	**UNCASE**	**UNGLUE**
YUCKERS	MULLING	GUMPING	UNCASED	UNGLUED
UDDERS	NULLING	HUMPING	UNCASES	UNGLUES
BUDDERS	PULLING	JUMPING	**UNCATE**	**UNGULA**
DUDDERS	WULLING	LUMPING	JUNCATE	UNGULAE
JUDDERS	ULLINGS	MUMPING	**UNCLES**	UNGULAR
MUDDERS	**ULOSES**	PUMPING	NUNCLES	**UNGYVE**
PUDDERS	DULOSES	RUMPING	**UNCLIP**	UNGYVED
RUDDERS	**ULOSIS**	TUMPING	UNCLIPS	UNGYVES
SUDDERS	DULOSIS	YUMPING	UNCLIPT	**UNHAND**
UGGING	**UMBERS**	**UMPIRE**	**UNCOES**	UNHANDS
BUGGING	CUMBERS	UMPIRED	BUNCOES	UNHANDY
FUGGING	LUMBERS	UMPIRES	JUNCOES	**UNHATS**
HUGGING	NUMBERS	**UNABLE**	UNCOEST	SUNHATS
JUGGING	**UMBLES**	TUNABLE	**UNCOPE**	**UNHEAD**
LUGGING	BUMBLES	**UNAKIN**	UNCOPED	BUNHEAD
MUGGING	FUMBLES	UNAKING	UNCOPES	UNHEADS
PUGGING	HUMBLES	**UNBALE**	**UNDATE**	**UNHELE**
RUGGING	JUMBLES	UNBALED	UNDATED	UNHELED

UNHELES	UNLIMED	UNROPES	**UNTUNE**	UPLEANT
UNHIVE	UNLIMES	**UNROVE**	UNTUNED	**UPLEAP**
UNHIVED	**UNLINE**	UNROVEN	UNTUNES	UPLEAPS
UNHIVES	UNLINED	**UNRULE**	**UNVAIL**	UPLEAPT
UNHOOD	UNLINES	UNRULED	UNVAILE	**UPMAKE**
NUNHOOD	**UNLIVE**	UNRULES	UNVAILS	UPMAKER
UNHOODS	UNLIVED	**UNSAFE**	**UNWIRE**	UPMAKES
UNIONS	UNLIVES	UNSAFER	UNWIRED	**UPPERS**
BUNIONS	**UNLOCK**	**UNSETS**	UNWIRES	CUPPERS
UNIQUE	GUNLOCK	SUNSETS	**UNWISE**	SUPPERS
UNIQUER	UNLOCKS	**UNSHED**	SUNWISE	**UPPILE**
UNIQUES	**UNLOVE**	DUNSHED	UNWISER	UPPILED
UNITED	UNLOVED	**UNSHIP**	**UNWIVE**	UPPILES
MUNITED	UNLOVES	GUNSHIP	UNWIVED	**UPPING**
UNITES	**UNMAKE**	NUNSHIP	UNWIVES	CUPPING
DUNITES	UNMAKER	UNSHIPS	**UNWOVE**	DUPPING
GUNITES	UNMAKES	**UNSHOE**	UNWOVEN	HUPPING
MUNITES	**UNNEST**	UNSHOED	**UNYOKE**	PUPPING
UNKING	DUNNEST	UNSHOES	UNYOKED	SUPPING
BUNKING	FUNNEST	**UNSHOT**	UNYOKES	TUPPING
DUNKING	UNNESTS	GUNSHOT	**UPBLOW**	UPPINGS
FUNKING	**UNPILE**	UNSHOTS	UPBLOWN	**UPRATE**
GUNKING	UNPILED	**UNSUIT**	UPBLOWS	UPRATED
JUNKING	UNPILES	SUNSUIT	**UPDATE**	UPRATES
UNKINGS	**UNPOPE**	UNSUITS	UPDATED	**UPRISE**
UNLACE	UNPOPED	**UNSURE**	UPDATER	UPRISEN
UNLACED	UNPOPES	UNSURED	UPDATES	UPRISER
UNLACES	**UNRAKE**	UNSURER	**UPDIVE**	UPRISES
UNLADE	UNRAKED	**UNTAME**	UPDIVED	**UPSIZE**
UNLADED	UNRAKES	UNTAMED	UPDIVES	UPSIZED
UNLADEN	**UNREAD**	UNTAMES	**UPDRAW**	UPSIZES
UNLADES	UNREADY	**UNTENT**	UPDRAWN	**UPTAKE**
UNLAST	**UNRIGS**	UNTENTS	UPDRAWS	UPTAKEN
UNLASTE	RUNRIGS	UNTENTY	**UPGAZE**	UPTAKES
UNLESS	**UNRIPE**	**UNTIES**	UPGAZED	**URALIS**
GUNLESS	UNRIPER	AUNTIES	UPGAZES	OURALIS
RUNLESS	**UNROBE**	PUNTIES	**UPGROW**	**URANIA**
SUNLESS	UNROBED	**UNTILE**	UPGROWN	URANIAN
UNLIKE	UNROBES	UNTILED	UPGROWS	URANIAS
NUNLIKE	**UNROOF**	UNTILES	**UPHROE**	**URANIC**
SUNLIKE	SUNROOF	**UNTINS**	EUPHROE	PURANIC
UNLIKED	UNROOFS	MUNTINS	UPHROES	**URARES**
UNLIKES	**UNROPE**	**UNTRUE**	**UPLEAN**	CURARES
UNLIME	UNROPED	UNTRUER	UPLEANS	**URARIS**

CURARIS	**USHERS**	**VALLAR**	**VERBID**	**VILEST**
OURARIS	BUSHERS	VALLARS	OVERBID	EVILEST
URATES	GUSHERS	VALLARY	VERBIDS	**VILLAN**
AURATES	HUSHERS	**VAMOSE**	**VERDIT**	VILLANS
CURATES	LUSHERS	VAMOSED	VERDITE	VILLANY
URBANE	MUSHERS	VAMOSES	VERDITS	**VIMINA**
URBANER	PUSHERS	**VANISH**	**VERISM**	VIMINAL
UREDIA	RUSHERS	EVANISH	VERISMO	**VISAGE**
UREDIAL	**UTASES**	**VAPOUR**	VERISMS	VISAGED
URENAS	MUTASES	VAPOURS	**VERMIL**	VISAGES
MURENAS	**UTILES**	VAPOURY	VERMILS	**VISING**
URGENT	RUTILES	**VARIES**	VERMILY	AVISING
SURGENT	**UTISES**	OVARIES	**VERMIN**	**VISITE**
TURGENT	CUTISES	**VAUNCE**	VERMINS	VISITED
URGERS	**UTMOST**	VAUNCED	VERMINY	VISITEE
BURGERS	OUTMOST	VAUNCES	**VERSET**	VISITER
PURGERS	UTMOSTS	**VAUNTS**	OVERSET	VISITES
SURGERS	**UTOPIA**	AVAUNTS	VERSETS	**VITTLE**
URGING	UTOPIAN	**VELATE**	**VERSIN**	VITTLED
GURGING	UTOPIAS	VELATED	VERSINE	VITTLES
PURGING	**UTTERS**	**VELURE**	VERSING	**VIZZIE**
SURGING	BUTTERS	VELURED	VERSINS	VIZZIED
URGINGS	CUTTERS	VELURES	**VERTED**	VIZZIES
URIALS	GUTTERS	**VELVET**	AVERTED	**VOIDED**
BURIALS	MUTTERS	VELVETS	EVERTED	AVOIDED
URINES	NUTTERS	VELVETY	**VESICA**	**VOIDER**
MURINES	PUTTERS	**VENGED**	VESICAE	AVOIDER
PURINES	RUTTERS	AVENGED	VESICAL	VOIDERS
URITES	**VACATE**	**VENGER**	VESICAS	**VOLANT**
CURITES	VACATED	AVENGER	**VETCHY**	VOLANTE
URNING	VACATES	VENGERS	KVETCHY	**VOLUME**
BURNING	**VADING**	**VENGES**	**VIATIC**	VOLUMED
DURNING	EVADING	AVENGES	AVIATIC	VOLUMES
GURNING	**VAGINA**	**VENTED**	VIATICA	**VOLUTE**
TURNING	VAGINAE	EVENTED	**VIATOR**	EVOLUTE
URNINGS	VAGINAL	**VENTER**	AVIATOR	VOLUTED
URPING	VAGINAS	EVENTER	VIATORS	VOLUTES
BURPING	**VAGUES**	VENTERS	**VIBRIO**	**VOLVED**
URTEXT	VAGUEST	**VENTRE**	VIBRION	EVOLVED
URTEXTE	**VAILED**	AVENTRE	VIBRIOS	**VOLVES**
URTEXTS	AVAILED	VENTRED	**VICTOR**	EVOLVES
USEFUL	**VALETE**	VENTRES	EVICTOR	**VOMICA**
MUSEFUL	VALETED	**VENUES**	VICTORS	VOMICAE
USEFULS	VALETES	AVENUES	VICTORY	VOMICAS

VOUDOU	SWAGGED	**WANDLE**	WARSLES	WEDGIES
VOUDOUN	**WAGGER**	WANDLED	**WASHED**	**WEEDER**
VOUDOUS	SWAGGER	WANDLES	SWASHED	WEEDERS
VOWERS	WAGGERS	**WANGLE**	**WASHER**	WEEDERY
AVOWERS	WAGGERY	TWANGLE	SWASHER	**WEEING**
VOWING	**WAGGLE**	WANGLED	WASHERS	SWEEING
AVOWING	WAGGLED	WANGLER	WASHERY	**WEENIE**
VOYAGE	WAGGLER	WANGLES	**WASHES**	TWEENIE
VOYAGED	WAGGLES	**WANKED**	SWASHES	WEENIER
VOYAGER	**WAGING**	SWANKED	**WASHIN**	WEENIES
VOYAGES	SWAGING	**WANKER**	WASHING	**WEEPER**
WABBLE	**WAITED**	SWANKER	WASHINS	SWEEPER
WABBLED	AWAITED	WANKERS	**WASPIE**	WEEPERS
WABBLER	**WAITER**	**WANNED**	WASPIER	**WEEPIE**
WABBLES	AWAITER	SWANNED	WASPIES	WEEPIER
WACKED	WAITERS	**WAPPED**	**WASTER**	WEEPIES
SWACKED	**WAITES**	SWAPPED	WASTERS	**WEETED**
WACKES	TWAITES	**WAPPER**	WASTERY	SWEETED
WACKEST	**WAKENS**	SWAPPER	**WATTER**	TWEETED
WADDIE	AWAKENS	WAPPERS	SWATTER	**WEETEN**
SWADDIE	**WAKING**	**WARBLE**	**WATTLE**	SWEETEN
WADDIED	AWAKING	WARBLED	TWATTLE	**WEETER**
WADDIES	WAKINGS	WARBLER	WATTLED	SWEETER
WADDLE	**WALIER**	WARBLES	WATTLES	TWEETER
SWADDLE	SWALIER	**WARDED**	**WAVIES**	**WEEVIL**
TWADDLE	**WALIES**	AWARDED	WAVIEST	WEEVILS
WADDLED	WALIEST	SWARDED	**WAYING**	WEEVILY
WADDLER	**WALING**	**WARDER**	SWAYING	**WEEWEE**
WADDLES	SWALING	AWARDER	**WEAKER**	WEEWEED
WADDLY	**WALLET**	WARDERS	TWEAKER	WEEWEES
TWADDLY	SWALLET	**WARMED**	**WEALTH**	**WEIGHT**
WADMOL	WALLETS	SWARMED	WEALTHS	WEIGHTS
WADMOLL	**WALLEY**	**WARMER**	WEALTHY	WEIGHTY
WADMOLS	WALLEYE	SWARMER	**WEARER**	**WEIRED**
WADSET	WALLEYS	WARMERS	SWEARER	SWEIRED
WADSETS	**WALLIE**	**WARNED**	WEARERS	**WELKIN**
WADSETT	WALLIER	AWARNED	**WEASEL**	WELKING
WAFFLE	WALLIES	**WARRAN**	WEASELS	WELKINS
WAFFLED	**WALLOW**	WARRAND	WEASELY	**WELLED**
WAFFLER	SWALLOW	WARRANS	**WEBBIE**	DWELLED
WAFFLES	WALLOWS	WARRANT	WEBBIER	SWELLED
WAGERS	**WAMBLE**	**WARSLE**	WEBBIES	**WELTED**
SWAGERS	WAMBLED	WARSLED	**WEDGIE**	SWELTED
WAGGED	WAMBLES	WARSLER	WEDGIER	**WELTER**

SWELTER	WIGGLER	WINGERS	**WISHES**	WORMERS
WELTERS	WIGGLES	**WINGES**	SWISHES	WORMERY
WESTER	**WIGHTS**	SWINGES	**WISSES**	**WOTTED**
WESTERN	TWIGHTS	TWINGES	SWISSES	SWOTTED
WESTERS	**WIGLET**	**WINIER**	**WISTED**	**WOULDS**
WHALER	TWIGLET	TWINIER	TWISTED	WOULDST
WHALERS	WIGLETS	**WINING**	**WITCHY**	**WOUNDS**
WHALERY	**WILING**	DWINING	SWITCHY	SWOUNDS
WHEELS	SWILING	TWINING	TWITCHY	**WRAXLE**
AWHEELS	**WILLED**	**WINISH**	**WITHER**	WRAXLED
WHEESH	SWILLED	SWINISH	SWITHER	WRAXLES
WHEESHT	TWILLED	**WINKED**	WITHERS	**WREATH**
WHEEZE	**WILLER**	SWINKED	**WITHIN**	WREATHE
WHEEZED.	SWILLER	TWINKED	WITHING	WREATHS
WHEEZER	WILLERS	**WINKER**	WITHINS	WREATHY
WHEEZES	**WILLIE**	SWINKER	**WITTED**	**WRETHE**
WHERES	WILLIED	WINKERS	TWITTED	WRETHED
WHERESO	WILLIES	**WINKLE**	**WITTER**	WRETHES
WHINGE	**WILLOW**	TWINKLE	TWITTER	**WRIEST**
WHINGED	WILLOWS	WINKLED	WITTERS	OWRIEST
WHINGER	WILLOWY	WINKLER	**WIVING**	**WRITHE**
WHINGES	**WILTED**	WINKLES	SWIVING	WRITHED
WHITES	TWILTED	**WINNED**	**WIZZES**	WRITHEN
WHITEST	**WIMBLE**	TWINNED	SWIZZES	WRITHER
WHOOMP	WIMBLED	**WINTER**	**WOBBLE**	WRITHES
WHOOMPH	WIMBLES	TWINTER	WOBBLED	**WUZZLE**
WHOOMPS	**WIMPLE**	WINTERS	WOBBLER	WUZZLED
WIBBLE	WIMPLED	WINTERY	WOBBLES	WUZZLES
WIBBLED	WIMPLES	**WINTLE**	**WOODIE**	**YABBIE**
WIBBLES	**WINDLE**	WINTLED	WOODIER	YABBIED
WIDDLE	DWINDLE	WINTLES	WOODIES	YABBIES
TWIDDLE	SWINDLE	**WIPERS**	**WOOLIE**	**YAFFED**
WIDDLED	WINDLED	SWIPERS	WOOLIER	NYAFFED
WIDDLES	WINDLES	**WIPING**	WOOLIES	**YAPPIE**
WIGGED	**WINDOW**	SWIPING	**WOONED**	YAPPIER
SWIGGED	WINDOWS	WIPINGS	SWOONED	YAPPIES
TWIGGED	WINDOWY	**WIRING**	**WOOSEL**	**YELLOW**
WIGGER	**WINERY**	TWIRING	WOOSELL	YELLOWS
SWIGGER	SWINERY	WIRINGS	WOOSELS	YELLOWY
TWIGGER	**WINGED**	**WISHED**	**WOPPED**	**YESSES**
WIGGERS	SWINGED	SWISHED	SWOPPED	OYESSES
WIGGERY	TWINGED	**WISHER**	**WORDED**	**YESTER**
WIGGLE	**WINGER**	SWISHER	SWORDED	DYESTER
WIGGLED	SWINGER	WISHERS	**WORMER**	YESTERN

YMPING	ZANIEST	ZIZZLES	**ZONULA**	ZONULET
GYMPING	**ZITHER**	**ZOARIA**	ZONULAE	**ZYMITE**
ZADDIK	ZITHERN	ZOARIAL	ZONULAR	AZYMITE
TZADDIK	ZITHERS	**ZONATE**	ZONULAS	ZYMITES
ZADDIKS	**ZIZZLE**	OZONATE	**ZONULE**	
ZANIES	ZIZZLED	ZONATED	ZONULES	

Unexpected -S hooks

In a game of Scrabble, it can be a great advantage to be able to surprise the opponent by making a play using an S that unexpectedly hooks an existing word that looks as if it is inextensible. There are four categories of such words selected here:

- Words that are past tenses in -ED that can be treated as a noun and therefore take an -S hook (eg MARRIED-S)

- Words that are irregular past tenses that can be treated as a noun, or that happen to be a noun with a totally different meaning, and therefore take an -S hook (eg WENT-S)

- Words that have already been pluralized with an S but which can then take a further S hook (eg CITES-S)

- Words that end in consonant followed by Y where the plural can be a straight -S, breaking the standard rule of converting Y to I and adding ES (eg TRILBY-S).

While these words of less than seven letters will also appear in their appropriate place within the hook word section, it is of value to have them all collected together here in one place, together with longer examples, for ease of learning.

Words ending in past tense –ED that take an –S

ASSURED -S	LAMED -S
BELOVED -S	LIMITED -S
BETROTHED -S	MALTED -S
CLASSIFIED -S	MARRIED -S
COLORED -S	MOPED -S
COLOURED -S	NEWLYWED -S
COMBINED -S	PUREBRED -S
CROSSBRED -S	SADDLEBRED -S
DECEASED -S	SIGNIFIED -S
DEPARTED -S	STANDARDBRED -S
ELEVATED -S	STRAIGHTBRED -S
FROSTED -S	UNDECIDED -S
HOMEBRED -S	UNEMPLOYED -S
ILLUSTRATED -S	UNINSURED -S
INBRED -S	UNLEADED -S
INCROSSBRED -S	UNMARRIED -S
INSURED -S	UNWASHED -S
INTENDED -S	WICKED –S

Words that are irregular past-tenses that take an –S

ATE -S	PENT -S
BOUGHT -S	RANG -S
BRED –S	SAID -S
CAME -S	SANG -S
CHOSE -S	SENT -S
DUG -S	SOLD -S
FED -S	SPRANG -S
FLEW –S	STANK -S
FORLORN –S	TORE -S
GIVEN -S	TROD -S
GREW -S	WENT -S
HAD –S	WOULD -S
HEARD -S	WOVEN -S
MET -S	

Words ending in an –S form that then take another –S

ABBES -S	BAS -S
ABYS -S	BIBLES -S
ACROS -S	BOS -S
ADVENTURES -S	BRAS -S
AMAS -S	BULGINES -S
AMIS -S	BUTTERINES -S
ASSES -S	CAMAS -S

CAPLES -S	MAS -S
CARES -S	MES -S
CARLES -S	MILLIONAIRES -S
CAVAS -S	MILLIONNAIRES -S
CHAPES -S	MIS -S
CITES -S	MORAS -S
COMBLES -S	MOS -S
COSINES -S	MUS -S
CUFFLES -S	NEEDLES -S
DAUPHINES -S	NERVINES -S
DEADLINES -S	OGRES -S
DECKLES -S	PHILOSOPHES -S
DOS -S	PIS -S
DURES -S	POS -S
ESQUIRES -S	POSSES -S
FAINNES -S	PRECES -S
FANGLES -S	PRELATES -S
FES -S	PRINCES -S
FOGLES -S	PROCURES -S
FOOTLES -S	PROS -S
FRAS -S	RANKLES -S
GAMINES -S	RAYLES -S
GARBLES -S	ROOTLES -S
GAUS -S	RUMPLES -S
GLASSINES -S	RUSTLES -S
GOS -S	SAGENES -S
GUES -S	SALTINES -S
HANDLES -S	SATYRES -S
HOMINES -S	SHINES -S
HOS -S	SIGHTLINES -S
HURTLES -S	SKIFFLES -S
INKLES -S	SOS -S
JOINTURES -S	SOUPLES -S
KAROS -S	SPARKLES -S
KAVAS -S	SPECKLES -S
KINDLES -S	SPRINGLES -S
KINGLES -S	SQUIRES -S
KIS -S	SUCKLES -S
KOS -S	TACKLES -S
LARGES -S	TAILLES -S
LAS -S	TARTINES -S
LOWNES -S	TAS -S
MAPLES -S	TIMELINES -S
MARQUES -S	TREADLES -S

TRICKLES -S
TYRANNES -S
USURES -S

WATTLES -S
WINDLES -S
ZEBRAS -S

Words ending in a consonant plus Y that take an –S

ABHENRY -S
ABY -S
BENDY -S
BIALY -S
BLOWBY -S
BY -S
CANTERBURY -S
COLBY -S
DARCY -S
DROSTDY -S
DRY -S
EMMY -S
FLYBY -S
GOODBY -S
HENRY -S
JANSKY -S

MILLIHENRY -S
MOLY -S
NY -S
PLATY -S
POLY -S
PRY -S
QWERTY -S
SHINDY -S
STANDBY -S
SWINGBY -S
TELLY -S
TREVALLY -S
TRILBY -S
WHY -S
ZLOTY -S

MISCELLANEOUS LISTS

- This section contains a variety of short lists that don't really have a home elsewhere in the book.

- Not all these lists are of great importance to Scrabble but they may appeal to some players.

- The section includes lists of place names and personal names that happen to be allowed words, and lists of allowable words whose origins are in overseas English-speaking regions of the world.

- Most of these lists do not aim to be exhaustive but the contents have been selected in order to maintain some relevance to Scrabble.

Place names

Some place names can also be valid Scrabble words, either because the word has a meaning related to that place or just through sheer coincidence. Here is a selection that may be of interest. The list is by no means exhaustive but represents a selection of words up to eight letters in length that have some value to the Scrabble player. (The assistance of David Sutton is acknowledged in generating this list.)

ACTON	a stuffed jacket worn under mail
ALAMO	a kind of poplar
ALASKA	a heavy fabric
AMAZON	a tall, powerful woman
AMMAN	a district magistrate
ANGOLA	relating to a fabric made from the wool of the Angora goat
ARMAGNAC	a kind of brandy
ASCOT	a type of necktie with broad ends
ASSAM	in Malaysia, tamarind as used in cooking
BABEL	a scene of confusion
BALBOA	the monetary unit of Panama
BALMORAL	a flat Scottish bonnet
BANGKOK	a straw hat
BARBICAN	an outer defensive work; esp a tower at a gate or bridge
BEDLAM	an asylum
BERLIN	a type of carriage
BLARNEY	to talk persuasively
BOHEMIA	a community of bohemians
BOLIVIA	a type of fabric
BOLOGNA	a kind of sausage
BOSTON	a card game
BOURBON	a kind of whisky
BOWERY	any area frequented by drunks
BRAZIL	a dyewood
BRENT	a kind of goose
BRISTOL	a smooth cardboard
BRUSSELS	a brussels sprout
CAMELOT	a strong waterproof fabric
CANADA	a narrow canyon
CHAD	a punched out piece of paper
CHANTILLY	as in chantilly lace
CHEDDAR	a type of cheese
CHESHIRE	a kind of pig
CHILE	chili
CHINA	fine porcelain ware
CHUR	New Zealand expression of agreement

COLOGNE	a perfumed liquid
COLORADO	refers to a medium strength cigar
CONGO	a kind of black Chinese tea
CORBY	a crow, a raven
CORDOBA	the standard monetary unit of Nicaragua
CREMONA	an ancient wind instrument
CREWE	a pot
DERBY	a kind of hat
DERRY	a dislike
DEVON	a breed of cattle from Devon
DONEGAL	a type of tweed
DOVER	to doze
ETNA	a vessel for heating liquids
FLORENCE	a former gold coin of Europe
FUJI	a silk fabric
FULHAM	a loaded die
GALILEE	a small chapel or porch at the western end of some medieval English churches
GALLOWAY	a breed of hornless beef cattle
GAMBIA	the inspissated juice of a plant growing in Malacca
GENEVA	a spirit distilled from gin
GENOA	a large jib which overlaps the mainsail
GERS	Mongolian tents
GOA	a kind of Tibetan gazelle with backward-curving horns
GOBI	Hindi word for cauliflower
GOSPORT	a communication device in an aeroplane
GREECE	a flight of steps
GUERNSEY	a woollen jersey
HACKNEY	a kind of cab
HAMBURG	a patty of ground beef
HARROW	a spiked frame for breaking up ground
HASTINGS	early fruit or vegetables
HAVERING	present participle of 'to haver'
HENLEY	a type of sweater
HOLLAND	a coarse cotton or linen
HOMBURG	a man's felt hat
ILLAWARRA	a breed of dairy cattle
INDIA	NATO alphabet code for letter i
JAFFA	a low-bowled ball in Cricket
JAPAN	to coat with glossy, black lacquer
JAVA	a kind of coffee
JERSEY	a close-fitting, knitted shirt
JORDAN	a chamber-pot
KASHMIR	a soft twilled fabric of goat's wool

KENT	to punt or pole
KIEV	a type of stuffed chicken dish
LABRADOR	a breed of dog
LANGLEY	a unit of illumination used to measure the temperature of a star
LEVANT	to abscond
LEWIS	a dovetailed iron tenon made to fit into a stone so that it can be hoisted
LIMA	a kind of bean
LUCERNE	a fodder plant
MACON	smoked salted mutton
MADEIRA	a white wine
MADISON	a type of cycle race, first staged in Madison Square Gardens
MADRAS	a cotton fabric
MALI	one of the gardener class in India
MANILA	a fibre used in making rope
MARGATE	a fish of the West Atlantic
MAYO	mayonnaise
MEDINA	in N. African cities, the ancient native quarter
MINORCA	a type of domestic fowl
MODENA	a dark purple colour
MOROCCO	a kind of leather
MUSCAT	muscatel wine; a musky variety of grape or its vine
MUSCOVY	a type of duck
NATAL	relating to birth
NELSON	a wrestling hold
NIAGARA	a deluge or outpouring
NIGER	a negro
NOME	a province or department esp. in ancient Greece
ORLEANS	a variety of plum
OXFORD	a type of shoe
PAISLEY	a patterned fabric
PANAMA	a kind of straw hat
PARIS	a European herb
PENNINE	a mineral of the chlorite group
PHOENIX	a mythological bird
PINNER	one who impounds cattle
POLISH	to make smooth and lustrous by rubbing
POPLAR	a kind of tree
PORTLAND	a kind of cement, having the color of the Portland stone
QUEBEC	NATO alphabet code for letter q
RABAT	to rotate into coincidence with another plane
RHINE	a drainage channel
RHONE	a roof-gutter
RIALTO	a theatrical district; a marketplace

RIOJA	a Spanish red wine
RIVIERA	any warm coastal district reminiscent of the Riviera
RUBICON	the winning of a game in piquet before one's opponent scores
RUSSIA	a kind of leather
SARK	a shirt, a chemise
SAUTERNE	a white wine
SEINE	to fish with a certain kind of net
SILESIA	a thin twilled cotton or linen
SODOM	any place notorious for vice
SOHO	a hunting cry
SOMERSET	a somersault
SPAIN	to wean
STEPNEY	a spare wheel
STROUD	a kind of coarse blanket made at Stroud
SUMATRA	a short, violent squall in or near the Straits of Malacca
SURREY	a horse-drawn carriage
TELFORD	a road made of stones
TEXAS	the uppermost structure on a steamboat
THEBES	plural of 'thebe', a monetary unit of Botswana
TILBURY	a light open two-wheeled carriage
TOLEDO	a sword made at Toledo
TONGA	a light two-wheeled Indian vehicle
TRIPOLI	an earthy substance originally brought from Tripoli, used in polishing stones and metals
TUPELO	a North American tree
TYNE	to lose
ULSTER	a kind of overcoat
VALENCIA	a kind of woven fabric
VICHY	a kind of mineral water
VICTORIA	a kind of open carriage
VIENNA	a type of steak
VIRGINIA	a type of flue-cured tobacco grown originally in Virginia
VOLTA	a lively Italian dance
WALES	weals
WALLSEND	a kind of coal
WANTAGE	a deficiency, a shortage
WARSAW	a kind of fish
WATERLOO	a decisive defeat or setback
WELS	an American catfish
WIGAN	a stiff plain-woven cotton
WOOMERA	a stick for launching a spear with greater force
WORTHING	present participle of 'worth', to be, to happen
YORK	to bowl a batsman with a YORKER
ZAIRE	a former monetary unit of what was Zaire

Personal names

Similarly, some personal names can also be valid Scrabble words, either because the familiar personal name has itself been derived from a word (such as girls' names that come from flowers) or because something has been named after someone, or just out of coincidence. Here is a selection that may be of interest. The list is by no means exhaustive but represents a selection of words up to eight letters in length that have some value to the Scrabble player. (The assistance of David Sutton is acknowledged in generating this list.)

ABIGAIL	a lady's maid
ALAN	a large hunting dog
ALBERT	a short kind of watch-chain
ALMA	Egyptian dancing girl
ANNA	a former coin of India
BASIL	an aromatic herb
BEN	a mountain peak
BENEDICT	a newly married man
BENJAMIN	benzoine, a gum resin
BENNY	an amphetamine tablet
BERTHA	a woman's deep collar
BETH	a Hebrew letter
BILL	to present for payment
BILLY	a metal container for cooking outdoors
BOBBY	a policeman
BONNIE	bonny (pretty)
BRAD	a thin nail
BUSTER	something large
CAL	short for calorie
CARL	a miser
CAROL	to sing joyously
CASSIE	a type of thorny shrub
CELESTE	a keyboard instrument
CHAD	a scrap of paper
CHARLEY	a fool
CHARLIE	a fool
CHUCK	to throw
CICERO	a typeface
CLARENCE	a closed carriage
CLEMENT	merciful
CLIFF	a high steep face of rock
CRISPIN	poetic for a shoemaker
DAISY	a flowering plant

DAPHNE	a flowering shrub
DAVY	a miner's safety lamp
DEXTER	situated on the right
DIANE	a kind of steak
DICK	a detective
DICKENS	a devil
DOLLY	a wheeled platform
DONNA	an Italian lady
DOTTY	crazy
DUSTY	full of dust
ERICA	a shrub of the heath family
FAGIN	one who trains young thieves
FANNY	the buttocks
FAY	to join closely
FELICITY	happiness
FLEUR	flower emblem used in heraldry
FLORENCE	a durable silk fabric
FLOSSIE	a floozy
FRANK	to mark for postage
FRITZ	a state of disrepair
GABBY	talkative
GILBERT	an electromagnetic unit of force
GILLY	to act as a hunting attendant
GLEN	a small valley
GLORIA	a halo
GRAHAM	wholewheat flour
GUY	chap, fellow
HANSEL	to inaugurate with a gift
HECTOR	to bully
HENRY	a unit of inductance
HERBY	abounding in herbs
HOMER	to hit a home run
HYACINTH	a type of flower
JACK	to raise with a type of lever
JACKY	a sailor
JADE	to weary
JAKE	a yokel
JANE	a girl or woman
JEAN	a durable cotton fabric
JEMIMA	an elastic-sided boot
JENNY	a travelling crane
JERRY	a builder of flimsy houses
JESS	to strap the legs of a hawk
JILL	a cart for carrying timber

JIMMY	to pry open with a crowbar
JO	a sweetheart
JOE	a sweetheart
JOEY	a young kangaroo
JOHNNY	a sleeveless hospital gown
JORDAN	a type of chamberpot
JOSEPH	a woman's long cloak
JOSH	to tease
JUDAS	a spyhole in a door
KELLY	a specialist drilling pipe
KELVIN	the SI unit of temperature
KEN	to know
KERRY	one of an Irish breed of cattle
KITTY	a fund of money
LANCE	to pierce with a lance
LAURA	a type of monastery
LOUIE	a lieutenant
LOUIS	a former gold coin of France
LUCIFER	a friction match
MARC	residue after pressing grapes
MARCEL	to give soft waves to hair with heated tongs
MARGE	margarine
MARIA	dark areas of the Moon or Mars
MARINA	a berthing area for yachts
MARTIN	a small bird
MARYJANE	marijuana
MATILDA	a hobo's bundle
MAXWELL	a unit of magnetic flux
MICHAEL	teasing (as in 'take the michael')
MICKEY	to drug someone's drink
MOLLY	a tropical fish
MORGAN	a type of saddle horse
MORRIS	an English folk dance
NANCY	an effeminate young man
NAPOLEON	a old French gold coin
NELLIE	a weak or foolish person
NELLY	a weak or foolish person
NEWTON	a unit of force
NOAH	a shark (Australian slang)
NOEL	any Christmas carol
OLIVE	a small fruit
OSCAR	cash
PAM	a type of card game
PATSY	one who is easily fooled

PATTY	a thin, flat cake of food
PETER	to diminish gradually
RALPH	to vomit
REG	a regulation
REX	a king
ROMEO	a swain, a beau
RUDY	a member of a youth movement originating in the 1960s
RUTH	compassion
SALLY	to rush out suddenly
SANDY	covered with sand
SHAW	a small wood
SHEILA	a young girl or a woman
SHELLY	abounding in seashells
SHERLOCK	a detective
SHYLOCK	a ruthless creditor
SIBYL	a female prophet
SONNY	a small boy
SPENCER	a short double-breasted overcoat
TAMMY	a fabric of mixed fibers
TEDDY	a furry, stuffed toy bear
TERRY	an absorbent fabric
TIFFANY	a thin, mesh fabric
TIMOTHY	a kind of grass
TINA	slang term for crystal meth
TITAN	anything gigantic
TOBY	a type of drinking mug
TOMMY	to oppress by paying in goods instead of money
TONY	stylish
TROY	a system of weights
VERA	very
VERONICA	a type of herb
VICTORIA	a gigantic water lily
WALDO	a remote control gadget
WALLY	something visually pleasing
WARREN	a place where rabbits live
WEBSTER	a weaver

Words from world English

One method of dealing with the awkward tile combinations that inevitably appear on your rack at some point in a game is to memorize a wide selection of words outside the core vocabulary of English. As the most widely spoken language in the world, English is rich in loan-words from other languages, and the versatility of the Roman alphabet and of English pronunciation means that these words tend to be assimilated without much corruption of their original sound. This means that there are many word in English that use 'foreign' letter combinations, which are ideal for Scrabble players. The following lists contain words from Australia, Canada, New Zealand and South Africa, as well as words from the main languages of the Indian Subcontinent – Hindi and Urdu – which have entered British English.

Australian words

Australian English is distinguished not only by the numerous Aboriginal terms for Australia's flora and fauna, but also by a great many shortened forms of commonplace English words. The Australian propensity to slang and short informal words is extremely useful to Scrabble players, especially as many of these words end in O, one of the most common tiles in the game. If you spot an O on the board when you have a difficult set of letters on your rack, there's a good chance that you'll be able to form an informal Aussie word. Native Australian words provide a range of unusual letter combinations, as well as a tendency to include double Os – so it's well worth acquiring some Antipodean vocabulary.

ADJIGO	yam plant
ALF	uncultivated Australian
ARVO	afternoon
ASPRO	associate professor
BARRO	embarrassing
BAUERA	small evergreen shrub
BEAUT	outstanding person or thing
BELAH	casuarina tree
BERKO	berserk
BIFFO	fighting or aggressive behaviour
BILBY	burrowing marsupial
BIZZO	empty and irrelevant talk
BOAB	baobab tree
BODGIE	unruly or uncouth man
BOGAN	fool
BOOBOOK	small spotted brown owl
BOOFY	strong but stupid
BOONG	offensive word for a Black person
BOOSHIT	very good
BORA	native Australian coming-of-age ceremony
BORAK	rubbish or nonsense
BRASCO	lavatory
BROLGA	large grey crane with red-and-green head
BRUMBY	wild horse

BUNYA	tall dome-shaped coniferous tree
BUNYIP	legendary monster
CADAGI	tropical eucalyptus tree
CARBY	carburettor
CHEWIE	chewing gum
CHIACK	tease or banter
CHOCO	conscript or militiaman
CHOOK	hen or chicken
CHOOM	Englishman
CONNIE	bus conductor
COMMO	communist
COMPO	compensation
CORREA	evergreen shrub
COUCAL	long-legged bird
COUGAN	rowdy person
COUTA	type of sailing boat
CRONK	unfit or unsound
CROOL	spoil
CROWEA	pink-flowered shrub
DACK	forcibly remove someone's trousers
DADAH	illegal drugs
DAGGY	untidy or dishevelled
DASYURE	small carnivorous marsupial
DELO	delegate
DERRO	vagrant
DINKUM	genuine or right
DOCO	documentary
DONGA	steep-sided gully
DORBA	stupid, inept, or clumsy person
DRACK	unattractive
DRONGO	slow-witted person
DROOB	pathetic person
DUBBO	stupid
DUGITE	venomous snake
DURRY	cigarette
EARBASH	talk incessantly
EUMUNG	type of acacia
EVO	evening
EXO	excellent
FASTIE	deceitful act
FESTY	dirty or smelly
FIBRO	house built of fibrocement
FIGJAM	very conceited person
FIZGIG	frivolous or flirtatious girl

FOULIE	bad mood
FRIB	short heavy-conditioned piece of wool
FUNDIE	fundamentalist Christian
FURPHY	rumour or fictitious story
GALAH	grey-and-pink cockatoo
GARBO	dustman
GEEBUNG	tree with edible but tasteless fruit
GIDGEE	small acacia tree that sometimes emits an unpleasant smell
GILGAI	natural water hole
GING	child's catapult
GNOW	ground-dwelling bird
GOANNA	monitor lizard
GOOG	egg
GOOLIE	stone or pebble
GUNYAH	bush hut or shelter
GYMPIE	tall tree with stinging hairs on its leaves
HAKEA	type of shrub or tree
HOSTIE	air hostess
HOVEA	plant with purple flowers
HUTCHIE	groundsheet draped over an upright stick as a shelter
JARRAH	type of eucalyptus tree
JEFF	downsize or close down an organization
JUMBUCK	sheep
KARRI	type of eucalyptus tree
KOORI	native Australian
KYBO	temporary lavatory
KYLIE	boomerang that is flat on one side and convex on the other
LOPPY	man employed to do maintenance work on a ranch
LOWAN	ground-dwelling bird
LUBRA	Aboriginal woman
MALLEE	low shrubby eucalyptus tree
MARRI	type of eucalyptus
MELBA	repeated farewell appearances
MIDDY	middle-sized glass of beer
MILKO	milkman
MOLOCH	spiny lizard
MOPOKE	small spotted owl
MOZ	hoodoo or hex
MUGGA	eucalyptus tree with pink flowers and dark bark
MULGA	acacia shrub
MULLOCK	waste material from a mine
MURREE	native Australian
MURRI	native Australian
MYALL	native Australian living independently of society

MYXO	myxomatosis
NANA	head
NARDOO	cloverlike fern
NEDDY	horse
NOAH	shark
NONG	stupid or incompetent person
NORK	female breast
NUMBAT	small marsupial with long snout
OCKER	uncultivated or boorish Australian
PIKER	wild bullock
PINDAN	desert region of Western Australia
PITURI	shrub with narcotic leaves
PLONKO	alcoholic, especially one who drinks wine
PLURRY	euphemism for bloody
PODDY	handfed calf or lamb
POKIE	poker machine
POON	stupid or ineffectual person
POONCE	male homosexual
POSSIE	position
PRELOVED	second-hand
QUOKKA	small wallaby
QUOLL	native cat
RANGA	offensive name for a person with red hair
RAZOO	imaginary coin
REFFO	offensive term for a European refugee after World War Two
REGO	registration of a motor vehicle
RESTO	restored antique, vintage car, etc
ROO	kangaroo
ROUGHIE	something unfair, especially a trick
SANGER	sandwich
SANGO	sandwich
SCOZZA	rowdy person
SCUNGY	miserable, sordid or dirty
SHARPIE	member of a teenage group with short hair and distinctive clothes
SHERANG	boss
SHYPOO	liquor of poor quality
SITELLA	small black-and-white bird
SKEG	rear fin on the underside of a surfboard
SKITE	boast
SMOKO	cigarette break
SMOODGE	smooch
SPAG	offensive term for an Italian
SPRUIK	speak in public

SWAGGIE	vagrant worker
SWAGMAN	vagrant worker
SWY	gambling game
TONK	effeminate man
TOOLIE	adult who gatecrashes Schoolies Week
TOOSHIE	angry or upset
TRIELLA	three horse races nominated for a bet
TROPPO	mentally affected by a tropical climate
TRUCKIE	truck driver
TRUGO	game similar to croquet
TUAN	flying phalanger
TUART	type of eucalyptus tree
UMPIE	umpire
UNCO	awkward or clumsy
UPTA	of poor quality
UPTER	of poor quality
UTE	utility
VAG	vagrant
VEGO	vegetarian
VIGORO	women's game similar to cricket
WADDY	heavy wooden club used by native Australians
WAGGA	blanket made of sacks stitched together
WANDOO	eucalyptus tree with white bark
WARATAH	shrub with dark green leaves and crimson flowers
WARB	dirty or insignificant person
WHARFIE	wharf labourer
WIDGIE	female bodgie
WILGA	small drought-resistant tree
WIRILDA	acacia tree with edible seeds
WTRRAH	saltwater fish with bright blue spots
WOF	fool or idiot
WOOMERA	spear-throwing stick
WURLEY	Aboriginal hut
YABBER	talk or jabber
YABBY	small freshwater crayfish
YACCA	grass tree
YACKA	grass tree
YARRAN	small hardy tree
YATE	small eucalyptus tree
YIKE	argument, squabble or fight
YUCKO	disgusting
YUMMO	delicious
ZAMBUCK	St John ambulance attendant
ZIFF	beard

Canadian words

Canadian English combines a broad range of British and US terms with words derived from Inuit, as well as from other Native American languages such as Algonquin. Canadian English incorporates many Canadian French words from Quebec, and there are also a number of recently coined Canadian terms. Inuit words can be helpful to Scrabble players because they tend to be quite vowel-heavy. K occurs frequently in Inuit terms, and sometimes appears twice. Such words require a blank tile for the second K if they are to be played during a game.

AGLOO	breathing hole made in ice by a seal
AGLU	breathing hole made in ice by a seal
AMAUT	hood on an Inuit woman's parka for carrying a child
AMOWT	hood on an Inuit woman's parka for carrying a child
ATIGI	Inuit parka
BABICHE	thongs or lacings of rawhide
BARACHOIS	shallow lagoon formed by a sand bar
BATEAU	light flat-bottomed boat
BAWK	type of Atlantic seabird
BIBE	in Newfoundland folklore, spirit whose wailing warns of a coming death
BEIGNET	deep-fried pastry
BOGAN	sluggish side stream
BREWIS	Newfoundland cod stew
BUMBLEBERRY	mixed berry pie filling
BUTTE	isolated steep-sided flat-topped hill
CANOLA	cooking oil extracted from a variety of rapeseed developed in Canada
CAYUSE	small Native American pony used by cowboys
CIPAILLE	type of pie traditional in Quebec
CRETONS	shredded pork spread
COULEE	dry stream valley
CUSK	gadoid food fish
DEKE	act or instance of feinting in ice hockey
ENDORSATION	approval or support
HOSER	unsophisticated rural person
ICEWINE	dessert wine made from frozen grapes
JOUAL	nonstandard Canadian French dialect
JUDICARE	state-paid legal services
KAMIK	Inuit boot made of caribou hide or sealskin
KLOOCH	North American Indian woman
KAMOTIQ	Inuit sled
KLOOTCH	North American Indian woman
KUDLIK	Inuit soapstone seal-oil lamp

LOGAN	backwater
LOONIE	Canadian dollar coin with loon bird on one face
MECHOUI	Canadian dish of meat roasted on a spit
MUCKAMUCK	food
MUCKYMUCK	very important person
MUKTUK	beluga skin used as food
NANOOK	polar bear
PANZEROTTO	baked turnover with savoury filling
PARFLECHE	dried rawhide
PARKADE	building used as a car park
PARKETTE	small public park
PLEW	beaver skin used as standard unit in fur trading
POGEY	financial relief for the unemployed
POGY	financial relief for the unemployed
POKELOGAN	backwater
POUTINE	chipped potatoes topped with curd cheese and tomato sauce
PUNG	horse-drawn sleigh
QAMUTIQ	Inuit sled
QAJAQ	a kayak
QUINZHEE	shelter made from hollowed-out snow
REDEYE	drink incorporating beer and tomato juice
RUBABOO	soup made by boiling pemmican
RUBBY	rubbing alcohol mixed with cheap wine for drinking
SKOOKUM	strong or brave
SNYE	side channel of a river
SPLAKE	hybrid trout bred by Canadian zoologists
STORMSTAYED	isolated due to adverse weather
SWILER	seal hunter
TILLICUM	friend
TOONIE	Canadian two-dollar coin
TULLIBEE	whitefish found in the Great Lakes
TUPEK	Inuit tent of animal skins
TUPIK	Inuit tent of animal skins
TURR	Newfoundland name for the guillemot
TWONIE	Canadian two-dollar coin
WAWA	speech or language
WENDIGO	evil spirit or cannibal

Hindi words

After Chinese, Hindi, the dominant language of India, is the most widely spoken language in the world. Many Hindi words entered British English during the Raj, and some have become everyday terms – BUNGALOW and PUNDIT, for example. Others are less common, but are useful to Scrabble players because they provide unusual letter combinations and thus solutions to difficult racks. Combinations such as BH, DH and KH are common in Hindi-derived words, and the preponderance of As, Is and Us can be very helpful in trying to balance a vowel-heavy rack. Above all, Hindi words are useful because they are quite unusual, and so provide a range of options for Scrabble players that aren't immediately obvious – front-hooking onto HANG with a B, for example, or end-hooking onto PUNK with an A. Committing some Hindi-derived words to memory will help to keep your opponents on their toes.

AKHARA	gymnasium
ALAP	vocal music without words
AMBARY	tropical plant
ANKUS	elephant goad
ANNA	old copper coin
ARTI	Hindu ritual
AYAH	maidservant or nursemaid
BABU	Mr
BAEL	spiny tree
BAHADUR	title for distinguished Indians during the Raj
BAHU	daughter-in-law
BANDH	general strike
BANYAN	tree with aerial roots
BHAI	form of address for a man
BHAJI	deep-fried vegetable savoury
BHANG	psychoactive drug made of hemp
BHANGRA	music combining traditional Punjabi music with Western pop
BHAVAN	large house or building
BHEESTY	water-carrier
BHINDI	okra used in cooking
BHISHTI	water-carrier
BINDI	decorative dot in middle of forehead
BOBBERY	mixed pack of hunting dogs
BUND	embankment
CHAI	tea, especially with added spices
CHAMPAC	tree with fragrant yellow flowers
CHAPATI	flat coarse unleavened bread
CHAPPAL	sandal
CHARAS	hashish
CHARKHA	spinning wheel
CHELA	disciple of a religious teacher
CHICHI	person of mixed British and Indian descent
CHILLUM	pipe for smoking cannabis
CHITAL	the axis deer
CHOLI	short-sleeved bodice

CHOWK	marketplace
CHUDDAR	large shawl or veil
CHUDDIES	underpants
CHUKAR	Indian partridge
COWAGE	tropical climbing plant with stinging pods
COWHAGE	tropical climbing plant with stinging pods
CRORE	ten million
CROREPATI	person who has ten million rupees
DACOIT	member of a gang of armed robbers
DACOITY	robbery by an armed gang
DAK	system of mail delivery
DAL	split grain
DATURA	plant with trumpet-shaped flowers
DEODAR	Himalayan cedar
DEWAN	chief minister of an Indian princedom
DHAK	tropical tree with red flowers
DHAL	curry made from lentils
DHARNA	method of obtaining justice by fasting
DHOBI	washerman
DHOTI	loincloth
DHOLAK	two-headed drum
DUPATTA	scarf
DURBAR	court of an Indian ruler
DURRIE	cotton carpet
DURZI	Indian tailor
GANJA	potent form of cannabis
GAUR	large wild cow
GARIAL	fish-eating crocodilian with long slender snout
GAVIAL	fish-eating crocodilian with long slender snout
GHARIAL	fish-eating crocodilian with long slender snout
GHARRI	horse-drawn vehicle for hire
GHARRY	horse-drawn vehicle for hire
GHAT	stairs or passage leading down to a river
GHEE	clarified butter
GHERAO	industrial action in which workers imprison their employers
GINGILI	oil obtained from sesame seeds
GORAL	small goat antelope
GUAR	plant that produces gum
GUNNY	coarse fabric used for sacks
HARTAL	act of closing shop or stopping work as a political protest
HOWDAH	seat for riding on an elephant's back
JAGGERY	coarse brown sugar
JAI	victory
JALEBI	type of sweet fried snack

KARAHI	bowl-shaped cooking pan
KHADDAR	cotton cloth
KHEDA	enclosure for captured elephants
KHEDAH	enclosure for captured elephants
KHEDDAH	enclosure for captured elephants
KIRANA	small, family-owned shop
KOEL	parasitic cuckoo
KOS	Indian unit of distance
KRAIT	brightly coloured venomous snake
KUKRI	Ghurka knife
KULFI	Indian dessert
KURTA	long loose garment like a shirt without a collar
LAC	resinous substance secreted by insects
LAKH	100,000
LANGUR	arboreal monkey
LASSI	yoghurt drink
LATHI	long heavy stick used as a weapon
LUNGI	long piece of cloth worn as loincloth or turban
MACHAN	platform used in tiger hunting
MAHANT	chief priest in a Hindu temple
MAHOUT	elephant driver
MAHSEER	large freshwater fish
MAKHANI	denoting a dish made with butter or ghee
MANDI	big market
MANDIR	Hindu or Jain temple
MAUND	unit of weight
MEHNDI	practice of painting designs on the hands and feet using henna
MELA	cultural or religious festival
MOHUR	old gold coin
MONAL	Asian pheasant
MORCHA	hostile demonstration against the government
MRIDANG	drum used in Indian music
NAUCH	intricate Indian dance
NAUTCH	intricate Indian dance
NAWAB	Muslim prince in India
NEEM	large tree
NILGAI	large Indian antelope
NULLAH	stream or drain
NUMDAH	coarse felt
OONT	camel
PACHISI	game resembling backgammon
PAISA	one hundredth of a rupee
PAKORA	dish of deep-fried chicken or vegetables
PANEER	soft white cheese

PARATHA	flat unleavened bread
PEEPUL	tree similar to the banyan
PUNKA	fan made of palm leaves
PUNKAH	fan made of palm leaves
PURDA	custom of keeping women secluded
PURDAH	custom of keeping women secluded
PURI	unleavened flaky bread
PUTTEE	strip of cloth wound around the leg
RAGGEE	cereal grass
RAGI	cereal grass
RAITA	yoghurt-and-vegetable dish served with curry
RAJ	government
RAJAH	ruler or landlord
RAMTIL	African plant grown in India
RANEE	queen or princess
RANI	queen or princess
RATHA	four-wheeled carriage drawn by horses or bullocks
ROTI	type of unleavened bread
RUPEE	standard monetary unit of India
RYOT	peasant or tenant farmer
SAMBAR	deer with three-tined antlers
SAMITI	political association
SAMOSA	triangular pastry containing spiced vegetables or meat
SARANGI	stringed instrument played with a bow
SARDAR	Sikh title
SARI	traditional dress of Indian women
SAROD	Indian stringed instrument
SWAMI	title for a Hindu saint or religious teacher
TABLA	pair of drums whose pitches can be varied
THALI	meal consisting of several small dishes
TIL	sesame
TOLA	unit of weight
TONGA	light two-wheeled vehicle
TOPEE	pith helmet
TOPI	pith helmet
URD	bean plant
VAHANA	vehicle in Indian myth
VANDA	type of orchid
VINA	stringed musical instrument
WALLAH	person in charge of a specific thing
ZENANA	part of a house reserved for women and girls
ZILA	administrative district in India
ZILLA	administrative district in India
ZILLAH	administrative district in India

New Zealand words

While New Zealand and Australian English have many words in common, the Kiwi lexicon is greatly enriched by New Zealand's Maori heritage. Maori-derived words are a marvellous resource for the Scrabble player, providing a wealth of unusual vowel combinations, and frequently using consonants that are rarer in European words, such as K, W and H. Maori words are especially good for balancing vowel-heavy racks, as many words use several As, Us or Is – sometimes with three vowels in a row. Relatively high-scoring consonants are also very common, especially K and H. Unfortunately, there is only one K in Scrabble, so many Maori words with two Ks are less useful than they might initially appear. Note that there are also some unusual words that have entered the vocabulary of New Zealanders from European or Asian languages.

ATUA	spirit or demon
BOOHAI	thoroughly lost
CHUR	expression of agreement
COOTIE	body louse
GOORIE	mongrel dog
GRAUNCH	crush or destroy
HAKA	war dance
HANGI	open-air cooking pit
HAPU	subtribe
HAPUKA	large fish
HAPUKU	large fish
HEITIKI	neck ornament
HIKOI	protest march
HOKONUI	illicit whisky
HONGI	nose-touching greeting
HUHU	hairy beetle
HUI	conference or meeting
HUIA	extinct New Zealand bird
JAFA	offensive term for someone from Auckland
JANOLA	household bleach
KAHAWAI	large fish
KAI	food
KAIK	village
KAINGA	village
KAKA	long-billed parrot
KAKAPO	ground-dwelling parrot
KARAKIA	prayer
KARANGA	call or chant of welcome
KATIPO	small venomous spider
KAUPAPA	strategy, policy or cause
KAURI	coniferous tree

KAWA	protocol or etiquette
KIEKIE	climbing bush plant
KOHA	gift or donation
KOKAKO	long-tailed crow
KONEKE	farm vehicle
KORU	curved pattern
KOWHAI	small tree
KUIA	female elder
KUNEKUNE	feral pig
KURI	mongrel dog
KUTU	body louse
MANUKA	myrtaceous tree
MATAI	evergreen tree
MIHI	ceremonial greeting
MOA	extinct large flightless bird
MOKI	edible sea fish
MOKO	Maori tattoo or tattoo pattern
MOOLOO	person from Waikato
MOPOKE	small spotted owl
MUNGA	army canteen
NGAI	clan or tribe
NGAIO	small tree
NGATI	tribe or clan
NIKAU	palm tree
PAKAHI	acid soil or land
PAKAPOO	Chinese lottery
PAKOKO	small freshwater fish
PAUA	edible abalone
PERFING	early retirement from the police force with financial compensation
PIKAU	rucksack
PIPI	shellfish
PIUPIU	leaf skirt
POI	ball of woven flax
PONGA	tall tree fern
PORAE	edible sea fish
PORANGI	crazy
PORINA	moth larva
POTAE	hat
POWHIRI	welcoming ceremony
PUGGY	sticky
PUHA	sow thistle
PUKEKO	wading bird
PURIRI	forest tree

RAHUI	Maori prohibition
RATA	myrtaceous forest tree
RAUPATU	seizure of land
RAURIKI	sow thistle
RONZ	rest of New Zealand
SHEEPO	person who brings sheep to the catching pen for shearing
TAIAHA	ceremonial fighting staff
TAIHOA	hold on!
TAKAHE	rare flightless bird
TANGI	Maori funeral ceremony
TANIWHA	legendary monster
TAONGA	treasure
TAPU	sacred or forbidden
TARSEAL	bitumen surface of a road
TAUIWI	non-Maori people of New Zealand
TIKANGA	Maori customs
TOETOE	type of tall grass
TOITOI	type of tall grass
TWINK	white correction fluid
WAKA	Maori canoe
WEKA	flightless bird
WERO	warrior's challenge
WETA	long-legged wingless insect
WHANAU	family
WHENAU	native land

South African words

South African English includes words from Nguni languages such as Xhosa and Zulu, as well as Afrikaans, amongst other languages. For Scrabble players, South African English offers a host of useful words for balancing vowel-heavy racks. Many Afrikaans-derived words contain a double A, while Nguni words often contain two or three As. It's a good idea, therefore, to have some South African words up your sleeve for when you find yourself with two or more As on your rack. There are also a lot of K words in South African English. As K can be an awkward letter to use effectively, these can come in very handy, as can the Afrikaans-derived words containing V, which are most helpful in trying to use that difficult tile.

AMADODA	grown men
AMANDLA	politcal slogan calling for power to the Black population
BAAS	boss
BABALAS	drunk or hungover
BAKGAT	excellent
BAKKIE	small truck

BONTBOK	type of antelope
BOYKIE	chap or fellow
BRAAI	grill or roast meat
BRAAIVLEIS	barbecue
BUNDU	wild, remote region
DAGGA	marijuana
DWAAL	state of befuddlement
FLATSTICK	with great speed
FOEFIE	rope along which a person suspended on a pulley may travel
GEELBEK	yellow-jawed fish
HAMBA	go away
JA	yes
JAAP	simpleton
JEREPIGO	heavy desert wine
JONG	friend
KAAL	naked
KEREL	chap or fellow
KRAAL	stockaded village
KWAITO	type of pop music
LEGUAAN	large monitor lizard
MEERKAT	sociable mongoose
MENEER	Mr or sir
MEVROU	Mrs or madam
MOOI	pleasing
MUTI	herbal medicine
NAARTJIE	tangerine
NEK	mountain pass
NKOSI	master or chief
OKE	man
OOM	title of respect
OUBAAS	person senior in rank or years
PADKOS	snacks for a long journey
PLAAS	farm
POTJIE	three-legged iron pot
ROOIKAT	lynx
SCAMTO	argot of urban South African Blacks
SKOLLY	hooligan
SNOEK	edible marine fish
SPEK	bacon, fat or fatty pork
STAFFRIDER	person who clings to the side of a train
STEEN	variety of white grape
STOKVEL	savings pool or syndicate
TIK	slang for crystal meth
UBUNTU	kindness

VLEI	area of marshy ground
VOEMA	vigour or energy
VOETSEK	expression of dismissal or rejection
VROU	woman or wife
WHOONGA	narcotic smoked as a recreational drug
YEBO	yes

Urdu words

Urdu, the official language of Pakistan and one of the official languages of India, is closely related to Hindi. Urdu, however, contains many more words derived from Arabic and Persian, and also uses a different system of writing from Hindi, lending a different character to the words that have entered English. Many Urdu culinary terms will be familiar to British Scrabble players from Indian restaurants, while most Anglo-Indian military vocabulary also derives from Urdu rather than Hindi. As with Hindi, the variant spellings of many Urdu words provide opportunities for Scrabble players, as does the frequency of the letter K.

BAGH	garden
BALTI	spicy Indian dish stewed until most liquid has evaporated
BASTI	slum
BEGUM	woman of high rank
BIRIANI	Indian dish of highly flavoured rice mixed with meat or fish
BIRYANI	Indian dish of highly flavoured rice mixed with meat or fish
BUSTEE	slum
BUSTI	slum
CHARPAI	bedstead of woven webbing on a wooden frame
CHARPOY	bedstead of woven webbing on a wooden frame
DAROGHA	manager
DHANSAK	Indian dish of meat or vegetables braised with lentils
INQILAB	revolution
IZZAT	honour or prestige
JACONET	light cotton fabric
JEMADAR	officer in the Indian police
KAMEEZ	long tunic
KHARIF	crop harvested at beginning of winter
KHAYAL	kind of Indian classical vocal music
KINCOB	fine silk fabric embroidered with gold or silver threads
KOFTA	Indian dish of seasoned minced meat shaped into balls
KOFTGAR	person skilled in inlaying steel with gold
KOFTGARI	art of inlaying steel with gold
KORMA	Indian dish of meat or vegetables braised with yoghurt or cream
LASCAR	sailor from the East Indies
MAIDAN	open space used for meetings and sports

MASALA	mixed spices ground into a paste
MOOLVI	Muslim doctor of the law
MOOLVIE	Muslim doctor of the law
MURDABAD	down with; death to
MUSTH	frenzied sexual excitement in male elephants
NUMDAH	coarse felt
QORMA	Indian dish of meat or vegetables braised with yoghurt or cream
RABI	crop harvested at the end of winter
SAHIB	title placed after a man's name
SAICE	servant who looks after horses
SARPANCH	head of a village council
SEPOY	Indian soldier in the service of the British
SHALWAR	loose-fitting trousers
SHIKAR	hunting
SHIKAREE	hunter
SHIKARI	hunter
SICE	servant who looks after horses
SUBADAH	chief native office in a company of sepoys
SUBADAR	chief native office in a company of sepoys
SUBAH	chief native office in a company of sepoys
SYCE	servant who looks after horses
TAHSIL	administrative division
TALOOKA	subdivision of a district
TALUK	subdivision of a district
TALUKA	subdivision of a district
TAMASHA	show or entertainment
TANDOORI	method of cooking on a spit in a clay oven